The Complete Book of
1940s Broadway Musicals

The Complete Book of 1940s Broadway Musicals

Dan Dietz

ROWMAN & LITTLEFIELD
Lanham • Boulder • New York • London

Published by Rowman & Littlefield
A wholly owned subsidiary of The Rowman & Littlefield Publishing Group, Inc.
4501 Forbes Boulevard, Suite 200, Lanham, Maryland 20706
www.rowman.com

Unit A, Whitacre Mews, 26-34 Stannary Street, London SE11 4AB

British Library Cataloguing in Publication Information Available

Library of Congress Cataloging-in-Publication Data

Dietz, Dan, 1945–
    The complete book of 1940s Broadway musicals / Dan Dietz.
        pages cm
    Includes bibliographical references and index.
    ISBN 978-1-4422-4527-3 (hardback : alk. paper) — ISBN 978-1-4422-4528-0
(ebook) 1. Musicals—New York (State)—New York—20th century—History
and criticism. I. Title.
    ML1711.8.N3D518 2015
    792.6'45097471—dc23   2014033040

∞™ The paper used in this publication meets the minimum requirements
of American National Standard for Information Sciences—Permanence of
Paper for Printed Library Materials, ANSI/NISO Z39.48-1992. Printed in the
United States of America

To the memory of my beloved parents, Celia and Frank
(Mother and Dad, the years of the 1940s
were in so many ways your decade.)

Contents

Acknowledgments   ix

Introduction   xi

Alphabetical List of Shows   xiii

BROADWAY MUSICALS OF THE 1940s

1940 Season   1

1940–1941 Season   29

1941–1942 Season   77

1942–1943 Season   113

1943–1944 Season   169

1944–1945 Season   233

1945–1946 Season   289

1946–1947 Season   349

1947–1948 Season   397

1948–1949 Season   443

1949 Season   493

APPENDIXES

A   Chronology (by Season)   519

B   Chronology (by Classification)   525

C   Discography   531

D   Gilbert and Sullivan Operettas   533

E   Filmography   535

F   Other Productions   537

G   Published Scripts   545

H   Theatres   547

Bibliography   551

Index   553

About the Author   593

Acknowledgments

I want to take this opportunity to thank my friends Mike Baskin and Ken DePew for their helpful comments and suggestions in the writing of this book.

Introduction

The Complete Book of 1940s Broadway Musicals examines in detail all 273 musicals that opened between January 1, 1940, and December 31, 1949. The musicals discussed are: eighty book musicals with new music; twelve with preexisting music; three operas; seven plays with incidental songs; fifty-seven revues; six personality revues; seven ice revues; four imports; twenty-nine revivals; twelve return engagements; and fifty-six pre-Broadway closings. For a quick rundown of these shows, see the Alphabetical List of Shows, appendix A (Chronology by Season), and appendix B (Chronology by Classification).

The purpose of this book is to present a complete picture of each musical, including technical information and commentary. My goal is to provide a handy reference source that examines technical aspects (cast and song listings, for example) as well as information that sheds new light on both familiar and forgotten musicals of the era. I've included obscure details about the productions because so often this kind of information personalizes a show and brings it to life. I've also examined the books and song structures of the musicals, and have noted the occasional curious choices made by a musical's creative team to give very little music to leading characters, decisions that seem antithetical for a musical (see entries for *Allegro* and *Lost in the Stars*).

The decade of the 1940s was a seminal period in the development of the American musical. The 1940–1941 season is perhaps the most remarkable one in the history of the American musical because within a period of three months three unusually strong book musicals premiered. All of them opened the door to a new chapter in the history of the musical. *Cabin in the Sky* was an adult fable about good and evil that utilized a generally well-developed book to tell its story, and its songs were used to develop character, further the plot, and create atmosphere. Two months later *Pal Joey* broke all the rules about musical comedy heroes: Joey was an unmitigated heel, an unpleasant and self-obsessed hoofer who cared about no one but himself. And *Lady in the Dark* explored the frustrations and unhappiness of a successful businesswoman who undergoes psychoanalysis; the sessions with her doctor develop into dreams and reveries that offer three mini-musicals in which the occurrences in her dreams mirror the events of her past and present.

Two seasons later, *Oklahoma!* institutionalized the new American musical as one that utilized plot, character, song, and dance to create a unified evening of storytelling. Following *Oklahoma!*, Broadway offered an array of musicals that built upon the structure and mechanics of the Richard Rodgers and Oscar Hammerstein II hit; some were dramatic (*Carousel, Street Scene, Brigadoon*), some satiric (*Finian's Rainbow*), and others old-fashioned larks (*Annie Get Your Gun, Kiss Me, Kate, Gentlemen Prefer Blondes*). But even the lighthearted offerings wove plot, character, song, and dance into a coherent entity.

The decade also saw the beginnings of the concept musical, a genre that flowered in the late 1960s and throughout the 1970s (including most of the Stephen Sondheim musicals of that period). The 1940s offered two flawed but ambitious concept musicals, *Allegro* and *Love Life*, and these were the forerunners of Sondheim's *Company, Follies,* and *Pacific Overtures* as well as *Hair* and *A Chorus Line*.

For this book, the technical information includes: name of theatre (including transfers, if applicable); opening and closing dates of production; number of performances (for consistency, I've used the performance numbers as reported by *Best Plays*); the show's advertising tag (including variations of the tag as used in a show's programs and flyers); names of book writers, sketch writers, lyricists, composers, directors, choreographers, musical directors, producers, and scenic, costume, and lighting designers. All the cast members are included, and each performer's name is followed by the name of the character portrayed (performers' names in italics reflect those billed above the show's title).

Also included are the number of acts; for book musicals, the time and locale of the show; and the titles of musical numbers are given by act (following each song title is the name of the performer, not the character, who introduced the song). If a musical is based on source material, such information is cited. Because programs sometimes didn't include every musical number, the song lists in this book reflect every musical sequence that was performed in a show, whether or not it was listed in the program. Also, if a song is known by a variant title, the alternate title is given in parentheses.

The commentary for each musical includes a brief plot summary (in the case of revues, representative sketches are discussed); brief quotes from the critics; informative trivia; details about London productions as well as New York revivals; and data about recordings, published scripts, and film, radio, television, and video versions. In most cases, the commentary also includes information regarding the show's gestation and pre-Broadway tryout history. Winners of the Tony Award, the New York Drama Critics' Circle Award, and the Pulitzer Prize are also cited. Throughout this book, bolded titles refer to productions that are discussed elsewhere in the text.

The book includes eight appendixes: a chronology by season; chronology by classification; a discography; a list of Gilbert and Sullivan revivals; a filmography; a special chronology of selected nonmusicals that opened during the decade and included incidental songs, dances, or background music; a list of published scripts; and a list of theatres where the musicals were performed.

The book also includes a bibliography. Virtually all the information in the book is drawn from such source materials as programs, souvenir programs, window cards (posters), flyers, recordings, scripts (both published and unpublished), and contemporary reviews.

As mentioned, of the 273 productions discussed in this book, 80 were book musicals that had new music. Of these new book musicals, 12 appear to have never been recorded in any fashion; and as far as location, New York City is the parish of choice, with 31 new musicals taking place in whole or in part in New York or the immediate surrounding area.

The decade had its amusing quirks. South American music was the rage during the era, and so an inordinate number of revues and musicals included Latin-styled songs in their scores. Even *Where's Charley?*, which was set in Oxford during the 1890s, managed to work in a Brazilian number ("Pernambuco"). Another trend during the era was the use of Russian dancers or, at least, dancers with Russian names; apparently a sprinkle of Russian names among the cast listing was considered a sign of High Culture. And so a dancer named Tillie Smith from Podunk might suddenly find herself billed as Tatiana Liefndeskya when she landed a dancing role in a Broadway musical (and, indeed, Marc Platt, the original Dream Curly in *Oklahoma!*, was for a time known as Marc Platoff).

During the decade, many dance numbers were called ballets, but many if not most of them weren't ballets in the accepted sense of that word. For the Broadway world of the 1940s (and for much of the 1950s, for that matter), the word *ballet* usually denoted an elaborate dance sequence that included dancing principals and chorus, and sometimes the stars. As the decades progressed, the word *ballet* wasn't used in the title of dance numbers (1961's dance "Subway Rush" from *Subways Are for Sleeping* might well have been called "The Subway Rush Ballet" if the musical had opened fifteen years earlier).

Alphabetical List of Shows

The following is an alphabetical list of all 273 musicals discussed in this book. There are multiple listings for those musicals that were produced more than once during the decade, and those entries are followed by the year of the production.

Adamant Eve	159	Blossom Time	181
A la Carte	513	Blue Holiday	278
Alaskan Stampede	284	Bonanza Bound!	436
Alice in Wonderland and Through the		Boys and Girls Together	36
Looking Glass	385	Brigadoon	380
Allah Be Praised!	214	Bright Lights of 1944	187
Allegro	404	By Jupiter	113
Alley Moon	435	Cabalgata	495
All for Love	478	Cabin in the Sky	42
All in Fun	57	Call Me Mister	330
Along Fifth Avenue	475	Caribbean Carnival	409
American Jubilee	15	Carib Song	295
American Sideshow	108	Carmen Jones (1943)	205
Angel in the Wings	411	Carmen Jones (1945)	277
Annie Get Your Gun	334	Carmen Jones (1946)	330
Are You With It?	305	Carousel (1945)	274
Around the World in Eighty Days	337	Carousel (1949)	480
Artists and Models	195	Chauve-souris of 1943	179
As the Girls Go	464	The Chocolate Soldier (1942)	117
Ballet Ballads (three one-act musicals:		The Chocolate Soldier (1947)	378
Susanna and the Elders; Willie the Weeper;		Cocktails at 5	160
and The Eccentricities of Davey Crockett		Concert Varieties	289
[as told by himself])	432	A Connecticut Yankee	199
Bal nègre	360	Count Me In	136
Banjo Eyes	91	The Cradle Will Rock	413
Barbara	392	Crazy with the Heat (includes revised version)	60
Barefoot Boy with Cheek	383	Curtain Time	223
Beat the Band	139	Dancing in the Streets	161
Beggar's Holiday	363	Dansation	108
Best Foot Forward	77	The Day before Spring	307
Big Time	223	The Desert Song	316
Billion Dollar Baby	309	Dream with Music	220
Bloomer Girl (1944)	240	The Duchess Misbehaves	322
Bloomer Girl (1947)	368	Earl Carroll Vanities	3

Early to Bed   171
The Eccentricities of Davey Crockett (as told
    by himself) (Ballet Ballads)   433
Edith Piaf and Her Continental Entertainers   408
Ed Wynn's Laugh Carnival   487
Everything's on Ice   393
Finian's Rainbow   372
The Firebrand of Florence   271
The Firefly   163
A Flag Is Born   354
Follow the Girls   212
The Foolies of 1949   488
For Your Pleasure   151
Full Speed Ahead   164
Funzapoppin   493
Gay New Orleans   31
Gentlemen Prefer Blondes   510
The Girl from Nantucket   303
Glad to See You   284
The Gypsy Baron (1944)   245
The Gypsy Baron (1945)   300
Gypsy Lady   356
Hairpin Harmony   190
Harlem Cavalcade   105
Hats Off to Ice   234
Headliners of '42   165
Heaven on Earth   452
Helen Goes to Troy   216
High Button Shoes   402
Higher and Higher   12
High Kickers   84
Hi Ya, Gentlemen   69
Hold It!   428
Hold on to Your Hats   34
Holiday on Broadway   424
Hollywood Pinafore   282
Hot from Harlem   70
Howdy, Mr. Ice   445
Howdy, Mr. Ice of 1950   485
Icetime   349
Icetime of 1948   390
If the Shoe Fits   361
In Gay New Orleans   393
Inside U.S.A.   425
It Happens on Ice (includes two editions)   38
Jackpot   207
John Henry   1
Johnny 2 x 4   102
Jump for Joy   108
Keep 'Em Laughing   104
Keep Off the Grass   17
Ken Murray's Blackouts of 1949   499
Kiss Me, Kate   472
La belle Helene   68

La vie Parisienne (1941)   86
La vie Parisienne (1942)   145
La vie Parisienne (1945)   267
The Lady Comes Across   94
Lady in the Dark (1941)   63
Lady in the Dark (1943)   153
A Lady Says Yes   265
Laffacade   438
Laffing Room Only   254
Laugh Time   183
Laugh, Town, Laugh   115
Lend an Ear   466
Let Freedom Sing   133
Let's Face It!   82
Liberty Jones   66
Life of the Party   165
The Little Dog Laughed   70
Look, Ma, I'm Dancin'!   418
Lost in the Stars   503
Louisiana Lady   397
Louisiana Purchase   21
Love in the Snow   340
Love Life   456
Lute Song   320
Magdalena   454
Make Mine Manhattan   416
Marching with Johnny   225
Marianne   224
Marinka   291
Maurice Chevalier—Songs and
    Impressions (1947)   377
Maurice Chevalier in an Evening of Songs
    and Impressions (1948)   424
The Medium (1947)   387
The Medium (1948)   470
Meet the People   50
Memphis Bound   280
Merry-Go-Rounders (aka The Merrymakers)   166
The Merrymakers (aka Merry-Go-Rounders)   167
The Merry Widow (1942)   126
The Merry Widow (1943)   176
The Merry Widow (1944)   243
Mexican Hayride   210
Miss Liberty   497
Morey Amsterdam's Hilarities   448
Mr. Strauss Goes to Boston   293
Mum's the Word   49
Music in My Heart   399
My Dear Public   184
My Romance   462
Nellie Bly   317
New Faces of 1943   146
The New Moon (1942)   127
The New Moon (1944)   219

New Priorities of 1943	129
Night of Love	59
Of "V" We Sing	99
Oklahoma!	154
Once Over Lightly	145
One Touch of Venus	192
On the Town	261
Oy is dus a leben!	138
Pal Joey	54
Panama Hattie	46
Paris Sings Again	438
Park Avenue	358
The Passing Show	341
Patricia	111
Polonaise	298
Porgy and Bess (1942)	97
Porgy and Bess (1943)	186
Pretty Penny	514
Priorities of 1942	101
The Rape of Lucretia	470
Raze the Roof	488
The Red Mill	301
Regina	505
Reunion in New York	9
Rhapsody	249
Rhapsody in Black	72
Robin Hood	243
Rosalinda	143
The Rose Masque	226
Run Little Chillun	177
Russian Bank	20
Sadie Thompson	246
Sally	430
Seven Lively Arts	251
The Shape of Things!	439
She Had to Say Yes	72
Shootin' Star	342
Show Boat (1946)	312
Show Boat (1948)	448
Show Time	131
Sim Sala Bim	33
Sing Out, Sweet Land!	258
Sleepy Hollow	443
Small Wonder	450
Something for the Boys	149
Song of Norway	236
Song without Words	343
Sons o' Fun	86
South Pacific	481
Spike Jones and His Musical Depreciation Revue	441
Spring in Brazil	345
Star and Garter	118
Stars on Ice (includes two editions)	120
Star Time	239
St. Louis Woman	326
Stovepipe Hat	227
Street Scene	369
The Student Prince	169
Sugar 'n' Spice	167
Sunny River	89
Susanna and the Elders (Ballet Ballads)	432
Sweet Bye and Bye	395
Sweethearts	375
Take a Bow	233
Tars and Spars	218
The Telephone (1947)	387
The Telephone (1948)	470
Texas, Li'l Darlin'	508
That's the Ticket	489
Theatre of the Piccoli	11
The Time, the Place and the Girl	141
They Can't Get You Down	111
This Is the Army	123
Three to Make Ready	324
Tidbits of 1946	351
'Tis of Thee	45
Tonight at 8:30 (revival; includes two double bills, each with three one-act plays, some with incidental songs)	421
Toplitzky of Notre Dame	366
Top-Notchers	107
Touch and Go	501
Tropical Pinafore	24
A Tropical Revue (1943)	189
A Tropical Revue (1944)	257
Two for the Show	6
Two Weeks with Pay	74
Under the Counter	400
Up in Central Park (1945)	267
Up in Central Park (1947)	389
Up to Now	516
A Vagabond Hero (aka The White Plume)	25
The Vagabond King	174
Vincent Youmans' "Fiesta"	228
Viva O'Brien	80
Walk with Music	29
The Waltz King	230
Watch Out, Angel!	286
What's Up	197
Where's Charley?	459
The White Plume (aka A Vagabond Hero)	25
Willie the Weeper (Ballet Ballads)	433
Windy City	347
Wine Women and Song	132
Winged Victory	202
You'll See Stars	148
Yours Is My Heart	352
Ziegfeld Follies	157

1940 Season

JOHN HENRY
"A NEW PLAY WITH MUSIC"

Theatre: 44th Street Theatre
Opening Date: January 10, 1940; *Closing Date*: January 15, 1940
Performances: 7
Book and *Lyrics*: Roark Bradford
Music: Jacques Wolfe
Based on the 1931 novel *John Henry* by Roark Bradford.
Direction: Uncredited; *Producer*: Sam Byrd (Fred Mitchell, Associate Producer); *Scenery*: Albert Johnson;
    Costumes: John Hambleton; *Lighting*: Uncredited; *Choral Direction*: Leonard dePaur; *Musical Direction*:
    Don Voorhees
Cast: Joshua White (Blind Lemon), Henrietta Lovelace (Julie Anne's Mamma), George Jones Jr. (Julie Anne's
    Papa), Ruby Elzy (Julie Anne), Minto Cato (Old Aunt Dinah), Robert Harvey (Hell Buster), Joe (Joseph)
    Attles (Man Named Sam, Bad Stacker Lee), Musa Williams (Ruby), *Paul Robeson* (John Henry), James
    Lightfoot (Deaf Man), Ray Yeates (A Rouster, Lead Heaver), Lloyd Howlett (Floyd), J. DeWitt Spencer
    (Nud, Mink Eye), Alexander Gray (Mate, Billie Bob Russell), Kenneth Spencer (Walking Boss), Myra John-
    son (Poor Selma), Merritt Smith (Member of Pimps' Quartette, Reader), Wyer Owens Handy (Member of
    Pimps' Quartette), Louis Gilbert (Member of Pimps' Quartette, First Caller), William Woolfolk (Mem-
    ber of Pimps' Quartette, Second Caller), Eva Vaughan (Member of Fancy Ladies' Octette), Alyce Carter
    (Member of Fancy Ladies' Octette), Mattie Washington (Member of Fancy Ladies' Octette), Benveneta
    Washington (Member of Fancy Ladies' Octette, Carrie), Alice White (Member of Fancy Ladies' Octette),
    Ruth Gibbs (Member of Fancy Ladies' Octette), Marie Fraser (Member of Fancy Ladies' Octette), Mildred
    Lassiter (Member of Fancy Ladies' Octette), C. W. Scott (Roustabout); Workers, Workers' Wives, Others:
    James Armstrong, Leona Avery, Ernest Baskette, Ella Belle Davis, Oscar Brooks, Maudine Brown, Jona-
    than Brice, Alyce Carter, George Dickson, John Diggs, Nora Evans, Marie Fraser, Samuel A. Floyd, Ruth
    Gibbs, Louis Gilbert, Samuel Gary, James B. Gordon, Edgar Hall, Claudia Hall, Kate Hall, Wyer Owens
    Handy, Lloyd Howlett, George Kennedy, Mildred Lassiter, James Lightfoot, Sadie McGill, Massie Patter-
    son, Bayard Rustin, C. W. Scott, Ernest Shaw, Anne Simmons, Maude Simmons, Randall Steplight, Eva
    Vaughan, Charles Welch, Benveneta Washington, Mattie Washington, Alice White, Frederick Wilkerson,
    William Woolfolk, Ray Yeates
The musical was presented in two acts.
The action takes place "in the Black River country" (of Wisconsin), in Argenta, Arkansas, on the Mississippi
    River, and in New Orleans.

Musical Numbers

Act One: "I'm Singing about a Man" (Joshua White); "How Come I'm Born wid a Hook in My Hand" (Paul Robeson); "All the People on the Levee" (Paul Robeson, Chorus); "Ya Gotta Bend Down" (Joshua White, Chorus); "How Come I'm Born wid a Hook in My Hand" (reprise) (Paul Robeson); "Coonjine" (Chorus); "Jaybird" (Minto Cato, Paul Robeson); "Got a Head Like a Rock" (Paul Robeson); "Whiffer's Song" (Joshua White); "Stingaree Song" (Myra Johnson); "Bad, Bad Stacker Lee" (Joe Attles); "Careless Love" (Ruby Elzy); "I've Trampled All Over" (Ruby Elzy, Paul Robeson); "Caught Ole Blue" (Joshua White, Chorus); "The Captain's Song" (Alexander Gray); "Old John Henry" / "Po' Lil' Frenchie" (Paul Robeson, Men); "Workin' on de Railroad" (Paul Robeson, Men); "High Ballin'" (Chorus)

Act Two: "Where Did You Get Dem High Heeled Shoes?" (Joshua White); "Let the Sun Sink Down" (Benveneta Washington, Chorus); "Ship of Zion" (Chorus); "No Bottom" (Chorus); "Lullaby" (Ruby Elzy); "Take Me a Drink of Whiskey" (Joe Attles, Musa Williams); "Sundown in My Soul" (Paul Robeson); "I'm Gonna Get Down on My Knees" (Robert Harvey, Chorus); "I Want Jesus to Walk with Me" (Robert Harvey, Chorus); "I'm Born in the Country" (Paul Robeson); "Now You Talks Mighty Big in the Country" (Joe Attles, Chorus); "So Stand Back, All You Bullies" (Paul Robeson); "Ship of Zion" (reprise) (Chorus); "I Don't Care Where They Buried My Body" (Chorus); "He Went to the East" (Chorus)

In the late nineteenth and early twentieth centuries, the respective legends of John Henry and Paul Bunyan came about. The former seems to have emanated from actual folk tales, while the latter's image was created for a sales product. But ersatz legend or not, Paul Bunyan quickly became part of American folklore, and he and John Henry were in many ways the white and black counterparts of the kind of powerful men needed to cultivate the land of a new country. Their almost superhuman strength cut swaths through forests as they downed towering trees as if they were no more than mere twigs.

And from the perspective of musical theatre, both men were themselves brought down when muscular strength became less important with the dawn of the industrial age. When John Henry dares to compete with the steam engine, he's not only defeated, he dies. In W. H. Auden and Benjamin Britten's opera *Paul Bunyan*, the hero is necessary for the development of a new nation; but when the land is settled and the country has matured, his physical force is no longer needed and he fades away (the opera premiered on May 5, 1941, at Brander Matthews Hall at Columbia University and is in many respects the first concept musical; see **Allegro** for more information about this genre).

The episodic *John Henry* told the familiar story of the fanciful feats of its hero (Paul Robeson), who orders the sun to shine, hauls bales of cotton without breaking a sweat, builds the railroads, and erects the levees on the Mississippi River. John Henry loves Julie Anne (Ruby Elzy), but becomes briefly infatuated with the scarlet big-city woman Poor Selma (Myra Johnson). Due to a foolish misunderstanding on his part, John Henry becomes jealous of Julie Anne and falls prey to the machinations of the evil Man Named Sam (Joe Attles). And when John Henry pits his strength against the steam engine, he loses the war with the machine age and dies. His body is placed on a bier of cotton bales, and in death he's joined by Julie Anne, who in grief has killed herself. Although John Henry dies, the story of his life takes on mythic proportion.

The critics were unanimous in their praise of Paul Robeson, whose powerful baritone and commanding physique were the perfect embodiment of the hero, but were less happy with the overall production. As a result, *John Henry* played for just seven performances and was the shortest-running musical of the season.

Richard Watts in the *New York Herald Tribune* said Robeson was "an actor of truly heroic presence" and "a sort of racial legend in himself," and Burns Mantle in the *New York Daily News* said Robeson was the "perfect choice" for John Henry (had he sung until midnight, the "crowd would still have demanded more"). But despite their accolades for Robeson, the critics were less than impressed with Roark Bradford's adaptation of his 1931 novel and the music composed by Jacques Wolfe. The libretto was found wanting with a number of "undramatic episodes" (per Watts), and Brooks Atkinson in the *New York Times* felt the book was "desultory," "underwritten," and "put together in perfunctory fashion." Richard Lockridge in the *New York Sun* said the musical was "skimpy" and "static," and seemed "too small" for its theme. As for the score, Mantle found it "nice" but "all in the same key and the same mood," and Watts said it was "unexceptional." But Atkinson said some of the music was "extraordinarily beautiful," and suggested if it were performed in concert it "might be better appreciated." The critics liked singer and banjo-player Joshua White (as Blind Lemon), who appeared throughout the evening as a kind of roving balladeer and sang five songs (including the first and second act opening numbers "I'm Singing about a Man" and "Where Did You Get Dem High Heeled Shoes?").

Wilella Waldorf in the *New York Post* also indicated the evening was more in the nature of a concert with "stage trappings," and felt she could "cautiously" recommend the musical only to those "who particularly enjoy Negro music and song." But audiences who demand "more drama" with their music might be disappointed. She mentioned that the musical had employed two directors (during the tryout and preview performances Anthony Brown and then Charles Friedman were credited), but noted the opening night program didn't credit anyone (Mantle said he had attended the first New York preview performance as well as the opening night, and at the preview Friedman had been officially credited with the direction).

Despite a general lack of enthusiasm for the score, a number of songs were singled out by the six critics, including "How Come I'm Born wid a Hook in My Hand," "Got a Head Like a Rock," "Sundown in My Soul," "Careless Love," and "I'm Born in the Country" (the latter was "triumphant," according to Atkinson). Although Robeson later recorded a song titled "John Henry" (which wasn't in the musical), it appears he never recorded any numbers from the score.

In 1931, Bradford's novel *John Henry* was published in hardback by The Literary Guild, and a year before the musical was produced its libretto was published in a hardback edition by Harper & Brothers. In 2008, Oxford University Press published a hardback edition that included the 1931 novel and the 1939 libretto.

Robeson had appeared in the original 1924 production of Eugene O'Neill's then-daring drama *All God's Chillun Got Wings* about an interracial romance. In 1924 and 1925, he starred in two Broadway revivals of O'Neill's 1920 drama *The Emperor Jones*, and was also in the 1933 film adaptation (Ruby Elzy, Robeson's costar in *John Henry*, also appeared in the film). Robeson's final New York performances were in the long-running 1943 Broadway revival of *Othello* (with José Ferrer and Uta Hagen) and a limited-run return engagement at City Center in 1945 (also with Ferrer and Hagan). He created the role of Joe for the 1928 London premiere of *Show Boat* and appeared in the 1932 Broadway revival of the musical. In 1936, he re-created the role for the film version (and with Hattie McDaniel introduced "Ah Still Suits Me," a new Oscar Hammerstein II and Jerome Kern song written especially for the film).

Joe (Joseph) Attles, who portrayed Man Named Sam and Bad Stacker Lee, appeared in musicals during a six-decade period. He made his Broadway debut in the hit revue *Blackbirds of 1928*, which played for 518 performances, and his final show was the long-running 1976 revue *Bubbling Brown Sugar*, which ran for 766 showings. Besides *John Henry*, his other musical appearances included the 1953 and 1965 revivals of *Porgy and Bess*, *Kwamina*, and *Tambourines to Glory*. He also appeared in such Off-Broadway musicals as the 1964 revival of *Cabin in the Sky*, the 1964 and 1968 productions of *Jerico-Jim Crow*, and *The Prodigal Son* (1965).

Roark Bradford had earlier written *Ol' Man Adam an' His Chillun*, a 1928 collection of short stories upon which Marc Connelly based his 1930 Pulitzer Prize–winning play-with-music *The Green Pastures*.

EARL CARROLL VANITIES
"AMERICA'S GREATEST REVUE"

Theatre: St. James Theatre
Opening Date: January 13, 1940; *Closing Date*: February 3, 1940
Performances: 25
Sketches: Archie Blyer
Lyrics: Dorcas Cochran, Mitchell Parrish, Charles Rosoff, and Al Stillman
Music: Nacio Herb Brown, Peter De Rose, Jararaca Paiva, and Vicente Paiva
Direction: Earl Carroll; *Producer*: Earl Carroll; *Choreography*: Eddie Prinz; *Scenery* and *Costumes*: Jean Le Seyeux; *Lighting*: Uncredited; *Musical Direction*: Lionel Newman
Cast: Susan Miller, Johnny Woods, Jerry Lester, Ygor and Tanya, Professor Lamberti, Norman Lawrence, Gary Stone, Topsy, Beryl Wallace, The Three Nonchalants, The Four Hot Shots, Don Milheim, Pat Lee, Clarence Low, Babe Westerlund, Nirska, Puddy Smith, Cass-Owen, Lela Moore, Ann Adams, Janet Atwater, Dale Wells, Ann Lynne, Yolande Donlan, Lorraine Gresh, Walter Norris, Herb Adams, The Most Beautiful Girls in the World: Muriel Barr, Kathleen Barclay, Joy Barlow, Dorothy Barrett, Mary Lou Bennett, Harriet Bennett, Anne Callahan, Jeanne Carroll, Carolyn Crumley, Florence Cubitt, Mary Daniels, Madeline

Elliott, Jean Frances, Katherine Grey, Rose Heitner, Jane Hughes, Bonnie Kildare, Roberta Lee, Patricia Lee, Dolores Loesch, Virginia Maples, Mildred Morris, Diana Mumby, Gwynne Norys, Lola Patten, Kay Pines, Bebe Porter, Rosemary Randall, Dorothe Small, Lanita Smith, Marna Stansell, Betty Stuart, Marlyn Stuart, Louise Wohl, Barbara Walters, Meriam Weller, Dale Wentworth, Lillian Girard, Susanne Jeanne The revue was presented in two acts.

Musical Numbers

Act One: Overture (Orchestra); "The Earl Carroll Theatre, Hollywood" (Norman Lawrence, Gary Stone); "Beauty on Parade"; "The Lady Has Oomph" (lyric and music by Dorcas Cochran and Charles Rosoff) (Beryl Wallace; The Oomph Girls: Muriel Barr, Harriet Bennett, Virginia Maples, Jean Frances, Rose Heitner, Patricia Lee, Barbara Walters, Jeanne Carroll); "Angel" (lyric by Mitchell Parrish, music by Peter De Rose) (Susan Miller); "Cascade of Plumes" (The Most Beautiful Girls in the World [for names of performers, see cast list above]); Jerry Lester (monologue); "Union Eyes" (sketch) (The Wife: Beryl Wallace; The Lover: Norman Lawrence; The Husband: Jerry Lester); "The Little Broadcast" (Johnny Woods); "Charming" (lyric and music by Dorcas Cochran and Charles Rosoff); "The Golden Garden" (dance) (Beryl Wallace); "Cigarettes in the Moonlight"; Specialty (Ygor and Tanya); "Fun in One" (Jerry Lester, Topsy); "The Corset Shop" (Salesman: Jerry Lester; Secretary: Topsy; Customer: Don Milheim; First Model: Pat Lee; Second Model: Virginia Maples; Third Model: Muriel Barr; Fourth Model: Jeanne Carroll; Premiere Model: Beryl Wallace; Another Customer: Clarence Low; Still Another Customer: Babe Westerlund; *Program Note*: "Corsets created by Hollywood Maxwell"); The Three Nonchalants; "Announcement" (Beryl Wallace); "The Starlit Hour" (lyric by Mitchell Parrish, music by Peter De Rose) (Gary Stone, Susan Miller, Norman Lawrence, Jeanne Carroll, Marlyn Stewart); "Fantasy of Feathers" (Gold Bird: Patricia Lee; Black Bird: Bebe Porter; Flamingo: Jean Frances; Hitlerio: Marna Stansell; Blue Bird: Betty Stuart; Swan: Harriet Bennett; Ostrich: Muriel Barr; Fire Bird: Barbara Walters; and The Crystal Ball Girls); "Harmony" (Three Lovely Ladies); "The Dance of Light" (butterfly dance "originated" by Nirska and performed by Nirska); "Announcement" (Miss Hollywood: Mary Daniels; Miss Los Angeles: Marlyn Stewart); "Musician Extraordinaire" (sequence included the song "Wishing"; Professor Lamberti; Stanley Livingston: Clarence Low, Babe Westerlund, and Don Milheim; Blue Allure: "Illustrated" by Rose Heitner; San Francisco Bay: Johnny Woods); "Westward Ho!" (lyric and music by Dorcas Cochran and Charles Rosoff); "Along the Road" (The Roller Skaters: Patricia Lee, Puddy Smith; Wholly Rollers: Cass-Owen, Topsy; The Cyclists: Jean Frances, Clarence Low, Babe Westerlund; The Hicyclist: Professor Lamberti; Bantam Auto: Johnny Woods; Grand Person: Jerry Lester); "Camera, Lights, Action" (Norman Lawrence, Gary Stone); "American Bolero" (music by Nacio Herb Brown) (Blue Tambourines: Mary Daniels, Mildred Morris, Gwen Norys, Bonnie Kildare, Dolores Loesch, Dorothy Barrett, Kathleen Barclay, Marlyn Stewart, Lela Moore; Gold Tambourines: Rosemary Randall, Madeline Elliott, Joy Barlow, Harriet Bennett, Marna Stansell, Jeanne Frances, Barbara Walters, Puddy Smith, Betty Stuart; Green Tambourines: Roberta Lee, Ann Adams, Diana Mumby, Muriel Barr, Jeanne Carroll, Virginia Maples, Patricia Lee, Bebe Porter, Ygor and Tanya; Red Tambourines: Janet Atwater, Dale Wells, Ann Lynne, Dorothy Barrett, Yolande Donlan, Lorraine Gresh, Kay Pines, Rose Heitner, Beryl Wallace); "Tapping the Tom-Toms" (The Four Hot Shots); Grand Finale

Act Two: "Can the Can-Can" (lyric and music by Dorcas Cochran and Charles Rosoff) (Susan Miller); "Can-Can Girls" (Rose Heitner, Virginia Maples, Muriel Barr, Jean Frances, Harriet Bennett, Barbara Walters, Patricia Lee, Dorothy Barrett); "Gay Paree"; "Isle of Capri" (Jerry Lester); "The Interrupted Broadcast" (Johnny Woods; Needle Salesman: Don Milheim; Palmist: Professor Lamberti); "I Want My Mama" (lyric by Al Stillman, music by Jararaca Paiva and Vicente Paiva; song otherwise known as "Mama Yo Quiero," Spanish lyric by Jararaca Paiva and Vicente Paiva) (Beryl Wallace, The Patticake Girls, Professor Lamberti); "Hot Feet" (The Four Hot Shots); "Mandalay" (Jerry Lester; First Chinaman: Walter Norris; Second Chinaman: Herb Adams); "Pretty Things" (Ted Lewis: Jerry Lester; Beautiful Hawaii: Beryl Wallace); "Angel" (reprise) (Susan Miller); "Beauty Empanelled" (Parade of Loveliness: The Girls); "Lovers' Lane" (First Bench: Beryl Wallace, Norman Lawrence; Second Bench: Muriel Barr, Gary Stone); "Dance of the Lovers" (choreography by Lela Moore) (Lela Moore); "Announcement" (Mary Daniels, Marlyn Stewart); "The Fortune Teller" (The Wife: Susan Miller; The Husband: Professor Lamberti; The Seer: Johnny Woods);

"The Glamour Parlor"; Specialty (Cass-Owen, Topsy, Jerry Lester); "Song of the Sarong" (lyric and music by Dorcas Cochran and Charles Rosoff) (Susan Miller, Gary Stone, Thirty-Six Tahitian Ladies); "Moon of Pepiti"; "Flaming Maraccas" ("A Vision in Radium"); "Messin' Around" (sketch by Archie Blyer); Grand Finale (Entire Company)

Earl Carroll's latest and final Broadway showing *Earl Carroll Vanities* (aka *Earl Carroll's Vanities*) lasted just three weeks. The impresario had produced eleven Broadway editions of his *Vanities* and *Sketch Books* between 1923 and 1935, and then headed for Hollywood where he opened his Earl Carroll Theatre-Restaurant, which offered patrons both dinner and a revue in a spectacular venue (walls of "masculine" wood were festooned with "feminine" dark green drapes). Because of the successes of his Hollywood revues, Carroll expanded his latest production and offered it to Broadway, which quickly sent it back to the West Coast.

In truth, the *Vanities* were more on the level of the *Passing Show* revues and never reached the heights of Florenz Ziegfeld's *Follies*, George White's *Scandals*, and Irving Berlin's *Music Box* revues, all of which offered memorable songs, sketches, and performances by the superstars of the era. Instead, the *Vanities* were obsessed with showgirls, showgirls, and more showgirls. Superior scores, sketches, and stars were less important than acres of feminine pulchritude, and, typical of Carroll's revues, the 1940 edition offered some three-dozen show girls in such numbers as "Cascade of Plumes," "The Oomph Girls," "The Corset Shop," "Fantasy of Feathers," "American Bolero," "Can-Can Girls," and "Song of the Sarong."

To be sure, there were other performers in the revue, including comics Jerry Lester and Professor Lamberti. The critics thought with better material the former had the makings of a star, and Brooks Atkinson in the *New York Times* liked his "funny" spoof of burlesque dancing; but Lester never enjoyed a major theatre career, and perhaps his biggest Broadway moment occurred when he was cast as one of Zero Mostel's replacements during the run of the original 1962 production of *A Funny Thing Happened on the Way to the Forum*. Others in the cast were singer Susan Miller, radio-personality-impersonator Johnny Woods, adagio dancers Ygor and Tanya, the acrobatic trio The Three Nonchalants, tap dancers The Four Hot Spots, and dancer Nirska (who according to John Mason Brown in the *New York Post* seemed to enjoy herself immensely as she waved huge chiffon wings and pretended to be a butterfly). And, *Hellzapoppin'*-style, there was a literal touch of audience participation when the customers were invited to play patticake with The Patticake Girls during the song "I Want My Mama." (But Burns Mantle in the *New York Daily News* noted that "timid" male customers were "noticeably shy" with the patticakers, and Sidney B. Whipple in the *New York World-Telegram* mentioned that the audience "sulked" when invited to patticake, the only exception perhaps being wealthy socialite Tommy Manville, who may have raised his hands in "self-defense.")

Richard Watts in the *New York Herald Tribune* said the evening was "exceptionally feeble and unimaginative" and lacked "zest, humor and tunefulness." He also noted the cast had an "almost pathetic eagerness to please," seemed to "beg" the audience to like them, and "effusively" thanked the audience for "whatever applause there may happen to be." Whipple found the material "banal," "stale," "unimaginative," "tedious," and "vapid," and sardonically noted that in a "burst of originality" the revue offered a can-can (he noted that Broadway had seen no more than four or five hundred can-can dances during the past three years); he also indicated the choreography seemed to be made up by the dancers as they went along. He and other critics complained about the show's length ("the long, long night of Jan. 13–14," noted Whipple, and Richard Lockridge in the *New York Sun* commented on the "extraordinary length" of the evening [including the overture, there were fifty-one individual numbers]). Mantle said the revue ran "pretty late," and reported that Carroll was going to trim the material (shortly after the opening, a few changes were made, including the omission of the first-act sketch "Union Eyes").

Many of the critics also complained that the revue was overly amplified, and Atkinson (who generally liked the evening but admitted it went on too long) suggested that the microphones were a "menace" that should "be yanked out and tossed in the alley."

Perhaps Brown best summed up the proceedings when he noted the evening was "strangely shoe-string" with "dented tin instead of glistening chromium."

Prior to the New York opening, one of Carroll's Hollywood editions included old-time comic Bert Wheeler as well as Bob Williams and his dog Red Dust (Wheeler, Williams, and Red Dust weren't in the New York production, but appeared in later Broadway revues of the era). The Hollywood editions included such numbers as "Tropical Moonlight" (with the Mandolin Girls), "Find Me a Beautiful Girl," "The Parasol Girls," "Blues on Parade," "Tower of Feathers," and "Pyramid of Beauty."

TWO FOR THE SHOW
"The Sparkling New Musical Revue" / "A New Revue" / "The New Musical Revue"

Theatre: Booth Theatre
Opening Date: February 8, 1940; *Closing Date*: May 25, 1940
Performances: 124
Sketches and *Lyrics*: Nancy Hamilton
Music: Morgan Lewis
Direction: "Entire production devised, staged and lighted" by John Murray Anderson (sketches directed by Joshua Logan); *Producers*: Gertrude Macy and Stanley Gilkey; *Choreography*: Robert Alton; *Scenery* and *Costumes*: Raoul Pene du Bois; *Musical Direction*: Ray Kavanagh
Cast: Eve Arden, Richard Haydn, Brenda Forbes, Betty Hutton, Eunice Healey, Nadine Gae, Keenan Wynn, Robert Smith, Alfred Drake, Tommy Wonder, Richard Smart, Frances Comstock, Kathryn Kimber, Austina McDonnell, William Archibald, Willard Gary, Norton Dean
The revue was presented in two acts.

Sketches and Musical Numbers

Act One: "The Show's the Thing" (sketch) (The Patient: Keenan Wynn; The Nurse: Brenda Forbes; A Visitor: Eve Arden; Other Visitors: Austina McDonnell, Frances Comstock, Nadine Gae, Eunice Healey, Betty Hutton, Kathryn Kimber, William Archibald, Alfred Drake, Willard Gary, Robert Smith, Tommy Wonder; The Doctor: Richard Smart; The New Arrival: Richard Haydn); "The Guess-It Hour" (sketch) (Radio Announcer: Robert Smith; Assistant Announcer: Richard Smart; Clifton Sharp: Alfred Drake; Bessie Bee Keesee: Frances Comstock; Mrs. Lilly Higgens: Brenda Forbes; George T. Barnswallow: Keenan Wynn); "Calypso Joe" (song/dance) (Betty Hutton; danced by Nadine Gae, Willard Gary, Eunice Healey, and Tommy Wonder; Calypso Joe: William Archibald); "This 'Merry' Christmas" (song) (Brenda Forbes); "The Age of Innocence" (sketch by Richard Haydn) (Aunt Lucy: Frances Comstock; Betty: Betty Hutton; First Scout: Robert Smith; Second Scout: Tommy Wonder; The Scout from Over-Seas: Richard Haydn); "That Terrible Tune" (song) (Robert Smith, Willard Gary, Eunice Healey, Tommy Wonder, and Richard Smart; danced by Eunice Healey); "Destry Has Ridden Again" (sketch) (Director: Keenan Wynn; Assistant Director: William Archibald; Cameraman: Robert Smith; Piano Player: Alfred Drake; Una: Kathryn Kimber; Destry: Norton Dean; A Maid: Austina McDonnell; Make-Up Expert: Richard Smart; Marlene: Eve Arden); "How High the Moon" (song) (Frances Comstock, Alfred Drake; An Air Raid Warden: Dean Norton; A "Lady" of the Town: Kathryn Kimber; A Diplomat: Richard Smart; A Young Girl: Austina McDonnell; An Aviator: Robert Smith; sequence includes The Costermongers: Eunice Healey and Tommy Wonder and "Danse Macabre," danced by Nadine Gae and William Archibald); "Painless Distraction" (sketch) (Dr. Fifer: Keenan Wynn; Miss Smith: Austina McDonnell; Mrs. Bullock: Eve Arden); "A House with a Little Red Barn" (song/dance) (Kathryn Kimber, Richard Smart; "swung" by Betty Hutton and Robert Smith and "danced" by "Soft Shoe" Nadine Gae and "Hot Foot" Tommy Wonder); "Cookery" (sketch by Richard Haydn) (Introduction: Keenan Wynn; Mr. Carp: Richard Haydn); "The All-Girl Band" (song) (Alfred Drake, with William Archibald, Willard Gary, Dean Norton, Richard Smart, Robert Smith, Tommy Wonder, and Keenan Wynn; The Owner of the Band: Keenan Wynn; The Leader of the Band: Eve Arden; Members of the International All-Girl Band—Miss Hungary: Frances Comstock; Miss American Indian: Nadine Gae; Miss Norway: Kathryn Kimber; Miss France: Austina McDonnell; Miss England: Brenda Forbes; Miss Ireland: Betty Hutton; Miss Scotland: Eunice Healey; The Mayor: Richard Haydn)

Act Two: "Where Do You Get Your Greens?" (sketch) (The Man in the Stocks: Richard Haydn; Tinker: Richard Smart; Tailor: William Archibald; Soldier: Robert Smith; Sailor: Tommy Wonder; Rich Man: Alfred Drake; The King: Keenan Wynn; Mistress Nell: Eunice Healey; The Cries of London—sung by "Sweet Lavender": Frances Comstock; "Cherry Ripe": Kathryn Kimber; "Strawberries": Austina McDonnell); "Little Miss Muffett" (song) (Little Miss Muffett: Betty Hutton; The Spider: Keenan Wynn); "To a Skylark" (sketch) (Adele: Nadine Gae; Mrs. Brewster: Brenda Forbes; Miss Torrence: Eve Arden; Tony: Alfred Drake); "At Last It's Love" (song/dance) (Kathryn Kimber, Richard Smart; Make-Believe Ballroom Dancers: Austina McDonnell, Nadine Gae, Eunice Healey, Betty Hutton, William Archibald, Alfred Drake, Robert Smith, Tommy Wonder; The Lady of the Favors: Frances Comstock; The Late-Comer: Willard Gary; sequence includes "The Jitter Dance," danced by Betty Hutton and Tommy Wonder, and "Waltz Variation," danced by Tommy Wonder [and uncredited partner]); "Song of Spain" (song) (The Infanta: Brenda Forbes; Courtiers: Frances Comstock, Richard Haydn); "Fool for Luck"(song/dance) (Kathryn Kimber, Robert Smith, Betty Hutton; danced by Nadine Gae and Willard Gary, and by Eunice Healey and Tommy Wonder); "Out of This World" (sketch) (Herbert: Richard Haydn; Miss Caruthers: Eve Arden; Madame Charlotte: Brenda Forbes); "Good Night, Mrs. Astor" (song) (Entire Company)

The intimate *Two for the Show* was the second of three title-connected revues with sketches and lyrics by Nancy Hamilton and music by Morgan Lewis. *One for the Money* had opened in 1939, and **Three to Make Ready** premiered in 1946. The program cover for *Two for the Show* listed the titles *One for the Money*, *Two for the Show*, and **Three to Make Ready**, as well as *And Four to Go*, but the series came to a halt after the third offering.

Two for the Show was a reunion for many of the participants of the earlier revue. It too was produced by Gertrude Macy and Stanley Gilkey (*One for the Money* was also coproduced by Robert F. Cutler), and like the first show it was devised, staged, and lighted by John Murray Anderson, choreographed by Robert Alton, designed by Raoul Pene du Bois, conducted by Ray Kavanagh, and opened at the Booth Theatre. Seven cast members from the first revue (Brenda Forbes, Frances Comstock, Alfred Drake, Robert Smith, Nadine Gae, William Archibald, and Keenan Wynn) joined the second production (others in the cast of *One for the Money* were Gene Kelly and sketch writer and lyricist Nancy Hamilton). *One* opened on February 4, 1939, and played for 132 performances, and *Two* opened almost exactly a year later (February 8, 1940) and ran for 124.

Three to Make Ready opened at the Adelphi Theatre on March 7, 1946, and had 327 showings; Gilkey returned as one of the producers, and was joined by Barbara Payne; again, the revue was directed by John Murray Anderson, and Brenda Forbes paid a third visit to the series. Others in the cast were Ray Bolger, Gordon MacRae, Bibi Osterwald, Harold Lang, Arthur Godfrey, and Carleton Carpenter.

Two for the Show offered a spoof of Gertrude Lawrence in her current hit play *Skylark*; titled "To a Skylark," Eve Arden was Miss Torrence. Another sketch kidded the popular film *Destry Rides Again*; as "Destry Has Ridden Again," Arden took on another legend, this time Marlene Dietrich. Betty Hutton's song "Little Miss Muffett" found her in pinafore, pantalets, and slippers; but here was no demure nursery-rhyme character: according to the lyric, when Hutton's Muffett encounters the spider (Keenan Wynn) she hits, bites, knicks, kicks, mars, scars, punches, crunches, and frightens him away (the stage directions noted that by the end of the song she has "literally mopped up the floor with him"). And the most enduring song from any of the *One-Two-Three* revues was the ethereal ballad "How High the Moon," sung by Alfred Drake and Frances Comstock in a sequence that took place during a London blackout. The song quickly achieved standard status, and in the 1950s became a hit all over again when it was recorded by Les Paul and Mary Ford. Another highlight of the evening was British monologist Richard Haydn, who in one sketch appeared as his popular character Mr. Carp and gravely lectured on the art of "Cookery" (he spoke of titillating the jaded palate with culinary cunning in the kitchen). In the 1939 revue *Set to Music*, Haydn's Carp dealt with the subject of fish ("Fish Mimicry"). The evening also offered jibes at George S. Kaufman, Jeanette MacDonald, and dental offices, various songs looked at all-girl bands and calypso music, and one dance sequence contrasted the jitterbug and the waltz.

The critics were generally pleased with the revue. Brooks Atkinson in the *New York Times* liked the "bright" score, but noted the sketches were "more clever than entertaining"; he praised the cast, and singled out Betty Hutton, who danced like a "mad sprite" and "sang breathlessly as though she enjoyed it." Richard Watts in the *New York Herald Tribune* said those who liked *One for the Money* would welcome its successor; he praised "How High the Moon," and while he enjoyed the "noisy and excitable" Hutton, he suggested she was "a little-goes-a-long-way girl."

Sidney Whipple in the *New York World-Telegram* felt the revue was "pleasant" enough, and said Betty Hutton was "the real discovery of the evening." Like the other critics, he was also taken with Brenda Forbes's skewed sense of the ridiculous, especially in her songs "This 'Merry' Christmas" (in which she portrayed a grumpy ornament on a Christmas tree) and "Song of Spain" (in which she played a sour Infanta). Burns Mantle in the *New York Daily News* praised the evening's "spirit and good taste" and liked the cast, especially the "riotous" Betty Hutton (but cautioned that "over-stimulated vanity is bad for talented youngsters").

Richard Lockridge in the *New York Sun* liked the "nice" revue with its "pleasant" score and the occasional "gay explosions" of Betty Hutton. Wilella Waldorf in the *New York Post* said the evening was a "considerable improvement" over *One for the Money* and noted the "often downright hilarious" show avoided the "faintly amateurish, afternoon-at-a-woman's-club quality" of the first revue. She hoped the series would become a Broadway annual, and said she'd be happy to sit through the show again (and would especially look forward to the sketch about Gertrude Lawrence).

During the tryout, the sketch "The French Lesson" and two monologues ("There's Been a Slump" for Richard Haydn and "Last Thursday" for Keenan Wynn) were dropped. "The French Lesson" seems to have been later revised as "The Russian Lesson" and was performed in **Three to Make Ready**.

In 1952, a softcover edition published by Samuel French offered sketch and song highlights from *One for the Money*, *Two for the Show*, and **Three to Make Ready**. Titled *Three to One*, the collection included five songs ("How High the Moon," "Calypso Joe," "Fool for Luck," "Little Miss Muffett," and "A House with a Little Red Barn") and one sketch ("To a Skylark") from *Two for the Show*. "How High the Moon" is included in Kaye Ballard's collection *The Ladies Who Wrote the Lyrics* (Painted Smiles LP # PSCD-1334); the standard has of course been widely recorded, and as noted above it again became a hit with Les Paul and Mary Ford's version during the early 1950s.

On January 13, 1972, the Equity Library Theatre presented the rather awkwardly titled *One for the Money Etc.*, an evening of highlights from the three revues. It later transferred Off Broadway to the Eastside Playhouse, where it opened on May 24, 1972, for twenty-three performances (the cast included Georgia Engel, Pat Lysinger, and Jess Richards). Numbers in the revue which had first been performed in *Two for the Show* were "The Guess-It Hour," "A Little House with a Red Barn," "How High the Moon," and "Goodnight, Mrs. Astor." In reviewing the production, Howard Thompson in the *New York Times* was glad the material hadn't been updated (he rhetorically asked if the evening was "square," and his answer was "You bet!").

With *Two for the Show*, Alfred Drake and Betty Hutton were on the brink of stardom. As the decade progressed, he starred in four musicals (**Oklahoma!**, **Sing Out, Sweet Land!**, **Beggar's Holiday**, and **Kiss Me, Kate**) and she was later a featured player in **Panama Hattie** (and from there became one of the most popular Hollywood personalities of the 1940s and early 1950s). Keenan Wynn (Ed Wynn's son) achieved solid second-banana status in films, and William Archibald wrote the book and lyrics for the exquisite score of *The Crystal Heart* (London, 1957; New York [Off Broadway], 1960), with music by Baldwin Bergersen (the two also collaborated on the 1945 Broadway musical **Carib Song** and the musical *Rosa*, which was presented in a showcase production in New York during 1978). Archibald also wrote the intriguing and stylized 1961 Off-Broadway drama *The Cantilevered Terrace*.

Eve Arden was already an established name, and over the years solidified her career as a wise-cracking comedienne in film and television. During the run of *Two for the Show*, Bill Johnson succeeded Richard Smart. Although he never became a household name, Johnson enjoyed a distinguished career on Broadway as the leading man in Cole Porter's **Something for the Boys** (with Ethel Merman, he introduced "Hey, Good Lookin'"), Alan Jay Lerner and Frederick Loewe's **The Day before Spring** ("God's Green World"), and Richard Rodgers and Oscar Hammerstein II's *Pipe Dream* (1955; as Doc, he introduced "All at Once You Love Her"). In 1947 he created the role of Frank Butler (opposite Dolores Gray) for the London premiere of Irving Berlin's **Annie Get Your Gun**, and in 1951 re-created Alfred Drake's role of Fred/Petruchio (opposite Patricia Morison) for the original London production of **Kiss Me, Kate**. He took on another role created by Drake when he appeared as Hajj in the national tour of *Kismet*. Johnson also had a leading role in Vernon Duke and John La Touche's Eddie Cantor vehicle **Banjo Eyes** (where he introduced "Not a Care in the World"). In late 1940, he appeared in the flop revue **All in Fun**; depending on which of the two opening night programs are referenced, he either did or did not appear as one of the featured players who introduced "It's a Big, Wide Wonderful World." Johnson was married to actress Shirl Conway, who brightened the 1955 musical *Plain and Fancy* as the wise-cracking New Yorker who visits Amish country. Sadly, Johnson died of a heart attack in 1957 at the age of forty-one, and four months after his death his twenty-four-year-old *Pipe Dream* costar Judy Tyler and her husband were killed in an automobile accident during their honeymoon.

REUNION IN NEW YORK

"A NEW MUSICAL REVUE" / "AN INTIMATE MUSICAL REVUE"

Theatre: Little Theatre
Opening Date: February 21, 1940; *Closing Date*: May 4, 1940
Performances: 89
Sketches: Richard Alma, Karl Don, David Greggory, Richard Holden, Hans Lefebre, Myron Mahler, Lothar Metzl, and Werner Michel
Lyrics: Peter Barry, Dorothy Fields, David Greggory, Milton Hindus, Lothar Metzl, Werner Michel, Jura Soyfer, and Auguste Spectorsky
Music: Peter Barry, Georges Bizet, Berenece Kazounoff, Fritz Kreisler, Werner Michel, and Andre Singer
Direction: Production "staged" by Herbert Berghof and Ezra Stone (production "supervised" by Ezra Stone and Marc Daniels); *Producer*: The American Viennese Group, Inc.; *Choreography*: Lotte Goslar; *Scenery*: Harry Horner; *Costumes*: Lester Polakov; *Lighting*: Uncredited; *Musical Direction*: Uncredited
Cast: Klaus Brill, Nelly Franck, Nell Hyrt, Vilma Kurer, Paul Lindenberg, Fred Lorenz, Katherine Mattern, Walter Martin, Elisabeth Neumann, Maria Pichler, Henry Peever, Lothar Rewalt, Edgar Vincent, Lotte Goslar, Annie Desser, Charlotte Krauss, Maria Temple, Leo Weith, Herbert Berghof, Anthony Scott, Leisl Paul, Herman Walter, Emery Gondor, Peter Koch; Orchestra: Hans Herberth (Piano), George Heinz (Piano), Bert Silving (Violin), Stanley Forbes (Accordion)
The revue was presented in two acts.

Sketches and Musical Numbers

Act One: "Hereinspaziert" (Host: Leo Weith; Hostess: Leisl Paul; Waiter: Anthony Scott; Salami Man: Herman Walter; Waitress: Annie Desser; Hat-Check Girl: Charlotte Krauss; Violinist: Bert Silving; Cartoonist: Emery Gondor; Lady: Maria Temple; Guide: Peter Koch); "At the Rail" (sketch and lyrics by Lothar Metzl and Werner Michel, music by Werner Michel) (The Viennese Group: Klaus Brill, Nelly Franck, Nell Hyrt, Vilma Kurer, Paul Lindenberg, Fred Lorenz, Katherine Mattern, Walter Martin, Elisabeth Neumann, Maria Pichler, Henry Peever, Lothar Rewalt, Edgar Vincent); "English in Six Easy Lessons" (sketch by Lothar Metzl and Werner Michel) (The Stranger: Fred Lorenz; Customs Officer: Henry Peever; Hotel Secretary: Nelly Franck; Bell-Boy: Klaus Brill; Detective: Lothar Rewalt; Passenger: Edgar Vincent; Girl in Park: Maria Pichler; Customer in Cafeteria: Paul Lindenberg; Passerby: Walter Martin); "Woodsprite" (dance) (Lotte Goslar); "Borderline" (sketch by Richard Alma, Lothar Metzl, and Werner Michel) (Paul: Paul Lindenberg; Milina: Maria Pichler; Officer of Pushia: Henry Peever; Officer of Kushia: Lothar Rewalt; Carol: Klaus Brill); "Stars in Your Eyes" (lyric by Dorothy Fields, music by Fritz Kreisler) (Charlotte Krauss); "Keep Laughing" (lyric and music by Lothar Metzl and Werner Michel) (Katherine Mattern, Walter Martin); "Where Is My Homeland?" (German lyric by Lothar Metzl, English lyric by Werner Michel and Auguste Spectorsky, music by Andre Singer) (Vilma Kurer, Maria Pichler, Nelly Franck); "The Pillmaker" (Fred Lorenz); "Waltz Mania" (dance) (Lotte Goslar); "Oratorium Salzburgiensis" (sketch and lyric by Lothar Menzl and Wernet Michel, music by Andre Singer; a program note thanked Edwin Kalser for the "valuable suggestions" he contributed to the number) (Narrator: Edgar Vincent; Mayor of Salzburg: Henry Peever; Cats: Nelly Franck, Elisabeth Neumann; The New Mayor: Paul Lindenberg; Trio: Vilma Kurer, Katherine Mattern, Henry Peever; Others: Klaus Brill, Nell Hyrt, Fred Lorenz, Walter Martin, Lothar Rewalt, Anthony Scott, Leo Weith)
Act Two: "Blitz-Carmen" (sketch and lyrics by Lothar Metzl and Werner Michel, with Richard Holden and Hans Lefebre, music by Georges Bizet arranged by Andre Singer) (Don Jose: Edgar Vincent; A Couple: Fred Lorenz, Charlotte Krauss; Carmen: Katherine Mattern; Two-Ton Tony of New Jersey: Paul Lindenberg; Two Magistrates: Walter Martin, Lothar Rewalt; The District Attorney: Henry Peever); "Modern Art" (sketch by Carl Don and Myron Mahler) (Guides: Vilma Kurer, Fred Lorenz); "Dachau" (German lyric by Jura Soyfer, English lyric by Milton Hindus, music by Andre Singer) (Herbert Berghof); "A Character in Search of a Character" (sketch and lyric by David Greggory, music by Berenece Kazounoff) (The Writer: Henry Peever; The Character: Vilma Kurer); "Chorus Girls" (a program note thanked Benny Goodman for the musical arrangement for this number) (Lotte Goslar, Nell Hyrt); "Shooting Gallery" (lyric by Lothar

Metzl and Werner Michel, music by Andre Singer) (Cupid: Nelly Franck; Franz: Edgar Vincent; Marie: Vilma Kurer; Baron Kalafati: Henry Peever; Track Walker: Fred Lorenz); "The Only Time of Day" (lyric by Richard Holden and Lothar Metzl, music by Andre Singer) (Paul Lindenberg); "I'm Going Crazy with Strauss" (lyric and music by Peter Barry and Werner Michel) (Vilma Kurer); "Vienna-Berlin Express" (based on an old Viennese folk tale) (Travelers: Paul Lindenberg, Fred Lorenz; An Officer: Walter Martin); "Ain't Love Awful?" (sketch by David Greggory) (Lieutenant: Lothar Rewalt; The Girls: Vilma Kurer, Katherine Mattern, Maria Pichler; The Boys: Paul Lindenberg, Fred Lorenz, Edgar Vincent; General: Walter Martin); "The Spinster" (dance) (Lotte Goslar); "A Party with Our Memories" (sketch and lyrics by Lothar Metzl and Werner Michel, music by Werner Michel) (Company)

The modest revue *Reunion in New York* was a sequel of sorts to *From Vienna*, which had opened at the Music Box Theatre on June 20, 1939, for seventy-nine performances. Both revues were by Austrian expatriates (theatre writers and performers all) who had left Europe because of the war. They were now settled in New York, and their revues looked back on the old life of Vienna and Europe and also looked forward to, and commented upon, life in the United States.

From Vienna was produced by The Refugee Artists Group, and by the time of the opening of *Reunion in New York* the company had changed its name to The American Viennese Group, Inc. Many of the performers and writers from the first revue participated in the second (there were only two carry-over numbers: *From Vienna*'s "Opening" sequence was retitled "At the Rail" for *Reunion*, and "English in Six Easy Lessons" was also retained).

The revue officially began at approximately 8:45 each evening, but about thirty minutes before the first act started, an informal sequence ("Hereinspaziert") took place in a Viennese wine garden. The cast members and the four-piece orchestra performed various songs, and a few in the cast joined the audience and handed out favors of candy (the sequence was eventually dropped).

The revue occasionally looked back on a nostalgic Old Vienna ("Where Is My Homeland?") and present-day Europe ("Dachau" as well as the matter of a constantly shifting "Borderline"), but in traditional-revue fashion spoofed theatre (William Saroyan was kidded in the sketch "A Character in Search of a Character"); movies (the current film *Dr. Ehrlich's Magic Bullet* became "Dr. Munison's Magic Handkerchief," which was added during the run); opera ("Blitz-Carmen" beat Oscar Hammerstein II's modern-day version of Bizet's opera by almost four years; here, Don José is a New York cop and Carmen a cigarette girl in a New York club); and interpretive dancing (Lotte Goslar's send-ups were "Woodsprite," "Waltz Mania," and "The Spinster"). There was also a comic look at new citizens learning to cope with English ("English in Six Easy Lessons"), and an amusing look at Picasso and "Modern Art."

Wilella Waldorf in the *New York Post* felt that the material was generally not up to the talents of the company, but she noted things began to pick up during the second act. She singled out the "lament" of "Where Is My Homeland?" and the "brash Broadway manner" of the Saroyan spoof. George Ross in the *New York World-Telegram* found the evening an "uneven potpourri," and felt the material and the players were better when they gazed back at the old world ("Broadway banter is not their idiom"); he enjoyed "Oratorium Salzburgiensis," which he described as a "lively spoof on the fate of Salzberg after the Germans clattered over the cobblestones."

Brooks Atkinson in the *New York Times* lamented that the world was "disintegrating," but he praised the Viennese expatriates for providing "consolation." He felt the revue was "more at home" than *From Vienna*, and the appropriately named Little Theatre was a more intimate venue than the Music Box; but overall the material was "more informal than brilliant." But he liked the players and wished them all "good luck." Richard Watts in the *New York Herald Tribune* suggested the evening was best enjoyed for its "informality, its spirit and its courage, rather than for any great excellence in its numbers." Burns Mantle in the *New York Daily News* enjoyed the "grotesquerie" of Lotte Goslar's interpretive dances, the "amusing account of the Saroyan ego," and thought there would be a "very numerous public" for the revue.

During the run, "Hereinspaziert" and "Stars in My Eyes" were dropped. The latter was replaced by "A Party with Our Memories," which had heretofore been performed during the finale and was now titled "Party with My Memories" (like "Stars," "Party" was performed by Charlotte Krauss). When "Party" was moved to the first act, a new finale was added ("After the Show," lyric by Lothar Metzl and Werner Michel, music by Werner Michel). "Vienna-Berlin Express" may have been rewritten, as later programs identified it as "Vienna-Berlin Express II."

There were two other numbers added during the run: "Dr. Munison's Magic Handkerchief" (sketch and lyric by Lothar Metzl and Werner Michel, music by Werner Michel) (Speaker: Walter Martin; Two Patients: Klaus Brill, Edgar Vincent; Dr. Edward G. Munison: Fred Lorenz; Mrs. Munison: Charlotte Kraus; Louis Pasteur: Henry Peever; Emile Zola: Leo Weth; Dr. Paul Ehrlich: Paul Lindenberg); and "America as She Is Spoke" (lyric by Karl Don and Werner Michel, music by Werner Michel) (sung by Fred Lorenz). "Dr. Munson's Magic Handkerchief" seems to have been a parody of three popular biographical films, *Dr. Ehrlich's Magic Bullet* (1940), *The Life of Emile Zola* (1939), and *The Story of Louis Pasteur* (1936).

THEATRE OF THE PICCOLI

Theatre: Majestic Theatre
Opening Date: March 21, 1940; *Closing Date*: April 6, 1940
Performances: 30
Direction: Vittorio Podrecca; *Producer*: Cheryl Crawford; *Scenery*: Bruno Angoletta; *Costumes*: Caramba of
    Scala Theatre Department, Milan; *Lighting*: Uncredited; *Musical Direction*: Angelo Canarutto
Cast: Puppeteers—Gorno, Braga, Donati, Forgioli, Possidoni, Fefe, Borda, Gamonet, and Ansaldo; Singers—
    Augusto Galli (Baritone), Rosa Giovonelli, Agostino Guidi (Tenor), Emma Lattuada (Soprano), Lia Po-
    drecca (Coloratura Soprano), Antonio Quaglia (Tenor), Mario Serangeli (Baritone), Dario Zani (Baritone),
    Alma Zatti (Soprano), and Irma Zappata (Soprano)
The revue was presented in two acts.

Musical Sequences

Act One: Overture to *L'italiana in Algeri* (music by Gioachino Rossini) (Orchestra); Prologue (Vittorio Po-
    drecca); The Piccoli Jazz Band; Tallerino and Canellone (Acrobats); *Cinderella* (the opera *Cendrillon*,
    music by Jules Massenet and libretto by Henri Cain; a version in four scenes, taking place in Cinderella's
    Home, The King's Palace, The Enchanted Coach, and The Magic Tree [all scenes designed by Grassi
    and Lefay]) (Puppet Voices—Cinderella: Emma Lattuada; Noemi: Alma Zatti; The Fairy: Lia Podrecca;
    Pandolfo: Dario Zani; Madame Haltiere: Irma Zappata; Dorothy: Rosa Giovonelli; The Prince Charming:
    Antonio Quaglia; The King: Mario Serangeli); Bil-Bal-Bul (Flying Trapeze Artist); Clowns with Heads and
    Without; Latin American Revue: (a) "Rancherita"(Argentine music by Buerrero and Lomuto); (b) "Mex-
    ico" ("Estrellita," music by Ponce; "The Jarabe Tapatio" [a popular dance]; (c) "Cuban Nights" ("Amor de
    mi bohio," music by Brito; "Rhumba" ["Congo Alegre"], music by Matamoros)
Act Two: "Waltztime" (music by Franz Schubert and Johann Strauss): (a) "Wine and Song"; (b) "Interlude"; (c)
    "The Voice of Spring" (Lia Podrecca); (d) Finale; "Men, Birds and Monkeys"; Aria from *Pagliacci* (music
    and words by Ruggero Leoncavallo) (Agostino Guidi); "Hollywood Party" (Impersonations); "The Concert
    Party" (music by Franz Liszt and other composers) (The Piccoli Pianist); Specialty: "Miss Skinny Lee"
    (Lia Podrecca)

Theatre of the Piccoli was a puppet revue, here making its fourth (and final) Broadway visit. Vittorio Podrecca's troupe of almost life-sized puppets was a bright addition to the season, and like the cast members of
Reunion in New York Podrecca was something of an émigré himself because he was forced to flee his homeland of Italy once the war began. As a result, he, his puppets, and his fellow puppeteers, singers, and musicians
performed on the stages of North and South America.

The evening began with the overture of Rossini's *L'italiana in Algeri*, which was followed by Podrecca,
who gave a brief curtain speech in "brokissimo" English. And then his puppets took over. (Besides the puppeteers, there were ten off-stage performers who were the speaking and singing voices of the puppets.)

The puppets offered their own version of Jules Massenet's opera *Cinderella* (replete with scenes depicting Cinderella's cottage, the castle, a stately carriage, and a magical forest; the sequence was like "a dream
out of Walt Disney," noted Louis Biancolli in the *New York World-Telegram*, and indeed Disney created his
own *Cinderella* a few years later with the release of his classic 1950 cartoon film); a torrid Latin American
rhumba (Brooks Atkinson in the *New York Times* remarked that the lady rhumba dancer was almost "too hot

to handle," thought the police might have to step in and stop the performance, and suggested she be packed in asbestos during the company's between-engagement travels); a jazz band; two acrobats (Biancolli said one of them coasted "in mid-air like a seagull"); Bil-Bal-Bul (a trapeze artist who appeared in all four New York productions); couples waltzing to Strauss ("with an ease worthy" of Arthur Murray graduates, according to John Mason Brown in the *New York Post*); a puppet Pagliacci; and an astounding danse macabre in which four clown puppets were dismembered as their heads and limbs suddenly flew apart, and, just as quickly, were re-assembled. There were also puppet impersonations of Charlie Chaplin, Greta Garbo, Mae West, Mickey Mouse, and the Three Marx Brothers (all the brothers' heads shared the same body).

Perhaps the most controversial sequence occurred during "Men, Birds and Monkeys" in which three black male puppets taught birds and monkeys how to dance. Burns Mantle in the *New York Daily News* stated that "colored brothers are sensitive about such contrasts" and suggested the scene might work better with three white dancing puppets. Biancolli found the number "satiric . . . showing evolution in reverse."

The critics agreed that the evening's highlight was a visit from the Piccoli Pianist, who had last been seen during the troupe's 1934 visit. Here was an irascible and temperamental master of the keyboard who clearly doesn't suffer bad singers gladly. Moreover, he acknowledges his audience with "humble grace" (per Mantle), tosses back his coat-tails, flips through his sheet music, deftly plays the piano, sometimes beats his knees against the instrument if the music is jazzy, and even occasionally falls asleep as he's playing. Atkinson said the character was a "masterpiece . . . a perfect puppet . . . mechanical at heart, he exudes personality." Richard Watts in the *New York Herald Tribune* said the pianist was the "best" performer in the show, for here was the "peak" of the evening in both "ingenuity and humor . . . an act to treasure."

Although the critics found much to like in the evening, a few had occasional reservations. Atkinson felt the show was "laboriously musical" and noted puppets were at their best satirizing humans and not the art of humans (such as opera). And Richard Lockridge in the *New York Sun* suggested the entertainment would have been more effective had it been shortened to one hour. While John Mason Brown in the *New York Post* felt the sketches could have been "more diversified" and "more sharply satiric," he nonetheless praised the "ingratiating" and "skillful" revue. As for puppet shows, Watts said he could "take them or leave them" but admitted there was "no doubt" Podrecca was "at the head of his ancient and honored profession."

Podrecca's first Piccoli visit was on September 10, 1923, when *The Marionette Players* opened at the Fulton Theatre for sixteen performances. *The Piccoli of Vittorio Podrecca* opened at the Lyric Theatre on December 22, 1932, for 141 performances, and with the same title opened at the Hudson Theatre on January 8, 1934, for forty-five performances.

HIGHER AND HIGHER
"RODGERS AND HART'S NEW MUSICAL COMEDY"

Theatre: Shubert Theatre
Opening Date: April 4, 1940; *Closing Date*: August 24, 1940
Performances: 108
Book: Gladys Hurlbut and Joshua Logan
Lyrics: Lorenz Hart
Music: Richard Rodgers
Based on an idea by Irvin Pincus.
Direction: Joshua Logan; *Producer*: Dwight Deere Wiman; *Choreography*: Robert Alton; *Scenery*: Jo Mielziner; *Costumes*: Lucinda Ballard; *Lighting*: Uncredited; *Musical Direction*: Al Goodman
Cast: Eva Condon (Hilda O'Brien), Robert Chisholm (Byng), Billie Worth (Dottie), Hilda Spong (Miss Whiffen), *Shirley Ross* (Sandy Moore), *Jack Haley* (Zachary Ash), Lee Dixon (Mike O'Brien), *Marta Eggerth* (Minnie Sorenson; *Note*: Some sources give her name as Marta Eggert, but Eggerth is the correct spelling.), Marie Louise Quevli (Scullery Maid), Gloria Hope (Nursemaid), Hollace Shaw (Nurseman), Jane Richardson (Nursemaid), Robert Rounseville (Soda Jerker, Truckman), Marie Nash (Ladies' Maid), Robert Shanley (First Cop), Joe Scandur (Cop, Truckman), Richard Moore (Cop), Carl Trees (Footman), Leif Erickson (Patrick O'Toole), Janet Fox (Ellen), Fin Olsen (Snorri), Sharkey (the seal, who portrayed himself), Frederic Nay (Handyman, Coachman), Ted Adair (Cat), Lyda Sue (Frog), Sigrid Dagnie (Bat), Joseph Granville (Gorilla), Jane Ball (Purity); Singing Girls: Kay Duncan, Gloria Hope, Marie Nash, Marie Louise Quevli,

Jane Richardson, Hollace Shaw; Singing Boys: William Geery, Joseph Granville, Richard Moore, Robert Rounseville, Joe Scandur, Robert Shanley; Specialty Girls: June Allyson, Irene Austin, Jane Ball, Ronnie Cunningham, Sigrid Dagnie, Eleanor Eberle, Vera-Ellen, Miriam Franklin, Marguerite James, Kay Picture, Lyda Sue; Specialty Boys: Ted Adair, Cliff Ferre, Bunnie Hightower, Louis Hightower, Michael Moore, Frederic Nay, Burton Pierce, Harry Rogue, Jack Seymour, Billy (William) Skipper Jr., Carl Trees
The action takes place in New York City.
The musical was presented in two acts.

Musical Numbers

Act One: Untitled Opening Dance (Dancers); "A Barking Baby Never Bites" (Jack Haley, Shirley Ross); "From Another World" (Marta Eggerth, Jack Haley, Shirley Ross, Eva Condon, Robert Chisholm, Company); "Morning's at Seven" (Lee Dixon, Billie Worth, Ensemble); "Nothing But You" (Marta Eggerth, Leif Erickson, Singers); "Disgustingly Rich" (Jack Haley, Shirley Ross, Lee Dixon, Eva Condon, Robert Chisholm, Hilda Spong, Billie Worth, Ensemble)

Act Two: "Blue Monday" (Robert Chisholm, Hollace Shaw, Marie Louise Quevli, Marie Nash, Ensemble); "Ev'ry Sunday Afternoon" (Marta Eggerth, Leif Erickson); "Lovely Day for a Murder" (Lee Dixon, Billie Worth, Ensemble); "How's Your Health?" (Jack Haley, Marta Eggerth, Leif Erickson); "It Never Entered My Mind" (Shirley Ross); "I'm Afraid" (Jack Haley, Shirley Ross, *Higher and Higher* Specialty Girls and Boys); "I'm Afraid" (development) (Shirley Ross, Janet Fox, Lee Dixon, Robert Chisholm, Eva Condon, Robert Shanley, Company); Finale (Entire Company)

Early in the 1939–1940 theatre season, Richard Rodgers and Lorenz Hart enjoyed a hit with their college football musical *Too Many Girls*, which garnered enthusiastic reviews and ran for 249 performances. However, *Higher and Higher*, their second musical of the season, received generally indifferent notices and in two slightly separated engagements managed just 108 showings. But both musicals enjoyed film versions (*Too Many Girls* received the more faithful adaptation), and each show boasted a song which became a standard (*Too Many Girls* offered the wistful "I Didn't Know What Time It Was" and *Higher and Higher* the sardonic torch song "It Never Entered My Mind"). Later in 1940, Rodgers and Hart bounced back with one of their longest-running hits, the ground-breaking **Pal Joey**.

Higher and Higher opened on April 4, 1940, and closed on June 15, for a total of eighty-four performances. After a summer hiatus of almost two months, the musical reopened on August 5 and then closed permanently on August 24, for a run of twenty-four more performances. For the second engagement, there was one major cast change when heretofore supporting player Marie Nash succeeded Marta Eggerth.

Although the musical had a relatively short run, the critics were generally pleased with the production, the cast, the choreography, the decor (which included two turntables, at least one of which rose above the stage and allowed Robert Alton's dancers to strut their stuff higher and higher), and the score (the critics singled out a total of seven of the score's eleven songs). But the evening's highest honors went to Sharkey, a show-stopping seal and a ham of the first order. During a second-act scene in the haunted quarters of a Manhattan mansion, Sharkey and Jack Haley indulged in comic folderol that centered on the former's particular delight in sneaking up on human types and nipping them by the literal seat of their pants. And, of course, Sharkey was not above accepting bribes from cast members when he was offered the occasional piece of succulent fish. So despite praise for the cast, scenery, songs, and dances, the musical had a definite problem: when a trained seal steals the show, that show is in trouble.

The musical played for less than thirteen weeks, but may have shown an ultimate profit when the film rights were sold to RKO (the movie was released in 1944; see below).

The slight plot dealt with the large staff of the wealthy Drake family, whose Manhattan mansion requires butlers, maids, footmen, handymen, coachmen, watchmen, and kitchen help. When the Drakes lose their fortune, their butler, Zachary Ash (Jack Haley), decides in Cinderella fashion to pass off scullery maid Minnie Sorenson (Marta Eggerth) as a debutante, the logic being that a society debutante will be courted by companies to endorse their products and thus her income will pay the staff's salaries. It's also hoped that Minnie will snag a millionaire, whose fortune will also bring in more money to pay the staff and keep the mansion going. But Minnie really loves watchman Patrick O'Toole (Leif Erickson), and so in one way or another things end well with the romantic pairings of Minnie and Patrick, and Zachary and Sandy Moore (Shirley Ross); and hopefully the staff finds financial security and Sharkey always has seafood to dine on.

As for the critics, it was Sharkey who walked, or waddled, away with the honors. Burns Mantle in the *New York Daily News* said the opening night customers were "in stitches" over his antics; Richard Watts in the *New York Herald Tribune* suggested that "Mr. Sharkey" should be called "the United States Marine Corps" because his entrance came along just in time to "save" the evening; John Mason Brown in the *New York Post* said Sharkey was the "Great Seal of the Republic"; Sidney B. Whipple in the *New York World-Telegram* stated the evening's "most hilarious" interlude was Sharkey's appearance (and suggested Sharkey had perhaps learned his trade by "attending burlesque shows too often"); and Richard Lockridge in the *New York Sun* noted that while Jack Haley didn't have to be fed fish, there was a "fine simplicity" in the way Sharkey went "straight to the point." Indeed, Sharkey was well aware that Haley was his stooge, and it was also clear Sharkey knew the details of his contract, including his inalienable right to snack on fish during his big scene.

And choreographer Robert Alton received praise for his dances. Lockridge said they were "ingeniously contrived and beautifully drilled"; Brooks Atkinson in the *New York Times* stated that Alton seemed "to have no end of ideas for stepping, skipping and whirling" and thus offered "some of the most joyous dancing in recent years"; Watts found the choreography "fresh," "imaginative," and "splendid"; Brown noted that Alton staged the dances with "unquestionable verve"; Whipple said the dances were the most "attractive" aspects of the show, noting the "tapping is expert" and the timing "in the more kaleidoscopic patterns is perfect"; and Mantle said the opening sequence (which wasn't listed in the program) offered a dozen couples "breaking through an international waltz" to offer specialty "bits," and this number was "as good as any musical comedy opening that I remember."

The critics were glad to see Haley back on Broadway, and found a lot to like in Broadway newcomers Shirley Ross and Marta Eggerth. Watts said the former contributed to the "good humors" of the evening, Whipple found her "breezy," and Mantle said her stage debut was "promising." Lockridge praised Eggerth, who "sings prettily and romps pleasantly," and Mantle liked her "warm soprano." But Atkinson found her "slightly mannered" and Watts noted she went "coloratura on us from time to time." In fact, Brown suggested she indulged in too many "lingual trills" and Whipple also noted she produced many "meaningless trills" (but said these trills had their compensation because Haley burlesqued them [during the trio "How's Your Health?"]).

Lockridge found the musical "glossy and expert" and Whipple said the evening was "well up" on his list of "preferred" musicals. But there was general grumbling about the evening's slow first act and the long waits between musical numbers. Watts was outright "disappointed" and Brown said the evening was "not a happy one." At least two of the critics quoted the musical's most memorable line: "Yale is the period in a man's life between the time his voice changes and the time be begins selling life insurance." The most curious critical comment was from Atkinson, who stated there was "quite a lot of normal masculinity in the cast."

During the tryout, two songs ("It's Pretty in the City" and "Life! Liberty!") were dropped. The collection *The Complete Lyrics of Lorenz Hart* includes all the songs from the show, including the two cut numbers.

During the run, one program included advertisements of various recordings from the score by Larry Clinton and His Orchestra ("From Another World" and "It Never Entered My Mind"), Leo Reisman and His Orchestra ("Nothing But You" and "Ev'ry Sunday Afternoon"), and Kitty Carlisle and Jessie Smith and His Music Box Orchestra ("Nothing But You" and "Ev'ry Sunday Afternoon"). Happily, Shirley Ross recorded four songs from the musical: "From Another World," "Nothing But You," "Ev'ry Sunday Afternoon," and "It Never Entered My Mind"; these can be heard in the collection *The Ultimate Rodgers & Hart* (Pearl Records CD # GEM-0118).

The cut song "Life! Liberty!" and the standard "It Never Entered My Mind" are included in the collection *The Broadway Musicals of 1940* (Bayview CD # RNBW019). The latter has been frequently recorded, and perhaps Ella Fitzgerald's rendition is the finest and most heartfelt version.

The musical marked a comeback of sorts for Haley, who had been visiting Hollywood for a few years, during which time he created his signature role of the Tin Man in the 1939 film *The Wizard of Oz*. As noted, Marta Eggerth and Shirley Ross made their Broadway debuts in *Higher and Higher*; during the 1940s, the former appeared in the long-running 1943 revival of **The Merry Widow** as well as the 1945 musical **Polonaise**, both with her husband, tenor Jan Kiepura, and Ross had previously appeared in films (with Bob Hope she introduced the standards "Thanks for the Memory" in *The Big Broadcast of 1938* and "Two Sleepy People" in *Thanks for the Memory* [1938]).

In the musical's chorus were up-and-coming June Allyson and Vera-Ellen, both of whom enjoyed popular film careers and in fact made guest appearances in the 1948 MGM Rodgers and Hart tribute *Words and Music*. In the film, Tom Drake portrayed Richard Rodgers and Mickey Rooney was Lorenz Hart; for the lyric of "Zip" from **Pal Joey**, Hart wrote that "Mickey Mouse and Rooney make me sicky," and so one wonders what he would have thought about the casting. Vera-Ellen and *Higher and Higher* cast member Robert Chisholm also enjoyed prominent roles in the 1943 revival of Rodgers and Hart's **A Connecticut Yankee**. Another distinguished cast member was Robert Rounseville, who created the title role in the 1956 classic musical *Candide* and later enjoyed a major role in the original 1965 production of *Man of La Mancha*. Supporting player Lee Dixon later created the role of Will Parker in Richard Rodgers and Oscar Hammerstein II's **Oklahoma!** *Higher and Higher*'s cast also included Hollace Shaw, who earlier in the season had appeared in Jerome Kern and Oscar Hammerstein II's *Very Warm for May*; in that musical, she was one of the original quartet who introduced what is perhaps the loveliest ballad in all musical theatre, "All the Things You Are"; in that musical she was also part of the trio who performed the jaunty "Heaven in My Arms"; and she sang the haunting and ethereal "In the Heart of the Dark."

In 1944, RKO released the film version of *Higher and Higher*, which generally followed the basic plot of the stage production. The movie marked Frank Sinatra's first major film role (he had previously been a vocalist sans dialogue in his first three movies). Jack Haley was also on board, but here his character was named Mike O'Brien; others in the cast were Michele Morgan, Barbara Hale, Leon Errol, Marcy McGuire, Dooley Wilson, Victor Borge, Mary Wickes, Mel Tormé, and Paul and Grace Hartman. The screenplay was by Jay Dratler and Ralph Spence (with additional dialogue by William Bowers and Howard Harris), and the direction by Tim Whelen. Only one song from the Broadway production was retained ("Disgustingly Rich"), and lyricist Harold Adamson and composer Jimmy McHugh provided eight new songs, a number of which became hits for Sinatra: "I Couldn't Sleep a Wink Last Night" (which was nominated for the Best Song Academy Award), "A Lovely Way to Spend an Evening," "The Music Stopped," "I Saw You First," "It's a Most Important Affair," "You're on Your Own," "Today I Am a Debutante," and a title number; Borge also contributed "Minuet in Boogie." The DVD was released by Warner Brothers (# 3000015692).

AMERICAN JUBILEE

Theatre: New York's World's Fair Grounds
Opening Date: May 12, 1940; *Closing Date*: October 2, 1940
Performances: 576 (estimated)
Book and *Lyrics*: Oscar Hammerstein II
Music: Arthur Schwartz
Direction: Leon Leonidoff; *Producer*: Albert Johnson; *Choreography*: Catherine Littlefield; *Scenery*: Albert Johnson; *Costumes*: Lucinda Ballard; *Lighting*: Uncredited; *Choral Direction*: Ken Christie; *Musical Direction*: Don Voorhees
Cast: Lucy Monroe, Ray Middleton, Paul Haakon, Wynn Murray, Gene Markey, Margret Adams, Joe Jackson, The Lime Trio, Harry Meehan, Nellie Durkin; "and an Ensemble of 350" (*Note*: See list of musical numbers for names of individual performers.)
The revue was presented in one act.

Musical Numbers

Prologue: The School Room; Song—"Another New Day" (Teacher: Margret Adams; Children: Lloyd Warren, Walter Kelly, Jeri Anne Raphael, Joan Flicker, Carol Renee, Gerry McMillan, Robert Jackson, Bonnie Baken, Gloria Carey, Marylin Jolie, Beryl Magee, Janet Regan, Billy Saunders, Howard Sherman); (I) *We Like It Over Here* (Tradesmen: Harold Crane, Ben Roberts, Eugene Keith, Donald Campbell, Milton Feher, Jesse Saunders, Andre Renald, Jerome Andrews, Evelyn Mills, Charles Burrows, Paul Wilson, Francis Carpenter, Tony Albert, Philip Gordon, Charles Pinckney, Parker Wilson, Vicki Michak, Charles Duncan, Allan Lee, Gerald Lysley, Ward Tallman, Fred Ardath, William Lane, Carl Clayton, Thomas Cannon, Robert Hauser, May Muth, Jane O'Gorman, Dorothy Calvert, Dolores Flanders, Frances Williams, Geraldine

Hamilton, Sally Billings, Gloria Hart, Erminie Randolph, Xenia Bank, Marjorie Nielson, Elinore Rutherford, Alice George, Anne Courtney, Wilma Simonson, Elise Eckert, Eleanor Brownell, Joyce Doncaster, Marie Fox, Mildred Talbot, Byrtie Ladd, Lucille Werner, Erika Zaranova, Diana Corday; Washington's Foot Guards: J. B. Laster, James Burrell, Sam Adams, Edward Heisler, Carter Farriss, Richard Browning, Wally Berg, Joseph Kendrick, Max Edwards, William Raible, Roy Williams, James Carroll, Bob Evans, Jack Wright, Roger Hill, Paul Kirk Giles, John Russell, Max Benson, Norman Van Emburgh, Frank Taylor, Erik (Eric) Brotherson, Bob Wayne, Tony Caridi, Jack Leslie, Finley Walker, Oscar Catoire, Frank Chamberlin, Ernest McLean, Norman MacKay, Bert Hillner, Henry Williamson, Kendall Crawford, Bruce Hamilton, Walter John, Larry Siegle, Philip Crosbie, Richard Reeves, Roy Johnston, Norman Farrow, James Allison, Leon Frank, John Fulco, Randolph Symonette, Murvyn Vye, Harold Gordon, Walter Searle, Rudy Williams, John Barry; Washington's Horse Guard: Tony Mongiello, Tony Orlando, Joe Brennan, Edgar Stone, Tom Early, Vince Burrell, William Lee, Don Pierce, Bill Kelly, John Ryan, Phil Coleman, Frank Basarab, Frank Godek, Sheldon Tapp, Buddy Baldwin, Babe Courvoisier, Frank Czyz, Vince Ferguson, Tony Madden, Andrew Alecks, Paul Forbes, Cedil Tatum, Lee Timmons, Larry O'Dell, Maynard Blanchard, Robert Gorham; George Washington: George L. Spaulding; Washington's Aides: Harry Meehan, Tony Blair; Guests on the Balcony: Jill Townsend, Nadine Cassel, Leslie Bryan, Mary Joan Punch, Juanita Bredt, Linda Faghn, Evelyn Eckhardt, Edith Vincent, Alice Talton, Mea Francyss, Nedra Harrison, Janice Parmenter, Marian Marvis, Charlotte Lorraine, Dale Preston, Jean Stanton, Carol Ann Brown, Evonne Kummer, Frances King, Bliss Farren, Elenor Moore, Marion Bailey, Marguerite Adams, Vera Divine; Civilians: Julia Sully, Viola Layton, Anna Minot, Helen Price, Janet Palmer, Betty Hull, Genevieve Frizzell, Vicki Michak, Evelyn Mills, Charles Duncan, Rudy Dalson; Song—"We Like It Over Here" (Ray Middleton) and "Flag Drill" (The Littlefield Ballet: Boy Dancers—Milton Feher, Jesse Saunders, Andre Renald, Jerome Andrews, Tony Albert, Philip Gordon, Charles Pinckney, Parker Wilson, William Lane, Carl Clayton, Thomas Cannon, Robert Hauser, Zachary Solov, George Hecht, Michael Kidd, Igor Meller, George Kiddon, Stephen Comfort, Teddy James, William Hecht, William Lang, Joseph Johnson, Leo Senweska, Joseph Bastian, Harry Grissin, Hugh O'Meagher; Girl Dancers—Virginia Rand, Hortense Kahrklin, Mary Heater, Norma Gentner, June Graham, Constance Love, Mary J. Woods, Kathleen McLean, Eleanor Boleyn, Selma Hoffman, Bernice Dollarton, Dorothy Swain, Maude Carroll, Barbara Bernard, Jane Johnstone, Helen Kramer, June MacLaren, Ruth Neslie, Lucille Bremer, Stephanie Cekan, Betty Gour, Patricia Deering, Tina Rigat, Paula Kaye, Luba Matiuk, Eleanor Fairchild, Dolores (Dody) Goodman, Rita Charise, Doris Call, Georgette Lampsi, Jeanette Lea, Louise Girard, Bobbie Howell, Alma Wertley, Joan Hope Lee, Blanche Fields, Kathryn Lozell, Jessie Fullum, Chula Morrow, Joan Patschke, Barbara Steele, Doris Guignet, Josephine McCann, Julie Stewart, Evelyn Foster, Dorothie Littlefield, Audrey Beggs, Betty Clary, Marion Warnes, Pamela Clifford, Janna Perlova; (II) *Union Forever* (Phineas T. Barnum: Jack Howard; Barker: Lee Fredrick); The Lime Trio (dance specialty); Song—"Jenny Lind" (Harry Meehan, The Male Singing Ensemble); Song—"How Can I Ever Be Alone?" (Jenny Lind: Lucy Monroe; Gene Marvey); "Waltz" (The Littlefield Ballet and Paul Haakon); The School Room: (a) Song—"Of the People" (Abraham Lincoln: Ray Middleton); (b) "Torchlight Parade"/ Song—"By the People" (The Male Singing Ensemble); and (c) Song—"For the People" (Ensemble); (III) *The Day Before Yesterday*: (1) Song—"My Bicycle Girl" (Gene Marvey); (2) "Bicycle Routine" (The Littlefield Ballet); (3) Specialty (Joe Jackson); (4) Song—"Struggle Buggy Days" (dance)/"Old-Time Automobile Parade" (Diamond Jim Brady: Tony Blair; Lillian Russell: Irene Christie; The Twenty-Four American Jubilee Beauties: Jill Townsend, Nadine Cassel, Leslie Bryan, Mary Joan Punch, Juanita Bredt, Linda Faghn, Evelyn Eckhardt, Edith Vincent, Alice Talton, Mea Francyss, Nedra Harrison, Janice Parmenter, Marian Marvis, Charlotte Lorraine, Dale Preston, Jean Stanton, Carol Ann Brown, Evonne Kummer, Frances King, Bliss Farren, Elenor Moore, Marion Bailey, Marguerite Adams, Vera Devine; (5) Song—"Tennessee Fish Fry" (May Irwin: Wynn Murray, The American Jubilee Singers); (6) "Cakewalk" (The Littlefield Ballet and Paul Haakon); and (7) "Equestrian Drill" (Teddy Roosevelt and His Rough Riders; Teddy Roosevelt: Fred Ardath); (IV) *Tomorrow* (The President: Ray Middleton); Song—"One in a Million" (during run, apparently replaced with "Who Will It Be?") (Wynn Murray, Harry Meehan, The Littlefield Ballet); Finale: "The Star-Spangled Banner" (lyric by Francis Scott Key, composer unknown) (Lucy Monroe, Entire Company)

The revue *American Jubilee* was presented during the second year of the New York World's Fair; the production previewed May 1–11, 1940; the official opening was on May 12; and the show closed on October 2 after approximately 576 performances (the revue was presented four times daily). The souvenir program stated the work was a "kaleidoscope" of American social and political history which was "embroidered with pageantry and song and shot through with homespun humor." Historical figures (George Washington, Abraham Lincoln, Teddy Roosevelt) and entertainment personalities (Jenny Lind, Lillian Russell) were featured in the production, which was also up-to-the-minute with its speculation about the upcoming presidential election (it appears that during the early weeks of the run, the song "One in a Million," which dealt with the election in a general manner, was replaced with a more specific one set in 1941 titled "Who Will It Be? (Roosevelt or Willkie)."

Brooks Atkinson in the *New York Times* said the evening was a "handsome and enjoyable" spectacle, a "lithographic sketchbook of American history" with a "good" book and a "rousing" score; Robert Coleman in the *New York Daily Mirror* described the production as one of "the great spectacles of all time"; Richard Watts in the *New York Herald Tribune* praised the "lively and colorful" show; John Chapman in the *New York Daily News* stated that "for gorgeous color and sweeping size [the show] is something this reporter has never seen approached"; John Mason Brown in the *New York Post* noted the evening was a "lightning bug's view of history" with "pretty" costumes and "agreeable" music; and Jack Pulaski in *Variety* said the forty-cent admission fee was "certainly worthwhile." But Wolcott Gibbs in the *New Yorker* said that despite "pretty" songs he "couldn't make a great deal out" of the revue and concluded that it was a "stately imbecile."

"Tennessee Fish Fry" is included in the collection *Arthur Schwartz Revisited* (Painted Smiles CD # PSCD-137). Except for the lyric of "Who Will It Be?" (which appears to be lost), all the lyrics are included in *The Complete Lyrics of Oscar Hammerstein II*.

The singing and dancing choruses of *American Jubilee* included Michael Kidd, Dody (here, Dolores) Goodman, Lucille Bremer, Eric Brotherson, and Murvyn Vye.

KEEP OFF THE GRASS
"THE NEW MUSICAL"

Theatre: Broadhurst Theatre
Opening Date: May 23, 1940; *Closing Date*: June 29, 1940
Performances: 44
Sketches: Mort Lewis, Reginald Beckwith, S. Jay Kaufman, Parke Levy and Alan Lipscott, and Norman Panama and Melvin Frank
Lyrics: Al Dubin; additional lyrics by Howard Dietz
Music: Jimmy McHugh; additional music by Vernon Duke
Direction: "Book directed" by Edward Duryea Dowling and "stage directed" by Fred de Cordova; *Producers*: The Messrs. Shubert; *Choreography*: George Balanchine; *Scenery* and *Costumes*: Nat Karson; *Lighting*: Edward Duryea Dowling; *Musical Direction*: John McManus
Cast: *Jimmy Durante, Ray Bolger, Jane Froman, Ilka Chase,* Betty Bruce, Nan Rae, Maude Davis, Larry Adler, Virginia O'Brien, John (Jack) McCauley, Sunnie O'Dea, Jack (Jackie) Gleason, The DeTuscans (Joanna and Bela), The Toreadors, José Limón, Daphne Vane, Robert Shackleton, Sid Walker, Peanuts Bohn, Hal Neiman, Emmet Kelly, Margery Moore, LaMotte Dodson's Monkeys (Blondie, Jiggs, Slats, and Louie), Saint Subber, Henry Dick; The Morelli Singers: Esta Elman, Virginia Burke, Martha Burnett, Imogen Carpenter, Lynn Lawrence, Jane Starner, Aileen Stone, Sylvia Stone, Frances Tannehill; Dancing Young Ladies: Billie Bernice, Mimi Berry, Gloria Clare, Harriet Clark, Margie Dale, Helen Devlin, Gloria Gaffey, Peggy Gallimore, June Leroy, Ann Lass, Peggy Littlejohn, Mary Joan Martin, Lois Martin, Jane Gray Petri, Mimi Walthers; Dancing Young Men: Ray Arnett, John Coy, Fred Deming, Jerry (Jerome) Robbins, Jerry Shepherd, Bob Sidney, Lee Tannen, Don Weissmuller
The revue was presented in two acts.

Sketches and Musical Numbers

Act One: "The Cabby's Serenade" (Jack Gleason, Bob Sidney, Peanuts Bohn, Hal Neiman, Emmet Kelly, Sid Walker); "This Is Spring" (Jane Froman, The Morelli Singers; danced by José Limón, Daphne Vane,

Margery Moore, The Dancing Ladies); "This Is Spring" (parody reprise) (Virginia O'Brien); "The Tree Doctor" (sketch by Mort Lewis) (Dr. Bush: John McCauley; Commissioner: Hal Neiman; Dr. Kildare: Jimmy Durante; Dr. Gillespie: Peanuts Bohn; Dr. Cyclops: Sid Walker; Dr. Watson: Robert Shackleton; Dr. Christian: Jack Gleason); "Crazy as a Loon" (Ray Bolger, Sunnie O'Dea; harmonica accompaniment by Larry Adler); "Romantique" (sketch by Mort Lewis and Reginald Beckwith) (She: Ilka Chase; He: John McCauley); "A Fugitive from *Esquire*" (lyric by Howard Dietz) (The Fugitive: Jimmy Durante; The Valets: Hal Neiman, Sid Walker, Jack Gleason, Peanuts Bohn); "I'll Applaud You with My Feet" (Betty Bruce, The Dancing Ladies and Gentlemen); "The Fountain" (sketch by Mort Lewis) (Thirsty Man: Ray Bolger; Thirsty Woman: Ilka Chase; The Cop: Jack Gleason; Park Attendant: Hal Neiman; Bootblack: Saint Subber; Park Strollers: Robert Shackleton, Peanuts Bohn, Lynn Lawrence, Esta Elman, Imogen Carpenter, Frances Tannehill, Aileen Stone, Bob Sidney); "Two in a Taxi" (lyric by Howard Dietz) (The Girl: Jane Froman; The Boy: Robert Shackleton); "The Old Park Bench" (lyric by Howard Dietz) (Jack Gleason, Larry Adler, Peanuts Bohn, Hal Neiman, Emmet Kelly, Sid Walker); "Misinformation, Please" (sketch by Parke Levy and Alan Lipscott) (Announcer: LaMotte Dodson; Clifton Fadiman: Jimmy Durante; Dorothy Thompson: Blondie; F.P.A.: Jiggs; John Kieran: Slats; Oscar Levant: Louie); "A Latin Tune, A Manhattan Moon, and You" (Ray Bolger, Betty Bruce, The Morelli Singers; danced by Ray Bolger, Betty Bruce, José Limón, Daphne Vane, Margery Moore, The Toreadors, The Dancing Ladies and Gentlemen); "Life with Mother" (sketch by Parke Levy and Alan Lipscott) (Hostess: Frances Tannehill; John: Jack Gleason; Elliot: Robert Shackleton; Franklyn Jr.: John McCauley; James: Sid Walker; Franklyn Sr.: Jimmy Durante; Eleanor: Ilka Chase; Porters: John Coy, Saint Subber; Western Union Boy: Peanuts Bohn; Waitresses: Lynn Lawrence, Mimi Walthers, Sylvia Stone; The Boss: Hal Neiman); Larry Adler; "Rhett, Scarlett & Ashley" (Rhett: Jimmy Durante; Ashley: Ray Bolger; Scarlett: Ilka Chase); "Clear Out of This World" (Jane Froman, Robert Shackleton, The Morelli Singers, The Dancing Ladies and Gentlemen); "Clear Out of This World" (parody reprise) (Virginia O'Brien)

Act Two: "Look Out for My Heart" (Jane Froman, Robert Shackleton, The Morelli Singers; fencing specialty by Joanna and Bela DeTuscan; danced by Betty Bruce, José Limón, The Dancing Ladies); "Museum Piece" (sketch by S. Jay Kaufman and Mort Lewis) (Guide: Jimmy Durante; Art Lovers: Ilka Chase, Jack Gleason, Peanuts Bohn, Robert Shackleton, Sid Walker, Emmet Kelly, Hal Neiman, Saint Subber); "Old Jitterbug" (Ray Bolger, Sunny O'Dea; danced by Ray Bolger, Sunnie O'Dea, Margery Moore, The Old Jitterbugs); "(I'm an) Old Jitterbug" (parody reprise) (Virginia O'Brien); "Birds" (The Lecturer: Nan Rae; The Interloper: Maude Davis; Bird Lovers: Esta Elman, Lynn Laurence, Frances Tannehill, Aileen Stone, Imogen Carpenter, Martha Burnett); "I'm in the Mood" (Jane Froman; danced Betty Bruce, Daphne Vane, José Limón, Henry Dick); "Shakespeare's-a-Poppin" (sketch by Mort Lewis) (Billings: John McCauley; White: Hal Neiman; McSwindle: Jimmy Durante; First Gravedigger: Peanuts Bohn; Juliet: Ilka Chase; Tybalt: Jack Gleason; Playgoer: Maude Davis); "Raffles" (dance) (music by Vernon Duke) (danced by Ray Bolger, Betty Bruce, Daphne Vane, Margery Moore, Bob Sidney, Henry Dick, Don Weissmuller, Fred Deming, The Dancing Ladies and Gentlemen); "The Old Park Bench" (reprise) (probably sung by Jack Gleason, Larry Adler, Peanuts Bohn, Hal Neiman, Emmet Kelly, Sid Walker); "Hormones" (sketch by Norman Panama and Melvin Frank) (Mulligan: Jimmy Durante; The Tiger: Ray Bolger; A Salesman: Jack Gleason); Virginia O'Brien; "This Is Winter" (Jane Froman; danced by Ray Bolger, José Limón, Daphne Vane, Margery Moore, Entire Company)

The short-lived revue *Keep Off the Grass* offered rowdy comics Jimmy Durante and Jack (Jackie) Gleason, acidic comedienne Ilka Chase, dead-pan singer Virginia O'Brien, straight-pan singers Jane Froman and Robert Shackleton, dancers Ray Bolger, José Limón, Betty Bruce, and Jerry (Jerome) Robbins (the latter in the chorus, but even so), choreography created by George Balanchine, harmonica virtuoso Larry Adler, clown Emmet Kelly, and future **Kiss Me, Kate**-*Out of This World*-*House of Flowers* producer (but now chorus boy) Saint Subber. Quite an impressive line-up! Plus there was Durante impersonating FDR (with a touch of Clarence Day's Father thrown in), Rhett Butler, a tree doctor named Kildare ("the Pasteur of the pastures," noted John Mason Brown in the *New York Post*), and MacBeth, not to mention a would-be fashion plate who can't understand why Lucius Beebe isn't impressed with his pink jacket, green plaid trousers, and canary yellow Alpine hat. *And* a monkey who impersonated Oscar Levant. All *this*—!?, and yet the show received indifferent reviews and was gone within six weeks!

Keep Off the Grass referred to Central Park, where most of the action took place among park strollers, cops, cabbies, and bird lovers, and some of the sketches occurred around a park fountain, in a taxi, and in the

Metropolitan Museum. There was an opening "Cabby's Serenade" sextet (which included Gleason), and later another sextet (again with Gleason) extolled the virtues of "The Old Park Bench." Two numbers ("Museum Piece" and "Look Out for My Heart") were set in the Metropolitan, the latter in the Armour Wing and included a fencing specialty by the team of Joanna and Bela DeTuscan; "Birds" dealt with bird lovers and their lecturer; "The Fountain" looked at the goings-on around a park fountain; and "The Tree Doctor" included Dr. Kildare (Durante), Dr. Gillespie (Peanuts Bohn), Dr. Watson (Robert Shackleton), and others examining the health of the park's trees.

And in true revue fashion, the evening included de rigueur looks at topical entertainments. The song "Rhett, Scarlett & Ashley" found Durante, Chase, and Bolger impersonating Margaret Mitchell's famous triangle (a few critics found the sequence tasteless; Burns Mantle in the *New York Daily News* said it was "coarse" and Brooks Atkinson in the *New York Times* pronounced it "malodorous"). The sketch "Life with Mother" spoofed both *Life with Father* and FDR (the Roosevelt clan sported bright red wigs, and Durante played the father-president). One or two of the aisle-sitters thought it went on too long, Richard Lockridge in the *New York Sun* said it "fell flat," and by the second week of the run the sketch was dropped. Ray Bolger's "Raffles" ballet (with music by Vernon Duke) gave him a dramatic dancing interlude as the dashing and slightly dangerous title character which had been portrayed by David Niven in the recent 1939 film.

Another spoof was "Shakespeare's-a-Poppin" in which the Bard meets Olsen and Johnson (Durante was McSwindle and Chase was Juliet). The revue also looked at the popular radio quiz program *Information, Please*, here called *Misinformation, Please*; Durante portrayed host Clifton Fadiman, and the four panelists were played by LaMotte Dodson's monkeys (Blondie, Jiggs, Slats, and Louie, the latter doing his impersonation of Oscar Levant). There was also the obligatory Latin American number (every other revue and musical of the era seemed to include one), here "A Latin Tune, a Manhattan Moon, and You"; and the ballad "Two in a Taxi" drove off with good notices from the critics.

Virginia O'Brien also scored. The MGM cut-up (whose shtick was that she never cut up) sang three songs in her famous dead-pan fashion; she'd follow up a straight ballad (such as Froman's "This Is Spring" and "Clear Out of This World") with her inimitable style of emotionless, monotone singing and her bland, frozen facial expression. Atkinson said she "convulses the audience by removing the ecstasy from high-pressure music," and Sidney Whipple in the *New York World-Telegram* found her contributions among the "dazzling moments" of the revue.

Perhaps the evening's highlight was Durante's song "A Fugitive from *Esquire*," in which he laments that his flashily colored outfits never win praise from such fashion experts as Lucius Beebe. Atkinson said he was hilarious in this sequence as he flounced about in clothes "with huge checks and swagger cuts." Richard Watts in the *New York Herald Tribune* said Durante was at his best in the "excellent" song (which had an "ingenious" lyric by Howard Dietz, according to Whipple). Beebe, incidentally, was dear to the hearts of the era's lyricists, composers, and sketch writers. He was also referenced in Richard Rodgers and Lorenz Hart's "Give It Back to the Indians" (*Too Many Girls*, 1939) and "Zip" (**Pal Joey**), Cole Porter's "I've Still Got My Health" (**Panama Hattie**), the notorious flop **Night of Love**, and Sid Kuller's sketch "Made to Order" (**Jump for Joy**).

Overall, Whipple found the evening "lusty and strong," and Lockridge said the entertainment was "bright and genial." And while Atkinson cautioned that the material was often "run-of-the-mire stuff," he nonetheless noted that Durante and Bolger were in "excellent form"; he mentioned that considering the current state of world affairs it was good the two of them had a chance to "cut loose" and entertain. Watts admitted the revue might well be "fairly routine," but with Durante in charge the show was a "springtime blessing." Brown suggested the evening lacked inspiration with a weak second act and a tendency "to repeat itself painfully"; but he suspected his opinion was likely to be a "minority report."

After the opening, the running order of the revue was altered; the sketch "Life with Mother," the song "I'm in the Mood," and the second-act reprise of the song "The Old Park Bench" were dropped; added to the second act were "Toscanini, Stokowski and Me" (which had been cut during the tryout) for Jimmy Durante (who was assisted by Jackie Gleason, Hal Neiman, Larry Adler, Peanuts Bohn, and Sid Walker) and a specialty spot for Larry Adler.

Besides "Toscanini, Stokowski and Me," the following numbers were deleted during the tryout: "Three Little Topical Debutantes" (lyric by Howard Dietz) for Ilka Chase, Nan Rae, and Maude Davis; "The Squaw-Women" for Nan Rae and Maude Davis; and "Cops and Robbers," which was sung by Ray Bolger and Betty Bruce and danced by them as well as José Limón, Daphne Vane, Margery Moore, and the Dancing Ladies and Gentlemen. Prior to Broadway, Sid Silvers was credited as one of the revue's sketch writers.

Cast members Jimmy Durante recorded "A Fugitive from *Esquire*" and Virginia O'Brien recorded "Clear Out of This World," "Two in a Taxi," "This Is Spring," and "(I'm an) Old Jitter Bug." The collection *The Broadway Musicals of 1940* (Bayview CD # RNBW019) includes "Two in a Taxi."

Cast member Jane Froman was the subject of the 1952 film *With a Song in My Heart* (in which Susan Hayward portrayed the singer, and whose vocals were dubbed by Froman herself); and Betty Bruce was a memorable Tessie Tura in the 1962 film version of *Gypsy*.

RUSSIAN BANK
"A New Play with Songs"

Theatre: St. James Theatre
Opening Date: May 24, 1940; *Closing Date*: June 1, 1940
Performances: 11
Play: Theodore Komisarjevsky and Stuart Mims
Songs: Mostly unidentified songs and dances, all arranged by Zinovy Kogan and Theodore Komisarjevsky (including the popular Russian ballad "Dark Eyes" and "Love Is [Such] a Cheat," the latter with lyric and music by Irving Caesar).
Direction and *Producer*: Theodore Komisarjevsky; *Scenery*: Louis Bromberg; *Costumes, Lighting,* and *Musical Direction*: Uncredited
Cast: Natasha Boleslavsky (Masha), Mikhail Rasumny (Serov, Shnizel), Natalie Harris (Serova, Katie), Josephine Houston (Natasha), James Rennie (Butienko), Ralph Morehouse (Patterson), Jeanne Palmer (Madame La Generale Denisova), Ernestine Stodelle (Valeria), Jay Mannering (Lisa), Roger Plowden (Baron Oeberg), Gerald Kean (Count Malsky), Tonio Selwart (Grand Duke Nikita), Elena Karam (Shubina), George Andre (Koulnis), John Adair (Cameron), Geena Goodwin (Petrova); Revolutionaries: Alexis Bolan, Michel Michon, Michel Greben, Arcady Stoyanovsky, Ivan Triesault, Boris Belostozky; Gypsy Man: Michel Michon; Gypsy Girl: Marjorie Tas; Gypsies: Ara Shvedova, Elena Arafelova, Natasha Boleslavsky, Gedda Petry, Evelyn Marsh, Arcady Stoyanovsky, Boris Belostozky, Alexis Bolan, Michel Greben, Feodor Zarkevitch; Marjorie Tas (Cleopatra), Effie Shannon (Mrs. Cameron), Arcady Stoyanovsky (Poushnoff), Alexis Bolan (Tipoff)
The play with music was presented in three acts.
The first act takes place in St. Petersburg, Russia, in 1917; the second act occurs there one year later; and the third act takes place on Long Island in 1933.

Ayn Rand's drama *The Unconquered* (which was based on her 1936 novel *We the Living*) opened on February 13, 1940, at the Biltmore Theatre to scathing reviews and a run of six performances. Directed by George Abbott, the story took place in the Stalinist Russia of 1924 and focused on former aristocrats Leo and Kira, who can't marry because of the former's poor health. In order to send Leo to Crimea for a rest cure, Kira sleeps with secret police agent Andrei. When the healthy Leo returns to Petrograd and discovers the nature of Kira's relationship with Andrei, he becomes a gigolo and Andrei commits suicide. Richard Watts in the *New York Herald Tribune* said the play was a "mishap," Wilella Waldorf in the *New York Post* found it "remarkably dull" and "embarrassing," and Richard Lockridge in the *New York Sun* indicated the "turgid" evening was "confused and directionless" as well as "singularly static."

When Theodore Komisarjevsky and Stuart Mims' *Russian Bank* opened some three months later and told a story similar to the one in *The Unconquered*, the critics said in comparison to the new offering *The Unconquered* wasn't so bad after all. Waldorf now felt *The Unconquered* was a "little gem" if not a "masterpiece," and Watts also decided that the earlier play now emerged as a "masterpiece."

Russian Bank begins in St. Petersburg in 1917, and centers on prima donna Natasha (Josephine Houston), who saves her lover the Grand Duke Nikita (Tonio Selwart) by becoming the mistress of Communist commissar Butienko (James Rennie). Mixed into this triangle are a group of merry gypsies who sing and dance at the drop of a hat, a comical spinster (who ends up marrying a half-dozen or so husbands during the course of the evening), a blustery and fusty banker, and many others who seem to have strayed in from a wandering operetta, including (according to Sidney Whipple in the *New York World-Telegram*) two "moth-eaten barons" and six "comedy Bolsheviks." In the second act, a year has gone by, but most of the characters are still hanging around St. Petersburg, including the madcap gypsies (Waldorf suspected they'd been hiding in a samovar). By the third act, it's 1933 and everyone is suddenly in a Long Island mansion, including those irrepressible gypsies. Natasha comes to realize that her true love is her former tormentor Butienko and not the Grand Duke. But all is well, for the Grand Duke is now interested only in his new fame as a radio star.

According to Whipple, "considerable music is injected into this confusion." And so the evening included songs and an occasional dance by the gypsies and various numbers for Houston, including "Dark Eyes" and "Love Is [Such] a Cheat" (the latter by Irving Caesar). Incidentally, Houston had earlier appeared as Lucy Brown in the first American production of *The Threepenny Opera* when it premiered on Broadway in 1933; during the same year she was in George and Ira Gershwin's *Pardon My English* and with George Givot introduced "Isn't It a Pity?," arguably the team's most lovely ballad.

Brooks Atkinson in the *New York Times* said there was nothing in the evening "to suggest mastery in any department," and except for some "wholly enchanting" Russian songs the work was "the quintessence of the commonplace." Watts noted you could easily tell the difference between the play's "heavy drama and gay banter" because the former was "funny" and the latter "grim." Whipple said *Russian Bank* was such a "weird" and "astoundingly bad" play that it was "hypnotic" and thus prevented the audience from rushing "madly into the night" between acts because there was an "irresistible curiosity" to see if the production was really some kind of "gigantic hoax."

Lockridge reeled from the madness of it all, and decided the "ludicrous" plot was in its "tormenting fashion" a classic of its kind; and he noted the "mad extravagance" of Komisarjevsky's direction was impossible to describe. In fact, "no words" could capture the "weird mixture of operetta sentiment, singing gypsies, melodramatic stratagems, and burlesque revolutionaries" in which "no two characters" seemed "even remotely in the same play." But he predicted the production would soon fade away, Josephine Houston would return to musicals, James Rennie would be seen in other plays, and the gypsies . . . ? Well, "there is no telling where they will go."

LOUISIANA PURCHASE

Theatre: Imperial Theatre
Opening Date: May 28, 1940; *Closing Date*: June 14, 1941
Performances: 444
Book: Morrie Ryskind
Lyrics and *Music*: Irving Berlin
Based on a story by B. G. (Buddy) De Sylva.
Direction: Edgar MacGregor; *Producer*: B. G. (Buddy) De Sylva; *Ballet Choreography*: George Balanchine; *Dance Choreography*: Carl Randall; *Scenery* and *Costumes*: Tom Lee; *Lighting*: Uncredited; *Musical Direction*: Robert Emmett Dolan
Cast: Georgia Carroll (Secretary), Sam Liebowitz (John Eliot), Robert Pitkin (Colonel Davis D. Davis, Sr.), Nicodemus (Abner), Ray Mayer (Davis D. Davis Jr.), Ralph Riggs (Dean Manning), Edward H. Robins (Police Captain Whitfield), *William Gaxton* (Jim Taylor), Carol Bruce (Beatrice), Nick Long Jr. (Lee Davis), April Ames (Emmy-Lou), *Vera Zorina* (Marina Van Linden), Irene Bordoni (Madame Bordelaise), *Victor Moore* (Senator Oliver P. Loganberry), Charles La Torre (Alphonse); The Martins: Hugh Martin, Ralph Blane, Jo Jean Rogers, Phyllis Rogers; The Buccaneers: John Panter, John Eliot, Don Cortez, James Phillips; Charles Laskey (Premiere Danseur); Louisiana Belles: Georgia Carroll, Judy Ford, Patricia Lee, Veva Selwood, Edith Luce; Dancing Girls: Helen Vincent, Dorothy Hall, Petra Gray, Rosemary Sankey, Anitra Upton, Betty Luster, Nancy Knott, Aleen Stewart, Althea Elder, Grace Gillern, Jean Scott, Zynade Spencer, Doris York, Mary Ganley, Leona Olsen, Dorothy Jeffers, Dorothy Barrett, May Hartwig, Virginia Morris; Dancing Boys: Harvey Mack, Charlie Curran, Clark Eggleston, James Leland, Douglas Dean, George Hunter, Jack McClendon, Kenneth Whelan, Henry Lahee, Richard Reed, Nicolai Popov, Dwight Godwin, Harold Haskins, Hubert Bland, Ned Coupland
The musical was presented in two acts.
The action takes place in New Orleans and Baton Rouge during the present time.

Act One: "Apologia" (in two parts, the opening includes "The Letter" and "It's News to Us") (Georgia Carroll, John Eliot, Ensemble); "Sex Marches On" (William Gaxton, Robert Pitkin, Ray Mayer, Ralph Riggs,

Edward H. Robins); "Louisiana Purchase" (Carol Bruce, Hugh Martin, Ralph Blane, Jo Jean Rogers, Phyllis Rogers, John Panter, John Eliot, Don Cortez, James Phillips, Ensemble); "Tomorrow Is a Lovely Day" (Irene Bordoni); "Louisiana Purchase" (reprise) (Carol Bruce, April Ames, Nick Long Jr., Hugh Martin, Ralph Blane, Jo Jean Rogers, Phyllis Rogers, Ensemble); "Outside of That, I Love You" (William Gaxton, Vera Zorina); "You're Lonely and I'm Lonely" (Victor Moore, Vera Zorina); Dance (Nicodemus); "Dance with Me (Tonight at the Mardi Gras)" (Hugh Martin, Ralph Blane, Jo Jean Rogers, Phyllis Rogers; Queen of the Mardi Gras: Vera Zorina; Premier Danseur: Charles Laskey; Queen of the Creoles: Vera Zorina); Finale ("Congratulations Are in Order") (Entire Company)

Act Two: "Opening" (Ensemble); "Latins Know How" (Irene Bordoni, Ensemble); "What Chance Have I (with Love)?" (Victor Moore); "The Lord Done Fixed Up My Soul" (Carol Bruce, Nicodemus, John Panter, John Eliot, Don Cortez, James Phillips, Ensemble); "Fools Fall in Love" (William Gaxton, Vera Zorina); "Old Man's Darling—Young Man's Slave?" (ballet Marina: Vera Zorina; Spirit of Jim Taylor: Charles Laskey; Spirit of Senator Loganberry: Harold Haskins); "You Can't Brush Me Off" (April Ames, Nick Long Jr., Hugh Martin, Ralph Blane, Jean Jo Rogers, Phyllis Rogers); Finale ("Somebody Handed Us a Ticket to Picket") (Entire Company)

Irving Berlin's delightful *Louisiana Purchase* received some of the best notices of the season and (not counting the World's Fair revue **American Jubilee** which gave four performances daily during its limited summer engagement) became its longest-running musical with 444 performances. With the new show, producer (and successful lyricist) B. G. (Buddy) De Sylva could boast the two biggest musical hits of the season; he had also brought in Cole Porter's *DuBarry Was a Lady*, which ran for 408 showings and was the final book musical of the 1930s. And a few months later he produced Porter's **Panama Hattie**, which topped out at 501 performances. During the early part of the decade, De Sylva's name was synonymous with lavish and somewhat saucy and risqué hit musicals.

With *Louisiana Purchase*, Morrie Ryskind again looked at politics from a generally genial and slightly satiric point of view. He and George S. Kaufman had written the book for George and Ira Gershwin's merry Pulitzer Prize–winning *Of Thee I Sing* (1931) and its somewhat sour sequel *Let 'Em Eat Cake* (1933), both of which starred William Gaxton and Victor Moore, the stars of *Louisiana Purchase*. For the new musical, Moore again portrayed a seemingly confused but essentially savvy politician (he was the hapless Vice President Alexander Throttlebottom in the two Gershwin musicals and was the U.S. Ambassador to Russia in Porter's 1938 musical *Leave It to Me!*) who according to Burns Mantle in the *New York Daily News* was "a match for any musical comedy crook ever invented."

The amiable romp dealt with New Hampshire Senator Oliver P. Loganberry (Moore), who goes to Louisiana on a fact-finding mission to investigate financial irregularities by the local political bosses (once there, he's informed that the best way to contact a politician is to call a certain phone number and ask for Mabel), one of whom (Jim Taylor, played by Gaxton) turns out to be not such a bad guy after all. In order to squelch Loganberry's investigation, the local politicos attempt to frame him in compromising relationships with various women, including the lovely Marina (Vera Zorina) and the worldly Madame Bordelaise (Irene Bordoni, affectionately dubbed "The Bordoni" by many of the New York critics). But the seemingly befuddled and bumbling Loganberry is a shrewd one, and he not only cleans up the local political machine but also finds himself a wife in Madame Bordelaise. Jim and Marina pair off as the second set of happy lovers, and a minor subplot included a third twosome, the young couple Emmy-Lou (April Ames) and Lee (Nick Long Jr.).

With its lighthearted plot, colorful production values (the scenery and costumes were designed by Tom Lee), choreography in the modern style by Carl Randall and ballet choreography by George Balanchine (who was married to Zorina), a good-natured cast (with Moore receiving the notices of his career), and a bandwagon of melodic songs from Irving Berlin's music box, the show was an instant hit. Further, the musical included the singing quartet The Martins (including Hugh Martin and Ralph Blane), and the swinging vocal arrangements were created by Martin.

Berlin's contributions were especially memorable. The irresistible title song was one of his very best, an insinuating, driving, and pulsating melody and the kind of number which practically defines the words "musical comedy," and "The Lord Done Fixed Up My Soul" was a swing-inflected gospel number, both excitingly performed by newcomer Carol Bruce (as Beatrice) and the chorus. "You're Lonely and I'm Lonely" was an appealing duet for Moore and Zorina, and his "What Chance Have I (with Love)?" was a gently bemused look at his lonely bachelor status (he notes that if Samson was weakened by a haircut, then he'd be murdered by a shave). The evening's two lovely ballads "Fools Fall in Love" and "Tomorrow Is a Lovely Day" were respectively sung by Gaxton and Zorina and by The Bordoni. The amusing opening number "Apologia" offered a disclaimer which instructed the audience that the stage goings-on in Louisiana were strictly fictitious and that Louisiana was indeed a "mythical" state and New Orleans an "invented" city.

For Berlin, the score was surprisingly naughty. Gaxton and a male trio informed us that "Sex Marches On"; The Bordoni made it clear that "Latins Know How"; Gaxton and Zorina's duet "Outside of That, I Love You" included a sly reference to those annoying "rubber things" men sometimes have to wear (suspenders, of course); and Bordoni's deleted number assured us that in the ways of romance knowing what to do comes naturally ("It'll Come to You"), and, of course, the song anticipated **Annie Get Your Gun**'s "Doin' What Comes Naturally."

Although a few critics thought the evening's satire could have been more pointed, they nonetheless gave the show unanimously enthusiastic reviews. Brooks Atkinson in the *New York Times* said the production was a "gay, simple, friendly" musical "with the accomplished ease of a thoroughbred." He noted the "good-humored and enjoyable" evening included such numbers as the title song (the "most beguiling" in the show), "Sex Marches On" (the "most comic"), and "The Lord Done Fixed Up My Soul" (an "excellent" spiritual). He also liked Moore's "What Chance Have I (with Love)?," an "amusingly plaintive ditty."

Mantle noted that if a musical was well staged and scored and "of average merit," it would rate three full stars. But for *Louisiana Purchase*, "What are you going to do?," he asked. And his answer was, "Give it three-plus obviously." Sidney Whipple in the *New York World-Telegram* reported that the new musical was "superb . . . a roaring smash," and said Berlin offered "some of the most entrancing tunes of recent years" (including "The Lord Done Fixed Up My Soul," "Tomorrow Is a Lovely Day," the rhumba "Latins Know How," and the "sweeping success" of the title song). Richard Lockridge in the *New York Sun* praised Berlin's "grand" music for the "superior," "luxurious," "handsome," and "likable" show, and concluded his review by noting that it "obviously" must be seen.

Richard Watts in the *New York Herald Tribune* suggested that the great Moore was somehow "even improving" as a comedian; heretofore, he was always funny, but now his strengths as an actor brought forth a "genuine, completely rounded and quite brilliant characterization." John Mason Brown in the *New York Post* noted that not since his Throttlebottom had Moore enjoyed "a better part or acted more creatively." Moore was still the master of comic shtick, but he had grown as an actor and now framed his comedy with characterization.

During the tryout, Emmy-Lou and Lee's "I'd Like (Love) to Be Shot from (out of) a Cannon (with You)" was cut (but their ingratiating "You Can't Brush Me Off" was retained) and as mentioned "It'll Come to You" was also dropped. Unused songs were "Wild about You," "I'm a Quaker's Daughter from the Latin Quarter," "The Waltz of Old Vienna," "You Must Catch a Senator with a Girl," "In an Old-Fashioned Parlor," and "We Might Have a Future." "Wild about You" had been originally intended for Berlin's 1935 film *Top Hat*; the song was included in the collection *Irving Berlin Revisited* (Painted Smiles CD # PSCD-118).

Besides a later 1951 television version of the musical with many of the original cast members, there was a film adaptation released in 1942 by Paramount with a screenplay by Jerome Chodorov and Joseph Fields and direction by Irving Cummings. Moore and Zorina reprised their stage roles and Gaxton's role was assumed by Bob Hope. The essential plot was retained, and the film was a fast-moving Technicolor feast. Surprisingly, the two main ballads ("Tomorrow Is a Lovely Day" and "Fools Fall in Love") were dropped (although the former was heard during the opening credits) and the obscure numbers "Apologia" and "You're Lonely and I'm Lonely" were retained along with the title song and "Dance with Me (Tonight at the Mardi Gras)." Dona Drake and Frank Albertson were the juvenile leads, and at one point seemed about to sing (perhaps "You Can't Brush Me Off"?), but suddenly an abrupt cut led to the next scene.

Louisiana Purchase marked the second time Bob Hope played a film role that had first been created on stage by William Gaxton. In 1934, Hope appeared in Warner Brothers' *Paree, Paree*, a short twenty-one-minute musical film version of Cole Porter's 1929 musical *Fifty Million Frenchmen* that had starred Gaxton (earlier, there had been a 1931 nonmusical film version of the stage production; titled *Fifty Million Frenchmen*, the movie included a Porter song or two as instrumental background music). (*Paree, Paree* is included in the bonus material of the DVD release of the 1957 film version of Porter's 1955 Broadway musical *Silk Stockings*.)

The musical was briefly revived in a limited engagement concert version at Carnegie Hall on June 19, 1996, for six performances with George S. Irving (Loganberry), Michael McGrath (Jim), Judy Blazer (Marina),

Taina Elg (Madame Bordelaise), and, in the Carol Bruce role, Debbie (Shapiro) Gravitte. The concert reinstated "It'll Come to You."

The television version was seen in 1951 with Moore, Gaxton, Bordoni, and Sandra Deel; the soundtrack of this production was briefly available on JJA Records (LP # JJA-19746A/B), and includes a number of bonus materials (including the unused "Wild about You") by Carol Bruce, Vera Zorina, Kate Smith, Dinah Shore, Janet Blair, and other artists. The 1996 concert was also recorded (DRG CD # 94766), and besides "It'll Come to You" (which had been included in the concert) the recording also offered the cut number "I'd Like to Be Shot from a Cannon." The scintillating recording is a must-have, and in the best Ethel Merman tradition Debbie (Shapiro) Gravitte blasts her songs into kingdom come.

The collection *The Complete Lyrics of Irving Berlin* includes all the songs, including the deleted and unused ones.

TROPICAL PINAFORE
"A Modern Rhythmical Version of Gilbert and Sullivan's *H.M.S. Pinafore*"

The musical opened at the Great Northern Theatre, Chicago, Illinois, on April 12, 1940, and played there for three weeks (it appears the musical's only engagement was in Chicago).
Libretto: W. S. Gilbert
Music: Arthur Sullivan
Direction: Victor Sutherland; *Producer*: The American Negro Light Opera Association; *Choreography*: Katherine Dunham; *Scenery*: Uncredited; *Costumes*: John Pratt; *Lighting*: Uncredited; *Musical Direction*: Ramon B. Girvin
Cast: Walter Vaughn (Boatswain's Mate), Frank Ferrel (Boatswain), Thelma Waide Brown (Little Buttercup), Napoleon Reed (Ralph Rackstraw), Don Pierson (Captain Corcoran), Frank Palmer (Dick Deadeye), La Julia Rhea (Josephine), George Bizzelle (Sir Joseph Porter, K.C.B.), Ernestine Lyle (Cousin Hebe), Carmella (Dance Soloist), Prince Antiga (Drummer), The Katherine Dunham Dancers—Dancing Girls: Frances Alexander, Lucille Ellis, Coclough Jackson, Mildred Johnson, Harriet Turner, Ehrai Walker; Dancing Boys: Morton Brown, Vernon Duncan, Laverne French, Joe Lewis, Frank Neal, Lowry Simms; Singing Ladies: Prossie Blue, Ruby Cameron, Lulu Case, Clarissa Cotton, Lela Davis, E. Ruth Downs, Beatrice Downs, Beatrice Gaines, Allie Mae Jones, Alice Lew, Lorraine Piggott, Hazel Reed, Nellie Russell, Mary Spraggin, Carlotta Stevens, Lulu Thomas, Rachel Wells, Clara M. White, Kathryn Williams; Singing Gentlemen: Edgar Blair, John Burdette, Clayton A. Calvin, Sanford Champion, William Houze, Fred Hudson, Alphonso Jones, Harold Kimbrough, John Kimbrough, Henry Markham, P.J. O'Dell, Joseph Samples, George Sanford, Gee Smith, Nathan Stubbs, Homer Lee Taylor, Talman Thomas, Roy Thompson, Joseph Vineyard, Albert Yarbrough
The musical was presented in two acts.
The action "might have taken place in the Caribbean."

Musical Numbers

Act One: "We Sail the Ocean Blue" (Male Chorus); "I'm Called Little Buttercup" (Thelma Waide Brown, Male Chorus); "The Nightingale's Song" (Napoleon Reed, Male Chorus); "A Maiden Fair to See" (Napoleon Reed, Male Chorus); "My Gallant Crew Good Morning" (Don Pierson, Male Chorus); "Sorry Her Lot" (La Julia Rhea); "Over the Bright Blue Sea" (Girls' Chorus); "Sir Joseph's Barge Is Seen" (Male Chorus, Girls' Chorus); "Now Give Three Cheers" (George Bizzelle, Ernestine Lyle, Chorus); "When I Was a Lad" (George Bizzelle, Chorus); "For I Hold That on the Seas" (George Bizzelle); "Admiral's Song" (Napoleon Reed, Frank Ferrel, Walter Vaughn, Male Chorus); "Refrain, Audacious Tar" (La Julia Rhea, Napoleon Reed); "Can I Survive This Overbearing" (Napoleon Reed); Act One Finale (Entire Company)
Act Two: "Fair Moon to Thee I Sing" (Don Pierson); "Things Are Seldom What They Seem" (Thelma Waide Brown, Don Pierson); "The Hours Creep on Apace" (La Julia Rhea); "Bell Trio" (La Julia Rhea, George Bizzelle, Entire Ensemble); "The Merry Maiden and the Tar" (Don Pierson, Frank Palmer); "Carefully on Tip Toe Stealing" (La Julia Rhea, Napoleon Reed, Ensemble); "He Is an Englishman" (La Julia Rhea, Napoleon

Reed, Don Pierson, Ensemble); "Farewell My Own" (La Julia Rhea, Napoleon Reed, Ensemble); "A Many Years Ago" (Thelma Waide Brown, Don Pierson); "Oh Joy Oh Rapture Unforeseen" (Entire Company)
The program also included the following separate list which featured the dances performed in the production, all of which were choreographed by Katherine Dunham:
Act One: "Opening Chorus" (Dancing Boys); "Buttercup Number" (Dance Ensemble); "Gaily Tripping" (Carmela, Dance Ensemble); "Monarch of the Seas" ("Sha-Sha" or "Shay-Shay" [two different spellings in program]) (Carmela, Dance Ensemble)
Act Two: "Opening" (Dancing Boys); "Things Are Seldom What They Seem" ("Voo-doo Scene") (Prince Antiga, Dancing Boys); "For He Is an Englishman" (Boys' Swing Chorus, Waltz, Boogie-Woogie); Finale (Calypso Carnival) (Dancers, Drummers)

W. S. Gilbert and Arthur Sullivan's *H.M.S. Pinafore*, or *The Lass That Loved a Sailor* first premiered at the Opera Comique in London on May 25, 1878, for 571 performances; the New York premiere took place at the Standard Theatre on January 15, 1879, for 175 performances.

Beginning in the late 1930s and continuing into the mid-1940s, a number of modern-day adaptations of Gilbert and Sullivan's operettas were produced in the United States. WPA's *The Swing Mikado* opened on Broadway at the New Yorker Theatre on March 1, 1939, and in two slightly separated engagements played for eighty-six performances. Later that month, on March 23, *The Hot Mikado* (with Bill "Bojangles" Robinson) opened at the Broadhurst Theatre for eighty-five performances, and then transferred to the New York World's Fair; it subsequently enjoyed a long national tour. On March 24, 1945, **Memphis Bound** (which was loosely based on both *Trial by Jury* and *H.M.S. Pinafore*) opened at the Broadway Theatre for thirty-six performances, and on May 31, 1945, George S. Kaufman's adaptation of *H.M.S. Pinafore* (titled **Hollywood Pinafore**, or **The Lad Who Loved a Salary**) opened at the Alvin Theatre for fifty-two showings.

Unlike the other four modern updates, *Tropical Pinafore* never made it to New York. Cecil Smith in *The Best Plays of 1939–1940* noted that the new adaptation of *H.M.S. Pinafore* lacked the "acumen" of the WPA production of *The Swing Mikado*.

Katherine Dunham choreographed *Tropical Pinafore*, and her dance troupe was part of the cast. Her breakthrough moment came later in the year when she created the role of Georgia Brown in the original production of **Cabin in the Sky**. Napoleon Reed, who played Ralph Rackstraw, was later in the original production of **Carmen Jones** and with Luther Saxon alternated in the role of Joe.

THE WHITE PLUME
"A Musical Play"

Theatres and *Dates*: The musical opened at the National Theatre in Washington, D.C., on December 25, 1939, and closed in Pittsburgh, Pennsylvania, on January 6, 1940.
Book and *Lyrics*: Charles O. Locke
Music: Samuel D. Pokrass and Vernon Duke
Based on Edmund Rostand's 1897 play *Cyrano de Bergerac*.
Direction: George Houston; *Producers*: The Messrs. Shubert; *Choreography*: Mme. Natalie Kamarova; *Scenery*: Watson Barratt; *Costumes*: Ernst Schrappro; *Lighting*: Uncredited; *Musical Direction*: Uncredited
Cast: Donald Green (Friar Joseph, Citizen, Third Apprentice), Joseph Holland (Comte de Guiche), Cornell Wilde (Vicomte de Valvert), Ruby Mercer (Roxane), Hal Forde (H.E. Cardinal Richelieu), Zella Russell (La Comtesse de Guiche, Old Woman), Earl McVeigh (Bellerose, Citizen), Maria Belita (Orange Girl), Ray MacDonald (Little Musketeer), Ruth Hovey (A Cocotte), Fred Harper (Ligniere), Eric Mattson (Baron Christian de Neuvillette), Douglas Leavitt (Ragueneau), Ed Roecker (Le Bret), Herbert Stark (Lackey), Hope Emerson (Roxane's Duenna), Valentina Litvinoff (Solo Dancer), Herbert Gubelman (Marquis de Quigy, A Capuchin Monk), Driscoll Wolfe (Marquis de Brissaille, First Apprentice), Truman Gaige (Montfleury, Messenger), George Huston (Cyrano de Bergerac), Fred Sherman (Meddler), Edward Constantine (D'Artagan), Robert Chisholm (Carbon de Castel Jaloux [Captain of the Gascons]), Wesley Bender (Citizen, Armand), Bill (William) Johnson (A Gascon, Second Apprentice), Betti Davis (A Citizeness, Sister Clair), Nina Olivette (Lisette), Louis A. Dmitri (Head Apprentice of Ragueneau's Bake Shop), Kay Kingsley (La Marquise de Montespan, Sister Martha), Evelyn Case (Mother Superior), Ellin Brooks (A Novice); Ladies

of the Ensemble: Betsey Berkley, Cynthia Cavanaugh, Barbara Elliot, Jill Gibson, Cornelia Fairley, Helen Hudson, Frances King, Ann Sande, Ailen Stone, Frances Tanner, Kay York, Jane Aldrich, Dolores Flanders, Stella Hughes, Maxine Moore, Jean Matus, Charlotte Orkin, Esta Elman, Hazel Graham, Gloria Hart, Lynn Lawrence, Erminie Randolph, Virginia Vonne, Marjorie Williamson; Gentlemen of the Ensemble: James Allison, John Barry, James Carroll, Edward Constantine, George Farrell, Joseph Granville, Karl Holly, Scott Ishmael, Robert Leffler, Thomas Mitchell, Jerry O'Rourke, Richard Reeves, Herbert Rissman, Harold Stark, Norman Van Emburgh, Roderick Williams, Henry Williamson, Philip Shafer, George Young; Ladies of the Corps de Ballet: Marilyn Brandberg, Doris Denton, Peggy Darcy, Marie Grey, Anna Lazarova, Ann Lee, Doris Padgett, Lillian Reilly, Charlotte Sumner, Janet Stull, Doris York

The musical was presented in two acts.

The action occurs over a period of fifteen years beginning in 1640, and is mostly set in Paris (and also in the vicinity of the village of Arras).

Musical Numbers

Note: An asterisk denotes music by Vernon Duke.

Act One: "Minuette" (Performers not credited); "The World Is Young" (Earl McVeigh); "The Play's the Thing" (Ensemble); "Cyrano" (Ed Roecker, Ensemble); "Pavane" (Valentina Litvinoff, Dancers); "My Nose" (George Houston, Ensemble); "Ballade of the Duel" (George Houston, Cornell Wilde); "Cyrano" (reprise) (George Houston, Ed Roecker, Ensemble); "What My Lips Can Never Say" (Ruby Mercer, Eric Mattson); "My Nose" (reprise) (George Houston, Fred Harper, Ensemble); "Little Musketeer" (dance) (Maria Belita, Ray MacDonald, Dancers); "Song of the Gascon Cadets" (Robert Chisholm, Gascon Cadets); "Dance of the Waitresses" (*) (Maria Belita, Dancers); "Bonjour, Goodbye" (*) (Nina Olivette, Louis A. Dmitri, Entire Ensemble); "Shadow of Love" (*) (lyric by Ted Fetter and Charles O. Locke) (George Houston); "Men of Jaloux" (George Houston, Cadets); "Letter Duet" (George Houston, Eric Mattson); "What My Lips Can Never Say" (reprise) (Eric Mattson, Ruby Mercer); "Shadow of Love" (*) (reprise) (George Houston)

Act Two: "Carnival" (*) (Maria Belita, Dancers, Entire Ensemble); "Peasant Harvest Dance" (*) (Valentina Litvinoff); "Tell Me of Love" (Ruby Mercer, Eric Mattson); "I Cling to You" (*) (lyric by Ted Fetter and Charles O. Locke) (Ruby Mercer); "Balcony Trio" (Ruby Mercer, Eric Mattson, George Houston); "Shadow of Love" (*) (reprise) (George Houston); Finaletto (Ruby Mercer, George Houston, Eric Mattson, Joseph Holland, Entire Ensemble); "Who Will Tie My Shoe" (*) (Ruby Mercer, Cadets); "Men of Jaloux" (reprise) (George Houston, Robert Chisholm, Ed Roecker, Cadets); "Gascon Voice from Beyond" (Eric Mattson, Cadets); "Gregorian Chant" (music by Vernon Duke and Giuseppe Bambuschek) (Evelyn Case, Sisters, Novices); "I Cling to You" (*) (reprise) (Ruby Mercer); "Gregorian Chant" (*) (reprise) (Sisters of the Convent); "The Song of the Gascon Cadets" (reprise) (Entire Company)

The White Plume was a musical version of Edmund Rostand's 1897 classic drama *Cyrano de Bergerac*, and it was one of the most misbegotten musicals of the era. During the 1932–1933 and 1939–1940 seasons it was mounted in two different productions under four different titles, and flopped each time. For its second version, Vernon Duke was brought in to bolster the score. But nothing worked, and the show finally closed for good in 1940. (But that didn't stop other composers from trying to convert the play into a successful musical; along with *Little Women*, *The Adventures of Huckleberry Finn*, and *The Adventures of Tom Sawyer*, *Cyrano de Bergerac* is one of the most frequently adapted of all literary works with a total of at least sixteen different lyric interpretations.)

As *Cyrano de Bergerac*, the self-described "Rollicking Romance" opened at the Colonial Theatre in Boston, Massachusetts, on October 31, 1932, then moved to Providence, Rhode Island, and finally closed in New Haven, Connecticut, on November 19, 1932 (prior to the tryout, the musical had been produced by St. Louis Municipal Opera Company). During the course of the three-week tryout, the title was changed to *Roxanne* (heretofore the heroine's name had been spelled Roxane). The book and lyrics were by Charles O. Locke, and the music by Samuel D. Pokrass; George Houston was Cyrano, Gladys Baxter was Roxane, Allan Jones was Christian, and others in the cast were Trueman (later Truman) Gaige and Nick Long Jr. *Variety* suggested the musical was promising but was in need of drastic cutting.

Gaige reprised his role of Montfleury for the 1939–1940 version, which was produced by the Shubert Organization at the National Theatre in Washington, D.C., on December 25, 1939. It was now titled *The White Plume*, the huge cast numbered ninety, and there were thirty-three individual musical numbers. From Washington, the musical traveled to Pittsburgh, Pennsylvania, where it closed permanently on January 6, 1940; there it had undergone its fourth and final change of title, to *A Vagabond Hero* (the third tryout stop in Philadelphia, Pennsylvania, was cancelled). Locke was still credited as book writer and lyricist, but this time around Vernon Duke was brought in to supplement Pokrass's score. Houston was again Cyrano (and was also the musical's director), and Ruby Mercer was Roxane. The cast included Eric Mattson (who later created the role of Mister Snow in **Carousel**) as Christian, Bill Johnson (see **Two for the Show** for more information about his career), and future film star Cornell Wilde. *Variety* said the musical was "overpowered" with songs and dances, and again urged that "a good deal of whittling" be done.

For the second production, nine numbers were retained from the first version: "The Play's the Thing," "Cyrano," "Pavane," "My Nose," "The Little Musketeer," "What My Lips Can Never Say," "Song of the Gascon Cadets," "Tell Me of Love," and "Song of the Balcony" (aka "Balcony Trio").

The original production of the drama *Cyrano de Bergerac* premiered in Paris on December 28, 1897, at the Theatre de la Porte Saint-Martin (the title role was created by Benoit Constant); the first Broadway production opened at the Garden Theatre on October 3, 1898, with Richard Mansfield. In later years, Jose Ferrer made the role his own in a long-running revival that played at the Alvin (now Neil Simon) Theatre for 195 performances beginning on October 8, 1946, and for the 1950 film version he won the Academy Award for Best Actor.

The first musical version of the play was *Cyrano de Bergerac*, which opened at the Knickerbocker Theatre on September 18, 1899, for twenty-eight performances; Victor Herbert composed the score. Next came Walter Damrosch's operatic adaptation *Cyrano*, which premiered at the Metropolitan Opera for six performances beginning on February 27, 1913 (Pasquale Amato sang the title role). Between the productions of *Cyrano de Bergerac/Roxanne* and *The White Plume/A Vagabond Hero*, Franco Alfano's operatic version premiered in 1936 (and was produced by the Met in 2005). From there, a Yale University production opened in 1958 with lyrics and book by Richard Maltby Jr., and music by David L. Shire; the cast included John Cunningham (in the title role), Richard (Dick) Cavett, Carrie Nye McGeoy, Bill Hinnant, Austin Pendleton, and Roscoe (Lee) Browne. In 1965, a children's version of the musical with lyrics and music by Judith Dvorkin premiered in North Carolina, and in 1967 and 1973 José Ferrer starred in an adaptation by Robert Wright and George Forrest that played in summer stock as *A Song for Cyrano*.

On May 13, 1973, *Cyrano* opened at the Palace Theatre for forty-nine performances; the book and lyrics were by Anthony Burgess, the music by Michael J. Lewis, and Christopher Plummer won the Tony Award for Best Leading Actor in a Musical. On November 21, 1998, a version which had previously been seen in the Netherlands in 1997 opened at the Neil Simon Theatre for 137 performances; titled *Cyrano—The Musical*, the score was by Ad Van Dijk and the lyrics were by Koen Van Dijk (the English lyrics were by Peter Reeves and Sheldon Harnick). In 1992, Reeves had been associated with an Australian version for which he wrote lyrics and music; it apparently went unproduced, but in 1994 he was involved in another musical version which was performed in Australia (the book and lyrics were by Hal Shaper, with music by Reeves). There have also been three other operatic versions of the story by Enio Tamberg, Marius Constant, and David DiChiera. The versions by Alfano, Maltby and Shire, Dvorkin, Lewis, Van Dijk, Reeves, Tamberg, and Constant have been recorded (both versions of Reeves' Australian versions were recorded, and there are two recordings of Van Dijk's adaptation, one a Netherlands cast recording and the other a symphonic version). In 2009, a musical version with book and lyrics by Leslie Bricusse and music by Frank Wildhorn opened in Tokyo, and a concept recording of the score has been announced for release by GlobalVision/Koch Records. Counting the Pokrass and later the Pokrass/Duke scores as two versions and the 1992 and 1994 productions by Reeves as two versions, there have been at least sixteen lyric adaptations of Rostand's play.

"I Cling to You" is included in the collection *Vernon Duke Revisited* (Painted Smiles CD # PSCD-138) and Hildegarde's *Songs from the Shows* (Vocalion CD # CDEA-6078). The latter collection indicates the song is from *Ziegfeld Follies of 1933* (there was a *Ziegfeld Follies of 1933–1934*, and while the song isn't listed in the revue's program, perhaps the music for the number had originally been intended for that production).

1940–1941 Season

WALK WITH MUSIC
"A New Musical Comedy"

Theatre: Ethel Barrymore Theatre
Opening Date: June 4, 1940; *Closing Date*: July 20, 1940
Performances: 55
Book: Guy Bolton, Parke Levy, and Alan Prescott (some sources cite Alan Lipscott)
Lyrics: Johnny Mercer
Music: Hoagy Carmichael
Based on the British play *Three Blind Mice* by Stephen Powys (aka Virginia de Lantz [Mrs. Guy Bolton])
Direction: "Book staged" by R. H. Burnside and "production under the supervision" of Rowland Leigh; *Producers*: Ruth Selwyn in association with the Messrs. Shubert; *Choreography*: "dance collaboration by" Anton Dolin and Herbert Harper; *Scenery*: Watson Barratt; *Costumes*: Tom Lee; *Lighting*: Uncredited; *Musical Direction*: Uncredited
Cast: Kitty Carlisle (Pamela Gibson), Mitzi Green (Rhoda Gibson), Betty Lawford (Carrie Gibson), Stepin Fetchit (Chesterfield), Lee Sullivan (Henry Trowbridge), Jack Whiting (Wing D'Hautville), Art Jarrett (Steve Harrington), Frances Williams (Polly Van Zile), Marty May (Conrad Harrington), Ted Gary (Bellboy), Barrie O'Daniels (House Detective), William Castle (Stuart Hobson); Alice Dudley and Kenneth Bostock; The Modernaires: Ralph Brewster, Bill Conway, Harold Dickinson, and Chuck Goldstein; Glamour Girls: Connie Constant, Althea Gary, Linda Lee Griffith, Betty Lynn, Maxine Martin, Renee Russell); Dancing Girls: Nancy Chaplin, Muriel Cole, Nona Field, Christine Gillespie, George Jarvis, Ruth Maitland, Eleanor Parr, Sylvia di Salvo, Lorraine Todd, Terry Kelly, Jean Trybon, Rose Tyrrell; Dancing Boys: Larry Baker, Ray Clarke, Frank Gagon, Phil King, Zoli Parks, Bob Pitts, Jack Richards, Sid Salzer
The musical was presented in two acts.
The action takes place in New York City, New Hampshire, Jacksonville and Palm Beach, Florida, and Havana, Cuba.

Musical Numbers

Act One: "Greetings, Gates" (Ensemble); "Today I Am a Glamour Girl" (Kitty Carlisle, Mitzi Green, Betty Lawford, The Glamour Girls, Ensemble); "Even If I Say It Myself" (Jack Whiting, Alice Dudley and Kenneth Bostock, The Modernaires, Ensemble); "I Walk with Music" (Kitty Carlisle, Jack Whiting, The Glamour Girls, Ensemble); "Ooh! What You Said" (Mitzi Green, The Modernaires, Ted Gary); "Everything Happens to Me" (Frances Williams); "Wait Till You See Me in the Morning" (Kitty Carlisle, Art Jarrett); "I Walk with Music" (reprise) (Kitty Carlisle); "Break It Up, Cinderella" (Mitzi Green, Jack Whiting, The Modernaires, The Glamour Girls, Ensemble)

Act Two: "Smile for the Press" (Kitty Carlisle, Jack Whiting, Art Jarrett, The Modernaires, The Glamour Girls); "Friend of the Family" (Kitty Carlisle, Jack Whiting, Art Jarrett); "Way Back in 1939 A.D." (Mitzi Green, Marty May, Alice Dudley and Kenneth Bostock, Ensemble); "How Nice for Me" (Kitty Carlisle); "Everything Happens to Me" (reprise) (Stepin Fetchit); "Today I Am a Glamour Girl" (reprise) (Kitty Carlisle, Mitzi Green, Betty Lawford, Jack Whiting, Art Jarrett, Marty May); "How Nice for Me" (reprise) (Kitty Carlisle); "The Rhumba Jumps" (Frances Williams, The Modernaires, The Glamour Girls, Ensemble); "Ooh! What You Said" (reprise) (Mitzi Green, Marty May); "What'll They Think of Next (Now That They've Thought of You)?" (Mitzi Green, Art Jarrett); Finale (Company)

Walk with Music told the familiar story of three young women in pursuit of rich husbands. In this case, the sisters Gibson (Pamela [Kitty Carlisle], Rhoda [Mitzi Green], and Carrie [Betty Lawford]) pool their resources and leave their New Hampshire farm for the big cities of New York, Palm Beach, and Havana, where they hope to snag millionaire husbands. Pamela poses as a society debutante, Rhoda pretends to be her maid, and Carrie her chaperone. Romance (from both millionaire and modest-income men) comes their way, and a happy ending is had by all.

The musical was the first of the 1940–1941 season, and had undergone one of the most grueling tryouts in years. As *Three After Three*, the musical's lengthy pre-Broadway tour began in late November 1939 and lasted until the following March (including engagements in New Haven, Boston, Baltimore, Washington, D.C., and eight other cities), but closed on the road for major rewriting and recasting. Pamela (Vivi during the tryout) had been played by Simone Simon, and Carrie by Mary Brian, and they were succeeded by Kitty Carlisle and Betty Lawford. The roles of Wing D'Hautville and Stuart Hobson were respectively performed by Earl Oxford and Hugh Martin on the road, and were played by Jack Whiting and William Castle for New York; Martin also appeared during the tryout with his quartet The Martins (which included Ralph Blane, Jo Jean Rogers, and Phyllis Rogers), but at some point the team left the production to join **Louisiana Purchase** (they were replaced with the big-band quartet The Modernaires, who soon joined the Glenn Miller Orchestra). Edward Clarke Lilley and Fred De Cordova were credited with the staging, but by New York R. H. Burnside and Rowland Leigh had succeeded them; the choreography was originally created by Boots McKenna, and for New York was credited to Anton Dolin and Herbert Harper; and while Lucinda Ballard designed the costumes for the tryout, Tom Lee was the designer of record for the New York premiere.

During the tryout, the following songs were deleted: "Put Music in the Barn," "Darn Clever, These Chinee (Chinese)," "Newsy Bluesies," "Boom, I'm off the Wagon," "Happy New Year to You," "Charm against Trouble," and "Amazing What Love Can Do." It's unclear if "Glamour Boys" was performed during the tryout.

Once the revised version opened in New York, a few critics wondered why the creators had bothered to trouble themselves with all the rewrites and recasting, and the indifferent and sometimes negative reviews relegated the show to a run of only six weeks. Burns Mantle in the *New York Daily News* liked the cast, including the dance team of Alice Dudley and Kenneth Bostock (he compared them to the incomparable Paul and Grace Hartman, who specialized in spoofs of popular dances) and the "colored boy" Stepin Fetchit (who was "droll" but "in need of direction"); but the musical itself was "frayed and pointless." Brooks Atkinson in the *New York Times* said that if not for the "mechanical complications" of the plot Carmichael's score would seem "gay and tingling"; the songs were full of "enjoyment" and Mercer's lyrics were "light-hearted." He singled out seven songs, and noted that Frances Williams "wrecks the theatre's cooling system" with "The Rhumba Jumps." Richard Watts in the *New York Herald Tribune* said the musical was "burdened with one of the dullest and most laborious books ever encountered in musical comedy," one which was "exceptionally fatuous"; he singled out "Way Back in 1939 A.D.," which he noted was enjoying "quite a radio run."

John Mason Brown in the *New York Post* said the musical was more "chore" than "entertainment," but praised Dudley and Bostock as old-timers-turned-jitterbugs in "Way Back in 1939 A.D." Sidney Whipple in the *New York World-Telegram* suggested there was "nothing extraordinary" about *Walk with Music*, but felt it was nonetheless a "pleasant evening." He said the score lacked distinction and complained that Carmichael's melodies emphasized rhythm over melody; but he admitted there were "good" songs in the show and assumed his readers had already heard "I Walk with Music" and "Ooh! What You Said" on the radio. As for the latter, he praised the dance number (and lead dancer Ted Gary) which followed the song, and mentioned that the musical found time for Mitzi Green to do a few of her celebrated impersonations (including ones of Greta Garbo, Fannie Brice's Baby Snooks, and a particularly "biting" one of Katharine Hepburn). Like Mantle, he compared Dudley and Bostock to the Hartmans, and suggested that both they and Ted Gary be given more to do.

The headline of Richard Lockridge's review in the *New York Sun* proclaimed that "*Walk with Music* Opens at the Barrymore Dragging Its Book Behind It." But he admitted the production had an "agreeable crispness" about it despite endless quips that reduced the progress of the plot "to a crawl." He stated "something" needed to be done about the books of musical comedies. And little did he know. Later in the season three superior book musicals would open: **Cabin in the Sky** told its touching fable with a relatively sturdy book (and of course a superior score); **Pal Joey** would turn musical theatre upside-down with its anti-hero and its adult situations; and **Lady in the Dark** took a decidedly adventurous turn when it examined an unhappy career woman who undergoes psychoanalysis in order to resolve her problems. And of course two seasons later **Oklahoma!** institutionalized a whole new way of looking at musicals when it unified its book, lyrics, music, and choreography into a cohesive whole.

Soon after the Broadway opening, Jack Whiting left the show to go into **Hold On to Your Hats** and was succeeded by Donald Burr, and two second-act reprises ("Everything Happens to Me" for Stepin Fetchit and "How Nice for Me" for Kitty Carlisle) were eliminated.

Numerous songs from the score have been recorded, including "Ooh! What You Said," "Way Back in 1939 A.D.," "The Rhumba Jumps," "What'll They Think of Next," "I Walk with Music," "How Nice for Me," and "Everything Happens to Me" (the first four are included in the collection *The Broadway Musicals of 1940* [Bayview CD # RNBW019]). The collection *Everyone Else Revisited* (Painted Smiles CD # PSCD-146) offers "I Walk with Music," "What'll They Think of Next," "Ooh! What You Said," and "Way Back in 1939 A.D." "The Rhumba Jumps" is also included in the collection *You Can't Put Ketchup on the Moon* (Rialto CD # SLRR-9201), and "How Nice for Me" and "I Walk with Music" can be heard in *Lost Broadway and More/ Volume Two* (Original Cast Records CD # OC-6830). For those songs that have surfaced, Carmichael's music comes across as breezy and tuneful, and all of Mercer's lyrics are alternately romantic and clever. Because *Walk with Music* was Carmichael's only book musical and because its score and lyrics are so pleasant in a light and topical vein, it's a shame some enterprising record company hasn't released a studio cast album (another 1940s score that deserves a recording is "Fats" Waller's **Early to Bed**).

The lyrics for the used, cut, and unused songs are included in the collection *The Complete Lyrics of Johnny Mercer*. The book reports that two songs are apparently lost: "Put Music in the Barn" (lyric by Johnny Mercer and Hugh Martin, music by Mercer) and "Happy New Year to You" (lyric by Mercer, music by Carmichael).

Stephen Powys's play *Three Blind Mice* was filmed in 1938 under that title and was later adapted into two musical film versions, *Moon over Miami* (1941) and *Three Little Girls in Blue* (1946). The 1953 film comedy *How to Marry a Millionaire* also utilized the theme of three girls on the prowl for millionaires (it was based on Zoe Atkins's 1930 play *The Greeks Had a Word for It*). Another variation of the story was Avery Hopwood's hit comedy *The Gold Diggers*, which opened in 1919 and ran for 720 performances. Stephen Powys was the nom de plume for Virginia de Lantz, who was married to the musical's co-librettist Guy Bolton (some sources cite Bolton as the author of *Three Blind Mice*).

Among the cast members of *Walk with Music* were Frances Williams, who introduced "Take Me Back to Manhattan" in *The New Yorkers* (1930), "As Time Goes By" (*Everybody's Welcome*, 1931), and "Fun to Be Fooled" (*Life Begins at 8:40*, 1934), and Betty Lawford, who created the role of the vamp Crystal in Clare Booth's *The Women* (1936) and who sported one of the play's most famous lines ("If Stephen doesn't like what I'm wearing, I just take it off"). William Castle later became famous as director and/or producer of a string of successful horror films (including *The House on Haunted Hill*, *The Tingler*, *Homicidal*, and *Rosemary's Baby*).

GAY NEW ORLEANS

Theatre and *Performance Dates*: The revue played at the Grover Whalen Playhouse at the New York World's
   Fair during the summer of 1940 (number of performances unknown).
Lyrics and *Music*: Allan Roberts, Buddy Bernier, and Jerome Brainin
Direction: Hassard Short; *Producer*: Michael Todd; *Choreography*: Uncredited; *Scenery*: Watson Barratt; *Costumes*: Irene Sharaff; *Lighting*: Uncredited; *Musical Direction*: Uncredited

Cast: See list of musical numbers below for credits.
The revue was presented in one act.

Musical Numbers

(I) "DuBarry Brown": (1) "DuBarry Brown" (Ann Lewis, St. Elmo Johnson Choir, The Bruce Dancers); (2) Specialty (The Zephyrs); (3) "I've Got a Job" (St. Elmo Johnson Choir, The Bruce Dancers); (4) Specialty (The Berry Brothers); (5) "Cotton's Up" (Ann Lewis, St. Elmo Johnson Choir, The Bruce Dancers); (6) "Dance, Children" (The Bruce Dancers, St. Elmo Johnson Choir, Ann Lewis, The Berry Brothers, The Zephrys); and (7) "Cotton's Up" (reprise) (Entire Company—The Bruce Dancing Girls: Geraldine Jones, Estelle Marrero, Juanita McGowan, Paulina Moore, Marguerite Pugh, Ferebee Purnell, Rosebud Thompson, Victoria Winston, Doris Winston, Gwendolyn Gill; The Bruce Dancing Boys: Walter Adams, Ronald Missick, Arthur Moore, George Jenkins, Alvin Padgett, Bennie Padgett, Julius Phillips, Lloyd Storey, LeRoy Smith; St. Elmo Johnson Boys: Mowbray Blackett, Claude Blackman, John Diggs, Vernon Ford, James Gordon, Walter Meadows, William Thompson, William Woolfolk; St. Elmo Johnson Girls: Margaret Dunkin, Virgie Augustine, Hazel Dykes, Hattie King Reavis, Urylee Leonardos, Vereda Pearson, Louise Kemp, Louise Twyman)

(II) "Sazerac" (Leading Performers: Mark Plant, Ruby Mercer, The Albertina Rasch Girls): (1) "Hello, Yankee" (The Albertina Rasch Girls, The Four Grand); (2) "It Wouldn't Be Love" (Mark Plant, Show Girls, The Four Grand); (3) "Sazerac" (Ruby Mercer, The Four Grand, Show Girls, The Albertina Rasch Dancers)—(a) Specialty (Carlos and Carita); (4) Specialty (The Oldfield's); (5) "I Touched a Star" (Mark Plant, Ruby Mercer, Show Girls, The Four Grand, The Albertina Rasch Girls); (6) Specialty (Ben Dova); and (7) "Who Can Deny" (Scarlett O'Hara: Ruby Mercer; Rhett Butler: Mark Plant; Belle Watling: Martha Errolle; Show Girls, The Albertina Rasch Dancers, The Four Grand: Tom Chetlin, Joe Frederick, George Jerstand, Jack Leslie; The Albertina Rasch Girls: Eleanor Brown, Marylin Brandberg, Marion Davison, Daline Ferguson, Helen Hyatt, Audrey Kent, Evelyn Lafferty, Margaret Miller, Carol Murphy, Juliette Michaelis, Ruth Ryder, Shirley Sheldon, Sonya Sorel, Ann Wilson, Mildred Thomas, Betty Yeager; Show Girls: Helen Cole, Eleanor Hall, Lee Frederick, Peggy Martin, Florence Moore, Josephine Russo, Estelle Searcy, Frances Smith, Mabel Shaw, Clara Waring)

(III) "Mardi Gras Frolic" (Leading Performers: The Flame Dancer—Muriel Page and The Wonder Woman—Carrie Finnell): (1) a—"Cotton's Up" (reprise) (St. Elmo Johnson Choir); b—"Dance, Childrin" (reprise) (The Bruce Dancers); c—"Cotton's Up" (reprise) (St. Elmo Johnson Choir, The Bruce Dancers); (2) "Hello, Yankee" (reprise) (The Albertina Rasch Girls); (3) "I Wouldn't Do That If I Were You" (Carrie Finnell, Show Girls); (4) "I Touched a Star" (The Albertina Rasch Girls, The Eaton Quartette) and (a) "Flame Dance" (Muriel Page); (5) Specialty (Ben Dova); (6) "Hail! To the King and Queen of the Mardi Gras" (Mark Plant, Ruby Mercer, The Eaton Quartette, The Albertina Rasch Girls, Show Girls, St. Elmo Johnson Choir, The Bruce Dancers); (7) "Harlequin" and (a) "I've Got a Job" (reprise) (The Albertina Rasch Girls, Show Girls); (8) Specialty (The Berry Brothers) and (a) "DuBarry Brown" (reprise); (9) "I Touched a Star" (reprise) (Entire Company); and (10) Finale Ultimo: "Hail! To the King and Queen of the Mardi Gras" (reprise) (Entire Company)

Michael Todd's *Gay New Orleans* was one of many musicals which opened at the New York World's Fair in 1939 and 1940, and with the exceptions of *Billy Rose's Aquacade* (1939) and **American Jubilee**, most were presented by Todd. His *The Hot Mikado* had opened on Broadway at the Broadhurst Theatre on March 23, 1939, and after its eighty-five-performance run transferred to the fairgrounds where it played for the summer of 1939. His *The Streets of Paris* followed *The Hot Mikado* at the Broadhurst, where it opened on June 19, 1939, and played there until February 10, 1940, for a total of 274 performances. And like *Mikado*, *Paris* transferred to the Fair when it opened on May 11, 1940, at the World's Fair Hall of Music (the venue later underwent a name change to Michael Todd's Hall of Music) where it was performed four times daily in a shortened one-act version. For *Paris*, Bud Abbott and Lou Costello reprised their Broadway roles and Gypsy Rose Lee joined the cast. In 1940, Todd also offered "Dancing Campus" at the Fair's Op'ry House; the evening was advertised as a production with "music by famous orchestras."

Gay New Orleans later played in Chicago and other cities, and for a time the touring company was headed by Gypsy Rose Lee; one song from the production ("It Wouldn't Be Love") is included in the collection *Mike Todd's Broadway* (Everest LP # LPBR-5011). Not to be confused with the later **In Gay New Orleans**.

SIM SALA BIM
"The Mystery Spectacle"

Theatre: Morosco Theatre
Opening Date: September 9, 1940; *Closing Date*: October 20, 1940
Performances: 54
Production conceived and produced by Dante (Harry A. Jansen)
Cast: *Dante*, Moi Yo Miller and Her Mystery Girls; Illusionists: Byron Cheu, Frank Curcio, William Eastley, Gregory Ferrer, Stanley Franklin, Leland Harris, Arrin Jackson, Gean Jordan, Harry Kellar, Joseph Keegan, Marty Faber, Nate Ward, George White, Allen Whitney, Paul Yoon; Illusionistas: Anabell Brooks, Diana Ferrer, Dorothy Kirby, Lynn Nelson, Mollie Sherman, Helen Shocket, Gloria Washburn, Harriet Williams
The revue was presented in two acts.

Magical and Musical Sequences

Note: Titles are followed by notes in program.
Act One: Overture; "Tricks of Past Masters/10 Surprises in 10 Seconds/If you nod to a friend you miss a trick": (1) "A Transparent Mystery" (Square Game); (2) "Collapsible Ducks" (Spoofology); (3) "Instantaneous Horticulture" (Not Important); (4) "Chef's Surprise" (That's a Good Trick, That Was); (5) "A Strange Nest" (More Spoof); (6) "Animal Tales" (Fathom this and you get a celluloid stove poker); (7) "Invisible Pigeons" (Aren't they pretty); (8) "Mysterious Motion" (Fast Work); (9) "A Shadeless Sunshade" (Marvellous! At least we think so); and (10) "The Vanishing Table" (A case on you); "Dante's $50,000 Hands"; "Sox Appeal"; "The Creation of a Woman" (From a rag, a bone and a hank of hair. Believe it or not. With apologies to Ripley); "Deft Demonstrations of Deceptive Dexterity" (And how); "Black and White"; "Breakaway" (Dante); "Painless Penetration"; "Television Outdone" (The visible transportation of a human being, or how to be in two places at the same time); "Separation, Mutilation, Confiscation, and Restoration"; "The Un-Sevilled Barber" (Dante); "A Barrel of Fun" (Dante); "The Great Triple Mystery" (Dante)
Act Two: "The Temple of Mystery" (Presenting a rapid series of bewildering sensations. The absolute climax in modern stagecraft. All natural laws are set aside. The unnatural becomes real. The unreal becomes commonplace. You see what you don't see, and don't see what you think you see); "Crushing a Woman" (From *Canterbury Times*, New Zealand: "The fakirs of India robbed of their secrets and the Doctors of Europe stripped of their cunning.") (Dante); "Backstage" (From King Hakon of Norway: "I saw it but I don't believe it") (Dante); "Magician's Rehearsal" (The last word in Spoofology) (Dante); "An Uncanny Manifestation" (Knot what you see, but what you are not; Hoots Mon); "Cabaret de la Mort" (Laughter born of bewilderment. A facsimile of séances as witnessed by Dante in the capital cities of the world; (a) Apparition; (b) Séance; (c) Decapitation; (d) Dancing Shoes; and (e) Impromptu (Note: In these manifestations Dante lays no claim to the supernatural. His object is merely to amuse and mystify.); "Magical Transportation"; "The Newest Hindu Rope Trick"; "The Mysterious Globe"; "The Indian Sedan Mystery" (And she lives); "Dante's Original Phantom Princess" (Or, A Woman Lost at Every Performance. She fades like a cloud); "A Light Affair, or The Roaming Candles" (The World's Newest and Fastest Illusion, The Mystery of the STRATOSPHERE/Dante's Latest Original Sensation GREATER THAN THE HINDU ROPE TRICK. Positively the last word in Modern Stagecraft. Protected by Patent); "A Knotty Problem"; "The Chest of Wonder"; "The Great Invisible Flight" (Causing the instantaneous and invisible transportation of a human being from a fully lighted stage to the dome of the Theatre); "Solid Through Solid" (The oldest trick in Magic made new by Dante; Hoops, my dear); "Three Cheers for Uncle Sam" (Yankee Doodle Dante); "The Star-Spangled Banner"

For *Sim Sala Bim* (which translates as "Thanks to you"), Danish magician Dante (Harry A. Jansen) offered "50 Mysteries" per the program, which announced that his was the "Most Travelled Theatrical Organization in the World Embodying: Transformations, Comedy, Magic, Novelty, Illusions, Skill, Quick Changes, and Transfigurations Extraordinary."

Like other performers of the era (such as the cast members of **Reunion in New York** and Vittorio Podrecca and troupe of the **Theatre of the Piccoli**), Dante was forced from his homeland because of the war. According to *The Best Plays of 1940–1941*, Dante's New York engagement was so well received that he cancelled a South American tour and instead booked a tour of U.S. cities.

L.N. (probably Lewis Nichols) in the *New York Times* said the revue was "marvelous . . . an echo of the Palace when the world was young and kind." Dante looked like a combination of Mephistopheles and Monty Woolley and he presided over a stage of ducks, pigs, girls in Spanish and Chinese costumes, mysterious trunks, rings, playing cards, skulls, and water tumblers, all the while orchestrating seemingly impossible tricks (such as "The Un-Sevilled Barber" in which as a barber he shaves a customer in full view of the audience and then suddenly he's the one in the chair being shaved). Herrick Brown in the *New York Sun* said it was "good news" that Dante was back on Broadway after thirteen years; the "superb magician" was also a "skillful showman," and "if it's magic you like, here's your banquet."

Wilella Waldorf in the *New York Post* said *Sim Sala Bim* provided "one of the merriest entertainments Broadway has boasted in some time." She praised Dante's boundless energy, noting the strain of performing so many tricks "must be worse than acting *Hamlet* unabridged, with *Cyrano de Bergerac* tossed in as a curtain-raiser." She described a jaw-dropping sequence ("Stratosphere") in which three members of the company ascend in a balloon, and then ten seconds after ascending were suddenly seen running down the aisles of the Morosco from the back of the house. Like the *Times*, she described Dante as a Mephistopheles type, but also one who looked like Uncle Sam (and for the finale, Dante appeared as Uncle Sam in a "valiantly" patriotic song titled "Three Cheers for Uncle Sam"). Sidney Whipple in the *New York World-Telegram* said the evening was a "wonderment" and that he had a "wonderful time." He noted that perhaps some of the magic tricks had been seen before, "but seldom have they been performed better, with more grace or with more geniality." He noted that one sequence ("Television Outdone") he "simply" did "not believe happened": in full view of the audience, Dante "broadcast" a girl from one place to another.

The program noted that "other new and original features" which might occasionally be introduced into the production were: "The Great Black and White Pony Mystery"; "A Mysterious Musical Record"; "The Vanishing Lion in Mid-Air"; "Decapitation"; "Hell's Gate"; "Vanishing Zeppelin"; "Fly-To"; "Cinderella's Dream"; "Vanishing Audience"; "Mystery of the Chinese Laundry Ticket"; "Magician's Bath Tub"; "Giving Away a Woman"; "Midget Villa"; "New Bridal Chamber"; "Crooked Croquet"; "Fakir of Oola"; and "many others."

HOLD ON TO YOUR HATS

Theatre: Shubert Theatre
Opening Date: September 11, 1940; *Closing Date*: February 1, 1941
Performances: 158
Book: Guy Bolton, Matt Brooks, and Eddie Davis
Lyrics: E. Y. Harburg
Music: Burton Lane
Direction: "Book staged" by Edgar MacGregor and "entire production under the supervision of" George Hale;
    Producers: Al Jolson and George Hale; *Choreography*: Catherine Littlefield; *Scenery* and *Costumes*: Raoul
    Pene du Bois; *Lighting*: Feder; *Musical Direction*: Al Goodman
Cast: Margaret Irving (Sierra), Gil Lamb (Slim), George Church (Lon), Jack Whiting (Pete), Martha Raye (Ma-
    mie), Jinx Falkenburg (First Dudette, Rita), Joyce Matthews (Second Dudette), Thea Pinto (Third Dudette),
    Lew Eckles (Sheriff), Arnold Moss (Fernando), *Al Jolson* (Lone Rider), John Randolph (Radio Announcer),
    Joe Stoner (Shep Martin), Marty Drake (Old Man Hawkins), Bert Gordon (Concho), George Maran (Sound
    Effects), Russ Brown (Dinky), Eunice Healey (Shirley), Sid Cassel (Luis), Will Kuluva (Pedro); The Tanner
    Sisters: Martha Tanner, Mickey Tanner, and Betty Tanner; The Radio Aces: Marty Drake, Lou Stoner, and
    Joe Stoner; The Ranchettes: Margie Greene, Anita Jakobi, Iris Wayne, and Janis Williams; Dudettes: Janet

Moore, Betty Jane Hess, Jean Ellis, Joyce Matthews, Thea Pinto, Ruthe Reid, Francisca Sims, Dorothy Wygal; Dancing Girls: Marjorie Baglin, Betty Boyce, Flora Bowes, Renee Cettel, Grace DeVita, Constance Dowling, Betty Ford, Jackie Gately, Betty Gavin, Marion Lulling, Joanne Marshall, Dorothy Thomas, Myra Weldin, Claire Wolf; Dancing Boys: Albert Amato, Alan Bandler, Frank Carey, Arthur Grahl, Randolph Hughes, Clarence Jaeger, Dave Jones, George Miller, Russ Milton, Bill Rettie, Jack Smith

The musical was presented in two acts.

The action occurs in New York City, Arizona, and Mexico.

Musical Numbers

Act One: "Way Out West Where the East Begins" (Martha Tanner, Mickey Tanner, Betty Tanner, Marty Drake, Lou Stoner, Joe Stoner, Boys); "Hold on to Your Hats" (Martha Raye, The Ranchettes, Ensemble); "Walkin' along Mindin' My Business" (Al Jolson); "The World Is in My Arms" (Jack Whiting, Eunice Healey, The Ranchettes, Martha Tanner, Mickey Tanner, Betty Tanner); "Would You Be So Kindly" (Al Jolson, Martha Raye, The Ranchettes, Ensemble); Dance (Gil Lamb); "Life Was Pie for the Pioneer" (Martha Raye, George Church, Boys); "Don't Let It Get You Down" (Jack Whiting, Eunice Healey, Russ Brown, Gil Lamb, Margaret Irving, Marty Drake, Lou Stoner, Joe Stoner, Martha Tanner, Mickey Tanner, Betty Tanner, Ensemble); "Don't Let It Get You Down" (reprise) (Al Jolson, Eunice Healey); "There's a Great Day Coming Manana" (Al Jolson, Ensemble)

Act Two: "Then You Were Never in Love" (George Church, Marty Drake, Lou Stoner, Joe Stoner, The Ranchettes. Ensemble); Dance (George Church); "Down on the Dude Ranch" (Al Jolson, Bert Gordon, Martha Raye); "She Came, She Saw, She Can Canned" (Martha Raye, Al Jolson, The Ranchettes, Ensemble); "The World Is in My Arms" (reprise) (Eunice Healey, Marty Drake, Lou Stoner, Joe Stoner, Boys); "Old-Timer" (Al Jolson, Boys); Specialty (Gil Lamb); Broadcast (sequence of standards originally introduced and/or popularized by Jolson; see list below) (Al Jolson); Finale (Entire Company)

Hold On to Your Hats had all the makings of a smash hit: Al Jolson was back on Broadway after nine years (he had last appeared in 1931's *The Wonder Bar*), the musical received good reviews, the songs were popular with the public, and thus a long run of a year or more wasn't unlikely. The musical reportedly enjoyed sell-out or near sell-out business, and on opening night the best seats sold for $8.80 apiece; one critic reported the standees were three-deep in the back of the house. But as the run progressed and the winter approached, Jolson the performer found the New York weather too hard on his health and so Jolson the coproducer decided to close the show.

The zany plot centered on radio's biggest cowboy star, The Lone Rider (Jolson). His image of a tough, macho cowboy (who bellows "Hi-yo, Goldie" to his horse) masks the fact he's never been farther west than New Jersey and faints at the sound of gunfire. When the Old West of 1940 is threatened by the bandit Fernando (Arnold Moss), The Lone Rider finds himself elected as the unlikely hero who must capture the varmint. Out in coyote country he meets dude ranch owner Mamie (Martha Raye) and other assorted Western types (including an Indian named Pancho [Bert Gordon, aka The Mad Russian] who sports an East Side accent). And the villain Fernando is of course brought to justice.

The critics were overjoyed to once again see Jolson on the Broadway stage. Here was our "First Minstrel" (per Richard Watts in the *New York Herald Tribune*), and Richard Lockridge in the *New York Sun* said the "pretty grand" Jolson was "back from limbo" (that is, Hollywood). John Mason Brown in the *New York Post* found him an "extraordinary entertainer," and Sidney B. Whipple in the *New York World-Telegram* said Jolson's appearance in a new musical made Broadway "look like Broadway again." Brooks Atkinson in the *New York Times* said *Hold on to Your Hats* was a "capital" show and one of the "funniest" musicals to "have stumbled on to Broadway in years." Here was an evening which "restored" the "magnetic minstrel" Jolson to his "former glory," and Burns Mantle in the *New York Daily News* said the show added "spicy seasoning" to the array of musicals playing in town.

Martha Raye may have been a bit overpowering with her unique brand of comedy, but Atkinson found her a "fantastic cut-up," Brown said her "goofy abandon" won her "salutes of laughter," and Mantle noted she "stopped the show on occasion and started it all over again." Watts said he had previously found her a "most distressing" movie comedienne, but admitted she was "three hundred times" better on stage than screen and thus added "zest" to the evening. Raye was a perfect foil for Jolson, and at one point in a perhaps calculated flub which took on the air of ad-libbing, she thanked Jolson for "saving the Jews" when she supposedly meant to say "saving the jewels"; Atkinson reported that the ensuing banter between Jolson and Raye erupted into "comic hysteria." And Atkinson said Jolson, Raye, and Bert Gordon's show-stopping trio "Down on the Dude Ranch" could "have gone on for a half hour if the verses had held out."

Of E. Y. Harburg and Burton Lane's twelve songs, six were singled out by the critics: Whipple noted that "Walkin' along Mindin' My Business" had the traditional "swing and lilting melody" characteristic of the typical Jolson song, and he found "The World Is in My Arms" the "best" ballad; "There's a Great Day Comin' Manana" was a jubilee of a show-stopper; and the aforementioned "Down on the Dude Ranch" was a grand comic moment. Other songs which pleased the critics were "Would You Be So Kindly" and "Don't Let It Get You Down."

Toward the end of the evening during the "Broadcast" sequence, Jolson performed a medley of his popular hits. The critics reported he sang "April Showers" (interpolated into the 1921 national tour of *Bombo*; lyric by B. G. [Buddy] De Sylva, music by Louis Silvers); "Sonny Boy" (1928 film *The Singing Fool*; lyric by Lew Brown, B. G. [Buddy] De Sylva, and Jolson, music by Ray Henderson); "Swanee" (*Capitol Revue* aka *Demi-Tasse Revue* [1919], and later interpolated into the national tour of *Sinbad* [also 1919]; lyric by Irving Caesar, music by George Gershwin); and "You Made Me Love You (I Didn't Want to Do It)" (the second edition of *The Honeymoon Express* [1913]; lyric by Joseph McCarthy, music by James V. Monaco). He also reportedly sang "My Mammy" (interpolated into the 1919 tour of *Sinbad*; lyric by Joe Young and Sam M. Lewis, music by Walter Donaldson).

Jack Whiting created the role of Pete during the early tryout performances but briefly left the show during the Boston tryout and was succeeded by Lee Dixon; Whiting was back in the musical for opening night and the entire New York run. Ruby Keeler left the musical during the Chicago tryout, and was succeeded by Eunice Healey (later in the year, Keeler and Jolson divorced). Keeler's most recent Broadway appearance had been in *Show Girl* in 1929, and *Hold On to Your Hats* would have marked her return to Broadway after almost a dozen years. As it turned out, forty-two years passed between *Show Girl* and her next Broadway musical, the smash hit revival of *No, No, Nanette* in 1971.

A 1980 studio cast album of the score was included in the collection *E. Y. Harburg Revisited* (Painted Smiles CD # PSCD-120) with a cast that included Carleton Carpenter, Helen Gallagher, and Arthur Siegel; all twelve songs are included on the recording.

Hold On to Your Hats is particularly important in the history of American musical theatre because with it co-librettists Guy Bolton and Eddie Davis began their grand tradition of assigning the name "Dinky" to one of their characters. Here, Dinky was played by Russ Brown. In **Follow the Girls**, Dinky was performed by Buster West, and two other characters were named Spud (Tim Herbert) and Goofy (Jackie Gleason). And *Ankles Aweigh* (1955) offered Dinky (Lew Parker) and Spud (Gabriel Dell). There's a message here, but perhaps one too subtle to understand.

BOYS AND GIRLS TOGETHER
"Hilarious Entertainment"

Theatre: Broadhurst Theatre
Opening Date: October 1, 1940; *Closing Date*: March 15, 1941
Performances: 191
"Talk": Ed Wynn and Pat C. Flick
Lyrics: Jack Yellen and Irving Kahal
Music: Sammy Fain
Direction: Ed Wynn; *Producer*: Ed Wynn; *Choreography*: Albertina Rasch; *Scenery*: Oden Waller; *Costumes*: Irene Sharaff; *Lighting*: Uncredited; *Musical Direction*: John McManus
Cast: Ed Wynn, Tony and Renee De Marco, Jane Pickens, Dave Apollon, Jerry Cooper, Walter Long, Al Baron, Jack Connover, Iris Marshall, Dell Parker, Kay Paulson, Mira Stephans, Lucienne and Ashour, Dot and Dick Remy, The Six Willys (Eugene, Ersilo, Willie, Hermina, Ebe, and Rosita), Paul and Frank La Varre, Marjorie Knapp, Edna Sedgwick, Sally Craven, Florence Foster, Phyllis Colt, Dorothy Koster, Lynn Lawrence, Ione Smith, Drucilla Strain; The Wynnsome Dancing Girls: Billie Bernice, Betty Bartley, Trudy

Burke, Eleanor Brown, Maude Carroll, Gloria Costa, Patricia Deering, Adair Dollar, Helen Devlin, Gloria Gaffey, Georgia Jarvis, Eleanore Marek, Mary Joan Martin, Hazel Nevin, Mary Ann Parker, Jane Petri, Davenie Watson

The revue was presented in two acts.

Sketches and Musical Numbers

Act One: "A Few Boys" (Express Boy: Al Baron; Storage Boy: Paul La Varre, Moving Boy: Eugene Willy; Helping Boy: Frank La Varre); "The Boy" (Ed Wynn); "Some Girls and a Boy" (A Singing Girl: Marjorie Knapp; A Dancing Boy: Walter Long; A Dancing Girl: Edna Sedgwick) and "Liable to Catch On" (Marjorie Knapp; danced by Walter Long and Edna Sedgwick; The Wynnsome Dancing Girls); "The Boy" (Ed Wynn; Another Boy: Walter Long; A Bunch of Boys: John McManus and Orchestra; A Call Boy: Jack Connover; Two More Boys: Musicians); "The Leading Girl" (Jane Pickens; The Boy: Ed Wynn) and "Tschaikowski" (Jane Pickens); "The Boy" (Ed Wynn); "The 'Cocktail Hour Girls'" (Miss Ritz Carlton: Dorothy Koster; Miss St. Regis: Drucilla Strain; Miss Stork Club: Lynn Lawrence; Miss El Morocco: Mira Stephans; Miss Monte Carlo: Iris Marshall; Miss Rainbow Room: Ione Smith; Miss Twenty-One Club: Kay Paulsen; Miss Versailles: Dell Parker; The Leading Boy: Jerry Cooper; The Boy: Ed Wynn); "Two Boys and a Girl" (The Leading Boy: Jerry Cooper; The Leading Girl: Jane Pickens; The Boy: Ed Wynn) and "Such Stuff as Dreams Are Made Of" (lyric by Irving Kahal) (Jerry Cooper, Jane Pickens); ""Dream Girls" (Night Girl: Sally Craven; A Dream Girl: Florence Foster; Other Dream Girls: The Wynnsome Dancing Girls); "Four Boys and a Girl" (The Police Boy: Ed Wynn; A Taxi Boy: Walter Long; A Nurse Girl: Dorothy Koster; Two Odd Boys: Paul and Frank La Varre); "The Charm Bracelet" and "A Charming Boy and Girl" (What Boy and Girl?: The De Marcos; The Boy: Ed Wynn) and "A Dance" (The De Marcos); "The Boy" (Ed Wynn); "Some New Boys and Girls" (Lots of Girls: The Wynnsome Dancing Girls; A Stout Girl: Dot Remy; A Helping Boy: Dick Remy; A French Girl: Lucienne; A French Boy: Ashour; A Dancing Boy: Walter Long; A Dancing Girl: Sally Craven; A Persistent Girl: Florence Foster; The Boy: Ed Wynn); "Boys and Girls Together" (A Latin Girl: Jane Pickens; A Sailor Boy: Walter Long; A Spicy Girl: Edna Sedgwick; Two Dazzling Dancing Girls: Sally Craven, Florence Foster; A Red Hot Pepper Boy and Girl: The De Marcos; Eight Cactus Flower Girls: Dorothy Koster, Drucilla Strain, Lynn Lawrence, Mira Stephens, Iris Marshall, Ione Smith, Kay Paulsen, Dell Parker); "Sixteen 'Down Mexico Way' Girls" (Billie Bernice, Betty Barclay, Helen Bennett, Trudy Burke, Eleanor Brown, Maude Carroll, Gloria Costa, Adair Dollar, Helen Devlin, Gloria Gaffey, Kay Gable, Mary Joan Martin, Hazel Nevin, Mary Ann Parker, Jane Petri, Davenie Watson); "Eight Conga Girls"; "The Boy" (Ed Wynn)/"The Latin in Me" (lyric by Irving Kahal) (Jane Pickens; danced by The De Marcos, Walter Long, Edna Sedgwick, Sally Craven, Florence Foster, The Conga Girls, and The Wynnsome Dancing Girls); Act One Finale

Act Two: "The Boy" (Ed Wynn); "Three Boys and Three Girls" (The Six Willys—Eugene, Ersillo, Willie, Hermina, Ebe, and Rosita; The Boy: Ed Wynn); "A Boy and Five Girls" (The Singing Boy: Jerry Cooper; The Dancing Girl: Edna Sedgwick; Other Girls: Eleanore Marik, Eleanor Brown, Billie Bernice, and Patricia Deering) and "I Want to Live (as Long as You Love Me)" (lyric by Jack Yellen) (Jerry Cooper); "A Girl and Two Boys" (The Leading Boy: Jerry Cooper; The Leading Girl: Jane Pickens; The Boy: Ed Wynn); "Boys and Girls Together" (A Tom Boy: Marjorie Knapp; A Rube Boy: Walter Long; A Rube Girl: Edna Sedgwick; a Bad Girl: Sally Craven; A Bad Boy: Florence Foster; A Boy and Girl: The De Marcos) and "Times Square Dance" (sung by Marjorie Knapp; danced by The De Marcos, Walter Long, Edna Sedgwick, Sally Craven, Florence Foster, "and about forty Boys and Girls"); "Four Boys" (One Boy: Dave Apollon; Another Boy: Frank La Varre; The Boy: Ed Wynn; A Wise Boy: Al Baron); "Five Girls and the Boy" (One Girl: Drucilla Strain; Another Girl: Kay Paulsen; A Girl: Mira Stephans; One More Girl: Lynn Lawrence; The Leading Girl: Jane Pickens; The Boy: Ed Wynn) and "Catsup on the Moon" (aka "You Can't Put Ketchup on the Moon") (Jane Pickens; "played" by Ed Wynn); "Boys and Girls Together" (The Leading Boy: Jerry Cooper; The Dancing Boy: Walter Long; The Leading Girl: Jane Pickens; A French Boy and Girl: Lucienne and Ashour; A Great Boy: Dave Apollon; A Ballet Girl: Sally Craven; A Blonde Girl: Florence Foster; A Little Girl: Marjorie Knapp; Some Boy and Some Girl: The De Marcos; The Dancing Girl: Edna Sedgwick; Three Boys and Three Girls: The Six Willys; The Boy: Ed Wynn; The Wynnsome Dancing Girls; The Cocktail Hour Girls) and "The Sun Will Be Up in the Morning" (lyric by Jack Yellen) (Jerry Cooper, Other Boys and

Girls; danced by The De Marcos, Walter Long, Edna Sedgwick, Sally Craven, Florence Foster, "and Loads of Boys and Girls") (Note in program at end of second-act song list: "To the Audience/Good Night/Boys and Girls/I Hope You Liked Us/Ed Wynn.")

Ed Wynn and his revue *Boys and Girls Together* received some of the best notices of the season. The self-described "Perfect Fool" Wynn had his winsome comic shtick down pat, and his fluttery gestures, wide-eyed bafflement, embarrassed chortles, and lisping voice were all in fine form, and of course he wore a succession of his trademark (and slightly surreal) hats and coats. Despite a large cast of comedians, acrobats, jugglers, mandolin players, singers, ballroom dancers, apache dancers, and other performers, Wynn was the whole show. He acted as a kind of dazed but delighted master of ceremonies, and when he wasn't the lead in a particular scene he was a welcome intrusion when others in the cast took the stage. Sometimes he became literally entangled with them, and at other times gazed at their performances with wide-eyed wonderment, appreciation, and perhaps even a bit of proud-poppa pride.

Brooks Atkinson in the *New York Times* proclaimed that on the evidence of *Boys and Girls Together* Ed Wynn was "the funniest man in the world." He was truly a "perfect fool out of a demented volume of Mother Goose" and his show was an "uproarious" entertainment. Atkinson noted that in one sequence with acrobats Paul and Frank La Varre, Wynn became hopelessly entangled with them and soon their six entwined legs became positive proof there was "no solution to this predicament." Burns Mantle in the *New York Daily News* said the evening was "the best revue we have had on Broadway in years," and he was amused when Wynn became involved in a juggling act (with The Six Willies) and an apache dance by Lucienne and Ashour (Wynn even found time to suggest ways for Lucienne to get even with her "brutal" partner).

Richard Lockridge in the *New York Sun* said Wynn had never been "more hilarious," and he liked the way Wynn cavorted about the stage on his invention of a bicycle-cum-piano. Lockridge also praised mandolin player Dave Apollon and the ballroom dancers The De Marcos, and said "Catsup on the Moon" was the best song of the evening. Richard Watts in the *New York Herald Tribune* said Wynn was a "superb" comic and his revue was "an entertainment to be cherished." He particularly enjoyed Wynn's screwball insistence that the revue would avoid boy-and-girl clichés, and so when such shenanigans occurred Wynn advised the audience that these antics were in no way part of the revue.

John Mason Brown in the *New York Post* proclaimed that Wynn was a "magician" of "nonsense." Sidney B. Whipple in the *New York World-Telegram* said the evening was a "great show" and that Wynn was at the height of his powers; his comic presence was simply "dazzling."

During the tryout, "The Latin in Me" was sung by Carolyn Marsh, who didn't appear during the New York run (for Broadway, the number was introduced by Jane Pickens). "Jitterbugging with the Young Folks" was cut during the tryout where it was sung by Phyllis Colt and danced by the chorus.

"The Cocktail Girls" saluted various New York hot spots (The Ritz-Carlton, the St. Regis, the Stork Club, El Morocco, Monte Carlo, the Rainbow Room, 21, and the Versailles); during the tryout and perhaps during the Broadway run, two other venues were honored, the Persian Room and the Waldorf-Astoria.

"Catsup on the Moon" was included in the collection *You Can't Put Ketchup on the Moon* (Rialto Recordings CD # SLRR-9201), and "The Latin in Me" is included in *The Broadway Musicals of 1940* (Bayview CD # RNBW019).

For *Boys and Girls Together*, Tony De Marco danced with his wife Renee. A year later he appeared in **Banjo Eyes** with his new wife (and dancing partner) Sally, and they were again seen on Broadway in the revues **Show Time** and **Star Time**.

IT HAPPENS ON ICE
"A MUSICAL ICETRAVAGANZA"

Theatre: Center Theatre
Opening Date: October 10, 1940; *Closing Date*: April 26, 1942
Performances: 662
Sketches: Joe Cook's comedy scenes "devised and written by" him in collaboration with Bud Pearson and Lester White
Lyrics: Al Stillman, Mitchell Parish

Music: Vernon Duke, Fred E. Ahlert, Peter De Rose; also by Morton Gould, Raymond Scott
Direction: Leon Leonidoff; *Producers*: Sonja Henie and Arthur Wirtz (Sonart Productions); *Choreography*: Catherine Littlefield (assisted by Robert Linden); *Scenery, Costumes*, and *Lighting*: Norman Bel Geddes; *Musical Director*: Erno Rapp (who was the conductor along with David Mendoza)
Cast: Joe Cook, Hedi Stenuf, The Caley Sisters, Le Verne, Jo Ann Dean, Mary Jane Yeo, Lloyd Baxter, Gene Berg, (Dr. A. Douglas) Arthur Nelles, The Four Bruises (Sid Spalding, Geoffe Stevens, Monte Scott, Buster Grace); Vocals: Joan Edwards, Felix Knight, Jack Kilty and The Buccaneers (for names of skaters, see list of skating sequences, below)

Skating, Sketches, and Musical Sequences

Act One: Overture (conducted by Erno Rapp); "Wintertime" (Their Partners: Arthur Erickson, Rudy Richards; Cocottes: Ethel Stout, Gweneth Butler, Edwina Blades; Flower Girls: Nancy Mae Woodbury, Hertha Grossman; A Gracious Lady: Kay Corcoran; Footman: John Dunaway; Three Laughing Girls: Angela Carson, Gladys Gooding, Eileen Brokaw; Footman: Charles Storey; A Roue: Charles Cavanaugh; Footman: Donald Arthur; A Mother: Margo Miller; Child: Peggy Fahy; The Father: Leon Kosofsky; Footman: John Anderson; Musician: Arthur Nelles; Policeman: Fred Marshall; Scamps: Neil Rose, Ian Grey, Jack Reese; Novice Skaters: Theckla Horn and Lyle Clark, Louise Clark and Scott Edwards, Janet Hester and Charles Hain, Audrey Butler and Albert McNulty; Expert Skaters: Lynn Clare and Edmund Rudnik; Eileen Thompson and Tex Mangrun, Helen Thompson and Meryl Baxter, Dorothy Chandler and Stan Skidmore; Nursemaid: Lillian Oldham; Two Small Girls: Trudy Schneider, Pearl Joseph; Balloon Man: Kenny Williams; Show-Off: Gene Berg; Two Admiring Girls: Jo Ann Dean, Mary Jane Yeo); "Joe Cook's Fountain in the Park" (Proprietor: Joe Cook; His Assistant: Senator Charles Senna; Customers: George Dewey, Marion Eddy, Gene Winchester, William Lilling, Geoffe Stevens, Montey Scott, Paul Castle); "Between You, Me, and the Lamp Post" (lyric by Al Stillman, music by Fred Ahlert) (sung by Joan Edwards and Felix Knight: Lamp Posts: Scott Edwards, John Anderson, Charles Storey, Edmund Rudink, Tex Mangrum, Meryl Baxter, Leon Kosofsky, Charles Hain, Lyle Clark, Arthur Erickson, Charles Cavanaugh, Rudy Richards; Sailors: Donald Arthur, Neil Rose, Ian Grey, Albert McNulty, Jack Reese, Fred Marshall; Girls: Ethel Stout, Peggy Fahy, Louise Clark, Janet Hester, Helen Thompson, Bernice Loughborough; A Park Bench: Margo Miller, Kay Corcoran, Dorothy Chandler; Another Bench: Ruth Noland, Jeanne Berman, Gladys Gooding; A Ladies' Maid: May Judels; A Statue: Lillian Oldham, Eileen Thompson, Theckla Horn; Chauffeur: Stan Skidmore; A Dog: Paul Castle; Drunks: Geoffe Stevens, Buster Grace); "Curlilocks and the Three Bears" (music by Morton Gould) (Curlilocks: Mary Jane Yeo; Father Bear: Arthur Nellis; Mother Bear: Kenny Williams; Baby Bear: Paul Castle); "Legend of the Lake" (Butterflies: Edwina Blades, Gweneth Butler, Theckla Horn, Patsy O'Day, Lucille O'Day, Lillian Oldham, Eileen Brokaw, Audrey Butler; Hunters: Tex Mangrum, Neil Rose, Ian Grey, Fred Marshall, Donald Arthur, Jack Reese, Lyle Clark, Stan Skidmore, Edmund Rudink, Meryl Baxter, Albert McNulty, Scott Edwards, Charles Hain, Arthur Erickson, Leon Kosofsky; Kabalo: Gene Berg; The Prince: Lloyd "Skippy" Baxter; The Princess: Hedi Stenuf; Swans: Janet Hester, Ruth Noland, Dorothy Chandler, Margo Miller, Louise Clark, Lynn Clare, Eileen Thompson, Peggy Fahy, Ethel Stout, Charlotte Weitzel, Kay Corcoran, Gladys Gooding, Trudy Schneider, Hertha Grossman, Angela Carson, Nancy Mae Woodbury, Florence Rohr); "As I See It" (Joe Cook; with the assistance of General Charles Senna; introducing the Absent-Minded Professor, Professor A. Douglas Arthur Nelles); "Fast Colors" (music by Raymond Scott) (Lucille O'Day, Helen Thompson, Ethel Stout, Janet Hester, Eileen Brokaw, Angela Carson, Theckla Horn, Kay Corcoran, Ruth Noland, Louise Clark, Patsy O'Day, Lynn Clare, Bernice Loughborough, Florence Rohr, Peggy Fahy, May Judels, Pearl Joseph, Eileen Thompson, Mary Jane Yeo, Jo Ann Dean); "The Moon Fell in the River" (lyric by Mitchell Parish, music by Peter De Rose) (sung by Joan Edwards and Felix Knight; Gweneth Butler and Trudy Schneider, Charlotte Weitzel, Nancy Mae Woodbury, Hertha Grossman, Dorothy Chandler, Margo Miller, Dorothy and Hazel Caley with Gene Berg and Meryl Baxter); "Captain Cook at the North Pole" (President of the Arctic Club: Marion Eddy; The Lecturer: Joe Cook; His Shadow: Colonel Charles Senna; Tourists: George Dewey, William Lilling; Vender: William Houston; Bathing Girl: Edwina Blades; and the following full-blooded Eskimos: Orville Race, Gene Winchester, Geoffe Stevens, Monte Scott, Sid Spalding, Buster Grace, Arthur Nelles, Paul Castle); "Don't Blow That Horn, Gabriel" (lyric by Al Stillman, music by Vernon Duke and Will Hudson) (Deacons: Rawdon Barnes, William Lilling, William Hanston, Orville Race; Sinners: May Judels, Lillian Oldham, Ruth Noland, Reszka Law, Florence Rohr, Jeanne Berman, Kay Corcoran, Audrey Butler, Theckla Horn, Gladys Gooding, Bernice Loughborough, Shirley Barney, Peggy Fahy, Pearl Joseph, Lucille O'Day, Patsy O'Day, Neil Rose, Jack Reese, Fred Marshall, Arthur Erickson, Charles Storey, Leon Kosofsky, Donald Arthur, Kenny Williams, Albert McNulty, Scott Edwards, Charles Hain, Ian Grey, Charles Cavanaugh, John Anderson, Lyle Clark, Rudy Richards; In the Groove: Jo Ann Dean and Gene Berg; Sister Susie: Le Verne; Gabriel: Jack Kilty; St. Pete: Felix Knight; Angels: Eileen Brokaw, Angela Carson; Cherub: Paul Castle)

Act Two: Entr'acte (Orchestra); "Your Presence Requested (R.S.V.P.)" and "Long Ago" (lyric by Al Stillman, music by Vernon Duke) (sung by Joan Edwards; Major-Domo: Gene Berg; Blackamoors: Patsy O'Day, Jeanne Berman, Kay Corcoran, Lillian Oldham, John Dunaway, John Anderson, Rudy Richards, Leon Kosofsky; Host: Lloyd "Skippy" Baxter; Hostess: Edwina Blades; Maids: Theckla Horn, Lucille O'Day, Eileen Brokaw, Angela Carson; Guests: Janet Hester, Ruth Noland, Dorothy Chandler, Margo Miller, Louise Clark, Lynn Clare, Eileen Thompson, Helen Thompson, Peggy Fahy, Charlotte Weitzel, Ethel Stout, Trudy Schneider, Hertha Grossman, Pearl Joseph, Audrey Butler, Nancy Mae Woodbury, Tex Mangrum, Neil Rose, Fred Marshall, Ian Grey, Donald Arthur, Jack Reese, Lyle Clark, Stan Skidmore, Edmund Rudink, Meryl Baxter, Albert McNulty, Scott Edwards, Charles Hain, Charles Storey, Arthur Erickson, Charles Cavanaugh); "Two of a Kind" (music by Fred Ahlert) (Dorothy and Hazel Caley); "Chief Cook and His Arctic Indians" (Joe Cook; The Indians: George Dewey ("with certain reservations"), Bill Dewey, and Andy McBann; A Half-Breed: Doctor Charles Senna); "Coquette" (Hedi Stenuf and Lloyd "Skippy" Baxter, with Albert McNulty, Scott Edwards, Lyle Clark, Edmund Rudink); "So What Goes" (lyric by Al Stillman, music by Fred Ahlert) (Jo Ann Dean and Gene Berg, assisted by Gladys Gooding, Audrey Butler, Bernice Loughborough, Florence Rohr, Kay Corcoran, Theckla Horn, Angela Carson, Peggy Fahy, Patsy O'Day, Jeanne Berman, Lucille O'Day, Janet Hester, Helen Thompson, Eileen Brokaw, Reszka Law, Ruth Nolan, Meryl Baxter, Donald Arthur, Jack Reese, Rudy Richards, Stan Skidmore, Fred Marshall, John Anderson, Tex Mangrum, Charles Cavanaugh, Arthur Erickson, Charles Hain, Kenny Williams, Leon Kosofsky, Ian Grey, John Dunaway, Neil Rose); "The 1941 Version of the Fuller Construction Company Symphony Orchestra" (William Lilling introducing Maestro Joe Cook and his sterling group of musicians, including George Dewey, Bill Dewey, Paul Castle, Gene Winchester, Andy McBann, and the Honorable Charles Senna); "The Ice Has 'It'" (music by Morton Gould) (Le Verne); "The Glamour Girls" (The Four Bruises [Sid Spalding, Geoffe Stevens, Monte Scott, and Buster Grace]); "What's on the Penny" (lyric by Al Stillman, music by Fred Ahlert) (sung by Jack Kilty, Joan Edwards, Felix Knight, and The Buccaneers) (The Girls: Lucille O'Day, Peggy Fahy, Eileen Brokaw, Janet Hester, Ruth Noland, Bernice Loughborough, Trudy Schneider, Gladys Gooding, Ethel Stout, Dorothy Chandler, Louise Clark, Angela Carson, Lynn Clare, Patsy O'Day, Florence Rohr, Theckla Horn, Margo Miller, Helen Thompson, Eileen Thompson, Kay Corcoran; The Boys: Rudy Richards, Charles Storey, Neil Rose, Ian Grey, Leon Kosofsky, Howard Bissell, Lyle Clark, Charles Cavanaugh, Albert McNulty, John Dunaway, Scott Edwards, James Wright, Donald Arthur, Stan Skidmore, Edmund Rudink, John Anderson, Tex Mangrum, Meryl Baxter, Charles Hain, Arthur Erickson; Drum Major: Kenny Williams; Le Verne, Hedi Stenuf, Lloyd "Skippy" Baxter, Dorothy Caley, Hazel Caley, Gene Berg, Jo Ann Dean, Mary Jane Yeo, Edwina Blades, Arthur Nellis, Gweneth Butler, May Judels, Paul Castle, Hertha Grossman, Nancy Mae Woodbury)

When the 1971 revival of *On the Town* opened on Broadway, a critic wondered why one sequence satirized ice revues. He had apparently forgotten that New York offered wall-to-wall ice revues for almost the entire decade of the 1940s. *It Happens on Ice* was the first, and was followed by **Stars on Ice** (1942), **Hats Off to Ice** (1944), **Icetime** (1946), **Icetime of 1948** (1947), **Howdy, Mr. Ice** (1948), and **Howdy, Mr. Ice of 1950** (1949). All seven musical ice revues were produced by Sonja Henie and Arthur Wirtz at Rockefeller Center's Center Theatre for a staggering run of 4,043 performances.

It Happens on Ice opened on October 10, 1940, and played until March 8, 1941, for a total of 180 performances; a second edition was presented a month later on April 4, 1941, and closed on June 14, 1941, after ninety-six additional showings; after a month's vacation, it resumed on July 15, 1941, when it played 386 additional performances before closing on April 26, 1942, for a grand total of 662 performances.

The critics generally enjoyed the revue, but complained it went on too long and the novelty and wonderment of spectacular ice skating began to pall after the first hour. Plus, it was difficult to keep the skaters straight. Was that Mary Jane Yeo in the last sequence, or was it Jo Ann Dean? Was that one Edmund Rudink, or was it Rudy Richards? (And, truly, were skaters Edwina Blades and Stan Skidmore really born with those almost too-perfect "ice-skating" names?) Further, the skating numbers were in many ways alike. George Jean Nathan once noted in his *Theatre Book of the Year* annuals that the skating sequences blended together and he was thus unable "to see anything remarkably different" when fifty skaters clad in white performed a "Jack Frost Ballet" than when clad in brown they performed an "Autumn Leaves Ballet."

Besides the skaters, the revue offered Broadway comic Joe Cook and other comedians in a few sketches, but their humor was in many ways lost within the confines of the enormous Center Theatre (which had some 3,700 seats). Further, the singers all but disappeared within the cavernous venue. The theatre had been problematic from the beginning, as it was clear that only huge, spectacle-like musicals could fill its large space, and so the theatre's first two tenants were the lavish operettas *The Great Waltz* (1934) and *White Horse Inn* (1936). They were followed by *Virginia* (1937), a musical that had been commissioned by the Rockefellers as a convenient tie-in with their recent restoration of Williamsburg into a popular tourist spot; George S. Kaufman and Moss Hart's pageant-like *The American Way* (1939); and the huge musical *Swingin' the Dream* (1939), which was loosely based on Shakespeare's *A Midsummer Night's Dream*. But it was the ice show format which really took off and gave the theatre a successful decade; for these ice shows, the Center's stage was expanded and it swept into the auditorium by gobbling up what had been the first eight or so rows of the orchestra section. Between the ice revue productions, there were occasional bookings of limited-run operas, but once the last ice revue closed, the theatre never again saw another production. After a few years as a television studio, the theatre was demolished in 1954 to make way for an office building.

Richard Lockridge in the *New York Sun* said the evening was "mechanically perfect" but also "abstract" and "distant and mathematical." He noted "perfect" skaters were followed by more perfect skaters who seemed to be doing "precisely" what the previous skaters had done (the costumes changed and "no doubt" the skaters, but "you couldn't prove it by me"). Richard Watts in the *New York Herald Tribune* praised Norman Bel Geddes's elaborate décor, and while he was glad to see Joe Cook back on stage, he felt the comedian wasn't given enough to do. He suggested the evening should have taken its cue from **Boys and Girls Together**, in which mainliner Ed Wynn was spelled by the chorus between his scenes; here, the skaters should have been the evening's glue by serving as brief entertainments between Cook's comic sketches.

John Mason Brown in the *New York Post* complained that Cook's personality was lost in the "chilling depths" of the huge theatre; and while he enjoyed the "Hans Brinker carnival" of a show, he noted that two hours of constant skating was "too much" and suggested the evening was a "frosted version" of Billy Rose's *Aquacade* at the World's Fair (but Billy Rose was to be congratulated for keeping the water revue down to one hour).

Burns Mantle in the *New York Daily News* liked the "grand" sequence "Your Presence Is Requested," which was decorated in blacks and whites. He also noted that "The Moon Fell in the River" threatened to be a "hit song" (but the song proved to hold back on such a threat). He noted that one of the lead skaters (Lloyd "Skippy" Baxter) was a "handsome young fellow," but said overall it was difficult to separate the skills of the individual skaters (some might do "a couple more twirls" than another, but he just "couldn't say"). Sidney B. Whipple in the *New York World-Telegram* praised the first-name-less Le Verne, who was "breathtaking" in "Don't Blow That Horn, Gabriel" and "The Ice Has 'It'"; he noted that "The Moon Fell in the River" offered a "haunting" melody; and was sorry that Cook's tour left him "lost in the icebergs" way up in the "frozen north."

Brooks Atkinson in the *New York Times* supposed there had never before been an ice show so "gorgeous" as *It Happens on Ice*, and said the Broadway "show-shops" probably didn't offer anything "more beautiful" than "The Legend of the Lake." But he regretted the evening didn't do "justice" to Joe Cook because the large theatre never really brought him into the revue's "carnival mood."

The producers clearly listened to the critics, because when the revue's second edition opened on April 4, 1941, Cook and his comic cronies were gone and the evening's hilarity was relegated to comic performances on the ice by The Four Bruises, who were back and now billed as "sensational" (they reprised their drag-routine-on-ice as scrubwomen in "The Glamour Girls"), and added to the comic mix were Freddie Trenkler, Fritz Dietl, Tommy Lee and Charlie Slagle, and, from the previous edition, Dr. A. Douglas Arthur Nelles, all billed as "The World's Funniest Ice Comedians."

The new edition brought back "Wintertime," "Curlilocks and the Three Bears," "Legend of the Lake," "Your Presence Requested," "The Moon Fell in the River," and "Between You, Me, and the Lamp Post," among others. But as noted there were now more comic ice routines, including The Four Bruises' "Horse-play" (which dealt with a horse and three drunks), bits with Tommy Lee and Charlie Slagle (as "The Skating Scamps"), Freddie Trenkler ("The Bouncing Ball of the Ice"), and Trenkler and Fritz Dietl in a "Down South" sequence with the former as Topsy and the latter as Simon Legree. The evening also offered an adagio number on skates performed by Betty Atkinson and Charles Hain. And, to prove the revue was up-to-the-minute, there was now a South American number, first titled "Heilo Caliente" (and a song, "Brazilian Nuts") and then later titled "Heilo Argentine." As the run progressed, "Cubana" (lyric and music by Joe Linz and Pembroke Davenport) was added to the score, and indeed throughout the remainder of the run new material was added and the running order of the routines was occasionally restructured.

In reviewing the second edition, Wilella Waldorf in the *New York Post* said she hadn't looked forward to seeing the show again because the first time around it was "very, very icy." But the new edition was "enjoyable," and while the departed Joe Cook had been "icebound" in the first edition, the new version wisely kept the comic routines on ice. She admitted that after two hours the "novelty" of an ice show wore off and became somewhat "repetitious," but noted the evening was now a "marked improvement . . . a cheering thought with hot weather just around the corner."

Sidney B. Whipple in the *New York World-Telegram* said the new edition was "brilliant" and "glittering," but admitted that one hour was really "sufficient" for ice skating ("the rest is redundant"). He was again happy to see "Legend of the Lake" (and Lloyd "Skippy" Baxter was here "more magnificent" than in the first edition) and "Wintertime" ("a kaleidoscopic picture" reminiscent of a Currier and Ives print, but "much more lively"). (Michael Todd's **Up in Central Park** also offered an homage to Currier and Ives in its celebrated dance number.) Whipple also liked Betty Atkinson, who was "tops" in her art of combined ice-adagio and baton-twirling, and comic skater Freddie Trenkler, who "stopped the show" with his clowning.

CABIN IN THE SKY
"A New Musical Play" / "The New Musical Triumph"

Theatre: Martin Beck Theatre
Opening Date: October 25, 1940; *Closing Date*: March 8, 1941
Performances: 156
Book: Lynn Root
Lyrics: John La Touche
Music: Vernon Duke
Direction: "Entire production staged" by George Balanchine and "dialogue directed" by Albert Lewis; *Producers*: Albert Lewis in association with Vinton Freedley; *Choreography*: George Balanchine; *Scenery* and *Costumes*: Boris Aronson; *Lighting*: Uncredited; *Musical Direction*: Max Meth
Cast: Katherine Dunham (Georgia Brown), Louis Sharp (Dr. Jones), J. Rosamond Johnson (Brother Green), Georgia Burke (Lily), *Ethel Waters* (Petunia Jackson), Rex Ingram (Lucifer Jr.), Dooley Wilson ("Little Joe" Jackson), Archie Savage (Imp), Jieno Moxzer (Imp), Rajah Chardieno (Imp), Alexander McDonald (Imp), Todd Duncan (The Lawd's General), Milton Williams (Fleetfoot), J. Louis Johnson (Dude), Earl Sydnor (First Henchman), Earl Edwards (Second Henchman), Maurice Ellis (Third Henchman), Al Stokes (Devil's Messenger), Wilson Bradley (Messenger Boy), Dick Campbell (Domino Johnson); Katherine Dunham Dancers: Claude Brown, Talley Beattey, Rita Christiana, Lucille Ellis, Lawaune Kennard, Roberta McLaurin, Alexander McDonald, Jiene Moxzer Harris, Rajah Ohardieno, Evelyn Pilcher, Carmencita Romero, Edith Ross, Archie Savage, Lavinia Williams, Thomas Woosley, J. Emanuel Vanderhans, Candido Vicenti; A. Rosamond Johnson Singers: Wilson Bradley, Rebecca Champion, Helen Dowdy, Clarence Jacobs, Ella MacLashley, Fradye Marshall, Arthur McLean, Louis Sharp, Eulabel Riley, Al Stokes, Laura Vaughns
The musical was presented in two acts.
The action takes place "somewhere in the South" and "at the Pearly Gates."

Musical Numbers

Act One: "The General's Song" (aka "Make Way" and "General's Entrance") (Todd Duncan, Saints); "Pay Heed" (aka "The Man Upstairs") (Todd Duncan, Saints); "Taking a Chance on Love" (lyric by John La

Touche and Ted Fetter) (Ethel Waters); "Cabin in the Sky" (Ethel Waters, Dooley Wilson); "Holy Unto the Lord" (Ethel Waters, Dooley Wilson, J. Rosamond Johnson, Church Members); "Dem Bones" (Ethel Waters, Helen Dowdy, Church Members); "Do What You Wanna Do" (Rex Ingram, Archie Savage, Jieno Moxzer, Rajah Chardieno, Alexander McDonald); "Taking a Chance on Love" (reprise) (Ethel Waters, Dooley Wilson)

Act Two: "Fugue" (Todd Duncan, Saints); "In My Old Virginia Home (on the River Nile)" (Ethel Waters, Dooley Wilson); "Egyptian Ballet" (aka "Vision") (The Katherine Dunham Dancers); "Love Me Tomorrow (but Leave Me Alone Today)" (Katherine Dunham, Dooley Wilson); "Love Turned the Light Out" (Ethel Waters); "Lazy Steps" (dance) (The Katherine Dunham Dancers); "Boogy Woogy" (dance) (The Katherine Dunham Dancers); "Honey in the Honeycomb" (Katherine Dunham, Boys); "Savannah" (lyric by John La Touche and Ted Fetter) (Ethel Waters; danced by Ethel Waters and Archie Savage); Finale

For its era, *Cabin in the Sky* was a charming fable about good and evil that took its story seriously and utilized song and dance to further the plot. This was no slapdash affair of clichéd musical comedy antics. The characterizations were shaped with thoughtfulness and the work's five major roles (three humans, two other-worldly ones) embodied the musical's opposing themes. Today the work may seem condescending to blacks, but there's no doubt it was conceived as a respectful and sometimes solemn story. Because of misguided po-litically correct notions, *Cabin in the Sky* will probably never be produced again, and the 1964 Off-Broadway revival will no doubt prove to be the musical's last major showing. But the 1943 film version as well as vari-ous recordings of the score will ensure the musical's place in Broadway history.

Sinner Little Joe (Dooley Wilson) is on his deathbed, and his wife Petunia (Ethel Waters) asks the Lord to give her husband a second chance. So Little Joe is granted an extension of six months to prove himself worthy of entering the pearly gates. The Lawd's General (Todd Duncan) and Lucifer's son (Rex Ingram) watch over the proceedings and each hopes he will be the one to win Little Joe's soul. Despite his second chance, Little Joe gives into temptation when he's vamped by the wicked Georgia Brown (Katherine Dunham), but all ends well when both Little Joe and Petunia are taken to that cabin in the sky.

All the critics praised Ethel Waters's alternately touching and jubilant performance, and agreed she was at the peak of her powers after an already legendary career (and she wowed them all over again a decade later with her masterful portrayal of Berenice in Carson McCullers's 1950 drama *The Member of the Wedding*). Most critics were impressed with the new musical, although some thought the second act was a let-down and one or two noted that a late second-act scene in which Waters cut loose in a barroom dance with Archie Savage seemed out of character.

Brooks Atkinson in the *New York Times* said Waters had never before given such a "rich" performance, and noted he had never heard any song performed as well as Waters sang "Taking a Chance on Love" (she deserved a Congressional Medal of Honor as a "reward" for standing the song "on its head"). He suggested the musical might be better, but couldn't imagine how. For here was an "original," "joyous," and "imagina-tive" show with an "extraordinarily fresh" book, "racy" music, and "crisp and jaunty" lyrics. He also noted Katherine Dunham played Georgia Brown as a "baggage at a blistering temperature."

Sidney Whipple in the *New York World-Telegram* advised his readers they'd be "taking no chances on anything" by seeing the "exuberantly" performed musical; he noted the evening occasionally dipped into *The Green Pastures* territory ("but not too much"), and he praised the "infectious jollity" of Waters's performance (he noted she sometimes danced "with all the agility of a mature Betty Hutton"). He said "Dem Bones" was a "sure-fire novelty number" and that "Taking a Chance on Love" was the score's best song. Burns Mantle in the *New York Daily News* stated that as of 10:30 on opening night the show was a "roaring success"; but noted the second act lost some of its "pace and substance" and veered into a **John Henry**–like conclusion. Otherwise, Waters was "perfection" and was "agreeably in command" of the evening.

Richard Lockridge in the *New York Sun* said the book often matched the "engaging originality" of its star and noted that Waters had "never been more engaging." He too thought there was a certain letdown in some of the second-act scenes, and suggested librettist Lynn Root might have had *The Green Pastures* in mind (there was a "comic innocence" in the musical that echoed the earlier play). John Mason Brown in the *New York Post* also noted influences from *The Green Pastures* and said the evening's "overlong struggle" between good and evil became tiresome. The musical's "promising beginning" became a "decided disappointment" and "something of a bore." But Waters radiated "geniality" as if the word were "spelled out in neon." She was "one of the truly grand performers of our stage."

Richard Watts in the *New York Herald Tribune* said the evening was "on the whole" a "lively musical show." It was at its peak in the gayer and lighter moments, but when it became serious it seemed like a "blackface *Liliom*." But Waters was "brilliant" and "one of the great women of the American stage." He also praised the "vigorous and rather striking" music and the "good" lyrics.

The combination of George Balanchine and Katherine Dunham and her troupe made for an evening of exciting dances. Mantle found some of the dances a "trifle orgiastic"; Atkinson noted there were "boogie-woogie orgies"; Lockridge said the evening was "sufficiently orgiastic in the fashion of Negro dancing shows"; and Brown described the dances as "orgiastic climaxes of extraordinary vigor." Watts said Dunham's "evil" character was so "exciting" that she "makes virtue " seem "dubious," and Whipple noted she provided much of the "zippier" dancing and was a "fiery little number." Mantle said she was a "siren with all the trimmings."

During the run, "It's Not So Good to Be Bad" was added (for Todd Duncan). "Taking a Chance on Love" had originally been written as "Foolin' Around with Love" by Duke and Ted Fetter for an unproduced musical. Three days before the New York opening, the creators realized a last-minute number was needed for Waters, Duke remembered the earlier song, and so La Touche revised the lyric. The song proved to be the biggest hit from the show and one of Broadway's evergreens.

Ethel Waters recorded four songs from the production ("Taking a Chance on Love," "Honey in the Honeycomb," "Love Turned the Light Out," and the title song), and Max Meth and the original Broadway orchestra members recorded the overture; all these were reissued on a CD released by AEI (# AEI-CD-017), which also includes numbers from **Carib Song** and *Porgy and Bess*. The 1943 film soundtrack was released by Rhino Movie Music (# R272245) and includes outtakes as well as extended versions of various songs.

The 1964 Off-Broadway revival opened at the Greenwich Mews Theatre on January 21 for forty-seven performances; the cast included Rosetta LeNoire (Petunia), Tony Middleton (Little Joe), Ketty Lester (Georgia Brown), and Sam Laws (The Lawd's General). Added to the production were: "Wade in the Water," "Gospel: Great Day," "Cross Over—Off to John Henry's," and "Living It Up" (all apparently with lyrics by Vernon Duke) as well as La Touche and Duke's "We'll Live All Over Again," which had been cut from the original production. The revival also included "Not a Care in the World" (from La Touche and Duke's **Banjo Eyes**). Retained for the revival were: "Taking a Chance on Love," "Cabin in the Sky," "Do What You Wanna Do," "Fugue," "Love Me Tomorrow (but Leave Me Alone Today)," "Love Turned the Light Out," "Honey in the Honeycomb," "Savannah," "Make Way" (aka "The General's Song" and "General's Entrance"), "The Man Upstairs" (aka "Pay Heed"), and "It's Not So Good to Be Bad" (here titled "Not So Bad to Be Good"). Unused in the revival were: "Holy Unto the Lord," "Dem Bones," and "In My Old Virginia Home (on the River Nile)" as well as three dance sequences ("Egyptian Ballet," "Lazy Steps," and "Boogy Woogy"). The revival was recorded by Capitol (LP # SW-2073; it was later issued on CD by Broadway Angel # ZDM-0777-7-64892-2-3, and then by DRG # 19088).

The 1943 MGM film version was produced by Arthur Freed, directed by Vincente Minnelli, and the screenplay was by Joseph Schrank, Eustace Cocrell, and Marc Connelly. Ethel Waters, Todd Duncan, and Rex Ingram reprised their stage roles, and the cast included Eddie "Rochester" Anderson (as Little Joe), Lena Horne (Georgia Brown), and Louis Armstrong (Trumpeter); others in the cast were John W. Bubbles (aka John William Sublett), Mantan Moreland, Willie Best, Butterfly McQueen, Duke Ellington and His Orchestra, and the Hall Johnson Choir.

The film retained "Taking a Chance on Love," "Honey in the Honeycomb," "Love Me Tomorrow (but Leave Me Alone Today)," "In My Old Virginia Home (on the River Nile)," and the title song. New songs added for the film (with lyrics by E. Y. Harburg and music by Harold Arlen) were "Happiness Is (Just) a Thing Called Joe" (which became a hit song), "Li'l Black Sheep," and "Life's Full o' Consequence" (aka "That Ole Debbil Consequence"); another new song ("Going Up") was by another Duke (Ellington). Two unused songs by Harburg and Arlen were "Ain't It the Truth" (for Horne) and "I Got a Song." The latter was filmed but cut prior to release and is included as a bonus on the film's DVD. The former was later sung by Horne in Harburg and Arlen's 1957 Broadway musical *Jamaica*, and the latter was included in Harburg and Arlen's score for **Bloomer Girl** (as a trio that included Dooley Wilson).

Of the original production's cast members, Dooley Wilson of course attained film immortality in the role of Sam when he sang "As Time Goes By" in *Casablanca* (1942), and Rex Ingram, who played Lucifer's son (with his father, he lives in an air-conditioned section of Hell), portrayed the Lord in the 1936 film version of *The Green Pastures*.

'TIS OF THEE
"AN INTIMATE REVUE"

Theatre: Maxine Elliott's Theatre
Opening Date: October 26, 1940; *Closing Date*: October 26, 1940
Performances: 1
Sketches: Sam Locke; additional sketches by Peter Barry, David Greggory (sometimes cited as David Gregory), and George Lloyd
Lyrics: Alfred Hayes; additional lyrics by Peter Barry, David Greggory (Gregory), and Mike Stratton
Music: Alex North and Al Moss; additional music by George Klinesinger (Kleinsinger), Richard Lewine, and Elsie Peters
Direction: Nat Lichtman; *Producer*: Nat Lichtman; *Choreography*: Esther Junger; *Scenery*: Carl Kent; *Costumes*: Uncredited; *Lighting*: Uncredited; *Musical Direction*: Alex Saron
Cast: Esther Junger, George Lloyd, Virginia Burke, Jane Hoffman, Jerry Munson, Mervyn Nelson, Sherle Hartt, Van Kirk, Laura Duncan, Capella and Beatrice, Alfred and Reese, Paul Roberts, Jack Berry, Arno Tanny, Vivian Block, Alfred Hayes, Jan Zerfing, Susan Remos, Saida Gerard, Ray Harrison, Daniel Nagrin, Bram Vanderberg, Al Moss, Frank Rogier
The revue was presented in two acts.

Sketches and Musical Numbers

Act One: "You've Got to Have Something to Sing About When You Sing" (lyric by Alfred Hayes, music by Al Moss) (Entire Company); "Case 305" (sketch by Sam Locke) (Mervyn Nelson, Sherle Hartt); "Darryl Zanuck Carries On" (sketch by Sam Locke) (Narrator: Paul Roberts; Tyrone Power: Jack Berry; Alice Faye: Jane Hoffman; Jean Hersholt: Arno Tanney; Sonya Henie: Vivian Block; Abe Lincoln: Alfred Hayes; Nurse: Virginia Burke); "Lupe" (lyric by Alfred Hayes, music by Alex North) (Lupe: Esther Junger; Dancers: Jan Zerfing, Susan Remos, Saida Gerard, Ray Harrison, Daniel Nagrin, Bram Vandenberg; Singers: Al Moss, Arno Tanny, Frank Rogier); "Hymn to a Stuffed Shirt" (sketch by Sam Locke) (Mr. Williamson: Jerry Munson; Miss Cavendish: Jane Hoffman; Davenport: Van Kirk); "What's Mine Is Thine" (lyric by Alfred Hayes, music by Al Moss) (Virginia Burke, George Lloyd); "Cantata" ("Saga of the Diamond") (lyric by Mike Stratton, music by George Klinesinger [Kleinsinger]) (Umpire: George Lloyd; Announcer: Jack Berry; Baseball Hero: Jerry Munson; His Girl: Vivian Block; Gangsters: Paul Roberts, Daniel Nagrin; The Mob: Company); "Case 306" (sketch by Sam Locke) (Mervyn Nelson, Sherle Hartt); "After Tonight" (lyric by Alfred Hayes, music by Al Moss) (Laura Duncan); "Prison Reformer" (sketch by Sam Locke) (Chairlady: Jan Zerfing; Mrs. Smiggens: Jane Hoffman); "Going South" (sketch by Sam Locke) (Clancy: Jack Berry; Salesmen: Paul Roberts, Arno Tanny; Customer: Mervyn Nelson); "Nerve Center" (sketch by George Lloyd) (George Lloyd); "Noises in the Street" (lyrics by David Greggory [Gregory] and Peter Barry, music by Richard Lewine) (Street Musician: Mervyn Nelson; Garbage Collector: Van Kirk; Doorman: Jerry Munson); "'Tis of Thee" (lyric by Alfred Hayes, music by Alex North) (Entire Company)

Act Two: "Barroom Ballads, or Virtue Rides Again" (music by Alex North) (dance) (Gambler's Mistress: Esther Junger; Gambler: Daniel Nagrin; The Stranger: Bram Vandenberg; Prospector: Ray Harrison; Lady in Green: Susan Remos; Lady in Plaid: Jan Zerfing; Lady in Purple: Saida Gerard; Waiter: Lloyd George; Drunk: Mervyn Nelson; Reformer: Jane Hoffman); "Imagination" (sketch by David Greggory [Gregory] and Peter Barry) (The Doctor: Arno Tanny; Mr. Peabody: Van Kirk); "Who Killed Vaudeville?" (Mervyn Nelson, Sherle Hartt); "The Lady" (lyric by Alfred Hayes, music by Elsie Peters) (Virginia Burke, Arno Tanny); "Telepathic Television" (sketch by David Greggory [Gregory] and Sam Locke) (Commentator: Jack Berry; danced by Cappello and Beatrice); "Case 307" (sketch by Sam Locke) (Mervyn Nelson, Sherle Hartt); "Hawaiian Ritual" (lyric by David Greggory [Gregory], music by Al Moss) (Chieftain: Jerry Munson; Maidens: Sherle Hartt, Jane Hoffman, Virginia Burke, Saida Gerard, Susan Remos, Jan Zerfing); "The Rhythm Is Red an' White an' Blue" (lyric by David Greggory [Gregory], music by Al Moss) (Laura Duncan, Alfred and Reese); "Life Covers Completely" (sketch by Sam Locke) (Mr. Creep: Mervyn Nelson; Mrs. Creep: Sherle Hartt; Reporter: Jack Berry; Photographers: Jerry Munson, Alfred Hayes; Second Reporter:

Atno Tanny); "String" (sketch by George Lloyd) (George Lloyd); "Tomorrow" (lyric by Alfred Hayes, music by Alex North) (Frank Rogier, Entire Company)

The hapless revue *'Tis of Thee* was the shortest-running musical of the season; it was gone after one performance, and not since *Hummin' Sam* in 1933 had a musical played for so short a run. It would be another twenty-five years before another musical (the notorious *Kelly*) played for a single stand on Broadway.

'Tis of Thee was conceived and directed by Nat Lichtman, who specialized in modest revues that he presented in summer camp theatres. During the summer of 1940, he assembled a group of sketch writers, lyricists, composers, and performers, and each weekend they presented a one-hour revue at the Times Square Unity House in Bushkill, Pennsylvania. For *'Tis of Thee*, he selected the "outstanding" numbers from these summer revues and unwisely assembled them for Broadway consumption.

Like **Two for the Show**'s sketch "Destry Has Ridden Again," there was here another spoof of the popular film *Destry Rides Again* with the number "Barroom Ballads, or Virtue Rides Again." The evening also kidded the movies ("Darryl Zanuck Carries On," which included impersonations of Tyrone Power, Alice Faye, Jean Hersholt, and Sonya Henie), *Life* magazine ("Life Covers Completely"), and vaudeville ("Who Killed Vaudeville?").

The evening's most controversial moments occurred with George Lloyd's monologues "Nerve Center" and "String." John Mason Brown in the *New York Post* said the "arch" and "boyish" Lloyd presented an "exhibition" of "coy toyings" with a piece of string that caused Brown and other audience members to become "sorely embarrassed" (but he noted that some gave the performer "vociferous applause"). Richard Watts in the *New York Herald Tribune* said the "painful" Lloyd was the "most annoying" performer of the season, one who "should be spoken to severely." Watts reported that with "String" Lloyd impersonated an insane man who hangs himself, and in "Nerve Center" played a psychopath; but Watts admitted that some in the theatre greeted his offerings with approval. Richard Lockridge in the *New York Sun* said Lloyd's "peculiar" monologues provided "pleasant shivers," and Sidney P. Whipple in the *New York World-Telegram* said Lloyd had an "agreeable manner, stage presence and considerable acting ability."

The critics decided that what had been amusing in the barn of a summer theatre was not necessarily so in a Broadway house. As a result, Atkinson found the revue "amateurish" with a "generally untalented cast" and "poor" material. Whipple said the troupe was "well-intentioned but sadly misguided," and the evening was "one of those pathetic theatrical orphans" that should never have attempted Broadway. Watts said the show was "hopelessly inept"; Lockridge noted there was "more pathos than entertainment" on display; Brown found the show "depressing"; and Burns Mantle in the *New York Daily News* emphasized that what looks "awfully good" in the summer theatre of August can seem "pretty terrible" on Broadway in October.

In June 1940, the summer stock revue **Two Weeks with Pay** opened and two of its numbers were later performed in *'Tis of Thee*: the sketch "Imagination" and the song "Noises in the Street." The latter was also performed in other revues (for more information, see **The Shape of Things!**).

One number in *'Tis of Thee*, "Cantata" ("Saga of the Diamond"), resurfaced as "Brooklyn Cantata" in the 1942 revue **Of 'V' We Sing**.

George Klinesinger (Kleinsinger) contributed the music of "Cantata" ("Saga of the Diamond"), and in 1957 composed the score for Broadway's revue-like *Shinbone Alley*. Jane Hoffman appeared in **One Touch of Venus** and also in a number of plays by distinguished playwrights, including Marc Connelly's *A Story for Strangers* (1948), Samuel Spewack's *Two Blind Mice* (1949), Horton Foote's *Borned in Texas* (1950), Tennessee Williams's *The Rose Tattoo* (1951), and Arthur Miller's *The Crucible* (1953).

PANAMA HATTIE

Theatre: 46th Street Theatre
Opening Date: October 30, 1940; *Closing Date*: January 3, 1942
Performances: 501
Book: Herbert Fields and B. G. (Buddy) De Sylva
Lyrics and *Music*: Cole Porter
Direction: Edgar MacGregor; *Producer*: B. G. (Buddy) De Sylva; *Choreography*: Robert Alton; *Scenery* and *Costumes*: Raoul Pene du Bois; *Lighting*: Uncredited; *Musical Direction*: Gene Salzer

Cast: Conchita (Mrs. Gonzalez), Eppy Pearson (Mac), Pat Harrington (Skat Briggs), Frank Hyers (Windy Deegan), Rags Ragland (Woozy Hogan), Nadine Gae (Chiquita), Linda Griffith (Fruit Peddler), Roger Gerry (Tim), Roy Blaine (Tom), Ted Daniels (Ted), Lipman Duckat (later known as Larry Douglas) (Ty), *Ethel Merman* (Hattie Maloney), Phyllis Brooks (Leila Tree), Elaine Shepherd (Mildred Hunter), Ann Graham (Kitty Belle Randolph), James Dunn (Nick Bullett), Betty Hutton (Florrie), Joan Carroll (Geraldine [Jerry] Bullett), Arthur Treacher (Vivian Budd), Hal Conklin (First Stranger), Frank DeRoss (Second Stranger), Jack Donahue (Mike), James Kelso (Whitney Randolph); Singing Girls: Janis Carter, Ann Graham, Marguerite Benton, Vera Deane; Dancing Girls: June Allyson, Irene Austin, Jane Ball, Mimi Berry, Betsy Blair, Lucille Bremer, Nancy Chaplin, Kathlyn Coulter, Ronnie Cunningham, Marrianne Crude, Doris Dowling, Vera-Ellen, Miriam Franklyn, Marguerite James, Pat Likely, Mary McDonald, Renee Russell, Audrey Westphal; Dancing Boys: Jack Baker, Cliff Ferre, Fred Nay, Harry Rogue, Jack Riley, Billy (William) Skipper, Art Stanley, Carl Trees, Don Weissmuller; Specialty Dancers: Lewis Hightower and Robert Hightower, Carmen D'Antonio

The musical was presented in two acts.

The action takes place in Panama City and in the Canal Zone.

Musical Numbers

Act One: Opening (aka "A Stroll on the Plaza Sant' Ana") (Singing Girls and Boys, Ensemble); "Join It Right Away" (Rags Ragland, Pat Harrington, Frank Hyers; Specialty: Nadine Gae, Lewis Hightower, Robert Hightower, Ensemble); "Visit Panama" (Ethel Merman, Four Men of Manhattan, Renee Russell, Ensemble; American Family: Marguerite Benton, Al Downing, and June Allyson); "My Mother Would Love You" (Ethel Merman, James Dunn); "I've Still Got My Health" (Ethel Merman, Ensemble; Specialty: Cliff Ferre and Miriam Franklyn); "Fresh as a Daisy" (Betty Hutton, Pat Harrington, Frank Hyers); "Welcome to Jerry" (Singing Girls and Boys, Ensemble; Specialty: Carmen D'Antonio, Lewis Hightower, Robert Hightower); "Let's Be Buddies" (aka "What Say, Let's Be Buddies") (Ethel Merman, Joan Carroll); "They Ain't Done Right by Our Nell" (Betty Hutton, Arthur Treacher); Specialty (Eppy Pearson, Nadine Gae); "I'm Throwing a Ball Tonight" (Ethel Merman, Ensemble); Conga (Ethel Merman, Nadine Gae, Lewis Hightower, Robert Hightower)

Act Two: Opening: (1) "We Detest a Fiesta" (Singing Girls and Boys, Ensemble); (2) "Who Would Have Dreamed?" (Janis Carter, Lipman Duckat); and (3) Specialty Dance (Ronnie Cunningham, Jack Baker); "Make It Another Old-Fashioned, Please" (Ethel Merman); "All I've Got to Get Now Is My Man" (Betty Hutton, Ensemble; Specialty: Harry Rogue); Street Scene: Dancer (Carmen D'Antonio); "You Said It" (Ethel Merman, Arthur Treacher, Rags Ragland, Frank Hyers, Pat Harrington); "Who Would Have Dreamed?" (waltz reprise) (Nadine Gae, Lewis Hightower, Robert Hightower, Ensemble); "Let's Be Buddies" (reprise) (Ethel Merman, Joan Carroll); "God Bless the Women" (Rags Ragand, Frank Hyers, Pat Harrington); Finale (Entire Company)

Cole Porter's South American carnival *Panama Hattie* was a smash hit and became the longest-running musical of the season. Ethel Merman received solo star billing for the first time in her career, and she made the most of one of her showiest roles as the alternately tough and tender title character. She introduced no less than seven songs in Porter's score, and while none became standards like those from her previous Porter outings (such as "I Get a Kick Out of You," "You're the Top," "Blow, Gabriel, Blow," and the title song from *Anything Goes* [1934]; "Down in the Depths [on the 90th Floor]," "It's De-Lovely," and "Ridin' High" from *Red Hot and Blue!* [1936]; and "Friendship" from *DuBarry Was a Lady* [1939]), her numbers were nonetheless salty and swinging, or sweet and sentimental.

The good-natured and gaudily dressed Hattie (whose outfits make Stella Dallas look positively demure) works at the Tropical Shore night spot, and while she enjoys socializing with sailors, particularly Woozy (Rags Ragland), Windy (Frank Hyers), and Skat (Pat Harrington), she nonetheless has a heart of brass. Although she's engaged to divorced Philadelphian mainliner Nick Bullett (James Dunn), she encounters a number of problems that threaten their upcoming marriage: first, she has insulted and infuriated Nick's boss; second, his eight-year-old daughter Jerry (Joan Carroll) can't stand her; and third, the scheming socialite Leila Tree (Phyllis Brooks) is trying to hook Nick. But when Hattie discovers that fifth columnists are planning to blow up the Panama Canal, she takes them on single-handedly and saves the day. So she's now in good with Nick's boss, has won over Jerry, and has sent Leila packing.

Porter's songs ran the gamut, from Hattie's merrily self-deprecating "I've Still Got My Health" and "I'm Throwing a Ball Tonight" to the torch song "Make It Another Old-Fashioned, Please" to the valentine sentiments of "My Mother Would Love You" (with Nick) and "Let's Be Buddies" (with Jerry). "I've Still Got My Health" was another jubilant Porter list song in which Hattie wryly comments on her low social standing (when she starts stripping at Minsky's, the crowd cries, "Put it on!," and when she holds teas, Lucius Beebe "ain't there").

Richard Lockridge in the *New York Sun* found the musical "particularly luxurious" with "gorgeous color," and noted Porter had provided plenty of chances for Merman to sing ("and a chance is all she ever needs"). Everything was "going great guns" at the 46th Street Theatre, but he noted that Betty Hutton needed to "calm down a little," if only "to the pace of a St. Vitus dance." Richard Watts in the *New York Herald Tribune* said *Panama Hattie* was a "phenomenal hit . . . a saturnalia at its peak," and Merman was "even better than ever." As for Hutton, he suggested she be relegated to one song per musical and should "work off her surplus energies elsewhere." He also praised the shrewd writing, which ensured that eight-year-old Joan Carroll wasn't on stage during the rowdy burlesque-styled scenes with the randy sailors (and he trusted she didn't spend her offstage time standing in the wings and overhearing the blue dialogue).

Brooks Atkinson in the *New York Times* mentioned that the pre-opening expectations for *Panama Hattie* were high, and he was happy to report the show was "equal" to its hype. Everything was "noisy, funny and in order." He noted that Merman sang "like a high-compression engine" and "hangs bangles" on her songs; the dancers were "forever whirling" through Robert Alton's routines; Raoul Pene du Bois' costumes were "most flamboyant"; and Herbert Fields and B.G. (Buddy) De Sylva's book was "roaring." He also noted that Hutton was a "blond vertigo."

Burns Mantle in the *New York Daily News* praised the entire show, and noted producer De Sylva had a winning formula for both the previous season's Porter and Merman haymaker (*DuBarry Was a Lady*) and the new musical by contrasting "sex with sentiment and burlesque with beauty." But he felt the direction let Betty Hutton down when it belittled her talent by allowing her to "unforgivably" overplay her role. John Mason Brown in the *New York Post* said Merman "had never been better" and that Broadway did "not often see a musical comedy more expertly done than" the "blushless" *Panama Hattie*. (And he noted that no one could accuse Hutton of "lacking energy.")

Sidney P. Whipple in the *New York World-Telegram* recalled Merman's naughty song "Katie Went to Haiti" from *Dubarry Was a Lady*, and suggested Katie-as-Hattie had moved to Panama. And with Merman, Porter, lavish décor, and "exciting" choreography, "who could ask for anything more?" Although Porter's score wasn't as "striking" as usual, it was nonetheless "brisk and fresh and crisp" and he noted the book offered "extraordinarily funny" dialogue.

The critics were particularly taken with one song in the score, "You Said It," which was a quintet for Merman, Treacher, Ragland, Hyers, and Harrington. Whipple said it was the show's "most entertaining" number and he praised its "tomfoolery." Mantle also singled it out, saying it was a song "for Broadway," Atkinson said it was one of many songs in the show which everyone would soon be hearing, and Watts stated it was his favorite song in the score and noted it was performed to "splendid" effect.

Soon after the opening, Betty Hutton's "They Ain't Done Right by Our Nell" was deleted (reportedly at Merman's insistence). During the tryout, "Americans All Drink Coffee" (for Arthur Treacher) was dropped, and "Welcome to Jerry" was titled "Ben Venida, Geraldina." "Here's to Panama Hattie" (for James Dunn) was cut during rehearsals.

Merman recorded four songs from the musical ("Make It Another Old-Fashioned, Please," "My Mother Would Love You," "I've Still Got My Health," and, with Joan Carroll, "Let's Be Buddies"); *12 Songs from Call Me Madam* (with Merman and a studio cast) includes these four numbers (MCA Classics CD # MCAD-10521). Live performances of Merman's singing "Make It Another Old-Fashioned, Please" and "I'm Throwing a Ball Tonight" are included in the collection *Cole Porter* (JJA Records LP # 19745A/B). The obscure songs "Visit Panama" and "All I've Got to Get Now Is My Man" are included in the collection *The Broadway Musicals of 1940* (Bayview CD # RNBW019) and "They Ain't Done Right by Our Nell" is included in the collections *Cole Porter Revisited Volume V* (Painted Smiles CD # PSCD-122) and *Keep Your Undershirt On!* (Rialto CD). The lyrics for the used, cut, and unused songs are included in *The Complete Lyrics of Cole Porter*.

The disastrous MGM film version went into production about midway through the Broadway run, and after a series of disappointing previews in late 1941 was put back into production and wasn't released until September 1942. Directed by Norman Z. McLeod (and then later by Roy Del Ruth and Vincente Minnelli), the movie was produced by Arthur Freed, who reportedly paid $130,000 for the film rights. Ann Sothern should have made a terrific Hattie, but the static and choppy film never really gave her a chance. The cast also included Dan Dailey, Red Skelton, Virginia O'Brien, Ben Blue, and, from the Broadway production, Rags Ragland. A handful of Porter's songs were retained ("I've Still Got My Health," "Fresh as a Daisy," and "Let's Be Buddies"), and a new one ("Did I Get Stinkin' at the Club Savoy" for Virginia O'Brien) with lyric by E. Y. Harburg and music by Walter Donaldson was added. When the film was re-shot, Lena was literally shoe-Horned into the plot with a specialty or two (including "Just One of Those Things" from Porter's 1935 Broadway musical *Jubilee*) and a last-minute patriotic finale "The Son-of-a-Gun Who Picks on Uncle Sam" (lyric by E. Y. Harburg, music by Burton Lane) was added. Reportedly "Make It Another Old-Fashioned, Please" was filmed (and may have been seen during the film's initial run); but the number is omitted from the DVD release (Warner Archive Collection).

A television adaptation produced by CBS on November 10, 1954, starred Merman, Ray Middleton (her leading man from the original 1946 stage production of **Annie Get Your Gun**), Jack Leonard, and Art Carney.

An undated program from a limited Off-Off-Broadway run by The Medicine Show includes "Americans All Drink Coffee" and "They Ain't Done Right by Our Nell." A Musicals Tonight! production, which was seen Off-Off-Broadway for a limited run October 12–23, 2010, included "They Ain't Done Right by Our Nell."

Deep in the cast listing of *Panama Hattie* were three chorus girls who would enjoy varying degrees of success in Hollywood. *Panama Hattie* was June Allyson's second Broadway appearance during the year (she had earlier been seen in **Higher and Higher**), and the following year would have her breakthrough success in **Best Foot Forward**. And indeed she went forward with a solid screen career that encompassed musicals, comedies, and dramas, many of them at MGM. The delightful if underrated 1974 Broadway musical *Over Here!*, which took place during the War Forties, offered a particularly memorable and almost surreal sequence ("Dream Drummin'" and "Soft Music") in which the characters see themselves as celebrities of the day (one beats the drums à la Gene Krupa, a treadmill allows another to "swim" as "Esther Williams," another assumes the iconic Betty Grable pin-up pose, etc.), and Phyllis Somerville's brief moment as "June Allyson" was quite memorable. Vera-Ellen also appeared in various MGM musicals, but she is best remembered for her appearance in Paramount's 1954 holiday musical *White Christmas*. And even Lucille Bremer had a brief MGM moment in the mid-1940s when she appeared as Judy Garland's older sister Rose in *Meet Me in St. Louis* (1944) as well as in *Yolanda and the Thief* (1945) and *Ziegfeld Follies* (1946); in the latter two films, she danced with Fred Astaire. Also in the chorus was Betsy Blair (who for a time was married to Gene Kelly), who later appeared opposite Ernest Borgnine in the 1955 Oscar-winning Best Picture *Marty*.

MUM'S THE WORD

Theatre: Belmont Theatre
Opening Date: December 5, 1940; *Closing Date*: December 14, 1940
Performances: 12
Sketches: "As imagined" by Jimmy Savo
Direction: Al Webster; *Producer*: Jimmy Savo
Cast: Jimmy Savo, Hiram Sherman, Herbert Kingsley (Pianist), and an unnamed performer who occasionally assisted Savo during the evening
The revue was presented in one act.

Sketches and Musical Numbers

Sketches: "Swedish Idyll"; "Singsong Mother Goose"; "The Emergency Call"; "Washerwoman in Love"; "Deep South Fever"; "Old-Fashioned Girl"; "Bourgeois Gentilhomme"; "Engagement at Sea"; "Chestnut Man"; "When Jokes Were Young"

Songs: "River, Stay Away from My Door" (lyric by Mort Dixon, music by Harry Woods); "Ol' Man River" (from *Show Boat*, 1927; lyric by Oscar Hammerstein II, music by Jerome Kern); "Lady Bird, Lady Bird, Fly Away Home" (traditional nursery rhyme); "Did You Ever See a Dream Walking?" (from 1933 film *Sitting Pretty*; lyric by Mack Gordon, music by Harry Revel); "Blue Moon" (lyric by Lorenz Hart, music by Richard Rodgers); "The Song of the Flea" (from 1846 cantata-cum-opera *La damnation de Faust*; original words and music by Hector Berlioz)

Diminutive comic Jimmy Savo had appeared in vaudeville and various revues, but probably his best-known role was Dromio of Syracuse in Lorenz Hart and Richard Rodgers's 1938 hit *The Boys from Syracuse*; with Wynn Murray he introduced the saucy duet "He and She," and with Eddie Albert the irresistible home-town tribute to "Dear Old Syracuse."

For *Mum's the Word*, Savo offered a few of his pantomime sketches and some songs (especially "River, Stay Away from My Door," which over the years had become his signature number). Savo had presented the revue in the straw-hat circuit the previous summer, and after its brief New York run he announced he would revise it, presumably in anticipation of a return engagement. But the revue was never again presented on Broadway.

Perhaps "mum" wasn't quite the word, for occasionally Savo sang a few songs. And Hiram Sherman appeared as master of ceremonies and gave impromptu-like introductions for each sequence. Further, Herbert Kingsley accompanied Savo on the piano and there was an unidentified stooge who occasionally helped out during the proceedings.

The one-act revue lasted approximately an hour and a half, and although the critics adored Savo's comical and occasionally serious cavorting, a few thought the evening went on a little too long.

Brooks Atkinson in the *New York Times* said the "wonderful" Savo presented theatergoers with a "rare and lovable" evening. He compared Savo to Chaplin, and noted that many had been "Savoyards" for years. He singled out a number of sketches, including a comic one in which a fisherman on a boat leaps into the water when an alluring mermaid swims by and a touching one about a hungry Bowery vagrant who looks longingly at a cart of roasting chestnuts for sale.

John Mason Brown in the *New York Post* said Savo was "Chaplinesque" in quality, and praised the Bowery sketch; the one in which Savo conjured up the image of a "Negro" singing "Ol' Man River"; and a look at Eve in which Savo had the particularly fey notion of impersonating her as a union worker in a pink suit (with a fig leaf sewed on it) who handles her long locks of hair as knitting wool and then as spaghetti. Sidney B. Whipple in the *New York World-Telegram* noted there were more laughs in the short evening than in a half-dozen typical Broadway comedies, and he noted the intimate Belmont Theatre was the perfect venue for the modest revue. Whipple singled out one particularly "brazen" sketch in which Savo portrayed a tipsy hospital porter who suddenly finds himself operating on a hapless patient.

Richard Lockridge in the *New York Sun* admitted Savo was one of Broadway's "funniest" performers, but felt the "perilous seas of solo entertainment" resulted in a show that became monotonous and required more variety (a "full evening" was "a long time to laugh at one man"). Richard Watts in the *New York Herald Tribune* also felt the revue offered "too much of a good thing" and noted the "cumulative effect" was one of "unhappy monotony." He disliked the "Chestnut Man" sketch, noting it was the second-most "uncomfortable pseudo-dramatic" sketch of the season (no doubt the other was George Lloyd's controversial "string" in **'Tis of Thee**).

Burns Mantle in the *New York Daily News* admitted the" little clown" had his "moments," but overall the evening should have been shortened by half. But he noted that for the curtain calls there was "friendly and numerous" applause for the beloved Savo.

MEET THE PEOPLE
"A Musical Revue" / "Liveliest Smartest Right on the Nosest Musical Revue"

Theatre: Mansfield Theatre
Opening Date: December 25, 1940; *Closing Date*: May 10, 1941
Performances: 160
Sketches: Ben Barzman, Sol Barzman, Henry Blankfort, Danny Dare, Edward Eliscu, Jack Gilford, Bert Lawrence, Henry Myers, Mortimer Offner, Mike Quin, and Arthur Ross

Lyrics: Henry Myers; other lyrics by Edward Eliscu, Ray Golden, and Sid Kuller
Music: Jay Gorney; other music by George Bassman, Ray Golden, Sid Kuller, Jacques Offenbach, and Giuseppe Verdi
Direction: Production staged by Danny Dare; sketches directed by Mortimer Offner; Edward Eliscu, "Revue Editor"; *Producer*: The Hollywood Theatre Alliance; *Choreography*: Uncredited; *Scenery*: Frederick Stover; *Costumes*: Gloria Vanderneers and Kate Lawson; *Lighting*: Carlton Winkler; *Musical Direction*: Archie Bleyer
Cast: Jack Gilford, Doodles Weaver, Nanette Fabares (Fabray), Elizabeth Talbot-Martin, Jack Williams, Peggy Ryan, Eddie Johnson, Jack Albertson, Barney Phillips, Marion Colby, Ted Arkin, Dorothy Roberts, Jack Boyle, Patricia Brilhante, Josephine Del Mar, Robert Nash, Virginia Bryan, Fay McKenzie, Marie DeForest, Robert Davis, Lois Paul, Angus Hopkins, Beverly Weaver, Sue Robin, Norman Lawrence, Beryl Carew, Kenneth Patterson, Michael Doyle, Rafe Eisenberg
The revue was presented in two acts.

Sketches and Musical Numbers

Act One: "The Legend of Sleeping Beauty" (sketch by Ben Barzman and Sol Barzman, music by George Bassman) (Princess: Fay McKenzie; Prince Charming: Barney Phillips; Ladies in Waiting: Marion Colby, Patricia Brilhante, Beryl Carew, Nanette Fabares, Sue Robin, Marie DeForest, Virginia Bryan, Lois Paul; First Newsboy: Eddie Johnson, Second Newsboy: Ted Arkin; Gangster: Jack Boyle; Policeman: Angus Hopkins; Fuehrer: Kenneth Patterson; Picket: Robert Davis; State Trooper: Michael Doyle; Radical: Dorothy Roberts; The Spirit of California: Rafe Eisenberg; Rosasharn: Beverly Weaver; Chef: Robert Nash; An Evangelist: Elizabeth Talbot-Martin; College Graduate: Jack Gilford; School Girl: Peggy Ryan; Man with Radio: Jack Albertson; Sailor: Doodles Weaver; Salesman: Jack Williams; Stenographer: Josephine Del Mar); "Meet the People" (lyric by Henry Myers, music by Jay Gorney) (Company); "Inquiring Reporter" (sketch by Mortimer Offner and Edward Eliscu, from an idea by Danny Dare) (The Inquirer: Jack Albertson; First American: Kenneth Patterson; Second American: Angus Hopkins; Innocent Bystanders, etc.); "Senate in Session" (lyric by Henry Myers, music by Jay Gorney) (The President: Doodles Weaver; Junior Senator: Jack Boyle; Senior Senator: Angus Hopkins; Senators: Robert Nash, Eddie Johnson, Barney Phillips; Secretaries: Patricia Brilhante, Marie DeForest, Peggy Ryan; Jitterbuggers: Dorothy Roberts, Ted Arkin); "The Stars Remain" (lyric by Henry Myers, music by Jay Gorney) (She: Beryl Carew; He: Robert Davis; Dancer: Marie DeForest; Another She: Marion Colby); "The Unwritten Law" (sketch by Ben Barzman and Sol Barzman) (Her: Nanette Fabares; Him: Jack Albertson; George: Kenneth Patterson); "Union Label" (lyric by Henry Myers, music by Jay Gorney) (First Girl: Fay McKenzie; Prince Charming: Barney Phillips; First Boy: Jack Williams; Second Girl: Peggy Ryan; Second Boy: Eddie Johnson; Boys and Girls); Elizabeth Talbiot-Martin; "The Lecture" (sketch by Henry Blankfort and Danny Dare) (Chairman: Robert Nash; Novelist: Kenneth Patterson; Members of Company Union: Robert Davis, Patricia Brilhante, Eddie Johnson, Peggy Ryan, Jack Gilford, Nanette Fabares, Ted Arkin, Dorothy Roberts, Angus Hopkins); Jack Williams; "The Dictator at Home" (sketch by Henry Blankfort and Bert Lawrence) (Pa: Jack Albertson; Ma: Dorothy Roberts; Ray: Fay McKenzie; Fay: Virginia Bryan; Kay: Marion Colby); "Hurdy Gurdy Verdi" (music by Giuseppe Verdi) (Nanette Fabares); "(It's) The Same Old South" (lyric by Edward Eliscu, music by Jay Gorney) (Mr. Mason: Eddie Johnson; Mr. Dixon: Jack Albertson); "The Bill of Rights" (lyric by Henry Myers, music by Jay Gorney) (Professor: Barney Phillips; Students and Co-eds); "How Movies Are Made" (sketch by Milt Gross) (Patron: Jack Gilford; Banker: Angus Hopkins; Producer: Eddie Johnson; Writer: Ted Arkin; Director: Jack Albertson; Exhibitor: Kenneth Patterson; Cashier: Marie DeForest) (*Note*: This sketch included the monologue "The Movie Fan," written and performed by Jack Gilford.); "American Plan" (lyric by Henry Myers, music by Jay Gorney) (Peggy Ryan, Angus Hopkins; The General: Barney Phillips; Cast)
Act Two: "Let's Steal a Tune from Offenbach" (lyric by Henry Myers, music by Jay Gorney; music based on Jacques Offenbach's 1858 operetta *Orphee aux enfers*) (Chopin: Angus Hopkins; Beethoven: Robert Nash; Tschaikowsky: Jack Boyle; Ravel: Barney Phillips; Sigmund: Robert Davis; His Girl Friend: Fay McKenzie; Offenbach: Ted Arkin; Spirit of Music: Patricia Brilhante); Doodles Weaver; "(It Seems There Was) A Fellow and a Girl" (sketch and lyric by Edward Eliscu, music by Jay Gorney) (Jane: Sue Robin; Bill: Jack

Williams; The Boss: Michael Doyle); Marion Colby (in one); "Have You Had Any Good Dreams Lately?" (sketch by Mortimer Offner and Henry Myers) (Nurse: Fay McKenzie; Doctor: Kenneth Patterson; Patient: Jack Gilford; Visitor: Marie DeForest); Elizabeth Talbot-Martin, with Jack Albertson; "No Lookin' Back" (lyric by Henry Myers and Edward Eliscu, music by Jay Gorney) (Michael Doyle); "Fancy Footwork" (Peggy Ryan; First Footworker: Patricia Brilhante; Second Footworker: Jack Boyle); "Light Meat or Dark" (sketch by Mike Quin) (Bongo: Barney Phillips; Wowzy: Kenneth Patterson); "In Chichicastenango" (lyric by Henry Myers, music by Jay Gorney) (La Chiquita: Josephine Del Mar; Americans: Robert Davis, Doodles Weaver; Guatemalans: Fay McKenzie, Marion Colby, Patricia Brilhante, Peggy Ryan, Sue Robin, Dorothy Roberts, Nanette Fabares, Beverly Weaver, Marie DeForest, Lois Paul, Eddie Johnson, Ted Arkin, Jack Boyle, Jack Williams, Robert Nash); "It's All Right, Joe" (sketch by Ben Barzman and Sol Barzman) (Joe: Jack Albertson; First Radio Voice: Angus Hopkins; Joe's Wife's Voice: Dorothy Roberts; Radio Voices: Eddie Johnson, Jack Boyle, Robert Davis, Barney Phillips, Fay McKenzie, Nanette Fabares, Robert Nash, Doodles Weaver, Elizabeth Talbot-Martin; The Hot Water Bottle: By Itself); "Elmer's Wedding Day" (lyric and music by Sid Kuller and Ray Golden) (Dowager: Nanette Fabares; Town Dude: Jack Gilford; Uncle: Robert Nash; Maiden Aunt: Elizabeth Talbot-Martin; Brat: Virginia Bryan; Village Idiot: Ted Arkin; His Yes-Man: Doodles Weaver; Elmer's Sister: Marie DeForest; Elmer's Brother: Jack Boyle; Elmer's Pa: Robert Davis; Elmer's Ma: Lois Paul; Zeke: Angus Hopkins; First Maid-in-Waiting: Fay McKenzie; Second Maid-in-Waiting: Peggy Ryan; Third Maid-in-Waiting: Beverly Weaver; Fourth Maid-in-Waiting: Sue Robin; Fifth Maid-in-Waiting: Beryl Carew; Sixth Maid-in-Waiting: Dorothy Roberts; Elmer Brown: Eddie Johnson; Eliza May: Patricia Brilhante; Parson: Jack Williams; Elmer's Landlord: Kenneth Patterson; Elmer's Boss: Michael Doyle; Banker: Barney Phillips; Doodles Weaver; "All This and Hollywood Too" (sketch by Arthur Ross) (J.R.: Kenneth Patterson; Joe: Angus Hopkins; Marilyn: Fay McKenzie); Finale (Company)

Meet the People was a slightly left-leaning revue that premiered in Los Angeles on December 25, 1939; produced by The Hollywood Theatre Alliance, a program note indicated the company's goal was the "formation of a permanent, democratic, professional, but non-profit alliance of all the cultural arts, and especially of the theatre." The program also mentioned that the revue gave a chance to those performers overlooked by "notoriously near-sighted talent scouts." The revue was surely inspired by the success of *Pins and Needles* (1937), but overall its material was more in keeping with traditional revue topics than social ones.

Because the revue had premiered on December 25, 1939, the producers insisted the New York opening take place exactly one year later. A major musical was scheduled to premiere on Christmas night (**Pal Joey**), but that didn't deter the revue's creators; and so while the regular newspaper critics reviewed the Rodgers and Hart show, the papers sent their second-string critics to assess the Hollywood revue. (When the Broadway production opened, the Los Angeles edition was beginning its second year in the film capital.)

The revue spoofed politics ("Senate in Session"), Hollywood ("How Movies Are Made"), the habit of adapting classical music into popular song ("Let's Steal a Tune From Offenbach"), and, this being the 1940s, there was the requisite South American number ("In Chichicastenango"). There was even a sketch about cannibalism ("Light Meat or Dark"). The revue's most serious moment occurred when the song "The Same Old South" described lynchings and discrimination.

Herrick Brown in the *New York Sun* liked Jay Gorney's "gay" score, but felt the quality of the sketches was a bit "uneven" (he noted the cannibal sketch had the "proper sting"). He liked Michael Doyle's "movingly" sung "No Lookin' Back," which was an homage to the spirit of John Steinbeck's *The Grapes of Wrath*, and he enjoyed Elizabeth Talbot-Martin's impersonations of Katharine Hepburn, Greta Garbo, and Eleanor Roosevelt as well as her burlesque of classical dancing. He also liked Marion Colby's "deadpan" singing style, but Wilella Waldorf in the *New York Post* noted that Virginia O'Brien had already perfected this shtick and thus it was no longer a novelty. Waldorf said the evening was occasionally "charming" and "clever," and felt the best of the serious moments occurred when Eddie Johnson (as Mr. Mason) and Frank Albertson (Mr. Dixon) saluted "dear old Dixieland" with the "blistering" lyrics of "The Same Old South" and its lynchings, child labor, and "Negro degradation."

J.P. in the *New York Herald Tribune* said the revue was a "poor man's *Hellzapoppin'*" with a score that fared better than the sketches, but L.N. (probably Lewis Nichols) in the *New York Times* praised the "good, very good" evening. George Ross in the *New York World-Telegram* said the score was "pleasant," Jack Williams was a "brilliant" dancer, and Jack Gilford's "drolleries" led the audience into "a state of near-hysteria." Overall, the evening was "affable" with an "adult point of view" and "not quite subversive enough" for Congress to investigate.

Robert Sylvester in the *New York Daily News* felt the first act went along "clicking with precision," but after intermission the evening seemed to "bog down." And while he liked Gorney's "fine" score, he mentioned that some of the entertainers were "pretty flimsy" and noted that the "good comrades" had tried "something that sounds like a *Daily Worker* editorial set to music."

During the run, the sketch "It's All Right, Joe" was dropped. Prior to New York, the sketch "Design for Earning a Living" (and its song "Voulez-vous, Mrs. Yifnif?," aka "May I Have the Next Waltz, Mrs. Yiffnif?") was dropped. For the post-Broadway tour, the sketches "A Bit of Americana" (by Joey Faye) and "Any Dependents?" (by Danny Dare) were added; besides Joey Faye, members of the tour included Betty Garrett and Henny Youngman.

The collection *The Broadway Musicals of 1940* (Bayview CD # RNBW019) includes "No Lookin' Back" and "We Have Sandwiches" (the latter seems to have been heard only in the Los Angeles production or the post-Broadway tour). *Everyone Else Revisited* (Painted Smiles CD # PSCD-146) includes "The Same Old South" and the title song; and the collection *Four Cast Recordings* (JJA Records LP # JJA-19752A/B) includes "The Bill of Rights" and the title number. The collection *Make Mine Manhattan and Great Revues Revisited* (Painted Smiles CD # PSCD-119) offers Gorney, Myers, and Eliscu's "Love in a Changing World" from their 1941 college musical **They Can't Get You Down**; the song was later heard in their 1943 revue **Marching with Johnny** (which seems to have been later revised as *The New Meet the People* for a brief national tour). The collection *Lost Broadway and More/Volume Three* (unnamed company and unnumbered CD) includes "You and Your Broken Heart"; the recording's liner notes indicate the song was heard in the second edition of *Meet the People* and was later used in **Marching with Johnny** and in *Meet the People of 1955*.

An in-name-only film version was released by MGM in 1944. Directed by Charles Riesner, choreographed by Sammy Lee and Charles Walters, produced by E. Y. Harburg, and with a screenplay by S. M. Herzig and Fred Saidy, the film starred Lucille Ball, Dick Powell, Virginia O'Brien, Bert Lahr, Rags Ragland, June Allyson, Robert (Bobby) Blake, Vaughn Monroe and His Orchestra, and Spike Jones and His City Slickers. The plot revolved around a musical comedy writer and shipyard welder (Powell) who insists that a Broadway star (Ball) is too snobbish to appear in his show; to prove she can "meet the people" she joins him in the shipyard and ends up not only on Broadway but with a husband to boot. None of the songs in the stage production were retained; a new title song (lyric by Ralph Freed, music by Sammy Fain) was included in the film's new score. A most pleasant surprise was the interpolation of "I Like to Recognize the Tune," Richard Rodgers and Lorenz Hart's sprightly song from their 1939 musical *Too Many Girls*. The very faithful film version of that musical didn't include "I Like to Recognize the Tune," and so its inclusion in *Meet the People* ensured that most of the songs from *Too Many Girls* made their way onto the screen in one way or another. *Meet the People* was released on DVD by the Warner Brothers Archive Collection.

Fifteen years after the revue opened on Broadway, Jay Gorney and Edward Eliscu wrote a sequel, *Meet the People of 1955*, which seems to have played only in regional theatres. Incidentally, Gorney's most memorable song was "Brother, Can You Spare a Dime?" (lyric by E. Y. Harburg), which became the unofficial anthem of the Depression years; it was first introduced in the 1932 revue *New Americana*.

The program for the Los Angeles and New York productions noted that many talented performers were overlooked by talent scouts. At least three in the New York cast found fame in the years following the revue's premiere. Jack Albertson became a familiar face in the theatre and in films, and in 1964 starred in the Pulitzer Prize-winning drama *The Subject Was Roses*; he appeared in the 1968 film version, and won the Academy Award for Best Supporting Actor. In the 1970s, he appeared in the original Broadway production of Neil Simon's *The Sunshine Boys* (opposite Sam Levene) and was "the man" in the successful NBC television series *Chico and the Man*. Nanette Fabares changed her last name to Fabray and soon appeared in supporting and later starring roles in musicals over a twenty-year period. In 1948, she won the Tony Award for Best Leading Actress in a Musical for her portrayal of Susan in Alan Jay Lerner and Kurt Weill's concept musical **Love Life**. And Jack Gilford became a Broadway favorite, too, and appeared in the original Broadway productions of *A Funny Thing Happened on the Way to the Forum* (1962) and *Cabaret* (1966) as well as the long-running revival of *No, No, Nanette* (1971).

PAL JOEY
"A NEW MUSICAL COMEDY"

Theatre: Ethel Barrymore Theatre (during run, the musical transferred to the Shubert Theatre and then to the St. James Theatre)
Opening Date: December 25, 1940; *Closing Date*: November 29, 1941
Performances: 374
Book: John O'Hara
Lyrics: Lorenz Hart
Music: Richard Rodgers
Based on a series of short stories by John O'Hara that were published in the *New Yorker* (the first story appeared in the October 22, 1938, issue); the collected stories were published in book format in 1939.
Direction: George Abbott; *Producer*: George Abbott; *Choreography*: Robert Alton; *Scenery* and *Lighting*: Jo Mielziner; *Costumes*: John Koenig; *Musical Direction*: Harry Levant
Cast: Gene Kelly (Joey Evans), Robert J. Mulligan (Mike Spears), Sondra Barrett (The Kid), June Havoc (Gladys), Diane Sinclair (Agnes), Leila Ernst (Linda English), Amarilla Morris (Valerie), Stanley Donan (Albert Doane), Vivienne Segal (Vera Simpson), Edison Rice (Escort), Jane Fraser (Terry), Van Johnson (Victor), John Clarke (Ernest), Jerry Whyte (Stagehand), Averell Harris (Max), Nelson Rae (The Tenor), Jean Casto (Melba Synder), Dummy Spevlin (Waiter), Jack Durant (Ludlow Lowell), James Lane (Commissioner O'Brien), Cliff Dunstan (Assistant Hotel Manager); Specialty Dancer: Shirley Page; Dancing Girls: Claire Anderson, Sondra Barrett, Alice Craig, Louise De Forrest, Enez Early, Tilda Getze, Charlene Harkins, Frances Krell, Janet Lavis, June Leroy, Amarilla Morris, Olive Nicolson, Mildred Patterson, Dorothy Poplar, Diane Sinclair, Mildred Solly, Jeanne C. Trybom, Marie Vanneman; Dancing Boys: Adrian Anthony, John Benton, Milton Chisholm, Stanley Donen, Henning Irgens, Van Johnson, Howard Ledig, Michael Moore, Albert Ruiz
The musical was presented in two acts.
The action takes place in Chicago during the late 1930s.

Musical Numbers

Act One: "You Mustn't Kick It Around" (Gene Kelly, June Havoc, Diane Sinclair, Sondra Barrett, Chorus Girls, Waiters); "I Could Write a Book" (Gene Kelly, Leila Ernst); "Chicago" (Michael Moore, Chorus Girls); "That Terrific Rainbow" (June Havoc, Van Johnson, Girls); "Love Is My Friend" (Vivienne Segal); "Happy Hunting Horn" (Gene Kelly, Jane Fraser, Chorus Girls, Boy Friends); "Bewitched, Bothered and Bewildered" (Vivienne Segal); "Joey Looks into the Future" (aka "Pal Joey" and "What Do I Care for a Dame?") (Gene Kelly, Shirley Paige, Company)
Act Two: "The Flower Garden of My Heart" (June Havoc, Nelson Rae, Shirley Paige, Ensemble); "Zip" (Jean Casto); "Plant You Now, Dig You Later" (Jack Durant, June Havoc, Ensemble); "In Our Little Den (of Iniquity)" (Vivienne Segal, Gene Kelly); "Do It the Hard Way" (Jack Durant, June Havoc, Claire Anderson, Ensemble); "Take Him" (Vivienne Segal, Leila Ernst, Gene Kelly); "Bewitched, Bothered and Bewildered" (reprise) (Vivienne Segal); "I Could Write a Book" (reprise) (Gene Kelly)

Pal Joey was a tough portrait of conceited, small-time hoofer Joey Evans (Gene Kelly) and his cheap world of seedy show business. In its first few lines of dialogue, the musical signaled that it wouldn't mince words: When a nightclub manager meets Joey, he offers him a drink, drugs, women . . . or, if he prefers, young men ("We have a band here. The drummer is just a boy"). Joey's ambition is to run his own nightclub, and so he sleeps with society matron Vera Simpson (Vivienne Segal) who agrees to bankroll him. He also becomes involved with the innocent Linda English (Leila Ernst). But by evening's end, both the worldly and amoral Vera and nice-girl Linda dump him.

Richard Rodgers and Lorenz Hart's brilliant score included Vera's lovely but very graphic "Bewitched, Bothered and Bewildered" (the lyric had to be sanitized for radio and recording consumption); Joey and Linda's touching ballad "I Could Write a Book" (Hart's lyric playfully puns "bookends" and "book ends"); Vera and Joey's naughty "In Our Little Den (of Iniquity)"; and Vera and Linda's "Take Him," in which they both give

Joey the gate. The musical also included parodies of nightclub routines (such as "Chicago," "That Terrific Rainbow," and "The Flower Garden of My Heart"), and one of the show's most memorable moments came out of nowhere when a minor character sang "Zip," a tongue-in-cheek salute to Gypsy Rose Lee (whose sister June Havoc was in the cast of *Pal Joey*) which managed to touch upon many of the era's cultural icons, such as William Saroyan, Tyrone Power, and "luscious Lucius" Beebe (not to mention Gypsy Rose Lee's fellow ecdysiasts Margie Hart, Sally Rand, and Lili St. Cyr).

One of the enduring legends of musical theatre is that the original production of *Pal Joey* was a failure that no one appreciated until the 1952 Broadway revival. Nothing is more misleading. When the musical closed in 1941, it was the *second*-longest-running of all the musicals by Rodgers and Hart, with a run of 374 performances. Only the team's 1927 *A Connecticut Yankee* had played longer, with 418 showings (in 1942, **By Jupiter** topped out as their longest-running show with a total of 427 performances).

In referring to his misgivings about a musical with an "odious" story and a leading character who is a "heel," a "punk," and a "rat infested with termites," Brooks Atkinson in the *New York Times* famously asked the most quoted question in the annals of theatre-reviewing: "Can you draw sweet water from a foul well?" But even his question is misleading, for Atkinson acknowledged that *Pal Joey* was "expertly done" and had a score of "wit and skill" (he singled out "Bewitched, Bothered and Bewildered" for its "scabrous" lyric and "haunting" music). He praised Robert Alton's "inventive" choreography, and said Gene Kelly's Joey hit the target with "remarkable accuracy . . . a brilliant tap dancer . . . if Joey must be acted, Mr. Kelly can do it."

Of the other five New York critics, two gave the musical raves. Richard Watts in the *New York Herald Tribune* found the evening a "hard-boiled delight . . . an outstanding triumph," and Sidney B. Whipple in the *New York World-Telegram* said the work was "bright, novel, gay and tuneful." Burns Mantle in the *New York Daily News* gave the musical three stars (out of four; it seems the highest he ever awarded a musical was three-plus stars) and noted *Pal Joey* heralded "signs of new life" for the American musical. And while John Mason Brown in the *New York Post* felt the show was "directionless" and its story "unimportant," he nonetheless admitted that the musical was an attempt to discard the "old conventions" of musical comedy in its depiction of a leading character who is a "bum." Overall, the critics singled out eight individual musical numbers as outstanding. So *Pal Joey* was hardly an overlooked and unappreciated musical.

Six months earlier when he reviewed **Walk with Music**, Richard Lockridge in the *New York Sun* noted that "something" needed to be done about the poor state of books written for musicals, and said this "unfinished business" needed to be addressed during the forthcoming Broadway season. So Lockridge was particularly happy with *Pal Joey* and noted that after a somewhat slow first act things started to pick up "wickedly" with the musical's "amusedly ruthless examination" of the title character, one of the "most substantial" and "funniest" characters to ever "stand among the shadows of musical comedy." Here was a musical which was always "lively" and "funny" with a "sharp, distinctive flavor."

When the musical was revived at the Broadhurst Theatre on January 3, 1952, it was a smash hit and ran for 540 performances. Vivienne Segal reprised her role of Vera, and Harold Lang, fresh from **Kiss Me, Kate**, played the title role; Helen Gallagher was Gladys (which June Havoc had played in the original production), and Pat Northrop was Linda. The revival won Tony Awards for Robert Alton for Best Choreography (Alton had also choreographed the original production); Helen Gallagher for Best Featured Actress in a Musical; and Max Meth for Best Conductor and Musical Director. The revival also won the New York Drama Critics' Circle Award for Best Musical of 1951–1952. This time around, Atkinson gave the show a rave, noting the 1940 production was a "pioneer" in the development of musicals that renewed "confidence in the professionalism of the theatre." Watts (now reviewing for the *New York Post*) said the rise and fall of a "nightclub insect" was the "best and most exciting" musical in New York and the "most hard-boiled musical play since *The Beggar's Opera*." The revival emanated from a 1950 studio cast recording of the musical by Columbia Records (LP # 4364; issued on CD by Sony Classical/Columbia/Legacy # SK-86856) which included Segal and Lang in the cast. The album sparked a regional production (with Bob Fosse in the title role) which eventually led to the Broadway revival.

During the tryout of the original production, "I'm Talking to My Pal" (which Gene Kelly sang just prior to the dance sequence "Joey Looks into the Future") was cut. A few weeks after the New York opening, the lyric of "Love Is My Friend" was rewritten as "What Is a Man?"

Unfortunately, Kelly never recorded any songs from the production; but for a radio broadcast in 1945 he re-created the so-called "pet shop scene" (the second scene of the first act) with Martha Tilden, who portrayed

Linda for the broadcast. The sequence is preserved in the collection *Rodgers & Hart Volume 3* (Pearl Records CD # GEM-0118).

There exists brief silent footage of a dance scene by Kelly that was surreptitiously filmed by an adventurous and daring audience member from a center orchestra seat during a live New York performance. (The fascinating sequence is probably from "Happy Hunting Horn.") This same person filmed brief sequences (some in color) from Broadway musicals of the 1930s and 1940s, from both orchestra and balcony seats. Footage from *Stars in Your Eyes* (1939) reportedly captures a moment in which an onstage Jimmy Durante suddenly notices that someone is filming the production and wags a finger in his direction as if saying, "That's a no-no." It's amazing that such footage of long-ago Broadway musicals exists, and it's also surprising that given the technology of the era (with its bulky and probably noisy film equipment) that the amateur filmmaker was able to get the apparatus into the theatre and then position it from his theatre seat to take footage, all apparently without ever being noticed (save for Durante's keen observation).

Besides Columbia's studio cast recording, there was an official cast recording of sorts for the 1952 revival (with Jane Froman and Dick Beavers substituting for Segal and Lang) released by Capitol (LP # 310; the CD was issued by Broadway Angel # ZDM-0777-7-64698-2-1). In 1952, a hardback edition of the script was published by Random House; the script was published in hardback in 2014 by the Library of Congress in a collection that includes the scripts of fifteen other musicals. The lyrics are included in the collection *The Complete Lyrics of Lorenz Hart*.

The first London production opened on March 11, 1954, at the Prince's Theatre for 245 performances and starred Lang and Carol Bruce (Vera). There were two institutional revivals produced by the New York City Center Light Opera Company. The first opened on May 31, 1961, for thirty-one performances; Bob Fosse was again Joey, and the cast included Carol Bruce (Vera), Christine Mathews (Linda), and Eileen Heckart (Melba). Fosse returned for the second revival, which opened on May 29, 1963, for fifteen performances; this time around, the cast included Viveca Lindfors (Vera), Rita Gardner (Linda), and Kay Medford (Melba).

Besides the 1952 revival, there were two other commercial revivals, both unsuccessful. On June 27, 1976, the musical opened at the Circle in the Square (Uptown) for seventy-three performances. During previews, Edward Vilella and Eleanor Parker were succeeded by Christopher Chadman and Joan Copeland; Janie Sell and Dixie Carter were also in the cast. On December 18, 2008, the musical was again revived, and played for eighty-four performances at Studio 54. Again, there was a major cast replacement during previews when Christian Holt was succeeded by Matthew Risch. Stockard Channing was Vera. This production included "I'm Talking to My Pal" as well as "Are You My Love?" (from Rodgers and Hart's 1936 film musical *Dancing Pirate*) and "I Still Believe in You" (from the team's 1930 musical *Simple Simon*; with a different lyric the song had also been heard as "Singing a Love Song" in their 1928 musical *Chee-Chee*, which was the first Broadway musical about castration, a theme which decades later was explored in such Off-Broadway musicals as *The Knife* [1987] and *Hedwig and the Angry Inch* [1998]).

A concert version of *Pal Joey* was given by Encores! on May 4, 1995, for four performances; the leads were Patti LuPone and Peter Gallagher, and Bebe Neuwirth was Melba; this version included "I'm Talking to My Pal," and the concert was recorded by DRG (CD # 94763).

A 1957 film adaptation by Columbia was considerably revised and softened, and here Joey (Frank Sinatra) was a singer instead of a hoofer. Sinatra was ideally cast as the brash title character as were Rita Hayworth as the worldly Vera and Kim Novak as the shy and demure Linda. The film retained a handful of songs from the stage production and interpolated numbers from various musicals by Rodgers and Hart. Taken on its own terms and in the context of 1950s film censorship, the film is entertaining and Sinatra is in top vocal form. The smoky nightclub scene in which he sings "The Lady Is a Tramp" (from the 1937 musical *Babes in Arms*) to Hayworth is strikingly photographed, edited, directed, and performed. This is one of the finest sequences in all Hollywood musicals, and if the entire film had matched this scene the final result would have been a great instead of a good movie. The soundtrack was released by Capitol (LP # DW-912), and the film's most recent DVD release (by Sony Pictures Home Entertainment # 25466) is included in the *Kim Novak Collection* (incidentally, the film's cast includes Barbara Nichols as chorus-girl Gladys; in the 1952 Broadway revival she had played the role of Valerie, another chorus girl).

ALL IN FUN
"A New Scintillating & Spectacular Revue"

Theatre: Majestic Theatre
Opening Date: December 27, 1940; *Closing Date*: December 28, 1940
Performances: 3
Sketches: Virginia Faulkner, Charles Sherman, and Everett Marcy
Lyrics: Virginia Faulkner, Irvin Graham, John Rox, S. K. Russel, and June Sillman
Music: Baldwin Bergersen; additional music by Glen Bacon, Will Irwin, and John Rox
Direction: "Staged" by Leonard Sillman with "additional direction" by John Murray Anderson; *Producer*:
    Leonard Sillman; *Choreography*: Marjery Fielding; *Scenery*: Edward Gilbert; *Costumes*: Irene Sharaff;
    Lighting: Uncredited; *Musical Direction*: Ray Kavanaugh
Cast: *Bill* ("Bojangles") *Robinson*, Imogene Coca, Pert Kelton, Wynn Murray, Red Marshall, Marie Nash, Paul
    Gerrits, David Morris, Don Loper, Maxine Barrat, Walter Cassel, Bill Johnson, Anita Alvarez, William
    Archibald, Candido Botelho; Specialty Dancers: Kirk Alyn, Henry Dick, Mildred Law, Jack Whitney, Ray
    Long, Puk Paaris, Nancy Noel, Orpha Dickey, Christopher Curtis, Dorothy Dennis, Beverly Whitney;
    Anna Marie Barrie, Eleanor Fairchild, Jane Fears, Betty Hull, Jane Johnstone, Peggy Littlejohn, Gertrude
    Nicols, Roberta Ramon, Miriam Seabold, Dorothy Speicher, Fred Deming, Hugh Ellsworth, David Pres-
    ton, Frank Milton, Stuart Ross, Theresa Mason; The Men of a Chord: Bob Oglesby, Bob Herring, Peter
    Holliday, and Ed (Edward) Platt
The revue was presented in two acts.

Sketches and Musical Numbers

Act One: "It's All in Fun" (lyric by S. K. Russel, music by Baldwin Bergersen) (Christopher Curtis, Bill John-
    son; danced by Anna Marie Barrie, Eleanor Fairchild, Jane Fears, Betty Hull, Jane Johnstone, Mildred Law,
    Peggy Littlejohn, Gertrude Nicols, Roberta Ramon, Miriam Seabold, Dorothy Speicher, Natalie Wynn,
    Fred Deming, Henry Dick, Hugh Ellsworth, Ray Long, David Preston, Jack Whitney); "Roll Out the
    Record" (sketch by Virginia Faulkner) (Dorothy Tom-Tom: Pert Kelton; Miss Pindicle: Orpha Dickey);
    "Where Can I Go from You?" (lyric by Virginia Faulkner, music by Baldwin Bergersen) (Wynn Murray,
    Bill Johnson, Bill Robinson; The Dancers: Mildred Law, Henry Dick); "Slowly I Turn" (sketch) (The Der-
    elict: Imogene Coca; The Samaritan: Red Marshall; The Bride: Dorothy Dennis; The Groom: Kirk Alyn);
    "Love and I" (lyric by Irvin Graham and June Sillman, music by Baldwin Bergersen) (The Singers: Marie
    Nash and Walter Cassel; The Dancers: Don Loper and Maxine Barrat with Anna Marie Barrie, Jane John-
    stone, Miriam Seabold, Dorothy Speicher, Peggy Littlejohn, Natalie Wynn, Kirk Alyn, Fred Deming, Jack
    Whitney, Ray Long, Hugh Ellsworth, David Preston); "Red Rails in the Sunset" (sketch) (Passenger: Red
    Marshall; Conductor: David Morris; Bride: Marie Nash; Groom: Bill Johnson; Brakeman: Frank Milton;
    French Girl: Pert Kelton); "April in Harrisburg" (lyric by Virginia Faulkner, music by Baldwin Bergersen)
    (Marie Nash; (a) "Dance Divertissement" by Jack Whitney, Anita Alvarez, and David Preston; (b) "Cake
    Walk" by Bill Robinson); "Neurosis Peddler" (sketch by Virginia Faulkner and Everett Marcy) (Paul Ger-
    rits); "Machine Age" (dance) (music by Glen Bacon) (Imogene Coca, Kirk Alyn, Hugh Ellsworth, David
    Preston, Jack Whitney); "Just Strollin'" (Bill Robinson); "That Man and Woman Thing" (lyric by John Rox,
    music by Baldwin Bergersen) (William Archibald; danced by Anita Alvarez and William Archibald); "Man-
    hattan Transfer" (sketch by Virginia Faulkner and Everett Macy [suggested by Albert Lewis]) (Announced
    by Paul Gerrits; Jen: Pert Kelton; Esther: Imogene Coca; Bert: David Morris; Ralph: Red Marshall); "It's
    a Big, Wide, Wonderful World" (lyric and music by John Rox) (Wynn Murray, Walter Cassel, Company;
    Note: See below for more information regarding which cast members introduced this song.)
Act Two: "How Did It Get So Late So Early?" (lyric by June Sillman, music by Will Irwin) (Marie Nash, Bill
    Johnson, Men of a Chord; danced by Don Loper and Maxine Barrat; Headwaiter: Ray Long); Pert Kelton
    (accompanied by Stuart Ross); "Young Man with a Reefer" (ballet music by Baldwin Bergersen) (Bill
    Robinson; The Apparition: Theresa Mason); "Where's the Boy I Saved for a Rainy Day?" (lyric by John
    Rox, music by Baldwin Bergersen) (Wynn Murray); "A Matter of Principle" (sketch by Charles Sherman;
    directed by Edward Clarke Lilley) (Counterman: Red Marshall; Mr. Jones: David Morris; Mrs. Jones:

Pert Kelton); "My Memories Started With You" (lyric by June Sillman, music by Baldwin Bergersen) (Bill Johnson, Dorothy Dennis, Men of a Chord; danced by Henry Dick, Mildred Law, Fred Deming, Ensemble); "Morning After of a Faun" (dance parody) (Nymph: Imogene Coca; Faun: William Archibald; Two Nymphs: Eleanor Fairchild, Miriam Seabold); Paul Gerrits (assisted by Puk Paaris); "Dr. Killjoy's Dilemma" (sketch) (Dr. Killjoy: David Morris; Patient: Frank Milton; Nurse: Orpha Dickey; Sufferer: Red Marshall); "Macumba" (lyric by June Sillman, music by Baldwin Bergersen) (Wynn Murray; danced by Anita Alvarez and William Archibald); this sequence included (a) New York—"L'Heure Bleu" by Virginia Faulkner (Mrs. Burton: Imogene Coca; Waiter: David Morris; Newsboy: Henry Dick; Cigarette Girl: Natalie Wynn; Flower Girl: Pert Kelton; Photographer: Orpha Dickey; Professor Mazotto: Frank Milton; Don Carlos: Kirk Alyn) and (b) Brazil (Candido Botelho); Bill Robinson (in one); "Quittin' Time" (lyric and music by John Rox) (Wynn Murray, Entire Company)

The revue *All in Fun* received devastatingly bad reviews and was gone after three performances. It covered many of the era's favorite revue topics, including spoofs of Hollywood ("Dr. Kiljoy's Dilemma") and modern dance, and of course there was the compulsory South American number ("Macumba"). And while **Keep Off the Grass** had kidded radio panelist Dorothy Thompson by having a monkey impersonate her, the new revue offered Pert Kelton in her portrayal of "Dorothy Tom-Tom."

Like all the critics, Brooks Atkinson in the *New York Times* was glad to see legendary tap dancer Bill "Bojangles" Robinson back on Broadway; and while his dancing moments were the high points of the evening, the aisle sitters regretted the sketches and songs didn't match his inimitable talents. And they generally liked comic Red Marshall, who was new to Broadway after making his name on the burlesque circuit. But Atkinson felt the revue held to "routine old patterns" and said there was "little talent and no freshness" on the stage. Burns Mantle in the *New York Daily News* found the material "spotty" and said Robinson wasn't seen to his best advantage.

John Mason Brown in the *New York Post* said there were "grim proceedings" on the stage of the Majestic, and even the great Robinson was "no more than a pleasant traveler who is lost in a desert." Among the low points of the evening were the Dorothy Thompson sketch and the song "April in Harrisburg," which he suggested was enough to "cause Pennsylvania to secede from the Union." Richard Watts in the *New York Herald Tribune* found the revue "singularly dull and unappetizing," and except for Robinson's contributions there was "very little else of good cheer" in the evening; Sidney B. Whipple in the *New York World-Telegram* said *All in Fun* was "the dullest" musical "to land—flat—on Broadway this season," and he felt the Thompson spoof was one of the "silliest and most distasteful" of sketches; but he liked the songs "How Did It Get So Late So Early?" and "April in Harrisburg." Richard Lockridge in the *New York Sun* said the evening "seldom rises above, and by no means always attains, mediocrity." But he praised Robinson's dancing, noted that Imogene Coca enjoyed "rages worthy of Donald Duck," and singled out "How Did It Get So Late So Early?"

"It's a Big, Wide, Wonderful World" became the score's most enduring song, but it was completely ignored by the critics. According to the opening night program, the number was performed as the first act finale and was sung by Wynn Murray, Walter Cassel, and the company (but a second four-page opening night program credited Murray and Cassel as well as Marie Nash, Bill Johnson, and the singing ensemble along with dancers Rosita Moreno, Anita Alvarez, William Archibald, and the Dancing Boys and Girls). John Rox's richly melodic song offered a sweeping melody and joyous lyric, and is one of the best theatre songs of the decade (and would make a nice companion piece to Richard Rodgers and Oscar Hammerstein II's later "It's a Grand Night for Singing" from their 1945 film musical *State Fair*). Much later, the number served as an ironic theme song for the 1962 film adaptation of Tennessee Williams' 1959 play *Sweet Bird of Youth*.

The four-page program may have been a corrected version of the regular program handed out to playgoers. While Bill Robinson was the sole performer billed above the title for the regular program, the four-page program billed Robinson, Imogene Coca, Red Marshall, and Pert Kelton above the title. The four-page program also credits the "book" (not sketches) to Virginia Faulkner and Everett Marcy; cites Edward Clarke Lilley as the sketch director (the regular program credited Leonard Sillman and John Murray Anderson with staging and direction); and includes a sketch not listed in the regular program, "Welles of Orson" ("announced" by Paul Gerrits, the sequence included Red Marshall, Nancy Noel, Natalie Wynn, Pert Kelton, and David Morris). Pert Kelton's early second-act "in one" sequence may have included a reprise of "Love and I."

For the Boston tryout, the revue's "book" was credited to Virginia Faulkner and Everett Marcy with "special material" by Blanche Merrill; and Edgar MacGregor was listed as the director of the sketches.

The collection *The Broadway Musicals of 1940* (Bayview CD # RNBW019) includes "How Did It Get So Late So Early?"

The very rotund singer Wynn Murray memorably introduced "Johnny One-Note" in Richard Rodgers and Lorenz Hart's 1937 musical *Babes in Arms*, and the following year was part of the show-stopping trio who sang "Sing for Your Supper" in the team's *The Boys from Syracuse* (and with Jimmy Savo she performed the naughty saga of "He and She," and with Teddy Hart complained about "What Can You Do with a Man?"). For *All in Fun*, she had reinvented herself, and was now trim and svelte. Instead of congratulating her, the critics actually took umbrage with her weight loss and grouchily complained that she was a pale imitation of her former self. Atkinson said she used to be "fat and cheerful" with the "genial amplitude" and "sunny good-humor of a fat girl," but now "oh, what a falling off is there!" Mantle noted that although she was now "slim and pretty," her former "charm has been sloughed off" and her "husky voice" hadn't profited from her dieting. Whipple said she had "thinned down almost to a wraith"; Brown complained that her new "sylph-like" appearance "reduced" his "enthusiasm" for her singing; and Watts said that with her weight loss she had also lost "much of her stage effectiveness."

The cast of *All in Fun* was an interesting one; besides Bill Robinson, Wynn Murray, and Imogene Coca, the participants included Bill Johnson, Anita Alvarez, Don Loper, William Archibald, and television's future *Get Smart* "Chief" Ed Platt.

NIGHT OF LOVE
"A MUSICAL PLAY"

Theatre: Hudson Theatre
Opening Date: January 7, 1941; *Closing Date*: January 11, 1941
Performances: 7
Book and *Lyrics*: Rowland Leigh
Music: Robert Stolz
Based on the 1930 play *Tonight or Never* by Lili Hatvany (as adapted by Frederic and Fanny Hatton from the original *Ma este vaga soha*).
Direction: Barrie O'Daniels; *Producers*: The Messrs. Shubert; *Choreography*: Uncredited; *Scenery*: Watson Barratt; *Costumes*: Ernest Schraps; *Lighting*: Uncredited; *Musical Direction*: Joseph Littau
Cast: Dorothy Sargent (Cleo de Francine), Martha Errolle (Madi Linden), Frank Hornaday (Rubero), Harrison Dowd (Rudig), George Spelvin (Call Boy), Robert Chisholm (Count Albert de Gronac), Helen Gleason (Nella Vago), Jack Blair (Andor), Melissa Mason (Lisel), Marguerite Namara (Marchesa Sangiovani), John Lodge (The Young Man [Jim]), Jann Moore (Tilly), Noel Cravat (Waiter)
The musical was presented in three acts.
The action takes place in June during the present time in Lucerne, Switzerland.

Musical Numbers

Act One: Overture (Orchestra); "My Loved One" (Aria) (Martha Errolle, Frank Hornaday); "Chiquitin' Trio" (Martha Errolle, Dorothy Sargent, Frank Hornaday); Musical Scene and Aria "I'm Thinking of Love" (Helen Gleason, Harrison Dowd, Martha Errolle); "I'm Thinking of Love" (reprise) (Frank Hornaday); Musical Scene (Helen Gleason, Robert Chisholm); "The One Man I Need" (Helen Gleason); Dance (Melissa Mason, Jack Blair); "Tonight or Never" (Helen Gleason, Melissa Mason, Harrison Dowd)

Act Two: Overture (Orchestra); "Serenade for You" (Helen Gleason, John Lodge); (a) "Melodrama" and (b) "Serenade for You" (reprise) (The Café Singer [performer unidentified]); "Without You" (Helen Gleason, John Lodge); "Tonight or Never" (reprise) (Helen Gleason, John Lodge)

Act Three: Overture (Orchestra); Reprise (unidentified song) (Helen Gleason, Melissa Mason); Musical Scene (Helen Gleason, Robert Chisholm); "Loosen Up" (Melissa Mason, Jack Blair); Reprise (unidentified song) (Helen Gleason, Melissa Mason); "Streamlined Pompadour" (Martha Errolle); (a) Finale (Ensemble) and (b) "Chiquitin'" Music and Finale (Ensemble)

The Shuberts brought in the short-lived modern-day operetta *Night of Love*, which had been based on the fairly successful Broadway comedy *Tonight or Never*, which opened at the Belasco Theatre on November 11, 1930, for a run of 232 performances; based on Lili Hatvany's *Ma este vaga soha*, the adaptation was by Frederic and Fanny Hatton and starred Helen Gahagan and Melvyn Douglas. A 1931 film version starred Gloria Swanson, with Douglas reprising his stage role.

The plot dealt with opera singer Nella Vago (Helen Gleason), who lacks the necessary operatic fire when she sings. It's suggested she take on a lover, since perhaps sex is what she needs to liven up her vocal chords. She meets a young man (Jim, played by John Lodge) whom she believes is a gigolo, and after a night of sex, her voice captures the required rapturous spirit of a true diva. And it turns out Jim isn't a gigolo at all, but a scout from the Metropolitan Opera. So Nella has a lover as well as an opera career.

The critics pounced on the new musical as one of the worst in memory, and were particularly disappointed because its composer Robert Stolz, a self-imposed exile from Austria, had previously written the hit song "Two Hearts in Three-Quarter Time."

The headline of Richard Watts's review in the *New York Herald Tribune* said the musical was "A Night of Dullness," and the critic noted the "incredibly tedious" evening set "new standards for dullness and ineptitude." Watts suspected Helen Gleason realized the hopelessness of it all and thus tended to "burlesque it a bit." John Mason Brown in the *New York Post* wasn't impressed with the musical's "ghoulish" attempts at "gaiety and romance" and proclaimed the evening could be "neither easily forgiven nor forgotten"; the score was "less a sedative than an interruption"; and the scenery seemed more "retrieved than designed" and (in a reference to the famous theatrical warehouse) more "Cain than able."

Sidney Whipple in the *New York World-Telegram* said the musical was "woodenly" acted, but praised the "attractive" song "I'm Thinking of Love" and a couple other "pleasant melodies." He noted when one performer spoke the line that "Madame might find it gayer in the main dining room," there was laughter from some in the audience, which was undoubtedly their "form of critical comment." Richard Lockridge in the *New York Sun* felt Rowland Leigh's book achieved nothing but "rather arresting vapidity" and wavered between "a kind of misty no-man's land" of both "drama and operetta." But he liked the "charming" songs (and singled out "I'm Thinking of Love" and "Without You") and two "amusing grotesque dances" by Melissa Mason and Jack Blair.

Louis Kronenberger in *PM* found the score "sometimes tuneful" and "always full of schmaltz," but nonetheless "pretty routine stuff." Further, the "outmoded" story offered coy and "twittery" acting, silly dialogue, "broken-down witticisms," and the "oddest" direction he'd seen in years. Burns Mantle in the *New York Daily News* commented that no one in the cast seemed "altogether happy," and thus the audience was "loyal" to the performers by being "depressed."

John Anderson in the *New York Journal-American* felt the before-and-after effects of Nella's night of love weren't believably acted by Gleason, who in her early scenes seemed "as cold and restrained and unawakened as a four-alarm fire," and after her title encounter had gone up a notch to a "five-alarm fire." He suggested her performance needed to begin in the refrigerator and end in the oven. And like Whipple he commented on the line about the dining room being gayer, and suspected that even the Hudson Theatre's lobby had its "advantages."

Brooks Atkinson in the *New York Times* said it was almost "admirable" how the new musical mixed the "exact" proportions of the "tawdriness to the trite." Here was a tired operetta way past its prime, and the Hudson's stage seemed "crowded with ghosts who had not heard the cock crow a decade or more ago."

The critics also felt the script needlessly and desperately tried to update the plot by including topical references to boogie-woogie, Hitler, LaGuardia, Willkie, and Lucius Beebe (historians, take note, for *Night of Love* was the fourth musical in eight months to reference Beebe; see **Keep Off the Grass**, **Panama Hattie**, and **Pal Joey**).

During the tryout, Marjorie Gainsworth was succeeded by Martha Errolle.

CRAZY WITH THE HEAT
"The New Musical Revue" / "1941's Merry Musical Revue"

Theatre: 44th Street Theatre
Opening Date: January 14, 1941; *Closing Date*: April 19, 1941

Performances: 99

Sketches: Mack Davis, Don Herold, Max Liebman, Robert Marko, H. I. Phillips, Arthur Sheekman, and Sam
   E. Werris; additional dialogue by Arthur Stander and Sydney Zelinka

Lyrics: Irvin Graham; additional lyrics by Kurt Kasznar, Carl Kent, Richard Kollmar, Walter Nones, Pete Kite
   Smith, and Maurice Vandair

Music: Irvin Graham; additional music by Walter Nones, William Provost, Rudi Revil, and Elsie Thompson,

Direction: Production staged by Kurt Kasznar; sketches staged by Arthur Sheekman; Willie Howard's sketches
   under the supervision of Eugene Howard; *Producer*: Kurt Kasznar; *Choreography*: Catherine Littlefield;
   Scenery and *Lighting*: Albert Johnson; *Costumes*: Lester Polakov and Maria Humans; *Musical Direction*:
   Harold Levey

Cast: *Willie Howard, Luella Gear*, Gracie Barrie, Richard Kollmar, Luba Rostova, Carl Randall, Marie Nash,
   Betty Kean, Don Cumming, David Rollins, Paul Bartels, Raymond Burr, William Howell, Ted Gary, Philip
   King, Frances Williams, Vera Deane, Thomas Mitchell, Marion Bailey, Helene (or Helen) Hudson, Jean
   Stanton, Eleanor Dawn, Evelyn Bonefine, Irene Reilly, Helenita Riordan, Frances O'Day, Harold Gary,
   Bobby Busch, Hildegarde Halliday, Edna Ward, Bobby Lane, Frank Cucksey, Harriet Clark, Al Kelly, Ed-
   die Eddy, Stapleton Kent, Vivienne Allen, Wilma Horner, Jane Hoffman, William Gordon, Harry Hale,
   Kay York; The Coronets: Frances Williams, Vera Deane, Thomas Mitchell, Bob (Robert) Evans; Dancing
   Ensemble: Kathryn Lazell, Marion Warnes (or Warness), Billie Dee, Ruth Neslie, Doris Call, Susan Scott,
   Rae McGregor, Lois Girard, Aileen Read, Barbara Bernard, Roberta Ogg, Pamela Clifford, Dale Priest, Mat-
   thew Bocchino, Hal Anthony, Philip Gordon, Remi Martel

Sketches and Musical Numbers

Act One: "This Way Out" (Footmen: David Rollins, Paul Bartels, Raymond Burr, William Howell, Philip
   King; Madame: Marie Nash; First Lady: Luba Rostova; Madame's Entourage—The Coronets; Ladies in
   the House of the Revue: Marion Bailey, Helene Hudson, Jean Stanton, Eleanor Dawn, Evelyn Bonefine,
   Irene Reilly, Helenita Riordan, Frances O'Day; Dancing Ensemble); "Man about Town" (Carl Randall);
   "It Should Happen to Me" (lyric by Richard Kollmar, music by Elsie Thompson) (She: Gracie Barrie; He:
   Richard Kollmar; Dancing Ensemble); "Call for Herbert Tilson" (sketch by Sam E. Werris) (Herbert Til-
   son: Willie Howard; Alice Tilson: Marie Nash; Jack: Harold Gary; Announcer: Bobby Busch; Neighbor:
   Hildegarde Halliday); "Sascha's Got a Girl" (The Tattletale: Gracie Barrie; Sascha: Ted Gary; Sascha's
   Girl: Betty Kean; Animals—Evelyn Bonefine (Zebra); Helene Hudson (Zebra), Edna Ward (Mama Monkey);
   Bobby Lane (Papa Monkey); Frank Cucksey (Offspring of Mama and Papa Monkey); Raymond Burr (Ac-
   tive Lion); David Rollins (Passive Lion); Dancing Ensemble; The Coronets); "Mental Giant" (sketch by
   H. I. Phillips) (The Wife: Luella Gear; The Husband: Willie Howard); Ted Gary; "Some Day" (lyric by Kurt
   Kasznar and Carl Kent, music by Rudi Revil) (Sailor: Richard Kollmar) and, "in the vision," "Il pleurait"
   (lyric and music by Rudi Revil and Maurice Vandair) (La Jeune Fille des Fleurs: Luba Rostova; Gendarme:
   David Rollins; La Blonde: Harriet Clark; La Masquereau: Thomas Mitchell; Le Musicien: Bob Evans; Le
   Garcon: Al Kelly; L'Assistante: Vera Deane; Boulanger: Bobby Busch; L'Homme Cacahouette: Eddie Eddy;
   L'Acrobat: Raymond Burr; Son Amie: Frances Williams; Les Dames de la Rue: Irene Reilly, Jean Stanton,
   Evelyn Bonefine, Helene Hudson; Les Apaches: Bobby Lane, Edna Ward; Les Tourists: Stapleton Kent,
   William Howell, Kathryn Lazell); "Butcher Boy" (sketch by Mack Davis) (Patient: Wilma Horner; Doctor:
   Harold Gary; Patient's Sister: Vivienne Allen; Butcher Boy: Willie Howard); "Time of Your Life" (lyric
   by Pete Kite Smith, music by William Provost) (The Maid: Gracie Barrie; The Lady in Red: Betty Kean;
   The Dancing Boys; Frank Cucksey); "Life without Father" (sketch by Robert Marko) (Mother: Luella
   Gear; Maid: Jane Hoffman; Father: Willie Howard; John: Richard Kollmar; Whitney: Harold Gary; Harlan:
   Philip Gordon; Junior: Bobby Busch; Cousin Gladys: Wilma Horner; Rodney: Bobby Lane); Don Cumming;
   "Morning Mist" (sketch by Sam E. Werris) (Announcer: Luella Gear; Ivan Roushinska: Willie Howard;
   Attendant: Don Cumming; Corps de Ballet); "Set to Music" (The Bride: Marie Nash; The Groom: Rich-
   ard Kollmar; The Bridesmaids: Jean Stanton, Helene Hudson, Helenita Riordan, Marion Bailey, Frances
   O'Day, Evelyn Bonefine, Irene Reilly, Eleanor Dawn; The Groom's Friends: Thomas Mitchell, Bob Evans,
   Raymond Burr, David Rollins); "Announcement to the Audience" (sketch by Don Herold) (Luella Gear);
   "Crazy with the Heat" (lyric by Irvin Graham, music by Rudi Revil) (Debutante: Gracie Barrie; Crazy with

Their Feet: Betty Kean, Carl Randall; Quartet: The Coronets; Doorman at Shapiro's: Harry Hale; Doorman at Cabana: David Rollins; Doorman at Typhoon: Stapleton Kent; Doorman at Zombie: Al Kelly; Shapiro's Eight Weaknesses: Marion Bailey, Helene Hudson, Irene Reilly, Jean Stanton, Eleanor Dawn, Helenita Riordan, Evelyn Bonefine, Frances O'Day; Dancing Ensemble)

Act Two: "No Smoking" (Ushers: Raymond Burr, David Rollins, Harry Hale, Thomas Mitchell, Bob Evans; The Audience: Marion Bailey, Helene Hudson, Irene Reilly, Jean Stanton, Eleanor Dawn, Helenita Riordan, Kay York, Frances O'Day, Paul Bartels, Dale Priest, Philip King, Matthew Boccino, Hal Anthony, William Howell, Philip Gordon, Remi Martel; The Victim: Bobby Busch; The Announcer: Luella Gear); "Twist of the Wrist" (Svengali: Richard Kollmar; Trilby: Gracie Barrie; Assistant Magician: Bobby Busch; Wire Walkers: Betty Kean, Ted Gary; Four Flying Aces: The Coronets; Dancing Ensemble); "A Voice of Experience" (sketch by Arthur Sheekman) (Professor Willie: Willie Howard; Announcer: Bobby Busch; Attendant: David Rollins; First Couple: Wilma Horner, Al Kelly; A Woman: Jane Hoffman; Strange Case: Harold Gary); "Yacht Song" (lyric and music by Walter Nones) (Luella Gear); "Fightin' for the Funnies" (Bobby Lane, Edna Ward); "Wine from My Slipper" (Ballerina: Luba Rostova; Singer: Marie Nash; Seducer: Philip Ogg; Ladies of the Can-Can: Billie Dee, Barbara Bernard, Ruth Neslie, Aileen Read, Roberta Ogg, Marion Warnes, Doris Call, Pamela Clifford, Susan Scott, Lois Girard, Kathryn Lazell, Rae McGregor, Ensemble); Betty Kean; "Music Hath Charms" (sketch by Max Liebman) (Alice: Wilma Horner; Charles: Richard Kollmar; Singer: Willie Howard; Proprietor: Harold Gary); "Set to Music" (reprise and finale) (Entire Company)

The revue *Crazy with the Heat* opened on January 14, 1941, and closed on January 21 after seven performances. Ed Sullivan saw something in the show that apparently no one else did, and so upon its closing he refinanced it (and apparently received some concessions by the unions). The revue was restaged by Lew Brown, and new cast members were added, and others left. The revised version opened on January 30, but it was all in vain; the revue permanently closed on April 19 after an additional ninety-two performances, for a total run of ninety-nine showings, and the two combined runs went down in a sea of red ink.

The first production, which lasted less than a week, received some of the season's poorest notices, and the critics were particularly disappointed that comic favorites Willie Howard and Luella Gear were given such weak material. Richard Watts in the *New York Herald Tribune* said the evening was a "lost cause" and would only be remembered because it was even worse than **All in Fun**, which had disappeared after three performances just two weeks earlier. John Mason Brown in the *New York Post* also recalled the earlier revue, and suggested that an argument over which was the worst was unnecessary because in both cases the "merits" of the two shows were "impossible to defend." But no one mentioned poor Marie Nash, who appeared in both flops, a distinction she probably wanted to forget because her program biography for *Crazy with the Heat* somehow omitted her appearance in **All in Fun**. Brown found *Crazy with the Heat* "pathetic" and Brooks Atkinson in the *New York Times* said the evening was "routine" and lacked "style, ideas and showmanship."

Richard Lockridge in the *New York Sun* said the leading performers were wasted in a show that was "thin" and offered "bad material"; Burns Mantle in the *New York Daily News* felt the evening was a "mistake"; John Anderson in the *New York Journal-American* said it was "depressing" to see so much talent wasted on "humdrum and tasteless material"; and Sidney B. Whipple in the *New York World-Telegram* said the revue wouldn't offer "active competition" to the other musicals in town.

Louis Kronenberger in *PM* went right for the jugular. The revue could be divided into four classifications: "indiscretions, misdemeanors, penitentiary offenses, and hanging matters."

The evening offered Broadway audiences yet another spoof of *Life with Father* (according to Watts, this was the revue's low point); Luella Gear sang "Yacht Song," which Mantle found a "brazenly coarse ditty"; Anderson said the title song offered nothing more than "mechanical exuberance" with a "weary bounce"; and "Wine from My Slipper" was according to the program "inspired" by Toulouse-Lautrec (the program also helpfully noted that he was a painter), and Anderson cautioned that the artist shouldn't be "blamed" for the sequence.

Another number (which combined "Some Day" and "Il pleurait") also looked toward Paris in its depiction of a young sailor (Richard Kollmar) on the New York docks who nostalgically gazes at the *Normandie* and recalls prewar Paris. A few months later saw the release of the MGM film musical *Lady, Be Good*, and it too offered a number that sentimentally embraced the Paris of old (with a lyric by Oscar Hammerstein II and music by Jerome Kern, "The Last Time I Saw Paris" won the Academy Award for Best Song).

To be sure, *Crazy with the Heat* had its moments. Willie Howard's fractured English was occasionally amusing, especially when he realizes he's inadvertently killed a relative (his very own fish and blood!), and in another sequence he appeared as a hapless ballet dancer in sagging tights and mournful air.

Poor Luella Gear was the evening's compere, and toward the end of the first act was saddled with a monologue in which she gave the audience advice on how to behave during intermission and cautioned them to be on time for the beginning of the second act. Anderson suggested this was "useless" on her part, because on opening night "many" in the audience never returned.

Hollace Shaw appeared in the revue during the tryout, and Luther Davis, John Cleveland, and Kay Kenney were among the credited sketch writers.

As mentioned, various new performers joined the revue upon its reopening, including dancers Mary Kaye and Naldi, singer Diosa Costello, Adele Gerard (a "swing harpist"), and, briefly, Carlos Ramirez, and the team of Tip, Tap and Toe. Among those who returned were Willie Howard, Luella Gear, and Jane Kean, and absent from this go-round were Richard Kollmar, Marie Nash, Carl Randall, and Luba Rostova. The sketch "Life without Father" was dropped, "Wine from My Slipper" was refashioned as "Les Rendezvous des Artistes," and the sketch "Butcher Boy" was retitled "Lamp Chops." New songs included "Yes, My Darling Daughter" (lyric and music by Jack Lawrence); additional choreography was now credited to Carl Randall, and "Begin the Beguine" was interpolated into the score (from *Jubilee*, 1935; lyric and music by Cole Porter).

In the chorus of the revue was Raymond Burr, who didn't have much in the way of a stage career, later played character roles in the movies (most memorably as the murderer in Alfred Hitchcock's 1954 thriller *Rear Window*), and ultimately found television immortality in the title roles of two long-running hit series (*Perry Mason* and *Ironside*).

LADY IN THE DARK
"A MUSICAL PLAY"

Theatre: Alvin Theatre
Opening Date: January 23, 1941; *Closing Date*: May 30, 1942
Performances: 467
Book: Moss Hart
Lyrics: Ira Gershwin
Music: Kurt Weill
Direction: "Staged by" Moss Hart and "production" and "musical sequences by" Hassard Short; *Producer*: Sam H. Harris; *Choreography*: Albertina Rasch; *Scenery*: Harry Horner; *Costumes*: Irene Sharaff (gowns by Hattie Carnegie); *Lighting*: Hassard Short; *Musical Direction*: Maurice Abravanel
Cast: Donald Randolph (Dr. Brooks), Jeanne Shelby (Miss Bowers), *Gertrude Lawrence* (Liza Elliott), Evelyn Wyckoff (Miss Foster, Sutton), Ann Lee (Miss Stevens), Margaret Dale (Maggie Grant), Natalie Schafer (Alison Du Bois), Danny Kaye (Russell Paxton, Beekman, Ringmaster), MacDonald Carey (Charley Johnson), Victor Mature (Randy Curtis), Ward Tallmon (Joe), Nelson Barclift (Tom), Bert Lytell (Kendall Nesbitt), Virginia Peine (Helen), Gedda Petry (Ruthie), Beth Nichols (Carol), Margaret Westberg (Marcia), Dan Harden (Ben Butler), Patricia Deering (Barbara), Davis Cunningham (Jack); The Albertina Rasch Group Dancers: Dorothy Bird, Audrey Costello, Patricia Deering, June MacLaren, Beth Nichols, Wana Wenerholm, Margaret Westberg, Jerome Andrews, Nelson Barclift, George Bockman, Andre Charise, Fred Hearn, John Sweet, William Howell; The Singers: Catherine Conrad, Jean Cumming, Carol Deis, Hazel Edwards, Gedda Petry, June Rutherford, Florence Wyman, Eric Brotherson, Davis Cunningham, Max Edwards, Len Frank, Gordon Gifford, Manfred Hecht, William Marel, Larry Siegle, Harold Simmons; The Children: Anne Bracken, Sally Ferguson, Ellie Lawes, Joan Lawes, Jacqueline Macmillan, Lois Volkman, Kenneth Casey, Warren Mills, Robert Mills, Robert Lee, George Ward, William Welch
The musical was presented in two acts.
The action takes place in New York City during the present time.

Musical Numbers

Act One: *Glamour Dream*: "Oh, Fabulous One (in Your Ivory Tower)" (Liza Elliott's Serenaders); "The World's Inamorata" (aka "Huxley") (Gertrude Lawrence, Evelyn Wyckoff); "One Life to Live" (Gertrude Lawrence, Danny Kaye); "Girl of the Moment" (Ensemble); "It Looks Like Liza" (Entire Company); and "Girl of the Moment" (reprise) (Ensemble); *Wedding Dream*: "Mapleton High Chorale" (The High School Graduates); "This Is New" (Victor Mature, Gertrude Lawrence); "The Princess of Pure Delight" (Gertrude Lawrence, Children); and "The Woman at the Altar" (Entire Company)

Act Two: *Circus Dream*: "The Greatest Show on Earth" (Danny Kaye, Ensemble); "Dance of the Tumblers" (Albertina Rasch Dancers); "The Best Years of His Life" (MacDonald Carey, Victor Mature); "Tschiakowsky" (Danny Kaye, Ensemble); and "The Saga of Jenny" (Gertrude Lawrence, Ensemble); "My Ship" (Gertrude Lawrence)

Lady in the Dark was the musical event of the season, and all its performances sold out, including standing room. Everyone knew this was *it*, the most modern of musicals in which a theatrical legend was giving the performance of her career. Gertrude Lawrence played what was (along with Rose in the later *Gypsy*) perhaps the Hamlet of female musical roles, and her contract gave her the summer off. So the musical played for 162 capacity performances, took an eleven-week vacation, and then reopened in the fall for an additional 305 performances (the combined runs totaled 467 showings). In 1943, Lawrence returned for a limited-run return engagement of eighty-three performances at the Broadway Theatre.

Lady in the Dark was both a drama and a musical. Except for the last scene, in which Lawrence sang "My Ship," the book scenes were played straight with no music. The songs were heard during three dream sequences that explore Liza Elliott's fears and frustrations that arise from her visits to psychoanalyst Dr. Brooks (Donald Randolph) and from her office reveries when she mulls over her sessions with the doctor.

Liza is the fabulously successful magazine editor of *Allure*, a chic woman's magazine that her married lover (whose wife won't give him a divorce) Kendall Nesbitt (Bert Lytell) has bankrolled for her. Liza has now come to the point where she breaks down for no reason, gets furious with subordinates at the drop of a hat, and can't even make a simple decision, such as choosing the cover for the magazine's Easter issue (should it be traditional or one with a circus motif?). With the magical effects of Harry Horner's four revolving sets, the scenes in the doctor's and Liza's offices instantly transported the audience into the worlds of Liza's dreams and memories, and the three sequences (the "Glamour Dream," "Wedding Dream," and "Circus Dream") were like Technicolor explosions of mini-musical comedies.

For its era, the musical was serious in its depiction of a successful career woman, but was simplistic in its Hollywood-like notions of psychiatry and women's liberation. That said, the musical knew its mind and didn't apologize. One reason Liza is unhappy is because she's not really committed to Kendall, and it takes her sessions with Dr. Brooks to realize she's actually in love with one of her staff members (Charley Johnson, played by MacDonald Carey). Here was a serious drama that utilized a unique framework of music to tell its story. Moss Hart's book was acerbic and to the point (if sometimes wordy and a bit obvious), Ira Gershwin's lyrics were among the most brilliant of his career, and Kurt Weill's score was magnificent. And with Gertrude Lawrence giving one of the all-time Broadway bravura performances, *Lady in the Dark* was a breakthrough musical with its intelligent characterizations, its daring use of psychiatry, and its innovative use of music and staging techniques.

The critics quickly realized that major changes were happening to the Broadway musical. Brooks Atkinson in the *New York Times* noted that the "splendors" of *Lady in the Dark* evolved from its drama, and that the season's earlier **Cabin in the Sky** and **Pal Joey** had been moving in that direction. And Sidney Whipple in the *New York World-Telegram* commented that like **Pal Joey** the new musical's book was "a piece of realism and not merely happy make-believe."

Richard Watts in the *New York Herald Tribune* noted the shifts between the drama's "realism" and the "musical gayety of the fantasy" were "shrewdly handled" (but he thought Hart's "psychoanalysis propaganda" was on the "primitive side"). That said, Gertrude Lawrence was "the greatest feminine performer" in the theatre and the "wonder girl" of the Broadway season. Burns Mantle in the *New York Daily News* gave the musical three-stars-plus, and noted it offered an "opulence in lighting and costumes" which were unequaled on the Broadway stage; further, Weill's music was "excellent," Gershwin's lyrics were "splendid," and Hart's book was an "inspiration."

Richard Lockridge in the *New York Sun* said Lawrence was "triumphant" with her "really admirable acting" and her "bubbling gayety"; but he cautioned that the book and musical sequences sometimes mixed like oil and water and didn't "really jell" because Hart wasn't "more honest" in his depiction of psychoanalysis. John Anderson in the *New York Journal-American* noted that Broadway had been on edge during the week preceding the musical's belated premiere of one week due to Lawrence's battle with the grippe; but all was well because she was "wonderful" on opening night and emerged triumphant in a "grueling and exhausting" role. The musical was "probably the most expensive way ever devised" to look into the mind of a woman, and while the book portions were sometimes "wearisomely long" and a "little pretentious," the evening was nonetheless a "triumph of stagecraft" which offered a "beautiful and imaginative" production.

John Mason Brown in the *New York Post* noted the evening was "too much of a muchness" but nonetheless deserved to be taken seriously as a "literary drama." He found Weill's music his "wittiest" and "most beguiling," Gershwin's lyrics gay, and he praised the "sheer mechanical wizardry of the production." As for Lawrence, she was "matchless" and ran the gamut of emotions "not only from A to Z but from Z to A."

Atkinson noted that the musical was a "work of theatre art" and Lawrence was "a goddess, that's all." Weill's music emerged as "the finest score written for the theatre in years," Gershwin's lyrics were "brilliant," and Horner's "whirling" décor gave the show a "transcendent loveliness." Despite a book which was sometimes "repetitious" and "interminable" in telling its story, Whipple said *Lady in the Dark* was "in many respects the most lavish and beautiful entertainment" to reach Broadway in years; it was a play with music rather than "just" a musical comedy, and its leading character was a "real, live, flesh-and-blood" woman.

Besides Gertrude Lawrence, Danny Kaye (in the role of the magazine's effeminate fashion photographer) was praised for his tongue-twisting "Tschiakowsky," in which he rattled off the names of some sixty Russian composers in not much more than sixty seconds. Whipple said Kaye was "extremely adept" at comedy; Atkinson found him "infectiously exuberant"; and Watts made the curious and rather interesting comment that although Kaye was "remarkable" as a "swishy" photographer, Kaye's performance indicated he was "pretty clearly . . . only acting."

During the tryout, "Bats about You" was cut, and "Unforgettable" (aka "You Are Unforgettable") was dropped during rehearsals. "Minstrel Dream" was refashioned as the "Circus Dream," but before it was abandoned an opening sequence had been written by Gershwin and Weill. An early version of the "Circus Dream" included the unused songs "The Unspoken Law," "No Matter under What Star You're Born," and "Song of the Zodiac"; the latter two were revised and combined into "You Have to Do What You Do Do" for *The Firebrand of Florence*. A fourth dream ("Hollywood Daydream") was written but went unused and included "The Boss Is Bringing Home a Bride," "Home in San Fernando Valley," and "Party Parlando" (aka "Hollywood Party").

Gertrude Lawrence recorded "The World's Inamorata," "One Life to Live," "This Is New," "The Princess of Pure Delight," "The Saga of Jenny," and "My Ship," and recordings also exist of a radio broadcast with scenes and songs from the musical (with Lawrence, MacDonald Carey, Hume Cronyn, and other performers). These can be heard on two AEI recordings (CD # AEI-CD-041 and CD # AEI-CD-003). The former includes the soundtrack of the 1954 television production (another CD of the television version was released by Sepia # 1052). Danny Kaye also recorded "Tschaikowsky" as well as "One Life to Live," "The Princess of Pure Delight," "The Saga of Jenny," "My Ship," and the cut song "It's Never Too Late to Mendelssohn." Spoken Arts (LP # 725) released a recording of Moss Hart reading excerpts from *Lady in the Dark* (and *The Man Who Came to Dinner*) as well as general commentary about his career. The unused "You Are Unforgettable" is included in the collection *Kurt Weill Revisited* (Painted Smiles CD # PSCD-108), and Hildegarde's *Songs from the Shows* (Vocalion CD # CDEA-6078) includes "The Saga of Jenny," "This Is New," "Girl of the Moment," "My Ship," and "One Life to Live."

The most complete recording of the score was released on a studio cast album by Columbia in 1963 (issued on CD by Sony Classical/Masterworks Heritage # MHK 62869); the sparkling cast includes Rise Stevens (Liza), Adolph Green (Beekman, Ringmaster), John Reardon (Randy Curtis), Kenneth Bridges (Charley Johnson), Roger White (Kendall Nesbitt), and Stephanie Augustine (Sutton, who reprised her role from the 1954 television version); the recording's orchestra and chorus were conducted by Lehman Engel.

The script was published in hardback by Random House in 1941; the book scenes are printed in black and the dream sequences in red. The hardback was republished in 1944 to coincide with the release of the film version. The script is also included in the hardback collection *Great Musicals of the American Theatre Volume Two* (1976), published by Chilton Book Company.

The lyrics of the used, cut, and unused songs are included in *The Complete Lyrics of Ira Gershwin*. Gershwin also includes some of the lyrics in his collection *Lyrics on Several Occasions*, and reports that for the musical's premiere performance in Boston Danny Kaye received a tremendous ovation after "Tschia-kowsky," which led the show's creators to worry that Lawrence's "The Saga of Jenny," the number which immediately followed it, would come across as a let-down; but Lawrence surprised everyone by incorporating bumps and grinds into the song and her ovation topped Kaye's. Gershwin also reports that in regard to the lyric of "My Ship" ("I can wait for years"), during rehearsals Lawrence asked him why "four" years, and thus he quickly changed the line to "I can wait the years."

The lavish but disappointing film version was released by Paramount in1944; directed by Mitchell Leisen, it was ideally cast with Ginger Rogers and Ray Milland (as Charley Johnson), who were supported by Warner Baxter, Jon Hall, Barry Sullivan, Gail Russell, and Mischa Auer. The Technicolor film (which sported costumes by Raoul Pene du Bois) eviscerated the score and offered just a handful of songs from the original production (including "One Life to Live" and "The Saga of Jenny") and only a snippet of "My Ship." A new song, "Suddenly It's Spring" (lyric by Johnny Burke and music by Jimmy Van Heusen), was added to the score.

A faithful television adaptation was shown by NBC on September 25, 1954, with Ann Sothern, Carleton Carpenter, James Daly, Shepperd Strudwick, Luella Gear, Robert Fortier, Stephanie Augustine, Bambi Linn, and Rod Alexander; Max Liebman directed, Rod Alexander choreographed, and Clay Warnick was the choral director. As noted above, the television soundtrack has been released on CD by Sepia and AEI (it was originally issued by RCA Victor LP # LM-1882).

Lady in the Dark: Biography of a Musical by Bruce D. McClung was published by Oxford University Press in 2007.

LIBERTY JONES
"A PLAY WITH MUSIC"

Theatre: Shubert Theatre
Opening Date: February 5, 1941; *Closing Date*: February 22, 1941
Performances: 22
Play: Philip Barry
Music: Paul Bowles
Direction: John Houseman; *Producer*: The Theatre Guild; *Choreography*: Lew Christensen; *Scenery* and *Costumes*: Raoul Pene du Bois; *Lighting*: Uncredited; *Musical Direction*: Daniel Mendelsohn
Cast: Nancy Coleman (Liberty Jones), William Lynn (Liberty's Uncle), Martha Hodge (Liberty's Aunt), John Beal (Tom Smith), Tom Ewell (Dick Brown), Howard Freeman (Harry Robinson), Katherine Squire (Nurse Cotton), Ivy Scott (Nurse Maggie); The Two Reporters: Don Glenn, Crahan Denton; The Two Dancers: Lew Christensen, Elise Reiman; The Three Shirts: Victor Thorley, Louis Polan, Richard Sanders; The Four Doctors, The Committee of Four, and The Four Policemen: Norman Lloyd, Murray O'Neill, Allan Frank, William Mende; The Five Singers: William Castle, Roy Johnston, Eva Burton, Ruth Gibbs, Alyce Carter; The Seven Friends: Lew Christensen, Joseph Anthony, Vincent Gardner, Craig Mitchell, William Castle, Roy Johnston, Jack Parsons; The Eleven Friends: Elise Reiman, Bedelia Falls, Caryl Smith, Honora Harwood, Ellen Morgan, Helen Kramer, Barbara Brown, Constance Dowling, Eva Burton, Ruth Gibbs, Alyce Carter
The play with music was presented in three acts.
The action takes place during the present time in and around Rock Creek Park in Washington, D.C.

Musical Sequences

Note: The program didn't cite musical numbers; the following list is taken from various newspaper reviews and reference sources.
Act One: "Close Your Two Eyes" (Lullaby) (Ivy Scott); "Comin' Through the Rye" (Norman Lloyd, Murray O'Neill, Allan Frank, William Mende; *Note*: It's unclear at which point in the play this number was performed)

Act Two: "Nurse and Intern Ballet" (Doctors, Reporters); "Close Your Two Eyes" (reprise) (Offstage Male Voice); "Cake Walk" (Dancers)

Act Three: "Sleep Walk" (Women's Voices); "Wedding Cake Song" (Ivy Scott); "Wedding Song" (Ushers, Bridesmaids); "Waltz" (Dancers)

Philip Barry's play-with-music *Liberty Jones* was a well-intentioned misfire that disappointed both audiences and critics, who expected something more impressive from the playwright who had given them the sparkling *The Philadelphia Story* two seasons earlier.

The play was a tiresome allegory in which Liberty (Nancy Coleman) is worried that her park (that is, the United States) is in danger from outside forces that will ask for just a tiny piece of the park before demanding all of it. Liberty is clearly sick and may die if she's neglected. But her ailing Uncle (Sam) (William Lynn) and various stalwarts of the realm, including the Doctors of Medicine, Letters, Divinity, and Law, are unable to revive her, and only when Tom Smith (John Beal) and his friends Dick (Tom Ewell) and Harry (Howard Freeman) recognize the urgency of the situation is Liberty saved (although Tom has to give his life for her). Hopefully the park will thrive when its keepers protect and nourish it.

Wilella Waldorf in the *New York Post* said Barry had undertaken a "tremendously dynamic theme" that he never developed, and so the evening was like a "high school pageant." The play lacked the "fire, drive and spirit" that a more "vigorous" writer might have brought to it. Brooks Atkinson in the *New York Times* complained that the characters were nothing more than symbols and the evening was "weighted down with symbolism" he couldn't understand. The play seemed to be a "complicated way of saying something" which should be "intelligible to all of us."

Louis Kronenberger in *PM* said Barry had written a "pretty little duck pond of a drama" that was "naïve and cute" and "extremely allegorical"; he even began to wonder if Liberty's carpet was really a symbol of the corn belt and whether the pills on her night table were symbols of the Republican Party. Kronenberger was all for blasting Fascism, but it was a "frightful idea to say it in baby talk."

Like Waldorf, Dorothy Kilgallen in the *New York Journal-American* said the evening came across like a high school pageant, and Barry's "personified abstractions" were either "so blatant" he seemed to be hitting the audience members on their heads or the abstractions were "so obscure" the audience needed a special libretto or appendix to explain them. George Ross in the *New York World-Telegram* also referred to the evening as an "earnest" high school pageant; Richard Lockridge in the *New York Sun* said the allegory came "perilously close to the ridiculous," sometimes the dialogue was "doggerel," and a sequence involving a literal and symbolic tin bridge confused him; and Richard Watts in the *New York Herald Tribune* was also perplexed by the tin bridge and confessed his bewilderment over its significance. He decided the play was "more lofty in purpose than triumphant in achievement."

Burns Mantle in the *New York Daily News* was kinder than most of the critics and gave it three stars. But he admitted the play would have to "struggle" to reach a wide audience and said its allegorical aspects weren't clear and direct.

Mantle noted that Paul Bowles's music was "original and fitting," and Ross said that while not "memorable" the score was nonetheless "fetching," and the dancing and pantomime sequences segued well into the fantasy. Waldorf complained that the "sing-song" aspects of the evening were "uninspiring," and noted there was much in the way of "dribbles" of older songs, nursery rhymes, childhood prayers, "and other scraps of Americana." But she was amused when the doctors of medicine, letters, divinity, and law went into a Gilbert and Sullivan-like quartet to the music of "Comin' Through the Rye."

Atkinson liked Bowles's "decorous" score, and noted Ivy Scott sang one number ("Close Your Two Eyes") with "considerable beauty"; Kronenberger found the music "pleasant and lively" with "sprightly" interludes in the manner of musical comedy; Kilgallen noted the second act offered a patriotic cake-walk; and Watts praised the "pleasantly staged" dances and Bowles's "attractive" music.

Two or three critics mentioned that Orson Welles was in the opening-night audience. Waldorf reported that he wore white tie and tails, and suggested he could have joined the cast as an allegorical symbol of a war profiteer.

The script was published in hardback by Coward-McCann in 1941.

LA BELLE HELENE

Theatres and *Performance Dates*: The musical opened on July 7, 1941, at the Westport Country Playhouse in Westport, Connecticut, and may have played at other summer-stock venues.
Book and *Lyrics*: A. P. Herbert
Music: Jacques Offenbach (music adapted by Herbert Kingsley)
Direction: Stewart Chaney; *Producers*: Demetrios Vilan and Stewart Chaney and "presented by" Lawrence Langner and Armina Marshall; *Choreography*: Felicia Sorel and Demetrios Vilan; *Scenery*: Stewart Chaney; *Costumes*: Karinska; *Lighting*: Uncredited; *Musical Direction*: Uncredited
Cast: Anne Brown (Helen of Troy), Hamtree Harrington (Menelaus), Kelsey Pharr (Paris), Avon Long (Orestes), Joe (Joseph) Attles (Calchas), Rosetta Le Noire (Bacchis), Bobbie Johnson (Mercury), Bruce Howard (Juno), Waldine Williams (Minerva), Idelle Pemberton (Venus), John Garth (Achilles), Lawrence Whisonant (Agamemnon), Randolph Sawyer (Ajax I, King of Salamis), Philander Thomas (Ajax II, King of the Locrians), P. Jay Sidney (Hector), Edith Ross (Alexandria Slave), Mable Hart and Al Bledger (Specialty Dancers), Ray Snead Jr. (Philocomus), Lynne King (Leanina), Winnie Johnson (Parthenes); Court Maidens: Muriel Gaines, Audrey White, Winnie Johnson, Amble Hart, Edith Ross, Tommy Lynn King, Pauline Meyers; Warriors: Amos Long, Al Bledger, Robert Dorsey, Bill O'Neill, Randolph Sawyer, Ray Snead Jr., Philander Thomas, Charles Weaver, Jimmy Wright, William Smith, John Edwards

Musical Numbers

Note: Division of acts and song assignments is unknown.
"To Thy Great Altars, Jove"; "O, God of Love"; "Saturday Night"; "I Carry the Mail"; "Pastorale"; "The Judgement of Paris"; "Such Exciting Rumors"; "Lovely One"; "Hail, Kings of Greece"; "Conference of the Kings"; "Off to Cnossus"; "Leda's Daughter"; "Alexandrian Dance"; "A Virtuous Wife"; "Bacchanale"; "Is It a Dream?"; "Love Fantasy"; "Great Kings, What Have You Done?"; "Lullaby"; "Darling, It's Too Early"; "Ten Long Years"; "Trojan Battle"; "Is This the Face That Launched a Thousand Ships?"

With Broadway's recent excursions into black swing adaptations of *The Mikado* (1939 saw dueling versions of *The Swing Mikado* and *The Hot Mikado*) and 1939's *Swingin' the Dream* (based on *A Midsummer Night's Dream*), it was probably a given that a black swing version of Jacques Offenbach's 1864 operetta *La Belle Helene* would come along because popular updated versions of the operetta had been seen in London in the early 1930s.

The new adaptation was clearly aimed at Broadway, and *Variety* noted that with its large production the evening was "definitely" looking toward a New York run but a "lot of effort" would be required before the musical could risk Broadway. As it turned out, the show never got closer to New York than Connecticut. Anne Brown, Broadway's original Bess, was Helen, and Avon Long and Joe (Joseph) Attles were also in the cast (some thirty-five years later Long and Attles were still cavorting around when they shared the stage in the long-running 1976 revue *Bubbling Brown Sugar*).

But the failure of *Helene* to reach New York didn't deter future producers. In 1944, **Helen Goes to Troy** (in a new musical adaptation by no less than Erich Wolfgang Korngold, who had been associated with the earlier London production of *Helen!* in 1932) went to Broadway for ninety-seven performances, and a 1962 version (with an adaptation by William Roy) titled *La Belle* closed during its pre-Broadway tryout.

Further, Rosetta Le Noire, who played Bacchis in the current Westport production, presented *La Belle Helene* at her AMAS Repertory Theatre on February 13, 1986, for sixteen performances; using Offenbach's music, the new book was by John Fearnley and the lyrics by David Baker.

Other musicals which sang the tale of Helen of Troy include the 1954 Off-Broadway (and later) Broadway *The Golden Apple* (with glorious music by Jerome Moross and witty lyrics by John La Touche); the merry 1961 Off-Broadway *Sing Muse!*; and *Helen*, a version of the story presented by the AMAS Repertory Theatre in 1978 (book by Lucia Victor and lyrics and music by Johnny Brandon).

There are various recordings of Offenbach's original *La Belle Helene* (but none of the current adaptation), including a 2-CD set on Erato/EMI Classics, and Kultur Video released a DVD of a contemporary adaptation of the operetta.

HI YA, GENTLEMEN
"A New Musical Comedy"

Theatres and *Performance Dates*: The musical opened at the Horace Bushnell Memorial Hall, Hartford, Connecticut, on November 29, 1940, and closed there on November 30; it then played the Colonial Theatre, Boston, Massachusetts, opening there on either December 2 (per the flyer) or December 3 (per the program) and seems to have permanently closed there on December 14.

Book: John Monks Jr., Fred F. Finklehoffe, and Sid Silvers
Lyrics: Harold Adamson
Music: Johnny Green
Direction: Edward Clarke Lilley; *Producers*: Alex A. Aarons and Robert G. Ritchie; *Choreography*: Bobby Connolly; *Scenery* and *Costumes*: Tom Lee; *Lighting*: Uncredited; *Musical Direction*: Johnny Green
Cast: Alfred Kappeler (Dean Parker), Erik Rhodes (Professor Cornwall, Referee), Jane Kean (Joan), Betty Jane Smith (Saundra), Ted Adair (Hunk), Renee Terry (Patsy), Ray McDonald (Christopher), Ella Logan (Binnie McDonald), Christina Lind (Martha Gilbert), Harry Stafford (Tony Murdock), Audrey Christie (Jessica Van Nye), Joe Kirk (Achilles Napolitano), Max Baer (Spinner Skinner), Sid Silvers (Googie), Owen Martin (Waldo), George M. Smith (The Colonel), Mary Roche (Secretary), Frank Gagan (Capra), Leon Alton (Riskin), Sid Salzer (G-Man), James Cushman (G-Man); The Quintones: June Hutton, Gene de Paul, Lloyd Hundling, Irving Deutch, Murray Deutch; The Sparks: Roy Melback, Eddie Mayo, Bob Coleman; The Townsmen: Ed Constantine, George Griffin, Harvey Harding, Arthur de Voss; Valerie: Valerie Thon; Bailey Basketball Team: Leon Alton, Ed Constantine, Art de Voss, Irving Deutch; Southeastern Basketball Team: Bob Beh, Lloyd Hundling, George Griffin, Harvey Harding, Sonny Qunn; Boy Students: Leon Alton, Larry Baker, Tony Barrett, Bob Beh, Jimmy Cushman, Frank Gagan, Bob Norris, Henry Quinn, Sid Salzer; Girl Students: Ruth Brady, Doris Donaldson, Marion Edell, Nona Feid, Kate Friedlich, Jessie Fullum, Amelia Gentry, Pearl Hales, Adele Hall, Marilyn Hall, Frances Hammond, Virginia Kepler, Georgette Lampsl, Jeanette Lea, June LeRoy, Charlotte Lorraine, Dona Massin, Eleanor Parr, Dorothy Reed, Tina Rigat, Paula Rudolph, Eileen Shirley, Sally Stiles, Rose Tyrrell, Sonny Wright
The musical was presented in two acts.
The action takes place on the campus of Bailey University.

Musical Numbers

Act One: "Ad Astra" (Alfred Kappeler, Erik Rhodes, The Quintones); "Hi Ya, Gentlemen" (Audrey Christie, Ella Logan, Christina Lind, Harry Stafford, Ray McDonald, Renee Terry, Alfred Kappeler, Jane Kean, The Townsmen, The Quintones, Students of Bailey University); "Down in Fraternity Row" (Audrey Christie, Ella Logan, Jane Kean, Students); "Never a Dull Moment" (Christina Lind, Harry Stafford, Ray McDonald, Renee Terry, The Quintones); "You're a Character" (Max Baer, Audrey Christie, Students); "Some Things You Can't Learn in College" (Audrey Christie, Girl Students; Dance Specialty by Ted Adair); "Up in Jessica's Room" (Sid Silvers, Max Baer, Audrey Christie); "Hi Ya, Gentlemen" (reprise) (Students at Bailey University); "Go 'Way Blues, Ya Bother Me" (Ella Logan, The Townsmen, The Quintones, Students; Dance Specialties by Ray McDonald, Ted Adair, and The Sparks); "Never a Dull Moment" (reprise) (Sid Silvers)
Act Two: "Whereas" (The Townsmen); "America Marches On" (Ella Logan, Harry Stafford, Christina Lind, The Townsmen, The Quintones, Students); "Some Things You Can't Learn in College" (reprise) (Audrey Christie, Harry Stafford); "I'll Take the High Note" (Sid Silvers, Ella Logan, Jane Kean, Erik Rhodes, Ray McDonald, Renee Terry, Max Baer, Audrey Christie); "I Heard You Were Lovely" (Christina Lind, Harry Stafford, Ray McDonald, Renee Terry, The Townsmen, Students; Specialty Dance by Valerie Thon); "Spinner Learned the Conga" (Audrey Christie, Max Baer, Girl Students); "Go 'Way Blues, Ya Bother Me" (reprise) (Betty Jane Smith, The Quintones); "See How They Run" (Christina Lind, Harry Stafford, Jane Kean, Renee Terry, Ray McDonald, The Townsmen, The Quintones); Finale (Entire Company)

Hi Ya, Gentlemen played tryout engagements in Hartford, Connecticut, and Boston, but after a total of two weeks on the road it collapsed. During the two or three days between its engagements in the two cities, the show added one song ("I Love Y-o-u") and dropped three ("Some Things You Can't Learn in College," "Up in Jessica's Room," and "Spinner Learned the Conga"). With the omission of the latter, the musical was without a South American number, certainly a daring move considering that during the era almost every revue and musical offered at least one such musical tribute.

The college musical included the requisite co-eds, college boys, and faculty members as well as some G-men and an Army man or two; and with popular 1934 Heavyweight Champion of the World Max Baer in the cast (the flyer noted that "Yes, Sir—himself IN PERSON—direct from the squared circle on to the stage"), there were a couple characters from the boxing world. The cast also included Ella Logan, Audrey Christie, Jane Kean, Erik Rhodes, Ray McDonald, Ted Adair, and Sid Silvers. Buried deep in the cast was Gene de Paul, who later composed the score for the classic 1954 MGM film musical *Seven Brides for Seven Brothers* and the hit 1956 Broadway musical *Li'l Abner*.

The musical was rich in music men: composer Johnny Green conducted the orchestra; vocal direction was by Hugh Martin, who with de Paul and Pete King also provided the vocal arrangements; and the orchestrations were by (Robert) Russell Bennett, Hans Spialek, and Don Walker.

One song in the musical's score enjoyed an afterlife. "I'll Take the High Note" (which was sung by Ella Logan, Jane Kean, Erik Rhodes, and others) was later included in the 1942 revue **Show Time**, where it was again performed by Ella Logan. The song had yet another moment, this time in the movies when it turned up as a major production number in the 1944 MGM film *Bathing Beauty*, where it was performed by Harry James and His Orchestra along with Helen Forrest, Red Skelton, Jean Porter, Janis Paige, organist Ethel Smith, and others.

HOT FROM HARLEM

Theatres and *Performance Dates*: The revue opened on May 13, 1941, in Bridgeport, Connecticut, and closed on August 30, 1941, in Atlantic City, New Jersey.
Lyrics and *Music*: Porter Grainger
Direction: Addison Kerry; *Producer*: Marty Forkins; *Choreography*: Unknown; *Scenery*: Kaj Velden and Seven Studio; *Costumes*: Mahlieu and Mme. Morgan; *Lighting*: Unknown; *Musical Direction*: Billy Butler
Cast: Bill "Bojangles" Robinson, Claudia McNeil, Edith Wilson, Apus and Estrellita, Freddie Robinson, Ada Ward, Naomi Price, Eubie Blake, George Wiltshire, Jeli Smith, Jimmie Baskett, Emory Evans, Alvin Cowens, Leon Warwick, Putney Dandridge, John Mason, Ferdi Lewis, Jackie Young, Juanita Williams, Ethel Fiddler, Ada Brown, The Musical Madcaps, The Sepia Brigade, Billy Butler's Swingphonic Orchestra

The black revue toured for over three-and-a-half months, but never tested the Broadway waters. And no doubt Bill "Bojangles" Robinson's name helped keep the show on the boards for so long (he bounced into *Hot from Harlem* just a few months after the debacle of **All in Fun**). Others in the cast were Claudia McNeil, Edith Wilson, Ada Ward, and composer Eubie Blake.

Variety noted the revue was "orthodox" in nature, but felt a shortened version might do well in "tab" bookings.

The musical sequences included "Ol' Man River" (from *Show Boat*, 1927; lyric by Oscar Hammerstein II, music by Jerome Kern); "Down by the Old Southern River"; and "Look What Love Done Done."

THE LITTLE DOG LAUGHED
"A MODERN MUSICAL COMEDY"

Theatres and *Performance Dates*: The musical opened on August 15, 1940, at the Garden Pier, Atlantic City, New Jersey, and closed on August 24, 1940, at the Shubert Theatre in Boston, Massachusetts.
Book: Joseph Schrank
Lyrics and *Music*: Harold Rome
Direction: Eddie Dowling; *Producer*: Eddie Dowling; *Choreography*: Chester Hale; *Scenery*: Jo Mielziner; *Costumes*: Nicholas De Molas; *Lighting*: Uncredited; *Musical Direction*: Lehman Engel

Cast: Paul Draper (Kip), Mili Monti (Hilda Pennypacker), Philip Loeb (Max Milch), Arthur Hunnicut (The Sad Man), Tess Gardella (Lucy Pennypacker), Ralph Bunker (Emile Pennypacker), Dennie Moore (Grace Pennypacker), Joseph Vitale (Lombardi), Loretta Sayers (The Witch), Augustin Duncan (Professor X), Gordon Gifford (Mr. Z), Fairfax (The Magician), Eric Roberts (Georgie Pennypacker), Louis Hightower (Herald, Prince Charming), Bunny Hightower (Herald), William Mende (Watchman), Albert Gifford (The Butcher), Joseph Scander (The Baker), Donald Bain (The Cabinet Maker), Roger Gerry (The Tailor), Dorothy Johnson (The Milkmaid), Jack Abbott (The Miller), Janice Chambers (The Seamstress), Michael Mann (The Sweeper), Edward Hedges (The Tavern Keeper), Al Sezton (Newsboy), Marjorie Bell (later known as Marge Champion) (Milkmaid, Snow White); Citizens: Wallace Seibert, Ted Lund; Girls: Jane Starner, Marion MacPherson; Maids: Gertrude Westmoreland, Christopher Curtis, Angele Morgensen, Dorothy Johnson, Roberta Welch, Zonia Porter, Janice Chambers; L. Arnold Grayson Jr. (The Giant); Dancers: Marjorie Bell, Tania Clell, Audrey Costello, Joan Engel, Alice Langford, Helene Marine, Marian MacPherson, Zonia Porter, Betty Schuller, Jack Abbott, Leon Barte, Edward Hedges, Bunny Hightower, Louis Hightower, Ted Lund, Michael Mann, Wallace Seibert; Singers: Joyce Allmand, Janice Chambers, Christopher Curtis, Dorothy Johnson, Angela Morgansen, Jane Starner, Robert Welsh, Gertrude Westmoreland, J. Raymond Baine, Jack Collins, Rodger Gerry, Albert Gifford, William Mende, Joseph Scander
The musical was presented in two acts.
The action takes place during the present time in Brooklyn and in a mythical kingdom.

Musical Numbers

Note: Division of acts and song assignments unknown.
"I Want Romance"; "You're Your Highness to Me"; "A Bunch of Cows"; "I'm a King"; "Court Dance"; "Beware the Dragon"; "Hail Number One"; "I'll Be a Hero, Too!"; "Happily Ever After"; "I'm Cynical"; "Some Things a Man Must Have"; "I Have a Song"' "Easy Does It"; "The Fairy Tales Are All Untrue"; "A Friend of Mine, a Hero"; "Of the People Stomp"; "Redheads"

After brief tryout engagements in Atlantic City and Boston, Harold Rome's satiric musical *The Little Dog Laughed* disappeared after two weeks. The story focused on Hilda Pennypacker (Mili Monti), a young woman from Brooklyn who dreams of romance. She and everyone she knows are soon transported to a mythical kingdom where love is outlawed and totalitarianism rules. But ultimately true love wins the day and Hilda finds the romance she's been seeking.

M. H. Orodenker in *Billboard* said the musical depicted "as fabulous a Hitlerland as Lewis Carroll or Walt Disney might have imagined," but noted the show clocked in at over three-and-a-half-hours and thus required judicious trimming. *Variety* praised the "good tunes," "superlative" dances, and "colorful" décor, but noted there was an "aimlessness" in the show's uneasy mixture of lighthearted satire and "serious propaganda."

The musical was bankrolled by a wealthy heiress as a showcase for her "discovery," a nightclub singer named Mili Monti, who seems to have disappeared once *The Little Dog Laughed* closed. The musical also featured dancers Paul Draper and Marjorie Bell. The latter eventually made a name for herself in the movies as Marge Champion (with her dancing partner and then husband Gower Champion, they appeared in six film musicals between 1951 and 1955). After *The Little Dog Laughed*, she appeared in **What's Up**, where she was known as Marjorie Beecher (her maiden name was Belcher), and for **Beggar's Holiday** she changed her name again, this time to Marjorie Belle.

The musical's song "Of the People Stomp" later surfaced in the 1942 revue **Let Freedom Sing**, where it was performed by Betty Garrett and the company for the show's finale. The number is included in the collection *You Can't Put Ketchup on the Moon* (Rialto CD # SLRR-9201).

The musical's title was probably inspired by the British revue *The Little Dog Laughed*, which opened at the London Palladium in 1939 and included Harold Rome's song "F.D.R. Jones" (which had originally been heard in the 1938 Broadway revue *Sing Out the News*).

Eight years later, Rome yet again met failure with another political satire, **That's the Ticket!**, which closed in Philadelphia after a handful of tryout performances.

RHAPSODY IN BLACK
"A SYMPHONY OF BLACK NOTES AND BLUE RHYTHM"

Theatres and *Performance Dates*: The revue was produced in Harlem's Apollo Theatre on August 30, 1940, and closed soon thereafter; it reopened on January 20, 1941, at the Erlanger Theatre in Philadelphia, Pennsylvania, where it closed permanently on January 25.
Sketches and *Dialogue*: Lew Leslie, Nat Dorfman, and Cecil Mack
Lyrics and *Music*: Johnny Mercer, Ruby Bloom, Dorothy Sacks, Louis Haber, Archie Guttler, Edgar Leslie, and George Gershwin
Direction: Lew Leslie; *Producer*: Rhapsody in Black, Inc.
Cast: Edith Wilson, Tim Moore, Hilda Rogers, Bland "Crack Shot" Hackley, Honi Coles, Joe Byrd, Sid Easton, Conway and Parks, Winfield and Ford, Cecil Mack's Famous International Choir, The Chocolateers, Billy Butler's Symphonic Swing Orchestra, Kate Hall, Jelli Smith, Musa Williams, Vivian Phillips, Gustave Burley, Clyde Parks; *Pianists*: Joseph A. Steel and Edward Rodgers

Musical Numbers

Note: Division of acts and song assignments unknown.
"Rhapsody in Black" (music by Ken Macomber and Pat Carroll); "Babylon Is Falling"; "Jericho"; "Just Walking through Mocking Bird Lane"; "Barber Shop Opera"; "Don't Advertise Your Man"; "Rhapsody in Blue" (music by George Gershwin); "St. James Infirmary" (lyric and music by Joe Primrose); "Dixie Isn't Dixie Anymore" (lyric by Johnny Mercer, music by Rube Bloom); "Refugees on Parade"; "Eli-Eli" (aka "Eili, Eili"); "America, I Love You" (lyric by Edgar Leslie, music by Archie Gottler); "Thursday" (lyric by Dorothy Sachs, music by Louis Haber); "Swing Struck" (lyric by Irving Taylor, music by Vic Mizzy)

Rhapsody in Black was a failed attempt by producer Lew Leslie to bring back his string of black revues to Broadway. He had produced the wildly successful *Blackbirds of 1928*, which played for 518 performances; and later produced a 1931 edition of *Rhapsody in Black*, which ran for eighty performances; his most recent Broadway effort had been a 1939 edition of *Blackbirds*, which closed after nine performances.

The new *Rhapsody in Black* opened at Harlem's Apollo Theatre on August 30, 1940; the flyer advised audiences to "see this show before it reaches Broadway." The seventy-five member cast included Billy Butler's Swing Symphonic Band, Cecil Mack's Choir, Ada Brown, Mae Diggs, Winfield and Ford, Estela and Pope, and Moore and Byrd. There were continuous performances given at the Apollo with admissions ranging from a quarter to fifty-five cents. After its run there, the revue seems to have closed for a few months while it underwent rewriting and recasting for a Philadelphia opening in January 1941 at the Erlanger Theatre. But after one week of performances, the revue permanently closed there. Linton Martin in the *Philadelphia Inquirer* said the singers, dancers, and musicians were the "mainstay" of the production; otherwise, the evening was "weak and negative" in its songs and sketches and the show lacked "zest and spontaneity."

The above credits and song list are from the Philadelphia production. Cast members who were in both the 1940 and 1941 versions included Cecil Mack's Choir, Billy Butler's Swing Symphonic Band, and the team of Winfield and Ford. Some cast members from both productions (including Ada May, Jelli Smith, and Billy Butler's Swingphonic/Symphony Swing Orchestra) had earlier appeared in **Hot from Harlem**.

The current *Rhapsody in Black* carried over three numbers from the 1931 production ("St. James Infirmary," "Eli-Eli," and the title song). From the 1939 *Blackbirds* were "Thursday" and "Swing Struck"; and "Dixie Isn't Dixie Anymore" had first been heard in the 1936 London edition of *Blackbirds*.

SHE HAD TO SAY YES
"A NEW MUSICAL COMEDY"

Theatres and *Performance Dates*: The musical opened on December 30, 1940, at the Forrest Theatre, Philadelphia, Pennsylvania, and permanently closed there on January 11, 1941.
Book: Bob Henley and Richard Pinkham

Lyrics: Al Dubin; additional lyrics by Irving Kahal
Music: Samuel (Sammy) Fain
Direction: Book staged by William Miles and production supervised by Dennis King; *Producer*: Dennis King; *Choreography*: Dances and ensembles by Charles Walters and ballets staged by Raoul Alba; *Scenery* and *Costumes*: Stewart Chaney; *Lighting*: Uncredited; *Musical Direction*: Jacques Rabiroff
Cast: John Wray Jr. (Private Homer Holliday), Warda Howard (His Mother), Robert Williamson (Station Master), Edwina Coolidge (Train Hostess), Paula Stone (Babs Anderson), Charles Walters (Tony MacFarland), Jimmy Banner (First Red Cap), Bobby Johnson (Second Red Cap), Wally Vernon (J. Spencer "Candy" Barr), Helen Raymond (Mrs. Matilda Townsend), Viola Essenova (Irina), Marcy Westcott (Joyce Townsend), Robert Sidney (First Reporter), Fred Newcomb (Second Reporter), Eldon Jones (Photographer), Richard Irving (Passerby), Al Renard (Passenger), Ralph Magelssen (Announcer), Joe Oakie (Irving Nussbaum), Leslie Austen (Chief Joe Broodhen Thompson), Richard Rober (Hymie McGinnis), *Dennis King* (Duke), Harry Bellaver (Taxi Driver), Olive Reeves-Smith (Madame O'Brien), Wyman Kane (Tailor); Mrs. Townsend's Guests: Joan Flagg, Ruth Gilman, Blanche Grady, Peggy Healey, Andrea Mann, Joan Mitchell, Adrienne Moore, Susan Paley; Mrs. Townsend's Dancers: Charlotte Alquist, Denise Brent, Tania Clell, Muriel Cole, Joy Coleman, Genevieve Cooke, Linda Grant, Rhoda Henderer, Peggy Holmes, Hortense Kahrlin, Evelyn Lafferty, Marion MacPherson, Doris Markell, Sonya Sorel, Edith Turgell, Virginia Wyckoff, Jack Abbott, Leif Argo, Richard Irving, Wyman Kane, Jerry Keith, Sam Martin, Peter Kite Smith, Frank Speers, Frank Worden, Gene Wright
The musical was presented in two acts.
The action takes place during the present time in New York City and environs.

Musical Numbers

Act One: Opening (Doris Markell, Ralph Magelssen, Edwina Coolidge, Ensemble); "Never Take No for an Answer" (Paula Stone, Charles Walters); "The Girl Who Works in a Laundry" (Marcy Westcott), "Spend Your Vacation on Broadway" (Paula Stone, Charles Walters, Wally Vernon; dance specialty by Jimmy Banner and Bobby Johnson); "Merrily on My Way" (lyric by Irving Kahal) (Dennis King); "Meet the Elite" (Paula Stone, Charles Walters, Ensemble); "The Men Who Came to Win 'Er" (Joe Oakie, Leslie Austen, John Wray Jr., Richard Rober); 'Between Romances" (Dennis King, Marcy Westcott); "Our Memoirs" (Wally Vernon, Dennis King); "Coney Island Ballet" (Viola Essenova, Robert Sidney, Corps de Ballet); "You for Me" (Marcy Westcott, Dennis King, Ensemble)

Act Two: Opening (The Junior Models); "The Customer's Always Right" (Olive Reeves-Smith, Models); "How Is Your Technique?" (Paula Stone, Applicants); "Stranger in the Mirror" (lyric by Irving Kahal) (Dennis King); "Stranger in the Mirror" (reprise) (Dennis King, Marcy Westcott); Specialty Dance Routine (Evelyn Lafferty, Edith Turgell, Tania Clell, Rhoda Henderer, Joy Coleman, Peggy Holmes, Doris Markell, Sonya Sorel, Frank Worder, Peter Kite Smith, Richard Irving, Leif Argo, Gene Wright, Jack Abbott, Sam Martin); "My DeeTees" (specialty dance) (Jimmy Banner, "assisted by Hives and Jives"); "Serenade to a Chambermaid" (Viola Essenova, John Wray Jr.); Specialty Dance (Wally Vernon, The Three Trojans); "Concerto in E-Flat Major" (Viola Essenova, Evelyn Lafferty, Robert Sidney, Corps de Ballet); "My Most Embarrassing Moment" (Paula Stone, Charles Walters, Helen Raymond, Wally Vernon, Dennis King, Marcy Westcott); Finale (Entire Company)

The light-as-air plot of *She Had to Say Yes* revolved around the plan of press agent J. Spencer "Candy" Barr (Wally Vernon) and Manhattan socialite Matilda Townsend (Helen Raymond) to promote Matilda's daughter Joyce (Marcy Wescott) as a debutante-like glamour girl who will endorse products on the radio. Complications ensue, as they say. In this case, due to a misunderstanding it is assumed Joyce is looking for a husband, and so various radio listeners "win" the chance to become her spouse, including on-his-uppers Duke (Dennis King). In one way or another, Joyce and Duke eventually find their way to the altar.

Variety felt the musical held promise but needed drastic revision, particularly in the book and choreography; there were two "spectacular" ballets, but because the ballets, dances, and choral numbers were staged by various creators they failed to "jell." After two weeks of performances in Philadelphia, the show shuttered for good.

Well, perhaps not "for good." One year later the musical's scenery was recycled for **The Lady Comes Across**, one of the biggest Broadway debacles of the era. The sets for *She Had to Say Yes* included a chic women's salon, a railroad station, a park, an estate, and a bedroom on the estate, and so the libretto of **The Lady Comes Across** worked in scenes that could utilize the existing sets of the earlier production.

Buried in the program notes for *She Had to Say Yes* was a reference to a first-act number titled "Border to Border"; but the song list itself wasn't listed in the program.

TWO WEEKS WITH PAY

Theatre and *Performance Dates*: The revue opened on June 24, 1940, at the Ridgeway Theatre in White Plains, New York, and permanently closed there on July 6.
Sketches, *Lyrics*, and *Music*: See list below for credits.
Direction: Production supervised by Felix Jacoves; *Producers*: Ted Fetter and Richard Lewine; *Choreography*: Gene Kelly; *Scenery*: Lawrence L. Goldwasser; *Costumes*: Marion Herwood; *Lighting*: Uncredited; *Musical Direction*: Alan Moran and Irving Brodsky at the pianos
Cast: Hiram Sherman, Marie Nash, Earl Oxford, Florence Lake, Pat Harrington, Maurice Kelly, Virginia Bolen, Dawn Roland, Melissa Mason, Bill Johnson, Ruth Mata, Eugene Hari, Lawrence Weber, Peter Barry, Marilyn Hale, Eileen Morrow, Lucille Rich, Doris Stuart, Key Taylor, Natalie Wynn, Charles Kraft, Frederic Nay, Sid Salzer, Julian Olney Jr., Robert McKelvey, Remo Bufano's Puppets
The revue was presented in two acts.

Sketches and Musical Numbers

Act One: "I Would Rather Be" (lyric by Peter Barry and David Greggory [sometimes cited as David Gregory], music by Baldwin Bergersen) (Broker: Earl Oxford; Teacher: Marie Nash; Ditch Digger: Pat Harrington; Glamour Girls: Eileen Morrow, Key Taylor, Virginia Bolen; Working Girls: Natalie Wynn, Marilyn Hale, Doris Stuart); "Come to Fuji Fuji" (sketch by Peter Barry and David Greggory [Gregory]) (Randolph: Pat Harrington; McPherson: Hiram Sherman; Kalano: Frederic Nay; A Native: Peter Barry; Jerrold: Eileen Morrow; Another Native: Julian Olney Jr.; Another Native: Robert McKelvey; Native Chief: Sid Salzer; Tourist: Eugene Hart; Another Native: Charles Kraft); "As Long as You're Along" (lyric by David Greggory [Gregory], music by Baldwin Bergersen) (Virginia Bolen, Bill Johnson; danced by Marilyn Hale, Eileen Morrow, Lucille Rich, Doris Stuart, Key Taylor, Natalie Wynn, Charles Kraft, Frederic Nay, Sid Salzer); "The Excursion" (sketch by Charles Sherman) (Station Announcer: Earl Oxford; Aunt Josie: Natalie Wynn; Uncle Phil: Peter Barry; Uncle Ben: Lawrence Weber; Aunt Sophie: Melissa Mason; Guard: Hiram Sherman; Alice: Florence Lake; Cousin Celia: Key Taylor; Cousin Maude: Eileen Morrow; Cousin Dick: Julian Olney Jr.; Tourists: Sid Salzer, Ruth Mata, Eugene Hari, Charles Kraft, Frederic Nay, Marilyn Hale, Doris Stuart, Lucille Rich); "Hey, Gal" (lyric by Peter Barry, music by Will C. K. Irwin) (Porto [Puerto] Rican Man: Earl Oxford; Porto Rican Girl: Ruth Mata; Broadway Man: Maurice Kelly; Frenchman: Eugene Hari; Englishman: Bill Johnson); "Dear Horse" (lyric by Ted Fetter, lyric by Richard Lewine) (Cowboy: Pat Harrington; Horse: Bill Johnson); "Just Another Page in Your Diary" (lyric and music by Cole Porter) (Virginia Bolen, Bill Johnson; Judge: Sid Salzer; danced by Marilyn Hale, Eileen Morrow, Lucille Rich, Doris Stuart, Key Taylor); "Ye Gypsy Crumpet Shoppe" (sketch by Peter Barry) (Girl: Ruth Mata; Lady: Florence Lake; Man: Hiram Sherman; First Gypsy: Peter Barry; Second Gypsy: Melissa Mason; Third Gypsy: Natalie Wynn; Fourth Gypsy: Marilyn Hale); "June, Moon, Spoon" (lyric and music by Herman Hupfield) (Pat Harrington, Bill Johnson, Earl Oxford, Sid Salzer, Dawn Roland, Frederic Nay, Maurice Kelly, Lawrence Weber, Natalie Wynn, Virginia Bolen, Hiram Sherman; Trio: Virginia Bolen, Marilyn Hale, Natalie Wynn); "Now That I Know You" (lyric by Lorenz Hart, music by Richard Rodgers) (Marie Nash, Earl Oxford); "The Jig Is Up" (lyric by Ted Fetter, music by Richard Lewine) (Melissa Mason, Hiram Sherman); "Imagination" (sketch by Peter Barry and David Greggory [Gregory]) (Peabody: Hiram Sherman; Doctor: Pat Harrington); "Praised Be Moses" (lyric by Charles Marvin, music by William Borden) (Marie Nash, Entire Company)

Act Two: "All That and Heaven Too" (lyric by Peter Barry and David Greggory [Gregory], music by Richard Lewine) (First Hostess: Virginia Bolen; Second Hostess: Dawn Roland; Third Hostess: Doris Stuart; Fourth Hostess: Marilyn Hale; Fifth Hostess: Lucille Rich; Sixth Hostess: Natalie Wynn; Seventh Hostess: Eileen Morrow; Eighth Hostess: Key Taylor; Passenger: Hiram Sherman); "Vacation" (sketch by Charles Sherman) (Manager: Hiram Sherman; Secretary: Florence Lake; Customer: Pat Harrington); "With You with Me" (lyric by Johnny Mercer, music by Johnny Green) (Marie Nash, Bill Johnson; danced by Dawn Roland and Maurice Kelly); "To the Futurama" (sketch by Peter Barry and David Greggory [Gregory]) (Woman: Melissa Mason; Girl: Florence Lake; Guard: Earl Oxford; Young Man: Hiram Sherman; Hot Dog Vendor: Charles Kraft; Man in a Bowler Hat: Pat Harrington; Colored Man: Peter Barry; Others: Frederic Nay, Lawrence Weber, Natalie Wynn); "Secret Sorrow" (lyric by Peter Barry and David Greggory [Gregory], music by Baldwin Bergersen) (Virginia Bolen; Second Little Girl: Key Taylor; Third Little Girl: Eileen Morrow; Camp Director: Natalie Wynn); "Once Upon a Morning" (by Peter Barry; music by Goetz Van Eyck) (Milk Maid: Ruth Mata; Shepherd: Eugene Hari; Man in a High Hat: Julian Olney Jr.; Tumbler: Lucille Rich; Drummer: Sid Salzer; Equestrian: Doris Stuart; Clown: Charles Kraft; Lion: Eileen Morrow; Rich Man: Frederic Nay; Rich Woman: Marilyn Hale; First Vendor: Key Taylor; Second Vendor: Natalie Wynn; Puppets by Remo Bufano); "The Gentleman in Tails" (sketch by Peter Barry and David Greggory [Gregory]) (Hiram Sherman); "Will You Love Me Monday Morning" (lyric by Ira Gershwin and E. Y. Harburg, music by Harold Arlen) (Marie Nash, Earl Oxford; danced by Dawn Roland and Maurice Kelly; Native Girls: Marilyn Hale, Eileen Morrow, Lucille Rich, Doris Stuart, Key Taylor, Natalie Wynn; Sailors: Charles Kraft, Frederic Nay, Sid Salzer; Vendors: Julian Olney Jr., Robert McKelvey); "Noises in the Street" (lyric by Peter Barry and David Greggory [Gregory], music by Richard Lewine) (Doorman: Earl Oxford; Street Musician: Hiram Sherman; Garbage Man: Pat Harrington; Boy: Julian Olney Jr.; Cop: Lawrence Weber); "Five-Cent Piece" (lyric by Ted Fetter, music by Richard Lewine) (Natalie Wynn, Bill Johnson; danced by Eileen Morrow and Doris Stuart; Lucille Rich and Sid Salzer; Marilyn Hale and Frederic Nay; Key Taylor and Charles Kraft; Quartet: Marilyn Hale, Natalie Wynn, Bill Johnson, Frederic Nay); Finale (Entire Company)

This summer stock revue took its title literally: *Two Weeks with Pay* played just two weeks at the Ridgeway Theatre in White Plains, New York, before calling it quits. It boasted a number of the era's up-and-coming performers, such as Bill Johnson and Hiram Sherman, and its choreography was created by Gene Kelly, who was six months away from his breakthrough title role of **Pal Joey**.

Two numbers briefly surfaced later in the season in the one-performance flop revue *'Tis of Thee*: the sketch "Imagination" (by Peter Barry and David Greggory [Gregory]) and the song "Noises in the Street" (lyric by Peter Barry and David Greggory, [Gregory] music by Richard Lewine). The latter was also performed in a number of other revues; for more information, see **The Shape of Things!**

Richard Rodgers and Lorenz Hart's ballad "Now That I Know You" recycled the same music as their two title songs for the 1937 musical *I'd Rather Be Right*. The first version of the title song (beginning with the refrain "Don't have to know much") was briefly heard during the tryout before it was replaced with a new lyric (its refrain began with "I'd rather be right than influential"). For the song's third version, the refrain began with the song's new title, "Now That I Know You."

Cole Porter's saucy "Just Another Page in Your Diary" had been intended for William Gaxton and Mary Martin to sing in *Leave It to Me!*, but the number wasn't used. As "A Weekend Cruise," the song "Will You Love Me Monday Morning (as You Did on Friday Night)?" (lyric by Ira Gershwin and E. Y. Harburg, music by Harold Arlen) had been heard in the 1934 revue *Life Begins at 8:40* where it had been performed by Frances Williams, Earl Oxford, Bert Lahr, and the ensemble (soon after the Broadway opening, the number was dropped; and the song isn't included in the 2010 recording of the score released by PS Classics). For *Two Weeks with Pay*, Oxford (along with other cast members of the summer revue) again sang the revised version of "A Weekend Cruise."

The revue also included "With You with Me," lyric by Johnny Mercer and music by Johnny Green.

1941–1942 Season

BEST FOOT FORWARD
"A New Musical Comedy"

Theatre: Ethel Barrymore Theatre
Opening Date: October 1, 1941; *Closing Date*: July 4, 1942
Performances: 326
Book: John Cecil Holm
Lyrics and *Music*: Hugh Martin and Ralph Blane
Based on John Cecil Holm's unpublished 1939 play *And One for the Lady*.
Direction: George Abbott; *Producer*: George Abbott; *Choreography*: Gene Kelly; *Scenery* and *Lighting*: Jo
  Mielziner; *Costumes*: Miles White; *Musical Direction*: Archie Bleyer
Cast: Jack Jordan Jr. (Dutch Miller), Gil Johnson (Fred Jones), Richard Dick (Freshman), Danny Daniels (Junior), Kenneth (Kenny) Bowers (Hunk Hoyt), Bobby Harrell (Satchel Moyer), Lee Roberts (Goofy Clark),
  Tommy Dix (Chuck Green), Fleming Ward (Dr. Reeber), Stuart Langley (Old Grad), June Allyson (Minerva), Victoria Schools (Ethel), Betty Anne Nyman (Miss Ferguson), Nancy Walker (Blind Date), Gil Stratton Jr. (Bud Hooper), Roger Hewlett (Professor Lloyd), Norma Lehn (Waitress), Marty May (Jack Haggerty),
  Rosemary Lane (Gale Joy), Vincent York (Chester Billings), Maureen Cannon (Helen Schlessinger), Robert
  Griffith (Professor Williams); Dancing Girls: Frances Bryan, Marianne Cude, Dorothy Eden, Bee Farnum,
  Mary Ganly, Anne Guier, Kay Guier, Rhoda Hoffman, Terry Kelly, Kaye Popp, Rosemary Schaefer, Rose
  Marie Schiller, Lenore Thomas, Doris York; Singing Girls: Eileen Barton, Peggy Ellis, Peggy Anne Ellis, Barbara Grant, Carol Horton, Beverly Hosier, Betty McCloskey, Elaine Miller, Penny Porter, Renee
  Rochelle, Marilyn Ross, Audrey Sperling; Dancing Boys: Buddy Allen, Wilbur Baron, William Baron, Gil
  Johnson, Kenneth Buffett, Danny Daniels, Richard Dick, Stanley Donen, Perry Jubelirer, Billy Parsons,
  George Staisey, Buddy Styles, Elmer Vernon, Art Williams; Singing Boys: Van Atkins, John Balian, Harvey
  Gould, Eugene Martin
The musical was presented in two acts.
The action takes place during the present time at Winsocki Prep School in Pennsylvania.

Musical Numbers

Act One: "Don't Sell the Night Short" (June Allyson, Nancy Walker, Students, Girls); "Three Men on a Date"
  (Gil Stratton Jr., Jack Jordan, Jr., Kenneth Bowers; The Dancer: Betty Anne Nyman; The Gay Blades: Stanley Donen, Buddy Allen, Art Williams; The Tap Dancers: George Staisey, Lee Roberts, Danny Daniels;
  The Acrobats: Gil Johnson, Bobby Harrell, Billy Parsons); "That's How I Love the Blues" (Rosemary Lane,
  Marty May); "The Three B's" (Victoria Schools, June Allyson, Nancy Walker; The Jury: Carol Horton,
  Beverly Hosier, Peggy Ellis, Elaine Miller, Penny Porter, Eileen Barton); "Everytime" (aka "Ev'ry Time")

(Maureen Cannon); "The Guy Who Brought Me" (Rosemary Lane, Marty May, Gil Stratton Jr., Jack Jordan Jr., Kenneth Bowers); "I Know You By Heart" (Gil Stratton Jr.); "Shady Lady Bird" (Maureen Cannon, Students); "Shady Lady Bird" (reprise) (Maureen Cannon, Ensemble)

Act Two: "Buckle Down, Winsocki" (Tommy Dix, Stuart Langley, Chorus); "My First Promise (at My First Prom)" (Victoria Schools, Singers); "What Do You Think I Am?" (June Allyson, Kenneth Bowers, Chorus; The Acrobats: Bobby Harrell, Gil Johnson); "Just a Little Joint with a Juke Box" (Nancy Walker, Kenneth Bowers); "Where Do You Travel?" (Marty May, Maureen Cannon, Betty Anne Nyman, Singers; danced by Betty Anne Nyman and Dancers); "Everytime" (reprise) (Rosemary Lane); "I'd Gladly Trade" (Rosemary Lane, Company)

Surprisingly, *Best Foot Forward* was the first book musical to open in New York in ten months; not since **Lady in the Dark** premiered in January had there been a new one on Broadway, and the ten-month period between the two musicals was the longest dry period in the history of Broadway musical comedy.

Producer and director George Abbott had visited a military academy in the comedy *Brother Rat* (1936), high school in the comedy *What a Life* (1938), college in the musical *Too Many Girls* (1939), and was now in prep school for his latest caper. *Best Foot Forward* was a typical Abbott show, with lots of young people scampering about in lighthearted, innocent hi-jinks. The plot centered on prep school student Bud Hooper (Gil Stratton Jr.) who jokingly invites famous movie star Gale Joy (Rosemary Lane) to be his date at the prom. To his shock, Gale accepts his invitation, not from altruism but for the sake of her slightly sagging film career. She and her agent Jack Haggerty (Marty May) decide her attendance at the prom will bring her welcome publicity.

But Bud already has a date for the prom with his girlfriend Helen Schlessinger (Maureen Cannon), and so there's much ado in the way of farcical proceedings until the final curtain when the juveniles' romantic misunderstandings are settled and Gale returns to Hollywood and a hopefully rejuvenated career.

The bright young cast (which included breakthrough roles for June Allyson and Nancy Walker, and featured future film director Stanley Donen and future stage choreographer Danny Daniels in the dancing chorus), Gene Kelly's lively choreography, Abbott's swift-paced direction, Jo Mielziner and Miles White's colorful décor and costumes, and a jukebox full of catchy songs by the team of Hugh Martin and Ralph Blane (including the hit "Buckle Down, Winsocki") ensured a long run of 326 performances. Other highlights of the score were the swinging "The Three B's" (the barrelhouse, the boogie-woogie, and the blues), the equally lively "What Do You Think I Am?," and the ballad "Everytime." (Officially, Martin and Blane took co-credit for lyrics and music, but usually each of their songs was written by one or the other and not jointly.)

The critics enjoyed the musical, although a few seemed a bit grumpy about so much *youth* on the stage. Wilella Waldorf in the *New York Post* noted that Abbott's **Pal Joey** was "not for children," and this time around he had gone to the "extreme" with a show "bursting with adolescence" in a performance that was "as deliriously amateur" as what the Winsocki students themselves might have put on in their gym. About thirty minutes of this "Youth Movement" was enough for her, and the "rest was boredom." Richard Watts in the *New York Herald Tribune* said that "within limits" he respected youth, but *Best Foot Forward* had too much of it and although the audience seemed to have a "wonderful time" he was able to contain himself with "comparative calmness." John Mason Brown in the *New York World-Telegram* said the new musical amounted to a "Children's Crusade" and he wondered if most of the cast arrived at the Ethel Barrymore Theatre on scooters; although they were "wonderfully expert and contagiously high-spirited," they didn't give him "the greatest of pleasure" and they didn't make youth all that "fascinating and enviable."

But Richard Lockridge in the *New York Sun* liked the "gay and comical" youngsters, said they made *Best Foot Forward* a "fresh and smiling" musical, and that twice Nancy Walker stopped the show "cold." John Anderson in the *New York Journal-American* reported that from the perspective of the first-nighters, the youthful "bright, breezy and brash" musical was just "the right kiddie kar entertainment for elderly tots romping in Broadway's hothouse nursery." He praised Walker's "tough" comedy, and said Gene Kelly's choreography offered the "dancingest youngsters around town" with their "exuberant rhythms and gyrations." They were quite a sight with the stage "heaving in full swing" during their dance routines.

Burns Mantle in the *New York Daily News* found the music "fresh and interesting," the lyrics "smart and timely," and the choreography full of "zip"; Louis Kronenberger in *PM* said the "pleasing," "lively," and "fresh" show was "sensationally youthful," and he liked the "fast and ingenious" dances as well as the score's "best" and most "infectious" song, "Buckle Down, Winsocki."

Brooks Atkinson in the *New York Times* praised the "good-humored" show with its "good" book, "excellent" score, and "droll and whirling" dances. He noted Nancy Walker was a "hard-boiled skirt" and June Allyson was a "sunny blonde with considerable charm."

During the tryout, "Alive and Kicking" (for Rosemary Lane, Marty May, Gil Stratton Jr., Jack Jordan Jr., and Kenneth Bowers) was deleted, and Lane's "Advice" seems to have been retitled "I'd Gladly Trade" for New York. "The Guy Who Brought Me" was added during the tryout; the lyric is by Richard Rodgers and Hugh Martin, and the music by Rodgers (who was a silent partner in the production of the musical).

The collection *Three by Hugh Martin* (JJA Records LP # JJA-19743A/B) includes four songs from the production performed by Nancy Walker ("What Do You Think I Am?," "Shady Lady Bird," "Just a Little Joint with a Juke Box," and "Every Time") and two by The Martins ("Just a Little Joint with a Juke Box" and "The Three B's"). *Everyone Else Revisited* (Painted Smiles CD # PSCD-146) includes "Don't Sell the Night Short" and "I Know You by Heart."

The jubilant and candy store-colored 1943 MGM film version was a faithful rendering of the show and boasted a number of the original cast members, including June Allyson, Nancy Walker, Kenneth (now Kenny) Bowers (Hunk on stage, and now playing Dutch Miller), Jack Jordan (Dutch Miller on stage, now playing Hunk), Tommy Dix (Chuck on stage, and now Bud Hooper [which was played on Broadway by Gil Stratton, who went uncredited in the film as an anonymous cadet]), and, in the chorus, Stanley Donen. The film also starred Gloria DeHaven and Virginia Weidler. For the role of Gale Joy, a glamorous Lucille Ball played herself as the movie star in search of publicity, and William Gaxton was her agent. And to make the film a truly 1940s moment, Harry James and His Music Makers were prominent in the film as the band that plays at the school prom.

The film was produced by Arthur Freed, directed by Edward (Eddie) Buzzell, choreographed by Charles Walters (and Jack Donohue and Stanley Donen), and the screenplay was by Irving Brecher and Fred F. Finklehoff. The film retained "Buckle Down, Winsocki," "Three Men on a Date," "Everytime," and "The Three B's"; and "Shady Lady Bird" and "I Know You by Heart" were heard as background music; "Wish I May" and "You're Lucky" were written for the film; and "Alive and Kicking," which had been cut during the pre-Broadway tryout, was now a show-stopping duet for Nancy Walker and Harry James. "What Do You Think I Am?" was filmed (with June Allyson and Kenny Bowers) but was dropped prior to the film's release; there were also two instrumental interpolations for James and his band, "Two O'Clock Jump" and "The Flight of the Bumblebee." Warner Brother released the DVD (# 79523); and the soundtrack was issued on CD by Rhino (# RHM2-7774). The CD includes "Shady Lady Bird," "I Know You by Heart," and "What Do You Think I Am?" as well as the two interpolations. "What Do You Think I Am?" resurfaced in the 1944 MGM musical *Broadway Rhythm* (which was based on Jerome Kern and Oscar Hammerstein II's 1939 Broadway musical *Very Warm for May*); here the song was performed by Gloria DeHaven and Kenny Bowers (the DVD was released by the Warner Brothers Archive Collection).

On November 20, 1954, a television adaptation was seen on NBC with Marilyn Maxwell, Robert Cummings, Pat Carroll, Jeannie Carson, Arte Johnson, Hope Holiday, and James (Jimmy) Komack; one of the script writers was Neil Simon.

The musical surprised everyone with a delightful Off-Broadway revival that opened at Stage 73 on April 2, 1963, for 224 performances and starred Liza Minnelli in her first New York stage role. Danny Daniels, who had been in the chorus of the original Broadway production, directed and choreographed the revival; besides Minnelli, the cast also included Ronald (later Christopher) Walken, his brother Glenn Walken, Karin Wolfe, Gene Castle, and Paula Wayne (as Gale Joy). During the run, Wayne was succeeded by an actual movie star of the 1940s when Veronica Lake assumed the role.

The revival retained "Three Men on a Date," "That's How I Love the Blues" (which wasn't listed in the program but was included in the "The Three B's" number), "Everytime," "The Guy Who Brought Me," "Shady Lady Bird," "Buckle Down, Winsocki," "What Do You Think I Am?," and "Just a Little Joint with a Juke Box"; the deleted song "Alive and Kicking," which had been added to the film version; the film's two new songs, "Wish I May" and "You're Lucky"; and two numbers from Martin and Blane's 1960 summer stock stage adaptation of their score for the 1944 MGM film musical *Meet Me in St. Louis*, "Raving Beauty" and "You Are for Loving." For the revival's CD release, Miles Kreuger reported that "The Old Hollywood Story" had originally been intended for Judy Garland to sing in the 1954 film musical *A Star Is Born*. The following numbers from the original production weren't included in the revival: "Don't Sell the Night Short," "I Know You by Heart," "My First Promise," "Where Do You Travel?," and "I'd Gladly Trade."

The revival was recorded by Cadence (LP # 24012), and later released on CD by Varese Sarabande (# 302-066-221-2); as bonus tracks, the CD includes two Cadence single releases of Minnelli singing "You Are for Loving" and "What Do You Think I Am?"

John Cecil Holm revised the musical's book as a nonmusical, and the play was published in paperback by The Dramatic Publishing Company in an undated edition.

Best Foot Forward chorus singer Eileen Barton later became a popular vocalist, and her recording of "If I Knew You Were Comin' (I'd've Baked a Cake)" (lyric and music by Bob Merrill, Albert Hoffman, and Al Trace) was a hit song in the early 1950s.

Featured player Maureen Cannon's entire Broadway career consisted of three musicals during the four-year period of 1941–1945: *Best Foot Forward* and **Up in Central Park** were hits, and in between came the legendary disaster **Hairpin Harmony**.

VIVA O'BRIEN
"A NOVEL MUSICAL COMEDY" / "AN AQUAMUSICAL"

Theatre: Majestic Theatre
Opening Date: October 9, 1941; *Closing Date*: October 25, 1941
Performances: 20
Book: William K. Wells and Eleanor Wells
Lyrics: Raymond Leveen
Music: Maria Grever
Direction: Robert Milton (comedy scenes staged by William K. Wells); *Producers*: Hickey, George Hale, Clark Robinson; *Choreography*: Chester Hale; *Scenery*: Clark Robinson; *Costumes*: John N. Booth Jr.; *Lighting*: The Century Lighting Company; *Musical Direction*: Ray Kavanaugh
Cast: Cyril Smith (Jeeves, Ship's First Officer), Milton Watson (Emilio Morales), Ruth Clayton (Betty Dayton), Roberto Bernardi (Manuel Estrada), Victoria Cordova (Lupita Estrada), Harold Diamond (Tom), Hugh Diamond (Dick, Gateman), Tom Diamond (Harry), Edgar Mason (J. Foster Adams), John Cherry (Professor Sherwood), Ann Dere (Mrs. Sherwood), Adelina Roatina (Senora Estrada), Gil Galvan (Pedro Gonzales, Vicente), Russ Brown (Don Jose O'Brien), Marie Nash (Carol Sherwood), Maria Lopez (Maria), Tanya Knight (Dolores), Rudy Williams (Ramon), Joe Frederic (Juan), Pete Desjardins (Native Carrier, Diver), James Phillips (Zambrano), Toni Oswald Labriola (Rani), Terry La Franconi (Secretary of Mexican Consulate), Ray Twardy (Diver), Betty O'Rourke (Diver); Male Singers: Terry La Franconi, Fred Kuhnly, Michael Singer, Frank E. Stafford; The Four Grand Quartette: Carter Ferris, Joe Frederic, Jack Leslie, Rudy Williams; The Senoritas: Deena Clark, Helena Goudvis, Dian Johnstone, Athalia Powell; Ballet Dancers: Patty Barker, Ann Marie Barrie, Marilyn Brandberg, Marjorie Castle, Muriel Cole, Jill De Sio, Carol Estes, Jane Fears, Dolores (Dody) Goodman, Helen Grayson, Betti Heart, Audrey Kent, Roberta Ogg, June Reynolds, Charlotte Sumner, Jean Van Buskirk, Betty Yeager
The musical was presented in two acts.
The action takes place in Miami Beach, Mexico, Yucatan, and on an airliner and a yacht.

Musical Numbers

Act One: "Mozambamba" (John Cherry, Ruth Clayton, Girls); "Don Jose O'Brien" (Russ Brown); "Mood of the Moment" (Marie Nash, Milton Watson, Girls, The Four Grand Quartette); "Mood of the Moment" (reprise) (Marie Nash, Milton Watson); "Mexican Bad Men" (Harold Diamond, Hugh Diamond, Tom Diamond); "Carinito" (Victoria Cordova, Ensemble); "Broken-Hearted Romeo" (Russ Brown); "Wrap Me in Your Sarape" (Marie Nash, Milton Watson, Ensemble); "Mood of the Moment" (reprise) (Milton Watson); "Yucatana" (Ruth Clayton, The Four Grand Quartette); "Ritual Dance" (Gil Galvan, Maria Lopez, Tanya Knight); "The Rain Ballet" (Ensemble)
Act Two: "Our Song" (Marie Nash, Senoritas, Ballet Dancers); "El matador terrifico" (Victoria Cordova); "How Long?" (Marie Nash, Milton Watson); "Matador Dance" (Gil Galvan); "To Prove My Love" (Russ

Brown, Victoria Cordova); "To Prove My Love" (reprise) (Victoria Cordova, Russ Brown); "The Sailors" (Harold Diamond, Hugh Diamond, Tom Diamond); Finale (Ensemble)

Viva O'Brien received some of the most scathing notices of the decade, and after its twenty performances on Broadway all but disappeared. But show music buffs speak its name in hallowed whispers, and along with **The Lady Comes Across, Hairpin Harmony, Allah Be Praised!, The Girl from Nantucket, The Duchess Misbehaves**, and **Louisiana Lady**, the musical has become something of a legend in its monumental awfulness (and in its memorably titled song "Wrap Me in Your Sarape").

And while many recall *Wish You Were Here* (1952) as Broadway's first swimming-pool musical, *Viva O'Brien* got there first with not only a pool but a waterfall, too. Well, not quite a waterfall: it was really a thirty-foot high sugarfall, as thousands of pounds of granulated sugar poured down on waving curtain-like material in order to give the effect of rushing water. Maybe you had to be there to appreciate it.

The title character (played by Russ Brown) is half-Irish and half-Spanish, and his dueling genes represent his alternately cowardly and brave sides. He's employed by a group of scientists to take them to Yucatan in search of a sacred wishing stone protected by angry natives. They find the stone and make wishes (the stone is particularly magical in its ability to instantly transport people anywhere they want to go), and so by the finale everyone eventually returns to Miami, where the show had started. The plot also focused on two love stories, one with a professor's daughter (Marie Nash) and her boyfriend (Milton Watson), who owns a silver mine without silver, and one with Don Jose and would-be Mexican spitfire (Victoria Cordova). And there's also a brief sojourn to a bull ring in Mexico City, where the title character finds himself in the unlikely role of a matador. But for all the travelling back and forth to Miami Beach, Mexico, and Yucatan, and with scenes aboard planes and ships, John Mason Brown in the *New York World-Telegram* said the "geographically" restless musical resulted in a dull cruise.

Brown was just one of many critics who wanted a wishing stone during the long evening at the Majestic. Since a wishing stone wasn't available, Brown said he rubbed his feet on the carpet and hoped it would "prove vehicular in its oriental way." He also noted the musical's swimming pool was "wet" and the book "wetter." The critics were at variance as to the musical's reported cost (apparently somewhere between $80,000 and $100,000), but Brown suggested the producers might as well have poured their money down a "rathole." As soon as the curtain rose on the first act, the book was "diving" and it was too late to call in the life guards. He also reported that heretofore the Ritz Brothers had topped his list of disagreeable family performers, but now the Diamond Brothers won top spot. *Viva O'Brien* was also at the top of the list of musicals he'd like to forget, and he concluded that its saga of a "rolling stone is one that gathers plenty of remorse."

Louis Kronenberger in *PM* said the musical was "brutal and bloody . . . incredibly dull, banal and fatuous"; John Anderson in the *New York Journal-American* found it an "irrigated bore"; and Richard Lockridge in the *New York Sun* couldn't recall a "worse" musical comedy plot.

Wilella Waldorf in the *New York Post* said the show was "one of the most childishly trying" she had encountered in years, and advised her readers that the Latins and the Americans in the musical were easy to spot because the former called Mexico "Mehico" and the latter "Mexico." Richard Watts in the *New York Herald Tribune* said the "terrible" musical had its characters running about in "tedium and apathy," and of the so-called jokes one character speculated on the value of "silver ore" and another responded with "Silver or what?" If this wasn't bad enough, someone said he got his suit of clothes "catch-as-catch-can," and another quipped that the suit looked as though it came from the "ash can."

Brooks Atkinson in the *New York Times* said the witless book, the "routine" music, and the "stuffy" production ideas were far too "ponderous" for the actors to "translate into entertainment." Burns Mantle in the *New York Daily News* liked the "rich and rare" costumes, the "expensive and rather attractive" décor, the "pleasantly unhackneyed and notably melodious" score (he wrongly told his readers they'd soon be hearing "Wrap Me in Your Sarape," "Mood of the Moment," and "To Prove My Love"), but, alas, the show had "one of the stupidest books in all Broadway history." But as "bad" as it was, *Viva O'Brien* was "visually still a lot of show for anything under $2.20."

As for the swimming pool, Waldorf reported it was briefly used by Olympic diving champion Pete Desjardins, comic swimmer Ray Twardy, and "watersprite" Betty O'Rourke, all of whom offered a "miniature Aquacade"—at least for those in the audience who returned after intermission. Lockridge also praised the swimming trio who entertained between 11:05 PM and 11:10 PM, but regretfully noted the musical itself had started at 8:30 PM.

During the tryout, the song "Sleepy Mexican" was dropped.

Russ Brown may have created the title role in a legendary flop, but he also acquitted himself with a Tony Award-winning performance as Best Featured Actor in a Musical when he appeared in *Damn Yankees* (1955) and was part of the quartet who introduced the show-stopping "Heart."

LET'S FACE IT!
"A NEW MUSICAL COMEDY"

Theatre: Imperial Theatre
Opening Date: October 29, 1941; *Closing Date*: March 20, 1943
Performances: 547
Book: Herbert Fields and Dorothy Fields
Lyrics and *Music*: Cole Porter
Based on the 1925 play *Cradle Snatchers* by Russell Medcraft and Norma Mitchell.
Direction: Edgar MacGregor; *Producer*: Vinton Freedley; *Choreography*: Charles Walters; *Scenery*: Harry Horner; *Costumes*: John Harkrider; *Lighting*: Uncredited; *Musical Direction*: Max Meth
Cast: Janice Joyce (Polly Lee), Marguerite Benton (Madge Hall), Helene Bliss (Helen Marcy), Helen Devlin (Dorothy Crowthers), Kalita Humphreys (Anna, Mrs. Wiggins), Mary Jane Walsh (Winnie Potter), Lois Bolton (Mrs. Fink), Margie Evans (Mrs. Wigglesworth), Sally Bond (Maid), Eve Arden (Maggie Watson), Joseph Macaulay (Julian Watson), Vivian Vance (Nancy Collister), James Todd (George Collister), Edith Meiser (Cornelia Abigal Pigeon), Fred Irving Lewis (Judge Henry Clay Pigeon), Marion Harvey (Molly Wincor), Beverly Whitney (Margaret Howard), Jane Ball (Ann Todd), Henry Austin (Phillip), Toni Caridi (Jules), Jack Williams (Eddie Hilliard), Benny Baker (Frankie Burns), Sunnie O'Dea (Muriel McGillicuddy), Nanette Fabray (Jean Blanchard), Houston Richards (Lieutenant Wiggins), *Danny Kaye* (Jerry Walker), Betty Moran (Gloria Gunther), Miriam Franklin (Sigana Earle), William Lilling (Master of Ceremonies), Fred Nay (Private Walsh); Dance Team: Mary Parker and Billy Daniel; The Royal Guards: Tommy Gleason, Ollie West, Roy Russell, Ricki Tanzi, Henry Austin, Tony Caridi; Vocalists: Marguerite Benton, Helene Bliss, Janice Joyce, Beverly Whitney, Lisa Rutherford, Frances Williams; Guests: Billie Dee, Mary Ann Parker, Sally Bond, Jane Ball, Peggy Carroll, Sandra Barrett, Jean Scott, Jean Trybom, Marilynn Randels, Marion Harvey, Miriam Franklin, Peggy Littlejohn, Pat Likely, Zynaid Spencer, Renee Russell, Pamela Clifford, Edith Turgell; Selectees: Garry Davis, George Florence, Fred Deming, Dale Priest, Mickey Moore, Jack Riley, Joel Friend, Fred Nay, Frank Ghegan, Randolph Hughes
The musical was presented in two acts.
The action takes place during the present in and around Long Island, including Southampton and Fort Roosevelt.

Musical Numbers

Act One: "Milk, Milk, Milk" (Guests at Milk Farm); "A Lady Needs a Rest" (Eve Arden, Vivian Vance, Edith Meiser); "Jerry, My Soldier Boy" (Mary Jane Walsh, Guests); "Let's Face It" (Tommy Gleason, The Royal Guards); "Farming" (Danny Kaye, Benny Baker, Jack Williams, Sunnie O'Dea, Nanette Fabray, Ensemble); "Ev'rything I Love" (Danny Kaye, Mary Jane Walsh); "Ace in the Hole" (Mary Jane Walsh, Sunnie O'Dea, Nanette Fabray, Ensemble); "You Irritate Me So" (Nanette Fabray, Jack Williams); "Baby Games" (Danny Kaye, Eve Arden, Benny Baker, Edith Meiser, Vivian Vance, Jack Williams); "Fairy Tale" (Danny Kaye); "Rub Your Lamp" (Mary Jane Walsh, Ensemble); Specialty Dance: "Cuttin' a Persian Rug" (Mary Parker, Billy Daniel)
Act Two: "I've Got Some Unfinished Business with You" (Mary Jane Walsh, Nanette Fabray, Sunnie O'Dea, Helen Devlin, Betty Moran, Joseph Macaulay, James Todd, Fred Irving Lewis); "Let's Not Talk about Love" (Danny Kaye, Eve Arden); "A Little Rumba Numba" (Tommy Gleason, Marguerite Benton, The Royal Guards; Specialty Dance: Mary Parker and Billy Daniel); "I Hate You, Darling" (Vivian Vance, James Todd, Mary Jane Walsh, Danny Kaye); "Melody in Four F" (Danny Kaye); Finale (Entire Company)

Let's Face It! came along as the third in a string of six solid hits by Cole Porter. It was preceded by *Leave It to Me!* (1938), *DuBarry Was a Lady* (1939), and **Panama Hattie**, and was followed by **Something for the Boys** and **Mexican Hayride**; all enjoyed long runs (five ran for over a year), and except for *Leave It to Me!*, all were filmed. Moreover, *Let's Face It!* became Porter's longest-running musical up to that time. There would be a couple of dry spots for him in the mid-1940s with **Seven Lively Arts** and **Around the World in Eighty Days**, but late in the decade he bounced back with his masterpiece **Kiss Me, Kate**.

Based on the hit 1925 comedy *Cradle Snatchers*, the lively musical dealt with three scheming wives, Maggie (Eve Arden), Nancy (Vivian Vance), and Cornelia (Edith Meiser) who decide to get even with their philandering husbands by taking on lovers from a nearby Army fort. Their victims are the hapless but willing Jerry (Danny Kaye), Frankie (Benny Baker), and Eddie (Jack Williams), who have girlfriends of their own, Winnie (Mary Jane Walsh), Muriel (Sunnie O'Dea), and Jean (Nanette Fabray). The only slightly naughty mix-ups were an excuse for an evening of merriment, and by the finale the ladies were back with their husbands and the soldiers with their girls.

Porter's contributions followed the pattern of most of his scores during the period. There weren't many classics of the "Night and Day" and "Begin the Beguine" variety, but there were pleasant ballads ("Ev'rything I Love"), clever songs about romance ("Let's Not Talk about Love" informed us that Bucks County was a "nest of nymphomania"), comedy songs that poked fun at the foibles of the day (such as celebrities' penchant for "Farming," which notes that Mae West is "at her best in the hay"), and the suggestive "Rub Your Lamp" (which notes your "vigor" will be "bigger" if you follow the advice of the song's title). With his tongue-twisting verbal acrobatics in "Tschiakowsky" from **Lady in the Dark**, Danny Kaye had become an overnight sensation, and thus enjoyed solo star billing in *Let's Face It!* Porter even allowed two interpolations into his score (both with lyrics by Kaye's wife Sylvia Fine and music by Max Liebman), "Fairy Tale" and "Melody in Four F." The critics were beside themselves over Kaye and these comedy songs, but like contortionist dancing this type of number doesn't go over well today and seems precious as well as tiresome.

Brooks Atkinson in the *New York Times* hailed the "wonderfully joyous" and "bright and brisk and continuously enjoyable" musical. Herbert Fields and Dorothy Fields offered an "impudent knockabout" book, Porter had "shaken good tunes and rhymes" from his "sophisticated jukebox," and Harry Horner had provided "gay-colored" décor. He noted the songs were "designed for enjoyment," and singled out "Jerry, My Soldier Boy" ("resounding band music"), "You Irritate Me So" (it was a "turned upside down" version of "You're the Top"), "Farming" (which "shakes a wry stick" at the smart set), and "Let's Not Talk about Love" ("restores the patter song to its ancient eminence").

Richard Watts in the *New York Herald Tribune* said the show could perhaps have reached a level of "slightly more satisfying entertainment," but there was no getting around the fact it was "bright, tuneful and enlivening"; Louis Kronenberger in *PM* praised Danny Kaye, and said Eve Arden's "acid manner is just right"; and Richard Lockridge in the *New York Sun* said the musical was "good for what ails you" and would be "radiant in any season."

Wilella Waldorf in the *New York Post* enjoyed Porter's "merry" songs, Charles Walters's "uncommonly pleasant dance routines," the "colorful" costumes, and the special dance routines contributed by the team of Mary Parker and Billy Daniel as well as the tap-dancing of Sunnie O'Dea.

John Anderson in the *New York Journal-American* said Broadway had been undergoing a "famine," and so the new musical looked "deliriously like a masterpiece." He liked Porter's score (and singled out six songs), the "lively and interesting" dances, the "gaily spirited" settings, and noted that Eve Arden, Vivian Vance, and Edith Meiser were "immensely amusing." John Mason Brown in the *New York World-Telegram* found the show a "smooth-running, uproarious and delectable affair with almost everything to recommend it." Porter's contributions were "diverting" and "rippling and pleasant," and the "rowdy" evening was "exuberant and irresistible" and didn't "hesitate to call a shovel a spade."

Burns Mantle in the *New York Daily News* praised the "generously and expertly selected" cast members, and noted that Eve Arden was "one of the literates of the better comedienne group."

As for Danny Kaye, he made his first-act entrance while driving an Army truck that crashes through the side of a building; another scene found him posturing as various statues in a war memorial; and in another one he impersonated Dracula. And of course he stopped the show with his two specialty numbers and participated in "Farming" and "Let's Not Talk about Love," two of Porter's best contributions. Atkinson said Kaye offered "highly original musical mummery"; Watts found him "brilliantly funny"; and Anderson said he was "terrific." Waldorf noted he was "refreshing," but indicated he might not be "everybody's dish." She quoted a theatergoer, whom she overheard as the audience was filing out of the theatre: "Insufferably cute! Altogether too much baby talk!"

During the tryout, the naughty "Get Yourself a Girl" was cut (it advised that if you have to "pet" yourself, then it's time to "get" yourself a girl). During rehearsals, "Revenge," "What Are Little Husbands Made Of?," and "Pets" were dropped; and "Make a Date with a Great Psychoanalyst" (which referenced *Lady in the Dark*, Gertrude Lawrence, and Moss Hart), "Up to His Old Tricks Again," and "You Can't Beat My Bill" weren't used. "Let's Not Talk about Love" was actually a two-part song that included "Let's Talk about Love," and while Kaye and Arden sang the first part, it isn't certain if they performed the latter.

When Kaye left the show toward the end of the run, he was succeeded by José Ferrer. With Kaye's departure, so went his two specialty numbers; and so Porter's "It Ain't Etiquette" from *DuBarry Was a Lady* was interpolated as a late second-act duet for Ferrer and Benny Baker (here it was titled "T'aint Etiquette").

Mary Jane Walsh recorded three songs from the musical ("Ev'rything I Love," "Ace in the Hole," and "I Hate You, Darling") all conducted by Max Meth, the conductor of the Broadway production. Danny Kaye recorded three as well ("Farming," "Let's Not Talk about Love," and "Melody in 4F"). These performances were collected in a recording issued under the Smithsonian's American Musical Theatre Series (LP # P-14944/R-018) and included songs from two other Porter musicals (*Red Hot and Blue!* and *Leave It to Me!*). The recording also offers two contemporary recordings by Hildegarde ("You Irritate Me So" and "A Little Rumba Numba"). "A Lady Needs a Rest," "Make a Date with a Great Psychoanalyst," and "What Are Little Husbands Made Of?" are included in the collection *Cole Porter Revisited Volume III* (Painted Smiles CD # PSCD-105), and "I've Got Some Unfinished Business with You" and "Revenge" were recorded for *Cole Porter Revisited Volume V* (Painted Smiles CD # PSCD-122).

The lyrics for all used, cut, and unused songs are included in *The Complete Lyrics of Cole Porter*.

Despite Bob Hope, Betty Hutton, ZaSu Pitts, Phyllis Povah, and Eve Arden reprising her stage role, Paramount's 1943 film version fell flat. Directed by Sidney Lanfield and scripted by Harry Tugend, the film retained just two of Porter's songs ("Let's Not Talk about Love" and the title number).

A television adaptation was seen on NBC's *Colgate Comedy Hour* on November 21, 1954; the production starred Dean Martin, Jerry Lewis, Vivian Blaine, Gene Nelson, Bert Lahr, and Betty Furness. Three songs from the stage production were retained ("You Irritate Me So," "Ev'rything I Love," and "Ace in the Hole") and two were interpolated from other Porter musicals ("It's De-Lovely" from *Red Hot and Blue!* and "I've Got You Under My Skin" from the 1936 film *Born to Dance*).

HIGH KICKERS
"AN AMERICAN MUSICAL COMEDY"

Theatre: Broadhurst Theatre
Opening Date: October 31, 1941; *Closing Date*: March 28, 1942
Performances: 171
Book: George Jessel, Bert Kalmar, and Harry Ruby
Lyrics and *Music*: Bert Kalmar and Harry Ruby
Based on a "suggestion" by Sid Silvers.
Direction: Production "directed by" Edward Sobol and "supervised by" Nat Karson; *Producer*: Alfred Bloomingdale; *Choreography*: Carl Randall; *Scenery*, *Costumes*, and *Lighting*: Nat Karson; *Musical Direction*: Val Ernie
Cast (in the prologue): Billy Vine (The Candy Spieler), The High Kickers Chorus (as themselves), Two American Showgirls: Joyce Mathews, Rose Teed; Joe Marks (Shultz), *George Jessel* (George M. Krause, Sr., aka Kelly), Mary-Robin Marlow (Sophia), Rollin Bauer (The Doctor), Dick Monahan (George M. Krause Jr.), The Stylish Four: Bob Shaw, Bob Bay, Harold Young, and Victor Griffin; Betty Bruce (Mamie); *Cast* (in the play): Sophie Tucker (as herself), George Jessel (George M. Krause Jr.), Jack Mann (S. Kaufman Hart), Lois January (Kitty McKay), Lee Sullivan (Jimmy Wilberforce), Franklyn Fox (Frank Whipple), Chick York (Mayor John Wilberforce), Rose King (Hortense Wilberforce), Jack Howard (Chief of Police), Betty Bruce (Betty), The Stuart Morgan Dancers (as themselves), Betty Jane Smith (Betty Jane), Ted Shapiro (The Pia-

nist), Chaz Chase (A Stage Hand); The Stuart Morgan Dancers: Showgirls—Sunny Ainsworth, Barbara Brewster, Gloria Brewster, Lucille Casey, Bonita Edwards, Eleanor Hall, Joyce Mathews, Betty Stewart, Rose Teed; Dancing Girls—Jean Anthony, Helen Barrie, Stephenie Cekan, Marilyn Hale, Frances Hammond, Ann Helm, Ellen Howard, Marjorie Jackson, Dorothy Jeffers, Mary-Robin Marlow, Ray McGregor, Bobby Prieser, Helen Spruill, Marion Warnes; Boys—Bob Bay, Bob Shaw, Harry Mack, Victor Griffin, Harold Young, Donald (Don) Weissmuller

The musical was presented in two acts.

The action takes place in 1910 and in 1941, in Paris, Panama, and Chambersville, Ohio.

Musical Numbers

Act One: Opening Chorus; "My Sweetheart Mamie" (Bob Shaw, Bob Bay, Harold Young, Victor Griffin, Betty Bruce); "Didn't Your Mother Tell You Nothing" (Sophie Tucker); "You're on My Mind" (Lois January, Lee Sullivan); Specialty: "Army and Navy Song" (lyric and music by Jack Yellen) (Sophie Tucker); Opening Chorus; Specialty (George Jessel); "Panic in Panama" (Lois January, Ensemble, Betty Bruce); "The Strip" (Sophie Tucker)

Act Two: "The Girls" (Betty Bruce); "Memories" (George Jessel); "Time to Sing" (Lois January, Lee Sullivan, Donald Weissmuller, Ensemble); "I Got Something" (Sophie Tucker); "Cigarettes" (Betty Bruce, Ensemble); "Waltzing in the Moonlight" (Lois January, Lee Sullivan, Ensemble); Dance (Stuart Morgan Dancers); "Some of These Days" (lyric and music by Shelton Brook) (Sophie Tucker); "Bits of What You've Heard" (that is, reprises) (Company)

High Kickers (or, as it was identified in the program, *George Jessel's High Kickers: An American Musical Comedy with Sophie Tucker*) enjoyed a modest run that lasted through much of the season and then toured. It was a loosely put-together affair that followed the history of a burlesque troupe run by George Krause and then later his son (both roles were played by George Jessel) from its palmy days in the early part of the century up to the present time when it's playing in a small Midwestern town. When the local sheriff discovers the nature of the troupe, he threatens to jail them, but Sophie Tucker (playing herself) saves the day when she recognizes the mayor's wife as an old friend and former stripper.

Wilella Waldorf in the *New York Post* was aghast by the tiresome goings-on. She reported that the opening night performance began thirty-five minutes late, and when she left the theatre to meet her newspaper's deadline, the show was still going "grimly forward." She noted she had to "pinch herself" to ensure she hadn't fallen asleep and gone into a *Hellzapoppin'* "nightmare." Among her descriptions were scenes with Sophie Tucker as the Statue of Liberty (which was preserved for posterity on the program's cover) while surrounded by chorus girls festooned with tanks-and-battleship head regalia; George Jessel doing imitations of Eddie Cantor and George M. Cohan; a comic (Chaz Chase) who ate lighted cigars and cigarettes; a comedian (Jack Mann) who spit water into hats; and a slapstick moment in which Tucker threw a pie in someone's face.

Louis Kronenberger in *PM* suggested "a strong whiff of the stockyards" blew through the evening, and noted there hadn't been such a "ham show" in years: some of it was "good" ham, but "most of it was bad." There was more vulgarity than humor, and the entire affair should have been "rattled off instead of ladled out." John Mason Brown in the *New York World-Telegram* said the "corny" evening seemed thrown together with "bad eggs and good," and noted that when scrambled the "good eggs do not win out." Brooks Atkinson in the *New York Times* said the "musical mélange is malodorous and mediocre"; Richard Lockridge in the *New York Sun* admitted there were "pleasures" in the show, with "the largest in all respects" being Sophie Tucker, but with that plot and "everything" else you are "left hardly strong enough to enjoy them"; and John Anderson in the *New York Journal-American* said the musical contained "in the exuberant poundage of Sophie Tucker one of our theatre's greatest shakers," but the show itself was "no great shakes."

Richard Watts in the *New York Herald Tribune* didn't mind rowdy humor, and in fact regretted the "ribald" jokes didn't "come fast and furiously enough." He suggested that if you thought it would be "inordinately comic" to watch Sophie Tucker do a strip-tease, then *High Kickers* was "exactly what you have been waiting for."

LA VIE PARISIENNE

Theatre: 44th Street Theatre
Opening Date: November 5, 1941; *Closing Date*: November 11, 1941
Performances: 7
Libretto: English version by Felix Brentano and Louis Verneuil, with lyrics by Marion Farquhar (based on the original French version by Henri Meilhac and Ludovic Helavy)
Music: Jacques Offenbach
Direction: Felix Brentano; *Producer*: The New Opera Company; *Choreography*: Igor Schwezoff; *Scenery* and *Costumes*: Marco Montedoro; *Musical Direction*: Antal Dorati
Cast: Carolina Segrera (Metella), Clifford Newdahl (Hutchinson), Ruby Mercer (Evelyn), Ralph Magelssen (Gardefeu), John Tyers (Boninet), George Rasely (Jackson), Ann Lipton (Gabrielle), Hugh Thompson (Gontran), Paul Best (Alphonse), Norman Roland (Georges), Leon Lischchiner (later Lishner) (Gaston), Igor Schwezoff (Dancing Master); Chorus: Vivian Bower, Louise Fearney, Marie Fox, Josephine Griffin, Meta Hartog, Marion Ross, Dorothy Starner, Dorothy Hartigan, Mary David, Dean Mundy, Alice Philipp, Margaret Omos, Anna Steck, Carol York, Cynthia Rose, Mary McKenna, Virginia Syms, Sam Adams, Hans Gareis, Hans Kuhn, Nathaniel Sprinzena, Elton Plowman, Eric Rautens, Franc Alden, Bertram Briess, John Reiff, Roneo Rim, Boris Vornovsky, Ludlow White, Anthony Scott, Leland Goodwin; Ballet Dancers: Maria Azrova, Phyllis Le Gassie, Julia Horvath, Sonia Orlova, Serge Ismailoff, Remington Olmstead, Miriam Oreck, George Grant, Angelo Rovida, Joan Schille, Edwina Seaver, Gemze de Lappe, Jack Abbott, Arlene Garver, Betty Nitsch
The operetta was presented in three acts.
The action takes place during the spring of 1866 in Paris.
There were no individual musical numbers listed in the program.

Jacques Offenbach's operetta *La vie parisienne* premiered on October 31, 1866, in Paris at the Theatre de Palais-Royal; the libretto was by Henri Meilhac and Ludovic Helavy. Originally produced in four acts, the work was revised by Offenbach in 1873 and condensed into three. The operetta was first seen in New York on March 29, 1868, at the Theatre Français, and the revised version was presented on June 12, 1876, at the Booth Theatre, with Offenbach himself conducting. (The Booth Theatre is not the same Booth which is located on West 45th Street and Shubert Alley.)

A lighthearted piece about romantic goings-on among Parisians and tourists, the new English version received a cool reception from Olin Downes in the *New York Times*, who complained that the production came across as an "inferior" version of an American musical. He felt few performers were "capable of giving the piece its native point and movement," and he noted the décor was "inadequate." But he was pleased the score was presented "virtually complete," and mentioned that music from other operettas by Offenbach (such as *La perichole*) had been interpolated into the score. The production played out its seven scheduled performances.

The New Opera Company revived the operetta two more times, on November 10, 1942, and on January 12, 1945 (for more information, see entries for each revival).

There are numerous recordings of the score, including a 2-CD set (with libretto) in French issued by EMI Classics; and a DVD of an updated adaptation set in contemporary Paris was released by Erato.

Among the cast members were Leon Lischchiner (later, Lishner), who had prominent roles in Gian-Carlo Menotti's *The Consul* (1950) and Marc Blitzstein's 1954 adaptation of Kurt Weill's *The Threepenny Opera*. John Tyers later introduced the ethereal "Haunted Heart" in Howard Dietz and Arthur Schwartz's 1948 revue **Inside U.S.A.**, and Gemze de Lappe was associated with Agnes De Mille and Jerome Robbins throughout her career. She had originally appeared as a replacement dancer in the original production of **Oklahoma!** and recreated De Mille's choreography for later revivals; was seen in the original productions of *Paint Your Wagon* (1952) and *Juno* (1959), both choreographed by De Mille; and was in the original production of *The King and I* (1951), which was choreographed by Robbins.

SONS O' FUN
"New Crazy Musical"

Theatre: Winter Garden Theatre (during run, the revue transferred to the 46th Street Theatre)
Opening Date: December 1, 1941; *Closing Date*: August 9, 1943

Performances: 742
Fun: Ole Olsen and Chic Johnson
Lyrics: Jack Yellen
Music: Sam E. (Sammy) Fain
Direction: "Fun staged" by Edward Duryea Dowling, production "supervised" by Harry Kaufman, and "additional fun" supervised by Hal Block; *Producers*: The Messrs. Shubert; *Choreography*: Robert Alton; *Scenery* and *Costumes*: Raoul Pene du Bois; *Lighting*: Edward Duryea Dowling; *Musical Direction*: John McManus
Cast: *Ole Olsen*, *Chic Johnson*, Carmen Miranda, Ella Logan, Frank Libuse, Rosario (Perez) and Antonio (Ruiz), The Pitchmen (Al Ganz and Al Meyers), Joe Besser, Lionel Kaye, (Paul) Walton and (Michael) O'Rourke, The Biltmorettes (Edna Mae Isenburg, Joan Baker, and Beverly Sweet), Ben Beri, Margot Brander, Milton Charleston, (William) Moran and (Al) Wiser, Valentinoff, James Little, Parker and Porthole, Ivan Kirov, Richard Craig, Martha Rawlins, Kitty Murray, Vilma Josey, Carter and Bowie, The Statler Twins (Jane and Jean), The Mullan Twins, The Crystal Twins, The Blackburn Twins (Royce and Ramon), (Helen) Magda and Springer; Frank Paxton, Don Gautier, Don Tompkins [sic] (Tomkins), Bruce Evans, Eddie Davis, John Howes, Gene Winchester, Paul Walton, Don Gautier, Bill Moran, "Shorty" Renna, Ernest D'Amato, Chu Chu Parr, John Keno, Catherine Johnson, Stan Ross; Ensemble: Tommy Adams, Alice Brent, Trudy Burke, Gloria Costa, Shannon Dean, Jean Elliott, Georgia Francis, Peggy Gallimore, Amelia Gentry, Emily Jewell, Kay Lazell, Joan Martin, Virginia McCurdy, Carol Murphy, Olive Nicholson, Eleanor Parr, Eileen Shirley, Diane Sinclair, Winifred Seeley, Al Anthony, Tony Barrett, Phil Clavadetscher, Cliffe Ferre, Henning Irgens, Jack McClendon, Peter Nielson, Albert Ruiz, Carl Trees
The revue was presented in two acts.

Sketches and Musical Numbers

Before the Show: "Fun on the Stage—Olsen & Johnson's Fun House" (Audience); "Fun in the Audience" (Head Usher: Frank Libuse; Where Do You Live? Chairman: Frank Paxton); "Fun in the Orchestra Pit—The Simp-Phony Orchestra" (Conductor: Maestro Frank Libuse)
Act One: "The Joke's on Us" (Stagehands, Usherettes, Chorus Girls, Vendors: The Girls and Boys of the Ensemble; Scrubladies: Don Gautier, Don Tomkins, Bruce Evans; The Attendants: Kitty Murray, Eddie Davis); "Those Sons o' Fun" (Ole Olsen and Chic Johnson, with Frank Libuse, Joe Besser, John Howes, Gene Winchester, Al Meyers, Al Ganz, Paul Walton, Martha Rawlins, Don Gautier, Bill Moran, James Little, "Shorty" Renna, Ernest D'Amato, Bruce Evans, Chu Chu Parr, Milton Charleston); "It's a New Kind of Thing" (Ella Logan; Couple: Diane Sinclair, Ivan Kirov; Maid: Kitty Murray; Jivers: Georgia Francis, The Blackburn Twins, Jean Elliott, Ensemble); "Fun in One" (Ole Olsen; Bowler: John Keno; Lena: Catherine Johnson; Maestro: Frank Libuse); "A Quiet Night in the Country" (Chic Johnson, Ole Olsen, Ella Logan, Frank Libuse, Joe Besser, James Little); "The Olsen & Johnson Mystery Hour"; "Meditation" (Divorcee: Vilma Josey; Husband: Ole Olsen; Dumbo: Chic Johnson); "The Pitchmen" ("Featuring the Sing-a-tina"); "Induction Center" (Captain: Ole Olsen; Sergeant: James Little; Navy Man: Milton Charleston; Volunteer: Don Tomkins; Conscientious Objector: Chic Johnson; Army Hostess: Eileen Shirley; Rookie: Joe Besser); "Oh, Auntie!" (The Niece: Ella Logan; Auntie: Valentinoff; Quartet: The Blackburn Twins, Cliff Ferre, Tony Barrett; The Redheads: The Crystal Twins; The Gymnasts: The Mullen Twins; The Blondes: The Statler Twins); "Moment Musicale" (At the Baby Grand: Frank Libuse; Soloist: Margot Brander; Valet: Ernest D'Amato); "Some More Fun in One" (Ole Olsen, Milton Charleston, Stan Ross, James Little, John Keno, Joe Besser, Virginia McCurdy, Catherine Johnson, Gloria Crystal); "Porthole and Poopdeck" (Porthole: A Dummy; Poopdeck: Chic Johnson; The Master Mind: Ole Olsen); "Thank You, South America" (Hattie: Ella Logan; Little Girl: Helen Magna: The Dancer: Valentinoff; Los Chavalillos: Rosario and Antonio); "Thank You, North America" (Carmen Miranda and Her Caballeros de Lua)
Intermission: Call Boy: Frank Libuse; also, Artists, Indians, F.B.I. Men
Act Two: "It's a Mighty Fine Country We Have Here" (Sheriff: Ella Logan; Little Nell: Diane Sinclair; Her Maw and Paw: Winifred Seeley and Don Gautier; Two Bandits: Valentinoff and Ivan Kirov; Madame La Rue: Shannon Dean; Cowgirls: The Biltmorettes); "*Hellzapoppin'* Night in Buckeye, Arizona" (Deadeye Dick: Chic Johnson; Gentleman Jim: Ole Olsen; Mexican Pete: "Shorty" Renna: Cowboy Joe: Joe Besser; Black Mike: Milton Charleston; Prospectors: Moran and Wiser; An Admiral: Don Tomkins; Bartender: James Little); "Hi-Ho, the Hoe-Down Way" (lyric by Irving Kahal) ("Every Man for Himself"); "Lena" (Catherine

Johnson); Walton and O'Rourke; "Manuelo" (lyric by Irving Kahal) (Carmen Miranda and Her Caballeros de Lua; Scene—A Cockfight, The Canary Islands: Gypsies—Rosario and Antonio; Fighters: Valentinoff, The Vanquished, and Ivan Kirov, The Victor, and Ensemble); "Tête à Tête" (Carmen Miranda, Ole Olsen, Chic Johnson); "Those Umbrella Men" (Frank Libuse, Joe Besser); "Fun in Bed" (Ole Olsen, Chic Johnson); Ben Beri; "Happy in Love" (Ella Logan; with The Blackburn Twins, The Crystal Twins, The Mullen Twins, The Biltmorettes, The Statler Twins, Diane Sinclair and Ivan Kirov, Shannon Dean and Valentinoff, Kitty Murray and Eddie Davis, Magna and Springer, Dancing Girls and Boys); "Olsen & Johnson's Surprise Party" (The Daffy Auctioneer: Lionel Kaye); "Let's Say Goodnight with a Dance" (Richard Craig and Emily Jewell); "A Very Pleasant Good Evening to You, One and All) (Ole Olsen, Chic Johnson, Carmen Miranda, Ella Logan, Frank Libuse, Rosario and Antonio, Joe Besser, Entire Company) *Note*: The program credited special dance music by Will Irwin which was interpolated into the following songs: "It's a Mighty Fine Country We Have Here," "The Joke's on Us," "Thank You, South America," and "Manuelo." Jay Levison (Livingston) and Ray Evans were credited for additional music.

Ole Olsen and Chic Johnson were surely daring pioneers of the American musical theatre. Unappreciated and virtually forgotten today, they were visionaries who foresaw what would happen to Broadway decades after they'd left it, and they gave the audiences of long ago a taste of what was to come. Yes, today there are those in the audience who have an almost neurotic need to be "part" of the show they're attending. It's no longer enough to buy a ticket, take a seat, enjoy the evening, and applaud during curtain calls. In order to prove they *truly* appreciate a show, these souls frantically applaud after every number, vociferously whistle and make "woo-woo" sounds, and like jack-in-box puppets stand with Pavlovian regularity at the curtain calls (and even after individual numbers). Not to mention singing (and even dancing) along, as a means of expressing their more-audience-member-than-thou attitude to the quiet ones sitting around them, who clearly aren't getting their money's worth out of the performance.

Imagine how happy these people would be if they found themselves in the Broadway world of Olsen and Johnson. Take *Sons o' Fun*, for example. When you walked into the theatre, you were met by a tough "policeman" who puffed away on his cigarette while warning you that smoking was absolutely forbidden inside. Then "ushers" took you to your seat, but the stooges guided you to the wrong one! And some ticketholders were led backstage, then *onto the stage itself* and through a Coney Islands fun-house maze before they were allowed to step off the stage and into the auditorium to (hopefully) find their seats. They were truly part of the show, and those in the audience who were already seated could enjoy watching them in their role of a hapless but rather thrilled theatergoer caught up in the madcap antics. There was also an "usher" who led stooges down the aisle and then offered them a convenient ladder to use in order to climb up to their box seats, and stooges seated near you would stand up and start removing some of their clothes. Yes, the lucky audience members of *Sons o' Fun* could immerse themselves in a roundelay of Pirandello-styled tomfoolery in which both audience and cast members alike were part of the zany fun.

Later, chorus girls came down from the stage and encouraged male victims in aisle seats to join them on stage for dancing (on opening night, former New York Governor Al Smith happily obliged). And before dancing, the chorus girls helped the gentlemen out of their jackets and then shuffled the jackets around. When the men returned to their seats, the critics reported oh such merry and wacky confusion when the gentlemen discovered they had the wrong jackets and must go in search of the right ones!

And sirens, gongs, horns, blank cartridges, and firecrackers would go off occasionally, just to make sure no one in the audience had fallen asleep. At one point, the theatre was completely darkened and strange wispy phosphorescent creatures flew over the heads of audience members to the soundtrack of horrific screams by terrified females. Soup beans were thrown down the backs of necks of lucky ticketholders, and chewing gum was dutifully distributed at various intervals. And during intermission scowling "Indians" and "G-Men" patrolled the aisles. And you could bet the rent that, a la Olsen and Johnson's earlier revue *Hellzapoppin'*, sooner or later another stooge carrying a huge potted palm tree would tramp between the rows of seats just to ensure that everyone sitting down was inconvenienced. And there was again that strange woman from *Hellzapoppin'* who roamed about the auditorium and shouted out for her elusive Oscar. This time around, she pushed a baby carriage, and each time she appeared the "baby" got bigger and bigger until it was a full-grown adult.

And the audience loved it. *Sons o' Fun* opened at the Winter Garden, ran two years, and became the season's longest-running musical; if it opened today it would probably outlast another show which years later opened at the same theatre and claimed it would run "now and forever."

Besides Olsen and Johnson and their zanies, the revue offered Carmen Miranda in all her fruit-salad-hat and sequined-pump-shoe glory, Scottish singer Ella Logan, the Latin dance team of Rosario and Antonio, juggling by Ben Beri, some puppet foolery by Walton and O'Rourke, and imitations by The Pitchmen. There were also spoofs of **Panama Hattie** and *Charley's Aunt* (Jose Ferrer had recently starred in a long-running Broadway revival of the comedy), and in one memorable sketch ("*Hellzapoppin'* Night in Buckeye, Arizona") Olsen and Johnson aimed shots at a picture of a battleship hanging over a bar: from within its frame, the battleship fired back at them and then promptly sank (the revue opened five days before Pearl Harbor, and after December 7 one wonders if this sequence of the sketch was cut).

Richard Lockridge in the *New York Sun* reported that half the show took place in the aisles, and so there was "no place to hide," and John Anderson in the *New York Journal-American* suggested that after the "hilarious asylum" of *Sons o' Fun*, audience members would want to return to *Hellzapoppin'* to "rest up" in a "nice, comfortable straitjacket." Once the evening was over, he was a "wreck" (but admitted that as soon as he pulled himself together he was going right back to another performance).

Wilella Waldorf in the *New York Post* said the evening was "seldom dull" because there was the chance you'd be hit by a flying hat, a dead bird, or an egg (a nearby stooge in the audience had a "babe" dropped in her lap by a flying stork). She said fans of Olsen and Johnson would have a "whale of an evening for their money." Richard Watts in the *New York Herald Tribune* noted the new revue was a "bedlam carnival" much more lavish than its predecessor; but for someone who had seen *Hellzapoppin'* twice and now *Sons o' Fun* once, he had to admit he found just a "minimum" of fun in the two shows and as such stood "somewhere outside of the human race."

John Mason Brown in the *New York World-Telegram* described the show as "part smoker, part burlesque show, part revue, part Hallowe'en party and all pandemonium" and was so worn out by it all that he needed his Vitamin B pills at intermission. He also noted that Carmen Miranda was amusing with her "Souse American ways" and that her "fascination remains undiminished." Burns Mantle in the *New York Daily News* noted that for the first-act finale Miranda was dressed in a silver outfit that (except for her towering headdress of fruit) made her look like an "animated sterling salt shaker."

Brooks Atkinson in the *New York Times* noted the revue was performed "in most parts" of the Winter Garden, throughout which Olsen and Johnson ensured that the gags kept coming "amid the luster of a handsome production." The evening was a *Hellzapoppin'* that had "come into a fortune and is putting on the dog."

When Carmen Miranda left the revue, the dance team of Rosario and Antonio was given more to do, and Wynn Murray eventually succeeded Ella Logan.

Cast member Don Tomkins (sometimes misspelled as Tompkins) was one of the college cut-ups in the original 1927 production of *Good News* who introduced the show-stopping "The Varsity Drag." In 1960, he stopped the show all over again when he and Lucille Ball made merry hi-jinks in "What Takes My Fancy" from *Wildcat*.

The era of *Hellzapoppin'* and *Sons o' Fun* marked Olsen and Johnson's heyday. *Hellzapoppin'* played for 1,404 performances and was for a time the longest-running musical in Broadway history, and *Sons o' Fun* ran for 742 performances. But **Laffing Room Only** played for just 233 showings, **Funzapoppin** for 37, and *Pardon Our French* (1950) for 100. **Laffacade** played briefly on tour in 1947 (but never attempted Broadway), and their revue *Pardon Our Antenna* closed during its pre-Broadway tryout in 1954. Their last New York performances were in a Broadway-styled revue which played the Palace for a one-month stand beginning March 11, 1952; the first half consisted of specialty acts, and the second was devoted to the antics of the two comics and their fellow zanies. But it's quite conceivable that if the team were with us today they'd be a Broadway hit all over again with their peculiar brand of rough and rowdy audience participation.

SUNNY RIVER
"A New Musical"

Theatre: St. James Theatre
Opening Date: December 4, 1941; *Closing Date*: January 3, 1942
Performances: 36
Book and *Lyrics*: Oscar Hammerstein II
Music: Sigmund Romberg

Direction: Production "supervised" by John Murray Anderson and "staged" by Oscar Hammerstein II; *Producer*: Max Gordon; *Choreography*: Carl Randall; *Scenery*: Stewart Chaney; *Costumes*: Irene Sharaff; *Lighting*: Uncredited; *Musical Direction*: Jacob Schwartzdorf

Cast: Carol Renee (Child), Joan Shepherd (Child), Edwin Bruce Moldow (Child), Richard Huey (Old Henry), Oscar Polk (Aristide), Ainsworth Arnold (Gabriel Gervais), Ivy Scott (Mother Gervais), Bob Lawrence (Jean Gervais), Donald Clark (Jim), George Holmes (Harry), Gordon Dilworth (Emil), Vicki Charles (Emma), Ethel Levey (Lolita), Dudley Clements (George Marshall), Frederic Persson (Judge Pepe Martineau), Muriel Angelus (Marie Sauvinet), Tom Ewell (Daniel Marshall), Helen Claire (Cecile Marshall), Byron Mulligan (Watchman), Joan Roberts (Madeline Caresse), Peggy Alexander (Martha), Jack Riano (Harlequin), Miriam LaVelle (Columbine), William O'Neal (Achille Caresse), Howard Freeman (The Drunk), Kenneth Tobey (The Doctor); Ladies: Barbara Barton, Henni Brooks, Betty Gilpatrick, Lodema Legg, Gwen Mann, Ann Morlowe, Helen Marshall, Mariquita Moll, May Muth, Ethel Taylor, Stephanie Turash, Helen Wagner; Gentlemen: James Allison, Jay Amiss, Russ Anderson, Alfredo Costello, Edward Dunbar, William Hearne, William Hogue, Philip Jones, John Marshall, Byron Mulligan, Robert Ormiston, Fred Peronne, Michael Sigel, Roy Williams, Buddy Worth

The musical was presented in two acts.

The action takes place in New Orleans in 1806, 1811, and 1815.

Musical Numbers

Act One: "Pictorial Overture" (aka "Symphonic Pantomime") (Ensemble); "My Girl and I" (Bob Lawrence); "Call It a Dream" (Muriel Angelus, Ensemble); "It Can Happen to Anyone" (Muriel Angelus, Ensemble); "The Butterflies and Bees" (aka "Observe the Bee") (Tom Ewell, Vicki Charles, Ethel Levey, Dudley Clements, Frederic Persson); "Along the Winding Road" (Muriel Angelus, Bob Lawrence); Finaletto (Muriel Angelus, Ethel Levey, Tom Ewell, Vicki Charles, Ensemble); Interlude; "Bundling" (Tom Ewell); "Along the Winding Road" (reprise) (Bob Lawrence); "Can You Sing?" (Muriel Angelus, Ensemble); "Making Conversation" (Muriel Angelus, Helen Claire, Ensemble); "Poem" (spoken by Helen Claire); "The Butterflies and Bees" (reprise) (Tom Ewell, Joan Roberts); "Let Me Live Today" (Muriel Angelus, Bob Lawrence, Ensemble)

Act Two: Entr'acte (Orchestra); "Bow-Legged Sal" (aka "Bow-Legged Gal") (Ensemble); "Sunny River" (Ethel Levey, Ensemble); "Call It a Dream" (reprise) (Muriel Angelus, Ensemble); "The Duello" (William O'Neal, Tom Ewell); "She Got Him" (Joan Roberts, Vicki Charles, William O'Neal, Tom Ewell, Ensemble); "My Girl and I" (reprise) (Bob Lawrence); "Time Is Standing Still" (Muriel Angelus, Bob Lawrence); "Let Me Live Today" (reprise) (Bob Lawrence, Muriel Angelus, Male Ensemble); Finaletto (Bob Lawrence, Howard Freeman); Finale Ultimo (Muriel Angelus, Helen Claire, Ethel Levey)

Oscar Hammerstein II and Sigmund Romberg's operetta *Sunny River* couldn't hold back the waters of critical apathy and shuttered after just thirty-six performances. Perhaps a star performer and a popular song would have helped, but maybe not. The musical was creaky in an old-hat genteel operetta style and probably didn't have much chance when up against the current rowdy Broadway world of **Panama Hattie** and **Sons o' Fun** and the ultra-elegant and modern **Lady in the Dark**.

The story took place in the New Orleans of the early nineteenth century, and centered on Marie Sauvinet (Muriel Angelus), who sings in a bordello run by Lolita (Ethel Levey, who had once been married to George M. Cohan and had appeared with him in a few earlier musicals, but hadn't been on Broadway since 1922). Marie and lawyer Jean Gervais (Bob Lawrence) are in love, but he's tricked ("by an antique lie," according to John Mason Brown in the *New York World-Telegram*) into marriage by the wealthy and scheming Cecile Marshall (Helen Claire). So Marie goes off to Europe and becomes a celebrated opera star. When she triumphantly returns to New Orleans, she and Bob fall in love all over again. But the War of 1812 rears its ugly head, and Bob is killed in an offstage Battle of New Orleans. At the final curtain, Marie and Cecile share their grief as well as Bob's sword and sash. For comic relief, Tom Ewell, a decade away from his breakthrough role as the hapless husband in *The Seven Year Itch*, played Cecile's randy brother Daniel. In another supporting performance was Joan Roberts, who created the role of Laurey in Oscar Hammerstein II's next musical, **Oklahoma!**

Brown said it would be an "understatement" to say the new musical "depressed" him. It was a "giant bore" of operetta clichés, of which he cataloged many of his dislikes: lovers torn apart by fate; "low comics" with predictable "wheezes" of jokes; atmospheric crowds of villagers and guests; "thumping" dancers of chorus boys trying to "be more male" than Ernest Hemingway; older characters "who get too gay"; jokes "tasteless as chalk"; "ridiculous" song cues; and "amorous" duets of lyrical and musical "maple sugar."

Wilella Waldorf in the *New York Post* found Hammerstein's book "stuffy and stilted" with "clumsy" direction, "mild" comedy, and little dancing. The evening's humor was relegated to one character saying, "Where have you been keeping yourself?" and the other replying, "What makes you think I've been keeping myself?" As for the great "Negro comedian" Oscar Polk, he was "completely wasted" (Waldorf reported that during the evening she had a "merry time" remembering Polk's performances in other productions). (Polk had also appeared in *Gone with the Wind*, in which he played the role of Pork.)

Richard Watts in the *New York Herald Tribune* said the evening was "weary," "dull," and "commonplace" with "conventional and synthetic" music; Louis Kronenberger in *PM* found the plot "terribly long-winded"; Burns Mantle in the *New York Daily News* said the story was "stupid"; Richard Lockridge in the *New York Sun* found the evening "reasonably coherent and pleasantly written," but felt the show lacked humor and "catchy" tunes; and John Anderson in the *New York Journal-American* said that while the stage burst with "splurging opulence," the work itself was just a "journeyman job" which was "synthetic and uninspired."

Brooks Atkinson in the *New York Times* said the musical was "workmanlike," and although it paid a "duty call on entertainment" it wasn't "really interested." Although he singled out a few songs (such as "Can You Sing It?," which had "genuine spirit," and the title number, "an excellent carnival tune"), he felt the music was for the most part "ponderous and pedestrian." But like one or two other critics, he was pleased with the unusual overture; while the orchestra played, the stage revealed the players pantomiming a promenade "along a watercolor street" in their "Delta finery."

As *New Orleans*, the musical had premiered at the Municipal Theatre Association of St. Louis (The Muny) on June 5, 1941, and was later seen in New Haven prior to the New York run. By the time the musical reached Broadway, its three acts had been compressed into two and there were major revisions in the plot. For the Muny engagement, the story took place during the 1850s and 1860s, and Jean was a defender of civil rights. A number of songs were cut during the pre-Broadway engagements, including: "Eleven Levee Street," "Lordy" (aka "Lordy, What a Sweet World!"), "When a Lark Learns to Fly," "Introduction into the Louisiana Lawyers' Club," "The Night Will Seem Long Ago," "The Men Are in the Dining Room," and "Let's Play We're Having Fun." Not used were "Doctors of Law" (an early version of the "Louisiana Lawyers' Club"), "Us Is Going to Have Us a Time," "What Makes You the Best?," "Nature Studies," "Her Name Was May," "For You," "I Don't Think of You as an Angel," and "Part of Me." All the lyrics for the used, cut, and unused songs are included in *The Complete Lyrics of Oscar Hammerstein II*; the collection also offers the lyrics of "Y'Better Not" and "I'm in Love with You," which reportedly were written for a proposed film version of the musical.

Despite its short Broadway run, *Sunny River* was produced in London on August 18, 1943, at the Piccadilly Theatre for two months. The cast included Evelyn Laye (Marie), Dennis Noble (Jean), Ena Burrill (Cecile), Edith Day (Lolita), and Don Avory (Daniel), and two songs were added ("Somebody Ought to Be Told" and "Madam") and one ("Eleven Levee Street") was reinstated into the score. "Somebody Ought to Be Told" had first been heard in Hammerstein and Romberg's 1935 Broadway musical *May Wine*; it's unclear if "Madam" was a new song or a revised version of an earlier one.

The collection *Oscar Hammerstein Revisited* (Painted Smiles CD # PSCD-136) includes "Eleven Levee Street" and "Along the Winding Road"; and the collection *Deep in My Heart/The Songs of Sigmund Romberg* (Living Era CD # CD-AJA-5642) includes "Lordy, What a Sweet World!"

BANJO EYES
"THE NEW MUSICAL COMEDY" / "AMERICA'S FAVORITE COMEDIAN IN HIS MOST SPECTACULAR MUSICAL COMEDY"

Theatre: Hollywood Theatre
Opening Date: December 25, 1941; *Closing Date*: April 12, 1942
Performances: 126

Book: Joe Quillan and Izzy Elinson
Lyrics: John LaTouche; additional lyrics by Harold Adamson
Music: Vernon Duke
Based on the 1935 play *Three Men on a Horse* by John Cecil Holm and George Abbott.
Direction: Staged by Hassard Short and "book directed" by Albert Lewis; *Producer*: Albert Lewis; *Choreography*: Charles Walters; *Scenery*: Harry Horner; *Costumes*: Irene Sharaff; *Lighting*: Hassard Short; *Musical Direction*: Ray Sinatra
Cast: Jacqueline Susann (Miss Clark), E. J. Blunkall (Mr. Carver), *Eddie Cantor* (Erwin Trowbridge), June Clyde (Sally Trowbridge), Richard Rober (Harry), Bill Johnson (Charlie), Virginia Mayo (Ginger), Sally and Tony De Marco (The De Marcos), Lionel Stander (Patsy), Ray Mayer (Frankie), Audrey Christie (Mabel), Tommy Wonder (Tommy), John Ervin (The General), James Farrell (The Captain), Ronnie Cunningham (The Filly), Nomi Morton and Virginia Mayo (Banjo Eyes); Dancing Trio: Lynn, Royce, and Vanya; Gloria Gilbert (specialty dancer); The Quartette: George Richmond, Phil Schafer, Doug Hawkins, George Lovesee; The Singing Show Girls: Ann Graham, Linda Griffeth, Adele Jurgens, Doris Kent, Florence Foster, Miriam Gwinn, Helene Hudson, Sherry Shadburne, Shirl Thomas; Dancing Girls: Betty Boyce, Norma Brown, Pamela Clifford, Kay Coulter, Doris Dowling, Kate Friedlich, Peggy Holmes, Mitzi Haynes, Leona Olsen, June Reynolds, Tina Rigat, Puddy Smith, Margie Young, Mimi Walthers, Evelyn Weiss, Audrey Westphal, Virginia Howe; Boys: Ray Arnett, Clark Eggleston, Arthur Grahl, Ray Harrison, Dick Irving, Ray Johnson, Rayford Malone, Jack Nagle, Remi Martell, John McCord, Bill (William) Skipper, Ray Weamer, Carl Eberle, Lynn Malone, Joseph Malvin
The musical was presented in two acts.
The action takes place in and around New York City.

Musical Numbers

Act One: "Opening" (E. J. Blunkall, Girls and Boys); The Greeting Cards—"Birthday Card" (Helene Hudson, Sherry Shadburne, Shirl Thomas); "Valentine's Day Card" (Bill Bailey); "Easter Greetings" (Linda Griffeth); "Merry Christmas" (George Richmond, Phil Schafer, Doug Hawkins, George Lovesee); and "Mother's Day" (Florence Foster); "I'll Take the City" (Eddie Cantor, Boys and Girls); "The Toast of the Boys at the Post" (lyric and music by George Sumner) (Audrey Christie, George Richmond, Phil Schafer, Doug Hawkins, George Lovesee); "I've Got to Hand It to You" (Tommy Wonder, Dancers); "A Nickel to My Name" (Bill Johnson, George Richmond, Phil Schafer, Doug Hawkins, George Lovesee); Dance (The De Marcos); "Who Started the Rhumba?" (Eddie Cantor, Virginia and Morton Mayo, Ensemble); Dance (Ronnie Cunningham); "It Could Only Happen in the Movies" (lyric by Harold Adamson) (Eddie Cantor, Audrey Christie)

Act Two: "Make with the Feet" (lyric by Harold Adamson) (Audrey Christie, The De Marcos); Dance (Lynn, Royce, Vanya); "We're Having a Baby" (lyric by Harold Adamson) (Eddie Cantor, June Clyde); "Banjo Eyes" (Ensemble); Dance (Gloria Gilbert); "We Did It Before and We'll Do It Again" (James Farrell, Boys); "Not a Care in the World" (Bill Johnson, Ensemble); Dance (The De Marcos); Eddie Cantor Medley (Eddie Cantor); Finale (Entire Company)

Like Al Jolson's **Hold on to Your Hats**, *Banjo Eyes* was an Event. For here was musical comedy legend Eddie Cantor returning to the New York stage for the first time since 1928, when he had starred in the hit musical *Whoopee*. Like Jolson's musical, Cantor's vehicle promised to be a long-running hit, but, like Jolson, Cantor's health (and perhaps the cold New York weather) forced him to leave the musical and head back home to California. So *Banjo Eyes* was gone in less than four months.

Banjo Eyes was Vernon Duke and John LaTouche's first musical since **Cabin in the Sky** had opened during the previous season. The team had the distinction of seeing two of their musicals open back to back during the 1941–1942 season: a few days after the premiere of *Banjo Eyes*, their troubled **The Lady Comes Across** opened and quickly closed after three performances. But both scores offered an array of pleasant songs, and over the years many have been recorded.

Despite Cantor's startling brown-button eyes, he didn't play the title role of Banjo Eyes, who was in fact a horse that was portrayed by the team of Mayo and Morton (that is, Virginia Mayo and Nomi Morton, who played both ends of the horse). As the Mayo Brothers, Morton and Virginia's brother-in-law Andy Mayo specialized in portraying horses on the vaudeville circuit while Virginia played their stooge (under her maiden name of Virginia Jones); when Virginia stepped in as part of the horse act, she changed her last name to Mayo so the team's name of Mayo and Morton could continue. Within a year after the closing of *Banjo Eyes*, she made her first film, and for the next two decades made over three dozen movies, including a leading role in the Oscar-winning Best Picture *The Best Years of Our Lives* (1946) and two films opposite Ronald Reagan, *The Girl from Jones Beach* (1949) and *She's Working Her Way Through College* (1952).

Based on the 1935 Broadway hit *Three Men on a Horse*, *Banjo Eyes* centered on meek and mild greeting-card-verse-writer Erwin Trowbridge (Cantor), who has the uncanny knack of picking the winning horse (but only if he himself doesn't place any bets). In a delightful conceit, the musical created the horse characters of Banjo Eyes and Filly (the latter played by Ronnie Cunningham), and in colorful Disney-like sequences Erwin meets the horses in "dream pastures" where they give him inside tips on the winning horses.

The critics weren't particularly bowled over by the score, but it yielded two eventual standards. Cantor's slightly sly "We're Having a Baby" was a delightful number in his "Makin' Whoopee" mode, and it found television immortality when Desi Arnaz (as Ricky Ricardo) sang it to Lucy (Lucille Ball) in a memorable television episode of *I Love Lucy*. And the jubilant jamboree "Not a Care in the World" is old-time Broadway razz-ma-tazz at its best (the song was later interpolated into the 1964 Off-Broadway revival of **Cabin in the Sky**).

Brooks Atkinson in the *New York Times* welcomed "very funny fellow" Eddie Cantor back to Broadway, saying the "uproarious" clown was an "excellent man" for a laugh and a "good time," and noted *Banjo Eyes* was "just" the show to "stretch around him." Atkinson praised Duke's "vibrant score of metallic music" and LaTouche's "witty handsprings for lyrics," and singled out "We're Having a Baby" and "I'll Take the City." Burns Mantle in the *New York Daily News* said the musical was "expansive and lavish," the score "lively," and the costumes "striking"; and he liked Hassard Short's "nice" turntable effects and "effective" lighting. He also praised the dance sequences: the trio Lynn, Royce, and Vanya's cleverly combined adagio with "a Hartman touch of burlesque"; Gloria Gilbert provided "faster whirls on a single toe" than anyone he'd ever seen; and The De Marcos (Tony, with his new wife and dancing partner Sally) offered traditional ballroom dancing.

Richard Watts in the *New York Herald Tribune* said Cantor was in the "great tradition" of musical comedy performers, and although the show itself wasn't "exceptional" it was nonetheless a "nice, lively carnival" with "agreeable, rather than distinguished" songs; Wilella Waldorf in the *New York Post* said the show had all the requisite "musical comedy fixings," but it was first and foremost Cantor's show "from start to finish"; and John Mason Brown in the *New York World-Telegram* liked the "remarkable" Cantor but said the "opulently staged" evening was "militantly routine."

John Anderson in the *New York Journal-American* was glad to see the "national institution" back on Broadway, but felt the "opulent" and "lovely and spectacular" musical didn't quite celebrate Cantor as well as it should; and while Louis Kronenberger in *PM* noted that with Cantor back on Broadway it was an "old-fashioned Christmas," he noted the "lively and entertaining enough" evening was nonetheless "a bad show but not a dull one."

Richard Lockridge in the *New York Sun* said *Banjo Eyes* offered "routine lavishness" and could best be described as a show that "needs" Eddie Cantor; he noted that the producers probably thought Eddie would "be enough to satisfy anybody and, come to think of it, I guess he is."

During the tryout, "Don't Let It Happen Again" was cut; songs dropped in preproduction were "Hush-a-Bye Land," "I Always Think of Sally," "Leave My Women Alone," "My Song without Words," and "What Every Young Man Should Know" (the latter surfaced briefly during the tryout of Duke and LaTouche's **The Lady Comes Across**, but was cut prior to the Broadway opening).

Like Jolson in **Hold On to Your Hats**, Cantor also sang some of his old songs toward the end of the show. In blackface, he serenaded the audience with such favorites as "April Showers" (added for the tour of *Bombo*, 1921; lyric by B. G. [Buddy] De Sylva, music by Louis Silvers); "Ida, Sweet as Apple Cider" (lyric and music by Eddie Leonard and Eddie Munson); "Margie" (interpolated into *Broadway Brevities of 1920*; lyric by Benny Davis, music by Con Conrad and J. Russel Robinson); "If You Knew Susie" (interpolated into *Kid Boots*, 1923; lyric by B. G. [Buddy] De Sylva, music by Joseph Meyer); and "Makin' Whoopee" (*Whoopee*, 1928; lyric by Gus Kahn, music by Walter Donaldson).

At least one source indicates "We Did It Before and We'll Do It Again" (lyric by Charles Tobias, music by Cliff Friend) was added to the show during its run, but two critics (Kronenberger and Waldorf) referenced the song in their opening night reviews (the number was later dropped from the production). Another source states "The Yanks Are on the March Again" was never heard in the show, but a program from late in the run lists this song in the spot where "We Did It Before" had been performed.

Note that future best-selling author Jacqueline Susann was in the cast of *Banjo Eyes*; throughout the first half of the decade her name would occasionally pop up in chorus and featured roles of the era's musicals. In 1946, she and Beatrice Cole cowrote the comedy *Lovely Me*, which briefly played on Broadway (see appendix F for "Other Productions").

Besides "We're Having a Baby" and "Not a Care in the World," other numbers that have surfaced from the score have proven delightful. The collection *Harold Arlen and Vernon Duke Revisited Volume II* (Painted Smiles PSCD-127) includes "I'll Take the City"; *Vernon Duke Revisited Volume III* (Painted Smiles PSCD-147) offers "Make with the Feet"; and "Not a Care in the World" is included in Richard Rodney Bennett's *Take Love Easy: The Lyrics of John LaTouche* (Audiophile Records LP # AP-206), which also has songs from **Cabin in the Sky**, **The Lady Comes Across**, *Polonaise*, **Beggar's Holiday**, and *The Golden Apple* (1954).

Twenty years after the opening of *Banjo Eyes*, there was a second musical adaptation of *Three Men on a Horse. Let It Ride!* opened at the Eugene O'Neill Theatre on October 12, 1961, for sixty-eight performances with a cast that included George Gobel (Erwin), Sam Levene (as Patsy, the role he created in the original 1935 production of the comedy), and Barbara Nichols. The tuneful if mostly unappreciated score (which included the show-stopping choral number for cops titled "Just an Honest Mistake" and the brassy ballad "Love, Let Me Know") was by Jay Livingston and Ray Evans, who a few weeks before the opening of *Banjo Eyes* had contributed songs to the hit revue **Sons o' Fun**.

THE LADY COMES ACROSS
"A NEW MUSICAL COMEDY"

Theatre: 44th Street Theatre
Opening Date: January 9, 1942; *Closing Date*: January 10, 1942
Performances: 3
Book: Fred Thompson and Dawn Powell
Lyrics: John LaTouche
Music: Vernon Duke
Direction: Book directed by Romney Brent and production supervised by Morrie Ryskind; *Producers*: George Hale in association with Charles R. Rogers and Nelson Seabra; *Choreography*: George Balanchine; *Scenery* and *Costumes*: Stewart Chaney; *Lighting*: Uncredited; *Musical Direction*: Jacques Rabiroff
Cast: Evelyn Wyckoff (Jill Charters), Ronald Graham (Tony Patterson), Joe E. Lewis (Otis Kibber), Morton L. Stevens (Elmer James), Betty Douglas (Mary), Stiano Braggiotti (Alberto Zorel), Four Shoppers: The Martins (Hugh Martin, Ralph Blane, Phyllis Rogers, Jo Jean Rogers); Ruth Weston (Mrs. Riverdale), Gower Champion (Campbell), Jeanne Tyler (Kay), Wynn Murray (Babs Appleway), Mischa Auer (Ernie Bustard), Helen Windsor (Baroness Helstrom), Eugenia Delarova (Ballerina Comique), Lubov Rostova (Ballerina), Marc Platt (The Phantom Lover); Models: Betty Douglas, Evelyn Carmel, Patricia Donnelly, Judith Ford, Dorothy Partington, Arline Harvey, Joan Smith, Drucilla Strain; Dancing Ensemble: Betty Apple, Mary Ann Crawford, Betty De Elmo, June Graham, Babs (Barbara) Heath, Phyllis Hill, Bettilu Ismailoff, Hortense Kharklin, Lorraine Latham, Edith Loumer, Claire Loring, Marian Lulling, Marjorie Moore, Elise Reiman, Aleen Stuart, Olga Suarez, Dorothy Thomas, Clarence Jaeger, Joseph Johnson, Roy Marshall, Bob Norris, Harry Pedersen, Peter Kite Smith, Zachary Solov, Ken Whelan
The musical was presented in two acts.
The action takes place in New York and a nearby estate.

Musical Numbers

Act One: "Three Rousing Cheers" (Souvenir Hunters, Autograph Seekers, Reporters, Others); "Feeling Lucky Today" (Evelyn Wyckoff, Joe E. Lewis); "Modes in Manhattan" (Models, Photographers); "You Took Me by Surprise" (Evelyn Wyckoff, Ronald Graham, The Martins); "Hit the Ramp" (Wynn Miller, Mischa Auer, Ensemble); "February" (lyric and music by Danny Shapiro, Jerry Seelen, and Lester Lee) (Joe E.

Lewis); "Eenie Meenie Minee Mo" (Mischa Auer, Wynn Miller, Joe E. Lewis, Ruth Weston); Tango (Mischa Auer, Eugenia Delarova, Ensemble); Reprise (song unknown) (Evelyn Wyckoff, Joe E. Lewis, Mischa Auer, Ensemble)

Act Two: "Lady" (Ronald Graham, The Models, Gower Champion, Jeanne Tyler, Ensemble); "The Queen of the Opera" (Ruth Weston); "Coney Island Ballet" (Ballerinas, Premiere Danseur, Ensemble); "This Is Where I Came In" (Wynn Miller, Gower Champion, Jeanne Tyler); "You Can't Get the Merchandise" (lyric and music by Danny Shapiro and Lester Lee) (Joe E. Lewis); "Summer Is a Comin' In" (The Martins, Ensemble); "Daybreak" (Evelyn Wyckoff, Marc Platt); Reprise

For years, hopes were high that British musical comedy star Jessie Matthews might one day team with Fred Astaire in a movie or return to Broadway in a musical (her most recent New York visit had been in Cole Porter's 1929 revue *Wake Up and Dream* in which she introduced "I Loved Him, but He Didn't Love Me"). She had also starred in Richard Rodgers and Lorenz Hart's 1930 London musical *Ever Green*, in which she and Sonnie Hale introduced the classic "Dancing on the Ceiling" and the delightful, almost art-deco piece of nonchalance "Dear! Dear!" (she and Hale also appeared in the 1934 film version).

A film with Matthews and Astaire never materialized, but in 1941 the lady came across the pond to America for her first Broadway book musical. Sadly, and despite some attractive songs by Vernon Duke, *The Lady Comes Across* was doomed from the beginning and had the shortest run of any of the season's musicals.

The musical's ramshackle book had been written around the left-over scenery from **She Had to Say Yes**, which had closed a year earlier during its pre-Broadway engagement in Philadelphia. Since that musical's sets had included scenes representing a chic fashion salon, a railroad station, a park, an estate, and a bedroom on the estate, the new musical necessarily had to ensure its story utilized the preexisting settings. There also must have been some trappings left over from a Coney Island scene, because Raoul Alba staged a "Coney Island Ballet" for **She Had to Say Yes**, and George Balanchine choreographed a "Coney Island Ballet" for *The Lady Comes Across*.

Further, Jessie Matthews wasn't in physical or emotional shape to perform in the show (she reportedly had a serious case of nerves brought on by the London Blitz), and so just days before the Broadway opening she was succeeded by Evelyn Wyckoff in the title role. Wyckoff had been seen in a supporting role in **Lady in the Dark**, and the replacement was so last-minute that the opening night program, which featured Wyckoff, also included an advertisement for the musical that touted Matthews as the show's star.

Like Liza in **Lady in the Dark** and Erwin in **Banjo Eyes**, Jill Charters (Wyckoff) has musical-comedy dreams. In her case, she dreams of being a U.S. secret agent for the FBI who ingeniously foils a Nazi plot. Sure enough, her dreams come true when she becomes involved with saboteurs, and she uses the clues in her dreams to uncover Fifth Column activities (a key plot point dealt with important and revealing "papers" which were hidden in the girdle of rich society matron Mrs. Riverdale, played by Ruth Weston). The story also found time for songs and comic shtick by popular nightclub comedian Joe E. Lewis (as Otis Kibber), film comedian Mischa Auer (as Ernie Bustard), and stalwart Broadway leading man Ronald Graham (not to be confused with Ronny Graham, who is best remembered for various *New Faces* and Off-Broadway revues of the 1950s) as Tony Patterson, Jill's love interest. If all this weren't enough, Auer had a drag scene, singer Wynn Murray was around for a song or two, The Martins supplied close-harmony vocalizing, Gower (Champion) and Jeanne (Tyler) presented ballroom-styled dances, and George Balanchine's troupe (with Marc Platt, formerly Marc Platoff) offered a few elaborate dance sequences. Platt played the Phantom Lover in Jill's dreams, and little more than a year later created the dancing role of the Dream Curly in **Oklahoma!**

Among Balanchine's contributions was a spoof of serious ballet. Wilella Waldorf in the *New York Post* thought the latter was "somewhat confused" and suggested it was better to just let ballet "go right on burlesquing itself," and Richard Watts in the *New York Herald Tribune* echoed her sentiments, saying he often couldn't tell "the humorous from the serious" when he attended the ballet. Richard Lockridge in the *New York Sun* liked a "fine, strange ballet" involving cats and black figures with umbrellas; John Anderson in the *New York Journal-American* enjoyed the surreal dances that depicted the heroine's dreams; and although Louis Kronenberger in *PM* praised the evening's earlier "light and imaginative" dances, he felt a later "pony-ballet extravaganza" was "too arty." Burns Mantle in the *New York Daily News* liked most of Balanchine's contributions, but thought the "Coney Island Ballet" was "pretty sad." Brooks Atkinson in the *New York Times* said Balanchine drained the "joy" from musical comedy dancing, and when his creations didn't resemble "intellectual persiflage" they took on "quotations from the 'Book of the Dead.'"

All the critics singled out three interpolations brought to the show by Joe E. Lewis: "February" (a lament for the short-changed month); "You Can't Get the Merchandise" (a slightly naughty laundry list of items that are hard to find because of the war); and "The H.V. Kaltenborn Blues" (an ode to the famous radio commentator). Although the first two were listed in the opening night program, the third wasn't (but four of the critics singled it out).

Ruth Weston had the curious and somewhat peripheral role of a society matron who doesn't know that the "papers" are hidden in her girdle; her big number was "The Queen of the Opera," a lament in which she admits she's a patron of the Met who hates opera.

Gower (Champion) and Jeanne (Tyler) received good reviews, but Waldorf complained that their routines involved small-talk conversation that took away from the pleasure of their dancing. For their next Broadway appearance (in **Count Me In**) they continued with lighthearted banter during their dances, and Waldorf again took them to task. The team appeared in a total of three Broadway musicals (the first was The Streets of Paris in 1939).

Atkinson found Wyckoff "enchanting"; John Mason Brown in the *New York World-Telegram* said she "agreeably" carried off her "difficult assignment"; and while Waldorf said she had no "bombshell personality," her material was such that the combination of Ethel Merman, Vera Zorina, and Katharine Cornell couldn't have salvaged it. Hollywood's Mischa Auer received mostly poor or indifferent notices; Watts found him lacking, and Atkinson said he spread "a canopy of dullness" in his scenes. But Waldorf said that in his drag scene he sprinted, leaped into the air, and kicked his heels, something she hadn't seen "since the days of the Keystone Cops."

Anderson felt the musical might have succeeded had a "lavish use" of scissors been applied to the book and the ballets, and suggested the show had "been taken off the assembly line too soon." He complained about "dat ole debbil book," and perhaps it all proved too much for him because he noted Ronald Graham had been one of the "redeeming features" of the previous month's **Sunny River** (only Graham was never in **Sunny River**).

Although Lockridge noted the evening offered a "good many plums," he felt the evening's overall effect suggested that the creators had worked "in separate and probably sound-proof rooms, each ignorant of the activities of the others"; Kronenberger said "the lady runs aground"; Mantle described the score as "'cold' Porter"; Watts found the show "mediocre"; and Brown said the evening was often "just one jump ahead" of the typical Hasty Pudding, Mask and Wig, and Princeton Triangle shows.

For **All in Fun**, poor Wynn Murray had been criticized for losing too much weight, and here a year later the critics were still carping about her diet. Anderson noted the "once ample" singer now had a "reduced" role "in line with her personal reduction," and Atkinson said she had recaptured some of her "old aplomb" (after her "shocking slenderizing") with "tolerable vigor" and suggested that next season she'd be "rolling" out songs with "complete gusto" if she kept on "feeding well."

During the tryout, the following songs were dropped: "Prairie Belle," "Upsala," "Let's Talk about the Weather," and "What Every Young Man Should Know." The latter had been written for, but not used in, Duke and LaTouche's **Banjo Eyes**, which had opened on Broadway a few days before the premiere of **The Lady Comes Across**.

Despite its obscurity and its reputation as one of the worst musicals of the decade, a surprising number of songs have been recorded from the musical, and they're all charming. The rather dark and intriguing "Lady" is included in the collection *Vernon Duke Revisited* (Painted Smiles CD # PSCD-138); *Harold Arlen and Vernon Duke Revisited Volume II* (Painted Smiles CD # PSCD-127) includes "This Is Where I Came In," "You Took Me by Surprise," and the deleted "Let's Talk about the Weather"; and Klea Blackhurst's *Autumn in New York: Vernon Duke's Broadway* (Ghostlight CD # 79155833022) offers "You Took Me by Surprise," which is also included in Richard Rodney Bennett's *Take Love Easy: The Lyrics of John LaTouche* (Audiophile Records LP # AP-206). As "Summer Is Icumen In," "Summer Is a Comin' In" was included in the 1956 Off-Broadway revue *The Littlest Revue* and can be heard on the cast album, which was originally released by Epic (LP # 3275) and later by Painted Smiles (CD # PSCD-112).

During the era, **Hairpin Harmony** and **Louisiana Lady** also borrowed scenery from earlier flops, and like *The Lady Comes Across* they too met with instant failure.

PORGY AND BESS

Theatre: Majestic Theatre
Opening Date: January 22, 1942; *Closing Date*: September 26, 1942
Performances: 286
Book: DuBose Heyward
Lyrics: DuBose Heyward and Ira Gershwin
Music: George Gershwin
Based on the 1927 play *Porgy* by Dorothy and DuBose Heyward (which in turn had been adapted from DuBose Heyward's 1925 novel *Porgy*).
Direction: Robert Ross; *Producer*: Cheryl Crawford; *Scenery*: Herbert Andrews; *Costumes*: Costumes supervised by Paul du Pont; *Lighting*: Uncredited; *Choral Direction*: Eva Jessye; *Musical Direction*: Alexander Smallens
Cast: Georgette Harvey (Maria), Helen Dowdy (Lily, Strawberry Woman), Catherine Ayers (Annie), Harriett Jackson (Clara), Edward Matthews (Jake), Avon Long (Sportin' Life), Jimmy Waters (Mingo), Henry Davis (Robbins), Ruby Elzy (Serena), Jack Carr (Jim), Robert Ecton (Peter), Todd Duncan (Porgy), Warren Coleman (Crown), Anne Brown (Bess), William Richardson (First Policeman), Paul du Pont (Second Policeman), Gibbs Penrose (Detective), John Garth (Undertaker), J. Rosamund Johnson (Nelson), William Woolfolk (Crab Man), Al West (Coroner); Residents of Catfish Row, Fishermen, Children, Stevedores, etc.: The Eva Jessye Choir—Eva Jessye, Lillian Cowan, Gladys Goode, June Hawkins, Louisa Howard, Alma Hubbard, Rosalie King, Assotta Marshall, Sadie McGill, Annabelle Ross, Musa Williams, John Diggs, Leslie Gray, Jerry Laws, Arthur MacLean, William McDaniel, William Smith, Charles Welch, Lawrence Whisonant; Children: Harvey McGill, Granville Williams, Lorraine Williams, Rosalie King, Naida King, Osbert Chevers
The opera was presented in three acts.
The action takes place in Catfish Row, Charleston, South Carolina, and on nearby Kittiwah Island (the original Broadway production's program indicated the time was "the recent past").

Musical Numbers

Act One: "Summer Time" (lyric by DuBose Heyward) (Harriett Jackson); "A Woman Is a Sometime Thing" (lyric by DuBose Heyward) (Edward Matthews, Ensemble); "They Pass by Singing" ("Entrance of Porgy") (lyric by DuBose Heyward) (Todd Duncan); "Crap Game Fugue" (lyric by DuBose Heyward) (Harriett Jackson, Ensemble); "Gone, Gone, Gone!" (lyric by DuBose Heyward) (Ensemble); "Overflow" (lyric by DuBose Heyward) (Ensemble); "My Man's Gone Now" (lyric by DuBose Heyward) (Ruby Elzy, Ensemble); "Leavin' fo' de Promis' Lan'" (Anne Brown, Ensemble)

Act Two: "It Takes a Long Pull to Get There" (lyric by Dubose Heyward) (Edward Matthews, Fishermen); "I Got Plenty o' Nuttin'" (lyric by Ira Gershwin and DuBose Heyward) (Todd Duncan); "Woman to Lady" (lyric by DuBose Heyward) (Todd Duncan, Anne Brown, A. Rosamund Johnson, Ensemble); "Bess, You Is My Woman Now" (lyric by DuBose Heyward and Ira Gershwin) (Todd Duncan, Anne Brown); "Oh, I Can't Sit Down" (lyric by Ira Gershwin) (Orphan Band, Ensemble); "It Ain't Necessarily So" (lyric by Ira Gershwin) (Avon Long, Ensemble); "What You Want with Bess?" (lyric by DuBose Heyward) (Warren Coleman, Anne Brown); "Time and Time Again" (lyric by DuBose Heyward) (Ruby Elzy, Ensemble); "Street Cries" (lyric by DuBose Heyward) (Helen Dowdy, William Woolfolk); "I Loves You, Porgy" (lyric by Ira Gershwin and DuBose Heyward) (Todd Duncan, Anne Brown); "Oh, de Lawd Shake de Heaven" (lyric by DuBose Heyward) (Ensemble); "A Red-Headed Woman" (lyric by Ira Gershwin) (Warren Coleman, Ensemble); "Oh, Doctor Jesus" (lyric by DuBose Heyward) (Principals, Ensemble)

Act Three: "Clara, Don't You Be So Downhearted" (lyric by Dubose Heyward) (Ensemble); "There's a Boat That's Leavin' Soon for New York" (lyric by Ira Gershwin) (Avon Long, Anne Brown); "Where's My Bess?" (lyric by Ira Gershwin) (Todd Duncan); "I'm On My Way" (lyric by DuBose Heyward) (Todd Duncan, Ensemble)

As of this writing, George Gershwin's masterpiece *Porgy and Bess* has been revived in New York sixteen times; including its original run, the work has enjoyed a total of 1,376 New York performances, a record for an American opera. Set in the environs of Charleston's Catfish Row and nearby Kittiwah Island, the folk-like story has taken on a mythic quality with its story of the crippled Porgy who against all odds and reason loves the selfish and sluttish Bess. When the demonic Sportin' Life seduces her with drugs and the promise of the "high life" in New York, she abandons Porgy without a qualm. With only a cart pulled by a goat, Porgy sets off from Charleston to New York to find her. Despite the soaring hopefulness of "I'm On My Way," one assumes Porgy is off on a futile quest which will only lead to more unhappiness and frustration for him.

The opera's world premiere took place at the Colonial Theatre in Boston, Massachusetts, on September 30, 1935, and the Broadway production opened on October 10 at the Alvin (now Neil Simon) Theatre for 124 performances. The current 1942 revival more than doubled the run of the original production with 286 showings, and for a time held the record for the longest-running New York revival of a musical. The opera returned to New York the following year for a showing of 24 performances, and in 1944 tallied up a total of 64 performances in two slightly separated engagements. The 1953 revival played for 350 performances with LeVern Hutcherson, Leontyne Price, and Cab Calloway in the leading roles, and still holds the record for the longest-running New York production of the work; this version restored cuts made to productions following the original version, and added about twenty minutes of music that heretofore hadn't been used in any of the previous productions. The opera was then seen at City Center four times (in 1961 for 16 performances; 1962, 6 performances; 1964, 17 performances; and 1965, 6 performances); the first three revivals were produced by the New York City Center Light Opera Company and the latter by the New York City Opera Company.

In 1976, the Houston Grand Opera's production opened on Broadway at the Uris (now Gershwin) Theatre for 122 performances, and in 1983 another revival was seen at Radio City Music Hall for 45 performances. On February 5, 1985, the work was produced for the first time by the Metropolitan Opera Company, and has since been revived there during the 1989–1990 and 1990–1991 seasons, for a total of 54 Metropolitan performances. A 2000 production by the New York City Opera Company played for 10 performances, and in 2002 the work was revived there for 3 more showings. The most recent Broadway revival opened in 2011 for 294 performances and won the Tony Award for Best Revival of a Musical (as did the 1976 revival).

The lavish 1959 film version released by Columbia was personally produced by Samuel Goldwyn and was directed by Otto Preminger; the cast reads like a Who's Who of the era's major black performers (many of whom were dubbed), including Sidney Poitier, Dorothy Dandridge, Sammy Davis Jr., Pearl Bailey, Diahann Carroll, and Brock Peters. The film has all but disappeared during the past few decades, reportedly because of the Gershwin estate's displeasure with the film (it has never been shown on cable television or issued on home video). The March 20, 2002, performance by the New York City Opera Company was shown live on public television.

Beginning in 1958, the libretto has been published in various paperback editions by the Chappell Music Company. The script is also included in the hardback collection *Ten Great Musicals of the American Theatre* (1973), published by Chilton Book Company (the collection isn't identified as volume one, but there was a later second volume in this series).

There are numerous recordings of the score, including one with many members of the original 1935 and 1942 casts, including Todd Duncan and Anne Brown (Decca LP # DL-7-9024); one of the most complete recordings is EMI's 1985 3-CD set (# CDS-7-49568-2). Joseph Horowitz's *On My Way: The Untold Story of Rouben Mamoulian, George Gershwin, and "Porgy and Bess"* was published in 2013 by W.W. Norton.

In order to relieve the work of its opera trappings, about forty-five minutes of recitative and other music was excised from the 1942 revival (as the decades passed, "opera" wasn't such a frightening word, and, as mentioned, future revivals happily restored the cuts and even added music that had been deleted during the original 1935 tryout). Although the 1942 revival had dropped the operatic framework and presented a production more in keeping with traditional musicals, the program curiously insisted on providing a detailed plot summary. In conjunction with the song list, this summary seems rather strange. The song "Summer Time" appears in the regular song listing, and the summary informs the audience that "Clara sings a lullaby to her baby." Later, the list includes "There's a Boat That's Leavin' Soon for New York," and the summary explains that "Sportin' Life tries to persuade Bess to go to New York with him."

The critics were glad to see the revival, and welcomed back Gershwin's score and original cast members Todd Duncan, Anne Brown, Ruby Elzy, Warren Coleman, Helen Dowdy, J. Rosamund Johnson, and Georgette Harvey (the latter has the distinction of appearing in both the original 1926 production of *Porgy* as well as the original 1935 musical adaptation). For the revival, Alexander Smallens was again the conductor, and the Eva Jessye Choir returned. New to the cast was Avon Long as Sportin' Life; Brooks Atkinson in the *New York Times* said he was "triumphantly vivid and entertaining," Louis Kronenberger in *PM* said he played the part with "great animation and a fine grotesquerie of style," and Burns Mantle in the *New York Daily News* said he had the "grace of a ballet dancer and the enthusiasm of an old-time cake walker." Mantle noted that Duncan and Brown were in "perfect" voice, and many of the critics thought their performances were now warmer and more authoritative.

For the revival, some of the critics rehashed the old is-it-opera-or-is-it-musical chant, something that seems a given for almost every revival of the work. In fact, Wilella Waldorf in the *New York Post* noted that when music critic Samuel Chotzinoff reviewed the original production for the newspaper, he said the work was a "hybrid" of "music-drama, musical comedy and operetta." As for Waldorf, she said Gershwin's music was "pleasant," but felt DuBose Heyward's original play *Porgy* was more compelling than the musical version; she also noted the current production seemed a "very long evening to this benighted reporter." Richard Lockridge in the *New York Sun* also mentioned the evening seemed "too long," but he nonetheless welcomed the "moving, bright-hued story" which, long or not, was an "event"; Richard Watts in the *New York Herald Tribune* enjoyed the "splendid production"; and John Anderson in the *New York Journal-American* felt that what had been "somewhat ponderous and dull" in 1935 was now a "great improvement" thanks to Cheryl Crawford's new production. Atkinson stated that during the years since the 1935 premiere the work's reputation had "grown beyond" any other Broadway musical, and only *Show Boat* enjoyed equal esteem.

Because the original production of *Porgy and Bess* had lost money, it was courageous for producer Cheryl Crawford to revive the work. But then Crawford was always an adventurous risk-taker, possibly the most daring and innovative producer Broadway has ever known. Many of her productions lost money, but they were nonetheless bold and challenging experiments that pushed the boundaries of traditional musical theatre with their staging, presentation, and subject matter: **Love Life**, **Regina**, *Flahooley* (1951), *Reuben Reuben* (1955), *Chu Chem* (1966), and *Celebration* (1969). While *Paint Your Wagon* (1951) wasn't a success, she enjoyed two out-and-out smash hits, **One Touch of Venus** and **Brigadoon**.

OF "V" WE SING

Theatre: Concert Theatre
Opening Date: February 11, 1942; *Closing Date*: April 25, 1942
Performances: 76
Sketches: Sam D. Locke; additional sketches by Al Geto
Lyrics: Alfred Hayes; additional lyrics by Lewis Allan, Norman Corwin, Joe Darian (Darion), Beatrice Goldsmith, Roslyn Harvey, Sylvia Marks, Mel Tolkin, and Arthur Zipser
Music: George Kleinsinger; additional music by Lewis Allan, Beau (Baldwin) Bergersen, Lou Cooper, Ned Lehack, Alex North, Toby Sacher, and Mel Tolkin
Direction: Lou Cooper; *Producers*: Alexander H. Cohen and Lennie Hatten (An American Youth Theatre Production); *Choreography*: Susanne Remos; *Musical Direction*: Lou Cooper
Cast: Phil Leeds, Betty Garrett, Curt Conway, Adele Jerome, Lee Barrie, Buddy Yarus, Robert Sharron, Susanne Remos, Lou Cooper, Perry Bruskin, Eleanor Bagley, Letty Stever, John Fleming, John Wynn, Daniel Nagrin, Diane Davis, Connie Baxter, Mary Titus, Ann Garlan, Byron Milligan; Pianists: Lou Cooper and Saul Davis
The revue was presented in two acts.

Sketches and Musical Numbers

Act One: "You Can't Fool the People" (lyric by Alfred Hayes, music by George Kleinsinger, coda by Lou Cooper) (Entire Company); "News Story" (sketch) (Phil Leeds, Adele Jerome); "NBC Goes to Broadcast" (sketch by Sam D. Locke) (Announcer: Curt Conway; M'sieur Jacquelon: Phil Leeds; Maid: Eleanor Bagley; News Announcer: Robert Sharron; Recruiting Officer: Buddy Yarus; Mayor: Perry Bruskin; Mayor's Assistant: Letty Stever; Second Announcer: John Wynn; Trio: Betty Garrett, Lee Barrie, and Adele Jerome;

Third Announcer: Daniel Nagrin; Kaltincuff: John Wynn); "Sisters Under the Skin" (lyric by Sylvia Marks, music by Beau [Baldwin] Bergersen) (Trio: Lee Barrie, Betty Garrett, Adele Jerome); "Rhumba" (danced and choreographed by Susanne Remos and Daniel Nagrin); "One Way Passage" (sketch by Sam D. Locke) (Angel: Phil Leeds; Senator: Curt Conway); "Red, White and Blues" (lyric and music by Lewis Allan) (John Fleming); "Mother Love" (lyric and music by Mel Tolkin) (Phil Leeds, Buddy Yarus); "Brooklyn Cantata" (lyric by Mike Stratton, music by George Kleinsinger) (Announcer: Curt Conway; Umpire: Phil Leeds; Drunk: John Wynn; Pinch Hitter: Buddy Yarus; Girl Friend: Eleanor Bagley; Company); "Take a Poem" (words by Norman Corwin, music by George Kleinsinger) (Robert Sharron); "Victory Conga" (lyric and music by Mel Tolkin) (Entire Company)

Act Two: "Priorities" (lyric by Roslyn Harvey, music by Lou Cooper) (Entire Company); "News Story" ("Again") (Phil Leeds, Adele Jerome); "Ivan the Terrible" (sketch by Al Geto) (Technician: Perry Bruskin; Announcer: John Wynn; Hitler: Phil Leeds; Off-Stage Voice of Ivan: Buddy Yarus); "Queen Esther" (lyric by Beatrice Goldsmith, music by George Kleinsinger) (Betty Garrett, Chorus); "Hy'a Joe" (sketch by Al Geto) (Curt Conway, Phil Leeds); "Gertie, The Stool Pigeon's Daughter" (lyric by Joe Darian [Darion], music by Ned Lehack) (Singer: Eleanor Bagley; Gertie: Lettie Stever; Bartender: Curt Conway; Company); "You've Got to Appease with a Strip Tease" (lyric by Lewis Allan, music by Toby Sacher) (Phil Leeds, Adele Jerome, Lee Barrie); "Belinda Blue" (sketch by Sam O. Locke) (Master of Ceremonies: Curt Conway; Movie Star: Betty Garrett; Ushers: Robert Sharron, Buddy Yarus; Company); "We Have a Date" (lyric by Roslyn Harvey, music by Lou Cooper) (First Couple: Diane Davis and Norman Lawrence; Second Couple: Connie Baxter and Robert Sharron; Third Couple: Lee Barris and Buddy Yarus); "Juke Box" (lyric by Alfred Hayes, music by Alex North) (Hep Cat: Phil Leeds; Proprietor: John Fleming; Waitress: Betty Garrett; Dancers: Susanne Remos. Daniel Nagrin, Adele Jerome, Lee Barrie, Buddy Yarus, Perry Bruskin, John Wynn); "Prologue to Finale" (poem by Walt Whitman, music by Lou Cooper) (Robert Fleming); "Of 'V' We Sing" (lyric by Arthur Zipser, music by Lou Cooper) (Entire Company)

The short-running revue *Of "V" We Sing* was sponsored by The American Youth Theatre; a program note described the company's mission as one that offered productions that "appeal to the widest possible audience, which reflect the times we live in and which further the principles of Democracy." As *"V" for Victory*, the revue had first been produced in New York at the Malin Studio Theatre in September 1941 and then gave al fresco performances in New York during the fall.

The revue touched upon topical foibles, such as Hollywood ("Belinda Blue"), radio ("NBC Goes to Broadcast"), politics ("One Way Passage"), the rage for strip-teasing ("You've Got to Appease with a Strip Tease"), popular music ("Juke Box"), vaudeville ("Mother Love"), and the era's obsession with Latin-American dances ("Victory Conga" and "Rhumba").

The headline of Brooks Atkinson's review in the *New York Times* was titled "Pins and People," and the critic noted that while the evening was in the idiom of both *Pins and Needles* (1937) and **Meet the People**, it was "inferior in material" to the former and "in personnel" to the latter. The intimate revue was "brighter in intention than in fact," but he singled out a lively jitterbug ("Juke Box") which was a "pleasure" to watch; an "amusingly-acted ballad" which satirized vaudeville ("Mother Love"); and "Brooklyn Cantata," a tone-poem that was "humorously enjoyable."

"Brooklyn Cantata" had been previously performed as "Cantata" ("Saga of the Diamond") in *'Tis of Thee*, which ran for one performance in 1940.

As the Youth Theatre, the company returned to Broadway a few months later with another revue, **Let Freedom Sing**. This time around, the company met with instant failure and the new production lasted only one week. Two numbers from *Of "V" We Sing* were retained for the second revue: the song "We Have a Date" and apparently the sketch "Hy'a Joe" (which was retitled "Tactics").

Alexander H. Cohen was one of the revue's coproducers, and over the decades produced an inordinate number of failed musicals, such as **Bright Lights of 1944** (1943), *Make a Wish* (1951), *Courtin' Time* (1951), *Rugantino* (1964), *Baker Street* (1965), *A Time for Singing* (1966), *Dear World* (1969), *I Remember Mama* (1979), and the out-of-town closings of *Hellzapoppin'* (both the 1967 and 1976 versions) and *Prettybelle* (1971). He was more successful when he produced intimate comedy revues along the lines of *An Evening with Mike Nichols and Elaine May* (1960), *Beyond the Fringe* (1962), and *Good Evening* (1973).

Lyricist Joe Darian (Darion) later wrote the lyrics for the long-running *Man of La Mancha* (1965), and his "The Impossible Dream" became one of the biggest hit songs in the history of the American musical.

PRIORITIES OF 1942

Theatre: 46th Street Theatre
Opening Date: March 12, 1942; *Closing Date*: September 6, 1942
Performances: 353
Lyrics and *Music* for The Versailles Beauties by Marjery Fielding and Charles Barnes
Direction: The Versailles Beauties directed by Marjery Fielding; *Producers*: Clifford C. Fischer by arrangement
    with the Messrs. Shubert; *Musical Direction*: Lou Forman
Cast: *Lou Holtz, Willie Howard, Phil Baker, Paul Draper,* Joan Merrill, Hazel Scott, The Helen Reynolds
    Skaters, The Nonchalants, Gene Sheldon and Loretta Fischer, The Barrys, Johnny Masters and Rowena
    Rollins, Diane Denise, Lari and Conchita, Beverley Lane, Al Kelly, Lora Saunders, Charles Senna, John
    Leopold; The Versailles Beauties: Hazel Baker, Michelle Magnin, Mary Lou Savage, Patricia Donnelly,
    Lillian O'Donell, Margaret Lane, Sheila Herman, Trudy Byers, Lee Loprete, Sonia Tanya, Murnai Pins, Lo-
    rayne Lloyd, Helen Wenzel, Gail Hereford, Helen Beck, Aleita Albert, Lee Myers, Joan Dare, Carol Gordon
The revue was presented in two acts.

Sketches and Musical Numbers

Act One: Overture (The Priorities Orchestra); "Vaudeville Is Back" (The Versailles Beauties); The Helen Reyn-
    olds Skaters; The Nonchalants; Willie Howard (assisted by Al Kelly, Lora Saunders, Charles Senna, and
    John Leopold); Joan Merrill; Phil Baker (assisted by Diane Denise); Johnny Masters and Rowena Rollins;
    "Brazilian Rhythms" (Lari and Conchita, Diane Denise, The Versailles Beauties)
Act Two: "I Waltzed with a Major" (The Barrys, Beverley Lane, The Versailles Beauties); Gene Sheldon and
    Loretta Fischer; Hazel Scott; Paul Draper (with Calvin Jackson at the piano); Willie Howard; Finale (Entire
    Company)

Clifford C. Fischer put together the inexpensive vaudeville-styled revue *Priorities of 1942*, and it proved to
be the surprise hit of the spring season and tallied up 353 performances. A few weeks later, Fischer brought in
another vaudeville evening, but ***Keep 'Em Laughing*** didn't, and a quickly revised version titled ***Top Notchers***
wasn't so top notch. Both revues totaled just 125 performances, and Fischer's ***New Priorities of 1943*** played
for 54 performances. The success of *Priorities of 1942* encouraged other producers to get on the variety-cum-
vaudeville bandwagon, and so the war years saw a number of such productions, including ***Harlem Cavalcade***,
Show Time, ***Wine Women and Song***, and ***Star Time***.
   The critics were glad to see such old friends as Lou Holtz (who acted as master of ceremonies), Willie
Howard, and Phil Baker, all of whom reprised their time-tested routines (but the reviewers noted that Baker
seemed somewhat tentative on opening night). They all enjoyed Hazel Scott's song stylings, but were a bit
cool to singer Joan Merrill. Besides the comics and singers, others on the bill were Conchita (a South American dancer), The Barrys (a dance team), The Nonchalants (acrobats), Gene Sheldon (a banjo-playing zany who
cavorted around in baggy pants), The Helen Reynolds Skaters (to be sure, roller skating, not ice skating), and
Johnny Masters and Rowena Rollins, who supplied a comic mélange of eccentric comedy, impersonations,
and dancing.
   One of the evening's highlights involved a sequence in which Holtz, Howard, and Baker got together and
took friendly pot shots at recent and current visitors to Broadway, including Eddie Cantor, George Jessel, and
Olsen and Johnson.
   But the star of the evening was tap dancer Paul Draper, whom the critics (and audiences) adored. According to Louis Kronenberger in *PM*, Draper stopped the show. His "clean and brilliant and completely individu-
alistic style" was "pretty wonderful." Robert Sylvester in the *New York Daily News* said he was the "best
solo dancer we have"; Richard Watts in the *New York Herald Tribune* noted he was "one of the superb dancers of the world"; and John Mason Brown in the *New York World-Telegram* said he had "charm and distinction" and was a "joy to watch." John Anderson in the *New York Journal-American* also reported that Draper
(who didn't come on until 11:00 and then proceeded to dance for thirty show-stopping minutes) was brilliant.
But Anderson couldn't understand why some in the audience felt the need to indulge in constant applause
and thus "break into such superb rhythms in sound and movements." Wilella Waldorf in the *New York Post*

echoed his sentiments, and suggested that an "astute manager" might place sharpshooters throughout the theatre in order to "pick off moronic individuals" who burst into applause during intricate dance routines.

The critics made several comments concerning the continuing invasion of microphones into the theatre. Brooks Atkinson in the *New York Times* was blunt about it: all microphones should be tossed in the alley. Anderson said they were a "metallic intrusion"; Brown wished that producers would "dispense with those troublesome and unnecessary amplifiers"; and Waldorf wondered if radio loud speakers, juke boxes, and movies had so "distorted" the taste of audiences that they now couldn't appreciate normal speaking and singing. She was so right, and little did she know what was to come.

Among the songs performed by Hazel Scott were "Dark Eyes" (lyric and music by A. Salama) and "Tea for Two" (from *No, No, Nanette*, 1925; lyric by Irving Caesar, music by Vincent Youmans); and Joan Merrill's interlude included "Blues in the Night" (1941 film *Blues in the Night*; lyric by Johnny Mercer, music by Harold Arlen). Later in the year, Merrill introduced the standard "There Will Never Be Another You" (lyric by Mack Gordon, music by Harry Warren) in the Sonja Henie film *Iceland*.

When Lou Holtz left the revue late in the run, he was replaced by Walter O'Keefe; Hazel Scott and Joan Merrill also departed, and such performers as Luba Malina and Billy Vine joined the cast. During the show's national tour, Holtz was back, along with Willie Howard and Phil Baker; this time around they were joined by the dancer Argentinita, and Bert Wheeler and Hank Ladd were later additions to the cast.

Priorities of 1942 gave sixteen performances a week (two daily plus an extra matinee on Sundays and a midnight performance on Saturdays). Matinee ticket prices ranged from fifty-five cents to $1.10, and top-priced tickets for evening performances were $2.20, except for Saturday nights when they skyrocketed to $2.75.

JOHNNY 2 X 4
"A NOVELTY MELODRAMA"

Theatre: Longacre Theatre
Opening Date: March 16, 1942; *Closing Date*: May 9, 1942
Performances: 65
Play: Rowland Brown; special material written by Frank Dolan
Direction: Anthony Brown; *Producer*: Rowland Brown; *Choreography*: Douglas Dean; *Scenery*: Howard Bay; *Costumes*: Rose Bogdanoff; *Lighting*: Century; *Musical Direction*: Merle Pitt
Cast: Lester Lonergan Jr. (Creepy), Lew Eckels (Pete), Yehudi Wyner (Bottles), Ralph Chambers (Mike Maloney), Jack Arthur (Johnny 2 x 4), Charles Adler, George Kelly, Rodney McLennan, and Don Richards (The Yacht Club Boys), Barry Sullivan (Coaly Lewis), Bert Reed (Beetle-Puss), Evelyn Wyckoff (Mary Collins), Jack Lambert (Dutch), Arthur L. Sachs (Martin), Isabel Jewell (Mabel), Harry Bellaver (Knuckles Kelton), Marie Austin (Butch), Douglas Dean (Rudy Denton), Sam Raskyn (Burns), Marianne O'Brien (B-Girl), Irene Collett (B-Girl), Josi Johnson (B-Girl), Muriel Cole (B-Girl), Natalie Draper (B-Girl), Carolyn Cromwell (B-Girl), Eddie Hodges (Ohio Customer), Bert Frohman (Midal), Leonard Sues (Apples), James La Curto (Billy the Booster), Al Durant (Harry), Monica Lewis (Cigarette Girl), Karen Van Ryn (Maxine), Wilma Drake (Dot), Russel Conway (Jerry Sullivan), Thom Conroy (Kean), Lance Elliot (Bottles [grown-up]); Bakery Men, Meat Men, Bodyguards, Guests: John Harvey, Syl Lamont, Charles L. Douglass, Chester Adams, Fred Catania, John Stark, Jack Parsons, William Sharon, Paul Clare, Victor Finney, Joseph Martel, James Falon, Stephen Morrow, Carmen Costi, Michel Spreder, William Forester, Eleanor Swayne, Carolyn Cromwell, Bea Barclay, Nancy Clark, Jordie McLean, Mary Martin, Eleanor Pryne, Ellwin Evans, Betty (Lauren) Bacall, Virginia Wyckoff, Maxine Sheppard, Ruth Maitland; Merle Pitt and His Music: Merle Pitt (Leader), Frank Froeba (Pianist), Sam Frey (Accordion), Terry Snyder (Vibraphones and Drums), Dick Kissinger (Bass), Mac Cappos (Violin)
The play with music was presented in two acts.
The action takes place in the Johnny 2 x 4 Club in Greenwich Village during the years 1926–1936.

Musical Numbers

Act One: Liszt's Tarantella (music by Franz Liszt) (Yehudi Wyner); "Close Your Eyes" (lyric and music by Bernice Petkere) (Evelyn Wyckoff); "Mother" (lyric by Howard Johnson, music by Theodore F. Morse) (Jack Arthur); Interlude of music by Frederic Chopin (Yehudi Wyner); "Ace in the Hole" (lyric and music by George D. Mitchell and James E. Dempsey) (Jack Arthur); "Down by the O-HI-O" (aka "O-H-I-O" and "Down by the O-H-I-O") (from *Ziegfeld Follies of 1920*; lyric by Jack Yellen, music by Abe Olman) (Marie Austin); "(In My) Solitude" (lyric by Eddie de Lange and Irving Mills, music by Duke Ellington) (Leonard Sues); "The Customer's Always Right" (The Yacht Club Boys); "Deep Night" (lyric by Rudy Vallee, music by Charlie Henderson) (Evelyn Wyckoff)

Act Two: "Between the Devil and the Deep Blue Sea" (*Rhyth-mania*, 1931; lyric by Ted Koehler, music by Harold Arlen) (Monica Lewis); "It's Been a Whole Year" (The Yacht Club Boys); "I Want a Girl" (lyric by William Dillon, music by Harry von Tilzer) (Marie Austin); "Hill and Dale" (The Yacht Club Boys); "Blue Prelude" (lyric and music by Joe Bishop and Gordon Jenkins) (Leonard Sues); "We Were Lucky Together" (lyric by Gladys Shelley, music by Harry Archer) (Evelyn Wyckoff)

Rowland Brown's *Johnny 2 x 4* was a play with music that nostalgically looked at the Prohibition era from the perspective of a speakeasy's heady days to its final end a few years later when the Volstead Act was repealed. It was a lavish and ambitious work, but unfortunately wasn't much of a play; instead of a compelling narrative, Brown's would-be epic looked at the Prohibition years with a series of colorful vignettes, most of them predictable and none of them particularly involving. The huge cast of sixty numbered more performers than many of the era's full-fledged musicals, and the characters included bartenders, waiters, cigarette girls, delivery men, mobsters, bodyguards, crooked cops, prostitutes, singers, dancers, musicians, and a flock of nightclub patrons who were essentially supernumeraries. There were so many of the latter that Richard Lockridge in the *New York Sun* was prompted to suggest that the police escort the leading actors to tables "reserved by the director for those with lines to say."

Designer Howard Bay created a cavernous and smoky basement nightclub with a huge staircase leading down from street level (could this have possibly inspired his Tony Award-winning set for *Man of La Mancha*?) His set for the Johnny 2 x 4 Club included a bar on one side of the stage, an orchestra on the other, and in between a dance floor as well as chairs and tables for the patrons.

Johnny (Jack Arthur) is the owner and sometime piano player of the speakeasy (the play's title was derived from his ability to play a portable piano). The club's singer Mary Collins (Evelyn Wyckoff, whose program biography said the show was her first featured Broadway appearance, apparently forgetting all about her roles in two "lady" musicals, **Lady in the Dark** and **The Lady Comes Across**, the latter of which had opened some two months earlier) is in love with Johnny's best friend, gangster Coaly Lewis (Barry Sullivan), a club habitué in the midst of a gangland feud with racketeer Midal (Bert Frohman). Eventually, Coaly is killed by Midal, who in turn is bumped off by the club's hot trumpet player Apples (Leonard Sues). By the third act, which served as a kind of wistful coda and contained no music, the club's glory days are long gone and those characters who are still alive mourn for the good old days.

More than half the critics compared the play to the similarly themed *Broadway*, Phillip Dunning and George Abbott's 1926 hit which played on Broadway for 603 performances. In fact, one critic said Rowland Brown should have revived the older play instead of writing and producing the current one.

John Anderson in the *New York Journal-American* found the evening "fadingly romantic," "faintly incredible," and "very, very dull." The play was "all atmosphere and no structure," and there were so many musical numbers the production threatened to become a "recital." Brooks Atkinson in the *New York Times* said the play was a conglomeration of "odds and ends of commonplace dialogue" with nightclub types, and the evening made him "homesick for *Pal Joey*." But he liked many of the musical sequences, including the "honeyed melancholy" of Evelyn Wyckoff's "Close Your Eyes," the "brilliant" trumpet solo of "strut music" by Leonard Sues, and the "husky, snarling gusto" of Marie Austin's "O-HI-O."

Louis Kronenberger in *PM* complained that the evening was a "rehash" (and "almost a take-off") of old gangster melodramas, and while Burns Mantle in the *New York Daily News* found the characters uninteresting he praised Bay's "solid and tricky" setting.

Richard Watts in the *New York Herald Tribune* said the play was "ramshackle" but nonetheless "disarmingly entertaining in its completely shameless way"; John Mason Brown in the *New York World-Telegram* said the sets were "lavish" but the script "parsimonious"; and Lockridge stated the play was a "ponderous nonentity" in which "thin slices of life" are "sandwiched in atmosphere." Although Wilella Waldorf in the *New York Post* found the play "largely tripe," she said it was a "nostalgic dip" into the recent past which was "often entertaining in its ginny fashion."

When Evelyn Wyckoff left the cast, her role was assumed by Victoria Cordova, who earlier in the season had appeared in **Viva O'Brien** (the name of Wyckoff's character was now changed to Maria Valdez). During the run, and all in the cause of economy, the twenty-eight performers who played various non-speaking roles were reduced to eighteen and a few speaking roles were also eliminated (although at least one new character was added). A few songs were dropped ("Ace in the Hole," "Between the Devil and the Deep Blue Sea," "Hill and Dale," and "We Were Lucky Together"), and others ("If I Had My Way," "Rock It," "Woo-Woo," "Spain," and "La Violetera") were added.

Buried deep in the cast list were Mary Martin and Betty Bacall. The former wasn't the musical comedy star, but the latter was indeed the later Lauren.

KEEP 'EM LAUGHING

Theatre: 44th Street Theatre
Opening Date: April 24, 1942; *Closing Date*: May 28, 1942
Performances: 77
Direction: Clifford C. Fischer; *Producers*: Clifford C. Fischer by arrangement with the Messrs. Shubert; *Scenery* (and draperies): Frank W. Stevens; *Musical Direction*: Phil Romano
Cast: *William Gaxton, Victor Moore, The Hartmans* (Paul and Grace Hartman), *Hildegarde*, Jack Cole and His Dancers (including Virginia Millar), Zero Mostel, The Stuart Morgan Dancers, The Bricklayers, Fred Sanborn, Miriam La Velle, Kitty Mattern, Shirley Paige, Peggy French, Jack Tyler, George E. Mack, Charles Lawrence, Phil Romano and His Orchestra; Al White Beauties: Alice Anthony, Paddy Barker, Eleanor Broun, Marji Beeler, Rita Berry, Cece Eames, Michael Neale, Isabel Rolfe, Lucy Lewis, Ellen Taylor, June Peiter, Edith Stromberg, Norma Richter, Kay Paige, Emily Fabian, Pinto, Ruth Joseph, Vera Devine
The revue was presented in two acts.

Sketches and Musical Numbers

Act One: Overture (Phil Romano and His Orchestra); "Al White Beauties"; Miriam La Velle; The Bricklayers; Sketch (by L. Metzl and W. Michel) (Kitty Mattern); "Authoritis" (sketch by Arthur Pierson) (William Gaxton, assisted by Peggy French, Jack Tyler, and George E. Mack); "Change Your Act or Back to the Woods" (sketch) (Victor Moore, assisted by Shirley Paige and Company); Jack Cole and His Dancers (music by Raymond Scott and Albert Ketelby); Fred Sanborn (assisted by Charles Lawrence); "Gay Nineties" (Al White Beauties); The Hartmans
Act Two: "Rainbow" (Al White Beauties); The Stuart Morgan Dancers; Zero Mostel; Hildegarde (assisted by Leo Kahn, pianist); "A Small Purchase" ("Not Louisiana") (sketch by Eddie Davis) (William Gaxton and Victor Moore); Finale

Producer Clifford C. Fischer had found success with his production of the vaudeville-styled revue **Priorities of 1942**, and so six weeks later put together another one. But *Keep 'Em Laughing* didn't, and so he soon revised the material and brought it back later in the season as **Top-Notchers**. But it too did not meet with the success of **Priorities of 1942**, which played for 353 performances; the other two vaudeville shows ran for just 77 and 48 respective showings.

William Gaxton and Victor Moore seemed to be sure-fire winners to headline the revue. The team had recently enjoyed one of their biggest successes in Irving Berlin's **Louisiana Purchase**, and so with Gaxton as master of ceremonies and the two of them participating in various sketches and songs, their casting seemed a natural. But the can-do-no-wrong Victor Moore was met with almost unanimously negative reviews, all of which focused on his classic 1920s comedy sketch "Change Your Act or Go Back to the Woods." The problem was that the antique sketch was no longer funny; John Anderson in the *New York Journal-American* found it "badly dated"; Richard Lockridge in the *New York Sun* suggested the "vintage" sketch had "been too long in the bottle"; and Richard Watts in the *New York Herald Tribune* felt the sketch had aged "far less pleasantly" than Moore himself. According to Wilella Waldorf in the *New York Post*, Gaxton's sketch "Authoritis," about a drunk Hollywood script writer, was "overlong" if "fairly amusing"; later in the evening he and Moore teamed up for the sketch "A Small Purchase," which John Mason Brown in the *New York World-Telegram* said showed the duo "to more than very mild advantage." As for Gaxton's hosting, Brown said he seemed "utterly lost" with such duties, and Louis Kronenberger in *PM* said there was a "terrific need" for a host along the lines of Lou Holtz.

Brown said the "uncomfortable" revue was "gasping" for its breath, and Anderson warned that it wasn't up to the pleasures of **Priorities of 1942**. But Brooks Atkinson in the *New York Times* found it "remarkably good vaudeville entertainment" and Watts recommended the "pretty good vaudeville show."

The evening also offered the Hartmans and their unique lampoons of ballroom dancing; acrobatic dancing by Miriam La Velle; song stylings by Hildegarde; exotic East Indian–styled dances set to swing music by Jack Cole and His Dancers; adagio turns by The Stuart Morgan Dancers; and comics Kitty Mattern and Fred Sanborn (the latter doing tricks on the xylophone).

Making his Broadway debut was radio and nightclub comedian Zero Mostel. Atkinson said the "zany" did "remarkably well" for his first appearance in a theatre; Robert Sylvester in the *New York Daily News* said he was a "sensation"; and Lockridge reported that the "amusing" Mostel worked himself "to the bone" (and for Mostel that was a "good distance"). Mostel's impersonations included Jimmy Durante, Charles Boyer, jitterbugs at Roseland, and politicians (Anderson said the latter was a "little masterpiece").

But the hit of the evening was the sequence that featured The Bricklayers, who were a team of trained dogs. These canines doggedly proceeded to put together (and then destroy) a house with all the necessary bricks, lumber, ladders, and scaffolds; one supposedly hurts himself, and then rolls over and plays dead throughout the scene (later, in widow's weeds, his spouse comes to mourn him); and another goes off and gets drunk, and returns to the stage completely pie-eyed. Anderson said the skit was "fantastic, fascinating and unbelievable" and "better than anything of its sort I have ever seen." Kronenberger also said the act was "unbelievable"; it was "the best and most delightful animal act in history," and the dogs had "perfect timing" and "immense charm." Watts found it "the best and most amusing dog act I have ever seen," and Waldorf said if she ever returned to *Keep 'Em Laughing* it would be only to see those dogs again.

Soon after *Keep 'Em Laughing* premiered, the first act was slightly re-structured, and acrobatic dancer Miriam La Velle was succeeded by Anita Jakobi.

Among the songs performed by Hildegarde were "Not a Care in the World" (from **Banjo Eyes**) and "I Said No" (from the 1942 film musical *Sweater Girl*, lyric by Frank Loesser and music by Jule Styne). And following their final sketch, Gaxton and Moore sang a medley of songs from some of their earlier successes, such as *Of Thee I Sing* (1931), *Anything Goes* (1934), and **Louisiana Purchase**.

The revue gave sixteen performances weekly (two apiece Mondays through Fridays, and three shows on Saturdays and Sundays).

For information about the revised version of *Keep 'Em Laughing*, see **Top-Notchers**.

HARLEM CAVALCADE

Theatre: Ritz Theatre
Opening Date: May 1, 1942; *Closing Date*: May 23, 1942
Performances: 49
Direction: Ed Sullivan and Noble Sissle; *Producer*: Ed Sullivan; *Choreography*: Leonard Harper; *Scenery*: Ed Sullivan and Noble Sissle; *Costumes*: Veronica; *Lighting*: Uncredited; *Musical Direction*: Bill Vodery
Cast: Noble Sissle, The Peters Sisters, Moke and Poke, Flournoy Miller, Tim Moore and Joe Byrd, Una Mae Carlisle, Red and Curley, (Monte) Hawley and (Johnny) Lee, Pops and Louie, The Miller Brothers and Lois, The Five Crackerjacks, Wini and Bob Johnson, The Four Gingersnaps, The Delta Rhythm Boys, Amanda Randolph, Tom Fletcher, Jesse Crior; Jimmie Daniels with pianists Garland Wilson and Edward Steele; The Sixteen Harlem Harlemaniacs: Claudia Heyward, Bee Williamson, June De Cuir, Julia Rogers, Jackie Bass, Cleo Haynes, Alyce Bishop, Olive Prince, Frances Jackson, Rusty Stanford, Mabel Garrett, Ruby Richards, Carolyne Rich, Ferebee Purnell, Nickey O'Daniel, Jackie Lewis

The revue was presented in two acts.

Sketches and Musical Numbers

Act One: "Bandana Days" (from *Shuffle Along*, 1921; lyric by Noble Sissle, music by Eubie Blake) (The Five Crackerjacks, Amanda Randolph, Jesse Crior, Tom Fletcher and the Sixteen Harlem Harlemaniacs); Pops and Louie; "John Doe Meets John Law" (sketch) (Monte Hawley and Johnny Lee); "Interlude in Harlem" (The Singer: Jimmie Daniels; The Pianists: Garland Wilson and Edward Steele; The Dancers: The Harlemaniacs; The Quartet: The Four Gingersnaps); Red and Curley; "Midnight Sonata" (Tim Moore, Joe Byrd); Moke and Poke; The Peters Sisters (sequence included "Embraceable You" from *Girl Crazy*, 1930; lyric by Ira Gershwin, music by George Gershwin); "His Honor, the Jedge" (The Jedge: Tim Moore; The Bailiff: Joe Byrd; The Lawyer: Maude Russell; Court Clerk: Jesse Crior; The Killer: Flournoy Miller; The Number Runner: Johnny Lee); Finale: "Pushin' the Sand" (The Peters Sisters, Moke and Poke, Wini and Bob Johnson, The Sixteen Harlemaniacs)

Act Two: Entr'acte (Jessie Crior); "I'm Just Wild about Harry" (*Shuffle Along*, 1921; lyric by Noble Sissle, music by Eubie Blake) (Noble Sissle, The Sixteen Harlemaniacs); Pops and Louie; Una Mae Carlisle (sequence included "Walkin' by the River," lyric and music by Una Mae Carlisle); "Drafting an Answer" (Flournoy Miller); "Melody in Sepia"; "Another Policy Game"(Flournoy Miller, Johnny Lee, Tim Moore, Joe Byrd, Amanda Randolph, The Four Gingersnaps); The Miller Brothers and Lois; Noble Sissle; Finale

The last half of the season offered a spate of vaudeville-styled revues, including **Priorities of 1942**, **Keep 'Em Laughing**, and **Top-Notchers**. During the previous season, Ed Sullivan had resurrected the ailing **Crazy with the Heat**, and now he decided to bring in a black revue. The result was *Harlem Cavalcade*, which lasted less than a month. Sullivan appeared in the revue on opening night to welcome the audience.

The critics were generally kind to *Harlem Cavalcade*, but felt it was too much of a good thing. Apparently tap number followed tap number followed tap number, and although they were expertly done, the critics were all tapped out and wished the evening had offered more variety.

The revue's cast included old-timers Flournoy Miller and Noble Sissle; Miller had co-written the book and Sissle the lyrics for the hit 1921 revue *Shuffle Along*, in which they both had starred. For *Harlem Cavalcade*, they reprised two songs from that classic revue, "Bandana Days" and "I'm Just Wild about Harry." The evening also offered two venerable sketches, "His Honor, the Jedge" and "Midnight Sonata," the latter updated to depict two air raid wardens who find themselves stationed in a graveyard. Another topical sketch was "Drafting the Answer." The first-act finale introduced "Pushin' the Sand," which the program identified as "Harlem's newest dance."

Wilella Waldorf in the *New York Post* found the evening a "pleasant sepia show" and commented that "the dark race" had a generally "simple, unforced quality about its fun-making." She also noted that the black comedians used blackface in some of the sketches. Waldorf mentioned that the "enormous" Peters Sisters were an "out-size" singing trio "with a rare assortment of double and triple chins" who sang with "gusto" and provided "something in the nature of an elephant ballet."

Burns Mantle in the *New York Daily News* thought Ed Sullivan had a "good idea" when he pulled together so many talented performers; but felt some of the routines went on too long. He noted the Peters Sisters called themselves a "ton of harmony and rhythm," and he praised the closing sequence in which Miller sang a "rousing" (unidentified) patriotic song. Richard Lockridge in the *New York Sun* felt the constant dancing fell victim to the law of diminishing returns because "monotony" soon set in; the performers were experts and the audience loved them, but for him the show went on too long and brought out his "hitherto unsuspected allergy" to too much tap dancing. Richard Watts in the *New York Herald Tribune* found the revue "pretty routine" and "commonplace," and noted the opening number was "so merry and frantic a carnival" that the rest of the evening could never quite match it. Like Lockridge, he felt the constant dancing became "monotonous." Louis Kronenberger in *PM* also felt the opening number's "dizzying display" of dancing offered the evening's best moments, but otherwise the revue should have offered some new songs in the class of "I'm Just Wild about Harry." As for the newest dance sensation "Pushin' the Sand," he said he "failed to find anything very new about it."

John Mason Brown in the *New York World-Telegram* also thought the "uniform excellence" of the dancing soon became "monotonous," and he complained that the evening offered too much of what he had previously seen in "every other Negro show." He thought the revue required more "originality," and while the program noted it was "subject to change" he regretfully noted that was "precisely" what he did not find.

But "L.N." (Lewis Nichols) in the *New York Times* said it's "the dancing that counts," and when the dancers took off, the Ritz Theatre "rocks and bounces," the drums "beat louder," the trumpets "howl," and thus vaudeville and *Harlem Cavalcade* more than held their own. Although The Delta Rhythm Boys weren't listed in the program, one or two critics referenced them in their reviews and Waldorf noted one of their songs was her "favorite" sequence in the show.

During the era, more and more critics complained about the growing use of microphones, and *Harlem Cavalcade* was no exception. Further, the reviewers sometimes grumbled about extended encores, and Burns Mantle noted that some performers just "can't let go" and thus "go on and on and on." It's clear the matter of encores was not always addressed by directors, and so many shows went on too long and lost their momentum due to overenthusiastic cast members who sometimes finished a number and then immediately proceeded to repeat it in its entirety. Curtain calls weren't always directed, either, but as the seasons progressed both encores and curtain calls soon became as fine-tuned as the shows themselves.

The revue gave sixteen performances a week (two shows Monday through Friday, and three shows on Saturdays and Sundays).

Flournoy and Sissle, along with Eubie Blake, the composer of *Shuffle Along*, appeared together in the 1952 in-name-only revival of *Shuffle Along*, and in the 1970s Blake enjoyed a re-discovery and was honored with *Eubie!*, a composer-tribute revue which opened on Broadway in 1978 and ran for 439 performances.

TOP-NOTCHERS

Theatre: 44th Street Theatre
Opening Date: May 28, 1942; *Closing Date*: June 20, 1942
Performances: 48
Direction: Clifford C. Fischer; *Producers*: Clifford C. Fischer by arrangement with the Messrs. Shubert
Cast: *Gracie Fields*, Argentinita (and Pilar Lopez and Federico Rey, with Carlos Montoya, Pablo Miquel, and Benigno Medina), The Hartmans (Paul and Grace Hartman), Zero Mostel, The Bricklayers, Al Trahan, Walter O'Keefe, "Think-A-Drink" Hoffman, A. Robins, Jack Stanton, The Six Willys, Marguerite Adams, Evelyn Brooks; Phil Romano and His Orchestra; The Al White Beauties: Alice Anthony, Paddy Barker, Eleanor Broun, Marji Beeler, Rita Berry, Cece Eames, Michael Neale, Isabel Rolfe, Lucy Lewis, Ellen Taylor, June Peiter, Edith Stromberg, Norma Richter, Kay Paige, Emily Fabian, Pinto, Ruth Joseph, Vera Devine
The revue was presented in two acts.

Sketches and Musical Numbers

Act One: Overture (a "British Victory Medley" arranged by R. Garrigan and dedicated to Gracie Fields) (Phil Romano and His Orchestra); Al White Beauties; Jack Stanton; The Six Willys; Walter O'Keefe; The Bricklayers; A. Robins; Zero Mostel; Walter O'Keefe; The Hartmans; Gracie Fields (with Ingolf Dahl at the piano)
Act Two: Al White Girls; Jack Stanton and Evelyn Brooks; Walter O'Keefe; Al Trahan (assisted by Marguerite Adams); Argentinita (with Pilar Lopez, Federico Rey, Carlos Montoya, Pablo Miquel, and Benigno Medina); "Think-A-Drink" Hoffman; Finale (reprise of "The Yanks Are Coming") (Company)

The critics had not been all that kind to Clifford C. Fischer's vaudeville-styled revue ***Keep 'Em Laughing***, and so he took it off the boards after seventy-seven performances and recast most of it with new performers. The previous production had offered the popular team of William Gaxton and Victor Moore, but they hadn't gone over well, and so now British music-hall singer Gracie Fields headlined the evening. Returning to the production were The Bricklayers, the dog act of all dog acts which had been a howling success in the earlier revue, and the canine crew was again joined by The Hartmans, Zero Mostel, and the Al White Beauties. Besides Gaxton and Moore, such cast members as Hildegarde, Jack Cole and His Dancers, and The Stuart Morgan Dancers didn't return for the second go-round, but among the newcomers were Al Trahan, Walter O'Keefe, "Think-A-Drink" Hoffman, and dancer Argentinita and her troupe of dancers and musicians.

Gracie Fields sang a number of songs, including Noel Coward's "London Pride" (from the 1941 return engagement of the London revue *Up and Doing*) and "The Yanks Are Coming Again" (lyric and music by Lew Pollack and Tony Stern), the words of which were included in the program. Argentinita (and her five-man troupe, which included soon-to-be-legendary flamenco guitarist Carlos Montoya) performed three dances ("Inca Indian Ritual Dance," "Malaguena," and "El Huayno"), Walter O'Keefe provided comedy, The Six Willys juggled, Jack Stanton offered songs and dances, A. Robins performed his clown act, and "Think-A-Drink" Hoffman conjured up his magical potions.

A few days after the revue opened, the program sequence underwent major reordering. Zero Mostel left the production after the first week, but Johnny Burke (the comedian; not the lyricist and sometime composer) joined the revue.

Keep 'Em Laughing had given sixteen performances a week, and *Top-Notchers* gave fifteen (two shows Monday through Saturday, and three shows on Sundays).

AMERICAN SIDESHOW

Theatre and *Performance Dates*: The revue opened on February 28, 1942, at the Civic Theatre, Chicago, Illinois, and closed there on February 29.
Sketches and *Lyrics*: Charles K. Freeman
Music: Sonny Vale
Producer: Charles K. Freeman
Cast: Billy Evenson, Lola Martini, Mickey Scharff, Ross Mendel, Irene Yablon, Charles Kolar, Wanda Sponder, Guy O'Neil, Howard Slavin, Jackie Harrison, Gary Temple, Charles Potts, Ruth Taron, Peggy Walsh, Sunny Burns, Jerry Burke, Mary Hall, Laurie Hunter, Jeanette Godley, Bill Hall, Morris Goodsen, Ann Huber, John Hoffstadt, Keith Hall, Burr Tillstrom

The obscure revue *American Sideshow* disappeared after two performances in Chicago. *Best Plays* reported the "home-written and home-acted" revue offered "puerile" material and performances. The premature closing resulted from the finding by Actors' Equity that producer Charles K. Freeman "had grossly violated union rules in engaging his cast."

DANSATION

Theatre and *Performance Dates*: *Dansation* played at the Colonial Theatre, Boston, Massachusetts, for one week beginning on December 29, 1941.

For the dance revue *Dansation*, the team of (Frank) Veloz and Yolanda (Casazza) created their own routines and were accompanied by Jerry Shelton (accordionist), Vicente Gomez (guitarist), and Harry and John Hynda (pianists). The production didn't reach New York, and it's unclear if it was seen in cities other than Boston. However, the evening was a forerunner of the team's "dance vaudeville" ***For Your Pleasure***, which opened at the Mansfield Theatre on February 5, 1943, for eleven performances; for the latter revue, Veloz and Yolanda were again accompanied by Jerry (Gene) Shelton and Vincente Gomez along with a small cadre of singers and musicians.

JUMP FOR JOY
"A Sun-Tanned Revusical"

Theatre and *Performance Dates*: The revue opened on July 10, 1941, at the Mayan Theatre in Los Angeles, California, and closed there on September 27 after 101 performances.

Sketches: Sid Kuller and Hal Fimberg

Lyrics: Paul (Francis) Webster

Additional lyrics and music by Sid Kuller, Otis Rene, Langston Hughes, Charles Leonard, Mickey Rooney, Sidney Miller, Ray Golden, Richard Weil, and Mercer Ellington

Music: Duke Ellington and Hal Borne

Direction: Production supervised by Henry Blankfort, staged by Nick Castle, and sketches directed by Sid Kuller and Everett Wile; *Producer*: The American Revue Theatre (Walter Jurmann, Chairman); *Choreography*: Nick Castle; *Scenery, Costumes,* and *Lighting*: Rene Hubert; *Musical Direction*: Duke Ellington

Cast: *Duke Ellington*, Dorothy Dandridge, Ivy Anderson, Herb Jeffries, Al Guster, The Rockets (Henry Roberts, Andrew Jackson), The Hi-Hatters (Clarence Landry, Vernod Bradley, Udell Johnson); Girls of the Ensemble: Artie Brandon, Lucille Battle, Avanelle Harris, Ethelyn Stevenson, Myrtle Fortune, Alice Key, Doris Ake, Hyacinth Cotton, Millie Munroe (or Monroe), Frances Neely, Louise Franklin, Pasty Hunter; Choir: Roy Glenn, Wesley Bly, Edward Short, Lawrence Harris, Louise Jones, Anna Dent, Evelyn Burwell (or Burrwell), Eloise Flenoury, Le Roy Antoine; Duke Ellington's Orchestra: Johnnie Hodge (Alto Saxophone), Barney Bigard (Tenor Saxophone), Ben Webster (Tenor Saxophone), Otto Hardwick (Alto Saxophone), Harry Carney (Baritone Saxophone), Rex Stewart (Trumpet), Ray Nance (Trumpet), Wallace Jones (Trumpet), Joe Nanton (Trombone), Lawrence Brown (Trombone), Juan Tizol (Valve Trombone), Jimmy Blanton (Bass Viol), Sonny Greer (Drums), Freddie Guy (Guitar); Other Musicians: LeRoy Antoine (Drums), Edward Short (Drums); Other Cast Members: Suzette Johnson, Marie Bryant, Paul White, Alice Key, Wonderful Smith, Garbo (dancer), Pot, Pan, and Skillet (Potts Jackson, Pans Ware, and Skillet Mayhand)

Sketches and Musical Numbers

Act One: "Sun-Tanned Tenth of a Nation" (lyric by Paul Francis Webster, music by Hal Borne and Otis Rene) (First Drummer: LeRoy Antoine; Second Drummer: Edward Short; Third Drummer: Sonny Greer; Pianist: Duke Ellington; Ivy Anderson, Dorothy Dandridge, Herb Jeffries, Roy Glenn, The Rockets, The Hi-Hatters, Choir, Ensemble); "Stomp Caprice" (dance) (music by Mercer Ellington) (Al Guster); "The Brown-Skinned Gal in the Calico Gown" (lyric by Paul Francis Webster, music by Duke Ellington) (The Boy: Herb Jeffries; The Girl: Dorothy Dandridge; Calico Girls: Artie Brandon, Lucille Battle, Avanelle Harris, Doris Ake, Myrtle Fortune, Suzette Johnson; danced by The Hi-Hatters); "Human Interest" (sketch by Hal Fimberg) (Charlie: Pot; Smithers: Roy Glenn; Baltimore: Skillet; Ohio: Pan; Old Man: Wonderful Smith); "Bli-Blip" (lyric by Sid Kuller, music by Duke Ellington) (Girl: Marie Bryant; Boy: Paul White); "I Got It Bad and That Ain't Good" (lyric by Paul Francis Webster, music by Duke Ellington) (Ivy: Ivy Anderson; A Friend: Alice Key); Wonderful Smith; "Cindy with the Two Left Feet" (lyric by Paul Francis Webster, music by Hal Borne) (Schoolboy: Paul White; Cindy: Dorothy Dandridge; First Sister: Avanelle Harris; Second Sister: Lucille Battle; Fairy Godmother: Evelyn Burwell; Prince Charming: Al Guster; Jitterbugs: The Rockets, The Hi-Hatters, Alice Brandon, Myrtle Fortune, Millie Munroe); "Bugle Break" (music by Duke Ellington) (Pot, Pan, and Skillet); "Flame Indigo" (lyric by Paul Francis Webster, music by Duke Ellington) (Garbo); "Mad Scene from Woolworth's" (sketch by Langston Hughes and Charles Leonard) (Cornelia: Ivy Anderson; Woman: Avanelle Harris; First Salesgirl: Suzette Johnson; Second Salesgirl: Alice Key; Manager: Al Guster; Passerby: Wonderful Smith); "Shhhh! He's on the Beat!" (sketch by Sid Kuller and Hal Fimberg, music by Duke Ellington) (Proprietor: Roy Glenn; Waitress: Marie Bryant; Bartender: Wonderful Smith; First Couple: Hyacinth Cotten and Andrew Jackson; Second Couple: Artie Brandon and Henry Roberts; Third Couple: Clarence Landry and Udell Johnson; Fourth Couple: Avanelle Harris and Pot; Cop: Pan); "I've Got a Passport from Georgia" (lyric by Paul Francis Webster and Ray Golden, music by Hal Borne) (The Traveler: Paul White); "Garbo and Hepburn" (sketch by Sid Kuller) (Garbo: Garbo; Hepburn: Marie Bryant); "The Emperor's Bones" (lyric by Paul Francis Webster, music by Otis Rene) (The Guide: Roy Glenn; Tourists: Artie Brandon, Louis Franklin, Patsy Hunter, Edward Short, Lawrence Harris; The Hi-Hatters, The Rockets); "Cymbal Sockin' Sam" (lyric by Sidney Miller, music by Mickey Rooney) (The Girl: Dorothy Dandridge; Sam: Sonny Greer); "Uncle Tom's Cabin Is a Drive-In Now" (Uncle Tom: Roy Glenn; Aunt Jemima: Evelyn Burwell; Waitress: Ivy Anderson; Second Waitress: Marie Bryant; Pot, Pan, and Skillet, The Hi-Hatters, The Rockets, Ensemble)

Act Two: "Jump for Joy" (lyrics by Sid Kuller and Paul Francis Webster, music by Duke Ellington) (Herb Jeffries, Choir, The Hi-Hatters, Ensemble); "Vignettes" (sketch by Sid Kuller) (First Couple: Dorothy Dandridge and Herb Jeffries; Second Couple: Marie Bryant and Udell Johnson); "Old-Fashioned Waltz" (lyric by Sid Kuller, music by Duke Ellington) (Herb Jeffries; Couples: The Hi-Hatters, Suzette Johnson, Millie Munroe, Avanelle Harris); "We Aim to Please" (sketch by Hal Fimberg and Sid Kuller) (Laughin' Andy: Roy Glenn; Ever Joyous: Paul White; Customer: Skillet; Smilin' Franky: Al Guster); "If Life Were All Peaches and Cream" (lyric by Paul Francis Webster, music by Duke Ellington) (First Couple: Dorothy Dandridge and Herb Jeffries; Second Couple: Marie Bryant and Paul White); "Rent Party" (sketch by Sid Kuller; sequence included "Concerto for Clinkers," music by Duke Ellington) (Hostess: Ivy Anderson; The Duke: Duke Ellington; Sonny Greer, Ray Nance, Jimmy Blanton, Rex Stewart, Roy Glenn, Henry Roberts, Suzette Johnson, Ensemble); "The Finished Symphony" (sketch by Richard Weil) (Tiger: Roy Glenn; Rough-House: Pan); "Chocolate Shake" (lyric by Paul Francis Webster, music by Duke Ellington) (Bartender: Paul White; Boy: Al Guster; Girl: Ivy Anderson; Cigarette Girl: Marie Bryant); "Hickory Stick" (lyric by Paul Francis Webster, music by Hal Borne) (Singer: Dorothy Dandridge; Dancer: Pete Nugent); "Resigned to Living" (sketch by Hal Fimberg) (Gertrude: Suzette Johnson; Noel: Al Guster; First Caller: Herb Jeffries; Second Caller: Henry Roberts; Man: Wonderful Smith); "Nothin'" (lyric by Sid Kuller and Ray Golden, music by Hal Borne) (Boy: Paul White; Girl: Ivy Anderson; The Rockets, The Hi-Hatters, Ensemble); "Made to Order" (sketch by Sid Kuller) (First Tailor: Pan; Second Tailor: Skillet; Customer: Pot); "Sharp Easter" (lyric by Sid Kuller, music by Duke Ellington) (The Loan Shark: Herb Jeffries; The Streetwalker: Marie Bryant; The Dandy: Andrew Jackson; The Sweetman: Henry Roberts; The Wolf: Garbo; The Customer: Pot; The Tailors: Pan and Skillet); Finale (Entire Company)

Jump for Joy was a black revue (with music mostly by Duke Ellington) which played during the summer of 1941 in Los Angeles, and although the production had Broadway in mind, it closed permanently in Los Angeles after 101 performances. It left behind one of the most achingly beautiful ballads in the American songbook, "I Got It Bad and That Ain't Good," which was introduced by Ivy Anderson. Among the revue's cast members was Dorothy Dandridge, who left the production during the run and was succeeded by Judy Carol.

The revue included a lavish assortment of songs, dances, and sketches, including a spoof of Greta Garbo and Katharine Hepburn; the sketch "Resigned to Living" kidded Noel Coward's *Design for Living* (Suzette Johnson was "Gertrude," and Al Guster was "Noel"); the song "I've Got a Passport from Georgia" depicted the excitement of a Southern black who looks forward to life in the North where signs proclaim "Out to Lunch" instead of "Out to Lynch"; the sketch "Made to Order" was yet another of the era's nods to the sartorially famous Lucius Beebe; and "Uncle Tom's Cabin Is a Drive-In Now" depicted a scene on the old plantation with Uncle Tom and Aunt Jemima which is magically transformed into a jive-hopping modern-day California fast-food joint.

Among the numbers dropped during the run were the Garbo-Hepburn spoof; the dance "Flame Indigo"; and "Cymbal Sockin' Sam" (which was composed by Mickey Rooney). A few weeks after the opening, Ellington wrote the lyric and music of "Rocks in My Bed," which was added to the score once blues singer Big Joe Turner joined the cast; the song emerged as the score's second standard.

In 1988, the Smithsonian released an archival recording of music from the production (Smithsonian Collection of Recordings LP # R-037/DMM-1-0722). The album includes Ivy Anderson's original cast performance of "I Got It Bad and That Ain't Good," and among the other numbers are "Stomp Caprice," "The Brown-Skinned Gal in the Calico Gown," "Bli-Blip," "Bugle Break," "Chocolate Shake," the title song, and Big Joe Turner's performance of "Rocks in My Bed." In the accompanying booklet for the album, Martin Williams notes that over the years five of Ellington's songs have completely disappeared ("Sharp Easter," "Flame Indigo," "Concerto for Clinkers," "Old-Fashioned Waltz," and "Shhhh! He's on the Beat!"); memorabilia from the production held by sketch writer and lyricist Sid Kuller and various cast members was either lost in storage vaults or stolen; and official photographs from the production were eventually sold for their silver nitrate content. Most tantalizing is silent footage taken from a live performance; it now seems to be in private hands and is unavailable for public viewing.

For the uninitiated, the program included a helpful glossary which translated various words and phrases (all reet = all right; dig you later = see you later; charge = marijuana; bust my conk = enjoy; skin = palm of hand; etc.).

PATRICIA

Theatre and *Performance Dates*: The musical opened at the Alcazar Theatre in San Francisco, California, on November 27, 1941, and closed there on December 20, 1941 (the production was briefly revived at the Alcazar in early 1942).
Book: Barry Connors
Lyrics: J. Keirn Brennan
Music: George Grandee
Based on the 1924 play *The Patsy* by Barry Connors.
Direction: Russell Fillmore; *Producer*: Henry Duffy; *Musical Direction*: Robert Nurok; other credits unknown
Cast: Dorothy Stone (Patricia Harrington), Charles Collins (Tony Anderson), Catherine Doucet (Mrs. Harrington), Jed Prouty (Mr. Harrington), Kathryn Mayfield (Grace Harrington), Reginald Craig (Billy Caldwell), Marjorie Wilson (Sadie Buchanan), Paul R. Maxey (Francis Patrick O'Flaherty)
The musical was presented in two acts.
The action takes place during the present time in Arizona.

Musical Numbers

Note: Division of acts and song assignments is unknown.
"Exquisite"; "To Know You Is to Like You"; "So Long, No Longer"; "Roll, Pony, Roll"; "Desert of Dreams"; Hot Dog, Mustard and You"; "Peguins"; "Nuggets"

Henry Duffy's production of *Patricia* was based on the 1924 play *The Patsy* by Barry Connors. The musical opened in late November 1941 and was met with middling reviews; it closed in late December, but Duffy brought it back in early 1942 before withdrawing it a second time.

Much later in the year Duffy resurrected the property with a new book, lyrics, and music. As **Life of the Party**, the musical played in Detroit for two months, but didn't risk New York; but the revised version is noteworthy because it marked the first collaboration of Alan Jay Lerner and Frederick Loewe. In this case, Lerner wrote the book, and Loewe the score (the lyrics were by Earle Crooker). For more information, see entry for **Life of the Party**.

THEY CAN'T GET YOU DOWN

Theatres and *Performance Dates*: The musical was first produced in Los Angeles, California, on October 27, 1941, and later played at the Studebaker Theatre, Chicago, Illinois, from January 25 to January 31, 1942 (between the Los Angeles and Chicago engagements, the musical probably played in other cities).
Book and *Lyrics*: Edward Eliscu and Henry Myers
Music: Jay Gorney
Direction: Unknown; *Producers*: Edward Eliscu, Henry Myers, Jay Gorney, Jack Kirkland, and Dwight Deere Wiman; *Choreography*: Danny Dare; *Scenery*: Frederick Stover; *Costumes*: Georgia Anderson; *Lighting*: Unknown; *Musical Direction*: Unknown
Cast: Julie Sherwin, Johnnie (Johnny) Johnston, Donald Brian, Berni Gould, Eve McVeagh, Edward Emerson, Glenn Turnbull, Eddie Johnson, Mary McCarty, James Griffith, Johnstone White, Eleanor Pryne, Mary Gilbert, Kathleen Reagan, Shirley Van, Gene Barry, Wally Castel, Bob Gallagher, Don Meyer, John Harvey, Ted Kneeland, Ross Murray (during the run, Jan Clayton and Peggy Ryan were also in the production)

Musical Numbers

Note: Division of acts and song assignments is unknown; the song list is given alphabetically.
"Ad Ripae Mildewensis Fluminis"; "It's No Fun Eating Alone"; "Love Can Settle Everything"; "Love in a Changing World"; "Mittel-Europa"; "More Mittel-Europa"; "Musical Chairs"; "On the Banks of the Mildew River"; "River to Dora Flora"; "Sir Pumphrey Mildew"; "Take Her, My Boy"; "They Can't Get You Down"; "Twenty-Five Bucks a Week"; "Twenty-One Bucks a Week"; "Unzer Amerika"; "You're Only a Barefoot Boy"

They Can't Get You Down was by Jay Gorney, Henry Myers, and Edward Eliscu, the creators of the revue **Meet the People**. In this case, the work was a book musical that kidded the genre of college musicals. Edwin Schallert in *Best Plays* said the show had "much originality" but "failed in actual construction." The plot was "hazily" written, and the evening's chief virtue was the score. In the same volume, Cecil Smith complained that the "entire book" contained as much "essential" entertainment as a single sketch in the "none too brilliant" **Meet the People**.

The musical provided early opportunities for such players as Jan Clayton, Mary McCarty, Johnny Johnson, and Gene Barry.

The song "Mittel-Europa" (aka "That Mittel-Europa Europe of Mine") was later interpolated into the score of the short-lived 1942 Broadway revue **Let Freedom Sing** and was then heard in Gorney, Myers, and Eliscu's 1943 revue **Marching with Johnny** during part of its pre-Broadway tryout (the revue closed prior to New York but apparently was revised and later toured as *The New Meet the People*). "Love in a Changing World" was also used in **Marching with Johnny**; the song is included in the collection *Make Mine Manhattan and Great Revues Revisited* (Painted Smiles CD # PSCD-119).

1942–1943 Season

BY JUPITER
"RODGERS AND HART'S NEW MUSICAL COMEDY"

Theatre: Shubert Theatre
Opening Date: June 3, 1942; *Closing Date*: June 12, 1943
Performances: 427
Book: Richard Rodgers and Lorenz Hart
Lyrics: Lorenz Hart
Music: Richard Rodgers
Based on the 1932 play *The Warrior's Husband* by Julian F. Thompson.
Direction: Joshua Logan; *Producers*: Dwight Deere Wiman and Richard Rodgers in association with Richard Kollmar; *Choreography*: Robert Alton; *Scenery* and *Lighting*: Jo Mielziner; *Costumes*: Irene Sharaff; *Musical Direction*: Johnny Green
Cast: Bob Douglas (Achilles), Mark Dawson (A Herald), Robert Hightower (Agamemnon, Slave), Jayne Manners (Buria), Rose Inghram (First Sentry), Martha Burnett (Second Sentry), Kay Kimber (Third Sentry), Monica Moore (Sergeant), Maidel Turner (Caustica), Margaret Bannerman (Heroica), Bertha Belmore (Pomposia), Don Liberto (First Boy), Tony Matthews (Second Boy), William Vaux (Third Boy), Benay Venuta (Hippolyta), *Ray Bolger* (Sapiens), Constance Moore (Antiope), Helen Bennett (A Huntress, Third Camp Follower), Flower Hujer (An Amazon Dancer), Ronald Graham (Theseus), Berni Gould (Homer), Vera-Ellen (Minerva, First Camp Follower), Lewis Hightower (Slave), Wana Wenerholm (Amazon Runner), Ralph Dumke (Hercules), Irene Corlett (Penelope), Ruth Brady (Second Camp Follower), Joyce Ring (Fourth Camp Follower), Rosemary Sankey (Fifth Camp Follower); Girls of the Ensemble: Helen Bennett, Ruth Brady, Betty Jo Creager, June Graham, Babs (Barbara) Heath, Janet Lavis, Virginia Meyer, Marjorie Moore, Mary Virginia Morris, Beth Nichols, Dorothy Poplar, Bobby Priest, Joyce Ring, Rosemary Sankey, Toni Stuart, Olga Suarez, Wana Wenerholm; Boys of the Ensemble: Ray Koby, Don Liberto, Michael Mann, Tony Matthews, George Schwable, William Silvers, Ken Whelan, Robert Wilson, William Vaux
The musical was presented in two acts.
The action takes place in ancient Greece.

Musical Numbers

Act One: "For Jupiter and Greece" (Bob Douglas, Mark Dawson, Greek Warriors); "Jupiter Forbid" (Benay Venuta, Martha Burnett, Rose Inghram, Kay Kimber, Monica Moore; danced by Marjorie Moore and Amazon Warriors; and by Robert and Lewis Hightower, Flower Hyjer, Ensemble); "Life with Father" (Ray Bolger); "Nobody's Heart Belongs to Me" (Constance Moore); "The Gateway of the Temple of Minerva" (Ronald Graham, Ensemble); "Life with Father" (reprise) (Bertha Belmore, Ray Bolger); "Here's a Hand" (Ronald Graham, Constance Moore); "No, Mother, No" (Ray Bolger, Ensemble)

Act Two: "The Boy I Left Behind Me" (Jayne Manners, Ensemble); "Nobody's Heart Belongs to Me" (reprise) (Ray Bolger); "Ev'rything I've Got (Belongs to You)" (Ray Bolger, Benay Venuta); "Bottoms Up" (Mark Dawson, Benay Venuta, Constance Moore, Berni Gould, Bob Douglas, Vera-Ellen, Flower Hujer, Robert and Lewis Hightower, Ensemble); "Careless Rhapsody" (Constance Moore, Ronald Graham); Finaletto (aka "The Greeks Have Got the Girdle") (Ray Bolger, Benay Venuta, Bertha Belmore, Ensemble); "Ev'rything I've Got" (reprise) (Benay Venuta); ("Wait Till You See Her" [Ronald Graham, Ensemble]; see below); "Now That I've Got My Strength" (Ray Bolger, Irene Corlett, Vera-Ellen, Ensemble); Finale (Entire Company)

Based on the 1932 play *The Warrior's Husband*, *By Jupiter* was a one-joke show. Set in ancient Greece, the women are tough-babe warriors and their somewhat sissified husbands stay home and cook supper. But in the expert hands of the musical's creators, the reversal-of-the-sexes theme resulted in a merry affair with romantic and comical songs by Richard Rodgers and Lorenz Hart, a fast-moving book (also by Rodgers and Hart) which included a war correspondent named Homer, lively dances by Robert Alton, lavish décor by Jo Mielziner and Irene Sharaff, and a cast that included a star turn by Ray Bolger.

No one knew it at the time, but *By Jupiter* was sadly the last new musical by Rodgers and Hart (the following year they teamed up for a revival of their 1927 hit *A Connecticut Yankee* and contributed a few new songs for the production). But *By Jupiter* ended their collaboration on a high note, and it became their longest-running musical with 427 performances (the original productions of *A Connecticut Yankee* and **Pal Joey** were runners-up with 421 and 374 respective performances).

The score offered a number of rapturous ballads, including "Nobody's Heart Belongs to Me," "Careless Rhapsody," and, maybe, the score's most well-known song, "Wait Till You See Her" (see below). "Ev'rything I've Got" was a sassy insult duet for Ray Bolger (Sapiens) and his wife Hippolyta (Benay Venuta); "Jupiter Forbid" was one of the most rhythmic and pulsating songs in the entire Rodgers and Hart songbook; Bolger's "Life with Father" made reference to the hit play and provided a show-stopping moment for him and Bertha Belmore (playing his mother Pomposia, the role she created in the straight play version *The Warrior's Husband*); "The Boy I Left Behind Me" emphasized the reversal-of-the-sexes theme; and the Greek Theseus (Ronald Graham) sang the amusing "In the Gateway of the Temple of Minerva" (where "she gave the gate to me").

Wilella Waldorf in the *New York Post* praised Bolger's "ingratiating" performance; said Venuta was "tough as raw venison"; and Graham looked "like Apollo, with a dash of Mars thrown in." The role of Antiope was created by Katharine Hepburn in *The Warrior's Husband*, and here it was "dashingly" played and "meekly" sung by Constance Moore; and Belmore was a "rare old girl" whose jitter-bugging *pas de deux* with Bolger was a "rare sight to see."

Barclay Hudson in the *New York World-Telegram* liked the "sparklingly told" story with its "catchy" score, and said Ronald Graham was "the epitome of what all musical comedy heroes should look and sound like"; Bertha Belmore stopped the show "for several minutes" with her jitterbug with Bolger; and Vera-Ellen was a "petite dancing doll." As for Constance Moore, "nothing so gorgeous has been seen on a Broadway stage for a couple of wars." Lewis Nichols in the *New York Times* suggested Moore was "more attractive than vocal"; that Bolger was "magnificent"; and that Belmore's dance "practically ends all dances." He noted that Bolger's "nancy role" might have proven "sudden death" had it had been overplayed.

John Anderson in the *New York Journal-American* said "by Jove!, and by all means" see *By Jupiter* because it offered "the speed, gaiety, and sophistication of Broadway's shiniest showmanship"; he praised the "fascinating knock-down and drag-out" catalog-of-insults "Ev'rything I've Got"; the "unforgettable steps" of Bertha Belmore's dance with Bolger; and the "beautiful" Constance Moore (but noted her voice was "hardly equal to the occasion").

Burns Mantle in the *New York Daily News* heralded the musical as a "rousing" hit and noted the book had "dirtied up the suggestions a bit" but "not too boldly"; he reported that Lorenz Hart had "vigorously denied" that John O'Hara and Marc Connelly worked on the book (Waldorf had mentioned that supporting actor Berni Gould had been "credited" with some of the lyrics which had "actually" been written by Hart). Mantle also noted that warrior women and male sissies offered "sure-fire" Broadway humor. Richard Watts in the *New York Herald Tribune* praised the "lavish, resplendent" and "entertaining" musical, and Richard Lockridge in the *New York Sun* said the "longish" show seemed "all too short," and it was "hard to give higher praise to a musical." He was also glad the sets and costumes hadn't been "rationed."

But Louis Kronenberger in *PM* said the show "gets by all right," but except for Bolger's stepping the musical "never goes to town." But he praised Bolger and Belmore's "extremely funny dance" and said it was one of the evening's best moments.

During the tryout, the musical was known as *All's Fair*; dropped prior to Broadway were "Fool Meets Fool," "Life Was Monotonous," and "Nothing to Do but Relax." The lyrics for the used and deleted songs are included in *The Complete Lyrics of Lorenz Hart*.

For a 1942 radio broadcast, Bolger performed "Ev'rything I've Got (Belongs to You)," and the sequence is preserved in the collection *Rodgers & Hart Volume 3* (Pearl Records CD # GEM-0118).

With the hit 1952 Broadway revival of *Pal Joey*, it was probably inevitable that another Rodgers and Hart show would be revived, and so two years later *On Your Toes* opened (and soon closed, after a disappointing two-month run). Similarly, the 1963 Off-Broadway revival of the team's *The Boys from Syracuse* was a long-running hit that tallied up five hundred performances, and so a few years later saw the surprise of a major Off-Broadway revival of *By Jupiter*, which opened at Theatre Four on January 19, 1967, for 118 performances. The production included all the songs from the original (although "No, Mother No" wasn't listed in the program, it was included as part of the first-act finale). The revival wasn't successful, but it left behind a delightful cast album (RCA LP # LOC/LSO-1137; issued on CD by DRG # DRG-CD-19105). Hildegarde's *Songs from the Shows* (Vocalion CD # CDEA-6078) includes four songs from the production ("Careless Rhapsody," "Jupiter Forbid," "Nobody's Heart," and "Ev'rything I've Got").

As for the glorious "Wait Till You See Her," it seems no one can agree whether or not the song was performed in the New York production. It was sung by Ronald Graham during the tryout, and the number is not only listed in the opening night Broadway program, it's also listed in the programs for most of the run. But legend has it that before the New York opening George Abbott was called in to critique the show, and he suggested the number be cut. The position of the song is interesting, because it's placed in the final scene of the show. With all the zany goings-on in the mad-cap story, this scene needed to resolve the plot's complications, including Sapiens's breakthrough moment when he asserts his manhood and sings "Now That I've Got My Strength." Perhaps the placement of the sweeping, romantic waltz "Wait Till You See Her" at this moment slowed down the action at a pivotal point that needed to focus on the story's resolution. Further, the musical included two other ballads ("Nobody's Heart Belongs to Me" and "Careless Rhapsody") and so maybe the deletion of a third was considered expedient since its omission tightened up the concluding minutes of the second act.

As for the song remaining in the program for most of the run, it may not have seemed all that important to remove it from the song listing. Errors and omissions sometimes occur in programs, and unless the production team rectifies the mistake, the error remains. For example, Irving Berlin's hit 1933 revue *As Thousands Cheer* included his classic "Easter Parade." But the song was never once listed as such in the program, which always referred to it as "Her Easter Bonnet." And *Half a Sixpence* (1965) offered the show-stopping dance sequence "Shop Ballet," but during the entire run the programs never listed the number. Further, *Cabaret* (1966) included two dances, the lighthearted "Fruit Shop Dance" and the rousing "Kickline" sequence, but they were never listed in the New York programs during the musical's long run.

Perhaps the best evidence that "Wait Till You See Her" wasn't sung in the Broadway production is from the critics themselves. This was an era when reviewers singled out songs and often made predictions as to which would most likely be heard in the nightclubs and on the radio, phonographs, and jukeboxes. Of the musical's twelve songs, the critics singled out nine numbers and not one of them mentioned "Wait Till You See Her."

LAUGH, TOWN, LAUGH (aka VAUDEVILLE 1942)

Theatre: Alvin Theatre
Opening Date: June 22, 1942; *Closing Date*: July 25, 1942
Performances: 65
Produced and *Directed* by Ed Wynn; *Scenery*: Frank W. Stevens; *Costumes*: Various gowns and costumes designed by Valentina, Saks Fifth Avenue, and Ernest Schrapps; *Musical Direction*: Emil Coleman
Cast: Ed Wynn, Jane Froman, Carmen Amaya (including her troupe Antonia, Leonor, Jose, and Paco, with guitarist Sabicas), Joe Smith and Charles Dale, Senor Wences, The Hermanos Williams Trio, Ken David-

son and Hugh Forgie, The Herzogs, The Volga Singers (Nicolas Vasilieff, Director, with Leonid Troyitsky, Boris Belostozky, Veacheslov Mamonuff, Stephen Slepushkui, Andrew Gregorioff, Michael Greben, Sasha Kuroschkin), The Mighty Nimrod, Hector and Pals (with Marion), Jerry Brannon, Eleanor Schramm, Ann Graham, Gene Wright, Gene Ashley, Emil Coleman and His Orchestra
The revue was presented in two acts.

Sketches and Musical Numbers

Act One: Overture (Emil Coleman and His Orchestra; the overture consisted of medleys from previous revues and musicals in which Ed Wynn had appeared); Ed Wynn, with "passersby" Eleanor Schramm, Ann Graham, Gene Wright, and Gene Ashley; The Herzogs (five female Australian trapeze artists); The Volga Singers (Russian choral group); Senor Wences (Portuguese [Spanish] puppeteer); Jane Froman (American singer); The Mighty Nimrod; Carmen Amaya (Spanish flamenco dancer and her troupe Antonia, Leonor, Jose, and Paco with guitarist Sabicas)
Act Two: Entr'acte (Emil Coleman and His Orchestra; with more medleys from earlier revues and musicals in which Wynn had appeared); The Hermanos Williams Trio (Argentinean singers and dancers); "A Little Bit of Fun" (Ed Wynn); Badminton Game (British Ken Davidson and Canadian Hugh Forgie; Sports Announcer: Jerry Brannon; "Dr. Kronkheit" (sketch) (Americans Joe Smith and Charles Dale); "From Here, There and Everywhere": Dog act Hector and Pals, with Marion; Finale (program note: "And That's 'Vaudeville')

Vaudeville and variety shows were all the rage during the War Forties, and Ed Wynn got on the bandwagon with *Laugh, Town, Laugh*, which the self-described Perfect Fool subtitled *Vaudeville 1942*. The program boasted "a galaxy of international stars" that included American comics Smith and Dale, American singer Jane Froman, the Russian Volga Singers, the Spanish dancer Carmen Amaya and her troupe, and even professional badminton champions British Ken Davidson and Canadian Hugh Forgie, who played a round of their game. The critics enjoyed the evening, but perhaps there was too much vaudeville in the current Broadway air, and so the revue closed after just a few weeks.

The program noted that as a "nimble mountain-goat leaps from crag to crag," the Perfect Fool would "leap from act to act." As he did in ***Boys and Girls Together***, Wynn ambled amiably along through the evening in his oversized coats and shoes, his undersized hats, and his strange contraptions (such as his famous piano-cum-bicycle as well as a cuckoo clock from which a cuckoo emerges every hour, looks around and shrugs, and then goes back into the clock). He often paused from the sidelines, watching the performers with childish glee and grandfatherly enthusiasm, and sometimes joined in the merriment. His classic persona was always present, and so he clucked and fussed and giggled and guffawed in self-effacing embarrassed bemusement. He indulged in his passion for puns, too. He made his first-act entrance by emerging from an erect, oversized cartoon of a hot-dog roll, and noted he was stepping out of his role.

The cast list for the opening night program included (Irish) Red Donohue and Uno, the latter a donkey. A few days before the opening, Wynn, Donohue, and Uno were rehearsing and Wynn had an unfortunate run-in with one Uno which severely hurt Wynn's hand. So it was announced that Red and Uno were temporarily out of the show and would join it later. In the meantime, the opening was postponed for a few days, and when the revue premiered Wynn performed with his hand in a rubber cast. But it seems Red and Uno never appeared in the revue, and two programs from later in the run don't list the twosome. However, a later program includes in the cast the team of Jayne and Adam DiGatano (who were from Holland and Scotland).

One source indicates that although Senor Wences was from Spain, the program bowed to the political sensibilities of the day by asserting that he was from Portugal. But, curiously, the same program had no problem stating Carmen Amaya was from Spain.

Wilella Waldorf in the *New York Post* said the revue made for "merry summer entertainment" and that Wynn was a "very funny fellow." She enjoyed the flamenco dancing of Carmen Amaya and her troupe, but noted an entire evening of them would have been monotonous; that Hector and his "cute" pooches were fine but that the inimitable Bricklayers of recent revues had taken the "edge" off other dog acts; and that Jane Froman's billing as "America's Leading Lady of Song" was an "exaggeration." Burns Mantle in the *New York Daily News* complained that Froman was "acquiring a collection of affectations"; said Senor Wences was "the greatest of modern ventriloquists"; and noted that with the worrisome war news on the front pages, the revue was "mighty welcome."

John Anderson in the *New York Journal-American* mentioned Wynn's fractured hand and stated "God help us" if he ever fractured his funny bone; he noted the badminton match between Ken Davidson and Hugh Forgie was "brisk" and "amusing," and that game announcer Jerry Brannon talked faster "than anybody outside a Gilbert and Sullivan patter song." Louis Kronenberger in *PM* said most of the acts were "remarkably good," and that at a $2.20 top ticket price the evening was "a buy." And Herrick Brown in the *New York Sun* noted he hadn't "run across any better cure for the blues" than *Laugh, Town, Laugh*.

Richard Watts in the *New York Herald Tribune* suggested the evening wasn't quite the "carnival" of Wynn's other shows, but noted Carmen Amaya brought "grim ferocity" and "bitter scorn" to her "violent and primitive dancing." An unsigned review in the *New York World-Telegram* mentioned that during intermission Wynn bantered about with audience members, including former governor Al Smith, who had also enjoyed a few moments in the spotlight during the opening night of **Sons o' Fun** (in honor of Smith, Wynn asked Emil Coleman and his orchestra to play "The Streets of New York").

Lewis Nichols in the *New York Times* said the evening was "practically the perfect vaudeville show," and he praised Carmen Amaya ("the frenzy of the flamenco"), and the Herzogs (the five female trapeze artists) who performed "incredible" feats up near the theatre's ceiling.

The critics reported that the Volga Singers sang (of course) "The Song of the Volga Boatmen," and that Jane Froman performed such numbers as "Don't Sit Under the Apple Tree" (1942 film *Private Buckaroo*; lyric by Lew Brown and Charles Tobias, music by Sam Stept); "Sleepy Lagoon" (lyric by Jack Lawrence, music by Eric Coates); and "Tea for Two" (*No, No, Nanette*, 1925; lyric by Irving Caesar, music by Vincent Youmans).

The hit of the evening occurred toward the end of the second act when old-timers Joe Smith and Charles Dale performed their classic sketch "Dr. Kronkheit." Anderson said this was one of the "vaudeville landmarks," and Kronenberger stated it was "one of the glories of the Palace era." In the sketch, the patient tells the doctor he's "dubious" about the "diogenes" the doctor has made, to which the doctor responds, "Glad to meet you, Mr. Dubious." The patient also complains that every time he eats a heavy meal "I don't feel so hungry."

Sadly, *Laugh, Town, Laugh* marked Ed Wynn's final appearance on Broadway. Al Jolson's last show had been **Hold on to Your Hats** and Eddie Cantor had bid farewell with **Banjo Eyes**. The great showmen of musical theatre were slowly but surely retiring, and the great era of Broadway clowns was gradually coming to a close.

THE CHOCOLATE SOLDIER

Theatre: Carnegie Hall
Opening Date: June 23, 1942; *Closing Date*: July 12, 1942
Performances: 24
Book and *Lyrics*: Stanislaus Stange (based on the original text by Rudolf Bernauer and Leopold Jacobson)
Music: Oscar Straus
Based on the 1894 play *Arms and the Man* by George Bernard Shaw.
Direction: John Pierce and José Ruben; *Producers*: Joseph S. Tushinsky and Hans Bartsch; *Choreography*: Unknown; *Scenery*: E. B. Dunkel Studios; *Costumes*: Paul DuPont; *Lighting*: Unknown; *Musical Direction*: Joseph S. Tushinsky
Cast: Helen Gleason (Nadina), Frances Comstock (Aurelia), Doris Patston (Mascha), Allan Jones (Lieutenant Bummerli), Detmar Poppen (Captain Massakroff), A. Russell Slagle (Colonel Popoff), Michael Fitzmaurice (Major Spiridoff), Tashamire (Ballerina), Peter Birch (Premier Dancer); *Note*: It seems that most of the chorus singers and dancers appeared in all three of Carnegie Hall's operetta revivals; for a list of these performers, see **The New Moon**.
The operetta was presented in three acts.
The action takes place in Bulgaria around 1885.

Oscar Straus's operetta *The Chocolate Soldier* was the first of three operettas presented at Carnegie Hall during the summer of 1942 under the auspices (and musical direction) of Joseph S. Tushinsky (the others in the series were **The Merry Widow** and **The New Moon**). All the productions employed full casts and singing and dancing choruses as well as a full orchestra. But production values were nil, and *Best Plays* described the scenery as "make-shift." In his annual seasonal summary, George Jean Nathan noted that despite some "jazzy liberties" taken with the score and occasional "arteriosclerotic" comedy, the "old warhorse delivered much of its familiar pleasure."

As *Der tapfere Soldat*, *The Chocolate Soldier* premiered in Vienna, Austria, on November 14, 1908, at the Theatre an der Wien, and its New York debut took place on September 13, 1909, at the Lyric Theatre for 296 performances. Since the Broadway premiere, the work has returned to New York seven times. The revivals opened on October 3, 1910, at the Circle Theatre (eight performances); on December 21, 1921, at the Century Theatre (83 performances); on January 27, 1930, at Jolson's Theatre (25 performances); on September 21, 1931, at Erlanger's Theatre (16 performances); and on May 2, 1934, at the St. James Theatre (13 performances). Following the current production, the work's most recent New York revival was in 1947 (see entry, which includes a list of the musical numbers).

The lighthearted plot of *The Chocolate Soldier* dealt with heroine Nadina who pines for a strong militaristic hero but finds herself falling in love with the title character, a devil-may-care soldier who'd rather nibble chocolates than spend time on the battlefield.

Because of legal issues raised by George Bernard Shaw, the 1941 MGM film *The Chocolate Soldier*, which starred Nelson Eddy and Rise Stevens, didn't utilize any of operetta's plot or its source material, Shaw's *Arms and the Man*; instead, the film was based on Ferenc Molnar's play *The Guardsman*, which had enjoyed a popular Broadway success in 1924 and is remembered for the first teaming of Alfred Lunt and Lynn Fontanne (the play was filmed in 1931, and it marks the couple's only major screen appearance). However, the film retained a few songs from *The Chocolate Soldier*, including "My Hero" and "Sympathy."

The 1947 revival, which played for seventy performances (see entry), used Stanislaus Stange's adaptation, which had been used in the original 1909 Broadway production as well as the Carnegie Hall revival.

There have been various recordings of the score, including a studio cast version released by RCA Victor (LP # LOP/LSO-1506; issued on CD by ArkivMusic/Sony Masterworks Broadway # SONY-81364) with Rise Stevens, Robert Merrill, Jo Sullivan, Peter Palmer, and Michael Kermoyan. The most complete version was issued by Newport Classics (CD # NPD-85650/2) in a two-CD set recorded live from a performance by the Ohio Light Opera.

STAR AND GARTER

Theatre: Music Box Theatre
Opening Date: June 24, 1942; *Closing Date*: December 4, 1943
Performances: 609
Sketches: H. I. Phillips
Lyrics: Irving Berlin, Al Dubin, Irving Gordon, Gypsy Rose Lee, Johnny Mercer, Harold J. Rome, Jerry Seelen, Al Stillman, Sis Willner
Music: Harold Arlen, Irving Berlin, Dorival Caymmi, Irving Gordon, Will Irwin, Gypsy Rose Lee, Lester Lee, James (Jimmy) McHugh, Harold J. Rome, Doris Tauber
Direction: Hassard Short; *Producer*: Michael Todd; *Choreography*: Al White Jr.; *Scenery*: Harry Horner; *Costumes*: Irene Sharaff; *Lighting*: Hassard Short; *Musical Direction*: Raymond Sinatra
Cast: Bobby Clark, Gypsy Rose Lee, Professor Lamberti, Georgia Sothern, Carrie Finnell, Pat Harrington, Eppy (Tiny) Pearson, Gil Maison (and his dogs and monkey, The Racketeers), Leticia, Marjorie Knapp, Juanita Rios, La Verne Lupton, Frank and Jean Hubert, Lynn, Royce, and Vanya, The Hudson Wonders (Ray and Geraldine Hudson), Joe Lyons, (George) Wayne and (Glenn) Marlin, Kate Friedlich and Bill (William) Skipper, Estelle Sloan, Richard Rober, Artie Conroy, Frank Price; Dancing Girls: Sunny Wright, Puddy Smith, Frances Hammond, Virginia Howe, Terry Lasky, Lorraine Latham, Janice Wallace, June Powers, Ruthe Reid, Jo Ann Flanagan, June MacLaren, Mimi Berry, Charlotte Lorraine, Betty Lee, Gloria Anderson, Margaret Kayes: Show Girls: June Sitarr, Andrea Mann, Helene Hudson, Audrey Westphal, Cynthia Cavanaugh, Lynn Powers, Adele Jurgens, Iris Marshall, Mary Lawrence, Ruth Josephs; Singers: Helen Price, Nina Dean, Carol Deis, Bob Lenn, Helen McCartney, Bill Marel, Richard Finney, Lipman Dukat
The revue was presented in two acts.

Sketches and Musical Numbers

Act One: "Star and Garter Girls" (lyric by Jerry Seelen, music by Lester Lee) (Gypsy Rose Lee, Star and Garter Girls); "The Sacred Gherkin" (sketch) (Mr. Wise: Joe Lyons; Biff: Gil Maison; Boff: Pat Harrington; First Girl: Juanita Rios; Second Girl: Geraldine Hudson); "Clap Yor (Your) Hands" (Georgia Sothern); "That Merry Wife of Windsor" ("stolen" from William Shakespeare) (Jennie Windsor: Gypsy Rose Lee; Andrew: Bobby Clark; Gus: Joe Lyons; Victor Windsor: Eppy "Tiny" Pearson); Gil Maison (and his dogs, The Racketeers); "Les Sylphides avec la Bumpe" (lyric and music by Irving Gordon) (Premier Dancer: Bill Skipper; Premiere Danseuse: Kate Friedlich; La Bumpe: La Verne Lupton; Second Premier Dancer: Wayne; Third Premier Dancer: Marlin; The Star and Garter Corps de Ballet); Wayne and Marlin; "In the Malamute Saloon" (music by Will Irwin) (The Ragtime Kid: Pat Harrington; The Bartender: Eppy "Tiny" Pearson; Dangerous Dan McGrew: Joe Lyons; The Lady That's Known as Lou: Gypsy Rose Lee; A Miner: Bobby Clark; Narrator: Richard Rober); "The Bunny" (aka "Bunny, Bunny, Bunny") ((lyric and music by Harold J. Rome) (Marjorie Knapp, The Star and Garter Girls; danced by The Hudson Wonders); Professor Lamberti (assisted by Dorothy Bigby); "The Girl on the *Police Gazette*" (from 1937 film *On the Avenue*; music and original and new lyric by Irving Berlin) (Singer: Frank Price; The Girl on the Police Gazette: Gypsy Rose Lee)

Act Two: "For a Quarter" (lyric by Jerry Seelen, music by Lester Lee) (The Candy Butchers: Bobby Clark, Pat Harrington, Eppy "Tiny" Pearson); "The Harem" (The Dancer: Leticia; The Sultan: Glenn Marlin; The Favorite Wife: Carrie Finnell; The Star and Garter Girls; this sequence included the song "Don't Take On More Than You Can Do," lyric and music by Irving Gordon); "I Can't Strip to Brahms" (lyric and music by Gypsy Rose Lee) (Gypsy Rose ["Authoress"] Lee); "Blues in the Night" (from 1941 film *Blues in the Night*; lyric by Johnny Mercer, music by Harold Arlen) (Ladies of the Night: June Sitarr, Lynn Powers, Ruth Josephs, Elnora Hayes, Cynthia Cavanaugh, Audrey Westphal, Iris Marshall, Adele Jurgens, Helene Hudson, Andrea Mann; The Evening Breeze: Leticia); "Robert the Roue" (aka "I'm Robert the Roue from Reading, Pa.") (from *Streets of Paris*, 1939; lyric by Al Dubin, music by Jimmy McHugh) (Bobby Clark, The Star and Garter Girls); "Aired in Court" (sketch by H. I. Phillips) (Court Clerk: Joe Lyons; Judge Gabby: Bobby Clark; District Attorney: Richard Rober; Gloria Pinknee: Gypsy Rose Lee; Council for the Defense: Eppy Tiny Pearson; William Abernathy: Pat Harrington; Court Recorder: Gil Maison); "I Don't Get It" (lyric by Sis Willner, music by Doris Tauber) (Marjorie Knapp; danced by La Verne Lupton); Lynn, Royce, and Vanya; "Brazilian Nuts" (lyric by Al Stillman, music by Dorival Caymmi) (Juanita Rios, Entire Company)

Under Mayor Fiorello H. LaGuardia, New York City's Commissioner of Licenses Paul Moss hadn't renewed licenses for theatres showing strip tease acts, but that didn't stop producer Michael Todd from getting on the vaudeville bandwagon with a lavish revue that incorporated old-time burlesque skits with traditional strip tease. Although the critics noted the show wasn't for children and that the second act was quite (shall we say) revealing, apparently the girls kept on enough tassels to ensure that the Music Box kept its license for the eighteen prosperous months that *Star and Garter* played.

Comic Bobby Clark (of the painted-on eyeglasses) was around for the jokes, and premier strip-tease queen Gypsy Rose Lee bumped around in sketches, songs, and her ladylike brand of stripping (in one song, she complained that "I Can't Strip to Brahms"). Another stripper of the era, Georgia Sothern, as well as a bevy of chorus girls, did what they could to shed as many costumes as possible, and apparently succeeded quite well. The evening also offered comedian Professor Lamberti (who believes the audience's applause is for his antics on the xylophone, and is completely oblivious to the fact they're applauding a strip-tease act going on behind him); Broadway high-steppers Kate Friedlich and Bill Skipper; more dancers with The Hudson Wonders; ballroom dancers Lynn, Royce, and Vanya; Frank and Jean Hubert's drunk act; muscle men George Wayne and Glenn Marlin; boyish tenor Frank Price; and Gil Maison and his dogs-and-monkey act, The Racketeers. And the evening ended with the required South American number (in this case, "Brazilian Nuts").

George Ross in the *New York World-Telegram* exclaimed that "happy-go-lucky rolling stone Michael Todd gathers no Moss of the license variety," and said the Minsky Brothers would be "green or magenta" with envy over the "most opulent" evening (he noted Irene Sharaff's costumes kept the chorus girls "unclothed in splendor"); Herrick Brown in the *New York Sun* said the revue was "fast-moving, sumptuous, dazzling and lusty"; and while Lewis Nichols in the *New York Times* felt the evening could have been more imaginative in its humor, he admitted the show was "sultry" with "blue flames" and the words of the lyrics offered both "one meaning" as well as nine others "lurking slyly behind."

Burns Mantle in the *New York Daily News* suggested the show's "anatomical twists" and "emotional bumps" could "excite license commissioners as well as refined but curious ladies from Dubuque." He reported that Bobby Clark was "riotous" and in the courtroom sketch had never "been funnier," and that Georgia Sothern had "no regard for anything much, including the law and her sacroiliac." Louis Kronenberger in *PM* said *Star and Garter* was a "leg-and-laugh show" filled with "plenty of good filthy fun." The revue didn't make a "lady" of burlesque, but it sure turned her into the "highest-stepping floozy" Broadway had seen in years. He cautioned that the "impressionable young" shouldn't stay for the second act, which contained "decidedly anatomical dances" and "equally anatomical quips."

Richard Watts in the *New York Herald Tribune* said *Star and Garter* was "rough, funny and unashamed . . . burlesque grown fancy but retaining its sense of humor." Gypsy Rose Lee was "the most dignified" of strip-teasers, and Georgia Sothern provided "hotter stripping." As for Bobby Clark, he was "one of the funniest men in the history of mankind" who could be "pretty rough" in his comedy. John Anderson in the *New York Journal-American* reported that Michael Todd had produced the season's "most anatomical spectacle" but cautioned that Todd had "stinted on nothing but imagination." Anderson found the comedy and the music wanting; he also noted that Harold J. Rome's "Bunny" offered "graceful" music and a "soiled" lyric.

Wilella Waldorf in the *New York Post* admitted the revue was "the most opulent burlesque show ever produced," but complained that Bobby Clark was "handicapped" by weak and often old material; at $4.40 for top seats (which had zoomed to $6.60 for the opening night!), she felt Todd should have ensured that the comedian had fresh material.

During the New York preview period, the following numbers were dropped: "Strong, Silent Men" (lyric by Jerry Seelen, music by Lester Lee) (for Bobby Clark and Gypsy Rose Lee); the sketch "Flugel Street" (by Billy K. Wells) which included the song "Noises in the Street" (lyric by Peter Barry and David Greggory [sometimes cited as David Gregory], music by Richard Lewine; see below); "The Kid's First and Last Fight" (sketch by Billy K. Wells); and "On a Saturday Night" (lyric by Jerry Seelen, music by Lester Lee).

During the run, the song "Don't Take on More Than You Can Do," which was sung during "The Harem" sketch, was dropped and replaced by "Turkish Oomph" (lyric by Jerry Seelen, music by Lester Lee), which itself seems to have been dropped later in the run. "The Bunny" (lyric and music by Harold J. Rome) was replaced by Rome's "Money" (see below), and it in turn was replaced by "It Was Marvelous" (lyric and music by Doris Fisher and Allan Roberts); all three numbers were performed by Marjorie Knapp, The Star and Garter Girls, and The Hudson Wonders. When Lynn, Royce, and Vanya left the revue, the sketch "Crazy House" (for Gypsy Rose Lee, Bobby Clark, Georgia Sothern, Pat Harrington, and other cast members) was substituted. Bobby Clark had originally introduced "Robert the Roue" (aka "I'm Robert the Roue from Reading, Pa.") in the 1939 revue *Streets of Paris*.

"Noises in the Street" had one of the busiest histories of all theatre songs. As noted in **Two Weeks with Pay**, the song surfaced in *'Tis of Thee* and then again during the preview period of *Star and Garter*; for more information, see **The Shape of Things!**

Harold Rome's "Money" is probably his later "Money Song" from **That's the Ticket!**

"The Girl on the *Police Gazette*" is included in the collection *Mike Todd's Broadway* (Everest LP # LPBR-5011).

STARS ON ICE
"A MUSICAL ICETRAVAGANZA"

Theatre: Center Theatre
Opening Date: July 2, 1942; *Closing Date*: April 16, 1944
Performances: 830
Lyrics: Al Stillman
Music: Paul McGrane
Direction: Staged by Catherine Littlefield, with skating direction by May Judels; *Producers*: Sonja Henie and Arthur M. Wirtz (A Sonart Production; William H. Burke, Executive Director); *Choreography*: Catherine Littlefield; *Scenery*: Bruno Maine; *Costumes*: Lucinda Ballard; *Lighting*: Eugene Braun; *Musical Direction*: David Mendoza

Cast: Carol Lynne, Lloyd "Skippy" Baxter, Twinkle Watts, Dorothy Caley, Mary Jane Yeo, The Brandt Sisters (Helga and Inge), Fritz Dietl, The Thaells (Edwina and Cliff), Bob and Peggy Whight, Mayita Montez, Hertha Grossman, Alex Hurd, Paul Castle, Paul Duke, The Three Rookies (Meryl Baxter, Don [Donald] Arthur, and Neil Rose), (Dr. A. Douglas) Arthur Nelles, Freddie Trenkler, The Sensational Four Bruises (Monte Stott, Sidney [Sid] Spalding, Geoffe Stevens, and Buster Grace); Vocals: Vivienne Allen, Jack Kilty; Ladies of the Ensemble: Irene Abitz, Jeanne Berman, Helen Bull, Jean Conrad, Irene Church, Corrynne Church, Dorothy Chandler, Kay Corcoran, Peggy Gordon, Janet Hester, Pearl Joseph, Billie Kling, Edith Kandel, Karen Lane, Ruth Noland, Patsy O'Day, Daphne Poole, Muriel Pack, Florence Rohr, Bing Stott, Trudy Schneider, Eileen Thompson, Helen Thompson; Male Ensemble (aka Speed Kings): Thomas DePauw, Rudolph VanDyke, James (Jimmie) Carter, Walter Hedberg, Peter Fenton, Fred Thompson, Charles Cavanaugh, Robert Coffman, Stan Skidmore, Ray Berg, James Sisk, Adolph Davidson, Willie Stikarowski, Bruce Clarke, Lyle Clark, Edward (Ed) Taylor, G. W. Bennett, Arthur Meehan, Ted Bruenn, Robert (Bob) Petrillo; Other Skaters: Meryl Baxter, Jean Conrad, Marta Dietl, Lucille O'Day, Walter Hedberg, Adolph Davidson, Rudy Richards, Jerry Decker, Bernice Stott, William (Billie) Taft, Kurt Fishman, Ralph Lippman, James Wright, Charles Slagle

The ice revue was presented in two acts.

Skating Sequences and Songs

Act One: Overture (Orchestra); "Stars on Ice" (Jack Kilty; Ladies of the Ensemble); Speed Kings; "Ten Easy Lessons" (Arthur Nelles); "Two of a Kind" (Helga Brandt and Inge Brandt); "Little Miss Muffet" (Little Miss Muffet: Twinkle Watts; Spider and Prince Charming: Meryl Baxter; Mushrooms: Peggy Gordon, Edith Kandel, Jeanne Berman, Jean Conrad, Marta Dietl, Karen Lane); "The Chase" (Fox: Buster Grace; Girls: Florence Rohr, Trudy Schneider, Pearl Joseph, Lucille O'Day, Helen Thompson, Kay Corcoran, Dorothy Chandler, Corrynne Church, Billie Kling, Helen Bull, Janet Hester, Muriel Pack, Patsy O'Day, Bing Stott, Eileen Thompson, Irene Abitz; Boys: Ray Berg, G. W. Bennett, William (Billie) Taft, Fred Thompson, Willie Stikarowski, Walter Hedberg, Adolph Davidson, Peter Fenton, Thomas DePauw, Rudy VanDyke, Rudy Richards, Bruce Clark, Robert Coffman, Charles Cavanaugh, Stan Skidmore, James Sisk; Grooms: Ted Bruenn, Jerry Decker, Robert Petrillo, Ed Taylor); "A Maid, a Cat and a Kitten" (Mary Jane Yeo, Neil Rose, Paul Castle) and "The Cavalier Cat" (Mary Jane Yeo); "Up and Over" (Alex Hurd); "Perfect Poise" (Edwina and Cliff Thaell); "Juke Box—Saturday Night" (Vivienne Allen; Mary Jane Yeo, Arthur Nelles, Rudy Richards, Paul Castle; Girls: Muriel Pack, Kay Corcoran, Patsy O'Day, Lucille O'Day, Pearl Joseph, Billie Kling, Bernice Stott, Helen Bull, Janet Hester, Dorothy Chandler, Helen Thompson, Daphne Poole, Ruth Noland, Florence Rohr, Trudy Schneider, Eileen Thompson, Corrynne Church, Irene Abitz, Jeanne Berman, Irene Church; Boys: Rudy Richards, Walter Hedberg, Robert Coffman, Fred Thompson, William Taft, Thomas DePauw, Charles Cavanaugh, Rudy VanDyke, Peter Fenton, James Sisk, Willie Stikarowski, Kurt Fishman, Robert Petrillo, Ray Berg, Bruce Clarke, Stan Skidmore, G. W. Bennett, Lyle Clark, Edward Taylor, Ralph Lippman); "Symphony in Smoke" (Paul Duke); "Russian Steppes" (Cossacks: Arthur Meehan, Ted Bruenn, Adolph Davidson, James Carter); "Bouncing Ball of the Ice" (Freddie Trenkler); "Jack Frost Reverie" (Jack Frost: Lloyd "Skippy" Baxter; Snow Queen: Hertha Grossman; Babies: Twinkle Watts, Paul Castle; Mother: Edwina Blades; Six Palette Boys: Rudy Richards, Bruce Clark, Rudy VanDyke, Fred Thompson, Robert Petrillo, Thomas DePauw; Snowflakes: Lucy O'Day, Muriel Pack, Pearl Joseph, Helen Bull, Ruth Noland, Billie Kling, Corrynne Church, Irene Abitz, Irene Church, Patsy O'Day, Eileen Thompson, Karen Lane, Helen Thompson, Dorothy Chandler, Bing Stott, Kay Corcoran, Trudy Schneider, Jean Conrad, Jeanne Berman, Daphne Poole) and "Little Jack Frost" (Vivienne Allen)

Act Two: Entr'acte (Overture); "Pan-Americana" (for this sequence, music of the song "Estrillita" by Ponce was used) (Castanet Group and Piano Accordion: Mary Jane Yeo, Muriel Pack, Rudy Richards, Helen Bull, Kurt Fishman; Girls: Peggy Corcoran, Eileen Thompson, Jeanne Berman, Edith Kardel, Kay Corcoran, Dorothy Chandler, Daphne Poole, Janet Hester, Bing Stott, Florence Rohr, Karen Lane, Patsy O'Day, Pearl Joseph, Trudy Schneider, Irene Church, Irene Abitz, Corrynne Church, Billie Kling, Jean Conrad, Helen Thompson; Boys: James Wright, Robert Petrillo, Willie Stikarowski, Ted Bruenn, Robert Coffman, Jerry Decker, Jimmie Carter, Arthur Meehan, Ralph Lippman, Stan Skidmore, Ray Berg, Fred Thompson,

Rudy VanDyke, Thomas DePauw, William Taft, Charles Cavanaugh, Adolph Davidson, Lyle Clark, Peter Fenton, Edward Taylor; Samba: Mayita Montez; Rhumba: Twinkle Watts and Paul Castle); "Syncro Style" (Dorothy Caley, Fritz Dietl); "Elevated Antics" (Buster Grace, Charles Slagle); "Autumn Leaves" (Chrysanthemum: Carol Lynne; The Wind: Lloyd "Skippy" Baxter; Autumn Leaves: Muriel Pack, Kay Corcoran, Ruth Noland, Billie Kling, Janet Hester, Eileen Thompson, Jeanne Berman, Helen Bull, Corrynne Church, Patsy O'Day, Peggy Gordon, Lucy O'Day, Trudy Schneider, Daphne Poole, Florence Rohr, Helen Thompson, Dorothy Chandler, Pearl Joseph, Irene Church, Bing Stott) and "Like a Leaf Falling in the Breeze" (lyric by Al Stillman, music by James Littlefield) (Jack Kilty, Mary Jane Yeo); The Three Rookies (Don Arthur, Meryl Baxter, Neil Rose); "Double Date" (Helga Brandt, Inge Brandt; Maids: Marta Dietl, Karen Lane); "Poetry of Motion" (Bob Whight, Peggy Whight); "Gin Rummy" (Players: Edwina Thaell, Cliff Thaell; The Joker: Don Arthur; The Deck: Ladies and Gentlemen of the Ensemble) and "Gin Rummy, I Love You" (Vivienne Allen, Jack Kilty); "Simon Legree and Topsy" (Freddy Trenkler, Fritz Diehl); "Smart Set" (Girls and Boys: Kay Corcoran and Bob Coffman, Janet Hester and Rudy Richards, Lucille O'Day and Fred Thompson, Muriel Pack and Bruce Clark, Peggy Gordon and Lyle Clark, Florence Rohr and Ray Berg, Daphne Poole and Kurt Fishman, Martha Dietl and James Carter, Jeanne Berman and Ed Taylor, Helen Bull and James Sisk, Corrynne Church and G. W. Bennett, Dorothy Chandler and Charles Cavanaugh, Eileen Thompson and Stan Skidmore, Helen Thompson and Willie Stikarowski, Ruth Noland and Robert Petrillo, Trudy Schneider and Ted Bruenn, Patsy O'Day and James Wright, Bing Stott and Rudy VanDyke, Irene Church and Walter Hedberg, Irene Abitz and Tommy DePauw) and "You're Awfully Smart" (Vivienne Allen, Jack Kilty); "A Gay Blade" (Lloyd "Skippy" Baxter); "Maids-A-Miss" (The Four Bruises: Sidney Spalding, Geoffrey Stevens, Monte Stott, Buster Grace); "Victory Ball" (Girls: Patsy O'Day, Martha Dietl, Irene Church, Peggy Gordon, Jeanne Berman, Kay Corcoran, Edith Kandel, Jean Conrad, Daphne Poole, Ruth Noland, Bing Stott, Corrynne Church, Muriel Pack, Janet Hester, Karen Lane, Irene Abitz, Trudy Schneider, Billie Kling, Lucille O'Day; Boys: Ralph Lippman, Peter Fenton, James Wright, Ed Taylor, G. W. Bennett, Walter Hedberg, Ray Berg, Bob Coffman, Adolph Davidson, Kurt Fishman, James Sisk, Lyle Clark, Jerry Decker, Ted Bruenn, Bruce Clark, James Carter, William Taft, Rudy VanDyke, Thomas DePauw, Robert Petrillo; Girl Principals: Helga Brandt, Inge Brandt, Edwina Blades, Dorothy Caley, Herta Grossman, Carol Lynne, Mayita Montez, Peggy Whight, Twinkle Watts, Mary Jane Yeo; Boy Principals: Bob Whight, Don Arthur, Lloyd "Skippy" Baxter, Meryl Baxter, Paul Castle, Fritz Diehl, Paul Duke, Buster Grace, Alex Hurd, Arthur Nelles, Neil Rose, Geoffrey Stevens, Sidney Spalding, Monte Stott, Charles Slagle, Cliff Thaell, Freddie Trenkler) and "Big Broad Smile" (Vivienne Allen, Jack Kilty)

The ice revue *Stars on Ice* opened on July 2, 1942, and ran through May 16, 1943, for a total of 427 performances; it closed for a one-month vacation and a second edition opened on June 24, and played through April 16, 1944, for 403 performances, for a grand total of 830 showings, the longest run of all the ice revues that played at the Center Theatre during the decade. The revue also boasted the only hit song from the series, "Juke Box—Saturday Night," which was popularized by Glenn Miller and His Band and remains one of the decade's most iconic numbers, a song that embodies the sound and even the attitude of the era's swing music.

In his seasonal summary, George Jean Nathan dubbed the show a "refrigerated spectacle" and voiced the old complaint that an entire evening of ice-skating was monotonous. He admitted that "little is more thoroughly graceful than professional rink movements," but two-and-a-quarter hours was more than he could "comfortably endure." He also cataloged the evening's lack of imagination, such as the inevitable skating waltz; a male skater in woman's clothes who falls down (apparently a drag outfit makes the fall funnier); the comic who skates rapidly toward the first row of the audience, suddenly stops before he crashes into them, and says, "I scared the hell outa you, eh?"; and the "repulsive" child skater who with the "self-assurance of a prima donna" proceeds to "grimly" twirl around a few times and then with "heavy humility coyly" acknowledges the audience's applause.

The second edition added such numbers as "Put Your Cares on Ice" (lyric and music by James Littlefield); "Waltz in Swingtime"; "South of the Border"; "The Dancing Lesson"; "Pied Piper of Rhythm"; "His Night Out"; "Salute to the Air Corps"; "Vintage of the Nineties"; "Valse Elegante," which included the song "You Must Be Part of a Dream" (lyric by Marten Lowell and music by James Littlefield); and "K. P. Kapers." Among the numbers that were deleted for the second edition were: "Little Miss Muffet"; "A Maid, a Cat and a Kitten"; "Gin Rummy, I Love You"; and "Smart Set."

THIS IS THE ARMY

"A New Soldier Show for the Benefit of Army Emergency Relief"

Theatre: Broadway Theatre
Opening Date: July 4, 1942; *Closing Date*: September 26, 1942
Performances: 113
Lyrics and *Music*: Irving Berlin
Direction: Staff Sgt. Ezra Stone; additional direction by Pvt. Joshua Logan; *Producer*: Uncle Sam; *Choreography*: Pvt. Robert Sidney and Cpl. Nelson Barclift (military formations directed by Cpl. Chester O'Brien); *Scenery* and *Costumes*: Pvt. John Koenig; *Lighting*: Uncredited; *Musical Direction*: Cpl. Milton Rosenstock
Cast (*Note*: When known, military ranks are given.): Pvt. Jus Addiss, Irving Albert, Cpl. Earl Allen, Sgt. Alan Anderson, Cpl. George Anderson, Sgt. Zinn Arthur, Pvt. Arthur Atkins, Charles Bacior, Pvt. Alan Bandler, Cpl. Nelson Barclift, Pvt. Kenneth Bates, Pvt. Herbert Beller, Samuel Benson, Pvt. Leonard Berchman, Pvt. Gene Berg, PFC Leander (Lee) Berg, Pvt. Richard Bernie, Pvt. Charles Blake, Sgt. Jack Brodmax, Pvt. Howard Brooks, Pvt. Marion "Spoons" Brown, Pvt. Richard Browning, Richard Burdick, Cpl. James Burrell, Pvt. Joseph Bush, Vance Campbell, Arturo Canzano, Pvt. Ted Cappy, Pvt. Samuel Carr, Pvt. Thomas Chetlin, Pvt. Stewart Churchill, Pvt. William Collier, PFC Joe Cook Jr., Pvt. Belmonte Cristiani, Cpl. James A. Cross, Pvt. Randolph Culley, Frank D'Elia, Pvt. Fred Deming, John C. Dempsey, Pvt. John Draper, Pvt. Bill Dutton, Pvt. Hercules Ecconomu, Pvt. Ross Elliot, Pvt. Derek Fairman, Pvt. Scott Farnworth, Pvt. James Farrell, Pvt. Cliffe (or Cliff) Ferre, Mario Fiorella, Bernard Frank, Leonard Fried, Pvt. Chick (Leo) Gagnon, Pvt. Larry Gengo, Marvin Goodis, Pvt. Ray (Benjamin) Goss, Murray Grubman, Cpl. Arthur Hatchett, Louis Hawkins, Pvt. Fred Hearn, Pvt. Hank Henry, Harold Hoha, Pvt. William Horne, Hyman Horowitz, Pvt. William (Billy) Howell, Pvt. Richard Irving, Pvt. Burl Ives, Pvt. Clarence Jaeger, Pvt. Eugene Jarvis, Pvt. Joseph Johnson, Cpl. Orlando Johnson, Pvt. Henry Jones, Pvt. Fred Kapner, PFC Fred Kelly, Pvt. Maurice Kelly, Pvt. Phil King, Pvt. Roger Kinne, Pvt. Stephen Lamarca, Pvt. Alfred Lane, Pvt. Richard Langdon, Pvt. Jack Lenny, Pvt. Earl Lippy, Pvt. Daniel Longo, Pvt. William Lynch, Pvt. Donald McCray, PFC James MacColl, Pvt. Ralph Magelssen, Pvt. Alan Manson, Jack Mendelsohn, Sgt. John Mendes, Pvt. Gary Merrill, Pvt. Pinkie Mitchell, Pvt. Howard Montgomery, Pvt. Robert Moore, Maurice Newman, Cpl. Chester O'Brien, Pvt. Edward O'Connor, Warren O'Harr, Pvt. Julie Oshins, Cpl. Earl Oxford, Pvt. Tileston Perry, Pvt. William Pillich, Pvt. Harvey Prael, Pvt. Orville Race, Pvt. Steve Ramos, Pvt. Charles Reade, Pvt. Richard Reeves, Pvt. John Riley, Pvt. Sydney Robin, Pvt. William Roerick, Milton Rogers, Pvt. Hayden Rorke, Henry Rosenblatt, Pvt. Anthony Ross, PFC Louis Salmon, Pvt. Sid Salzberg, Pvt. Nicholas Sassi, Pvt. Stanley Saloman, David Schoenfeld, Pvt. Robert Shanley, Pvt. Robert Sidney, Gerald Simini, Pvt. Stanley Sirois, Sgt. Arthur Steiner, Pvt. Benjamin Stermer, Sgt. Ezra Stone, Pvt. Norman Stuart, Sid Tamber, Cpl. Philip Truex, Sgt. Clyde Turner, Pvt. Norman VanEmburgh, Pvt. Claude Watson, Pvt. George Watson, Pvt. Larry Weeks, Pvt. Larry Weill, Bernard Welansky, Pvt. Albert Whitley, James Wiggins, Pvt. Joseph Wojcikowski, Pvt. William Wyckoff; The Allon Trio; Members from the original production of *Yip, Yip, Yaphank*: Peter J. Burns, Dan Healy, Harold Kennedy, John Murphy, Peter O'Neill, and Jack Riano; and Irving Berlin; Orchestra: First Violins—Acting Cpl. and Assistant Conductor Elias Dan, Pvt. Max Miller, Pvt. Harry Rosoff, Pvt. Nathan Gottschalk, Pvt. Herbert Sorkin, Cpl. Carl Ottobrino, Pvt. Louis Feldman, Pvt. Abner Silverstein; Second Violins—Pvt. Genc (or Gene) Rubin, Pvt. Peter Mesrobian, Pvt. Harold Silverstein, Pvt. Irving Merlin; Third Violins—Oscar Kraut, Pvt. Martin Samel, Walter Horton, Nathan Freeman; Violas—Pvt. Thomas Lanese, Pvt. Harry Kolstein, Pvt. Paul Israel; Cellos—Pvt. Cesare Pascarella, Pvt. Joseph Tekula, Pvt. Jesse Ehrlick; Saxophones—Pvt. Saul Levy, Pvt. John Meunzenberger, Pvt. Emil Weissfeld, Pvt. Joseph Guidice, Pvt. John Towne; Piano—Cpl. Morton Kahn; Percussion—Pvt. Philip Kraus, Pvt. Charles DeMilt; Basses—Pvt. Lester Braun, Pvt. Abe Siegal; Woodwinds—Flute, Pvt. Edward LeVanda; Oboe, Pvt. Benedict Kaufman; Bassoon, PFC Leonard Sharrow; French Horns, Pvt. Lester Salomon, Pvt. Christian G. Woehr; Trumpets—PFC Ronald Synder, Cpl. James Morreale, Pvt. Ralph Kessler, PFC Willard Jones; Trombones—Don Matteson, Pvt. Seymour Goldfinger, Pvt. Herbert Pine
The revue was presented in two acts.

Sketches and Musical Numbers

Act One: "A Military Minstrel Show" (dialogue by Pvt. Jack Mendelsohn, PFC Richard Burdick, Pvt. Tom McDonnell) (First Interlocutor: Pvt. Gary Merrill; Captain: Pvt. Ralph Magelssen; Guards: Pvt. Tileston Perry and Pvt. Edward O'Connor): (a) Opening Chorus (two sequences, "The Army and the Shuberts Depend on You" and "Some Dough for Army Relief") (Minstrel Men); (b) "This Is the Army, Mister Jones" (Selectees: Pvts. Ross Elliot, Nicholas Sassi, Henry Jones, Charles Blake, Sydney Robin, William Roerick, Stanley Saloman, Kenneth Bates, Herbert Beller; Guards: Pvt. John Draper. Cpl. Chester O'Brien; Second Interlocutor: Pvt. Alan Manson); (c) "I'm Getting Tired So I Can Sleep" (Pvt. William Horne; Octette: Sgt. Zinn Arthur, Cpl. James Burrell, Pvts. Orville Race, James Farrell, Thomas Chetlin,, William Collier, Earl Lippy, Donald McCray; End Man: Sgt. Richard Bernie); (d) "My Sergeant and I Are Buddies" (Pvt. Pinkie Mitchell; End Man: PFC James MacColl, assisted by Pvt. Leonard Berchman; Messenger: PFC Louis Salmon); (e) "I Left My Heart at the Stage Door Canteen" (Cpt. Earl Oxford and Company; Guards: PFC Louis Salmon, Pvt. Ross Elliott; Third Interlocutor: Cpl. Philip Truex; End Men: Pvt. Julie Oshins, Sgt. Ezra Stone); (f) "The Army's Made a Man Out of Me" (Sgt. Ezra Stone, Cpl. Philip Truex, Pvt. Julie Oshins); and (g) "Mandy" (dance choreographed by PFC Fred Kelly) (Banjoists: Pvts. Samuel Carr and Claude Watson; Mandy: Pvt. Richard Irving; Her Boy Friend: PFC Fred Kelly; Mandy Girls: Pvts. Larry Gengo, Nicholas Sassi, Charles Reade, Eugene Jarvis, Jack Lenny, Stanley Sirois; Mandy Boys: Pvts. Stephen Lamarca, Fred Deming, Joseph Wojcikowski, Benjamin Stermer, Phil King, Harvey Prael); "A Military Vaudeville Show": (a) Pages: Pvts. Ray Goss and William Pillich; (b) Kitchen Police: Pvts. Larry Weeks and Hank Henry; (c) Inspection: Sgt. John Mendes, Pvt. Ross Elliott; and (d) Manoeuvers: The Allon Trio and Sgt. Arthur Steiner, PFC Leander Berg, Pvts. Belmonte Cristiani and Pinkie Mitchell; "Ladies of the Chorus" (Girls: Pvts. Burl Ives, Alan Manson, Alfred Lane, Robert Moore, Anthony Ross, Scott Farnworth, Larry Weill, Sydney Robin; Boys: Pvts. Edward O'Connor, Stanley Saloman, Richard Browning, Kenneth Bates, Richard Reeves, John Draper, Alan Bandler, Daniel Longo); "That Russian Winter" (Pvt. Julie Oshins; Specialty Dance: Pvt. Leonard Berchman; Girls: Cpl. Nelson Barclift, Pvt. Robert Sidney, Pvt. Clarence Jaeger; Boys: Pvt. Charles Reade, PFCs Gene Berg and Fred Kelly, Pvts. Fred Deming, Joseph Wojcikowski, Maurice Kelly, Richard Irving, Phil King, William Pillich, Arthur Steiner, Cliff Ferre; Russian Winter Ensemble: Benjamin Stermer, Harvey Prael, Charles Reade, Ray Goss, Chick Gagnon, William Lynch, Richard Langdon, Sid Salzberg, Billy Howell, Ted Cappy); "That's What the Well-Dressed Man in Harlem Will Wear" (Specialties: Cpl. James A. Cross, Pvts. Marion "Spoons" Brown and William Wyckoff; sung and danced by Sgts. Clyde Turner, Jack Brodmax, Cpls. Orlando Johnson, Arthur Hatchett, George Anderson, Earl Allen, Pvts. John Riley, Randolph Culley, Steve Ramos, George Watson); "How About a Cheer for the Navy?" (Chorus); Finale Act One (This Is the Army Quartet: Pvts. Tileston Perry, Anthony Ross, Joseph Bush, and Hank Henry; Stage Manager: Sgt. Alan Anderson; Shore Policemen: Pvts. Hayden Rorke, Jus Addiss, Howard Brooks, Entire Company)

Act Two: "Stage Door Canteen" (dialogue and direction by PFC James MacColl; sequence includes "Jane Cowl Number") (Jane Cowl: Pvt. Alan Manson; Sergeant: Sgt. Ezra Stone; Joe Cook: PFC Joe Cook Jr.; Vera Zorina: Cpl. Nelson Barclift; Noel Coward: Pvt. Hayden Rorke; Gypsy Rose Lee: Pvt. Julie Oshins; Lynn Fontanne: Pvt. Tileston Petty; Alfred Lunt: PFC James MacColl; Eileen: Cpl. Philip Truex; Soldier: Cpl. Earl Oxford; Hostesses: Pvts. Alan Bandler, Scott Farnworth, Clarence Jaeger, William Roerick, Fred Kapner, John Draper, Norman Stuart, Albert Whitley, Larry Gengo, Howard Montgomery, Larry Weill, Charles Blake, Cpl. Chester O'Brien; Stage Door Canteen Soldiers: Vance Campbell, Sid Tamber, Richard Burdick, Jack Mendelsohn, Derek Fairman, Murray Grubman, Hercules Ecconomou, Sgt. Zinn Arthur, Joseph Bush, William Collier, Thomas Chetlin, Leonard Fried, Bernard Frank, Frank D'Ella, Ray Goss, Louis Hawkins, Harold Hoha, Burl Ives, Anthony Ross, Ralph Magelsson, Arturo Canzano, James Wiggins, Richard Browning, Stewart Churchill, Henry Rosenblatt, Orville Race, Maurice Newman, Milton Rogers, Richard Reeves, Marvin Goodis, William Horne, Arthur Atkins, Samuel Benson, Charles Bacior, Mario Fiorella, Louis Salmon, David Schoenfeld, Bernard Welansky, Gerald Simini, Irving Albert, Warren O'Harr, Hyman Horowitz, John C. Dempsey; "I'm Getting Tired So I Can Sleep" (reprise) (Cpl. Nelson Barclift, Pvts. Robert Sidney, Maurice Kelly, and Cpl. Chester O'Brien); "American Eagles" and "With My Head in the Clouds" (Air Corps; Soloist: Pvt. Robert Shanley); "Aryans Under the Skin" (Japs: Cpl. Philip Truex, Pvts. Robert Moore, Pinkie Mitchell, Arthur Atkins; Germans: Pvts. Richard Reeves, Norman VanEmburgh, Burl Ives, Roger Kinne); "A Soldier's Dream" (Pvt. Stewart Churchill; Sergeant: Arthur Steiner; Soldiers: PFC Fred Kelly, Pvts. William Howell, Hercules Ecconomu, Maurice Kelly, Joseph Wojcikowski, Fred Deming, Cliff Ferre; Gypsy Violinists: PFC Louis Salmon, Pvt. William Roerick; Valets: PFC Sid Salzberg, Richard Langdon, William Lynch, Scott Farnworth, Derek Fairman, Howard Montgomery, Albert Whitley; Waitresses: Pvts. Leo Gagnon, Harvey Prael, Benjamin Goss, Benjamin Stermer, Richard Irving, William Pillich, Bill Dutton; Dream Girls: Cpl. Nelson Barclift, Pvts. Joseph Johnson, Clarence Jaeger, Robert Sidney, Phil King, Lee Berg, Fred Hearn); "Yip,Yip, Yaphanker's Introduction" (introduced by Pvt. Gary Merrill; Peter O'Neill, Peter J. Burns, Dan Healy, John Murphy, Jack Riano, Harold Kennedy) ; "Oh! How I Hate to Get Up in the Morning" (Irving Berlin); "This Time" (Entire Company)

A program note stated that *This Is the Army* "was conceived and produced at the request and for the benefit of The Army Emergency Relief Fund by Irving Berlin as a successor to his World War I soldier show, *Yip, Yip, Yaphank*." The goal was to raise $1 million, and the opening night performance alone took in $45,000, due to the high cost of opening-night tickets (up to $27.50 per), including two for which Kate Smith paid $10,000. On the night of the premiere, news leaked out that a pre-opening film sale to Warner Brothers brought in $250,000, and so by opening night the revue had already reached about a third of its million-dollar goal. (Reportedly, the final profit for the Broadway and touring productions and the film was more than $2 million.) The Broadway production's all-military cast and orchestra numbered almost two hundred, and the backstage personnel of stage managers, electricians, property men, carpenters, sound technicians, photographers, and other staff were also military members.

The revue was originally scheduled to play a limited four-week engagement, but the Broadway run was extended by almost two months, and then the show embarked on a national and then eventually overseas tour, including a stop at the London Palladium. The production was virtually critic-proof, and the New York reviewers wrote valentines to Berlin and the all-Army company. Richard Watts in the *New York Herald Tribune* said it was "one of the greatest musical shows of any description ever produced in this country"; George Ross in the *New York World-Telegram* said the "grand and glorious show" was a "smashing victory"; and an unsigned review for the *New York Times* (probably written by Lewis Nichols) hailed the evening as "the best show of a generation."

Burns Mantle in the *New York Daily News* gave the evening one of his rare four stars; Wilella Waldorf in the *New York Post* noted the revue was a "delirious and unforgettable evening in the theatre"; Louis Kronenberger in *PM* said it was a "whale of a show"; Herrick Brown in the *New York Sun* called the revue "top-notch"; and John Anderson in the *New York Journal-American* noted that as of opening night the revue had already raised $300,000 and after seeing the show he suspected it "could raise anything, including the roof."

The revue kidded Army life in "This Is the Army, Mister Jones" "My Sergeant and I Are Buddies," "The Army's Made a Man Out of Me," and "I'm Getting Tired So I Can Sleep"; offered a tribute to a black Army unit in "That's What the Well-Dressed Man in Harlem Will Wear"; a stirring march in "This Time"; a sentimental ballad in "I Left My Heart at the Stage Door Canteen"; tributes to the other military services ("American Eagles," "Head in the Clouds," and "How About a Cheer for the Navy?"); "That Russian Winter" was a topical jab at Hitler's retreat from Russia; and there was a special slap at the Japs and the Germans, in which the former assure the latter that they are "Aryans Under the Skin." There were also the required drag numbers in which muscular, hairy-chested soldiers paraded about (with Burl Ives in drag, "Ladies of the Chorus" must have been memorable; and "Stage Door Canteen" included impersonations of Gypsy Rose Lee, Vera Zorina, Lynn Fontanne, Alfred Lunt, and Noel Coward).

In 1918, Irving Berlin had written a revue similar to *This Is the Army*. *Yip, Yip, Yaphank* opened at the Century Theatre on August 19, 1918, for thirty-two performances; presented by "Uncle Sam," the profits of the revue were "In Aid of the Fund to Establish a Community House at Camp Upton for the Wives, Mothers and Sweethearts Who Visit Their Boys at Camp." *This Is the Army* retained three songs from *Yaphank*: "Oh! How I Hate to Get Up in the Morning"; the well-known version of "Mandy" (which was first heard as "The Sterling Silver Moon" in *Yaphank*; the popular version of the song was introduced in *Ziegfeld Follies of 1919*); and *This Is the Army*'s "Ladies of the Chorus" was based on material from the first Army show.

The London production of *This Is the Army* premiered at the Palladium on November 10, 1943; a new Berlin song was added for this version ("Don't Sing, Go into Your Dance") and "My British Buddy" (which had been introduced by Berlin prior to the London opening) was interpolated into the score. A later overseas tour of the revue also included the new songs "The Kick in the Pants" and "Daddy's Coming Home on a Furlough." The 1943 film version included one new song, "What Does He Look Like (That Boy of Mine)?"

(introduced by Frances Langford). Other songs written for but unused in *This Is the Army* are "Officer's Speech," "Dressed Up to Kill" (as "Dressed Up to Win," the number was incorporated into the film's finale "This Time"), and "England and America." In February 1943, the revue was heard on a *Lux Radio Theatre* broadcast which included a new song, "Ve Don't Like It." As for "How About a Cheer for the Navy?," *The Complete Lyrics of Irving Berlin* notes that Berlin wanted the song to be a surprise for the audience, and thus it wasn't listed in the program (it seems to have been performed immediately before the first act finale).

A recording of some of the revue's songs was released by Decca on a 78 RPM set, and for later issuances the set was either paired with other military show cast albums which were recorded by Decca (*Winged Victory* and *Call Me Mister*) or with Decca's cast recording of *Texas, Li'l Darlin'*. The recordings of *This Is the Army*, *Winged Victory*, and *Call Me Mister* are collected on Decca Broadway (CD # B0000831-02). The selections from *This Is the Army* are the overture (which includes the title song, "I Left My Heart at the Stage Door Canteen," and "That Russian Winter"), "I'm Getting Tired So I Can Sleep," "I Left My Heart at the Stage Door Canteen," "The Army's Made a Man Out of Me," "What the Well-Dressed Man in Harlem Will Wear," "How About a Cheer for the Navy," "American Eagles," "With My Head in the Clouds," and "Oh! How I Hate to Get Up in the Morning." A release by Jasmine (CD # JASCD-115) includes the cast recordings of *This Is the Army* and *Call Me Mister*, and bonus tracks for *This Is the Army* include recordings of Berlin's renditions of "This Is the Army" and "My British Buddy" as well as the Cote Glee Club's "This Time." The lyrics of all the songs for *This Is the Army* (as well as for those of *Yip, Yip, Yaphank*) are included in *The Complete Lyrics of Irving Berlin*.

Released by Warner Brothers in 1943, the colorful, entertaining, and historic film version was directed by Michael Curtiz from a screenplay by Casey Robinson and Captain Claude Binyon; the choreography was by Robert Sidney (who co-choreographed the stage production) and Leroy Prinz. The film included many of the soldiers who appeared in the stage production, including principal singers Earl Oxford, Julie Oshins, and Ezra Stone. A newly created plot revolved around a group of soldiers who are part of the show, and their romantic problems (the Hollywood cast included Ronald Reagan, George Murphy, and Joan Leslie with guest appearances by Kate Smith, Frances Langford, and Gertrude Niesen). And, as he did for the stage production, Irving Berlin sang "Oh! How I Hate to Get Up in the Morning." The film's final sequence takes place in and around the National Theatre in Washington, D.C. The DVD *Warner Bros. and the Homefront Collection* (#30000163-93/94/95) includes *This Is the Army*, *Thank Your Lucky Stars*, and *Hollywood Canteen*; *This Is the Army* includes the overture and exit music along with one song ("My British Buddy") which was seen only in non-U.S. showings of the film.

THE MERRY WIDOW

Theatre: Carnegie Hall
Opening Date: July 15, 1942; *Closing Date*: August 16, 1942
Performances: 39
Book: Victor Leon and Leo Stein
Lyrics: Adrian Ross
Music: Franz Lehar
Direction: John Pearce and Felix Brentano; *Producers*: Joseph S. Tushinsky and Hans Bartsch; *Scenery*: Artistic supervision by Richard Eichberg; *Costumes*: Costumes and gowns by Eaves Costume Company; *Lighting*: Uncredited; *Musical Direction*: Joseph S. Tushinsky
Cast: Michael Fitzmaurice (St. Brioche), Elizabeth Houston (Natalie), Felix Knight (Camille de Jolidon), George Mitchell (Cascada), Elaine Ellis (Olga), Neil Fitzgerald (Novakovich), Roy M. Johnston (Khadja), John Cherry (Nish), Eddie Garr (Baron Popoff), Helen Gleason (Sonia), Wilbur Evans (Prince Danilo), Harriet Borger (Madam Khadja), Carl Nelson (Head Waiter), Diana Corday (Zo Zo), Peter Birch (Premier Dancer); *Note*: It seems that most of the chorus singers and dancers appeared in all three of Carnegie Hall's summer series of operetta revivals; for a list of these performers, see **The New Moon**.
The operetta was presented in three acts.
The action takes place in and around Paris in the early 1900s.

Franz Lehar's *The Merry Widow* was the second of three operettas that were revived by Joseph S. Tushinsky at Carnegie Hall during the summer of 1942; it followed **The Chocolate Soldier** and preceded **The New Moon**.

In his annual summary of the season, George Jean Nathan noted that Helen Gleason and Wilbur Evans "were immensely more suitable" in the roles of Sonia and Prince Danilo than were Ethel Jackson and Donald Brian, who created the roles for the first Broadway production in 1907. But he felt the revival "monkeyed" with the book and allowed Eddie Garr (Baron Popoff) to "run amuck." Further, he noted the dialogue included such lines as "It's the nuts" and "That's all, brother!" and there were allusions to priorities, Frankie and Johnny, and the conga. And in the scene at Maxim's he was certain he heard a character mention hot dogs.

The following season the New Opera Company offered another revival of *The Merry Widow* with a new book by Sidney Sheldon and Ben Roberts; the lyrics were still credited to Adrian Ross, and Felix Brentano returned as director. The production was a surprise hit and played for 322 performances (see entry for more information, including song list).

As *Die lustige witwe*, the operetta premiered in Vienna, Austria, at the Theater an der Wien on December 30, 1905, with Mizzi Gunther (Sonia) and Louis Treumann (Prince Danilo). Lehar's melodic score and Viktor Leon and Leo Stein's libretto told the story of the impoverished Ruritanian land of Marsovia and the attempts of its politicians to see that the fortune of Sonia, its wealthiest citizen, will remain in the country. To this end, Prince Danilo is sent to Paris to woo her into marriage and thus ensure the financial solvency of the nation. Of course, the two fall in love and so their romantic happy ending is also a financially happy one for the coffers of the Marsovian government.

The operetta has enjoyed some twenty-one productions in New York; as mentioned, Ethel Jackson and Donald Brian were the stars of the first one, which opened at the New Amsterdam Theatre on October 21, 1907, for 416 performances.

There have been various film versions, the most memorable one directed by Ernst Lubitsch for MGM in 1934 with Jeanette MacDonald and Maurice Chevalier (most of the lyrics were by Lorenz Hart, and additional music was by Richard Rodgers and Herbert Stothart).

There are numerous recordings of the score, including the cast recording of the 1964 Music Theatre of Lincoln Center production which starred Patrice Munsel and Bob Wright (RCA Victor LP # LOC/LSO-1094; the CD was released by Sony Masterworks Broadway # 88697-88567-2).

THE NEW MOON

Theatre: Carnegie Hall
Opening Date: August 18, 1942; *Closing Date*: September 6, 1942
Performances: 24
Book: Oscar Hammerstein II, Frank Mandel, and Laurence Schwab
Lyrics: Oscar Hammerstein II
Music: Sigmund Romberg
Direction: Production staged by John Pierce and supervised by Richard Eichberg; *Producer*: Joseph S. Tushinsky; *Choreography*: Uncredited; *Scenery*: Draperies by Supreme Scenery Studios and Encore Studio; *Costumes*: Eaves Costume Company and Brooks Costume Company; *Lighting*: Equipment by Duwico; *Musical Direction*: Joseph S. Tushinsky
Cast: Doris Patston (Julie), George Leonard (Beaunoir), Gene Barry (Captain Duval), Marcel Journet (Vicomte Ribaud), Carl Nelson (Fouchette), Wilbur Evans (Robert Mission), Teddy Hart (Alexander), Paul Reed (Besac), George Mitchell (Jacques), Ruby Mercer (Marianne Beaunoir), Everett West (Philippe), Walter Munroe (Doorman, Captain De Jean), Joan Benoit (Flower Girl), Peter Birch (Spaniard, Premiere Dancer), Viola Essenova (Spanish Dancer, Premiere Danseuse), John Edwards (Proprietor), Paul Wendel (A Man), Joan Wheatley (A Girl), Hope Emerson (Clotilde), Robert Tower (Brunet); Singers: Joan Benoit, Harriet Borger, Lucy Lee, Irene Carroll, Joyce Doncaster, Sally Hadley, Katherine Lester, Emily Marsh, May Muth, Marvel Skeels, Joan Wheatley, Jimmy Allison, Ray Cook, Robert Curi, Arthur Davies, Edward Dunbar, Joseph Monte, Carl Nelson, Larry Shindel, Richard Torigi, Robert Tower, Paul L. Wendel; The Dancers: Harriet Adler, Lief Argo, Deanne Benmore, Dan Denton, Nicoli Fatula, Marie Grey, Eddie Howland, Emily Jewell,

Audrey Kent, Anna Konstance, Ann Kus, Marion Lynn, Ruth Mann, Eileen McBride, Irving Rapee, Mary Lou Reed, Arleen Robinson, Grace Rudder, Judy Sargent, John Schindehette, Peter Kite Smith
The musical was presented in three acts (the original production was in two).

The action takes place during 1791 and 1792 (1792 and 1793 in the original production) in New Orleans, on the high seas, and on the Isle of Pines.

Musical Numbers

Act One: Overture (Orchestra); Opening (aka "Dainty Wisp of Thistledown") (Girl Ensemble); "Marianne" (Wilbur Evans); "Entrance of Marianne" (Ruby Mercer, Ensemble); "The Girl on the Prow" (Ruby Mercer, Paul Reed, George Mitchell, Ensemble); "Gorgeous Alexander" (Doris Patston, Teddy Hart); Tavern Scene ("Tavern Song") (Ensemble); "Spanish Dance" (Viola Essenova, Peter Birch); "Softly, as in a Morning Sunrise" (Everett West, Ensemble); "Stouthearted Men" (Wilbur Evans, Everett West, Men); Tango (aka "Sweet Creole Lady") (Viola Essenova); "One Kiss" (Ruby Mercer, Girls); "The Trial" (aka "Ladies of the Jury") (Teddy Hart, Doris Patston, Hope Emerson, Girls); Finale and Duet (sequence includes "Gentle Airs, Courtly Manners" and "Wanting You") (Ruby Mercer, Wilbur Evans, Ensemble)
Act Two: Opening (aka "Chanty") (Paul Reed, Peter Birch, Men); "Funny Little Sailor Men" (Paul Reed, Hope Emerson, Ensemble); Dance (Viola Essenova, Peter Birch); "Lover, Come Back to Me" (Ruby Mercer); Finale and Drill
Act Three: Marriage Number and "Try Her Out at Dances" (Doris Patston, Teddy Hart, Peter Birch, Ensemble); "One Kiss" (reprise) (Wilbur Evans, Ruby Mercer); Finale (Entire Company)

During the summer of 1942, Carnegie Hall under the auspices of musical conductor Joseph S. Tushinsky presented limited-engagement revivals of three venerable operettas, **The Chocolate Soldier**, **The Merry Widow**, and *The New Moon* (the series was officially titled "Festival of Famous Musical Comedies"). The 1940s saw a number of revivals of operettas, including **The Student Prince** (its original title was *The Student Prince in Heidelberg*), **The Vagabond King**, **Blossom Time**, **Robin Hood**, **The Gypsy Baron**, **The Red Mill**, **Sweethearts**, and lavish productions of *Die Fledermaus* (now titled **Rosalinda**) and **The Merry Widow** by the New Opera Company.

The era of the mid- and late 1920s was the last hurrah for the operetta, and *The New Moon* was one of many that enjoyed long and successful runs. Others of the era were Rudolf Friml and Herbert Stothart's *Rose-Marie* (1924, 557 performances; lyrics by Otto Harbach and Oscar Hammerstein II); Sigmund Romberg's *The Student Prince in Heidelberg* (1924, 608 performances; lyrics by Dorothy Donnelly); Friml's *The Vagabond King* (1925, 511 performances; lyrics by Brian Hooker and W. H. Post); Romberg's *The Desert Song* (1926, 471 performances; lyrics by Otto Harbach and Oscar Hammerstein II); Harry Tierney's *Rio Rita* (1927, 494 performances; lyrics by Joseph McCarthy); Romberg's *My Maryland* (1927, 312 performances; lyrics by Dorothy Donnelly); and Friml's *The Three Musketeers* (1928, 318 performances; lyrics by P. G. Wodehouse and Clifford Grey).

Set in the New Orleans of 1792, the plot of *The New Moon* focused on Frenchman Robert Mission who has been accused by his home country of killing a member of the royalty in a revolutionary fracas. He's captured by the French who plan to return him to France for trial, and when the *New Moon* sets sail for France, Robert discovers that his love Marianne Beaunoir is also aboard. He eventually escapes with his followers (and Marianne) to an island where they establish a colony for all those who seek liberty.

Best Plays said producer (and musical director) Joseph S. Tushinsky was "brave" to stage his series of three operettas on Carnegie Hall's concert stage (and with "make-shift" scenery); but the gamble paid off, and the popularly priced series was a success. But George Jean Nathan in his season's annual said the "beer-weeping" operetta was no better now than it had been in 1928; even back then its book was "dull," its humor "corny," and the score "saloon-piano" and "derivatively familiar." He suggested the current revival took place "musically in a juke-box," that the scenery was apparently designed by the Acme Colored Postcard Company, and the costumes were created "by Joseph S. Tushinsky's Aunt Becky." (Nathan seemed to forget that while he was cool to the score, his original 1928 review stated the musical was "so greatly superior to the other new musical exhibitions that I commend it to your notice.")

The following songs from the original Broadway production were omitted from the concert version: "An Interrupted Love Song," "Love Is Quite a Simple Thing," and "Never for You." The program listed a "Marriage Number" for the beginning of the third act, and while it's unclear what specific song is being referred to, the sequence might have included "Love Is Quite a Simple Thing."

The New Moon was one of the last successful operettas of the 1920s; it opened at the Imperial Theatre on September 19, 1928, for 509 performances. To be sure, there would be many more operettas, but musical comedies and musical plays became the fashion, and even old-fashioned musicals that flirted with the operetta form (such as **Up in Central Park**) could arguably be classified as musical comedy. By the 1950s, the critics were vigilant in damning any musical that even whispered the dreaded "O" word, and they seemed to find vestiges of operetta in what were truly musical comedies or musical plays. In the 1950s, Brooks Atkinson became particularly cold if not frigid to the operetta format, and so the genre all but faded, and even revivals of traditional operetta warhorses went out of fashion.

Despite the initial success of *The New Moon*, it has never enjoyed a full-scale commercial revival on Broadway. Besides the scaled-down concert-styled revival at Carnegie Hall, the operetta was seen at City Center in a limited-run revival by the Belmont Operetta Company in 1944 (see entry), and then four decades later was produced in repertory by the New York City Opera Company in 1986 and 1988 for a total of twenty-three performances. Encores! presented a concert version on March 27, 2003, for five performances, and the cast album of that production by Ghostlight (CD # 4403-2) is the most complete recording of the score.

The New Moon began life in 1927 as *Marianne* (not to be confused with the 1929 film musical *Marianne* or the 1944 **Marianne**, which closed during its pre-Broadway tryout). The troubled pre-Broadway engagement closed in January 1928, underwent drastic rewriting and recasting, and resumed its tryout in August of that year. It was well received by the critics (Brooks Atkinson in the *New York Times* praised its "good" book and "full-bodied" score). The cast included Evelyn Herbert and Robert Halliday, and the melodious score included the typical virile male marching song ("Stouthearted Men"), the inevitable ode to drink ("Tavern Song"), and lush ballads ("Softly, as in a Morning Sunrise," "Lover, Come Back to Me," "Wanting You," and "One Kiss").The London production (with Evelyn Laye and Howett Worster) opened at the Drury Lane in 1929.

There were two major film versions, both produced by MGM and both titled *New Moon*. The 1930 film, which starred Grace Moore and Lawrence Tibbett, dropped the plot of the stage version and created an entirely new one set mostly in Russia. The1940 adaptation starred Jeanette MacDonald and Nelson Eddy and was more in keeping with the plot of the original.

The script was published in paperback by Chappell & Co. Ltd. (London) in 1935, and the lyrics are included in *The Complete Lyrics of Oscar Hammerstein II*.

NEW PRIORITIES OF 1943
"The Star Studded Laff-A-Riot"

Theatre: 46th Street Theatre
Opening Date: September 15, 1942; *Closing Date*: October 11, 1942
Performances: 54
Ensemble Lyrics and *Music*: Lester Lee and Jerry Seelen
Direction: Jean Le Seyeux; *Producers*: Clifford C. Fischer by arrangement with the Messrs. Shubert; *Choreography*: Truly McGee; *Scenery*: Supervised by Edouard Halouze; *Costumes*: Mahieu; *Musical Direction*: Lou Forman
Cast: *Harry Richman, Bert Wheeler, Carol Bruce*, Hank Ladd, Henny Youngman, Johnny Burke, The Bricklayers, The Radio Aces, Sally Keith, Harrison and Fisher, The Acromaniacs, Francetta Malloy, Imogen Carpenter, Ted Adair, Dorothy Partington; *Dancing Priorettes*: Vela Ceres, Paddy Barker, Ruth Ryder, Olga Roberts, Norma Holt, Shirley Gordon, Mary Jan Pieter, Toni Traub, Carmelita Lanza, Betty De Elmo, Xenia Astafieva, Molly Pierson, Lee Mayer; *Priorette Show Girls*: Beatrice Ratcliffe, Roy Standish, Lucille Casey, Mary Siem, Theo Willis, Pamela De Vorne
The revue was presented in two acts.

Sketches and Musical Numbers

Act One: "It's Mental" (lyric and music by Lester Lee and Jerry Seelen) (The Priorettes); The Acromaniacs; Henny Youngman; Johnny Burke; The Bricklayers; Carol Bruce; Bert Wheeler and Hank Ladd, with Francetta Malloy; Harry Richman (with Jack Golden at the piano); "Heigh Ho, Tra, La, La, La" (lyric and music by Lester Lee and Jerry Seelen) (Carol Bruce, Imogen Carpenter); "Song of the WAAC's" (lyric and music by Lester Lee and Jerry Seelen) (Sally Keith)

Act Two: Harrison and Fisher; Henny Youngman; "I Like Your Style" (lyric and music by Lester Lee and Jerry Seelen) (Harry Richman, Ted Adair, Dorothy Partington); Bert Wheeler; The Radio Aces; Finale

Producer Clifford C. Fischer jump-started the trend of variety and vaudeville-styled revues that popped up regularly during the War Forties. His **Priorities of 1942** was an out-of-nowhere hit that ran for 353 performances, and a few weeks after it opened he offered **Keep 'Em Laughing** and then later its revised version **Top-Notchers**, both of which closed in the red after disappointing runs of 77 and 48 performances. His optimistically titled *New Priorities of 1943* was his fourth offering of 1942, and like his second and third revues it lasted only a few weeks and never saw the light of 1943.

The headline of Louis Kronenberger's review in *PM* stated "Vaudeville Takes a Terrific Spill," and the critic noted the performers lacked a certain amount of sparkle; in fact, the "best" the evening could offer was "second best." Kronenberger noted the first act's "patriotic intentions" were "obliterated" and made "downright enigmatic" by the "bodily contortions" of a performer who must have seen one of the acts in **Star and Garter** and then decided to "outdo" it. (John Mason Brown in the *New York World-Telegram* said she was quite a "tassel-tosser.")

Howard Barnes in the *New York Herald Tribune* said the evening was "bad vaudeville," and only old-timer Bert Wheeler's "engaging presence" offered a few "bright moments"; but the "great" dog-act The Bricklayers was back, The Acromaniacs (a tumbling group) were "fairly impressive," and the team of Harrison and Fisher danced "effectively." Like most of the critics, Brown complained that the revue lacked a master of ceremonies on the order of Lou Holtz to give the evening shape and continuity, and although Henny Youngman was "droll, very droll," he left "much, if not most, to be desired." Brooks Atkinson in the *New York Times* said the revue was "flat and dull," but he had "modest appreciation" for Bert Wheeler and Henny Youngman. While John Anderson in the *New York Journal-American* was glad to see the "wonderful" Bricklayers back and found occasional "hilarious passages" throughout the evening, he noted that while vaudeville wasn't "dead," it certainly did "sleepeth."

Richard Lockridge in the *New York Sun*, however, found *Priorities* "generous entertainment," and Wilella Waldorf in the *New York Post* found the evening "intermittently amusing." Burns Mantle in the *New York Daily News* said the "lively" revue made up in "quantity" what it lacked in "class."

The revue featured singers Harry Richman and Carol Bruce. Richman's songs included Irving Berlin's "Puttin' on the Ritz," which he had introduced in the 1930 film of the same name. Bruce sang medleys of George Gershwin and Irving Berlin, including numbers from **Louisiana Purchase**, some of which she had introduced in that musical. The critics had liked her in the Berlin show and would later praise her Julie in the 1946 revival of **Show Boat**; but for *Priorities* some were in a rather grumpy mood and took her to task (John Anderson in the *New York Journal-American* said she needed "showmanship," Kronenberger said she'd lost some of her "freshness and vividness," and Barnes found her lusterless).

New Priorities of 1943 gave thirteen performances a week (the ticket prices ranged from fifty-five cents to $3.30). Among its other cast members were monologist Hank Ladd and comedian Johnny Burke (the latter wasn't the well-known lyricist and sometime composer).

Perhaps the highlight of the evening was a sale of bonds and war stamps. Harry Richman introduced a chorus girl who wore only corsages of stamps and bonds, and the gentlemen in the audience were asked to place bids (for the bonds and stamps). As the corsages were sold, the young woman became (according to Waldorf) "nuder and nuder," and Lockridge reported that finally there was just one "crucial" corsage left (with a starting bid of ten dollars). It was then that the bidding became frantic. Playboy Tommy Manville bid $110, then film stock pioneer Jules Brulatour offered $1,000 and then $2,000, and soon Brulatour and toy manufacturer Louis Marx started a bidding war that ended when Marx won the corsage for $25,000. Mantle reported that when the corsage was removed, the chorus girl was wearing "a small adhesive plaster" on which was written "Buy Bonds." Waldorf then reported that the girl rushed into the wings in a state of "patriotic confusion."

SHOW TIME
"A Variety Show" / "Uproarious Variety Revue"

Theatre: Broadhurst Theatre
Opening Date: September 16, 1942; *Closing Date*: April 3, 1943
Performances: 342
Producer: Fred F. Finklehoffe (later, Finklehoff); *Scenery*: Scenery for the De Marco's sequence by Kaj Velden; *Costumes*: Various clothing and shoes credited to Mme. Fiffi, Delamn's from Bergdorf Goodman, and Lily Dache
Cast: *George Jessel, Jack Haley, Ella Logan, The De Marcos* (Tony and Sally De Marco), The Berry Brothers, Bob Williams, Con Colleano, Olsen and Shirley, Lucille Norman
The revue was presented in two acts.

Sketches and Musical Numbers

Act One: George Jessel (Conferencier); Jack Haley; Lucille Norman; Olsen and Shirley; Con Colleano; The De Marcos
Act Two: George Jessel; Ella Logan; Jack Haley; The Berry Brothers; Bob Williams

After the success of the long-running *Priorities of 1942*, vaudeville and variety revues sprouted up all over Broadway. Most were mildly or indifferently received by critics and audiences, almost all of them lost money, and one (**Wine Women and Song**) received particularly scathing notices. But *Show Time* (which was first produced in California) proved to be a hit with everyone, and its 342-performance run was the longest of the era's two-a-day revues (the self-described "variety show" gave twelve performances weekly). For more information about Finklehoff and his occasional partner Paul Small's vaudeville revues, see **Laugh Time**.

Brooks Atkinson in the *New York Times* said the revue was a "rattling good evening of entertainment," one which was "refreshing and relaxing" and in the hands of enthusiastic professionals, and John Mason Brown in the *New York World-Telegram* found it a "first-rate" evening. And while John Anderson in the *New York Journal-American* said the production had the "air of spontaneous good humor and high spirits," he suggested the show needed "sharper timing and drastic control of the encores."

Atkinson (as well as Burns Mantle in the *New York Daily News*) noted that George Jessel (who was described in the program as the evening's conferencier) and Jack Haley had been let down by their recent book musicals (**High Kickers** and **Higher and Higher**, respectively) and so the current revue was the perfect conduit for their unique talents. Jessel pleased everyone with his old but still refreshing routines, and as of yore phoned in to report to his mamma. He also revived his shtick as the visiting lecturer from Czechoslovakia (which he had also performed in **High Kickers**).

Brown noted he hadn't always been taken with Jessel, but *Show Time* cured him of this "allergy" and so from now on he would enter Jessel's "cheering section cheering." In fact, Anderson also admitted that Jessel had never seemed all that "richly comic" before, but had now reached "a new level" as an entertainer.

Jack Haley revived his beloved routine of kidding opera (including an operatic burlesque of "Chattanooga Choo-Choo" which Atkinson noted was "unlike anything else in the world of music"), and the critics liked the friendly-insult camaraderie between Haley and Jessel. Richard Lockridge in the *New York Sun* said Haley was an "amiable comedian" who was "agreeable" to be around, and when he and Ella Logan joined forces in a couple of numbers "the two of them go places." Brown noted that Logan stopped the show, for she had "the energy of a hurricane" and an "irresistible way with a song"; Howard Barnes in the *New York Herald Tribune* said she sang with "her accustomed enthusiasm"; and Anderson too noted she stopped the show. But Louis Kronenberger in *PM* said "her charm continues to elude me."

Others on the bill were The De Marcos, whom Anderson praised for their "glossy and graceful precision" (*Show Time* marked Tony De Marco's second Broadway appearance with his new wife and dance partner,

Sally; they had previously danced in **Banjo Eyes**, and would later appear in the revue **Star Time**); the contortionists-cum-dancers Olsen and Shirley (a "superior team," according to Mantle); wire-walker Con Colleano (Barnes praised his "remarkable feats of balance"); singer Lucille Norman (Anderson noted her "pleasant enough thrush-work"); the Berry Brothers (an "agile Negro dancing trio," per Wilella Waldorf in the *New York Post*); and Bob Williams and his disinterested dog Red Dust (Atkinson reported that the "lazy chow mongrel performs no feats whatsoever" and Waldorf said the red setter "just sits and looks bored to death" while to no avail Williams "shrieks and coos and endeavors to induce" the dog to do a few tricks).

Ella Logan was rather strangely described in the program as the "Glasgow grenade," perhaps a description wartime audiences didn't really want to hear. Among her selections were "The Shady Side of the Street" and "It's a Long Way to Tipperary" (the latter with lyric and music by Jack Judge and Henry James "Harry" Williams). She also sang "I'll Take the High Note" (lyric by Harold Adamson, music by Johnny Green), which she had introduced in **Hi Ya, Gentlemen**, and "Something I Dreamed Last Night" (lyric by Jack Yellen and Herb Magidson, music by Sammy Fain), another song she had previously introduced (in the 1939 edition of *George White's Scandals*). Haley's "Chattanooga Choo-Choo" (lyric by Mack David, music by Harry Warren) had first been heard in the 1941 film *Sun Valley Serenade*.

WINE WOMEN AND SONG

Theatre: Ambassador Theatre
Opening Date: September 28, 1942; *Closing Date*: December 3, 1942
Performances: 150 (see below)
Direction: Ensembles staged by Truly McGee; *Best Plays* noted the production was supervised by Max Liebman; *Producer*: Uncredited (see below); *Scenery*: Frederick Fox; *Costumes*: Margie Hart's costumes designed by Ernest Schraps; *Lighting*: Uncredited; *Musical Direction*: Murray Friedman
Cast: *Margie Hart, Jimmy Savo*, The Wesson Brothers (Eugene and Richard), Pinky Lee, Herbie Faye, Marian Miller, Isabelle Brown, Noel Toy, The Don Ritz Favorettes, Murray Briscoe, Evelyn Farney, Ruth Mason, Billy and Buster Burnell, Murray White; Dancing Chorus: Elita Albert, Rita Carmen, Maude Carroll, Muriel Cole, Dolores (Dody) Goodman, Virginia Grimes, Lucy Lewin, Sylvia Mettler, Tola Nelson, Gloria Page, Lenore Thall, Gail Vaughn; Show Girls: Patsy Ann, Connie Constant, Bobbe Jason, Margaret Lane, Kay Mallah, Pat Marlan, Florence Moore, Rene Stahl
The revue was presented in two acts.

Sketches and Musical Numbers

Act One: "This Is Not a Play by Saroyan" (lyric and music by Irvin Graham) (Margie Hart); Queen of Quiver (Marian Miller); "Shore Leave" (Pinky Lee, Murray White, Margie Hart); Noel Toy; "Confidential Loan" (Herbie Faye, Murray Briscoe, Ruth Mason, Eugene Wesson); The Don Ritz Favorettes; "52nd Street" (Jimmy Savo, Margie Hart, Murray Briscoe, Murray White); "It's Smart to Be Stupid" (Herbie Faye, Ruth Mason); "Strawberry Blonde" (The Don Ritz Favorettes, Billy and Buster Burnell, Girls); The Wesson Brothers; "Jitterbug Wedding" (Billy and Buster Burnell, Girls)
Act Two: "Starry Night" (Murray White, Isabelle Brown, Girls); "Taking Her Home" (Herbie Faye, Margie Hart); "New York Cowboy" (Murray White, Evelyn Farney, Girls); "Hands Off" (Isabelle Brown); Jimmy Savo; Margie Hart (who sang an untitled song by Irvin Graham and who was assisted by The Don Ritz Favorettes); "Jivin' Around" (Pinky Lee, Murray Briscoe, Girls); Finale (Entire Company)

With Broadway suddenly offering a spate of variety-and-vaudeville-styled revues and with the success of Michael Todd's lavish burlesque and strip tease show **Star and Garter** (which headlined the premier stripper of them all, Gypsy Rose Lee), it wasn't surprising someone brought in a cheap, quickie revue that combined both vaudeville and strip tease elements. *Wine Women and Song* not only filled the bill for such a specialized subgenre of musical theatre but also managed to offend just about everyone, including the police (see below).

In **Pal Joey**'s "Zip," a reporter sang that Gypsy Rose Lee wondered if William Saroyan would "ever write a great play" and asked "Who the hell is Margie Hart?" For *Wine Women and Song*, Broadway (as opposed to burlesque) audiences got a chance to see Margie Hart, who opened the show with the helpfully titled song "This Is Not a Play by Saroyan." Since Saroyan's *Hello Out There* opened the day after the premiere of *Wine Women and Song*, perhaps Margie Hart wanted to ensure that audiences didn't confuse the two shows.

Brooks Atkinson in the *New York Times* suggested the "monotonous" *Wine Women and Song* was a "fire-sale" **Star and Garter**. Under Mayor Fiorello H. LaGuardia, the New York City Commissioner of Licenses Paul Moss had refused to renew the licenses for burlesque theatres, and so Atkinson reported he merely "peeked through his fingers" at the proceedings on the Ambassador's stage. John Mason Brown in the *New York World-Telegram* said burlesque died a "painful and lingering death" at the hands of the unnamed producers who wouldn't own up to their "shoddy" offering in which burlesque impersonated vaudeville in order to ensure "its rolling rhinestones would gather no Commissioner Moss." He noted that Margie Hart had a "larger following than a wardrobe," and while her "chassis" was fine she lacked the "style, the nonchalance, the nuance and the classicism" of Gypsy Rose Lee.

Howard Barnes in the *New York Herald Tribune* said theatrical "low-water" marks weren't always easy to chart, but *Wine Women and Song* was "right in there with the worst ebb tides of taste, imagination and craftsmanship"; Burns Mantle in the *New York Daily News* reported the first-night audience "seemed more stunned than startled" with the offering, and in comparing Miss Lee to Miss Hart he said the former is "exposure touched with art" while the latter "is exposure under a spotlight"; and Wilella Waldof in the *New York Post* noted that since there were no producers listed in the program, the revue was a "mistake" which "just happened."

Richard Lockridge in the *New York Sun* said the sketches and jokes were often "remarkably vulgar," and advised his readers to "pretend none of it happened"; John Anderson in the *New York Journal-American* said Hart's "disrobing" had all the "allurement of a tired salesclerk taking off a mannequin in a Fifth Avenue window," and noted that what was supposed to "throw the customers in the aisles" instead landed them "into the dumps"; and Louis Kronenberger in *PM* said the evening was one of the "unhappiest" of "recent Broadway experiences" and was a "horrible" mistake.

The revue also offered Marian Miller, whom Lockridge said was "known dreadfully" as the self-described "Queen of Quiver," and Kronenberger said those three words absolutely described it all; Noel Toy performed a fan dance; the Wesson Brothers performed impersonations (including the Roosevelts); various comedians offered jokes that pronounced "hors d'oeuvres" as "horse derbies"; and Kronenberger noted four young women offered a "frolicksome" moment (set to of all things Liszt's "Second Hungarian Rhapsody") which had "all the merry roguishness of a skit at a Mt. Holyoke chafing-dish party in 1882."

As for Jimmy Savo, the beloved comedian could normally do no wrong, but on this occasion he received a number of sour notices. Lockridge said he used to enjoy Savo's shticks, but now they were "tepid"; Anderson said when Savo sang his classic version of "River, Stay Away from My Door," the fun nonetheless stayed "stubbornly at low tide"; and Brown said Savo wasn't enough to prevent "dullness" from staying away from his usually "entertaining" door (in fact, the critic noted Savo was "as grubby as the show," and he never thought Savo's stage presence would make him "indifferent" to the comedian).

During the run, the sketch "Madame Concentrate" was added (for Herbie Faye, Ruth Mason, and Murray Briscoe). Savo's classic "River, Stay Away from My Door" (lyric by Mort Dixon and music by Harry Woods) had also been heard in **Mum's the Word**.

Although the program didn't credit a producer, *Best Plays* later reported the revue was sponsored by Lee Shubert, I. H. Herk, and Max Liebman. The annual also noted that the police soon "interfered" with the "pretty coarse" revue, but with "the aid of injunctions and other court delays" the show was able to hang on for several weeks (the annual credited the revue with both 150 and 112 performances). Because the show was performed sixteen times weekly, the former figure seems the more reliable one.

LET FREEDOM SING
"A NEW MUSICAL REVUE"

Theatre: Longacre Theatre
Opening Date: October 5, 1942; *Closing Date*: October 10, 1942
Performances: 8

Sketches: Sam Locke; additional sketch by Al Geto

Lyrics: Harold Rome; additional lyrics by Lewis Allen (aka Abel Meeropol), Marc Blitzstein, Edward Eliscu, David Greggory (aka Gregory), Roslyn Harvey, Henry Meyers, and Hy Zaret

Music: Harold Rome; additional music by Marc Blitzstein, Lou Cooper, Jack Gerald, Jay Gorney, Walter Kent, and Earl Robinson

Direction: Joseph C. Pevney; *Producer*: Youth Theatre; *Choreography*: Dan Eckley; additional choreography by Ken Whelan; *Scenery*: Herbert Andrews; *Costumes*: Paul du Pont; *Lighting*: Uncredited; *Musical Direction*: David Mordecai

Cast: *Mitzi Green*, Berni Gould, Lee Sullivan, Betty Garrett, Phil Leeds, Mordecai Bauman, Jane Johnstone, Margie Jackson, Marion Warnes, Ethel Sherman, Lois Girard, Pat Shibley, Remi Martel, Buddy Yarus, Harry Mack, Joan Dexter, Jack Baker, Jules Racine, Bob Davis, Bill Randall, Ruth Cavanaugh, Molly Hoban, Sally Gracie

The revue was presented in two acts.

Sketches and Musical Numbers

Act One: "Ring Up the Curtain" (lyric and music by Harold Rome) (Entire Company); "It's Fun to Be Free" (lyric and music by Harold Rome) (Entire Company); "Tactics" (sketch by Al Geto) (First Man: Berni Gould; Second Man: Phil Leeds); "The Lady Is a WAAC" (lyric and music by Harold Rome) (Mitzi Green; danced by Jane Johnstone, Margie Jackson, Marion Warnes, Ethel Sherman, Lois Girard, Pat Shibley); "A Night in Washington" (sketch) (Landlady: Betty Garrett; Mr. Dwerp: Phil Leeds; Jenkins: Remi Martel; Judd: Berni Gould; Smith: Buddy Yarus; Secretary: Margie Jackson; Leon Henderson: Harry Mack; Senator: Mordecai Bauman; Spy: Joan Dexter; F.B.I. Man: Jack Baker; Dollar-a-Year Men: Jules Racine, Bob Davis; Congressman: Bill Randall); "I Did It for Defense" (lyric and music by Harold Rome) (Mitzi Green); "We Have a Date" (lyric by Roslyn Harvey, music by Lou Cooper) (Joan Dexter, Lee Sullivan; danced by Jane Johnstone, Jack Baker, Company); "Be Calm" (lyric and music by Harold Rome) (Chairlady: Betty Garrett; Senator: Berni Gould; Attendants: Jules Racine, Bob Davis); "Congress" (sketch) (First Senator: Jack Baker; Second Senator: Mordecai Bauman); "History Eight to the Bar" (lyric and music by Harold Rome) (Teacher: Betty Garrett; Students: Ensemble); Mitzi Green; "Little Miss Victory Jones" (lyric and music by Harold Rome) (Lee Sullivan, Entire Company)

Act Two: "Give a Viva!" (lyric and music by Harold Rome) (Betty Garrett, Entire Company); "How Do I Get There?" (sketch by Al Geto) (First Man: Berni Gould; Second Man: Phil Leeds); "The Little Things We Like" (lyric by Roslyn Harvey, music by Lou Cooper) (Mitzi Green, Lee Sullivan); "Flowers in Bloom" (lyric by David Greggory aka Gregory, music by Jack Gerald) (Phil Leeds); "Women in Uniform" (sketch) (Captain Flagg: Betty Garrett; Sergeant Quirt: Mitzi Green; Blotto: Berni Gould; WAAC Girls: Jane Johnstone, Margie Jackson, Marion Warnes, Ethel Sherman, Lois Girard, Pat Shibley); "Blackout Blackout" (sketch) (Buddy Yarus, Mordecai Bauman, Ruth Cavanaugh, Remi Martel, Harry Mack, Molly Hoban, Bill Randall, Lois Girard, Sally Gracie); "The House I Live In" (lyric by Lewis Allen, music by Earl Robinson) (Mordecai Bauman); "Grandpa Guerrilla" (lyric by Hy Zaret, music by Walter Kent) (Mitzi Green, Entire Company); "Johnny Is a Hoarder" (lyric and music by Harold Rome) (Johnny: Phil Leeds; Janie: Betty Garrett); "Mittel Europa" (lyric by Henry Meyers and Edward Eliscu, music by Jay Gorney) (Berni Gould, with Jack Baker, Harry Mack, Remi Martel, Jules Racine); "Fraught" (lyric and music by Marc Blitzstein) (Mitzi Green, with Phil Leeds); "Of the People Stomp" (lyric and music by Harold Rome) (Betty Garrett, Entire Company)

The revue *Let Freedom Sing* was the (American) Youth Theatre's second Broadway production following *Of "V" We Sing*, which had opened earlier in the year and played for almost ten weeks. Unfortunately, the critics were mostly unforgiving with the quality of the new revue's material, and so *Freedom* sang for just one week. Among the cast members who returned for the second go-round were Betty Garrett and Phil Leeds, who were now joined by Mitzi Green, who received star billing.

The evening spoofed the crowded conditions of wartime Washington ("A Night in Washington"), which later in the season was the subject of Howard Dietz and Vernon Duke's *Dancing in the Streets*, which closed during its tryout. Other topical subjects covered in the revue were hoarding (the song "Johnny Is a Hoarder");

blackouts (the sketch "Blackout Blackout"); women in the armed services (the sketch "Women in Uniform" as well as Mitzi Green's "The Lady Is a WAAC," which didn't match the popularity of "The Lady Is a Tramp," which she had introduced in Richard Rodgers and Lorenz Hart's 1937 Broadway hit *Babes in Arms*); the sketch about military "Tactics"; a send-up of Hitler, Mussolini, and Hirohito in "It's Fun to Be Free"; "I Did It for Defense" (in which a girl gives a soldier her most prized possession, the last of her tin foil); South American numbers ("Give a Viva!"); the ballad "We Have a Date"(in which a boy and girl look forward to life after the war); a patriotic hurrah ("Of the People Stomp"); and a patriotic hymn to the homeland ("The House I Live In").

There was also a look at American history through the prism of jive music ("History Eight to the Bar") and a sketch in which a senator beseeches everyone to "Be Calm" and ends up so upset that attendants escort him away in a straitjacket. Rome also offered a patriotic ditty called "Little Miss Victory Jones" which was in some ways cousin to his other "Jones" song "F.D.R. Jones" (*Sing Out the News*, 1938), although Louis Kronenberger in *PM* suggested it was less cousin and more "the puniest sort of stepsister." There was also the typical "New York" sketch, Al Geto's "How Do I Get There?," which focused on helpful people giving confusing subway directions (the sketch was a forerunner of Betty Comden, Adolph Green, and Jule Styne's amusing "Subway Directions" from their 1961 musical *Subways Are for Sleeping*).

"The House I Live In" is the revue's most famous and enduring song. In 1945, RKO released *The House I Live In*, a ten-minute film version that starred Frank Sinatra; it won a special Golden Globe Award in 1946, and in 2007 was included in the National Film Registry. The song was also heard in the 1945 revue **Blue Holiday**.

Herrick Brown in the *New York Sun* noted the revue had a "friendly jauntiness" about it, and despite "spotty" material the evening offered "plenty of fun" if you didn't set your hopes "too high." But most of the critics were less than happy. While he found some of the sketches "amiable," John Anderson in the *New York Journal-American* said the evening lacked "distinctive material"; Howard Barnes in the *New York Herald Tribune* said the revue offered "no hits, no runs and a multitude of errors," and while it might "get by in a high school auditorium, it is embarrassing on Broadway"; and Burns Mantle in the *New York Daily News* was sorry the young cast wasn't "able to make the best" of their material, and he felt Harold Rome's score wasn't up to his contributions for *Pins and Needles* (1937) and *Sing Out the News* (1938). But all the critics liked Betty Garrett. Wilella Waldorf in the *New York Post* found her "versatile"; Barnes said she had "zest and excitement"; Anderson liked her "mischievous manner"; and Brown found her "vivaciously engaging."

Kronenberger in *PM* was disappointed that the revue lacked a single "witty" skit, and he noted the evening's "satiric side" was a "complete bust"; but the "fresh and pretty and likable" Betty Garrett came "closest to giving something to Broadway." John Mason Brown in the *New York World-Telegram* said the evening had "no bite" and was all "gums and gawkishness"; but Betty Garrett was a "happy exception" and she had "genuine and engaging" talent. (Despite Mitzi Green's theatrical background and top billing, most of the reviewers were generally cool toward her and felt she did little to lift her material out of the doldrums.)

Brooks Atkinson in the *New York Times* said a "faint touch of the synthetic" permeated the revue, but he for one liked Mitzi Green ("a talented, good-hearted girl who knows her business") and said Betty Garrett came in a "close second." Atkinson singled out "The House I Live In" as the score's best song; it was "a quiet and homely invocation to America" and was sung by Mordecai Bauman with "earnest sincerity."

A few of the revue's numbers had been performed in earlier productions. "Of the People Stomp" was from Rome's 1940 musical **The Little Dog Laughed**, which closed prior to its Broadway opening; Rome's "History Eight to the Bar" had been heard as "Victory Symphony, Eight to the Bar" in the earlier 1942 morale-and-propaganda revue *Lunchtime Follies*, which had been presented at Brooklyn's Todd Shipyards; Jay Gorney's "Mittel Europa" had been heard in **They Can't Get You Down**, which closed during its tryout during the 1941–1942 season; and Marc Blitzstein's "Fraught" had first been introduced by Carol Channing in Marc Blitzstein's *No for an Answer* (1941); for more information about *No for an Answer*, the reader is referred to the author's *Off-Broadway Musicals, 1910–2007*. The song "We Have a Date" had been heard in **Of "V" We Sing**, and it appears Al Geto's sketch "Tactics" (with Phil Leeds and Curt Conway) was also performed in that revue (as "Hy'a Joe," where it was played by Leeds and Berni Gould).

"The House I Live In" has been recorded by various artists, and of course Frank Sinatra's version is the best known. "Of the People Stomp" is included in the collection *You Can't Put Ketchup on the Moon* (Rialto CD # SLRR-9201), and Carol Channing's "Fraught" can be heard on the original cast album of *No for an Answer* (Box Office LP # JJA-19772A/B).

The revue shouldn't be confused with the special one-performance revue *Let Freedom Sing*, which was presented at the Imperial Theatre on May 25, 1941. Produced by the Committee to Defend America by Aiding the Allies, the revue's cast included Irving Berlin, William Gaxton, Jack Norworth, Irving Caesar, Harland Dixon, Harry von Zell, and Noble Sissle and His Band. In 1987, another revue titled *Let Freedom Sing!* played at the American Music Theatre Festival in Philadelphia, Pennsylvania. Subtitled "A Constitutional Revue," the production included sketches by David Crane, Marta Kauffman, and Paul Lazarus; lyrics and music by a variety of writers and composers including Sheldon Harnick, Stephen Schwartz, Alan Menken, Larry Grossman, Ellen Fitzhugh, Doug Katsaros, and Jonathan Sheffer; and the cast included David (James) Carroll.

COUNT ME IN
"THE ALL-AMERICAN MUSICAL COMEDY"

Theatre: Ethel Barrymore Theatre
Opening Date: October 8, 1942; *Closing Date*: November 28, 1942
Performances: 61
Book: Walter Kerr and Leo Brady
Lyrics and *Music*: Ann Ronell; dance music by Don Walker
Direction: Production supervised by Harry A. Kaufman and book staged by Robert Ross; *Producers*: The Messrs. Shubert and Ole Olsen and Chic Johnson in association with Krakeur and Schmidlapp; *Choreography*: Robert Alton; *Scenery*: Howard Bay; *Costumes*: Irene Sharaff; *Lighting*: Uncredited; *Musical Direction*: John McManus
Cast: Charles Butterworth (Papa Brandywine), Luella Gear (Mama Brandywine), Hal LeRoy (Alvin York Brandywine), June Preisser (Tommy), Mary Healy (Sherry Brandywine), Gower Champion (Teddy Roosevelt Brandywine), Jeanne Tyler (in an unspecified but probably all-dancing role), Melissa Mason (Priscilla), Alice Dudley (Aunt Carrie Brandywine, Nurse, Columbia), Milton Watson (Dr. Heart), The Ross Sisters (Betsy, Vicki, and Dixie, who also played Bandagers), The Rhythmaires (Robert Bay, Don Weissmuller, Robert Shaw, Victor Griffin; the foursome also played The Four Japs), Jack McCauley (Radio Voice, First Examiner, Sergeant, First Officer), Joe E. Marks (Fourth Draftee, Mr. Moto), Alfred Latell (Sad Eyes, Ticketyboo), Don Richards (Coordinator, Richard), Willard Woolsey (Cadet Brandywine, Runner), Dorothy Griffin (Marianne, Private Simpson), Margaret Ryan (Hilda), Elizabeth Ryan (Hulda), Mary Alice Bigham (Olga), Buddles Mandl (Dolores), June Kim (Lotus), Janie New (Janie), Jean Arthur (Jean, Private McMullen), Carolyn Ayers (Carolyn), William Sharon (Second Examiner, Third Officer), Willis Claire (Third Examiner), Whit (Whitney) Bissell (First Draftee, Australian Announcer, Lowell Cabot, U.S.N.), Gibbs Penrose (Second Draftee, F.B.I. Man, Chinese Laundryman), Jack Lambert (Third Draftee, Benny the Gut, U.S.N.), Harry Rogue (Fifth Draftee), Danny Daniels (Sixth Draftee), Jean Darling (Aide), Agnes Kane (Aide), Lew Eckles (F.B.I. Man), Stanley Jessup (F.B.I. Man), Willis Claire (American Announcer, Second Officer), Richard Brasno (Ickety Tickeyboo), Jack Lambert (Chinese Laundryman), Alice Tyrell (Private Sweeney), Julie Colt (Susy Phillips), Olga Novosel (Wilma), Cookey Kley (Private Vanderhoff), Marian Sumetz (Private Hamilton); The Singing Girls: Julie Colt, Jean Darling, Agnes Kane, Cornelia Kilbourn, Johanna Gillman, Olga Novosel, Marian Sumetz, Alice Tyrell; The Dancing Girls: Jean Arthur, Carolyn Ayers, Mary Alice Bigham, Kay Coulter, Dorothy Griffin, Cookey Kley, June Kim, Kay Lewis, Claire Loring, Bubbles Mandl, Dolores Milan, Janie New, Jeane Owens, Margaret Ryan, Elizabeth Ryan, Nina Starkey, Pat Weakley, Marie Wilson; The Dancing Boys: Leonard Adriance, Jim Barron, Vincent Carbone, Danny Daniels, Charles Julian, William O'Shay, Jack Riley, Harry Rogue, Joe Viggiano
The musical was presented in two acts.
The action takes place in the present time in Connecticut, Australia, Virginia, and Washington, D.C.

Musical Numbers

Act One: "All-Out Bugle Call" (The Rhythmaires, The Singing Girls, The Dancing Girls, The Dancing Boys); "The Way My Ancestors Went" (Charles Butterworth; The Rhythmaires—General Brandywine/Revolutionary War: Robert Bay; Captain Brandywine/War of 1812: Don Weissmuller; Lieutenant Brandywine/

Civil War: Robert Shaw; Private Brandywine/Spanish-American War: Victor Griffin; Cadet Brandywine: Willard Woolsey; Aunt Carry Brandywine: Alice Dudley); "Someone in the Know" (June Preisser, Hal LeRoy; The Ross Sisters; Dancers: Harry Rogue, Girls, Boys); "On Leave for Love" (Luella Gear); "You've Got It All" (Mary Healy, Milton Watson); "Why Do They Say They're the Fair Sex?" (Don Richards, The Rhythmaires, The Singing Girls; danced by Gower and Jeanne, Girls, Boys); "We're Still on the Map" (dance music by Don Walker) (Mary Healy, Milton Watson; Coordinator: Don Richards; The West: Melissa Mason, The Rhythmaires; The North: Mary Healy, Milton Watson, Jack McCauley, Alfred Latell; The South: Gower and Jeanne, Gibbs Penrose, Willard Woolsey; The Southwest: Luella Gear, Richard Brasno, The Rhythmaires; Dancers: Hal LeRoy, June Preisser, The Rhythmaires, Girls, Boys)

Act Two: "Ticketyboo" (Don Richards, Singing Girls; danced by Alice Dudley, Gower and Jeanne, Girls, Boys; Ticketyboo: Alfred Latell; Ickety Ticketyboo: Richard Brasno); "Who Is General Staff?" (Joe E. Marks, The Rhythmaires); "Why Do They Say They're the Fair Sex?" (reprise) (danced by Hal LeRoy); "The Woman of the Year" (dance music by Don Walker) (Mary Healey, Singing Girls; Columbia: Alice Dudley; The Dancers: The Rhythmaires, Girls, Boys); "You've Got It All" (reprise) (Mary Healey, Milton Watson); "On Leave for Love" (reprise) (Melissa Mason, with Whit Bissell and Jack Lambert); Finale (Entire Company)

The almost revue-like structure of *Count Me In* dealt with an American family doing its bit for the war effort. Mama Brandywine (Luella Gear) is a WAAC, daughter Sherry—yes, that's Sherry Brandywine—(Mary Healy) works in a hospital dispensing first aid, one son Alvin York (Hal LeRoy) is an air warden, and another son, Teddy Roosevelt Brandywine (Gower Champion) is with the air brigade. Everyone in the family is happily and industriously busy except for Papa (Charles Butterworth), a mapmaker who is all at sea when it comes to war work. (Later in the season, ***Dancing in the Streets*** also looked at this dilemma when three military retirees feel they have nothing to contribute to the current conflict; the theme also seems to have surfaced in a revue sketch or two, such as "Grandpa Guerrilla" in ***Let Freedom Sing***.)

But Papa soon devises a scheme in which he creates a phony map citing a place called Shangri-La, goes to Australia and environs, purposely gets himself captured and interned by the Japanese, deceives them with the map, and thus fools them into invading an area already held by the Allies, where the Japanese are thoroughly shellacked. Papa is first assumed to be a traitor, but the U.S. government soon absolves him and crowns him a hero. All ends well when Papa—you can now count him in—returns home for a victory celebration at the local Village Green Canteen.

Wilella Waldorf in the *New York Post* said the musical began with "plenty of snap" and the first three or four songs promised a "smartly" fashioned "bright" and "topical" show; but the evening soon ran out of inspiration and repeated itself. The show offered an occasional "surprise package" but also "a lot of junk." She liked the "graceful stepping" of Gower Champion and Jeanne Tyler, but noted (as she did in her review of ***The Lady Comes Across***) they'd be more effective if they'd drop the business of exchanging lighthearted banter during their dance routines.

Burns Mantle in the *New York Daily News* regretted that the usually delightful dead-pan Charles Butterworth and the eternally acerbic Luella Gear didn't have better material, but he praised five numbers from Ann Ronell's score ("You've Got It All," "On Leave for Love," "Tickeyboo," "Who Is General Staff?," and "The Woman of the Year"). Brooks Atkinson in the *New York Times* also liked "You've Got It All" (a "sweet melody") and "Who Is General Staff?" (it had "pace and humor"), but overall felt her work was "mostly imitative." He said the book was "industrious" but "busily useless"; praised Robert Alton's "brisk and exhilarating" choreography (especially the "half-wry humors" for the "grinning Jap quartet," which made for "crisp and shrewd vitality"); and the "brilliant and stunning" costumes by Irene Sharaff (who even made Uncle Sam's utilitarian uniforms "blend into the fantasy" of musical comedy).

John Anderson in the *New York Journal-American* said the book was more of a "loose-leaf folder," and he regretted that superb comic Charles Butterworth was a man "script-wrecked on a desert libretto"; Richard Lockridge in the *New York Sun* felt that nothing was missing in the musical except "entertainment" because the book was "almost too vague to grasp" and the score was "uneventful"; John Mason Brown in the *New York World-Telegram* said the "alleged" book made *The Trojan Women* seem like a "hilarious lark"; Howard Barnes in the *New York Herald Tribune* said "all that is wanting is a show"; and Louis Kronenberger in *PM* apologized for the "obvious" when he said to "count me out."

While Butterworth and Gear were shortchanged with their material, the critics felt tap dancer Hal LeRoy and the ballroom dancing team of Gower and Jeanne shined. As for the three Ross Sisters, Anderson said he didn't admire lady contortionists, and "the better they are the worse" they seemed. Brown suggested the "unbearably pretzel-like" trio required "a stiff dose of mothersill" in order to "look at them in comfort." As for June Preisser, he noted she was "on hand if this by any chance should bring you pleasure."

The program credited Don Walker with the dance music of "The Woman of the Year," the first act finale ("We're Still on the Map"), "First Aid Ballet," and "Please Take Papa Away." The latter two weren't listed among the song numbers, but it's likely the "First Aid Ballet" was performed in the first act's fifth scene during the "You've Got It All" sequence. The program also thanked songwriters Lester Lee and Jerry Seelan for uncredited assistance (a few weeks earlier, the team had contributed four songs to the revue **New Priorities of 1943**). During the run, Gower and Jeanne left the production and were succeeded by Elaine and Fred Barry; and Jack Gilford and Johnny Burke joined the cast in unspecified roles (the latter was a comedian, and not the well-known lyricist and sometime composer).

Among the chorus members were future Broadway choreographer Danny Daniels and future film character actor Whit Bissell. Marie Wilson is the same performer who later excelled in wacky dumb-blonde roles, but chorus girl Jean Arthur isn't the same as the celebrated film actress. And of course co-librettist Walter Kerr became one of the most important New York theatre critics.

Earlier in the year, the musical had been first produced by the Reverend G. V. Hartke at Catholic University in Washington, D.C. The critics suspected the home-grown version was more satiric, and that during the gestation of the musical's trek to Broadway the pointed humor had been leavened out and more traditional musical comedy seasoning had been added.

OY IS DUS A LEBEN!
"A MUSICAL CAVALCADE"

Theatre: Molly Picon Theatre
Opening Date: October 12, 1942; *Closing Date*: February 6, 1943
Performances: 139
Book: Jacob Kalich
Lyrics: Molly Picon
Music: Joseph Rumshinsky
Direction: Jacob Kalich; *Producer*: Edwin A. Relkin; *Choreography*: David Lubritzky and Lillian Shapiro;
    Scenery: Harry Gordon Bennett
Cast: Prologue—Leon Gold (Theatre), David Lubritzky (Achashverosh), Jennie Casher (Vaschti) Esta Saltzman (Vaizuso), Boris Auerbach (Jacob P. Adler), Izidor Casher (David Kessler), Sam Kasten (Sigmund Mogilesco), Michael Wilenski (Boris Tomashefsky), Tillie Rabinowitz (Bessie Tomashefsky), Celia Pearson (Keni Lipzin); The Play—Molly Picon (Molly), Jacob Kalich (Mr. Kay), Dora Weissman (Mrs. Picon), Izidor Casher (Ziggie), Anna Appel (Rosalia), Leon Gold (Misha), Sam Kasten (A Comedian), Esta Saltzman (Sylvia), Jennie Casher (Nadya), Tillie Rabinowitz (Zelda), Rosa Greenfield (Rebbitzen), Charles Cohen (Schlome), David Lubritzky (Zalmyn), Boris Auerbach (Getzel), Rebecca Weintraub (Chayeh-Sura), Morris Friedman (Policeman), Samuel Mlanock (Policeman), Sam Milman (Judah), Herbert Cohen (Israel)
The musical was presented in two acts. (*Note*: The program didn't list musical numbers.)
The action takes place during the years 1912–1942 in Boston, Philadelphia, the Catskills, and New York City as well as in Bucharest, Romania, and Galicia, Poland.

Oy is dus a leben! (*Oh, what a life!*) was performed in Yiddish and followed the saga of star Molly Picon's theatrical life, from her stage debut in Philadelphia to her years playing in Boston and in the Catskills, and then her theatrical experiences in Europe and finally her heyday as one of the most famous stars of New York's Yiddish theatre. The musical's book was written by Picon's husband Jacob Kalich, who also appeared in the production.

Perhaps the musical's most interesting review was by George Jean Nathan, who reviewed the New York newspaper critics who reviewed the musical. In his annual survey of the season, he noted that his knowledge of Yiddish was confined to the words *Ish kabibble*, and so despite the program's English synopsis, he felt unqualified to review the musical. But the other New York critics were "apparently familiar with Yiddish since early childhood," and thus "Yiddish scholar" Richard Lockridge (*New York Sun*), "Yiddish authority" Wilella

Waldorf (*New York Post*), "Yiddish expert" John Mason Brown (*New York World-Telegram*), "Yiddish honor scholar" Burns Mantle (*New York Daily News*), "Yiddish salon" Joseph Pihodna (*New York Herald Tribune*), "Yiddish luminary" Robert Coleman (*New York Mirror*), and that "Yiddish medallist" Brooks Atkinson were all qualified to write about a production which was spoken entirely in Yiddish.

Lockridge reported that the "grand" Molly Picon proves "all over again why her fame has spread so very far from Second Avenue"; Waldorf said the descriptions of Picon's early career days were presented with "carefree insouciance" but was "only intermittently interesting," while her European experiences "offered some fantastic clowning"; Brown said Picon's "unpretentious biography" was "colorful, amusing, even exciting," with "broad" comedy and "unblushing" sentiment; Mantle praised Picon's sense of "comedy and drama"; Pihodna said Picon was "justly honored" by the production; Coleman said the evening "sets a new high" for Yiddish theatre and was a "big hit"; and Atkinson said Picon ran "the whole gamut in her autobiography" and thus could underplay when necessary and then would "break your heart" with a love song.

The production's musical numbers included "I Don't Want to Be a Man" and the title song. The Molly Picon Theatre was the temporary name for Jolson's 59th Street Theatre. During the venue's thirty-odd years of life, it was renamed the Central Park Theatre, Shakespeare Theatre, Venice Theatre, Molly Picon Theatre, and New Century Theatre. It was the original home of *The Student Prince* (1924), *The Cradle Will Rock* (1937), **Follow the Girls**, **Up in Central Park**, **High Button Shoes**, **Inside U.S.A.**, **Kiss Me, Kate** (which was the theatre's biggest hit), *Out of This World* (1950), and the legendary flops *Buttrio Square* (1952) and *Carnival in Flanders* (1953) (the latter was the theatre's final tenant).

In 1961, Picon marked her fiftieth year in show business by appearing in Jerry Herman's first Broadway musical *Milk and Honey*, which ran for 543 performances. Playing a Jewish widow vacationing in Israel and on the look-out for a second husband, she had two show-stoppers in "Chin Up, Ladies" (in which she encouraged fellow widows to "climb every mountain to find your Mister Snow") and "Hymn to Hymie" (an amusing one-sided discussion with her late husband). John McClain in the *New York Journal-American* said she defied "both Christian and Hebrew calendars" with her "sprightly kicks and buck-and-wing antics." For a taste of Picon's special brand of comedy, note her appearance in the 1963 film version of Neil Simon's 1961 play *Come Blow Your Horn*; the film's plot literally stops for a few minutes to give Picon a monologue-like shtick in which she tries to take messages from a barrage of incoming phone calls.

Rose Leiman Goldemberg's play-with-music *Picon Pie* was a tribute to the legendary fixture of the Yiddish and Broadway stage; it was first seen in New York in a 2004 Off-Off-Broadway production that ran for an estimated 200 performances, and then later played a regular Off-Broadway engagement in 2005 for 121 showings (for Off Broadway, June Gable was Molly Picon and Stuart Zagnit played the role of Jacob Kalich).

BEAT THE BAND
"A New Musical Comedy" / "A Sophisticated New Musical Comedy"

Theatre: 46th Street Theatre
Opening Date: October 14, 1942; *Closing Date*: December 12, 1942
Performances: 68
Book: George Marion Jr., and George Abbott
Lyrics: George Marion Jr.
Music: Johnny Green
Direction: George Abbott; *Producer*: George Abbott; *Choreography*: David Lichine; *Scenery*: Samuel Leve; *Costumes*: Freddy Wittop; *Lighting*: Uncredited; *Musical Direction*: Archie Bleyer
Cast: Romo Vincent (Buster de Costa), Joan Caulfield (Veronica), Jerry Lester (Hugh Dillingham), Toni Gilman (Willow Willoughby), Ralph Bunker (Mr. Pirosh), Eunice Healey (Princess), Jack Whiting (Damon Dillingham), James Lane (Doorman), Johnny Mack (Drummer), Leonard Sues (Trumpet Player), Evelyn Brooks (Band Girl), Juanita Juarez (Mamita), Susan Miller (Querida), Averell Harris (Don Domingo), Brian Connaught (First Detective), John Wray (Second Detective), Cliff Dunstan (Hotel Manager), Doris Dowling (Bell Girl), John Clarke (Hotel Owner); Dancing Girls: Dorothy Barrett, Tessie Corrano, Eileen Devlin, Doris Dowling, Marilyn Hightower, Rhoda Hoffman, Muriel Hunt, Terry Kelly, Margaret Long, Mary MacDonnell, Frances Martone, Judy O'Brien, Ellen Taylor, Mimi Walthers, Doris York; Singing Girls: Anita Dillon, Dolores Gaylord, Rosalind Madison, Leonore Rae, Jane Starner, Roberta Welch, Nellilew

Winger, Beverly Whitney; Dancing Boys: Jack Allen, Richard Andre, Larry Baker, Bob Copsey, Stanley Donen, Sidney Gordon, Harold Haskin, Herb Lurie, Robert McKernan; Damon Dillingham's Band: Johnny Mack (Drums), Leonard Sues (Trumpet), Steady Nelson (Trumpet), Clarence Willard (Trumpet), Ford Leary (Trombone), Spud Murphy (Trombone), Pete Pumiglio (Clarinet), Dave Harris (Tenor Sax), Dick Kissinger (Bass), David Le Winter (Piano)

The musical was presented in two acts.

The action takes place during the present time in New York City and Washington, D.C.

Musical Numbers

Act One: "Down Through the Agents" (Romo Vincent, The Wiman Girls, The Cole Porter Girls, The Script Girls, The Bistro Girls, The Ballet Boys, Male Quartet, The Saroyan Boy); "Free, Cute, and Size Fourteen" (Jerry Lester, Eunice Healey; danced by Ensemble and Eunice Healey); "Song of Two Islands" (Susan Miller); "Keep It Casual" (Jack Whiting, Susan Miller; danced by Johnny Mack, Dancing Girls and Boys); "Proud of You" (Jack Whiting); "Break It Up" (Romo Vincent, Damon Dillingham's Band; Trumpet Solo: Leonard Sues); "Let's Comb Beaches" (Jack Whiting, Susan Miller); "The Swimmers" (dance) (Doris York, Marc Platt, Ensemble); "America Loves a Band" (Susan Miller, Jack Whiting, Eunice Healey, Romo Vincent, Juanita Juarez, Jerry Lester, Ensemble, Damon Dillingham's Band)

Act Two: "The Afternoon of a Phoney" (Romo Vincent, Clients; danced by Eunice Healey and Marc Platt); "Men" (Juanita Juarez, Susan Miller); "Steam Is on the Beam" (Eunice Healey, Evelyn Brooks, Jack Whiting, Romo Vincent, Leonard Sues, Johnny Mack, Marilyn Hightower, Larry Baker, Damon Dillingham's Band, Ensemble); "I'm Physical, You're Cultured" (Jerry Lester, Toni Gilman); "Every Other Heartbeat" (Susan Miller, Jack Whiting, Leonard Sues, Singing Girls); "The Four Freedoms—Calypso" (Juanita Juarez, Jack Whiting, Jerry Lester, Romo Vincent, Entire Company); The Encore (Susan Miller)

There are many unrecorded musicals worthy of studio cast recordings. **Walk with Music** (with lyrics by Johnny Mercer) was Hoagy Carmichael's only full-length Broadway score, **Early to Bed** (lyrics by George Marion Jr.) was "Fats" Waller's final Broadway offering, and *Beat the Band* (lyrics also by Marion) was Johnny Green's only Broadway outing. The songs that have emerged from these shows are melodious and inventive, and one suspects they'd make terrific recordings. It appears that *Beat the Band*'s unique score might well be a defining moment that took the traditional format of a Broadway score and married it to the contemporary sound of the era's popular music, much in the way Burt Bacharach's score for *Promises, Promises* encapsulated the sound of late 1960s pop music.

Beat the Band is especially intriguing because Johnny Green's score made a more than usual impact upon the critics, both negatively and positively. Brooks Atkinson in the *New York Times* seems to have been the most conflicted of the reviewers. He said Green's score of "tornadoes" ran up a "considerable temperature" and was composed "on the downbeat in the idiom of tomorrow." Here was "super-heated" music by a composer in "top form" who liked his profession and thus kept every musical instrument in the orchestra "working at top efficiency." Recently, only Irving Berlin had composed music with such "enthusiasm," and so it was a "pleasure" to encounter Green. *But*—Green's musical style was not "particularly good for singing"; some songs were so "civilized" they seemed to lack notes, and with vocals his music was less song and more a "clearing of the throat." He concluded that Green was "more technician than musician." Howard Barnes in the *New York Herald Tribune* said the score was "first rate" and a "humdinger," and from the "standpoint of melody and syncopation" it was "captivating"; Richard Lockridge in the *New York Sun* found the songs "pleasing and tuneful" but not "particularly memorable"; and George Ross in the *New York World-Telegram* praised the "superior" music.

Burns Mantle in the *New York Daily News* found "little to enthuse" about in regard to the "dull" and "unmelodious" score, said he supposed the composer hailed "from the hot spots," and as far as he was concerned he could live for "years and years" without ever hearing another note of jive; John Anderson in the *New York Journal-American* said the score was "agreeable"; Louis Kronenberger in *PM* said the music was "pretty undistinctive"; and Wilella Waldorf said the score had a "distressing tendency to blend in with the general mediocrity" of the show.

Of the musical's fourteen songs, seven were singled out by the critics. Waldorf said the "peppiest" number was the boogie-woogie "hot stuff" of "Steam Is on the Beam"; Kronenberger said the song was "hot and lusty"; Barnes said the number was a "knockout" (it offered "exuberance, high spirits and whirling spectacle"); and Ross said the song and "America Loves a Band" were "splendid and exciting." As for the latter, Anderson said it provided a "whammo" first-act finale. Atkinson said "Song of Two Islands" was "superb" in its "vein of brass-tongued romance"; Kronenberger found "Every Other Heartbeat" a "catchy" (but "commonplace") ballad, while Mantle said it was one of the "best" songs in the score. Anderson liked "Song of Two Islands" and "Let's Comb Beaches," both of which were "Cole Porterish"; Lockridge liked the "graceful" songs "Every Other Heartbeat" and "Keep It Casual"; and Ross said "Let's Comb Beaches" and "The Afternoon of a Phoney" were "impish."

The trifling if somewhat confusing plot dealt with American heiress Querida (Susan Miller) who has lived on a Caribbean island and is now in New York to visit her godfather (and chaperone) Hugh Dillingham (Jerry Lester), whom she's never met. Hugh has temporarily moved into the penthouse apartment of his half-brother, temperamental bandleader Damon Dillingham (Jack Whiting) who is on the outs with his fiancé Willow (Toni Gilman). When Querida assumes Damon is her godfather, he decides to go along with her mistaken impression, but Willow is still on the scene, and so much of the evening's humor derived from Damon and Hugh's efforts to keep Querida and Willow from meeting one another. Further, there was much would-be comic business which involved passing off members of Damon's jazz orchestra as wealthy Manhattan socialites. Added to the mix were comic Romo Vincent as a casting agent: dancers Marc Platt, Eunice Healey, and Johnny Mack; Juanita Juarez as a fiery Latin; and trumpeter Leonard Sues (who had made quite an impression in *Johnny 2 x 4*). Anderson said Sues could "probably give Gabriel lessons on the trumpet," and Kronenberger suggested that "a mere echo of his blasts would have done all that was needed at Jericho."

Waldorf found the story "monotonous," and felt Marion strained in his lyrics and rhyme schemes, especially when in "Down Through the Agents" Romo Vincent scolded a group of chorus girls for being "morons" because they'd never equal Gertrude "Lawrence"; Anderson said the book was so "unsafe" the performers probably suffered from "plot fright"; Barnes suggested the "attractive" evening could have been "far better"; and despite its book troubles Ross thanked George Abbott for supplying "some much-longed-for-gaiety upon the town."

Lockridge liked Freddy Wittop's "bright" costumes and Sam Leve's "clever" sets, and Anderson praised David Lichine's "lively" choreography. Further, Mantle found Jack Whiting "likable" and Ross said Susan Miller's way with a song was reminiscent of Ethel Merman's style.

"Steam Is on the Beam," which was performed in a scene which took place in the boiler room of a hotel, is included in the collection *Life's a Funny Present* (Rialto CD # SLRR-9306).

Beat the Band never caught on, and disappeared after two months. Well, not quite disappeared. In 1947, RKO filmed the musical (advertised as "A Musical Love Story in Laughtime!") with Frances Langford, who was backed by Gene Krupa and His Band; others in the cast were Ralph Edwards and Phillip Terry, and the direction was by John H. Auer. The altered plot found Langford as opera student Ann Rogers who prefers boogie-woogie to Bellini; she's misled into believing Damon Dillingham (Terry) is really a classical voice teacher; conveniently, he's the leader of a swing band, and after much mistaken identity nonsense as well as various misunderstandings the twosome find themselves making sweet music on the bandstand. No songs from the stage production were used. Mort Greene and Leigh Harline wrote three numbers for the film: "Kissin' Well," "I'm in Love," and "I've Got My Fingers Crossed," the latter the score's highlight (except for its title, it bore no relation to Jimmy McHugh and Ted Koehler's equally ingratiating song from the 1936 film musical *King of Burlesque*). Krupa and his band performed the specialty "Shadow Rhapsody," and "I Couldn't Sleep a Wink Last Night" (lyric by Harold Adamson, music by Jimmy McHugh) was borrowed from the 1944 film version of *Higher and Higher*. One source indicates Greene and Harline wrote a title song for the film, but if so the number wasn't performed; it may have been filmed and cut prior to release, or perhaps it was used as instrumental background music. Like the stage production, the film also utilized a musical scene that took place in a hotel's boiler room.

THE TIME, THE PLACE AND THE GIRL
"A MUSICAL COMEDY"

Theatre: Mansfield Theatre
Opening Date: October 21, 1942; *Closing Date*: October 31, 1942
Performances: 13

Book: Revised book by Will Morrissey and John Neff
Lyrics: William B. Friedlander
Music: Joe Howard
Based on the 1907 musical *The Time, the Place and the Girl*, original book and lyrics by Will M. Hough and
    Frank R. Adams and music by Joe (Joseph E.) Howard
Direction: William B. Friedlander; *Producer*: Georges D. Gersene; *Choreography*: Carl Randall; *Scenery*:
    Amend; *Costumes*: Paul duPont; *Lighting*: Uncredited; *Musical Direction*: Louis Katzman
Cast: Evelyn Case (Mrs. Talcott), Vickie Cummings (Molly Kelly), Joe Howard (Joe Howard), James Phillips (A
    Guide, A Policeman), Lee Sullivan (Tom Cunningham), "Red" Marshall (Johnny Hicks), Rolfe Sedan (Mr.
    Duval), Fred Kuhnly (An Attendant), Richard Worth (Lawrence Farnham), Irene Hilda (Margaret Howard),
    Duke Norman (Willie Talcott), Rae McGregor (Ballerina);The Buccaneers: James Phillips, Wilson Lang,
    Fred Kuhly, Robert Douglas; The Sophisti-Kids: Irene Carroll, May Muth, Terry Saunders, Doris Pare,
    Jimmy Allison, Ray Cook, Gene Stern, Andrew Thurston; Specialty Dancers: Kendrick Coy, William
    Weber; The Girls: Olga Alexandrova, Kay Dowd, Rhoda Gerard, Sheila Herman, Marion Lulling, Peggy
    Lynn, Ruth Mitchell, Dorothy Ostrander, Connie Sheldon, Dot Sloane, Fanette Stalle, Dorothy Stirwalt,
    Helen Zurad
The musical was presented in two acts.
The action takes place in the early 1900s at a sanitarium and hotel in the mountains of Virginia.

Musical Numbers

Act One: Overture (Orchestra); "There's a Little Man on My Shoulder" (danced by Duke Norman; sung by
    The Buccaneers, The Sophisti-Kids, Ensemble); "Ocarina" (Evelyn Case, The Sophisti-Kids, The Bucca-
    neers); "Travelling Man" (Richard Worth, The Buccaneers, The Sophisti-Kids); "Something in My Eye"
    (according to program, song written by Joe Howard, Randolph and Britten) (Irene Hilda, Dancing Ensem-
    ble); "Dr. Keeley" (Vickie Cummings, Red Marshall); "Will-o'-the-Wisp" (Evelyn Case, The Sophisti-Kids;
    danced by Rae McGregor, Kendrick Coy, William Weber, Ensemble); Dance (Duke Norman); "A Penny for
    Your Thoughts, Junior Miss" (Irene Hilda, Lee Sullivan, The Sophisti-Kids, Dancing Girls); Finale of Act
    One: "The Custom of Dressing for Dinner" (Evelyn Case, Ensemble; danced by Rae McGregor, Kendrick
    Coy, William Weber)
Act Two: "The Custom of Dressing for Dinner" (reprise) (Evelyn Case, Ensemble; danced by Rae McGregor,
    Kendrick Coy, William Weber); "Work Eight Hours" (Lee Sullivan, Ensemble); "Treason" (Irene Hilda,
    Richard Worth); "Rations" (Vickie Cummings, Red Marshall, Dancing Ensemble); "I Can't Get Along
    without You" (Irene Hilda, Lee Sullivan); Song Hits Medley (Joe Howard)

Although the record books (including this one) cite *The Time, the Place and the Girl* as a revival, it was
pretty much one in name only. The musical had originally been produced in Chicago for a year's run, but
its Broadway production, which opened on August 5, 1907, at Wallack's Theatre, played for just forty performances. The original book and lyrics were by Will M. Hough and Frank R. Adams, and the score was by Joe
Howard. For the current production, the revised book was credited to Will Morrissey and John Neff; a completely new score was written by Howard with lyrics by William N. Friedlander. Howard also portrayed himself in the musical (he hadn't been slated to appear, but stepped in when the original performer bowed out).

The program included an insert sheet by producer Georges D. Gersene, who noted the revival's creators
had "not attempted to make it into a modern musical comedy," and thus the production was "presented" in
the style of the period of forty years earlier "with costumes and scenery in vogue then." But if the show wasn't
supposed to be "modern" and if the work was presented with décor from decades earlier, why were there such
topically titled songs as "Rations" and "A Penny for Your Thoughts, Junior Miss"? (Jerome Chodorov and
Joseph Fields's hit 1941 comedy *Junior Miss* was about halfway through its 710-performance run when the
current production of *The Time, the Place and the Girl* opened.)

While the revival didn't include any songs from the original version, the program noted that the overture
itself was a medley of songs from the 1907 production. Joe Howard didn't sing until the very end of the evening when he performed a medley of his old songs (but none from the musical's original production), which

probably included his hits "I Wonder Who's Kissing Her Now," "Good-by, My Lady Love," and "Hello, My Baby."

Like the original, the revival was set at a hotel and sanitarium in the mountains of Virginia for patients in advanced stages of delirium tremens. Two college playboy types hang out at the hotel and become involved in romantic misadventures. Wilella Waldorf in the *New York Post* reported that one character (played by the musical's leading eccentric dancer) was "not only eccentric but balmy," and Burton Rascoe in the *New York World-Telegram* noted the dancer mimicked "the droolings of an imbecile."

Waldorf said the evening was an "embarrassing bore" replete with "persistent encores accorded everything regardless of applause or lack of it"; she noted she had chided George Marion Jr. for his lyrics in **Beat the Band**, but after listening to William B. Friedlander's lyrics, she declared Marion was a "gifted poet." Richard Lockridge in the *New York Sun* said the evening was "odd" and "discouraging," with a story "incredible beyond description" and encumbered by "dullness beyond belief"; Rascoe noted the audience had "come to cheer and remained to yawn"; and Burns Mantle in the *New York Daily News* noted that with the "guerre" going on, "bombings from the air" were possible, and there could be theatrical ones as well.

John Anderson in the *New York Journal-American* said he hoped never to remind himself where he was "last night between 8:45 and 11:00," for the evening was like a "peculiarly unpleasant hallucination"; he was thankful that fellow critics Howard Barnes, Wilella Waldorf, Louis Kronenberger, and George Jean Nathan were all there to assure him that they too had seen the same show, else he would "have summoned a straitjacket in the belief that I had lost my mind."

Louis Kronenberger in *PM* suggested that those who thought the gas-lit era a romantic one should stay away from *The Time, the Place and the Girl*, and then noted his readers should "stay away from it in any case" (he also shared the show's idea of humor: "Did you graduate from college?" "No, I quit after five years"); Howard Barnes in the *New York Herald Tribune* said when the evening was "not downright embarrassing, it is incredibly dull"; and Brooks Atkinson in the *New York Times* noted that for the years 1907 to 1942 Broadway had somehow gotten along without a production of *The Time, the Place and the Girl*, and in retrospect this was "one of the most celestial periods in New York history."

ROSALINDA

Theatre: 44th Street Theatre (during run, the operetta transferred to the Imperial Theatre, then back to the 44th Street Theatre, and then to the 46th Street Theatre)

Opening Date: October 28, 1942; *Closing Date*: January 22, 1944

Performances: 521

Book: Original libretto by Karl Haffner and Richard Genee; English adaptation by Gottfried Reinhardt and John Meehan Jr. (based on an adaptation by Max Reinhardt)

Lyrics: Paul Kerby

Music: Johann Strauss

Direction: Felix Brentano; *Producers*: Produced by Lodewick Vroom for The New Opera Company (Mrs. Lytle Hull, President, and Mme. Yolanda Mero-Irion, General Manager); *Choreography*: George Balanchine; *Scenery*: Oliver Smith; *Costumes*: Ladislas Czettel; *Lighting*: Jean Rosenthal; *Musical Direction*: Erich Wolfgang Korngold

Cast: Everett West (Alfredo Allevanto), Ernest McChesney (Gabriel Von Eisenstein), Virginia MacWatters (Adele), Dorothy Sarnoff (Rosalinda Von Eisenstein), Leonard Stocker (Blint), Gene Barry (Falke), Paul Best (Dr. Frank), Shelly (Shelley) Winter (Winters) (Fifi), Oscar Karlweis (Prince Orlofsky), Edwin Fowler (Aide de Camp), Louis Sorin (Frosch), José Limón (Premier Dancer), Mary Ellen (Premiere Danseuse); Ladies of the Ensemble: Nina Allen, Thelma Altman, Betty Baker, Xenia Bank, Nancy Baskerville, Jeanne Beauvais, Lillian C. Bennett, Betty Billings, Diana Corday, Anne Dawson, Camille Fischelli, Lucy Marshall, Frances McCann, Joan O'Neil, Dorothy Ramsey, Loretta Schere, Joan Wheatley, Jane Whyte; Gentlemen of the Ensemble: Marden Bate, Edwin Fowler, David Goldstein, Harold Gordon, William Hearne, Alfred Kunz, Lawrence Lieberman, Alfred D. Morgan, Benjamin Siegel, Robert Tower, Bernard Tunisse, George V. Vincent, Alan Winston; Corps de Ballet: Lillian Lanese, Yvonne Patterson, Phyllis Hill, Joyce Hill, Elise Reiman, Betty Lou Reed, Yvonne Tibor, Anne Wiman, Julia Horvath, Sonya Orlova, Mary Ellen Moylon,

Douglas Caudy, Todd Bolender, Herbert Bliss, Jack Gansaert, Edward Bigelow, Jean Faust, Simon Sadoff; William Dollar (Ballet Master)

The operetta was presented in a prologue and three acts.

The action takes place in a summer resort near Vienna in 1890.

The program didn't list individual musical numbers.

Johann Strauss' *Die Fledermaus* (*The Bat*) premiered on April 5, 1874, at the Theatre an de Wien in Vienna, Austria, and became one of the most popular operettas ever written. Strauss's lush melodies are perfectly wedded to the lighthearted story of amorous misbehavior, marital deceptions, and mistaken identities.

The operetta was first seen in New York at Brooklyn's Thalia Theatre on October 18, 1879, for 7 performances in repertory, and the first English adaptation (by Sydney Rosenfeld) opened at the Casino Theatre on March 16, 1885, for 42 performances. The work has been revived in New York many times in both German and English, including a number of notable American adaptations: *The Merry Countess* (Casino Theatre, August 20, 1912, for 135 performances; adaptation by Gladys Unger, lyrics by Arthur Anderson); *A Wonderful Night* (Majestic Theatre, October 31, 1929, for 125 performances; adaptation by Fanny Todd Mitchell [the cast included Archie Leach, who later changed his name to Cary Grant]); and *Champagne, Sec* (Morosco Theatre, October 30, 1933, for 113 performances; adaptation by Alan Child [Lawrence Langner], lyrics by Robert A. Simon).

Rosalinda was by far the most successful American version, with a total run of 521 performances. George Marion Jr., had originally been set to adapt the operetta, but presumably his involvement with **Beat the Band** caused him to bow out. *Rosalinda* was based on a European revival by Max Reinhardt and Erich Wolfgang Korngold (who conducted the current production), and the new book was by Gottfried Reinhardt (Max's son) and John Meehan Jr., with lyrics by Paul Kerby. The production interpolated other music by Strauss, including the waltzes "Tales of the Vienna Woods" and "Wine, Women and Song" as well as an interpolation from Strauss's opera *Knight Pazman*. *Rosalinda* was originally scheduled to be performed in repertory with other operas produced by The New Opera Company, but it was so successful that it offered eight weekly performances and stayed on Broadway for fifteen months.

For most of the critics, the song was the thing, not the plot. But the story never overwhelmed the music, and with good solid voices, a lavish production, and an especially brilliant second act that emphasized George Balanchine's swirling choreography, the revival received good reviews. Howard Barnes in the *New York Herald Tribune* said the book was "obvious and stuffy" and thus the singers had to "muddle through" the dialogue; but when everybody sang, all was forgiven. Virgil Thomson was the newspaper's music critic, and he felt the performers weren't up to the rigors of acting their roles and thus the production "looked and sounded amateurish" in contrast to the "superb control and rhythmic power" of Korngold's orchestra. But when the dancers took over in the ballroom scene at Prince Orlofsky's palace at the end of act two, "everything fell into the groove" because the dancers "had style and knew what they were doing."

Burns Mantle in the *New York Daily News* noted the story had always been "pretty soggy," but he felt the new book was "serviceable" and even added a "modest disrobing number" for Dorothy Sarnoff which came across as a "sort of striptease of the '90s." Louis Kronenberger in *PM* felt the evening sparkled in the second act ballroom sequence; the music was "irresistible" and the dancers "foamed out into effective full-stage waltz patterns." John Anderson in the *New York Journal-American* commented on how many versions of the operetta had recently appeared on Broadway and suggested producers believed "if you build a better *Fledermaus*-trap" the audiences will come; as for the current revival, it had a "nit-wit" plot but the music was "lovely," especially the second act's "climax of swooning sound."

The critics also commended Ralph Herbert, who literally at the last minute took over the role of Von Eisenstein from the ailing Ernest McChesney. Robert Bagar in the *New York World-Telegram* offered "special words of praise" to Herbert for stepping in so quickly, and he praised Dorothy Sarnoff in the title role. She was a "lovely soprano" who sang the music "fascinatingly." Olin Downes in the *New York Times* said her voice was the "greatest" of the evening and noted she had "marked dramatic talent."

When *Rosalinda* was about ten months into its Broadway run, another version of *Die Fledermaus* hit the boards in a West Coast production titled **The Rose Masque**. It clearly hoped to capitalize on the current success of the operetta in New York, but stalled permanently after its San Francisco and Los Angeles engagements.

There isn't a recording of *Rosalinda* per se, but there are a number of recordings of *Die Fledermaus*. And while there wasn't a film version directly based on the current revival, a musical version set in contemporary

Vienna was released in Great Britain as *Oh, Rosalinda!!* (aka *Oh . . . Rosalinda!!*) in 1955 by The Archers/ABPC. The film starred Ludmilla Tcherina, Anthony Quayle, Dennis Price, Michael Redgrave, and Mel Ferrer, and was codirected and co-scripted by Michael Powell and Emeric Pressburger. The soundtrack was released by Mercury Records (LP # MG-20145).

LA VIE PARISIENNE

Theatre: Broadway Theatre
Opening Date: November 10, 1942; *Closing Date*: December 7, 1942
Performances: 17
Libretto: English version by Felix Brentano and Louis Verneuil, with lyrics by Marion Farquhar and additional dialogue by Frank Torloff and Leo Riskin (based on the original French version by Henri Meilhac and Ludovic Helavy)
Music: Jacques Offenbach
Direction: Felix Brentano; *Producer*: The New Opera Company; *Scenery* and *Costumes*: Marco Montedoro; *Lighting*: Uncredited; *Musical Direction*: Paul Breisach
Cast: Stanley Carlson (Station Master, Revolutionary), Donald Burr (Comte Raoul de Gardefeu), Wilbur Evans (Baron Bobinet), Paul Reed (Jackson), Carolina Segrera (Metella), Paul Kwartin (Gontran, Alphonse), Virginia Card (Evelyn), Hugh Thompson (Mr. Hutchinson), Andzia Kuzak (Gabrielle); Tradespeople: Mary Davis, Cynthia Rose, Josephine Griffin; Chorus: Mary Davis, Josephine Griffin, Margaret Ormos, Cynthia Rose, Freda Starr, Carol Yorke, Alice Philipps, Julia Beoletto, Marian Ross, Maria Orleos, Marie Fox, Zadah Guerian, Meta Hartog, Louise Fearney, Patricia Neway, Elsa Fiore, Hans Kuhn, Elton Plowman, Eric Rautens, Nathaniel Sprinzena, Samuel Adams, Carter Farriss, Franz George, Roger Hill, Bertram Breiss, Walter Graf, Romeo Rim, Boris Brown, Ludlow White, Sebastian Engelberg, Tony Gardell, Raymond Pach; Ballet Dancers: Gisella Caccialanza (Premiere Danseuse), Anne Barlow, Margit DeKova, Arlene Garver, Pauline Goddard, Georgia Hiden, Miriam Oreck, Mary Jane Shea, Beatrice Tompkins, Jane Ward, Nora White, Baret Cummings, Nicholas Magallanes, Frank Moncion, Stanley Zompakos
The operetta was presented in three acts.
The action takes place during the spring of 1866 in Paris.
There were no individual musical numbers listed in the program.

The current revival of Jacques Offenbach's 1866 operetta *La vie Parisienne* by The New Opera Company played for seventeen performances in repertory. For more information about the work, see entries for the company's 1941 and 1945 revivals.

In the current production, Wilbur Evans appeared in a major role, and as the decade progressed he made his mark as the leading man in two hit musicals, Cole Porter's **Mexican Hayride** and Sigmund Romberg's **Up in Central Park**. In the chorus was Patricia Neway, who became an important figure in American operas and musicals; she created the role of Magda Sorel in the original production of Gian-Carlo Menotti's *The Consul* (1950), and in 1959 won the Tony Award for Best Featured Actress in a Musical when she created the role of the Mother Abbess in Richard Rodgers and Oscar Hammerstein II's *The Sound of Music* (she introduced "Climb Every Mountain" and, with Mary Martin, the duet "My Favorite Things"). Paul Reed probably had his greatest stage moment as Mr. Macy, when he sang the jubilant "That Man Over There" in Meredith Willson's 1963 musical *Here's Love*.

ONCE OVER LIGHTLY
"THE NEW MUSICAL PLAY"

Theatre: Alvin Theatre
Opening Date: November 19, 1942; *Closing Date*: November 22, 1942
Performances: 6
Book and *Lyrics*: New version of the original libretto by Laszlo Halasz; dialogue and solos written by Louis Garden, and ensembles written by George Mead; additional dialogue by Robert Pierpont Forshew

Music: Gioachino Rossini
Based on the 1816 opera *Il barbiere di Siviglia* (*The Barber of Seville*), libretto by Cesare Sterbini and music by Gioachino Rossini.
Direction: Robert H. Gordon; *Producer*: Saul Colin; Henry Leiser, Associate Producer; *Scenery*: Richard Rychtarik; *Costumes*: Uncredited; *Lighting*: Uncredited; *Musical Director*: Laszlo Halasz
Cast: Igor Gorin (Figaro), Grace Panvini (Rosina), Felix Knight (Count Almaviva), Carlos Alexander (Don Basilio), Richard Wentworth (Dr. Bartolo), Ardelle Warner (Bertha), Myron Szandrowsky (Fiorella); Musicians and Soldiers: Van Atkins, Max Birnbaum, Dick Bracken, Anthony Musarra, Frank E. Price, Martin Stewart; during the run, the following performers alternated with the opening-night cast: John DeSurra (Figaro), Frances Watkins (Rosina), Robert Marshall (Almaviva), Harold Kravitt (Don Basilio), Carlos Alexander (Dr. Bartolo), and Nord Vernellj (Fiorella)
The musical was presented in a prologue and two acts.
The action takes place in Seville.

Musical Numbers

Prologue: "Dawn Is Approaching" (Felix Knight); "I'm the Most Popular Barber in Town" (Igor Gorin); Duet (Felix Knight, Igor Gorin)
Act One: Musical Interlude; "When a Maiden Must Decide" (Grace Panvini); "Slander's Whisper" (Carlos Alexander); "I'm a Man of Reputation" (Carlos Alexander)
Act Two: "When You Find a Man of Forty" (Ardelle Warner); Musical Interlude

Once Over Lightly was a failed attempt to update Gioachino Rossini's 1816 opera *The Barber of Seville* into an "Americanized" version. While the new book and lyrics utilized American slang ("it is my motto, never be blotto") and supposedly up-to-date dialogue ("I'm the well-known barber of Seville who gets in everybody's hair"), the musical was still set in Seville. In his 1942–1943 annual, George Jean Nathan said it made as much sense to produce a Broadway version of *The Barber of Seville* as for the Metropolitan Opera Company to perform its own adaptation of **Beat the Band**.

Once Over Lightly (not to be confused with the 1955 Off-Broadway revue of the same name) was gone in less than a week. But the following season another Americanized adaptation of a venerable opera (**Carmen Jones**) did very well; however, *My Darlin' Aida* (1952) floundered after a few weeks on Broadway.

Although he wasn't named on the pages of the program's cast listing, John Tyers was listed as Figaro in the biography section of the program.

NEW FACES OF 1943

Theatre: Ritz Theatre
Opening Date: December 22, 1942; *Closing Date*: March 13, 1943
Performances: 94
Sketches: John Lund; additional sketches by William Callanan, June Carroll, Sidney Carrol, Bus Davis, Nannie Foster, J. B. Rosenberg, Charles Sherman, Lee Wainer, and Harry Young
Lyrics: John Lund; additional lyrics by June Carroll, J. B. Rosenberg, and Dorothy Sachs
Music: Lee Wainer; additional music by Will Irwin
Direction: Production supervised by Leonard Sillman and sketches directed by Laurence Hurdle; *Producer*: Leonard Sillman; *Choreography*: Charles Weidman and John Wray; *Scenery* and *Costumes*: Edward Gilbert; *Lighting*: Carlton Winkler; *Musical Direction*: Lee Wainer
Cast: Evelyn Brooks, Irwin Corey, Diane Davis, Dorothy Dennis, Doris Dowling, Laura Deane Dutton, Kent Edwards, Tony Farrar, Blanche Fellows, Hie Thompson, Ilsa Kevin, Ralph Lewis, John Lund, Marie Lund, Mervyn Nelson, Alice Pearce, Ann Robinson, Bernard (Bernie) West, Robert Weil, Leonard Sillman
The revue was presented in two acts.

Sketches and Musical Numbers

Act One: Opening (lyric by John Lund, music by Lee Wainer) (The Producer: Leonard Sillman; Mr. Priddis: John Lund; The Stagehand: Kent Edwards; The Showgirl: Doris Dowling; The Dancers: Ilsa Kevin, Tony Farrar, Diane Davis, Hie Thompson; The Comics: Mervyn Nelson, Bernard West); "We'll Swing It Through!" (lyric by John Lund, music by Lee Wainer) (Company); "*Cue* Says—Go!" (sketch by John Lund and J. B. Rosenberg) (Miss *Cue*: Marie Lund; Lecturer at Museum of Modern Art: Alice Pearce; At the Automat: Evelyn Brooks, Kent Edwards, John Lund, Diane Davis, Bernard West, Alice Pearce; At the Colony: Leonard Sillman, Kent Edwards; At *Star and Garter*: Blanche Fellows, Bernard West; At *Life with Father*: Diane Davis, Hie Thompson, Bernard West, Kent Edwards; At the Copacabana: Bernard West, Ralph Lewis, Evelyn Brooks); "Animals Are Nice" (lyric by J. B. Rosenberg, music by Lee Wainer) (The Pony: Evelyn Brooks; The Flamingo: Ilsa Kevin; The Tiger: Hie Thompson; The Skunk: Tony Farrar; The Cat: Doris Dowling; The Deer: Diane Davis; The Donkey: Kent Edwards; Tap Specialty: Hie Thompson); "Welles of Loneliness" (sketch by John Lund and Sidney Carrol) (The Psychiatrist: Kent Edwards; The Producer: John Lund; The Director: Leonard Sillman; The Writer: Bernard West; The Actor: Ralph Lewis); "Richard Crudnut's Charm School" (lyric by June Carroll and John Lund, music by Lee Wainer) (Heddy Schwarz: Alice Pearce; Basil: Mervyn Nelson; Miss Fairfield: Ilsa Kevin; Elizabeth: Evelyn Brooks; Dorothy: Marie Lund; Helena: Diane Davis; Mr. Beecher: Kent Edwards; Physical Instructor: Ralph Lewis; Dancing Master: Hie Thompson); Showgirl (Doris Dowling); "Quiet Zone" (sketch by John Lund and J. B. Rosenberg) (Orderly: Hie Thompson; Receptionist: Marie Lund; Dr. Scalpel: John Lund; Dr. Forceps: Ilsa Kevin; Dr. Clystra: Ralph Lewis; Expectant Father: Mervyn Nelson; Emergency Case: Leonard Sillman; Interne: Tony Farrar; Nurse: Diane Davis); "Love, Are You Raising Your Head?" (lyric by June Carroll, music by Lee Wainer) (The Girl: Evelyn Brooks; The Man: Ralph Lewis; The Dancers: Ilsa Kevin, Hie Thompson); Reprise (song not listed; probably "Love, Are You Raising Your Head?") (Ann Robinson); "Far above Angustora's Bitters" (sketch by John Lund) (Professor: John Lund; Binion: Mervyn Nelson; Bunion: Leonard Sillman; Manion: Bernard West; Olsen: Tony Farrar); "Yes, Sir, I've Made a Date" (lyric by J. B. Rosenberg, music by Lee Wainer) (The Boy: Hie Thompson; The Girl: Diane Davis; The Boy's Parents: Marie Lund, John Lund; The Girl's Parents: Evelyn Brooks, Ralph Lewis); "Showgirl" (Doris Dowling); "The Skin of Your Life" (sketch by John Lund) (Introduction by the Showgirl: Doris Dowling; Mordkin: Mervyn Nelson; Bodkin: Kent Edwards; Barber: Ralph Lewis; Groyn: John Lund; Julie: Ilsa Kevin; Messenger: Bernard West; Catharties: Hie Thompson; Gorilla: Hie Thompson; Drunken Woman: Marie Lund); Tony Farrar (sequence danced and choreographed by Tony Farrar); "Travel, Travel, Toil and Travel" (sketch by Sidney Carrol) (Ed: Ralph Lewis; Joe: John Lund; Lady: Alice Pearce [this sketch included the song "Radio City, I Love You," lyric by June Carroll, music by Lee Wainer]); "Land of Rockefellera" (lyric by John Lund, music by Lee Wainer) (Lieutenant: Kent Edwards; Tourist: Alice Pearce; Dowager: Marie Lund; Captain: John Lund; Mature: Bernard West; Sergeant: Leonard Sillman; Lieutenant Lipschitz: Mervyn Nelson); Mervyn Nelson; "Shoes" (lyric by June Carroll, music by Will Irwin) (Evelyn Brooks, Ann Robinson, Ilsa Kevin, Hie Thompson, Entire Company)

Act Two: "Shoes" (reprise) (Entire Company); "Back to Bundling" (lyric by Dorothy Sachs, music by Lee Wainer) (Leonard Sillman, Hie Thompson, Doris Dowling, Diane Davis, Marie Lund, Ralph Lewis, Kent Edwards, Tony Farrar; Tap Specialty: Hie Thompson); Showgirl (Doris Dowling); "Help Wanted" (sketch by J. B. Rosenberg and Nannie Foster) (Miss Swerk: Marie Lund; Miss Swenson: Ilsa Kevin; Mrs. Astor: Diane Davis; The Marquise: Alice Pearce; Flunkeys: Hie Thompson, Kent Edwards); Bernard West; "Whither America!" (Switchboard Operator: Diane Davis; Typist: Marie Lund; Swami: Leonard Sillman); "Hey, Gal!" (lyric by June Carroll, music by Will Irwin) (The Gal: Ilsa Kevin; The Singers: Kent Edwards, Evelyn Brooks, Hie Thompson, Ralph Lewis, John Lund); "Nearsighted Bullfighter" (Tony Farrar); "Vacation Sketch" (sketch by Charles Sherman and Harry Young) (Manager: Bernard West; Secretary: Blanche Fellows; Mr. Jones: Mervyn Nelson); "Ten Percenters" (dialogue and music by Lee Wainer) (A Voice: John Lund; An Agent: Mervyn Nelson; A Band Leader: Kent Edwards; A Hoofer: Hie Thompson; A Torch Singer: Ilsa Kevin; A Comic: Bernard West); "Well, Well!" (lyric by June Carroll, music by Lee Wainer) (Ann Robinson, Entire Company); Reprise (song not listed; probably "Well, Well!") (Diane Davis); "The Star's the Thing" (sketch by John Lund, William Callanan, and Bus Davis) (Scoggins: Marie Lund; Wigby: Leonard Sillman; Millicent: Alice Pearce; Bolingbroke: Ralph Lewis; Strangeways: Bernard West); "Musical Chairs" (finale) (Entire Company)

The revue *New Faces of 1943* (its complete title was *Leonard Sillman's New Faces of 1943 in New Shoes*) was Sillman's third of seven occasional *New Faces* revues that were produced on Broadway over a thirty-four-year period. The following are the others in the series, with their year, number of performances, and names of some of the new faces: 1934, 149 performances (Henry Fonda, Imogene Coca); 1936, 193 performances (Van Johnson and Karl Swenson, who in 1944 created the title role in Arthur Miller's first Broadway play *The Man Who Had All the Luck*); 1952, 365 performances (Eartha Kitt, Carol Lawrence, Alice Ghostley, Paul Lynde); 1956, 221 performances (Maggie Smith, Jane Connell, Inga Swenson); 1962, 28 performances (Marian Mercer); and 1968, 52 performances (Madeline Kahn, Robert Klein). Sillman also produced non-*New Faces* revues (such as **All in Fun** and *Mask and Gown* [1957], the latter a showcase for female impersonator T. C. Jones) and book musicals (**If the Shoe Fits** and *Happy as Larry* [1950]).

The revue included a spoof of Orson Welles ("Welles of Loneliness"); one skit laughed at both Thornton Wilder and William Saroyan ("The Skin of Your Life"); Broadway agents were the target of "Ten Percenters"; "Quiet Zone" satirized the medical field in its depiction of a "shirt hospital" where an ailing shirt undergoes an operation; New York institutions were kidded in both "Radio City, I Love You" and "Land of Rockefellera"; and beauty-instruction schools were at the mercy of the sketch "Richard Crudnut's Charm School."

Wilella Waldorf in the *New York Post* liked the "pleasant" if "hardly world-shattering" score, an occasional "laughable" sketch, "agile" dancing, and a "general air of insouciance." However, a "faintly amateurish, prep-schoolish quality" worked against the evening and made it an uneasy contender against the more "slick, ultra-professional" competition.

Waldorf noted that Harlem singer Ann Robinson "picked up the show and carried it around with her whenever she came on"; apparently Robinson's scat-singing style was something new to the critics, and Waldorf described it as a "curious rhythmic exercise" called "riffing." Burton Rascoe in the *New York World-Telegram* explained her style from a program description which stated she "improvises" her melodies as she sings. Burns Mantle in the *New York Daily News* said Robinson seemed to be the overwhelming favorite of the first-night audience, while Lewis Nichols in the *New York Times* liked her "gay breezy style" and noted her songs received a "workout."

The critics also liked pantomime Tony Farrar (who at one point impersonated a nearsighted bull fighter), Irwin Corey (who scored with his comic lecture about *Hamlet*), and acerbic comedienne Alice Pearce. The latter two of course parlayed their eccentric talents into popular careers, and performer and co-writer John Lund enjoyed a number of film appearances in which he often played a stuffy but handsome leading man (*To Each His Own*, *A Foreign Affair*, *No Man of Her Own*, *The Mating Season*, and *High Society*).

During the run, the sketch "Welles of Loneliness" and the song "Back to Bundling" were dropped; "Vacation Sketch" was retitled "The Assembly Line," and "The Star's the Thing" was retitled "Tea for Three."

YOU'LL SEE STARS

Theatre: Maxine Elliott's Theatre
Opening Date: December 29, 1942; *Closing Date*: January 2, 1943
Performances: 4
Book and *Lyrics*: Herman Timberg
Music: Leo Edwards
Direction: Herman Timberg and Dave Kramer; *Producer*: Dave Kramer; *Choreography*: Eric Victor ("George Jessel" choreography by Sam Carlton); *Scenery*: Perry Watkins; *Costumes*: Eaves; *Lighting*: Uncredited; *Musical Direction*: Charles S. Sanford
Cast: (*Note*: Sources disagree on who performed which roles on opening night, and even on the correct spelling of some of the performers' names; to be as inclusive as possible, the following list includes the names of all cited performers, and variant spellings [not all listed performers may have been seen on opening night].) Jackie Green (Eddie Cantor), Jackie Michaels (George Jessel), Alan Lester or Alan Ray (Gus Edwards), Irving Freeman (Walter Winchell), Lou Dahlman (Groucho Marx), Fene Bayliss or Arnold Stang (Herman Timberg; Stang may also have played the role of Patrick Levy), John (Stuart) Briter (or John Stuart Breiter) (Willie Hammerstein, Radio Announcer), George Lyons (Harpo Marx), Sal La Porta (Chico Marx, Perry, Zuccini Dokes, Tony), Eugene Martin (Zeppo Marx), Ronny Carver (Bob Williams, Joseph Kelly), Gordon King (Johnny Boston Beans), Jack Matis (Biff Dugan, The Tough Kid), Maurice Dover (or Maurice Doner) (Pisha Pasha, Yasha Kasha), Buddy Simon (or Buddy Swan) (Georgie Price), Norma Shea (Mary Jones), Patricia Bright (Hildegarde), Reni (or Renee) Rochelle (Lola Lane), Joan Barry (or Joan Barrie)

(School Teacher), Phyllis Baxter (Cuddles aka Lila Lee), Pat Marshall (Vera Nulty), Dorothy Dale (Jane Nulty), Harriet Greene (Ann Little), Betty May Lee (Hazel Nulty), Eric Victor (Ray Bolger), Norma Shea (Maggie Grabenheimer, Judy Williams), Audrey Burkes (Sue), Honey Murray or Arlene Robinson (Sassie/Sassy Little; Honey Murray may have also played role of Freshie Buttinsky), Edith Russell (Daisy Fair), Iris Karyl (Rajah), Dan Marshall (Carl Dashshundt, Jack), Claire Harvey (Ima Hog), Peggy Fisher (Ura Hog), George Lyons (Tommy Tatters), Jimmy Smith (Specialty)

The musical was presented in two acts.

The action takes place in New York City.

Musical Numbers

Act One: "Future Stars" (Alan Ray); "America" (Company); "Time and Time Again" (Joan Barry [possibly Barrie]); "By the Light of the Silvery Moon" (originally introduced in vaudeville, the song was later performed in *Ziegfeld Follies of 1909*; lyric by Edward Madden, music by Gus Edwards) (Honey Murray, Company); "It Could Happen, It's Possible" (Ronny Carver, Norma Shea); "All You Have to Do Is Stand There" (Irving Freeman, Lou Dahlman, Norma Shea, Eric Victor); "Dancing on a Rainbow" (Eugene Martin, George Lyons, Boys, Girls)

Act Two: "Jelly Beans at Walgreen's" (Honey Murray, Boys, Girls); "Betcha I Make Good" (Norma Shea, Pat Marshall, Company); "Swinging the Bhumba" (Reni [possibly Renee] Rochelle; Dancers: Arlene Robinson, Dan Marshall, Boys, Girls); "What a Pretty Baby You Are" (Patricia Bright); "School Days" (aka "Readin', Writin' and 'Rhythmatic'") (lyric by Will D. Cobb, music by Gus Edwards) (Norma Shea, Company)

You'll See Stars should perhaps have been titled *You'll See Very Bad Impersonations of Stars*. The hapless evening was supposedly a tribute to old-time vaudevillian and songwriter Gus Edwards (1879–1945), whose discoveries on the vaudeville circuit included such future headliners as Eddie Cantor, George Jessel, Ray Bolger, and The Marx Brothers, all of whom "appeared" in *You'll See Stars* via impersonations by young performers who were hopelessly out of their element in carrying off such assignments. Edwards was also a composer, and his compositions include "By the Light of the Silvery Moon," "In My Merry Oldsmobile," and "School Days" ("dear old golden rule days"). *The Star Maker*, a 1939 Hollywood film of Edwards's life and career, starred Bing Crosby.

Louis Kronenberger in *PM* reported that no sooner had he made a New Year's resolution to be "kind and courteous," he was faced with having to write a review of *You'll See Stars*. He noted the 8:40 curtain rose at 9:17, at 9:18 "matters started taking a downward turn," at 9:23 had "dropped way below sea level," and at 9:31 "began the descent into Avernus." By 10:36—well, he "was no longer around" by then because he had "just swallowed poison." According to Lewis Nichols in the *New York Times*, to say the musical was "bad" was to underestimate it (he noted that half the audience left at intermission, and the remaining customers were left "in a state of profound melancholy").

Howard Barnes in the *New York Herald Tribune* said the evening fell with a "dull thud" that plunged into "the lowest depths of dramatic ineptitude" with "fumbling" performers and material. The impersonations were "genuinely embarrassing" and "uniformly terrible." Richard Lockridge in the *New York Sun* predicted that the new year of 1943 "or any year in the future" would never see "anything" as "unnerving" as *You'll See Stars* (but of course he couldn't have anticipated **Hairpin Harmony**). He noted that the impersonation of Groucho Marx was played "as badly as anyone has ever played anything."

Burton Rascoe in the *New York World-Telegram* said the evening was "pitiful," a "ghastly debacle" which "opened cold and gathered icicles." Burns Mantle in the *New York Daily News* said the impersonations were "all quite terrible," and when he escaped at intermission he "could already see stars, but they were not on the stage."

You'll See Stars had perhaps just one distinction: it was the season's shortest-running musical.

SOMETHING FOR THE BOYS

Theatre: Alvin Theatre
Opening Date: January 7, 1943; *Closing Date*: January 8, 1944

Performances: 422
Book: Herbert Fields and Dorothy Fields
Lyrics and *Music*: Cole Porter
Direction: Staged by Hassard Short and book directed by Herbert Fields; *Producer*: Michael Todd; *Choreography*: Jack Cole; *Scenery*: Howard Bay; *Costumes*: Billy Livingston; *Lighting*: Hassard Short; *Musical Direction*: William Parsons
Cast: Paula Laurence (Chiquita Hart), Jed Prouty (Roger Calhoun), Allen Jenkins (Harry Hart), *Ethel Merman* (Blossom Hart), Bill Johnson (Staff Sergeant Rocky Fulton), Stuart Langley (Sergeant Laddie Green), Betty Garrett (Mary-Frances), Betty Bruce (Betty-Jean), Bill Callahan (Corporal Burns), Anita Alvarez (Micheala), The Barnes Twins (Lois and Lucille), Jack Hartley (Lieutenant Colonel S. D. Grubbs), William Lynn (Mr. Tobias Twitch), Remi Martel (Sergeant Carter), Frances Mercer (Melanie Walker), Walter Rinner (Burke), Madeline Clive (Mrs. Grubbs), The De Marlos; Dancing Girls: Alice Anthony, May Block, Jean Coyne, Betty Deane, Patricia Dearing, Ruth Godfrey, Dolores (Dody) Goodman, Betty Heather, Margie Jackson, Jean Owens, Leslie Shannon, Ethel Sherman, Puddy Smith, Nina Starkey, Patricia Welles, Helen Wenzel, June Wieting; Dancing Boys: Stanley Catron, Bob Davis, Denny DeSio, Jerry Florio, Albert Gaeta, Aaron Gobetz, Ray Harrison, David Mann, Remi Martel, Paul Martin, Duncan Noble, Ricky Riccardi, William Vaux, Joe Viggiano, William Weber, Lou Wills Jr., Parker Wilson; Singing Boys: Jimmy Allison, Joseph Bell, Alan Fleming, Richard Harvey, Buddy Irving, Art Lambert, Bruce Lord, Paul Mario, John W. Mayo, Joseph Monte, Walter Rinner, Murvyn Vye; Band: Bill Dreslin, Ted Fischer, Ken Snell, Jimmy Hanson, Wally Barron, Tony Frasetti
The musical was presented in two acts.
The action takes place in Kansas City, Missouri, New York City, Newark, New Jersey, Kelly Field, Texas, and in and around San Antonio, Texas.

Musical Numbers

Act One: "Announcement of Inheritance" (Jed Prouty, Paula Laurence, Allen Jenkins, Ethel Merman); "See That You're Born in Texas" (Ensemble); "When My Baby Goes to Town" (Bill Johnson; danced by Anita Alvarez and Ensemble); "Something for the Boys" (Ethel Merman, Boys); "When We're Home on the Range" (Ethel Merman, Paula Lawrence, Allen Jenkins); "Could It Be You?" (Bill Johnson, Boys); "Hey, Good Lookin'" (Ethel Merman, Bill Johnson); "Hey, Good-Lookin'" (reprise) (Betty Bruce, Bill Callahan, Girls, Boys); "He's a Right Guy" (Ethel Merman); "Assembly Line" (Allen Jenkins, Betty Garrett, Anita Alvarez, Girls); "The Leader of a Big-Time Band" (Ethel Merman; danced by Bill Callahan, Ensemble)
Act Two: "I'm in Love with a Soldier Boy" (Betty Garrett, Girls, Boys); "There's a Happy Land in the Sky" (Ethel Merman, Paula Laurence, Allen Jenkins, William Lynn, Bill Johnson); "He's a Right Guy" (reprise) (Ethel Merman); "Could It Be You?" (reprise) (Bill Johnson, Ensemble); "By the Mississinewah" (Ethel Merman, Paula Laurence); "Square Dance" (The De Marlos, Ensemble); Dance (Anita Alvarez, Boys); Finale (Ethel Merman, Entire Company)

Known in preproduction as *Jenny, Get Your Gun*, Cole Porter's *Something for the Boys* was a popular and critical hit that ran for one year and marked Ethel Merman's fifth and final appearance in a Porter musical. Michael Todd's lavish production offered a lighthearted wartime-related plot that involved soldiers, their wives and girlfriends, defense plants, and even the novelty of a secret "weapon" to win the war.

The plot dealt with three cousins Blossom (Ethel Merman), Chiquita (Paula Laurence), and Harry (Allen Jenkins), all strangers to one another who jointly inherit a huge estate in Texas that is located next to a military base. The three turn the dilapidated mansion into a boarding house for servicemen's wives as well as a kind of defense plant in which the wives make airplane parts. Blossom and soldier Rocky Fulton (Bill Johnson) fall in love, but jealous society girl Melanie Walker (Frances Mercer) tries to break up the romance by suggesting to Army officials that the boarding house is another kind of house. But in the happy and illogical ways of musical comedy plots, it seems a filling in one of Blossom's teeth acts as a conduit for radio transmissions, and so the military, which has discovered that the activities on the estate are innocent, uses Blossom's suggestion that soldiers' teeth be filled with corborundum so they can become their own radio transmitters in the war.

Although Cole Porter's score didn't yield any standards, it offered an array of both sweet and swinging ballads, including "Hey, Good-Lookin'," "He's a Right Guy," "Could It Be You?," and "I'm in Love with a Soldier Boy." Further, "When My Baby Goes to Town" and the title song were lively numbers, and the evening's showstopper was Merman and Laurence's out-of-nowhere comedy number "By the Mississinewah." One of the score's highlights was Merman's "The Leader of a Big-Time Band," a wry and naughty salute to the bandleaders of the day (when Dorsey tilts his horn about, Mrs. Vanderbilt bumps herself out; and when Goodman starts "blowin' blue," those "rum-ridden debutramps nearly come to").

Lewis Nichols in the *New York Times* proclaimed that all season the world had been waiting for a "big, fast, glittering" musical, and *Something for the Boys* was that musical; Porter's songs were from his "topmost drawer" (and "By the Mississinewah" was "the funniest moment in a musical show in years"); Herbert Fields and Dorothy Fields had written a book with "words better than most"; Billy Livingston's costumes were "magnificent"; Howard Bay's settings were "superb"; and Merman's performance suggested that all her previous ones had been "just practice."

Richard Lockridge in the *New York Sun* suggested that if you didn't like Porter's songs (he singled out six) and the evening's "high polish" and "general dash," then you were no doubt "allergic" to musicals. As for "Mississinewah," it was a "curious," "highly comical," and "strangely mad song." Wilella Waldorf in the *New York Post* found the evening "tuneful," "handsome," and "one of the funniest musicals Broadway has seen in some time." She noted that Merman and Laurence were a "riot" in the "idiotic" "Mississenewah"; and after the debacles of **Of "V" We Sing** and **Let Freedom Ring**, it was good to see Betty Garrett show her stuff in a hit (it was clear she was "on her way to bigger things"). Burton Rascoe in the *New York World-Telegram* said the show was "top among the current offerings of words and music." And Howard Barnes in the *New York Herald Tribune* said the "tonic entertainment" was one of the "delights" of the Broadway season, noting the production's "handsome trappings" even offered the sight of a bomber roaring across the Alvin's stage (as for "Mississinewah," the "marvelous" song was "daffy and irrelevant" and his "favorite" moment in the show). Louis Kronenberger in *PM* said Merman and Laurence had a "field day" with "Mississinewah," a "pileup of insanity" that "brought down the house."

During the tryout, "Riddle-Diddle Me This" and "So Long, San Antonio" were cut; deleted during pre-production and rehearsals were "Washington, D.C.," "Oh, How I Could Go for You," "Texas Will Make You a Man," "Well, I Just Wouldn't Know," "Wouldn't It Be Crazy?," and "Carborundum." The lyrics for used, deleted, and unused songs are included in *The Complete Lyrics of Cole Porter*.

Selections from a 1943 radio broadcast of the musical (which starred Merman and Bill Johnson) along with contemporary recordings of songs from the score by Betty Garrett and Paula Laurence were compiled and released by Sound/Stage (LP # Z305) and AEI (LP # AEI-1157; later issued on CD # AEI-CD-004). The collection *Cole Porter Volume 4* (Pearl Records CD # GEM-0195) includes the radio broadcast and other contemporary recordings (twelve numbers in all), and *Cole Porter/Overtures and Ballet Music* (EMI Classics CD # CDC-7-54300-2, and conducted by John McGlinn) includes the musical's overture.

The 1997 San Francisco production by the 42nd St. Moon company was recorded by Music Box (CD # MBR-42001) and includes such esoterica as the "Announcement of Inheritance" sequence; the deleted song "Washington, D.C."; and two interpolations, "There Must Be Someone for Me" (from **Mexican Hayride**) and "Coffee" (from the unproduced musical *Ever Yours*, which had been slated for production in 1934).

The candy-colored film version released by Twentieth Century-Fox in 1944 starred Vivian Blaine (Blossom), Carmen Miranda (Chiquita), and Phil Silvers (Harry); others in the cast were Perry Como, Sheila Ryan, and Michael O'Shea. Only one song was retained (the title number), and lyricist Harold Adamson and composer Jimmy McHugh contributed new ones, including "I Wish We Didn't Have to Say Goodnight." The DVD was released on Twentieth Century-Fox Home Video's Marquee Musicals series.

FOR YOUR PLEASURE
"THE NEW MUSIC-DANCE SHOW"

Theatre: Mansfield Theatre
Opening Date: February 5, 1943; *Closing Date*: February 13, 1943
Performances: 11

Direction: Frank Veloz; *Producers*: George M. Gatts and Frank Veloz; *Costumes*: Gowns by Katherine Kuhn; *Musical Direction*: Jerry (Gene) Shelton
Cast: *Veloz* (Frank Veloz) and *Yolanda* (Yolanda Casazza Veloz), Susan Miller, The Golden Gate Quartet (Willie Johnson, Orlandus Wilson, Clyde Riddick, and Henry Owens), Jerry (Gene) Shelton, Bill Gary, Al and Lee Reiser (Pianos), Vicente Gomez
The revue was presented in two acts.

Musical Numbers

Act One: Overture (Al and Lee Reiser); Part One—Veloz and Yolanda: (1) "Moonlight Madonna" (music by Fibich); (2) "Darktown Strutters' Ball" (lyric and music by Sheldon Brooks); and (3) "Carnival" (music by Ann Ronell); Bill Gary; Vicente Gomez; Part Two—Veloz and Yolanda: (1) "Caprice" (music by Schonberger); (2) "Rhumba (Son)" (music by J. Fernandez); and (3) "Dance of Mistakes" (music by Frank Veloz); The Golden Gate Quartet; "Chiapenecas" (Mexican folk dance) (Veloz and Yolanda)
Act Two: "Gitanerias" (music by Ernesto Lecuona) (Al and Lee Reiser, Bill Gary); "Capriccio Espagnole" (music by Rimsky-Korsakoff) (Al and Lee Reiser, Bill Gary); Part Three—Veloz and Yolanda: (1) "Blue Danube" (music by Johann Strauss); (2) "The Maxixa" (music by Philipo Mendez); and (3) "Minuet?" (music by S. Henry); Susan Miller; Jerry (Gene) Shelton; Part Four—Veloz and Yolanda: (1) "Three Easy Lessons" (lyric by Frank Veloz); (2) "Alexander's Ragtime Band" (lyric and music by Irving Berlin); (3) "Samba" (music by Arroyo); and (4) "Tango Yolanda" (music by Frank Veloz)

For Your Pleasure was a tasteful and classy dance-and-music revue that in an earlier version had toured as **Dansation**. The critics noted the revue was so daring it didn't include dog acts, rowdy comedians, and a master of ceremonies. Instead, the married dance team of Veloz and Yolanda offered a variety of fourteen dances in four sections throughout the two acts, including a waltz, a rhumba, a tango, a samba, and a Mexican folk dance; occasionally Veloz would explain the background of a particular dance. Interspersed among the dance sequences were singer Susan Miller (late of **Beat the Band**), ballet-tap dancer Bill Gary, the pianists Al and Lee Reiser, guitarist Vicente Gomez, accordionist Jerry Sheldon, and the black spiritual group The Golden Gate Quartet.

The critics were a bit conflicted. Some found it refreshing to see a streamlined revue that avoided the clichés of vaudeville, but others felt the evening wasn't varied enough and needed more variety. Most felt there was too much emphasis on dancing, and suggested Veloz and Yolanda would have been more effective in smaller doses.

Louis Kronenberger in *PM* admitted Veloz and Yolanda were "among the best ballroom dancers of our time," but he grew tired of the evening's sameness. It was like "a meal made up of rice, potatoes, noodles and macaroni." Continuing in this culinary vein, G. E. Blackford in the *New York Journal-American* said the evening was "too much sugar and not enough spice" because it offered non-stop music and dancing without the "leavening" effects of slapstick; the evening was too much of a good thing because even "the finest steak" needed mustard sauce, Bernaise, Worcestershire, or "lowly" catsup to bring out the flavor.

Lewis Nichols in the *New York Times* also complained about the lack of variety. The artists were "impeccable" but their show wasn't "good" because it lacked comic relief, and he suggested that someone should page Ed Wynn. Howard Barnes in the *New York Herald Tribune* found the evening "repetitious" and "remarkably tiresome"; while he enjoyed Veloz and Yolanda's "grace and precision," he noted the evening belonged in a night club and not in a Broadway theatre. Ward Morehouse in the *New York Sun* enjoyed the "beautifully and excitingly" danced numbers, but missed the comedy and "a little patter here and there."

Burns Mantle in the *New York Daily News* praised the "gifted" and "graceful" Veloz and Yolanda, and suggested that those who liked dance revues would enjoy the evening. He also complimented Vicente Gomez (the "best guitarist" he'd ever heard), said Paul Draper himself would approve of young ballet-tap dancer Bill Gary, and enjoyed the "finely blended" voices of The Golden Gate Quartet. Burton Rascoe in the *New York World-Telegram* said accordionist "virtuoso" Jerry Shelton was the "envy" of all accordionists because "he can make it sound like every instrument and all instruments except the accordion as amateurs play it."

The critics liked Susan Miller, but suggested she ditch the microphone. Among her songs were "Brazil" (lyric and music by Ary Barroso; English lyric by S. K. Russsell); "Easy to Love" (1936 film *Born to Dance*;

lyric and music by Cole Porter), and "Summer Time" (*Porgy and Bess*, 1935; lyric by DuBose Heyward and music by George Gershwin). According to Waldorf, Miller announced the latter was one of Gershwin's "most beautiful" songs, and then proceeded to sing it with "boop-boop-a-doop trimmings" (the critic noted that singing it "that way" didn't make it one of Gershwin's best songs). The Golden Gate Quartet's offerings included the spiritual "I'm Listenin', Lord" and one of their own compositions called "Stalin Wasn't Stallin'" which was a timely look at Hitler's withdrawal from Russia.

Tickets for the revue ranged from eighty-five cents to $3.30.

LADY IN THE DARK
"A MUSICAL PLAY"

Theatre: Broadway Theatre
Opening Date: February 27, 1943; *Closing Date*: May 15, 1943
Performances: 83
Book: Moss Hart
Lyrics: Ira Gershwin
Music: Kurt Weill
Direction: Play staged by Moss Hart and musical sequences staged by Hassard Short; *Producer*: Sam H. Harris; *Choreography*: Albertina Rasch; *Scenery*: Harry Horner; *Costumes*: Irene Sharaff (gowns designed by Hattie Carnegie); *Lighting*: Hassard Short; *Musical Direction*: Maurice Abravanel
Cast: Richard Hale (Dr. Brooks), Jeanne Shelby (Miss Bowers), *Gertrude Lawrence* (Liza Elliott), Gedda Petry (Miss Foster, Sutton), Adrienne Moore (Miss Stevens), Margaret Dale (Maggie Grant), Ann Lee (Alison du Bois), Eric Brotherson (Russell Paxton, Beekman, Ringmaster), Hugh Marlowe (Charley Johnson), Willard Parker (Randy Curtis), Edward Browne (Joe), Walter Stane (Tom), John Leslie (Kendall Nesbitt), Helene Young (Helen), Rose Marie Elliott (Ruthie), Margaret Gibson (Carol), Christine Horn (Marcia), Nicholas Saunders (Liza's Father), Lee Bergere (Ben Butler), Jane Davies (Barbara), Lynn Alden (Jack); Soloists: Arthur Davies, Warren Jones, Byron Milligan; The Albertina Rasch Dancers: Rita Charise, Anne Helm, Joan Lee, June MacLaren, Christine Horn, Margaret Gibson, Alla Shishkina, Edward Browne, Richard D'Arcy, Nikolai Fatula, John Scott, Walter Stane, Scott Merrill, George Martin; The Mapleton High Glee Club: Adelaide Abbot, Florence Wyman, Ingebord Bransen, Jean Cumming, Joyce Doncaster, Rose Marie Elliott, Jane Irving, Lynn Alden, Ken Black, Jack Collins, Arthur Davies, Warren Jones, Byron Milligan, Fred Perrone, Edwin Ziegler, Matthew Ferrugio; The Children: Bonnie Baker, Anne Bracken, Phyllis de Bus, Sally Ferguson, Louise Pearl, Janice Smith, Edward Tappa, Robert Allen, William Welch
The musical was presented in two acts.
The action takes place during the present time in New York City.

Musical Numbers

Act One: *Glamour Dream*: "Oh, Fabulous One (in Your Ivory Tower)" (Liza Elliott's Serenaders); "The World's Inamorata" (aka "Huxley") (Gertrude Lawrence, Gedda Petry); "One Life to Live" (Gertrude Lawrence, Eric Brotherson); "Girl of the Moment" (Ensemble); and "It Looks Like Liza" (Entire Company); *Wedding Dream*: "Mapleton High Chorale" (The High School Graduates); "This Is New" (Willard Parker, Gertrude Lawrence); "The Princess of Pure Delight" (Gertrude Lawrence, Children); and "This (The) Woman at the Altar" (Entire Company)
Act Two: Overture (Orchestra); *Circus Dream*: "The Greatest Show on Earth" (Eric Brotherson, Ensemble); "Dance of the Tumblers" (The Albertina Rasch Dancers); "The Best Years of His Life" (Hugh Marlowe, Willard Parker); "Tschaikowsky" (Eric Brotherson, Ensemble); and "The Saga of Jenny" (Gertrude Lawrence, Jury, Ensemble); "My Ship" (Gertrude Lawrence)

The current production of *Lady in the Dark* was a limited-run return engagement of the national touring company between road engagements, and it provided New Yorkers one last chance to see Gertrude Lawrence in one of her greatest roles. For more information about the musical, see entry for the original 1941 production.

OKLAHOMA!
"A MUSICAL PLAY"

Theatre: St. James Theatre
Opening Date: March 31, 1943; *Closing Date*: May 29, 1948
Performances: 2,212
Book and *Lyrics*: Oscar Hammerstein II
Music: Richard Rodgers
Based on the 1931 play *Green Grow the Lilacs* by Lynn Riggs.
Direction: Rouben Mamoulian; *Producer*: The Theatre Guild; *Choreography*: Agnes De Mille; *Scenery*: Lemuel Ayers; *Costumes*: Miles White; *Lighting*: Uncredited; *Musical Direction*: Jacob Schwartzdorf
Cast: Betty Garde (Aunt Eller), Alfred Drake (Curly), Joan Roberts (Laurey), Barry Kelley (Ike Skidmore), Edwin Clay (Fred), Herbert Rissman (Slim), Lee Dixon (Will Parker), Howard da Silva (Jud Fry), Celeste Holm (Ado Annie Carnes), Joseph Buloff (Ali Hakim), Jane Lawrence (Gertie Cummings), Katharine Sergava (Ellen), Ellen Love (Kaye), Joan McCracken (Sylvie), Kate Friedlich (Armina), Bambi Linn (Aggie), Ralph Riggs (Andrew Carnes), Owen Martin (Cord Elam), George Church (Jess), Marc Platt (Chalmers), Paul Shiers (Mike), George (S.) Irving (Joe), Hayes Gordon (Sam); Singers: Elsie Arnold, Harvey Brown, Suzanne Lloyd, Ellen Love, Dorothea MacFarland, Virginia Oswald, Faye Smith, Vivienne Simon, John Baum, Edwin Clay, Hayes Gordon, George Irving, Arthur Ulisse, Herbert Rissman, Paul Shiers, Robert Penn; Dancers: Diana Adams, Margit DeKova, Bobby Barrentine, Nona Fied, Rhoda Hoffman, Maria Harriton, Kate Friedlich, Bambi Linn, Joan McCracken, Vivian Smith, Billie Zay, Rosemary Schaeffer, Kenneth Buffet, Jack Dunphy, Gary Fleming, Eddie Howland, Ray Harrison, Erik Kristen, Kenneth LeRoy
The musical was presented in two acts.
The action takes place in the Indian Territory (now Oklahoma) just after the turn of the twentieth century.

Musical Numbers

Act One: "Oh, What a Beautiful Mornin'" (Alfred Drake); "The Surrey with the Fringe on Top" (Alfred Drake, Joan Roberts, Betty Garde); "Kansas City" (Lee Dixon, Betty Garde, Boys); "I Cain't Say No" (Celeste Holm); "Many a New Day" (Joan Roberts, Girls; danced by Joan McCracken [as The Girl Who Falls Down], Kate Friedlich, and Katharine Sergava); "It's a Scandal! It's a Outrage!" (Joseph Buloff, Boys, Girls); "People Will Say (We're in Love)" (Alfred Drake, Joan Roberts); "Pore Jud" (Alfred Drake, Howard da Silva); "Lonely Room" (Howard da Silva); "Out of My Dreams" (Joan Roberts, Girls); "Laurey Makes Up Her Mind" (ballet) (Laurey: Katharine Sergava; Curly: Marc Platt; Jud: George Church; The Child: Bambi Linn; Jud's Post Cards: Joan McCracken, Kate Friedlich, Margit DeKova; Laurey's Friends: Rhoda Hoffman, Rosemary Schaeffer, Nona Feid, Maria Harriton, Diana Adams, Billie Zay; Cowboys: Gary Fleming, Erik Kristen, Jack Dunphy, Ray Harrison, Kenneth LeRoy, Eddie Howland, Kenneth Buffet; Other Post Cards: Bobby Barrentine, Vivian Smith)
Act Two: "The Farmer and the Cowman" (Ralph Riggs, Betty Garde, Alfred Drake, Lee Dixon, Celeste Holm, Edwin Clay, Ensemble; danced by Marc Platt); "All er Nothin'" (Celeste Holm, Lee Dixon; danced by Joan McCracken and Kate Friedlich); "People Will Say (We're in Love)" (reprise) (Alfred Drake, Joan Roberts); "Oklahoma" (Alfred Drake, Joan Roberts, Betty Garde, Barry Kelley, Edwin Clay, Ensemble); "Oh, What a Beautiful Mornin'" (reprise) (Joan Roberts, Alfred Drake, Ensemble); Finale (Ensemble)

Probably even Richard Rodgers and Oscar Hammerstein II were surprised at the rapturous reception accorded *Oklahoma!* Hammerstein seemed to have been in a rut with a series of failed musicals (*Gentlemen Unafraid* [1938], *Very Warm for May* [1939], and **Sunny River**) and here was Rodgers composing music without his longtime collaborator, lyricist Lorenz Hart. And instead of a snazzy wartime musical dealing with such topical matters as rationing, priorities, jitterbugging, and South American carnival numbers, here was a slice of Americana which was based on an almost forgotten play from the early 1930s. Moreover, the musical had no headliners in its cast: there were no Mermans, Jolsons, or Cantors here, and instead the musical offered a crop of relatively unknown performers such as Alfred Drake, Joan Roberts, and Celeste Holm. And the plot? Forget it. Boiled down to essentials, the first act dealt with the heroine's dilemma of choosing her escort to a picnic. And the second act had the temerity to kill off one of the major characters (and no less than by the musical's hero). But the elements all came together in a crowd-pleaser that not only became the longest-running musical of the season but also the longest of the decade; and when *Oklahoma!* closed in 1948, it had the distinction of being the longest-running musical in the history of the American theatre, a title it held until *My Fair Lady* (1956) surpassed its run in 1961.

Oklahoma! told a simple story with disarming simplicity. The first act didn't begin with a bevy of chorus girls gaily singing about the upcoming picnic; instead, the hero strolled on and sang the virtues of a beautiful morning. Virtually all the songs—ballads, comedy numbers, and expansive ensembles—served to establish mood, define character, and further the plot. Even the dances evolved from the story, and Agnes De Mille's iconic first-act-curtain ballet "Laurey Makes Up Her Mind" was a phantasmagoria in which Laurey dreams of her conflicted relationship with Curly and her fear of Jud Fry, a dream peopled with dancing cowboys and naughty French postcard girls.

The critics praised the evening, but it's worth noting some had slight reservations. The opening scene in front of Laurey's farm house seemed to go on too long, and then after the climactic title song late in the second act, the plot meandered a bit more than necessary. There was definitely a feeling the first and last scenes could have been trimmed. Wilella Waldorf in the *New York Post* said the opening sequence was "mild" and "somewhat monotonous" with everyone "warbling" in front of the farm house (she noted that life on the old farm was apt to grow a bit "tiresome"), but midway through the first act the musical grew "steadily more entertaining" and became "gay and colorful"; in fact, the show was "the most original and entertaining" evening offered by the Theatre Guild in some time.

Howard Barnes in the *New York Herald Tribune* also felt the evening got off to a "slow start," but even so *Oklahoma!* was a "superb" musical in which song, story, and dance had been "triumphantly blended" into a "jubilant and enchanting" production. John Anderson in the *New York Journal-American* suggested that the long first act should undergo some tightening, but otherwise here was a "fresh and imaginative" and "enchanting" musical. He praised Lemuel Ayers's "handsome" scenery, and he and others compared it to the paintings of Grant Wood and Thomas Benton.

In his annual, George Jean Nathan said the evening offered "agreeable entertainment," and Rodgers' score was "one of his best." But he felt De Mille's choreography leaned toward the "arty" and said that after the "rousing" title song there was an "extension of the action" that "loses the audience."

Louis Kronenberger in *PM* praised the "charming" score, "picturesque and lively" dances, and "attractive sets" and felt the musical was "just different enough" to give Broadway a "lift"; but he noted the book "is just one of those things, if that." Lewis Nichols in the *New York Times* reported that the "truly delightful musical play" could be called a "folk operetta"; but "whatever" it was, it was "very good." Burton Rascoe in the *New York World-Telegram* said the "fresh, lively, colorful and enormously pleasing" musical also boasted "one of the finest musical scores any musical play ever had."

Burns Mantle in the *New York Daily News* said *Oklahoma!* was the "most thoroughly and attractively American musical" since *Show Boat* (1927). It was "different—beautifully different," and was a "mighty sweet joining of the arts of drama and the dance."

When the musical began tryout performances it was titled *Away We Go!* Dropped during the tryout was Curly and Laurey's second-act ballad "Boys and Girls Like You and Me" (which was replaced by a reprise of "People Will Say We're in Love"). Judy Garland sang the deleted number in the 1944 MGM film *Meet Me in St. Louis*, but the song was cut prior to release; it was later used in MGM's 1949 musical *Take Me Out to the Ball Game*, where it was sung by Frank Sinatra, and again the song was cut prior to release. The DVD of the former includes Garland's soundtrack recording, which is accompanied by a photo re-creation of the scene; and the DVD release of the latter includes the complete deleted outtake of Sinatra's rendition of the number.

Songs dropped during preproduction were "Someone Will Teach You," "We Will Be Together," "Why, Oh Why," "You Are My Girl," and "When Ah (I) Go Out Walkin' with Mah (My) Baby." The latter (along with "Boys and Girls Like You and Me") was interpolated into the 1996 Broadway stage version of *State Fair* and is also included in the collection *Lost in Boston III* (Varese Sarabande CD # VSD-5563); both songs were recorded for the cast album of *State Fair* (DRG Records CD # 94765).

As of this writing, *Oklahoma!* has been revived in New York nine times. The first visit was a limited-engagement by the musical's national touring company on May 29, 1951, for seventy-two performances at the Broadway Theatre; the cast included Ridge Bond (Curly) and Patricia Northrop (Laurey). The next five revivals were produced by the New York City Center Light Opera Company, and opened on August 31, 1953, for forty performances (Bond was again Curly; Florence Henderson, Laurey; Barbara Cook, Ado Annie); on March 19, 1958, for fifteen performances (Herbert Banke, Curly; Lois O'Brien, Laurey; Helen Gallagher, Ado Annie; Betty Garde reprised her original role of Aunt Eller; and Gene Nelson appeared as Will Parker, the role he performed in the 1955 film version); on February 27, 1963, for fifteen performances (Peter Palmer, Curly; Louise O'Brien, Laurey; Betty Garde, Aunt Eller); on May 15, 1963, for fifteen performances (again with Palmer, O'Brien, and Garde); and December 15, 1965, for twenty-four performances (John Davidson, Curly; Susan Watson, Laurey; Karen Morrow, Ado Annie; Ruth Kobart, Aunt Eller; Jules Munshin, Ali Hakim).

The next revival opened for 88 performances on June 23, 1969, at the New York State Theatre in a Music Theatre of Lincoln Center production (Bruce Yarnell, Curly; Lee Beery, Laurey; Lee Roy Reams, Will Parker; Spiro Malas, Jud Fry; Margaret Hamilton, Aunt Eller). The superb 1979 revival, which opened on December 13 at the Palace Theatre for 301 performances, was especially memorable for its slightly dark and brooding atmosphere. Martin Vidnovic was especially striking in his unusual approach to Jud Fry, for here was a Jud who was young, handsome, and sexually charged. Others in the splendid cast were Laurence Guittard (Curly), Christine Andreas (Laurey), Christine Ebersole (Ado Annie), Mary Wickes (Aunt Eller), Harry Groener (Will Parker), and Bruce Adler (Ali Hakim).

The work's most recent revival (which was based on a 1998 London production) opened on March 21, 2002, at the Gershwin Theatre for 388 performances (Patrick Wilson was Curly, and from the London cast was Josefina Gabrielle as Laurey).

The script of the musical was published in hardback by Random House in 1943, and was also included in the same publisher's hardback collection *Six Plays by Rodgers and Hammerstein* (released in hardback in 1959, the volume also includes the scripts of **Carousel**, **Allegro**, **South Pacific**, *The King and I*, and *Me and Juliet*). In 2010, another edition of the script was published in softback by Applause Theatre & Cinema Books; and the script was published in hardback in 2014 by the Library of Congress in a collection that includes the scripts of fifteen other musicals. The lyrics of the musical are included in the collection *The Complete Lyrics of Oscar Hammerstein II*. Max Wilk's *Ok! The Story of 'Oklahoma!'* was published by Grove Press in 1993, and in 2002 was republished by Applause Books. In 2007, Yale University Press published Tim Carter's *Oklahoma! The Making of an American Musical*.

There are numerous recordings of the score, but the essential one is the original Broadway cast album by Decca (LP # DL-8000; the CD by MCA Classics # MCAD-10798 includes an alternate take as well as the complete version of "Pore Jud"). As a runner-up, the recording of the 1979 revival is highly recommended (RCA Victor LP # CBL1-3572). The cast album of the original 1943 production is historic, for here was the first time a Broadway musical had been recorded with the original cast and orchestra and sold in a mass-market collection. From your living room, you could actually hear what a Broadway musical sounded like in the theatre, a truly remarkable experience which had never occurred before. Here was the biggest hit musical in years, and you could easily buy its recording and listen to it whenever you wished.

To be sure, there had been occasional single recordings of Broadway songs by the performers who first introduced them (such as Gertrude Lawrence, Ethel Merman, Danny Kaye, and others) and Marc Blitzstein's *The Cradle Will Rock* and *No for an Answer* had been recorded with their original casts. But with *Oklahoma!*, the record-buying public was able to buy all the major songs of a musical, and with production photos and an informative booklet to boot. The recording forever changed the American musical, and paved the way for the preservation of music and performances of untold shows to come.

Oklahoma! was first seen in London at the Drury Lane on April 29, 1947, where it played for 1,548 performances (Howard Keel was Curly and Betty Jane Watson was Laurey). The most recent London production opened on July 15, 1998, at the Royal National Theatre with Hugh Jackman (Curly) and Josefina Gabrielle. This revival was released on DVD by Image Entertainment (# ID1055700KDVD).

The 1955 film version was filmed twice, for both the Todd-AO and CinemaScope processes; the roadshow release in Todd-AO was released by Magda Theatre Corporation, and RKO Radio Pictures distributed the CinemaScope version. The casting is notable for both the traditional (Gordon McacRae [Curly] and Shirley Jones [Laurey] and offbeat (Rod Steiger [Jud Fry] and Gloria Grahame [Ado Annie]). Except for Lonely Room and It's a Scandal! It's a Outrage!, the entire score was retained. Twentieth Century-Fox distributed the home video releases, and the DVD (# 0-24543-20843-3) includes both versions of the film. A Japanese production by the Takarazuka company was released on DVD (Takarazuka Creative Arts Co. Ltd. # TCAD-149).

ZIEGFELD FOLLIES
"A National Institution Glorifying the American Girl"

Theatre: Winter Garden Theatre
Opening Date: April 1, 1943; *Closing Date*: July 22, 1944
Performances: 553
Sketches: Lester Lawrence, Lester Lee, and Jerry Seelen; additional material by Joseph Erens (supervised by Harry A. Kaufman)
Lyrics: Jack Yellen; additional lyrics by Bud Burtson and Jerry Seelen
Music: Ray Henderson; additional music by Baldwin Bergersen, Bud Burtson, Lester Lee, and Dan White
Direction: Staged by John Murray Anderson; dialogue directed by Arthur Pierson and Fred De Cordova; *Producers*: The Messrs. Shubert in association with Alfred Bloomingdale and Lou Walters by arrangement with Billie Burke Ziegfeld; *Choreography*: Robert Alton; *Scenery*: Watson Barratt; *Costumes*: Miles White; *Lighting*: Uncredited; *Musical Direction*: John McManus
Cast: Milton Berle, Ilona Massey, Arthur Treacher, Jack Cole, Sue Ryan, Nadine Gae, Tommy Wonder, Dean Murphy, Christine Ayers, The Rhythmaires (Robert Bay, Victor Griffen, Bob Shaw, and Don Weissmuller), Jack McCauley, Imogen Carpenter, Jay Martin, Katherine Meskill, Bil and Cora Baird, Arthur Maxwell, Charles Senna, The Jansleys, Ben Yost's Vi-Kings (Eddie [Edward] Hayes, Manfried Hecht, Howard Jackson, Robert Rippy, Edmund [Bob] Lyndeck, and Theodore Teddick), Ray Long, Mary Ganley, Patricia Hall, Penny Edwards, Dixie Roberts, Ruth Rowan; The Ziegfeld Follies Show Girls: Bea Bailey, Doris Brent, Veronica Byrnes, Josine Cagle, Ann Connolly, Betty Douglas, Eleanor Hall, Yvonne Kummer, Renee Riley, Betty Stuart, Rose Teed; The Ziegfeld Follies Dancing Girls: Carolyn Ayers, Mary Alice Bigham, Virginia Cheneval, Skippy Cekan, Grace DeWitt, Gretchen Houser, Marilyn Hightower, Jerry Koban, Kay Lewis, Bubbles Mandel, Mary McDonnell, Janie New, Marianne O'Brien, Rosaleen Simpson, Ila Marie Wilson, Mimi Walthers, Doris York; The Messrs.: Jack Allen, Ray Arnett, Jim Barron, Bob Copsy, Ray Cook, David Gray, Arthur Grahl, Bruce Davison, Howard Ludwig, Michael Pober, Tom Smith
The revue was presented in two acts.

Musical Numbers

Act One: Prologue (sketch by Jerry Seelen and Lester Lee; lyrics by Jerry Seelen, music by Lester Lee) (Nadine Gae, Tommy Wonder, Imogen Carpenter, Jay Martin): (a) Vignette after Cole Porter (Christine Ayers, Mary Ganley, Dixie Roberts, Michael Pober, Penny Edwards, Jim Barron, Bob Copsy, Ben Yost's Vikings); (b) Vignette after Ernest Hemingway (The Hero: Jack McCauley; The Bellringer: Jerry Jansley); (c) Vignette after William Saroyan (A Character: Manfried Hecht; Another Character: Charles Senna; Still Another Character: Bil Baird); and (d) Vignette after Irving Berlin (The Ziegfeld Follies Show Girls, The Ziegfeld Follies Dancing Girls; The Messrs.); "Something for the Berles" (Milton Berle); "Thirty-Five Summers Ago" (Ilona Massey, Jay Martin, The Ziegfeld Follies Show Girls); Ben Yost's Vi-Kings); "Good God Godfrey" (sketch by Bud Pearson and Les White) (Mr. Tappan: Jack McCauley; Mrs. Tappan: Katherine Meskill; Godfrey: Arthur Treacher); "This Is It" (Arthur Maxwell, Imogen Carpenter; danced by Nadine Gae, Penny Edwards, Patricia Hall, Dixie Roberts, Mary Ganley, The Ziegfeld Dancing Girls and Boys, The Rhythmaires, Tommy Wonder); "Counter Attack" (sketch by Charles Sherman and Harry Young) (Cecil: Milton Berle; Mr. Andrews: Jack McCauley; Mrs. Andrews: Sue Ryan); "The Wedding of a Solid Sender" (music by Baldwin Bergersen) (choreographed by Jack Cole) (The Groom: Jack Cole; The Bride: Rebecca Lee; Bridesmaids: Virginia Miller, Ruth Rowan; Congregation: Carolyn Ayers, Mary McDonnell, Mimi Walthers, Marilyn Hightower); "The Merchant of Venison" (sketch by Lester Lee and Jerry Seelen) (J. Pierswift Armour: Milton Berle); "Love Songs Are Made in the Night" (Ilona Massey, Jay Martin)— (a) Romantic Ballet (Nadine Gae, The Rhythmaires); (b) Rhythmic Ballet (Christine Ayers, Ray Long, Ensemble); Sue Ryan (untitled song with lyric by Bud Burtson, music by Dan White); Ben Yost's

Vi-Kings; "Come Up and Have a Cup of Coffee" (Arthur Maxwell, Imogen Carpenter, Ben Yost's Vi-Kings, The Ziegfeld Show Girls; danced by Dixie Roberts, Mary Ganley, Patricia Hall, Penny Edwards, The Rhythmaires, The Ziegfeld Follies Dancers, Nadine Gae, Tommy Wonder); "Loves-a-Poppin" (sketch by Ray Golden and Sid Kuller) (Gertrude Olsen: Ilona Massey; Perry Johnson: Milton Berle; Crumpet: Arthur Treacher); "Carmen in Zoot" (Prologue: Jay Martin, Kay Lewis; "The Saga of Carmen" sung by Sue Ryan; A Fortune Teller: Christine Ayers; A Smuggler: Ray Long; The Bull: Nadine Gae; A Toreador: Tommy Wonder; Michala: Ilona Massey; Don Jose: Arthur Treacher; Matadors: The Rhythmaires; Carmen: Sue Ryan; Picadors: Ben Yost's Vi-Kings; Escamillio: Milton Berle; Entire Company)

Act Two: "Swing Your Lady, Mr. Hemingway" (sung and danced by Sue Ryan, Ray Long, The Rhythmaires, Christine Ayers, Doris Brent, Jack McCauley, Marilyn Hightower, Nadine Gae, Tommy Wonder, Ensemble); The Jansleys; "Once a Butler" (sketch by Lester Lawrence) (Himself: Arthur Treacher; His Wife: Katherine Meskill; Mr. Smith: Jack McCauley); Dean Murphy; "Back to the Farm" (lyric and music by Bud Burtson) (Sue Ryan, with Christine Ayers and The Ziegfeld Follies Show Girls); "Mr. Grant Goes to Washington" (sketch by Joseph Erens) (Charlie Grant: Milton Berle; Mary Grant: Katherine Meskill; Bell Boy: Charles Senna; Hotel Manager: Jack McCauley); Bil and Cora Baird; "Hindu Serenade" (Ilona Massey, Jay Martin; danced by Jack Cole, Rebecca Lee, Virginia Miller, Ruth Rowan); "The Micromaniac" (lyric and music by Harold J. Rome) (Milton Berle); "Hold That Smile" (Nadine Gae, Tommy Wonder, Jay Martin, Imogen Carpenter, Milton Berle, Ilona Massey, Arthur Treacher, Mary Ganley, Entire Company)

In reviewing *Ziegfeld Follies* for *PM*, Louis Kronenberger reported that shortly before the opening night performance began, Moss Hart said to him and Lillian Hellman, "Who'd have thought we'd see another *Follies*?" To which Hellman replied, "What makes you think we will?" And Hellman was right. What everyone saw was a warmed-over revue with spotty sketches and songs. It was nothing like the old days when such legendary performers as Eddie Cantor and Al Jolson and Fannie Brice and Will Rogers and Marilyn Miller headlined the *Follies* and introduced songs that became synonymous with old-time Broadway.

But the new *Follies* was large and lavish and it starred Milton Berle, who would soon become one of the all-time great television comedians. And, in truth, Berle in zoot-suit-by-way-of-old-Seville must have been a riot. He clowned throughout the evening, acted as a genial host, and, Ed Wynn-style, gamely took part in a few of the acts. After an opening number which spoofed Cole Porter and Irving Berlin musicals, Hemingway's novels, and Saroyan's plays, the Ziegfeld Follies Show Girls, The Ziegfeld Follies Dancers, and the chorus boys (here called The Messrs.) paraded on stage. And then suddenly one of the chorus boys stepped forward. It was Berle, making a surprise entrance. The stage cleared, and Berle was off and running with a fast-and-furious monologue ("Something for the Berles") in which he chatted up the audience. When he spied playboy Tommy Manville in the crowd, he asked if Manville was in the eighth row with his sixth wife, or was he in the sixth row with his eighth wife? And when something suddenly crashed backstage, Berle quipped that Lee Shubert's teeth had just fallen out. Yes, it was that kind of evening, and the public, if not all the critics, ate it up. Of the twenty-five *Follies* produced on Broadway from 1907 to 1957, the 1943 edition became the longest-running of them all.

The revue looked at topical subjects such as rationing (in the sketch "The Merchant of Venison," Berle was J. Pierswift Armour who with bodyguards in attendance deposits a package of meat in a bank vault); crowded wartime Washington (in "Mr. Grant Goes to Washington," Berle is a hapless bridegroom who books a hotel room for his wedding night, only to discover the government has proclaimed the day as "Loveless Tuesday"); and jive dancing ("The Wedding of a Solid Sender" was choreographed and performed by Jack Cole). For the sketch "Counter Attack," Berle was the proprietor of a diner who hates his customers and "Loves-a-Poppin" (a nod to Ole Olsen and Chic Johnson, whose *Hellzapoppin'* and **Sons O' Fun** had held court at the Winter Garden for almost six years [Berle referred to the Winter Garden as Olsen and Johnson's National Bank]) was a madcap sketch which combined Olsen and Johnson–styled antics with sophisticated Noel Coward drawing-room comedy. With Arthur Treacher on hand, there were of course a couple of sketches that revolved around butlers; Hollywood's Ilona Massey came on for a few songs; Nadine Gae and Tommy Wonder provided dance interludes; The Jansleys were a group of tumblers; Dean Murphy impersonated the Roosevelts, Wendell Willkie, Bette Davis, Clark Gable, Joe E. Brown, and (in what seemed to be the umpteenth impression of her in Broadway revues) Katharine Hepburn; and marionettes Bil and Cora Baird offered a sequence with their enchanting "little people." Only a dog act was missing.

Lewis Nichols in the *New York Times* said "funny fellow" Berle was "luckily" in almost everything that transpired on the stage and his "extemporaneous" chats with the audience exemplified his "brash, casual" humor which "perfectly" complemented the revue format; Ward Morehouse in the *New York Sun* said it was clear "a lot" of money had been spent on the big and lavish revue and he predicted the production would be a "wallop" at the box office; and Burns Mantle in the *New York Daily News* said Berle was one of the "smartest" and "most industrious" of the "patter monologists," but he found Arthur Treacher's material sadly lacking in humor; otherwise, the huge revue could fill about "six floor shows and a couple of large back rooms."

John Anderson in the *New York Journal-American* said the evening was "large, lavish, opulent and optical," and he was glad to see a topical revue tackle such "pertinent matters" as jive dancing; "Carmen in Zoot" offered "zoot-suited frenzies of bizarre Bizet," and poor Arthur Treacher kept his "noble nostril appropriately uplifted," no doubt because he "had just detected his material." Howard Barnes in the *New York Herald Tribune* said the evening offered "rewarding entertainment" and praised the "comely" girls and Berle's "comic buoyancy"; and Wilella Waldorf in the *New York Post* "shuddered" to imagine what the revue would have been like without Berle and his "much-needed comic relief"; the production was too often brought down by "poor material" and Treacher was given very few moments to shine. As for Ilona Massey, Waldorf was certain she was "doubtless very good in films."

Burton Rascoe in the *New York World-Telegram* felt the material was "unbelievably obvious, crude, cheap and witless," and said the "saving merit" of the revue could be summed up in two words: Milton Berle. The comedian was "talented and ingratiating," but Rascoe suggested his mother "wash his mouth out with lye soap and disinfectant" after each performance. For all that, he predicted the Shuberts would "make scads of dough out of the show."

During the tryout, the following numbers were cut: two special bits for Arthur Treacher ("That Creature Treacher" and "The Deliberate Delineator," the latter by David Greggory); the sketch "Taxes" (by Irving Brecher); the sketch "L'Honour de Chez de Lang" (by Jerry Seelen and Lester Lee); and the song "Hep Hot and Solid Sweet" (for Betty Kean and other cast members, including The Ziegfeld Jitterbugs). By the time the revue reached New York, Kean was no longer in the show. During the tryout, "Thirty-Five Summers Ago" was titled "Summer Roses."

The collection *Broadway Musicals of 1943* (Bayview CD # RNBW015) includes the revue's finale, "Hold That Smile."

Berle became so popular through television that he was soon crowned "Mr. Television" by the press and the public, and a few years later on that very Winter Garden stage "Uncle Miltie" was the in-all-but-name subject of the musical *Top Banana*, in which Phil Silvers portrayed a manic, free-wheeling top television comedian. This time around it was Berle, not Manville, in the opening night audience and William Hawkins in the *New York World-Telegram and Sun* reported that Berle was "sitting down front" and "laughing his head off."

ADAMANT EVE
"A COMEDY WITH MUSIC"

Theatre and *Performances Dates*: The play with music opened at the Curran Theatre in San Francisco, California, on November 2, 1942, for what *Best Plays* referred to as a "brief sojourn."
Play (and apparently lyrics): Francis Edwards
Music: Henry Holt
The play with music was based on the 1880 play *Divorçons* by Victorien Sardou and Emile de Najac.
Direction: Eugene S. Bryden; *Producers*: Eugene S. Bryden; N. H. Rappaport, Associate Producer; *Scenery*: Ernest Glover; *Costumes*: Western Costume Co.; *Lighting*: Uncredited; *Musical Direction*: Paul Schoop and Nilo Menendez at the twin pianos
Cast: Nola Chilton (Josepha), Guy Kingsford (Jean), Carol Stone (Cyprienne), Barry Norton (Maurice), Norma Varden (Estelle De Brionne), June Cooper (Mme. Duchatel), Jacqueline De Wit (Mme. Valfontaine), Stephanie Bachelor (Mlle. Lusignan), Edward Cooper (Clavignac), Rex O'Malley (Adhemar), Fred Essler (Adolphe), Elmer Jerome (Gendarme)
The play with music was presented in three acts.
The action takes place in Paris during the 1890s.
The program did not list musical numbers.

Adamant Eve was based on the 1880 comedy *Divorçons* (*Let's Get a Divorce*) by Victorien Sardou and Emile de Najac which dealt with merry marital mishaps. It was later the basis for Ernst Lubitsch's 1941 film *That Uncertain Feeling*. The current adaptation included songs, most of them sung by Carol Stone, the daughter of legendary Broadway comedian Fred Stone and the sister of actresses Dorothy and Paula Stone.

The work was intended for Broadway, but never made it beyond San Francisco (the production canceled its other tryout stops in Los Angeles, Chicago, and Detroit). *Best Plays* reported that of the three productions that premiered in San Francisco during the season (the revue **Show Time**, the drama *The Barber Had Two Sons*, and *Adamant Eve*), only the first two made it to Broadway. The annual praised Carol Stone's "beauty and charm" and the "valiant" acting of Rex O'Malley and Barry Norton.

An unsigned article in the *Los Angeles Examiner* reported on the San Francisco opening night, and it reads like a puff piece. It stated that Carol Stone "demonstrated her right to stardom in one of the most difficult roles ever essayed by an actress" and "scored an outstanding success" with her "personal triumph."

COCKTAILS AT 5
"A NEW MUSICAL COMEDY"

Theatre and *Performance Dates*: The musical opened on July 19, 1942, at the Erlanger Theatre in Chicago, Illinois, for one week before it permanently closed.
Book and *Lyrics*: Rowland Leigh
Music: Jean Schwartz
Direction: Rowland Leigh; *Producer*: The Messrs. Shubert; *Choreography*: Boots McKenna; *Scenery* and *Costumes*: Stage Costumes, Inc.; *Lighting*: Uncredited; *Musical Direction*: Irving Actman
Cast: Jack Coyle (Mr. Black), Ruth Bond (Patsy), Jack Good (Andy), Bobbie Morris (Bagsy), Ty Kearney (Stagehand), Vicki George (Claudette Bretanne), Loraine DeWood (Lorraine), Chet Bree (Henry Crane), Morton Bowe (Leon Lambert), George Dill (Inspector), Ernie DiGennaro (Waiter), Norma Riley (Flo Flo), Kay Paige (Nanatee), Frances King (Evelyn), Betty Lou (Street Urchin), Hal Conklin (Paul Raymond), Shelly (Shelley) Winter (Winters) (Norma DuBois, Julie), Charlotte Lansing (Gertrude LaMont), Joseph E. Marks (Louis Condor), Evelyn Oaks (High School Girl), Charmaine (Society Girl); Show Girls: Dorothea Pinto, Norma Riley, Barbara Thurston, Fredi Sears, Kay Paige, Alice Perlin, Ann Hudlin, Frances King; Dancing Girls: Sylvia Mettler, Virginia McKay, Eza Coleman, Helen Luther, Carolyn Ayers, Ruth Ryder, Maude Carroll, Ruth Mitchell, Peggy Lynn, Jean Lollie, Ruth Blake, Edna Paine, Betty Greene, Betty Granger, Francine Warner, Lucille Franchon; Dancing Boys: Robert McKernan, Pack Purcell, Sidney Enkowe, Robert Davis, Ernie DiGennaro, Robert Copsy, Ty Kearney, William O'Shea
The musical was presented in two acts.
The action takes place during the present time in New Orleans.

Musical Numbers

Act One : "Grind and Bump" (Ruth Bond, Ensemble); "Lovey Dovey" (Loraine Dewood, Show Girls); "Revelation" (Charmaine); "Mardi Gras" (Shelly Winter, Dancing Girls and Boys); "Home from Home" (Vicki George, Morton Bowe); "The Lights Went Out" (Ruth Bond); "Chez Claudette" (Jack Good, Dancing Girls and Boys); "My Gink" (Vicki George); "Lily of the Gutter" (Hal Conklin, Vicki George, Ruth Bond); "(You've) Got to Be Fast" (Ruth Bond, Jack Good, Dancing Girls and Boys); "Charm" (Hal Conklin, Vicki George); "Time Out for Romance" (Chet Bree, Morton Bowe); "My Gink" (reprise) (Vicki George); Finale Act One (Vicki George, Ruth Bond, Hal Conklin, Entire Ensemble)
Act Two: "Together" (Loraine DeWood, Dancing Boys and Girls, Show Girls); "I'm So Glad" (Morton Bowe, Ruth Bond); "Yes, Mrs. Lamont" (Charlotte Lansing, Maids); "Times May Change" (Charlotte Lansing, Morton Bowe); "She Can't Make Coffee" (Jack Good, Dancing Girls); "As Long as We Love" (Vicki George, Hal Conklin); "All the Time" (Vicki George); "Chez Claudette" (reprise) (Betty Lou, Dancing Girls and Boys, Show Girls); Specialty Dance (Betty Lou, Dancing Boys); "Creole Samba" (Vicki George, Dancing Girls and Boys); Specialty Dance (Ruth Bond); Finale (Entire Company)

The musical *Cocktails at 5* was a show business saga that took place among the theatres and cafes of New Orleans, particularly those that specialized in acts of the strip-tease variety. According to *Best Plays*, the "dismal warehouse musical" played in Chicago for one "desolate" week before it disappeared forever (as a result, show-tune buffs were forever deprived of hearing such songs as "Bump and Grind," "Lily of the Gutter," "Lovey Dovey," "My Gink," and "Mardi Gras"). But then the musical never really had much of a chance because it was set in the unfriendly musical-comedy territory of New Orleans, a locale that more often than not dooms a musical to Cain's warehouse.

Among the cast members of *Cocktails at 5* was Shelly Winter who went on to bigger and better things (including two Academy Awards) as Shelley Winters.

The musical was a revised version of *Cocktails From 5 to 7*, which briefly toured in 1935 without ever braving the Broadway waters; this version seems to have been set in Paris. Songs from the first go-round which didn't make it to the Chicago version were "Paris in Spring," "Paris Police," "Take Love While You May," "Twilight Rhythms," and "Whoops, My Dear."

Later in the season, three songs ("I'm So Glad," "You've Got to Be Fast," and "She Can't Make Coffee") and possibly a fourth ("Creole Samba," which probably became "Brazilian Samba") from *Cocktails at 5* turned up in Rowland Leigh, Jean Schwartz, and Irving Actman's **Full Speed Ahead**, which also closed prior to its Broadway opening.

In 1945, the play-with-music **A Gift for the Bride** (see appendix F, "Other Productions") included three songs from *Cocktails at 5*, "Home from Home," "Charm," and "All the Time."

DANCING IN THE STREETS
"A NEW MUSICAL COMEDY"

Theatres and *Performance Dates*: The musical opened on March 23, 1943, at the Shubert Theatre, Boston, Massachusetts, and permanently closed on April 10, 1943, at the Boston Opera House.
Book: John Cecil Holm and Matt Taylor
Lyrics: Howard Dietz
Music: Vernon Duke
Based on a short story by Matt Taylor.
Direction: Edgar MacGregor; *Producer*: Vinton Freedley; *Choreography*: Robert Alton; *Scenery* and *Lighting*: Robert Edmond Jones; *Costumes*: Kiviette (Mary Martin's costumes designed by Valentina); *Musical Direction*: Max Meth
Cast: Eddie Green (Jeff), Mary Wickes (Louella Briggs), Helen Raymond (Agatha Windrop), Cora Witherspoon (Mabel Windrop), Dudley Digges (Admiral Downey Windrop, USN), Jack Smart (Colonel Waverly Smithers, USMC), Ernest Cossart (General Leonidas Perkins, USA), Jack Kilty (Lieutenant Tom Crawford), *Mary Martin* (Mary Hastings), Betty Allen (Judy), Mildred Law (Mildred), Charlotte Maye (Charlotte), Billie Worth (Billie), Mavis Mims (Mavis), Kay Aldridge (Kay), Aina Constant (Aina), Drucilla Strain (Drucilla), Paul Mann (Rex Dunlop), Mark Dawson (Buddy McGraw), Lucille Bremer (Lucille), Peggy Maley (Peggy), George E. Mack (Senator "Petroleum" Tiffenberry), Carl Carelli (Telegraph Boy); Newsreel Men: Bill Cadmus, James Harkins, Fred Peters, Oliver Boersma; Reporters: Jack Merkel, Joe LeClaire; The Boy Friends: Johnny Coy, Jere McMahon, Don Liberto, Bobby Harrell, Burt Harger, William Archibald; White Collar Girls: Billie Worth, Mavis Mims, Mildred Law, Jeanne Blanche, Charlotte Maye; Guests: Helen Bennett, Eleanor Boleyn, Marianne Cude, Dolores Milan, Mary Virginia Morris, Kaye Popp, Jean Scott, Toni Stuart, Evelyn Ward; Selectees: Oliver Boersma, Fred Peters, David Hartley, Jack Allen, Ray Arnette, Clark Eggelston, George Hunter, Larry Evers, Tom Powers, Robert Trout, Jack Wilkens, Jack Rosenmerkel, James Harkins, William Cadmus, Joseph LeClaire, Carl Carelli
The musical was presented in two acts.
The action takes place during the present time in Washington, D.C.

Musical Numbers

Act One: "Swattin' the Fly" (Eddie Green); "We've Been Through the Mill Together" (Dudley Digges, Ernest Cossart, Jack Smart); "The Comforts of Home" (Mary Martin, Girls); "Tallahassee" (Mary Martin, Girls);

"A Friendly Bar" (Mark Dawson, Dudley Digges, Boys); "Indefinable Charm" (Jack Kilty, Mary Martin); "Keep Your Amateur Standing" (Betty Allen, Girls); "Kiss Your Baby Goodbye" (Mary Martin, Jack Kilty, Paul Mann); "Hip!" (Mary Martin, Girls); "Dancing in the Streets" (Mary Martin, Ensemble)

Act Two: "Got a Bran' New Daddy" (Mary Martin, Girls); "Irresistible You" (Betty Allen, Paul Mann); "Irresistible You" Specialty Dance (Don Liberto and Jeanne Blanche, Jere McMahon, Charlotte Maye and Burt Harger, Johnny Coy and Billie Worth); "Bay of Botany" (Mark Dawson, Boys); "Can-Can" (aka "Can-Can in the Canteen") (Mary Martin, Boys, Girls); "In My Dreams" (Mary Wickes, Helen Raymond, Cora Witherspoon); Dance (Mavis Mims); "Indefinable Charm" (reprise) (Jack Kilty, Mary Martin); Finale (Entire Company)

The housing shortage during wartime Washington, D.C., was a favorite subject of movies and plays during the era, most notably in Joseph Fields's amusing 1942 hit comedy *The Doughgirls* and the classic 1943 George Stevens film comedy *The More the Merrier*. *Dancing in the Streets* told the familiar story from a musical-comedy perspective, but unfortunately it closed after the second week of its Boston tryout and canceled its scheduled May opening on Broadway at the Imperial Theatre. Today *Dancing in the Streets* is most likely remembered as the show Mary Martin chose to do after turning down an item called *Away We Go!*, which later changed its name to **Oklahoma!** (for one week during March 1943, the Boston tryouts of both musicals overlapped). But Mary Martin was destined for a date with the Imperial, and later in the year she opened there in the title role of the hit musical **One Touch of Venus**.

Most of *Dancing in the Streets* took place in and around a Washington, D.C., mansion owned and lived in by three high-ranking retired military officers; bored because they're not part of the current conflict, they decide to do their bit by turning their home into bachelor quarters for young officers. But through those confusing circumstances that occur only in musical comedies, a swarm of government girls move in and force the three men to barricade themselves on the grounds of their estate. Ultimately, the girls are evicted, but not before they're honored by the government for helping to solve the wartime housing shortage. So the three officers welcome the girls back to the mansion, and the officers themselves are now officially in charge of a newly created government bureau called the Office of the Mobilization of Private Homes for War Workers (or, in government acronym style, The OOMPH).

Variety seemed certain that with proper revisions *Dancing in the Streets* would "click" in New York, but Elinor Hughes in the *Boston Herald* said that in the musical's "present state" a visit to Broadway would be "hazardous." One critic indicated Mary Martin was now appearing in her first leading role in a musical, apparently forgetting that in 1939 she was the leading lady of *Nice Goin'*, which also floundered in Boston and never made it to New York.

The musical marked the first of three Broadway collaborations by composer Vernon Duke and lyricist Howard Dietz; all were failures, but their scores for **Jackpot**, **Sadie Thompson**, and *Dancing in the Streets* left behind many pleasant, and a few outstanding, songs. They also wrote the score for the Coast Guard recruiting revue **Tars and Spars** which toured throughout the country, including a limited New York engagement.

Strange as it seems, during the two-week tryout the musical moved from the Shubert Theatre to the Boston Opera House; the program for the latter indicates that by the show's second tryout week two songs were dropped (the opening sequence which included "Swattin' the Fly" and "We've Been through the Mill Together").

A number of songs have surfaced from the musical, all of them quite delightful. Klea Blackhurst's *Autumn in New York/Vernon Duke's Broadway* (Ghostlight CD # 79155833022) includes "Indefinable Charm"; *Dawn Upshaw Sings Vernon Duke* (Nonesuch CD # 79531-2) offers "Swattin' the Fly"; *Vernon Duke Revisited Volume III* (Painted Smiles CD # PSCD-147) includes a medley of songs from the show ("Indefinable Charm," "Irresistible You," and the title number); and the collection *You Can't Put Ketchup on the Moon* (Rialto CD # SLRR-9201) also includes the title song.

Chorus singer Billie Worth was occasionally associated with Mary Martin throughout both their careers. Worth appeared in the chorus and occasionally had featured-player roles in such musicals as *Very Warm for May* (1939), **Higher and Higher**, **Bright Lights of 1944**, **Jackpot**, and **Seven Lively Arts** (for the latter, she was part of the quintet who introduced Cole Porter's tongue-twisting ode to jive talk "Hence It Don't Make Sense"). Besides singing in the chorus of *Dancing in the Streets*, Worth was also Martin's understudy; Worth had a secondary lead in the national touring company of **Annie Get Your Gun** which starred Martin, and when the latter left the tour, Worth assumed the title role and played it for almost a year on the road. She was later Martin's stand-by in **South Pacific** and went on for a few performances when Martin took ill. In 1951, Worth had a leading role in *Courtin' Time*; during the tryout, she was billed below the title, but because of her great reviews, she was soon listed above the title along with Joe E. Brown. Brooks Atkinson in the *New York Times* praised her performance and said she "sparkled" and would "keep on making friends whenever she appears on a stage." Unfortunately, *Courtin' Time* marked her last appearance in a Broadway musical. In 1957, she starred in Robert Wright and George Forrest's *The Carefree Heart*, but the show closed during its pre-Broadway tryout.

THE FIREFLY

Theatres and *Performance Dates*: The revival opened on November 21, 1942, at the Horace Bushnell Memorial Hall in Hartford, Connecticut, opened in Baltimore, Maryland, on November 23, 1942, and then opened on December 1, 1942, at the Majestic Theatre, Boston, Massachusetts, where it permanently closed.

Book and *Lyrics*: Otto Harbach

Music: Rudolf Friml

Direction: Barrie O'Daniels; *Producers*: The Messrs. Shubert; *Choreography*: Boots McKenna; *Musical Direction*: Irving Actman; other credits unknown

Cast: Emma Otero (Nina), Gordon Gifford (Lieutenant Jack Temple), Jack Good (Jenkins), Leonard Ceeley (Doctor Franz), Olive Reeves-Smith (Mrs. Van Dare), Ruth Bond (Sybil Van Dare), Helen Arthur (Geraldine), Perry Askam (Roger Thurston), Bobby Morris (Chips), Naomi Saunders (Dolores), Seymour Penzner (Pedro), Ruth Mitchell (Tony Columbo), Dorothea MacFarland (Carlotta), Jacqueline Susann (Wilma Loraine), Barbara Blaine (Diana Thurston), George Dill (Captain), Richard Worth (Slugger, Police Officer), Helene LeBerthon (Mrs. Barry), George Spelvin (Mr. Barry), Jessie Cemberg (Bozo); Chorus: Lillie Lawrence, Deana Kemble, Martha Ashley, Helene LeBerthon, Lilo Hunter, Jacqueline Susann, Dorothea MacFarland, Nona Feid, Edna Groove, Deanne Benmore, Olga Roberts, Audrey Kent, Ruth Mitchell, Rusha Jojson, Vern Hopkins, Ann Neville, Frances Lee, Floryne Newbar, Peggy Lynn, Cal Reiter, Frank Panzo, William LeConac, Teddy Dixon, Bob Dowling, Edward Harrington, Roger Sullivan, Warren Lane

The operetta was presented in three acts.

The action takes place in New York City and Miami.

The original production of Rudolf Friml's operetta *The Firefly* opened on December 2, 1912, at the Lyric Theater for 120 performances. Among its memorable songs were "Love Is Like a Firefly," "Giannina Mia," "Sympathy," and "When a Maid Comes Knocking at Your Heart." It was filmed in name only by MGM in 1937 with Jeanette MacDonald and Allan Jones because the new plot wasn't based on the original stage production. But a few of Friml's songs were retained, some with revised lyrics by Robert Wright and George Forrest; and the film enjoyed a hit song with Jones's "The Donkey Serenade" (lyric by Wright and Forrest, and music based on a 1920 solo piano piece by Friml titled "Chanson").

The current revival of *The Firefly* dimmed out on the road, but reopened a month later with many of the same cast members in a production so completely revised that it wasn't a revision of *The Firefly* at all, but an entirely new musical under the title of **Full Speed Ahead**. But **Full Speed Ahead** stalled, and like *The Firefly* it too closed during its tryout.

The revival of *The Firefly* starred Cuban soprano Emma Otero, and appearing again in a small role in an early 1940s musical was future best-selling author Jacqueline Susann.

In 1947, the Shuberts again revived *The Firefly*, this time for a national tour. The original production took place in 1912 and was set in New York City and Bermuda; both the 1942 and 1947 revivals took place in New York and Miami (the 1947 production interpolated "The Donkey Serenade").

A complete recording of *The Firefly* by the Ohio Light Opera was released on a 2-CD set by Albany Records (# TROY-891/92).

FULL SPEED AHEAD

Theatre and *Performance Dates*: The musical opened at the Forrest Theatre, Philadelphia, Pennsylvania, on December 25, 1942, and permanently closed there on January 2, 1943.
Book and *Lyrics*: Rowland Leigh
Music: Jean Schwartz; additional music by Irving Actman and H. Leopold Spitainy
Direction: Rowland Leigh and Barrie O'Daniels; *Producers*: Producers Associates, Inc., and J. J. Shubert; *Choreography*: Boots McKenna; *Musical Direction*: George Hirst; other credits unknown
Cast: Emma Otero (Juanita Cardoza), Jack Good (Benson), Leonard Ceeley (Pedro Cardoza), Olive Reeves-Smith (Mrs. Fellows), Ruth Bond (Peggy Fellows), Helen Arthur (Constance Fellows), Gordon Gifford (Colonel Cardew), Naomi Saunders (Dolores), Hal Conklin (Peter), Dorothea MacFarland (Carlotta), Jacqueline Susann (Wilma Loraine), Barbara Blaine (Diana), Fred Catania (Killer McGee), Bobby Morris (Chips), Richard Worth (Slugger), John A. Lorenz (Captain Gintner), Helene LeBerthon (Mrs. Barry), Richard Worth (Brazilian Policeman), Betty Allen (Julia Starr), Barry English (Hotel Manager), Jesse Cimberg (Bozo), Neville (as himself); Chorus: Lillie Lawrence, Helene LeBerthon, Lilo Hunter, Jacqueline Susann, Dorothea MacFarland, Sidney Brown, Hyla Carpenter, Lennie Leeds, Nona Feid, Edna Groove, Deanne Benmore, Olga Roberts, Audrey Kent, Ruth Mitchell, Rusha Jojson, Vera Hopkins, Ann Neville, Frances Lee, Floryne Newbar, Peggy Lynn, Cal Reiter, Frank Ponzo, William LeConac, Teddy Dixon, Bob Dowling, Edward Harrington, Roger Sullivan, Warren Lane
The musical was presented in two acts.
The action takes place in New York City, Brazil, and Trinidad.

Musical Numbers

Note: Division of acts and song assignments is unknown.
"Brazilian Samba"; "I Don't Repent"; "I'm a Sailor"; "Senorita"; "First Love"; "Tropicana"; "You've Got to Be Fast"; "I'm on My Way to Paradise"; "Happiness Calling"; "In Trinidad"; "Romp in the Hay"; "Ruisenor"; "Gorgeous to Gaze At"; "I'm So Glad"; "Got a New Boy Friend"; "If Only You"; "You've Got to Pay"; "Dream Dance"; "She Can't Make Coffee"

When the tryout of *The Firefly* flickered out in early December 1942, the production was completely revamped and brought to life later in the month as *Full Speed Ahead*, which is sometimes erroneously assumed to be a revised version of *The Firefly*. In truth, the new production dropped all of Rudolf Friml's score and the operetta's book, and brought in a new team of writers to create an entirely new story and score (well, an almost new score; see below). But it appears that *The Firefly*'s decor was recycled for *Full Speed Ahead* because the former took place in New York and Miami (the original production was set in New York and Bermuda) and the latter's action occurred in New York, Trinidad, and Brazil. And most of the cast members of *The Firefly* appeared in *Full Speed Ahead*, including Cuban soprano Emma Otero and bit player and future best-selling author Jacqueline Susann.

The flimsy plot dealt with an unknown Brazilian singer who falls in love with a scion from a rich old New York family. She follows him from Brazil to Trinidad, where she somehow becomes involved with Nazi spies. But she's proven innocent of any wrongdoing, becomes a famous singer, eventually performs in New York, and is happily reunited with her blueblood.

Billboard stated it was "*Full Speed Ahead* to oblivion," and Philadelphia's *Daily News* said the musical was "the theatrical counterpart of what has become tradition for a Thanksgiving feast."

Rowland Leigh and Jean Schwartz (along with Irving Actman) wrote the score for *Full Speed Ahead*. Earlier in the season, Leigh and Schwartz had written the songs for *Cocktails at 5*, which, like *Full Speed Ahead*, closed during its tryout after one week of performances. For *Full Speed Ahead*, they salvaged three songs from the earlier debacle ("I'm So Glad," "You've Got to Be Fast," and "She Can't Make Coffee") and possibly a fourth ("Brazilian Samba" was probably the new title for the earlier "Creole Samba").

Four songs in the production had lyrics by Rowland Leigh and music by H. Leopold Spitainy: "Senorita," "First Love," "I'm on My Way to Paradise," and "If Only You."

HEADLINERS OF '42

Theatre and *Performance Dates*: The revue opened on June 10, 1942, at the Grand Opera House, Chicago, Illinois, and closed there on June 27, 1942 (the revue seems to have closed permanently in Chicago).
Producers: Alfred Bloomingdale and Nat Karson
Cast: Bert Lahr, Joe E. Lewis, Bert Wheeler, Romo Vincent, Hank Ladd, The Biltmorettes, Francetta Malloy, Paul Sydell and Spotty, Mary Raye and Naldi, Peg Leg Bates and Lynn, Royce and Vanya

This was the era of vaudeville-styled revues, but despite a cast that included Bert Lahr, Joe E. Lewis, and Bert Wheeler, *Headliners of '42* seems to have closed permanently after its Chicago engagement (the production was the last one to be booked at the Grand Opera House, which soon became a movie theatre). *Best Plays* remarked that the variety revue was "badly paced and crudely put together."

Lewis, Wheeler, Hank Ladd, and others in the cast were familiar visitors to the vaudeville entertainments that regularly popped up on Broadway during the war years.

LIFE OF THE PARTY

Theatre and *Performances Dates*: The musical opened on October 8, 1942, in Detroit, Michigan, at the Wilson Theatre and permanently closed there on December 6, 1942.
Book: Alan Jay Lerner
Lyrics: Earle Crooker
Music: Frederick Loewe
Based on the 1924 play *The Patsy* by Barry Connors.
Direction: Russell Fillmore; *Producer*: Henry Duffy; *Choreography*: Theodore Adolphus; *Scenery, Costumes, Lighting*, and *Musical Direction*: Unknown
Cast: Dorothy Stone (Patricia Harrington), Charles Collins (Tony Anderson), Helen Raymond (Mrs. Harrington), Harry Antrum (William Harrington), Dean Norton (Billy Caldwell), Louise Kirtland (Grace Harrington), Dudley Clements (Mr. O'Flaherty), Trudy Byers (Rose), Betty Leighton (Alice), Vera Teatom (Adrienne), Helen Luther (Hope), Josephine McCann (Louise), Elaine Meredith (Judy), Adela Clark (Greta), Leonora Niece (Eloise), Muriel Breunig (Jane), Iris Manning (Lois), Lucille Fanchon (Eve), Lillian Hulit (Marge), Marty Allen (Earl), Terry Tankerslay (Hugh), Gene Banks (Ed), Thomas Kenny (Ralph), Brett Woods (Andy), Howard Ludwig (Dick), Arthur Laurent (Jack), George Holmes (Jim), Lewis Appleton (Jeff), Al Burger (Josh)
The musical was presented in two acts.
The action takes place during the present time in Arizona.

Musical Numbers

Note: Division of acts and song assignments is unknown.
"The West Is Best"; "One Robin Doesn't Make a Spring"; The Hand-Me-Down"; "Alone in a Crowd"; "El Rancho"; "No Olive in My Martini"; "The Hot Gavotte"; "Life of the Party"; "Wearin' the Grin"; "Sunny Day"; "I'll Tell the World"; "Somehow"; "Let's Waltz and Whistle"; "Night After Night"

During the 1941–1942 season, the 1924 comedy *The Patsy* by Barry Connors was adapted as the musical **Patricia**; produced by Henry Duffy, the lyrics were by J. Keirn Brennan and the music by George Grandee. Although the musical closed after its only tryout engagement (in San Francisco), Duffy didn't give up. A year later he produced a completely new version of the play, this time around titled *Life of the Party*; the book was by Alan Jay Lerner, the lyrics by Earle Crooker, and the music by Frederick Loewe. Loewe and Crooker had been previously represented on Broadway with the 1936 revue *The Illustrators' Show* and the 1938 book musical *Great Lady*, both of which quickly closed after five and twenty respective performances.

Life of the Party is historic because it marks Lerner and Loewe's first collaboration (albeit here Lerner supplied the book and not the lyrics); like its successor *Patricia*, *Life of the Party* closed on the road. Lerner and

Loewe faltered with their first Broadway collaboration **What's Up**, enjoyed a *succès d'estime* with **The Day before Spring**, and then found their stride in **Brigadoon**. But their output was surprisingly small, and after *Brigadoon* they collaborated on just three more Broadway musicals (*Paint Your Wagon* [1951], *My Fair Lady* [1956], and *Camelot* [1960]. They also wrote two film musicals (*Gigi* [1958] and *The Little Prince* [1974]), and contributed a few new songs when the former was adapted for the stage in 1973.

The Patsy centered around Patricia (Pat) Harrington, who puts up with her selfish sister Grace, even though the latter has stolen both money and a beau from her. But Pat gets a backbone and is a patsy no more: she wins the love of Tony Anderson, whom she's loved from afar and who was temporarily taken in by Grace's graceless would-be charms.

During the tryout of *Life of the Party*, choreographer Theodore Adolphus was replaced by Larry Caballos, and the performers Helen Raymond, Harry Antrum, and Louise Kirtland were respectively succeeded by Margaret Dumont, Charles Ruggles, and Jane Lawrence. During the course of the Detroit run, the songs "Wearin' the Grin," "I'll Tell the World," "Let's Waltz and Whistle," and "Somehow" were cut. While Len G. Shaw in the *Detroit Free Press* found the musical "colorful" and "tuneful," Russell McLauchlin in the *Detroit News* reported there was too much plot and the "endless, explanatory dialogue" needed to be trimmed.

Two songs from *Life of the Party* ("Somehow" and "One Robin Doesn't Make a Spring") had previously been heard in Lerner and Crooker's *Salute to Spring*, which had been produced by the St. Louis Municipal Opera in 1937.

MERRY-GO-ROUNDERS (aka THE MERRYMAKERS)

Theatres and *Performance Dates*: As *Merry-Go-Rounders*, the revue began its tryout on March 18, 1943, at the Shubert Lafayette Theatre, Detroit, Michigan, and as *The Merrymakers* permanently closed at the National Theatre, Washington, D.C., where it played from May 17 through May 29, 1943.

Merry-Go-Rounders

Producer: Henry Duffy; *Choreography*: Fred Evans; *Musical Direction*: Ray Kavanaugh
Cast: El Brendel, Flo Bert, Chick York, Rose King, Dan Daniels, Will Ahern, Eola Galli, Ming, Ling, and Hoo-Shee, George Moore, Fred Evans, Gladys Ahern, John Masters, Rowe Collins; The Ten Debutantes: Penny Drake, Joan Dale, Loraine Todd, Eileen Messina, Helen Virginia, Bunny Higgins, Jet Dumas, Gem Dumas, Bernice Harnig, Nancy Hanks
The revue was presented in two acts.

Sketches and Musical Numbers

Act One: Overture (Ray Kavanaugh and His Orchestra); The Ten Debutantes; Dan Daniels ("The Dancing Fool"); Will Ahern (Master of Ceremonies); Eola Galli ("The Captivating Singing Star"); El Brendel ("Star of Stage, Screen and Radio"); Ming, Ling, and Hoo-Shee ("Oriental Oddities"); El Brendel, assisted by Flo Bert ("Sip a Hoy"); Chick York and Rose King ("Old-Fashioned Tintypes")
Act Two: Dan Daniels, assisted by The Ten Debutantes; "Casey at the Bat" (sketch by El Brendel) (Casey: El Brendel; Base Ball Fan: Flo Bert; Pitcher: Dan Daniels; Catcher: George Moore; Umpire: Fred Evans); Will and Gladys Ahern ("In Their Original Offering"); Eola Galli ("With Songs You Like to Hear"); Chick York and Rose King ("Necking Time"); John Masters and Rowe Collins ("in 'Jest as You Like It'"); "Hurry Up Honeymoon" (sketch by El Brendel) (Bridegroom: El Brendel; Bride: Nancy Hanks; Bellboy: John Masters; Sleep Walker: Dan Daniels); Finale (Entire Company)

The Merrymakers

"A Hurricane of Unrationed Laughter"

Producer: Uncredited; *Musical Direction*: Ray Kavanaugh
Cast: Maysy and Brach (also cited as Broch), Jay C. Flippen, Sid Marion and Cliff "Sharlie" Hall, Jane Fraser and The Roberts Sisters; Douglas Keaton, Marie Windsor, The Three Sailors, "Think-a-Drink" Hoffman, Salici's Puppets, Harris and Shore, Susan Miller, Zoraster and Zendavesta
The revue was presented in two acts.

Sketches and Musical Numbers

Act One: Overture (Ray Kavanaugh and His Orchestra); Maysy and Brach ("World's Most Sensational Uni-cycle Act"); Jay C. Flippen (Master of Ceremonies); Sid Marion and Cliff "Sharlie" Hall; Jane Fraser and The Roberts Sisters; "The Old Army Game" (sketch) (Operator: Cliff Hall; Passerby: Sid Marion; Another Passerby: Douglas Keaton; A Girl: Marie Windsor); The Three Sailors; Marie Windsor; "Think-a-Drink" Hoffman
Act Two: Salici's Puppets; "Stand In" ("A Story of Hollywood"); Jay C. Flippen; Harris and Shore; Susan Miller ("Late Star of George Abbott's *Beat the Band*"); Sid Marion and Cliff "Sharlie" Hall (in "The Crazy House"); Finale

Merry-Go-Rounders was one of the era's many variety-cum-vaudeville revues, and while it never reached New York it holds a certain distinction because during its tryout it not only changed titles (to *The Merry-makers*) but also replaced every single cast member. The programs from the revue's opening in Detroit to its closing in Washington, D.C., show that only the revue's musical director Ray Kavanaugh remained. In fact, the Washington program didn't even list a producer. **Sugar 'n' Spice** hadn't credited a director in its program (which is never a good sign), but *The Merrymakers* went a step further by omitting the name of its producer (which perhaps is more disconcerting to the cast than the audience, especially when payday rolls around).

Early in the revue's run, Belle Baker was part of the company, and sang a number of standards (including Irving Berlin's "Blue Skies," which she had first introduced in Richard Rodgers and Lorenz Hart's 1926 Broadway musical *Betsy*).

For the first run, Hollywood comic El Brendel (a trial for some and a guilty pleasure for others) was the master of ceremonies, but as the revue continued he was succeeded by Jay C. Flippen who, like Baker, sang a few old favorites.

After Washington, D.C., the revue was scheduled for a Philadelphia engagement prior to opening in New York; but as noted the production closed permanently after the D.C. run.

SUGAR 'N' SPICE

Theatre and *Performance Dates*: The revue opened on May 26, 1943, at the Copley Theatre in Boston, Mas-sachusetts, where it played for one week (the production may have played in other cities before closing during its pre-Broadway tour).
Sketches: Charles Sherman; other material by Joe Meyers and Lou Daly
Lyrics: Norman Zeno
Music: Al Schofield (some sources cite last name as Scofield)
Direction: Uncredited; *Producer*: Edward Gould; *Choreography*: Don Liberto; *Scenery*: Clarence Hanson (drapes and curtains designed by Raoul Pene du Bois); *Costumes*: Mahieu, Inc.; *Lighting*: Uncredited; *Musical Direction*: Phil Saltman
Cast: David Brooks, Nat Burns, Hal Conklin, Shirley Devon, Dorothy Eaton, Ann (Anne) Francine, Ann Franklin, Fred Keating, Elizabeth Keen, Don Liberto, Larry Martin, Lucille Matthews, Hilda Morse, Edna Russell, Norma Shea, Arthur Simmons, Ruth Tremaine, Murial Williams
The revue was presented in two acts.

Sketches and Musical Numbers

Act One: "We're Not Going to Talk about It" (Murial Williams, Edna Russell, Hilda Morse, Lucille Matthews, Dorothy Eaton, Ruth Tremaine, Shirley Devon, Norma Shea, Hal Conklin, Don Liberto, David Brooks); "Lucky Winner" (Fred Keating, Larry Martin, Hal Conklin, Nat Burns); "You Are All" (Don Liberto, Norma Shea, Lucille Matthews, David Brooks, Nat Burns, Hilda Morse); "All Done" (Ann Francine); "Lost in a Dimout" (Larry Martin, Elizabeth Keen, David Brooks, Ann Francine, Nat Burns, Ann Franklin, Murial Williams, Hal Conklin, Ruth Tremaine); "Behind the Gun" (Fred Keating); "Whistling" (Larry Martin, Edna Russell, Ann Francine, Elizabeth Keen, Arthur Simmons, Lucille Matthews, Norma Shea, Murial Williams, David Brooks, Ruth Tremaine, Dorothy Eaton); "Shadows in the Evening" (David Brooks, Hilda Morse); "The Doctor Gets Better" (Larry Martin, Nat Burns, Murial Williams); "Lick & Riff" (Lucille Matthews, Hilda Morse, Ann Francine); "Smoke" (David Brooks, Don Liberto, Arthur Simmons, Shirley Devon, Ruth Tremaine, Norma Shea, Edna Russell); "Ration Inflation" (Ann Francine, Larry Martin); "Circus" (Entire Cast)

Act Two: "Sugar 'n' Spice" (Fred Keating, Girls); "So Near" (Hal Conklin); "Taxi" (sketch by Charles Sherman and Joseph Erens) (Fred Keating, Ann Francine); "In My Mind" (David Brooks, Don Liberto, Lucille Matthews, Norma Shea); "Murder" (Larry Martin, Ann Francine, Nat Burns, Hal Conklin, David Brooks, Murial Williams, Elizabeth Keen, Sandra Devon, Ruth Tremaine); "Old Way" (Lucille Matthews, Ruth Tremaine); "Lady in the Dark" (Hilda Morse, Company); "Lil" (Lucille Matthews, Company); "Little WAAC" (Don Liberto, Norma Shea); Finale (Entire Company)

The intimate revue *Sugar 'n' Spice* played just one week in Boston and then gave up the notion of heading to Broadway. The evening specialized in topical sallies ("Lost in a Dimout," "Little WAAC," "Ration Inflation," and "Lick & Riff") and at least one Broadway spoof (of **Lady in the Dark**). During the following season, "Lick & Riff" was heard as "A Lick, and a Riff, and a Slow Bounce" in the short-lived Broadway production **Bright Lights of 1944**.

Cast member David Brooks was in various flops during the decade (*Sugar 'n' Spice*, **Marching with Johnny**, and **Shootin' Star**), but also enjoyed leading-man roles in the hit musicals **Bloomer Girl** and **Brigadoon**. Don Liberto and Ann (later Anne) Francine also had lengthy careers on the New York stage, and the latter was a particularly memorable Vera Charles during the original Broadway run of *Mame*.

1943–1944 Season

THE STUDENT PRINCE

Theatre: Broadway Theatre
Opening Date: June 8, 1943; *Closing Date*: October 2, 1943
Performances: 153
Book and *Lyrics*: Dorothy Donnelly
Music: Sigmund Romberg
Based on the 1901 play *Alt-Heidelberg* by Wilhelm Meyer-Forster (which in turn was adapted from Meyer-Forster's 1898 novel *Karl Heinrich*).
Direction: J. J. Shubert; *Producers*: The Messrs. Shubert; *Choreography*: Ruthanne Boris and Alexis Dolinoff; *Scenery*: Watson Barratt; *Costumes*: Stage Costumes, Inc.; *Lighting*: Uncredited; *Musical Direction*: Program credited both Pierre de Reeder and Fred Hoff for musical direction
Cast: Howard Roland (First Lackey), Dennis Dengate (Second Lackey), Fred Lane (Third Lackey), Ken Harlan (Fourth Lackey), William Pringle (Prime Minister Von Mark), *Everett Marshall* (Doctor Engel), Frank Hornaday (Prince Karl Franz), Walter Johnson (Ruder), Ann Pennington (Gretchen), Nathaniel Sack (Toni), Roy Barnes (Detlef), Lyndon Crews (Von Asterberg), Daniel De Paolo (Lucas), Barbara Scully (Kathie), Detmar Poppen (Lutz), Jesse M. Cimberg (Hubert), Nina Varela (Grand Dutchess Anastasia), Helene Arthur (Princess Margaret), Charles Chesney (Captain Tarnitz), Helena Le Berthon (Countess Leydon), Herman Magidson (Rudolph), Jimmy Russell (Postillion); Ladies of the Ensemble: Judy Turnbull, Phyllis Manning, Gloria Hope, Marilyn Merkt, Harriet Williams, Elaine Haslett, Page Morton, Shirley Gordon, Carol Hunter, Jacqueline Max, Helena Le Berthon; Gentlemen of the Ensemble: Colin Harvey, Eden Burrows, Ernst Nibbe, George Tallone, Kent Williams, Elliott Robertson, Gurney Bowman, Jimmy Russell, Herman Magidson, Howard Roland, Don Powell, Fred Lane, Dennis Dexgate, Ken Harlan, Robert LaMarr, George Lombroso, Anthony Coffaro, Dale Spangler, Fred Catania, Andrew Thurston, Stanton Barrett
The operetta was presented in four acts.
The action takes place during the years 1830–1832 in Karlsburg and Heidelberg, Germany.

Musical Numbers

Act One: "By Our Bearing So Sedate" (Howard Roland, Dennis Dengate, Fred Lane, Ken Harlan); "Golden Days" (Frank Hornaday, Everett Marshall); "To the Inn We're Marching" (Roy Barnes, Lyndon Crews, Daniel de Paolo, Barbara Scully, Students); "Drinking Song" (aka "Drink, Drink, Drink") (Roy Barnes, Lyndon Crews, Daniel de Paolo, Students); "You're in Heidelberg" (Frank Hornaday, Everett Marshall); "Welcome to Prince" (Barbara Scully, Walter Johnson, Ann Pennington, Girls); "Deep in My Heart, Dear" (Frank Hornaday, Barbara Scully); "Serenade" (aka "Overhead the Moon Is Beaming") (Frank Hornaday, Everett Marshall, Roy Barnes, Lyndon Crews, Daniel De Paolo, Students); Finale ("Come, Sir, Will You Join Our Noble Saxon Corps") (Frank Hornaday, Barbara Scully, Roy Barnes, Lyndon Crews, Daniel De

Paolo, Walter Johnson, Detmar Poppen, Everett Marshall, Ann Pennington, Jesse M. Cimberg, Students, Girls)

Act Two: "I've Never Heard about Love" (Everett Marshall, Students); "Student Life" (Frank Hornaday, Barbara Scully, Everett Marshall, Roy Barnes, Ann Pennington, Lyndon Crews, Daniel De Paolo, Students); "Golden Days" (reprise) (Everett Marshall); "Deep in My Heart, Dear" (reprise) (Frank Hornaday, Barbara Scully); Finale (Frank Hornaday, Barbara Scully, William Pringle, Everett Marshall)

Act Three: "Waltz Ensemble" (Ambassadors, Officers, Helena Le Berthon, Baron Arnheim [Performer Unknown], Ladies of Court); "Just We Two" (Helene Arthur, Charles Chesney, Officers); "Gavotte" (Frank Hornaday, Helene Arthur, Helena Le Berthon, Charles Chesney); "What Memories" (aka "Thoughts Will Come Back to Me of Days Gone By") (Frank Hornaday); Finale ("Never More Will Come Again Those Days of Youth") (Frank Hornaday, Barbara Scully, Everett Marshall)

Act Four: "Sing a Little Song" (Students and Girls); "To the Inn We're Marching" (reprise) (Roy Barnes, Lyndon Crews, Students); "Serenade" (reprise) (Roy Barnes, Lyndon Crews, Students, Frank Hornaday); "Come, Boys, Let's All Be Gay, Boys" (Roy Barnes, Lyndon Crews, Students); "Deep in My Heart, Dear" (reprise) (Frank Hornaday, Barbara Scully, Herman Magidson, Ann Pennington, Jesse M. Cimberg, Detmar Poppen, Nina Varela, Roy Barnes, Lyndon Crews, Entire Ensemble)

As *The Student Prince in Heidelberg*, Sigmund Romberg's richly melodic operetta opened in New York on December 2, 1924, at Jolson's Theatre for 608 performances; Howard Marsh (who later created the role of Gaylord Ravenal in the original production of *Show Boat*) was Prince Karl, Ilse Marvenga was Kathie, and Greek Evans was Doctor Engel. From Romberg's sweetly nostalgic music box poured forth one of Broadway's most gorgeously romantic scores: the glorious ballads "Deep in My Heart, Dear" and "Serenade" (aka "Overhead the Moon Is Beaming"), the lilting waltz "Just We Two," the stirring march "To the Inn We're Marching," the carefree and lighthearted "Student Life," and perhaps the ultimate Broadway salute to drinking, the rich male chorus "Drinking Song" (aka "Drink, Drink, Drink"). And serving as a theme song throughout the evening was the bittersweet "Golden Days."

The simple story, told straight and without a touch of the tongue-in-cheek, centered on Prince Karl, who attends school at Heidelberg University for a few months and falls in love with the barmaid Kathie, who works at the nearby Three Gold Apples Inn. But royal duty calls: when his father dies, he becomes king and must enter into an arranged marriage with a princess.

At a $2.75 top, the revival of *The Student Prince* seems to have been a bargain. It offered a large cast and chorus, and was reasonably faithful to the original production. If some of the critics weren't overwhelmed by Frank Hornaday's Prince Karl and Barbara Scully's Kathie, others were. Burns Mantle in the *New York Daily News* found the cast "entirely adequate" and said Hornaday was "equal" to the role's vocal demands and Scully was a "lively and active" young singer; Wilella Waldorf in the *New York Post* found Hornaday "extremely uneven" and Scully somewhat "shrill"; and Louis Kronenberger in *PM* said Hornaday's voice "never quite finds itself" and Scully was "vocally not very satisfying." But Burton Rascoe in the *New York World-Telegram* devoted two effusive paragraphs to Scully; he said she was "the loveliest, the most exquisite, the most gracious and the most talented apparition that has adorned the New York stage since Marilyn Miller melted" Broadway hearts many years earlier.

Howard Barnes in the *New York Herald Tribune* felt the operetta was somewhat "ponderously" revived in a "routine" manner; Kronenberger said the evening was not "inspired"; and Waldorf felt the "good old" Romberg songs were "pretty shabbily treated." But Herrick Brown in the *New York Sun* noted that while the revival wasn't the "sprightliest," it nonetheless was one of the "most tuneful" musicals on Broadway.

Burns Mantle seemed a bit uncomfortable with the German setting and its students, and noted that "today German students just aren't popular." And John Anderson in the *New York Journal-American* said that while Heidelberg may have lost its "romantic glamour" because of the Nazis, the Old Heidelberg of the operetta was laid in a Ruritanian "Never-Never Land" of "broken hearts and gold braids." But as if to emphasize the world situation, two or three critics noted that during the performance "screaming" air-raid siren tests on the streets filtered into the theatre.

The revival included two favorites from the past, Metropolitan Opera singer Everett Marshall (in the role of Doctor Engel) and former Broadway dancer Ann Pennington (as Gretchen, one of the maids at the Three Gold Apples Inn). Pennington had appeared in numerous editions of both the *Ziegfeld Follies* and *George White's Scandals*; in the 1926 edition of the *Scandals* she introduced "The Black Bottom," and was one of the quartet (with ensemble) that introduced "Take Me Back to Manhattan" in Cole Porter's 1930 revue *The New Yorkers*.

The current production omitted a few songs from the original production of *The Student Prince*, including "Garlands Bright," "Farmer Jacob," and "Farewell, Dear."

Prior to the 1943 production, the operetta had been revived on Broadway at the Majestic Theatre on January 29, 1931, for forty-five performances. The work was later revived five times by the New York City Opera Company at the New York State Theatre: on August 29, 1980 (thirteen performances); on August 27, 1981 (six performances); on July 5, 1985 (nine performances); on July 7, 1987 (fourteen performances); and on August 14, 1993 (fifteen performances). For the company's 1985 revival, Jerry Hadley was Prince Karl.

The London premiere took place at His Majesty's Theatre on February 3, 1926, for ninety-six performances (Ilse Marvenga reprised her role of Kathie, and Prince Karl was played by Allan Prior).

The operetta was filmed by MGM in 1928 and 1954. The first was a silent version directed by Ernst Lubitsch, and the cast included Ramon Novarro (Prince Karl) and Norma Shearer (Kathie). The second adaptation, directed by Richard Thorpe, was colorful and melodic and had an old-fashioned charm about it. Mario Lanza had been scheduled to play the title role, but was replaced by Edmund Purdom (whose singing voice was dubbed by Lanza); Ann Blyth was Kathie, and others in the cast were Louis Calhern, S. Z. "Cuddles" Sakall, Edmund Gwenn, John Williams, Evelyn Varden, and Betta St. John. The film included three pleasant new songs, "Summertime in Heidelberg," "I'll Walk with God," and "Beloved" (lyrics by Paul Francis Webster and music by Nicholas Brodszky). Lanza later recorded songs from the film (including the three new ones), and these were released with other Lanza vocals by Sepia (CD # 1200).

The most complete recording of the score was released by That's Entertainment Records on a 2-CD set (# CDTER2-1172).

Alt-Heidelberg was first seen on Broadway as *Heidelberg, or When All the World Was Young*; it opened at the Princess Theatre on December 15, 1902; another version of the drama was produced as *Old Heidelberg* at the Lyric Theatre on October 12, 1903.

Romberg's version of *Alt-Heidelberg* wasn't the first lyric adaptation of the material. The opera *Eidelberga mia* premiered in Genoa, Italy, in 1908 (music by Ubaldo Pacchierotti and libretto by Alberto Colantuoni).

EARLY TO BED
"A New Musical Comedy" / "A Fairy Tale for Grown-Ups"

Theatre: Broadhurst Theatre
Opening Date: June 17, 1943; *Closing Date*: May 13, 1944
Performances: 382
Book and *Lyrics*: George Marion Jr.
Music: Thomas "Fats" Waller; special ballet music by Baldwin Bergersen
Direction: Dialogue directed by Robert Alton; production under the supervision of Alfred Bloomingdale; during run, direction credited to Richard Kollmar; *Producer*: Richard Kollmar; *Choreography*: Robert Alton; *Scenery*: George Jenkins; *Costumes*: Miles White; *Lighting*: Uncredited; *Musical Direction*: Archie Bleyer
Cast: Ruth Webb (Opal), Anthony Blair (Bartender), John Lund (O'Connor), David Bethea (Gardener), Maurice Ellis (Gendarme), Jeni Le Gon (Lily Ann), Ralph Bunker (Mayor), Louise Jarvis (Marcella), Choo Choo Johnson (Pauline), Peggy Cordrey (Interlude), Mary Small (Jessica), Eleanor Boleyn (Butch), Helen Bennett (Duchess), Honey Murray (Minerva), Harold Cromer (Caddy), Muriel Angelus (Madame Rowena), Angela Green (Isabella), Bob Howard (Pooch), George Zoritch (Pablo), Richard Kollmar (El Magnifico), Jane Deering (Lois), Jimmy Gardiner (Wilbur), George Baxter (Coach), Jane Kean (Eileen), Charlotte Maye (Charlotte), Burt Harger (Burt), Evelyn Ward (Naomi), Charles Kraft (Charles), Harrison Muller (Junior), Franklyn Fox (Admiral Saint-Cassette); Dean Murphy (Radio representation of President Roosevelt's voice); Pigeons: Deanne Benmore, Helen Bennett, Eleanor Boleyn, Marianne Cude, Kay Dowd, Marge Ellis, Claire Loring, Virginia McGraw, Dolores Milan, Olive Nicolson, Helen Osborne, June Reynolds, Olga Roberts, Isabel Rolfe, Jean Scott, Toni Stuart, Evelyn Ward; Track Team: George Hunter, Thomas Kenny, Charles Kraft, John Martin, Harrison Muller, Tom Powers, Robert Trout, Jack Wilkins
The musical was presented in two acts.

The opening scene of each act takes place in the present time in New York City; otherwise all the action occurs in prewar Martinique.

Musical Numbers

Act One: "A Girl Who Doesn't Ripple When She Bends" (Mary Small, Honey Murray, Girls, Harold Cromer); "There's a Man in My Life" (Muriel Angelus); "Me and My Old World Charm" (Richard Kollmar); "Supple Couple" (Mary Small, Jeni Le Gon, Bob Howard, Richard Kollmar); "Slightly Less Than Wonderful" (Jane Deering, George Zoritch); "Slightly Less Than Wonderful" (reprise) (Jeni Le Gon, Bob Howard, Harold Cromer, David Bethea, Maurice Ellis); "This Is So Nice (It Must Be Illegal)" (Richard Kollmar); "Hi-De-Ho High" (Bob Howard, Jeni Le Gon, Harold Cromer, David Bethea, Maurice Ellis, Evelyn Ward, Charles Kraft, Ensemble); "The Ladies Who Sing with a Band" (Mary Small, Muriel Angelus, Jane Kean, Jane Deering); "There's 'Yes' in the Air" (Richard Kollmar, Mary Small, Jane Kean, Jane Deering, Burt Harger, Charlotte Maye, Honey Murray, Ensemble)

Act Two: "Get Away, Young Man" (Jane Kean, Harrison Muller, Charles Kraft, Jimmy Gardiner, Ensemble); "Long Time No Song" (Richard Kollmar, Muriel Angelus); "Early to Bed" (Mary Small, Jane Deering, George Zoritch, Burt Harger, Charlotte Maye, Harold Cromer, Ensemble); "There's a Man in My Life" (reprise) (Muriel Angelus); "When the Nylons Bloom Again" (Bob Howard, Jeni Le Gon); Finale (Entire Company)

Early to Bed was one of the season's hits, and ran for almost a year. But considering the subject matter of George Marion Jr.'s book, it wasn't a likely candidate for a Hollywood film adaptation or even a national tour. The setting was prewar Martinique, where Madame Rowena (Muriel Angelus) runs a bordello called the Angry Pigeon with her brood of young-lady pigeons. When an old flame (and former matador) El Magnifico (Richard Kollmar) shows up, she leads him to believe her establishment is a girls' finishing school and hotel. Soon El Magnifico's son Pablo (George Zoritch) and nightclub singer Lois (Jane Deering) are involved in a car accident and are carried unconscious into the Angry Pigeon; when they awake, they too think they're recuperating in a hotel. And then there's a group of visiting California college boys, all members of the track team on a goodwill tour, and of course they and their coach are also under the impression the Angry Pigeon is a hotel (but presumably the boys quickly size up the situation).

The evening was clearly a one-joke show, but its ribald humor and situations went over well with wartime audiences. There was lavish and colorful décor by set-designer George Jenkins and costumer Miles White, lively dances by Robert Alton, and a large and game company which added merriment to the charade. It also didn't hurt the show's publicity machine when during the Boston tryout the censors demanded wholesale cuts to the musical in order to preserve the sensibilities of Boston audiences; and so for Boston the Angry Pigeon was a gambling casino instead of a sporting house. But the show's publicists comfortingly assured Broadway audiences that once the musical moved to New York all the deleted lines and situations would be restored to their full and former glory.

"Fats" Waller's score was the highlight of the musical; the songs which have surfaced are bright and tuneful, and cry out for a studio cast recording from an enterprising record company. "The Ladies Who Sing with a Band" is the score's gem, one of those self-assured struts which practically define the words "musical comedy"; its insinuating and irresistible melody and clever lyric make it easy to see why it was one of the era's showstoppers. Other memorable songs are the comedy numbers "When the Nylons Bloom Again" (a song dear to the hearts of the women in the wartime audience) and "Hi-De-Ho High"; the soft and sinuous ballad "There's a Man in My Life"; and the upbeat ballads "Slightly Less Than Wonderful" and "This Is So Nice (It Must Be Illegal)." Of the musical's thirteen songs, eleven were singled out by the critics (only "A Girl Who Doesn't Ripple When She Bends" and "Supple Couple" weren't mentioned, and they sure have terrific titles).

The critics complained that the musical's one joke was stretched almost to the breaking point, but they nonetheless admitted the show was lavish, lively, and colorful. Lewis Nichols in the *New York Times* said the chorus was "the most beautiful in the land," the décor was "definitely pre-priority," and Robert Alton's choreography for the first act finale ("There's 'Yes' in the Air") was excellent. He also praised "There's a Man in My Life" ("a pretty love song"), "Hi-De-Ho High" ("good Waller"), "The Ladies Who Sing with a Band" (an "excellent parody"), and singled out two others ("Slightly Less Than Wonderful" and "This Is So Nice").

G. E. Blackford in the *New York Journal-American* found the evening "a lot of fun—bright, lively, smart," with a book "risqué enough to spice up the proceedings." Waller's songs were "delightful," and he singled out "Me and My Old World Charm," "Slightly Less Than Wonderful," "Hi-De-Ho High," "Get Away, Young Man," and "When the Nylons Bloom Again" (he noted the latter reached a "pinnacle in rhythm and rhyme"). But it was "The Ladies Who Sing with a Band" which took "top honors"; it was a "hum-dinger, a dilly of the first order."

Howard Barnes in the *New York Herald Tribune* said the evening was "lively, tuneful and vulgar," and predicted the show with its "very tasteless" book would "catch on as a bit of escapist hot-cha"; he liked "Hi-De-Ho High," "Long Time No Song," "There's a Man in My Life," and the title number, and found "The Ladies Who Sing with a Band" a "delight." Louis Kronenberger in *PM* said Waller's score was "acceptable," by "no means exciting," but nonetheless "agreeable," and "The Ladies Who Sing with a Band" was the "live-liest" in its "amusing if ear-splitting spoof of the girls who murder the mike"; he also noted that "There's a Man in My Life" was the evening's "torchiest" song. Burns Mantle in the *New York Daily News* said the evening was "noisy, gorgeous, leggy and without wit." He commented that Waller's songs were "brisk and singable" but seemed "curiously unmusical," and suggested this was because the singers "shouted" too much; he predicted the "lively" songs would no doubt improve upon a second hearing.

Herrick Brown in the *New York Sun* warned that *Early to Bed* was not for the "squeamish"; as for Waller's score, "The Ladies Who Sing with a Band" was the evening's show-stopper; "Slightly Less Than Wonderful" and "Hi-De-Ho High" were bound to be popular; the other songs were "lively" and rhythmic enough "to set toes to tapping on stage and off"; and "There's 'Yes' in the Air" was an "especially spectacular and eye-filling delight."

Burton Rascoe in the *New York World Telegram* found the musical "immensely pleasing" and noted the décor's color effects were "prismatic and opalescent." From out-of-town reports, he had feared the score would be all "jive and jamboree," but was pleasantly surprised to discover it was the kind of music you could whistle, and "from the overture to the finale" the audience's eardrums would be "pleasantly tickled and caressed." Three songs ("This Is So Nice," "Slightly Less Than Wonderful," and "Hi-De-Ho High") were "dandies" and two other "song hits" were "There's a Man in My Life" and "When the Nylons Bloom Again." But it was "The Ladies Who Sing with a Band" that knocked him out: it was "one of the funniest musical numbers you ever heard."

Although the musical wasn't her "dish," Wilella Waldorf in the *New York Post* noted the evening offered "sultry tropical scenery," "colorful" costumes, "torrid" dances, and "agreeable" music. And, oh, yes, the "One Joke" show was able to squeeze "double, triple, sometimes even quadruple" meanings out its One Joke. She was surprised to note the loudest applause was for the smoothly shifting and changing scenery. Indeed, the audience was in "such a state of ecstasy" over these maneuvers that she was surprised the stagehands didn't move the scenery around again for an encore. Since songs could be reprised, why not scenery? But she supposed there was some rule in the stagehands' union contract which prevented encores for scenery changes.

"The Ladies Who Sing with a Band" is included in the collection *Broadway Musicals of 1943* (Bayview CD # RNBW-015), and "Slightly Less Than Wonderful," "Hi-De-Ho High," and "This Is So Nice" are included in the collection *Everybody Else Revisited* (Painted Smiles CD # PSCD-146). And throughout the marathon 1,604-performance run of *Ain't Misbehavin'* (Broadway's 1978 tribute to "Fats" Waller) two songs from *Early to Bed* were included (and can be heard on RCA Victor's cast recording), "The Ladies Who Sing with a Band" and "When the Nylons Bloom Again."

During the Boston tryout, "On Your Mark" (which featured the college boys) was cut; and George Marion Jr., was credited with the staging of the dialogue sequences.

During the show-stopping "The Ladies Who Sing with a Band," Mary Small, Muriel Angelus, Jane Kean, and Jane Deering also offered brief interpolations of popular songs (no doubt to show how lady band singers demolish the tunes), such as "Jim," "You Made Me Love You (I Didn't Want to Do It)," "Love Is the Sweet-est Thing," "Wanting You," "Love Me or Leave Me," "All of Me," "Love, Your Magic Spell Is Everywhere," "That Old Black Magic," "I Want My Mama," "Oh, Johnny, Oh," and "What Is This Thing Called Love?" "The Ladies Who Sing With a Band" makes a good pairing with Richard Rodgers and Lorenz Hart's "I Like to Recognize the Tune" from *Too Many Girls* (1939), which, like *Early to Bed*, had a book by George Marion Jr.

Incidentally, the musical was bookended with scenes that took place in a New York bar. You see, some-one in the bar was telling the tale of the Angry Pigeon, a story that never really happened (as the show's tag warned, the musical was a "fairy tale for grown-ups").

About halfway through the musical's run, "Fats" Waller unexpectedly died. His score for *Early to Bed* is not only a delightful one, it's also historic: it appears to be the first musical by a black composer that was specifically written for white characters (albeit a few of the musical's characters were black). Later, Duke Ellington's musical **Beggar's Holiday** featured a mostly all-white cast, and his *Pousse-Café* (1966) had an all-white cast.

THE VAGABOND KING
"A MUSICAL PLAY"

Theatre: Shubert Theatre
Opening Date: June 29, 1943; *Closing Date*: August 14, 1943
Performances: 56
Based on the 1901 play *If I Were King* by Justin Huntly McCarthy.
Book and *Lyrics*: Brian Hooker and Russell Janney
Music: Rudolf Friml
Direction: Staged by George Ermoloff and entire production under the supervision of Russell Janney; *Producer*: Russell Janney; *Scenery*: Raymond Sovey; *Costumes*: James Reynolds; *Lighting*: Uncredited; *Musical Direction*: Joseph Majer
Cast: Artells Dickson (Rene de Montigny), Bert Stanley (Casin Cholet), George Karle (Jehan Le Loup), Jann Moore (Margot), Evelyn Wick (Isabeau), Rosalind Madison (Jehanneton), Arline Thomson (Huguette Du Hamel), Will H. Philbrick (Guy Tabarie), Douglas Gilmore (Tristan L'Hermite), Jose Ruben (Louis XI), John Brownlee (Francois Villon), Frances McCann (Katherine De Vaucelles), Ben Roberts (Thibaut D'Aussigny), Charles Henderson (Captain of Scotch Archers), Franz Bendtsen (An Astrologer), Teri Keane (Lady Mary), Dan Gallagher (Noel of Anjou), Curtis Cooksey (Oliver Le Dain), Earl Ashcroft (Herald of Burgundy), Betty Berry (The Queen), Craig Newton (The Hangman), Vincent Henry (The Cardinal); Premier Dancers: Julia Harvath, Dorothee Littlefield, and Peter Birch; Two Dice Players: Kenneth Sonnenberg, Birger Hallderson; Corps de Ballet: Franca Baldwin, Sally Sheppard, Carlye Ramey, Patricia Leith, Muriel Breunig, Anna Jacqueline, Ginee Richardson, Davide Daniel; Ladies of the Ensemble: Ruth Barber, Muriel Blane, Zola Palmer, Helen Carlson, Claire Wells, Ann Garland, Betty Berry, Doris Blake, Linda Kay, Katrina Van Oss, Rosalind Madison, Iris Howard, Helen George, Evelyn Wick, Mary David, Shirley Conklin, Mary Burns, Bernice Hoffman, Joan Barrie, Mary Ellen Bright; Gentlemen of the Ensemble: Frederick Langford, Vincent Henry, Charles Arnold, Robert Kimberly, Kenneth Sonnenberg, Chris Gerard, Earle Ashcroft, Al Bartolet, William Gephart, Jay Patrick, Birger Hallderson, George Walker, Norvel Campbell, Max Plagmann, Ernest Pavano, George Beach, Otto Simetti, Jerry Madden, Graham Alexander, Jerry Clayton, Harry Nordin, Charles Trott
The operetta was presented in four acts.
The action takes place in Old Paris during the period of Louis XI.

Musical Numbers

Act One: Overture (Orchestra); Opening Chorus ("Life Is Like a Bubble in Our Glasses") (Ensemble); "Love for Sale" (Arline Thomson; danced by Peter Birch, Dorothee Littlefield, Ballet Dancers); "Drinking Song" (aka "A Flagon of Wine") (Will H. Philbrick, Male Chorus); "Song of the Vagabonds" ("Onward! Onward! Swords against the Foe!") (John Brownlee, Chorus); "Some Day" (Frances McCann); "Only a Rose" (Frances McCann, John Brownlee); "Fight Music" and Finaletto (Entire Company)
Act Two: "Hunting Number" ("Men Hunt Today for a Wilder Sort of Game") (Dan Gallagher, Ensemble); Ballet (Diana: Julia Horvath; Count Etienne: Peter Birch; Ballet Dancers); "Tomorrow" (Frances McCann, John Brownlee, Women's Chorus); Finale (Entire Company)
Act Three: "Nocturne" ("In the Night, while the Winds Are Murmuring Low") (Ensemble; Obligato: Helen George and Fred Langford); "Tarantella" (Dorothee Littlefield, Julia Horvath, Peter Birch, Ballet Dancers); "Serenade" ("Lullaby! Plim-plum") (Will H. Philbrick, Curtis Cooksey, Teri Keane); "Waltz Huguette"

("Hearts May Flower—for an Hour") (Arline Thomson, Dan Gallagher, Julia Horvath, Dorothee Little-field, Ballet Dancers); "Love Me Tonight" (Frances McCann, John Brownlee); Finale (Entire Company)
Act Four: "Te Deum" (Ensemble); "Victory March" (reprise of "Song of the Vagabonds") (Ensemble); Finale Ultimo ("Only a Rose" reprise) (Frances McCann, John Brownlee, Entire Company)

Rudolf Friml's operetta was one of the most popular of the 1920s. When it opened at the Casino Theatre on September 21, 1925, it ran for 511 performances with Dennis King in the title role. Friml's richly melodic score included such ballads as "Some Day," "Only a Rose," and "Love Me Tonight," and of course there was a lovely waltz ("Huguette Waltz"), a stirring march ("Song of the Vagabonds" ["Onward! Onward! Swords against the Foe!"]), and a hearty "Drinking Song" (aka "A Flagon of Wine").

The vagabond king is no less than French poet Francois Villon. He's involved with the tragic Huguette but loves noblewoman Katherine de Vaucelles, who is related to King Louis XI. In disguise at an inn, the king hears Villon making fun of him and, upon consultation with his astrologer, Louis decides to make Villon king for a day, with the idea that Villon's last act as king will be to condemn Villon to the gallows. But Villon rises to the occasion, and because the Duke of Burgundy and his followers hope to overthrow Louis, Villon and his "lousy rabble of low degree" overcome the dissenters and thus save both the nation and the crown. Huguette has meanwhile committed suicide, and Villon can marry Katherine since he's proven himself a hero to King Louis.

Russell Janney, the operetta's original producer (and the work's co-librettist and co-lyricist), revived the musical with a sumptuous production. But the critics were less than impressed with the casting, and were a bit disappointed with Metropolitan Opera singer John Brownlee, whom they felt lacked the dash and elan that Dennis King had brought to the role. Despite generally good reviews for the overall production, the revival closed after a disappointing seven weeks. (With the exception of "The Song of the Archers," it appears the entire score was retained for the revival; and except for a comment about meat shortages, there were no topical sallies added to the script.)

Lewis Nichols in the *New York Times* predicted the operetta would be around for a long spell; he praised the lavish décor, noting Janney was not one to offer "drooping" scenery and "tattered" costumes; further, the "splendid" score was well sung and acted by Brownlee, and Frances McCann made an impressive Katherine. Of course, the book was sometimes "tiresome" and the comedy was regrettably "this side of perfect," but the evening on the whole was redeemed by the "excellent" singers and the colorful sets and costumes. But Wilella Waldorf in the *New York Post* felt the musical "inclined to become a bit wearisome" and "uncommonly silly"; for pace, she suggested Janney combine the second and third acts; and she noted that Brownlee sang "far better" than any Broadway baritone she could remember, but felt his acting skills were lacking.

Howard Barnes in the *New York Herald Tribune* said the "second-rate" operetta was "on the sorry side," and concluded that the evening was a "theatrical left-over" with "not much left over"; and Louis Kronen-berger in *PM* felt that while the revival had no "particular distinction," it nonetheless had a "certain vigor"; it lacked "style" but had "schmaltz enough," and "if you liked it once, you'll like it again." Although Burton Rascoe in the *New York World-Telegram* had reservations about Brownlee and some of the staging choices, he assumed the otherwise "fine production" would enjoy a prosperous run.

John Anderson in the *New York Journal-American* felt the singing left "something to be desired" and noted some of the basic plot points were essentially foolish; but he said the opening night audience "gave resounding evidence" that they enjoyed the revival. Burns Mantle in *PM* said the libretto offered a more "lively romance" than the ones depicted in **The Student Prince** and **Blossom Time**; that the evening's comedy was superior to the other two; and Friml's score was "rich in melody and satisfying in body." In all, the venerable operetta was "superior" to "most of the jive and jingle stuff of this day."

The London production opened at the Winter Garden Theatre on April 19, 1927, for 480 performances.

The musical was filmed twice by Paramount, in 1930 and 1956. The first version was photographed in gorgeous Technicolor and retained six songs from the original production ("Huguette Waltz," "Love Me To-night," "Nocturne," "Only a Rose," "Some Day," and "Song of the Vagabonds") as well as a few new ones that weren't composed by Friml; Dennis King reprised his stage role of Villon, and the cast included Jeanette MacDonald (Katherine) and Lillian Roth (Huguette); Ludwig Berger directed. The second adaptation was directed by Michael Curtiz and choreographed by Hanya Holm. It starred Oreste (aka Oreste Kirkop), Kathryn Grayson (Katherine), Rita Moreno (Huguette), Sir Cedric Hardwick, and Walter Hampden. Four songs from the original production were retained ("Huguette Waltz," "Only a Rose," "Some Day," and "Song of the Vagabonds"); and Friml wrote five new ones (all with lyrics by Johnny Burke), "Bon Jour," "Vive La You," "This Same Heart," "Companions," and "Watch Out for the Devil." It appears a sixth song ("Lord, I'm Glad I Know Thee," lyric by Burke and music by Victor Young) was considered for the film.

A complete 2-CD of the score by the Ohio Light Opera was released by Troy/Albany Records (CD # TROY-738-39); there was no soundtrack album released of the 1956 film version, but Oreste (and Jean Fenn) recorded many songs from the score, including a few of the new ones written for the film (RCA Victor LP # LM-2004). The script was published in softcover by Samuel French in an undated edition (probably 1956).

THE MERRY WIDOW

Theatre: Majestic Theatre
Opening Date: August 4, 1943; *Closing Date*: May 6, 1944
Performances: 322
Book: Adaptation by Sidney Sheldon and Ben Roberts from the original libretto by Victor Leon and Leo Stein
Lyrics: Adrian Ross (from the original lyrics by Victor Leon and Leo Stein); special lyrics by Robert Gilbert
Music: Franz Lehar (music adapted by Robert Stolz)
Direction: Felix Brentano; *Producers*: Yolanda Mero-Irion (A New Opera Company Production); *Choreography*: George Balanchine; *Scenery*: Howard Bay; *Costumes*: Walter Florell; *Lighting*: Uncredited; *Musical Direction*: Robert Stolz
Cast: Karl Parkas (The King), Melville Cooper (Popoff), Robert Field (Jolidon), Ruth Matteson (Natalie), Ethelyne Holt (Olga Bardini), Ralph Dumke (General Bardini), Gene Barry (Novakovich), Alex Alexander (Cascada), Arnold Spector (Khadja), Josephine Griffin (Guest), Mark Farrington (Guest), David Wayne (Nish), *Marta Eggerth* (Sonia Sadoya), *Jan Kiepura* (Prince Danilo), Lisette Verea (Clo-Clo), Wana Allison (Lo-Lo), Bobbie Howell (Frou-Frou), Babs Heath (Do-Do), Lubov Roudenko (Premiere Danseuse), Milada Mladova (Premiere Danseuse), Chris Volkoff (Premier Dancer), James Starbuck (Premier Dancer), Karl Farkas (Gaston); Ladies of the Ensemble: Janie Janvier, Doris Pape, Birute Ramoska, Renee Rochelle, Peggy Turnley, Marya Woczeska, Frances Yeend, Marie Fox, Arline Carmen, Josephine Griffin, Florence McGovern, Irene Jordan; Gentlemen of the Ensemble: Jerome Cardinale, Frank Finn, John Harrold, Robert La Marr, Albert Schiller, Nathaniel Sprinzena, Edward Visca, Mark Farrington, Nicholas Torzs, Robert Tower, Alan Vaughan, Dennis Dengate; Ballet Dancers: Wana Allison, June Graham, Babs (Barbara) Heath, Bobbie Howell, Zoya Leporsky, Jayne Ward, David Ahdar, Alan Banks, Nicholas Nagallenes, Frank Moncion, Stanley Zompakos, James Starbuck; Lackies: Morgan Kendall, George Buzante, Eddie Dane
The operetta was presented in three acts.
The action takes place in Paris during the summer of 1906.

Musical Numbers

Act One: "A Dutiful Wife" (Ruth Matteson, Robert Field); "In Marsovia" (Marta Eggerth, with Ralph Dumke, Alex Alexander, and Male Chorus); "Maxim's" (Jan Kiepura); "Polka" (Lubov Roudenko, James Starbuck); Finale (Jan Kiepura, Marta Eggerth, Melville Cooper, Ralph Dumke, Alex Alexander, Ensemble)
Act Two: "Vilia" (Marta Eggerth); "Marsovian Dance" (Milada Mladova, Chris Volkoff, Corps de Ballet); "The Pavilion" (Jan Kiepura); "The Women" (a) Melville Cooper, Ralph Dumke, Robert Field, David Wayne, Arnold Spector, Gene Barry, and Alex Alexander; (b) The above, with June Graham and Babs Heath; and (c) Josephine Griffin, Renee Rochelle, Arlene Carmen, Marya Woczeska, Doris Pape, Janie Janiver; "I Love You So" (Jan Kiepura, Martha Eggerth; danced by Milada Mladova, Chris Volkoff, Corps de Ballet); Finale (Entire Company)
Act Three: "The Girls at Maxim's (Lisette Verea; danced by Lubov Rubov Roudenko and Ballet Girls); "Kuiawiak" (music by Henri Wieniawski) (sung in Polish by Jan Kiepura); "I Love You So" (reprise) (Jan Kiepura, Marta Eggerth); Finale (Entire Company)

The New Opera Company's lavish production of Franz Lehar's *The Merry Widow* was a long-running and prosperous follow-up to their **Rosalinda**, which had opened almost a year earlier. Although revivals of such

American operettas as **The Student Prince**, **The Vagabond King**, and **Robin Hood** didn't do well during the period, there was a definite market for the European variety.

The critics praised the décor and costumes and George Balanchine's dancers, but were somewhat mixed in their feelings about Marta Eggerth and Jan Kiepura. Ward Morehouse in the *New York Sun* said Kiepura gave Prince Danilo a "vocal power" the role usually never enjoyed, and Wilella Waldorf in the *New York Post* said his singing was "immense" but too much in the tradition of grand opera and thus needed a lighter touch. John Chapman in the *New York Daily News* suggested everyone in the production was "too serious"; Kiepura seemed to feel the need to sing "the hell out of his role," but he really should have had "some fun" with it, too.

Burton Rascoe in the *New York World-Telegram* said Kiepura seemed nervous during the first act and his pitch was too high; but he sang "beautifully" and perhaps his best moment was an interpolation in Polish ("Kuiawiak") which "was just as understandable as his songs in English." Waldorf noted his accent was so "intense" she actually thought for a moment he was singing "Kuiawiak" in English.

Rascoe also noted Kiepura was "too young and innocent looking," and thus his "sweet, babyish sort of face" made it difficult to believe he was the dashing man-about-town involved in amorous pursuits with a bevy of Parisian lovelies. Further, he couldn't really dance, and thus playgoers were denied the pleasure of watching Danilo and Sonia take the floor with the famous merry widow waltz; instead, they took a few tentative steps and then the dancers took over.

Lewis Nichols in the *New York Times* said Eggerth was "beautiful" but failed to put over "Vilia"; and Waldorf noted she sang of "Vilia the Vitch." Chapman said she was "quite beautiful"; Howard Barnes in the *New York Herald Tribune* noted she sang "charmingly"; and Louis Kronenberger in *PM* said she was "attractive" and "sang pleasantly."

Waldorf noted the production was the "most opulent" she'd ever seen of the operetta; and Morehouse said the production had "color, beauty, ballet effects and imagination." As for Balanchine's choreography, G. E. Blackford in the *New York Journal-American* felt it was "perfectly tuned to the tempo and spirit" of the story and provided a "kaleidoscopic mélange of grace and beauty." Rascoe said the can-can at Maxim's was "nifty," and Nichols said the can-can was "fast" and the waltzes "graceful."

The production marked early Broadway appearances by Gene Barry and David Wayne. The conductor was composer Robert Stolz, who had conducted the premiere performance of the operetta in Vienna in 1905. Kronenberger said the orchestra played with "dash and zip," and Chapman said the music was "under [his] loving and knowing direction," which included "a honey of a string section."

In an interesting side note, Kronenberger reported there was one "unpleasant" aspect to the music because he understood Lehar had "played ball" with the Nazis. But the critic took some satisfaction that the composer wouldn't receive any royalties from the current production.

For more information about the operetta, see entry for the 1942 revival.

RUN LITTLE CHILLUN

Theatre: Hudson Theatre
Opening Date: August 11, 1943; *Closing Date*: August 26, 1943
Performances: 16
Book, *Lyrics*, and *Music*: Hall Johnson
Direction: Clarence Muse (production supervised by Lew Cooper); *Producers*: Lew Cooper in association with Meyer Davis and George Jessel; *Choreography*: Felicia Sorel; *Scenery* and *Costumes*: Perry Watkins; *Lighting*: Uncredited; *Musical Direction*: Hall Johnson
Cast: Bessie Guy (Sister Mattie Fullilove), Bertha Powell (Sister Flossie Lou Little), Rosalie King (Sister Mahalie Ockletree), Maggie Carter (Sister Judy Ann Hicks), Eloise Uggams (Sister Lulu Jane Hunt), Eva Vaughan (Sister Susie May Hunt), Robert Harvey (Brother Esau Redd), Wardell Saunders (Brother Bartholomew Little), William O. Davis (Brother Goliath Simpson), Randall Steplight (Brother Jeremiah Johnson), Elijah Hodges (Brother George W. Jenkins), Helen Dowdy (Ella Jones), Edward Roche (Clarence Jackson), Miriam Burton (Bessiola), Awilda Frazier (Organist), Olive Ball (The Reverend Sister Luella Strong), Louis Sharp (Reverend Jones), Caleb Peterson (Jim), Charles Holland (Charlie), Edna Mae Harris (Sulamai), Violet McDowell (Sister Mary Lou Mack), Service Bell (The Elder Tongola), P. Jay Sidney (Brother Moses), Maude

Simmons (Mother Kanda), Fredye Marshall (Sister Mata), Walter Mosby (Brother Jo-Ba), Gertrude Saunders (Mag), Viola Anderson (Belle), Myrtle Anderson (Mame), Lulu B. King (Sue Scott), Adolph Henderson (Sexton of the Hope Baptist Church), Roger Alford (Brother Absalom Brown), Clarence Harris (Blind Man), Charles Hopkins ("Run Little Chillun" Singer); Dancers: Olive Gordon, Roxie Foster, Norma Miller, Norma Ross, Nyoka Pleasant, Robert Lopez, Joseph Noble, Geraldine Prillerman, Mable Hart, Enid Williams, James Riley, Alfred Bledger, Lillian Roberts, Frank Green, Joan Smith, Bill O'Neill, Dorothy Williams, Garfield Ritter; Novitiates of the Pilgrims of the New Day: James Jones, Roger Alford, Wardell Saunders, Andrew Taylor, W. O. Davis, Elijah Hodges; Young People's Choir: Ruth Collins, Howard Carter, Miriam Burton, Eddie Roche; Rhythm Beaters: Thornton Cherokee, Martin James, Means Mases, Sylvanna Cole, John Adele, Okey Lawson

The play with music was presented in two acts.

The action takes place "somewhere in the South" during the present time.

Musical Numbers

Act One: "Church in the Dale" (Choir); "Bye and Bye" (music by Hall Johnson) (Charles Hopkins); "Song of the Hill" (music by Hall Johnson) (Charles Hopkins); "Processional" / "Credo" / "Moon-Music" / "Tangola Dance-Music" (music by Hall Johnson) (Fredye Marshall, Inez Matthews)

Act Two: "I Can't Stay Here by Myself" (Bertha Powell); "Song of the Hill" (reprise) (Charles Howard): Sung by The Choir: "Steal Away"; "Amazing Grace"; "Oh, Jesus, Come Dis-a-Way"; "Done Written Down-a My Name"; "I'll Never Turn Back No Mo'"; "Oh, My Lovin' Brother"; "Do You Love My Lord?"; "Great Gettin' Up Mornin'"; and "Nobody Knows de Trouble I See"; "Run Little Chillun" (music by Hall Johnson) (Charles Hopkins); Sung by The Choir: "So Glad"; "Return, Oh Holy Dove"; and "Lord, Oh Have Mercy on Me"

The original production of Hall Johnson's folk-like tale *Run Little Chillun* opened as *Run, Little Chillun!* at the Lyric Theatre for 126 performances beginning on March 1, 1933. That production advertised the evening as "A Negro Folk Drama," and the program's title page warned: "Run, little chillun, run! Fo' de devil's done loose in de lan.'" Due to mostly indifferent reviews (plus perhaps a New York heat wave and a recalcitrant air-cooling system in the Hudson Theatre), the revival wasn't able to muster more than two weeks of performances.

The basic plot of *Run Little Chillun* was somewhat reminiscent of the later **Cabin in the Sky**. The play with music contrasted Christianity as practiced by the members of the Hope Baptist Church with the pagan rituals performed in the woods by the worshippers of the New Day Pilgrims. Specifically, the evening centered on the soul of Jim, the son of Reverend Jones, the minister of the Hope Baptist Church, and the temptress Sulamai who participates in orgies in the woods with her fellow New Day Pilgrims and who attempts to seduce Jim and bring him into their fold. But good wins the day: the evil Sulamai is struck by lightning, and Jim rejoins the Hope Baptist Church.

A program note indicated the New Day Pilgrims believe that "black people . . . sorely need a new religion based upon and developed out of their own essential nature and not grafted on through contact with other peoples." As a result, "sin" doesn't exist as "fact" but only as "a sense of guilt." But the program cautions that man shouldn't live "on the plane of the lower animals" and should instead cultivate his "laudable ambitions and right desires."

Hall Johnson was himself the son of a minister, and in 1925 organized the Hall Johnson Negro Choir; he also served as the director of the spirituals that were heard in *The Green Pastures*.

Louis Kronenberger in *PM* noted that as drama the evening was "inept or absurd" and its "crude" story of sex and religion was so confused it was "hard to tell one from the other"; he enjoyed the songs, but felt the evening was a "bad play with music" and not a "real" musical. He concluded that Johnson the composer was "done in" by Johnson the playwright. Ward Morehouse in the *New York Sun* said the show wasn't a play, not "even half a play"; it offered "exciting moments" when the choir sang, but otherwise was a "bad" play. John Chapman in the *New York Daily News* found the "overlong" evening "pretty silly," with a "badly acted plot" (he also noted the theatre was "steaming" due to the breakdown of its cooling system). And Howard Barnes in the *New York Herald Tribune* suggested the work was more concert than play; he also suggested the "fragments" of the plot should have been worked into a "consecutive and motivated background for the musical numbers."

Like Kronenberger, Lewis Nichols in the *New York Times* felt Johnson's musical talents outweighed his dramatic ones and certain scenes assumed "the aspect of the ridiculous" and drew unintended laughs from the audience. Louis Sobel in the *New York Journal-American* said the evening would be a success if Johnson abandoned the book and concentrated on the music, for the dialogue portions were "dreary gabble-gabble" with a "skimpy" and "uninspired plot" (and like Chapman he remarked upon the intense heat in which "rivers of sweat drenched audience and actors alike").

Wilella Waldorf in the *New York Post* said the early part of the evening was "slow going," but the "brilliant dramatic and tonal" effects of the singing were "tremendously impressive." She noted the evening began with a kind of overture in which the Hall Johnson Choir sang "The Star-Spangled Banner" as she had "never heard it sung before" because they made "something genuinely spine-tingling out of the National Anthem" (Sobel said he had never realized the anthem had such a "magnificent" melody, and suggested it should also be sung at the end of the evening); like some of the other critics, Waldorf also commented upon how "very hot" it was in the theatre.

Unlike the seven other critics, Burton Rascoe in the *New York World-Telegram* gushed over the production. He was "profoundly and humbly grateful" to Hall Johnson, because the work was "one of the most beautiful, most thrilling, most touching" shows he had ever seen. He was so carried away by the performance that its "spell" made it difficult for him to write his review. The show was an "incomparable work of art" and not since *The Green Pastures* had he been so "excited" about a theatrical presentation.

CHAUVE-SOURIS OF 1943

Theatre: Royale Theatre
Opening Date: August 12, 1943; *Closing Date*: August 21, 1943
Performances: 12
Lyrics: English lyrics by Irving Florman
Music: Music compiled and arranged by Gleb Yellin
Direction: Entire production devised and supervised by Leon Greanin; production staged by Michel Michon; *Producer*: Leon Greanin (by arrangement with Mme. Nikita Balieff); *Choreography*: Vecheslav Swoboda and Boris Romanoff; *Scenery* and *Costumes*: Serge Soudeikine; *Lighting*: Uncredited; *Musical Direction*: Gleb Yellin
Cast: Leon Greanin, Marusia Sava, Zinaida Alvers, Vera Pavlovska, Tatiana Pobers, Jeanne Soudeikina, Dania Krupska, Georgiana Bannister, Norma Slavina, Georges Doubrovksy, Michael Dalamatoff, Simeon Karavaeff, Michel Michon, Arcadi Stoyanovsky, Jack Gansert, Vladimir Lazarev, Leo Resnickoff, Arsen Tarpoff, Leo Vlassoff, Nicholas Dontzoff, George Yurka, Florence Berline, Cyprienne Gabelman, Audrey Keane, Blanche Sanborska, Fern Sironi, Nicolas Dontzoff, Olga Nicolaeva, Nicholas Yourovsky, Sergei Zdanoff, Lev Xanoff
The revue was presented in two acts.

Musical Numbers

Act One: Overture (music taken from Russian classics) (Orchestra); "Russian Shawls" (Songs of Babi with greetings from Russia; lyric by Michel Michon) (Marusia Sava, Zinaida Alvers, Georgiana Bannister, Vera Pavlovska, Tatiana Pobers; solo sung by Jeanne Soudeikina); "The Parade of the Wooden Soldiers" (music by Leon Jessel; setting by Serge Soudeikine after M. Narbout) (Arcadi Stoyanovsky, Jack Gansert, Florence Berline, Cyprienne Gabelman, Audrey Keane, Dania Krupska, Blanche Sanborska, Fern Sironi, Norma Slavina); "Victory Parade" (Michael Dalmatoff, Nicolas Dontzoff, George Doubrovsky, Leo Resnickoff, Arsen Tarpoff, Leo Vlassoff, George Yurka); "Song of the Flea" (music by Modest Moussorgsky) (Mephistopheles: Georges Doubrovsky); "Trepak" (folk dance; choreography by Boris Romanoff) (Cyprienne Gabelman, Audrey Keane, Dania Krupska, Blanche Sanborska, Fern Sironi, Simeon Karavaeff, Jack Gansert); "Love in the Ranks" ("The Daughter of the Regiment in Old St. Petersburg") (music by Alexei

Archangelsky) (staged by Boris Romanoff) (scenery and costumes by Serge Soudeikine, after N. Benois) (The Daughter of the Regiment: Vera Pavlovska; The Corporal: Arcadi Stoyanovsky; The Lieutenant: Arsen Tarpoff; The Captain: Michel Michon; The Major: Georges Doubrovsky; The General: Michael Dalmatoff); "The Nightingale" (music by A. Alabieff-Liszt; choreography by Vecheslav Swoboda) (danced by Norma Slavina); "A Russian Sailor in New York" (The Sailor: Simeon Karavaeff); "Hobo-Genius Chorus in 4F" (Georges Doubrovsky, Nicholas Dontzoff, Simeon Karavaeff, Michel Michon, Leo Resnickoff, Arcadi Stoyanovsky, Arsen Tarpoff, Leo Vlassoff, George Yurka; under the leadership of Michael Dalmatoff); "Song of Chauve-souris 1943" (Vera Pavlovska); "Harvest Festival" (music inspired by contemporary Russian composers) (choreography by Vecheslav Swoboda): (a) "Song of the Fields" (music by L. Knipper); (b) "United Nations" (music by Dmitri Shostakovich) (Zinaida Alvers, Georges Doubrovsky); (c) "Balalaikas" (music by H. Dounaevsky); (d) "Oh, My Heart!" (music by H. Dounaevsky); (e) "Strolling Home" (music by V. Zakharoff); and (f) "Electric Lights Come to the Village" (music by Dmitri Shostakovich and V. Zakharoff) (Jeanne Soudeikina) (Marusia Sava, Zinaida Alvers, Georgiana Bannister, Florence Berline, Cyprienne Gabelman, Audrey Keane, Dania Krupska, Vera Pavlovska, Tatiana Pobers, Blanche Sanborska, Fern Sironi, Norma Slavina, Jeanne Soudeikina, Olga Nicolaeva, Michael Dalmatoff, Georges Doubrovsky, Nicholas Dontzoff, Jack Gansert, Simeon Karavaeff, Vladimir Lazarev, Michel Michon, Leo Resnickoff, Arcadi Stoyanovsky, Arsen Tarpoff, Leo Vlassoff, Lev Xanoff, Nicolas Yourovsky, George Yurka, Sergei Zdanoff)

Act Two: Overture (music taken from contemporary Russian composers) (Orchestra); "The Gypsies" (Original Gypsy Romances) (songs arranged by Mme. Nastia Poliakova) (First Gypsy Soloist: Marusia Sava; Second Gypsy Soloist: Zinaida Alvers; Third Gypsy Soloist: Tatiana Poberts; Fourth Gypsy Soloist: Jeanne Soudeikina; Minstrel: Michel Michon; Hussar: Georges Doubrovsky; Gypsies: Georgiana Bannister, Cyprienne Gabelman, Florence Berline, Leo Resnickoff, Nicolas Dontzoff, Arsen Tarpoff, Leo Vlasoff, George Yurka (chorus under the leadership of Michael Dalmatoff); "A la Polka" (choreography by Vecheslav Swoboda) (Audrey Keane, Norma Slavina, Jack Gansert); "Romances of Tschaikovsky" (Peter Ilich Tchiakovsky: Michel Michon; duet sung by Zinaida Alvers, Vera Pavlovska); "Katinka's Birthday" ("Katinka Is Sweet Sixteen") (lyric by Michel Michon and Robbins) (Katinka's polka by Boris Romanoff) (Katinka: Dania Krupska; Mother: Jeanne Soudeikina; Father: Leo Vlassoff; Aunt: Georgiana Bannister; Bridegroom: Arsen Tarpoff; Uncle: Arcadi Stoyanovsky; Portrait: Georges Doubrovsky; Statue: Michel Michon; Little Brother: Blanche Sanborska); "Night Idyl" (staged by Mme. Elena Balieff) (setting by Serge Soudekine after N. Remisoff) (The Girl: Marusia Sava; The Boy: Arcadi Stoyanovsky; Musical Echoes: Jeanne Soudeikina, Georgiana Bannister, Simeon Karavaeff, Leo Resnickoff; Accordionist: Nicolas Dontzoff; Guitarist: George Yurka); "Wedding in Ukraine" (Original Ukrainian folk songs and dances) (choreography for "Hopak" by Boris Romnoff) (Bride: Vera Pavlovska; Groom: Vladimir Lazarev; Mother: Jeanne Soudeikina; Father: Michael Dalmatoff; First Best Man: Simeon Karavaeff; Second Best Man: Michel Michon; Priest: Georges Doubrovsky; Bridesmaids, Neighbors, Friends, and Guests: Entire Company)

The revue *Chauve-souris* (*The Bat*) originated in Moscow where it was created by Nikita Balieff; he and other players of the Moscow Art Theatre first performed their material as an after-hours amusement for themselves. After the Russian Revolution, the émigrés re-created their revues in Paris and London, and on February 4, 1922, *Chauve-souris* opened in New York at the 49th Street Theatre for 520 performances (during this run, a succession of new editions were presented). Despite the enormous success of the production in New York, the law of diminishing returns soon set in. The second *Chauve-souris* opened on October 21, 1931, at the Ambassador Theatre for only 29 performances, and the current and final *Chauve-souris* closed after just 12 showings. Balieff had appeared as performer and conferencier in the 1922 and 1931 engagements, and the new edition was presented "by arrangement" with his widow.

The critics were merciless in their reviews of the new offering. They missed moon-faced Bailieff, who used to wander in and out of the proceedings and introduce the musical sequences in his funny and fractured English (Wilella Waldorf in the *New York Post* fondly remembered how he "recklessly" battled "English idioms in an accent that became more intricate and more hilarious as the years passed"). For the new edition, producer Leon Greanin assumed Bailieff's old role as the evening's master of ceremonies, but the critics were less than impressed with his efforts (Ward Morehouse in the *New York Sun* said he lacked the "charm" and "magic" of his predecessor). Burton Rascoe in the *New York World-Telegram* reported the opening night was somewhat chaotic, and Greanin didn't seem to realize things weren't going smoothly backstage. He would introduce a number that didn't materialize, and sometimes he and the orchestra conductor seemed to be literally on the wrong page. Further, five sequences in the "Harvest Festival" number weren't performed, and three complete numbers in the second act "dropped out."

The evening offered folk songs and dances as well as two numbers ("The Parade of the Wooden Soldiers" and "Katinka's Birthday") which were based on sequences seen in the original 1922 production. But to ensure that the revue was up to date, there were numbers such as "A Russian Sailor in New York" (on the town, no doubt); "Hobo-Genius Chorus in 4F"; and a number about an American WAC and a Russian sniper. Lewis Nichols in the *New York Times* didn't identify the last (it was probably "Love in the Ranks"), but said it was "dreadful." And the very title of "Electric Lights Come to the Village" seems to be the kind of number Cole Porter satirized when he wrote "Ode to a Tractor" for *Silk Stockings* (1955).

Louis Kronenberger in *PM* regretfully noted that Greanin was "not quite funny" and the revue was "not quite fun"; and Louis Sobel in the *New York Journal-American* said Greanin was up there on the Royale's stage "trying to convince me I was having a good time. He was wrong. I wasn't." Howard Barnes in the *New York Herald Tribune* said the production was "embarrassingly dull" and the performers were "generally stymied"; and Waldorf found the "dull" evening a "disappointment" that was often "poorly staged" with a hoped-for "informality" that resulted in "embarrassing amateurishness."

One or two critics noted that much of the material and some of the performers had been seen at Kretchma, a Russian restaurant located on 14th Street; perhaps smaller doses of the material in an intimate setting worked better than on the stage of a large Broadway house.

The revue is notable as one of Dania Krupska's earliest New York appearances (here, she danced the title role in "Katinka's Birthday"). She worked steadily on Broadway as both a dancer (*Can-Can* [1953], *The Girl in Pink Tights* [1954]) and choreographer (*Seventeen* [1951], *The Most Happy Fella* [1956], *The Happiest Girl in the World* [1961]).

BLOSSOM TIME

Theatre: Ambassador Theatre
Opening Date: September 4, 1943; *Closing Date*: October 9, 1943
Performances: 47
Book and *Lyrics*: Dorothy Donnelly
Music: Franz Schubert and Heinrich Berte (music adapted and augmented by Sigmund Romberg)
Based on the 1916 operetta *Das Dreimaderhaus*.
Direction: J. J. Shubert; *Producers*: The Messrs. Shubert; *Scenery*: Watson Barratt; *Costumes*: Stage Costumes, Inc.; *Lighting*: Uncredited; *Musical Direction*: Pierre de Reeder
Cast: Alexander Gray (Franz Schubert), Doug Leavitt (Christian Kranz), Roy Cropper (Baron Schober), Robert Chisholm (Scharntoff), Barbara Scully (Mitzi), Adelaide Bishop (Fritzi), Loraine Manners (Kitzi), Helene Arthur (Bellabruna), Helen Thompson (Flower Girl aka Emmy), Zella Russell (Mrs. Kranz), Jacqueline Susann (Greta), Helena LeBerthon (Rosie), Pamela Dow (Mrs. Coburg), Roy Barnes (Vogel), George Mitchell (Von Schwindt), Nord Cornell (Kuppelweiser), Harry K. Morton (Novotny), Walter Johnson (Domeyer), George Beach (Erkman), John O'Neill (Binder), Alice Drake (Waitress); Flower Girls and Bridesmaids: Gloria Sterling, Marcella Markham, Edith Vincent, Jay Flower, V. Stowe; Ballet Girls: Jacqueline Jacoby, Aura Vainio, Virginia Meyer, Mary Grey, Frances Spelz, Greta Borjosen, Lola Balser
The musical was presented in three acts.
The action takes place in Vienna during 1826.

Musical Numbers

Act One: Opening (Helen Thompson, Nord Cornell, George Mitchell, Roy Barnes, Ensemble); "Melody Triste" (Helene Arthur, Robert Chisholm); "Three Little Maids" (Barbara Scully, Adelaide Bishop, Loraine Manners, Chorus); "Serenade" (Alexander Gray, Nord Cornell, Roy Barnes, Roy Cropper, George Mitchell); "My Springtime Thou Art" (Roy Cropper, Alexander Gray, Roy Barnes, Nord Cornell, George Mitchell, Corps de Ballet, Ensemble); "Song of Love" (Alexander Gray, Barbara Scully); Finale (Entire Company)

Act Two: "Hark! The Lark" (Entire Ensemble); "Interlude Musicale" (Alexander Gray, Girls); "Love Is a Riddle" (Roy Cropper, John O'Neill, George Beach, Barbara Scully, Adelaide Bishop, Loraine Manners); "Let Me Awake" (Helene Arthur, Roy Cropper); "Tell Me, Daisy" (Barbara Scully, Alexander Gray); "Only One Love Ever Fills My Heart" (Barbara Scully, Roy Cropper); Finale (Barbara Scully, Alexander Gray, Roy Cropper)

Act Three: "Keep It Dark" (Helene Arthur, Roy Barnes, George Mitchell, Nord Cornell); "Lonely Heart" (Barbara Scully, Alexander Gray); Finale (Entire Company)

The venerable operetta *Blossom Time* was a fictionalized account of Austrian composer Franz Schubert's unrequited love for Mitzi, who falls in love with his best friend Von Schober. The story was a piffle, and the evening was mainly an excuse to hear Schubert's music.

The work first premiered in Vienna on January 15, 1916, as *Das Dreimaderhaus*; for this production, Schubert's music was adapted by Heinrich Berte, and the libretto was by Alfred M. Willner and Heinz Reichert (the operetta had been based on the 1912 novel *Schwammerl* by Rudolf Hans Bartsch). The original Broadway production (which like the current revival opened at the Ambassador Theatre) premiered on September 29, 1921, for 576 performances. For the American version, the Shuberts brought in Sigmund Romberg to adapt some of Schubert's music, and for the opening night of the 1943 revival Romberg himself was in the audience. In the 1921 production, Roy Cropper created the role of Vogel, and for the current revival he was Baron Schober.

Another version of the material was *Lilac Time*, which opened in London at the Lyric Theatre on December 22, 1922, for 626 performances; this production utilized Berte's musical adaptation for the 1916 Austrian production.

The current production was the operetta's seventh (and still most recent) Broadway revival. The first and second revivals both opened on May 21, 1923, when the Shuberts presented them across the street from one another, one at the Shubert and the other at the 44th Street Theatre (for twenty-four and sixteen respective performances); the third opened at Jolson's Theatre on May 19, 1924, for twenty-four performances; again at Jolson's Theatre, this time on March 8, 1926, for sixteen performances; then at the operetta's original home of the Ambassador Theatre on March 4, 1931, for twenty-nine performances; and at the 46th Street Theatre on December 26, 1938, for nineteen performances.

Wilella Waldorf in the *New York Post* noted that the uninspired direction of the current revival resorted to lining up the cast in threes, fours, and so on, and then having them "pace up and down before the footlights in time to the music." As for the "senile" comic scenes, she noted that one tipsy character scratches a table's leg instead of his own and then cries out, "My God! I'm dead!" Waldorf also reported that one musical number in the program ("Ballet a la Degas") wasn't performed on opening night. A later program doesn't include the number, and so it apparently was never performed during the revival's short six-week run.

Robert Garland in the *New York Journal-American* commented that the book made Schubert a "sentimental sap . . . a misty, if music-minded, moron." But the evening was "pleasantly familiar," and he praised the "lovely and melodious" Barbara Scully, whom the Shuberts brought over from the current revival of **The Student Prince**, where she had been playing the role of Kathie; Howard Barnes in the *New York Herald Tribune* found the music "rather adequately" performed, but the dramatic side of the evening left "almost everything to be desired." John Chapman in the *New York Daily News* said the production was "strictly standard," but he noted Schubert's music offered "gentle hits" with no hints of "boogie-woogie or Sinatra Apassionata in them."

Lewis Nichols in the *New York Times* complained that the work had "one of the dreariest books in the world" and that the revival itself lacked "sparkle" and "luster"; but Burton Rascoe in the *New York World-Telegram* was still swooning over Barbara Scully, noting that she "adorned" the revival and that at her birth the "good fairies" had given her "beauty, grace, sweetness," as well as the "instincts and perceptions of a born actress" and a "melodious" and "incredibly powerful" voice.

Ward Morehouse in the *New York Sun* said the cast was "serviceable," the production's look was strictly from "stock-company," the book became "steadily wearisome," and his overall impression was that the revival had been "carelessly put together." Louis Kronenberger in *PM* said the "distinctly dated" operetta offered "foolish" dialogue and "desperate" comedy, and while these stale conventions were once "merely what you expected" from an operetta, they were now "worse than you feared."

The most complete recording of *Blossom Time* is from an Ohio Light Opera Company production which was recorded on a 2-CD set by Albany Records (# TROY-1401/02).

Another musical adaptation of the original operetta, and also titled *Blossom Time*, was adapted by Sydney Box, with lyrics by G. H. Clutsam, John Drinkwater, and H. V. Purcell; the musical adaptation of Schubert's music was by Clutsam. This version, which seems to have been partially adapted from *Lilac Time*, was produced in Great Britain in 1936, and the script was published in paperback by Samuel French the following year.

LAUGH TIME
"A VAUDEVILLE SHOW"

Theatre: Shubert Theatre (during run, the revue transferred to the Ambassador Theatre)
Opening Date: September 8, 1943; *Closing Date*: November 20, 1943
Performances: 126
Producers: Paul Small and Fred F. Finklehoff (Finklehoffe); *Scenery*: R. L. Grosch & Sons; *Musical Direction*: Lou Forman
Cast: *Frank Fay, Ethel Waters, Bert Wheeler,* Jane and Adam Di Gatano, Buck and Bubbles, Adriana and Charly, Lucienne and Ashour, Jerri Vance, Warren Jackson, The Bricklayers; Pianist Reginald Beane accompanied Ethel Waters
The revue was presented in two acts.

Sketches and Musical Numbers

Act One: Frank Fay (Host); Adriana and Charly; Buck and Bubbles; The Bricklayers; Jane and Adam Di Gatano; Frank Fay and Bert Wheeler
Act Two: Bert Wheeler; Frank Fay; Ethel Waters; Lucienne and Ashour; Frank Fay; Finale

Laugh Time was a vaudeville-styled revue produced by Paul Small and Fred F. Finklehoff, the latter of whom had previously enjoyed the long-running success of the similarly styled **Show Time**. These revues began on the West Coast, but unlike **Show Time** and *Laugh Time*, their **Big Time** and Small's **Curtain Time** didn't reach Broadway. Later on, there was also Small's **Star Time**, which did. Anyone who can describe in under three minutes the specific differences of **Show Time**, *Laugh Time*, **Big Time**, **Curtain Time**, and **Star Time** deserves an autographed opening night program of **Hairpin Harmony**.

The program notes said *Laugh Time* would prove that the "burial of vaudeville" in 1932 was "premature." It also stated that Frank Fay's monologues would explain "a few of his theories about cosmic problems" and later he and Bert Wheeler would "conspire in something that defies Roget." As for the finale, it would *not* offer a spiral stairway, adagio dancers, or chorus girls "symbolizing the Four Freedoms."

Burton Rascoe in the *New York World-Telegram* said the evening offered "as good a vaudeville bill as you ever saw, no matter how old you are." Ward Morehouse in the *New York Sun* found the revue "excellent" and suspected it would "bring further stampedes to Forty-fourth street, a thoroughfare that is already booming." And Robert Garland in the *New York Journal-American* also said the evening was "excellent . . . a vaudeville show well worth seeing."

Frank Fay was the evening's master of ceremonies, and his understated humor worked well. His comments included the news that he'd recently been to a nightclub with a newspaper woman. Pause. "She owns a stand." And later he tore into a chorus of "Tea for Two" (*No, No, Nanette*, 1925; lyric by Irving Caesar and music by Vincent Youmans). John Chapman in the *New York Daily News* said Frank Fay and Bert Wheeler made a great team who traded casual insults. They had perfect timing, and sensed the "tempo" of their audience; they could slowly "feel their way along" and then once the customers were into their shtick the two comedians picked up speed to match the audience. Chapman noted their act was a "demonstration of the most difficult of all vaudeville tricks, timing."

Ethel Waters sang many of her standards, including "Am I Blue?" (1929 film *On with the Show*; lyric by Grant Clarke, music by Harry Akst); "Dinah" (interpolated into *Kid Boots*, 1923; lyric by Sam Lewis and Joe

Young, music by Harry Akst); "Heat Wave" (*As Thousands Cheer*, 1933; lyric and music by Irving Berlin); "Stormy Weather" (*Cotton Club Parade*, 1933; lyric by Ted Koehler, music by Harold Arlen); "Taking a Chance on Love" and "Cabin in the Sky" (**Cabin in the Sky**, 1940; music by Vernon Duke; lyric for the former by Ted Fetter and John LaTouche and the latter by LaTouche); as well as "Happiness Is Just a Thing Called Joe" (written especially for the 1943 film version of *Cabin in the Sky*; lyric by E. Y. Harburg, music by Harold Arlen). Lewis Nichols in the *New York Times* decided that "happiness in vaudeville is a name called Ethel," and Garland said she was the "outstanding hit" of the show.

The revue included the indomitable dog act The Bricklayers (Nichols said the pooches were the "best in the business"); the black song-and-dance comedy team of Buck and Bubbles ("up to their customary antics," noted Wilella Waldorf in the *New York Post*); the tumblers Adriana and Charly; the ballroom dancers Jane and Adam Di Gatano; and Apache dancers Lucienne and Ashour (Lucienne surprised everyone with a welcome twist when she turned the tables on Ashour).

The revue gave twelve performances weekly.

MY DEAR PUBLIC
"A Revusical Story"

Theatre: 46th Street Theatre
Opening Date: September 9, 1943; *Closing Date*: October 16, 1943
Performances: 45
Book: Irving Caesar and Charles Gottesfeld
Lyrics and *Music*: Irving Caesar, Sam Lerner, and Gerald Marks
Direction: Edgar MacGregor; *Producer*: Irving Caesar; *Choreography*: Felicia Sorel; Henry Le Tang, Assistant Choreography; *Scenery*: Albert Johnson; *Costumes*: Lucinda Ballard; *Lighting*: Uncredited; *Musical Direction*: Harry Levant
Cast: David Burns (Walters), Georgie Tapps (Tapps), Nanette Fabray (Jean), Ethel Shutta (Daphne Drew), *Willie Howard* (Barney Short), Renee Russell (Renee), Louise Fiske (Louise), Mitzi Perry (Mitzi), Eric Brotherson (Byron Burns), Sherle North (Lulu), Gordon Gifford (Gordon), William Nunn (Playwright), Jesse White (Gus Wagner), Al Kelly (Kelly), Rose Brown (Rose Brown), Dave Hamilton (Announcer), Janice Wallace (Ruth), Edith Laumer (Edith), Monica Boyer, Lee Varrett, Della Lorrie, Harry Day, The Harmoneers (Dave Hamilton, Louise Rose, Bill Jones, and Michael Kojak), The Crandall Sisters (Truda, Mickey, and Heather), Helene (and her violin); Girls: Renee Russell, Marylin Johnson, Zynaid Spencer, Ann Middleton, Betty Burns, Virginia Stevens, Janice Wallace, Joan Sommers, Mitzi Perry, Edith Laumer, Louise Fiske, Marjorie Gaye, Betty Laighton, Jean Cooke, Dorothy Thomas, Billie Ferguson, Robin Marlowe, Vivian Newell, Dorothy Hyatt, Lorene Gray, Ginger Lynne; Boys: Jack Lyons, Richard Andre, Paul Vincent, Ernie Di Gennaro, Larry Evers, William Hunter, William Lundy
The musical was presented in two acts.
The action takes place during the present time in New York City.

Musical Numbers

Act One: "Feet on the Sidewalk (Head in the Sky)" (lyric by Sam Lerner, music by Gerald Marks) (Georgie Tapps, Nanette Fabray, The Crandall Sisters, Monica Boyer, The Harmoneers, Boys and Girls); "My Dear Public" (Gordon Gifford, Sherle North, Jesse White, Monica Boyer, Lee Varrett, Marlynn Arden, Truda Crandall, Mickey Crandall, Heather Crandall, The Harmoneers); "Last Will and Testament" (Eric Brotherson); "Little Gamins" (Ethel Shutta, Ensemble); "(This Is) Our Private Love Song" (lyric by Irving Caesar, music by Sam Lerner) (Eric Brotherson, Nanette Fabray; Violin Solo: Helene); "My Spies Tell Me (You Love Nobody but Me)" (lyric by Irving Caesar and Sam Lerner, music by Gerald Marks) (David Burns, Sherle North, The Crandall Sisters); "Color Line" (aka "There Ain't No Color Line Around the Rainbow") (lyric by Irving Caesar and Sam Lerner, music by Gerald Marks) (Rose Brown); "If You Want a Deal with Russia" (Willie Howard); "May All Our Children Have Rhythm" (George Tapps, Nanette Fabray, The Crandall Sisters, The Harmoneers, Della Lorrie, Harry Day, Girls and Boys)

Act Two: "Pipes of Pan Americana" (lyric by Irving Caesar, music by Gerald Marks) (Gordon Gifford, The Harmoneers, Monica Boyer, Della Lorrie, Harry Day, Boys and Girls); "Rhumba Jake" (Willie Howard, Ethel Shutta); "Lulu" (David Burns, Sherle North); "Love Is Such a Cheat" (lyric by Irving Caesar, music by Irma Hollander and Gerald Marks) (Ethel Shutta, The Harmoneers, Helene); Ballet (music based on Enesco's Rumanian Rhapsody No. 1) (Marlyin Arden, Helene, Boys and Girls); "I Love to Sing the Words (While We're Dancing)" (lyric by Irving Caesar and Sam Lerner, music by Gerald Marks) (Nanette Fabray, Georgie Tapps, Boys and Girls); "Our Private Love Song" (reprise) (probably sung by Eric Brotherson and Nanette Fabray); Finale (Entire Company)

My Dear Public received some of the worst notices of the era, but somehow managed to hang on for six weeks. It's not that the show didn't try. It had originally been produced a year and a half earlier and had bombed on the road. But producer and cowriter Irving Caesar didn't give up, and so eighteen months later the revised version opened on Broadway. Louis Kronenberger in *PM* said it was "one of the most terrific bores" he'd ever seen; it was "relentlessly undiverting," and while "suspicious" minds might have scented a "conspiracy," he was content to believe it was all a "mistake."

The 1942 production billed itself as a musical comedy, but the constant rewrites and recasting and postponements probably led the creators to realize they hadn't much in the way of a book musical. As a result, they perhaps tried to apologize for their final product by calling it a "revusical." But whether the show was a "musical comedy" or a "revusical," Lewis Nichols in the *New York Times* said "new words cannot disguise old dullness."

The plot concerned zipper manufacturer Barney Short (Willie Howard) and his wife Daphne Drew Short (Ethel Shutta) who wants him to back a musical so she can star in it. So Barney meets up with arty Village playwright-director Byron Burns (Eric Brotherson), but Burns is more interested in seeing that his girlfriend Jean (Nanette Fabray) gets a leading role in the show. Burton Rascoe in the *New York World-Telegram* commented that Brotherson was offstage for such long periods that it became easy to forget exactly which role he was playing. Others who roamed in and out of the action were comedian David Burns, tap-dancer Georgie Tapps, and black singer Rose Brown. Many of the musical numbers were performed during the rehearsals of the show-within-a-show.

The critics felt the material never gave comedian Willie Howard a chance to shine, but they liked "If You Want a Deal with Russia," which capitalized on Howard's famous repertoire of accents. Rascoe enjoyed the "very witty" number, and also praised Brotherson's "satirical" song "Last Will and Testament." John Chapman in the *New York Daily News* suggested "Feet on the Sidewalk" was the show's best number, and Nichols thought many of the songs would have shined under better circumstances (including the "good popular"-styled "Our Private Love Song" and "I Love to Sing the Words"; the "good boogie-woogie" "My Spies Tell Me"; and the "better than average" "There Ain't No Color Line Around the Rainbow").

But the vaporous book did the show in. Ward Morehouse in the *New York Sun* said the musical was "routine and unexciting," and Howard Barnes in the *New York Herald Tribune* said "all that is wanting is an amusing show." Robert Garland in the *New York Journal-American* reported that the Drama Critics' Circle was considering an award for the worst show of the 1943–1944 season, and if so the booby prize should go to *My Dear Public*.

Kronenberger noted that there seemed to be a semblance of plot early on, but after awhile the musical didn't "seem to be about anything." He also said the songs were "uninspired," and the "best" of them was "Our Private Love Song" (which sounded like "once-upon-a-time Cole Porter"). Wilella Waldorf in the *New York Post* found the musical "tedious," but liked "If You Want a Deal with Russia" ("funny") and "There Ain't No Color Line Around the Rainbow" ("throbbing"). Otherwise, she noted that ever since *Very Warm for May* (1939) she nursed a suspicion "that it is very difficult to put on a musical show about people trying to put on a musical show."

The critics were glad to see veteran Ethel Shutta back on stage after fifteen years (her most recent appearance had been opposite Eddie Cantor in 1928's *Whoopee*), but apparently the debacle of *My Dear Public* discouraged her, because it took twenty years for her to return, when she played Mary Martin's mother in *Jennie* (1963). But Broadway glory and immortality were patiently waiting. In 1971, she appeared in Stephen Sondheim's monumental *Follies* and stopped the show cold with her fervent wish to be a "Broadway Baby." Shutta and Willie Howard had both appeared in *The Passing Show of 1922*, but, unlike Shutta, Howard never again enjoyed a later success to match his earlier ones. After *My Dear Public*, he was seen on Broadway just once more, in the failed 1948 revival of **Sally** (he died during the tryout of the 1949 revue ***Along Fifth Avenue*** and was replaced by Jackie Gleason).

As mentioned, the first production of *My Dear Public* closed during its tryout. It had been presented two seasons earlier, opening at the Shubert Theatre in New Haven on March 5, 1942, and closing in Philadelphia on March 28. The writers, composers, and producer were still the same, but Joseph Pevney was the director and Carl Randall the choreographer. The cast included Joe Smith (Barney Short), Cora Witherspoon (Daphne), Mitzi Green (Jean), and John Buckmaster (Byron). Others in the cast were Smith's vaudeville partner Charles Dale, Tamara, The Martins (Hugh Martin, Ralph Blane, Phyllis Rogers, and Jo Jean Rogers), and Rose Brown, who appeared in the Broadway version. In the minor role of a waiter was Karl Malden, and, last but certainly not least, was the team of The Revuers (Betty Comden, Adolph Green, Judy Tuvim [Holliday], John Frank, and Alvin Hammer), who played themselves and contributed three sequences, "We Had a Show," "Variety," and "The Baroness Bazooka." When the musical finally opened on Broadway, The Revuers and their material were not part of the show. Comden and Green performed "The Baroness Bazooka" in both the original 1958 production and the 1977 revival of their retrospective revue *A Party with Betty Comden and Adolph Green*. Both productions were recorded live and the number can be heard on both cast albums.

Songs in the 1942 production that weren't used on Broadway were: "Buy a Song," "Rain on the Sea" (lyric by Irving Caesar and Sam Lerner, music by Gerald Marks), "Spanish Joke," "Breakfast with Hazel," "The Honeymoon of Pancho Pincus," and "Now That I'm Free" (lyric by Irving Caesar and Sam Lerner, music by Irma Hollander).

PORGY AND BESS

Theatre: 44th Street Theatre
Opening Date: September 13, 1943; *Closing Date*: October 2, 1943
Performances: 24
Theatre: City Center
Opening Date: February 7, 1944; *Closing Date*: February 19, 1944
Performances: 16
Reopening Date: February 28, 1944; *Final Closing Date*: April 8, 1944
Performances: 48
Libretto: DuBose Heyward
Lyrics: DuBose Heyward and Ira Gershwin
Music: George Gershwin
Total Performances: 88
Based on the 1927 play *Porgy* by Dorothy and DuBose Heyward (which in turn had been adapted from DuBose Heyward's 1925 novel *Porgy*).
Direction: Robert Ross; *Producers*: Cheryl Crawford (John J. Wildberg, Associate Producer); *Scenery*: Herbert Andrews; *Costumes*: Costumes supervised by Paul du Pont; *Lighting*: Uncredited; *Musical Direction*: Alexander Smallens
Cast: Georgette Harvey (Maria), Catherine Ayers (Lily, Strawberry Woman), Musa Williams (Annie), Harriet Jackson (Clara), Edward Matthews (Jake), Avon Long (Sportin' Life), Jerry Laws (Mingo), Henry Davis (Robbins), Alma Hubbard (Serena), William C. Smith (Jim), George Randol (Peter), Todd Duncan (Porgy), Warren Coleman (Crown), Etta Moten (Bess), Kenneth Konopka (Policeman), Richard Bowler (Detective), Coyal McMahan (Undertaker), Charles Welch (Lawyer Frazier), Charles Colman (Nelson), Edward Tyler (Crab Man), Don Darcy (Coroner); Residents of Catfish Row, Fishermen, Children, Stevedores, etc.—The Eva Jessye Choir: Virginia Girvin, Gladys Goode, Eulabel Riley, Louisa Howard, Assotta Marshall, Sadie McGill, Annabelle Ross, Zelda Shelton, Eloise Uggams, Musa Williams, John Diggs, Leslie Gray, Jerry Laws, William C. Smith, Harold Desverney, Velda Shelton, Roger Aeford, Charles Colman, Coyal McMahan, Edward Tyler, William O'Neal; Children: Robert Tucker, Ruthetta Anderson, Kenneth Tucker, Thomas Tucker, Douglas Rice, Patricia Rice
The opera was presented in three acts.
The action takes place in Catfish Row, Charleston, South Carolina, and on nearby Kittiwah Island (the original Broadway production's program indicated the time was "the recent past").

Musical Numbers

Act One: "Summer Time" (lyric by DuBose Heyward) (Harriet Jackson); "A Woman Is a Sometime Thing" (lyric by DuBose Heyward) (Edward Matthews, Ensemble); Entrance of Porgy: "They Pass by Singing" (lyric by DuBose Heyward) (Todd Duncan); "Crap Game Fugue" (lyric by DuBose Heyward) (Harriet Jackson, Ensemble); "Gone, Gone, Gone!" (Ensemble); "Overflow" (lyric by DuBose Heyward) (Ensemble); "My Man's Gone Now" (lyric by DuBose Heyward) (Alma Hubbard, Ensemble); "Leavin' fo' de Promis' Lan'" (lyric by DuBose Heyward) (Etta Moten, Ensemble)

Act Two: "It Takes a Long Pull to Get There" (aka "Rowing Song") (lyric by DuBose Heyward) (Edward Matthews, Fishermen); "I Got Plenty o' Nuttin'" (lyric by Ira Gershwin and DuBose Heyward) (Todd Duncan); "Woman to Lady" (lyric by DuBose Heyward) (Todd Duncan, Etta Moten, Charles Welch, Ensemble); "Bess, You Is My Woman Now" (lyric by DuBose Heyward and Ira Gershwin) (Todd Duncan, Etta Moten); "Oh, I Can't Sit Down" (lyric by Ira Gershwin) (Orphan Band, Ensemble); "It Ain't Necessarily So" (lyric by Ira Gershwin) (Avon Long, Ensemble); "What You Want with Bess?" (lyric by DuBose Heyward) (Warren Coleman, Etta Moten); "Time and Time Again" (lyric by DuBose Heyward) (Alma Hubbard, Ensemble); "Street Cries" (lyric by DuBose Heyward) (Catherine Ayers, Edward Tyler); "I Loves You, Porgy" (lyric by Ira Gershwin and DuBose Heyward) (Todd Duncan and Etta Moten); "Oh, de Lawd Shake de Heaven" (lyric by DuBose Heyward) (Ensemble); "A Red-Headed Woman" (lyric by Ira Gershwin) (Warren Coleman, Ensemble); "Oh, Doctor Jesus" (lyric by DuBose Heyward) (Principals, Ensemble)

Act Three: "Clara, Don't You Be Downhearted" (lyric by DuBose Heyward) (Ensemble); "There's a Boat That's Leavin' Soon for New York" (lyric by Ira Gershwin) (Avon Long, Etta Moten); "Where's My Bess?" (lyric by Ira Gershwin) (Todd Duncan); "I'm On My Way" (lyric by DuBose Heyward) (Todd Duncan, Ensemble)

Cheryl Crawford's successful 1942 revival of George Gershwin's *Porgy and Bess* more than doubled the run of the original 1935 production. The current 1943 return engagement at the 44th Street Theatre was a limited run of twenty-four performances that Crawford brought to Broadway just prior to the musical's national tour. On February 7, 1944, Crawford again brought the opera to New York, where it played at City Center through February 19, and then reopened there on February 28 and played through April 8, for a total of sixty-four City Center showings. All told, the opera gave eighty-eight performances during the 1943–1944 season.

The above cast and credits represent the September 1943 performances. With the major exception of Todd Duncan, the 1944 cast remained the same; for the 1944 performances, William Franklin succeeded Duncan in the role of Porgy. (The program for the 44th Street Theatre revival noted the next attraction to play there would be Crawford's new musical **One Touch of Venus**, which instead opened at the Imperial.)

BRIGHT LIGHTS OF 1944
"An Intimate Musical Revue"

Theatre: Forrest Theatre
Opening Date: September 16, 1943; *Closing Date*: September 18, 1943
Performances: 4
Dialogue: Norman Anthony and Charles Sherman; additional dialogue by Joseph Erens
Lyrics: Mack David; additional lyrics by George Blake, Dorothy Fields, Teddy Hall, Glenn Herbert, James P. Johnson, Dick Leibert, Al Scofield (some sources cite last name as Schofield), and Norman Zeno
Music: Jerry Livingston; additional music by George Blake, Teddy Hall, Glenn Herbert, James P. Johnson, Dick Leibert, Jimmy McHugh, Al Scofield, and Norman Zeno
Direction: Dan Eckley; *Producers*: Alexander H. Cohen in association with Martin Poll and Joseph Kipness; *Choreography*: Truly McGee; *Scenery* and *Costumes*: Perry Watkins; *Lighting*: Al Alloy; *Musical Direction*: Max Meth
Cast: James Barton, Frances Williams, Joe Smith and Charles Dale, Buddy Clark, Jayne Manners, John Kirby and His Orchestra, The Royal Guards (Thomas Gleason, Arthur Barry, John Hamill, Carlton Male), Billie Worth, Jere McMahon, Renee Carroll, Elaine Miller, John A. Lorenz, Sollen Burry, Dave Leonard, Don Roberts, Russell Morrison, Kathryn Barton, Mimi Lynne; The Dancing Girls: Janet Joy, Cece Eames, Betty

de Elmo, Darlene Francys, Murnai Pins, Rose Marie Magrill; John Kirby and His Orchestra (John Kirby, Charles Shavers, Russell Procope, Clyde Hart, William Bailey, and William Beason)
The revue was presented in two acts.

Sketches and Musical Numbers

Act One: Outside Sardi's (Cop: John A. Lorenz; Out-of-Towner: Cece Eames); Inside Sardi's (The Boy: Jere McMahon; The Girl: Billie Worth; First Waiter: Joe Smith; Second Waiter: Charles Dale; Levy: Sollen Burry; Farquardt: Dave Leonard; Marquardt: Don Roberts); "Haven't We Met Before?" (sung and danced by Billie Worth and Jere McMahon); James Barton (who performed the songs "Damned Ole Jeeter," lyric and music by Dick Leibert and George Blake, and "I Can't Give You Anything but Love, Baby," from *Blackbirds of 1928*; lyric by Dorothy Fields, music by Jimmy McHugh); Inside Sardi's (Mr. Potts: Russell Morrison; Miss Miller: Elaine Miller; Renee Carroll [Herself]; Buddy Clark [Himself]; "You'd Better Dance" (sung and danced by Billie Worth and Jere McMahon); "Thoughtless" (Buddy Clark); "Don't Forget the Girl from Punxsutawney" (Jayne Manners, The Royal Guards, Chorus); "The Pest" (sketch by James Barton) (The Pest: James Barton; Gert: Kathryn Barton; Charlie: John A. Lorenz); "That's Broadway" (lyric and music by Gene Herbert and Teddy Hall) (Frances Williams); John Kirby and His Orchestra; "We're Having Our Fling" (Entire Company)
Act Two: "Back Bay Beat" (Frances Williams, John Kirby and His Orchestra, The Dancing Girls); The Royal Guards;"Your Face Is Your Fortune" (Jere McMahon, Billie Worth, Frances Williams, Buddy Clark, The Dancing Girls); "Yes, I Love You, Honey" (lyric and music by James P. Johnson) (James Barton, John Kirby and His Orchestra); "Dr. Kronkite" (Joe Smith, Charles Dale); "Frankie and Johnny" (Frances Williams; Frankie: Jayne Manners; Johnny: James Barton; Nelly Bly: Mimi Lynne; Ensemble); Jere McMahon; "A Lick, and a Riff, and a Slow Bounce" (lyric by Norman Zeno, music by Al Scofield [Schofield]) (Frances Williams, Jayne Manners, Billie Worth); Finale (Entire Company)

Shortly before the Broadway opening and on a decidedly optimistic note, the creators of the revue changed its name from *Bright Lights* to *Bright Lights of 1944*. But it didn't do any good. The revue opened on September 16, 1943, dimmed out after four performances, and never saw September 19, 1943, let alone January 1, 1944. It seems that somewhere in the revue's past was the semblance of a book musical. The first act took place in Sardi's Restaurant and revolved around three producers who hope to present a musical on Broadway. They have a potential backer, and so they outline the book, lyrics, and music of the show to him, only to have him back out. But two of Sardi's waiters (Joe Smith and Charles Dale) come up with the necessary capital, and, presto, act two of *Bright Lights of 1944* was the show itself.

To add complete verisimilitude to the evening, Renee Carroll, who was in real life a hatcheck girl at Sardi's, portrayed herself during the first act scenes which were set in the restaurant.

Despite its short run and its reputation as one of the horrors of the era, the revue received some surprisingly gentle notices. Ward Morehouse in the *New York Sun* said the evening was "no prize winner" but noted there was a "certain freshness" about it. The second act was a "decided and welcome improvement" over the first, the dancing was "all right," and he enjoyed the songs "Don't Forget the Girl from Punxsutawney" and "Your Face Is Your Fortune." Robert Garland in the *New York Journal-American* found the evening "curiously uneven," but nonetheless the "salon swing" of John Kirby and His Orchestra and the "hot and unbothered" pit orchestra conducted by Max Meth provided "as much fun as anything of its kind in town." He noted that Frances Williams, Jayne Manners, and Billie Worth won over the audience with "A Lick, and a Riff, and a Slow Bounce," and he also singled out the "equally unusual" songs "That's Broadway," "Back Bay Beat," "Yes, I Love You, Honey," "We're Having Our Fling," and the two numbers praised by Morehouse.

Louis Kronenberger in *PM* suggested that after **My Dear Public** and *Bright Lights of 1944*, a moratorium should be placed on musicals about people producing musicals. He noted the dialogue in the Sardi's scenes was "spectacularly ghastly," but on the plus side John Kirby's orchestra served up "some fair hot jazz." In regard to the "spectacularly ghastly" dialogue, Lewis Nichols in the *New York Times* quoted one exchange: "Who's your backer?" "The angel Gabriel." "Oh, a trumpet player."

John Chapman in the *New York Daily News* said the evening was "structurally a mess," but praised Smith and Dale's venerable "Dr. Kronkite" sketch (which was updated to include the doctor warning the patient to be quiet "or I'll give you gas," to which the patient retorts, "I'll take eight gallons") and James Barton's old sketch "The Pest" (about a drunk); Chapman also mentioned that at one point during the revue Barton joined John Kirby's orchestra for a jam session that included his "whapping the drums and playing boogie-woogie piano." As for the songs, Chapman said, "damned if I can remember any."

Wilella Waldorf in the *New York Post* said the comic material was generally "poor" and "meagre," and the songs "seedy." But the "Dr. Kronkite" sketch was still amusing, and John Kirby's band pepped up the proceedings. Howard Barnes in the *New York Herald Tribune* noted the "ragged little entertainment" offered little in the way of "sustained merriment." But Barton's drunk sketch and his "first rate" jive session were highlights, along with Smith and Dale's routine.

During the marathon run of *Tobacco Road*, James Barton succeeded Henry Hull in the role of Jeeter Lester and reportedly played the character 1,899 times in New York. One of his songs in *Bright Lights of 1944* was a tribute to the character ("Damned Ole Jeeter"). One or two of the critics also made note of the ballad "Thoughtless," which included the line, "Although I was thoughtless, it didn't mean I thought less of you."

As "Lick & Riff," the song "A Lick, and a Riff, and a Slow Bounce" had been heard in the previous season's **Sugar 'n' Spice**, which closed during its pre-Broadway tryout.

A TROPICAL REVUE

Theatre: Martin Beck Theatre (during run, the revue transferred to the Forrest Theatre)
Opening Date: September 19, 1943; *Closing Date*: December 4, 1943
Performances: 87
Direction and *Choreography*: Katherine Dunham; *Producer*: S. Hurok; *Scenery* and *Costumes*: John Pratt; *Lighting*: Dale Wasserman; *Musical Direction*: Albert Arkuss
Cast: *Katherine Dunham*, Roger Ohardieno, Lucille Ellis, Tommy Gomez, Lavinia Williams, Laverne French, Syvilla Fort, Claude Marchant, Lawaune Ingrim, Lenwood Morris, Maria Montiero, Vanoye Aikens, Ramona Erwin, Andre Drew; The Leonard Ware Trio; Gaucho Vanderhans (Drums), Candido Vicenty (Drums); Albert Arkuss (First Piano); Paul Barragan (Second Piano)
The dance revue was presented in three acts.

Musical Numbers

Act One: "Primitive Rhythms": (a) "Rara-Tonga" (music by Paquita Anderson) (The Chosen Woman: Lavinia Williams; The God: Roger Ohardieno; The Jealous Husband: Tommy Gomez); (b) "Tempo-Son" (Possessed Dancer: Lucille Ellis); and (c) "Tempo-Bolero" (music by Paquita Anderson) (Lavinia Williams, Tommy Gomez, Group); "Rumba Suite": (a) "Concert Rumba" (music by Morejon) (Katherine Dunham with Syvilla Fort, Lavinia Williams, Claude Marchant, and Tommy Gomez); (b) "Rumba with a Little Jive Mixed In" (music by Andre) (Lucille Ellis, Laverne French, and Claude Marchant); (c) "Brazilian Carnival Macumba" (Katherine Dunham with Lenwood Morris, Andre Drew, Laverne French, and Tommy Gomez); (d) "Santos Ritual" (Syvilla Fort, Roger Ohardieno); and (e) "Mexican Rumba" (from the "Rumba Symphony") (music by Harl MacDonald) (Katherine Dunham, Tommy Gomez, Group)
Act Two: "Rites of Passage": (a) "The Fertility Ritual" (Maiden in the Community: Lavinia Williams; Man in the Community: Laverne French); (b) "Male Puberty Ritual" (Boy Initiate: Tommy Gomez; Warrior: Roger Ohardieno); and (c) "Death Ritual" (Matriarch: Katherine Dunham); "Rhythm Interlude" (Lucille Ellis; Drums: Gaucho Vanderhans and Candido Vicenty); "Bahiana" (music by Don Alfonso) (Katherine Dunham with Roger Ohardieno, Claude Marchant, Tommy Gomez, Lenwood Morris); "Tropics—Shore Excursion" (music by Paquita Anderson; percussion by Gaucho Vanderhans) (Woman with the Cigar: Katherine Dunham)
Act Three: "Plantation Dances" from "Br'er Rabbit an' de Tah Baby" (Interlocutor: Katherine Dunham; Field Hands: Claude Marchant, Tommy Gomez, Roger Ohardieno, Lenwood Morris, and Vanoye Aikens); "Strutters' Ball" (Helen Dowdy, Singer); Couple from Memphis: Syvilla Fort and Laverne French);

Square Dance, Juba, Jennie Cooler, Palmer House, Pas Mala, Ballin' de Jack, Strut, and Cakewalk (dances) (Company); The Leonard Ware Trio; "Jazz Hot": (a) "Variations on the Theme Boogie Woogie" (music by Lewis, Ammons, and Smith) (Lucille Ellis, Group); (b)"Barrel House" ("Florida Swamp Shimmy") (music by Lewis and Ammons) (Katherine Dunham and Roger Ohardieno); and (c) "Honky-Tonk Train" (music by Lewis) ("Cokey" Brakeman: Laverne French; Lady Passenger: Lucille Ellis)

Katherine Dunham and her company appeared on Broadway in a number of dance revues over a period of almost twenty years; she recycled many of the dances from revue to revue. During the 1944–1945 season, Dunham and her troupe returned in another dance revue (also titled **A Tropical Revue**), and it included at least seven dance sequences that had been performed in the earlier edition. When the first edition toured and played a four-week engagement at the Blackstone Theatre in Chicago, Claudia Cassidy in *Best Plays* noted the revue was "brilliant" (it had been revised since New York, and included new material).

None of Dunham's revues had particularly long runs (and perhaps some were intended as limited engagements). She first made her mark as Georgia Brown in **Cabin in the Sky**; thereafter she appeared mostly in revues, with an occasional involvement in a book musical. Prior to **Cabin in the Sky** she had created the choreography for a song added to the 1937 labor revue *Pins and Needles*. After *Cabin*, she was represented as director, choreographer, and performer in a number of productions. Following the 1943 *Tropical Revue*, her Broadway credits are as follows: a return engagement of a revised version of **Tropical Revue** (1944; twenty-four performances; director, choreographer, performer); **Blue Holiday** (1945; eight performances; she created the choreography for the sequences in which her company appeared; among the troupe's members were Eartha Kitt and Talley Beatty); **Concert Varieties** (1945; thirty-six performances; choreography for the sequences in which her company appeared; she was also a dancer in this production); the book musical **Carib Song** (1945; thirty-six performances; choreographer, codirector, performer; the cast members included her troupe of dancers); **Bal Negre** (1946; fifty-four performances; director, choreographer, performer; company included her dancers); *Katherine Dunham and Her Company* (1950; thirty-seven performances; director, choreographer, performer); *Katherine Dunham and Her Company* (1955; thirty-two performances; director, choreographer, performer); and *Bamboche!*, her final Broadway appearance (1962, eight performances; director, choreographer, performer). Dunham also created the choreography for the 1946 book musical **Windy City**, which closed during its pre-Broadway tryout.

HAIRPIN HARMONY
"MUSICAL FARCE" / "MANHATTAN'S MERRIEST MUSICAL!"

Theatre: National Theatre
Opening Date: October 1, 1943; *Closing Date*: October 2, 1943
Performances: 3
Book, *Lyrics*, and *Music*: Harold Orlob; additional dialogue by Don Witty
Direction: Dora Maugham; production supervised by Mack Hilliard; *Producer*: Harold Orlob; *Choreography*: Uncredited; *Scenery*: Donald Oenslager; *Costumes*: Mahieu; *Lighting*: Jeanette Hackett; *Musical Direction*: Uncredited
Cast: Lennie Kent (Bill Heller), Carlyle Blackwell (Howard Swift), Gil Johnson (Chet Warren), Maureen Cannon (Reenie Franton), Teri Keane (Jackie Stevens), Karen Conrad (Evelyn), Gay Gaynor (Betty), The Clawson Triplets—Barbara, Doris, Dorothy (June, Ruth, Sue), Smiles & Smiles (Cobalt and Looseknit), Irene Corlett (Racey Corday), Don Valentine (Reverend Doctor Brown), Ving Merlin (Buddy Roc), Margaret Irving (Mrs. Warren), David Leonard (Inspector), Clair Kramer (State Trooper); The Hairpin Harmonettes: Rochelle Kritchmar (Piano), Esther Shure (Violin), Esther Rabiroff (Violin), Susanne Sprecher (Harp and Violin), Thelma Fitch (Bass), Julia Goldman (Drums and Violin), Nadine Winstead (Saxophone), L'Ana Hyams (Saxophone), Muriel Burns (Saxophone), Leona May Smith (Trumpet), Elvira Rohl (Trumpet), Elaine Fitch (Trombone)
The musical was presented in two acts.
The action takes place during the present time.

Musical Numbers

Act One: Opening (The Hairpin Harmonettes); "Hairpin Harmony" (Maureen Cannon, The Clawson Triplets); "You're the Reason" (Gil Johnson, Maureen Cannon, The Clawson Triplets, Cobalt); "What-a-Ya-Say" (Lennie Kent, Gil Johnson, Maureen Cannon, Teri Keane, The Clawson Triplets); "I'm Tickled Pink" (Teri Keane, The Clawson Triplets); "I'm a Butter Hoarder" (Gil Johnson); "Without a Sponsor" (Lennie Kent, The Clawson Triplets; danced by Karen Conrad); Tango (Karen Conrad)

Act Two: Trumpet Solo (Leona May Smith); "You're the Reason" (reprise) (Ving Merlin; the reprise included a violin solo); Dance (Karen Conrad); "I Can Be Like Grandpa" (Gil Johnson, Maureen Cannon); "Without a Sponsor" (reprise) (Maureen Cannon, Gil Johnson); "That's My Approach to Love" (Teri Keane, Lennie Kent); Violin Solo (Ving Merlin); "Piccaninny Pie" (Smiles & Smiles); "That's My Approach to Love" (reprise) (Teri Keane, Lennie Kent, The Clawson Triplets); "What Do the Neighbors Say?" (Maureen Cannon, Teri Keane, Karen Conrad, Gay Gaynor, The Clawson Triplets); "You're the Reason" (reprise and finale) (Entire Cast)

There are flops and there are flops, but perhaps Harold Orlob's *Hairpin Harmony*, which the advertisements touted as "Manhattan's Merriest Musical!," is the ultimate Broadway bomb. It certainly doesn't hold the record for having lost the most money, and of course there were other musicals that ran for fewer than three performances. But in sheer terms of jaw-dropping mediocrity and tastelessness, *Hairpin Harmony* has a special place in the rarified club of truly terrible musicals that have absolutely no redeeming qualities.

There is little that remains of the musical. The Library of Congress has no record of it in its database, and because there's no copyright, there's no script in the archives. There doesn't seem to have been any sheet music published from the score, and the show is one of a handful of book musicals in recent decades for which not a single song has been recorded (apparently the radios and jukeboxes of 1943 weren't playing "Pickaninny Pie" and "I'm a Butter Hoarder"). Besides its program and its window card, all that really exists of this legendary disaster is what the critics wrote about it. And they all had something to say.

The plot dealt with baby-food manufacturer Howard Swift (Carlyle Blackwell) who wants to sponsor a radio show in order to advertise his product. Bill Heller (Lennie Kent) comes to his rescue with the suggestion of a music show that features an all-girl band, The Hairpin Harmonettes (the poster artwork describes them as an "All-Girl Orchestra of Musical Charmers"). To make matters even better, Bill has the unusual ability to imitate a baby's voice with falsetto touches, and thus his presence on the program will help sell baby food. At one point he impersonates a baby, even down to wearing diapers (when viewing the diaper-clad Bill in an over-sized baby carriage, a character uttered the immortal line, "But that baby needs a shave!").

Further, the book offered four sequences that George Jean Nathan in his annual seasonal summary reported were of "an indelicacy seldom encountered in the theatre, even on the old burlesque show stages at their dirtiest." As a result, many women in the audience headed for the exits. Of all the critics, only Nathan was somewhat specific about the evening's tastelessness when he described a scene in which a young woman sits on a lawman's lap amid dialogue about his loaded gun.

If the ridiculous plot and the gamy humor weren't enough, the musical offered a variety of songs, many of which have tantalizing titles: "What-a-Ya-Say," "I'm Tickled Pink," "I'm a Butter Hoarder," and, especially, "Piccaninny Pie," which was sung and danced by the black duo of Smiles & Smiles, who played the roles of Cobalt and Looseknit.

Nathan said *Hairpin Harmony* was "beyond any possible doubt one of the worst musical shows ever to have been shown in the whole history of the American theatre." Even **You'll See Stars** and **My Dear Public** couldn't "have been so dreadful as they unquestionably were."

Wilella Waldorf in the *New York Post* said the evening was "acutely embarrassing" and noted Broadway seldom offered "anything as doggedly amateurish . . . any college dramatic society would be ashamed to own it." The thought of returning to the show after intermission was "too horrible to contemplate" and so she fled down 41st Street for home. John Chapman in the *New York Daily News* also confessed he left at intermission and stated that the musical shouldn't have been produced "anywhere, let alone in a good playhouse in the theatre metropolis of the Western Hemisphere." Louis Kronenberger in *PM* said other shows during the season might have been dull or silly, but none of them had been "even remotely as unprofessional" as *Hairpin Harmony*; at one point, the dialogue convinced him that both his morals and his sanity "would best be served" if he said "aloha" to the show, and he noted that some of the other critics had "beat it much earlier."

Ward Morehouse in the *New York Sun* found the evening "pretty terrible" and said it was the "worst" he'd seen since his high school days in Guyton, Georgia, when *St. Elmo* ("or was it *Lena Rivers*?") was produced; Howard Barnes in the *New York Herald Tribune* said if worse musicals had ever been produced, he had missed them, for *Hairpin Harmony* was "all of a piece and it is all awful"; and Lewis Nichols in the *New York Times* said many words could describe the musical, but "dreadful" would do; and he noted that many in the audience left early during the "witless, vulgar, inept and tasteless" evening.

Robert Garland in the *New York Journal-American* said he'd been attending the theatre since he was a boy, but nothing in his theatergoing experience could match the "ineptitude" of *Hairpin Harmony*, which managed "to live down to its title." He noted Harold Orlob had been involved with *Listen Lester* (1918) and *Yes, Yes, Yvette* (1927), and suggested someone should have told him, "Listen, Harold, 'No, No, *Hairpin Harmony*'."

Burton Rascoe in the *New York World-Telegram* had believed it "impossible" for anything to equal **You'll See Stars** in mediocrity. But when Orlob made the "grievous error" of opening *Hairpin Harmony*, the disaster of **You'll See Stars** seemed "almost bright in comparison." He noted that about half the audience failed to return after intermission, and said besides being "unbelievably dull, unorganized and tasteless," the "offensive" musical required some of the Hairpin Harmonettes to utter lines that implied "they had the morals of alley cats."

Many of the critics noted the musical had undergone numerous postponements, rewriting, recasting, and a change of directors, and Morehouse suggested the show should have stayed in Bridgeport, Connecticut (or at least "Bridgeport should have warned us").

Sam Zolotow in the *New York Times* reported that after the "barrage" of negative reviews, Orlob closed the show after three performances and stated, "I couldn't combat that sort of criticism." The musical had been capitalized at $37,000, and for the three performances took in a total of $2,160 in ticket sales. It was the season's shortest-running musical, but, ironically, the season's longest-running musical, **Follow the Girls**, is today probably just as obscure as *Hairpin Harmony*.

The production presumably saved some money with its single set because Donald Oenslager's setting had been previously used in the 1941 six-performance comedy *Pie in the Sky*. Waldorf reported that in order to avoid seeing and hearing what was occurring on the National's stage, she started concentrating on the set, "which began to look too familiar." She then realized the now somewhat "dingy" scenery had been used in the earlier "turkey."

The artwork for the musical's newspaper advertisements showed the faces of singing Hairpin Harmonettes (although they appear to be howling rather than singing); the artwork for the window card showed a trumpet-playing Hairpin Harmonette in her scanties (perhaps she's the forerunner of *Gypsy*'s Miss Mazeppa).

ONE TOUCH OF VENUS

Theatre: Imperial Theatre (during run, the musical transferred to the 46th Street Theatre)
Opening Date: October 7, 1943; *Closing Date*: February 10, 1945
Performances: 567
Book: S. J. Perelman and Ogden Nash
Lyrics: Ogden Nash
Music: Kurt Weill
Based on the 1885 novel *The Tinted Venus* by F. Anstey (Thomas Anstey Guthrie).
Direction: Elia Kazan; *Producer*: Cheryl Crawford (John Wildberg, Associate Producer); *Choreography*: Agnes De Mille; *Scenery*: Howard Bay; *Costumes*: Paul du Pont and Kermit Love (Mary Martin's gowns by Mainbocher); *Lighting*: Uncredited; *Musical Direction*: Maurice Abravanel
Cast: *John Boles* (Whitelaw Savory), Paula Laurence (Molly Grant), Teddy Hart (Taxi Black), Harry Clark (Stanley), *Kenny Baker* (Rodney Hatch), *Mary Martin* (Venus), Florence Dunlap (Mrs. Moats), Sam Bonnell (Store Manager, Anatolian), Lou Wills Jr. (Bus Starter), Zachary A. Charles (Sam), Helen Raymond (Mrs. Kramer), Ruth Bond (Gloria Kramer), Bert Freed (Police Lieutenant), Jane Hoffman (Rose), Harold J. Stone (Zuvetli), Johnny Stearns (Dr. Rook), Matthew Farrar (Anatolian), Sono Ostao (Premiere Danseuse); Singers: Jane Davies, Beatrice Hudson, Rose Marie Elliot, Julie Jefferson, Willa Rollins, Betty Spain, Lynn Alden, Arthur Davies, Matthew Farrar, Jeffrey Warren; Dancers: Nelle Fisher, Ruth Harte, Jinx Heffelfinger, Jean Houloose, Ann Hutchinson, Pearl Lang, Allyn Ann McLerie, Lavina Nielsen, Ginee Richardson,

Patricia Schaeffer, Kirsten Valbor, Carle Erbele, Robert Pageant, Peter Birch, William Garrett, Ralph Linn, Duncan Nobl, Kevin Smith, William Weber, Lou Wills, Jr., Parker Wilson
The musical was presented in two acts.
The action takes place during the present time in New York City.

Musical Numbers

Act One: "New Art Is True Art" (John Boles, Chorus); "One Touch of Venus" (Paula Laurence, Girls); "How Much I Love You" (Kenny Baker); "I'm a Stranger Here Myself" (Mary Martin); "Forty Minutes for Lunch" (ballet) (danced by Mary Martin, Sono Osato, Peter Birch, Dancers); "West Wind" (John Boles); "Way Out West in Jersey" (Helen Raymond, Ruth Bond, Kenny Baker; danced by Ruth Bond and Lou Wills Jr.); "Foolish Heart" (Mary Martin; danced by Sono Osato and Robert Pageant); "The Trouble with Women" (Kenny Baker, John Boles, Teddy Hart, Harry Clark); "Speak Low" (Mary Martin, Kenny Baker); "Dr. Crippen" (John Boles, Dancers)

Act Two: "Very, Very, Very" (Paula Laurence); "Speak Low" (reprise) (Kenny Baker, Mary Martin); "Catch Hatch" (John Boles, Paula Laurence, Ensemble); "That's Him" (Mary Martin); "Wooden Wedding" (Kenny Baker); "Venus in Ozone Heights" (ballet) (Children: Ruth Harte, Jean Houloose, Ralph Linn, Lou Wills Jr.; Shy Girls: Diana Adams, Allyn Ann McLerie; The Head Nymph: Sono Osato; The Jumping Nymphs: Nelle Fisher, Kirsten Valbor, Pearl Lang; The Aviator and His Girl: Kevin Smith and Patricia Schaeffer; Gods: Robert Pageant; Fauns, Nymphs, Satyrs, Gods); Finale ("Speak Low") (Kenny Baker)

The saucy fantasy *One Touch of Venus* was not only one of the longest-running musicals of the season, it also marked the longest run of any of Kurt Weill's Broadway musicals. The story dealt with mild-mannered barber Rodney Hatch (Kenny Baker) who brings a statue of Venus (Mary Martin) to life when he places a ring intended for his shrewish fiancée Gloria Kramer (Ruth Bond) on the statue's finger. The statue has just been delivered to a modern art museum owned by Savory Whitelaw (John Boles), who has bought the statue because it reminds him of a lost love.

With the statue missing from its pedestal, it's assumed Rodney must have had something to do with its disappearance. Only Rodney knows about the transformation, and Venus (being Venus, after all) is in hot pursuit of him and can't understand his reluctance to bed her (she says love isn't the sound of a "distant violin—it's the triumphant twang of a bedspring"). In "I'm a Stranger Here Myself" she sings of her bewilderment over the nature of modern love, where "gender is just a term in grammar." So problems romantic and otherwise abound: Rodney is pursued by Venus, Gloria, and the police; and Savory is after Venus as well as his statue (not realizing they are really one and the same).

Rodney soon finds himself falling in love with Venus, and looks forward to their life together in suburban Ozone Heights. But a dream that depicts ordinary, everyday life on Earth closes in on Venus; the script notes that for her Ozone Heights suddenly becomes the "myth" and Ancient Greece the reality, and so she returns to the gods and her statue materializes on its pedestal in the museum. But all is not lost. As Rodney gazes at the statue, a girl (Martin) walks in who looks just like Venus. Rodney asks her if she likes Ozone Heights and she replies it's the only place to live; he tells her his name, and she begins to tell him hers before he shushes her and says he knows. They walk off together as the curtain falls.

S. J. Perelman and Ogden Nash's book was one of the wittiest of the era, and Nash's lyrics were both romantic and cynical. In the title song, Savory's secretary Molly (Paula Laurence) suggests that for a girl with a touch of Venus life is "a goddess damsel cinch," and the barbershop quartet "The Trouble with Women" catalogs the problems with the fair sex, and concludes that the trouble with women is . . . men. Rodney's "How Much I Love You" depicted his conflicted relationship with Gloria and clearly showed he wasn't in love with her (he loves her more than a hangnail hurts, more than a dachshund hates revolving doors, even more than boring commercials). (Incidentally, a few lines of Nash's lyric were later used for a Valentine card issued by Hallmark/Contemporary Cards # 60KV-103-1/99-16.)

The haunting and richly melodic "Speak Low" became a standard, and "Foolish Heart" and "West Wind" were other distinguished ballads in the score. "That's Him" was an especially felicitous moment that found Martin sitting alone on the stage languorously and amusingly ruminating over the vagaries of love and the irony that the goddess Venus herself is in love with a man not "arty" or "actory" but definitely "satisfactory."

Further, Agnes De Mille's choreography offered two elaborate dance sequences, the humorous if somewhat extraneous "Forty Minutes for Lunch" (which described a hectic Manhattan lunch break) and the plot-driven "Venus in Ozone Heights."

After a rash of disappointing musicals (***My Dear Public***, ***Bright Lights of 1944***, and ***Hairpin Harmony***), the critics were glad to welcome a savvy and entertaining new show. Quite a few complained that the opening scenes were sluggish, but all agreed the show soon picked up the pace and offered melodic songs, amusing dialogue, entertaining dances, and a star performance by Mary Martin, who had appeared on Broadway just once before in Cole Porter's *Leave It to Me!* (1938) where she had introduced the show-stopping "My Heart Belongs to Daddy" (between the Porter musical and *One Touch of Venus*, two of her Broadway-bound musicals, *Nice Goin'* [1939] and ***Dancing in the Streets***, had closed in Boston).

Wilella Waldorf in the *New York Post* said the musical was "adult, professional, often comic and genuinely amusing"; it was Weill's "best" score and she noted it had been a long time since she'd heard a "new and modern score in musical comedy that struck" her "as something at once popular and unusually fine." At their best, Nash's lyrics were often "very diverting and even witty," and in their less-inspired moments came across as "rather tired Cole Porter." John Chapman in the *New York Daily News* said Weill's style was "hard to put a finger on"; it wasn't Tin Pan Alley, it was "elusive" and "tricky" but not "smarty," and it wasn't "lush and fruity"; it "teases you along," and he noted "Speak Low" would soon have the "swoon crooners fainting all over the broadcast band." As for Nash's lyrics, he commented that first-nighter Cole Porter had given an "attentive ear" to the "smartly turned" lyrics.

Louis Kronenberger in *PM* suggested the book's "cleverness" was sometimes "too literary," but he noted the show spurned the "easy formulas of Broadway" and had "personality and wit and genuinely high moments of music and dancing"; he also commented that De Mille's dances were "even bolder" than those she created for *Oklahoma!* Lewis Nichols in the *New York Times* said *One Touch of Venus* made theatre-going a "pleasure" again, for here was a musical "complete with freshness, an adult manner and lavishness of display" (he noted that the "engaging" Mary Martin had the rare ability to toss a song across the footlights, which was "the only place to send a song," and suggested the "beautiful" and "graceful" dancer Sono Osato would likely be "the toast of the autumn").

Robert Garland in the *New York Journal-American* said the show was a "smash hit," and noted the lyric of "The Trouble with Women" had been restored after a brush with the Boston censors during the tryout. Ward Morehouse in the *New York Sun* felt the musical wasn't always up to the standards of its cast, but it was clear the show was a "definite hit" and he praised the "catchy" music and "devastating" lyrics. Howard Barnes in the *New York Herald Tribune* said *One Touch of Venus* "proved an occasion for rejoicing" and noted that after a "slow start" it "strikes fire." He praised the "resounding hit" and said De Mille's choreography gave the evening its "peculiar charm" (like most of the critics, he singled out Sono Osato); he also commented that Elia Kazan had directed with "finish and tempo."

But Burton Rascoe in the *New York World-Telegram* said the musical wasn't "bad," just "disappointing"; he noted he could feel the disappointment in the audience and the principals ("you could see it in their faces and in their lack of animation—the sense that the show was dying on its feet"). The second act perked up, but the "only distinct hit" of the evening was Sono Osato. He suggested the show's creators had never decided what the show was about. Was it to be "arty, sophisticated and abstract"? Or "something like a Minsky burlesque only more literate"? But he said the evening offered "some of the brightest and most singable songs you ever heard" (and singled out eight numbers).

The musical marked the first time soon-to-be-legendary Elia Kazan helmed a musical. He would do so once more, again in collaboration with Kurt Weill, when he directed the ground-breaking ***Love Life***, one of the first concept musicals.

During the tryout, the following songs were cut: "Simply Paranoia" (for John Boles and chorus); "The Modest Goddess" (for Paula Laurence and chorus); and "Who Am I?" (for John Boles); "Way Out West in Jersey" was titled "Oh, New Jersey." Songs dropped during rehearsals and preproduction were: "Vive La Difference," "The Jersey Plunk," "Bacchanale Ballet," "Fresh Air and Exercise," "It Must Be Ernie," "Same Time, Same Place," "Too Soon," "Who Dealt?," "You'll Find It on the Bill," and "Love in a Mist" (which was the musical's title during preproduction).

Decca recorded nine numbers (and the finale) from the musical, including shortened versions of the ballets "Forty Minutes for Lunch" and "Venus in Ozone Heights"; Mary Martin and Kenny Baker (and chorus) performed all the songs, and Maurice Abravanel conducted. The CD was released by MCA Classics/Broadway

Gold (# MCAD-11354) and is coupled with selections from **Lute Song**, which also starred Martin. *Kurt Weill Revisited* (Painted Smiles CD # PSCD-108) includes original cast member Paula Laurence singing the title song as well as the unused "Vive La Difference"; also included in the collection are "Dr. Crippen" and the unused "Love in a Mist." *Kurt Weill Revisited Volume II* (Painted Smiles CD # PSCD-109) includes "Way Out West in Jersey." The collection *Tryout* (DRG CD # 904) offers private rehearsal recordings of Weill singing "West Wind," "Very, Very, Very," "Wooden Wedding," "Speak Low," "The Trouble with Women," and the cut "The Jersey Plunk."

A two-CD studio cast recording released by Jay Records (# CDJAY2-1362) offers the entire score, including the complete dance music, encores, reprises, underscoring, and the entr'acte as well as three deleted songs ("Vive La Difference," "Who Am I?," and "Love in a Mist"). The featured singers are Melissa Errico, Brent Barrett, Ron Raines, Victoria Clark, and Judy Kaye.

The script was published in hardback by Little, Brown and Company in 1944. The script is also included in the hardback collection *Ten Great Musicals of the American Theatre* (1973), published by Chilton Book Company (the collection isn't identified as volume one, but there was a later second volume in this series).

The 1948 film version by Universal-International was perfectly cast with film goddess Ava Gardner in the title role (she was dubbed by Eileen Wilson), and she was ably supported by Robert Walker, Eve Arden, Tom Conway, Dick Haymes, and Olga San Juan; the screenplay was by Harry Kurnitz and Frank Tashlin, and the direction by William A. Seiter. Although the adaptation is more of a comedy with incidental songs, the mild film has a modest and rather cozy black-and-white charm. Only a handful of songs were retained: "Speak Low"; "Foolish Heart" (with a new lyric by Ann Ronell, the latter was heard as "Don't Look Now but My Heart Is Showing"); "West Wind" (with Ronell's new lyric, the song was heard as "My Week"); "That's Him" (with a revised lyric by Ronell); and "The Trouble with Women," briefly heard during the opening credits. The DVD was released by Republic Pictures/Lionsgate (# NYSE-LGF), and the soundtrack was issued in the collection *Kurt Weill in Hollywood* (Ariel Records LP # KWH-10).

An NBC television adaptation directed by George Schaeffer and choreographed by Edmund Balin was seen on August 27, 1955, with Janet Blair, Russell Nype, George Gaynes, Laurel Shelby, Iggie Wolfington, Mort Marshall, Louis Nye, and Arnie Freeman; the DVD of the production was issued by Video Artists International (# 4568). The telecast was more faithful than the film version and included "How Much I Love You," "I'm a Stranger Here Myself," "Forty Minutes for Lunch," "West Wind," "One Touch of Venus," "Foolish Heart," "The Trouble with Women," "Speak Low," "Catch Hatch," "That's Him," "Wooden Wedding," and "Venus in Ozone Heights."

ARTISTS AND MODELS
"A Revue"

Theatre: Broadway Theatre
Opening Date: November 5, 1943; *Closing Date*: November 27, 1943
Performances: 28
Dialogue: Lou Walters, Don Ross, and Frank Luther
Lyrics and *Music*: Dan Shapiro, Milton Pascal, and Phil Charig
Direction: Dialogue directed by Jack Kennedy (production staged by Lou Walters); *Producers*: Lou Walters and Don Ross in association with E. M. Loew and Michael Redstone); *Choreographer*: Natalie Kamarova (assisted by Lauretta Jefferson); *Scenery*: Watson Barratt; *Costumes*: Kathryn Kuhn; *Lighting*: Uncredited; *Musical Direction*: Max Meth
Cast: *Jane Froman*, Frances Faye, Jackie Gleason, Marty May, Colette Lyons, Billy Newell, The Radio Aces (Joe Stoner, Lou Stoner, and Marty Drake), Nick Long, Carol King, The Peters Sisters, Harold and Lola, The Worth Sisters (Toni and Mimi), Ben Yost, Don Saxon, Mayla, Mildred Law, The Three Businessmen of Rhythm and Pearl, Billie Boze, Barbara Bannister, The Ben Yost Singers (aka The Ben Yost Octet: Albert Cazentre, William Hogue, Alfred Jimenez, Arthur Laurent, Jack Leslie, Fred Peters, Jack Paddock, and Torine Rella), Mary Raye and Naldi, Sheila Bond, Gloria LeRoy, Jeanne Blanche, Lee Lopret, The Mullen Twins, The Christiani Troupe, Gertrude Erdey, Betty Jane Hunt, Patsy LuRains, The Harp Ensemble; Wally Wanger's American Beauties; Specialty Dancers: Sheila Bond, Jeanne Blanche, Gertrude Erdey, Lee Loprete, Betty Jane Hunt, The Mullen Sisters, Patsy LuRains, and Mary-Jo Ball; Dancing Girls: Ellen

Taylor, Maureen Cunningham, Wynn Stanley, Lillian Moore, Edna Ryan, Helen Heller, Grace DeWitt, Frances Gardner; Ballet Girls: Carmelita Lanza, Virginia Harriot, Jane Sproule, Patti Robbins, Irene Vernon, Nancy Newton, Didi Foret, Margret Neil, Leandra Hines, and Anita Divine; Models: Iris Amber, Gail Banner, Nancy Callahan, Ruth Dexter, Lana Holmes, Jackie Jordan, Joan Myles, Velvet Knight; Aerial Ballet: Chat Chilvers, Betty Hackett, Corinne Rose, Florence Walsh; Ballet Boys: Charles Beckman, Joseph Hahn, Harold Haskin, Slava Toumina

The revue was presented in two acts.

Sketches and Musical Numbers

Act One: "Parade of Models" (Velvet Night: Mira Stephans; Garden Day: Nancy Callahan; My Sin: Jackie Jordan; Midnight Madness: Joan Myles; Melody Mood: Ruth Dexter; Star Sapphire: Gail Banner; Tempest Topaz: Lana Holmes; Amber Glow: Iris Amber; Bridal Blush: Helen Heller; Coral Crown: Edna Ryan; Blithe Harbor: Lillian Moore; Rose Bloom: Grace DeWitt; Blue Heaven: Maureen Cunningham; Dusky Dawn: Patti Robins; Radiant Ruby: Carmelita Lazna); Prologue (Jackie Gleason, Marty May, Billy Newell); Minstrelsy—"Way Up North in Dixieland" (Marty May, Jackie Gleason, Billy Newell, The Radio Aces, The Three Businessmen, The Peters Sisters, Minstrel Men, Minstrel Girls, Ensemble); "Swing Low, Sweet Harriet" (Jane Froman); Burlesque—Candy Butcher: Jackie Gleason; "How'ja Like to Take Me Home" (Collette Lyons); "Strip Tease" (The Worth Sisters); Pages: The Mullen Twins; "Taken for a Ride"—Boze-O-Snider: Jackie Gleason; Sliding Willie Weston: Marty May; Mick Specks: Billy Newell; Gypsy Rose Corio: Collette Lyons; Margie Smart: Billie Boze; Georgia Sudden: Barbara Bannister); Hollywood—*The Road to Manasooris* ("A Super-Duper Epic in Technicolor")—Virgin Princess: Mayla; Chief Danasooris: Jackie Gleason; Beachcomber: Don Saxon; Kay Townsend: Mildred Law; Margie (Boo-Boo) Le May: Collette Lyons; Bob Stevens: Nick Long; Girls of Manasooris: Bille Boze, Barbara Bannister, Grace DeWitt; Schwartzerooris: The Peters Sisters; Captain of Marines: Ben Yost; "Isle of Manasooris" (Mayla, Island Beauties); "Sears Roebuck" (Jackie Gleason, Collette Lyons); "Lover's Tryst Narrative": Mayla; "Dance of the Cobra" (Harold and Lola); Resume for Latecomers—Marty May; Concert—Frances Faye and Harps in Swing: Helen Thomas, Margaret Ross, Catherine Johnk, Ann Roberts; Vaudeville—"North Dakota, South Dakota Moon" (Jackie Gleason, Marty May, Billy Newell); "My Heart Is on a Binge Again" (Jane Froman); Ballet—"New York Heartbeat" (music by Georges F. Kamaroff) (Nick Long, The Worth Sisters, Mayla, The Three Businessmen of Rhythm and Pearl, The Yost Singers, Corps de Ballet, Dancing Girls, Specialty Girls, American Beauties; Ballerina: Carol King; Dancer: Slava Tourmine)

Act Two: Circus—Equestriennes: Sheila Bond, Jeanne Blanche, Gertrude Erdey, Lee Loprete; Jungle Denizens: Mira Stephans, Ruth Dexter, Lana Holmes, Iris Amber, Joan Myles, Jackie Jordan, Gail Banner, Nancy Callahan; Ponies: Ballet and Dancing Girls; Birds of Paradise: The Worth Sisters; Carnivori: Betty Jane Hunt, The Mullen Twins, Patsy LuRains; Clowns: The Ben Yost Octet; Aerial Ballet: Chat Chilvers, Betty Hackett, Corine Rose, Florence Walsh; Trainer: Joseph Hahn; Lion Tamer: Mildred Law; The Christiani Troupe; Questionnaire—"What Does the Public Want?" (special material by Bud Burtson) (The Radio Aces); Revue—"You Are Romance" (Jane Froman, Don Saxon, The Ben Yost Octet, Dancers, Specialty Girls, Ballet Boys, Mary Raye and Naldi); Afternoon Tea—Collette Lyons; Drama—"Submarine U Boat X37" (Captain Anchluss: Jackie Gleason; Lieutenant Eingamacht: Billy Newell; Bystander: Marty May; Seamen: Lou Stoner, Marty Drake; Boatswain: Joe Stoner; Stowaway: Billie Boze); Specialty (Gloria Le-Roy); Songs—"Let's Keep It That Way" (lyric by Milton Berle and Ervin Drake, music by Abner Silver) (Jane Froman); Finale ("Every Show Has One")

The lavish *Artists and Models* didn't survive beyond a month. The revue was overloaded with performers, and perhaps there was too much of everything. The evening was hosted by Jackie Gleason, Marty May, and Billy Newell, and they explained that the producers differed on what the revue should be about, and so they threw in every kind of conceivable act: minstrels, burlesque, vaudeville, ballet, concerts, the movies, the circus, the drama, songs, and dances.

After an opening parade of models (who promenaded about in perfumed fashion under such monikers as Tempest Topaz, Coral Brown, Bridal Blush, and Rose Bloom [not to mention the appropriately named Amber Glow, who was played by Iris Amber]), it was announced that from here on in the revue had no connection to its title. But it was all too much, and Louis Kronenberger in *PM* noted the "vastness" of the undertaking didn't leave the writers time to find a single good joke (the humor, such as it was, ran along the lines of, "They're debutantes. They came out in 1941 and haven't been home since"). As for the burlesque spoof, the reigning queens of the strip tease were kidded ("Gypsy Rose Corio," "Margie Smart," and "Georgia Sudden") and for Hollywood the *Road* movies were mocked in *The Road to Manasooris*, subtitled "A Super-Duper Epic in Technicolor." This last sequence included the Peters Sisters (who had earlier appeared in **Harlem Cavalcade**); their program bio noted they were "ebon of hue" and in the spoof they appeared as "Schwartzersooris."

Kronenberger noted the evening was a "pretty awful mess," but admitted it was "cheerful and fairly high-spirited." However, he was bewildered by the ballet "New York Heartbeat," an "astounding venture into choreography." He couldn't figure it out, and finally decided it was an attempt to "cram" into ten minutes every ballet in existence along "with quite a few that have never been dreamt up." Lewis Nichols in the *New York Times* found the revue "tedious" and a "little windy," but suggested no one could say they didn't get enough show for their money. Wilella Waldorf in the *New York Post* said the evening seemed like a series of night club turns, and if *Artists and Models* offered a "fair sample" of nitery floorshows then she was glad she hadn't been to a night spot in a long time.

Ward Morehouse in the *New York Sun* liked the minstrel song "Way Up North in Dixieland" and the vaudeville number "North Dakota, South Dakota Moon," and noted that of the comedians Jackie Gleason fared best. John Chapman in the *New York Daily News* said the revue wasn't "much good . . . just a lot of stuff"; and he too suggested most of the material was best suited for a nightclub. Burton Rascoe in the *New York World-Telegram* said the evening was a "green persimmon" which belonged in a "high-class saloon." He noted that Max Meth and his orchestra had been just about the "only good thing" in **Bright Lights of 1944**, and with *Artists and Models* Meth and his musicians were again "superb."

Howard Barnes in the *New York Herald Tribune* found the songs "melodic and catchy," but regretted the evening was "lean on fun"; like his fellow critics, he said the revue was a glorified floor show. For Robert Garland in the *New York Journal-American*, the evening was a "long, luxurious and not very funny extravaganza," but he seemed to feel it was enjoyable enough. He and all the critics praised Jane Froman, who sang four songs throughout the evening. During the previous winter she had been seriously hurt in a plane crash with major leg and other injuries, and so she was seated while she performed her songs. The trauma of the plane wreck and her injuries haunted her for the remainder of her life; in 1952, Hollywood depicted her life and career in *With a Song in My Heart*, which starred Susan Hayward (whose vocals were dubbed by Froman).

During the tryout, "Art for Artists and Models Sake" and "Blowing the Top" were deleted; also cut was a sketch "Winter Garden Vikings," a spoof of the 1943 **Ziegfeld Follies** in which Jackie Gleason impersonated Milton Berle.

WHAT'S UP
"A MERRY NEW MUSICAL COMEDY" / "A NEW MUSICAL"

Theatre: National Theatre
Opening Date: November 11, 1943; *Closing Date*: January 4, 1944
Performances: 63
Book: Alan Jay Lerner and Arthur Pierson
Lyrics: Alan Jay Lerner
Music: Frederick Loewe
Direction: Book directed by Robert H. Gordon and production staged by George Balanchine; *Producer*: Mark Warnow; *Choreography*: George Balanchine; *Scenery*: Boris Aronson; *Costumes*: Grace Houston; *Lighting*: Al Alloy; *Musical Direction*: Will Irwin
Cast: Mary Roche (Jayne), Pat Marshall (Susan), Mitzi Perry (Eleanor), Lynn Gardner (Margaret), Claire Meade (Harriett Spinner), Honey Murray (Pamela), Sondra Barrett (Louise), Sara Macon (Martha), Marjorie Beecher (aka Marge Champion) (May), Phyllis Hill (Jennifer), Frank Kreig (Doctor), Larry Douglas (Sergeant Willie Klink), Rodney McLennan (Captain Robert Lindsay), Jack Baker (Sergeant Henry Wagner), Robert Bay (Second Lieutenant Murray Bacchus), Don Weissmuller (First Lieutenant Ed Anderson), Johnny Morgan

(Sergeant Moroney), Helen Wenzel (Judy), William Tabbert (Sergeant Dick Benham), Gloria Warren (Virginia Miller), Jimmy Savo (The Rawa of Tanglinia), Kenneth Buffett (Sergeant Jimmy Stevenson)

The musical was presented in two acts.

The action takes place during the present time at Miss Langley's School for Girls in Crestville, Virginia.

Musical Numbers

Act One: "Miss Langley's School for Girls" (Mary Roche, Girls); "From the Chimney to the Cellar" (Mary Roche, Girls); "You've Got a Hold on Me" (Gloria Warren, Lynn Gardner, Larry Douglas); "A Girl Is Like a Book" (Rodney McLennan); "Joshua" (Lynn Gardner; danced by Girls and Fliers); "Three Girls in a Boat" (Lynn Gardner, Mary Roche, Pat Marshall); Ballet (Jimmy Savo, Phyllis Hill); "How Fly Times" (Larry Douglas, William Tabbert, Flyers; danced by Don Weissmuller); "My Last Love" (Mary Roche, Larry Douglas, Lynn Gardner, Johnny Morgan, William Tabbert, Gloria Warren)

Act Two: "You Wash and I'll Dry" (Lynn Gardner, Larry Douglas, Pat Marshall, Robert Bay; danced by Sondra Barrett, Kenneth Buffett, Honey Murray; Duo Dance by Marjorie Beecher and Rodney McLennan); "You Wash and I'll Dry" (reprise) (Gloria Warren); "The Ill-Tempered Clavichord" (Mary Roche, Pat Marshall, Gloria Warren; danced by Fliers and Girls; Specialty Dance by Robert Bay); "You've Got a Hold on Me" (reprise) (Gloria Warren, William Tabbert, Fliers, Girls; danced by Phyllis Hill and Jack Baker); Finale (Entire Company)

One of the eternal verities of musical theatre is that mistaken identity is a sure-fire way to ignite a plot. A sub-verity of this theme is that an establishment run by or for women is comic fodder for misinterpretation of the establishment's true nature. The bordellos run in **Early to Bed** and **Louisiana Lady** were sometimes mistaken by characters for schools or hotels for women, and at other times an innocent boarding house for servicemen's wives (**Something for the Boys**) or the telephone services provided by the Susanswerphone company (*Bells Are Ringing* [1956]) were open to salacious speculation. But wasn't it Freud who once said that sometimes a girls' boarding school is just a girls' boarding school? That was the case for *What's Up* because Alan Jay Lerner and Arthur Pierson's book was daringly original in its groundbreaking plot. A military plane crash lands on the grounds of an exclusive girls' boarding school in Virginia, and not once did the servicemen assume they'd come upon a fancy house in an upscale red-light district; they took the school at face value and never cracked wise about whether the school girls might be other kinds of girls.

The plane not only carries military men; the passengers also include Middle Eastern potentate The Rawa of Tanglinia (Jimmy Savo), who speaks no English, and his secretary Virginia Miller (Gloria Warren), who does. When someone comes down with measles, the students, the soldiers, and the visiting dignitary and his secretary are quarantined on the campus, all of which leads to innocent romantic and comic episodes. Because Savo excelled in pantomime, his role was a perfect one that allowed him to mostly pantomime and gesture his thoughts and words. His pantomime revue **Mum's the Word** had a short run, and his appearance in the burlesque revue **Wine Women and Song** received mostly negative notices. So he must have felt his current role in a traditional book musical was perfectly tailored for his specialized talents and that he'd enjoy his first Broadway success since *The Boys from Syracuse* in 1938. But *What's Up* lasted just two months, and with its closing the comic bid farewell to the Broadway stage.

The critics said the mild-mannered musical needed a stronger plot and more comic routines for Savo. Howard Barnes in the *New York Herald Tribune* said the evening was "derivative but generally diverting," and while it lacked inspiration it was likely to do well at the box office; Burton Rascoe in the *New York World-Telegram* "wholeheartedly" recommended the show despite its wispy plot; and singled out Don Weissmuller's dancing ("his glissandos in tap were unearthly in cadence and precision"), the "eminently singable" score (especially "Joshua" and "My Last Love"), and praised Savo (but suggested the clown omit his first-act curtain line, which sounded as though it had been suggested by Milton Berle); and Louis Kronenberger in *PM* said the "pint-sized" musical was too full of cute and peppy youngsters and thus needed a "hatchet-faced old maid" or a "besotted old man" to spice up the proceedings (he also suggested that "boarding school capers" were perhaps not George Balanchine's "long suit").

Ward Morehouse in the *New York Sun* said the George Abbott-like show had an occasional "deadly lull" in its book, but otherwise the musical interludes came "zestfully" to the rescue, and he singled out the dances and score, including "Joshua," "You Wash and I'll Dry," and "You've Got a Hold on Me"; but Robert Garland in the *New York Journal-American* found the musical "betwixt and between" and noted that Savo spoke just two English words during the entire evening (these must have been the ones that offended Rascoe, but now the words are lost to theatrical history because none of the critics got specific about just what Savo uttered).

John Chapman in the *New York Daily News* suggested some of the songs and dances needed trimming so that more stage time could be allotted to Savo, but otherwise he enjoyed the "really funny" spoof of dream ballets (with only two performers, one of which was diminutive Savo in eternal pursuit of a dancer so tall he has to carry around a chair to stand on in order to try and hold her). He also mentioned a second-act dance, a sort of early pajama game, in which the soldiers in pajamas and the girls in nighties danced away the night (it was "all right in a gentle sort of way"); this would probably make an interesting companion piece to the "Pajama Dance" in **Look, Ma, I'm Dancin'!** Chapman also noted the male performers managed to come across as soldiers, and in view of Broadway's manpower shortage this was "an achievement." As for the score, he found it "fresh" and "tuneful," and singled out "Miss Langley's School for Girls" and "You Wash and I'll Dry." But "A Girl Is Like a Book" was "off-color" and seemed out of place in the surroundings.

Lewis Nichols in the *New York Times* found the songs "fairly catchy," including "How Fly Times," "Joshua," and "You've Got a Hold on Me." But overall the show was "curiously lacking" and he suspected a few more weeks on the road might have improved matters. Wilella Waldorf in the *New York Post* said the musical was as "pretty and sweet" as a Hollywood starlet, and just as "vapid"; and the score was "pretty and sweet" as well, but like Hollywood ingénues "a little hard to tell apart." Waldorf noted that one of the more comic sequences occurred when the Rawa's mousey secretary calls President Roosevelt and asks for romantic advice.

During the tryout, the following songs were cut: "Just Then," "Natural Life," and "Love Is a Step Ahead of Me."

What's Up marked Lerner and Loewe's first Broadway collaboration. Lerner had written the book and Loewe the music for their first joint venture **Life of the Party**, which closed during its pre-Broadway tryout. Despite the failures of their first two musicals, they were on their way: **The Day before Spring** ran just a few months and lost money, but it offered an impressive score and was one of the most imaginative musicals of the era; and it was followed by their first hit, the long-running **Brigadoon**.

What's Up also marked early appearances by a number of performers who made their marks in later musicals. William Tabbert introduced Cole Porter's "Frahngee-Pahnee" in **Seven Lively Arts**, created the roles of Lieutenant Joseph Cable in Richard Rodgers and Oscar Hammerstein II's **South Pacific** (where he introduced "Younger Than Springtime" and "You've Got to Be Carefully Taught") and Marius in Harold Rome's *Fanny* (1954) (where he introduced "Restless Heart" and the title song). Larry Douglas later created the role Lun Tha in Rodgers and Hammerstein's *The King and I*, and with Doretta Morrow introduced "We Kiss in a Shadow" and "I Have Dreamed." Pat Marshall had a leading role in **The Day before Spring** and later appeared in *Mr. Wonderful* (1956); perhaps she's now best remembered as June Allyson's nemesis in the 1947 film version of *Good News*. The production's cast also included Marge Champion, who as Marjorie Bell had appeared in **The Little Dog Laughed** in 1940. Here she was billed as Marjorie Beecher (a variation of her maiden name, Belcher), and for **Beggar's Holiday** she utilized a variant of her first stage name and was known as Marjorie Belle.

The collections *Broadway Musicals of 1943* (Bayview CD # RNBW-015) includes "You Wash and I'll Dry" and "My Last Love," and *Alan Jay Lerner Revisited* (Painted Smiles CD # PSCD-141) includes "You've Got a Hold on Me" and "My Last Love." The lyrics of "You Wash and I'll Dry," "My Last Love," and "You've Got a Hold on Me" are included in *A Hymn to Him/The Lyrics of Alan Jay Lerner*.

A CONNECTICUT YANKEE
"A New Musical Adaptation" / "A New Musical"

Theatre: Martin Beck Theatre
Opening Date: November 17, 1943; *Closing Date*: March 11, 1944
Performances: 135
Based on the 1889 novel *A Connecticut Yankee in King Arthur's Court* by Mark Twain.
Book: Herbert Fields

Lyrics: Lorenz Hart
Music: Richard Rodgers
Direction: John C. Wilson; *Producer*: Richard Rodgers; *Choreography*: William Holbrook and Al White Jr.;
    Scenery, *Costumes*, and *Lighting*: Nat Karson; *Musical Direction*: George White Jr.
Cast: In Hartford, Connecticut—Robert Byrn (Lieutenant [J. G.] Kenneth Kay, U.S.N.), John Cherry (Judge
    Thurston Merrill), Robert Chisholm (Admiral Arthur K. Arthur, U.S.N.), Chester Stratton (Ensign Ger-
    ald Lake, U.S.N.), Jere McMahon (Ensign Allan Gwynn, U.S.N.), Dick Foran (Lieutenant Martin Barratt,
    U.S.N.), Stuart Casey (Captain Lawrence Lake, U.S.N.), Vivienne Segal (Fay Merrill, W.A.V.E.), Julie
    Warren (Alice Courtleigh); In Camelot—Robert Byrn (Sir Kay), Dick Foran (Martin), Julie Warren (The
    Demoiselle Alisande La Courtelloise [aka Sandy]), Robert Chisholm (King Arthur), John Cherry (Merlin),
    Katherine Anderson (Queen Guinevere), Stuart Casey (Sir Lancelot), Chester Stratton (Sir Galahad), Mimi
    Berry (Angela), Vivienne Segal (Queen Morgan La Fay), Jere McMahon (Sir Gawain), Vera-Ellen (Evelyn La
    Rondell); Dancing Girls: Dorothy Blute, Carole Burke, Eleanor Eberle, Bee Farnum, Virginia Gorski (later,
    Gibson), Janet Joy, Rose Marie Magrill, Frances Martone, Mary McDonnell, Beth Nichols, Murnai Pins,
    Dorothy Poplar, Joyce Ring, Rosemary Sankey, Helen Vent, Violetta Weems, Doris York; Dancing Boys:
    Tad Bruce, Buster Burnell, Pittman Corry, Frank deWinters, Bob Gari, William Hunter, Hal Loman, Wil-
    liam Lundy, Jack Lyons; Singing Girls: Marjorie Cowen, Toni Hart, Linda Mason, Martha Emma Watson;
    Singing Boys: Lester Freedman, Vincent Henry, Craig Holden, Wayne McIntyre
The musical was presented in two acts (with a prologue and an epilogue).
The action of the prologue and epilogue takes place in Hartford, Connecticut, during the present time; the
    action for the two acts takes place in England in 543 AD.

Musical Numbers

Prologue: "This Is My Night to Howl" (Vivienne Segal, Ensemble); "My Heart Stood Still" (Dick Foran, Julie
    Warren)
Act One: "Thou Swell" (Dick Foran, Julie Warren); "At the Round Table" (Company); "On a Desert Island
    with Thee" (Chester Stratton, Vera-Ellen, Jere McMahon, Ensemble); "To Keep My Love Alive" (Vivienne
    Segal); "My Heart Stood Still" (reprise) (Dick Foran, Julie Warren); Finale (aka "Ibbidi Bibbidi Sibbidi Sab")
    (Dick Foran, John Cherry, Principals, Ensemble)
Act Two: "Ye Lunchtime Follies" (Chester Stratton, Ensemble); "Can't You Do a Friend a Favor?" (Vivienne
    Segal, Dick Foran); "Thou Swell" (reprise) (Dick Foran, Julie Warren); "I Feel at Home with You" (Chester
    Stratton, Vera-Ellen, Jere McMahon, Ensemble); "You Always Love the Same Girl" (Dick Foran, Robert
    Chisholm); "The Camelot Samba" (Jere McMahon, Ensemble)
Epilogue: Finale (Company)

The original production of Richard Rodgers and Lorenz Hart's *A Connecticut Yankee* opened on November 3, 1927, at the Vanderbilt Theatre for 418 performances; only the team's **By Jupiter** enjoyed a longer New
York run. In reviewing the original production, Brooks Atkinson in the *New York Times* said the musical
offered an "intelligent" book, "fresh and lilting" music, and "well-turned" lyrics, and Robert Benchley in *Life*
noted that "My Heart Stood Still" was "the loveliest musical comedy song in recent years."
    In the current revised version, the prologue is set in 1943 and Martin Barrett (Dick Foran) is celebrating his
forthcoming marriage to Fay Merrill (Vivienne Segal) at a tipsy bachelor party. When Fay discovers him in the
arms of Alice Courtleigh (Julie Warren), she hits him on the head with a champagne bottle, and while knocked
out he dreams he's living in Camelot during the era of King Arthur. Everyone there reminds him of people
he knew in 1943, including the lovely Alisande (or Sandy) (Julie Warren), King Arthur (Robert Chisholm), and
Arthur's evil sister Morgan La Fay (Vivienne Segal). When Martin awakes from his dream, he discovers it is
Alice, not Fay, whom he really loves.
    During the course of the evening, Martin introduces modern 1943 technology to King Arthur, his knights,
and their ladies, and soon everyone is riding around in jeeps, using walkie-talkies, working on swing shifts in
defense factories, hanging out at canteens, and dancing the samba. And the spoofy "Ye Lunchtime Follies"
had Sir Galahad (Chester Stratton) indulging in some Sinatra-styled crooning into a microphone which had

the court ladies swooning like Forties' bobbysoxers. Much of the humor derived from these anachronisms, including verbal ones, such as the line "Thou hast put me on the beam."

The revival retained six songs from the original production ("My Heart Stood Still," "Thou Swell," "At the Round Table," "On a Desert Island with Thee," "I Feel at Home with You," and the first act finale) and added six ("This Is My Night to Howl," "To Keep My Love Alive," "Ye Lunchtime Follies," "Can't You Do a Friend a Favor?," "You Always Love the Same Girl," and "The Camelot Samba"). Songs from the original production that were omitted in the revival were: "A Ladies' Home Companion," "Nothing's Wrong," "The Sandwich Men," and "Evelyn, What Do You Say?"

Louis Kronenberger in *PM* said the revival was "entertaining, likable and warm-voiced," but he could have done without so much "methinksy and forsoothy"; the dances had "liveliness and zest," and the "un-abashedly gaudy" costumes suggested Camelot was more circus than court. John Chapman in the *New York Daily News* praised the "beautiful" production with its "boldly colorful and imaginatively contrived" décor; but he felt the show could have been a bit funnier and admitted he grew weary of the "half-modern, half-Arthurian argot."

The critics generally felt Dick Moran and Julie Warren were somewhat tentative in their roles, but almost everyone agreed that dancers Vera-Ellen and Jere McMahon were terrific, that Chester Stratton offered nice singing, and that Vivienne Segal stopped the show with one of the greatest Broadway comedy songs "To Keep My Love Alive," in which she cataloged her long list of deceased husbands and justified her good reasons for speeding each one to his heavenly reward.

As for Moran, Burton Rascoe in the *New York World-Telegram* suggested he wipe the "red stuff" off his lips because it made him "look like a sissy" and noted Segal delivered "To Keep My Love Alive" to "hilarious effect." Ward Morehouse in the *New York Sun* suggested his readers might become a bit "fretful" about the show's book, but they'd nonetheless enjoy the "beautifully mounted" production. Lewis Nichols in the *New York Times* found the book "feeble," but said the show "was pretty to look at and agreeable to hear"; he also noted that Vera-Ellen "put the most life into" the evening and was "one of the world's most engaging performers as a dancer or minor comedienne."

Howard Barnes in the *New York Herald Tribune* found the evening "ponderous" but paradoxically a "delight," "very good," and "pleasant to watch," and he praised the "expert" choreography and the "rather sensational" Vera-Ellen; Robert Garland in the *New York Journal-American* found the show "a good deal skimpier in humor" than the original production, but the revival was "big, handsome and melodious"; he said Vivienne Segal was the show's "outstanding" performer and that Vera-Ellen and Jere McMahon were "skillful and likable dancers."

Wilella Waldorf in the *New York Post* felt the book was somewhat collegiate and she was disappointed with Dick Foran and Julie Warren (their renditions of "My Heart Stood Still" and "Thou Swell" had "all the vitality and zip of lukewarm soda pop"); but Vivienne Segal excelled in "To Keep My Love Alive" and Vera-Ellen and Jere McMahon were "two uncommonly beguiling" dancers.

Decca recorded the cast album (which was later released by Decca Broadway CD # 440-013-560-2); the album contains the overture and finale as well as seven songs, four from the 1927 production ("My Heart Stood Still," "Thou Swell," "On a Desert Island with Thee," and "I Feel at Home with You") and three of the six songs written for the revival ("To Keep My Love Alive," "Can't You Do a Friend a Favor?," and "You Always Love the Same Girl"). AEI released the 1955 television soundtrack (CD # AEI-CD-043) which includes songs from both the original ("My Heart Stood Still," "Thou Swell," "At the Round Table," "On a Desert Island with Thee," "I Feel at Home with You," and the first act finale) and revival ("This Is My Night to Howl," "To Keep My Love Alive," "Ye Lunchtime Follies," "Can't You Do a Friend a Favor?," "You Always Love the Same Girl," and "The Camelot Samba").

The lyrics for all the songs from both the 1927 and 1943 productions are included in *The Complete Lyrics of Lorenz Hart.*

There were two film versions of Twain's novel. A non-musical adaptation (as *A Connecticut Yankee*) with Will Rogers was released in 1931, and in 1949 a musical version (as *A Connecticut Yankee in King Arthur's Court*) was released by Paramount with Bing Crosby (lyrics by Johnny Burke and music by Jimmy Van Heusen).

The above-mentioned television adaptation of *A Connecticut Yankee* was presented by NBC on March 12, 1955; the cast included Eddie Albert (Martin), Janet Blair (Sandy), Gale Sherwood (Fay), Boris Karloff

(Arthur), John Conte (Sir Kay), and Leonard Elliott (Merlin); the leading dancers were Bambi Linn and Rod Alexander. The teleplay was by William Friedberg, Neil Simon, Al Schwartz, and Will Glickman; the direction was by Max Liebman and William Hobin; and the choreography was created by Rod Alexander.

On February 8, 2001, Encores! presented a concert revival of the musical at City Center for five performances; the cast included Steven Sutcliffe (Martin), Judith Blazer (Sandy), Christine Ebersole (Morgan Le Fay), and Henry Gibson (Arthur). For this version, the prologue and epilogue remained in 1927, but all the numbers from the 1943 production were retained ("This Is My Night to Howl," "To Keep My Love Alive," "Ye Lunchtime Follies," "You Always Love the Same Girl," The Camelot Samba," and "Can't You Do a Friend a Favor?") and seven songs from the 1927 production were used ("My Heart Stood Still," "Thou Swell," "At the Round Table," "On a Desert Island with Thee," "I Feel at Home with You," "The Sandwich Men," and the first act finale). Unused from the 1927 production were "A Ladies' Home Companion," "Nothing's Wrong" and "Evelyn, What Do You Say?" The song "I Blush" had been cut during the 1927 tryout, and was reinstated for the concert along with "Here's Martin the Groom"; the latter had been written for the 1943 production but seems never to have been performed (it wasn't listed in the programs for the 1943 tryout, Broadway production, and post-Broadway tour). "I Blush" is included in the collection *Rodgers and Hart Revisited* (Painted Smiles CD # PSCD-116).

Two years after the opening of the original Broadway production, the musical was presented in London as *A Yankee at the Court of King Arthur*; it opened at Daly's Theatre on October 10, 1929, for forty-three performances; the cast included Harry Fox (Martin), Constance Carpenter (here reprising her original New York role of Sandy), Norah Robinson (Morgan Le Fay), and Sam Livesey (Arthur). Surprisingly, "My Heart Stood Still" was omitted from the production and was replaced with a new song "I Don't Know How" (lyric and music by Vivian Ellis and Desmond Carter).

A Connecticut Yankee chorus member Virginia Gorski later changed her last name to Gibson. She was one of the seven brides in the 1954 MGM film musical *Seven Brides for Seven Brothers*, and in 1956 she was Ethel Merman's daughter in *Happy Hunting* and the two introduced the popular song "Mutual Admiration Society."

Sadly, five days after the opening of the revival, Lorenz Hart died, and so Broadway would never again hear new lyrics by one of the masters of the form.

WINGED VICTORY
"A PLAY"

Theatre: 44th Street Theatre
Opening Date: November 20, 1943; *Closing Date*: May 20, 1944
Performances: 212
Play: Moss Hart
Music: Sgt. David Rose
Direction: Moss Hart; *Producer*: The U.S. Army Air Forces; *Scenery*: Sgt. Harry Horner; *Costumes*: Sgt. Howard Shoup; *Lighting*: Sgt. Abe Feder; *Musical Direction*: Sgt. Norman Leyden; *Choral Direction*: Second Lt. Leonard de Paur
Cast: Cpl. Mark Daniels (Allan Ross), Pvt. Dick Hogan (Frankie Davis), Pvt. Don Taylor (Danny "Pinky" Scariano), Phyllis Avery (Dorothy Ross), Virginia Hammond (Mrs. Ross), Pvt. Red Buttons (Whitey [An Andrews Sister]), Pvt. Bert Hicks (Fred Cassidy), Pfc. Kenneth Forbes (Eddie Borden), Pvt. William Nash (Tommy Gregg), Sergeant Kevin McCarthy (Ronny Meade), Pvt. Elliot Sullivan (Sergeant Casey), Pvt. Barry Nelson (Bobby Grills), Pfc. Edmond O'Brien (Irving Miller), Sergeant Rune Hultman (Dave Anderson), Sergeant Edward Reardon (Sergeant Everett), Pvt. Alan Baxter (Major Halper), Pvt. Whitner (Whit) Bissell (Lt. Jules Hudson), Pvt. Grant Richards (Captain Elkton), Cpl. Edward Ashley (Captain Payne), Pvt. Henry Rowland (Captain Speer), First Lieutenant William Neil (Lt. Johnson), Pvt. Harry Lewis (Peter Clark), Pvt. Paul Kaye (Lieutenant McCarthy), Pvt. John Elliott (Henry Larsen), Sergeant Gilbert Frye (A.L. Simpson), Sergeant Frank Kane (Ed Slater), Captain Russell W. Drewes (Russell Chandler), Pvt. Hayes Gordon (Gordon Williams), Cpl. Don Richards (Mark Walton), Staff Sergeant Daniel Scholl (Al Black), Pvt. John R. Kearney (Gilbert Paxton), Pvt. Stuart Langley (Bob Chapman), Sergeant Robert Willey (Jim Gardner), Pfc. Anthony Ross (Mr. Gardner), Laura Pierpont (Mrs. Gardner), Pvt. Michael Harvey (Lieutenant

Stevens), Pvt. Kent Morrison (Ed Ried), Mary Lenhardt (Sally), Jean McCoy (Jane), Cpl. Gary Merrill (Captain McIntyre), Sergeant David Calvin (Dick Talbert), Pvt. Cy Perkins (Nick Bush), Cpl. Ira Cirker (Gordon Cantrell), Pfc. Edward McMahon (Mack Hall), Sergeant David Durston (Sid Marshall), Pvt. James Engler (Ralph Stevens), Pfc. Donald Hanmer (Leo Nadler), Pfc. Thomas Dillon (David Michaelson), Pvt. Phillip Bourneuf (Colonel Gibney), Sgt. George Reeves (Lieutenant Thompson), Pvt. Walter Reed (Jerry Ellison), Sergeant Zeke Manners (Russ Coleman), Pvt. Ray Merrill (George Morse), Cpl. Jerry Hilliard Adler (Sid Green), Pfc. Ray McDonald (Fred Kelly), Sergeant Victor Young (Lee), Cpl. Fred Cotton (Chaplain), Second Lieutenant Gilbert Herman (Lieutenant Reynolds), Pvt. Damian O'Flynn (Colonel Ross), Sergeant Ray Middleton (Lieutenant Sperry), First Lieutenant George Hoffmann (Lieutenant Rayburn), Pvt. William Marshall (Major Burke), Captain Raye Bidwell (Charles Jordan), Captain Sidney Bassler (The Mayor), Sergeant Joseph Meyer (Mr. Grills), Elisabeth Fraser (Helen), Genevieve Frizzel (Helen), Pvt. Richard Beach (The Minister), Pvt. George Petrie (Barker), Pvt. Alfred Ryder (Milhauser), Pvt. Karl Malden (Adams), Staff Sergeant Peter Lind Hayes (O'Brien), Pfc. Martin Ritt (Gleason), Olive Deering (Ruth), Sergeant John Ademy (Radio Announcer), Pvt. Archie Robbins (Glenn Barrows [Master of Ceremonies]), Pvt. Jack Powell Jr. (Paul Conway [Drummer]), Staff Sergeant Sascha Brastoff (Miguel Lopez [Carmen Miranda]), Pvt. Henry Slate (Sam Preston [An Andrews Sister]), Pvt. Jack Slate (Harry Preston [An Andrews Sister]), Second Lieutenant Donald Beddoe (Colonel Blakely), Pvt. John Tyers (Corporal Regan), Pvt. Barry Mitchell (Jack Browning), Mary Cooper (Miss Aldridge), Pvt. Lee J. Cobb (Doctor Baker), Pvt. Michael Duane (Milton Benson); Army Air Force Personnel (portraying Soldiers, Civilians, Aviation Students, Mechanics, Pilots): Pvt. John Andes, Cpl. Richard Annis, Cpl. Etienne Bauer, Pfc. Kenneth Black, Pvt. Ramon Blackburn, Pvt. Royce Blackburn, Pvt. Robert Blakeman, Sergeant Horace Brynolfson, Pfc. Thomas Burdick, Pfc. James Burke, Cpl. Robert Cantell, Sergeant Frank Chamberlin, Pfc. Dick Chandlee, Pfc. Thomas Charlesworth, Pvt. Alfred Cocozza, Sergeant Howard Cranford, Staff Sergeant Frank Davis, Pfc. John Deane, Cpl. Milton Douglas, Cpl. Russell Drewes, Pvt. George Edwards, Second Lieutenant Frank Egan, Cpl. Tommy Farrell, Pvt. Arthur Finne, Pvt. John Ford, Pvt. John Forsythe, Sergeant D.J. Fradenberg, Sergeant Carl Fredickson, Pvt. Dave Gaber, Staff Sergeant Gordon Gaines, Cpl. Charles Gavek, Sergeant Thomas Grace, Pvt. A. L. Green, Pfc. John Green, Sergeant George Griffin, Pvt. Hayes Gordon, Pfc. Pitt Herbert, T/5 Jay Hyde, Cpl. Donald Hultgren, Pvt. Milton Hultgren, Pfc. Alan Jason, Pvt. James Keogan, Pvt. Alfred Kunz, Cpl. James Larmore, Cpl. John Lawlor, Pvt. Louis Magyar, Pvt. James Mattingly, Pfc. Robert Mauch, Pfc. William Mauch, Pfc. Norman Mendelson, Pvt. Robert Nash, Cpl. James Polack, Sergeant. Jack Proctor, Pvt. James Rafferty, Sergeant Salvatore Randazzo, Cpl. Earl Redding, First Lieutenant Carroll C. Riddle, Pvt. Robert Rose, Pfc. David Scott, Sergeant Wilbur Sheibels, Pfc. Douglas Sibole, Pvt. Dan Stanley, Pvt. Robert Stevens, Pvt. Julian Stockdale, Pvt. Claude Stroud, Cpl. Frederick Sullivan, Cpl. David Sureck, Pfc. Forrest Thompson, Pfc. James Thompson, Pfc. Kenneth Utt, Pvt. Howard Vanderberg, Pvt. George Wainwright, Cpl. Finley Walker, Sergeant Fred Weiberg, Sergeant Frank Whitmore, Pvt. Jack Williams, Cpl. Joseph Williams, Pvt. Jack Willey, Sergeant Jerome Zimmerman; Civilian Members (portraying WACs, Soldiers' Wives, Mothers): Miss Florence Aquino, Mrs. Edward Ashley, Miss Faith Avery, Miss Matilde Baring, Mrs. Alan Baxter, Miss Joan Black, Mrs. Robert L. Braun, Mrs. William Cahan, Miss Shirley Chambers, Mrs. Thomas Charlesworth, Mrs. Mark Daniels, Mrs. Milton Douglas, Mrs. Michael Duane, Miss Katherine Eames, Miss Helen Eastman, Mrs. James Engler, Mrs. Abe Feder, Miss Elfin Finn, Mrs. Arthur Finne, Mrs. Thomas Grace, Mrs. William Justice, Mrs. Herman Kantor, Mrs. Paul Kaye, Mrs. Maurice La Pue, Mrs. Stuart Langley, Mrs. John Macmillan, Mrs. Edward McMahon, Mrs. Norman Mendelson, Mrs. Gary Merrill, Miss Ellen Miller, Mrs. William Neil, Miss Margaret Parmentier, Mrs. Jack Proctor, Mrs. George Reeves, Mrs. Carroll Riddle, Mrs. Archie Robbins, Miss Elsa Ryan, Mrs. Julian Stockdale, Mrs. Claude Stroud, Mrs. Elliott Sullivan, Miss Laura Walker, Mrs. Robert Willey; Choral Group: Sergeant John Ademy, Pvt. John C. Andes, Cpl. R. H. Annis, Pfc. Kenneth Black, Cpl. Etienne Bauer, Sergeant H. W. Brynolfson, Sergeant F. Chamberlain, Pfc. T. E. Charlesworth, Pvt. A. A. Cocozza, Pvt. Eugene Conley, Staff Sergeant R. Davis, Pfc. E. J. Deane, Cpl. Milton Douglas, Sergeant Dave Durston, Second Lieutenant Frank Egan, Private Arthur Finne, Private J. A. Ford, Sergeant D. J. Fradenburg, Sergeant D. Fredickson, Staff Sergeant Gordon Gaines, Cpl. C. S. Gavek, Pvt. Hayes Gordon, Sergeant George Griffen, Cpl. Donald Hultgren, Pvt. A. P. Kunz, Private Stuart Langley, Cpl. John Lawler, Pvt. J. E. MacMillan, Pvt. L. J. Magyar, Pfc. N. M. Mendelson, Cpl. Eugene Nelson, Cpl. James Polack, Sergeant Jack Proctor, Pvt. J. A. Rafferty, Sergeant Salvatore Randozzo, Cpl. E. W. Redding, Cpt. Donald Richards, Pvt. E. N. Rosenberg, Staff Sergeant Daniel Scholl, Sergeant W. A. Sheibels, Pfc. D. E. Sibols, Pvt. R. H. Stevens, Pvt. John Tyers, Pfc. K. C. Utt, Pvt. Howard Vanderberg, Pvt. George Wainwright, Cpl. Finley Walker, Sergeant Fred Weisberg, Sergeant Frank Whitmore, Cpl. Joseph Williams; Orchestra: Flutes—Staff Sergeant Martin Heylman, Pfc. Francis P. Taylor; Clarinets—Pvt. Samuel L. Arons, Sergeant Stanley W. Aronson, Sergeant Robert A. Bunch, Cpl. Harold H. J. Dankers; Bassoon—Cpl. Robert J. Wisneskey; Oboe—Sergeant Arnold Koblentz; French Horns—Pfc. Michael Glass, Pfc. Arthur B. Holmes, Pfc. William Lebedeff, Pfc. Lester Salomon; Trumpets—Cpl. Sidney Baker, Staff Sergeant Milton Bloom, Pvt. Stephen J. Lipkins, Pfc. Joseph Perrin, Staff Sergeant Ruben Weinstein; Trombones—Sergeant Joseph C. Clements, Sergeant Phillip Croughan, Sergeant Marvin W. Long, Staff Sergeant Henry M. Singer; Drums—Pvt. Alan I. Abel, Pvt. Max E. Albright; Violins—Cpl. Julius Arluck, Pfc. Noah Bielski, Sergeant James Caesar, Staff Sergeant Elias Dan, Private Bernard Gerrard, Cpl. Leon Goldstein, Sergeant Jacque Gorodetsky, Cpl. Jasper A. Hornyak, Pvt. Saul Pavlow, Pvt. David Sarser, Pvt. Eugene Shepherd, Pvt. Robert J. Sushel; Violas—Sergeant Jerome J. Lipson, Pfc. Joseph F. Maita, Pvt. Joseph Reilich, Pvt. Samuel Ross; Cellos—Pvt. Claus Adams, Cpl. Edward Cresswell, Cpl. Cesare A. Pascarella; Basses—T/Sergeant Edward Gilbert, Sergeant Harry Goodman; Piano—Master Sergeant Joseph Bushlik; Harp—Pvt. Abraham Rosen

The play was presented in two acts.

The action takes place during the war years in such locales as Ohio, Oregon, California, and the South Pacific.

Musical Numbers

Note: The program didn't list the musical numbers.

Act One :"Gee, Mom, I Want to Go Home" (Air Force Choral Group); "When the War Is Over" (lyric by Jerome Lawrence and Robert E. Lee, music by Carmen Dragon) (Air Force Choral Group); "Mademoiselle from Armentiers" (Air Force Choral Group)

1. **Act Two:** "The Army Air Corps" ("Off We Go, into the Wild Blue Yonder") (lyric and music by Robert Crawford) (Air Force Choral Group); "Pennsylvania Polka" (lyric and music by Lester Lee and Zeke Manners) (performed à la The Andrews Sisters by Pvt. Henry Slate, Pvt. Red Buttons, and Pvt. Jack Slate); "Chica Chica Boom Chic" (1941 film *That Night in Rio*; lyric by Mack Gordon, music by Harry Warren) (performed à la Carmen Miranda by Staff Sergeant Sascha Brastoff); "Silent Night" (traditional Christmas carol; lyric and music by Joseph Mohr and Franz Gruber) (John Tyers); "Winged Victory" (lyric and music by David Rose) (Air Force Choral Group); "The Star-Spangled Banner" (finale) (Entire Company) (Also performed in the play were "My Dream Book of Memories," lyric and music by David Rose, and "The Whiffenpoof Song," lyric inspired by Rudyard Kipling and rewritten by Meade Minnigerode and George S. Pomeroy, music by Guy H. Scull; during preproduction, the song "You're So Nice to Remember," lyric by Leo Robin and music by David Rose, was cut).

Moss Hart's drama *Winged Victory* was in its way a companion piece to Irving Berlin's **This Is the Army**. But *Winged Victory* wasn't a musical, although it included incidental songs, both original and interpolated. Like its Army counterpart, all the male roles were performed by active-duty servicemen (for *Winged Victory*, the female roles were played by civilians); and like the Berlin revue, in which all the proceeds went to the The Army Emergency Relief Fund, the proceeds for *Winged Victory* went to the U.S. Army Air Forces Relief Fund.

Although the production included over three hundred performers, the basic story line followed six young men (Mark Daniels, Dick Hogan, Rune Hultman, Barry Nelson, Edmond O'Brien, and Don Taylor) from their days as civilians when they eagerly await news from the Army Air Force about their applications for pilot training. Once they're inducted, the play follows them through classification and processing, then to lectures and training and exams, and finally to the time when they earn their wings and head for action in the South Pacific. Not all of them make it; one doesn't pass pilot training (but becomes a gunner), and another dies during a test flight. The evening presented a mosaic of patriotic young men with their camaraderie, their passion for flying, and their willingness to sacrifice their lives if it means a better life for future American generations. The work also included roles for female civilians, who played WACs, mothers, wives, and sweethearts, and the critics praised one particularly effective scene which took place in a shabby hotel where three of the soldiers' wives (Phyllis Avery, Elisabeth Fraser, and Olive Deering) try to deal with the war and the possibility they may never again see their husbands.

Ward Morehouse in the *New York Sun* said *Winged Victory* was a "play and spectacle that dwarfs all else of the current season and beside which the majority of productions of the present decade and century shrink to mediocrity"; Howard Barnes in the *New York Herald Tribune* found the evening a "great and profoundly moving war play" and a "major theatrical event"; and Burton Rascoe in the *New York World-Telegram* said Hart's work offered "thrilling spectacle, full of emotional drive." But perhaps Louis Kronenberger in *PM* had the best perspective of the topical and timely play when he noted it "belongs utterly in the moment—not merely the moment in history, but also the moment when you sit before it." Otherwise, the play's "force starts evaporating as you exit" the theatre. But if the play was "so wholly divorced from art," then it was also "partly exempted from criticism."

Lewis Nichols in the *New York Times* noted that one scene in the "wonderful show" took place in Mapleton, Ohio, and mentioned this was the fourth time the town of Mapleton popped up in a work by Hart, including *The American Way* and *The Man Who Came to Dinner* (both 1939, and both of which Hart cowrote with George S. Kaufman) and **Lady in the Dark** (but the town of Mesalia, not Mapleton, seems to be the only small town mentioned in *The Man Who Came to Dinner*). Wilella Waldorf in the *New York Post* commented that one of the best lighthearted moments in the play occurred when Sascha Brastoff did a "side-splitting" impersonation of Carmen Miranda; in this case, instead of fruit, "Carmen" was bedecked with pots and pans. The critics also praised Harry Horner's scenery, which employed five revolving stages to facilitate the sweep of the story's locales and the movement of its three-hundred-member cast. Rascoe reported the curtain calls went on for fifteen minutes, and John Chapman in the *New York Daily News* noted that when Moss Hart was asked to make a curtain speech, it was short and succinct: "I have just heard over the radio that Berlin has been bombed. That's what this play is about."

The cast members included three future Best Supporting Actor Academy Award winners (Karl Malden, Edmond O'Brien, and Red Buttons) as well as an array of names who would make their marks on stage, screen, and television, including Barry Nelson, Kevin McCarthy, Gary Merrill, Peter Lind Hayes, Whit Bissell, George Reeves, John Forsythe, Ed Asner, Martin Ritt, Victor Young, John Tyers, Don Richards, Ray McDonald, and Danny Scholl. Veteran Broadway performer Ray Middleton was also in the production.

Gary Merrill appeared in both **This Is the Army** and *Winged Victory*. He was a private when he appeared in the former in 1942, and was now a corporal.

The script was published in hardback by Random House in 1943. Decca recorded four numbers from the play ("My Dream Book of Memories," "The Whiffenpoof Song," "The Army Air Corps," and the title song) and these were included in the "serviceman" collection of *This Is the Army*, *Winged Victory*, and *Call Me Mister* released by Decca Broadway (CD # B0000831-02).

The film version was released in 1944 by Twentieth Century-Fox; directed by George Cukor and scripted by Moss Hart, the cast included Lon McCallister, Edmond O'Brien, Don Taylor, Lee J. Cobb, Peter Lind Hayes, Red Buttons, Barry Nelson, Karl Malden, Gary Merrill, Martin Ritt, Kevin McCarthy, Keith Andes, Martin Balsam, Mario Lanza, Jeanne Crain, and Judy Holliday. The film never seems to show up on cable television, and has never been released on home video.

CARMEN JONES

Theatre: Broadway Theatre
Opening Date: December 2, 1943; *Closing Date*: February 10, 1945
Performances: 503
Book and *Lyrics*: Oscar Hammerstein II
Music: Georges Bizet (new orchestrations by Robert Russell Bennett)
Based on the 1875 opera *Carmen* (music by Georges Bizet, libretto by Henri Meilhac and Ludovic Halevy), which in turn was based on the 1845 story *Carmen* by Prosper Merimee.
Direction: Libretto directed by Charles Friedman; staged by Hassard Short; *Producer*: Billy Rose; *Choreography*: Eugene Loring; *Scenery*: Howard Bay; *Costumes*: Raoul Pene du Bois; *Color Schemes*: Designed by Hassard Short; *Lighting*: Hassard Short; *Musical Direction*: Joseph Littau; *Choral Direction*: Robert Shaw
Cast: Napoleon Reed (Corporal Morrell; alternate, Robert Clarke), Robert Clarke (Foreman, Soldier; alternate for Foreman, George Willis), Carlotta Franzell (Cindy Lou; alternate, Elton J. Warren); Jack Carr (Sergeant Brown), Luther Saxon (Joe; Napoleon Reed, alternate); Muriel Smith (Carmen; Muriel Rahn, alternate);

Sibol Cain (Sally, Card Player), Edward Roche (T-Bone), William Jones (Tough Kid), Cozy Cole (Drummer), Melvin Howard (Bartender, Tough Kid), Edward Christopher (Waiter), June Hawkins (Frankie), Jessica Russell (Myrt), Edward Lee Tyler (Rum), Dick Montgomery (Dink), Glenn Bryant (Husky Miller), J. Flashe Riley (Boy), Royce Wallace (Girl), William Woolfolk (Soldier), George Willis (Soldier), Elijah Hodges (Soldier), P. Jay Sidney (Mr. Higgins), Fredye Marshall (Mrs. Higgins), Alford Pierre (Photographer), Urylee Leonardos (Card Player), Ethel White (Card Player), Ruth Crumpton (Dancing Girl), William Dillard (Poncho), Sheldon B. Hoskins (Dancing Boxer), Randolph Sawyer (Dancing Boxer), Tony Fleming Jr. (Referee): Soldiers, Factory Workers, Socialites: Viola Anderson, Lee Allen, Carmine Brown, William Archer, Miriam Burton, Sibol Cain, Clarice Crawford, Ruth Crumpton, Robert Clarke, Anne Dixon, Marguerite Duncan, Edwina Divers, Richard DeVaultier, George Dosher, William Davis, Awilda Frasier, Elijah Hodges, Melvin Howard, Clarence Jones, Elsie Kennedy, Fredye Marshall, Theresa Merritte, Vivienne Mussenden, Maithe Marshall, Bertha Powell, Alford Pierre, Fred Randall, Chauncey Reynolds, Edward Roche, Randall Steplight, Andrew Taylor, Harold Taylor, Audrey Vanterpool, Ethel White, George Willis, Robert Woodland, William Woolfolk, Howard Carter, Urylee Leonardos, Wilbur Marshall; Dancers: Valerie Black, Al Bledger, Edward Christopher, Posie Flowers, Tony Fleming, Jr., Audrey Graham, J. Prioleau Gray, Frank Green, Erona Harris, Mabel Hart, Sheldon B. Hoskins, Rhoda Johnson, Richard James, Dorothy McNichols, Vera McNichols, Betty Nichols, Frank Neal, Joseph A. Noble, Bill O'Neil, Evelyn Pilcher, Edith Ross, J. Flashe Riley, Randolph Sawyer, Randolph Scott, Royce Wallace; Children: Albert Bailey, Robert Bailey, Raymond Brooks, William Jones, Joe Green, Gilbert Irvis, Richard Granady, Oliver Hamilton, Arthur Rames, Robert Smith, LeRoy Westfall, Carlos Van Putten, Delano Vanterpool, James Holman

The musical was presented in two acts.

The action takes place during the present time in a Southern town and in Chicago.

Musical Numbers

Act One: Prelude; Opening Scene (aka "Send Along Anudder Load," "Cain' Let You Go," and "I Like Your Eyes") (Napoleon Reed, Carlotta Franzell, Workmen); "Lift 'Em Up and Put 'Em Down" (Street Boys); "Honey Gal o' Mine" (Workers); "Good Luck, Mister Flyin' Man" (Ensemble, Dancers); "Dat's Love" (Muriel Smith, Ensemble); Scene: Joe and Cindy Lou ("I tol' your maw") (Luther Saxon, Carlotta Franzell); "You Talk Just Like My Maw" (Luther Saxon, Carlotta Franzell); Finale of Scene One (aka "Murder, Murder" and "You Ain't a Police'm") (Muriel Smith, Luther Saxon, Jack Carr, Sibol Cain, Ensemble); "Carmen Jones Is Goin' to Jail" (Ensemble); "Dere's a Café on de Corner" (Muriel Smith, Luther Saxon); Finaletto and Entr' Scene; "Beat Out Dat Rhythm on a Drum" (June Hawkins, Cosy Cole, Dancers, Ensemble); "Stan' Up and Fight" (Glenn Bryant, Ensemble); "Whizzin' Away Along de Track" (Edward Lee Tyler, Dick Montgomery, June Hawkins, Jessica Russell, Muriel Smith); Scene: Carmen and Joe ("Thinkin' 'bout you all the time") (Muriel Smith, Luther Saxon); "Dis Flower" (Luther Saxon); "If You Would Only Come Away" (Muriel Smith, Luther Saxon); Finale of Act One ("Joey, It's Time for You to Go") (Muriel Smith, Ensemble)

Act Two: Entr'acte music based on music between Acts III and IV of *Carmen*; "De Cards Don't Lie" (Jessica Russell, June Hawkins, Card Players); "Dat Ol' Boy" (Muriel Smith); "Poncho De Panther from Brazil" (Jessica Russell, June Hawkins, Glenn Bryant, Edward Lee Tyler, Ensemble); "My Joe" (Carlotta Franzell); Finale of Scene One ("Your maw is lonesome") (Muriel Smith, Luther Saxon, Carlotta Franzell, Glenn Bryant, Edward Lee Tyler, Dick Montgomery, Jessica Russell, June Hawkins); "Get Yer Program for de Big Fight" (Ensemble); "Dat's Our Man" (Ensemble); Scene: Joe and Carmen (Luther Saxon, Muriel Smith) ("But All I Want to Do Is Love You Like I Useter"); Finale ("Stan' up an' Fight" and "String Me High on a Tree") (Ensemble, Luther Saxon)

Carmen Jones was the surprise hit of the 1943–1944 season. Oscar Hammerstein II's modern-day adaptation of Georges Bizet's 1875 opera *Carmen* opened at the huge Broadway Theatre on December 2, 1943, and played for 503 performances. For the leading roles of Carmen and Joe, Muriel Smith and Muriel Rahn, and Luther Saxon and Napoleon Reed, alternated performances; for opening night, Smith and Saxon sang the roles.

The story was shifted to the American South of 1943 where femme fatale Carmen Jones works in a war factory that manufactures parachutes. Although Army MP Joe is engaged to Cindy Lou, Carmen seduces him and he's so inflamed with desire he deserts both Cindy Lou and the Army. He and Carmen head off for Chicago, but once there Carmen becomes bored with him and drops him for the flashy boxer Husky Miller. In a jealous rage, Joe stabs Carmen to death.

The production received generally favorable reviews, with Lewis Nichols in the *New York Times* saying it was "wonderful, quite wonderful" and "beautifully done in every way," and Howard Barnes in the *New York Herald Tribune* found the "triumphant" evening "as wonderful and exciting as it is audacious," and noted that Hammerstein had "brilliantly translated" the original libretto. But Wilella Waldorf in the *New York Post* cautioned that the production was a "half-and-half affair," complaining that the singers were no more than "passable" and noting you could see "just as stiff acting at the Metropolitan" where the singers were "generally much better." But she noted that Howard Bay's scenery was "attractive," and Raoul Pene du Bois' costumes made *Carmen Jones* "something to look at" if not "always something to listen to." She praised Hammerstein's "neatly done" lyrics (which were a relief after the typical "It is the umbrella of my grandfather" translations of operas into English) and said she wished he'd consider writing "'straight' English versions of grand opera."

John Chapman in the *New York Daily News* was beside himself; the show was "enchantingly beautiful," "musically exciting," "visually stirring," Muriel Smith's Carmen was the best he'd ever seen, and the "superb" choral singing was "better than any I ever heard at the Met." Robert Garland in the *New York Journal-American* predicted the "milestone" event would go down in "theatrical history"; it was "a great theatrical achievement" and he noted the famous story was now "retold in the lovely dialect of our North Carolina colored people." Louis Kronenberger in *PM* found the evening "exciting and richly colored," and said Muriel Smith brought to the role a "lustful, taunting arrogance."

Herrick Brown in the *New York Sun* said *Carmen Jones* was a "brilliant idea brilliantly carried out"; it was "lavish" and out of the "top drawer"; and Alton Cook in the *New York World-Telegram* suggested the evening was "such a startling and unexpected departure" from anything he'd ever seen before and thus there was "the air of a dream production, a mighty nice dream, too."

The musical was revived at City Center three times; the first two revivals were presented by Billy Rose, and the third by the New York City Center Light Opera Company. The first opened on May 2, 1945, for twenty-one performances (Muriel Smith/Inez Matthews, Napoleon Reed/LeVern Hutcherson); the second on April 7, 1946, for thirty-two performances (Muriel Smith/Urylee Leonardos, Napoleon Reed/LeVern Hutcherson); and the third on May 31, 1956, for twenty-four performances (Muriel Smith/Gwendolyn Belle, William DuPree/Jon White). (See separate entries for the 1945 and 1946 revivals.)

The script was published in hardback by Alfred A. Knopf in 1945, and the lyrics are included in *The Complete Lyrics of Oscar Hammerstein II*. The latter contains unused and early draft versions of twenty-two songs, including those for the character Hepcat Miller (in early drafts, the Escamillo character from the opera was envisioned as a jive bandleader; Hammerstein later changed the character and his profession, and he became the boxer Husky Miller).

The original cast album was released by Decca (LP # DL-8014; later issued on CD by Decca Broadway # 440-066-780-2, which includes a bonus track of Kitty Carlisle singing "Beat Out Dat Rhythm on a Drum").

The 1954 film version produced by Twentieth Century-Fox was directed by Otto Preminger and starred Dorothy Dandridge (whose singing voice was dubbed by Marilyn Horne) and Harry Belafonte (who was dubbed by LeVern Hutcherson); others in the cast were Olga James, Diahann Carroll, Pearl Bailey, and Brock Peters. The DVD was released by Twentieth Century-Fox Home Entertainment (# 2001883).

JACKPOT
"A New Musical Comedy"

Theatre: Alvin Theatre
Opening Date: January 13, 1944; *Closing Date*: March 11, 1944
Performances: 69
Book: Guy Bolton, Sidney Sheldon, and Ben Roberts
Lyrics: Howard Dietz
Music: Vernon Duke

Direction: Roy Hargrave; *Producer*: Vinton Freedley; *Choreography*: Dances by Lauretta Jefferson and ballet by Charles Weidman; *Scenery*: Raymond Sovey and Robert Edmond Jones; *Costumes*: Kiviette; *Lighting*: Uncredited; *Musical Direction*: Max Meth

Cast: Althea Elder (Peggy, Tot Patterson), Billie Worth (Billie, Nurse), Morton L. Stevens (Mr. Dill), Ben Lackland (Bill Bender), Mary Wickes (Nancy Parker), Nanette Fabray (Sally Madison), Houston Richards (Dexter De Wolf), Jacqueline Susann (Edna), Helena Goudvis (Hedy), John Kearny (Hawley), Walter Monroe (Assistant Bartender), Jerry Lester (Jerry Finch), Benny Baker (Winkie Cotter), Allan Jones (Hank Trimble), Flower Hujer (Girl), Bill Jones (Reporter), Wendell Corey (Sergeant Naylor), Betty Garrett (Sergeant Maguire), Frances Robinson (Helen Westcott), Bob Beam (Sniper), Edith Turgell (Edith), Eva Barcinska (Accordionist), Drucilla Strain (Monica), Pat Ogden (Pat), Betty Stuart (Betty), Sherry Shadburne (Sherry), Marie Louise Meade (Mary Lou), Connie Constant (Connie); Hostesses: Cece Eames, Virginia Barnes, Diane Chase, Gene Cooke, Billie Dee, Marion Harvey, Marion Lulling, Edith Laumer, Dorothy G. Thomas, Dorothy Matthews, Aileen Reed, Ellen Taylor, Sally Tepley, Dorothy Thomas, Edith Turgell, Jeanne C. Trybom, Lorraine Todd, Georginia E. Yeager; Vocalists: Fague Springman, Robert Beam, George Frank, Mario Pichler, Bill Jones, Michael Kozak, Roger E. Miller, John Hamill; Marines: Ray Cook, Lawrence Evers, Bob Ferguson, T. C. Jones, Walter Koremin, Jack McCaffrey, Robert Sullivan, Joe Wismak, Frank Westbrook

The musical was presented in two acts.

The action takes place during the present time in South Carolina.

Musical Numbers

Act One: "The Last Long Mile" (Nanette Fabray, Althea Elder, Billie Worth, Factory Workers); "Blind Date" (Nanette Fabray, Factory Workers); "I Kissed My Girl Goodbye" (Allan Jones, Marines); "A Piece of a Girl" (Allan Jones, Jerry Lester, Benny Baker); "My Top Sergeant" (Jerry Lester, Betty Garrett, Boys); "Sugar Foot" (Betty Garrett, Mary Wickes, Jerry Lester, Benny Baker, Ensemble; Specialty Dance: Don Liberto); "I Kissed My Girl Goodbye" (reprise) (Marines); "What Happened?" (Nanette Fabray, Allan Jones); "Sugar Foot" (reprise) (Betty Garrett, Jerry Lester, Benny Baker); "Grist for De Mille" (choreographed by Charles Weidman) (Mary Wickes, Ensemble; Cowboy: Peter Hamilton; Nymph: Florence Lessing; Pagan Girl: Flower Hujer)

Act Two: Opening (Eva Barcinska); "He's Good for Nothing but Me" (choreographed by Charles Weidman) (Betty Garrett, Ensemble, Dancers: Don Liberto, Billie Worth, and Althea Elder); "What's Mine Is Yours" (Jerry Lester, Benny Baker); "What Happened?" (reprise) (Allan Jones); "It Was Nice Knowing You" (Nanette Fabray, Allan Jones); "Nobody Ever Pins Me Up" (Mary Wickes, Ensemble); "I've Got a One-Track Mind" (Allan Jones; danced by Florence Lessing and Peter Hamilton); "There Are Yanks (from the Banks of the Wabash)" (Betty Garrett. Ensemble); Finale (Entire Company)

Jackpot was an attempt to create a far-fetched but lighthearted topical wartime musical about defense worker Sally (Nanette Fabray), who agrees to be the marriage prize in a war-bond raffle. Three Marines, Hank (Allan Jones), Jerry (Jerry Lester), and Winkie (Benny Baker), jointly buy a bond, and when they're declared the winners each one finds himself as the owner of a "piece of a girl." But in typical musical comedy fashion, Hank soon pairs off with Sally, Jerry with female sergeant Maguire (Betty Garrett), and Winkie with Nancy (Mary Wickes). There are the usual complications and misunderstandings, but by the finale everything is straightened out.

The musical reportedly played very well and was extremely funny at times; and Vernon Duke and Howard Dietz's score was praised (those songs which have surfaced from the show are quite delightful). And while "Grist for De Mille," a spoof of musical comedy ballets, wasn't all that well received, one suspects it offered amusing moments. Further, the show was peopled by pleasant singers and clowns. But it all went down after two months, and today what's perhaps most remembered about the show are some of its more obvious comic moments, such as one in which the Marines are on maneuvers and assume camouflage, as trees. One Marine says he'd like to be a birch, but another tells him he's more like an ash. Further, there was a bit of silent business: a Marine assumes full tree-drag, and then a woman walks onstage with her dog.

Producer Vinton Freedley had enjoyed a successful string of musicals (including *Lady, Be Good!*, *Oh, Kay!*, *Funny Face*, *Girl Crazy*, *Anything Goes*, *Leave It to Me!*, **Cabin in the Sky**, and **Let's Face It!**). But his two attempts at topical wartime musicals failed; **Dancing in the Streets**, which dealt with crowded wartime Washington and also had a score by Duke and Dietz, closed on the road, and *Jackpot* managed just two months on Broadway. Freedley had been one of the co-owners of the Alvin Theatre (he was the second syllable of the theatre's name), and the failure of his newest project must have been a severe disappointment.

Louis Kronenberger in *PM* said the "completeness of the disaster" was hard to understand given the talented cast and creators, but here was a musical that was a "complete frost, an unmitigated bore, an ocean-crossing of tedium" (he managed to praise two songs, "Sugar Foot" and "I Kissed My Girl Goodbye"); Robert Garland in the *New York Journal-American* found the "dull" evening "too long, too complicated, too lacking in wit and humor"; but the décor was "handsomely pictorial," the costumes were "expensively colorful," and "I've Got a One-Track Mind" was "lovely . . . a fetching ballad sung with effect and feeling" by Jones which "you'll be taking home with you. It really is something!"; and Burton Rascoe in the *New York World-Telegram* said a "first-rate" production had been squandered on a "third-rate" show; although he didn't care for Duke's score, he noted that when Max Meth's orchestra played the overture (which had been orchestrated by others than Duke) the music was "lively, melodious and rhythmically infectious."

John Chapman in the *New York Daily News* said Meth's orchestra was so good that "you get to thinking the songs are better than they really are"; he noted that "Grist for De Mille" drew some welcome "steam" from the generally cool first-night crowd which for the most part had been only "perfunctorily" applauding. The sequence burlesqued De Mille's choreography for both **Oklahoma!** and **One Touch of Venus** in an amusing mix of dancing cowboys and Grecian nymphs, and Chapman said that although choreographer Charles Weidman had provided some "genuinely humorous" ideas, the number lacked "good enough" dancers.

Lewis Nichols in the *New York Times* said *Jackpot* wasn't a "very good show" and probably should have stayed on the road longer. He noted that Betty Garrett and Mary Wickes lacked good material, and that Allan Jones sang well but didn't have the "bounce" for musical comedy. But he predicted "Sugar Foot" was "destined for fame," and also praised "I've Got a One-Track Mind," "I Kissed My Girl Goodbye," and "What Happened?" Wilella Waldorf in the *New York Post* stated that around the middle of the first act she realized she was "slowy petrifying with boredom"; later she went "numb all over" and felt that if something "violently amusing" didn't happen soon she'd no doubt have to be carried out of the theatre. But all was not lost: the book writers brought in a secondary character named Dexter De Wolf (Houston Richards) who had just divorced his sixth or seventh wife and who was a spoof of Tommy Manville. Compared to what had previously gone on all evening, Waldorf found the sequence "highly diverting" and after a "vigorous stamping" of her feet to rid them of pins and needles she was able to leave the theatre under her own power.

Ward Morehouse in the *New York Sun* said the musical was at its best when it danced, and while it never rose to Freedley's normally high standards it was nonetheless "funny in spots, frisky at times, always good to look at, occasionally tuneful," and he singled out four songs ("Sugar Foot," "My Top Sergeant," "I Kissed My Girl Goodbye," and "It Was Nice Knowing You"). He suggested that comics Jerry Lester and Benny Baker were "occasionally successful"; that Fabray was "only passable"; and that Jones had a "good voice" but couldn't carry the show through its sagging moments. But Betty Garrett was "quite zestful all the way."

During the tryout, the following songs were deleted: "I Wanna Go Back," "An Hour Ago," "In a Dear Little Cottage," "A Girl with a Green Eye," and "There's Room for All of Us."

The collection *Vernon Duke Revisited* (Painted Smiles CD # PSCD-138) includes "Sugar Foot"; *Vernon Duke Revisited Volume III* (Painted Smiles CD # PSCD-147) includes "What Happened?"; and *Life's a Funny Present* (Rialto CD # SLRR-9306) offers "I've Got a One-Track Mind" and "There Are Yanks (from the Banks of the Wabash)."

Decades after *Jackpot* closed, one of its book writers and one of its cast members enjoyed lucrative careers as novelists. Co-librettist Sidney Sheldon enjoyed a string of best-sellers, including *The Other Side of Midnight*, and bit player Jacqueline Susann wrote the best-selling *Valley of the Dolls*, which reportedly sold over thirty million copies. Others in the cast of *Jackpot* were future film actor Wendell Corey and future female impersonator T. C. Jones (the latter was in *New Faces of 1956*, and in 1957 starred in his own revue *Mask and Gown*).

MEXICAN HAYRIDE

Theatre: Winter Garden Theatre (during run, the musical transferred to the Majestic Theatre)
Opening Date: January 28, 1944; *Closing Date*: March 17, 1945
Performances: 481
Book: Herbert Fields and Dorothy Fields
Lyrics and *Music*: Cole Porter
Direction: Book directed by John Kennedy and entire production staged by Hassard Short; *Producer*: Michael Todd; *Choreography*: Paul Haakon; *Scenery*: George Jenkins; *Costumes*: Mary Grant; *Lighting*: Hassard Short; *Musical Direction*: Harry Levant
Cast: George Givot (Lombo Campos), Jean Cleveland (Mrs. Augustus Adamson), Edith Meiser (Eadie Johnson), Eric Roberts (Augustus Jr.), William A. Lee (Mr. Augustus Adamson), *Bobby Clark* (Joe Bascom [alias Humphrey Fish]), June Havoc (Montana), Horton Henderson (Picador, Second Merchant), Jerry Sylvon (Picador, Fourth Merchant), Bill Callahan (Billy), David Leonard (Senor Martinez), Sergio DeKarlo (Miguel Correres), Wilbur Evans (David Winthrop), Byron Halstead (Henry A. Wallace), Raul Reyes (Jose, First Merchant), Larry Martin (A. C. Blumenthal), Lois Bolton (Tillie Leeds), Virginia Edwards (Lydia Toddle), Arthur Gondra (Carol [Ex-King of Roumania]), Dorothy Durkee (Mme. Lepescu), Corinna Mura (Lolita Cantine), Luba Malina (Dagmar Marshak), Alfonso Pedroza (Bolero), Richard Bengali (Chief of Police), Hank Wolff (Lottery Boy), Jeanne Shelby (Mrs. Molly Wincor), Ben Hernandez (Third Merchant), Bobby Lane (Fifth Merchant), Claire Anderson (Woman Vendor), Eva Reyes (Lottery Girl), Paul Haakon (Paul), Eleanor Tennis (Eleanor), Marjorie Leach (Lillian), Marta Nita, Luisillo and Rosa; Show Girls: Anita Arden, Cynthia Cavanaugh, Mildred Hughes, Andrea Mann, Nancy Callahan, Martha McKinney, Candy Jones, Gail Banner; Singing Girls: Doris Blake, Jean Cummings, Lydia Fredericks, Perdita Hanson, Barbara Jevne, Rose Marie Patane, Gedda Petry, Naomi Sanders, Grace Martin; Dancing Girls: Margaret Cuddy, Malka Farber, Marjorie Gaye, Janet Gaylord, Peggy Holmes, Audrey Howell, Dorothy Hyatt, Alicia Krug, Ramona Lang, Dean Mylas, Vera Teatom, Aura Vainio, Betty Williams; Dancing Boys: Richard Andre, Thor Bassoe, Aleks Bird, John Conrad, Edmund Howland, Joey Gilbert, James Lanphier, Ted Lund, Jimmy Russell, Eric Schepard, Pat Vecchio, Leonard Bushong, Donald Powell; Singing Boys: Morton Beck, Danny Leeds, James Mate, Roy Mantelman, Tony Montell, Gar Moore, Armando Sisto, Robert Tavis; Mariachi Players: Manuel San Miguel, Frank Guzzardo, Ben Hernandez, Nuncio Di Bonis, Savino Lucatorto, Sara Mercado; Children: Jimmy Dutton, Louis Altmark, Hank Wolf, Francine Fernandez
The musical was presented in two acts.
The action takes place during the present time in Mexico.

Musical Numbers

Act One: "Entrance of Montana" (Principals, Girls, Boys); Dance (directed by Dan Eckley) (Girls and Boys); Dance (Bill Calhoun); "Sing to Me, Guitar" (Corinna Mura, Ensemble); Dance (Luisillo and Rosa); "The Good-Will Movement" (dance directed by Virginia Johnson and Dan Eckley) (Wilbur Evans, Ensemble); Dance (Marta Nita, Bill Calhoun, Girls and Boys); "The Good-Will Movement" (reprise) (Wilbur Evans, Girls); "I Love You" (Wilbur Evans); Dance (Paul Haakon, Eleanor Tennis); "I Love You" (reprise) (Wilbur Evans); "There Must Be Someone for Me" (June Havoc); "Carlotta" (Corinna Mura, Ensemble); Dance (Girls and Boys); "Girls" (directed by Lew Kesler) (Bobby Clark, Girls)
Act Two: "What a Crazy Way to Spend Sunday" (Girls and Boys); Dance (Bobby Lane, Claire Anderson); "Abracadabra" (directed by Lew Kesler) (June Havoc, Boys); "I Love You" (reprise) (Wilbur Evans); Dance (Girls and Boys, The Mariachi Players); Dance (Raul and Eva Reyes); "Count Your Blessings" (June Havoc, Bobby Clark, George Givot); "Toreador Ballet" (Paul Haakon, Ensemble); Finale (Entire Company)

Mexican Hayride was a lavish jamboree that gave Bobby Clark (he of the painted-on glasses, the cane, the cigar, the strut, and the leer) ample opportunities to cavort through a series of comical shenanigans. As Joe Bascom (alias Humphrey Fish), amiable con-man Bobby is on the lam in Mexico because American authorities want him for running a numbers racket in five states; and soon he's also pursued by the Mexican police because he's started his own lottery to compete with the government's.

While watching a bullfight, Bobby is the unwitting recipient of a bull's ear, which female matador Montana (June Havoc) inadvertently tosses to him instead of to her boyfriend, David Winthrop (Wilbur Evans), who just happens to be one of those U.S. government officials looking for Bobby. Because the attendant publicity surrounding the bull's ear has made Bobby a hero and the target of too much publicity, he dons disguises in order to avoid the police. In one episode, he masquerades as a member of a mariachi band, but perhaps isn't wise in choosing the flute as his instrument of choice. Then in drag he poses as a Mexican woman with huge false teeth who runs a tortilla-tamale-and-enchilada stand. One of the evening's best visual jokes occurred when he turned around and revealed a baby in his papoose who also sports painted-on spectacles.

A few critics said the opening scenes were too slow, but noted the evening picked up when Wilbur Evans sang Porter's ethereal ballad "I Love You" and then hit its stride once Bobby let loose with his comic shtick and various disguises. The evening was another hit for producer Michael Todd, and Burton Rascoe in the *New York World-Telegram* described *Mexican Hayride* as "one of the most beautiful spectacles ever seen on the stage," and, in the lingo of the day, said the show was "on the beam and going places." Ward Morehouse in the *New York Sun* found the musical a "big and beautiful fiesta," one in which Todd had "outdone himself." The show was a "Ziegfeldian eyeful" that was "spectacularly beautiful"; the designers had "splashed color all over the stage" and Porter had provided such "first-rate" songs as "I Love You," "Count Your Blessings," and "There Must Be Someone for Me." Howard Barnes in the *New York Herald Tribune* said the "big, brash and generally undistinguished extravaganza" was redeemed by Bobby Clark, whose "wonderful cavorting" made the "carnival" a "rousing success."

Louis Kronenberger in *PM* noted that during its early scenes the evening threatened to be a "sumptuous bore," but once Bobby took over the musical was on its way. He delighted in Bobby's mariachi scene (he came across like a "missing Marx Brother"), and praised "I Love You," "Count Your Blessings," "There Must Be Someone for Me," and "Abracadabra." John Chapman in the *New York Daily News* noted the musical was the first in twelve years to sell its best tickets at a $5.50 top, but he was certain the show would pay off. He reported the first-nighters were "enthralled" with the "smooth, easy-running" ballad "I Love You"; this "certain hit" was in the category of Porter's "Night and Day" and "Begin the Beguine." Rascoe also compared the song to "Night and Day" and said it "touches the heart and spine—hummable, singable, catchy, exciting—a hit song not of the show, but of the year." Robert Garland in the *New York Journal-American* said Bobby Clark had never been "more hilarious" and the "large, luxurious and laugh-filled entertainment" was an "earful, an eyeful and an uproarious rowdy-dow."

Wilella Waldorf in the *New York Post* was disappointed with the first act (a "beautiful bore"), but cautioned her readers to hang on after intermission because the superior second act sparkled with Bobby Clark's comic routines. He popped up in "hilarious" disguises, and the evening's "high point" was watching him in drag while he peddled tortillas. It suddenly occurred to Waldorf that with his wig and huge false teeth he "bore a haunting resemblance to Katharine Hepburn." As a result, the "torture" of the first act was worth it, "if only for a chance to see Bobby wear those teeth."

During the tryout, the following songs were cut: "Hereafter," "It Must Be Fun to Be You," "Here's a Cheer for Dear Old Ciro's," and "Tequila." Dropped during rehearsals or in pre-production were: "We're Off for a Hayride in Mexico," "He Certainly Kills the Women," "A Humble Hollywood Executive," "It's a Big Night," "It's Just Like the Good Old Days," "It's Just Yours," "Octet," "Put a Sack Over Their Heads," "A Sightseeing Tour," "That's What You Mean to Me," "I'm Afraid I Love You," and "I'm So Glahd to Meet You." It's interesting that sixteen numbers weren't used in the Broadway production, and that Porter's contributions for the final version amounted to just ten songs (and three reprises) plus ten separate dance numbers. All the used, cut, and unused songs are included in *The Complete Lyrics of Cole Porter*.

The cast recording was released by Decca (LP # DL-5232; issued on CD by Decca Broadway # B0003125-02); except for "Entrance of Montana" and "The Good-Will Movement," all the songs were recorded (Clark didn't appear on the recording, and so "Girls" was sung by Wilbur Evans and "Count Your Blessings" by Havoc and a male quartet). The unused song "That's What You Mean to Me" is included in the collection *Cole Porter Revisited Volume 5* (Painted Smiles CD # PSCD-122), and the cut "It Must Be Fun to Be You" and the unused "It's Just Yours" can heard in *Lost Broadway and More/Volume Two* (Original Cast Records CD # OC-6830).

There was an in-name-only film version released in 1948 by Universal-International as a vehicle for Bud Abbott and Lou Costello that dealt with the boys on the loose in Mexico in search of a lost mine. Virginia Grey was Montana, and from the stage production was Luba Malina. Directed by Charles T. Barton, scripted by Oscar Brodney and John Grant, and produced by Robert Arthur, the comedy didn't include any songs. The film is included in *The Complete Abbott & Costello Universal Pictures Collection* (Universal 15-DVD set # 2007808).

FOLLOW THE GIRLS
"A NEW MUSICAL COMEDY"

Theatre: New Century Theatre (during run, the musical transferred to the 44th Street Theatre and the Broadhurst Theatre)
Opening Date: April 8, 1944; *Closing Date*: May 18, 1946
Performances: 882
Book: Guy Bolton and Eddie Davis; additional dialogue by Fred Thompson
Lyrics and *Music*: Dan Shapiro, Milton Pascal, and Phil Charig
Direction: Harry Delmar (a note in the program thanked Fred Thompson for "his assistance in the direction of the book"); *Producers*: Dave Wolper (Albert Borde, Associate Producer); *Choreography*: Catherine Littlefield; *Scenery* and *Lighting*: Howard Bay; *Costumes*: Lou Eisele; *Musical Direction*: Will Irwin
Cast: Bill (William) Tabbert (Yokel Sailor), Ernest Goodhart (Doorman), Terry Kelly (First Girl Fan), Rae MacGregor (Second Girl Fan), Frank Parker (Bob Monroe), Irina Baronova (Anna Viskinova), Jackie Gleason (Goofy Gale), Frank Kreig (Seaman Pennywhistle, Archie Smith), Geraldine Stroock (Catherine Pepburn), Val Valentinoff (Sailor Val, Felix Charrel), Charles Conaway Jr. (Marine), Gertrude Neisen (Bubbles LaMarr), Kathryn Lazell (Cigarette Girl), Tim Herbert (Spud Doolittle), Buster West (Dinky Riley), Dorothy Keller (Peggy Baker), Toni Gilman (Phyllis Brent), Robert Tower (Dan Daley), Lee Davis (Petty Officer Banner), Walter Long (Captain Hawkins), George Spaulding (Officer Flanagan), Dell Parker (Flirtatious Miss); Dance Team at the Canteen: The DiGatanos (Jayne and Adam); Dancing Girls: Lillian Moore, Rae MacGregor, Ruth Rathbun, Renee Russell, Kathryn Lazell, Ruthe Reid, Nancy Newton, Mitzi Perry, Lee Mayer, Virginia Harriot, Virginia Conrad, Edna Ryan, Terry Kelly, Sherri Phillips, Myra Weldon, Patricia Martin, Merritta Moore; Dancing Boys: Roy Andrews, Dave Pullman, Francois Brouillard, George J. Sabo Jr., Ben Piazza, Bob Emmett, Walter Hastings, Ray Hamilton, Arthur Randy, Danny Aiello, Albert Bahr, Don Miraglia, Erik Kristen, Henry Tatler, Ken Tibbetts, Herbert Ross; Singing Men: Benard Kovler, Robert Thomas, Bill (William) Tabbert, Richard Harvey, Frank Touhey, Larry Leiberman, Larry Mayo, George Lambrose, John O'Neill, Charles Marten; Show Girls: Ruth Joseph, Dorothea Pinto, Norma Amigo, Joan Mylers, Dell Parker, Dorothy Wygal, June Sitar, Kay Crespi
The musical was presented in two acts.
The action takes place in August 1943 in New York City and Great Neck, Long Island.

Musical Numbers

Act One: "At the Spotlight Canteen" (Soldiers, Sailors, Marines); "Where You Are" (Frank Parker, Irina Baronova); "You Don't Dance" (Dorothy Keller, Val Valentinoff, Boys and Girls); "Strip Flips Hip" (Gertrude Neisen, Boys); "Thanks for a Lousy Evening" (Tim Herbert, Dorothy Keller, Buster West); "You're Perf" (Gertrude Neisen, Jackie Gleason, Boys and Girls); Dance (Irina Baronova); "Twelve O'Clock and All Is Well" (Gertrude Neisen); "Out for No Good" (Buster West); Dance (Dorothy Keller); "You Don't Dance" (waltz reprise) (Boys and Girls); Dance (The DiGatanos); "Where You Are" (reprise) (Frank Parker, Irina Baronova); "Flamingo Dance" (Irina Baronova); "Follow the Girls" (Gertrude Niesen, Entire Company)
Act Two: "John Paul Jones" (Frank Parker, Boys and Girls; danced by Val Valentinoff, Boys and Girls); "Where You Are" (reprise) (Frank Parker, Irina Baronova); "I Wanna Get Married" (Gertrude Niesen, Bridesmaids); "Today Will Be Yesterday Tomorrow" (Frank Parker, Marines); "You're Perf" (reprise) (Boys and Girls; danced by Irina Baronova); Specialty Dance (Tim Herbert, Dorothy Keller); "A Tree That Grows in Brooklyn" (Gertrude Niesen, Jackie Gleason, Tim Herbert, Buster West); Finale (Entire Company)

Follow the Girls was a fast-and-loose musical comedy that today seems to have been an anomaly. Truly, did it actually happen? Was it really produced? For the musical has become something of a joke among theatre lovers as one of those shows that could only have happened in the War Forties, and boy it must have been terrible. Many of the musical's writers created the same kind of story ten years later, but *Ankles Aweigh* became a legendary bomb, and no doubt many assumed *Follow the Girls* was in the same category. But *Follow the Girls* was a huge wartime hit, and received surprisingly good notices from the critics. When it closed after 882 performances it was not only the longest-running musical of the season, it was also the *second*-longest-running book musical in Broadway history, after **Oklahoma!** Of course, one might say, "What book?" because the musical for all purposes disintegrated into a glorified nightclub show.

The free-wheeling script covered such topical matters as wartime canteens, randy servicemen, and a strip-tease queen who seems to be a forerunner of *Guys and Dolls'* Miss Adelaide with her nightclub career and her pursuit of a wedding band. The show was an excuse for a variety of comic turns, lighthearted songs, and numerous dance numbers, and is clearly not revivable (although a concert version would probably prove to be an amusing frolic). The musical opened in an era when cast albums of hit musicals were being recorded by Decca on a somewhat regular basis, but only a single from *Follow the Girls* was released (of Gertrude Niesen's show-stopping "I Wanna Get Married"). So that one saucy song is the only original cast recording from one of the decade's biggest hits and longest-running shows. The title song is included in the collection *Everyone Else Revisited* (Painted Smiles CD # PSCD-146).

There was virtually no plot, and the evening revolved around the almost revue-like antics of on-the-town soldiers, sailors, and marines in their amorous pursuits in wartime New York. Most of the action took place in a canteen, where stripper Bubbles LaMarr (Gertrude Neisen) is doing her patriotic best to entertain the boys. She's pursued by her 4-F boyfriend Goofy Gale (Jackie Gleason), and there were a couple of spies thrown into the mix for good measure. (Did the canteen-and-spies story inspire the creators of *Over Here!*, which was one of the funniest and most enjoyable musicals of the 1970s?)

The evening evolved into a nightclub revue, but occasionally gave a nod to the plot. The spirit of the musical is perhaps best exemplified in a scene in which the spies are finally caught. The first-night audience was well into the evening's fun and games and suddenly began to hiss the villains. In an apparently impromptu moment, the performers who played the spies walked to the footlights and started hissing back. It was that kind of show, one that critics liked and audiences loved.

Besides its broad comedy, including a sequence that found Jackie Gleason in WAVE drag (Wilella Waldorf in the *New York Post* reported he was more than a WAVE, he was a "tidal WAVE"), the evening allowed for a number of ballads and comedy numbers, and an array of dances, many of which were clever variations of the hornpipe. But once the musical's post-Broadway tour was over, the show was gone forever and became a footnote in an era of such classics as **Oklahoma!, Bloomer Girl**, **On the Town**, **Carousel**, **Annie Get Your Gun**, **Finian's Rainbow**, **Brigadoon**, **Kiss Me, Kate**, and **South Pacific** (some of which had shorter runs than *Follow the Girls*).

John Chapman in the *New York Daily News* said the new musical was by "no means" the best show in town, but it offered a "generous" evening of "superior" dances, "brilliantly colored and sexy" costumes, "the most beautiful" show girls in New York, and in Gertrude Niesen a leading lady whose "dirty song" ("I Wanna Get Married") had the first-nighters begging for more after "she had run through umpteen verses." Howard Barnes in the *New York Herald Tribune* found the "rowdy and engaging" show "a spring-time delight" and he predicted the "vastly amusing" evening would be around "for a long time to come." Robert Garland in the *New York Journal-American* felt the musical would be more at home in a nightclub with attendant "food and drink, cigarettes and sotto voce conversation." But the "handsome, haphazard and not overly hilarious" show had its "mainstay" in Gertrude Neisen who made every song her own, including "Twelve O'Clock and All Is Well" (a "doleful ditty"), "A Tree That Grows in Brooklyn" ("nifty"), and "I Wanna Get Married" ("brazen").

Louis Kronenberger in *PM* was less than impressed with the book and music, but noted the show offered a "general atmosphere of bustle and good humor." The choreography had "zest and liveliness," the chorus girls were lookers, and the décor was "handsome and stylish." And Niesen made an "engaging toughie," emphasizing the "ribaldries" of "I Wanna Get Married," "brandishing sex" in "Strip Flips Hip," and "bounding around with the boys" in "A Tree That Grows in Brooklyn." The latter was of course a reference to Betty Smith's best-selling novel, and it sang the praises of the Brooklyn borough where "Mother Nature slipped Mother Earth a Mickey Finn" and where there's always a nearby tree when you walk your dog; and "Strip Flips Hip" was Bubbles' entrance number which describes her art in *Variety* lingo. Another clever number was the opening sequence "At the Spotlight Canteen," in which the servicemen catalog the visiting celebrities (no one can take out the garbage like Orson Welles; Charles Boyer's soufflé is "distingue"; and no one serves a "keener weener" than Myrna Loy).

Lewis Nichols in the *New York Times* found the show "easy and agreeable," and noted that while Niesen was known as a good singer, many didn't realize she was a comedienne of "many and considerable talents." In the words of one of the song titles, the musical wasn't "perf," but it was "good Broadway." He liked Gleason, but felt the material let him down; but he predicted that "some day when he gets the words he will be wonderful instead of just very good."

Burton Rascoe in the *New York World-Telegram* said the "fast-paced" and "generally infectious gaiety" was "ingratiating, iridescent and entertaining"; the "hit song" was "I Wanna Get Married" and the "most melodious" one was "You Don't Dance." Ward Morehouse in the *New York Sun* said the "suggestions" of a book were salvaged by Jackie Gleason's comic routines and Catherine Littlefield's good dance numbers. Further, Gleason was in "top form" and Neisen "stampeded" over the house with "I Wanna Get Married." He noted the show was "funnier" than **Mexican Hayride**; it was a "gay and fast and funny romp" which couldn't "possibly miss."

Waldorf said the evening was the "brightest and giddiest" musical in months and said to "see it, if you can get in." With its "light-hearted, tongue-in-cheek, attractively goofy" quality, it was "beautiful" to look at; and Niesen was "rough but rollicking" and had both the company and the audience in a "happy state of inebriation." The show offered "merry material," "tuneful" music, "amusing" lyrics, "good" dancing, and "some of the handsomest scenic effects" ever designed by Howard Bay "or anybody else."

Late in the run, "Strip Flips Hip" was cut from the show, and associate producer Albert Borde stepped up as the producer of record. The musical included early appearances by William Tabbert, Ben Piazza, and future Broadway choreographer Herbert Ross.

The musical opened at the refurbished Century Theatre, now called the New Century (the venue had originally opened in 1921 as Al Jolson's 59th Street Theatre). Garland said the theatre had "been redecorated beyond recognition" and was now "one of the most splendid and spacious show-shops in Manhattan."

The London production opened at His Majesty's Theatre on October 25, 1945, for a long run of 572 performances; the leads were Evelyn Dall (Bubbles) and Arthur Askey (Goofy), and others in the cast were Wendy Toye and Vic Marlowe. The script was refashioned to depict a visit to New York by the Royal Navy sailors. The second act opening "John Paul Jones" was changed to "Brave Jack Tar"; "Strip Flips Hip" became "Strip Tease Girl"; the songs "A Tree That Grows in Brooklyn" "Out for No Good," and "Today Will Be Yesterday Tomorrow" were omitted; "Story of a Girl" (music by Freddie Bretherton) was added as well as "Going Adrift," "The Debut," "Inspection with the Feet," and a dance sequence ("Beguine").

ALLAH BE PRAISED!
"An Exotic and Exciting Musical Comedy" with "A Haremful of Delightful Eyefuls"

Theatre: Adelphi Theatre
Opening Date: April 20, 1944; *Closing Date*: May 6, 1944
Performances: 20
Book and *Lyrics*: George Marion Jr.
Music: Don Walker and Baldwin Bergersen
Direction: Staged by Robert H. Gordon and Jack Small; entire production under the supervision of Alfred Bloomingdale; *Producer*: Alfred Bloomingdale; *Choreography*: Jack Cole; *Scenery* and *Lighting*: George Jenkins; *Costumes*: Miles White; *Musical Direction*: Ving Merlin
Cast: Jack Albertson (Caswell, Bulbul), Helen Bennett (Receptionist, Matron), Edward Roecker (Tex O'Carroll), Sheila Bond (Clerk), Joey Faye (Citizen, Youssouf, Sludge), Sid Stone (Abdul), Mary Jane Walsh (Carol O'Carroll), Margie Ellis (Roberta), Lee Joyce (Paula), Mary McDonnell (Doris), Anita Alvarez (Tubaga), John Hoysradt (Emir), Milada Mladova (Zarah), Pittman Corry (Nij O'Carroll), Margie Jackson (Dulcy Robot), Beatrice Kraft (Beatrice), Evelyne Kraft (Evelyne), Patricia Morison (Marcia Mason Moore), Jayne Manners (Mimi McSlump), Tom Powers (Merchant); Girls About Teheran: Eleanor Hall and Louise Jarvis; Trainees: Lee Joyce, Susan Scott, Marge Ellis, Mari Lynn, Natalie Wynn, Barbara Neal, Alice Anthony, Olga Suarez, Margie Jackson, Mary McDonnell, Dorothy Bird, Ila Marie Wilson, Grace Crystal, Gloria Crystal, Hazel Roy, Muriel Breunig, Pat Welles; Photographers: Mischa Pompianov, Ray Arnett

Jr., Remi Martel, Jack Baker, Jacy McCord, Johnny Oberon, Tom Powers, Jack L. Nagle, William Lundy, Forrest Boncher

The musical was presented in two acts.

The action occurs in 1948 in New York City, Sultanbad (or Teheran), and Hollywood.

Musical Numbers

Act One: "Persian Way of Life" (Mary Jane Walsh), "Allah Be Praised" (choreographed by Dan Eckley) (Edward Roecker; danced by Sheila Bond and Pittman Corry); "What's New in New York" (Mary Jane Walsh); "Leaf in the Wind" (Patricia Morison; danced by Evelyne Kraft and Beatrice Kraft); "Katinka to Eva to Frances" (John Hoysradt; danced by Anita Alvarez); "Let's Go Too Far" (Edward Roecker, Patricia Morison; danced by Milada Mladova and Pittman Corry); Finaletto and Ballet (Entire Company)

Act Two: "Getting Oriental Over You" (Mary Jane Walsh; danced by Sheila Bond, Milada Mladova, Beatrice Kraft, Evelyne Kraft); "Let's Go Too Far" (reprise) (Joey Faye, Jayne Manners); "Secret Song" (Patricia Morison, Edward Roecker); "Sunrise on Sunset" (Edward Roecker); Finale (Entire Company)

The story goes that when producer Alfred Bloomingdale realized *Allah Be Praised!* was going down as a major flop, he asked a friend what he should do. The reply: Close the show and keep the store open nights.

But *Allah Be Praised!* had a lot going for it: the critics liked the lavish production values, the constant flow of dances (which gave choreographer Jack Cole yet another opportunity to indulge his particular and somewhat peculiar fancy for dances with Middle Eastern motifs), and a generally lively score that boasted one of the most splendid list songs in all of musical comedy ("What's New in New York" noted that girl bands at the Stork make the town "a holiday for G strings").

Robert Garland in the *New York Journal-American* said he wished "you wouldn't" ask him what the plot was about; he said he didn't know and he didn't care. In fact, the more the critics tried to describe the plot, the less it made sense. James Aronson in the *New York Post* noted the cast "struggled valiantly to get out from between the covers of the book, a ponderous volume."

The 1944 musical took place in 1948, and was mostly set in Sultanbad (or possibly Teheran, because the program didn't quite seem to make up its mind; there were also side trips to New York City and Hollywood). It seems that a Dartmouth grad (John Hoysradt) once went to Persia as a tutor and ended up as an emir with a harem of American girls, 365 of them (one for each day of the year, with an extra one just for leap year). For some reason, United States Senator Marcia Mason Moore (Patricia Morison) goes to Persia (even then, American politicians couldn't leave the Middle East alone), perhaps on a fact-finding mission, but perhaps not. Also arriving in Persia is another senator (Edward Roecker) along with his brother and sister as well as two comic types named Sludge (Joey Faye) and McSlump (Jayne Manners). Others arriving in town include a bevy of young American women who seem hell-bent on becoming members of the emir's harem. Ultimately, the wispy plot all but disintegrated and the emir went into a lengthy but by all accounts amusing parody that described an evening in a typical tiny New York night club (Burton Rascoe in the *New York World-Telegram* found this the "funniest" part of the show).

The critics singled out seven of the musical's nine songs. There were ballads (Ward Morehouse in the *New York Sun* said "Secret Song" and "Let's Go Too Far" were "pleasant," and Aronson said the latter "should be on somebody's hit parade before long") and comedy songs (Lewis Nichols in the *New York Times* found "Getting Oriental Over You" a "jingley" number; John Chapman in the *New York Daily News* said "What's New in New York" was "clever"; and Morehouse said the latter and "Katinka to Eva to Frances" were "excellent"). Rascoe noted that the overture "puts you in a happy mood of expectation," and the opening song "Persian Way of Life" was the "best" in the show. A seventh song, "Leaf in the Wind," was praised by Nichols.

Morehouse said Jack Cole's choreography was "excellent" (the musical offered six separate dance numbers, and Cole must have been happy with the Middle Eastern setting, given that throughout his career he flavored his dance creations with oriental touches), and he and other critics were especially taken with the satiric "Katinka to Eva to Frances" which depicted a slow-motion softball game played by the harem. Rascoe said Cole's contributions were "fetching" and Chapman liked his "interesting" dance patterns.

Diminutive Joey Faye and the Amazonian Jayne Manners (who had in fact played an Amazon in *By Jupiter*) made an interesting visual pair. He was quite short, and she was over six feet tall (Aronson said she was "extremely well-proportioned every inch of the distance"). Chapman noted she was "probably the most beautiful tall girl in the world or the tallest beautiful girl," and when she swished her bare thighs at Faye "Alexander Calder's mobiles quiver over at the Museum of Modern Art." But the critics felt the show didn't exploit the inherent humor of these two clowns. And that was really the whole problem with *Allah Be Praised!* It was loaded with talented performers, ingratiating songs, lively and ingenious dances, and lavish décor and costumes, but the book was unable to pull it all together into an enjoyable evening. As a result, Bloomingdale did indeed close the show (after twenty performances) and perhaps decided to extend the store's hours during the evenings.

The irresistibly melodic and lyrically clever "What's New in New York" has been recorded on two collections: *Life's a Funny Present* (Rialto CD # SLRR-9306) and *Everyone Else Revisited* (Painted Smiles CD # PSCD-146). "Let's Go Too Far" is included in the collection *Lost Broadway and More/Volume Three* (unnamed and unnumbered CD).

HELEN GOES TO TROY
"Operetta"

Theatre: Alvin Theatre
Opening Date: April 24, 1944; *Closing Date*: July 15, 1944
Performances: 97
Book: Gottfried Reinhardt and John Meehan Jr.
Lyrics: Herbert Baker
Music: Jacques Offenbach (musical adaptation by Erich Wolfgang Korngold)
Based on the 1864 operetta *La belle Helene* (libretto by Henri Meilhac and Ludovic Halevy, music by Jacques Offenbach).
Direction: Production staged by Herbert Graf; dialogue directed by Melville Cooper; *Producer*: Yolanda Mero-Irion for The New Opera Company; *Choreography*: Leonide Massine; *Scenery* and *Lighting*: Robert Edmond Jones; *Costumes*: Ladislas Czettel; *Musical Direction*: Erich Wolfgang Korngold; *Choral Direction*: Irving Landau
Cast: George Rasely (Philocomus), Ralph Dumke (Calchas), *Jarmila Novotna* (Helen), Donald Buka (Orestes), Doris Blake (Parthenis, Minerva), Phyllis Hill (Laena), William Horne (Paris), Rose Inghram (Discordia), Rosalind Nadell (Juno), Peggy Corday (Venus), Michael Mann (Policeman), John Guelis (White Wing), Jesse White (Ajax 1), Alfred Porter (Ajax 2), Ernest Truex (Menalaus), Gordon Dilworth (Agamemnon), Hugh Thompson (Achilles), Jane Kiser (Lady-in-Waiting); Premiere Danseuses: Katia Geleznova, Kathryn Lee, Nancy Mann; Premier Dancers: Michael Mann, John Guelis, George Chaffee; Lillian Andersen (alternate for Jarmila Novotna for matinee performances); Joseph Laderoute (alternate for William Horne); Ladies of the Ensemble: Johnsie Bason, Peggy Blatherwick, Louise Fagg, Elizabeth Giacobbe, Eleanor Jones, Nancy Kenyon, Jeanne Stephens, Virginia Beeler, Anne Bolyn, Louise Newton, Maria Orelo, Matilda Strazza, Betty Tucker, Leona Vanni; Gentlemen of the Ensemble: Sam Adams, George Crawford, William Golden, John Gould, Vincent Henry, Robert Marco, Edwin Alberian, Paul Campbell, Robert Kirland, Seymour Osborne, Gordon Richards, Irving Strull; Ballet Dancers: Galina Razoumova, Lee Lauterbur, Rickey Soma, Edwina Seaver, Jane Kiser, Claire Pasch, Katherine Clark, Ricia Orkina, Nina Frenkin, Nicholas Beriozoff, Sviatoslav Toumine, Todd Bolender, David Adhar, Ricardo Sarroga
The musical was presented in two acts.
The action takes place in Ancient Greece.

Musical Numbers

Act One: "Scenic Overture: Antiquity Awakes" (danced by Michael Mann, Nicholas Beriozoff, Sviatoslav Toumine, John Guelis, Kathryn Lee, Edwina Seaver, Ballet Dancers); "Come to the Sacrifice" (George Rasely, Chorus); "Where Is Love?" (Jarmila Novotna, Ladies-in-Waiting, Ballet Dancers); "Tsing-la-la" (Donald Buka, Ralph Dumke, Phyllis Hill, Doris Blake, George Rasely, Chorus, Ballet Dancers); "Take My Advice" (Jarmila Novotna, Donald Buka); "The Shepherd Song" (William Horne); "The Judgment of

Paris" (William Horne, Rose Inghram, Doris Blake, Rosalind Nadell, Peggy Corday); "What Will the Future Say?" (Ralph Dumke); "Extra! Extra!" (George Rasely, Michael Mann, Chorus, Ballet Dancers); "Ajax 1 and Ajax 2" (Jesse White, Alfred Porter); "Sweet Helen" (Jarmila Novotna, William Horne); "Entrance of the Kings" (Entire Company); First Act Finale: (a) "Entrance of the Kings"; (b) "Dance of Procreation"; (c) "Opera Parody"; and (d) "Go to Naxos" (Entire Company)

Act Two: Prologue to Second Act (Rose Inghram); "Dance of the Ladies-in-Waiting" (Katia Geleznova, Ballet Dancers); "Love at Last" (Jarmila Novotna); "Baccanale": (a) "Bring on the Concubines" (Cast, Chorus); (b) "Waltz" and "Can-Can" (Doris Blake, Kathryn Lee, Donald Buka, Ballet Dancers); (c) "If Menelaus Only Knew It" (Kings, Ralph Dumke, Chorus); and (d) "Drinking Song" and Dance (William Horne, Kings, Ralph Dumke, Kathryn Lee, Michael Mann, John Guelis, Ballet Dancers); Reprise (Ernest Truex); "Is It a Dream?" (Jarmila Novotna, William Horne); "A Little Chat" (Donald Buka, Gordon Dilworth, Ernest Truex, Chorus); "Advice to Husbands" (Jarmila Novotna, Chorus); "Grecian Frieze" (Entire Company); "Come with Me" (Jarmila Novotna, William Horne, Ernest Truex, Company); Second Act Finale (Entire Company)

The New Opera Company enjoyed tremendous successes with **Rosalinda** and **The Merry Widow**, and with glowing notices for *Helen Goes to Troy* it seemed the organization was posed for its third major hit in a row. To be sure, there were some minor reservations from a few of the aisle-sitters, but overall they showered the musical with great notices, the kind that would normally guarantee long lines at the box office and a year's run on Broadway. But the public didn't come, and so the melodious and tongue-in-cheek look at the goings-on in Ancient Greece lasted for just ninety-seven performances.

Jacques Offenbach's 1864 operetta *La belle Helene* had been seen earlier in the decade in an all-black version, but Herbert Kingsley's adaptation never made it to Broadway (see **La belle Helene** for more information, including other *Helene*-related musicals which were based on Offenbach's scores as well as those which offered new music, such as 1954's *The Golden Apple*). Another Broadway musical that employed Offenbach's music was 1961's *The Happiest Girl in the World*, based loosely on *Lysistrata*; like *Helen Goes to Troy*, it lasted three months in New York for a total run of ninety-six performances.

Helen Goes to Troy was based on Max Reinhardt's famous European adaptation of *La belle Helene*, which was produced as *Helen* and for which Erich Wolfgang Korngold adapted the music. In many respects, the evening was in the nature of Offenbach's greatest hits; fourteen numbers were from other operettas by Offenbach (including *La perichole, Genevieve de Brabant, La docteur Ox, La roi Carotte, Robinson Crusoe*, and *Sissy*). The famous "Barcarolle" from *Die Rheinnixen* (which was later interpolated into *Les contes d'Hoffman*) was adapted as "Love at Last." Music retained from the original *La belle Helene* were Helen's entrance; "Tsing-la-la"; "The Judgment of Paris"; the dream-duet ("Is It a Dream?"); the concert-overture; and the two finales. Offenbach's serenade from *La pont de soupirs* was converted into the fox-trot "What Will the Future Say?"

The musical lampooned the story of the beautiful Helen (Jarmila Novotna), who is married to the elderly Menelaus (Ernest Truex) and is seduced by the young and handsome Paris (William Horne). That the triangle caused the tragedy of the Trojan War was overlooked, and the evening concentrated on humor and lively melody. And of course there were almost de rigueur anachronisms (such as a reference to meat shortages and a comment that someone was "sold down the Styx"), there was Discordia (the Goddess of Mischief), and one character was given the title of Assistant Seer. Nothing was taken too seriously, and the evening abounded in lavish décor, lively dances, amusing performances, and Offenbach's sparkling music. Like **Sunny River**, the evening's overture (titled "Scenic Overture: Antiquity Awakes") was unusual in that it was danced.

Lewis Nichols in the *New York Times* said the evening was one of the "pleasures" of Broadway; it was "one of the most spectacular productions of the season" and its décor was "excellent," the costumes employed "wonderful color schemes," and Metropolitan soprano Jarmilla Novotna had an "ease of manner" for the operetta genre and made an "agreeable" Helen (he noted she would probably be responsible for making the barcarolle "Love at Last" a hit all over again). He found the book somewhat long and labored, but predicted the wooden horse and the Greek soldiers would no doubt "capture all of Broadway by this morning."

Oscar Thompson in the *New York Sun* praised the "sumptuous spectacle" which was "handsomely" produced by The New Opera Company; the headline of Howard Barnes' review in the *New York Herald Tribune* announced that "A Hit Is Launched"; he noted the evening was a "blithesome blend of arias, ballets and clowning" with "expensive and tasteful" décor, and concluded that the operetta was an "exceedingly satisfying entertainment" which was "good-looking, tuneful and great good fun"; and Harriet Johnson in the

New York Post said the "colorful spectacle" offered scenery, costumes, and lighting that were "brilliantly effective in the extravagant manner of" **Rosalinda** and **The Merry Widow**; the dialogue was "vastly superior" to most operettas, and the "glamorous" Novotna "had plenty of zip" and put "her lines across with a keen sense of showmanship."

Burton Rascoe in the *New York World-Telegram* said the operetta was an "unmitigated delight" for those seeking "jollity and sensuous relaxation" and predicted ticket-buyers would be "storming" the Alvin's box office for months to come. He noted the evening was a "mile above" the "nauseous" book of **By Jupiter**, and praised the "opalescent and sensual" settings and the "rich and voluptuous" costumes; John Chapman in the *New York Daily News* found the operetta "opulent" and "dazzlingly beautiful," a "spectacle" with "lithe and lovely" dancers and "smartly beautiful" settings; but he noted the evening needed better humor and perhaps a bit of tightening; Louis Kronenberger in *PM* found the evening "well out of the ordinary" but cautioned that Helen "only goes to Troy—not to town" because the book needed better pace and comedy; and Robert Garland in the *New York Journal-American* said the production was "handsome" but "somewhat heavy"; he praised the "melodious" and "beautiful" Novotna and said Ernest Truex made a "frequently funny" and "mouse-like" Menalaus.

In 1948, Novotna made a rare film appearance when she starred opposite Montgomery Clift in the gripping 1948 postwar drama *The Search* in which she portrayed a distraught mother trying to find her little boy among the survivors of the concentration camps. Directed by Fred Zinnemann, the film won the Academy Award for Best Story.

TARS AND SPARS
"The Coast Guard Show" / "A Tabloid Musical Revue"

Theatre: Strand Theatre
Opening Date: May 5, 1944; *Closing Date*: Unknown
Performances: Unknown
Book (*Sketches*) and *Lyrics*: Howard Dietz
Music: Lieutenant Vernon Duke, USCGR(T)
Direction: Max Liebman; *Producer*: The United States Coast Guard; *Choreography*: Ted Gary, BM2c; *Musical Direction*: Ben Harrod, GM1c
Cast: Tars—Fay Alexander, Mus1c, Marc Ballero, QM2c, Larry Burns, MM2c, Sidney (Sid) Caesar, Sea1c, Gower Champion, Sea1c, Edwin Clay, HA1c, Warren Davis, RM1c, Byron Evans, BM1c, Robert Fallow, Sea1c, Frank Fuentes, Sea1c, Ted Gary, BM2c, Peta Gladke, SK3c, Harry Halicki, BM2c, Charles Hogg, SK2c, Russell Lewis, SM2c, Ted Lybarger, Mus1c, Joe Pettillo, BM2c, Charles Pettillo, BM2c, Bill (William, Billy) Skipper, PhM2c, Bill Snyder, Mus1c, Benny Yaffee, Sea2c; Spars—Coralee Burson, Y3c, Arline (Arlene) Dahl, Sea1c, Collette Ford, Sea1c, Alice Frantz, Y3c, Jeanne Freed, SK3c, Lois Geisguth, Sea1c, Jinx Jarvi, Y3c, Dorothy Kachele, Sea1c, Nell Keith, Sea1c, Shirley Kephart, Y3c, Dorothy Kerfoot, Sea1c, Julie Litwin, Sea1c, Melba Martindale, PhM3c, Lee Parisi, Y3c, Arline E. Peirce, Y2c, Kathryn Pence, Sea1c, Audrey Pettersen, Y3c, Bette Powell, Y3c, Lynn Roberts, Sea1c, Edith Rosencrans, Sea2c, Thelma Smith, PhM3c, Gloria Tickell, Sea1c, Lorraine Whitney, Sea1c; The Coast Guard Invaders Orchestra— Ben Harrod, GM1c, Conductor; Saxophones: Bertil Kempel, Mus3c, Dominic Capone, RM2c, John Smith, Mus1c, Clifton Case, CM1c, John Drake, Mus2c, Andrew Fitzgerald, Mus2c; Piano: John Brogan, RM2c; Trumpets: Bernard Savodnick, Mus1c, Barney Zudekoff, Mus1c, Blaine Houserman, SK3c; Trombones: Paul Gilmore, Mus1c, Warren Covington, Mus3c; Drums: Michael Fuchs, MM2c; Bass: Richard Neumann, Mus1c
The revue was presented in one act.

Sketches and Musical Numbers

Overture (The Coast Guard Invaders Orchestra); "Get Out to Sea" (Tars and Spars); "Stepping Out" (Bill Skipper, PhM2c); "(You Gotta Have a Reason to Be a) Civilian" (Draftee: Ted Gary, BM2c; Tar: Marc Ballero, QM2c; Spar: Kay Pence, Sea1c; Out Front: Ed Clay, HA1c; danced by Robert Fallow, Sea1c and Benny

Yaffee, Sea2c); "Recruiting" (Recruit: Sidney [Sid] Caesar, Sea1c; Spars: Lorraine Whitney, Sea1c and Melba Martindale, PhM3c); "Arm in Arm" (Charles Hogg, SK2c, alternating with Warren Davis, RM1c; Audrey Pattersen, Y3c); "48-Hour Liberty" (choreography by Gower Champion, Sea1C; Accompaniment by John Brogan, RM3c) (danced by Gower Champion, Sea1c, Coralee Burson, Y3c, and Jeanne Freed, SK3c); The Coast Guard Invaders Orchestra ("Direct from Three Invasions Aboard the U.S.S. *Samuel Chase*"); "Apprentice Seaman" (Charles Hogg, SK2c; Chief: Marc Bellero, QM2c); "Palm Beach" (Marjorie Parker, SK3c, and Spar Quintette [Lorraine Whitney, Sea1c; Kathryn Pence, Sea1c; Julie Litwin, Sea1c; and Alice Frantz, Y3c]; danced by Ted Gary, BM2c, alternating with Russell Lewis, SM2c; Specialty Dancers: Bill Skipper, PhM2c, alternating with Peta Gladke, SK3c); "Acrobatricks" (The DeWaynes: Ted Lybarger, Mus1c, Bill Snyder, Mus1c, and Fay Alexander, Mus1c); "Cigarette Dance" (danced by Gower Champion, Sea1c; accompanied by Barney Zudekoff, Sea1c); "Celebrities at the Biltmore" (Marc Ballero, QM2c); "Philharmonicas" (Joe Pitello, BM2c, Charles Pitello, BM2c, and Harry Halicki, BM2c); "The Silver Shield" (Vic [Victor] Mature, CBM; sung by Ed Clay, HA1c, and Tars and Spars)

Tars and Spars, like **This Is the Army** and **Winged Victory**, was a tribute to service personnel; the cast and orchestra were all TARS and SPARS (that is, men and women members of the Coast Guard), and while the other two productions were designed to raise money for the Army Relief programs, *Tars and Spars* was a short one-act revue that according to its program notes was designed "to further the recruiting program of the Coast Guard Women's Reserve, the SPARS."

The revue played for a limited engagement in New York at the Strand Theatre, which was located at the corner of Broadway and West 47th Street. The theatre was primarily a film house, although throughout its early history it occasionally hosted vaudeville-style shows (it opened in 1914, and was demolished in 1987). (Some sources indicate the revue may have also briefly played at the Plymouth Theatre.) Besides New York, the revue played throughout the country in order to entertain audiences and to introduce the Coast Guard to young men and women.

The revue included Coast Guard members Vic (Victor) Mature, Gower Champion, Sidney (Sid) Caesar, Bill (William) Skipper, and Arline (Arlene) Dahl. In the production, Champion danced with Jeanne Freed, who wasn't part of the team of Champion and Jeanne (Gower Champion and Jeanne Tyler) who had earlier part-nered in three Broadway musicals (*The Streets of Paris*, **The Lady Comes Across**, and **Count Me In**).

During the course of the tour, the "Acrobatricks" and "Philharmonicas" sequences as well as the "Ciga-rette Dance" were deleted, and "Harmonics" (sung by Harry Blumenthal, Y3c, and danced by Gower Champion, Sea1c) was added. Apparently during the course of the show's tour, the ballad "Farewell for a While" was also added.

A 1946 film version was released by Columbia; directed by Alfred E. Green and choreographed by Jack Cole, the now-obscure film didn't utilize any of Howard Dietz and Vernon Duke's score and instead included new songs with lyrics by Sammy Cahn and music by Jule Styne. The story wasn't in revue format and the film's plot dealt with the romantic complications of a TAR and SPAR; the leads were Alfred Drake (in his only film appearance), Janet Blair, Marc Platt, and Ray Walker. From the stage production, Sid Caesar made an appearance in which he performed a one-man encapsulation of a typical war movie, here called *Wings Over Boomerschnitzel*.

Caesar and *Tars and Spars'* director Max Liebman teamed up again for the hit revue **Make Mine Manhat-tan**, and in the early 1950s made television history with their legendary series *Your Show of Shows*.

THE NEW MOON
"An Operetta"

Theatre: City Center
Opening Date: May 17, 1944; *Closing Date*: June 24, 1944
Performances: 53
Book: Oscar Hammerstein II, Frank Mandel, and Laurence Schwab
Lyrics: Oscar Hammerstein II
Music: Sigmund Romberg

Direction: Jose Ruben; *Producer*: The Belmont Opera Company; *Choreography*: Charles Weidman; *Scenery*: Oliver Smith; *Costumes*: Brooks Costume Company; *Lighting*: Uncredited; *Musical Direction*: Charles Blackman

Cast: Elizabeth Houston (Julie), Laurence Hayes (Monsieur Beaunoir), George Mitchell (Captain Duval), Harold Gordon (Vicomte Ribaud), Carl Nelson (Fouchette), Earl Wrightson (Robert), Johnny Morgan (Alexander), Hamilton Benz (Besac), Frederick Poller (Jacques), Dorothy Kirsten (Marianne Beaunoir), William Sutherland (Doorkeeper of Tavern), Ludlow White (Tavern Proprietor), Peter Hamilton (A Spaniard), Zoya Leporsky (A Dancer), John Hamill (Philippe), Dorothy Ramsey (Clotilde Lombaste), Hall Carnegie (Emile), Vaughn Trinnier (Brunet), Ralph Sassano (Latouche), John Scott (Gervais), George Bruno (A Sailor), Dick Todd (Captain De Jean); Ladies: Harriet O'Neill, Jeanne Gordon, Jeanne Beauvais, Molly Consley, Elline Walther, Lucille Barton, Alice Richmond, Donna Gardner, Villetta Russell, Margit Fisher, Martha King, Betty Leighton, Ann Jackson, Virginia Barnes, Patricia Leith, Ann Winters, Roberta Casell, Zoya Leporsky; Gentlemen: William Sydenstricker, John Jackson, Vaughn Trinnier, Ludlow White, G. Raymond Breit, John P. Sheridan, Jerry Davenport, Carl Nelson, William Sutherland, John Scott, Ralph Sassano, Kenneth Renner, Joe Monte, Everett S. Anderson, John Duane, David Raher, Aaron Girard

The operetta was presented in three acts (the original production was in two).

The action takes place in the early 1790s in New Orleans, on the high seas, and on the Isle of Pines.

Musical Numbers

Act One: "A Dainty Wisp of Thistledown" (Guests); "Marianne" (Earl Wrightson, Dorothy Kirsten, Ensemble); "The Girl on the Prow" (Dorothy Kirsten, Hamilton Benz, Ensemble); "Gorgeous Alexander" (Elizabeth Houston, Johnny Morgan, Girls); "An Interrupted Love Song" (George Mitchell, Dorothy Kirsten, Earl Wrightson); "Tavern Song" (Flower Girl, Ensemble; tango danced by Peter Hamilton and Zoya Leporsky); "Softly, As in a Morning Sunrise" (John Hamill, Ensemble); "Stouthearted Men" (Earl Wrightson, Ensemble); "One Kiss" (Dorothy Kirsten, Ensemble); "Wanting You" (Dorothy Kirsten, Earl Wrightson, Ensemble)

Act Two: "Chanty" (Hamilton Benz, Men); "Lover, Come Back to Me" (Dorothy Kirsten); Finale (Ensemble)

Act Three: Marriage Number (Elizabeth Houston, Johnny Morgan, Ensemble); "Try Her Out at Dances" (Elizabeth Houston, Johnny Morgan, Ensemble); "Softly, As in a Morning Sunrise" (reprise) (John Hamill, Men); "Lover, Come Back to Me" (reprise) (Earl Wrightson); Finale (Entire Company)

Sigmund Romberg's 1928 operetta *The New Moon* had last been presented by Joseph S. Tushinsky at Carnegie Hall in 1942 (for more information about that revival, see entry which also contains background information about the operetta). The current production was produced at City Center under the auspices of The Belmont Opera Company.

DREAM WITH MUSIC
"A MUSICAL FANTASY" / "A NEW MUSICAL COMEDY"

Theatre: Majestic Theatre
Opening Date: May 18, 1944; *Closing Date*: June 10, 1944
Performances: 28
Book: Sidney Sheldon, Dorothy Kilgallen, and Ben Roberts
Lyrics: Edward Eager
Music: Clay Warnick (most of the songs were adapted by Warnick from the music of classical composers; see song listing for specifics; other music used for the production were Beethoven's First Symphony and Wagner's "Ride of the Valkyries"; and probably some music was by Warnick himself)
Direction: Richard Kollmar; *Producer*: Richard Kollmar; *Choreography*: George Balanchine; tap routines by Henry Le Tang; *Scenery*: Stewart Chaney; *Costumes*: Miles White; *Lighting*: Uncredited; *Musical Direction*: Max Meth

Cast: In Reality—Betty Allen (Ella), *Joy Hodges* (Marian), *Vera Zorina* (Dinah). Alex Rotov (Western Union Boy), *Ronald Graham* (Michael), Robert Brink (Robert); In the Dream—Vera Zorina (Scheherazade), Joy Hodges (Jasmin), Robert Brink (Sultan), Alex Rotov (Wazier), Marcella Howard (Mispah, Mrs. Owl), Janie Janvier (Hispah, Mrs. Lion), Lois Barnes (Rispah, Twin, Leopard), Lucille Barnes (Tispah, Twin, Ermine), Jane Hetherington (Fispah, Mrs. Fox), Donna Devel (Kispah, Rabbit), Ronald Graham (Aladdin), Ray Cook (Rug Merchant, Wolf), Robert Beam (Perfume Merchant, I. J.), Michael Kozak (Fakir, Tiger), Bill Jones (Candy Salesman, Unicorn), John C. Panter (Musical Instrument Merchant), Byron Milligan (Snake Charmer, Mr. Owl), Ralph Bunker (Sand Diviner, Mr. Panda), Leonard Elliott (Sinbad), Betty Allen (Mrs. Sinbad), Dave Ballard (Genie), Jerry Ross (Guard, Monkey, Chinese Masseur), Larry Evers (Guard), Bill Weber (Guard, Penguin, Aladdin's Aide), Parker Wilson (Guard), Dorothy Babb (The Little One, Lamb), Dee Turnell (The Blonde One), Sunny Rice (The First Hot One, Night), Dixie Roberts (The Second Hot One, Mrs. Panda), Mavis Mims (The Slender One), Dolores Milan (The Tall One), Tari Vance (The One with the Pug Nose), Peter Birch (Day, Lion), Buddy Douglas (Mouse); Corps de Ballet: Jacqueline Cezanne, Betty Claire, Dorothy DeMolina, Georgia Hiden, Carmelita Lanza, Margaret Murray, Toni Stuart, Dee Turnell, Larry Evers, Jerry Ross, Bill Weber, Parker Wilson; Singers: Lois Barnes, Lucille Barnes, Donna Devel, Jane Hetherington, Marcella Howard, Janie Janvier, Robert Beam, Ray Cook, Bill Jones, Michael Kozak, Byron Milligan, John C. Panter; The Caryatids: Mae Francis, Beatrice Griffith, Roseler Joynes, Rosemary Mitchell, Gladys Pollard, Bonita Purdue
The musical was presented in two acts.
The action takes place in New York City at the present time, and in Dinah's dreams.

Musical Numbers

Act One: "Scheherazade's Dance" (music based on a theme from Nikolai Rimsky-Korsakov's *Scheherazade*) (Vera Zorina, Singing Ensemble); "Be Glad You're Alive" (music based on a theme from Camille Saint-Saens' Violin Concerto in B Minor) (Joy Hodges, Singing Ensemble, Alex Rotov, Peter Birch, Dancing Ensemble); "I'm Afraid I'm in Love with You" (music based on a theme from Rimsky-Korsakov's *Scheherazade*) (Robert Brink); "Baby, Don't Count on Me" (music based on a theme from Franz Shubert's Ninth Symphony) (Ronald Graham, Singing Ensemble); "Give, Sinbad, Give" (music based on a theme from Ludwig van Beethoven's Seventh Symphony) (Leonard Elliott, Singing Ensemble); "I'll Take the Solo" (music based on a theme from Carl Maria von Weber's *Oberon*) (Betty Allen, Tap Specialty Girls: Sunny Rice, Mavis Mims, Dixie Roberts, Dorothy Babb, Tari Vance, and Dolores Milan, The Barnes Twins, Corps de Ballet); "Love at Second Sight" (music based on a theme from Edvard Grieg's Piano Concerto) (Joy Hodges, Robert Brink); "Relax and Enjoy It" (Vera Zorina, Joy Hodges, Robert Brink, Betty Allen, Leonard Elliott); "Come with Me"(music based on a theme from Alexander Borodin's *Prince Igor*) (Ronald Graham, Vera Zorina); "Battle of the Genie" (music based on a theme from Modest Mussorgsky's "Night on Bald Mountain") (Alex Rotov, Dave Ballard, Larry Evers, Jerry Ross, Bill Weber, Parker Wilson); "Mr. and Mrs. Wrong" (Betty Allen, Leonard Elliott); "Ballet in the Clouds" (music based on a theme from Frederic Chopin's Twenty-four Preludes) (Vera Zorina, Peter Birch, Sunny Rice, Corps de Ballet, Singing Ensemble)
Act Two: "The Lion and the Lamb" (music based on a theme from Christoph Willibald Gluck's "Ballet Suite") (Donna Devel, Ensemble); "Mouse Meets Girl" (music based on a theme from Robert Schumann's Piano Concerto) (Vera Zorina, Buddy Douglas); "Baby, Don't Count on Me" (reprise) (Sunny Rice); "Love at Second Sight" (reprise) (Joy Hodges); "The Moon Song" (music based on a theme from Frederic Chopin's Prelude No. 4) (Ronald Graham); "Woman against the World" (music based on a theme from Joseph Haydn's First Symphony) (Vera Zorina, Jerry Ross, The Barnes Twins, The Tap Specialty Girls, Singing Girls); "The Ballet"" (Leonard Elliott); "Dinah's Nightmare" (music based on themes from Pyotr Ilyich Tschiakovsky's *Nutcracker Suite*) (Entire Company)

The musical fantasy *Dream with Music* took a page out of the book of **Lady in the Dark**, and dealt with another unhappy and frustrated Manhattan career woman. Like Liza Elliott, Dinah is at the top of her profession. She's a successful script writer of radio soap operas, but churning them out day after day becomes too much. And, like Liza, she's involved with two men, a newspaper correspondent and an advertising man who represents one of the sponsors of her radio show. Dinah escapes from reality by dreaming she's Scheherazade, who must conjure up tale after tale for the sultan (Robert Brink) lest she be beheaded. In her stories, she meets such Arabian types as rug and perfume merchants, snake charmers, wazirs, fakirs, and genies, takes rides on magic carpets, and meets such famous names as Aladdin (and his lamp from Cartier) and Sinbad. Her glamorous dreams take place in palaces, Bagdad bazaars, and even an enchanted forest where she encounters pandas, owls, unicorns, penguins, and other assorted show business–styled animals.

Lewis Nichols in the *New York Times* noted the promising script (by future best-selling novelist Sidney Sheldon, future-columnist and television personality Dorothy Kilgallen [who was also married to Richard Kollmar, the musical's producer], and Ben Roberts) never lived up to its potential; as a result, the "dull" musical lacked comedy and liveliness and resorted to the insertion of topical humor into the fantasy. He also noted the conceit of adapting classical composers into musical comedy numbers didn't come off, and only one song was hummable ("Love at Second Sight," based on musical themes by Edvard Grieg, who would be re-adapted all over again the following season when **Song of Norway** opened). But Nichols praised the lavish production, which ranked near the top of all Broadway musicals. Stewart Chaney's décor was a "display of color" and his effects even offered a flying carpet ride for Zorina and Ronald Graham. As for costumer Miles White, he "mixed all the primary and secondary colors and then added some of his own." For *Dream with Music* the "wrappings," not the musical itself, were the thing.

Nichols mysteriously referred to "backstage" problems on opening night, and Robert Garland in the *New York Journal-American* shed some light on the subject. Actually, it was a lack of light because the theatre's lighting equipment literally blew a master fuse. And as far as the look of the musical, it was definitely a "fuse-blower." Louis Kronenberger in *PM* said the designers had created a "playground of charming color and design" and thus no other musical during the season looked "prettier." He admitted the show's conception was "imaginative," but regretted that the "unrewarding" music and "tiresome" book never offered much in the way of fun. He too noted the "serious" lighting problems and also mentioned "scene-shifting trouble." Burton Rascoe in the *New York World-Telegram* said Zorina and the other performers provided "valiant services" for "hopeless tasks"; but he too praised the designers for creating "one of the most beautiful visual backgrounds seen on the stage in recent years."

John Chapman in the *New York Daily News* reported that not since *Fioretta* (a lavish 1929 flop produced by Earl Carroll) "had so elaborate a load been dumped on a stage." The show had "everything—everything but spirit," and as it "unfolded, rolled, and even slid" on the Majestic's stage it provided "splendors" that were "vast, but its torpor was vaster." Howard Barnes in the *New York Herald Tribune* noted that while the musical had "fancy trimmings," it also needed "good songs" and "comic nonsense." Herrick Brown in the *New York Sun* said the show had "serious book trouble" and thus the "lavish and eye-filling and beautiful" production was "often ponderous" and lacked humor.

Wilella Waldorf in the *New York Post* explained to her readers that after the show's writers concocted the basic outline of the plot, they were "apparently so completely exhausted by the mental effort that they were unable to contribute much of anything else." She praised the "eye-filling" décor, but as for the jokes, "Banish them, Aladdin!" She noted the $175,000 production included a scene in which two chorus girls scampered around Old Bagdad carrying a "conspicuously labeled" brand of popular soap powder. Here was an early example of product placement, and Waldorf hoped the revenue from the promotion would help the producer toward the recoupment of the musical's costs.

During the Boston tryout, the following songs were cut: "Gory Lullaby" (music based on a theme from Rimsky-Korsakov's *Scheherazade*); "Sinbad's in Bad" (music based on a theme from Wagner's "Siegfried Idyll"); "Old Love" (music based on a theme from Wagner's "Siegfried Idyll"); and "Just Like a Man" (music based on a theme from Dvorak's "New World Symphony"). In Boston, "The Moon Song" was titled "I Wished for the Moon," and June Knight was succeeded by Joy Hodges.

One of the New York critics noted that an unacknowledged but well-known song by Richard Rodgers and Lorenz Hart was heard in the production; perhaps it was from the team's 1938 musical *I Married an Angel*, which had starred Zorina.

The collection *Life's a Funny Present* (Rialto CD # SLRR-9306) includes "Love at Second Sight" and both *You Can't Put Ketchup on the Moon* (Rialto CD # SLRR-9201) and *Lost Broadway and More/Volume 3* (unnamed company and unnumbered CD) includes "I'm Afraid I'm in Love with You."

BIG TIME
"A VARIETY REVUE" / "HILARIOUS VARIETY REVUE"

Theatres and *Performance Dates*: The revue premiered in San Francisco, California, and played at various venues around the country including two weeks at the Shubert Theatre, Boston, Massachusetts, beginning on August 30, 1943, and one week at the National Theatre, Washington, D.C., beginning on September 20, 1943.
Producers: Fred F. Finklehoff and Paul Small; *Draperies*: R. L. Grosh & Sons, Hollywood; *Lighting*: Duweco; *Musical Direction*: Waldemar Guterson
Cast: *Ed Wynn*, Cross & Dunn, Marie Nash, Bob DuPont, Paul La Varre & Brother, Coleman Clark & Co., Con Colleano, Eleanor Niles, Nancy Hill, Nina Crane, Paul Haakon and Patricia Bowman
The revue was presented in two acts.

Sketches and Musical Numbers

Act One: Ed Wynn; Coleman Clark & Co.; Con Colleano; Paul La Varre & Brother; Marie Nash; Paul Haakon and Patricia Bowman
Act Two: Ed Wynn; Bob DuPont, Cross & Dunn, Eleanor Niles, Nancy Hill, Nina Crane; "And a few final moments of impromptu amusement"

Big Time, which starred Ed Wynn, was one of five vaudeville-styled revues presented together or singly by producers Fred F. Finklehoff and Paul Small (for more information about their revues, see **Laugh Time** as well as **Show Time**, **Star Time**, and **Curtain Time**). **Show Time**, **Laugh Time**, and **Star Time** made it to New York, but **Big Time** and **Curtain Time** floundered on the road.

A program note indicated there was "happily" no script or story and thus no one ("least of all, Mr. Wynn") had to "worry about plots and such contraptions." The Perfect Fool "acts as master of hilarities to tie the various stars and performers together. They in turn also serve, after a fashion, to tie Mr. Wynn's jibes and improvisations together."

The revue included singer Marie Nash and dancers Paul Haakon and Patricia Bowman.

During the course of the national tour, various acts were seen in the revue; the cast list above reflects those who performed during the Washington, D.C., run. In Boston, the cast included Frieda Hempe, Capt. Proske's Tigers, Red & Curley, Polly Miller, and Sue Taylor.

CURTAIN TIME
"THE REVUE"

Theatre and *Performance Dates*: The revue opened at the Curran Theatre, San Francisco, California, on December 27, 1943, for a six-week run. Other venues (if any) are unknown.
Producer: Paul Small; *Scenery* and *Draperies*: R. L. Grosh & Sons, Hollywood; *Musical Direction*: Waldeman Guterson
Cast: *Chico Marx*, *Connee Boswell*, Diosa Costello, Jayne and Adam DiGatano, Think-a-Drink Hoffman, The Three Swifts, Gene Sheldon, The Miller Brothers and Lois, Pupi, The Whitney Sisters, Buck and Bubbles
The revue was presented in two acts.

Sketches and Musical Numbers

Act One: The Miller Brothers and Lois; Diosa Costello and Pupi; Think-a-Drink Hoffman; Gene Sheldon; Buck and Bubbles; Jayne and Adam DiGatano
Act Two: The Three Swifts; The Whitney Sisters; Connee Boswell; Chico Marx

Curtain Time was one of five vaudeville-styled revues presented together or singly by Fred F. Finklehoff and Paul Small (for more information about their revues, see *Laugh Time* as well as *Show Time*, *Star Time*, and *Big Time*). *Show Time*, *Laugh Time*, and *Star Time* made it to New York, but *Big Time* and *Curtain Time* closed prior to their Broadway openings.

A program note indicated the evening was strictly "for the complete enjoyment and relaxation of theatergoers." The show was for "fun, and fun only" and there were "no morals, historical or political messages to get across via the footlights."

MARIANNE
"A NEW MUSICAL PLAY"

Theatres and *Performance Dates*: The musical opened at the Shubert Theatre, New Haven, Connecticut, on December 30, 1943; at Ford's Theatre in Baltimore, Maryland, on January 3, 1944; and at the National Theatre, Washington, D.C., on January 10, where it permanently closed on January 15, 1944.

Book: Sylvia Regan and Kenneth White

Lyrics: Beatrice Metzl, Lothar Metzl, and Robert B. Sour

Music: Abraham Ellstein

Direction: Marion Gering; *Producers*: B. P. Schulberg and Marion Gering; *Choreography*: Helen Tamiris; *Scenery*: Frederick Fox; *Costumes*: Ken Barr; *Lighting*: Uncredited; *Musical Direction*: Abraham Ellstein

Cast: Stanley Bell (Rene), Gregory Robins (Bobo), Lewis Rose (Jacques), Jean Darling (Villager), Marjorie Hayward (Villager), Ernest Treux (Monsieur Pichon), Mary Sargent (Madame Pichon), Mary Jane Walsh (Suzanne), Paul Reed (Rafael), Helen Wagner (Lizette), Virginia MacWatters (Martine), Jerry Wayne (Toni Robert), Elizabeth Malone (Grandmother Robert), Guy Samsel (Father Robert), Ethel Strickland (Mother Robert), Val Valentinoff (Francois Robert), Harold Patrick (Doctor Marcel Du Bois), William Malone (Village Drunkard), Robert Vivian (Grandfather Robert), Gloria Vale (Henriette), Jimmie Allen (Jean); Dancers: Dorothy Bird, Kathleen O'Brien, Charles Bockman, Vivian Cherry, Clara Cordery, Lidija Franklin, Joseph Gifford, Miriam Kornfield, Olga Lunich, Daniel Nagrin, Hazel Roy, Emy St. Just, Ida Soyer, Jack Star, Barbara Bray

The musical was presented in two acts.

The action takes place in France during the present time.

Musical Numbers

Note: * denotes lyrics by Robert Sour and ** denotes lyrics by Beatrice Metzl and Lothar Metzl.

Act One: "What Do I Have to Do" (*) (Mary Jane Walsh, Val Valentinoff); "The Kind of a Man" (*) (Virginia MacWatters, Jerry Wayne); "Vive Pichon" (**) (Entire Company); "Marianne" (**) (Mary Jane Walsh); "Always Goodbye" (*) (Jerry Wayne, Virginia MacWatters); "Crepe Suzette" (**) (Mary Jane Walsh)

Act Two: "No More" (**) (Virginia MacWatters); "The Germ in the German" (*) (Harold Patrick, Villagers); "Out of the Dark" (*) (Jerry Wayne); "Always Goodbye" (reprise) (ballet) (Dancers); "The Pom Pom on Your Hat" (*) (Mary Jane Walsh, Val Valentinoff); "My Heart Is Like a Bird" (*) (Virginia MacWatters); "The Black Horsemen" (**) (Entire Company)

The musical's title, and its title song, didn't refer to a heroine named Marianne; *La marianne* took its name from an anti-French government movement in the early 1850s, a name that was later adopted during World War II for a French underground society that plotted against the German invaders. A note in the program stated "the story of the play is based upon an actual incident that occurred at the occupation of France by the Nazis in 1942."

Because the musical's hero Toni (Jerry Wayne) belongs to *La marianne*, he's unable to share his secret with his girlfriend Martine (Virginia MacWatters) and his mysterious disappearances lead her to believe he's involved with another woman. The "actual incident" referred to in the program was a clever ruse in which all the able-bodied young men in the village fake their deaths by the concoction of a phony disease. The Nazis are completely fooled by their "funerals," not realizing the young men are now in a figurative and not literal underground.

Variety said the musical "not only failed to score a bull's eye," it "almost missed the target completely." The reviewer noted the book wasn't particularly "cheerful" and lacked comic relief.

During the course of the three-city tryout, the songs "The Locusts and the Rabbits," "Godspeed in Your Flight," "We Are Not Alone," and "You've Got to Build Up Your Resistance" were cut (the latter may have been an early title for, or an early version of, "The Germ in the German").

MARCHING WITH JOHNNY
"New Exciting Musical Revue"

Theatres and *Performance Dates*: The revue opened on November 22, 1943, at the Mosque Theatre in Newark, New Jersey, and closed permanently in Philadelphia, Pennsylvania, on December 25; between these two engagements, the revue played in at least one other venue when it opened at the Klein Memorial Auditorium in Bridgeport, Connecticut.
Sketches and *Lyrics*: Henry Myers, Edward Eliscu, Leonard Keller, Robert Meltzer
Music: Jay Gorney; additional music by Phil Moore
(The revue also included unidentified songs and sketches by William Copeland, Searle Kramer, and Stella Bloch.)
Direction: Philip Loeb and Robert H. Gordon; *Producer*: The National Congress of Industrial Organizations War Productions; *Choreography*: Dan Eckley (Charles Weidman, supervision of choreography); *Scenery* and *Lighting*: Howard Bay; *Costumes*: Rose Bogdanoff; *Musical Direction*: Pembroke Davenport
Cast: David Brooks, Beatrice Kay, Jack Marshall, Norman Lloyd, Rosetta LeNoire, April Ames, Mervyn Nelson, Coby Ruskin, Billy Newell, Gil Johnson, Beau Jenkins, Mary Sutherland, Virginia Bolen, Ginger Dulo, Harold Gordon, Jean Tighe, The Three Poms, The Showmen, The Tio Trio, The Louis Reed Quartet, Wally Coyle, Bob Wattoff, Jerry Gilbert, Charles Dubin, Sibyl Warner, Geraldine Ball, Ludie Jones, Mildred Jocelyn, John Miccio, Lilias MacLellan, Gordon Clark, George Farrell, Arthur Craig, Suzanne TaFel, Joan Chandler, Anita Carroll, Kate Carroll, Kate Harkin, Maya Herne, Marjorie Johnstone, Virginia Conrad, Doris Jean Rothman, Betty Leighton, Harriet Waite, Margaret Gibson, Marie von Behren, Dodo Wicker, Nancy McCabe, Carol Ossman, Jean Witlow, Helen Shepard, Ernie DiGennaro, Lawrence Ehrlich, Fred Bernaski, Johnny Lane

Sketches and Musical Numbers

The following list is given alphabetically; song assignments and division of acts are unknown.
"Crispus Attucks" (lyric by Edward Eliscu and Robert Meltzer, music by Phil Moore); "Damn the Torpedoes (Full Speed Ahead)"; "Early Monday Morning"; "The Four Rivers"; "He Was All Right Here (He'll Be All Right There)"; "Let's Go Out and Ring Doorbells"; "Lincoln and Juarez"; "Love in a Changing World"; "Marching with Johnny"; "Mamma, It's Saturday Night"; "Mr. Roosevelt and Mr. Churchill"; "That Mittel-Europa Europe of Mine" (aka "Mittel-Europa"); "You and Your Broken Heart"; "You're Good for My Morale"

The advertisements for the hopefully morale-boosting revue *Marching with Johnny* stated the show was "more than just a sparkling, youthful, happy revue—it is a real contribution to the victory spirit that animates America today." But the production quickly disappeared and never opened in New York (where it was scheduled to play at City Center beginning on December 29, 1943, for a limited engagement of two months).

"You and Your Broken Heart" is included in the collection *Lost Broadway and More: Volume Three* (unnamed company and unnumbered CD); the recording's liner notes indicate the song was added to a second edition of **Meet the People** and was later included in *Meet the People of 1955*.

The revue was by the creators of **Meet the People**, which had enjoyed a five-month run on Broadway after a successful West Coast engagement; they had followed up that hit with the book musical **They Can't Get You Down**, a spoof of college musicals that closed during its pre-Broadway tryout and had included two songs

("That Mittel-Europa Europe of Mine" [aka "Mittel-Europa"] and "Love in a Changing World") that were recycled for *Marching with Johnny* (it appears the former song was dropped at some point during the tryout of *Marching with Johnny*). In between the productions of **They Can't Get You Down** and *Marching with Johnny*, "Mittel-Europa" was also heard in the short-lived 1942 Broadway revue **Let Freedom Ring**. "Love in a Changing World" is included in the collection *Make Mine Manhattan and Great Revues Revisited* (Painted Smiles CD # PSCD-119).

The revue had been conceived by the National CIO War Productions as a patriotic revue by mostly union labor talent. Although *Variety* found the show "engaging and frequently thrilling," it nonetheless felt its potential was only "partially realized." Linton Martin in the *Philadelphia Inquirer* said the revue was a "shoddy, shabby" evening that seemed to have been "slapped together from odds and ends right off the remnant counter."

Ken Bloom's *American Song* indicates *Marching with Johnny* was later revised as *The New Meet the People*, which apparently toured (but was never seen on Broadway). Incidentally, years later Jay Gorney and Edward Eliscu offered *Meet the People of 1955*, which, like *The New Meet the People*, played only on tour.

THE ROSE MASQUE
"An Operetta"

Theatres and *Performances Dates*: The operetta opened at the Curran Theatre in San Francisco, California, on August 23, 1943, and at the Philharmonic Auditorium in Los Angeles, California, on September 27, 1943.
Book: Erich Weiler
Lyrics: Erich Weiler and Thomas Martin
Music: Johann Strauss
Direction: Reinhold Schunzel; *Producers*: L. E. Behymer in association with The Comic Opera Theatre; *Choreography*: William Christensen; *Scenery*: Stewart Chaney; *Costumes*: Goldstein & Co.; *Lighting*: Uncredited; *Musical Direction*: Walter Herbert
Cast: John Garris (Alfred Allevanto), Joseph Sullivan (Gabriel Von Eisenstein), Marita Farell (Rosalinda Von Eisenstein), Margaret Spencer (Adele), George Burnson (Blint), Ruby Asquith (Piccolo, Premiere Danseuse), John Shafer (Falke), Gerhard Pechner (Dr. Frank), James Westerfield (Frosch), Sue Bell Browne (Ida), John Wengraf (Prince Orlofsky), Robert Ainsley (Aide de Camp), Frank Marasco (Premier Dancer), Charles Goodwin (Major Domo); Ladies of the Ensemble: Jean Forward, Betty Ivers, Gwen Jones, Laura Lyons, Peggy Engel, Audrey Deardon, Barbara Boudwin, Gloria Martin; Gentlemen of the Ensemble: Jack Garland, Martin Jenkins, Charles Goodwin, Wilton Clary, John Dickens, Edward Haas, Cameron Grant, Russell Heath; Corps de Ballet: Mattlyn Gevurtz, Natalie Carr, Celina Cummings, Lois Treadwell, Onna White, Mildred Ferguson, Beatrice Tompkins, Rosalie Prosch, Peggy Swift, Jocelyn Vollmar, Beverlee Bozeman, Josef Carmassi, Rudolfo Silva, Mark Lintz, Robert Hansen, Robert Tucker
The operetta was presented in three acts.
The action takes place in Vienna during the year 1890.

Musical Numbers

Act One: Overture; "Rosalind Dear" (John Garris); "Dancing Duet" (Joseph Sullivan, John Shafer); "Ballet of the Waiters" (Ruby Asquith, Corps de Ballet); "Oh Me, Oh My" (Marita Farell, Margaret Spencer, Joseph Sullivan); "Drinking Song" and Finale (John Garris, Marita Farell, Gerhard Pechner)
Act Two: Introduction and Gallop (Corps de Ballet, Chorus); "Gambling Polka" (Chorus); "Laughing Song" (Margaret Spencer); "Each One to His Taste" (John Wengraf); "Csardas" (Marita Farell); "Champagne Song" (Joseph Sullivan, Margaret Spencer, John Shafer); "You Are the Dream" (Marita Farell, Joseph Sullivan); "Brother Mine" (John Shafer, Entire Ensemble); "Grand Waltz" (Ruby Asquith, Corps de Ballet); Finale
Act Three: "Frank's Nightmare" (Gerhard Pechner, Corps de Ballet); "Adele's Audition" (Margaret Spencer); Trio (Marita Farell, John Garris, Joseph Sullivan); "You Forgive Me, I Forgive You" (Marita Farell, Joseph Sullivan); Finale

With the New Opera Company's Broadway success of **Rosalinda**, it was probably inevitable that another adaptation of Johann Strauss' *Die Fledermaus* would soon come along. In fact, The Comic Opera Theatre's *The Rose Masque* was produced on the West Coast when **Rosalinda** was some ten months into its Broadway run. But *The Rose Masque* never tested the Broadway waters and seems to have closed for good after its San Francisco and Los Angeles engagements.

Listed among the members of the corps de ballet was future choreographer Onna White, who created the dances for many Broadway productions (for more information, see **Hold It!**). For more information about *Die Fledermaus* and **Rosalinda**, see entry for the latter.

STOVEPIPE HAT
"A LEGEND WITH MUSIC"

Theatres and *Performances Dates*: The musical opened on May 18, 1944, at the Shubert Theatre, New Haven, Connecticut, and closed there on May 20; it opened at the Shubert Theatre, Boston, Massachusetts, on May 23, and permanently closed there on May 27, 1944.
Book and *Lyrics*: Walter F. Hannan, Edward Heyman, and Harold Spina
Music: Harold Spina
Direction: Robert Ross; entire production under the supervision of Harold Spina; *Producer*: Carl E. Ring; *Choreography*: Helen Tamiris; *Scenery*: Lucinda Ballard and A. A. Ostrander; *Costumes*: Lucinda Ballard; *Lighting*: Uncredited; *Musical Direction*: Albert Richard Wagner
Cast: Stanley Nelson (Josh, Southern Senator), Georgia Simmons (Ma, Emmy Smoots, First Townswoman), Marsha Norman (Nancy Hanks Lincoln), Jonathan Harris (New Man, Officer, A Telegrapher), Morton Da Costa (Joe, Professor Clip), Seymour Penzner (Charlie, Mr. Applegate), Sam Kramer (George, Strongheart), Bernard Griffen (Woodcutter), Joan Chandler (Ann Rutledge), Liam Dunn (Hank Smoots), Duval Springman (Jack Armstrong, Itinerant Singer, Ike), Rem Olmstead (Bil Clary, Geronimo), Morton L. Stevens (Dan Potter, Marshall Lamon, Judge Cleaver, Sergeant), Frederica Going (Mrs. Miller, Third Townswoman), Lulu Bell Clarke (Miss Cogsdale, Second Townswoman), Homer Miles (Mentor Grahame, Senator, Second Townsman), Jack Lee (Eb), Paul Ransom (Paul, Dolin), Lila King (First Girl), Jimmie Elliott (First Boy, A Boy, Another Boy, Office Boy), Eleanor Dennis (Second Girl), Harold Schlegel (Second Boy), Bob Kennedy (Johnny Drummer), Ann Warren (Barbara), Frederic Tozere (William Herndon, Doc Barker), Alan Dreeban (John Hay, Willie), Charles Hart (Hannibal Hamlin), David Kurlan (General, Jeb), Joy Geffen (Lucy), Ruth White (Mary Todd Lincoln, Mrs. Bixby), Madeleine Clive (Mrs. Stuart), Clarence Foster (Servant), David Perry (Servant), Oscar Brooks (Servant), Parker Fennelly (A Reverend, Farmer), Grace Carroll (A Small Girl), William Carroll (A Small Boy), Daniel Nagrin (Townsman), Eric Martin (Lieutenant), John Garth III (Singer); The Richard A. Gordon Choir: Anita Bensing, Shirley Conklin, Eleanor Dennis, Bernard J. Griffen, Holly Harris, Elwin Howland, Dorothy Johnson, Lila King, Adele Lambert, Robert Lenn, Jacqueline Geffen, Brayton Lewis, Lucille Lewis, Doris Link, Fred Langford, Paul Phillips, Terry Saunders, Harold Schlegel, Garry Sherwood, Kent Williams, Eleanor Winter; The Helen Tamiris Dancers: Mary Anthony, Richard Beard, Aleks Bird, George Bachman, Vivian Cherry, Clara Cordery, Lidija Franklin, Joseph Gifford, Eric Martin, Lavinia Nielsen, Daniel Nagrin, Kathleen O'Brien, Emy Saint-Just, Mary Tiffany; The Eva Jessye Choir: Lavetta Albright, Rosamond Boxill, Oscar Brooks, Evelyn Davis, Clarence Foster, Virginia Girvin, St. Clair George, Francis Kairson, Ruthena Matson, David Perry, Harry Nash, Nelle Plante, Virtis Reese, Catherine Van Buren, Phyllis Walker
The musical was presented in two acts.
The action takes place during the span of Abraham Lincoln's life (1809–1865) in Kentucky, Illinois, Washington, D.C., "somewhere down South," "somewhere in the Middle West," and Gettysburg, Pennsylvania.

Musical Numbers

Act One: "A Mother's Prayer" (lyric by Edward Heyman) (Marsha Norman); "Six Foot of Hick'ry" (lyric by Harold Spina) (Seymour Penzner); "Honest Abe" (lyric by Walter F. Hannan) (Duval Springman, Rem Olmstead, Lulu Belle Clarke, Stanley Nelson, Liam Dunn, Joan Chandler, Ensemble); "An Illinois

Republican" (lyric by Walter F. Hannan) (Ensemble); "There's Trouble Brewin'" (lyric by Harold Spina) (Duval Springman); "Lady Lovely" (lyric by Edward Heyman) (Cotillion); "The Great Man Says" (lyric by Edward Heyman) (John Garth III, The Eva Jessye Choir)

Act Two: "Ghost of Gettysburg" (lyric by Walter F. Hannan) (Bob Kennedy); "He Walks across the Sky" (lyric by Edward Heyman) (Soloist: Marsha Norman; Entire Ensemble)

Stovepipe Hat was an epic and episodic attempt to depict Abraham Lincoln's life from his birth to his assassination. The events of his days as a young lawyer and his eventual emergence into public office, his engagement to Ann Rutledge, his marriage to Mary Todd, his presidency, the Civil War, and the Emancipation Proclamation, were all part of a mosaic that employed drama, music, and dance with a huge company of more than seventy performers. But missing from the entire evening was Lincoln himself. The concept was that Lincoln never appeared; he was the subject of the songs and scenes, but except for his stovepipe hat, which was placed on a chair and visually dominated each scene, the man himself was never onstage. The idea may have seemed promising in conception, but the lack of an actual flesh-and-blood leading character probably doomed the show and kept it confined within its somewhat abstract framework. The man himself was never allowed to speak, and so it was left to other characters to define and describe the emotional and dramatic arcs of his life.

The musical also included a generic young soldier named Johnny Drummer (played by Bob Kennedy) who weaved in and out of the proceedings and who eventually dies at Gettysburg (he seems to be a forerunner of the nameless Young Soldier in *Mata Hari* [1967] who sings "Maman" and the one who is the subject of the song "Momma, Look Sharp" in *1776* [1969]).

Elinor Hughes in the *Boston Herald* felt the "novel" musical was well-intentioned but "badly confused" and "episodic and vague," and Elliot Norton in the *Boston Post* said the "melodious" score and "first-class" singers were lost amid a "confusing and disappointing" story.

The production cancelled its scheduled June 5, 1944, tryout in Philadelphia and closed in Boston on May 27 at a reported loss of $125,000. At its final Boston performance, the musical was retitled *Johnny Drummer* at the insistence of producer Carl E. Ring. William Torbert Leonard in *Broadway Bound* reports another civil war of sorts erupted offstage when Ring and composer and co-lyricist-and-librettist Harold Spina collided over their differing views about the musical.

Other songs that may have been heard during the tryout were "Softly My Heart Is Singing" (lyric by Edward Heyman), "O' Queen of Victory" (lyric by Harold Spina), and "I Know a Man" (lyric by Harold Spina).

In 1961, the musical was briefly revived at the Music Box Theatre in Hollywood, California, with Tex Ritter (Frank Cardinale played the role of Johnny Drummer).

VINCENT YOUMANS' "FIESTA"
"A NEW BALLET REVUE"

Theatres and *Performance Dates*: The revue opened on January 27, 1944, at the Lyric Theatre in Baltimore, Maryland, played in Toronto, Canada, and then at the Boston Opera House, Boston, Massachusetts, where it closed on February 19, 1944.

Lyrics: Marla Shelton, Gladys Shelley
Music: Nikolai Rimsky-Korsakov, Maurice Ravel, and Ernesto Lecuona
Choreography: Leonide Massine and Eugene Van Grona; *Producer*: Vincent Youmans; *Scenery*: Woodman Thompson; *Costumes*: John N. Booth Jr.; *Lighting*: Uncredited; *Musical Direction*: Max Goberman
Cast: Massine's Corps de Ballet—Principals: Kathryn Lee, Alexander Iolas, Ivan Kirov, Katia Geleznova, David Ahdar, Jean Guelis, Monica Lind; Ensemble: Nina Frenkin, Jacqueline Cezanne, Elana Keller, Lee Lauterbur, Jeanne Mikupa, Recia Orkina, Claire Pasch, Carol Percy, Galina Razoumova, Theodora Roosevelt, Edwina Seaver, Rickey Soma, Nikolas Berezoff, Ivan Boothby, George Chaffee, Harold Haskin, Vladimir Nijinsky, Andrew Ratousheff, Ricardo Sarroga, Andor Silva, Sviatoslav Toumine, Parker Wilson, Jane Kiser; Van Grona's Dancers—Principals: Diana Gary, Toni and Mimi Worth, Otto Garcia, Dulcina Garcia, Freida Dova, Herbert Ross; Ensemble: Aza Bard, Ida Bildner, Irene Bonney, Betty Clary, Helen Franklin, Phyllis Gehrig, Saida Gerrard, Betty Killingsworth, Marian Lawrence, Sonia Levanskaya, Eda

Lioy, Louise Schmid, Forrest Bonshire, Alfred DeMolli, John Kopera, Joe Viggiano, John Ward, Ronald Verne; Singers: Olga Coelho, Nestor Chayres, Esther Borja
The revue was presented in two acts.

Dances

Act One: "Antar" (music adapted from Nikolai Rimsky-Korsakov's Second Symphony) (choreographed by Leonide Massine) (Antar: Ivan Kirov; The Princess: Katia Geleznova; The Bird: Jean Guelis; Massine's Corps de Ballet); "Frog Song," "Copias," and "Lemon Tree" (Olga Coelho [Brazilian Soprano-Guitarist]); "Valencia Mora" (music by Ernesto Lecuona) and "Mexico Canta" (Nestor Chayres [Mexican Tenor]); "Rapsodia negra" ("Black rhapsody") (ballet) (music by Ernesto Lecuona) (choreography by Eugene Van Grona) (Diana Gary, Toni and Mimi Worth, The Van Grona Dancers); "Zambra Gitana" (music by Ernesto Lecuona) (choreography by Eugene Van Grona) (Diana Gary, Toni and Mimi Worth, Freida Dova, Otto Garcia, Herbert Ross, The Van Grona Dancers; sung by Esther Borja [Cuban Soprano] and Nestor Chayres)
Act Two: "Daphnis and Chloe" (music by Maurice Ravel) (choreography by Leonide Massine) (Chloe: Kathryn Lee; Daphnis: Alexander Iolas; Pan: Ivan Kirov; Andor Silva (Father), Monica Lind (Mother), Theodora Roosevelt (Bacchante), Galina Razoumova (Bacchante), Massine's Corps de Ballet); "Murcia" (music by Lara), "Tu nombre" ("Your name"), and "La morena de mi copla" ("Brunette of my song") (Nestor Chayres); "In the Silence of the Night" (music by Rachmaninoff), "French Song of Marie Antoinette," and "Xango" (Brazilian song) (Olga Coelho); "Rowlandson Comic Ballet" (music by Ernesto Lecuona) (choreography by Leonide Massine) (based on the caricature of "The Unfortunate Painter" by Thomas Rowlandson) (The Unfortunate Painter: David Ahdar; His Wife: Monica Lind; The Baby: Andrew Ratousheff; The Lover: Jean Guelis; Massine's Corps de Ballet); "Rhumba Ballet" (music by Ernest Lecuona) (choreography by Eugene Van Grona) (Massine's Corps de Ballet and The Van Grona Dancers)

Vincent Youmans's ill-fated production was one of the most disastrous of the era and reportedly lost over $200,000. After a turbulent three-week tryout in Baltimore, Toronto, and Boston, the show permanently closed without risking New York.

During preproduction the revue was known as *Good Neighbor*, *Vincent Youmans' Concert Revue*, *Vincent Youmans' Revue*, and *Concert Grand*. When it began its Baltimore tryout, it was called *Vincent Youmans' Ballet Revue*; in Toronto it was titled *Fiesta* and then *Ballet Revue*; and when it opened in Boston it was known as *Vincent Youmans' 'Fiesta'* and was subtitled "A New Ballet Revue." The changes of title reflect both the chaos of the revue's genesis and short life as well as its lack of focus in regard to what the show was about. The titles were generally misleading because words such as "concert" and "ballet" perhaps frightened away regular theatergoing audiences, who assumed it was an evening of classical-styled music and dance. And yet with Youmans' name featured in some of the titles, prospective ticket buyers probably assumed the show featured songs by the composer of "Tea for Two," "I Want to Be Happy," "Without a Song," "More Than You Know," "The Carioca," and "Great Day." As it turned out, not a note of Youmans's music was used in the revue (but the production offered songs and dance music by a number of other composers and lyricists).

William Torbert Leonard in *Broadway Bound* reports that early performances utilized a plot of sorts, which was scripted by screenwriter Eric Hatch. Apparently **Lady in the Dark** inspired the notion of a man who tries to forget his unhappy marriage by escaping into dreams; but his dreams sound like a nightmare, because he and everyone he knows are transformed into puppets (enacted by The Frank Paris Puppeteers). Further, Gerald Bordman in *Days to Be Happy, Years to Be Sad: The Life and Music of Vincent Youmans* reports that critic and composer Deems Taylor was brought in as the evening's master of ceremonies, and when performances conflicted with his schedule he was replaced by a life-sized puppet that spoke his prerecorded lines. Soon Youmans discarded the sketch-like plot, the puppets, and the notion of utilizing a narrator, and as the tryout progressed from city to city it evolved into a revue of unrelated songs and dances. At some point during the Boston run, Imogene Coca and John Sebastian joined the cast; since ballet spoofs were one of Coca's specialties, it seems likely she appeared in the "Rowlandson Comic Ballet" sequence.

In reviewing the Baltimore tryout, *Variety* said "it's going to take plenty of handling and maximum showmanship" to salvage the evening. But despite major changes in the show's concept, nothing could save it.

The above credits and song list reflect the final version of the revue when it played in Boston.

THE WALTZ KING
"LIFE, LOVES AND MUSIC OF JOHANN STRAUSS"

Theatres and *Performance Dates*: The musical opened on September 13, 1943, in Los Angeles, California, and then opened at the Civic Opera House, Chicago, Illinois, on November 1, 1943, where it closed on November 27, 1943.

Book and *Lyrics*: Boris Morros, Theodore Bachenheimer, and Aubrey Stauffer; additional dialogue by Bert Levine; additional lyrics by Mort Greene

Music: Johann Strauss (music adapted by Boris Morros and Fritz Berens)

Direction: Theodore Bachenheimer (dialogue direction by Serege Bertens); *Producer*: Boris Morros; *Choreography*: David Lichine; *Scenery*: Boris Leven; *Costumes*: Western Costume Company (ballet costumes by Travilla, and Irra Petina's gowns designed by Santiago); *Lighting*: Adrian Awan; *Musical Direction*: Fritz Berens; *Vocal Direction*: Hugo Strelitzer

Cast: Nina Ferova (Alma, Russian Lady), Anthony Marlowe (Peter), Virginia Card (Vicki), Max Willenz (Mandel), *Richard Bonelli* (Johann Strauss), Marjorie Cooke (Fritzi), Leon Belasco (Prime Minister), Randolph Symonette (Coachman), *Irra Petina* (Henrietta), Charles LaTorre (Count Polesky), Edna Harris (French Lady, Waitress), Betty Benee (British Lady), Judy Landon (American Lady); Corps de Ballet: Tatiana Riabouchinska, Walter Stane, Marilyn Radcliffe, Marjorie Tallchief, Beverly Braisier, Maisie Carter, Betty Hannon, Gloria Maggenette, Mildren Mauldin, Svieltana McLee, Diane Meroff, Rod Alexander, Pierre Andre, Edward Browne, Allan Cooke, Clair Freeman, George Martin, G. Tony Saylor, Robert Tucker, Virginia Morris, Patricia Overbey, Betty Scott, Lois Smith, Paula Stacey, Doria Yrys

The musical was presented in two acts.

The action takes place during one day in the summer of 1872 in Vienna.

Musical Numbers

Act One: "Pantomime Dance" / "Early in the Morning" (Four Maids: Marjorie Tallchief, Marilyn Radcliffe, Beverly Braisier, Cynthia Revere; Postman: Allan Cooke; Servant: Edward Browne); "Where Is Johann Strauss?" (Anthony Marlowe); "Who Is His New Lorelei?" (Virginia Card, Anthony Marlowe); "Try to See Clearly" (Richard Bonelli, Virginia Card); "I Dreamed of You Again Last Night" (lyric by Mort Greene) (Richard Bonelli, Anthony Marlowe); "The Naughty, Naughty Polka" (Marjorie Cooke, Anthony Marlowe; Ballet Dancers: Mildred Mauldin, Cynthia Revere, Doria Yrys, Diane Meroff, Betty Hannon, Betty Scott, Paula Stacey, Svieltana McLee, Lois Smith, Gloria Maggenette); "Don't Blame the Girl—Blame the Gown" (Virginia Card, Marjorie Cooke); Quartet (Leon Belasco, Virginia Card, Anthony Marlowe, Max Willenz); "Lost Paradise" (Irra Petina); First Act Finale: "Don't Blame the Girl—Blame the Gown" (reprise) (Virginia Card, Marjorie Cook; Modistes: Mildred Mauldin, Cynthia Revere, Doria Yrys, Diane Meroff, Betty Hannon, Betty Scott, Paula Stacey, Svieltana McLee, Lois Smith, Gloria Maggenette)

Act Two: "Polonaise" (Ladies and Gentlemen of the Court: Charles LaTorre, Edna Harris, Cynthia Reeves, Betty Benee, Judy Landon, Doria Yrys, Betty Scott, Paula Stacey, Svieltana McLee, Edward Browne, Robert Tucker, George Martin, Nina Ferova); "Waltz of Love" (lyric by Mort Greene) (Irra Petina, Richard Bonelli; Ballet: Marjorie Tallchief, Marilyn Radcliffe, Beverly Braisier, Maisie Cater, Betty Hannon, Gloria Maggenette, Mildred Mauldin, Svieltana McLee, Diane Meroff, Mary Morris, Patricia Overbey, Cynthia Revere, Betty Scott, Lois Smith, Paula Stacey, Doria Yrys); "Deep in Love Again" (Richard Bonelli); "I Dreamed of You Again Last Night" (reprise) (Marjorie Cooke, Richard Bonelli); "Chick, Chick, Chickadee" (Anthony Marlowe, Virginia Card); "The Emperor's Ballet" (Lead Dancers: Tatiana Riabouchinska, assisted by Walter Stane)—(a) "Emperor's Waltz" (Tatiana Riabouchinska); (b) "Chimes in Vienna" (Tatiana Riabouchinska, Walter Stane, Marjorie Tallchief, Marilyn Radcliffe, Maisie Carter, Beverly Brasier, Paula Stacey, Doria Yrys, Patricia Overbey, Virginia Morris); (c) "Voice of Spring" (Marjorie Tallchief, Marilyn Radcliffe, Maisie Cater, Beverly Braisier, Paula Stacey, Doria Yrys, Patricia Overbey, Virginia Morris, Allan Cooke, Clair Freeman, George Martin, Rod Alexander, Edward Browne, Tony Saylor,

Pierre Andre, Robert Tucker); (d) "Polka" (Tatiana Riabouchinska, assisted by Walter Stane); (e) "Little Soldiers" (Lois Smith, Cynthia Revere, Mildred Mauldin, Betty Hannon, Svieltana McLee, Diane Meroff, Gloria Maggenette, Betty Scott); and (f) Finale; "You'll Remember Vienna" (Virginia Card); Sextet (Leon Belasco, Virginia Card, Irra Petina, Marjorie Cooke, Anthony Marlowe, Richard Bonelli); Finale for Scene One: "Life's a Song" (Entire Company); Interlude (The Imperial Court Orchestra); "Drinking Song" (Leon Belasco); "Peasants' Dance" (Cynthia Revere, Diane Meroff, Lois Smith, Gloria Maggenette, Mildred Mauldin, Betty Hannon, Rod Alexander, Clair Freeman, Edward Browne, Allan Cooke, Robert Tucker, George Martin); "To You! To You!" (Irra Petina, Leon Belasco, Anthony Marlowe, Virginia Card, Richard Bonelli, Marjorie Cooke); Finale (various reprises) (Entire Company)

The Waltz King utilized the music of Richard Strauss in order to relate its account of the purported romantic dalliances of the married composer (Richard Bonelli) with various women, including ballerina Vicki (Virginia Card), who really prefers the attentions of his servant Peter (Anthony Marlowe), and then the young model Fritzi (Marjorie Cooke). And all the while his wife Henrietta (Irra Petina) has to deal with the waltz king's roving eye. In true operetta fashion, there are romantic misunderstandings, mistaken identities, and songs with such titles as "The Naughty, Naughty Polka," "Don't Blame the Girl—Blame the Gown," and "Chick, Chick, Chickadee." Of course, everything ends happily, although perhaps on a twinkling arch note: for when Strauss and Henrietta take off for a tour of the United States, he promises her he won't stray over there, or at least not until he learns English.

Variety suggested the operetta's appeal might be "limited," and any possible New York production would have to hold its own against shows that weren't "so dated." But the ballets as well as the costumes had "showmanly spectacular appeal" in their "rare beauty in color and shading."

One of the production's principal dancers was Marjorie Tallchief, who was the sister of Maria Tallchief.

The operetta closed in Chicago, although a year later it reopened on August 28, 1944, in San Francisco, and then again played in Chicago, where it opened at the Great Northern Theatre on December 25, 1944, and permanently closed there five days later. Most of the creative team joined the second production, which was produced by the Universal Light Opera Company. Richard Bonelli reprised the title role (for matinees he was spelled by Victor Carell), and Marjorie Cooke was again Fritzie. Others in the cast were Margit Bokor (Henrietta) and Litzie Helm (Vicki). For the Boston engagement, it appears Bonelli was no longer with the company and was succeeded by John Shafer.

There have been at least two film versions that utilized the title of the operetta, but that were otherwise unrelated to it. Both were television productions, and rather than looking at Strauss's romantic life they instead focused on the relationship between Johann Strauss *pere* and *fils*. The first version was presented in two parts by NBC on *Walt Disney's Wonderful World of Color* on October 27, 1963, and November 3, 1963 (and was later released theatrically in Europe). The second was produced by BBC in 2005.

The Waltz King ended with Strauss taking off for the United States, and in 1945 the short-lived Broadway musical **Mr. Strauss Goes to Boston** speculated on his romantic life upon his arrival there.

1944–1945 Season

TAKE A BOW

Theatre: Broadhurst Theatre
Opening Date: June 15, 1944; *Closing Date*: June 24, 1944
Performances: 12
Lyrics: Benny Davis
Music: Ted Murray
Direction: Wally Wanger; *Producer*: Lou Walters; *Choreography*: Marjery Fielding; *Scenery*: Kaj Velden; *Costumes*: Ben Wallace; *Lighting*: Uncredited; *Musical Direction*: Ray Kavanaugh
Cast: *Chico Marx, Gene Sheldon, Jay C. Flippen*, Think-a-Drink Hoffman, Pat Rooney, Johnny Mack, Alan Cross and Henry Dunn, The Murtah Sisters (Kate-Ellen, Jean, and Onriett), Mary Raye and Naldi, Loretta Fischer, The Four Whitson Brothers; The Marjery Fielding Dancers: Gloria Riley, Helen Simpson, Dede Barrington, Amita Artega, Kathryn Reed, Rae Hardin; Ladies of the Ensemble: Elaine Singer, Bee Farnum, Kay Popp, Doris Call, Rosemary Ryan, June Powers, Betty Francys, Marion Kay, Darlene Zito, Betty Baussher, Charlotte Lorraine, Elaine Meredith
The revue was presented in two acts.

Sketches and Musical Numbers

Act One: "Take a Bow" (The Marjery Fielding Dancers); Jay C. Flippen (Master of Ceremonies) and Chico Marx (The Man in the Box); Gene Sheldon, assisted by Loretta Fischer (banjo and pantomime act); Jay C. Flippen; The Whitson Brothers (acrobats); Johnny Mack (tap dancer), assisted by The Marjery Fielding Dancers; Chico Marx and Gene Sheldon (poker game sketch from 1925 musical *The Cocoanuts*); Jay C. Flippen; Alan Cross and Henry Dunn (singers), assisted by Newman Fear at the piano; Jay C. Flippen; Pat Rooney, The Marjery Fielding Dancers (sequence included "The Daughter of Rosie O'Grady," lyric by Monty C. Brice, music by Walter Donaldson) (dancing and reminiscing); Jay C. Flippen; Think-a-Drink Hoffman (comedy sketch); Jay C. Flippen
Act Two: "The Hollywood Jump" (The Marjery Fielding Dancers); Jay C. Flippen; Gene Sheldon (burlesque of classical dance) with female performer; Mary Raye and Naldi (ballroom dancers); The Murtah Sisters (singers); Jay C. Flippen; Chico Marx (at the piano); The Whitson Brothers (acrobats); Jay C. Flippen

Of the era's vaudeville-styled revues, many were lucky and enjoyed long runs while others disappeared almost as soon as they opened. *Take a Bow* (which in an earlier incarnation was known as *Slap Happy*) was one of the latter, and so the cast had only twelve performances in which to take their bows. The star of the evening was Chico Marx, who performed his standard piano routines and, with Gene Sheldon, reprised the poker game scene from the 1925 musical *The Cocoanuts*, in which he had appeared with his brothers Groucho, Harpo, and Zeppo as well as their eternal lady-stooge Margaret Dumont. Jay C. Flippen was the master of ceremonies, and other performers in the revue were the singing trio The Murtah Sisters; the acrobatic quartet The Whitson Brothers; ballroom dancers Mary Raye and Naldi; comedian, banjo player, and pantomimist Gene Sheldon; tap dancer Johnny Mack; singers Alan Cross and Henry Dunn; comedian Think-a-Drink Hoffman (in what seemed to be his umpteenth appearance in the decade's revues); and old-timer Pat Rooney, who was celebrating his fiftieth year in show business and who indulged in a bit of nostalgia with his singing and dancing (and, proving he was a modern-day hepcat, also joined a chorus girl for some jitterbugging).

John Chapman in the *New York Daily News* thought the revue started snappily with the overture, the opening title song, the comedy of Gene Sheldon, and the acrobatic team of the four Whitson Brothers; but after that, the evening "collapsed" and lost its sense of "speed and economy"; Robert Garland in the *New York Journal-American* found the "potpourri" a "tedious" one which seemed like a "memory-haunted floor show"; and Lewis Nichols in the *New York Times* concurred that the "tedious" show belonged in a nightclub.

Burton Rascoe in the *New York World-Telegram* felt the "lifeless" evening had been "thrown together haphazardly and without taste"; further, Flippen's material consisted of three jokes, all of them "familiar," "corny," and "dirty." He also noted Gene Sheldon was a good banjo player, but otherwise his routines dealt with "involuntary facial contortions and epileptic muscular movements" of someone who was a "drooling mental defective"; and while he didn't go into details, the critic noted that some of the routines were "revolting" and "sickening." Louis Kronenberger in *PM* elaborated on what apparently grossed out Rascoe: in one scene Sheldon pretended to remove his eyeballs, then plucked them in again and emerged cross-eyed. Kronenberger found Sheldon something less than a "riot" with his "rowdy" and somewhat "macabre" humor, and he noted the "pallid" evening "dwindles into routine nightclub stuff, or actually drops into limbo."

Although Herrick Brown in the *New York Sun* admitted the evening offered "familiar" material, he said the revue offered plenty of laughter and that the first-night audience "applauded vigorously and kept calling for more." He also reported that during the ballroom dancing of Mary Raye and Naldi, the former underwent (in today's parlance) a wardrobe malfunction in which the strap of her gown almost led to an inadvertent moment of strip tease. He also noted that the self-described "inimitable" three singing Murtah Sisters "grimaced" and "warbled" with "more gusto than charm." Howard Barnes in the *New York Herald Tribune* found the "high-class" revue "familiar, fast-paced and funny" and a "welcome addition" to the current Broadway scene; in fact, it offered "far more" entertainment than many recent productions. As for Chico Marx, the critic noted his piano playing executed "allegro pizzicato" with "a side dish of macaroni."

Wilella Waldorf in the *New York Post* said the revue offered "gayer entertainment" than many of the town's more recent musicals, but noted the Murtah Sisters made "extraordinary faces" and did indeed "murtah" several songs.

HATS OFF TO ICE
"A MUSICAL ICETRAVAGANZA"

Theatre: Center Theatre
Opening Date: June 22, 1944; *Closing Date*: April 27, 1946
Performances: 889
Lyrics and *Music*: James Littlefield and John Fortis
Direction: Catherine Littlefield; *Producers*: Sonja Henie and Arthur M. Wirtz (A Sonart Production) (William H. Burke, Executive Director); *Choreography*: Catherine Littlefield, assisted by Dorothie Littlefield; *Skating Direction*: May Judels; *Scenery*: Bruno Maine; *Costumes*: Grace Houston; *Lighting*: Eugene Braun; *Musical Direction*: David Mendoza
Cast: Freddie Trenkler, Carol Lynne, Lucille Page, The Caley Sisters (Dorothy and Hazel), The Brandt Sisters (Helga and Inge), Geoffe Stevens, Rudy Richards, James Caesar, Paul Castle, Jean Sturgeon, Clare Wilkins, Robert and Gretle Uksila, Peggy Whight and Bob (Robert) Ballard, Jimmy Sisk, Joe Shillen; Vocals: Pat Marshall, Don Loring Rogers, and The Top Hatters (Andrei Kristopher, John Patteson, and Everett Anderson); Octette: Bing Stott, Janet Hester, Barbara Johnson, Clare Wilkins, James Carter, Harper Flaherty, Alex Lindgren, John Roach; James Kenny, Robert Payne, Bernard Feldman, Fred Griffith, Virginia Litz, Charley Storey, Alice Farrar, Lucille Risch, Ruth Noland, Julian Apley, Charles Cavanaugh, Jack Raffloer, Fred Griffith, Kay Corcoran, Billy Kling, Charles Storey, Robert Petrillo, Eileen Thompson, Jean Sakovich, Ladies of the Ensemble: Katherine Arnaiz, Nancy Adamack, Margaret Barry, Jean Conrad, Helen Carter,

Jeanne Crystal, Helen Dutcher, Edith Kandcl, Billy Kling, Marian Lulling, Annette Lawrence, Sharlene Munster, Kay Corcoran, Ruth Noland, Berenice O'Dell, Jane Petri, Theresa Rothacker, Lela Rolontz, Ragna Ray, Jean Sakovich, Dorothy Thomas, Sally Tepley, Eileen Thompson, Helen Thompson, Michelle Winters; Gentlemen of the Ensemble: James Black, William Campbell, William Carvel, Manuel Del Toro, Jere Decker, Joachim Dietl, Gordon Harris, Fred Kaufman, Garry Kerman, Alfred Kutchy, Bert Pegram, Gordon Holley, Harvey Wolfers, George Wagner, Tom Travers, Arthur Meheen

The revue was presented in two acts.

Musical Numbers

Act One: Overture (Orchestra); "Hats Off to Ice" (Pat Marshall, Don Loring Rogers, The Top Hatters; Octette; Ladies of the Ensemble, Gentlemen of the Ensemble); "Little Red Riding Hood" (Jean Sturgeon; Woodchoppers: James Kenny, Robert Payne; Wolf: Bernard Feldman); "Double Vision" (Helga Brandt and Inge Brandt); "Nautical Nonsense" (Olive Oyle: Gretle Uksila; Pop-Eye: Robert Uksila); "Love Will Always Be the Same" (Pat Marshall, Don Loring Rogers; King: Fred Griffith; Queen: Virginia Litz; Princess: Barbara Johnson; White Prince: Harper Flaherty; Black Prince: Charley Storey; Heralds: Alice Farrar, Janet Hester, Lucille Risch, Bing Stott, Ruth Noland; Hand Maidens: Kay Corcoran, Margaret Barry, Ragna Ray, Eileen Thompson; Knights: Julian Apley, William Carvel, Manuel Del Toro, Garry Kerman, James Kenny, Alfred Kutchy, Alex Lindgren, George Wagner); "Sophisticated Lady" (Lucille Page; Boys: James Carter, Charles Cavanaugh, Joachim Dietl, Bernard Feldman, Robert Payne, Jack Raffloer, John Roach, Harvey Wolfers); "Goddess of the Hunt" (Diana: Carol Lynne; Maidens: Kay Corcoran, Barbara Johnson, Virginia Litz, Eileen Thompson); "The Skating Rileys" (Mother: Virginia Litz; Father: Fred Griffith; Sweetheart: Jean Sturgeon; Junior: Paul Castle); "The Boogie Bachelor" (Bachelor: Rudy Richards; Chorines: Ragna Ray, Alice Farrar; Debs: Janet Hester, Bing Stott; Herself: Clare Wilkins); "They've Got What It Takes" (Swingtime: Dorothy Caley, Hazel Caley) and "You've Got What It Takes" (Pat Marshall, Don Loring Rogers); "Bouncing Ball of the Ice" (Freddie Trenkler; Lovelies: Barbara Johnson, Virginia Litz, Sharlene Munster, Eileen Thompson); "Slavic Rhapsody" (The Flame: Carol Lynne; Gypsy Girls: Janet Hester, Barbara Johnson, Clare Wilkins; Gypsy Boys: James Carter, Harper Flaherty, Jack Raffloer, John Roach; Peasant Girls: Katherine Arnaiz, Nancy Adamack, Margaret Barry, Jean Conrad, Kay Corcoran, Jean Crystal, Helen Dutcher, Edith Kandel, Billy Kling, Marian Lulling, Annette Lawrence, Sharlene Munster, Ruth Noland, Berenice O'Dell, Jane Petri, Theresa Rothacker, Lela Rolontz, Ragna Ray, Jean Sakovich, Dorothy Thomas, Sally Tepley, Helen Thompson, Michelle Winters; Peasant Boys: William Campbell, William Carvel, Jere Decker, Joachim Dietl, Bernard Feldman, Gordon Harris, James Kenny, Fred Kaufman, Garry Kerman, Alfred Kutchy, Arthur Meehan, Gordon Holley, Harvey Wolfers, Robert Payne, George Wagner, Tom Travers

Act Two: Entr'acte (Orchestra); "Isle of the Midnight Rainbow" (sung by Pat Marshall, Don Loring Rogers, The Top Hatters; Drum Dancer: Clare Wilkins; Drum Dancer: Clare Wilkins; Mayor: Geoffe Stevens; Warriors: James Kenny, Charles Storey, Robert Petrillo; Native Boys: Alex Lindgren, Gordon Holley; Hula Dancers: Alice Farrar, Janet Hester, Ragna Roy, Lucille Risch, Bing Stott, Katherine Arnaiz, Nancy Adamack, Margaret Barry, Jean Conrad, Helen Carter, Helen Dutcher, Edith Kandel, Marian Lulling, Annette Lawrence, Sharlene Munster, Ruth Noland, Berenice O'Dell, Jane Petri, Theresa Rothacker, Lela Rolontz, Jean Sakovich, Dorothy Thomas, Sally Tepley, Helen Thompson, Michelle Winters, Kay Corcoran; Boys: James Black, William Campbell, William Carvel, Manuel Del Toro, Joachim Dietl, Gordon Harris, Garry Kerman, Alfred Kutchey, Arthur Meehan, Bert Pegram, Harvey Wolfers, George Wagner, Tom Travers, Julian Apley, Charles Cavanaugh); "Russian Rhythm" (Dorothy Caley, Hazel Caley); "Over the Jumps" (James Caesar); "Pathway to the Stars" (song "With Every Star," sung by Pat Marshall; skated by Ladies of the Ensemble); "Out of the Blue" (Peggy Whight and Robert Ballard); "The Lazy Q" (song "Headin' West" sung by Don Loring Rogers and The Top Hatters; Cowgirls: Janet Hester, Alice Farrar, Ragna Ray, Lucille Risch, Bing Stott; Twins: Helga Brandt and Inge Brandt; Cowhand: Geoffe Stevens; The Horse: Joe Shillen and James Sisk; Tenderfoot: Lucille Page; Cowboys: James Kenny, Robert Payne, Bernard Feldman); "A Persian Legend" (Prince: Fred Griffith; Genii: James Caesar; Peri: Carol Lynne; Attendants of the Prince: Katherine Arnaiz, Helen Carter, Berenice O'Dell, Theresa Rothacker, Jean Sakovich, Michelle Winters; Odalisques: Clare Wilkins, Janet Hester, Sally Tepley, Alice Farrar, Bing Stott, Ragna Ray, Lucille Risch, Dorothy Thomas, Helen Thompson, Ruth Noland, Jane Petri, Marian Lulling, Annette Lawrence, Eileen

Thompson, Edith Kandel, Margaret Barry, Helen Dutcher, Lela Rolontz, Sharlene Munster, Jean Conrad, Nancy Adamack; Boys: James Kenny, Fred Kaufman, Robert Payne, Julian Apley, Garry Kerman, Joachim Dietl, Tom Travers, Gordon Holley, Gordon Harris, Harvey Wolfers, Jack Raffloer, Jere Decker, Manuel Del Toro, Bert Pegram, James Black); "Shore Leave" (Geoffe Stevens, Joe Shillen, Jimmy Sisk; Pin-Up Girls: Margaret Barry, Ruth Noland, Helen Thompson); "Cocktail Time in Rio" (Caballero: Rudy Richards; Octette Girls; Octette Boys; Show Girls: Edith Kandel, Helen Dutcher, Margaret Barry, Sally Tepley, Marian Lulling, Virginia Litz; Boys and Girls of the Ensemble); "G.I. Nuisance" (The Nuisance: Freddie Trenkler; Sergeant: Charley Storey; Squad: Charles Cavanaugh, Joe Shillen, Jimmy Sisk; "Here's Luck" (sung by Pat Marshall, Don Loring Rogers, The Top Hatters; Ensemble; Helga and Inge Brandt, Dorothy and Hazel Caley, May Judels, Carol Lynne, Lucille Page, Jean Sturgeon, Gretle Uksila, Peggy Whight, Clare Wilkins, James Caesar, Paul Castle, Rudy Richards, Joe Shillen, Jimmy Sisk, Geoffe Stevens, Freddie Trenkler, Robert Uksila, Fred Griffith)

Hats Off to Ice was another successful entry in Sonja Henie and Arthur M. Wirtz' series of ice-skating revues at Rockefeller Center's Center Theatre, and while it didn't boast a hit song like "Jukebox Saturday Night" (which had been introduced in the previous entry **Stars on Ice**), it nonetheless managed to achieve the longest run of all the ice shows with 899 performances.

To prove the series was up to date, it included "Shore Leave," which depicted three sailors on the town and on the ice who meet three pinup girls on ice (**Follow the Girls**, which dealt with gobs and gals in the big city had opened a few months earlier; *Fancy Free*, Jerome Robbins's ballet about three sailors on the town, had premiered at the Metropolitan Opera House the month before; and later in the year the ballet was the inspiration for **On the Town**, and so sailors on leave in the big city was definitely a popular theme in 1944). Other topical items were "The Boogie Bachelor" and "G.I. Nuisance," and of course there was the requisite South American number, here "Cocktail Time in Rio." Freddie Trenkler supplied comedy-on-ice routines, and there was also a look at fairy tales ("Little Red Riding Hood") and the American west ("The Lazy Q") as well as the usual ersatz exotica ("Slavic Rhapsody," "Isle of the Midnight Sun," and "A Persian Legend").

In his annual look at the season, George Jean Nathan suggested the popularity of ice revues was due to "the American admiration of monotony." As usual, the skaters twirled and whirled and raced "for dear life hell-bent for nowhere," and except for changes of title all the sequences were basically just the same as the ones presented in the earlier ice excursions. As a matter of fact, a viewing of *Hats Off to Ice* offered irrefutable proof of the theory of "spiral time," because while he watched *Hats Off to Ice* Nathan realized he had gone back in time and had returned to 1940 where he was again sitting in the Center Theatre and watching **It Happens on Ice** all over again.

SONG OF NORWAY
"A New Operetta Based on the Life and Music of Edvard Grieg" / "The Musical Triumph"

Theatre: Imperial Theatre (during run, the musical transferred to the Broadway Theatre)
Opening Date: August 21, 1944; *Closing Date*: September 7, 1946
Performances: 860
Book: Milton Lazarus
Lyrics: Robert Wright and George Forrest
Music: Edvard Grieg (musical adaptation by Robert Wright and George Forrest)
Based on an unproduced play by Homer Curran.
Direction: Charles K. Freeman; *Producer*: Edwin Lester; *Choreography*: George Balanchine; *Scenery*: Scenery designed by Lemuel Ayers and supervised by Carl Kent; *Costumes*: Costumes designed by Robert Davison and executed by Walter J. Israel; *Lighting*: Howard Bay; *Musical Direction* and *Choral Direction*: Arthur Kaye
Cast: Janet Hamer (Sigrid), Kent Edwards (Einar), Robert Antoine (Eric), William Carroll (Gunnar), Patti Brady (Grima), Jackie Lee (Helga), Robert Shafer (Rikard Nordraak), Helena Bliss (Nina Hagerup), Lawrence Brooks (Edvard Grieg), Walter Kingsford (Father Grieg), Philip White (Father Nordraak), Ivy Scott (Mother Grieg), Frederic Franklin (Freddy), Sig Arno (Count Peppi Le Loup), Irra Petina (Louisa Giovanni), Ewing Mitchell (Faculty Member), Audrey Guard (Faculty Member), Paul De Poyster (Faculty Member),

Lewis Bolyard (Inn Keeper), Doreen Wilson (Frau Professor Norden), Sharon Randall (Elvera), Karen Lund (Hedwig), Gwen Jones (Greta), Ann Andre (Marghareta), Elizabeth Bockoven (Hilda), Sonia Orlova (Miss Anders), Dudley Clements (Henrik Ibsen), Frederic Franklin (Tito), Robert Bernard (Maestro Pisoni), Cameron Grant (Butler), Alexandra Danilova (Adelina), Nora White (Maid), Barbara Boudwin (Signora Eleanora); Children: Sylvia Allen, Grace Carroll, Pat O'Rourke, Shannon Randolph; Dancing Peasants, Employees of Tito's, The Ballet of the Teatro Reale (The Italian Opera Ballet Company), and the Characters of the Fantasy: Performed by the artists of the Ballet Russe de Monte Carlo (Sergei J. Denham, Director): Alexandra Danilova, Frederic Franklin, Nathalie Krassovska, Leon Danielian, Maria Tallchief, Ruthanna Boris, Alexander Goudovitch, Mary Ellen Moylan, Serge Ismailoff, Anna Istomina, Nicholas Magallanes, Michael Katcharoff, Julia Horvath, Peter Deign, Allan Banks, Herbert Bliss, Vida Brown, Alfredo Corvino, Pauline Goddard, Helen Kramarr, Karel Shook, Gertruda Swobodina, Nikita Talin, Nora White; Singing Peasants, Guests and Faculty at Copenhagen, and Guests at the Villa Pincio: Performed by the Singing Ensemble of the Los Angeles and San Francisco Civic Light Opera Company: Girls—Ann Andre, Elizabeth Bockoven, Barbara Boudwin, Mary Bradley, Shirley Conklin, Kaye Connors, Audrey Dearden, Audrey Guard, Leone Hall, Gwen Jones, Karen Lund, Sharon Randall, Margaret Ritte, Mary Walker, Doreen Wilson; Boys—Robert Bailes, Lewis E. Bolyard, Frank Brenneman, John Chaloupka, Paul de Poyster, Cameron Grant, Larry Haynes, Hal Horton, Raymond Keast, Hal McMurrin, Arthur Waters, Maurice Winthrop, Stanley Wolfe, Walter Young

The musical was presented in two acts.

The action takes place during the 1860s in Bergen and Copenhagen, Norway, and in Rome, Italy.

Musical Numbers

Note: Following the individual songs titles are the original musical sources from which they are adapted.

Act One: Prelude: "The Legend" (adapted from Grieg's A-Minor Concerto) (Orchestra) and "Hill of Dreams" (A-Minor Concerto) (Helena Bliss, Lawrence Brooks, Robert Shafer); "In the Holiday Spirit" (dance) (Dancing Peasants); "Freddy and His Fiddle" ("Norwegian Dance") (Kent Edwards, Janet Hamer, Frederic Franklin, Singing Townspeople); "Now" (Waltz Opus 12, Number 12; and the Violin Sonata No. 2 in G Major) (Irra Petina, Townspeople); "Strange Music" ("Nocturne" and "Wedding in Troldhaugen") (Lawrence Brooks, Helena Bliss); "Midsummer's Eve" ("'Twas on a Lovely Eve in June" and "Scherzo") (Robert Shafer, Irra Petina); "March of the Trollgers" (aka "The Cake Lottery") ("Mountaineers' Song," "Halling" in G Minor, and "March of the Dwarfs") (Entire Ensemble); Finale of Act One: (a) "Hymn of Betrothal" ("To Spring") (Ivy Scott, Villagers); (b) "Strange Music" (reprise) (Lawrence Brooks, Helena Bliss, Chorus); and (c) "Midsummer's Eve" (reprise) (Robert Shafer, Helena Bliss, Chorus)

Act Two: Introduction—"Papillon"; "Bon Vivant" Part I ("Water Lily") (Lawrence Brooks, Girls) and "Bon Vivant" Part II ("The Brook" from the Haugtussa Cycle) (Sig Arno, Lawrence Brooks, Sonia Orlova, Girls); "Three Loves" ("Albumblatt" and "Poem Erotique") (Irra Petina, Lawrence Brooks); Finaletto: (a) "Down Your Tea" ("Springtide") (Irra Petina, Faculty Members, Guests); (b) "Nordraak's Farewell" ("Springtide") (Robert Shafer); and (c) "Three Loves" (reprise) (Irra Petina, Helena Bliss, Ensemble); "Chocolate Pas de Trois" ("Rigaudon" and "From Monte Pinco") (Frederic Franklin, Employees); "Waltz Eternal" ("Waltz Caprice") (Ladies and Gentlemen); "Peer Gynt": (a) "Solvejg's Melody"; (b) "Hall of the Dovre King"; and (c) "Anitra's Dance" (Ballet of the Italian Opera); "I Love You" ("Ich Liebe Dich") (Helena Bliss); "At Christmastime" ("Woodland Wanderings") (Philip White, Ivy Scott, Helena Bliss); "Midsummer's Eve" (reprise) (Lawrence Brooks, Helena Scott); "Strange Music" (reprise) (Lawrence Brooks, Helena Bliss); "The Song of Norway" (Piano Concerto) (Lawrence Brooks, Ballet Dancers)

Song of Norway was one of the biggest hits of the decade, and when it closed was the third-longest-running book musical in Broadway history (after ***Oklahoma!*** and ***Follow the Girls***). It was one of those Great Composer biographical musicals so beloved by Broadway and Hollywood, and it purported to tell the life story of Norwegian composer Edvard Grieg (Lawrence Brooks). In his small village, he courts Nina Hagerup (Helena Bliss), who later becomes his wife, and is friend to Rikard Nordraak (Robert Shafer), a poet who writes of their native country. Soon the invented character of tempestuous opera star Louisa Giovanni (Irra Petina) enters the picture, and she cajoles Grieg into going with her to Rome, where he will undoubtedly be inspired to write music in the great European tradition rather than composing music that reflects the folk music and legends of his native country. But when in Rome, Grieg eventually realizes he's untrue to his musical self. And the death of Rikard leads him to the realization that he must return to his Norwegian roots.

The book was a bit top-heavy with dialogue, and some of the lines were groan-inducing: Father Grieg wants his son to go into the family fish business, not the world of music ("Only a few people want music, but everybody eats fish"); when Grieg faces a personal crisis, he says "I will never write again"; and, in the tradition of Great Composer Musical name-dropping, Henrik Ibsen makes a brief appearance (and when on-lookers admire Edvard and Nina's Christmas tree, someone notes that one of the Christmas presents is from the "Russian composer Tschiakowsky"). (Decades later, in a variant of Great Composer Musicals' name-dropping, the Son Of such musicals paid tribute to popular singers, singing groups, lyricists, or composers, and they too followed the strict rules of the genre; as a result, "Judy Garland" and "Liza Minnelli" appear in *The Boy from Oz* [2003] and "Joe Pesci" has a walk-on in *Jersey Boys* [2005].)

Song of Norway had been highly successful in Los Angeles and San Francisco, and producer Edwin Lester brought the entire production intact to New York during the dog days of August 1944. It received surprisingly good reviews and became a hit with audiences; further, Grieg's "Nocturne" and "Wedding in Troldhaugen" became the basis for the soaring ballad "Strange Music," which emerged as a hit song.

Grieg's music was adapted by the Hollywood team of lyricists and composers Robert Wright and George (Chet) Forrest. Among other songs, they had written the lyric for the popular "Donkey Serenade" (music by Rudolf Friml) for the 1937 film *The Firefly*, and in 1940 wrote their lush Academy Award–nominated "It's a Blue World" for *Music in My Heart* (not to be confused with **Music in My Heart**, the 1947 Great Composer Musical purportedly based on Tschaikowsky's love life, or lack thereof). After *Song of Norway*, Wright and Forrest adapted the works of classical composers for their musicals or created scores with original songs. (For a list of their works, see below.)

Wilella Waldorf in the *New York Post* noted the musical didn't quite have a point of view. Sometimes the book was tongue-in-cheek, but often it bowed to formulaic operetta staging conventions, such as having chorus singers wave their hands in the air after finishing a song, and, when the lights dimmed and spotlighted one singer, the chorus stood and watched "as in a trance."

Howard Barnes in the *New York Herald Tribune* said the musical's book was "lamentable" and resulted in a "dramatic dud" of an evening that was redeemed by "sprightly" musical numbers. Louis Kronenberger in *PM* noted the musical was "purely formula stuff, without style or originality"; he was disappointed with George Balanchine's choreography, but noted that besides being in "good voice" Irra Petina had a "likeable personality" and "a nice comedy manner."

Otherwise, the remaining critics were more receptive to the operetta. Burton Rascoe in the *New York World-Telegram* told his readers the musical was "something you should count on seeing," and he praised the "excellently played and sung" principal roles. He noted that Irra Petina "scored the greatest personal triumph" of the evening and had a field day with her flirtations and temperamental displays of a "self-indulgent and resourceful artiste." He also liked Robert Bernard, who portrayed a comically flustered impresario who must live "in a hell of prima donnas and prima ballerinas." Ward Morehouse in the *New York Sun* said the book sometimes dragged, but otherwise the "creditable and charming" evening had "great vitality" and was "as pretty as it is melodious." John Chapman in the *New York Daily News* admitted the musical had its "sobersided stretches," but Petina's temperamental diva and Sig Arno's "mincing" husband offered welcome comic relief; further, the evening was "lovely," "ambitious," and often "thrilling."

Lewis Nichols in the *New York Times* said the musical offered "great cheer" with Grieg's "beautiful" music and a chorus and orchestra that ensured the composer wasn't "cheated of his rights." As for Petina, he liked the "gay air" about her and noted she was "pretty special"; he mentioned that in one number ("Now") she combined a "perfect blend" of both opera and Tin Pan Alley, and when she was "on the prowl" she was reminiscent of Mae West.

Robert Garland in the *New York Journal-American* said the plot "was manipulated and more than a little clumsy," but these were minor matters because the combination of Grieg's music, a first-rate cast, and Balanchine's choreography provided the season with its first "head-in-the-air" production.

During the tryout, Walter Cassell was succeeded by Lawrence Brooks, and the song "The High Cost of Loving" (for Sig Arno) was dropped.

There have been at least six recordings of the score, including the original cast album released by Decca (LP # DL-79019; later issued on Decca Broadway CD #B0002471-02; for the recording, Kitty Carlisle substituted for Irra Petina, reportedly because the album's producer didn't like the "foreign" sound of Petina's voice) and a 1959 Jones Beach production recorded by Columbia (LP # CS-8135) included John Reardon, Brenda Lewis, William Olvis, and, from the original Broadway company, Helena Bliss and Sig Arno. The most complete recording was issued by That's Entertainment Records (CD # CDTER2-1173) on a two-CD set by a studio cast.

The script was published in paperback by Chappell & Co. Ltd. (London) in an undated edition.

The musical was revived on Broadway by the New York City Opera Company at the New York State Theatre on September 3, 1981, for fourteen performances. The London production opened at the Palace Theatre on March 7, 1946, for 527 performances; the cast included John Hargreaves, Halina Victoria, Janet Hamilton-Smith, and Arthur Servent.

The 1970 film version was released by ABC Pictures Corporation with Toralv Maurstad, Florence Henderson, Christina Schollin, Frank Porretta, Oscar Homolka, Robert Morley, Edward G. Robinson, and Harry Secombe; the direction and screenplay were by Andrew L. Stone and the choreography was by Lee (Becker) Theodore. In his *Movie Guide*, Leonard Maltin gives the movie a "BOMB" rating, and notes that the "dud" is "beautiful to look at" but otherwise a "poor" biography with "weak" interpretations of Grieg's music. The soundtrack was released by ABC Records (LP # ABCS-OC-14).

Among the musical's dancers in the Ballet Russe de Monte Carlo was Maria Tallchief. Eleven years after the premiere of *Song of Norway*, Robert Shafer enjoyed another huge hit when he created the role of the older Joe Hardy in *Damn Yankees* (1955).

After *Song of Norway*, Wright and Forrest's other Broadway musicals were **Magdalena** (1948; 88 performances; music by Heitor Villa-Lobos); *Kismet* (1953; 583 performances; adapted from music by Alexander Borodin); *Kean* (1961; 92 performances; original score); *Anya* (1965; 16 performances; adapted from music by Sergei Rachmaninoff); and *Grand Hotel* (1989; 1,018 performances; original score). The latter had been originally produced as *At the Grand* in 1958, but closed during its pre-Broadway engagement; the 1989 version included some of the team's songs from the 1958 production, a few of which were revised by Maury Yeston, and new songs by Yeston. The team also wrote original scores for **Spring in Brazil** and *The Carefree Heart* (1957), both of which closed during their pre-Broadway tryouts. *The Carefree Heart* was later produced in London as *The Love Doctor* in 1959. Another original musical by the team was *A Song for Cyrano*, which played on the summer stock circuit in the 1960s and 1970s. Wright and Forrest also wrote the new lyrics for **Gypsy Lady** (1946; 79 performances) which was based on Victor Herbert's scores for *The Serenade* (1897) and *The Fortune Teller* (1898); the team also staged the production, but in this case Herbert's music was adapted by Arthur Kay.

STAR TIME
"The Hilariously Happy Revue" / "An Hilarious Revue"

Theatre: Majestic Theatre
Opening Date: September 12, 1944; *Closing Date*: December 9, 1944
Performances: 120
Producer: Paul Small; *Draperies* and *Scenery*: R. L. Grosh & Sons; *Musical Direction*: Waldemar Guiterson.
Cast: *Lou Holtz, Benny Fields, Tony and Sally De Marco*, Shirley Dennis, The Berry Brothers, Jimmy and Mildred Mulcay, The Whitson Brothers (Lester and Buddy), Armand Cortes, Francine Bordeaux, George Prospery
The revue was presented in two acts.

Sketches and Musical Numbers

Act One: Lou Holtz; The Whitson Brothers; Shirley Dennis; Jimmy and Mildred Mulcay; Armand Cortes and Francine Bordeaux; Tony and Sally De Marco (The De Marcos were accompanied by Alan Moran at the piano)
Act Two: Lou Holtz; Benny Fields; The Berry Brothers
Note: The program stated that between the two acts there would be an intermission, "just as in *Othello*."

Producer Paul Small (sometimes in conjunction with Fred F. Finklehoff) presented a series of modest vaudeville-styled revues that enjoyed success in Los Angeles, San Francisco, and other stops on the road; three (**Show Time**, **Laugh Time**, and the current *Star Time*) opened in New York, but two others (**Big Time** and **Curtain Time**) never came in. Because the revues employed a handful of performers and offered negligible production values, some wags referred to the productions as *Small Time*.

For *Star Time*, comedian Lou Holtz was master of ceremonies and sometimes joined the other acts for a bit of horseplay, including dancing on a pogo stick with The Berry Brothers; the other performers were singer and comedian Benny Fields, ballroom dancers Tony and Sally De Marco, singer Shirley Dennis, black acrobatic dancers The Berry Brothers, the acrobats The Whitson Brothers, and harmonica players Jimmy and Mildred Mulcay. Wilella Waldorf in the *New York Post* said Lou Holtz was ingratiating as both a performer and master of ceremonies, and she suggested the evening be titled *Holtz Time*; she also praised The De Marcos, The Whitson Brothers, and The Berry Brothers, but complained that the other performers were too "mike-bound" for comfort.

Ward Morehouse in the *New York Sun* noted the revue wasn't the best he'd ever seen, but was "all right." Benny Fields sang a number of patriotic songs, and Morehouse said his version of "Over There" was "thrilling." Shirley Dennis's repertoire included numbers from *Show Boat*. John Chapman in the *New York Daily News* apologized for being churlish, but he just didn't appreciate Benny Fields and his microphone, the mike that Waldorf had so deplored; in fact, Chapman felt like telling Fields what Groucho Marx had once said to Chico: "If you get near a tune, play it." Chapman was also annoyed with a trombone player in the orchestra pit who loudly fanned himself with sheet music and thus "killed" a couple of Holtz's jokes.

Burton Rascoe in the *New York World-Telegram* found the evening "pleasant, friendly and decorously informal," and while there was nothing to get "enthusiastic" about there was also nothing to "disapprove" of; and Howard Barnes in the *New York Herald Tribune* said the revue was no "great shakes" but was "sprightly and sometimes genuinely amusing."

But Lewis Nichols in the *New York Times* felt the revue lacked "sprightliness," and while the "old" acts and manners were present they unfortunately didn't offer "energy, gaiety and pleasure." He also suggested that Shirley Dennis and Benny Fields "keep away from that damned microphone." Louis Kronenberger in *PM* found the evening "generally dreary and occasionally dreadful," but he liked Holtz's way with one-liners, such as when he told the audience he sincerely hoped "your marriage lasts as long as mine seems." But Robert Garland in the *New York Journal-American* was having none of it. The "long-drawn, unhappy" revue proved vaudeville was dead, and if Holtz was indeed receiving three-thousand dollars per week to appear in the production, then Holtz should be "ashamed" of himself for telling "smutty" and "dull and dirty wisecracks." Garland said that whenever he woke up from the goings-on, Holtz always seemed to be relating "shabby" gags in the nature of "the guy-who-had-to-go." Finally, Garland said he'd had enough and so didn't return after intermission.

BLOOMER GIRL
"A New Musical"

Theatre: Shubert Theatre
Opening Date: October 5, 1944; *Closing Date*: April 27, 1946
Performances: 654
Book: Sig Herzig and Fred Saidy
Lyrics: E. Y. Harburg
Music: Harold Arlen
Based on an unproduced play by Lilith and Dan James.
Direction: Production staged by E. Y. Harburg and book directed by William Schorr; *Producers*: John C. Wilson in association with Nat Goldstone; *Choreography*: Agnes De Mille; *Scenery* and *Lighting*: Lemuel Ayers; *Costumes*: Miles White; *Musical Direction*: Leon Leonardi
Cast: Mabel Taliaferro (Serena), Pamela Randell (Octavia), Claudia Jordan (Lydia), Toni Hart (Julia), Carol MacFarlane (Phoebe), Nancy Douglass (Delia), Joan McCracken (Daisy), Matt Briggs (Horatio), John Call (Gus), Celeste Holm (Evelina), Robert Lyons (Joshua Dingle), William Bender (Herman Brasher), Joe E. Marks (Ebenezer Mimms), Vaughn Trinnier (Wilfred Thrush), Dan Gallagher (Hiram Crump), Margaret

Douglass (Dolly), David Brooks (Jeff Calhoun), Lee Barrie (Paula), Eleanor Jones (Prudence), Arlene Anderson (Hetty), Eleanor Winter (Betty), Blaine Cordner (Hamilton Calhoun), Dooley Wilson (Pompey), Charles Howard (Sheriff Quimby), John Byrd (First Deputy, State Official), Joseph Florestano (Second Deputy), Ralph Sassano (Third Deputy), Hubert Dilworth (Augustus), Richard Huey (Alexander), Butler Hixon (Governor Newton); Singers: Eleanor Jones, Matilda Strazza, Arlene Anderson, Terry Saunders, Alice Richmond, Eleanor Winter, Lee Barrie, Ralph Sassano, Ray Cook, Henry Roberts, Byron Milligan, Joseph Fiorestano, Alan Gilbert; Dancers: Peggy Holmes, Dorothy Hill, Betty Low, Carmelita Lanza, Elena Karina, Joan Mann, Phyllis Gehrig, Theresa Gushurst, Emy St. Just, Lidija Franklin, Kathleen O'Brien, Art Partington, Richard D'Arcy, Frank DeWinters, James Mitchell, William Weber, Jack Starr, Arthur Grahl

The musical was presented in two acts.

The action takes place during spring 1861 in the small Eastern manufacturing town of Cicero Falls.

Musical Numbers

Act One: "When the Boys Come Home" (Mabel Taliaferro, Pamela Randell, Claudia Jordan, Toni Hart, Carol MacFarlane, Nancy Douglass); "Evelina" (David Brooks, Celeste Holm); "Welcome Hinges" (Mabel Taliaferro, Matt Briggs, Pamela Randell, Claudia Jordan, Toni Hart, Carol MacFarlane, Nancy Douglass, Robert Lyons, William Bender, Joe E. Marks, Vaughn Trinnier, Dan Gallagher, Celeste Holm, David Brooks); "The Farmer's Daughter" (Robert Lyons, William Bender, Joe E. Marks, Vaughn Trinnier, Dan Gallagher); "It Was Good Enough for Grandma" (Celeste Holm, Bloomer Girls); "Dance Specialty" (Joan McCracken, Dancers); "The Eagle and Me" (Dooley Wilson); "Right as the Rain" (David Brooks, Celeste Holm); "T'morra', T'morra'" (Joan McCracken); "The Rakish Young Man with the Whiskers" (Celeste Holm, David Brooks); "Pretty as a Picture" (Male Ensemble); Waltz (Dancers; The Waltzers: Lidija Franklin and James Mitchell with Joan Mann, Theresa Gushurst, Kathleen O'Brien, Betty Low, Phyllis Gehrig, Richard D'Arcy, Arthur Grahl, William Weber, Art Partington); "Style Show Ballet" (Principals, Dancers)

Act Two: "Sunday in Cicero Falls" (Principals, Company); "I Got a Song" (Richard Huey, with Hubert Dilworth and Dooley Wilson); "Lullaby" (aka "Satin Gown and Silver Shoe") (Celeste Holm); "Simon Legree" (Joseph Florestano); "Liza Crossing the Ice" (Emy St. Just, Ensemble); "I Never Was Born" (Joan McCracken); "Man for Sale" (Alan Gilbert); "Civil War Ballet" (Dancers; Woman in Black and Red: Betty Low; Girl in Rose: Lidija Franklin; Her Soldier: James Mitchell); "The Eagle and Me" (reprise) (Ensemble); "When the Boys Come Home" (Entire Company)

With E. Y. Harburg as its lyricist and also credited with the musical's staging (although William Schorr was listed in the program for "book direction"), it's no wonder *Bloomer Girl* had a political agenda; but perhaps the agenda was too broad in its attempt to deal with the rights of women, the issue of slavery, and the evil of war. All these subjects may have been more than the book's structure could handle, especially since there had to be room for romantic ballads ("Evelina" and "Right as the Rain"), comedy songs (such as "T'morra', T'morra'"), charm numbers ("Sunday in Cicero Falls"), a "Civil War Ballet," and (seven years before *The King and I*'s ballet "The Small House of Uncle Thomas") a mini-musical version of *Uncle Tom's Cabin* (which included the songs "Simon Legree," "Liza Crossing the Ice," "I Never Was Born," and "Man for Sale").

Dolly Bloomer (Margaret Douglass) is a champion of women's rights, and to that end believes that hoop skirts should be abolished in favor of pantalettes (or bloomers). It isn't clear if her goal is to *make* all women wear bloomers, or to give them the *choice* of hoop skirts or bloomers. (If the musical's production photos are any indication, there is clearly *no* choice: the bloomer outfits on the performers make them look embarrassingly foolish and thus unwittingly make the unwieldy hoop skirts seem more attractive than ever.) Dolly's niece Evelina is the daughter of a hoop skirt manufacturer, but Evelina sides with her aunt on the bloomers issue and also agrees with her aunt's abolitionist views. The latter causes romantic problems because Kentuckian Jeff Calhoun is a slave owner and one of his escaped slaves is now in Cicero Falls thanks to the efforts of Dolly and the Underground Railroad. There's also an insufferably cute and coy character (Daisy, played by Joan McCracken) who seems to be out of *Oklahoma!* by way of Ado Annie. And if all this isn't enough, there's the Civil War to deal with.

Bloomer Girl was Arlen's longest-running Broadway musical with 654 performances, and his 1957 musical *Jamaica* came in second with 555 showings. But ironically his two biggest hits had generally mild scores that aren't remotely in the same league with his two masterpieces, **St. Louis Woman** and *House of Flowers* (1954). Even his final musical, the generally ignored *Saratoga* (1959), has more interesting and melodic songs than the ones in *Bloomer Girl* and *Jamaica*. *Bloomer Girl* offered a couple of passable if pallid ballads ("Evelina" and "Right as the Rain"), an obvious comic song ("It Was Good Enough for Grandma"), and one that is so tiresome it almost defies description ("Welcome Hinges"). Even the would-be-thrilling anthems "The Eagle and Me" and "I Got a Song" missed the mark (although, to be sure, these last two have their advocates).

Burton Rascoe in the *New York World-Telegram* said *Bloomer Girl* was no **Oklahoma!**; it wasn't even a **Song of Norway**; in fact, it was "probably the least entertaining musical in town"; the lyrics and music lacked "distinction" and some of the songs were decidedly "third rate"; the book was "awful"; and "T'morra', T'morra'" was an attempt to give Joan McCracken a song in the manner of "I Cain't Say No" (and he noted she was "so damned busy being cute" she became "irritating"). Wilella Waldorf in the *New York Post* reported that the show took an "unconscionably long time" to get going, and the first act was a "big, beautiful bore" with the décor the only positive aspect; but the second was better because it was shorter and "livelier." She remarked that had she composed the score, she would have been distressed over how poorly most of it was sung and would have been found dead by her own hand in Shubert Alley. As for the choreography, she predicted Broadway was in for "several seasons of intensely old-fashioned quaintness" with choreography mostly by Agnes De Mille. As for "Sunday in Cicero Falls," she was certain that Sunday couldn't be "that long, even in Cicero Falls." John Chapman in the *New York Daily News* liked the show, but noted it often had a "ponderous lack of pace" and he got "downright restless" during the "Civil War Ballet" because the dancers fought the "whole darn" war during the course of the piece. But he concluded the evening was a "bountiful hit" even though it wasn't as "swift and light-hearted" as it could have been.

Louis Kronenberger in *PM* found *Bloomer Girl* "unusually good," but noted the score was "not distinguished," the book was "far from inspired" but "less insipid" than most, and the evening lacked humor. Ward Morehouse in the *New York Sun* liked the "melodious and beautiful" musical, but cautioned that the book was "ambling" and more humor "wouldn't hurt" it. Lewis Nichols in the *New York Times* liked the "good" show and the "eminently serviceable" songs, but he mentioned that the book was "not the show's most sturdy beam." Howard Barnes in the *New York Herald Tribune* pronounced the musical an "event" that was "enchanting" and an "entertainment to remember"; and Jim O'Connor in the *New York Journal-American* praised the "fabulous" musical, which was "fresh, vigorous, radiant, enchanting and thoroughly American."

Celeste Holm had received great reviews for her supporting role of Ado Annie in **Oklahoma!**, but as *Bloomer Girl*'s leading lady some of the critics were disappointed with her weak singing. Waldorf asked the "lovely" performer and "nice" actress to "go back to the drama where you belong" because in musicals "you're killing us." Rascoe noted that everyone was aware she had no real singing voice, and reported that during a duet with David Brooks she suddenly veered into a different melody from the one he was singing. Kronenberger also said she wasn't much of a singer but was definitely "acquiring a real gift" for "putting over" a number (but her "Satin Gown and Silver Shoe" was a "downright mistake"). After *Bloomer Girl*, Holm created just one more role in a Broadway musical when thirty-five years later she appeared in Clark Gesner's *The Utter Glory of Morrissey Hall*, which closed after just one performance in 1979. In the interim, she appeared in *The King and I* (1951) and *Mame* (1966) during their Broadway runs as a replacement, and in two original film musicals, *Three Little Girls in Blue* (1946) in which she portrayed an Ado Annie–type character who sings "Always a Lady," and in Cole Porter's *High Society* (1956) in which she and Frank Sinatra introduced the merry duet "Who Wants to Be a Millionaire?"

"I Got a Song" had been written for the film version of **Cabin in the Sky**; although the song was filmed, it was cut prior to the film's release (but is included on the DVD).

The cast album was released by Decca (78 RPM # DA-381; LP # DL-8015; and CD by Decca Broadway # 440-013-561-2, which includes bonus tracks of three of the score's songs by Bing Crosby and Russ Morgan). For the cast album, Arlen sang "Man for Sale" (which had been performed by Alan Gilbert on the stage), and (for the CD release) Arlen is also heard in the "Sunday in Cicero Falls" sequence. "The Civil War Ballet" (with original orchestrations by Robert Russell Bennett and arranged for two pianos by Richard Rodney Bennett) is included in the collection *Special Occasions: Richard Rodney Bennett Plays the Ballet Music of Cole Porter, Harold Arlen and Richard Rodgers* (DRG Records LP # 6102).

The musical was revived at City Center for a limited engagement when the national touring company (with Nanette Fabray, who had succeeded Holm during the New York run) played there on January 6, 1947, for forty-eight performances (see entry). Encores! presented a concert revival on March 22, 2001, for five performances. A revival at the Goodspeed Opera House on September 16, 1981, included the non-show song "Promise Me Not to Love Me" (for Dolly).

On February 28, 1956, the musical was presented by NBC on *Producers' Showcase* with direction by Alex Segal and a teleplay by Leslie Stevens. The cast included Barbara Cook, Keith Andes, Patricia Hammerlee, Rawn Spearman, Paul Ford, Carmen Matthews, and Brock Peters; the "Civil War Ballet" included a few of the dancers from the original Broadway production, including James Mitchell and Lidija Franklin.

In the mid-1960s, Twentieth Century-Fox announced it would film *Bloomer Girl* with Shirley MacLaine and Harry Belafonte; perhaps a film musical about women's and blacks' rights seemed a natural for the era; but, for whatever reason, the project was shelved and the musical has never been filmed.

THE MERRY WIDOW

Theatre: City Center
Opening Date: October 7, 1944; *Closing Date*: November 4, 1944
Performances: 32
Book: Adaptation by Sidney Sheldon and Ben Roberts from the original libretto by Victor Leon and Leo Stein
Lyrics: Adrian Ross (from the original lyrics by Victor Leon and Leo Stein); special lyrics by Robert Gilbert
Music: Franz Lehar (music adapted by Robert Stolz
Direction: Felix Brentano; *Producer*: The New City Opera (Yolanda Mero-Irion, Director); *Choreography*: George Balanchine; *Scenery*: Howard Bay; *Costumes*: Walter Florell; *Lighting*: Uncredited; *Musical Direction*: Fritz Zweig
Cast: John Harrold (The King, Gaston), Karl Farkas (Popoff), Nils Landin (Jolidon), Xenia Bank (Natalie), Lucy Hillary (Olga Bardini), Gordon Dilworth (General Bardini), Alan Vaughan (Novakovich), Dennis Dengate (Cascada), Alfred Porter (Khadja), Connie Clark (Guest), Ward Richard (Guest), Norman Budd (Nish), Marta Eggerth (Sonia Sadoya), Jan Kiepura (Prince Danilo), Lisette Verea (Clo-Clo), Annette Norman (Lo-Lo, Jou-Jou), Mary Broussard (Frou-Frou), Babs (Barbara) Heath (Do-Do, Premiere Danseuse), Alice Borbus (Margot), Nina Popova (Premiere Danseuse), Jack Gansert (Premier Dancer); Ladies of the Ensemble: Connie Clark, Irene Gans, Leona Vanni, Georgette Rolandez, Maxine Schraeder, Jan Rankin, Doris Parker, Dorothy Ramsey, Katherine Borron, Beatrice Gordon, Mary Rankin; Gentlemen of the Ensemble: Alfred Morgan, George Karle, Joseph Monte, Ward Richard, Joseph Bellafiore, Louis Fried, Colin Harvey, Stanton Barrett, Jon Carlson; Ballet Dancers: Mary Broussard, Teddi Sanders, Alice Borbus, Rita Charise, Barbara Gaye, Annette Norman, Alice Tisen, Aleks Bird, Jeffery Longe, Stanley Zompakos, Terry Townes, Ernest Richman, Bruce Laffey, Charles Chartier
The operetta was presented in three acts.
The action takes place in Paris during the summer of 1906.

In 1943, The New Opera Company presented its new version of Franz Lehar's 1905 operetta *Die lustige witwe*; the production was well-received and played for 322 performances with Marta Eggerth (Sonya) and Jan Kiepura (Danilo) in the leading roles. The current revival by the company played at City Center for a limited engagement of thirty-two performances, with Eggerth and Kiepura reprising their roles from the previous year's production. For more information about the 1943 revival, see entry; for more information about the operetta in general, see entry for an earlier (1942) revival.

ROBIN HOOD
"Reginald DeKoven's Romantic Comic Opera"

Theatre: Adelphi Theatre
Opening Date: November 7, 1944; *Closing Date*: November 18, 1944
Performances: 15

Book and *Lyrics*: Harry B. Smith
Music: Reginald DeKoven
Direction: R. H. Burnside; *Producer*: R. H. Burnside; *Choreography*: Uncredited; *Scenery*: United Studios;
   Costumes: Veronica; *Lighting*: Uncredited; *Musical Direction*: Roger P. Vene
Cast: Robert Field (Robert of Huntington [later Robin Hood]), George Lipton (Sheriff of Nottingham), Frank
   Farrell (Sir Guy of Gisborne), Harold Patrick (Little John), Wilfred Glenn (Will Scarlett), Jerry Robbins
   (Friar Tuck), Edith Herlick (Allan-a-Dale), Barbara Scully (Lady Marian Fitzwalter [later Maid Marian]),
   Zamah Cunningham (Dame Durden), Margaret Spencer (Annabel); Milk Maids: Lucille Barton, Virginia
   Chestnutt, Susan Corey, Frances Joslyn, Helena Kozlowsky, Gloria Marshall, Margaret McKenna, Beatrice
   Miller, Wanda Owen, Jane Riehl, Ruth Simas, Doris Sward; Sheriff's Men: Edgar Joseph, Philip Lowry,
   William Nuss, Raymond Vincent; King's Men: Roy Ballard, Tom Kelly, Stanley Turner, Louis Vern; Vil-
   lagers and Archers: Gerda Christensen, Frances Fleming, Florence Hurst, Adele Jakiel, Ethel Johnson,
   Gloria Laflin, Jean Lawrence, Jeanne Lee, Jane Moses, Arlene Ross, Jane Shelby, Norine Winters; Villagers
   and Outlaws: Lee Edwards, Herman Glazer, Steven Kent, Jerry Madeira, Gerry Sherwood, Dale Sommer,
   Milton Vaughn, Melville Veitch, Allan Whitman
The musical was presented in three acts.
The action takes place in England during the reign of Richard I.

Musical Numbers

Act One: Overture (Orchestra); Introduction and Opening Chorus; "The Milkmaids' Song" (Milk Maids);
   "Come the Bowmen in Lincoln Green" (Robert Field); "My Dream Has Come True" (Robert Field, Barbara
   Scully); "I Am the Sheriff of Nottingham" (Frank Farrell, George Lipton, Chorus); "Churning" (George
   Lipton, Frank Farrell, Barbara Scully); Finale
Act Two: "It Takes Nine Tailors to Make a Man" (Wilfred Glenn, Ensemble); "Brown October Ale" (Harold
   Patrick, Chorus); "Oh, Promise Me" (Edith Herlick); "The Tinker Song" (George Lipton, Frank Farrell,
   Tinkers); "See the Little Lambkins Play" (Sextette); "The Forest Song" (Barbara Scully); "The Serenade"
   (Robert Field); "Revenge Is Mine" (Edith Herlick, Wilfred Glenn, Robert Field, Barbara Scully); Finale
Act Three: "The Armorer's Song" (Wilfred Glenn); "When a Maiden Weds" (Margaret Spencer); "The Legend
   of the Chimes" (Edith Herlick, Chorus); "Quintette" (Margaret Spencer, Zamah Cunningham, Frank Far-
   rell, George Lipton, Jerry Robbins); Finale

Reginald DeKoven's operetta *Robin Hood* had enjoyed many decades of revivals and audience popularity,
but the current production seems to have done it in. The setting was Nottingham and Sherwood Forest and it
told the familiar story of Robin Hood, Maid Marian, the Sheriff of Nottingham, Little John, and Friar Tuck. It
was first seen in New York at the Standard Theatre on September 28, 1891, for a limited engagement of thirty-
five performances. Its score offered a number of standards, including the drinking song "Brown October Ale"
and the wedding song "Oh, Promise Me," which had been added to the production after its world premiere in
Boston (with a lyric by Clement Scott, it had been written by Scott and DeKoven as an independent song in
1887). Including the current production, the operetta was revived on Broadway a total of thirteen times (prior
to 1944, its most recent revival had opened in New York on January 27, 1932, at the Erlanger's Theatre for
twenty-nine performances).

But the critics weren't kind to the current revival, and it seems the evening's inordinate length (due to
poor direction that allowed the performers to indulge in endless encores) was particularly annoying to the
reviewers. Despite their enjoyment of the score and their general praise for the singing leads, the production
lasted just two weeks and, as far as Broadway was concerned, the operetta disappeared.

Robert Garland in the *New York Journal-American* found the revival "long-drawn and unfunny" but
noted the score was still "fresh and lilting." He liked Robert Field in the title role and said Barbara Scully's
Maid Marian was "personable," "sweet," and "winning" but noted her riding costume was at least three-
hundred years ahead of its time. Burton Rascoe in the *New York World-Telegram* said Scully was the "only
reason" to see the "draggy, spiritless and old-fashioned" operetta, and he noted the first-nighters "walked out
in droves."

Wilella Waldorf in the *New York Post* reported that for some songs the cast began encores before the audience had a chance to applaud, and when there was applause the encores were again repeated; so she feared if someone in the theatre shouted "Bravo!" the cast might go back to the first scene and start the show all over again. Lewis Nichols in the *New York Times* said the encores "considerably" slowed down the action and suggested the encores "be fixed with firmness," and Louis Kronenberger in *PM* said the encores overworked the songs and overextended the performance.

Howard Barnes in the *New York Herald Tribune* said many of the songs received "perfunctory" vocals and "slip-shod" delivery, and noted the singers and orchestra were "rarely" in tune with one another; as a result, the revival was a "rather sorry exhumation" of a "solid" operetta; Nichols found the evening sometimes "long and incredibly tedious" and the dialogue intruded upon the score like commercials on the radio; Chapman noted that by "today's standards" the book was "terrible—but at least they get it over with fast"; and Kronenberger summed up the evening as one with "tuneful music" and "very tiresome folderol."

AEI Records (CD # AEI-CD-032) released a collection of songs from the operetta, including recordings made in 1898, 1906, and 1919. The most complete recording is from an Ohio Light Opera production that was released on a two-CD set by Albany Records (# TROY-712-713).

An advertisement in the revival's opening night program stated that "America's Most Beloved Operetta" offered a "singing cast of 110." But a count of the listed performers shows a total of fifty-one in the production. Note that cast member Jerry Robbins is not the well-known choreographer Jerome Robbins. The production was Barbara Scully's swan song to Broadway; critic Burton Rascoe had touted her voice and beauty in the previous year's revivals of **The Student Prince** and **Blossom Time**, but after the closing of *Robin Hood* she never again appeared on Broadway.

THE GYPSY BARON
"An Opera"

Theatre: City Center
Opening Date: November 14, 1944; *Closing Date*: December 3, 1944
Performances: 11 (in repertory)
Based on *Saffi* by Mor Jokai.
Libretto: Ignaz Schnitzer (current revival revised and adapted into English by George Mead)
Music: Johann Strauss
Direction: Stage direction by William Wymetal and dialogue direction by Jessie Royce Landis; *Producer*: The New York City Center Opera Company (Laszlo Halasz, Director); *Choreography*: Ballet choreography by Helene Platova; *Scenery*: H. A. Condell; *Costumes*: Van Horn & Son; *Lighting*: Uncredited; *Musical Direction*: Thomas Philipp Martin
Cast: William Horne (Sandor Barinkay), Polyna Stoska (Saffi), Alice Howland (Czipra), Marjorie King (Arsena), Stanley Carlson (Kalman Zsupan), Arthur Ulisse (Ottokar), Paul Dennis (Carnero), Carlton Gauld (Count Homonnay), Ruth Harris (Solo Dancer for czardas and waltzes), Tashamira (Solo Dancer for gypsy dances); Villagers, Gypsies, Hussars, Vivandieres, Soldiers, Citizens, Town Folk, etc.: The New York City Center Opera Company Chorus; *Note*: During the run, Marguerite Piazza also sang the roles of Saffi and Arsena; Elizabeth Wysor, Czipra; Thomas Hayward, Ottokar; Emile Renan, Carnero; and Laszlo Halasz and Julius Rudel also conducted
The operetta was presented in three acts.
The action takes place during the nineteenth century in Budapest, Hungary; in the Transylvanian countryside; and in Vienna.
Note: The program didn't list individual musical numbers.

As *Der Zigeunerbaron*, Johann Strauss's operetta *The Gypsy Baron* had its world premiere on October 24, 1885, at the Theatre an der Wien in Vienna; the libretto was by Ignaz Schnitzer. The work received its first American showing on February 15, 1886, at the Casino Theatre, where it played for three months. For the current revival, the operetta was revised and adapted into English by George Mead.

The lighthearted story took place in the romantic operetta world of Budapest, the Transylvanian countryside, and Vienna, where the formerly exiled but now pardoned rebel Sandor Barinkay is again a citizen who can claim his birthright. He discovers that a band of gypsies is living on his family's estate and that local farmer Kalman Zsupan has taken over much of the property; in order to placate Barinkay, Zsupan offers his daughter Arensa to him in marriage. But Arsena loves Ottokar! And romantic complications ensue. Soon Barinkay is crowned a gypsy baron and becomes involved with Saffi, the daughter of a gypsy fortune teller. It turns out she is actually of royal blood, and ultimately they marry; and the gypsy baron asks Zsupan to allow Arensa to wed Ottokar.

The current production was revived by the New York City Center Opera Company during the 1945–1946 season (see entry). (The company later altered its name to the New York City Opera, but continued to perform at City Center for the next two decades; when Lincoln Center was built, the New York State Theatre became the company's new home.)

There are many recordings of *The Gypsy Baron*, including a two-CD release (in German) by Elektra with Wolfgang Holzmair conducting the Vienna Symphony Orchestra. The operetta has also been released on DVD (in German, by Deutsch Grammophon).

The operetta's source is *Saffi* by Hungarian novelist and playwright Mor Jokai, who in 1854 wrote *Zoltan Kapathy* (one wonders if the character is a rude and dreadful pest who oozes charm from every pore).

SADIE THOMPSON
"A MUSICAL PLAY"

Theatre: Alvin Theatre
Opening Date: November 16, 1944; *Closing Date*: January 6, 1945
Performances: 60
Based on W. Somerset Maugham's 1921 short story "Miss Thompson" and its 1922 stage adaptation *Rain* by John Colton and Clemence Randolph.
Book: Howard Dietz and Rouben Mamoulian
Lyrics: Howard Dietz
Music: Vernon Duke
Direction: Rouben Mamoulian; *Producer*: A. P. Waxman (A Rouben Mamoulian Production); *Choreography*: Edward Caton; *Scenery*: Boris Aronson; *Costumes*: Motley; June Havoc's costumes designed from studies by Azadia Newman from her painting *Sadie Thompson*; *Lighting*: Rouben Mamoulian; *Musical Direction*: Charles G. Sanford; *Choral Direction*: Millard Gibson
Cast: Ralph Dumke (Joe Horn), Daniel Cobb (Corporal Hodgson), Norman Lawrence (Private Griggs), James Newill (Sergeant Tim O'Hara), Grazia Narciso (Ameena), Beatrice Kraft (Honeypie), Zolya Talma (Mrs. Alfred Davidson), Doris Patston (Cicely St. Clair), Remington Olmsted (Lao Lao), June Havoc (Sadie Thompson), Walter Burke (Quartermaster Bates), Lansing Hatfield (Reverend Alfred Davidson), Milada Mladova (Polynesian Girl), Chris Volkoff (Polynesian Boy); Singers: Ann Browning, Arlene Carmen, Paula Carpino, Mollie Causley, Ethel Greene, Marilyn Merkt, Dorris Moore, Linda White, Jimmy Allison, Anthony Amato, Adolph Anderson, John (Jack) Cassidy, Neil Chirico, Delmar (Del) Horstmann, Robert Lawrence, Alan Noel; Dancers: Vivian Cherry, Faith Dane, Toni Darnay, Andrea Downing, Joan Dubois, Mary Grey, Lil Liandre, Virginia Meyer, Theodora Roosevelt, Anna Scarpova, Alla Shishkina, Ruth Sobotka, Natalie Wynn, Vanessi, Fred Bernaski, Bob Gari, T. C. Jones, William Lundy, Mischa Pompianov, Igor Tamarin, William Vaux, John Ward; Polynesian Musicians: Wasantha Singh and His Group—Minakshi, S. R. Mandel, Frank da Silva, Karla Margot Pries
The musical was presented in two acts.
The action takes place during the present time in Pago Pago in the South Seas.

Musical Numbers

Act One: Polynesian Scene; "Barrel of Beads" (Norman Lawrence, Beatrice Kraft); "Fisherman's Wharf" (June Havoc); "When You Live on an Island" (James Newill, Choral Ensemble); "Poor as a Church Mouse" (June Havoc); "Jungle Dance"—(a) Beatrice Kraft, Natives and (b) Milada Mladova, Chris Volkoff, Natives; "The

Love I Long For" (June Havoc, James Newill); "Dance to the Sun God" (Remington Olmstead, Vanessi, Natives); "Garden in the Sky" (Lansing Hatfield)

Act Two: "Dancing Lesson" (Doris Patston, Native Girls); "Siren of the Tropics" (Beatrice Kraft, Walter Burke, Norman Lawrence, Daniel Cobb); "Life's a Funny Present from Someone" (June Havoc); "Born All Over Again" (Lansing Hatfield); "Sailing at Midnight" (James Newill, June Havoc); "Montage: Sadie's Conversion" (a) The Inner Voices: James Newill, Lansing Hatfield; (b) Hot Spot: June Havoc, William Newill; (c) Sunflowers—The Young Sadie: Milada Mladova; The Boy: Chris Volkoff; That Man: Remington Oldstead; (d) The Lamplit Street: June Havoc, Mischa Pompianov, William Vaux, William Lundy; (e) Kangaroo Farm: June Havoc, James Newill; (f) Prison and Conversion: June Havoc, Lansing Hatfield, James Newill); (g) The Living Curtain: Choral Group, Dancers; "The Mountains of Nebraska" (ballet) (Lansing Hatfield; Davidson's Other Self: Chris Volkoff; and various Sadie Thompsons danced by Milada Mladova and other female dancers); "Fisherman's Wharf" (reprise) (June Havoc); "When You Live on an Island" (reprise) (Company, Ensemble)

Sadie Thompson told the story of a prostitute who is drummed out of San Francisco and heads off for Sydney, Australia. But the threat of cholera forces her and other shipboard travelers to temporarily take refuge at a ramshackle hotel on Pago Pago in the South Sea Islands. There she becomes involved with a group of Marines, particularly Sergeant Tim O'Hara. Also staying at the hotel are missionaries Reverend Davidson and his wife; Davidson wants Sadie driven out of the hotel and off the island, but eventually tries to redeem her soul. He seems to temporarily succeed, but his baser instincts take over and he rapes her. And then he commits suicide. The next morning Sadie reverts to her old ways and heads off for Sydney, saying "I guess I'm sorry for everybody in the world."

As soon as *Sadie Thompson* began rehearsals it stumbled and never recovered. Ethel Merman agreed to appear in the show, but during the first week of rehearsals she suddenly objected to Howard Dietz's lyrics and left the production. She was succeeded by June Havoc, and despite a tumultuous tryout in which at least seven songs were deleted and a number of dance sequences underwent major revisions, the musical wasn't ready to face the critics on opening night. But perhaps this musical would never have been ready. Its structure veered from intimate, straight storytelling (the Sadie-Davidson-O'Hara characters) to lavish production numbers that included extraneous jungle dances. Nothing quite meshed, and it often seemed to be two musicals in one. Further, the critics felt the strong dialogue scenes were too frequently interrupted with less-than-compelling songs. Extracted from the musical, Dietz and Vernon Duke's songs are actually quite interesting; but with one or two exceptions they never quite jell into theatrically exciting material. The major exception is Sadie and O'Hara's hauntingly lovely "Sailing at Midnight," a quiet introspective song that seems perfectly right for the moment and the characters and is one of the most beautiful and touching Broadway songs of the era.

Lewis Nichols in the *New York Times* noted that musical comedy–minded audiences would have to sit through "long stretches" of dialogue, and those interested in the work as a drama would "find the numerous songs an annoyance." Even a director the caliber of Rouben Mamoulian couldn't find a way to handle "the gap which develops when a serious play is stopped dead for a light song." Ward Morehouse in the *New York Sun* found the "costly" and "colorful" musical "very dull" with an awkward mix of a serious story poorly blended with ballads and jungle ballets. Robert Garland in the *New York Journal-American* also complained that the "ballets interfere with the story, the story interferes with the ballets, and the musical-comedy songs just don't belong." Louis Kronenberger in *PM* echoed these sentiments, saying the story, dances, and songs all interrupted one another and thus the evening of "starts and stops" resulted in a "mess."

But Howard Barnes in the *New York Herald Tribune* found the musical "distinguished and exciting," with a "crafty blend of song, dance and theatre"; here was a "happy musical resurrection of a somewhat archaic play." Wilella Waldorf in the *New York Post* said the musical was a "good show," a "success" that "proved uncommonly enjoyable"; and Burton Rascoe in the *New York World-Telegram* went all out, proclaiming that *Sadie Thompson* was "in a class with *Oklahoma!*" and was "one of the most beautifully integrated shows of its kind I have ever seen and heard" (and noted he was taking *Show Boat* into account).

The critics were further divided on the merits of the score. Barnes found the music "melodious" and the lyrics "dandy"; Rascoe said the score was "full of heavenly sounds" that were "pulse-quickening" and "ear-caressing"; the "enchanting" music offered "original but lovely" syncopation with rhythm-breaks that "surprised" you but that "were perfect" in their melodic development. But Waldorf said Duke's songs would never cause a "major riot" in Tin Pan Alley and noted the choral and ballet music offered more "distinction" than the principals' songs. Nichols said the music was "undistinguished" and Dietz's lyrics were not written with his "sharpest pencil"; Morehouse also found the score "undistinguished." Chapman said the show had everything but music, for Duke's contributions were "heavy and dull and of scant variety"; and Kronenberger found the score "commonplace." Of the individual songs, "The Love I Long For," "Life's a Funny Present," "When You Live on an Island," "Fisherman's Wharf," "Born All Over Again," and "Poor as a Church Mouse" garnered most of the critical praise.

The critics liked the singing of Metropolitan baritone Lansing Hatfield, but most felt his acting was weak. As for June Havoc, they were impressed with her performance and the emotional arc she created for the character (but noted her singing voice wasn't always strong). Waldorf said her "surprisingly effective" portrayal was a "worthy successor" to Jeanne Eagels; Chapman found her "truly touching"; Garland said her performance "stood up bravely" with the Sadies of Jeanne Eagels, Gloria Swanson, and Joan Crawford; Barnes said she built the role of the prostitute into "rather triumphant dimensions" with the "gradations" she created in the development of her character; Kronenberger praised her "engaging quality" and said she was the musical's most "enjoyable" aspect; and Rascoe praised the "consummate skill of her artistry."

During the run, Sadie's "Fisherman's Wharf" and its second act reprise were deleted and replaced by "If You Can't Get the Love You Want."

During the tryout, the following numbers were cut: "Join the Marines," "You, U.S.A," "The Weeping Sky," "Any Woman Who Is Willing Will Do," "The Key to the Gates," "Deep Down Inside You," and "Hurdy Gurdy." For the tryout, "Sadie's Conversion" was titled "Sadie's Struggle" and it included the song "I Lived in a House with a Piano"; "Dancing Lesson" was titled "Dancing Politely"; and "Jungle Dance" was divided into two separate sequences a scene or two apart, titled "Dance in the Jungle" (Part I) and "Dance in the Jungle" (Part II); for Broadway, "Jungle Dance" was performed by the island's natives, but for the tryout's Part I sequence the dance also included beachcombers. For Broadway, the first musical number was titled "Polynesian Scene" for which no performers were credited; for the tryout, the number was titled "Polynesian Opening" and included five characters as well as children, a native band, the chorus, and the ballet dancers.

In 2002, Original Cast Records (CD # OC-6042) released a most welcome studio cast recording of the score with Meilssa Errico (Sadie), Ron Raines (Davidson), and Davis Gaines (O'Hara). The recording included six songs from the Broadway production ("When You Live on an Island," "Fisherman's Wharf," "The Love I Long For," "Sailing at Midnight," "Garden in the Sky," and "Life's a Funny Present"); six which had been dropped during the tryout ("Join the Marines," "The Weeping Sky," "You, U.S.A.," "Hurdy Gurdy," "The Key to the Gates," and "I Lived in a House with a Piano"); and five which were apparently dropped in preproduction ("Cradle to the Grave," "Back in Circulation," "Where the Sun God Walks," "Below the Equator," and "Circles Under Your Eyes"). Numbers heard in the Broadway production that weren't represented on the recording are: "Barrel of Beads," "Poor as a Church Mouse," "Siren of the Tropics," "Born All Over Again," "The Mountains of Nebraska," and all the dance and ballet music; further, "If You Can't Get the Love You Want" (which was added after the Broadway opening) is not included on the recording.

The collection Vernon Duke Revisited (Painted Smiles CD # PSCD-138) includes "If You Can't Get the Love You Want" (sung by Tammy Grimes) and "Life's a Funny Present" (Joan Rivers); Vernon Duke Revisited Volume II (Painted Smiles CD # PSCD-127) offers "Sailing at Midnight" and "Poor as a Church Mouse" (both performed by Dolores Gray); Klea Blackhurst's Autumn in New York: Vernon Duke's Broadway (Ghostlight CD # 79155833022) also includes "Sailing at Midnight" and "Poor as a Church Mouse"; Dawn Upshaw Sings Vernon Duke (Nonesuch CD # 795312) has "The Love I Long For"; and "Life's a Funny Present" is included in Life's a Funny Present (Rialto CD # SLRR-9306).

Sadie Thompson first began life as the 1921 short story "Miss Thompson" by W. Somerset Maugham; it was then adapted by John Colton and Clemence Randolph for the stage in 1922 as Rain, and played for 648 performances with Jeanne Eagels reportedly giving one of the era's legendary performances. The play was revived in 1935 with Tallulah Bankhead, and then twice Off Broadway, in 1972 with Madeleine le Roux (an unknown John Travolta played one of the Marines) and in 1984 with Sabra Jones.

There were three nonmusical film adaptations of the play: in 1928, Gloria Swanson starred in a silent version titled Sadie Thompson; in 1932, Rain starred Joan Crawford; and in 1946 an all-black version called Dirty Gertie from Harlem, U.S.A. featured Francine Everett as Gertie La Rue.

There have been four lyric adaptations of the work. A few years after the 1944 musical closed, Vernon Duke revisited the material in his 1952 Broadway revue Two's Company; with lyrics by Ogden Nash, the revue offered a mini-musical version called "Roll Along, Sadie" with Bette Davis (Duke didn't use any music from the 1944 production); the cast album was released on RCA Victor (LP # LOC-1009; the CD was issued by Sepia # 1047). In 1953, the film *Miss Sadie Thompson* (with Rita Hayworth, José Ferrer, and Aldo Ray) included four songs (lyrics by Alan Roberts and Ned Washington, music by Lester Lee), "A Marine, A Marine, A Marine" (aka "Marine Song"), "Hear No Evil," "The Heat Is On," and "Blue Pacific Blues." "The Heat Is On" is one of the steamiest musical numbers ever captured on film, and the torchy "Blue Pacific Blues" is a ravishingly melodic song, one of the era's finest. The soundtrack was released by Mercury (ten-inch LP # MG-25181). *Rain* was Richard Owens's operatic adaptation, which premiered in February 2003 at Alice Tully Hall in Lincoln Center; a two-CD set of the opera was released by Albany Records (# TROY-623/24).

In his autobiography *Passport to Paris*, Vernon Duke noted that Gypsy Rose Lee threw an opening-night cast party for *Sadie Thompson*, which of course starred her sister June Havoc, who had taken over the title role when Ethel Merman left the show. Fifteen years later, Gypsy, June, and Ethel's paths would again cross when they were associated with one of the greatest of all Broadway musicals, and *Sadie Thompson* chorus girl Faith Dane would be memorably associated with the show as well. As *Gypsy*'s Miss Mazeppa, she was one of the trio of strippers who stopped the show with "You Gotta Have a Gimmick" (and she later reprised her role for the 1962 film version).

Also in the chorus of *Sadie Thompson* was Jack Cassidy, who had one of the most remarkable careers in musical theatre, appearing in the original productions of seventeen musicals and revues: *Sadie Thompson* (1944); *The Firebrand of Florence* (1945); *Marinka* (1945); *Spring in Brazil* (1945; closed prior to New York); *Around the World in Eighty Days* (1946); *Music in My Heart* (1947); *Inside U.S.A.* (1948); *Small Wonder* (1948); *Alive and Kicking* (1950); *Wish You Were Here* (1952); *Sandhog* (1954); *Shangri-La* (1957); *She Loves Me* (1963); *Fade Out—Fade In* (1964); *Pleasures and Palaces* (1965; closed prior to New York); *It's a Bird It's a Plane It's SUPERMAN* (1966); and *Maggie Flynn* (1968; in which he appeared with his then wife Shirley Jones). He was also a replacement performer in the original productions of *Something for the Boys* (1943) and *South Pacific* (1949), and in 1957 appeared in the New York City Center Light Opera Company's revival of *The Beggar's Opera* with Shirley Jones. *Wish You Were Here* marked his breakthrough role, and he introduced the popular title song (which became a hit for Eddie Fisher). In the 1960s he memorably played a series of "cad" roles in *She Loves Me*, *Fade Out-Fade In*, and *It's a Bird It's a Plane It's SUPERMAN* (for *She Loves Me*, he won the Tony Award for Best Featured Actor in a Musical). For Columbia Records in the 1950s he was the leading male singer in a number of memorable studio cast albums, including *Oh, Kay!*, *Roberta*, *Jumbo*, *On Your Toes*, *Babes in Arms*, *The Boys from Syracuse*, and *Brigadoon*. In later years he was in the cast of *Sondheim: A Musical Tribute*, which took place at the Shubert Theatre on March 11, 1973 (the concert was recorded and later released by RCA Victor).

RHAPSODY
"FRITZ KREISLER'S NEW OPERETTA"

Theatre: New Century Theatre
Opening Date: November 22, 1944; *Closing Date*: December 3, 1944
Performances: 13
Book: Leonard Louis Levinson and Arnold Sundgaard
Lyrics: John LaTouche; additional lyrics by Russell Bennett and Blevins Davis
Music: Fritz Kreisler; music adapted by Russell Bennett
Based on an original story by A. N. Nagler.
Direction and *Choreography*: David Lichine; *Producers*: Blevins Davis in association with Lorraine Manville Dresselhuys; *Scenery*: Oliver Smith; *Costumes*: Frank Bevan; *Lighting*: Stanley McCandless; *Musical Direction*: Fritz Mahler
Cast: John Cherry (Lotzi Hugenhaugen), Gloria Story (Lili Hugenhaugen), John Hamill (Charles Eckert), Bertha Belmore (Frau Tina Hugenhaugen), Patricia Bowman (Ilse Bonen), Mildred Jocelyn (Greta), Eddie Mayehoff (Casanova), Rosemarie Brancato (Madame Boticini), Mister Johnson (Demi-Tasse), George Zoritch (Ivan), Alexandra Denisova (Sonya), George Young (Emperor Francis I), Annamary Dickey (Empress Maria Theresa), Randolph Symonette (Captain of the Palace Guard), Nicolas Beriozoff (Rickshaw Man), Jerry Ross (The Dandy), Robert W. Kirland (Jailer); Court Octette: Barbara Jevne, Muriel O'Malley, Lucille Shea, Camille Fischelli, Carl Anders, William Hearne, Gordon Gaines, Gar Moore; Maywine Octette: Angela

Carabella, Evelyn Keller, Mildred Joycelyn, Nina Allen, John Henson, Thomas La Monaco, Harry Ward, Rudy Rudisill; Rhapsody Double Quintette: Betty Baker, Bette Van, Stephanie Turash, Ella Mayer, Maxine Dorelle, Lewis Rose, Robert Marco, Tony Coffaro, Robert W. Kirland, Rudolph Bain; Corps de Ballet: Adele Bodroghy, Leslie Cater, Joan Collonette, Joan Hansen, Betty Jayne, Jane Kiser, Irene Larson, Kirra Lehachova, Marina Lvova, Cecile Mann, Ann Mauldin, Dorothy Scott, Pat Sims, Sally Sorvo, Yvonne Tibor, Janie Ward, Betty Yeager, Charles Bockman, Jack Donald Claus, Walter Roberts, Igor Storojeff
The musical was presented in two acts.
The action takes place during the eighteenth century in and around Vienna from noon to midnight during the reign of Empress Maria Theresa.

Musical Numbers

Act One: "They're All the Same" (Eddie Mayehoff, Gloria Story, Nina Allen, Angela Carabella, Camille Fischelli, Marina Lvova, Ella Mayer, Yvonne Tibor, Stephanie Turash, Janie Ward); "My Rhapsody" (Gloria Story, John Hamill); "Scherzo" (Rosemarie Brancato); "Heaven Bless Our Home" (George Young); "The World Is Young Again" (Annamary Dickey, Ladies of the Court); "Presentation" (Annamary Dickey, George Young, Rosemarie Brancato, Randolph Symonette, Ensemble); "Chinese Porcelain Ballet" (Patricia Bowman, George Zoritch, Nicolas Beriozoff, Ladies of the Corps de Ballet); "To Horse" (Rosemarie Brancato, Eddie Mayehoff, Bertha Belmore, John Cherry); "The Dandy's Polka" (Jerry Ross); "May Wine Polka" (Corps de Ballet, Ensemble); "Take Love" (Gloria Story, John Hamill, Ensemble); "The Hunt" (Patricia Bowman, Corps de Ballet, Ensemble); "The Roulette Game" (Alexandra Denisova, assisted by Nicolas Beriozoff, Corps de Ballet, Ensemble); "Song of Defiance" (John Hamill, Ensemble)
Act Two: "Because You're Mine" (John Hamill); "When Men Are Free" (John Hamill, Ensemble); "Happy Ending" (Annamary Dickey); "Rosemarin" (Rosemarie Brancato); "Caprice Viennois" (Annamary Dickey, George Young); "Midnight Ballet" (Patricia Bowman, George Zoritch, Alexandra Denisova, Corps de Ballet); Finale (Entire Company)

The music for the operetta *Rhapsody* was taken from various musical compositions by Fritz Kreisler, who attended the opening night performance. To provide a framework for his music, librettists Leonard Louis Levinson and Arnold Sundgaard concocted a story that took place during a twelve-hour period on the birthday of Empress Maria Theresa (Annamary Dickey). Amid court intrigues and romantic complications, the character of a villainous Casanova (Eddie Mayehoff) was somehow shoehorned into the confusing plot, and, according to *Best Plays*, a "gorgeously dressed" company found themselves "floundering in a sea of expensive scenery." But they didn't flounder for long, because the musical was gone in less than two weeks.

The critics noted that *Rhapsody* had been seen in various pre-Broadway engagements and had continually postponed its New York opening. After finally viewing the production, they wondered why the producers had bothered to bring it in. The story was slight, dull, and decidedly unfunny, and Kriesler's melodic score was out of place in an eighteenth-century setting and would have been more at home in the late 1800s. They also noted that the stirring "When Men Are Free" was awkwardly introduced into the plot, but, this being wartime, the song offered a welcome message.

Wilella Waldorf in the *New York Post* thought the idea of using Kreisler's music in a new operetta was an "enchanting" idea, but unfortunately the new work was a "ponderous, pretentious, preposterous mess" with an "appalling" book and "nauseous, coyly leering" and "laboriously smutty and monumentally dull" lyrics.

Ward Morehouse in the *New York Sun* said the book was the "dreariest within memory" and the evening provided every indication of being a "theatrical calamity of major proportions." However, the costumes were "dazzling" and the décor was "massive" if "ponderous"; the "May Wine Polka" was "attractive and colorful"; and Jerry Ross performed an "excellent" acrobatic dance ("The Dandy's Polka"). Regarding the latter's solo dance, Burton Rascoe in the *New York World-Telegram* reported that Ross took an "extraordinary leap" in which his feet touched the back of his head; otherwise, the "bad" book stuck out "like a goiter." He reported there were a few encores, and the ballet dancers were greeted with a "claquelike applause"; but overall the audience's response to the proceedings was "ghastly" and the walk-outs were "legion."

Louis Kronenberger in *PM* said the "splurgy" evening was "overripe operetta" which offered "lavishness without style"; the "dreadful" book and its terrible puns sank the musical "under its own weight" and was a "travesty of grand-scale operetta." John Chapman in the *New York Daily News* found the book and lyrics "quaintly awful" but noted Oliver Smith's "brooding" prison scene was done in variations of red and had the kind of "heroic quality" that many grand operas "deserved" but never got; and he praised Smith's "mirror-lined, many-arched, crystal-hung" décor for the evening's final ballet sequence.

Robert Garland in the *New York Journal-American* said *Rhapsody* was an "off-stage misdemeanor," a "masterpiece" of what money couldn't buy; and he noted the show actually managed to "live down" to the negative rumors that preceded it to New York. He concluded that in all his theater-going, he had never seen a "big-time" musical "so misbegotten, so flat-footed, so pretentious." Lewis Nichols in the *New York Times* found the production "top heavy and weighty," and while Kriesler's music called for "gaiety, sparkle, and charm" and might one day find itself the proper musical framework for an operetta, *Rhapsody* was not that operetta. He also noted that the "ponderous" physical production offered mirrors, chandeliers, lights, and backgrounds that stretched "roughly to the infinity of the Century Theatre." Howard Barnes in the *New York Herald Tribune* said the "pretentious" musical established "something of a low for libretto fabrication," and the direction was as "bad" as the book.

Dancer Jerry Ross appeared in a few of the era's musicals, and received especially good notices for *Rhapsody*; he's not the Jerry Ross who with Richard Adler cowrote the lyrics and music for *The Pajama Game* (1954) and *Damn Yankees* (1955).

Supporting player Bertha Belmore had charmed the critics when she jitterbugged with Ray Bolger in **By Jupiter**, and the critics were disappointed that *Rhapsody* failed to give her good material. But the older, portly performer seems to have had one good sequence when she donned a tutu and tried in vain to perform light-footed pirouettes under the tutorage of a stern, no-nonsense ballet mistress.

SEVEN LIVELY ARTS

Theatre: Ziegfeld Theatre
Opening Date: December 7, 1944; *Closing Date*: May 12, 1945
Performances: 183
Sketches: Beatrice Lillie's sketches by Moss Hart; other sketches by George S. Kaufman and Charles Sherman; Don Rockwell's comments by Ben Hecht
Lyrics and *Music*: Cole Porter; ballet music by Igor Stravinsky
Direction: Sketches directed by Philip Loeb; production staged by Hassard Short; *Producer*: Billy Rose; *Choreography*: dances choreographed by Jack Donohue and ballets choreographed by Anton Dolin; *Scenery*: Norman Bel Geddes; *Costumes*: Mary Grant; modern gowns by Valentina; *Lighting*: Hassard Short; *Musical Direction*: Maurice Abravanel; *Choral Direction*: Robert Shaw
Cast: Beatrice Lillie, Bert Lahr, Benny Goodman, Alicia Markova, Anton Dolin, Doc Rockwell, Nan Wynn, Jere McMahon, Paula Bane, Billie Worth, Bill (William) Tabbert, Dolores Gray, Mary Roche, Albert Carroll, Michael Barrett, Dennie Moore, Thomas Kenny, Edward Hackett, King Ross, Teddy Wilson, Red Norvo, Morey Feld, Sid Weiss, Robert Austin; Corps de Ballet: Franca Baldwin, Virginia Barnes, John Begg, Angelina Buttignol, Phyllis Brown, Evangeline Colis, Margarita de Valera, Bettye Durrence, Adriana Favaloro, Louise Ferrand, Jerry Florio, Nina Frenkin, Helen Gallagher, Arlene Carver, Mimi Gomber, Edward Hackett, Jean Harris, Ray Johnson, Harriet Katzman, Thomas Kenny, Lee Lauterbur, Constance Love, Richard Martini, Paul Olson, Michael Pober, Lester Russon; Singers: Robert Austin, Johnsie Bason, Charlotte Bruce, Irene Carroll, Nina Dean, Rose Marie Elliott, Paul Fairleagh, Vincent Henry, Bob Herring, Raynor Howell, Stella Hughes, Jimmy Kane, Robert Kimberly, Mary Ann Krejci, Ethel Madson, John Mathews, Helen Molveau, Louise Newton, Richmond Page, Allen Sharp, Gordon Taylor, William Utley, Martha Emma Watson; Page Boys: Charles Franklin Beck, Sonny Cavell, Alan Grossman, Barry Laffin, Buddy Millard, Dickie Millard, Donald Rose; Ladies of Fashion: Savona King, Jean Colleran, Alma Holt, Cissy Smith, Truly Barbara, Viki Maulsby, Gwen Shirey, Susan Blanchard, Adrian Storms, Paddy Ellerton, Gayle Mellott, Temple Texas
The revue was presented in two acts.

Sketches and Musical Numbers

Act One: Overture: "Frahngee-Pahnee" (Orchestra); "Big Town" (Mr. Audience: Doc Rockwell; The Young Hopefuls—Painter: Nan Wynn; Tap Dancer: Jere McMahon; Radio Singer: Paula Bane; Ballet Dancer: Billie Worth; Playwright: Bill Tabbert; Movie Actress: Dolores Gray; Stage Actress: Mary Roche; Ensemble); "Is It the Girl? (or Is It the Gown?)" (Dolores Gray; The Ladies of Fashion); "Local Boy Makes Good" (sketch by George S. Kaufman) (The Secretary: Billie Worth; The Producer: Albert Carroll; The Agent: Michael Barrett; The Stagehand: Bert Lahr); "Ev'ry Time We Say Goodbye" (The Girl: Nan Wynn; The Boy: Jere McMahon; Ensemble); "There'll Always Be an England" (sketch by Moss Hart) (Lady Carleton: Dennie Moore; Lady Agatha Pendleton: Beatrice Lillie; First Soldier: Thomas Kenny; Second Soldier: Edward Hackett; Colonel Charteris: Albert Carroll; Third Soldier: Michael Barrett); "Only Another Boy and Girl" (The Girl: Mary Roche; The Boy: Bill Tabbert; Fragonard in Pink: Beatrice Lillie, Bert Lahr, Ensemble); "Wow-ooh-wolf!" (Nan Wynn, Dolores Gray, Mary Roche); "Ticket for the Ballet" (sketch by Moss Hart) (The Customer: Beatrice Lillie; The Box Office Man: Michael Barrett; The Manager: Albert Carroll; A Man in the Line: King Ross); "Drink" (Bert Lahr, Male Ensemble); "When I Was a Little Cuckoo" (Beatrice Lillie); "Billy Rose Buys the Metropolitan Opera House!" (Benny Goodman, Teddy Wilson, Red Norvo, Morey Feld, Sid Weiss; Ensemble; sequence included "Toreador Dance," danced by Jere McMahon)

Act Two: "Scene de Ballet" (excerpts) (music by Igor Stravinsky) (Alicia Markova, Anton Dolin, Corps de Ballet); Untitled song performed by Beatrice Lillie; "The Great Man Speaks" (sketch by Charles Sherman) (The Nurse: Billie Worth; The Doctor: Albert Carroll; The Patient: Bert Lahr); "Concertina for Clarinet" (music by Weber) (Clarinet Solo played by Benny Goodman); "Frahngee-Pahnee" (Bill Tabbert, Ensemble); "Dancin' to a Jungle Drum (Let's End the Beguine)" (Beatrice Lillie); "Hence It Don't Make Sense" (Nan Wynn, Mary Roche, Dolores Gray, Billie Worth; danced by Jere McMahon and Billie Worth); "Heaven on Angel Street" (sketch by Moss Hart) (Mr. Manningham: Anton Dolin; Mrs. Manningham: Beatrice Lillie; Mr. Clarence Day: Bert Lahr; Mrs. Day: Dennie Moore; Dude Lester: Michael Barrett; Jester Lester: Albert Carroll; George Jean Nathan: Robert Austin; The Maid: Paula Bane); "Is It the Girl? (or Is It the Gown?)" (reprise) (Dolores Gray; with lecture by Doc Rockwell); "Pas de Deux" (danced by Alicia Markova and Anton Dolin); "They All Made Good" (Doc Rockwell, The Young Hopefuls); Finale (Doc Rockwell, Entire Company)

Billy Rose's production of *Seven Lively Arts* was one of the decade's event musicals. Rose had bought the Ziegfeld Theatre and had refurbished it, and the revue was the first production to play there under his ownership. Opening night tickets cost a then unheard-of $24.00 apiece, and during intermission the audience was served complimentary champagne. On exhibit in the theatre's lower lobby was a display of seven especially commissioned paintings by Salvador Dali which depicted his "surrealist conception" of the seven lively arts. It was estimated that the purchase of the theatre itself, its refurbishment, and the cost of the revue totaled two million dollars. The revue offered new sketches by Moss Hart and George S. Kaufman (each writing separate, not collaborative, sketches) and songs by Cole Porter (and with original ballet music by Igor Stravinsky). The revue starred Beatrice Lillie, Bert Lahr, and Benny Goodman, and prominent among the featured performers were Dolores Gray and Bill (William) Tabbert.

The production had originally been conceived as a book musical that dealt with seven young hopefuls who go to New York in search of fame in the seven areas of the arts: painting (Nan Wynn), tap dancing (Jere McMahon), radio singing (Paula Bane), ballet dancing (Billie Worth), play writing (Bill Tabbert), film acting (Dolores Gray), and stage acting (Mary Roche). The concept was soon dropped and the evening evolved into a revue, but the basic hook of the seven young hopefuls was retained for the opening (the song "Big Town") and closing (the overall sequence titled "They All Made Good"). And throughout the evening, these seven performers took part in most of the songs and dances. By the end of the run, the closing sequence had been dropped. And when Dolores Gray left the production, she wasn't replaced for a long period and so for a while there were just six hopefuls; and thus the trio "Wow-ooh-wolf!" for Wynn, Gray, and Roche became a duet for Wynn and Roche. When Benny Goodman left the production, he was replaced by The Cozy Cole Quintet (which besides Cole included among others Tiny Grimes, Don Byas, and Billy Taylor). Throughout the evening, Doc Rockwell served as a kind of master of ceremonies and chatted up the audience with occasional bits of humor.

The critics agreed that Beatrice Lillie's sparkling performance was the revue's finest, and her sketches (all by Moss Hart) were the best of the evening. In "There'll Always Be an England," she portrayed the clueless British spinster Lady Agatha who visits a canteen for American servicemen; she's made a careful study of American lingo and tries to be "one of the boys" with her slang. But she doesn't realize her expressions don't mean what she thinks they mean, and thus her sexual innuendo sends the young American doughboys reeling in shock. In "Ticket for the Ballet" she played another clueless character, this time a customer waiting in line to buy a ticket to the ballet; she doesn't know much about dancing, but thinks the ballet "S. Hurok" might be interesting to see. And the sketch "Heaven on Angel Street" managed to intertwine the plots of *Angel Street*, *Life with Father*, and *Tobacco Road* into one play and also worked in some swipes about the critics (one performer played the role of George Jean Nathan). She also excelled in a mad little song that exemplified her brand of musical humor in "When I Was a Little Cuckoo," and in "Dancin' to a Jungle Drum (Let's End the Beguine)" she expressed her weariness with South Sea Island romance music.

Unfortunately, Bert Lahr was short-changed in his material, and Lillie clearly outshone him. His high point was "Drink," a hilarious drinking song for him and the male chorus (three different critics used the same description when they said it was the "drinking song to end all drinking songs"). Otherwise, the evening offered a bit of classical ballet (with original music by Igor Stravinsky) and swing music by Benny Goodman. The latter and his musicians took part in the first act finale, which kidded Rose with the sequence "Billy Rose Buys the Metropolitan Opera House!"

Burton Rascoe in the *New York World-Telegram* said Beatrice Lillie was "glorious . . . the world's greatest satiric comedienne, the incomparable empress of witty pantomime"; and he noted that as Lady Agatha she "shocked" the servicemen "to death" with her inadvertent ribaldry; he also noted the physical production was lavish in its "breath-taking dream-world." Wilella Waldorf in the *New York Post* said the "mammoth musical" was apparently conceived as an entertainment with "something for just about everybody," and she guessed this idea was "probably sound" because it offered "so many different moods." Ward Morehouse in the *New York Sun* praised the "whopping show," which was "big and beautiful" with "elaborate special effects" in "the tradition of Ziegfeld lavishness"; and he noted the "perfect clown" Lillie was in "great form." He singled out a number of "nice" Porter songs, including "Is It the Girl? (or Is It the Gown?)," "Hence It Don't Make Sense," "Only Another Boy and Girl," and "Wow-ooh-wolf!"

Robert Garland in the *New York Journal-American* said the evening was "long, opulent," and "beautiful" but not as "tuneful" and "laughable" as it might have been; but there was enough "first-rate material for a history-making enterprise." He liked Lahr in the sketch "Local Boy Makes Good," in which Lahr portrays a fellow who has indeed risen to the heights of money and power in the theatrical profession . . . you see, he's a stagehand (at one point, he's shocked *shocked* to think he's supposed to pick up a prop chair *all by himself*). Garland also noted the Lady Agatha sketch had been "cleaned up" since the Philadelphia tryout.

Despite the revue's "extravagance of talent and production pomp," Howard Barnes in the *New York Herald Tribune* found the evening "ordinary" and "disappointing" (but noted Lillie accented the "high points" with her "stunning and brilliantly variegated musical pot-pourri" whenever she appeared on the stage). John Chapman in the *New York Daily News* said Lillie had never been funnier and that he liked Lahr as the stagehand who hates scenery, and he singled out Porter's "really witty" song "Wow-ooh-wolf!" But he noted the evening was too long and needed to pick up some speed; nonetheless, he guaranteed that "if you can get in" you'd get your money's worth.

Lewis Nichols in the *New York Times* said the evening "was undoubtedly Miss Lillie's"; as for the revue itself, it needed cutting because there was too much of everything (but he quickly noted that "more than enough of it is good"). While he felt Porter's songs were "not his best," he nonetheless singled out "Ev'ry Time We Say Goodbye" and "Frahngee-Pahnee." Louis Kronenberger in *PM* said there was much that was "wrong" with *Seven Lively Arts*, but "all in all it's a darn good show." Lillie was the evening's "great personality" and she was "as wonderful as ever." He felt Porter had done "nothing overpowering" with the songs, but noted "Ev'ry Time We Say Goodbye" was "pleasant" and "Wow-ooh-wolf!" was "rather amusing."

In his annual review, George Jean Nathan said the revue was "in large part a dandy," was "handsomely" staged by Hassard Short, and was "no less handsomely set and costumed." He noted many highlights, including the Lady Agatha sketch in which Lillie's clueless American lingo "startles the boys out of their wits with its sexual double entendre" and Lahr's drinking song. He said that one of the evening's "lowlights" was the sketch in which he himself was spoofed; he found it "too strainedly polite" and suggested it required a "more hearty impudence and vulgarity."

"The Band Started Swinging a Song" was performed during the tryout by Nan Wynn in the "They All Made Good" sequence; it wasn't listed in the early New York programs, but eventually was. *The Collected Lyrics of Cole Porter* suggests the number was either added after the New York opening or was perhaps inadvertently omitted from early programs. Similarly, "The Big Parade"/"Yours for a Song" sequence may have been part of the skit "Billy Rose Buys the Metropolitan Opera House!"

Deleted during the tryout was "Pretty Little Missus Belle"; songs dropped during preproduction were: "Dainty, Quainty Me," "I Wrote a Play," "If I Hadn't a Husband," "Where Do We Go from Here?," and "Café Society Still Carries On." "Let's End the Beguine" was rewritten as "Dancin' to a Jungle Drum."

All the used, deleted, revised, and unused songs are included in *The Collected Lyrics of Cole Porter*.

The only song from the score that has emerged as a standard is the ethereal "Ev'ry Time We Say Goodbye," which has been frequently recorded. Over the years, a number of other songs from the production have been recorded, including the shimmering and velvety "Frahngee-Pahnee," the tongue-twisting, jive-talking verbal pyrotechnics of "Hence It Don't Make Sense" (which irrefutably proves that a skunk isn't French perfume), "Is It the Girl? (or Is It the Gown?)" (which opens up all sorts of possibilities in its suggestion that some men may prefer a girl's "exquisite" gown to the girl herself), "Big Town," and the somewhat simpering "Only Another Boy and Girl."

Cole Porter Revisited Volume III (Painted Smiles CD # PSCD-105) includes the deleted "I Wrote a Play" and the cut "Pretty Little Missus Belle." Dolores Gray re-created her original performance of "Is It the Girl? (or Is It the Gown?)" for the collection *Cole Porter Revisited Volume IV* (Painted Smiles CD PSCD-117). The collection *Cole Porter Volume 4* (Pearl Records CD # GEM-0195) includes "Only Another Boy and Girl" (The Benny Goodman Quintet with vocal by June Harvey) and "Ev'ry Time We Say Goodbye" (The Teddy Wilson Quintet with vocal by Maxine Sullivan), and *Cole Porter (Music and Lyrics)* (JJA Records LP # 19745) includes "Is It the Girl? (or Is It the Gown?)" and "Frahngee-Pahnee" (both sung by Thomas L. Thomas), "Ev'ry Time We Say Goodbye" and "Only Another Boy and Girl" (Dorothy Kirsten), and "Hence It Don't Make Sense" (Tony Pastor). *Thomas Hampson Sings Cole Porter* (EMI Classics # CDC-7-54203-2; conducted by John McGlinn) includes "Drink."

Incidentally, just how often do the words "banyan tree" pop up in the lyrics of musicals? And what are the chances that one performer would be given two songs in two musicals that include those words? "Banyan tree" is part of "Frahngee-Pahnee," which Bill Tabbert sang in the revue; and later in the decade (as William Tabbert) he introduced "My Girl Back Home" in **South Pacific**, in which he again sang of banyan trees (the song was cut during the tryout but was reinstated for the 1958 film version). But for *Pippin* (1972), it was Ben Vereen, not Tabbert, who mentions a banyan tree in Stephen Schwartz's song "Simple Joys."

LAFFING ROOM ONLY
"THEIR NEW MUSICAL MADHOUSE"

Theatre: Winter Garden Theatre
Opening Date: December 23, 1944; *Closing Date*: July 14, 1945
Performances: 233
Sketches: Ole Olsen, Chic Johnson, and Eugene Conrad
Lyrics and *Music*: Burton Lane
Direction: Production staged by John Murray Anderson, supervised by Harry Kaufman, and comedy directed by Edward Cline; *Producers*: The Messrs. Shubert, Ole Olsen, and Chic Johnson; *Choreography*: Robert Alton; *Scenery*: Stewart Chaney; *Costumes*: Billy Livingston; *Lighting*: Uncredited; *Musical Direction*: John McManus
Cast: *Ole Olsen, Chic Johnson*, Frank Libuse, Betty Garrett, Willie West and McGinty, Mata and Hari, Margot Brander, Ethel Owen, William Archibald, Kathryn Lee, Pat Brewster, Ida James, O'Donnell Blair, Bruce Evans, Robert Breton, Lou Wills, Jr., Harry Burns, Penny Edwards, Billy Young, Joe Young, Charles Senna, Ernest (Ernie) D'Amato, Kenny Buffett, Frances Henderson, Jean Moorehead (Moorhead), Shannon Dean, Catherine Johnson, Tom McKee and Sam Kramer, Stanley Stevens and "Big Boy," Virginia Barrett, Eddie Vincent with Chico and Coco, Dippy Diers, Billy West, Mary La Roche, Charles O'Donnell, Gus Stevens, John Stevens, Jennie Lewis, Andrew Ratousheff, Susan West, Ted McGinty, Francis Henderson, Tom Fletcher, Robert Breton, Rhythm Red; The Glee Club: Ruth Cottingham, Johanna Gillman, Betty Gilpat-

rick, Jocelyn McIntyre, Lewis Appleton, George Beach, Gerard Bercier, Gene Bone, Francis Cooke, Burk Esaias, John Ferguson, Jerry Gilbert, James Kovach, Allan Leonard, Roger Miller, Fred Peters, Roy Russell, Edward Sanders, Otto Simanek, Tommy Thompson; Dancers: May Block, Jean Bortz, Lillian Cross, Dotty Dee, Eloise Farmer, Virginia Gorski (Gibson), Gae Hess, Penny Holt, Gretchen Houser, Elana Keller, Marjorie Johnstone, Lee Joyce, Eleanor Leaman, Patricia Lenn, Marcia Maier, June Walker, Doris York, Ray Arnett, Forrest Bonshire, Ronny Chetwood, Norman Drew, Jack Pierce, Kenneth (Ken) Peterson, J. C. McCord, Budd Rogers, Herbert Ross

The revue was presented in two acts.

Sketches and Musical Numbers

Act One: Before the Show: In the Lobby—Dippy Diers, Billy West, Harry Burns; In the Audience—Frank Libuse; Overture (The Conductor: Frank Libuse; Stage Manager: Charles Senna; Company Manager: Fred Peters); "The Russian Art Players" (Anna: Catherine Johnson; Sonya: Mary La Roche; Count Dimitri Resluvsky: Robert Breton; Prince Vasiloff: Bruce Evans); "Hooray for Anywhere" (Pat Brewster, The Glee Club; danced by Frances Henderson, Kenny Buffett, Dancers); Ole Olsen and Chic Johnson; "The White House" Guests and Tourists: Frank Libuse, Margot Brander, Pat Brewster, Charles O'Donnell, Joe Young, Shannon Dean, Charles Senna, Harry Burns, Stanley Stevens, Ernie D'Amato, Billy Young, Jean Moorehead, Penny Edwards, Bruce Evans, Frances Henderson, Betty Gilpatrick, Doris York, Lee Joyce; and Olsen and Johnson); "Go Down to Boston Harbor" (ballet music by Alan Moran) (Betty Garrett; danced by Kathryn Lee, William Archibald, J. C. McCord; British Soldiers: Norman Drew, Herbert Ross, Ronny Chetwood, Kenneth Peterson; Conspirators: Elana Keller, J. C. McCord; Girl Patriots: Gae Hess, Marcia Maier, Lillian Cross, Eleanor Leaman, Eloise Farmer; Corps de Ballet; General Duquesne: Chic Johnson); "The Russian Art Players" (Colonel: Bruce Evans; Firing Squad: Francis Cooke, John Ferguson, Jerry Gilbert); Mata and Hari; "An Apartment in 1980" (Real Estate Agent: Ole Olsen; Mr. Tenant: Chic Johnson; Mrs. Tenant: Ethel Owen; Miner: Frank Libuse; Stanley, Gus, and John Stevens, Dippy Diers, Jennie Lewis, Andrew Ratousheff, Harry Burns, Billy Young, Susan West, Bruce Evans, Shannon Dean, Pat Brewster, Charles Senna, Ted McGinty; Eddie Vincent with Chico and Coco); "Moments Musical" (Harpist: Frank Libuse; Soprano: Margot Brander; Flutist: Tom McKee; Cellist: Sam Kramer); "Stop That Dancing" (Betty Garrett; The Sailor: William Archibald; In Central Park: Penny Holt, Jack Pierce; On Broadway: Eleanor Leaman, Ronny Chetwood, Lillian Cross, Herbert Ross; In Greenwich Village: Frances Henderson, Forrest Bonshire, Gae Hess, J. C. McCord, Marcia Maier; At El Morocco: Penny Edwards, Kenny Buffett, Marjorie Johnstone, Virginia Gorski, May Block, Dotty Dee; In Harlem: Gretchen Houser, Ken Peterson, Ray Arnett, Lee Joyce; The Glee Club and The Corps de Ballet); "Pocatello, Idaho" (Ole Olsen, Joe Young, Chic Johnson); "The Russian Art Players"; "The Ghost Train (A Night on a Union Pacific Pullman)" (Ole Olsen, Chic Johnson; O'Donnell Blair, Ernie D'Amato, Billy West, Fred Peters, Tom McKee, Virginia Barrett, Shannon Dean, Tom Fletcher, Billy Young, Joe Young, Jean Moorehead, Penny Edwards, Susan West, Harry Burns, Jennie Lewis, Frances Henderson, Pat Brewster, Ethel Owen, Charles Senna, Roy Russell); "This Is as Far as I Go" (Betty Garrett; Ray Arnett, Forrest Bonshire, Ronny Chetwood, Norman Drew, Kenneth Peterson, Jack Pierce, J. C. McCord, Budd Rogers, Herbert Ross); Willie West and McGinty; Stanley Stevens and "Big Boy"; "Fussin', Feudin' and Fightin'" (Pat Brewster, The Glee Club; danced by Kathryn Lee, William Archibald, and The Corps de Ballet; Mother Hatfield: Eleanor Leaman; Grandmother: June Walker; Daughter: Kathryn Lee; Father: Herbert Ross; Uncles: Ronny Chetwood, Norman Drew; McCoy Son: William Archibald; Maw McCoy: Ethel Owen; Child: Jean Moorehead; Neighbors: Stanley Stevens, Virginia Barrett, Billy Young; Judge: Bruce Evans; Bridegroom: Ole Olsen; Paw: Harry Burns; Bride: Chic Johnson; Sons: Robert Breton, Charles Senna, Ernie D'Amato); "Gotta Get Joy" (Entire Company); In the Box—Frank Libuse, Margot Brander, Virginia Barrett, Andrew Ratousheff, Dippy Diers

Act Two: "Got That Good Time Feelin' (Mississippi)" (Ida James, The Glee Club; First Ballerina: Kathryn Lee; The Beau: Kenny Buffett; The Suitor: Ronny Chetwood; The Corps de Ballet); "The Piano Movers" (Ole Olsen, Chic Johnson, O'Donnell Blair, Lou Wills, Jr.); "Sunny California" (Betty Garrett; The Hollywood Star: Penny Edwards; The Hollywood Producer: William Archibald; The Cameraman: Lewis Appleton; Chauffer: Rhythm Red; Ensemble, Mata and Hari); "In a Radio Station" (Radio Announcer: Ole Olsen; The Glee Club; The Sound Man: Chic Johnson; Ethel Owen, Billy Young, Charles Senna, Jean Moorehead,

Shannon Dean, Jennie Lewis, Andrew Ratousheff, Tom Fletcher, Susan West, Virginia Barrett, Bruce Evans, Tom McKee, Gretchen Houser); "The Hellzapoppin' Polka" (danced by Virginia Barrett, Ruth Cottingham, Jean Moorehead, Doris York, Shannon Dean, Betty Gilpatrick, Johanna Gillman, Mary La Roche, Jocelyn McIntyre, Penny Holt, Susan West, Jennie Lewis, Frances Henderson); "The Steps of the Capitol" (Betty Garrett, Pat Brewster, The Glee Club)

Ole Olsen and Chic Johnson's revue *Laffing Room Only* (which was sometimes advertised with an exclamation point) managed a seven-month run on Broadway, turned a profit, and then played a lengthy national tour with many of the original cast members, including Olsen, Johnson, and Betty Garrett (the latter was eventually succeeded by Mary La Roche). As noted in the entry for the team's **Sons o' Fun**, the comedians were active in theatrical revues for over fifteen years, but the law of diminishing returns set in and the runs became shorter and shorter (in 1954, their final offering *Pardon Our Antenna* closed prior to its Broadway opening).

Laffing Room Only opened at the Winter Garden Theatre, the home of Olsen and Johnson's earlier hits *Hellzapoppin'* (1938) and **Sons o' Fun**, but this time around the critics were less than enthusiastic and suggested the broad, madcap shenanigans were wearing out their welcome. But enough audiences showed up in New York and on the road to put the revue into the hit column.

The revue was perhaps more structured than the team's previous outings, and so there were more standard sequences of song and dance, with most of the numbers performed by Betty Garrett, who, like Nanette Fabray, was becoming a fixture in the era's revues and musicals (including two replacement roles, Fabray appeared in eight musicals during the decade and Garrett was in six). But there were still the comics who roamed about the theatre before the show and during intermission, and the audience was treated to a midget dressed in diapers who grabbed at the legs of hapless customers; comics who sprayed seltzer bottles at one another; a man who called out for "Harvey, Harvey" as he carried live rabbits in his arms; and Big Boy, a live six-hundred-pound bear (according to Ward Morehouse in the *New York Sun*, Big Boy was "amiable" and John Chapman in the *New York Daily News* reported he had "a sense of humor"); and male cast members in servicemen's uniforms who then added bras, panties, and girdles to their uniforms and proceeded to cavort about the auditorium.

Shots of gunfire crackled throughout the evening; blackouts were punctuated with the blood-curdling screams of unseen women; and audience members were asked to wave their handkerchiefs back and forth in the air and to sometimes join in a community sing (and lucky ones received gifts from the cast members, such as cans of Esso lubricating oil). And let's not forget the sausage, which throughout the evening was passed around from one audience member to another; and beer, candy (some of which was stuffed with sawdust), and toupees (the latter for follically challenged gentlemen in the audience) were also handed out.

A stooge in one of the box seats shouted that he was going to shoot the rat who invaded his home; later, there was a pistol shot and when a spotlight shone upon the man, he proudly held aloft a huge stuffed rodent. Another performer picked up his telephone to order whiskey and soda, and then was sprayed by the liquid as it spurted through the phone; and, ignoring the rule of fool-me-once, he then ordered a cup of coffee, and it too sprayed him. One performer is "plastered" in the mode of Rodin's statue "The Thinker," and at one point is shown seated on a toilet, and in another sequence a Scot in a kilt goes into a ladies' room, only to be kicked out (he thought he was in the "laddies' room"). A few critics reported that on opening night the stagehands became confused (and with all the goings-on, no wonder) and so one first-act sequence ("Moments Musical") was stopped in its tracks and was only resumed once the second act got under way.

Some critics objected to the "bad taste" of having a performer appear throughout the evening wearing a mask with huge false teeth that represented Eleanor Roosevelt (it was "shamelessly vulgar ridicule," according to Burton Rascoe in the *New York World-Telegram*), and some questioned why a religious hymn was used as the catalyst for a spray of gunfire (chorus members in choir-boy outfits began to sing "Silent Night" and then shot off blank cartridges). There was also some off-color humor, including a segment in which male members of the cast carry drooping rubber rifles; but at the sight of an almost naked woman, the rifles magically become firm and erect.

The revue also poked fun at the McCoy and Hatfield feud (in the sequence that included "Fussin', Feudin' and Fightin'") and gave Chic Johnson the opportunity to don drag as a hillbilly bride. There were also looks at apartment living in the future ("An Apartment in 1980") and a comical train trip ("The Ghost Train," or "A Night on a Union Pacific Pullman").

Howard Barnes in the *New York Herald Tribune* said nothing could make a "purse" out of the revue; it lacked "fun or taste" and only a "smattering" of it could be "vaguely" termed as "entertainment"; Louis Kronenberger in *PM* stated Olsen and Johnson were not his "feedbag," but like most of the reviewers he predicted the show would be a hit (but Rascoe noted that the "arithmetical retrogression" of the runs of *Hellzapoppin'* and **Sons o' Fun** suggested that *Laffing Room Only* wouldn't last as long as its predecessors and would in fact play for just 396 showings [it actually played for 233]).

James Aronson in the *New York Post* said the material was familiar but still "pretty funny," and noted the humor was "strictly" from Minsky and sometimes from "low" in the "barrel"; Chapman suggested the evening was OK, but you definitely had to be "in the mood" for it; and Morehouse noted that while the "cannonading" went on for three hours, the "fun" was considerably shorter than that, and so he only "intermittently" enjoyed himself.

Garland said the evening was "tactless, tasteless and tiresome"; Olsen and Johnson had heretofore been "corny but contagious cut-ups" and were now "irksome, mechanical and off-key"; but Lewis Nichols in the *New York Times* felt it was "good" to have the team back on Broadway, and while he noted the evening was sometimes "tiresome" it was nonetheless in the team's familiar mold of "big and loud, gaudy and not infrequently vulgar" humor.

During the tryout, the sketch "Balloons!" was dropped, and "The Hellzapoppin' Polka" was titled "The Pocatello Polka." At some point during the post-Broadway tour, "The Hellzapoppin' Polka" was eliminated and "The Doolittle Hop" was substituted.

Although composer Burton Lane was officially credited with the revue's lyrics, Steven Suskin in *Show Music* reports the lyrics were by Al Dubin with possibly an assist from Frank Loesser (including "Fussin', Feudin' and Fightin'"). The latter became a hit song a few years after the revue closed, and is the only song from any of the Olsen and Johnson revues to achieve popularity.

John Murray Anderson's assistant was Arny (Arnold) Saint-Subber, who as Saint Subber later produced such musicals as **Kiss Me, Kate**, *Out of This World* (1951), and *House of Flowers* (1954).

The Olsen and Johnson revues were of their moment, and shows of their ilk could never be profitably produced today (but with the almost obsessive need of modern audiences to be "part" of the theatrical experience, you never know . . .). Certainly one shtick in *Laffing Room Only* would be welcome today: during the revue's overture, the conductor occasionally turned around, faced the audience, and told them to *shut up*.

A TROPICAL REVUE

Theatre: New Century Theatre
Opening Date: December 26, 1944; *Closing Date*: January 13, 1945
Performances: 24
Direction: Dale Wasserman; *Producer*: S. Hurok; *Choreography*: Katherine Dunham; *Scenery* and *Costumes*: John Pratt; *Lighting*: Dale Wasserman; *Musical Direction*: Martin Gabowitz
Cast: *Katherine Dunham*, Helen Dowdy, Roger Ohardieno, Tommy Gomez, Talley Beatty, Claude Marchant, Lucille Ellis, Lavinia Williams, Syvilla Fort, Lenwood Morris, Vanoye Aikens, Lawaune Ingram, Ramona Erwin, Bobby Capo, Rosalia King, Howard Carlos, Oliver Busch, Andre Drew, Eddy Clay, Ora Lee, Richardena Jackson, Dolores Harper, Gloria Mitchell; *Percussion*: Astrada; *Drums*: Oscar Estrada, Julio Mendez, Candido Vicenty
The revue was presented in two acts.

Musical Numbers

Act One: "Rara Tonga" (music by Paquita Anderson) (The Chosen Woman: Ramona Erwin; The God: Roger Ohardieno; The Jealous Husband: Tommy Gomez; Narrator: Katherine Dunham); "Cuban Slave Lament" (The Singer: Bobby Capo; Possessed Dancer: Lucille Ellis); "Moorish Bolero" (music by Paquita Anderson) (Lavinia Williams, Tommy Gomez, Group); "Choro" (Katherine Dunham, Syvilla Fort, Lenwood Morris, Tommy Gomez); "Rumba with a Little Jive Mixed In" (music by Andre) (Lucille Ellis, Vanoye Aikens, Claude Marchant); "Bahiana" (music by Don Alfonso) (Katherine Dunham with Roger Ohardieno, Vanoye

Aikens, Talley Beatty, Tommy Gomez); "Tropics—Shore Excursion" (music by Paquita Anderson) (Woman with Cigar: Katherine Dunham; Dockhand: Roger Ohardieno; Percussionist: Astrada); "Para que tu veas" (Bobby Capo); "Promenade—Havana 1910" (music by Mercedes Navarro) (Katherine Dunham, Company, Bobby Capo, The Dowdy Quartet)

Act Two: "L'Ag'Ya" (music by Robert Sanders) (Loulouse: Katherine Dunham; Alcide: Vanoye Aikens; Julor: Claude Marchant; Roi Zombie: Roger Ohardieno; Fishermen, Street Vendors, Zombies, Townspeople of Vauclin: The Katherine Dunham Company); "Street Scene—Port au Prince" (Lucille Ellis, Astrada, Julio Mendez); "Strutters' Ball" (Helen Dowdy, Rosalia King, Howard Carlos, Oliver Busch); "Cakewalk" (Syvilla Fort, Vanoye Aikens, Company); "Barrel House" ("A Florida Swamp Shimmy") (music by Meade Lux Lewis and Albert Ammons) (Katherine Dunham, Roger Ohardieno); "Flaming Youth—1927" (music by "Brad" Gowans) (Blues Singer: Helen Dowdy; Kansas City Woman: Lucille Ellis; with Tommy Gomez); "Charleton," "Black Bottom," "Mooch," and "Fishtail" (Lawaune Ingram, Claude Marchant, Ensemble); Finale (The Katherine Dunham Dancers)

Katherine Dunham's *A Tropical Revue* had opened on Broadway the previous season; the current production was technically a return engagement, but about 60 percent of the material was new, and much of it would surface again in her later Broadway engagements (for a list of Dunham's other Broadway visits, see entry for the 1943 production).

SING OUT, SWEET LAND!
"A SALUTE TO AMERICAN FOLK AND POPULAR MUSIC" / "THE NEW MUSICAL HIT"

Theatre: International Theatre
Opening Date: December 27, 1944; *Closing Date*: March 24, 1945
Performances: 102
Book: Walter Kerr
Lyrics and *Music*: *Note*: See song list for credits (the music was arranged by Elie Siegmeister).
Direction: Book directed by Walter Kerr; production staged by Leon Leonidoff; and production supervised by Lawrence Langner and Theresa Helburn; *Producer*: The Theatre Guild; *Choreography*: Doris Humphrey and Charles Weidman; *Scenery*: Albert Johnson; *Costumes*: Lucinda Ballard; *Lighting*: Uncredited; *Musical Direction*: Elie Siegmeister; *Choral Direction*: Verse Chorus directed by Arthur Lessac and Spiritual Ensemble coached by Juanita Hall
Cast: Alfred Drake (Barnaby Goodchild), Burl Ives, Bibi Osterwald, Alma Kaye, Philip Coolidge (Killjoy), Jack McCauley, Robert Penn, James Westerfield, Peter Hamilton, Irene Hawthorne, Ethel Mann, Jules Racine, Ted Tiller, Adrienne Gray, Charles Hart; Vocal Ensemble: Dorothy Baxter, Cathleen Chambers, Marjorie Chandler, Carol Hall, Irene Jordan, Selma Rogoff, Phyliss Wilcox, Maria Wilde, George Cassidy, Charles Ford, Lawrence Gilbert, Sam Green, Calvin Harris, Edwin Marsh, Fred Rivetti, Ludlow White, Fred Kohler; Dancers: Peggy Campbell, Roberta Cassell, Margaret Cuddy, Ann S. Halprin, Christine Karner, Ethel Mann, Patricia (Pat) Newman, Miriam Pandor, Frances Rainer, Harriett Roeder, Helen Waggoner, Ann Williams, Kendrick Coy, Joseph Gifford, Joseph Landis, Robert Mayo, Joseph Precker, Sam Steen, Bill Summer, Bill Weaver; Verse Chorus: Morty Halpern, Ellen Love, Dorothy Baxter, Carol Hall, Irene Jordan, Christine Karner, Ethel Mann, Patricia Newman, Frances Rainer, George Cassidy, Joseph Gifford, Sam Green, Robert Mayo, Fred Rivetti, Ludlow White; Spiritual Ensemble: Juanita Hall, Rhoda Boggs, Claretta Freeman, Massine Patterson, Hercules Armstrong, Harry Bolden, Oscar Brooks, James Gordon, Vitres Reese, Wilson Woodbeck, William Sol
The musical was presented in two acts.
The action takes place throughout the United States (and on an aircraft carrier overseas) from the Puritan era to the present time.

Musical Numbers

Act One: "Who Is the Man" (Puritan hymn, authorship unknown) (Vocal Ensemble); "As I Was Going Along" (by Elie Siegmeister and Edgar Eager, based on a folk song [authorship unknown]) (Alfred Drake); "Way

Down the Ohio" (folk song, authorship unknown) (Alfred Drake);"Mountain Whirlpool" (poem by Stephen Vincent Benet) (recited by Alfred Drake); "Country Dance" (choreographed by Charles Weidman) (Dancing Ensemble); "When I Was Single" (folk song, authorship unknown) (Bibi Osterwald); "Foggy, Foggy Dew" (folk song, authorship unknown) (Burl Ives); "Hardly Think (I Will)" (folk song, authorship unknown) (Adrienne Gray, Ted Tiller); "The Devil and the Farmer's Wife" (folk song, authorship unknown) (Alfred Drake, Ensemble); "Little Mohee" (Kentucky mountain ballad, authorship unknown) (Alfred Drake, Alma Kaye); "Oregon Trail" (poem by James Marshall) (recited by Ellen Love and Verse Chorus); "Oh Susannah" (lyric and music by Stephen Foster) (Vocal Ensemble); "Springfield Mountain" (authorship unknown) (Alfred Drake); "Hammer Ring" (work chant, authorship unknown) (Spiritual Ensemble); "Watermelon Cry" (authorship unknown) (Juanita Hall); "You Better Mind" (spiritual, authorship unknown) (Spiritual Ensemble); "Didn't My Lord Deliver Daniel" (spiritual, authorship unknown) (Spiritual Ensemble); "The Roving Gambler" (ballad, authorship unknown) (Jack McCauley, Alma Kaye, Ellen Love); "Louisiana Gals" (minstrel song, lyric and music by Cool White) and "Camptown Races" (lyric and music by Stephen Foster) (Vocal Ensemble; choreography by Charles Weidman, and danced by Peter Hamilton, Irene Hawthorne, Dancing Ensemble); "Frankie and Johnny" (folk song, authorship unknown) (staged by Walter Kerr) (Burl Ives, Alma Kaye, Jack McCauley, Philip Coolidge, Christine Karner, Ted Tiller); "Polly Wolly Doodle" (folk song, authorship unknown) (staged by Doris Humphrey) (Company)

Act Two: "Cap't Jinks" (Civil War song, authorship unknown) (Male Ensemble); "Blue Tail Fly" (Civil War song, authorship unknown) (Burl Ives); "Marching Down This Road" (folk song, authorship unknown) (Alfred Drake, Burl Ives); "Casey Jones" (lyric by Wallace Saunders and Lawrence Seibert, music by Eddie Newton) (Bibi Osterwald, James Westerfield, Morty Helpern); "Rock Candy Mountain" (hobo song, authorship unknown) (Burl Ives); "I Have Been a Good Boy" (folk song, authorship unknown) (Jack McCauley); "Wanderin'" (hobo song, authorship unknown) (Alfred Drake); "Hallelujah, I'm a Bum" (hobo song, lyric by Joe Hill [not the title song from Richard Rodgers and Lorenz Hart's 1933 film]) (Alfred Drake); "Jesse James" (poem by William Rose Benet) (staged by Charles Weidman) (recited by Morty Halpern, Verse Chorus; danced by Peter Hamilton); "While Strolling Through the Park One Day" (lyric and music by Ed Haley) (Vocal Ensemble); "Bicycle Built for Two" (aka "Daisy Bell") (lyric and music by Harry Dacre) (Alma Kaye, Ted Tiller); "Heaven Will Protect the Working Girl" (lyric by Smith and Sloane) (Alma Kaye, Ted Tiller); "There'll Be a Hot Time in the Old Town Tonight" (lyric by Joe Hayden, music by Theodore August Metz) (Alfred Drake, Burl Ives, Alma Kaye, Ted Tiller); "Trouble, Trouble" (blues, authorship unknown) (Ruth Tyler); Ragtime Sequence (choreographed by Doris Humphrey): (a) "By the Sea" (aka "By the Beautiful Sea") (lyric by Harold B. Atteridge, music by Harry Carroll); (b) "Come Josephine in My Flying Machine" (lyric by Alfred Bryan, music by Fred Fisher); and (c) "Maxixe" (lyric and music by Tracy and Walker); "Funny Bunny Hug" (lyric and music by W. Raymond Walker and Tracy) (Alfred Drake); "Temptation Rag" (lyric and music by Henry Lodge) (performer[s] unknown); "Hey, Mr. Bossman" (jail song, lyric and music adapted from a folk theme by Elie Siegmeister) (Ruth Tyler); "Basement Blues" (blues, lyric and music by W. C. Handy) (Ruth Tyler, Spiritual Ensemble; danced by Dancing Ensemble); "Some of These Men" (blues, authorship unknown) (Ruth Tyler, Ensemble); "I Got Rhythm" (from *Girl Crazy*, 1930; lyric by Ira Gershwin, music by George Gershwin) (choreographed by Charles Weidman) (Dancing Ensemble); "At Sundown" (lyric and music by Walter Donaldson) (Alfred Drake); "My Blue Heaven" (lyric by George A. Whiting, music by Walter Donaldson) (Alfred Drake); "Yes, Sir, She's My Baby!" (lyric by Gus Kahn, music by Walter Donaldson) (Bibi Osterwald); "Charleston" (*Runnin' Wild*, 1923; lyric by Cecil Mack, music by James P. Johnson) (choreographed by Charles Weidman) (danced by Peter Hamilton, Irene Hawthorne, Dancing Ensemble); "Sea Chanty" (authorship unknown) (Burl Ives); "Where" (lyric by Edward Eager, music by John Mundy) (Alfred Drake); "More Than These" (lyric by Edward Eager, music by John Mundy) (staged by Doris Humphrey) (Alfred Drake, Entire Company)

With its enormously successful **Oklahoma!** in the second year of its marathon five-year run, the Theatre Guild offered up another slice of Americana with *Sing Out, Sweet Land!*, a retrospective of American folk songs and popular music. This was indeed the era that offered nostalgic looks at the country's past; besides **Oklahoma!**, **Bloomer Girl** had opened earlier in the season and **Up in Central Park** and the Theatre Guild's **Carousel** were just around the corner. But *Sing Out, Sweet Land!* was more in the nature of a revue and was a musical and spiritual granddaddy to the 1964 World's Fair revue *To Broadway with Love* as well as various tributes to American music that surfaced during the nation's Bicentennial, such as *Music! Music!* (which opened at City Center in 1974 for thirty-seven performances); *A Musical Jubilee* (St. James Theatre, for ninety-two performances in 1975); and *Sing America Sing*, which briefly toured in 1975 with John Raitt but wisely never braved New York.

Although the program referred to Walter Kerr's "book," the evening was for the most part an almost plotless revue-like series of musical numbers that depicted America's music from the Puritan era in New England through the period of the Civil War and into the present-day War Forties with a scene on an aircraft carrier. In between, there were stops in the Illinois Wilderness, the Oregon Trail, the South, and the Mississippi River, and visits to Texas, city parks, and even a speakeasy. (Wilella Waldorf in the *New York Post* noted that perhaps the only momentous American event not covered during the evening was the opening of the Erie Canal.)

In order to provide continuity for the evening's cavalcade of songs, Kerr created the role of Barnaby Goodchild (Alfred Drake), who is first seen in a stockade during Puritan times when he's punished by Parson Killjoy (Philip Coolidge) for the crime of singing. Throughout the show, and the centuries, the ageless and free-spirited singer Barnaby is always pursued by Killjoy. But, guess what: the music wins out. (The critics described Barnaby as both a Paul Bunyan and Johnny Appleseed type, and Robert Garland in the *New York Journal-American* said he was a sort of "Wandering Gentile.")

The critics felt that an entire evening of mostly familiar folk songs and other popular music became somewhat monotonous, and said the slender Barnaby-Killjoy thread soon grew tiresome. But they praised the singers, and in particular singled out Burl Ives.

Lewis Nichols in the *New York Times* said the evening was generally "disappointing" because Walter Kerr's "coy, cute" and "often childish" book had the choice of burlesquing the material or playing it straight for nostalgic appeal; unfortunately, Kerr chose the former path and thus the show could have been titled *Swing Out, Sweet Land!* Further, Drake's character should have been Bunyanesque but was instead a "tiresome" and "playful sophomore." Waldorf said the endless stream of folk songs spread "deadly monotony" over the evening, and soon there was even "too much" of Drake. Ward Morehouse in the *New York Sun* said the show provided "wonderful moments" when it sang, but otherwise the narrative sequences were "quite ponderous"; but he noted Burl Ives stopped the show with such numbers as "Rock Candy Mountain" and "Blue Tail Fly." Louis Kronenberger in *PM* understood that the narrative was "connective tissue" between the musical sequences, but nevertheless found the dialogue "depressingly coy, corny and thin-blooded" in its presentation of American history in the "form of juvenile burlesque."

But Burton Rascoe in the *New York World-Telegram* stated the Theatre Guild had added a "precious gem to its crown of theatrical glories," and the evening was "richly rewarding . . . a thing of beauty, dignity and taste, simple, homely and refreshing." Howard Barnes in the *New York Herald Tribune* found Kerr's book "obvious" and not always effective, and admitted the evening was sometimes repetitive and could have used some pruning; but even so, the show was a "musical delight" in its "captivating cavalcade" of American music. As for Garland, he was an in exclamatory mood: the musical was "IT!" and he could "never expect to get enough of it!" He found the "new and fresh and fascinating" presentation a "happy American fusion of drama, dance and music."

The musical included four new songs: "Where" and "More Than These" (lyrics by Edward Eager, music by John Mundy); "As I Was Going Along" (lyric by Edward Eager, music by Elie Siegmeister; the music for this song was based on a nameless folk music theme); and "Hey, Mr. Bossman" (lyric and music by Elie Siegmeister).

The cast album was recorded by Decca (LP # DL-74304; later issued by AEI on LP # 1137) and offers seventeen numbers from the score, including three of the new songs ("Where," "More Than These," and "As I Was Going Along"). The script was published in softcover by Baker's Plays in 1949.

During the tryout, a number of songs were cut, including: "Going to Boston," "The Revolutionary Rising," "The Girl I Left Behind Me," "The Liberty Song," "Yankee Doodle," "He's Gone Away," "Tenting Tonight," "When Johnny Comes Marching Home," "It Takes a Worried Man," and "Love Song." There was even a sequence about Jesse James (who was danced by Peter Hamilton) titled "The Cows Can Have the Cowboys" (lyric by Walter Kerr, with music based on a folk theme adapted by Elie Siegmeister). In her review of the opening night Boston tryout performance, Helen Eager in the *Boston Traveler* noted Bibi Osterwald made a "big hit" with this number. Eager also mentioned that Drake played the role of Barnaby with "easy grace, ingratiating charm and sure voice" and created a character who was a combination of Johnny Appleseed and Peter Pan. But she said the first act scenes "limp lethargically"; and while the second act was an "improvement," she cautioned that the evening's "high anticipation as a successor to *Oklahoma!* was far from realized."

Eleven months before *Sing Out, Sweet Land!* opened on Broadway, Elie Siegmeister presented and directed *The American Ballad Singers*, an evening of native American music which played for a limited engagement of two performances at City Center on February 6, 1944. The evening was in some respects an early run-through of the current American music retrospective.

With Burl Ives's iconic dramatic role of Big Daddy in the 1955 stage production and subsequent 1958 film version of Tennessee Williams's *Cat on a Hot Tin Roof* and his portrayal of a ruthless rancher in the 1958 film *The Big Country* (which earned him an Academy Award for Best Supporting Actor), it's sometimes easy to overlook his musical side. He performed and recorded numerous folk, children's, and holiday songs. His first Broadway appearance was in the original 1938 production of Richard Rodgers and Lorenz Hart's *The Boys from Syracuse*, and he was also in the original cast of **This Is the Army**. He later appeared as Ben Rumson in the national tour of Alan Jay Lerner and Frederick Loewe's 1951 musical *Paint Your Wagon*, and in 1954 was Captain Andy in the New York City Opera Company's production of Jerome Kern and Oscar Hammerstein II's *Show Boat*. He also starred in the charming 1948 Walt Disney film *So Dear to My Heart*, where he introduced the popular song "Lavender Blue (Dilly, Dilly)."

The cast also included dancer Irene Hawthorne, who in 1946 appeared in **Windy City**, which closed during its pre-Broadway tryout. In 1956, she choreographed and starred in her dance program *Autobiography*, which played at the Booth Theatre for six performances and was conducted by her husband Kurt Adler.

The International Theatre had opened in 1903 as the Majestic and was located at Columbus Circle (the theatre isn't to be confused with the Majestic Theatre on West 44th Street). Among the early hits of the playhouse were the musicals *The Wizard of Oz* and *Babes in Toyland* (both 1903), but with its out-of-the-way location the theatre was relegated to a kind of theatrical limbo (the flyer of *Sing Out, Sweet Land!* assured potential ticket-buyers that the theatre was "serviced by *all* subways, trolleys and bus lines"). It underwent various management changes as well as name changes and besides plays and musicals its checkered history also offered burlesque, vaudeville, ballet, and movies. **Caribbean Carnival** was the last musical to play there, and during the first week of 1949 the theatre permanently closed its doors after the final showing of N. Richard Nash's drama *The Young and the Fair*. During its final years, the venue served as an NBC television studio, and Sid Caesar's legendary *Your Show of Shows* was telecast from there. In 1954, the theatre was demolished.

ON THE TOWN

Theatre: Adelphi Theatre (during run, the musical transferred to the 44th Street Theatre and then to the Martin Beck Theatre)
Opening Date: December 28, 1944; *Closing Date*: February 2, 1946
Performances: 463
Book and *Lyrics*: Betty Comden and Adolph Green; additional lyrics by Leonard Bernstein
Music: Leonard Bernstein
Based on an idea by Jerome Robbins (and his 1944 ballet *Fancy Free*).
Direction: George Abbott; *Producers*: Oliver Smith and Paul Feigay; *Choreography*: Jerome Robbins; *Scenery*: Oliver Smith; *Costumes*: Alvin Colt; *Lighting*: Sam Amdurs; *Musical Direction*: Max Goberman
Cast: Marten Sameth (Workman, Actor), Frank Milton (Second Workman, Master of Ceremonies), Herbert Greene (Third Workman, Waiter, Conductor), Lavina Nielson (Girl in Yellow), Adolph Green (Ozzie), Cris Alexander (Chip), Lyle Clark (Sailor), John Battles (Gabey), Frank Westbrook (Andy), Richard D'Arcy (Tom, Sailor in Blue), Cyprienne Gabelman (Girl in Green, First Ballet Girl), Don Weissmuller (Sailor, Penny Arcade Boy), Florence MacMichael (Flossie), Marion Kohler (Flossie's Friend), Larry Bolton (Bill Poster), Maxine Arnold (Little Old Lady), Lonny Jackson (Policeman), Milton Taubman (S. Uperman), Nancy Walker (Hildy), Roger Treat (Policeman), Remo Bufano (Figment), Betty Comden (Claire), Nelle Fisher (High School Girl), Susan Steell (Maude P. Dilly), Sono Osato (Ivy), Alice Pearce (Lucy Schmeeler), Malka Farber (Lady in Red), Robert Chisholm (Pitkin), Frances Cassard (Voice, Singer [Diana Dream]), Dorothy Johnson (Singer [Dolores Dolores]), Sam Adams (Musician, Rajah Bimmy), Carle Erbele (Musician), Jeanne Gordon (Spanish Singer), Ben Piazza (Boy), Allyn Ann McLerie (Second Ballet Girl, Doll Girl), Ray Harrison (The Great Lover), Robert Lorenz (Bimmy); Dancers: Barbara Gaye, Lavina Nielsen, Atty Vandenberg, Dorothy

McNichols, Cyprienne Gabelman, Jean Handy, Virginia Miller, Nelle Fisher, Royce Wallace, Allyn Ann McLerie, Malka Farber, Aza Bard, Ray Harrison, Frank Neal, Carle Erbele, James Flashe Riley, Ben Piazza, Douglas Matheson, Duncan Noble, Frank Westbrook, John Butler, Richard D'Arcy, Lyle Clark; Singers: Frances Cassard, Jeanne Gordon, Lila King, Frances Leger, Marion Kohler, Dorothy Johnson, Regina Owens, Shirley Ann Burton, Frank Milton, Roger Treat, Martin Sameth, Benjamin Trotman, Milton Taubman, Herbert Greene, Lonny Jackson, Melvin Howard, Sam Adams, Robert Lorenz

The musical was presented in two acts.

The action takes place during the present time in New York City within the period of twenty-four hours.

Musical Numbers

Act One: "I Feel Like I'm Not Out of Bed Yet" (Martin Sameth, with Frank Milton and Herbert Greene); "New York, New York" (John Battles, Cris Alexander, Adolph Green); "Miss Turnstiles" (dance) (danced by Sono Osato, Frank Westbrook, Lyle Clark, John Butler, Duncan Noble, Don Weissmuller, Richard D'Arcy; Radio Announcer: Robert Lorenz); "Come Up to My Place" (Nancy Walker, Cris Alexander); "I Get Carried Away" (Betty Comden, Adolph Green; danced by Malka Farber, Cyprienne Gabelman, Atty Vandenberg, John Butler, Lyle Clark, Duncan Noble); "Lonely Town" (John Battles, Chorus); "Lonely Town Pas de Deux" (danced by Nelle Fisher and, Richard D'Arcy; followed by dance sequence by Ballet Dancers); "Do, Re, Do" (aka "Carnegie Hall Pavane" and "Do-Do-Re-Do") (Susan Steell, Sono Osato, Girls; danced by Sono Osato); "I Can Cook, Too" (lyric by Leonard Bernstein; additional lyric by Betty Comden and Adolph Green) (Nancy Walker); "Lucky to Be Me" (John Battles, Chorus); "Sailors on the Town" (aka "Times Square Ballet") (Dance Ensemble; Penny Arcade Boy: Don Weissmuller)

Act Two: "So Long" (aka "So Long, Baby") (Lavinia Nielsen, Aza Bard, Cyprienne Gabelman, Atty Vandenberg, Malka Farber, Allyn Ann McLerie, Frances Cassard, Jeanne Gordon); "I'm Blue" (aka "I Wish I Was Dead") (Frances Cassard, Jeanne Gordon); "You Got Me" (aka "Ya Got Me") (Nancy Walker, Betty Comden, Adolph Green, Cris Alexander); "I Understand" (aka "Pitkin's Song") (Robert Chisholm, Alice Pearce); "Subway to Coney Island" (danced by Royce Wallace, Allyn Ann McLerie, Frank Neal, Frank Westbrook, Malka Farber); "Gabey in the Playground of the Rich" (aka "The Imaginary Coney Island Ballet" and "The Dream Coney Island Ballet") (the sequence includes the dances "The Great Lover Displays Himself" and "Pas de Deux") (danced by Sono Osato and Ray Harrison; and Lavina Nielsen, Aza Bard, Nelle Fisher, Virginia Miller, Barbara Gaye, Cyprienne Gabelman, Lyle Clark, Richard D'Arcy, John Butler, Don Weissmuller, Duncan Noble, and Carle Erbele); "Some Other Time" (Betty Comden, Adolph Green, Nancy Walker, Cris Alexander); "Coney Island" (aka "The Real Coney Island") (Rajah Bimmy: Sam Adams; Cooch Girls: Allyn Ann McLerie, Aza Bard, Sono Osato); "New York, New York" (reprise) (Lyle Clark, Frank Milton, Don Weissmuller, Entire Company)

Along with **Song of Norway**, **Bloomer Girl**, **Up in Central Park**, and **Carousel**, *On the Town* was one of five hit musicals that opened during the 1944–1945 season; while its run was the shortest of the five, *On the Town* (along with **Carousel**) is the only musical from the season that is regularly revived on Broadway and in regional theatre.

The musical was inspired by the 1944 ballet *Fancy Free* (music by Leonard Bernstein and choreography by Jerome Robbins), which depicted three sailors on the town during shore leave. The ballet premiered at the Metropolitan Opera House on April 18, 1944, with Harold Lang, Jerome Robbins, John Kriza, Muriel Bentley, Janet Reed, and Shirley Eckl as the sailors and their girls.

Within eight months of the ballet's premiere, the musical comedy version was on Broadway. Bernstein and Robbins returned as composer and choreographer, and Oliver Smith, who had designed the setting for the ballet, performed the same duty for the musical (and, with Paul Feigay, he was also the show's coproducer). Betty Comden and Adolph Green wrote the book and lyrics (as part of the nightclub act The Revuers, they had performed and written their own material, and here for the first time they were represented on Broadway as librettists, lyricists, and performers). Added to the mix were George Abbott (director), Alvin Colt (costume designer), and a youthful cast that besides Comden (as Claire) and Green (Ozzie) also included Nancy Walker (Hildy), John Battles (Gabey), Cris Alexander (Chip), Alice Pearce (Lucy Schmeeler), and, last but not least, dancer Sono Osato (Ivy), whose stunning beauty made it clear why Gabey falls in love with her the instant he sees her poster photo as "Miss Turnstiles of the Month."

The musical took place during the sailors' twenty-four-hour shore leave, and much of it was devoted to Gabey's search for the elusive Ivy. Eventually he and she pair up, as do Claire and Ozzy and Hildy and Chip. But the unspoken background of the war hovers over the proceedings, and soon the three couples must part, hoping they'll meet again "Some Other Time," which was a lovely, understated ballad performed at the end of the musical.

The score also offered two spectacular ballads for Gabey, the blues "Lonely Town" and the joyous "Lucky to Be Me"; amusing comedy songs (two raucous ones for Hildy, "Come Up to My Place" and "I Can Cook, Too," and Claire and Ozzie's mock-operetta spoof "I Get Carried Away"); and a satire of nightclub songs and singers ("I'm Blue" aka "I Wish I Was Dead") performed first by sultry Veronica Lake wannabe Diana Dream and then in a Spanish version by hot tamale Dolores Dolores. The musical's most famous song is Gabey, Chip, and Ozzie's jubilant trio "New York, New York" ("it's a helluva town") in which they salute the city and its heady promise of sex (and maybe even romance). Moreover, Bernstein created alternately bluesy and swinging ballet music to depict a lively evening in Times Square ("Sailors on the Town" aka "Times Square Ballet"), a subway trip to Coney Island, and then both an imaginary and real Coney Island, the first a playground of the rich (which the script describes as a "dreamy void of blue" in which sophisticated men and "unattainable" women dance "easily and coldly") and the other a "gaudy honky-tonk sort of place."

Wilella Waldorf in the *New York Post* found the "attractive, tremendously good-natured" musical a "slap-happy," "often rather juvenile," and "sometimes downright amateurish affair" which was nonetheless "ingratiating"; the "plotlet" served as background for "lovely" songs and "merry" choreography; and Ward Morehouse in the *New York Sun* said the "brisk and festive" evening had "freshness, originality and vitality." Burton Rascoe in the *New York World-Telegram* found the "fast-paced, jazzy and tuneful" show reminiscent of **Follow the Girls**, and while he liked the "better than average" tunes he complained that Robbins's choreography was sometimes "plastic rather than rhythmical and completely uninspired"; further, there was "too much" in the way of dancing and "not enough" comedy (but he noted Nancy Walker had the audience "howling," and it was she who carried the show).

Howard Barnes in the *New York Herald Tribune* noted Abbott's "shrewd" direction made the most of "scant" material with a plot that had "all the attributes of a Class B picture"; but the evening offered some "crisp and imaginative" moments, and overall the "jubilance and enthusiasm" overcame the musical's "defects." Robert Garland in the *New York Journal-American* said that overall the musical didn't live up to its parts, but he praised the "tuneful and amazingly orchestrated" score; the "generally mocking" and "frequently shocking" book and lyrics; the "ingenious" choreography; the "stunning" décor; and the "impressive" costumes. But he felt Abbott hadn't pulled everything together and, curiously, he seemed to think the evening offered "too much" in the way of youth and "exuberance," "enthusiasm," and "animal spirits."

But Louis Kronenberger in *PM* said *On the Town* was not only the best musical of the season, it was also "one of the freshest, gayest, liveliest" musicals he'd ever seen, and the book was the best since **Pal Joey**; moreover, Bernstein's music was "unhackneyed without being highbrow" and Robbins's dances were "crisp, humorous, fast," and "exciting," and only in the dream Coney Island sequence did it become "arty." Lewis Nichols in the *New York Times* said the musical was the "freshest and most engaging" to open in New York since **Oklahoma!** The dances were "perfect" and it had been "a long time" since audiences had "been allowed to enjoy a musical comedy book."

But John Chapman in the *New York Daily News* said the musical was "dullish" if "serviceable"; the lyrics and music were "almost always disappointing"; and there were "of course" ballets, and he moaned, "Cripes, what I wouldn't give to see a good old hoofing chorus again!"

During the tryout, the songs "The Intermission's Great," "Say When," and "Gabey's Comin'" were cut (the latter was restored for the 1997 and 1998 revivals). The music for "The Intermission's Great" was later heard in Robbins's 1946 ballet *Facsimile*. The song "Ain't Got No Tears Left" was dropped in preproduction, and its music was recycled into Bernstein's 1952 symphony *Age of Anxiety*. "Dream with Me" was also dropped in preproduction (along with "Another Love," "I'm Afraid It's Love," "Lonely Me," and "The Nicest Time of the Year"), and was later used in Bernstein's 1950 version of *Peter Pan*, where it was again cut.

The musical did well during its initial Broadway run and played for nearly 500 performances. But almost as soon as the show closed in New York, it fell victim to a kind of hex. Thanks to the popular film version, it's a musical everyone seems to know, but for some reason it's never been successfully revived: critics don't get particularly excited about it, and audiences stay away.

The national tour starred Nancy Walker, but did indifferent business and soon closed. Two Broadway revivals were quick failures. Despite choreography by Ron Field and a cast that included Donna McKechnie (Ivy), Phyllis Newman (Claire), Bernadette Peters (Hildy), Ron Husmann (Gabey), Remak Ramsay (Ozzie), Jess Richards (Chip), and Marilyn Cooper (Lucy Schmeeler), and a dancing company that included Carole (Kelly) Bishop, John Mineo, and Tony Stevens, the first (which opened at the Imperial Theatre on October 31, 1971) closed after seventy-three performances; and the second (at the Gershwin Theatre on November 19, 1998) played for sixty-five showings; it was choreographed by Keith Young, and while it offered amusing performances by Lea DeLaria (Hildy), Annie Golden (Lucy Schmeeler), and Mary Testa (Maude P. Dilly), many of the leads were somewhat indifferently cast. The most notable aspect of the evening was Adrianne Lobel's décor which nostalgically evoked the look of long-ago New York City through the use of old-time crayon-colored-styled post cards. A third Broadway revival opened on October 16, 2014, at the Lyric Theatre. Ben Brantley in the *Times* said the "jubilant" revival with "jelly bean hues" made "vintage Techicolor look pallid."

The 1998 revival was first seen Off-Broadway when it was produced by the Public Theatre at the Delacorte Theatre on August 1, 1997, for twenty-five performances (with choreography by Eliot Feld). An earlier Off-Broadway visit opened at the Carnegie Hall Playhouse on January 15, 1959, for seventy performances; the cast included Harold Lang (Gabey), William Hickey (Ozzie), Joe Bova (Chip), Wisa D'Orso (Ivy), and Pat Carroll (Hildy).

The belated London production was also a failure. It opened at the Prince of Wales Theatre on May 30, 1963, for fifty-three performances; the cast included Elliott Gould (Ozzie), and Joe Layton created the direction and choreography. The production was designed by Oliver Smith, and the costumes were by Cynthia Tingey. The cast album was recorded by CBS Records (LP # SAPG-60005), and the CD (Masterworks Broadway/Arkiv Music) was released by Sony (# 500728).

The 1949 film version by MGM is notable for a sparkling cast which includes Gene Kelly (Gabey), Frank Sinatra (Chip), Jules Munshin (Ozzie), Vera-Ellen (Ivy), Ann Miller (Claire), Betty Garrett (Hildy), and, reprising her Broadway role, Alice Pearce as Lucy Schmeeler. In a major departure from sound-stage-bound filming, some scenes were actually filmed in New York, and the real and studio New York locations blend well together and the film has the look of a Technicolor dream. Unfortunately, just three songs were retained from the stage production ("New York, New York," "Come Up to My Place," and, surprisingly, "I Feel Like I'm Not Out of Bed Yet"), along with some of Bernstein's dance music. Comden and Green supplied lyrics for new songs which were composed by Roger Edens; the new ones were pleasant enough, but not particularly distinguished.

Decca recorded only a handful of songs from the stage production and included a mix of Broadway cast (Betty Comden, Adolph Green, and Nancy Walker) and non-cast members (including Mary Martin, who sang John Battles' songs!). The album was released on LP (# DL-8030) along with seven numbers from **Lute Song**, which had opened on Broadway in 1946 with Martin. The film's soundtrack album was issued by Show Biz Records (LP # 5603); the London cast by CBS Records (LP # SAPG-60005); a studio cast by Stet (LP # DS-150129) included many of the songs written for the film; a 1993 concert production was released by Deutsch Grammophon (CD # 437-516-2) in the late but unlamented era of "crossover" recordings (in this case, everyone from Samuel Ramey and Evelyn Lear to David Garrison to Cleo Laine to Tyne Daly); a complete two-CD 1996 studio cast recording issued by Jay (# CDJAY2-1231) even includes the almost-forgotten "I Understand" (aka "Pitkin's Song"). The unused song "Ain't Got No Tears Left" is included in the collection *Leonard Bernstein's New York* (Nonesuch CD # 79400-2), and "Dream with Me" has surfaced on at least two collections, including *Leonard Bernstein/Arias and Barcarolles/Songs and Duets* (Koch CD # 3-7000-2).

The best recording of the score is a 1960 release by Columbia (LP # OL-5540/#OS-2028; issued by Sony Classical/Columbia/Legacy on CD # SK-60538) which includes Broadway cast members Betty Comden, Adolph Green, Nancy Walker, and Cris Alexander as well as John Reardon and Michael Kermoyan; Leonard Bernstein conducts the score.

The script was published in hardback in 1997 as part of the collection *The New York Musicals of Comden and Green* (Applause Books), which also includes the scripts of *Wonderful Town* (1953) and *Bells Are Ringing* (1956), both of which had originally been published in hardback by Random House; unfortunately the volume ignores the team's *Subways Are for Sleeping* (1961). The script was published in hardback in 2014 by the Library of Congress in a collection that includes the scripts of fifteen other musicals.

Comden and Green wrote a sequel of sorts to *On the Town*. In 1955, their MGM film musical *It's Always Fair Weather* looked at three servicemen in 1945 who agree to meet ten years after the war. But a decade later they're different people with little in common with one another, and a pervasively sour and sad mood settled over the film. The leads were Gene Kelly, Dan Dailey, and Michael Kidd; Comden and Green wrote the screenplay and lyrics, and Andre Previn the score; Gene Kelly and Stanley Donen codirected and co-choreographed. The film's highlights were a split screen sequence ("I Shouldn't Have Come," set to the music of the "Blue Danube" waltz) in which in voice-over the three former servicemen cringe over the awkwardness of their reunion; some sweeping solo dances for Kelly; and, best of all, a knowing performance by Dolores Gray as the hostess of a reality-styled television show that will surprise the trio by reuniting them live on national television (and Gray stopped the show with her dazzling "Thanks a Lot but No Thanks," a production number in which she kills off the men in her life as she sings of her love for material things).

A LADY SAYS YES
"A New Musical"

Theatre: Broadhurst Theatre
Opening Date: January 10, 1945; *Closing Date*: March 25, 1945
Performances: 87
Book: Clayton Ashley (a pseudonym for plastic surgeon Dr. Maxwell Maltz)
Lyrics: Stanley Adams
Music: Fred Spielman and Arthur Gershwin
Direction: Uncredited; *Producers*: J. J. Shubert in association with Clayton Ashley; *Choreography*: Dances choreographed by Boots McKenna and ballets choreographed by Natalie Kamarova; *Scenery*: Watson Barratt; *Costumes*: Lou Eisele; *Lighting*: Uncredited; *Musical Direction*: Ving Merlin
Cast: In 1945—Helene LeBerthon (First Nurse), Sue Ryan (Licetta), Jackson Jordan (Second Nurse), Blanche Grady (Third Nurse), Jack Albertson (Doctor), Bobby Morris (Scapino), Carole Landis (Ghisella), Christine Ayers (Christine), Jacqueline Susann (Hildegarde), Arthur Maxwell (Lieutenant Anthony Caufield, U.S.N.R.), Earl McDonald (Doctor Gaspare), Martha King (Isabella), Pittman Corey (Captain Gordon); In 1545—Pittman Corey (Captain Desiri), Helene LeBerthon, (Francesca), Blanche Grady (Rosa), Jackson Jordan (Carmela), Jack Albertson (Doctor Bartoli), Martha King (Isabella), Bobby Morris (Scapino), Arthur Maxwell (Anthony Gaspare), Christine Ayers (Christine), Jacqueline Susann (Hildegarde), Sue Ryan (Licetta), Earl McDonald (Gaspare), Fred Catania (Killer Pepoli), Al Klein (Second), Steve Mills (Pantaloon), Carole Landis (Ghisella), Francelia Schmidt (Page Boy), Tatiana Grantzeva, Ronnie Cunningham; Ladies of the Ensemble: Maika Beranova, Doris Brent, Jan Brooks, Jane Cleaveland, Betty Greene, Lola Kendrick, Marguerite Kimball, Pat Leslie, Candace Montgomery, Cecilia Nielsen, Shirley Norman, Olivia Russell, Exilona Savre, Fredi Sears, Tiigra, Eileen K. Upton; Dancers: Bunnie Brady, Fena Cella, Madeleine Detry, Sheila Herman, Albertina Horstmann, Jacqueline Jones, Jacqueline Karsh, Carol Keyser, Virginia Lee, Patricia Leith, Jeanne Lewis, Elaine Meredith, Cammy O'Brien, Susan Pearce, Deiree Rockafellow, Francelia Schmidt, Helen Schmidt, Alice Swanson, Lucas Aco, Jack Allen, Peyton Blowe, Corbett Booth, Dick Hayes, Eddie Miller, Joseph O. Paz, Eddie Wells
The musical was presented in a prologue and two acts.
The action takes place in 1945 in Washington, D.C., and in 1545 in Venice and China.

Musical Numbers

Prologue: "Viva Vitamins" (sung and danced by the Ensemble); "A Lesson in Terpsichore" (Christine Ayers and Bobby Morris)
Act One: "You're the Lord of Any Manor" (sung and danced by the Ensemble); "Take My Heart with You" (Martha King, Arthur Maxwell; danced by Pittman Corry, Tatiana Grantzeva, Ensemble); "Without a Caress" (Carole Landis, Ladies of the Ensemble); "I Wonder Why You Wander" (Sue Ryan, Bobby Morris); "I Don't Care What They Say About Me" (Arthur Maxwell, Ensemble); "A Hop, A Skip, A Jump, A Look" (Judges: Jack Allen, Peyton Blowe, Lucas Aco, Corbett Booth, Eddie Miller, Eddie Wells); "A Pillow for

His Royal Head" (Chambermaids: Fena Cella, Francelia Schmidt, Helen Schmidt, Alice Swanson, Elaine Meredith, Virginia Lee; danced by Ronnie Cunningham); Dance (Christine Ayers); "Don't Wake Them Up Too Soon" (Carole Landis, Ladies of the Ensemble); Finaletto (Entire Company)

Act Two: "Carnival Dance" (Pittman Corry, Ronnie Cunningham, Ensemble); "You're More Than a Name and an Address" (Carole Landis, Arthur Maxwell); "Brooklyn, U.S.A." (lyric and music by Will Morrissey) (Sue Ryan); "Chinese Ballet" (music by George Kamaroff) (Boy: Pittman Corry; Princess: Tatiana Grantzeva; Emperor: Lucas Aco; Slave Girl: Virginia Lee; Executioner: Al Klein; Gong Girls: Francelia Schmidt, Helen Schmidt, Alice Swanson; Monkeys: Bunnie Brady, Jeanne Lewis, Patricia Leith; Commentator: Bobby Morris); "I'm Setting My Cap for a Throne" (Carole Landis); "Leave Us Let Things Alone Like They Was" (lyric by Bud Burton, music by Harold Cohen) (Sue Ryan); "It's the Girl Everytime, It's the Girl" (Arthur Maxwell, Ladies of the Ensemble); "You're More Than a Name and an Address" (reprise) (Carole Landis, Arthur Maxwell); Finale (Entire Company)

A Lady Says Yes began in the present year of 1945 when Navy Lieutenant Anthony Caufield (Arthur Maxwell) undergoes plastic surgery in order to enlarge his nose. Although the critics danced around the subject and were never quite direct about the ultimate intent of the operation, it appears the lieutenant and his doctors believe that a large nose gives rise to a larger manhood, and thus will enable Anthony to emerge as a virile lover for his soon-to-be bride Licetta (Sue Ryan). While he's under the knife, he dreams he's gone back in time to the Venice of 1545, where he meets everyone he knows in 1945 as Venetians, including Ghisella (Carole Landis), who was once a hospital attendant and is now a courtesan. After a merry old time of Venetian carnivals and dances and prize fights and an ode to the delights of Brooklyn, U.S.A., Anthony and the Venetians are transported to ancient China, where they have a merry old time with Chinese ballets. After all this globe-trotting, Anthony's operation is over, he's back in 1945, and everyone's at a chic garden party in Washington, D.C. Anthony is presumably the proud owner of an enlarged manhood, which he can share with Ghisella, for in his dreams he realized it was she, and not Licetta, whom he really loves.

The musical received a terrible drubbing from the critics, who lambasted the weak story line and the even weaker jokes (examples: "Do you like Kipling?" "I don't know. I've never kippled" and "Marco Polo is here." "I thought marco polo was something you played on horses with sticks"; not to mention that a female comic is described as being "nuts" because she has chestnut hair, hazel eyes, and a walnut complexion). A few songs were praised (such as "You're More Than a Name and an Address" and what seems to have been the requisite Brooklyn number for many of the shows of the era, in this case "Brooklyn, U.S.A."), and screen actress Carole Landis, here making her stage debut, was game enough in her role (but had a small singing voice, and soon after the opening her only solo number was dropped). The cast also included future celebrity author Jacqueline Susann in yet another appearance in a 1940s musical. Considering the critical brickbats and the lack of a hit song, the show somehow managed to run ten weeks, probably on the strength of Carole Landis's Hollywood celebrity.

Louis Kronenberger in *PM* said the musical was the season's worst; it wasn't just "old stuff," it was "fourth-rate " and "dull smutty" stuff. The headline of Howard Barnes's review in the *New York Herald Tribune* proclaimed that "This Critic Says 'No'"; he said the evening was a "big and rather bewildering bore" with "dull" music (cowritten by George and Ira's brother Arthur Gershwin) and "lamentable" lyrics (but he liked the "considerable bounce" of the interpolated "Brooklyn, U.S.A."); and Lewis Nichols in the *New York Times* suggested the "at best second-rate" show had a book "which well might drive a saint to drink"; he liked the ballad "You're More Than a Name and an Address" but commented that Landis was giving a "personal appearance" rather than a performance.

Burton Rascoe in the *New York World-Telegram* said he'd written down some of the jokes, but many would be squelched by his editor because the *World-Telegram* was a family newspaper; he also described a strange scene involving an "electrical contraption" that transfers ailments from a patient to a dummy; unfortunately, the lead comic is sitting in the dummy's seat and so becomes victim to stuttering, androgynous traits, and, oh, yes, "is about to become pregnant." Rascoe reported that many in the audience didn't return for the second act.

Wilella Waldorf in the *New York Post* said the evening was "thoroughly undistinguished" and noted that at times the performers playfully condemned the book. Robert Garland in the *New York Journal-American* also commented that the musical "tries to kid itself and dies in the attempt to do so"; he also said the dances were "mediocre" and that the musical couldn't begin to compete with ***Follow the Girls*** and ***On the Town***, two other musicals that dwelt on "sailors and how they got that way." John Chapman in the *New York Daily News* noted the evening consisted primarily of "a series of entrances and exits, with the exits being generally the better," but said "Brooklyn, U.S.A." was a "show-stopper"; and Ward Morehouse in the *New York Sun* said the score was generally "routine," there was "plenty of book trouble," and overall the show was "definitely humdrum."

During the run, Carole Landis's only solo ("I'm Setting My Cap for a Throne") was dropped, as was Sue Ryan's engagingly titled "Leave Us Let Things Alone Like They Was"; and a dance ("Minuet in Swing") was added for Ronnie Cunningham.

During the tryout, the musical was titled *A Lady of ?*, and the numbers "Gossip Is the Thing" and "Ethiopian Dance" were cut. The musical's tryout and New York programs didn't list a director; Edgar MacGregor apparently left the show during rehearsals, and J. J. Shubert unofficially succeeded him.

LA VIE PARISIENNE

Theatre: City Center
Opening Date: January 12, 1945; *Closing Date*: February 10, 1945
Performances: 37
Libretto: English version by Felix Brentano and Louis Verneuil, with lyrics by Marion Farquhar (based on the original French version by Henri Meilhac and Ludovic Helavy)
Music: Jacques Offenbach (new musical adaptation by Antal Dorati)
Direction: Ralph Herbert; *Producer*: The New Opera Company (Yolanda Mero-Irion, Director); *Choreography*: Leonide Massine; *Scenery*: Richard Rychtarik; *Costumes*: Ladislas Czettel; *Lighting*: Uncredited; *Musical Direction*: Antal Dorati; *Choral Direction*: Irving Landau
Cast: Phillip George (Stationmaster), Roy Ballard (Policeman), Irene E. Sherrock (Newsboy), Loretta Schere (Flower Girl), Brian Lawrence (Comte Raoul de Gardefeu), Edward Roecker (Baron Bobinet), Marion Carter (Metella), Lee Edwards (Gontran, Alphonse), David Morris (Jackson), Lillian Andersen (Evelyn), Arthur Newman (Mr. Hutchinson), Anna Istomina (Premiere Danseuse), Elena Kramarr (Premiere Danseuse), James Lyons (Premier Dancer), Nicholas J. Insardi (Custom Inspector), Sylvan Evans (Custom Inspector), Frances Watkins (Gabrielle); Delivery People: George Bakos, Doris M. Sward, Bonnie Murray, Jeannette Weise; Chorus: Louise Barnhart, Charlotte Cheney, June Dunn, Patricia Glennon, Rosalind Guest, Jean Mary Lawrence, Millicent Lewis, Bonnie Murray, Flora Previn, Loretta Schere, Irene E. Sherrock, Doris M. Sward, Jeannette Weise, Mary Lou Wallace, George Bakos, Roy Ballard, Salvatore Cosentno, William Peen Bradford, Sylvan Evans, Nicholas J. Insardi, John J. Girt, William G. Schwarz, Barkev Vartanyan, Phillip George; Ballet Dancers: Jeanne Reeves, Jane Kiser, Irene Larson, Aline DuBois, Gloria Morgan, Jane Rattinger, Kirra LeHachova, Deanne Benmore, Elmer Maddox, Julian Mitchell, Stephen Billings, Rex Harrower
The operetta was presented in three acts.
The action takes place during the spring of 1866 in Paris.
Note: There were no individual musical numbers listed in the program.

The current revival of Jacques Offenbach's 1866 operetta *La vie Parisienne* by The New Opera Company played for thirty-seven performances. For more information about the operetta, see entries for the company's 1941 and 1942 revivals.

UP IN CENTRAL PARK

Theatres: New Century Theatre (during run, the musical transferred to the Broadway Theatre)
Opening Date: January 27, 1945; *Closing Date*: April 13, 1946
Performances: 504
Book: Herbert Fields and Dorothy Fields
Lyrics: Dorothy Fields
Music: Sigmund Romberg

Direction: John Kennedy; *Producer*: Michael Todd; *Choreography*: Helen Tamiris; *Scenery* and *Lighting*: Howard Bay; *Costumes*: Grace Houston and Ernest Schraps; *Musical Direction*: Max Meth
Cast: Bruce Lord (A Laborer), Walter Burke (Danny O'Cahane), Charles Irwin (Timothy Moore), Betty Bruce (Bessie O'Cahane), Maureen Cannon (Rosie Moore), Wilbur Evans (John Matthews), Maurice Burke (Thomas Nast), John Quigg (William Dutton, Headwaiter), Robert Field (Andrew Munroe), Paul Reed (Vincent Peters), Rowan Tudor (Mayor A. Oakey Hall), George Lane (Richard Connolly), Harry Meehan (Peter Sweeney), Noah Beery, Sr. (William Marcey Tweed), Herman Glazer (Butler), Lydia Fredericks (Mildred Wincor), Fred Barry (Joe Stewart), Harry Matlock (Porter), Delma Byron (Lotta Stevens), Kay Griffith (Fanny Morris), Martha Burnett (Clara Manning), Watson White (James Fisk, Jr.), Daniel Nagrin (Daniel), Louise Holden (Governess), Ann Hermann (First Child), Joan Lally (Second Child), Janet Lally (Third Child), Mary Alice Evans (Fourth Child), Henry Capri (Page Boy), Wally Coyle (Arthur Finch), Elaine Barry (Ellen Lawrence), Stanley Schimmel (Bicycle Rider), Guy Standing Jr. (George Jones); Bagpipe Players: Isobel Glasgow, James McFadden, Thomas Lorimer; Newsboys: Kenneth Casey, Teddy Casey; Organ Grinders: William Nuss, Charles Wood; Singing Men: Phil Lowry, Charles W. Wood, Jerome Cardinale, Kenneth Renner, Leonard Daye, Stanley Turner, Bruce Lord, Bob Woodward, James Caputo, William Nuss, Rudy Rudisill, Harry Matlock, Sidney Paul, William Sydenstricker; Dancers: Daniel Nagrin, Saul Bolasini, George Bockman, Henri Capri, Wally Coyle, Payne Converse, Gregor Taksa; Singing Girls: Martha Burnett, Beatrice Lind, Mildred Jocelyn, Elyse Jahoda, Lillian Horn, Claire Saunders, Rose Marie Patane, Donna Hughes, Lydia Fredericks, Joan Gladding; Dancers: Wana Allison, Joan Dubois, Margaret Gibson, Miriam Kornfield, Rebecca Lee, Ruth Lowe, Penny Ann Nilsson, Hazel Roy, Evelyn Shaw, Gloria Stevens, Natalie Wynn
The musical was presented in two acts.
The action takes place in New York City during the years 1870–1872.

Musical Numbers

Act One: "Up from the Gutter" (Betty Bruce); "Up from the Gutter" (reprise) (Betty Bruce, Maureen Cannon, Walter Burke, Charles Irwin); Dance (Betty Bruce, Maureen Cannon, Walter Burke, Charles Irwin, Singers and Dancers); "Carousel in the Park" (Maureen Cannon); "It Doesn't Cost You Anything to Dream" (Maureen Cannon, Wilbur Evans); "It Doesn't Cost You Anything to Dream" (reprise) (Maureen Cannon, Betty Bruce, Wilbur Evans); "Boss Tweed" (Noah Berry, Sr., Rowan Tudor, George Lane, Harry Meehan, Robert Field, Paul Reed, Charles Irwin, Men); Opening, Scene Three (Singing Girls and Boys); "When She Walks in the Room" (Wilbur Evans); "Currier and Ives" (Betty Bruce, Fred Barry); "Currier and Ives Ballet" (Betty Bruce, Fred Barry, Daniel Nagrin, Dancers); "Close as Pages in a Book" (Maureen Cannon, Wilbur Evans); "Rip Van Winkle" (Maureen Cannon, Betty Bruce, Noah Berry, Sr., Wilbur Evans, Fred Barry, Paul Reed, Singers and Dancers); Dance (Daniel Nagrin, Dancers); "Close as Pages in a Book" (reprise) (Wilbur Evans); Opening, Scene Five (Dancers); "The Fireman's Bride" (Maureen Cannon, Betty Bruce, Fred Barry, Daniel Nagrin, Dancers); "The Fireman's Bride" (reprise) (Principals, Singing Girls and Boys)
Act Two: "When the Party Gives a Party" (Singing Girls and Boys, Paul Reed, Rowan Tudor, Robert Field, Harry Meehan, Charles Irwin, Walter Burke); "Maypole Dance" (Dancers); Specialty (Fred Barry, Elaine Barry); "The Big Back Yard" (Wilbur Evans, Singing Girls and Boys); "April Snow" (Maureen Cannon, Wilbur Evans); Finaletto, Scene One (Dancers, Singing Girls and Boys); "The Birds and the Bees" (Maureen Cannon, Betty Bruce, Charles Irwin, Walter Burke); Specialty (Betty Bruce); "The Big Back Yard" (reprise) (Orchestra); "Close as Pages in a Book" (Maureen Cannon, Wilbur Evans); Finale (Entire Company)

Up in Central Park was another of the era's musicals that offered up a slice of Americana, in this case the New York City of the 1870s with its corrupt politicians of the Tammany machine, including Boss Tweed (Noah Beery, Sr.) and his cronies. Central Park is New York's "big back yard," and the politicians ensure they get hefty cuts of public monies that have been earmarked for development of the park. Rosie Moore (Maureen Cannon), an ambitious would-be opera singer in the Jenny Lind tradition whose father is a park subcontractor, is unaware of the underhanded goings-on of graft and political conniving. *New York Times'* reporter John

Matthews (Wilbur Evans) and *Harper's Weekly* cartoonist Thomas Nast (Maurice Burke) are investigating the political scandals of the Tammany gang, and when John and Rosie meet, they fall in love. But Tweed cohort Richard Connolly (George Lane) lures Rosie with the promise of wealth and a singing career, and, Rosie, in part to avenge John for his investigative exposures, which affected her father, marries Richard. Almost immediately she discovers Richard is not only another politician on the take, but also a bigamist. When he's killed in an accident, Rosie comes to realize how close she came to being caught up in his system of corrupt values. A year later, she and John accidentally meet at a Fourth of July band concert, and there in the park they reunite.

Most of the critics agreed that Dorothy and Herbert Fields's book took on fresh subject matter, but some felt that typical operetta conventions and a lack of humor prevented the musical from being a complete success. In fact, one or two critics suggested the corrupt goings-on of Tammany Hall and Boss Tweed had the makings of a satiric operetta, and because of the enjoyable performance by Noah Beery, Sr., they regretted he didn't have more stage time. But the reviewers were in agreement that Michael Todd's lavish production offered a cook's tour of Little Old New York, compliments of scenic designer Howard Bay and costume designers Grace Houston and Ernest Schraps. The audience was treated to views of the park, including its gardens, its bird house, an ice-skating pond in the winter, and a bandstand on the Fourth of July as well as the Stetson Hotel, which was located in the park. Further, Helen Tamiris's dance routines (particularly a maypole dance and of course the celebrated "Currier and Ives Ballet") were icing on the cake of a melodious evening that offered a number of catchy old-fashioned ballads by Sigmund Romberg ("Close as Pages in a Book," "When She Walks in the Room," and, especially, the shimmering "April Snow," the musical's finest song), comedy numbers ("The Fireman's Bride," "The Birds and the Bees"), and choral groupings ("The Big Back Yard," "When the Party Gives a Party").

Louis Kronenberger in *PM* suggested school children could learn a lot about American history by attending the current crop of Broadway musicals (**Oklahoma!**, **Bloomer Girl**, **Sing Out, Sweet Land!**, and now *Up in Central Park*). But unfortunately the book was so intent on being a history lesson that it forgot to be humorous. The evening was clearly produced with "taste" and was most likely the season's "most charmingly mounted" musical, but no one "bothered to animate" it. He noted that Bay's "stylish, glossy and amusing" sets were the "real hero" of the evening, and concluded that while the show made a "commendable departure" from run-of-the-mill musical comedy it had "only the haziest idea of its destination." James Aronson in the *New York Post* said the musical was "pleasant" but sometimes slowly paced; its humor was of the "begorra-begorra, back-of-me-hand-to-ye school"; and its "vaudeville brogue" was "so thick you couldn't smell the flowers in the park for the corned beef and cabbage."

Lewis Nichols in the *New York Times* found the musical "long" and "pretty dull"; he admitted there were "several good songs," but the evening grew "monotonous" and the score and the choreography had a "sameness" about them. Although the show was "pretty to watch" like a "lace Valentine" on Currier and Ives prints, the prints never came to life. But Burton Rascoe in the *New York World-Telegram* said *Up in Central Park* was "one of the most charming musicals ever staged" and would become a classic; he noted the snowfall effects for "April Snow" made for one of the "most enchanting scenes ever devised for the stage" and the music itself was "ravishment to the ears."

Otis L. Guernsey in the *New York Herald Tribune* noted the book never matched Michael Todd's "flawless" production, but the score was "lovely," the costumes were "gay" and "varicolored," and the décor was "tasteful." However, "a dose of rip-roaring villainy" could have "welded" the show's elements together and allowed the evening to move faster. But even so, "two-thirds" of the musical was "charming" and thus worth "100% of a ticket." John Chapman in the *New York Daily News* noted that Howard Bay's sets offered a "souvenir album of picture postcards" and Romberg contributed a "memory-book of songs"; as a result, the evening was "warm, gentle and affectionate" (he also noted that Noah Beery, Sr., was a "happy stroke" of casting, and his "Boss Tweed" number was one of the evening's "high spots"). Ward Morehouse in the *New York Sun* admitted the book had its "labored moments," but overall *Up in Central Park* was Todd's "most ambitious" production with a "first-rate" score, "lovely" scenery, and "colorful" costumes.

Robert Garland in the *New York Journal-American* went all-out. The musical was a "miracle" as "miraculous" as *Show Boat* and **Oklahoma!** put together. It was an "out-of-the-world concoction," a musical "pretty near perfection," and a "flawless honest-to-Todd production." And just to ensure everyone understood his feelings about the show, he stated it was "one of the best words-and-music get-togethers ever assembled in America."

During the tryout, the musical was titled *Central Park*; Rose Inghram, who played the role of Rosie, was replaced by Maureen Cannon; and the following numbers were dropped: "Christmas Eve," "Can-Can," "Bessie's Wedding Day," "Passing of a Year," and "Street Singer."

As was typical of many Decca cast albums of the era (**Oklahoma!** and **Carousel** were major exceptions), the cast recording of *Up in Central Park* didn't include the entire score, and some of the singers were non-cast members. Eight songs were recorded ("Carousel in the Park," "It Doesn't Cost You Anything to Dream," "When She Walks in the Room," "Currier and Ives," "Close as Pages in a Book," "The Fireman's Bride," "The Big Back Yard," and "April Snow"), and the performers include original cast members Wilbur Evans and Betty Bruce as well as non-cast members Eileen Farrell (replacing Maureen Cannon) and Celeste Holm performing one song. The recording was issued on 78 RPM # DA-395, on LP # DL-8016, and by Decca Masterworks CD # B0000554-02 (the latter also includes Decca's cast album of *Arms and the Girl* [1950]).

The disappointing film version was released by Universal-International in 1948. In preproduction, the film must have seemed promising. The cast included Deanna Durbin as the heroine, Albert Sharpe (fresh from creating the title role of Finian in **Finian's Rainbow** the previous year) as her father, Dick Haymes as the hero and investigative reporter, and Vincent Price as the villainous Boss Tweed (the characters of Bessie O'Cahane and Thomas Nast were eliminated from the screenplay). Two busy Broadway dancers from the era (William Skipper and Nelle Fisher) were signed as the leads for the "Currier and Ives Ballet"; Helen Tamiris re-created her stage choreography for the ballet (which is the film's highlight; but her choreography for the floorshow at a hotel is one of the strangest of the era and the dance movements border on the weird); the show's set designer Howard Bay was brought to Hollywood to create the decor; and Broadway costume designer Mary Grant created the opulent fashions. Moreover, the screenplay by Karl Tunberg (who also produced the film) retained the basic plot of the Broadway production. William A. Seiter directed.

Eight numbers from the stage production were prerecorded (including the "Currier and Ives Ballet"), and most if not all seem to have been filmed (production stills exist for some of them). But the final release print retained just two songs from the Broadway score ("Carousel in the Park" for Durbin and Haymes and "When She Walks in the Room" for Haymes) and the ballet. Sigmund Romberg and Dorothy Fields wrote two new numbers for the movie ("Tammany Hall Song" for the chorus and "Oh, Say Can You See" for Durbin; the latter is also known as "Oh, Say Do You See What I See") and "Pace, pace, mio Dio" (from Verdi's *La forza del destino*) was interpolated for Durbin. But the following songs, which were recorded (and apparently filmed), went unused: "It Doesn't Cost You Anything to Dream," "Close as Pages in a Book," "April Snow," "The Big Back Yard," and "Rip Van Winkle." The film was released on videocassette by Universal (# 81459) and on DVD by the Universal Vault Collection (# 61122066). Note that one or two sources indicate the film includes "Close as Pages in a Book"; the song may have been heard during the film's initial release and then cut; if so, the sequence seems to be lost and isn't included in the video release.

In 2012, Sepia (CD # 1203) issued the soundtrack album, which includes the above-mentioned eight numbers from the Broadway production as well as the two new ones written especially for the film. The recording also offers six songs from the musical which were recorded by Jeanette MacDonald and Robert Merrill (including "The Fireman's Bride") as well as one selection from the original cast album (Betty Bruce's "Currier and Ives").

The musical was revived at City Center on May 19, 1947, by Michael Todd when he presented a return engagement with the national touring company for sixteen performances; the cast included Earle MacVeigh, Maureen Cannon, and Betty Bruce. A limited engagement was presented by the Equity Library Theatre on March 8, 1984, for thirty performances and included "Christmas Eve" and "Bessie's Wedding Day." Musicals Tonight! also presented a limited run that played March 29–April 10, 2011; this revival included "Christmas Eve" as well as "You Can't Get Over the Wall" (the latter may have been dropped before or during rehearsals of the original production).

Choreographer Helen Tamiris's husband, dancer Daniel Nagrin, was in *Up in Central Park*, and he appeared in six other musicals that she choreographed: the Broadway productions of **Show Boat** (1946 revival), **Annie Get Your Gun**, **Touch and Go**, and *Plain and Fancy* (1955) as well as two that folded on the road during the 1943–1944 season, **Marianne** and **Stovepipe Hat**.

THE FIREBRAND OF FLORENCE
"A New Musical"

Theatre: Alvin Theatre
Opening Date: March 22, 1945; *Closing Date*: April 28, 1945
Performances: 43
Book: Edwin Justus Mayer and Ira Gershwin
Lyrics: Ira Gershwin
Music: Kurt Weill
Based on the 1924 play *The Firebrand* by Edwin Justus Mayer.
Direction: Book directed by John Haggott and production staged by John Murray Anderson; *Producer*: Max
    Gordon; *Choreography*: Catherine Littlefield; *Scenery* and *Lighting*: Jo Mielziner; *Costumes*: Raoul Pene
    du Bois; *Musical Direction*: Maurice Abravanel
Cast: Randolph Symonette (Hangman), Don Marshall (Tartman), Bert Freed (Souvenir Man), Boyd Heathen
    (Maffio), Jean Guelis (Arlecchino), Norma Gentner (Columbina), Eric Kristen (Pierot), Diane Meroff (Flo-
    mina), Hubert Bland (Pantalone), Mary Alice Bingham (Florinetta), Kenneth Le Roy (Gelfomino), Mary
    Grey (Rosania), William Vaux (Dottore), Marion Green (Magistrate), Earl Wrightson (Cellini), Charles
    Sheldon (Captain of the Guard), Ferdi Hoffman (Ottaviano), James Dobson (Ascanio), Gloria Story (Eme-
    lia), Beverly Tyler (Angela), Paul Best (Matquis), Melville Cooper (Duke), Billy (Dee) Williams (Page), Lotte
    Lenya (Duchess), Walter Graf (Major-Domo), Alan Noel (Clerk of the Court); Models: Yvette Heap, Doris
    Blake, Marya Iversen, Gedda Petry, Rose Marie Elliot, Perdita Chandler; Apprentices: John (Jack) Cassidy,
    Lynn Alden, Walter Rinner, Frank Stevens; Soldiers, Promenaders, Courtiers: Susie Baker, Joan Bartels,
    Lisa Bert, Angela Carabella, Jean Crone, Gay English, Donna Gardner, Frances Joslyn, Julie Jefferson, Lily
    Paget, Stephanie Turash, Evelyn Ward, John Henson, Frank Stevens, Paul Mario, Eric Sander, Gayne Sulli-
    van, Edwin Alberian, Jimmy Allison, Ray Bessmer, Tony Collaro, Thomas La Monaco, Ralph Lee, William
    Sutherland; Duchess's Sedan Chair Bearers: George McDonald, Walter Korman
The musical was presented in two acts.
The action takes place during 1535 in and around Florence, Italy, and in Paris, France.

Musical Numbers

Act One: Opening Sequence: (a) "Song of the Hangman" ("When the Bell of Doom Is Clanging") (Randolph
    Symonette, His Two Assistants); (b) Civic Song: "Come to Florence" (Randolph Symonette, Choral En-
    semble, Jean Guelis, Norma Gentner, Commedia Dell' Arte Dancers); (c) Aria: "My Lords and Ladies"
    (Earl Wrightson, John Cassidy, Lynn Alden, Walter Rinner, Frank Stevens, Choral Ensemble); and (d) Fare-
    well Song: "There Was Life, There Was Love, There Was Laughter" (Earl Wrightson, Choral Ensemble);
    Duet: "Our Master Is Free Again" (Gloria Story, James Dobson); Arietta: "I Had Just Been Pardoned" (Earl
    Wrightson); Love Song: "You're Far Too Near Me" (Beverly Tyler, Earl Wrightson); The Duke's Song:
    "Alessandro the Wise" (Melville Cooper, Choral Ensemble); Finaletto: "I Am Happy Here" (Melville Coo-
    per, Ferdi Hoffman, Earl Wrightson, Beverly Tyler, Paul Best, Gloria Story, Choral Ensemble); "Duchess's
    Entrance" (Billy Williams); "The Duchess's Song: Sing Me Not a Ballad" (Lotte Lenya, Four Courtiers);
    Madrigal: "When the Duchess Is Away" (Charles Sheldon, Melville Cooper, Gloria Storey, Choral En-
    semble); Love Song: "There'll Be Life, Love and Laughter" (Earl Wrightson, Beverly Tyler); Trio: "I Know
    Where There's a Cozy Nook" (aka "Cozy Nook Trio") (Melville Cooper, Beverly Tyler, Earl Wrightson);
    First Act Finale: Night Music (a) "The Nightime Is No Time for Thinking" (Gloria Story, Melville Cooper,
    Beverly Tyler, Choral Ensemble); (b) "Tarantella" (Dancers); (c) "Dizzily, Busily" (Gloria Story, Choral
    Ensemble, Jean Guelis, Norma Gentner, Commedia Dell' Arte Dancers); and (d) "This Night in Florence"
    (Choral Ensemble)
Act Two: Reprise: "You're Far Too Near Me" (Beverly Tyler, Earl Wrightson); Cavatina: "The Little Naked
    Boy" (Beverly Tyler, Female Choral Ensemble); Letter Song: "My Dear Benvenuto" (Earl Wrightson, Bev-
    erly Tyler); March of the Soldiers of the Duchy: "Just in Case" (Charles Sheldon, Soldiers of the Duchy);
    Ode: "A Rhyme for Angela" (Melville, Poets, Ladies in Waiting); Procession: (a) "Souvenirs" and (b) "Hear
    Ye! Hear Ye!" (Vendors, Randolph Symonette, Apprentices, Models, Clerks); Chant of Law and Order: (c)

"The World Is Full of Villains" (Clerks, Magistrates, Melville Cooper, Choral Ensemble); and Trial by Music: (d) "You Have to Do What You Do Do" (Earl Wrightson, Melville Cooper, Paul Best, Lotte Lenya, Ferdi Hoffman, Marion Green, Choral Ensemble); Arietta: "How Wonderfully Fortunate" (Beverly Tyler); Duet: "Love Is My Enemy" (Earl Wrightson, Beverly Tyler); Reprise: "The Little Naked Boy" (Lotte Lenya, Beverly Tyler); Civic Song: "Come to Paris" (Paul Best, Two Ladies of Paris, Choral Ensemble); Finale: (a) "Gigue" (The Commedia Dell' Art Dancers); (b) "Saraband" (Choral Ensemble); and (c) "There'll Be Life, Love and Laughter" (Entire Ensemble)

Based on Edwin Justus Mayer's 1924 play *The Firebrand*, Kurt Weill and Ira Gershwin's *The Firebrand of Florence* was one of the most lavish productions of the era, and with a reported investment of $225,000 also one of its most costly failures. But its richly melodic and ambitious music and witty and literate lyrics are arguably the best heard on Broadway during the 1940s, and the score's only equal came along eleven years later when Leonard Bernstein's comic operetta *Candide* premiered. There are many wonderful theatre scores, but only a handful of truly great ones: *Show Boat* (1927), *Porgy and Bess* (1935), **Pal Joey** (1940), **Lady in the Dark** (1941), *The Firebrand of Florence*, **Street Scene** (1947), *The Golden Apple* (1954), *House of Flowers* (1954), *Candide* (1956), *Juno* (1959), *Gypsy* (1959), *Greenwillow* (1960), *Follies* (1971), *The Voyage* (1992), and *Floyd Collins* (1996). *The Firebrand of Florence* is a brilliant cornucopia of gorgeously textured and beautifully orchestrated songs, and the sweeping score carries one along on a tide of irresistibly insinuating and expansive melody that perfectly captures the romantic intrigues of the leading characters and the atmosphere of old Florence with its hangmen, tart sellers, and souvenir hawkers.

The story centered on Florentine sculptor Benvenuto Cellini (Earl Wrightson) who has been sentenced to hang by the Duke of Florence (Melville Cooper) but is temporarily pardoned because he hasn't completed one of the Duke's commissions. The artist is in love with his model Angela (Beverly Tyler), who is being pursued by the married Duke, whose wife, the Duchess (Lotte Lenya), has designs on Cellini. The amorous goings-on were indeed in keeping with the musical's pre-Broadway title *Much Ado about Love*. And of course Cellini's date with the hangman is soon forgotten amid a mélange of sex, swordplay, and song.

Weill and Gershwin wrote thirty-four separate numbers to tell the story, and the bounteous score featured expansive musical sequences as well as ballads, comedy songs, and rousing choral numbers. The brilliant opening was twenty minutes in length and included four separate musical numbers ("Song of the Hangman," "Come to Florence," "My Lords and Ladies," and "There Was Life, There was Love, There Was Laughter"), which introduced the main story line with lush melodies and incisive lyrics. The first act finale was also presented as an extended four-part musical sequence ("The Nighttime Is No Time for Thinking," "Tarantella," "Dizzily, Busily," and "This Night in Florence") as was the second act's trial sequence ("trial by music") ("Souvenirs," "Hear Ye! Hear Ye!," "The World Is Full of Villains," and "You Have to Do What You Do Do").

"You're Far Too Near Me," "Sing Me Not a Ballad" (the musical's best-known song), and the ethereal "Love Is My Enemy" were gorgeous ballads, and "I Know Where There's a Cozy Nook" and "A Rhyme for Angela" exploded with Ira Gershwin's playful lyrics. The "trial by music" sequence offered especially impressive verbal pyrotechnics on Gershwin's part. Every song and song sequence was perfectly right in both music and lyric, and the result is one of the most thrilling scores ever written for the American musical stage. Over the years, occasional songs from the score surfaced, and they all proved tantalizing. But for those who hadn't seen the original production, the full glory of the score wasn't in evidence until John McGlinn's CD collection *Kurt Weill on Broadway* was released in 1996. It included forty minutes of music (including the sweeping opening sequence) and was beautifully sung and played. Then in 2003, the release of the complete score as performed by the BBC Singers and BBC Symphony Orchestra emphasized what had been so evident in the McGlinn release: here was quite simply one of the towering achievements of the American musical (for more information about these recordings, see below).

The musical's five-week run leads one to suspect the show received unanimous pans, but some of the critics were enthusiastic. Overall, however, they were unimpressed with the score and thought the proceedings tiresome and lacking in comic strength. There was also a great deal of grumbling over the leading players, particularly the weak singing voices of Beverly Tyler and Lotte Lenya. Louis Kronenberger in *PM* said Tyler was "no more than an adequate ingénue" and Wilella Waldorf in the *New York Post* said the "pretty" performer had an often "painful" singing voice and a "stage deportment" that was "deploringly amateur." (But Howard Barnes in the *New York Herald Tribune* found her "comely and very pleasant to hear.") John Chapman in the *New York Daily News* thought that Lenya was "unhappily cast," and noted "Sing Me Not a Ballad" (the "best" of "many excellent" songs) was all wrong for her but would have been a "wow" for Ethel Merman.

Burton Rascoe in the *New York World-Telegram* said Wrightson sang "fairly well" but had a speaking voice that was "flat" and "nasal" and thus made him seem "a little preposterous in the swashbuckling romantic role." Waldorf liked his singing, but noted he wasn't much of an actor and thus offered as much "Florentine fire" as an American boy choir singer.

As for Melville Cooper, the critics liked him, but many felt he was short-changed with too little in the way of comedy. But Barnes noted the book allowed him to come "charging to the rescue with captivating flippancies and pantomime" which brought the second act to a "stunning climax"; and Garland mentioned Cooper had two excruciatingly funny scenes that kept the audience "doubled up with laughter." Rascoe mentioned that Cooper was in a "very bad voice" on opening night, due perhaps either to a cold or to his indifference to the song he was performing.

Barnes said the show was a "rare delight" of "melodic eloquence" and "lyrical felicity." Gershwin's lyrics were "singularly singable" and "vastly entertaining" and Weill's score was his "finest" with such "enchanting" songs as "You're Far Too Near Me" and "Love Is My Enemy." He also noted the choral ensembles were "brilliant." Kronenberger said Weill has created a "big romantic score" of "full-bodied" and "tuneful" songs; Chapman praised the "lovely score" written in "lush operetta style"; Waldorf said the musical was "distinguished by one of Kurt Weill's finest scores"; Robert Garland in the *New York Journal-American* said the music was often "lovely" (and singled out eight "superior" songs); and Lewis Nichols in the *New York Times* said many of the songs had a "good rhythm" and others had a "tinkling, gay charm"; but the remainder were "casual and not distinguished" (he singled out five numbers, including "Sing Me Not a Ballad" and "You Have to Do What You Do Do"). But Rascoe found the music "definitely liturgical" and "watered Massenet."

Waldorf mentioned that the opening sequence offered "movement and color," but then the evening bogged down with a "clumsy air" about it; Garland felt the story was "old-fashioned" and "unduly dated"; Nichols said the "slowly paced and ambling" evening lacked "sparkle, drive or just plain nervous energy"; and Rascoe found the musical "dreary, vapid and inept." But Barnes said the production was "just what the spring season needed."

Waldorf praised the "lovely" Renaissance-inspired scenery by Jo Mielziner and costumes by Raoul Pene du Bois; Garland said the production values were "opulent"; Chapman found the sets beautiful and the company "enchantingly costumed"; Kronenberger also noted the "brilliantly colored costumes"; Nichols said the production was "beautiful" to look at with its décor and "brilliant" costumes; and Morehouse also complimented the "beautiful" scenery and costumes. But Rascoe at least partially dissented, finding the scenery "drab and uninteresting" (but he praised the "sumptuous" costumes "in red and yellow, with all the chromatic variations").

It's unclear if "Our Master Is Free Again," "I Had Just Been Pardoned," and "How Wonderfully Fortunate" were performed in the New York production; although they weren't listed in the program, editor Robert Kimball in *The Complete Lyrics of Ira Gershwin* suggests the first number was probably heard, but the other two may have been dropped in Boston. (All three are heard on the Capriccio recording.) "You Have to Do What You Do Do" was adapted from "No Matter Under What Sign You're Born" and "Song of the Zodiac," both of which had been intended for the "Circus Dream" in **Lady in the Dark** (they were replaced by "The Saga of Jenny").

The musical was revived in concert format for just one performance on March 12, 2009, at Alice Tully Hall at Lincoln Center; Roger Rees narrated the production, and the cast included Nathan Gunn (Cellini), Anna Christy (Angela), Terrence Mann (The Duke), and Victoria Clark (The Duchess).

As mentioned, the 1996 collection *Kurt Weill on Broadway* (Angel CD # 7243-5-55563-2-5) includes almost forty minutes of music from the production (John McGlinn is the conductor, and the principal singers are Thomas Hampson and Elizabeth Futral). A 2000 British concert by the BBC Singers and BBC Symphony Orchestra (conducted by Sir Andrew Davis) was released in 2003 on a two-CD set by Capriccio (# 60-091); the singers include Rodney Gilfry (Cellini), Lori Ann Fuller (Angela), George Dvorsky (The Duke), and Felicity Palmer (The Duchess). Lotte Lenya recorded "Sing Me Not a Ballad," and Gershwin (vocals) and Weill (piano) recorded eight numbers from the musical.

It's fascinating to note how many leading characters in Weill's European and Broadway musicals are arrested, incarcerated, brought to trial, or placed on parole, including Macheath (*The Threepenny Opera*), Jimmy Mahoney (*The Rise and Fall of the City of Mahagonny*), David Orth and Johann Mattes (*Die Burgschaft*),

Severin (*Der Silbersee*), Juan Santos (*Der Kuhhandel*), Johnny Johnson (*Johnny Johnson*), Joe Dennis and Helen (*You for Me*), Brom Broek (*Knickerbocker Holiday*), Liza Elliott (**Lady in the Dark**), Cellini (*The Firebrand of Florence*), Frank Maurrant (**Street Scene**), and Absalom Kumalo (**Lost in the Stars**). Even hapless Rodney Hatch in **One Touch of Venus** is pursued by both police and private detectives when it's assumed he's somehow responsible for the theft of the statue of Venus.

There have been at least three other lyric versions of Cellini's life. Hector Berlioz's opera *Benvenuto Cellini* (libretto by Leon de Wailly and Henri Auguste Barbier) premiered in 1838 (and was first produced by the Metropolitan Opera Company in 2003); *The Dagger and the Rose* (book by Isabel Leighton, lyrics by Edward Eliscu, and music by Eugene Berton) was produced in 1932 and closed in Atlantic City during its pre-Broadway tryout (like *The Firebrand of Florence*, it too was based on Mayer's play *The Firebrand*); and the 1979 Off-Broadway musical *Not Tonight, Benvenuto!* (book, lyrics, and music by Virgil Engeran) played for just one performance.

CAROUSEL
"A New Musical Play"

Theatre: Majestic Theatre
Opening Date: April 19, 1945; *Closing Date*: May 24, 1947
Performances: 890
Book and *Lyrics*: Oscar Hammerstein II
Music: Richard Rodgers
Based on the 1909 play *Liliom* by Ferenc Molnar (as adapted by Benjamin Glazer).
Direction: Rouben Mamoulian; *Producer*: The Theatre Guild (A Lawrence Langner and Theresa Helburn Production); *Choreography*: Agnes De Mille; *Scenery*: Jo Mielziner; *Costumes*: Miles White; *Lighting*: Uncredited; *Musical Direction*: Joseph Littau
Cast: Jean Darling (Carrie Pipperidge), Jan Clayton (Julie Jordan), Jean Casto (Mrs. Mullin), John Raitt (Billy Bigelow), Robert Byrn (First Policeman), Franklyn Fox (David Bascombe), Christine Johnson (Nettie Fowler), Eric Mattson (Enoch Snow), Murvyn Vye (Jigger Craigin), Annabelle Lyon (Hannah), Peter Birch (Boatswain), Connie Baxter (Arminy), Marilyn Merkt (Penny), Joan Keenan (Jennie), Ginna Moise (Virginia), Suzanne Tafel (Susan), Richard H. Gordon (Jonathan), Larry Evers (Second Policeman), Blake Ritter (Captain), Jay Velie (First Heavenly Friend, Minister), Tom McDuffie (Second Heavenly Friend), Russell Collins (Starkeeper), Bambi Linn (Louise), Ralph Linn (Enoch Snow, Jr.), Robert Pagent (Jimmy), Lester Freedman (Principal); Singers: Martha Carver, Iva Withers, Anne Calvert, Connie Baxter, Glory Wills, Josephine Collins, Marilyn Merkt, Joan Keenan, Ginna Moise, Beatrice Miller, Suzanne Tafel, Verlyn Webb, Joseph Bell, Robert Byrn, Tom Duffey, Blake Ritter, Charles Leighton, Louis Freed, Neil Chirico, Lester Freedman, Richard H. Gordon, John Harrold; Dancers: Pearl Lang, Andrea Downing, Margaret Cuddy, Polly Welch, Diane Chadwick, Ruth Miller, Lu Lauterbur, Margaretta DeValera, Lynn Joelson, Sonia Joroff, Elena Salamatova, Marjory Svetlik, Ernest Richman, Tom Avera, Larry Evers, Ralph Linn, Tony Matthews, David Ahdar
The musical was presented in two acts.
The action takes place in Maine during the period 1873–1888.

Musical Numbers

Act One: "Waltz Suite: Carousel" (Orchestra; pantomimed by principals); "You're a Queer One, Julie Jordan" (Jean Darling, Jan Clayton); "When I Marry Mister Snow" (Jean Darling); "If I Loved You" (John Raitt, Jan Clayton); "Give It to 'Em Good, Carrie" and "June Is Bustin' Out All Over" (Christine Johnson, Jean Darling, Ensemble; Pearl Lang [Lead Dancer aka June Girl], Dancing Ensemble); "When I Marry Mister Snow" (reprise) (Jean Darling, Eric Mattson, Girls); "When the Children Are Asleep" (Eric Mattson, Jean Darling); "Blow High, Blow Low" (Murvyn Vye, John Raitt, Male Chorus; "Hornpipe Dance" (led by Annabelle Lyon and Peter Birch, and Dancing Ensemble); "Soliloquy" (John Raitt); Finale (John Raitt, Murvyn Vye, Christine Johnson, Chorus)

Act Two: "This Was a Real Nice Clambake" (Jean Darling, Christine Johnson, Jan Clayton, Eric Mattson, Ensemble); "Geraniums in the Winder" (Eric Mattson); "There's Nothin' So Bad for a Woman" (aka "Stonecutters Cut It on Stone") (Murvyn Vye, Ensemble); "What's the Use of Wond'rin'" (Jan Clayton); "You'll Never Walk Alone" (Christine Johnson); "The Highest Judge of All" (John Raitt); Ballet (Louise: Bambi Linn; A Younger Miss Snow: Annabelle Lyon; The Brothers and Sisters Snow: Margaretta de Valera, Lynn Joelson, Sonia Joroff, Polly Welch, Diane Chadwick; Badly Brought Up Boys: Ralph Linn, Ernest Richman; A Young Man Like Billy: Robert Pagent; A Carnival Woman: Pearl Lang; Members of the Carnival Troupe: Robert Pagent, Pearl Lang, Andrea Downing, Larry Evers, Lee Lauterbur, Tony Matthews, Marjory Svetlik, David Ahdar, Margaret Cuddy, Tom Avera); "If I Loved You" (reprise) (John Raitt); "You'll Never Walk Alone" (reprise) (Company)

Carousel is perhaps the masterwork of the Richard Rodgers and Oscar Hammerstein II collaborations (of all his musicals, *Carousel* was reportedly Rodgers's favorite). The sad, bittersweet story centered on the romance and brief marriage of irresponsible carousel barker Billy Bigelow (John Raitt) and meek millworker Julie Jordan (Jan Clayton), a marriage that ends in Billy's death when he chooses suicide over imprisonment after a botched robbery attempt with petty criminal Jigger Craigin (Murvyn Vye). Julie is left alone and pregnant, but years later Billy is allowed to return to Earth for one day in order to give hope and courage to his unhappy and ostracized daughter Louise (Bambi Linn).

The score was expansive and began with a swirling calliope-inflected waltz prelude (otherwise known as the "Carousel Waltz") that the orchestra played while the principal characters wordlessly swarmed about the colorful amusement park in what the script describes as "pantomimic action synchronized to the music" but was "in no sense a ballet treatment." After this prelude soon followed the famous park bench scene between Julie and Billy in which music and dialogue flowed back and forth and then flowered into the glorious "If I Loved You." Later, when Billy discovers he's to become a father, his lengthy, free-ranging "Soliloquy" expresses his fears, misgivings, and ultimate determination to give his unborn child a better life than his own. The score also included the inspirational, hymn-like "You'll Never Walk Alone"; two gorgeous melodies for the secondary characters Carrie Pipperidge (Jean Darling) and Enoch Snow (Eric Mattson), first her "When I Marry Mister Snow" and then their duet "When the Children Are Asleep"; the male chorus's virile hornpipe "Blow High, Blow Low"; and the jubilant "June Is Bustin' Out All Over."

It was inevitable that critics and audiences compared *Carousel* to **Oklahoma!**, and not just because they were playing across the street from one another. Both musicals shared the same librettist, lyricist, composer, director, choreographer, costume designer, lead female dancer, and producer, and both were set in a nostalgic American past. There were grumblings that perhaps *Carousel* borrowed a little too heavily on its predecessor: the flighty Ado Annie and the giddy Carrie Pipperidge were very much kissing cousins; the wiser and older characters of Aunt Eller and Nettie Fowler could have been sisters; and Jud Fry and Jigger Craigin were both villains. Further, both musicals killed off a leading character (Jud and Billy), and both included elaborate ballets by Agnes De Mille. Moreover, each musical celebrated nature ("Oh, What a Beautiful Mornin'" and "June Is Bustin' Out All Over"); both centered on outdoor get-togethers (a picnic for **Oklahoma!**, a clam bake for *Carousel*); and both offered tentative, almost in-denial love songs ("People Will Say We're in Love" and "If I Loved You"). When **Oklahoma!**'s Will Parker comes back from the big city, he extols its virtues in "Kansas City," and for a while there it seemed as if Carrie would do the same about her visit to New York City (but thankfully her "I'm a Tomboy, I'm a Madcap Maiden from Broadway" was never developed into a full-fledged number).

But despite their similarities, the two musicals are very much dissimilar in style: **Oklahoma!** is an essentially sunny and optimistic musical comedy, and *Carousel* is a dark and brooding musical play. And the length of their New York runs is quite telling: **Oklahoma!** played more than twice as long as *Carousel*, with 2,212 performances for the former and 890 for the latter. Many audience members clearly enjoyed the laughter of **Oklahoma!** more than the tears of *Carousel*. It's notable that in his opening night review Louis Kronenberger in *PM* predicted that *Carousel* might not run for "years and years" but would probably "seem more of a milestone in the years to come."

As for the score, the critics were generally pleased, but a first-hearing of new music can be deceptive. Most completely ignored the waltz prelude and the "Soliloquy," two of *Carousel*'s most famous musical sequences. Further, an unsigned notice in the *New York World-Telegram* (the reviewer was substituting for an ailing Burton Rascoe) said that "What's the Use of Wond'rin'" and "You'll Never Walk Alone" were "cheerful" songs;

but the former is sad, wistful, and introspective, and the latter is a church-like inspirational choir song, and certainly the word "cheerful" doesn't define either one of them.

The second-act ballet (unimaginatively titled "Ballet") was one of the most wearisome moments of the evening. No matter who seems to choreograph the sequence (De Mille, of course, for the original production and for most subsequent revivals, and Kenneth MacMillan for the 1994 New York revival), it comes across as obvious (and furthermore is too long). During the tryout, the sequence was titled "Billy Makes a Journey" and was divided into two parts, "The Birth of Billy's Child" and "The Childhood." The final version of the ballet cut the first part and concentrated on the second.

Kronenberger said the musical was "lovely and touching," "an occasion in the theatre," and made "no obeisances to routine musical-comedy demands"; and Rodgers's music was the "best" aspect of the evening (Rodgers incidentally watched the opening night performance from backstage because of a recent back injury). De Mille's first-act hornpipe had "wonderful liveliness and freshness," and while the second-act ballet was "very good" it was in her "slightly too familiar style." Ward Morehouse in the *New York Sun* found *Carousel* "memorable" theatre and said the "touching and affecting" production would "be around for a long time." Robert Garland in the *New York Journal-American* said the musical offered "an evening of sheer theatrical enchantment," and he had just two quibbles: he wished the opening waltz prelude had been longer, and that the unnamed second-act ballet had been shorter.

Lewis Nichols in the *New York Times* found the musical "on the whole delightful" with one of the most "beautiful" Rodgers scores and some of Hammerstein's "best" lyrics; but he noted the first few scenes moved "a little slowly," that Raitt was not as good an actor as a singer, and that De Mille's second-act ballet was "perhaps not up" to her usual creations. Otis L. Guernsey Jr. in the *New York Herald Tribune* praised the "lovely" score and noted the evening's "brilliant diamond" was "If I Loved You," which deserved to be hailed as "the song of the Broadway musical year." John Chapman in the *New York Daily News* said the work was "one of the finest musical plays I have seen and I shall remember it always."

Wilella Waldorf in the *New York Post* said the score was "fine" but felt the music was shortchanged because some of cast members were no "vocal treat"; she suspected the music would have been "more haunting" with better singers. As for comparisons with **Oklahoma!**, she noted some of *Carousel*'s performers could walk across the street to the St. James and "without undue comment" could easily mingle with that cast during a performance. Otherwise, the **Oklahoma!** formula was becoming "a bit monotonous" and so were De Mille's ballets (and she concluded her review with "All right, go ahead and shoot").

Carousel was the season's longest-running musical. During its run, chorus member Iva Withers succeeded Jan Clayton in the role of Julie, and later performed the part for the national tour and the London production. Howard Keel followed John Raitt as Billy Bigelow, and on tour Stephen Douglass played the role. The London production opened at the Drury Lane on June 7, 1950, for 566 performances, and the cast included Douglass and Withers, Margot Moser (Carrie), and, from the original cast, Bambi Linn and Eric Mattson.

The 1956 film version was released by Twentieth Century-Fox and starred Gordon MacRae (Billy), Shirley Jones (Julie), Barbara Ruick (Carrie), Robert Rounseville (Mister Snow), and Susan Luckey (Louise) (later that year, Rounseville created the title role in the Broadway production of *Candide*). Frank Sinatra had originally been signed for Billy, but left the filming when he discovered each scene would have to be filmed twice, for both the CinemaScope and CinemaScope 55 processes. After his departure, a new technology allowed the film to be shot simultaneously in both screen processes, and so unlike the screen version of **Oklahoma!** (which was filmed in both CinemaScope and Todd-AO, and thus required that each scene be filmed twice), there weren't two separate film versions of *Carousel*.

The final release print omitted "You're a Queer One, Julie Jordan" and "Blow High, Blow Low," both of which had been filmed and were shown in early screenings (and which were included on the film's soundtrack album); the numbers were effective because the first established Julie's character and the second gave some musical weight to Jigger, but the cut footage seems permanently lost. Two others songs, "Geraniums in the Winder" and "The Highest Judge of All," weren't filmed. The DVD was released by Twentieth Century-Fox Home Entertainment (# 24543-38147).

A television version directed by Paul Bogart was presented by ABC on May 7, 1965, with Robert Goulet (Billy), Mary Grover (Julie), Pernell Roberts (Jigger), Marilyn Mason (Carrie), Charles Ruggles (The Starkeeper), and Patricia Neway (Nettie). The teleplay was by Sidney Michaels, and the choreography by Edward Villella.

As of this writing, the musical has been revived in New York six times, including four productions at City Center, three of which were produced by the New York City Center Light Opera Company (NYCCLOC).

The first revival (which played at City Center but was produced by the Theatre Guild) opened on January 25, 1949, and soon transferred to the Majestic Theatre, home of the original 1945 production; at the two theatres it played for a total of forty-nine performances, and the cast included Stephen Douglass and Iva Withers; others in the company had either appeared in the original production or would later appear in the London edition (see entry for more information about the 1949 revival).

The first revival by the NYCCLOC opened on June 2, 1954, for seventy-nine performances; the cast included Chris Robinson (Billy), Jo Sullivan (Julie), Barbara Cook (Carrie), John Conte (Jigger), and Bambi Linn (Louise); during the run, Robinson was succeeded by David Atkinson; the second was seen on September 11, 1957, for twenty-four performances, with Howard Keel as Billy, and, this time around Barbara Cook was Julie, not Carrie; the cast also included Russell Nype (Mister Snow), Marie Powers (Nettie), Kay Medford (Mrs. Mullins), and Bambi Linn (Louise); the third NYCCLOC revival took place on December 15, 1966, for twenty-two performances and starred Bruce Yarnell (Billy), Constance Towers (Julie), Nancy Dussault (Carrie), Patricia Neway (Nettie), and Michael Kermoyan (Jigger).

Between the second and third NYCCLOC revival came the Music Theatre of Lincoln Center's production, which opened at the New York State Theatre on August 10, 1965, for forty-eight performances; John Raitt recreated his role of Billy from twenty years earlier, and others in the company were Eileen Christy (Julie), Susan Watson (Carrie), Reid Sheldon (Mister Snow), Katherine Hilgenberg (Nettie), Jerry Orbach (Jigger), Benay Venuta (Mrs. Mullins), and Everett Edward Horton (The Starkeeper).

The most recent New York revival was seen at Lincoln Center's Vivian Beaumont Theatre on March 24, 1994, for 322 performances. Based on a revival by the Royal National Theatre of Great Britain, Nicholas Hynter's production was stunningly designed by Bob Crowley and offered a breathtaking opening sequence. As the music of the waltz prelude begins, the factory girls are seen at work as a huge clock hovers over them; when their work day ends, the clock dissolves into a gigantic moon and the girls head off for the carnival as the carousel is dazzlingly constructed before the audience.

Crowley's scenic designs offered even more delights, and it was his vision that made the revival truly memorable. Unfortunately, the production was somewhat indifferently cast, and Michael Hayden's Billy was criticized because of his average singing voice. But his Billy was the heart and soul of the evening because his acting was magnificent. Here was a tough, brooding, and vulnerable Billy in full young-Marlon-Brando mode, and his boyishly handsome looks clearly showed why women were attracted to him, from the middle-aged and hard-boiled Mrs. Mullins to the young and naïve Julie Jordan.

The score has been recorded a number of times, but the best version is that of the original cast (released by Decca LP # DL-8003 and on CD by MCA Classics # MCAD-10799, which includes a bonus track of an alternate and more complete version of the "Carousel Waltz").

The script was published in hardback by Alfred A. Knopf in 1946, and the lyrics are included in *The Complete Lyrics of Oscar Hammerstein II*.

Awards

New York Drama Critics' Circle Award (1945–1946): Best Musical (**Carousel**)

CARMEN JONES

Theatre: City Center
Opening Date: May 2, 1945; *Closing Date*: May 19, 1945
Performances: 21
Book and *Lyrics*: Oscar Hammerstein II
Music: Georges Bizet (new orchestrations by Robert Russell Bennett)
Based on the 1875 opera *Carmen* (music by Georges Bizet, libretto by Henri Meilhac and Ludovic Halevy), which in turn was based on the 1845 story *Carmen* by Prosper Merimee.
Direction: Libretto directed by Charles Friedman; staged by Hassard Short; *Producer*: Billy Rose; *Choreography*: Eugene Loring; *Scenery*: Howard Bay; *Costumes*: Raoul Pene du Bois; *Color Schemes*: Designed by Hassard Short; *Lighting*: Hassard Short; *Musical Direction*: David Mordecai; *Choral Direction*: Robert Shaw

Cast: Robert Clarke (Corporal Morrell, Soldier), George Willis (Foreman), Elton J. Warren (Cindy Lou; alternate for Cindy Lou, Carlotta Franzel), Jack Carr (Sergeant Brown), LeVern Hutcherson (Joe; alternate for Joe, Napoleon Reed), Muriel Smith (Carmen; alternate for Carmen, Inez Matthews), Sibol Cain (Sally, Card Player), Edward Roche (T-Bone), Carlos Van Putten (Tough Kid), Cozy Cole (Drummer), Maithe Marshall (Bartender), Edward Christopher (Waiter), June Hawkins (Myrt), Theresa Merritte (Frankie), John Bubbles (Rum), Ford Buck (Dink), Bill O'Neil (Boy), Erona Harris (Girl), Glenn Bryant (Husky Miller), Ruth Crumpton (Dancing Girl), Elijah Hodges (Poncho, Soldier), Lee Allen (Bullet Head), Randall Steplight (Soldier), George Willis (Soldier, Photographer), George Spelvin (Mr. Higgins), Fredye Marshall (Mrs. Higgins), Urylee Leonardos (Card Player), Doris Brown (Card Player), Sheldon B. Hoskins (Dancing Boxer), Randolph Sawyer (Dancing Boxer), Tony Fleming Jr. (Referee); Soldiers, Factory Workers, Socialites: Anne Dixon, Urylee Leonardos, Fredye Marshall, Doris Brown, Ida Johnson, Mattie Washington, Margaret Eley, Elsie Kennedy, Mary Graham, Sibol Cain, Clarice Crawford, Ruth Crumpton, Lee Allen, Robert Clarke, Elijah Hodges, Randall Steplight, Maithe Marshall, Chauncey Reynolds, Edward Roche, Richard de Vaultier, George Willis, Clarence Jones, Andrew J. Taylor, Harold Taylor; Dancers: Evelyn Pilcher, Edith Ross, Dorothy McDavid, Hedye Brown, Carmencita Romero, Westleen Foster, Posie Flowers, Audrey Graham, Erona Harris, Mabel Hart, Rhoda Johnson, Vera McNichols, Edith Hurd, Randolph Sawyer, Charles Williams, Daniel Lloyd, Walter Smith, Edward Christopher, Ivan Gittens, Gilbert Rivera, Tony Fleming, Clifton Gray, Sheldon Hoskins, Smalls Boykins, Joseph Noble, Bill O'Neil; Children: Lawrence Drayton Jr., Earl Drayton, Gilbert Irvis, Albert Smith, Carlos Van Patten, James Holeman, Melba Evelyn Hawkins, Roger Smith

The musical was presented in two acts.

The action takes place during the present time in a Southern town and in Chicago.

Carmen Jones, Oscar Hammerstein II's modern-day adaptation of Georges Bizet's 1875 opera *Carmen*, opened at the Broadway Theatre on December 2, 1943, and played for 503 performances before closing on February 10, 1945. Some three months after the production closed, producer Billy Rose brought the musical to City Center, where it played for an additional 21 performances as the first stop of a one-year, twenty-six-city tour (for the last stop of the tour, the company returned to City Center for another limited engagement; see separate entry for the 1946 visit).

The current production featured Muriel Smith and Glenn Bryant, who reprised their original roles of Carmen and Husky Miller, and LeVern Hutcherson was Joe. For more information about the musical, including a list of musical numbers, see entry for the 1943 production.

BLUE HOLIDAY
"A NEW VARIETY SHOW"

Theatre: Belasco Theatre
Opening Date: May 21, 1945; *Closing Date*: May 26, 1945
Performances: 8
Lyrics and *Music*: Al Moritz
Direction: Monroe B. Hack; *Producers*: Irvin Shapiro and Doris Cole; *Choreography*: "Fiji Island" and "Voodoo in Haiti" choreographed by Katherine Dunham; *Scenery*: Perry Watkins; *Costumes*: Kasia; *Lighting*: Uncredited; *Musical Direction*: Billy Butler; *Choral Direction*: Hall Johnson
Cast: Ethel Waters, Josh White, Willie Bryant, Timmie Rogers, The Katherine Dunham Dancers, The Hall Johnson Choir, Mary Lou Williams, Lillian Fitzgerald, The Three Poms, Evelyn Ellis, Mildred Smith, Josephine Premice, The Chocolateers; The Katherine Dunham Dancers: Lavinia Williams, Talley Beatty, Florence Moriles, Roxie Foster, Wilbur Bradley, Teppy Fletcher, Jesse Hawkins, Victoria Henderson, Richard James, Eartha Kitt, Alveta Hudson, Albert Popwell, Eugene Robinson, Joe Smith, J. DeWitt Spencer, John Weaver, Enid Williams, and Henri Augustine (Drummer); The Hall Johnson Choir: Laura Adamson, James Armstrong, Olive Ball, Mabel Bergen, Maudiva Brown, William Davis, Bessie Guy, Lola Hayes, Willie Mays, Ruthena Matson, Violet McDowell, Massie Patterson, Bertha Powell, George Rayston, Jessie Williams, Robert Woodland

The revue was presented in two acts.

Sketches and Musical Numbers

Act One: "The Star-Spangled Banner" (The Hall Johnson Choir); "Blue Holiday" (lyric and music by Al Moritz) (Lillian Fitzgerald); Willie Bryant; The Three Poms; "Voodoo in Haiti" (choreographed by Katherine Dunham) (The Katherine Dunham Dancers, Josephine Premice; sequence included "Chant," sung by the Hall Johnson Choir); Timmie Rogers; Scenes from *Mamba's Daughters* by DuBose and Dorothy Heyward (Hagar: Ethel Waters; Gilly Bluton: Willie Bryant; Mamba: Evelyn Ellis; Lissa: Mildred Smith; sequence included song "Sleep Time Lullaby," lyric and music by Al Moritz,, which was sung by Ethel Waters); Josh White: "Hard Time Blues" (lyric and music by Josh White and Warren Cuney); "Evil-Hearted Man" (traditional song arranged by Josh White); "The House I Live In" (lyric by Lewis Allen, music by Earl Robinson); "(I'm Gonna Move to the) Outskirts of Town" (lyric by Andy Razaf, music by William Weldon); and "One Meat Ball" (lyric by Hy Zaret, music by Lou Singer)

Act Two: "Fiji Island" (music by Herbert Kingsley; choreographed by Katherine Dunham) (The Katherine Dunham Dancers, featuring Lavinia Williams and Talley Beatty; for matinees, Lavinia Williams was spelled by Roxie Foster); Mary Lou Williams: sequence included "Limehouse Blues" (from 1922 London revue *A to Z*, and later heard in the 1924 Broadway revue *Andre Charlot's Revue of 1924*; lyric by Douglas Furber, music by Philip Braham); a medley of songs by Duke Ellington; and a medley of her own (mostly boogie-woogie) songs; Josephine Premice (who performed Haitian songs and dances): "Philomene, The Lazy Girl"; "Angelico"; and "Nibo—Carnival"; The Hall Johnson Choir: "I Got a Mule" (traditional); "Fare Ye Well" (traditional); and "St. Louis Blues" (lyric and music by W. C. Handy); The Chocolateers; Ethel Waters (accompanied by Marian Roberts at the piano); Waters's medley included "Stormy Weather" (*Cotton Club Parade*, 1933; lyric by Ted Koehler, music by Harold Arlen) and "Happiness Is Just a Thing Called Joe" (written especially for the 1943 film version of *Cabin in the Sky*; lyric by E. Y. Harburg, music by Harold Arlen); "The Free and Equal Blues" (lyric by E. Y. Harburg, music by Earl Robinson) (Entire Company)

Despite a cast that included Ethel Waters, the Katherine Dunham Dancers, and The Hall Johnson Choir, the revue *Blue Holiday* lasted just one week and became the season's shortest-running musical. The self-described variety show also included comedian (and master of ceremonies) Willie Bryant; comedian Timmie Rogers; the dance groups the Three Poms and the Chocolateers; singer Josh White; singer and dancer Josephine Premice; and pianist Mary Lou Williams.

Many of the critics noted the revue's original opening night had been postponed because the show was too long and that producer Jed Harris along with Monroe B. Mack had been called in at the last minute to reposition the songs and dances and to shorten the evening. But even with thirty minutes cut out, the revue was still lengthy, and so on opening night Ethel Waters didn't begin her song medley until 10:55 PM (which according to Herrick Brown in the *New York Sun* was "a late hour to start saving a production").

Brown also noted that some cast members extended their stage time by performing encores the moment they heard an "encouraging handclap." Prolonged encores were a complaint throughout the decade. It was one thing for a star of Ethel Merman's stature to sing an extra chorus or two of a Cole Porter patter song; but it was another matter when routine Broadway performers overextended their welcome by drawing out what was already a prolonged evening. It appears that some of the era's directors didn't focus on the issue of encores and apparently applause buttons weren't used to first encourage and then end an encore if it went on too long.

Robert Garland in the *New York Journal-American* reported that the programs handed out at the Belasco weren't necessarily indicative of what was actually performed on the stage. And so it wasn't always easy to figure out who was performing what at any given moment (he noted that a group of dancers could have been the Three Poms, but maybe not, and so he concluded that "perhaps I'll never know"). The above song list is a composite listing that reflects both the numbers listed in the opening night program as well as songs mentioned by the critics in their reviews. One critic reported that the title song wasn't heard at the premiere performance, and another indicated that "The Free and Equal Blues" was sung as the first (not the second) act finale; the above list gives the numbers as they appear in the program, but with the caveat that other songs that were performed are also listed.

Besides complaining about the overly long evening, some of the critics had major reservations about Ethel Waters. They felt the scenes from her 1939 drama *Mamba's Daughters* (by Dorothy and DuBose Heyward) were out of place in the revue, and their context wasn't always clear unless one had seen the drama and had a clear memory of it. As for her song medley, many said she was too stylized and thus failed to project her songs in her well-known direct, forthright, and clarion manner.

John Chapman in the *New York Daily News* suggested *Blue Holiday* was less an organized and well-paced revue than an "old-style Sunday Night Concert"; Burton Rascoe in the *New York World-Telegram* said that with *Blue Holiday* "vaudeville raised its feeble head" and then "sank right back into a coma"; the evening was one of the "dullest" and "most discomforting" of efforts to bring back vaudeville to Broadway; Howard Barnes in the *New York Herald Tribune* said the show was "monotonous and a bit tiresome"; Louis Kronenberger in *PM* found the evening often "heavy and monotonous" and thus "the greater part of it" was a "bore"; and Wilella Waldorf in the *New York Post* said the revue was more in the nature of a "series of recitals."

Like some of the other critics, Lewis Nichols in the *New York Times* suggested the best parts of the evening were better suited to a nightclub presentation, and he also noted the show seemed "insufficiently rehearsed." He mentioned that Waters's singing was too mannered, that she was "vocally sedate," and "accented her gestures." Kronenberger mentioned she had "very misguidedly gone cute instead of really singing"; and Garland said her "heart-warming simplicity" had become "fussy, foolish and unfamiliar."

The critics liked Josh White and his then well-known comedy song "One Meat Ball," about a man who has just fifteen cents and thus can't afford a large dinner. In light of the present-day meat shortages, Waldorf suggested White revise the words of the song to reflect that bread is plentiful but that now you can't even get one meat ball.

The revue included "The House I Live In," which previously had been heard in **Let Freedom Sing** (for more information about the song, see entry for the earlier revue).

MEMPHIS BOUND
"The Musical Smash" / "A New Musical Comedy"

Theatre: Broadway Theatre (during run, the musical transferred to the Belasco Theatre)
Opening Date: May 24, 1945; *Closing Date*: June 23, 1945
Performances: 36
Book: Albert Barker and Sally Benson
Lyrics: W. S. Gilbert; new lyrics by Clay Warnick
Music: Arthur Sullivan; new music by Don Walker
Based in part on W. S. Gilbert and Arthur Sullivan's 1878 operetta *H.M.S. Pinafore, or The Lass That Loved a Sailor*; and some music from the team's 1875 operetta *Trial by Jury* was also used in the musical.
Direction: Directed by Robert Ross and under the personal supervision of Vinton Freedley; Eva Jessye was the assistant director; *Producer*: John Wildberg; *Choreography*: Al White Jr.; *Scenery* and *Lighting*: George Jenkins; *Costumes*: Lucinda Ballard; *Musical Direction*: Charles Sanford
Cast: William C. Smith (Hector), Edith Wilson (Melissa Carter aka Aunt Mel), Ann Robinson (Chloe), Billy Daniels (Roy Baggott), Ada Brown (Mrs. Paradise), Sheila Guys (Lily Valentine), Ida James (Penny Paradise), Thelma Carpenter (Henny Paradise), Frank Wilson (Mr. Finch), Avon Long (Winfield Carter aka Windy), *Bill Robinson* (Pilot Meriwether aka Pops), Timothy Grace (Timmy), Oscar Plante (Sheriff McDaniels), Joy Merrimore (Eulalia), Harriet Jackson (Sarabelle), Charles Welch (Bill), William Dillard (Gabriel); The Delta Rhythm Boys: Traverse Crawford, Rene De Knight, Carl Jones, Kelsey Pharr, Lee Gaines; Members of the Calliboga Social Drama Center: Lee Eberlee, Ethel White, Joy Merrimore, Eulabel Riley, Nell Plante, Marion Bruce, Harriet Jackson, Mary Lewis, Muriel Watkins, John Diggs, Leslie Gray, William C. Smith, Oscar Plante, Roy White, William Archer, David Perry, Rodesta Timmons, Lulling Williams, Charles Welch, Theodore Brown, William Dillard; Dancing Girls: Sophia Miller, Louise Patterson, Lula Hill, Bethesta Williamson, Laura Catherell, Mitzi Coleman, Clarice Cook, Eleanor Brown, Mimi Williams, Jacqueline Petty, Jackie Lewis, Joan Cooper, Charlotte Saunders, Libby Parker; Dancing Boys: Prince Hall, William Chapman, Toni Thompson, Morton Brown, Wilson Young, Abe Moore, Charles Keith, John Smith, Andrew Drew; Children: Ann Timmons, Jeanne Petti, June Fussell, Marliene Strong, Richard Reed, Neils LeRoy, Timothy Grace, James Worden
The musical was presented in two acts.
The action takes place during the present time near Calliboga, Tennessee.

Musical Numbers

Act One: "Big Old River" (Ensemble); "Stand Around the Bend" (Avon Long, The Delta Rhythm Boys, Ensemble); "Old Love and Brand New Love" (Billy Daniels, Avon Long, Sheila Guys); "Growing Pains" (Bill Robinson); From the performance of *H.M.S. Pinafore* by the members of the Calliboga Social Drama Center: "We Sail the Ocean Blue" (Sailors); "I'm Called Little Buttercup" (Ada Brown, The Delta Rhythm Boys); "A Maiden Fair to See" (Billy Daniels, Sailors); "I Am the Captain of the Pinafore" (Avon Long, Sailors); "Sorry Her Lot" (Sheila Guys, Ida James, Thelma Carpenter); "Over the Bright Blue Sea" (Ensemble); "I Am the Monarch of the Sea" (Bill Robinson, Ensemble); "The Ruler of the Queen's Navee" (Bill Robinson); "The Nightingale, the Moon and I" (Billy Daniels); Finale (Ensemble)

Act Two: "The Gilbert and Sullivan Blues" (Ann Robinson); *Note*: Most of the remainder of the second act was a continuation of the performance of *H.M.S. Pinafore*: "Farewell, My Own" (Bill Robinson, Billy Daniels, The Beer Garden Four); "Fair Moon" (Avon Long, The Delta Rhythm Boys, Ensemble); "Love or Reason" (Sheila Guys, Ida James, Thelma Carpenter); "Things Are Seldom What They Seem" (Bill Robinson, Avon Long); "Trial by Jury" (Bill Robinson, Avon Long, Edith Wilson, Frank Wilson, William Dillard, Ensemble); "The Nightingale, the Moon and I" (reprise) (Billy Daniels, Sheila Guys, Ensemble); "Old Love and Brand New Love" (reprise) (The Delta Rhythm Boys, Ensemble); "A-Many Years Ago" (Ada Brown, The Delta Rhythm Boys); "Ring the Merry Belles" (Bill Robinson); Finale (Company)

In the late 1930s, Broadway's *The Swing Mikado* and *The Hot Mikado* were dueling black adaptations of Gilbert and Sullivan's *The Mikado*; and late in the 1944–1945 season two adaptations of the team's *H.M.S. Pinafore* opened within a week of one another, first *Memphis Bound* and then **Hollywood Pinafore**; both were quick failures that closed after thirty-six and fifty-three respective performances.

Memphis Bound dealt with a group of black players headed down the Mississippi on the show boat *Calliboga Queen* in order to give a performance of *H.M.S. Pinafore* in Memphis. When the vessel runs aground on a sandbar, the players must give an impromptu performance of the operetta in order to raise funds to dislodge the boat. The evening offered both "book" songs (lyrics by Clay Warnick and music by Don Walker) as well as numbers from Gilbert and Sullivan, and so unlike *Hollywood Pinafore* the evening wasn't a strict adaptation of the original operetta with an updated story and lyrics; instead the original operetta appeared as a show-within-the-show.

Wilella Waldorf in the *New York Post* and other New York critics noted that Bill Robinson, the celebrated tap dancer and star of the new musical, would be celebrating his sixty-seventh birthday on the day after the opening. But no one could really believe it. Waldorf said he was in "wonderful form" as he cavorted through the evening; Lewis Nichols in the *New York Times* said the musical found a way to work in Robinson's celebrated staircase dance, and he tapped up and down the stairs "with an agility that would dizzy a grandchild"; Burton Rascoe in the *New York World-Telegram* said Robinson was the "top man" in the field of tap who danced with "unearthly ease and dexterity" and provided "tingling" thrills when he went into his dance four times during the course of the evening; and John Chapman in the *New York Daily News* said Robinson's feet provided "inimitably clear patterns of tap" and the stair routine had "lost none of its capacity to astonish."

Waldorf noted that Avon Long (as Captain Corcoran) wore a lavender outfit and did a "mild swish" around the deck while the sailors waved handkerchiefs at him; and three chorus girls jointly performed the role of Josephine because all had been promised the part, and they had been practicing a la the Andrews Sisters, anyway. So the evening wavered between the Tennessee troupe's quirky conception of how to play *H.M.S. Pinafore* and a "sophisticated Broadway exercise in modern rhythms." Nichols noted the musical hesitated a bit and sometimes didn't seem to know what to do next, but he liked Don Walker's "*Pinafore*, eight to the bar" (per one of Clay Warnick's lyrics) with its dashes of boogie-woogie, jazz, and "even" Arthur Sullivan. Howard Barnes in the *New York Herald Tribune* found the musical's "fragments curiously unrelated and discordant" but noted the evening was most successful when it "hops up" Sullivan with a "bit of off-beat" (he singled out "The Gilbert and Sullivan Blues," noting it was "spectacular").

Rascoe complained that the musical lacked "zip and zingo" and the cast was left to "sadly" search for a book that had little humor; but he noted the evening was "very clean—good-natured, informal and inoffensive." Herrick Brown in the *New York Sun* praised the "catchy" new songs by Walker and Warnick, and enjoyed the Sullivan music "jazzed up to the mood of 125th Street." Chapman was glad to see a musical reminiscent of the old days; here there was no solemn plot with artistic ballets; instead, *Memphis Bound* was a breezy show with "zip," "stomp," and "whoosh"; and he praised Avon Long as "a brown-skinned Clifton Webb." Robert Garland in the *New York Journal-American* praised the "resplendent" musical; it "couldn't be improved upon" and it provided a "memorable" entertainment from "the Land of Professional Make-Believe."

Clay Warnick and Don Walker's new songs were "Big Old River," "Stand Around the Bend," "Old Love and Brand New Love," and "Growing Pains." As mentioned, Warnick updated some of Gilbert's lyrics (and also provided the vocal arrangements), and Walker adapted Sullivan's score (and provided the orchestrations).

The collection *Life's a Funny Present* (Rialto CD # SLRR-9306) includes "The Nightingale, the Moon and I."

HOLLYWOOD PINAFORE (or THE LAD WHO LOVED A SALARY)

Theatre: Alvin Theatre
Opening Date: May 31, 1945; *Closing Date*: July 14, 1945
Performances: 53
Book and *Lyrics*: George S. Kaufman (*Program Note*: "With the deepest apologies to W. S. Gilbert")
Music: Arthur Sullivan
Based on W. S. Gilbert and Arthur Sullivan's 1878 operetta *H.M.S. Pinafore*, or *The Lass That Loved a Sailor*; the production also included music from the team's other operettas.
Direction: George S. Kaufman; production supervised by Arnold Saint-Subber; *Producer*: Max Gordon (in association with Meyer Davis); *Choreography*: Ballet choreographed by Antony Tudor and Ensemble Dances choreographed by Douglas Coudy; *Scenery* and *Lighting*: Jo Mielziner; *Costumes*: Modern Costumes by Kathryn Kuhn and Period Costumes by Mary Percy Schenck; *Musical Direction*: George Hirst
Cast: *Victor Moore* (Joseph W. Porter), George Rasely (Mike Corcoran),Gilbert Russell (Ralph Rackstraw), *William Gaxton* (Dick Live-Eye), Annamary Dickey (Brenda Blossom), Shirley Booth (Louhedda Hopsons), Russ Brown (Bob Beckett), Mary Wickes (Miss Hebe), Diana Corday (Miss Gloria Mundi), Pamela Randell (Miss Beverly Wilshire), Ella Mayer (Little Miss Peggy), Dan De Paolo (Doorman), Jackson Jordan (Secretary), Eleanor Prentiss (Secretary), Drucilla Strain (Secretary), Ernest Taylor (Guard); The Lyn Murray Singers: Sally Billings, Florence George, Jane Hansen, Lucy Hillary, Josephine Lambert, Margaret McKenna, Candace Montgomery, Jeanne North, Annette Sorell, Mary Williams, Dean Campbell, Harold Cole, Jack Collins, Charles Dubin, Silas Engum, Howard Hoffmann, Barry Kent, James Mate, John Mathews, Larry Stuart, Jeffrey Warren; Dancers: Eleanor Boleyn, Helene Constantine, Barbara (Babs) Heath, Virginia Meyer, Ann Newland, Mary Alice Bingham, John Butler, Ronny Chetwood, Stanley Herbert, Shaun O'Brien, Jack Purcell, Regis Powers
The musical was presented in two acts.
The action takes place during the present time at Pinafore Pictures Studio in Hollywood, California.

Musical Numbers

Note: The program didn't list most of the musical numbers; the following is compiled from the script, newspaper reviews, reference sources, and the program.
Act One: "We Are Simple Movie Folk" (Girls: Diana Corday, Pamela Randall, Ella Mayer; Ensemble); "Little Butter-Up" (Shirley Booth); "An Agent's Life (Lot) Is Not a Happy One" (William Gaxton); "A Maiden Often Seen" (Gilbert Russell, Chorus); "I'm a Big Director at Pinafore" (George Rasley, Chorus); "Here on the Lot" (Annamary Dickey); "Joe Porter's Car Is Seen" (Chorus); "I Am the Monarch of the Joint" (Victor Moore, Mary Wickes, Ensemble); ""When I Was a Lad" (Victor Moore, Ensemble); "A Writer Fills the Lowest Niche" (aka "Studio Writers' Song") (Russ Brown, Gilbert Russell, Ensemble); "Never Mind the Why and Wherefore" (William Gaxton, Ensemble); "Refrain, Audacious Scribe" (Annamary Dickey); "Proud Lady, Have Your Way" ("This Very Night") (Gilbert Russell, Annamary Dickey); Act One Finale (includes "Studio Writers' Song") (Entire Cast)
Act Two: "Fair Moon" (George Rasley); "I Am the Monarch of the Joint" (reprise) (Victor Moore, Mary Wickes, Ensemble); "Success Story" (ballet) (Viola Essen; Other Little Maids: Barbara Heath, Helene Con-

stantine; Talent Scout: Regis Powers; Her True Love: Ronny Chetwood; Two More Boys: Shaun O'Brien, Jack Purcell; Armand, The Movie Hero: John Butler; Director: Stanley Herbert; Studio Assistants: Eleanor Boleyn, Ann Newland, Virginia Meyer; Soloists: Lucy Hillary, John Mathews); "Hollywood's a Funny Place" (Shirley Booth, Victor Moore); "To Go upon the Stage" (Annamary Dickey); "He Is a Movie Man" (William Gaxton, Victor Moore, Ensemble); "The Merry Maiden and the Jerk" (William Gaxton, Victor Moore); "Carefully on Tiptoe Stealing" (Annamary Dickey, Gilbert Russell, William Gaxton, George Rasley, Ensemble); "Pretty Daughter of Mine" (George Rasley, Gilbert Russell, Mary Wickes, Victor Moore, William Gaxton, Ensemble); "Farewell, My Own" (Gilbert Russell, Annamary Dickey, Mary Wickes, Victor Moore, Shirley Booth, Russ Brown, Ensemble); "This Town I Now Must Shake" (Shirley Booth, Ensemble); Act Two Finale ("We Are Simple Movie Folk") Entire Company)

George S. Kaufman's adaptation of Gilbert and Sullivan's *H.M.S. Pinafore* into a satiric look at the Hollywood studio system seemed like a sure thing. The characters included Joseph W. Porter, the head of Pinafore Pictures (Victor Moore); agent Dick Live-Eye (William Gaxton), who is more than happy to give his clients 90 percent of what they make; gossip columnist Louhedda Hopsons (Shirley Booth); director Mike Corcoran (George Rasley), who "no, never, well, hardly ever" makes a flop; film star Brenda Blossom (Annamary Dickey); screenwriter Ralph Rackstraw (Gilbert Russell); press agent Bob Beckett (Russ Brown); Porter's secretary Miss Hebe (Mary Wickes); and an assortment of secretaries and yes men, all of whom are sisters, cousins, and aunts of Porter and thus receive exorbitant salaries for doing absolutely no work. Among Kaufman's conceits was the notion that scriptwriters are the lowest form of Hollywood life, and so at studio meetings the writers wear convict black-and-white striped clothing and are bound and gagged during conferences. Further, when star Brenda Blossom announces she's in love with screen writer Ralph Rackstraw, it's virtually tantamount to career suicide (if they wed, it will be in secret and they'll tell only the *New York Times*).

With the team of Victor Moore and William Gaxton in the leading roles, Kaufman's adaptation and direction, and Jo Mielziner's sumptuous (if ultimately confining) single set, which depicted the magnificent Pinafore Studios' main entrance and office, *Hollywood Pinafore* promised a wicked evening of satire. But most of the critics were severely disappointed with the musical. With Moss Hart, Kaufman had written the devastating Hollywood spoof *Once in a Lifetime* in 1930, and fifteen years later a satiric look at tinsel town didn't seem all that fresh and exciting, especially since now even the movies themselves kidded Hollywood.

Further, Moore excelled in bumbling characterizations fringed with pathos, and the role of a powerful studio head (who states that the sun must start setting in the east so that his office can have more afternoon light) didn't quite jibe with his well-known stage personality. Gaxton was well-cast as the sly agent, but the role wasn't equal to his billing, and so "The Policemen's Lot" (from Gilbert and Sullivan's *The Pirates of Penzance*) was interpolated for him (as "The Agent's Lot"). (The second act ballet "Success Story," which depicted how a starlet can rise to the top of the Hollywood firmament, borrowed music from a number of Sullivan's compositions, including *The Mikado, Iolanthe*, and *The Yeomen of the Guard* as well as Sullivan's song "The Lost Chord.") The musical even suffered from being somewhat set-bound, as all the action took place in the main office and conference room of Pinafore Studios (when the ballet broke loose from the confines of the conference room, one critic noted the audience wildly applauded because everyone was clearly ready for a change of scene). And many of the critics didn't understand why Kaufman occasionally employed archaic phrases ("Wouldst you know"; "What, pray?"; "Methinks"; "Naught else matters"; "Hast ever thought"), none of which blended well with the otherwise modern jargon.

In regard to Mielziner's set, the script described walls done up in gray satin and red marble with a center staircase that led to right and left balconies; two large curved desks conformed to the shapes of the curving rails of the staircase; and on each desk were three telephones in various colors. Thus Mielziner's designs made a sly reference to the setting of the poop deck of the H.M.S. *Pinafore*.

As a result of the mixed critical notices and the lack of audience interest, *Hollywood Pinafore* (like **Memphis Bound**, another adaptation of *H.M.S. Pinafore* that had opened a week earlier) closed within a few weeks. In 1940, **Tropical Pinafore**, another modern-day adaptation of the operetta, closed prior to Broadway.

Wilella Waldorf in the *New York Post* found Kaufman's "somewhat sophomoric" adaptation a "sad disappointment," and it was her "reluctant duty" to report it "almost never comes off. What never? Well, hardly ever"; Lewis Nichols in the *New York Times* also said the musical was "disappointing," and while there were occasional "sharp, devastating" lines the evening was too one-note in its depiction of Hollywood; Robert Garland in the *New York Journal-American* felt the musical was "better in theory than in performance";

although Kaufman was in a "collegiate" mood, the adaptation would have been "cute" only if undertaken by "college boys" and as an evening of Broadway entertainment, the production was "somewhat juvenile"; John Chapman in the *New York Daily News* said the first twenty minutes of the show were "grand," and then "disappointment" set in with Kaufman's "old-hat" burlesque of Hollywood; and while Louis Kronenberger in *PM* noted the production had its "virtues," it wasn't "much fun" and was more clever than entertaining; but like all the critics he praised Shirley Booth, who brought "satiric insight and skill" to her role of a Hollywood gossip columnist.

But Burton Rascoe in the *New York World-Telegram* said the musical hit the "jackpot" and was "one of the finest New York has ever seen"; and he complimented Mielziner's "properly garish and splendiferous" décor; Herrick Brown in the *New York Sun* noted the evening might well be a "theatrical stunt" but was nonetheless in the "upper brackets" of Broadway entertainment; and Howard Barnes in the *New York Herald Tribune* said the "gaily impudent" musical was "audacious and vastly entertaining"; and "right up there at the top" was Shirley Booth's Louhedda Hopsons, whose "Little Butter-Up" was the high point of the first act, and who brought the second act to a close on a "note of high gaiety."

An abridged version of the script was published in hardback by St. Martin's Press in 1979 in *By George: A Kaufman Collection* (edited by Donald Oliver). "Little Butter-Up" is included in the collection *Life's a Funny Present* (Rialto CD # SLRR-9306).

ALASKAN STAMPEDE

Theatre and *Dates*: The ice revue opened on June 16, 1944, at the Coliseum, Chicago, Illinois, and closed there on July 15, 1944.
Book: Leo A. Seltzer and Harold M. Sherman
Music: Leonard Whitcup and Wilson Sawyer
Producer: Leo A. Seltzer
Cast: The cast included Margaret Spencer, Earl Covert, Wini Shaw, Evelyn Chandler, Bruce Mapes, and Mimi.

Alaskan Stampede was described as a "musical extravaganza on ice" by the *Chicago Stagebill Yearbook*. Claudia Cassidy in *Best Plays* reported that the "gold rush musical on ice turned out to be cold storage turkey." It's unclear if the ice show played in other cities.

GLAD TO SEE YOU
"A NEW MUSICAL COMEDY"

Theatres and *Performance Dates*: The musical opened on November 13, 1944, at the Shubert Theatre, Philadelphia, Pennsylvania, and then played at the Boston Opera House, Boston, Massachusetts, where it permanently closed on December 30, 1944.
Book: Fred Thompson and Eddie Davis
Lyrics: Sammy Cahn
Music: Jule Styne
Direction: Busby Berkeley; *Producer*: David Wolper; *Choreography*: Valerie Bettis; *Scenery* and *Lighting*: Howard Bay; *Costumes*: Travis Banton; *Musical Direction*: Max Meth
Cast: Beverly Michaels (Reception Clerk), Charles Conoway (Director), Kenny Bowers (Nick Lee), *Jane Withers* (Pat Rennie), *Eddie Davis* (Danny Riddle), Joseph Macaulay (Lorenzo Merlin, and later Charles Merlin, Sandy McMerlin, Ben Ali Merlin, and Luigi Merlino), Eric Roberts (Horace Merlin, and later Elmer Merlin, Angus McMerlin, Hassim Merlin, and Dominic Merlin), Patsy O'Shea (Caroline Merlin, and later Dora Merlin, Jeannie McMerlin, Fatima Merlin, and Maria Merlino), Alexis Rotov (Mr. Trotter), Gloria McGehee (Secretary), Nancy Donovan (Betty Saunders), Sammy White (Corky Corcoran), Gene Barry (Flight Lieutenant Don Neil, R.A.F.), *June Knight* (Louise Rockaway), Lew Eckels (Bartender), Walter Rinner (Voice on Loud Speaker), Michael Mauree (Mauree), Sid Lippe (Bell Hop), Peter Kehrlein (Agmar), John (Red) Kullers (Peddler), Slam Stewart (Genie), Jayne Manners (Zuleika), Valerie Bettis (The Embodiment of Pat's Emotions), Maria Monez (Fruit Girl), Paul Mario (Waiter), The Whitney Sisters; "Those with the Gift

of Dancing": Eleanor Boleyn, Clara Cordery, Jane Dodge, Oolan Farley, Betty Jane Hunt, Jeanne Ivory, Pan Leslie, Lucy Lewin, Olga Lunick, Gloria McGehee, Nancy Newton, Janet Pearsall, Olga Roberts, Gisella Svetlik, Marjorie Svetlik; "Those with the Gift of Singing": Diana Carlton, Richard Clemens, Jack Harney, Marian Hughes, Judith F. Kean, Gordon Leigh, Herbert Leighton, Paul Mario, Walter Rinner, Richard Spencer, Ellen Wilkes, Mary Williams; "Those with the Gift of Beauty": Gale Bennett, Lynn Carol, Doris Claire, Mildred Mahaney, Jeanne Martyn, Michael Mauree, Beverly Michaels, Maria Monez, Marge Pemberton, Myra Stephens

The musical was presented in two acts.

The action takes place during the present time in New York City, on an island in the Azores, in Loch Lomond, Scotland, in Algiers, in Italy, and in Monte Carlo.

Musical Numbers

Act One: "Give Us Dames" (Soldiers; Dancers—Ballerina: Nancy Newton; Leapers: Oolan Farley and Olga Lunick; Sister Act: The Whitney Sisters; Acrobat: Betty Jane Hunt; Dance Ensemble); "Just for You" (Jane Withers, Kenny Bowers); "I Murdered Them in Chicago" (Eddie Davis); "Horta Interlude" (The Whitney Sisters, Ensemble); "What Did I Do?" (Gene Barry, Officers); "Ladies Don't Have Fun" (Eddie Davis, June Knight); "I Don't Love You No More" (Kenny Bowers, Jane Withers; danced by Jane Withers, Kenny Bowers, The Whitney Sisters, Marjorie Svetlik, Gisella Svetlik, Lucy Lewin, Eleanor Boleyn, Oolan Farley, Olga Lunick, Nancy Newton, Clara Cordery); "I Don't Love You No More" (reprise) (danced by Alexis Rotov); "Most Unusual Weather (for This Time of Year)" (June Knight, Ensemble; interlude dance by Eleanor Boleyn, Olga Lunick, Nancy Newton); "Any Fool Can Fall in Love" (Gene Barry, June Knight, Ensemble; samba danced by The Whitney Sisters); "Classical Medley in a Bath" (pantomimed by Sammy White); "Come On! Come On!" (Nancy Donovan, Ensemble; danced by Eleanor Boleyn, Oolan Farley, Olga Lunick, Nancy Newton, Jeanne Ivory, Clara Cordery, Jane Dodge, Marjory Svetlik, Gisella Svetlik, Lucy Lewin, Olga Roberts, Betty Jane Hunt, Janet Pearsall); "Any Fool Can Fall in Love" (reprise) (Kenny Bowers); "B Apostrophe, K Apostrophe, L-Y-N" (Eddie Davis, Joseph Macaulay, Jane Withers, June Knight, Ensemble; danced by Ladies on Horseback: Eleanor Boleyn, Jane Dodge, and Olga Lunick; danced by Jitterbugs: Jane Hunt and Janet Pearsall; danced by Sharpie: Alexis Rotov)

Act Two: "I Lost My Beat" (Kenny Bowers, Slam Stewart, Ensemble; danced by The Whitney Sisters, Olga Roberts, Gloria McGehee, Dance Ensemble); "Guess I'll Hang My Tears Out to Dry" (Jane Withers, Ensemble; danced by Valerie Bettis); "I'll Hate Myself in the Morning" (Eddie Davis, Jayne Manners; danced by Eleanor Boleyn, Oolan Farley, Nancy Newton, Marjorie Svetlik); "So This Is Italy" (Gene Barry, Nancy Donovan, Officers); "I'm Laying Away a Buck" (June Knight); "Grown-Ups Are the Stupidest People" (Jane Withers, Kenny Bowers, Eddie Davis, June Knight, Sammy White); "Love and I Went Waltzing" (Gene Barry, Nancy Donovan, Ensemble; danced by Alexis Rotov, The Whitney Sisters; Wallflowers: Gisella Svetlik, Marjory Svetlik, Lucy Lewin, Jeanne Ivory, Betty Jane Hunt, Janet Pearsall; Dance Ensemble); Finale (Entire Company)

The title of *Glad to See You* (sometimes cited as *Glad to See You!*) was taken from a catch phrase popularized by and associated with comedian Phil Silvers, who couldn't appear in the musical because he was contracted to Twentieth Century-Fox at the time. If *Glad to See You* had opened on Broadway, it would have been Jule Styne's first full-length Broadway musical; as things turned out, Styne's first Broadway show was the long-running hit **High Button Shoes**, which premiered three years later and which starred Phil Silvers. In 1960, Silvers starred in Styne's *Do Re Mi*, a raucous satire of the jukebox and recording industries.

The musical marked screen child actress Jane Withers in her musical debut and in a grown-up acting role. She received good reviews, and introduced the haunting "Guess I'll Hang My Tears Out to Dry," one of the best torch songs ever written. The musical also gave Gene Barry one of his first leading roles, and the cast included June Knight (who introduced "Begin the Beguine" and "Just One of Those Things" in Cole Porter's 1935 musical *Jubilee*) and Eddie Davis, who was the musical's co-librettist and had also cowritten the book of **Follow the Girls**. But a week into the musical's tryout, Davis was seriously injured in an automobile accident; lyricist Sammy Cahn took over the role for a few performances, and then late in the Philadelphia run Eddie Foy Jr. assumed the role for the remainder of the tryout. The role of Louise had been scheduled to be played by Lupe Velez, but because of personal circumstances she bowed out and was replaced by June Knight (Velez committed suicide during the time of *Glad to See You*'s tryout).

The musical's scattershot plot sounds promising, in a farcical kind of way. Three magicians (Lorenzo, Horace, and Caroline Merlin, played by Joseph Macaulay, Eric Roberts, and Patsy O'Shea) are stalked for death by a worldwide organization seeking revenge because Lorenzo cheated his extended family out of an inheritance. When the trio flees New York, they leave their passports behind, which are found by three entertainers (Danny Biddle, Pat Rennie, and Nick Lee, played by Eddie Davis, Jane Withers, and Kenny Bowers) who use the passports to join a world tour that entertains soldiers overseas. But once overseas, the "organization" assumes Danny, Pat, and Nick are the Merlins, and so everywhere they go they're marked for, and barely escape from, death. (The organization's leading members were also played by Macaulay, Roberts, and O'Shea, who are now respectively Charles Merlin, Sandy McMerlin, Ben Ali Merlin, and Luigi Merlino; Elmer Merlin, Angus McMerlin, Hassim Merlin, and Dominic Merlino; and Dora Merlin, Jeannie McMerlin, Fatima Merlin, and Maria Merlino). Also figuring into the plot are R.A.F. Flight Lieutenant Don Neil (Gene Barry) and troupe singer Louise Rockaway (June Knight). Of course, by the finale all ends well and no tears are hanging out to dry.

Variety liked Jane Withers (she had the "ease and aplomb of a finished trouper"), and praised the score, choreography, and décor as well as the show's topical references and blue humor. But the trade paper felt the book never settled on a tone and a coherent viewpoint and thus the creators faced the "tricky job" of pulling the script together in order to get the show ready for Broadway.

William Torbert Leonard in *Broadway Bound* reports the musical (whose original title was *Have a Good Time*) lost approximately $250,000.

An advertisement for *Glad to See You* in the Boston program of *A Lady of ?* (later, **A Lady Says Yes**) noted that even though the musical was still in tryout, two of its songs had already "attained national fame": "Guess I'll Hang My Tears Out to Dry" had been performed by Frank Sinatra on a radio broadcast, and Kate Smith was scheduled to sing it on her radio show as well. And "B Apostrophe, K Apostrophe, L-Y-N" was going to be adopted by Brooklyn as its "city anthem" and "it is expected that this rousing, gay paean to New York's most populous borough will become as celebrated and cherished for generations as is 'The Sidewalks of New York' in Manhattan or even 'Dixie' in the Southland." The advertisement was correct about "Guess I'll Hang My Tears Out to Dry": this fabulous torch song has indeed become a standard. But poor "B Apostrophe, K Apostrophe, L-Y-N" seems to have gone nowhere.

There are numerous recordings of "Guess I'll Hang My Tears Out to Dry"; the song "I'm Laying Away a Buck" is included in the collection *Lost Broadway and More Volume 5* (unnamed company and unnumbered CD).

Joseph Macaulay played five roles in the Jule Styne musical, and he's sometimes confused with Jack (also known as John) McCauley, who appeared in Styne's **High Button Shoes** and **Gentlemen Prefer Blondes**. Macaulay and McCauley appeared together in **Spring in Brazil**, which closed during its pre-Broadway tryout.

WATCH OUT, ANGEL!
"A New Musical Comedy" / "Sparkling Musical Cocktail!"

Theatre and *Performance Dates*: The musical opened on April 3, 1945, at the Curran Theatre, San Francisco, California, and permanently closed there after a three-and-a-half-week run.
Book: Isabel Dawn and David Alison
Lyrics: Eddie de Lange
Music: Josef Myrow
Based on an original story by David Alison.
Direction: Harry Howell; *Producer*: David Alison; *Choreography*: Aida Broadbent; *Scenery*: Richard Jackson; *Costumes*: Martingale; *Lighting*: Uncredited; *Musical Direction*: Charles Hathaway
Cast: Marilyn Hare (Eleanor Wyatt), Danny Jackson (Danny "Red" Underwood), Jim Nolan (Preston Prescott), Eden Nicholas (Jerry Jackson), Parker Gee (Tommy Conway), Barbara Perry (Sandra), Heidi Olsen (Kathe), Irene Thomas (Dolores), Carol Haney (Genevieve), Donald Kerr (Barry), Lester Allen (Val), William O'Neal (John McIntyre), Anne Triola (Gaby Todd), Lucien Littlefield (Oscar Stone), Terry Randall (Jackie), Barbara Hipp (Peggy), Ruth Walton (Lois), Stephanie Stevens (Manila), Raisa (Zany Girl); Dancing Girls and Boys

in Tommy Conway's Production of *What's New in New York*: Elaine Corbett (Myrtle), Terry Randall (Jackie), Barbara Hipp (Peggy), Beverly Billman (Babs), Elise Rhea (Darlene), Irene Thomas (Dolores), Jean Foreman (Olive), Stephanie Stevens (Laura), Virginia King (Maizie), Georgia Reed (Priscilla), Ruth Walton (Lois), Vicki Mallory (Dorothy), Ronnie Stanton (Jimmy), Rodolfo Silva (Johnny), Ray Dolciame (Kenny), Jerry Antes (Sid)

The musical was presented in two acts.

The action takes place in New York City in 1945.

Musical Numbers

Act One: Overture (Orchestra); "Where Is the Boss?" (Marilyn Hare, Ronnie Stanton, Jerry Antes, Maids); "I Love You but Good" (Eden Nicholas, Marilyn Hare); "It's a Great Life If You Weaken" (Barbara Perry, Parker Gee, Irene Thomas, Ensemble); "To Be Young" (Heidi Olsen, Ensemble; Kathe, age sixteen: Elaine Corbett; Kathe, age twenty-one: Stephanie Stevens); "It's a Great Life If You Weaken" (reprise) (Marilyn Hare, Eden Nicholas); "Half a Dream to Go" (Eden Nicholas); "It's a Great Life If You Weaken" (reprise) (Donald Kerr, Lester Allen); "Watch Out, Angel!" (Anne Triola); "Publicity" (Danny Jackson, Jim Nolan, Anne Triola); "Co-op-hooray-shun" (Barbara Perry, Danny Jackson, Ensemble)

Act Two: Entr'acte (Orchestra); "Publicity" (reprise) (Jim Nolan, Danny Jackson, Ensemble); "Short and Sweet" (Barbara Perry, Donald Kerr, Lester Allen, Ensemble); "Don't You Believe It" (Anne Triola); "Everybody Wants to Get Into the Act" (Anne Triola, Ensemble); "Watch Out, Angel!" (reprise) (Eden Nicholas); "What's New in New York?" (Marilyn Hare); "Joyride" (Ensemble); "To Be Young" (reprise) (Lester Allen); "Co-op-hooray-shun" ("Mexican Boogie" reprise) (Barbara Perry); "What's New in New York?" (reprise) (Marilyn Hare); "Five A.M. Ballet" (Street Girl: Carol Haney; Sailor: Rodolfo Silva; Dancing Ensemble); "I Love You but Good" (reprise) (Marilyn Hare, Eden Nicholas); Finale—Medley (Entire Company)

Watch Out, Angel! dealt with the mounting of a new Broadway musical called *What's New in New York*. *What's New in New York* may have been successful, but *Watch Out, Angel!* stumbled badly and permanently closed during its San Francisco run. *Best Plays* reported the critics were "unanimous in their blasting of the total outcome in all departments" and the show was "thinly patronized." As a result, future audiences were denied hearing such song as "Co-op-hooray-shun" (and its "Mexican Boogie" reprise version), "I Love You but Good," and the title song, which was performed three times during the evening.

Each act included a big production number. The first act's "To Be Young" focused on aging star Kathe (an "erstwhile primadonna," according to the program) who dreams of her girlhood as a "teenage romanticist" and relives "the heights of her stage successes." The dance sequence included a Dream Kathe (at age sixteen) and another Dream Kathe (at twenty-one).

The second act featured the "Five A.M. Ballet," which included lead dancer Carol Haney (as a "street girl") in one of her first prominent roles. The program described the dance as follows: "Typifying musically the sounds common to the dawn of a great city we see a street girl, a policeman, a sailor, defense workers off the night shift; a ballerina with a rich admirer, tired chorus girls, secretaries with their escorts, and night club habitués dancing their rhythmic way until the 5 o'clock chimes bring on the rush and clamor of a metropolis awakening from its slumber."

For part of the run, the song "Out of My Mind" (for Marilyn Hare and Eden Nicholas) was performed.

Composer Josef Myrow was a two-time Best Song Oscar nominee, and his best known song is "You Make Me Feel So Young" from the 1946 film musical *Three Little Girls in Blue*. Lyricist Eddie de Lange enjoyed a number of hit songs during his career, including "Moon Glow," "Darn That Dream," "A String of Pearls," and "(In My) Solitude."

1945–1946 Season

CONCERT VARIETIES
"An Entertainment"

Theatre: Ziegfeld Theatre
Opening Date: June 1, 1945; *Closing Date*: June 28, 1945
Performances: 36
Direction: Technical direction by Carlton Winkler; *Producer*: Billy Rose; *Musical Direction*: Pembroke Davenport
Cast: Katherine Dunham and Her Dance Company, Deems Taylor, Rosario (Perez) and Antonio (Ruiz), Eddie Mayehoff, The Salici Puppets, Zero Mostel, Jerome Robbins and Company, Imogene Coca, William Archibald, Albert Ammons, Pete Johnson, and Sidney Catlett, Nestor Chayres; The Katherine Dunham Dancers: Vanoye Aikens, Talley Beatty, Eddy Clay, LaVerne French, Tommy Gomez, Lenwood Morris, Roger Ohardieno, Lucille Ellis, Syvilla Fort, Dolores Harper, Richardena Jackson, Ora Leak, Gloria Mitchell, Candido Vicenty (Drummer), La Rosa Estrada (Drummer), and Julio Mendez (Drummer); The Jerome Robbins Dancers: Jerome Robbins, Janet Reed, John Kriza, Michael Kidd, Muriel Bentley, Rozsika Sabo, Bettina Rosay, Erik Kristen, and Tibor Krizma (Pianist)
The revue was presented in two acts.

Musical Numbers

Act One: The Salici Puppets; Eddie Mayhoff; Rosario and Antonio: "Caprice Espagnol" (music by Rimsky-Korsakoff) and "A Spanish Dance"; Nestor Chayres; Rosario and Antonio: "Dansa Ritual del Fuego" (music by Manuel de Falla) and "Fire Dance"; Imogene Coca; "Interplay" (ballet choreographed by Jerome Robbins) (music by Morton Gould; based on his "American Concertette," a piano concerto which had first been performed in 1943): (1) "Free Play" (The Jerome Robbins Dance Company); (2) "Horse Play" (Jerome Robbins); (3) "By Play" (Janet Reed and John Kriza); and (4) "Team Play" (The Jerome Robbins Dance Company)
Act Two: Katherine Dunham and Her Dance Company: (1) "Callate" (Brazil) (music by Candido Vicenty) (Katherine Dunham, Candido Vicenty, Vanoye Aikens, Roger Ohardieno, Eddy Clay); (2) "Rhumba" (Mexico) (music by Harl MacDonald) (Katherine Dunham, Talley Beatty, Ensemble); and (3) "Tropics" (Martinique) (music by Paquita Anderson) (Katherine Dunham, Roger Ohardieno, Company) (Drummers: Candido Vincenty, La Rosa Estrada, and Julio Mendez; Dancers: Vanoye Aikens, Talley Beatty, Eddie Clay, La Verne French, Tommy Gomez, Lenwood Morris, Roger Ohardieno, Lucille Ellis, Sylvilla Fort, Dolores Harper, Richardena Jackson, Ora Leak, Gloria Mitchell); "Dance Divertissement" ("Morning After of a Faun," a dance parody of "Afternoon of a Faun"; music by Claude Debussy) (Imogene Coca with William Archibald); Albert Ammons, Pete Johnson, and Sidney Catlett; Zero Mostel; Rosario and Antonio: "Jota de la Dolores" (music by Tomas Breton) and "Peasant Dance"; Nestor Chayres; Rosario and Antonio: "Canasteros de Triana" (music by Curritos-Matos-Villacanas) and "Flirtation Dance"; Finale

Producer Billy Rose brought opera to the masses with **Carmen Jones**, Oscar Hammerstein II's successful modern-day adaptation of Georges Bizet's *Carmen*. And so Rose decided that concert-hall recitals perhaps needed the common touch by including occasional vaudeville-styled entertainers along with the more serious performers. So his notion of a typical evening of "concert varieties" would feature both kinds of entertainment, and each month he planned to offer a new program of artists from the concert stage and from the worlds of Broadway and nightclubs. *Concert Varieties* was scheduled to be the first of the proposed series, but generally cool reviews along with audience indifference put a quick end to the short-lived series and it never went beyond its first installment.

Deems Taylor served as the evening's master of ceremonies (and had briefly performed the same duties during part of the pre-Broadway tryout of **Vincent Youmans' "Fiesta"**), and soon after the opening act of the Salici Puppets it quickly became clear the revue offered more dancing than anything else. In fact, Wilella Waldorf in the *New York Post* suggested the show should have been titled *Dance Varieties*. And, indeed, there were seven separate dance items in the program: four sequences (which included a total of eight dances) by the nightclub and Broadway team of Rosario and Antonio; Jerome Robbins's ballet "Interplay"; a sequence that included three dances by Katherine Dunham and Her Dance Company; and a dance spoof by Imogene Coca and William Archibald. There were also comic monologues from nightclub and Broadway entertainers Eddie Mayehoff and Zero Mostel, songs from Mexican tenor and nightclub entertainer Nestor Chayres, and the nightclub trio of drummer Sidney Catlett and pianists Albert Ammons and Pete Johnson.

One wonders just why Billy Rose thought the evening presented a varied look at entertainers from both the concert hall and the variety stage, because only the intimate ballet "Interplay" came close to a Town Hall or Carnegie Hall offering. Most of the other performers were familiar faces in nightclubs and on Broadway, and because many of them trudged out their tried-and-true and all-too-familiar routines, it appears the evening was quickly thrown together. And so Zero Mostel again did his impersonation of a Southern senator, Imogene Coca reprised her dance parody of "Afternoon of a Faun," and Katherine Dunham and company hauled out what amounted to the "greatest hits" from their recent **A Tropical Revue**.

To be sure, some of the critics were generous in their appraisal of the evening. Robert Garland in the *New York Journal-American* said it was the "best vaudeville show" he'd ever seen, and John Chapman in the *New York Daily News* found it "more lively" than **Seven Lively Arts**. The former said "Interplay" was "fresh, imaginative and colorful," but he didn't care for the comedians Eddie Mayehoff and Zero Mostel (Eddie was "unedifying" and Zero "lives up to his given name"). Chapman said "Interplay" was the "best" of the evening, and he was glad to see Imogene Coca again ("the most undiscovered comedienne of the last 15 years").

Burton Rascoe in the *New York World-Telegram* said the Salici Puppets were the "most extraordinary" marionettes he'd ever seen; Coca reminded him of a "female Harpo Marx" and a "second-rate Fannie Brice"; the "story and pattern" offered by Dunham and her dancers "always seem to be the same"; and while the audience found Mostel funny (including his impersonation of a coffee percolator), Rascoe was not amused. Herrick Brown in the *New York Sun* felt the evening failed to "blend" the entertainments of the concert hall and the variety stage, and thus Billy Rose "still has to prove his point." Lewis Nichols in the *New York Times* suggested the revue was too "polite" and needed a "good, roaring comedian to give it oomph." As for Coca, Mayehoff, and Mostel, their humor was more suited to the nightclub than the stage.

Louis Kronenberger in *PM* said the evening didn't "come off," lacked variety, and danced itself "into the doldrums." The revue was "neither good highbrow nor good lowbrow," neither "real art" nor "real entertainment," and thus existed in a "kind of cultural half-world." He found the Salici puppets "enchanting" and noted that "Interplay" offered the "best dancing" in the revue; but Dunham's contributions were "pretty unrewarding" and Coca was "not quite big-league stuff." Howard Barnes in the *New York Herald Tribune* said the evening was "slip-shod and wearisome," but "Interplay" was "brilliant" and "remarkably fluent and eloquent."

Waldorf said the Salici Puppets received her vote as the revue's "most entertaining" offering; otherwise, the evening was "monotonous" with too much dancing and too little in the way of comedy. Mostel's "inevitable" senator routine had been around "far too long now," and the least he could have done was focus on a representative from the House; Mayehoff was a Mostel-type "without so much talent or perspiration"; and the "undistinguished" Mexican tenor Nestor Chayres "no doubt" had a "nightclub background." In his seasonal summary, George Jean Nathan suggested the concert-like aspects of the evening were fine; but the variety offerings should have gone all-out with "good, juicy, old-fashioned custard pie acts." He felt the current "Rose mixture of Deems and dems only too naturally was followed by doze."

One of Rosario and Antonio's dances was Manuel de Falla's "Dansa Ritual del Fuego," and the music was heard again later in the season when it was used as the background for "Dance of the Matador" in **The Duchess Misbehaves**.

Clearly, the most successful segment of the evening was Robbins's "Interplay," which used the music of Morton Gould's short piano concerto "American Concertette" (which had premiered in April 1943 when it was presented by Jose Irurbi and the NBC Symphony). The concerto was divided into four movements: (1) with drive and vigor; (2) gavotte; (3) blues; and (4) very fast. The ballet was divided into four parts as well: "Free Play," "Horse Play," "By Play," and "Team Play," and the through-theme of the ballet was that of children at play. Robbins himself and Janet Reed were the principal dancers, and they were supported by Muriel Bentley, Rozsika Sabo, Bettina Rosay, Erik Kristen, and future Broadway choreographer Michael Kidd. "Interplay" has become a staple in ballet repertoire, and has been recorded numerous times. One of the most recent versions of the score was heard in the collection *Morton Gould* (Albany Records CD # TROY-1174), which was performed by the Albany Symphony Orchestra.

MARINKA
"A New Romantic Musical" / "The Romantic Musical HIT!"

Theatre: Winter Garden Theatre (during run, the musical transferred to the Ethel Barrymore Theatre)
Opening Date: July 18, 1945; *Closing Date*: December 8, 1945
Performances: 165
Book: George Marion Jr. and Karl Farkas
Lyrics: George Marion Jr.
Music: Emmerich Kalman
Direction: Hassard Short; *Producers*: Jules J. Leventhal and Harry Howard; *Choreography*: Albertina Rasch;
    Scenery: Howard Bay; *Costumes*: Mary Grant; *Lighting*: Hassard Short; *Musical Direction*: Ray Kavanaugh
Cast: Ruth Webb (Nadine), Elline Walther (Countess Von Diefendorfer), Romo Vincent (Bratfisch), Harry Stockwell (Crown Prince Rudolph), Taylor Holmes (Count Lobkowitz), Noel Gordon (Naval Lieutenant), Paul Campbell (Count Hoyos), Leonard Elliott (Francis), Ronnie Cunningham (Tilly), Joan Roberts (Marinka), Ethel Levey (Madame Sacher), Luba Malina (Countess Landovska), Jack Leslie (Waiter), Bob Douglas (Lieutenant Baltatzy), Reinhold Schunzel (Emperor Franz Josef), Adrienne Gray (Countess Huebner), Michael Barrett (Sergeant Negulegul), Jack Gansert (Lieutenant Palafy); Ladies of the Ensemble: Suzie Baker, Ethel Madsen, Jane Reihl, Gloria A. Tromara, Elline Walther, Donna Gardner, Lois Eastman; Gentlemen of the Ensemble: Jimmy Allison, Paul Campbell, John (Jack) Cassidy, Richard Clemens, Edwin Craig, Noel Gordon, Lynn Alden, Vincent Henry; Dancing Girls: Tessie Carrano, Muriel Bruenig, Aline DuBois, Phoebe Engel, Marie Fazzin, Albertina Horstmann, Ann Hutchinson, Jeanne Lewis, Thea Lind, Franca Baldwin, Judith Sargent, Nathalie Kelepovska, Alla Shishkina, Aura Vainio, Betty Williams, Carol Keyser, Anna Scarpova; Dancing Boys: Stanley Zompakos, Robert Armstrong, Lee Michel, Edmund Howland, Ted Lund, George Tomal, John Begg, Francisco Xavier
The musical was presented in two acts.
The action takes place during the present time in Connecticut and in Austria and Hungary in the years 1888 and 1889.

Musical Numbers

Act One: "One Touch of Vienna" (Romo Vincent, Girls); Ballet (Ronnie Cunningham, Ballet Girls); "The Cab Song" (Romo Vincent, Ronnie Cunningham, Leonard Elliott); "My Prince Came Riding" (Joan Roberts, Debutantes); "If I Never Waltz Again" (Joan Roberts, Harry Stockwell); "The Cab Song" (reprise) (Ronnie Cunningham, Elline Walther, Debutantes); "Turn on the Charm" (Romo Vincent); "One Last Love Song" (Joan Roberts, Harry Stockwell); "Old Man Danube" (Romo Vincent, Officers); "Hungarian Dance" (Ronnie Cunningham, Jack Gansert, Dancers); "Czardas" (Luba Malina, Officers); "Sigh by Night" (Joan Roberts, Harry Stockwell); "One Last Love Song" (reprise) (Joan Roberts, Harry Stockwell); "Paletas" (dance) (Jack Gansert, Dancers)

Act Two: "Treat a Woman Like a Drum" (Joan Roberts, Ronnie Cunningham, Romo Vincent, Leonard Elliott, Jack Gansert); Dance (Ballerinas, Sailors); "When I Auditioned for the Harem of the Shah" (Luba
Malina); "Young Man Danube" (Leonard Elliott, Ronnie Cunningham, Jack Gansert, Ensemble); "Turn
on the Charm" (reprise) (Joan Roberts, Harry Stockwell); "Sigh by Night" (reprise) (Joan Roberts, Harry
Stockwell); "One Last Love Song" (reprise) (Joan Roberts, Harry Stockwell)

Marinka took place in the Austria and Hungary of the late 1880s, and despite a story that centered on the
tragic and mysterious Mayerling affair, the musical was strictly from operetta territory. And with settings in
such locales as Vienna's famed Sacher Restaurant, a park pavilion in Old Budapest, and the private gardens of
the Imperial Palace; with one character impersonating a waiter in order to keep an eye on various restaurant
patrons; with fusty comic types as Bratfisch (the coachman, portrayed by Romo Vincent); with characters
such as the cigar-smoking Madame Sacher (Ethel Levey) and the smoldering, tempestuous, and would-be
blackmailer Countess Landovska (Luba Malina); and with such song titles as "One Touch of Vienna," "My
Prince Came Riding," "Old Man Danube," "Young Man Danube," "Czardas," "Sigh by Night," and "Treat a
Woman Like a Drum," how could the evening have been other than a stuffy operetta?

Mayerling was the Austrian hunting lodge where the bodies of Crown Prince Rudolph (Harry Stockwell)
and his mistress, the commoner Marinka (Joan Roberts), were found. Was it murder and suicide? Or two
murders arranged to look like a double suicide? But wait. According to the musical *Marinka*, the prince and
his mistress didn't die at all; they fled Austria in order to defy convention and have a life of their own, and
the prince's father Emperor Franz Josef (Reinholt Schunzel) was left to concoct a fabrication to explain their
disappearance. All this was framed by scenes set in 1945 when a group of teenagers, tearful because they've
seen a movie of the Mayerling story, are told the "true" version by their school bus driver, whose father just
happened to be Prince Rudolph's coachman and thus knows the "real" story. Hence the two-act flashback
which sugar-coated history with the frills and flourishes of old-hat operetta.

The musical received cool but surprisingly gentle reviews and lasted five months on Broadway. Harriett
Johnson in the *New York Post* said the book played "somersaults" with history, but the music "trots innocu-
ously along" and the "beautiful" production was "superbly" lighted and lush with "intriguing and artistic
color blends." But she warned that the musical was enjoyable only if you let your brain, memory, and critical
faculties "take a little snooze." Louis Kronenberger in *PM* noted the show wasn't "very dreadful," but there
was "nothing favorable" about it either, it was just a "harmless bore." He mentioned that the atmosphere
of Old Vienna was lacking, and here the Old World had "all the elegance of Weehawken." The score was
"pretty" and "melodious" in its "familiar way" and could have "come out of any operetta written since
McKinley was in the White House."

Lewis Nichols in the *New York Times* complained that the evening was out of "stock operetta" with
"maddening" dialogue and weak comedy. There was a "general sameness" about the songs, and the choreography was only "serviceable without being outstanding." And like most of the critics, he noted that Joan
Roberts and Harry Stockwell were not well-suited to their roles; both had appeared in ***Oklahoma!***: she was of
course Broadway's first Laurey, and he succeeded Alfred Drake in the original production. Unfortunately the
two of them brought a mid-American touch to the proceedings, which was out of the place in late nineteenth-
century Austria. Robert Garland in the *New York Journal-American* said the evening offered both positive and
negative attributes, and thus the musical neither added nor detracted from the Broadway season. Burton Rascoe in the *New York World-Telegram* felt the musical was the victim of "poor timing" because the country
had just fought a war against an Austrian named Adolf Hitler and thus it was somewhat "repulsive" to offer
a musical about an Austrian prince who was little more than a "royal bum." But he praised Luba Malina's
"When I Auditioned for the Harem of the Shah" (he noted "she stopped the show with repeated curtain calls,"
and Johnson reported there were seven ovations in all).

Howard Barnes in the *New York Herald Tribune* pronounced the musical a "satisfying if somewhat silly
entertainment," and while it was "remote and a bit rusty" it was still a "welcome" addition to the season;
much of the score was "clumsily derivative" but would probably produce a few hit songs, and he noted
that Luba Malina was responsible for giving the musical a "casual and captivating" quality, and her "Shah"
number was "strictly a honey." Ward Morehouse in the *New York Sun* had enjoyed "far better" shows, but
Marinka was nonetheless "tolerable." It offered a "fairly pleasant" score, "excellent" décor, "fetching,"

"gay," and "imaginative" costumes, but a "dullish" and "cumbersome" book and "labored" humor. Further, the players were not all that "exciting." Joan Roberts seemed miscast and "out of place in the Austrian locale" and Harry Stockwell was "only moderately good." But Luba Malina had "all the exuberance in the world" and was "quite a show-stopper."

Both Roberts and Stockwell left the show about midway through its five-month run, and by early fall Edith Fellows was Marinka and Jerry Wayne Prince Rudolph. By November, Roberts was back on Broadway in the modern-day carnival world of **Are You With It?**, but after her two 1945 musicals she never again created a role in a Broadway musical (she later succeeded Nanette Fabray in **High Button Shoes**, and then after a half-century returned to Broadway as Heidi in the 2001 revival of Stephen Sondheim's *Follies*). As for Stockwell, after *Marinka* he never again appeared on Broadway (incidentally, he was the father of actor Dean Stockwell).

During the run, "I Admit" was added to the second act for Prince Rudolph. During the tryout, Hassard Short received staging credit and librettists George Marion Jr., and Karl Farkas were listed as directors of the book; by New York, Short was still credited for the staging, but there was no credit for book direction.

In 2008, the Operetta Foundation released a full-length recording of the complete score (Operetta Archives CD # OA-1021), including the added song "I Admit"; an unused number ("Brave New World"); and the overture, entr'acte, dance music, scene-change music, and reprises (many of the original orchestrations are apparently lost, and the recording used a two-piano accompaniment for the singers). The collection *Broadway Musicals of 1945* (Bayview CD # RNBW-039) includes "Turn on the Charm" and "Sigh by Night." For the recording *Joan Roberts Sings Her Hit Songs & Frank Crumit and Julia Sanderson—Famous Songs from Their Best Known Musical Comedies* (CD released by Original Cast Records), Roberts performs two songs from the production ("Sigh by Night" and "Treat a Woman Like a Drum").

MR. STRAUSS GOES TO BOSTON
"A ROMANTIC COMEDY WITH MUSIC"

Theatre: New Century Theatre
Opening Date: September 6, 1945; *Closing Date*: September 15, 1945
Performances: 12
Book: Leonard L. Levinson
Lyrics: Robert Sour
Music: Robert Stolz
Based on an original story by Alfred Gruenwald and Geza Herczeg.
Direction: Felix Brentano; *Producer*: Felix Brentano; *Choreography*: George Balanchine; *Scenery*: Stewart Chaney; *Costumes*: Walter Florell; *Lighting*: Uncredited; *Musical Direction*: Robert Stolz
Cast: Ralph Dumke (Dapper Dan Pepper), Brian O'Mara (Policeman McGillicudy), Don Fiser (Inspector Gogarty), Dennis Dengate (First Reporter), Larry Gilbert (Second Reporter), Joseph Monte (Third Reporter), Florence Sundstrom (Pepi), Frank Finn (Bellhop), George Rigaud (Johann Strauss), Edward J. Lambert (Elmo Tilt), Lee Edwards (Hotel Manager, Aide to President), Virginia MacWatters (Brook Whitney), Paul Mario (Waiter, Man in Overalls), Lailye Tenen (Mrs. Dexter), Rose Perfect (Mrs. Blakely), Sydney Grant (Mr. Whitney), Arlene Dahl (Mrs. Taylor), Selma Felton (Mrs. Hastings), Marie Barova (Mrs. Iverson), Cecile Sherman (Mrs. Byrd), John Oliver (Butler), Jay Martin (Tom Avery), John Harrold (Photographer), Brian O'Mara (Earl), Ruth Matteson (Hetty Strauss), Norman Roland (President Grant); Solo Dancers: Harold Lang, Babs (Barbara) Heath, Margit Dekova; Singing Ensemble: Nancy Baskerville, Jeanne Beauvais, Arlene Carmen, Doris Elliott, Alma Fernandez, Lucy Hillary, Olga Pavlova, Mia Stenn, Mary Lou Wallace, Dennis Dengate, Lee Edwards, Frank Finn, Larry Gilbert, John Harrold, Philip Harrison, Paul Mario, Joseph Monte, John Oliver, Brian O'Mara; Corps de Ballet: Mary Burr, Jacqueline Cezanne, Sylvia de Penso, Andra Downing, Helen Gallagher, Arlene Garver, Mary Grey, Fiala Mraz, Virginia Poe, Stephen Billings, Paul Olson, William Sarazen, Tilden Shanks, Terry Townes
The musical was presented in two acts.
The action takes place in 1872 in New York City and in Boston.

Musical Numbers

Note: An asterisk denotes music by Johann Strauss as arranged by Robert Stolz and George Lessner; otherwise, all music is by Robert Stolz.

Act One: "Can Anyone See" (Ensemble); "Radetsky March-Fantasie" (*) (Dancing Girls); "For the Sake of Art" (Ralph Dumke, Reporters, Girls); "Laughing-Waltz" (*) (Virginia MacWatters); "Mr. Strauss Goes to Boston" (Ralph Dumke, Florence Sundstrom, Edward J. Lambert); "Down with Sin" (Ralph Dumke, Edward J. Lambert, Boston Ladies); "Who Knows?" (Virginia MacWatters); "Midnight Waltz" (*) (danced by Babs Heath, Harold Lang, Corps de Baller); "Into the Night" (Jay Martin); "Coloratura Waltz" (*) (Virginia MacWatters); "The Gossip Polka" (*) (Ensemble; danced by Babs Heath, Harold Lang, Corps de Ballet)

Act Two: "Dream Scene" (Ensemble); "Going Back Home" (Ruth Matteson); "You Never Know What Comes Next" (Florence Sundstrom); "Mr. Strauss Goes to Boston" (reprise) (George Rigaud, Ruth Matteson, Ralph Dumke); "You Never Know What Comes Next" (reprise) (danced by Harold Lang); "Into the Night" (reprise) (Jay Martin, Ensemble; ballet danced by Harold Lang, Margit Dekova, Corps de Ballet); "What's a Girl Supposed to Do?" (Virginia MacWatters, Jay Martin); "The Grand and Glorious Fourth" (Ensemble; danced by Harold Lang, Helen Gallagher, Corps de Ballet); "Who Knows?" (reprise) (Virginia MacWatters); "Waltz Finale" (*) (Entire Company)

A program note stated that "any similarity between *Mr. Strauss Goes to Boston* and actual history is coincidental." Well, yes, we figured that out. We didn't really believe that President Grant stepped in as a marriage counselor for Johann Strauss and his Missus.

In 1872, Johann Strauss the younger (George Rigaud) is the Frank Sinatra of his day, and fans clamor to see the famous composer during his celebrity tour of the United States. Because his handlers want Strauss to maintain a romantic image, they hide the fact he's actually married and that his wife Hetty (Ruth Matteson) lives in Vienna. When the roving-eye composer arrives in Boston to conduct a concert for the World Peace Jubilee, he dallies with Beacon Hill blueblood Brook Whitney (Virginia MacWatters), who of course has no idea he's married. When Hetty gets wind of what's going on, she hightails it to Boston in order to rein in her wayward husband, apparently with a little assist from President Ulysses S. Grant, who is in Boston to attend the jubilee (in an early script of the musical, he says "Bully" and notes he knows only two songs: one is "Yankee Doodle" and "the other isn't").

The musical contained a mixture of new songs composed by Robert Stolz (who also conducted) as well as music by Strauss (which was adapted by Stolz and George Lessner). Excluding reprises, there were eighteen numbers, twelve by Stolz and six by Strauss. The critics pounced on the lethargic entertainment, and one or two gratefully noted the musical was relatively short and that the final curtain went down before eleven (Burton Rascoe in the *New York World-Telegram* reported the total playing time of "the agony" was just under two hours). Dancer Harold Lang walked away with the evening's best notices (Rascoe suggested he was a "good" dancer but not as good as his "noisy claque" would have one believe); otherwise, the reviewers complained about the evening's lack of entertainment values and groaned over the weak humor ("This is my coming out dress" / "You're certainly coming out of it" and "I'm homesick" / "I wish you were home, sick").

Even Walter Florell's costumes were criticized, as they over-emphasized the bustles on the women's dresses. John Chapman in the *New York Daily News* said the women looked like "ostriches in an air-raid shelter," and thus it seemed every girl wore a hat on her behind (and "this is the wrong place for hats"); further, Florell mixed "his colors rather unattractively." Rascoe said the bustles were "garish and absurd, without being funny," and Louis Kronenberger in *PM* noted that unlike the costumes in most period musicals, the ones in *Mr. Strauss* were not attractive. Lewis Nichols in the *New York Times* said they "are forgotten too easily and soon," and Howard Barnes in the *New York Herald Tribune* wondered if Florell had been occasionally napping during the preproduction phase of the musical. Wilella Waldorf in the *New York Post* commented that even for the Fourth of July sequence that took place on the banks of the Charles River, the costumes didn't jibe: most of the cast wore casual "sports"-like costumes, but Strauss wore a full evening dress of white tie and tails.

In his annual summary, George Jean Nathan said he was tired of leading men "so pretty" he couldn't tell if they were portraying composers or movie actors, and he wondered how a musical's hero could possibly fall in love with a coloratura heroine who is depicted as "loudly gargling her way, while grinning like a triumphant hyena, to a high C." Rascoe said the "pretty stupid" musical was a "bore" with an "atrocious, vulgar, cheap and smutty" book, and even the familiar waltzes were played "without fire or feeling." Kronenberger said the book was "dreadful" in a "dark brown fog" kind of way; eventually he found himself disinterested in the show, and for all he cared it could have morphed into **Marinka**.

Chapman said Strauss "should have stood in Vienna"; Nichols said the evening was "tired" and "old"; Barnes found the musical a "shabbily pretentious entertainment" which fell to pieces "with a frightening acceleration"; and Ward Morehouse in the *New York Sun* noted the new theatre season had begun "dolefully" with a "costly mistake" (the musical reportedly cost $180,000), and his verdict was a "vehement no."

South American–born actor George Rigaud (who spent many of his early years in France) seems to have been a handsome and swaggering leading man, but was apparently ill at ease with English (he had been contracted to star with Claudette Colbert in the 1939 film *Midnight*, but was replaced because of his problems with English). Nichols noted Rigaud was "perhaps not as easy" in the role of Strauss as he might have been; Morehouse found him "clumsy"; Chapman said he was "amiable but not startling"; Waldorf said Rigaud never indicated he had "ever heard of Vienna," and since he didn't sing and his acting was "routine," she suspected he was cast because of his "romantic mien"; and Robert Garland in the *New York Journal-American* wished him "better luck" next time.

For the second and final week of the musical's run, an extra scene was added for the second act, after the "Waltz Finale"; it took place at the Jubilee Concert a few minutes after the previous scene and included "Jubilee Concert" and a reprise of the "Waltz Finale" (both numbers were performed by the entire company).

Dropped in preproduction were the songs "A Breeze Blew Up Boylston Street," "Long Ago" and "Not Allowed" (the latter for Strauss and his female fans, who sing to him that "t'was your baton that put us in the mood"). One of the musical's songs, "For the Sake of Art," states that sex is what inspires Strauss: when the Duke of Brabante "caught Strauss without a panty" it was "merely the andante" of the composer's Opus Number five; and regarding Queen Eugenie, Strauss will "waltz her," but if he "assaults her" it's only for the sake of art.

During the tryout, choreographer Edward Caton was succeeded by George Balanchine.

The collection *You Can't Put Ketchup on the Moon* (Rialto CD # SLRR-9201) includes "What's a Girl Supposed to Do?"

CARIB SONG
"A MUSICAL PLAY OF THE WEST INDIES" / "A NEW MUSICAL PLAY"

Theatre: Adelphi Theatre
Opening Date: September 27, 1945; *Closing Date*: October 27, 1945
Performances: 36
Book and *Lyrics*: William Archibald
Music: Baldwin Bergersen
Direction: Book directed by Mary Hunter and production staged by Katherine Dunham and Mary Hunter; *Producer*: George Stanton; *Choreography*: Katherine Dunham; *Scenery* and *Lighting*: Jo Mielziner; *Costumes*: Motley; *Musical Direction*: Pembroke Davenport
Cast: Harriet Jackson (The Singer), Eulabel Riley (The Friend), Mary Lewis (Another Friend), Mable Sanford Lewis (The Fat Woman), Mercedes Gilbert (The Tall Woman), William Franklin (The Husband), Avon Long (The Fisherman), Katherine Dunham (The Woman), Elsie Benjamin (The Fishwoman); Byron Cuttler (The Madras Seller), La Rosa Estrada (The Shango Priest), Tommy Gomez (The Boy Possessed by a Snake), Vanoye Aikens (Leader of the Shango Dancers), Lucille Ellis (Another Leader of the Shango Dancers); The Village Friends: Lucille Ellis, Roxie Foster, Lauwane Ingram, Richardena Jackson, Eartha Kitt, Ora Leak, Mary Lewis, Gloria Mitchell, Eulabel Riley, Priscilla Stevens, Enid Williams, James Alexander, Eddy Clay, Norman Coker, Byron Cutler, John Diggs, Jesse Hawkins, Julio Mendez, Lenwood Morris, Eugene Lee Robinson, William C. Smith, Charles Welch; The Katherine Dunham Dancers: Lucille Ellis, Lenwood Morris, Tommy Gomez, Vanoye Aikens, Lauwane Ingram, Richardena Jackson, Gloria Mitchell, Ora Leak, Eddy Clay, Byron Cutler, James Alexander, Roxie Foster, Eugene Robinson, Eartha Kitt, Jesse Hawkins, Enid Williams; Drummers: La Rosa Estrada, Julio Mendez, Norman Coker; Singing Ensemble: Mary Lewis, Eulabel Riley, Priscilla Stevens, John Diggs, William C. Smith, Charles Welch
The musical was presented in two acts.
The action takes place in a village in the West Indies.

Musical Numbers

Act One: "Go Sit by the Body" Chant (Company); "Legba" (Charles Welch, Company); "This Woman" (William Franklin, William C. Smith, Charles Welch, Company); "Water Movin' Slow" (William Franklin); "Basket, Make a Basket" (Katherine Dunham; Dancers: Lucille Ellis, Lauwane Ingram, Richardena Jackson, Tommy Gomez, Lenwood Morris, Vanoye Aikens; Singers: Eartha Kitt, Mary Lewis, Eulabel Riley, Priscilla Stevens, John Diggs, Jesse Hawkins, William C. Smith, Charles Welch); "Congo Paillette" (dance) (Katherine Dunham, Company); "Woman Is a Rascal" (Avon Long, William C. Smith, Charles Welch); "A Girl She Can't Remain" (Katherine Dunham, La Rosa Estrada, Byron Cutler, James Alexander); "Shango Ritual" (dance) (La Rosa Estrada, Tommy Gomez, Katherine Dunham, Avon Long, Vanoye Aikens, Company)

Act Two: "Market Song" (Mable Sanford Lewis, Company); "Sleep, Baby, Don't Cry" (Harriet Jackson); "Things Remembered" (ballet) (Katherine Dunham, Lucille Ellis, Richardena Jackson, Ora Leak, La Rosa Estrada, Lauwane Ingram, Vanoye Aikens, Gloria Mitchell, Lenwood Morris); "Today I Is So Happy" (William Franklin); "Can't Stop the Sea" (John Diggs); "Forest at Night" (dance) (Katherine Dunham, Lenwood Morris, Vanoye Aikens, James Alexander, Byron Cutler, Tommy Gomez); "You Know, Oh Lord" (William Franklin); "Go to Church Sunday" (Company); "Go Down to the River" (aka "The Washer Women's Song") (Priscilla Stevens, Eulabel Riley, Mary Lewis, Mable Sanford Lewis); "Washer Women's Dance" (Lauwane Ingram, Lucille Ellis, Roxy Foster, Richardena Jackson, Eartha Kitt, Ora Leak, Gloria Mitchell, Enid Williams); "Oh, Lonely One" (Katherine Dunham, Harriet Jackson)

In his annual review of the season, George Jean Nathan noted that Katherine Dunham wasn't much of an actress and singer, but her "capricious determination" to be both led her to the "misadventure" of *Carib Song*, which was really part **A Tropical Revue** with a dash of *Porgy and Bess* thrown in. The entire evening was "excessively dull" and monotonous. He suggested that for evenings of this nature, producers should stop kidding their audiences with "herring-trail" program notes explaining the religious and ritualistic nature of the dances; because with their "profusion of mammary gland agitations, hip rollings and posterior undulations," the dances were clearly all about sex.

He also noted that Dunham's program biography stated she had been "permitted to witness secret ceremonials never before seen by strangers"; but Nathan suggested the "secret" ceremonies in Cuba, Jamaica, Haiti, and other islands in the West Indies must have been witnessed by thousands, and at "ringside" the crowds were so numerous they "often resembled" those attending a prize fight at Madison Square Garden.

Carib Song was the kind of show in which the characters had descriptive rather than real names. And so there is "The Husband" (William Franklin) who is married to "The Woman" (why not "The Wife"?) (Katherine Dunham) who sleeps with "The Fisherman" (Avon Long), and although she repents, The Husband kills her anyway. Besides this triangle there were such characters as "The Fat Woman," "The Tall Woman," "The Boy Possessed by a Snake," and other Nameless Ones.

Lewis Nichols in the *New York Times* suspected the dances were "born in" and destined for the concert hall. He suggested that as an actress Dunham could settle for "less posturing"; and he asked for "less repetition" because the "sameness" of her material was becoming very familiar. The evening was written in pidgin English ("perhaps for verisimilitude"), the show suffered from a lack of inventiveness, and the "siesta" nature of the proceedings made for an "unhappy" evening of "good theatre." Louis Kronenberger in *PM* found the "childish and contrived" and "blatantly undramatic" evening an exercise in such garnishments as voodoo, corn-sorting, church-going, clothes-washing, and other "not very advanced subjects." As for Dunham, she was "too conscious of her charm."

Howard Barnes in the *New York Herald Tribune* said the musical was often "pretentious" and "tedious," but noted the occasionally "repetitious" dancing gave the evening "slight distinction"; he reported that the characters spoke lines such as "I ain't know" and "I ain't like," and as a reviewer he concluded that he too "ain't like" the show. Ward Morehouse in the *New York Sun* found the entertainment on the "skimpy" side and predicted the "listless" show would be unsuccessful; he also commented that Dunham's singing and acting weren't in the league of her dancing. Robert Garland in the *New York Journal-American* said the evening was lost in a "maziness of monotony"; the book, music, costumes, choreography, and scenery were "monotonous" on their own and in conjunction with one another. Dunham's dances were "overly familiar" and she gave him the impression she didn't "in the least care whether the show goes on or whether the show goes off."

Wilella Waldorf in the *New York Post* felt that an aura of "tropical lethargy" engulfed the stage; the evening was "tastefully presented" and included some "charming" scenes, but the book was "very slender" and lacked "variety." Soon even the dances began "to look and sound very much alike." But she praised the show's best song ("Sleep, Baby, Don't Cry," which was also singled out by five other reviewers), and she noted that Avon Long stopped the show with "Woman Is a Rascal." In fact, the audience wouldn't let him go, and so the song and its encores lasted a full twenty minutes. Barnes also said Long sang and danced "brilliantly," and John Chapman in the *New York Daily News* said the "fascinating" Long stopped the show (in fact, he stopped it "just a little bit too long") with his "delightful" number.

Chapman was quite taken with the musical, and said it was "not like any Negro show you ever saw before"; he also praised the "brooding, tropical and evocative" décor by Jo Mielziner and said the "very, very good" score was "above average in grace and charm." But he noted the evening sometimes had a "sameness" about it. Burton Rascoe in the *New York World-Telegram* confessed he'd never before cared for Dunham's "pseudo-cultural cavortings," but now she had "knocked a home run" and he was her "ardent" fan. The "very unusual and entrancing operetta" also offered the "superb" Avon Long (who had the "spontaneity and rhythmic sense of Fred Astaire") and overall the entertainment was "beautifully done" with its "skillful" blend of book, lyrics, music, and choreography, all of it set against Mielziner's "impressionistic and moody" décor.

Lyricist William Archibald and composer Baldwin Bergersen recorded six songs from the musical which were originally released on a 78 RPM set by International Records; the recordings are included in a collection titled *Porgy and Bess, Cabin in the Sky,* and *Carib Song* (AEI CD # AEI-CD-017). The numbers are: "Basket, Make a Basket," "Woman Is a Rascal," "Sleep, Baby, Don't Cry," "Go Down to the River" (aka "The Washer Women's Song"), "If," and "The Insect Song." The latter two were dropped in preproduction. The collections *Everybody Else Revisited* (Painted Smiles CD # PSCD-146) and *Unsung Musicals II* (Varese Sarabande CD # VSD-5564) include "Sleep, Baby, Don't Cry."

With *Carib Song*, the luckless Adelphi Theatre began another bad season. But then it always had bad seasons. Seven name changes during its forty-two-year life didn't help (it opened as the Craig, was known as the Adelphi for most of its history, and during its last years was re-named the 54th Street Theatre and then finally the George Abbott). Not being centrally located in the traditional theatre district was the usual reason given for the venue's almost uncanny knack for booking flops; but the theatre was just around the corner from Seventh Avenue, and its nearest neighbor the Ziegfeld was even further down the street on Sixth Avenue, and that didn't prevent the Ziegfeld from hosting a number of hits, including both the original and long-running 1946 revival of **Show Boat**, **Brigadoon**, **Gentlemen Prefer Blondes**, and *Kismet* (1953).

No, it wasn't so much the location as it was the fact that flop musicals seemed to know the Adelphi was their destiny, and so they dutifully opened there so that they could quickly close. If a hit accidentally premiered there (such as **On the Town**, **Three to Make Ready**, and *No Strings* [1962]), it quickly moved to another theatre, and already established long-running musicals (like *Damn Yankees* [1955], *Bye Bye Birdie* [1960], *Do Re Mi* [1960], and *Golden Rainbow* [1968]) which had opened at other theatres and were now winding down their Broadway runs would move to the Adelphi before their final stop at Cain's warehouse.

The 1945–1946 semester was an especially dismal one for the Adelphi, with five flop musicals: *Carib Song* (36 performances), **The Girl from Nantucket** (12 performances), **Nellie Bly** (16 performances), **The Duchess Misbehaves** (5 performances), and **Around the World in Eighty Days** (75 performances). The doomed **Polonaise** had opened at the Alvin, but soon headed for the Adelphi to run out its short life of 113 performances. And the aforementioned **Three to Make Ready** played its first few weeks at the Adelphi before transferring to the Broadhurst, where it ran for an additional seven months. It's ironic that the musical *What Makes Sammy Run?* (1964), which played all its 540 performances at the theatre (and which thus holds the record as the venue's longest-running musical) was nonetheless a financial failure (at 580 performances, *No Strings* is technically the theatre's long-run champ, but the musical played at the venue for only a third of its seventeen-month Broadway run).

In 1958, the Adelphi was host to *Portofino*, which with **Hairpin Harmony** probably ranks as one of the most dismal Broadway musicals of all time (Walter Kerr famously said he couldn't state for certain that *Portofino* was the worst because he'd only been seeing musicals since 1919). Other flops that later played at the theatre were *Happy Town* (1959; 5 performances); *13 Daughters* (1961; 28); *Kwamina* (1961; 32); *The Student Gypsy*, or *The Prince of Liederkranz* (1963; 16); *La Grosse Valise* (1965; 7); *Darling of the Day* (1968; 33); and *Buck White* (1969; 7). And in its early years, the theatre had played host to *Jonica* (1930; 40); *The Well of Romance*; 8); *Swing It* (1937; 36); *A Hero Is Born* (1937; 50); *Sing for Your Supper* (1939; 60); **Allah Be Praised!**

(1944; 20); and the revival of **Robin Hood** (1944; 15). The final show to play at the theatre was the musical *Gantry* (1970), which opened and closed on February 14, 1970.

POLONAISE
"A New Musical"

Theatre: Alvin Theatre (during run, the musical transferred to the Adelphi Theatre)
Opening Date: October 6, 1945; *Closing Date*: January 12, 1946
Performances: 113
Book: Gottfried Reinhardt and Anthony Veiller
Lyrics: John LaTouche
Music: Frederic Chopin (musical adaptation by Bronislaw Kaper); new music by Bronislaw Kaper
Direction: Book directed by Stella Adler; *Producer*: Harry Bloomfield; *Choreography*: David Lichine; *Scenery*: Howard Bay; *Costumes*: Mary Grant; *Lighting*: Uncredited; *Musical Direction*: Ignace Strasfogel; *Choral Direction*: Irving Landau
Cast: John V. Schmidt (Captain Adams), Josef Draper (General Washington, Count Casimir Zaleski), Martin Lewis (Colonel Hale), *Jan Kiepura* (General Thaddeus Kosciusko), Curt Bois (Sergeant Wacek Zapolski), Sidney Lawson (Private Tompkins), Arthur Lincoln (Private Skinner), Martin Cooke (Private Motherwell, Blacksmith), *Marta Eggerth* (Marisha), Rem Olmsted (Wladek), Tania Riabouchinska (Telca), Harry Bannister (General Boris Volkoff), Lewis Appleton (Peniatowski), Andrew Thurston (Kollontaj), Gary Green (Potocki), Rose Inghram (Countess Ludwika Zaleski), Larry Beck (Butcher), Larry O'Dell (Priest), Zadel Skolovsky (Pianist), James MacColl (King Stanislaus Augustus), Walter Appler (Count Gronski), Candy Jones (Princess Margarita), Leta Mauree (Princess Lydia), Sherry Shadburne (Princess Lania), Martha Emma Watson (Princess Anna), Betty Durrence (Peasant Girl); Singers: Eileen Ayers, Joan Bartels, Marjorie Chandler, Jean Cumming, Ann Dennis, Leigh Hoffman, Mary McQuade, Mary Woodley, Barbara Barlow, Jeanette Weiss, Lewis Appleton, Oakley Bailey, Larry Beck, Oliver Boersma, Martin Cooke, Gary Green, Raynor C. Howell, Arthur Lincoln, Sidney Lawson, Larry O'Dell, John Schmidt, Otto Simanek, Andrew Thurston, Michael Vertzilous, Tony Montell; Dancers: Virginia Barnes, May Block, Adele Bodroghy, Jane Collenette, Betty Durrence, Jean Harris, Pamela Kastner, Alicia Krug, Dorothy Love, Ruthanna Mitchell, Ruth Riekman, Dorothy Scott, Amalia Velez, Hubert Bland, Jay Dowd, Jerry Florio, Sergei Ismaeloff, Martin Kraft, Tangi Nicelli, Shaun O'Brien, Martin Schneider, Marc West
The musical was presented in two acts.
The action takes place during 1783 at West Point, New York City, Cracow, Poland, Warsaw, Poland, and Philadelphia.

Musical Numbers

Act One: Overture (Orchestra); "Autumn Songs" (Marta Eggerth, Rem Olmsted, Peasants); "Laughing Bells" (music by Bronislaw Kaper) (Tania Riabouchinska, Curt Bois); "O, Heart of My Country" (from Chopin's Nocturne in E-Flat) (Jan Kiepura); "Stranger" (music by Bronislaw Kaper) (Marta Eggerth); "Au Revoir, Soldier" (music by Bronislaw Kaper) (Rose Inghram); "Meadow-lark" (from Chopin's Mazurka in B Flat) (Jan Kiepura, Peasants); "Mazurka" (from various themes by Chopin) (Tania Riabouchinska, Rem Olsted); "Hay, Hay, Hay" (Curt Bois); "Just for Tonight" (from Chopin's Etude in E) (Jan Kiepura, Marta Eggerth); "Midnight Soliloquy" (from Chopin's Nocturne in F Sharp Major) (Tania Riabouchinska); Finale (from Chopin's Polonaise in A Flat and the Revolutionary Etude)
Act Two: "Gavotte" (from Chopin's Variations on a French Air) (Courtiers); "Exchange of Lovers" (ballet) (from various themes by Chopin) (Corps de Ballet, including—The Princess: Ruth Riekman; The Prince: Shawn O'Brien; The Highwayman: Sergei Ismaeloff; The Page: Amalia Valez; The Ballerinas: Jean Harris, Virginia Barnes, Adele Bodroghy, Joan Collenette); "Polonaise" (from Chopin's Polonaise in A Flat) (piano interlude by Zadel Skolovsky); "Now I Know Your Face by Heart" (from Chopin's Waltz in D Flat) (Jan Kiepura, Marta Eggerth); "The Next Time I Care" (music by Bronislaw Kaper) (Rose Inghram); "Tecla's Mood" (from various themes by Chopin) (Tania Riabouchinska, Girls); "Motherhood" (music by Broni-

slaw Kaper) (Curt Bois, Candy Jones, Leta Mauree, Sherry Shadburne, Martha Emma Watson); "Wait for Tomorrow" (from various themes by Chopin) (Jan Kiepura); "I Wonder as I Wander" (from Chopin's Waltz in A Minor and Fantasia Impromptu) (Marta Eggerth); "Battle Ballet" (from Chopin's Four Etudes) (Spirit of the Flag: Tania Riabouchinska; Spirit of the Soldier: Rem Omsted; Bugler: Sergei Ismaeloff; Drummer: Hubert Bland; Corps de Ballet); "Just for Tonight" (reprise) (Jan Kiepura, Marta Eggerth); "Wait for Tomorrow" (reprise) (Jan Kiepura); Finale

For *Polonaise*, Bronislaw Kaper adapted music by Frederic Chopin to tell the true story of Polish patriot Thaddeus Kosciusko (Jan Kiepura), who aided General Washington during the Revolutionary War. Once he helped the colonists, Kosciusko returned to Poland and found himself in another struggle for independence, this time by his fellow countrymen. From there, the musical invented a subplot in which Kosciusko falls in love with peasant girl Marisha (Marta Eggerth).

Although much of the evening's music was adapted from Chopin, Kaper wrote original music for five songs, including the most acclaimed one of the evening, Rose Inghram's show-stopping "The Next Time I Care." And, for those who care, Chopin's Waltz in A Minor and Fantasia Impromptu, which had been adapted by Harry Carroll into the hit song "I'm Always Chasing Rainbows" for *Oh, Look!* in 1918, was heard in *Polonaise* as "I Wonder as I Wander."

The married Kiepura and Eggerth had enjoyed an almost one-year run in the successful 1943 revival of **The Merry Widow**; but their new venture received cool reviews, and, for Kiepura, particularly scathing ones. But somehow the musical was able to hang on for three months before closing, and despite the short run it nonetheless managed to get the financing for a post-Broadway tour.

Wilella Waldorf in the *New York Post* said the musical was a "stupid, inept, often embarrassingly ludicrous spectacle" and noted the "Battle Ballet" (in which Howard Bay's "majestic" décor was "gorily flooded in red light") was the sort of sequence that if not "superlatively done" was "apt to seem rather silly." Further, John LaTouche's lyrics were the "best-kept secret" of the evening because most of the stage was "hip-deep in broken English." Louis Kronenberger in *PM* found the musical "quite deplorable," but because it was so appalling it actually kept his attention. Ward Morehouse in the *New York Sun* noted the evening was "routine and lifeless" with "long stretches of unrelieved tedium"; John Chapman in the *New York Daily News* said the musical was a "disappointment," and mentioned that Curt Bois was saddled with "what may be the longest and most unfunny comedy number in music-show history" (possibly "Hay, Hay, Hay," which Howard Barnes in the *New York Herald Tribune* noted "no one seems to want to take credit for," but more likely "Motherhood," of which Robert Garland in the *New York Journal-American* quoted the line "Father is a bother, but sister is a blister").

Lewis Nichols in the *New York Times* felt the evening was like an "old-fashioned pageant"; the basic story had the makings of a possibly "stirring" musical, but *Polonaise* wasn't it; he also noted the "Battle Ballet" could easily have been mistaken for "parody" (and suggested it needed Fannie Brice to make an entrance, crying out "Rewolt! Rewolt!"). Barnes said a "constant pall" hovered over the production, which was "unkempt and tedious"; Garland described the evening as a "hodgepodge" of "history" and "hokum"; and Burton Rascoe in the *New York World-Telegram* said the book reeked of the "odor of dry-rot and mothballs"; he noted that for the most part the audience members "sat on their hands" and the evening's "travesty of history" brought forth many "disrespectful giggles" from the first-nighters.

But the reviews for the musical were kind and gentle when compared to the critics' comments about Kiepura (and, to a lesser extent, Eggerth). Everyone agreed he could sing; it was his stage deportment that drove them up the wall. Waldorf noted he couldn't act, but that was the least of it: he was an "exhibitionist" who utilized "puppet-show gestures" in the "worst operatic tradition" and he unwittingly became a more "devastating caricature of a pompous *tenore robusto* than any satiric impressionist" could ever hope to emulate. Kronenberger said Kiepura seemed "carved out of wood," and Morehouse reported that when responding to the audience's applause after a song, the tenor walked to the very edge of the stage, struck a pose, and stood there beaming in "utterly transfixed delight." Chapman said he didn't act, he posed, and noted the singer's favorite spot was "the middle of the stage at the edge of the apron" (Chapman surmised there must have been a mark on the stage floor to ensure Kiepura wouldn't fall into the orchestra pit).

Nichols noted that despite Kiepura's "good voice," he was "one of the most wooden actors imaginable"; Rascoe too appreciated his "great range and magnificent lung power," but noted Kiepura was "stiff" and "awkward" and shouldn't be cast in "romantic or heroic" roles; instead, his "natural qualifications as a comedian" could turn him into a Victor Moore with a Polish accent. Rascoe also noted that Rose Inghram's show-stopping "The Next Time I Care" was apparently "so distressing" to Kiepura that when he came on for the next number he sang himself "blue in the face." One of the sub-headlines in Garland's review simply stated: "Ham and Eggerth."

As for Eggerth, there was too much of the opera house about her performance. And Barnes noted that when she and Kiepura were on the stage it was almost impossible to discern what language they were speaking and singing. Waldorf suggested Eggerth needed to rid herself of her "stage smile," and noted that at times there was a shrill and metallic quality about her singing. But Wardhouse said she sang "nicely," was "easy" with dialogue, and he very much liked her "I Wonder as I Wander."

During the run, some of the musical numbers were reordered, a few were dropped, and others added: "Meadow-Lark," "Motherhood," and the late second act reprise of "Just for Tonight" were cut; "Mazurek" (for Kiepura) and "An Imperial Conference" (for James MacColl, Walter Appler, and Leta Mauree) were added; and a reprise of Rose Inghram's show-stopping "The Next Time I Care" was added . . . for Kiepura and Eggerth.

A studio cast album of seven songs from the score (which was paired with Victor Herbert's 1917 musical *Eileen*) was recorded by RCA Camden (LP # CAL-210) by The Harold Coates Orchestra and Chorus with Soloists (the selections are "Polonaise," "O, Heart of My Country," "Mazurka," "Just for Tonight," "Now I Know Your Face by Heart," "The Next Time I Care," "I Wonder as I Wander," and a finale sequence). The collection *Broadway Musicals of 1945* (Bayview CD # RNBW-039) includes "Wait for Tomorrow"; and Richard Rodney Bennett's *Take Love Easy: The Lyrics of John LaTouche* (Audiophile Records LP # AP-206) includes "The Next Time I Care."

As mentioned, despite its short run *Polonaise* nonetheless embarked on a national tour (with Kiepura). The tour's advertisements touted that "America's loveliest operetta" was "direct from a triumphant New York engagement," was a "record-breaking musical hit," and that Kiepura was "one of the best loved singing actors of the current theatre."

THE GYPSY BARON
"An Opera"

Theatre: City Center
Opening Date: October 6, 1945; *Closing Date*: November 10, 1945
Performances: 4 (in repertory)
Libretto: Ignaz Schnitzer (current revival revised and adapted into English by George Mead)
Music: Johann Strauss
Based on *Saffi* by Mor Jokai.
Direction: Leopold Sachse; *Producer*: The New York City Opera Company (Laszlo Halasz, Director); *Choreography*: Carl Randall; *Scenery*: H. A. Condell; *Costumes*: Unknown (probably Van Horn & Son); *Lighting*: Unknown; *Musical Direction*: Julius Rudel
Cast: Gordon Dilworth (Barinsky), Enid Szantho (Czipra), Brenda Lewis (Saffi), George Lipton (Zsupan), Helen George (Arsena), John Harrold (Ottokar), Nathaniel Sprinzena (Ottokar, Alternate), Hubert Norville (Carnero), Grant Garnell (Count Homonnay); Villagers, Gypsies, Hussars, Vivandiers, Soldiers, Citizens, Town Folk, etc.: The New York City Opera Company Chorus
The operetta was presented in three acts.
The action takes place during the nineteenth century in Budapest, Hungary; in the Transylvanian countryside; and in Vienna.
The program didn't list individual musical numbers.

The New York City Opera Company's revival of Johann Strauss's operetta *The Gypsy Baron* played four performances in repertory. The work rarely had been produced in New York since its first showing in 1886, and the current 1945 production marks its most recent revival to date.

For more information about the operetta, see entry for the 1944 revival.

THE RED MILL

Theatre: Ziegfeld Theatre (during run, the musical transferred to the 46th Street Theatre)
Opening Date: October 16, 1945; *Closing Date*: January 18, 1947
Performances: 531
Book: Original book by Henry Blossom
Lyrics: Henry Blossom; additional lyrics by Forman Brown
Music: Victor Herbert
Direction: Stage direction by Billy Gilbert; vocal numbers staged by George Cunningham; *Producers*: Paula Stone and Hunt Stromberg Jr.; *Choreography*: Aida Broadbent; *Scenery* and *Lighting*: Adrian Awan; scenic sketches for act one by Arthur Lonergan, and scenic sketches for act two by Richard Jackson; *Costumes*: Walter Israel; *Musical Direction*: Edward Ward
Cast: Billy Griffith (Town Crier, Pennyfeather), Hal Price (Willem), George Meader (Franz), Dorothy Stone (Tina), Tom Halligan (Bill-Poster), Hope O'Brady (Flora), Lois Potter (Lena), Mardi Bayne (Dora), Frank Jaquet (The Burgomaster), Thomas Spengler (A Sailor), Lorna Byron (Juliana), Michael O'Shea (Con Kidder), Eddie Foy Jr. (Kid Conner), Ann Andre (Gretchen), Robert Hughes (Hendrik Van Damn), Charles Collins (Gaston), Odette Myrtil (Madame La Fleur), Phyllis Bateman (Georgette), Nony Franklin (Suzette), Kathleen Ellis (Fleurette), Jacqueline Ellis (Nanette), Patricia Gardner (Lucette), Joan Johnston (Yvette), Edward Dew (The Governor), Singing Ensemble: Girls—Mardi Bayne, Jane Bender, Betty Bursher, Charlotte Christman, Kathleen Ellis, Jacqueline Ellis, Nony Franklin, Betty Galavan, Patricia Gardner, Carol Johnston, Joan Johnston, Hope O'Brady, Lois Potter, Patsy Tingstrom; Boys—Lloyd R. Bell, Gordon Boelzner, Pete Civello, Kenneth Davies, Tom Decker, Jack Garland, Elton Howard, Leland Ledford, Wally Mohr, Tom Spengler, Calvin Swihart, Michael King; Girls of the Ballet: Dorothy Bauer, Elaine Corbett, Gloria DeWerd, June Fitzpatrick, Irene Hall, Georgia Reed, Doris Walcott, Patricia Sims, Mildred Ann Mauldin, Donna Birock, Barbara Penland, Barbara Hallstone, Jackie Lindberg, Jacqueline Dupont; Ballet Soloists: Mildred Ann Mauldin, Dorothy Bauer, Patricia Sims, Tom Halligan, Elton Howard
The musical was presented in two acts.
The action takes place around 1900 in Katwyk-ann-Zee, Holland.

Musical Numbers

Act One: "Opening Chorus" (aka "By the Side of the Mill") (Village Girls, Boys, Artists); "Mignonette" (Dorothy Stone, Boys, Dancing Girls); "Whistle It" (Michael O'Shea, Eddie Foy Jr., Dorothy Stone); "In the Isle of Our Dreams" (Ann Andre, Robert Hughes); "The Dancing Lesson" (Charles Collins, Ballet Dancers); "The Streets of New York:" (aka "In Old New York") (Michael O'Shea, Eddie Foy Jr., Dancers); "When You're Pretty and the World Is Fair" (Odette Myrtil, Billy Griffith, Ensemble); "Moonbeams" and First Act Finale (Ann Andre, Robert Hughes, Ballet Dancers, Dorothy Stone, Charles Collins, Frank Jaquet, Ensemble)
Act Two: Opening: (a) "Why the Silence?" (aka "Gossip Song") (Boys and Girls) and (b) "The Legend of the Mill" (Lorna Byron, Ensemble, Ballet Dancers); "Every Day Is Ladies' Day with Me" (Edward Dew, Male Chorus, Madame's Daughters); "I Want You to Marry Me" (Ann Andre, Robert Hughes); "Al Fresco" (Dorothy Stone, Charles Collins); "Because You're You" (Edward Dew, Lorna Byron, Dancing Boys and Girls); "Romanza?" (Eddie Foy Jr., Odette Myrtil); "Wedding Bells" (Guests, Bridesmaids, Edward Dew, Odette Myrtil, Lorna Byron, Frank Jaquet, Ann Andre, Robert Hughes); Finale (Entire Company)

Although today it's generally regarded as an operetta, Victor Herbert's 1906 musical *The Red Mill* is really more in the mode of traditional musical comedy. It takes place in what was then virtually contemporary Holland, and while it had its share of romantic folderol, it avoided tear-jerking love affairs, encounters with royalty, and overly fusty humor (but there appears to have been a merry villager or two).
The central characters were two wise-cracking New Yorkers (Kid Connor and Con Kidder, played by David Montgomery and Fred A. Stone in the original production and by Eddie Foy Jr. and Michael O'Shea in the revival) who find themselves stranded in Holland and thus have to work at the local inn (Kid as a waiter, Con as an interpreter for tourists) in order to pay their hotel bills and save enough money for the trip home.

Further, Kid and Con have promised the innkeeper's daughter Tina that they'll take her to New York and make her a star. The Burgomaster's daughter Gretchen is in love with a sailor (Van Damm, but Van Damn for the revival) and defies her father's command that she marry the Governor, who is really in love with Bertha, the Burgomaster's sister. Gretchen hides in the *moulin rouge*, which is said to be haunted, and the Burgomaster hires two detectives (Kid and Con, disguised as Sherlock Holmes and Doctor Watson) to "find" Gretchen, although of course Kid and Con know she's hiding in the red mill. But all is resolved when a veiled Bertha takes Gretchen's place at the wedding, and so Bertha and the Governor become one; and it's happily revealed that Van Damm is the son of wealthy parents, and so he and Gretchen can wed. And presumably Kid and Con and Tina head off for little old New York where "the peach crop's always fine."

The musical was first seen in New York at the Knickerbocker Theatre on September 24, 1906, for 318 performances. It was an immediate hit and had the longest run of the season, played on Broadway for nine months, enjoyed a number of popular hit songs, and toured for some two years with Stone and Montgomery. Its score included "Moonbeams," "Because You're You," "In the Isle of Our Dreams," "Whistle It," and the especially delightful "Every Day Is Ladies' Day with Me" and "The Streets of New York" (aka "In Old New York") (the latter notes that "you cannot see in gay Paree, in London or in Cork / The queens you'll meet on any street in old New York").

A note in the program from the 1907 tour states the musical was probably "the first time that a play devoted exclusively to the portrayal of Dutch character and location has been submitted to the American public." Further, the musical offered a "quaint atmosphere" of "dikes, windmills and wooden shoes." In the original production, the interior of the burgomaster's home was designed by the Delft Company in the style of delft blue.

The New York revival was set for a limited engagement of two months at the Ziegfeld; Burton Rascoe in the *New York World-Telegram* said an eight-week run was "unfair" and he planned to picket the Ziegfeld and demand a year's run because the musical was "something to be treasured in memory." Rascoe got more than his wish because the revival played for fifteen months. But after its initial two-month booking, the show had to transfer to the 46th Street Theatre because the Ziegfeld had already been booked for the upcoming revival of **Show Boat**.

Rascoe said the evening offered "fun and music" and "color and excitement"; he had seen the original production on tour when he was a "kid," and the new version was "immensely, insuperably better." And he praised Eddie Foy Jr. (who at one point toward the end of the evening announced to the audience, "And that's the plot"), and wondered where "they" had been keeping him. For here was a natural comic, "one of the great comedians of our time" and the "only man living to dispute Bobby Clark's position as the ace zany" of the stage.

Wilella Waldorf in the *New York Post* noted that Broadway had recently offered "lamentable tripe" such as **Mr. Strauss Goes to Boston** and **Polonaise** and thus it was in no position to look down on the revival whose "greatest charms" are "old-fashioned atmosphere and style." She predicted *The Red Mill* would again be a big hit during its limited New York run and "should do well" on the road. As for Eddie Foy Jr., he brought a "Mad Hatter quality" to his role and was "persistently ingratiating." She also enjoyed the "snappy twirling" dances by Dorothy Stone and Charles Collins, which were a great relief after the "solemn toe work" offered in recent musicals, including "all the Battle Ballets" (the last reference to the "Civil War Ballet" in **Bloomer Girl** and the "Battle Ballet" in **Polonaise**). Ward Morehouse in the *New York Sun* found the evening an "agreeable surprise" and said Foy was "outstanding." Here was a comedian who was "droll, likeable and acrobatic," and his tasty performance led Morehouse to wonder "if he hasn't been shockingly neglected" by Broadway producers.

John Chapman in the *New York Daily News* said the show was "surprisingly pleasant," and Robert Garland in the *New York Journal-American* noted the revival had been produced with "pride and taste and affectionate understanding" and was a "delightful evening's entertainment."

But Lewis Nichols in the *New York Times* found the evening "amiable but dated" and "slow rather than sprightly"; it was "much better" than **Mr. Strauss Goes to Boston**, but it still didn't offer a "full measure" of entertainment. Howard Barnes in the *New York Herald Tribune* was mainly indifferent to the evening's charms but he admitted it was a "pleasant contrast to some of the drivel that has been dished out recently."

Louis Kronenberger in *PM* said he couldn't "conscientiously" call the revival a "full evening's entertainment," but he liked the score and Foy's clowning and thus didn't "particularly suffer." Compared to **Mr. Strauss Goes to Boston** and **Polonaise**, the revival could "more than hold its head up," but nonetheless it was "still not too much of a show."

The revival was coproduced by Paula Stone, Fred A. Stone's daughter, and one of the leads in the production was Dorothy Stone, another daughter of Stone's (Dorothy's husband Charles Collins was also prominently featured in the cast in the newly created role of Gaston). Stone himself was in the opening night audience along with his wife Aline Crater Stone, who had originated the role of Bertha in the 1906 production.

The revival omitted five songs from the original ("You Can Never Tell about a Woman," "A Widow Has Ways," "Always Go While the Goin' Is Good," "An Accident," and "Good-a-bye, John"), and added two numbers ("Al Fresco" and "Romanza?") which may have been in the original production and were now outfitted with new lyrics by Forman Brown.

The most complete recording is by the Ohio Light Opera on a two-CD set that was released by Albany Records (# TROY-492/493). Other versions of the score were released by Decca (six songs on LP # DL-8016; which is paired with *Up in Central Park*) with Wilbur Evans, Eileen Farrell, and Felix Knight; by RCA Camden (eight songs on LP # CAL-437) with such singers as Earl Wrightson along with Al Goodman and His Orchestra; and by Turnabout (twelve songs on LP # TV-34766) by various artists including the Gregg Smith Singers.

A charming silent film adaptation was released by Cosmopolitan Productions and MGM in 1927 with a cast that included Marion Davies, Owen Moore, Louise Fazenda, and George Siegmann; it was directed by Roscoe "Fatty" Arbuckle under the name of William B. Goodrich (the film is available from the Warner Brothers' Archive Collection).

A television adaptation was produced by CBS on the *DuPont Show of the Month* on April 19, 1958, with direction by Delbert Mann and teleplay by Robert Alan Aurthur; the cast included Shirley Jones, Donald O'Connor, Harpo Marx, Mike Nichols, Elaine May, Elaine Stritch, Edward Andrews, and Evelyn Rudie. This was the season for "Dutch" musicals. Two months earlier, on February 9, 1958, NBC's *Hallmark Hall of Fame* had presented Tab Hunter in *Hans Brinker, or the Silver Skates* with lyrics and music by Hugh Martin.

THE GIRL FROM NANTUCKET
"The Modern Musical Comedy" / "A New Musical Comedy of Today" / "A New Musical Comedy"

Theatre: Adelphi Theatre
Opening Date: November 8, 1945; *Closing Date*: November 17, 1945
Performances: 12
Book: Paul Stanford and Harold Sherman; additional dialogue by Hy Cooper
Lyrics: Kay Twomey; additional lyrics by Burt Wilson
Music: Jacques Belasco
(Additional lyrics and music by Hughie Prince and Dick Rogers.)
Based on a story by Fred Thompson and Berne Giler.
Direction: Book directed by Edward Clarke Lilley and production staged by Henry Adrian; *Producer*: Henry Adrian; *Choreography*: Val Raset; *Scenery* and *Lighting*: Albert Johnson; *Costumes*: Lou Eisele; *Musical Direction*: Harry Levant
Cast: Bob Kennedy (Michael [Mike] Nicolson), Adelaide Bishop (Betty Ellis [evening performances]), Pat McClarney (Betty Ellis [matinee performances]), George L. Headley (Tom Andrews), Marion Niles (Ann Ellis), Jane Kean (Dodey Ellis), Helen Raymond (Keziah Getchel), John Robb (Judge Peleg), Billy Lynn (Captain Matthew Ellis), Jack Durant (Dick Oliver), Richard Clemens (Enrico Nicoletti), The Corporation played by The Four Buccaneers (Paul Shiers, John Panter, Don Cortez, Joseph Cunneff), Johnny Eager (Roy, Caleb, and "Several Other Fellows"), Connie Sheldon (Mary), Kim and Kathy Gaynes (Dance Specialists), Tom Ladd (Solo Dancer), Rapps and Tapps; The Nantucket Guides: Claire Weidener, Deanne Benmore, Marilyn Pendry, Mary Bernice Brady, Madeleine Detry, Gloria Evans, Lee Joyce, Zelda Allen, Fran Celia, Kay Popp, Louise Harris, Aleen Frank, Sylvia Mehler; The Vacationists: Bettina Theyer, Ruth Vrana, Jeanne North, Geraldine Willier, Harriet Pegors, Linda Hayes; The Townfolk: Jean D'Arcy, Doris Claire, Rita Rallis, Lee Dennis, Vicky Raaf, Jerry Daily, Sherry Stevens, Francis Pruitt, Temple Texas Norma Hetzler, Panette Piper, Francis Kiernan, Allan Waine, Mischa Pompianov, Randolf Hughes; The Fishermen: Erno Czako, Gerald Scima, Robert Vaden, Neal Towner, Jack Riley, T. C. Jones, Terry Dawson
The musical was presented in two acts.
The action takes place during the present time in New York City and in Nantucket, Rhode Island.

Musical Numbers

Act One: "I Want to See More of You" (Adelaide Bishop, Bob Kennedy); "Take the Steamer to Nantucket" (The Vacationists and The Guides); Dance Specialty (Kim and Kathy Gaynes, Marion Niles); "What's He Like?" (Adelaide Bishop, Jane Kean, Girls); "What's a Sailor Got?" (Billy Lynn, Ensemble); "Magnificent Failure" (lyric and music by Hughie Prince and Dick Rogers) (Jack Durant); "Hurray for Nicoletti" (lyric by Kay Twomey and Burt Milton) (Jack Durant, Entire Ensemble); Dance Specialty (Marion Niles, Rapps and Tapps); "When A Hick Chick Meets a City Slicker" (lyric by Burt Milton) (Jane Kean, Jack Durant); "Your Fatal Fascination" (Adelaide Bishop, Bob Kennedy, Kim and Kathy Gaynes, Marion Niles, Ensemble); "Let's Do and Say We Didn't" (lyric and music by Hughie Prince and Dick Rogers) (Jack Durant, Girls); "Nothing Matters" (Connie Sheldon, Girls); Dance Specialty (Rapps and Tapps); "Sons of the Sea" (George L. Headley, Fishermen); "Whalers' Ballet—A Page from Old Nantucket" (ballet's narrative written by Mary Carroll) (Monologue: George L. Headley; The Sea: Kathy Gaynes; The Whale: Kim Gaynes; Tom: Tom Ladd)

Act Two: "Isn't It a Lovely View?" (Adelaide Bishop, The Vacationists); "Isn't It a Lovely View?" (reprise) (Adelaide Bishop); "From Morning Till Night" (Adelaide Bishop, Bob Kennedy); "I Love That Boy" (Jane Kean, Jack Durant); "I Love That Boy" (reprise) (Bob Kennedy); "(A) Hammock in the Blue" (Adelaide Bishop, Bob Kennedy, Ensemble); "Boukra Fill Mish Mish" (Billy Lynn, Tom Ladd, Ensemble); Dance Specialty (Jack Durant, Billy Lynn); Reprise (song unknown); Finale

During its tryout, *The Girl from Nantucket* was subtitled "The Modern Musical Comedy" and a later New York advertisement billed it as "A New Musical Comedy of Today." But considering the production's hopelessly old-hat shtick, cooler heads prevailed and the show's tag line was officially changed to "A New Musical Comedy," which even then was no doubt overselling the evening. James Barton (as the Captain, and who was billed above the title) and Evelyn Wyckoff (as Betty Ellis) left the show during the Philadelphia tryout; the former was succeeded by Billy Lynn (who didn't receive star billing) and Wyckoff was followed by both Adelaide Bishop (for evening performances) and Pat McClarney (for matinees). Among the songs cut prior to the New York run were: "Morning in Manhattan," "I Live across the Street," "That's How I Know That I'm in Love," "It's the New England in Me," and "Tendin' to My Knittin'" (the lyric for the latter was by Kay Twomey and Burt Milton). The tryout's "A Sailor's Serenade" became "What's a Sailor Got?" for New York. "Muriel" (as in "A Mural of Muriel") with lyric by Burt Wilton may have been dropped in preproduction.

The plot dealt with Manhattan house painter Mike Nicolson (Bob Kennedy) who in Peeping Tom fashion likes to look into the window of a comely young woman named Betty Ellis (Adelaide Bishop) while she dresses and undresses (this naturally leads into the song "I Want to See More of You"). An in-his-cups Nantucket ex-sea captain (Billy Lynn) mistakes Mike for the artist Enrico Nioletti (Richard Clemens), and offers him $1,000 to do some painting. When Mike arrives in Nantucket, he discovers the job is not to paint houses but to paint a mural for the local museum. Luckily, it turns out that Betty is a painter and so she takes over the job as muralist.

Nothing much in the way of action occurred, and so the evening presented out-of-nowhere (but welcome) dance routines by the black duo Rapps and Tapps; offered weak humor (along the lines of: "Are you taking along a bag?" / "No, she's not coming with me"); tired visual humor, which included a scene in which a male comedian attempts to put on a brassiere; and smarmy songs such as "Let's Do and Say We Didn't." Today the musical is mostly remembered for its pretentious ballet "A Page from Old Nantucket," in which one dancer portrayed "The Sea" and another "The Whale." The twelve-performance fiasco lost a reported $365,000, an enormous sum for the era.

Willela Waldorf in the *New York Post* managed to sit through the first act before she fled to the sanity of West 54th Street. She said if the producers wanted to lift a quote from her review, she had one for them: "It lacks everything." Lewis Nichols in the *New York Times* suggested the musical wasn't "the worst seen since the beginning of understanding" but "for at least part of the time it runs a good race. It is bad enough for the moment." Burton Rascoe in the *New York World-Telegram* said the musical had "no book in the usual sense, and no music in any sense at all." The "bawdy" lyrics of "Let's Do and Say We Didn't" made **Follow the Girls'** "I Wanna Get Married" sound "like a Sunday school hymn" and two dance routines by Kim and Kathy Gaynes "would have made the Minsky brothers blush."

John Chapman in the *New York Daily News* found the musical "90% torture," and noted the ballet "A Page from Old Nantucket" was "a gem of horrid pretentiousness" in which the dancers "nearly bust their suspenders being symbolic." Howard Barnes in the *New York Herald Tribune* said the book was "bad," Kay Twomey was "to blame" for the lyrics, and the ballet was "weirdly dull"; but he noted Rapps and Tapps lent the evening some "fleeting distinction" with their hoofing, Jane Kean emerged as the best of the principals (even though she had to sing "such doggerel" as "When a Hick Chick Meets a City Slicker"); and Jack Durant was stuck with the "spluttering" "Let's Do and Say We Didn't." Like Lewis Nichols, Louis Kronenberger in *PM* mentioned that producer Henry Adrian had also offered the terrible comedy *Victory Belles* two years earlier. That comedy was one of the "worst of all straight plays," and now *Nantucket* was "one of the sorriest" of all musicals. He suggested Adrian should have titled the musical *The Girl from Death Valley*; the evening was full of "macabre doings," and he felt sorry for Jane Kean, who was forced to speak "awful dialogue" and sing "smutty" songs.

Robert Garland in the *New York Journal-American* suggested the musical was an "endurance contest" between the audience and the performers. But the cast had to remain on stage throughout the performance, while the lucky audience members could at least keep "going out and out." The "musical misdemeanor" was the kind of show only its backers could love.

Ward Morehouse in the *New York Sun* said the "awkward and disconnected" musical was one of the "very worst." The "overpoweringly dull" evening offered a "routine" score and a "dreadful" book, and so it made him think that perhaps **Mr. Strauss Goes to Boston** wasn't all that bad. In his summary of the season, George Jean Nathan said *The Girl from Nantucket* closely followed **Hairpin Harmony** and **The Duchess Misbehaves** as the decade's "worst." The music sounded like the result of "hitting a wash-boiler alternately with a saxophone and a potato-masher," the scenery was what you'd come across in "summer hotel shows," and the performances were mostly "out of the road grab-bag." But he noted the evening had one "sole virtue": during the twenty-five minute ballet, a performer sat on a papier-mâché rock and explained to the audience what the ballet was all about. This was helpful because without such exposition Nathan would have assumed the dance was about a man in brown tights who fought a woman in green before another man in a college sweater hit him in the jaw; he never would have understood that the ballet was *really* about the battle of a whale and a fisherman for the "fickle affections of the sea."

The collection *The Broadway Musicals of 1945* includes "From Morning Till Night" (Bayview CD # RNBW-039).

ARE YOU WITH IT?
"A Bright New Musical"

Theatre: New Century Theatre (during run, the musical transferred to the Shubert Theatre)
Opening Date: November 10, 1945; *Closing Date*: June 29, 1946
Performances: 267
Book: Sam Perrin and George Balzer
Lyrics: Arnold B. Horwitt
Music: Harry Revel
Based on the 1941 novel *Slightly Perfect* by George Malcolm-Smith.
Direction: Edward Reveaux; *Producers*: Richard Kollmar and James W. Gardiner; *Choreography*: Jack Donohue; *Scenery* and *Lighting*: George Jenkins; *Costumes*: Willa Kim (from sketches by Raoul Pene du Bois); *Musical Direction*: Will Irwin
Cast: Jane Dulo (Marge Keller), Sydney Boyd (Mr. Bixby), Johnny Stearns (Mr. Mapleton, Barker), Johnny Downs (Wilbur Haskins), Joan Roberts (Vivian Reilly), Duke McHale (Policeman), Lew Parker (Goldie), Lou Wills Jr. (Bartender), Lew Eckels (Carter), Jane Deering (Snake Charmer's Daughter, Aerialist), Bunny Briggs (Cicero), June Richmond (Cleo), Mildred Jocelyn (Balloon Seller), Dolores Gray (Bunny La Fleur), Diane Adrian (Sally Swivelhips), Buster Shaver (Georgetta), Olive (Olive), George (George), Richard (Richard), William Lundy (Strong Man), Hal Hunter (Office Boy), Lou Hurst (First Musician), David Lambert (Second Musician), Jerry Duane (Third Musician), Jerry Packer (Fourth Musician), Loren Welch (Loren); Quartette: Jerry Duane, Lou Hurst, David Lambert, Jerry Packer; Girls: Dorothy Bennett, Vivian Cook, Jeanne Coyne, Pompey Cross, Dorothy Drew, Suzanne Graves, Beth Green, Betty Heather, Penny Holt,

Gretchen Houser, Jo Ann Kavanagh, Charlotte Lorraine, Pat Marlowe, June Morrison, Renee Russell, Bette Valentine, Doris York; Boys: Jimmy Allen, Jerry Ames, Eddie Feder, Bill Julian, John Laverty, William Lundy, Don Miraglia, Tommy Morton, George Thornton

The musical was presented in two acts.

The action takes place during the present time in Hartford and Bushnell Park, Connecticut.

Musical Numbers

Act One: "Five More Minutes in Bed" (Jane Dulo, Ensemble; Dancer: Jane Deering); "Nutmeg Insurance" (Johnny Downs, Jane Dulo, Sydney Boyd, Johnny Stearns, Ensemble); "Slightly Perfect" (Joan Roberts, Johnny Downs); "When a Good Man Takes to Drink" (Joan Roberts, Duke McHale); "When a Good Man Takes to Drink" (reprise) (Joan Roberts, Duke McHale, Lou Wills Jr.); "Poor Little Me" (June Richmond); "Are You With It?" (Dolores Gray, The Quartette, Ensemble); "This Is My Beloved" (Joan Roberts, Johnny Downs); "Slightly Slightly" (Olive, George, Richard); Dance (Buster Shaver, Olive); "Vivian's Reverie" (music adapted by Will Irwin from themes by Harry Revel) (Jane Deering, William Lundy, Circus Performers)

Act Two: "Send Us Back to the Kitchen" (Jane Dulo, Girls); "Here I Go Again" (Joan Roberts, The Quartette); "You Gotta Keep Saying 'No'" (Dolores Gray); "Just Beyond the Rainbow" (June Richmond, Ensemble; danced by Bunny Briggs); "In Our Cozy Little Cottage of Tomorrow" (Dolores Gray, Lew Parker); Finale (Entire Company)

Are You With It? was an old-fashioned musical comedy set in the world of the carnival. When insurance actuary Wilbur Haskins (Johnny Downs) accidentally misplaces a very important decimal point, he's fired from the Nutmeg Insurance Company. He then becomes the accountant for a touring carnival, and while he and his girlfriend Vivian Reilly (Joan Roberts) are the musical's conventional "serious" romantic couple, midway barker Goldie (Lew Parker) and carnival dancer Bunny La Fleur (Dolores Gray) provide the evening's comic moments. When Wilbur uncovers an insurance fraud and is able to save his former company a large amount of money, all is forgiven and he's welcomed back into the world of the Nutmeg.

Are You With It? opened the same night as Robert Sherwood's drama *The Rugged Path*, which marked Spencer Tracy's return to Broadway after a fifteen-year absence. The first-string critics reviewed the drama, and the second-stringers covered the musical.

Alton Cook in the *New York World-Telegram* noted the weather outside was rainy and windy, but all was "snug and comfortable" inside the New Century Theatre. The musical was "prodigal" with talented cast members, offered lots of dancing, and had plenty of slyness in the book and lyrics (he singled out the anti-feminist song "Send Us Back to the Kitchen," in which the chorines sang, "Let us learn to be adept / In the art of being kept"). Robert Sylvester in the *New York Daily News* said the musical was the first "good" old-fashioned show since **Panama Hattie**. The cast was "refreshing" and "talented," the evening moved quickly, and whatever the show lacked was "happily overlooked" amid the lighthearted proceedings. He said Joan Roberts could take her place as "the town's No. 1 musical gal"; he praised "roly-poly Negro singer" June Richmond, who did a "great job" with the blues "Poor Little Me"; Gray and Parker's "In Our Cozy Little Cottage of Tomorrow" was "more amusing than most such Porterish novelties"; and the dancing midget trio of Olive, George, and Richard stopped the show "cold."

Ben Rosenberg in the *New York Post* predicted the musical would be around for a "long time"; it offered "lively, tuneful" and "fast-paced" songs, "rollicking" comedy, and a "good story." Otis L. Guernsey in the *New York Herald Tribune* noted the evening was sometimes in "bad taste" and was occasionally the victim of "weak material," but overall the show was a "riot of color" with a "syncopated" score and a talented company. Herrick Brown in the *New York Sun* said the "bright" musical was a "fast-stepping and colorful" one that had a "gay and easy" score. Jim O'Connor in the *New York Journal-American* mentioned that "no expense" had been spared on the lavish production, which sported "gorgeous" costumes and "striking" sets. *Are You With It?* was a "good show, a very good show—a musical comedy with music and with comedy"; and Lewis Funke in the *New York Times* said that here was a musical comedy "that knows the full meaning of the term." The book was "better than ordinary"; the lyrics were "smart and right"; the music was "tuneful" and "rhythmic"; the choreography offered dance sequences of "verve and dash"; and the décor was appropriately "garish." He singled out seven songs, including June Richmond's show-stopping "Poor Little Me" and "Just Beyond the Rainbow" and Dolores Gray's "You Gotta Say 'No'" and "In Our Cozy Little Cottage of Tomorrow."

But Robert A. Hague in *PM* said Broadway was still waiting for a good musical. *Are You With It?* began promisingly, but as the evening progressed the players found themselves "stranded" with indifferent material. And in his seasonal summary George Jean Nathan stated he was not all that amused: but he was thankful for Dolores Gray (she was "something") and he was grateful the plot didn't require Johann Sebastian Bach to fall in love with Joan Roberts.

Many of the critics had particular praise for the musical's opening number "Five More Minutes in Bed," which depicted a scene in silhouette of boarding-house dwellers waking up for the day. Rosenberg said with this "clever" sequence the show began in "high gear," and predicted the song would be heard often. Hague also praised the number and said it offered a "fascinating realism" with its early-morning peek of the world waking up; after this pantomimic sequence, Jane Dulo and the "fast-stepping" chorus sang of their wish for those five more minutes of sleep.

"Five Minutes More in Bed" was part of a mini-trend in mid-1940s musicals that depicted the early morning hours of the big city. **On the Town** began with the song "I Feel Like I'm Not Out of Bed Yet" and its view of the sailors let loose from their ship at 6:00 AM in order to enjoy the pleasures of "New York, New York." **Watch Out, Angel!** included the "Five A.M. Ballet," which the program described as "typifying musically the sounds common to the dawn of a great city," including such types as a street girl (danced by Carol Haney) and a sailor (Rodolfo Silva). Even **The Duchess Misbehaves** offered "Morning in Madrid."

During the run, "Slightly Slightly" was dropped and in its place Bunny Briggs performed a solo (and untitled) dance.

The collection *Broadway Musicals of 1945* (Bayview CD # RNBW-039) includes "Here I Go Again" and "Slightly Perfect." The recording *Joan Roberts Sings Her Hit Songs & Frank Crumit and Julia Sanderson—Famous Songs from Their Best Known Musical Comedies* (released on CD by Original Cast Records) includes Roberts's "This Is My Beloved"; *Lost Broadway and More/Volume Three* (unnamed company and unnumbered CD) also includes "This Is My Beloved"; and the collection *Keep Your Undershirt On!* (Rialto CD) offers "Slightly Perfect."

The film version (which was advertised as "The Biggest Fun Show on Earth!") was released by Universal-International in 1948, and is one of the most obscure of all Broadway adaptations; it never shows up on cable television and hasn't been released on home video. The cast includes Lew Parker from the Broadway production, along with Donald O'Connor, Olga San Juan, Martha Stewart, and Walter Catlett. The direction was by Jack Hively, the choreography by Louis Da Pron, and the screenplay by Oscar Brodney. Although the plot followed the basic outline of the stage production, a completely new score was written for the film (lyrics and music by Sidney Miller and Inez James).

THE DAY BEFORE SPRING
"A New Musical" / "The Witty New Musical"

Theatre: National Theatre
Opening Date: November 22, 1945; *Closing Date*: April 14, 1946
Performances: 165
Book and *Lyrics*: Alan Jay Lerner
Music: Frederick Loewe
Direction: Book directed by Edward Padula and production staged by John C. Wilson; *Producer*: John C. Wilson; *Choreography*: Antony Tudor; *Scenery*: Robert H. Davison; *Costumes*: Miles White; *Lighting*: Uncredited; *Musical Direction*: Maurice Abravanel
Cast: Irene Manning (Katherine Townsend), John Archer (Peter Townsend), Bert Freed (Bill Tompkins), Lucille Benson (May Tompkins), Bill Johnson (Alex Maitland), Karol Loraine (Marie), Bette Anderson (Lucille), Lucille Floetman (Leonore), Estelle Loring (Marjorie), Arlouine Goodjohn (Susan), Betty Jean Smythe (Anne), Tom Helmore (Gerald Barker), Don Mayo (Joe McDonald), Robert Field (Harry Scott), Dwight Marfield (Eddie Warren), Patricia Marshall (Christopher Randolph), Mary Ellen Moylan (Katherine [in the book]), Hugh Laing (Alex [in the book]), Paul Best (Voltaire), Ralph Glover (Plato), Hermann Leopoldi

(Freud); Vocal Ensemble: Nina Dean, Arlouine Goodjohn, Karol Loraine, Estelle Loring, Bette Anderson, Lucille Floetman, Shirley Dean, Betty Jean Smythe, Ernest Taylor, Jeffrey Warren, Alfred Sukey, Tommy Matthews, Robert Lussier, Paul Mario, Kenny McCord, Bernard Tunis; Dancers: Janice M. Cioffi, Mattlyn Gevurtz, Isabel Mirrow, June Morris, Eva Soltesz, Eleanor Treiber, Sonja Tyven, Bruce Cartwright, Ronny Chetwood, Erik Kristen, Jack Miller, Frank Westbrook, Richard Astor

The musical was presented in two acts.

The action occurs within a period of twenty-four hours in June of the present year in both New York City and in and around Harrison University.

Musical Numbers

Act One: "The Day before Spring" (Irene Manning); "The Invitation" (Bert Freed); "God's Green World" (Bill Johnson, Ensemble; A Girl: Eleanor Treiber; A Boy: Ronny Chetwood; Another Boy: Jack Miller); "You Haven't Changed at All" (Irene Manning, Bill Johnson); "My Love Is a Married Man" (Patricia Marshall); "The Day before Spring" (reprise) (Irene Manning, Bill Johnson); "Ballet of the Book According to Alex" (Katherine: Mary Ellen Moylan; Alex: Hugh Laing); "Katherine Receives Advice" (Hermann Leopoldi, Ralph Glover, Paul Best); Finale (Ensemble)

Act Two: "Friends to the End" (Bert Freed, Don Mayo, Robert Field, Tom Helmore, Alumni); "A Jug of Wine" (Patricia Marshall); "The Book" (narrated by John Archer): (1) "I Love You This Morning" (Irene Manning, Bill Johnson, Ensemble) and (2) "The Day before Spring" (reprise) (Bill Johnson, Irene Manning); "Where's My Wife?" (John Archer); "This Is My Holiday" (Irene Manning); "Ballet of the Book According to Gerald" (Katherine: Mary Ellen Moylan; Alex: Hugh Laing); Finale (Principals, Company)

Alan Jay Lerner and Frederick Loewe's second Broadway musical was the ambitious and truly original *The Day before Spring*, which was light-years ahead of their first collaboration, the old-fashioned **What's Up**. And while their new musical wasn't a hit, it was a *succes d'estime* (although Lerner reportedly joked that it was a success that ran out of steam), played for 165 performances, received many good reviews, briefly toured, and was even sold to the movies (but went unfilmed).

Although *The Day before Spring* opened in the era when cast albums of new musicals were being recorded on a somewhat regular basis, the show went sadly unrecorded. Its melodic and ambitious score deserves to be preserved, and if happy surprises like recordings of **Sadie Thompson**, **The Firebrand of Florence**, **Marinka**, and **Sweet Bye and Bye** occasionally come along, who knows, maybe one day we'll see a release of this important score. Thankfully, a number of songs from the musical have surfaced (see below), but the ballet music, the college drinking-buddy number "Friends to the End," the apparently quite witty patter song "Where's My Wife?" ("a very amusing buzz of a ditty," according to Louis Kronenberger in *PM*), and the musical interlude in which the heroine consults Plato, Voltaire, and Freud for advice, have gone unrecorded.

The plot takes place within a twenty-four hour period. Katherine Townsend (Irene Manning) and her husband Peter (John Archer) drive up from New York City to attend their tenth college reunion at Harrison University. A decade earlier, Katherine had planned to elope with classmate Alex Maitland (Bill Johnson), but their plans went awry, and Katherine met, fell in love with, and married Peter. Now Alex is a successful novelist, and his recent best-seller *The Day before Spring* is a thinly veiled account of his romance with Katherine. At the reunion, Alex and Katherine fall in love all over again and they again plan to elope. But the past repeats itself, and Katherine realizes that it is Peter, not Alex, whom she loves. There were dance sequences that depicted the romantic conflicts of the principals, and the song "Katherine Receives Advice" took place in the college library where statues of Plato, Voltaire, and Freud come to life and give advice to the heroine (the first tells her to keep her relationship with Alex on a platonic level; the Frenchman suggests she enjoy both Peter and Alex; and Freud urges her to run off with Alex).

The musical included roles for Tom Helmore (as Gerald Barker, Alex's secretary-cum-valet) and Patricia Marshall (as Christopher Randolph, who carries a torch for Peter). Marshall had also appeared in Lerner and Loewe's **What's Up**, and so has the distinction of creating leading roles in the team's first two Broadway musicals.

Burton Rascoe in the *New York World-Telegram* found the musical "sweet and charming" with a book of "substance," lyrics that were an "integral part" of the book and that were "clean as fresh snow on a hillside and almost as brilliantly textured as snow crystals." He singled out eight songs (five "romantic and haunting," three "witty and amusing"), and mentioned that Lerner and Loewe showed the kind of creative harmony that marked the collaboration of Richard Rodgers and Oscar Hammerstein II. John Chapman in the *New York Daily News* said the musical was "urbane, humorous," and "tuneful," and noted that the plot was "interesting, integrated and full of pleasant surprises"; further, the lyrics were "much better than average" and the music was "generous and beguiling." Robert Garland in the *New York Journal-American* praised the "fresh" and "delightfully disarming" musical as a "welcome addition" to Broadway's "top musicals." Here was a show that was "adult and affable" and "gay and gracious."

But Wilella Waldorf in the *New York Post* said the "tedious" evening was a "curious mixture" of the "pseudo-sophisticated" and the "collegiate" (and commented that Loewe's score was "pleasant" if "hardly exciting"); Ward Morehouse in the *New York Sun* found the "pleasant and generally likable" musical one of "excellent taste," and he noted the music was "nice" and the book "serviceable" but "humorless"; and Kronenberger said the musical never quite reached the level of sophistication it aimed for; Loewe's music was "buoyant and bright" if "not too original"; and while the show had a "nice look and spirit" it never quite jelled into a satisfying evening of entertainment.

Howard Barnes in the *New York Herald Tribune* liked the "melodious" score but felt the "slight and brittle" book could have offered more in the way of humor; the songs were "fresh and amusingly lyrical" and he noted there was a "nice interweaving" of the musical sequences and the libretto. Lewis Nichols in the *New York Times* was glad to hear "cheerful" music and see a "smart" production that was created with "care and integrity." But overall the book was "heavy" and "austere" and thus the "good" things in the musical didn't add up to a "satisfactory evening."

During the tryout, "Happy, Happy, Happy" (for Irene Manning) was cut.

In *The Movies' Greatest Musicals*, Hugh Fordin reports that in 1946 and in 1960 MGM had planned to film the musical, but of course the proposed film versions never came to fruition. The first had a screenplay by George Oppenheimer and I. A. L. Diamond, with eight new songs (lyrics by Frank Loesser and music by Johnny Green); *The Collected Lyrics of Frank Loesser* includes six of the eight songs written for the project. The second proposed film was an adaptation by Joseph Stein of Lerner's script that retained the original Lerner and Loewe songs.

The collection *Alan Jay Lerner Revisited* (Painted Smiles CD # PSCD-141) includes seven songs from the score ("I Love You This Morning," "This Is My Holiday," "God's Green World," "You Haven't Changed at All," "A Jug of Wine," "My Love Is a Married Man," and the title number); *Lyrics by Lerner* (DRG CD # 5246) includes "A Jug of Wine"; *Broadway Musicals of 1945* (Bayview CD # RNBW-039) includes "You Haven't Changed at All"; and *Life's a Funny Present* (Rialto CD # SLRR-9306) offers "This Is My Holiday" and "God's Green World."

The collection *A Hymn to Him: The Lyrics of Alan Jay Lerner* includes the lyrics of "You Haven't Changed at All," "A Jug of Wine," "God's Green World," "I Love You This Morning," "This Is My Holiday," "My Love Is a Married Man," and the title song.

BILLION DOLLAR BABY
"A MUSICAL PLAY OF THE TERRIFIC TWENTIES"

Theatre: Alvin Theatre
Opening Date: December 21, 1945; *Closing Date*: June 29, 1946
Performances: 220
Book and *Lyrics*: Betty Comden and Adolph Green
Music: Morton Gould
Direction: George Abbott; *Producers*: Paul Feigay and Oliver Smith; *Choreography*: Jerome Robbins; *Scenery*: Oliver Smith; *Costumes*: Irene Sharaff; *Lighting*: George Schaff; *Musical Direction*: Max Goberman
Cast: Emily Ross (Ma Jones), William David (Pa Jones), Shirley Van (Esme), Maria Harriton (Neighbor, Chorine), Edward Hodge (Neighbor), Howard Lenters (Neighbor), Douglas Deane (Neighbor, Comic), Helen Gallagher (Neighbor, Chorine), Beverly Hosier (Neighbor), Danny Daniels (Champ Watson), Anthony Reed (Photographer), Alan Gilbert (Reporter, Marathon M.C.), Joan McCracken (Maribelle Jones), Douglas Jones (Newsboy), Richard Thomas (Newsboy), Richard Sanford (Master of Ceremonies, Rodney Gender),

Althea Elder (Miss Texas), Mitzi Green (Georgia Motley), Tony Gardell (Violin Player, Danny), Don De Leo (Jerry Bonanza), David Burns (Dapper Welch), William Tabbert (Rocky Barton), Jeri Archer (Cigarette Girl), David Thomas (Waiter), Robert Chisholm (M. M. Montague), Joan Mann (Chorine), Lorraine Todd (Chorine), Virginia Gorski (aka Virginia Gibson) (Chorine), Virginia Poe (Chorine), Horace Cooper (J. C. Creasy), Eddie Hodge (Art Leffenbush), Robert Edwin (Watchman), James Mitchell (The Dancing Rocky), Howard Lenters (Policeman); Dancers: Jacqueline Dodge, Helen Gallagher, Virginia Gorski (Gibson), Maria Harriton, Ann Hutchinson, Cecille Mann, Joan Mann, Virginia Poe, Lorraine Todd, Lucas Aco, Allan Waine, Douglas Deane, Fred Hearne, Joe Landis, Arthur Partington, William (Bill) Skipper, Bill Sumner; Singers: Peggy Anne Ellis, Jeri Archer, Future Fulton, Lyn Gammon, Doris Hollingsworth, Beverly Hosier, Sydney Wylie, Betty Saunders, Thelma Stevens, Beth Shea, Tony Caffaro, Tony Gardell, Robert Morrissey, Franklin Powell, Anthony Reed, David Thomas, Philip La Torre

The musical was presented in two acts.

The action takes place during 1928 and 1929 in Staten Island, Atlantic City, New York City, and Palm Beach.

Musical Numbers

Act One: "Million Dollar Smile" ("Billion Dollar Baby") (Voice on the Radio: Alan Gilbert); "Who's Gonna Be the Winner?" (Joan McCracken, Althea Elder, Beverly Hosier, Betty Saunders, Doris Hollingsworth, Bathing Beauties); "Dreams Come True" (Joan McCracken, James Mitchell, Fred Hearne, Bill Skipper); "Charleston" (Dance) (Cop: Arthur Partington; Three Flappers: Virginia Gorski, Helen Gallagher, Lorraine Todd; Rich Girl: Joan Mann; Playboy: Fred Hearne; A Timid Girl: Ann Hutchinson; Good-Time Charlie: Bill Skipper; Collegiates: Virginia Poe and Douglas Deane; Younger Generation: Bill Sumner and Maria Harriton; Older Generation: Jacqueline Dodge and Joe Landis; Two Gangsters: Lucas Aco and Allan Waine; Two Bootleggers: Anthony Reed and Alan Gilbert); "Broadway Blossom" (Mitzi Green); "Speaking of Pals" (David Burns, Don De Leo, David Thomas, Tony Gardell, William Tabbert, Ensemble); "There I'd Be" (Mitzi Green, Robert Chisholm); "One-Track Mind" (Shirley Van, Danny Daniels); "Bad Timing" (William Tabbert, Joan McCracken); "The Marathoners" (Dance Ensemble); "A Lovely Girl" (Mitzi Green, Joan McCracken, The Jollities Beauties)

Act Two: "Funeral Procession" (The Mob); "Havin' a Time" (Mitzi Green); "The Marathon Dance" (Danny Daniels); "Faithless" (Robert Chisholm, Joan McCracken); "I'm Sure of Your Love" (William Tabbert); "A Life with Rocky" (Joan McCracken; The Wealthy Ones: Jacqueline Dodge, Douglas Deane; Rocky: James Mitchell; Two Cops: Joe Landis, Allan Wayne; Passerby: Arthur Partington; Bartender: Fred Hearne; Two Thugs: Lucas Aco, Bill Sumner; Their Molls: Joan Mann, Lorraine Todd; Leader of Thugs: Bill Skipper); "The Wedding" (Entire Company)

Billion Dollar Baby was a reunion of sorts for many of the team members who put **On the Town** together: producers Paul Feigay and Oliver Smith; librettists and lyricists Betty Comden and Adolph Green; director George Abbott; choreographer Jerome Robbins; scenic designer Oliver Smith; musical director Max Goberman; and even cast member Robert Chisholm. But lightning didn't strike twice, the musical didn't make much of an impression, and it closed after six months (although it reportedly returned its initial investment and even made a small profit). The show didn't enjoy a national tour, a London production, a film version, or a hit song, but it has a way of occasionally popping up: a rare summer stock revival in 1961; a re-creation of its "Charleston" number in the long-running 1989 dance revue *Jerome Robbins' Broadway*; a limited-engagement 1998 Off-Broadway production; and a 2000 cast recording that was partially based on the 1998 production.

The musical looked at the era of the flapper-laden Twenties with its speakeasies, bootleggers, gangsters, marathon dances, Atlantic City beauty contests, old-time Broadway revues (here, the *Jollities*), and, yes, the stock market crash. At the story's center is Maribelle Jones (Joan McCracken), a hard-as-nails gold-digger who literally wants to be a billion-dollar baby. She runs through a series of men: marathon dancer Champ Watson (Danny Daniels); bootlegger Jerry Bonanza (Don De Leo); gangster Dapper Welch (David Burns); Welch's bodyguard Rocky Barton (William Tabbert); and finally the rich and older M. M. Montague (Robert Chisholm, here in the sixth of seven musicals he appeared in during the decade), whom she marries. But the stock market crash leaves Montague broke, and so the sour ending finds Maribelle as destitute as she was at the beginning of the show. Along the way, first-billed Mitzi Green played a Texas Guinan type (here, Georgia Motley), who didn't have much to do during the musical but enlivened the proceedings whenever she appeared.

Despite lavish production values, a generally game cast, and Robbins's highly praised dance numbers, the musical didn't quite catch the brass ring. A show that called itself a musical of the "terrific Twenties" promised lighthearted gaiety, and perhaps audiences were surprised and put off by the avaricious, back-stabbing title character. Later in the decade, **Gentlemen Prefer Blondes** covered much of the same territory with its affectionate look at the 1920s. But that musical's gold-digger Lorelei Lee was a genuinely comic creation, and Carol Channing's droll and madcap impersonation made her immensely likable. Further, *Blondes* offered tasty and tuneful music by Jule Styne, while Morton Gould's score for *Billion Dollar Baby* was sometimes pleasant but generally unimpressive (Gould's second and final Broadway score was 1950's *Arms and the Girl*, and it too was lackluster).

It may be that Joan McCracken wasn't ideally cast in the leading role, and she may have been unable to soften the harsh aspects of her character. She excelled in supporting roles, but perhaps the leading one of a female Pal Joey was beyond her capabilities. Her two film appearances (in *Hollywood Canteen* and *Good News*) indicate she was an enjoyable and talented dancer who nonetheless came across as somewhat remote and slightly robotic. She had first appeared on Broadway in the original production of Richard Rodgers and Oscar Hammerstein II's **Oklahoma!**, in which she had a small but showy dance sequence; from there she was featured in Harold Arlen's **Bloomer Girl** and introduced "T'morra', T'morra'"; and she later had major roles in the revue *Dance Me a Song* (1950) and in Rodgers and Hammerstein's *Me and Juliet* (1953). In the dancing chorus of *Dance Me a Song* was Bob Fosse, her future husband. He was married to three Broadway dancers: his first wife was Mary Ann Niles, who was also in *Dance Me a Song*; then he later married McCracken; and of course he and Gwen Verdon eventually married and during their professional and personal relationship joined forces to create five hit musicals over a twenty-year period.

Louis Kronenberger in *PM* said Maribelle was a "bitch fiendishly on the make," and this "Pal Josie" was "almost excessively hard and cold." But he felt McCracken was "engaging" despite "being the worst kind of female heel." The musical fell a "trifle short," however, and while it was more "ambitious" than **On the Town** it was "far less successful." He noted that Comden and Green's book could never decide whether it wanted to burlesque the twenties or to create a "real quality" of melodrama that encapsulated the era. He noted that Robbins's contributions were "lively and amusing," and that the "Charleston" was his favorite dance. Burton Rascoe in the *New York World-Telegram* felt the evening lacked humor and let down Mitzi Green with poor material; Gould's score was "stunty" and unmelodic; and he noted the "little morality play" owed much to Jerome Robbins' choreography which was able to overcome a "thin" book and "sparse" lyrics.

Lewis Nichols in the *New York Times* admitted the musical was "off the beaten track," but unfortunately it didn't "completely come off"; further, the book wavered between a satiric bent and one that dealt in the "solemnities" of "formal musical comedy." He noted Maribelle was a "toughie like a female Pal Joey" and it was probably not McCracken's fault that as written her character lacked a certain consistency.

Robert Garland in the *New York Journal-American* mentioned that the musical was "not entirely unrelated to *Pal Joey*," and while he liked McCracken, it was Mitzi Green who walked away with the show. As for the score, it was probably "not up anybody's Tin Pan Alley." His harshest comments were for the late second-act ballet "A Life with Rocky," in which Maribelle envisions her life with a man who is both poor and part of the underworld. The number was "pedestrian" and the musical never recovered from it. But Howard Barnes in the *New York Herald Tribune* said the ballet was "enchanting"; Gould's score was "rich and varied"; the "Charleston" was "full of caustic commentary"; and thus the evening was "great good fun."

Ward Morehouse in the *New York Sun* found the musical "spotty but generally satisfactory," and although it "flounders frequently," it nonetheless offered "pace" and "vitality." The ballet "A Life with Rocky" was a "genuinely imaginative" sequence, and he said McCracken was at her "best" in the dancing department and "only moderately successful" as a singer and actress. John Chapman in the *New York Daily News* had a "very fine time" watching the new musical, and while the cast was good (Mitzi Green in particular was "quite remarkable"), the "real stars" of the show were Robbins's dances, Abbott's fast-paced direction, and Smith's décor. He noted that in the past he had found Gould's brand of music on the "syrupy, over-orchestrated" side, but here his score was "funny," "terse," and "fruity."

The musical was a reunion of sorts for Robbins and Gould, as their ballet "Interplay" had premiered earlier in the season in the short-running **Concert Varieties**. The musical marked another welcome appearance by Mitzi Green, and offered an opportunity for the up-and-coming Helen Gallagher, who two years later had her breakthrough role as a tango dancer in Robbins's **High Button Shoes**. William Tabbert had featured singing roles in Alan Jay Lerner and Frederick Loewe's **What's Up** and Cole Porter's **Seven Lively Arts**, and would later create the roles of Cable in Richard Rodgers and Oscar Hammerstein II's **South Pacific** and Marius in Harold Rome's *Fanny*. David Burns also continued making favorable impressions in plays and musicals, and a dozen or so years later would enjoy a string of musical comedy successes (two of which garnered him Tony Awards) when he appeared in three back-to-back smash hits, *The Music Man* (1957), *A Funny Thing Happened on the Way to the Forum* (1962), and *Hello, Dolly!* (1964).

Danny Daniels later choreographed such musicals as *High Spirits* (1964) and *Walking Happy* (1966); James Mitchell was the lead dancer in various musicals, including **Brigadoon**; and chorus singer Jeri Archer became immortal when she portrayed Belle Poitrine in the hilarious photographs that accompanied Patrick Dennis's *Little Me*, a 1961 spoof of tell-all Hollywood autobiographies (which was adapted into a Broadway musical the following year).

A 1961 summer stock revival of *Billion Dollar Baby* was presented by the Dallas State Fair Musicals and starred Eileen Rodgers (Georgia Motley), Reginald Denny (M. M. Montague), and Wisa D'Orso (Maribelle Jones). Robbins's choreography was re-created by Joan Mann, who had appeared in the original production.

The dance revue *Jerome Robbins' Broadway* opened at the Imperial Theatre on February 26, 1989, and included the complete "Charleston" dance number, which was recorded for the revue's two-CD cast album by RCA Victor (# 60150-2RC). The revue played for 634 performances and won the Tony Award for Best Musical.

The Off-Broadway production enjoyed a limited engagement as part of the York Theatre Company's Musicals in Mufti series; it opened on September 11, 1998, and inspired a 2000 recording released by Original Cast Records (CD # OC-4304) that features Kristin Chenoweth, Debbie Shapiro, Marc Kudisch, and Richard B. Schull. The collection *Broadway Musicals of 1945* (Bayview CD # RNBW-039) includes "Bad Timing."

SHOW BOAT
"KERN AND HAMMERSTEIN'S NEW PRODUCTION"

Theatre: Ziegfeld Theatre
Opening Date: January 5, 1946; *Closing Date*: January 4, 1947
Performances: 418
Book and *Lyrics*: Oscar Hammerstein II
Music: Jerome Kern
Based on the 1926 novel *Show Boat* by Edna Ferber.
Direction: Staged by Hassard Short and book directed by Oscar Hammerstein II; *Producer*: Jerome Kern and Oscar Hammerstein II; *Choreography*: Helen Tamiris; *Scenery*: Howard Bay; *Costumes*: Lucinda Ballard; *Lighting*: Uncredited; *Musical Direction*: Edwin McArthur
Cast: Scott Moore (Windy), Robert Allen (Steve), Seldon Bennett (Pete), Helen Dowdy (Queenie), Ethel Owen (Parthy Ann Hawks), Ralph Dumke (Captain Andy), Colette Lyons (Ellie), Buddy Ebsen (Frank), Francis X. Mahoney (Rubber Face), Carol Bruce (Julie), Charles Fredericks (Gaylord Ravenal), Ralph Chambers (Vallon), Jan Clayton (Magnolia, Kim [in her twenties]), Kenneth Spencer (Joe), Howard Frank (Backwoodsman), Duncan Scott (Jeb), Pearl Primus (Sal, Dahomey Queen), Laverne French (Sam), Hayes Gordon (Barker), Jeanne Reeves (Fatima), Willie Torpey (Old Sport), Paula Kaye (Strong Woman), Congress of Beauties: Andrea Dowling (Spanish), Vivian Cherry (Italian), Janice Bodenhoff (French), Elana Keller (Scotch), Audrey Keane (Greek), Marta Becket (English), Olga Lunick (Russian), Eleanor Boleyn (Indian), Alma Sutton (Ata), Claude Marchant (Mala), Talley Beatty (Bora), Sara Floyd (Landlady), Assota Marshall (Ethel), Sheila Hogan (Sister), Iris Manley (Mother Superior), Alyce Mace (Kim, as a child), Max Showalter (Jake), Jack Daley (Jim), Tom Bowman (Man with Guitar), William C. Smith (Doorman at Trocodero), Paul Shiers (Drunk), Nancy Kenyon (Lottie), Lydia Fredericks (Dolly), Bettina Thayer (Sally), Frederica Slemons (Old Lady on Levee), Charles Tate (Jimmy Craig); Singers: Carmine Alexandria, Grace Benton, Clarise Crawford, Lydia Fredericks, Adah Friley, Marion Hairston, Katie Hall, Marion Holaves, Jean Jones, Frances Joslyn, Charlotte Junius, Assota Marshall, Linda Mason, Eulabel Riley, Agnes Sundgren, Bettina Thayer, Fannie Turner, Ethel Brown White, Evelyn Wick, Jerome Addison, Gilbert Adkins, William Bender, Thomas Bowman, Robert Bulger, Glenn Burris, Edward Chappell, William Cole, Erno Czako, Richard DiSilvera, John Garth III, Hayes Gordon, George H. Hall, Thomas Jordan, Robert Kimberly, James Lapsley, Albert

McCary, William McDaniel, Bowling H. Mansfield, Walter Mosby, Clarence Redd, Paul Shiers, William C. Smith, William Sol, Rodester Timmons, David Trimble; Dancers: Marta Becket, Elmira Jones Bey, Janice Bodenhoff, Eleanor Boleyn, Vivian Cherry, Andrea Dowling, Betty Jane Geiskopf, Carol Harriton, Vickie Henderson, Audrey Keane, Elana Keller, Orak Leak, Olga Lunick, Lean Reeves, Alma Sutton, Viola Taylor, Yvonne Tibor, Paula Kaye, Talley Beatty, Terry Dawson, Laverne French, Eddie Howland, Gerard Leavitt, Claude Marchant, William Miller, Nick Nadeau, Joseph Nash, Stanley Simmons, William Weber, Henry Wessell, Francisco Xavier; Children: Betty Barker, Dolores Gamble, Carol Lewis, Miriam Quinn, Sybil Stocking, Billy DeForest, Roland Gamble, Edward Hayes, Bobby O'Connor, Eugene Steiner

The musical was presented in two acts.

The action takes place from the 1880s to the 1920s, principally in Mississippi and Chicago.

Musical Numbers

Act One: "Cotton Blossom" (Entire Ensemble); "Show Boat Parade" and "Ballyhoo" (Ralph Dumke, The Show Boat Troupe, Townspeople); "Only Make Believe" (Charles Fredericks, Jan Clayton); "Ol' Man River" (Kenneth Spencer, Stevedores); "Can't Help Lovin' Dat Man" (Carol Bruce, Helen Dowdy, Jan Clayton, Kenneth Spencer, Quartette); "Life upon the Wicked Stage" (Colette Lyons, Ensemble); "No Gems, No Roses, No Gentlemen" (dance) (Colette Lyons, Stage Door Admirers); "Ballyhoo" (aka "Queenie's Bally-hoo" and "C'mon, Folks") (Helen Dowdy, Ensemble); "No Shoes" (dance) (Pearl Primus, Laverne French, Theatre-Goers); "You Are Love" (Jan Clayton, Charles Fredericks); Finale (Entire Ensemble)/"Levee Dance" (Talley Beatty, Claude Marchant, Laverne French, Levee Dancers)

Act Two: "At the Fair" (aka "The Sports of Gay Chicago") (Sightseers, Barkers, Ushers); "Congress of Beauties" (dance) (Beauties, Ushers); "Why Do I Love You?" (Jan Clayton, Charles Fredericks, Ensemble); "In Dahomey" (Dahomey Villagers), including "Dance of the Dahomeys" and "Avenue A Release" (Pearl Primus, Villagers, Alma Sutton, Claude Marchant, Talley Beatty); "Bill" (lyric by P. G. Wodehouse) (Carol Bruce); "Can't Help Lovin' Dat Man" (reprise) (Jan Clayton); Service and Scene Music at St. Agatha's Convent (Orchestra); "Only Make Believe" (reprise) (Charles Fredericks); "Goodbye, My Lady Love" (lyric and music by Joseph E. Howard) and "Cakewalk" (dance) (Buddy Ebsen, Colette Lyons); Magnolia's Debut at the Trocadero Music Hall: "After the Ball" (lyric and music by Charles K. Harris) (Jan Clayton); "Ol' Man River" (reprise) (Kenneth Spencer); "You Are Love" (reprise) (Charles Fredericks); "Nobody Else but Me" (Jan Clayton); "Dance 1927" (Jan Clayton, Charles Tate, Flappers, Cake Eaters, Levee Dancers); Finale (Entire Company)

In his program notes for the 1946 revival of *Show Boat*, Oscar Hammerstein II wrote that he and Jerome Kern (who had died a few weeks before the revival opened) had kept the musical "substantially" as it had been presented in 1927. He mentioned that a "front scene" (in front of the curtain) had been eliminated along with "three minor" songs; and that a new one had been written for the revival, "Nobody Else but Me" (which was the last song Kern ever wrote).

Of the "three minor" numbers that were eliminated, there were actually four: Gaylord's "Where's the Mate for Me?" and "Till Good Luck Comes My Way"; Ellie and Frank's "I Might Fall Back on You"; and Queenie's "Hey, Feller." And it's questionable if all were "minor," especially Gaylord's introspective "Where's the Mate for Me?" and the sweeping expectation of his thrilling "Till Good Luck Comes My Way," which are character-establishing songs for one of the most enigmatic roles in the musical. Incidentally, for the current revival there was a curious penchant for naming all the dance numbers, most of which were just dance accompaniments to the songs which had just preceded them (for example, Ellie sings "Life Upon the Wicked Stage," and the dance which immediately follows it is titled "No Gems, No Roses, No Gentlemen").

The revival didn't have a pre-Broadway tryout; instead, the $275,000 production played for two preview performances before its official opening night, and among the cast members was Francis X. Mahoney, who had originated the role of Rubber Face in the 1927 production. The revival was partially backed by MGM, which later offered a mini-version of *Show Boat* in *Till the Clouds Roll By*, its 1947 biography of Jerome Kern (the *Show Boat* sequence included Kathryn Grayson, Tony Martin, Lena Horne, and Virginia O'Brien) and then released the third film version of the musical in 1951 (Grayson reprised her role of Magnolia, and others in the cast were Howard Keel, Ava Gardner, and William Warfield). The 1946 revival (which opened at the Ziegfeld Theatre where the original 1927 production had premiered) played on Broadway for a full year, and two national companies toured the country for a total of sixteen months (the second company kicked off its tour with a two-week engagement at City Center in 1948; see entry).

It had been fifteen years since the last New York revival of *Show Boat*, and the critics were glad to see it again. A few quibbled about the company. Some said the new cast members were better than the originals, while others felt they weren't up to their memories of the 1927 cast. In some cases, one wonders exactly what the critics saw during the opening night performance. Charles Winninger had played Captain Andy in the 1927 production, and he had a special way of saying "Happy New Year" (he broke the word "happy" into two words by emphasizing the first syllable and then pausing for a moment before saying the second syllable). Burton Rascoe in the *New York World-Telegram* complained that the current Captain Andy (Ralph Dumke) "hasn't learned . . . how to say" the phrase properly; but John Chapman in the *New York Daily News* said it was "fun" to hear Dumke "explode" the word "Happy" so "ingratiatingly."

Further, Robert Garland in the *New York Journal-American* felt Jan Clayton wasn't "up" to the role of Magnolia, at least "not yet," and Rascoe found her a "disappointment" and suggested she "should take voice instruction." But John Chapman in the *New York Daily News* said she was "touching," and Lewis Nichols in the *New York Times* stated the "fresh-looking" performer possessed a "clear" voice and conveyed "the various moods of the part." (*The Rodgers and Hammerstein Fact Book* reports that Clayton left the production in April, four months after the opening.) Wilella Waldorf in the *New York Post* liked Carol Bruce (Julie) and Kenneth Spencer (Joe), but otherwise noted that the rest of the cast were "up and down, some very down indeed." But overall the critics praised Clayton, Charles Fredericks (Gaylord), Carol Bruce, and Kenneth Spencer.

The reviewers couldn't quite agree on the merits of Howard Bay's scenery and Lucinda Ballard's costumes. Rascoe said he hadn't seen "such garish, preposterous, [and] inappropriate" costumes since **Memphis Bound**, and the sets weren't "appropriate" either. But Garland liked Ballard's creations and noted they were "colorful" and in a "mocking mood." He also mentioned that while Bay's sets "adorned" the production, they didn't always quite fill the large stage of the Ziegfeld. Louis Kronenberger in *PM* said the sets and costumes allowed Bay and Ballard to "dabble in charm and wallow in wonderful bad taste."

The critics praised the now familiar score. Waldorf said the musical was distinguished by "really superior" music; John Chapman in the *New York Daily News* stated Kern and Hammerstein had written the "most bountiful score ever put into one musical"; and Howard Barnes in the *New York Herald Tribune* said the show's "hardy perennials . . . constituted a prodigal score for any musical comedy."

Nichols said the "near-classic" was presented in an "excellent" production, and Ward Morehouse in the *New York Sun* noted the musical had been "magnificent" in 1927, had again been magnificent in its 1932 revival, and magnificent it always would be. It offered "beauty, pathos, nostalgia," and a "panoramic pattern" that was adorned by a score that "will endure for as long as the theatre exists."

A few critics noted the second act sagged and offered a few too many reprises (there were four in all); further, there was the problematic 1920s section of the musical, which historically has always been bothersome (all the characters have aged, and the scenes focus on Magnolia and Gaylord's daughter Kim, who is now a Broadway star [traditionally, the same actress who plays Magnolia also plays Kim]). For the 1927 tryout, the insinuating and irresistible "It's Getting Hotter in the North" was used in the Twenties section, but for Broadway the number was eliminated and instead the production capitalized on the ability of Norma Terris (the original Magnolia) to perform impersonations of celebrities of the era; the London production introduced a new song ("Dance Away the Night") for the sequence; the 1936 film incorporated yet another new song ("Gallavantin' Aroun'") into the Twenties sequence; the 1946 production offered another new one ("Nobody Else but Me"); and the 1994 Broadway revival created a choreographed sequence of 1920s dance routines. The 1951 film version dispensed with the 1920s altogether and compressed the story's action into about a ten-year period from the late 1880s into the 1890s, and thus Kim seems to be about six or seven years old in the film's final scene.

Garland mentioned the "last-act trouble" (which he said was a direct quote from the musical's original producer, Florenz Ziegfeld) and noted the musical "starts a story it never really finishes." Waldorf said that even in 1927 she had found the story occasionally "ponderous" and overly "sentimental," and she remarked that the scenes in the 1920s had the "old folks" wearing a "bevy of white wigs that might have been borrowed from one of the French courts."

The original production opened at the Ziegfeld Theatre on December 27, 1927, for 572 performances. It was groundbreaking in its depiction of racism, miscegenation, and unhappy marital relationships, and was further ahead of its time in its sad and bittersweet survey of the passing of time (the story takes place over a period of forty years) and the general unhappiness of the major characters, some of whom drift away without neatly orchestrated explanations of their fates (hence Garland's complaint that the musical's story "never really finishes").

The musical was revived on Broadway in 1932 for 180 showings; and as mentioned a return engagement of the 1946 production by the national touring company played at City Center in 1948 for sixteen performances. Three interrelated productions (produced by the New York City Opera Company and the New York City Center Light Opera Company) were seen in New York during 1954 for a total of twenty performances; the latter company also revived the work in 1961 for fourteen performances; and in 1966 the Music Theatre of Lincoln Center presented a lavish production with Barbara Cook and Stephen Douglass in the leading roles for a total of sixty-four showings. There were also two commercial Broadway revivals, in 1983 (seventy-three performances) and 1994 (949 performances). The latter was the most definitive production seen since the original, and included the deleted "Mis'ry's Comin' 'Round," which foreshadowed the unhappiness in store for many of the major characters. The song had been previously performed just one time, at the musical's first tryout performance at the National Theatre in Washington, D.C., on Tuesday, November 15, 1927 (by the next day's matinee, the song, along with "Cheer Up," "My Girl," "Coal Black Lady," "Bully Song," "Hello, My Baby," and the splendid shuffle for the 1920s sequence, "It's Getting Hotter in the North," were cut from the production). But "Mis'ry's Comin' 'Round" remained in the overture and along with "Ol' Man River" summarized how the overpowering forces of fate and nature control the destinies of helpless mortals.

The definitive book about the history of the musical is Miles Kreuger's *Show Boat: The Story of a Classic American Musical*, which was published by Oxford University Press. Oxford also published *Show Boat: Performing Race in an American Musical* by Todd Decker. The script of the 1932 London production was published in paperback in Great Britain by Chappell & Co. Ltd., and the script was published in hardback by the Library of Congress in 2014 (along with the scripts of fifteen other musicals). The lyrics are included in *The Complete Lyrics of Oscar Hammerstein II*.

The most complete recording is a lavish 1988 three-CD set by EMI (# CDS-7-49108-2), which was conducted by John McGlinn and includes Frederica Von Stade, Jerry Hadley, and Teresa Stratas. The set includes a number of songs deleted from the original production's tryout as well as songs written for the 1928 London production ("Dance Away the Night"), the 1936 film version ("I Have the Room Above Her," "Ah Still Suits Me," and "Gallavantin' Aroun'"), and the 1946 revival ("Nobody Else but Me"). There are also a few recordings of songs by members of the original Broadway and London companies, and of the numerous versions of the score, the 1962 studio cast album released by Columbia is a particular standout with Barbara Cook, John Raitt, William Warfield, and Anita Darian (LP # OL-5820/OS-2220; issued on CD by Sony Classical/Columbia/Legacy # SK-61877).

The 1946 revival was recorded by Columbia Records (LP # ML-4058), and the CD was released by Sony Broadway (# 53330).

The musical has been filmed three times: a part-silent, part-talkie released in 1929; the faithful and very entertaining 1936 version by Universal, which starred Irene Dunne, Allan Jones, Helen Morgan, Paul Robeson, and Hattie McDaniel; and a misguided adaptation by MGM in 1951, which as mentioned above compressed the action into about a ten-year period and thus completely lost the epic sweep of the story. Both the 1936 and 1951 versions are available on DVD (the former was released by the Warner Brothers' Archive Collection and the latter by Warner Home Video # 3000032268).

The lyric of "Bill" was written by P. G. Wodehouse; the lyric of "Goodbye, My Lady Love" by Joseph E. Howard; and the lyric and music of "After the Ball" by Charles K. Harris (the latter had been interpolated into the long-running 1891 Broadway hit *A Trip to Chinatown*).

Sadly, Wilella Waldorf's review of the 1946 revival of *Show Boat* was her last; she had been ill for some time, and two months later on March 12 she died. Besides being the first woman who was a full-time, first-string theatre reviewer for a New York newspaper, she was also one of the wittiest, most entertaining, and most perceptive of all American theatre critics, and her reviews (along with those of Brooks Atkinson, Walter Kerr, Martin Gottfried, and the *Chicago Tribune*'s Claudia Cassidy) deserve to be published in a volume all their own.

THE DESERT SONG

Theatre: City Center
Opening Date: January 8, 1946; *Closing Date*: February 16, 1946
Performances: 45
Book: Otto Harbach, Oscar Hammerstein II, and Frank Mandel
Lyrics: Otto Harbach and Oscar Hammerstein II
Music: Sigmund Romberg
Direction: Sterling Holloway; *Producers*: Russell Lewis and Howard Young; *Choreography*: Aida Broadbent; *Scenery*: Boris Aronson; *Costumes*: Uncredited; *Lighting*: Nels Petersen; *Musical Direction*: Waldemar Guterson
Cast: Edward Wellman (Mindar), Richard Charles (Sid El Kar), Keith Gingles (Ahmed), Jack Saunders (Omar), Thayer Roberts (Hassi), Walter Cassel (Pierre Birabeau [The Red Shadow]), Jack Goode (Benjamin "Bennie" Kidd), William Bower (Sentinel), Wilton Clary (Captain Paul Fontaine), Joseph Claudio (Sergeant LeVerne), Antonio Rovano (Sergeant De Boussac), Clarissa (Azuri), Tamara Page (Edith), Sherry O'Neil (Susan), Barbara Bailey (Mardi), Bettina Orth (Florette), Maria Taweel (Yvonne), Dorothy Sandlin (Margot Bonvalet), Lester Matthews (General Birabeau), Jean Bartel (Clementina), Richard Hughes (Harem Guard), George Burnson (Ali Ben Ali), Louis DeMagnus (Nogi), Paul Ruth (Riff Runner); French Girls, Natives, and Ladies of the Harem: Joan Bishop, Lillian Bloch, Beth Alba Cushing, Georgine Dwyer, Florette Hillier, Rosemary Leisen, Doris Luff, Suzette Meredith, Tamara Page, Margaret Smitherum, Helen Vey, June Walks; Riffs and French Legionnaires: William Bower, Fred Butterworth, Warren Christian, Arthur Couture, John Donaty, Charles Fries, Louis DeMagnus, Dean Etmund, Keith Gingles, Sterling P. Hall, Richard Hughes, Joseph Malpasuto, Allan Mars, Antonio Rovano, Paul Ruth, Russell Sanders, Harvey Sauber, Jack Saunders, Walter Swanson, Edward Wellman, Stanley Wolfe; Dancing Girls: Barbara Bailey, Natalie Carr, Rita Currier, Jean Caples, Barbara Downie, Lynn Hunt, Bettina Orth, Dorothy Jean Sheppard, Betty Slabe, Marie Taweel
The musical was presented in two acts.
The action takes place during 1925 in North Africa.

Musical Numbers

Act One: Prelude and Opening (aka "High on a Hill" and "Feasting Song") (Chorus); "The Riff Song" (aka "Ho!") (Walter Cassel, Richard Charles, Riffs); "Margot" (Wilton Clary, Soldiers); "I'll Be a Bouyant Girl" (aka "I'll Be a Bouyant Gal") (Sherry O'Neil, Tamara Page, Dancers); "Why Did We Marry Soldiers?" (Girls); "The French Military Marching Song" (Dorothy Sandlin, Girls, Soldiers); "Romance" (Dorothy Sandlin); "Then You Will Know" (Dorothy Sandlin, Walter Cassel); "I Want a Kiss" (Dorothy Sandlin, Wilton Clary, Walter Cassel, Chorus); "Tropics" (Jack Goode, Sherry O'Neil); "The Desert Song" (aka "Blue Heaven and You and I") (Dorothy Sandlin, Walter Sandlin); "Morocco Dance of Marriage" (Clarissa, Richard Charles, Dancing Girls); "The Desert Song" (reprise) (Walter Cassel, Dorothy Sandlin)
Act Two: "My Little Castagnette" (Harem Girls); "Song of the Brass Key" (Jean Bartel, Girls); "Spanish Dance" (Dancing Girls); "One Good Boy Gone Wrong" (Jack Goode, Jean Bartel); "Eastern and Western Love" (*Note*: The songs in this three-part sequence were backed by a male chorus.): (1) "Let Love Go" (George Burnson); (2) "One Flower Grows Alone in Your Garden" (Richard Charles); and (3) "One Alone" (Walter Cassel); "En Route a la Bain" (Damsels of the Harem); "The Sabre Song" (Dorothy Sandlin, Walter Cassel); Finaletto (Walter Cassel, Dorothy Sandlin); "Farewell" (Walter Cassel, Riffs); Opening (aka "All Hail the General") (Lester Matthews, Girls); "Tropics" (reprise) (Jack Goode, Sherry O'Neil, Dancing Girls); Finale

When Sigmund Romberg's operetta *The Desert Song* premiered in 1926, it was actually a contemporary piece that was very loosely based on then-current political events in North Africa. The musical centered on the mysterious Red Shadow, described as a "Riff Robin Hood" who leads the rebellious Riff tribes against the Europeans in Morocco. The Red Shadow is actually Pierre Birabeau, the son of Governor-General Birabeau, and Pierre poses as a meek and mild-mannered introvert in order to protect his identity as the Red Shadow.

As Pierre, his attempts to court the beautiful Margot Bonvalet are doomed because she wants to escape her "humdrum world" and find a "rough and ready" man who will "master" her, not some wispy bookworm like Pierre. So as the Red Shadow, Pierre abducts her and thus fulfills her dreams of romantic adventure. But when his father wants to duel the Red Shadow, Pierre of course can't agree to it and thus disappears, much to the chagrin of Margot, who now believes her hero has turned coward. Later, Pierre "kills" the Red Shadow, and when he brings the Red Shadow's clothes to the French headquarters he's considered a hero. Meanwhile, Pierre's father realizes his son is the Red Shadow and comes to understand that with Pierre's help the Moroccans and the Europeans can peaceably coexist. And when Pierre is alone with Margot he dons his mask and cape, and she realizes the wimpy Pierre is truly the "rough and ready" man of her dreams.

During its tryout, the musical was known as *Lady Fair*; the original production, which starred Robert Halliday and Vivienne Segal, opened at the Casino Theatre on November 30, 1926, for 471 performances and became one of the era's most popular operettas. The score offered lushly romantic melodies such as "Romance," "The Desert Song" (aka "Blue Heaven and You and I"), and a fascinating three-part sequence with the overall title "Eastern and Western Love" (which included "Let Love Go," "One Flower Grows Alone in Your Garden," and "One Alone"). There were also stirring choral numbers ("Ho!" aka "The Riff Song" and "The French Military Marching Song") and some surprisingly sly ones (a salute to Elinor Glyn and that "indefinable thing" known as "It," "One Good Boy Gone Wrong," and "Then You Will Know").

The musical was filmed three times by Warner Brothers (in 1929, with John Boles and Carlotta King; in 1943, in an updated adaptation that included Nazis in North Africa, with Dennis King and Irene Manning; and 1953, with Gordon MacRae and Kathryn Grayson). An NBC television adaptation by William Friedberg, Neil Simon, and Will Glickman was aired on May 7, 1955, with Nelson Eddy and Gale Sherwood. After the current 1946 production, the operetta was seen in New York just one more time in an entertaining and well-sung revival that opened at the Uris Theatre on September 5, 1973, for fifteen performances (the cast included David Cryer and Chris Callan). The original London production opened at the Drury Lane on April 7, 1927, for 432 performances (with Harry Welchman and Edith Day).

The script was published in softcover by Samuel French in 1954, and the lyrics are included in *The Collected Lyrics of Oscar Hammerstein II*. There are numerous recordings of the score, including a studio cast by RCA Victor (released on ArkivMusic/RCA Masterworks Broadway CD # 88725-42771-2) with Giorgio Tozzi, Kathy Barr, and Peter Palmer. A delightful recording with Mario Lanza and Judith Raskin was also released by RCA (LP # LM-2440).

The current revival omitted "It"; in the same spot where "It" had originally been performed by Bennie and Susan, the number "Tropics" was sung by the same two characters, and so it's possible "Tropics" was a revised version of "It." The revival also added "Spanish Dance" and "En Route a la Bain," both of which probably used music from other songs in the score.

In his seasonal summary, George Jean Nathan dismissed the current revival, which belonged to the "turban period" of entertainment when male performers of the Valentino variety wore such headgear and induced swoons among their female admirers. It was a "wretched" production that offered musical "mayonnaise" and a book and lyrics written with pens "dipped in artificial and synthetic moonlight."

NELLIE BLY
"A New Musical Comedy" / "The 'Round-the-World Musical Comedy"

Theatre: Adelphi Theatre
Opening Date: January 21, 1946; *Closing Date*: February 2, 1946
Performances: 16
Book: Joseph Quillan
Lyrics: Johnny Burke
Music: James (Jimmy) Van Heusen
Direction: Dialogue directed by Edgar MacGregor; *Producers*: Nat Karson and Eddie Cantor; *Choreography*: Edward Caton and Lee Sherman; *Scenery, Costumes,* and *Lighting*: Nat Karson; *Musical Direction*: Charles Drury
Cast: Walter Armin (Pulitzer, French Mayor, Czar), Edward H. Robins (Bennett, Second Sheik), William O'Shay (Newsboy), *William Gaxton* (Frank Jordan), Fred Peters (Ferry Captain, Santos Dumont, Russian

Captain), Harold Murray (Deckhand, Official), *Victor Moore* (Phineas T. Fogarty), Robert Strauss (First Reporter, First Sheik), Artells Dickson (Murphy), Jack Voeth (Wardheeler), Larry Stuart (Second Reporter, Stewart, Third Sheik), Eddy Di Genova (Third Reporter), Joy Hodges (Nellie Bly), Benay Venuta (Battle Annie), Doris Sward and Jack Voeth (Honeymoon Couple), Drucilla Strain (French Girl), Luboy Roudenko (Grisette), Jack Whitney (French Dandy), The Debonairs (Reporters), Suzie Baker (Copygirl); Members of the Choir: Marjorie Anderson, Suzie Baker, Johnsie Bason, Jeannine Burke, Betty de Cormier, Margaret Lide, Betty Spain, Drucilla Strain, Ruth Strickland, Doris Sward, Julie van Dusen, Eddy Di Genova, William Golden, Bernard Griffin, Alfred Homan, Karl Newart, Merrill Shea, Larry Stuart; Dancing Ensemble: Charlotte Burgmeier, Faith Dane, Mimi Gomber, Mary Grey, Sandra Scott, Dorothy Jeffers, Nathalie Kelepovska, Terry Lasky, Michael Neale, Nancy Newton, Mitzi Perry, Rita Barry, Ronan York, Ed Dragon, Bob Gari, William O'Shay, Jack Richards, William Segar, Kenny Springer

The musical was presented in two acts.

The action takes place in 1889 in New York City, on the Atlantic Ocean, in Paris, in the stratosphere, in Moscow, in Aden, and Texas.

Musical Numbers

Act One: "There's Nothing Like Travel" (Ensemble, Victor Moore); "All Around the World" (William Gaxton, Joy Hodges); "Fogarty the Great" (Victor Moore, Fogarty Boosters); "That's Class" (Benay Venuta); "Nellie Bly" (Nellie Bly Social Club); "Nelly Bly" (reprise)/"Fogarty the Great" (reprise) (Ensemble); "May the Best Man Win" (Entire Cast); "How About a Date?" (Suzie Baker, Johnsie Bason, Sandra Scott, Drucilla Strain, The Debonairs); "You Never Saw That Before" (Benay Venuta); "L'Exposition Universalle" (Lubov Roudenko, Jack Whitney, Ensemble); "Sky High" (William Gaxton, Joy Hodges, Ensemble)

Act Two: "No News Today" (The Debonairs, *New York Herald* Employees); "Choral Russe" (Walter Armin, Officers, Guards, Muscovites); "Just My Luck" (William Gaxton, Joy Hodges, Ensemble); ""Aladdin's Daughter" (Benay Venuta); "Start Dancing" (William Gaxton, Benay Venuta, Lubov Roudenko, Jack Whitney, Ensemble); "Harmony" (William Gaxton, Victor Moore); Finale (Entire Company)

Nellie Bly was the eighth and final Broadway appearance by the celebrated team of William Gaxton and Victor Moore. Their first collaboration was in George and Ira Gershwin's Pulitzer Prize-winning *Of Thee I Sing* (1931), where they created the roles of Wintergreen and Throttlebottom, and they revisited these roles in the Gershwins' sequel *Let 'Em Eat Cake* (1933); they then appeared in Cole Porter's *Anything Goes* (1934) and *Leave It to Me!* (1938) and in Irving Berlin's **Louisiana Purchase**. Their final three joint stage appearances were in the short-running **Keep 'Em Laughing**, **Hollywood Pinafore**, and *Nellie Bly*. The team had earlier starred in the 1932 film *Ladies Not Allowed* (with Lois Moran, who had appeared with them in *Of Thee I Sing* and *Let 'Em Eat Cake*), and in 1943 they starred opposite Mae West in *The Heat's On*, which also featured trumpeter Leonard Sues, who had impressed the critics in **Johnny 2 x 4** and **Beat the Band**.

Nellie Bly was the season's first of two failed musicals about an around-the-world race (here between Nellie Bly and Phineas T. Fogarty); a few months later and at the same theatre, Orson Welles and Cole Porter's **Around the World in Eighty Days** opened and quickly closed (here the race was between Phileas Fogg and Dick Fix). In 1962, **Around the World in 80 Days** opened at the Jones Beach Marine Theatre (with lyrics by Harold Adamson and music by Sammy Fain); the musical returned there the following summer, and then had a brief life in summer stock. The character of Nellie Bly later surfaced in *Nellie*, a 1997 Off-Off-Broadway musical.

The plot centered on a publicity stunt concocted by the *New York World*, which sent its reporter Nellie Bly (Joy Hodges) on an around-the-world trip that would hopefully beat the record of Jules Verne's fictitious character Phileas Fogg, who took eighty days to make the journey. When the *New York Herald* gets wind of the stunt, it too sponsors a traveler to beat Fogg's record (and to outrun Nellie Bly as well), in this case the hapless landlubber Phineas T. Fogarty (Victor Moore), who is accompanied by *Herald* reporter Frank Jordan (William Gaxton). Apparently everyone breaks Verne's record and makes the trip in seventy-five days (but Robert Garland in the *New York Journal-American* said the musical made the trip seem "a whole lot longer"). (At least three musicals during the era, **Up in Central Park**, *Nellie Bly*, and **Miss Liberty**, centered on either dueling newspapers after a scoop or investigative newspaper reporters in search of scandal.)

Ward Morehouse in the *New York Sun* said the new musical lagged, dragged, and crawled and thus made "a long, long trip around the world." The lyrics and music were "routine," the book "dull," and overall the evening was "cumbersome" and "completely lifeless." Further, Gaxton didn't "seem to have his heart in" the show, and Moore was "let down dreadfully" by the authors. Louis Kronenberger in *PM* said the "hollow" musical never came to life, and the book was "forever around, and forever in trouble"; Gaxton's role never really gave him any good moments, but occasionally Moore had an amusing routine or two (such as when he dons drag as a woman in a harem). Howard Barnes in the *New York Herald Tribune* found Nellie's trip a "rough voyage" of "embarrassingly dull" proceedings; the evening was a "sad waste" with "uniformly terrible" jokes, "moss-covered" stage business, and "undistinguished" and "uninspired" songs (but he liked "Just My Luck").

John Chapman in the *New York Daily News* found the evening "more than ordinarily dull," but singled out the "sprightly" lyric of Benay Venuta's "That's Class." Vernon Rice in the *New York Post* noted the musical had serious book trouble, and mentioned that despite playing the title role Joy Hodges didn't have much to do (but he praised her for doing "very well indeed," considering she had taken over the role [from Marilyn Maxwell] just one week before the Broadway premiere). "Musical globaloney" was the verdict of *Time*.

Garland said the book was "unwise and witless," the lyrics "forced and feeble," the music "tuneless and tiresome," and the choreography "just isn't!" From Garland's reportage, apparently everyone knew the show was doomed: coproducer Eddie Cantor had decamped for Hollywood without attending the New York opening, and Gaxton told another theatre professional the musical was for audiences, not critics (and Gaxton seems to have been in a foul mood, for he referred to the luckless Adelphi Theatre as "the dump of dumps").

But Burton Rascoe in the *New York World-Telegram* saw something completely different from the other aisle-sitters. The authors had written an "extraordinarily funny" book that was "full of wit and humor," and the show offered "voluptuousness in costume, scenery, and music." He therefore left the theater "happy, contented and full of celestial vitamins."

For the opening-night program, the last number in the second act was listed as "Finale" (sung by the entire company); for the second (and final) week's program, the last number performed in the second act was listed as "You May Not Love Me," sung by William Gaxton, Joy Hodges, and the entire company.

As mentioned, Marilyn Maxwell played the title role during the tryout, and was replaced by Joy Hodges. Sig Herzig was cited as the librettist, but for New York Eddie Quillen was the writer of record; Nat Karson received credit for staging, and Edgar MacGregor for dialogue direction (for New York, MacGregor's credit still held, but Karson's name was omitted from staging credits). Further, the choreography was credited to Edward Caton, but for New York both Caton and Lee Sherman were cited.

The tryout's cast also included Bil and Cora Baird (and their puppets), who performed the number "Hong Kong to Hoboken"; both they and the song were dropped for New York. Other songs cut prior to Broadway were: "A Very Silly Story," "I've Got to Get Somewhere with You," and "In Less Than Eighty Days" (the latter for Teddy Roosevelt, who was played by Robert Strauss; although the character and the song were dropped, Strauss remained in the show and played two other roles).

The team of Johnny Burke and Jimmy Van Heusen made their mark in Hollywood with a succession of cleverly written and richly melodic songs for various films, including "But Beautiful," "It Could Happen to You," "Like Someone in Love," "Aren't You Glad You're You?," "Moonlight Becomes You," "Personality," and their Academy Award-winning song "Swinging on a Star" from *Going My Way* (1944). Their 1953 Broadway musical *Carnival in Flanders* had an even shorter run than *Nellie Bly*'s sixteen performances, but that score yielded one of Broadway's classic torch songs in "Here's That Rainy Day." Very little of their score for *Nellie Bly* has surfaced; there were contemporary recordings of two numbers, "Just My Luck" and "Harmony"; the former was recorded by Bing Crosby and is included in his collection *Bing Sings Broadway* (MCA Records LP # MCL-1730).

Johnny Burke wrote the lyrics and music for *Donnybrook!* (1961), one of the best Broadway scores of the 1960s (it included one of the all-time great Broadway comedy songs, "Sad Was the Day," the gorgeous ballad "He Makes Me Feel I'm Lovely," and, with its Irish folk music air, the haunting lament "The Day the Snow Is Meltin'" could have found its place in John McCormack's repertoire).

With other lyricists, Van Heusen wrote "Darn That Dream," "The Second Time Around," "My Kind of Town (Chicago Is)," "Ain't That a Kick in the Head?," "Love and Marriage," "A Pocketful of Miracles," "(Love Is) The Tender Trap," and "Come Fly with Me." And in later years he won three more Best Song Academy Awards: "All the Way" (*The Joker Is Wild*, 1957); "High Hopes" (*A Hole in the Head*, 1959); and "Call Me Irresponsible" (*Papa's Delicate Condition*, 1963).

LUTE SONG
"A LOVE STORY WITH MUSIC"

Theatre: Plymouth Theatre
Opening Date: February 6, 1946; *Closing Date*: June 8, 1946
Performances: 142
Book: Sidney Howard and Will Irwin
Lyrics: Bernard Hanighen
Music: Raymond Scott
Based on the play *Pi-Pa-Ki* by Kao-Tong-Kia (an adaptation of the play was presented as early as 1404).
Direction: John Houseman; *Producer*: Michael Myerberg; *Choreography*: Yeichi Nimura; *Scenery*, *Costumes*, and *Lighting*: Robert Edmond Jones; Mary Martin's costumes designed by Valentina; *Musical Direction*: Eugene Kusmiak
Cast: Clarence Derwent (The Manager, The Honorable Tschang), Yul Brynner (Tsai-Yong), Augustin Duncan (Tsai), Mildred Dunnock (Madame Tsai), *Mary Martin* (Tchao-Ou-Niang), McKay Norris (Prince Nieou [The Imperial Preceptor]), Helen Craig (Princess Nieou-Chi), Nancy Davis (Si-Tchun), Pamela Wilde (Waiting Woman), Sydelle Sykovna (Waiting Woman), Blanche Zohar (Hand Maiden, Child), Mary Ann Reeve (Hand Maiden, Child), Rex O'Malley (Youen-Kong), Diane De Brett (Marriage Broker), Jack Amoroso (Messenger), Ralph Clanton (The Imperial Chamberlain, Genie), Gene Galvin (Food Commissioner, A Bonze), Max Leavitt (First Clerk, Li-Wang), Bob Turner (Second Clerk, Rich Man), Tom Emlyn Williams (First Applicant, Priest of Amida Buddha), Michael Blair (Second Applicant, Secretary), John Robert Lloyd (Imperial Guard), John High (Imperial Guard, Merchant), Gordon Showalter (Imperial Attendant), Ronald Fletcher (Imperial Attendant), Lisa Maslova (The White Tiger, Phoenix Bird), Lisan Kay (The Ape, Phoenix Bird), Joseph Camiolo (A Lesser Bonze), Leslie Rheinfeld (A Lesser Bonze), Donald Rose (Little Boy), Walter Stane (Lion), Albert Vecchio (Lion), Teddy Rose (Child); Travellers on the North Road, Beggars, Guards, Attendants, Gods, Others: Mary Burr, Arlene Garver, Sydelle Sylvona, Pamela Wilde, Alan Banks, Victor Burset, Jack Amoroso, Joseph Camiolo, Jack Cooper, Ronald Fletcher, John High, John Robert Lloyd, Lang Page, Bernard Pisarski, Leslei Rheinfeld, Gordon Showalter, Walter Stane, Alberto Vecchio
The musical was presented in three acts.
The action takes place many centuries ago in the Chinese village of Tchin-lieou, on the road to the Capital, and in the Capital itself.

Musical Numbers

Act One: Introduction to Act One; "Mountain High, Valley Low" (Mary Martin, Yul Brynner); "North Road"; "Imperial March"; "Monkey See, Monkey Do" (Mary Martin); "Where You Are" (Mary Martin); "Eunuch Scene"; "Marriage Music"
Act Two: Introduction to Act Two; "Willow Tree" (Yul Brynner); "Beggars' Music"; "Vision Song" (Mary Martin, Yul Brynner); "Chinese Market Place" and "Bitter Harvest" (Mary Martin); "Dirge Song"; "Genie Music"
Act Three: Introduction to Act Three; "Phoenix Dance" (Lisa Maslova, Lisan Kay); "Mountain High, Valley Low" (Mary Martin); "Lion Dance" (Walter Stane, Alberto Vecchio); "Imperial March" (reprise); "Lute Song" (Mary Martin)

The classic Chinese play *Pi-Pa-Ki* was written by Kao-Tong-Kia, and an adaptation of the work was presented as early as 1404. The play's title roughly translates as *Lute Song*.

Lute Song represented New York's first look at the play, and despite lavish production values (with an initial investment of $185,000; for comparison purposes, three years earlier it had cost $83,000 to open **Oklahoma!**) as well as Mary Martin in the lead and the then unknown Yul Brynner in a supporting one, the offbeat musical played for just four months. Besides Martin and Brynner, the cast also included Helen Craig, who created the leading role in *Johnny Belinda* (1940). In a secondary role, future First Lady Nancy Davis (Reagan) was Si-Tchun. Toward the end of the run, Mary Martin left the production and was succeeded by Dolly Haas (wife of famed caricaturist Al Hirschfeld); later, the musical toured with Haas and Brynner in a slightly revised version which was presented in two acts.

Advertised as "A Love Story with Music," the plot centered on Tchao-Ou-Niang (Mary Martin), whose husband Tsai-Yong (Yul Brynner) is called from his village to study in the capital, where he's forced to marry Princess Nieou-Chi (Helen Craig). Now living in the palace, he's unaware that a famine has plagued his village, his parents have died of starvation, and Tchao-Ou-Niang has become a beggar in order to survive. She eventually makes her way to the capital, and when the princess realizes how much Tchao-Ou-Niang loves Tsai-Young, she releases him from his marriage vows so that the young couple can be reunited. Most of the musical sequences were presented as incidental interludes that provided atmospheric background as well as accompaniment for dance music.

The critics noted the musical was a labor of love on behalf of producer Michael Myerberg, but most felt the work was more pageant than play. The stylized conventions of the evening caused the story to feel remote, and sometimes the production couldn't decide on its tone and point of view.

Burton Rascoe in the *New York World-Telegram* said he was more "educated" than "entertained" by the musical, and mentioned that with the "gong beating, dragon processions, exorcisms of the devil with blue lights" as well as smoke and masks, he found the story difficult to follow. He also noted that Mary Martin in beggar mode wore a "gorgeous" white silk gown by Valentina, and in "another number" by Valentina was shown selling her hair in order to give her in-laws a decent burial, and in "still another Valentina special" she walked hundreds of miles from her village to the capital and arrived there without a "speck of dust and pretty as a picture." (All of Martin's costumes were designed by Valentina, and the rest of the company were costumed by Robert Edmond Jones; as for Martin, besides her exclusive gowns by Valentina, the program credited her shoes by I. Miller and her makeup by Perc Westmore and the House of Westmore.)

Vernon Rice in the *New York Post* noted the creators had "been busily at work" to create *Lute Song*, but it "scarcely seemed worth the effort." But for all its pageantry, "spectacular" costumes, and "breath-taking" décor, there hung a "shroud of dullness" over the evening. Robert Garland in the *New York Journal-American* said the musical was really a "decorator's show," and otherwise the "little play" lost inside the pageantry kept intruding upon the "high, wide and handsome holiday," which Robert Edmond Jones had created with his décor, costumes, and lighting. Lewis Nichols in the *New York Times* stated the evening's décor and costumes raised a bar for beauty that would "not soon be equaled"; but the musical's "intentions" were "more worthy" than their fulfillment. Further, the evening couldn't decide upon its tone, and so the sumptuous décor was "alien" to the "simplicity" of the story, and Raymond Scott's score was too much in the "modern" mode; and while most of the characters spoke in "artificial" dialogue, one of them delivered his lines "after the manner of *The Mikado*." He noted that "on the whole" Martin did well with her "difficult" part, and Brynner was "satisfactory."

Louis Kronenberger in *PM* felt Martin's role didn't suit her particular talents, and while Brynner had "looks and grace," he wasn't "much of an actor" and wasn't up to the evening's "dramatic demands." The musical itself was the kind of show that "must walk among eggs" because its framework demanded "delicately stylized treatment," and he suggested the material would have been better served had it been presented as a "kind of magnificently pictorial ballet." Ward Morehouse in the *New York Sun* commented that it had taken *Pi-Pa-Ki* "several centuries" to reach Broadway, and the "staggering expense" of the production offered a "spectacle" of "surpassing loveliness." But the narrative was weak and "overpowered by the pageantry."

Howard Barnes in the *New York Herald Tribune* said the musical offered "rare theatrical excitement," and while the early parts of the evening were somewhat "top-heavy," the production had "bounce and exquisite pageantry." Like most of the critics, he singled out "Mountain High, Valley Low"; and he noted Martin's presence could easily have come across as a "stunt," but instead she gave "lovely support" to the production (and Brynner did "about as well as could be expected" with his "awkward assignment"). Although John Chapman in the *New York Daily News* found *Lute Song* "one of the most exquisite and most exciting things" he'd ever seen, the evening was something of a "pose." It was "arty as all hell" and reminded him of the "annual June play at a girls' school."

During the tryout, "Bang Went the Cymbal" (for Rex O'Malley), "Pan-Ku" (for Mary Martin), and "Spring Thunder" (for Yul Brynner) were deleted.

The musical was revived by the New York City Center Light Opera Company on March 12, 1959, for a limited run of fourteen performances; Dolly Haas was again Tchao-Ou-Niang, and Clarence Derwent, Gene Galvin, and Tom Emlyn Williams reprised their roles from the original production.

The script was published in paperback by the Dramatic Publishing Company in 1955. A selection of seven songs and instrumental sequences was released by Decca (LP # DL-8030), with Martin, which also included numbers from *On the Town*. The *Lute Song* tracks were also included on the CD release of the Broadway cast album of *One Touch of Venus* (MCA Classics/Broadway Gold # MCAD-11354).

THE DUCHESS MISBEHAVES
"A FROLICSOME MUSICAL COMEDY"

Theatre: Adelphi Theatre
Opening Date: February 13, 1946; *Closing Date*: February 16, 1946
Performances: 5
Book and *Lyrics*: Gladys Shelley; additional dialogue by Joe Bigelow
Music: Frank Black
Direction: Martin Manulis; production supervised by Chet O'Brien; *Producer*: A. P. Waxman; *Choreography*: George Tapps; *Scenery*: A. A. Ostrander; *Costumes*: Willa Kim; *Lighting*: Carlton Winckler; *Musical Direction*: Charles Sanford
Cast: In Carlton's Department Store—Grace Hayle (Woman), Buddy Ferraro (Franchot), Elena Boyd (First Sister), Mildred Boyd (Second Sister), Edith Boyd (Third Sister), Penny Edwards (Butterfly), Larry Douglas (Paul), James MacColl (Fitzgerald), Joey Faye (Woonsocket), Gail Adams (First Girl), Ethel Madson (Second Girl), Paula Lawrence (Miss Kiester), Audrey Christie (Crystal Shalimar), Al Downing (Reporter), Philip Tonge (Neville Goldglitter); In Spain—Larry Douglas (Pablo), Grace Hayle (Amber), Joey Faye (Goya), Joanne Jaap (Model), James MacColl (Roberto), Audrey Christie (Duchess of Alba), Penny Edwards (Mariposa), Paul Marten (Barber), Joanne Jaap (Manicurist), Ken Martin (Tailor), Bernie Williams (Assistant Tailor), Buddy Ferraro (Messenger), Victor Clark (First Student), Jess Randolph (Second Student), Philip Tonge (Duke of Alba), The Boyd Triplets (Ladies in Waiting), Paula Lawrence (Queen of Spain), Norma Kohane (A Model), George Tapps (Matador), Al Downing (Jose), Mata Monteria (Dancer), Jean Handzlik (The Woman), George Tapps (Her Man); Models: Joanne Jaap, Norma Kohane, Ann Miller, Lillian Moore; Singing Girls: Gail Adams, Adele Lulince, Ethel Madson, Jane Riehl; Singing Boys: Victor Clark, Vincent Henry, Jerry O'Rourke, Jess Randolph; Dancing Girls: Jane Atwood, Trudy Cirrito, Theo Denis, Helen Devlin, Gertrude Gibbons, Eleanore Gregory, Freddie Grey, Janet Joy, Beverly Joyce, Mary Jane Kersey, Anna Konstance, Dorothy Matthews, Marilyn Pendry; Dancing Boys: Dan Karry, Walter Koremin, Paul Marten, Anthony Sherman, Merritt Thompson, Bernie Williams
The musical was presented in two acts.
The action takes place in the present time in Carlton's Department Store in New York City and in Madrid around 1800.

Musical Numbers

Act One: "Art" (James MacColl; danced by George Tapps and Ensemble); "My Only Romance" (Larry Douglas, Singing Girls, Dancing Girls); "Broadminded" (Joey Faye, Show Girls); "I Hate Myself in the Morning" (Audrey Christie, Students); "Men" (Paula Lawrence, The Boyd Triplets); "Couldn't Be More in Love" (Larry Douglas, Penny Edwards); "Dance of the Matador" (music based on Manuel de Falla's "Ritual Fire Dance") (George Tapps); "Ole' Ole'" (Joey Faye, Ensemble); "Katie Did in Madrid" (Audrey Christie, Singers, Dancing Boys and Girls)
Act Two: "Morning in Madrid" (Entire Ensemble); "Lost" (Jean Handzlik, George Tapps); "Honeymoon Is Over" (Paula Lawrence, Penny Edwards, Dancers); "Nuts" (Audrey Christie); "Fair Weather Friends" (Larry Douglas, Penny Edwards); "The Nightmare" (Joey Faye, Paula Lawrence, Audrey Christie, Dancers and Singers); "Art" (reprise) (Entire Company)

During its tumultuous tryout, *The Duchess Misbehaves* lost its star Jackie Gleason (who left the show just before the New York opening and was replaced by Joey Faye) and one song ("Would You Rather Love Me"). Faye was a literal last-minute replacement, and so the New York programs still included an advertisement touting Gleason as the star of the musical. Although Gleason never made it to the Adelphi's stage in *The Duchess Misbehaves*, he was there in 1955 and 1956, for it was during those years that the theatre temporarily became a television studio where Gleason's classic thirty-nine episodes of *The Honeymooners* were filmed.

With just a five-performance run and a unanimous drubbing by the critics, the production was the season's shortest-running musical and one of the decade's major flops. It cost (and lost) a reported $230,000, a staggering sum for the era (for comparison purposes, three years before *The Duchess Misbehaves* was produced, **Oklahoma!** had cost $83,000 and ten years later *My Fair Lady* was capitalized at $360,000).

The opening scene took place in one of those musical-comedy art galleries (this one located in a department store), the kind that got Rodney Hatch into so much trouble in **One Touch of Venus**. Sign painter Woonsocket (Joey Faye) is conked on the head, and in typical musical-comedy dream fashion (*DuBarry Was a Lady* [1939], **A Connecticut Yankee**, **Dream with Music**, and **A Lady Says Yes**) he's immediately transported to another time and place. Instead of Old France, Old England, Old Persia, Old Italy, or Old China, Woonsocket finds himself in Old Madrid where he's now the famous artist Francisco Goya. Everyone he knew in 1946 has an eighteenth-century counterpart, including his fiancée Crystal Shalimar (Audrey Christie), who is now the Duchess of Alba and has posed for Goya in the nude. In order to escape the wrath of her husband the Duke (Philip Tonge), Goya claims another woman was his model for the portrait and says all he can remember is that the woman had a mole on her posterior. And of course this results in a search for a substitute model who must of course sport a mole on her hip. Goya also meets up with the Queen of Spain (who insists he fight a bull) as well as a bevy of models, matadors, and other Old Madrid types. At the end of the musical he wakes up and finds he's back in the safe and comfortable world of 1946.

The headline of Louis Kronenberger's review in *PM* proclaimed that "Horror Reigns at the Adelphi." The musical was a "noisy and witless mess" with an "abysmal" and "tormentingly broad and lowdown" book, "anemic" and "no worse than utterly commonplace" music, "schoolboy" lyrics (which included "Broadminded," "Katie Did in Madrid," and "I Hate Myself in the Morning"), and "absurdly pretentious" and "rubbishly fancy" choreography. Lewis Nichols in the *New York Times* said Gladys Shelley's book came from a "lower shelf," and facetiously noted the musical's most "magnificent moment" (the search for a substitute mole woman) stretched "into hours" and thus the libretto offered a certain amount of "macabre" interest. As for the jokes, they dropped "with the solid ring of a falling pancake."

Howard Barnes in the *New York Herald Tribune* found the evening "tasteless and turgid" with a book "as disconnected as a cross-word puzzle." The dialogue fell with a "dull thud" and the "pretentious" dances had "no more bounce than a croquet ball." He noted the musical's tag line described it as "frolicsome," and if *The Duchess Misbehaves* was frolicsome, then he'd "take a steam-shovel." John Chapman in the *New York Daily News* said the musical was more a "misdemeanor than a misbehavior," and when Shelley's lyrics rhymed "anguish" and "language," he stated, "And I just languish." He noted that for the second act a character named The Woman (portrayed by Jean Handzlik) who heretofore had not appeared in the show and suddenly came out of nowhere, proceeded to sing "Lost," a torch song he found reminiscent of "Body and Soul" (Nichols mentioned the "haunting" song reminded him of "Bill"; and Ward Morehouse in the *New York Sun* reported Handzlik "created something" of a "tumult" with the "bewildering" number). Burton Rascoe in the *New York World-Telegram* said a "flagrant aesthetic misdemeanor" had been committed on the Adelphi's stage; the evening was like a series of "filthy pictures," but the "dirt is mainly vocal." When the overture began, he was briefly misled into thinking the evening might promise "some nice music," but his hopes were soon dashed (and he noted he couldn't print some of the song titles because he wrote for a family newspaper).

Morehouse reported the "long and dreary" evening was "overpoweringly dull" with "mediocre" music and "silly and tiresome" book and lyrics. He noted the show belonged in the category of **Nellie Bly** . . . "or worse." That ill-fated musical had of course opened at the Adelphi a few weeks earlier, and Robert Garland in the *New York Journal-American* also referenced it by proclaiming that if someone formed a "Bring Back *Nellie Bly* to the Adelphi Club" he would sign up as a charter member. He concluded his review by stating, "Come back, *Nellie Bly*. You are forgiven."

In his annual seasonal summary, George Jean Nathan reported the lyrics were of the "spouse"-"louse" variety, and the jokes were along the lines of "Oh, Señor, don't go, you bewitch me" / "Aw, I'll be wit' choo later" and "I'm a great bull fighter" / "Well, you can certainly throw the bull."

Vernon Rice in the *New York Post* said that "almost since its inception" the musical had been beset with "misfortune"; but its "greatest misfortune" was that "it opened." The book and lyrics were as "unsubtle and distasteful" as any heard during the Broadway season, and in the spirit of the show's idea of humor he predicted *The Duchess Misbehaves* "will Goya way soon."

THREE TO MAKE READY
"A NEW REVUE"

Theatre: Adelphi Theatre (during run, the musical transferred to the Broadhurst Theatre)
Opening Date: March 7, 1946; *Closing Date*: December 14, 1946
Performances: 327
Sketches and *Lyrics*: Nancy Hamilton
Music: Morgan Lewis
Direction: Production devised and staged by John Murray Anderson; sketches directed by Margaret Webster;
    Producers: Stanley Gilkey and Barbara Payne; *Choreography*: Robert Sidney; *Scenery*: Donald Oenslager;
    Costumes: Audre; *Lighting*: Uncredited; *Musical Direction*: Ray (M.) Kavanaugh
Cast: *Ray Bolger*, Brenda Forbes, Arthur Godfrey, Rose Inghram, Gordon MacRae, Bibi Osterwald, Harold
    Lang, Jane Deering, Garry Davis, Althea Elder, Joe Jonson, Meg Mundy, Carleton Carpenter, Mary Alice
    Bingham, Martin Kraft, Mary McDonnell, Jack Purcell, Edythia Turnell, Irwin Charles, Candace Montgomery, Jimmy Venable, Iris Linde, Jim Elsegood
The revue was presented in two acts.

Sketches and Musical Numbers

Act One: "It's a Nice Night for It" (Gordon MacRae; Wardrobe Mistress: Bibi Osterwald; Stage Manager: Garry Davis; Stagehand: Carleton Carpenter; Ballerina: Jane Deering; Ballet Dancer: Harold Lang; Mary Alice Bingham, Althea Elder, Mary McDonnell, Candace Montgomery, Meg Mundy, Edythia Turnell, Irwin Charles, Joe Jonson, Martin Kraft, Jack Purcell, Jimmy Venable); "Post Mortem" (He: Ray Bolger; She: Rose Inghram; Alexandre Bernier: Garry Davis; Bellboy: Carleton Carpenter); Arthur Godfrey (monologue); "There's Something in My Program" (Juliet: Jane Deering; Romeo: Harold Lang; The Nurse: Candace Montgomery; The Capulets: Mary McDonnell, Edythia Turnell, Mary Alice Bingham, Althea Elder; The Montagues: Jimmy Venable, Jack Purcell, Martin Kraft, Joe Jonson); "The Shoe on the Other Foot" (Lady: Brenda Forbes; Salesman: Ray Bolger); "Tell Me the Story" (Rose Inghram, Gordon MacRae); "The Old Soft Shoe" (Ray Bolger; Jitterbugs: Mary McDonnell, Jack Purcell; Samba Dancers: Mary Alice Bingham, Joe Jonson); "The Russian Lesson" (Mrs. Budge: Rose Inghram; Mrs. Wattrous: Bibi Osterwald; Mrs. Pelloble: Meg Mundy; Miss Umstedder: Brenda Forbes); "Barnaby Beach" (Gordon MacRae, Althea Elder; danced by Jane Deering and Harold Lang); Arthur Godfrey (monologue); "Housing Shortage" (aka "Cold Water Flat") (Jo: Ray Bolger; Mary: Rose Inghram); Arthur Godfrey (monologue); "Wisconsin" or "Kenosha Canoe" (Auntie Plum: Bibi Osterwald; Clyde Griffiths: Ray Bolger; Roberta: Rose Inghram; June Alden: Jane Deering; Ido Wanny: Brenda Forbes; Mr. Snow: Gordon MacRae; Yellow Belly: Garry Davis; Judge: Irwin Charles) and "Kenosha Canoe Ballet" (Harold Lang, Cowboys, Children, Strumpets)
Act Two: "If It's Love" (Rose Inghram, Gordon MacRae; danced by Ray Bolger, with Mary Alice Bingham, Edythia Turnell, Althea Elder, and Mary McDonnell; and Jane Deering and Ensemble); "The Story of the Opera" (Marilyn: Brenda Forbes; Lucy: Bibi Osterwald; Waiter: Martin Kraft); "A Lovely Lazy Kind of Day" (Arthur Godfrey; danced by Ray Bolger in a reprise of his "Scarecrow Dance" from the 1939 film *The Wizard of Oz*; Milkmaid: Bibi Osterwald); "And Why Not I?" (aka "Born for Better Things") (Brenda Forbes); "The Sad Sack" (The Sack: Ray Bolger; Sergeant: Garry Davis; Joe: Joe Jonson; Goldbricks: Irwin Charles; Slug: Carleton Carpenter; Lieutenant: Harold Lang; M.P.: Martin Kraft; Captain: Arthur Godfrey; Colonel: Arthur Godfrey; General: Arthur Godfrey; Sleeper: Jimmy Venable; Greeley: Jack Purcell); Ray Bolger (in an unnamed ballroom dance sequence); Finale (Entire Company)

With the opening of the revue *Three to Make Ready*, the luckless Adelphi Theatre finally found a hit. Earlier in the season, *Carib Song* (36 performances), *The Girl from Nantucket* (12 performances), *Nellie Bly* (16 performances), and *The Duchess Misbehaves* (at 5 performances, the season's shortest running musical) had played there as well as the flop **Polonaise** (which had transferred to the Adelphi from the Alvin Theatre and which totaled up 113 showings at the two theatres) and later in the season **Around the World in Eighty Days** (75 performances, and the shortest-running of all Cole Porter's musicals). But the theatre that William Gaxton had referred to as "the dump of dumps" was still luckless. Because a few weeks after *Three to Make Ready* opened and was clearly an established hit, it moved to the more desirable Broadhurst Theatre, leaving the Adelphi briefly dark until Orson Welles and Porter's adaptation of Jules Verne's novel opened.

Three to Make Ready was the third in Nancy Hamilton and Morgan Lewis's occasional series of intimate revues. *One for the Money* (1939) and **Two for the Show** (1940) enjoyed modest runs, and the latter introduced "How High the Moon," one of the finest of all theatre ballads. *Three to Make Ready* was more elaborate than its predecessors, and with Ray Bolger it for the first time offered a name star in its cast. It wasn't a blockbuster, but it played for the remainder of the year, turned a profit, had a national tour, and "The Old Soft Shoe" enjoyed a certain amount of popularity on the radio. But after the third edition, the series disappeared and Broadway never saw *And Four to Go*.

The production received mixed revues, but everyone agreed Bolger was the mainstay of the evening. Otherwise, most of the aisle sitters felt the material let him and the cast down. In fact, with just two exceptions the critics were so generally unhappy with the revue that it's surprising it lasted for nine months and made a profit.

Everyone agreed Bolger's best moments were "The Old Soft Shoe" and a reprise of his dancing Scarecrow from the 1939 film *The Wizard of Oz* (which was part of the "A Lovely Lazy Kind of Day" sequence). Otherwise, the critics were turned off by the "bathroom" sketch "Housing Shortage" (aka "Cold Water Flat"), which they found somewhat tasteless. And many felt the sketches "The Shoe on the Other Foot" (about a woman wasting a salesman's time in a shoe store); "The Russian Lesson" (about a group of housewives who decide to learn a foreign language); and "The Story of the Opera" (which had first been performed in *One for the Money* and which centered on a woman who describes a Wagnerian opera she has seen) were generally flat and obvious.

Further, the Noel Coward spoof "Post Mortem" was weak, and although Bolger's impersonation of Sergeant George Baker's funny-paper character "The Sad Sack" should have been a winner (and certainly Bolger's mien was perfect for it), it was apparently too mild. And "Wisconsin" or "Kenosha Canoe" (with its "Kenosha Canoe Ballet") should have been one of the evening's high spots with its speculation of how Richard Rodgers and Oscar Hammerstein II would have adapted Theodore Dreiser's *An American Tragedy* as a musical in the style and outlook of **Oklahoma!** and **Carousel** (it also included a special swipe at Agnes De Mille's brand of choreography). But in the main the reviewers found it lacking. In this sequence, Gordon MacRae played the leading man, "Mr. Snow," and of course about a decade later he played the leading roles of Curly and Billy Bigelow in the film adaptations of the two Rodgers and Hammerstein musicals.

John Chapman in the *New York Daily News* said the material was "uneven," and the evening "awkwardly" wavered between an intimate revue and a lavish one. And while he liked the songs "Barnaby Beach" and "A Lovely Lazy Kind of Day," he felt Morgan Lewis's score was "nothing remarkable"; further, Donald Oenslager's sets were "all right" but "not particularly witty." Lewis Nichols in the *New York Times* noted the revue's creators had surrounded Bolger with "indifferent" material and as a result the evening was a "disappointment." The bathroom sketch was one in which Bolger "should have no part in," and in "The Sad Sack" he was "not too happy." But the old-time salute to vaudeville "The Old Soft Shoe" was one of the "high moments" of current theatergoing.

Robert Garland in the *New York Journal-American* said it was Bolger who helped the revue shed its "amateur aspect," and suggested "The Old Soft Shoe" was reason enough to see the show. He criticized the "nonprofessional" words by Nancy Hamilton and the "non-professional" music by Morgan Lewis, all of it "no more than collegiate entertainment." But he praised Rose Inghram, who sang "as if she had never heard of Jan Kiepura" (earlier in the season, Inghram had appeared with Kiepura and his wife Marta Eggerth in **Polonaise**, and it was Inghram and Inghram alone who stopped that show with her song "The Next Time I Care").

Burton Rascoe in the *New York World-Telegram* found the revue "careless" and "semi-amateur" in "nature." But when Bolger went into "The Old Soft Shoe," the audience "went crazy"; otherwise, the evening was "dreary, tawdry and amateurish." Ward Morehouse in the *New York Sun* noted the "long-suffering" Adelphi Theatre now had "somewhat better luck" with the new revue. It was "very spotty" with an only "fair" score and "weak" sketches (some of which were "dreadfully tedious"), but it had Bolger, who stopped the show with "The Old Soft Shoe." Louis Kronenberger in *PM* found the evening "very disappointing," and even though the season's previous musicals might suggest one shouldn't be too choosy, there was no getting around the fact that *Three to Make Ready* was "still not good enough." The music was "ineffectual" and the sketches mostly "fell flat." Besides Bolger, the only other pleasant aspect of the evening was "Barnaby Beach," which was "charmingly staged."

But Howard Barnes in the *New York Herald Tribune* found the evening a "stunning" one that had "pace, excitement and wit" and the kind of dancing that hadn't "been seen in many a moon." While most of the critics had been less than impressed with the Rodgers and Hammerstein spoof, he found "Wisconsin" a "wonderfully funny" (but not "downright malicious") take-off. And Vernon Rice in the *New York Daily News* said the revue was a "handsome, giddy affair" and a "solid hit." He said "Wisconsin" brought down the house, and the Noel Coward sketch was "devastating." And while everyone knew Bolger could dance, it was worth noting that now he had developed into a "first-rate comedian."

Radio star Arthur Godfrey appeared in the revue, offering monologues and serving as a kind of master of ceremonies. Barnes suggested his "brief" monologues could have been briefer; Morehouse said Godfrey's material led him to "wander about rather helplessly"; and Kronenberger said Godfrey was one of the revue's "mistakes." Rice also noted that Godfrey wandered in and out throughout the evening, and Chapman said he "ambles in now and again" and was "likeable" if not "exactly forceful."

During the tryout, the following numbers were cut: the songs "After You," "Oh, You're a Wonderful Person," "Desert Isle," "Furnished Bed," and "Rushing the Growler"; the dance "New Clothes" (for Harold Lang); and the sketches "Bertie, The Sewing-Machine Girl" and "Mrs. Doakes Becomes an American." For the tryout, most of Arthur Godfrey's monologues had titles ("Quick Change," "To the Rescue," "For the Guild," and "Our Little Sandpiper"). It also appears that the "If It's Love" sequence underwent major changes; for the tryout, it included spoofs of **Lute Song** and the recent revivals of *Antigone* and Maurice Evans's G.I. version of *Hamlet*, but these take-offs were apparently dropped prior to the New York opening.

During the run, Arthur Godfrey left the show, and the song "Hot December" (for Bibi Osterwald) was added; incidentally, the sketch "The Story of the Opera" had first been performed in *One for the Money*. The sketch "The Russian Lesson" is probably the earlier "The French Lesson," which was dropped from **Two for the Show** during its tryout. For the post-Broadway tour, Kaye Ballard joined *Three to Make Ready* and sang two new numbers, "The Apartment" and "I Found Him Under a Log"; and the sketch "There'll Come a Day" (written by Gwen Rickard) was added.

"The Old Soft Shoe" and "He's a Millionaire" are included in Kaye Ballard's collection *The Ladies Who Wrote the Lyrics* (Painted Smiles LP # PS-1334); the album credits the latter to *Three to Make Ready*, but it's not listed in various tryout, Broadway, and post-Broadway tour programs, and may have been cut during the preproduction phase of the revue.

In 1952, a paperback edition published by Samuel French included sketch and song highlights from the *One-Two-Three* revues. Titled *Three to One*, the collection includes the following numbers from *Three to Make Ready*: the sketches "The Shoe on the Other Foot," "Cold Water Flat" (aka "Housing Shortage") and "Wisconsin" or "Kenosha Canoe" and the songs "The Old Soft Shoe" and "And Why Not I?" (here titled "Born for Better Things").

In 1972, the rather awkwardly titled Off-Broadway revue *One for the Money Etc.* offered a "best of" evening that presented songs and sketches from all three of the *One-Two-Three* revues (for more information, see **Two for the Show**). Numbers heard in this revue that had been performed in *Three to Make Ready* are: "Post Mortem," "And Why Not I?" (aka "Born for Better Things"), "Wisconsin" or "Kenosha Canoe," "If It's Love," "The Old Soft Shoe," and "The Russian Lesson" (as mentioned above, this last is probably a revised version of "The French Lesson," which had been dropped from **Two for the Show**). The Off-Broadway production also included "The Story of the Opera," which had first been performed in *One for the Money* and was reprised for **Two for the Show**.

ST. LOUIS WOMAN
"A New Musical Comedy About the Gaudy Nineties" / "A New Musical Play"

Theatre: Martin Beck Theatre
Opening Date: March 30, 1946; *Closing Date*: July 6, 1946
Performances: 113

Book: Arna Bontemps and Countee Cullen
Lyrics: Johnny Mercer
Music: Harold Arlen
Based on the 1931 novel *God Sends Sunday* by Arna Bontemps.
Direction: Rouben Mamoulian; *Producer*: Edward Gross; *Choreography*: Charles Walters; *Scenery* and *Costumes*: Lemuel Ayers; *Lighting*: Uncredited; *Musical Direction*: Leon Leonardi
Cast: Robert Pope (Badfoot), Harold Nicholas (Little Augie), Fayard Nicholas (Barney), June Hawkins (Lila), Louis Sharp (Slim), Pearl Bailey (Butterfly), Ruby Hill (Della Green), Rex Ingram (Biglow Brown), Elwood Smith (Ragsdale), Merritt Smith (Pembroke), Charles Welch (Jasper), Maude Russell (The Hostess), J. Mardo Brown (Drum Major), Milton J. Williams (Mississippi), Frank Green (Dandy Dave), Juanita Hall (Leah), Joseph Eady (Jackie), Yvonne Coleman (Celestine), Herbert Coleman (Piggie), Lorenzo Fuller (Joshua), Milton Wood (Mr. Hopkins), Creighton Thompson (Preacher), Carrington Lewis (Waiter); Choral Group: Olive Ball, Rhoda Boggs, Miriam Burton, Rosalie King, Maude Russell, Zelda Shelton, Lori Wilson, J. Mardo Brown, John Diggs, Leon Edwards, Lorenzo Fuller, Theodore Hines, Jerry Laws, Arthur Lawson, Merritt Smith, Charles Welch; Dancers: Rita Garrett, Dorothea Greene, Gwendolyn Hale, Betty Nichols, Marguerite Roan, Royce Wallace, Enid Williams, Theodore Allen, Smalls Boykins, Norman DeJoie, Frank Green, Lonny Reed, Arthur Smith, George Thomas
The musical was presented in three acts.
The action takes place during 1898 in St. Louis, Missouri.

Musical Numbers

Act One: Overture (Orchestra); "Li'l Augie Is a Natural Man" (Robert Pope); "Limericks" (aka "Sweet'nin' Water") (Robert Pope, Fayard Nicholas, Louis Sharp, Ruby Hill, Male Ensemble); "Any Place I Hang My Hat Is Home" (Ruby Hill); "I Feel My Luck Comin' Down" (Harold Nicholas); "I Had Myself a True Love" (June Hawkins); "Legalize My Name" (Pearl Bailey); "Cakewalk Your Lady" (Drum Major: J. Mardo Brown; Quartet: Rhoda Boggs, Rosalie King, Robert Pope, Milton J. Williams; Competing Couples: (1) Betty Nichols and Smalls Boykins; (2) Rita Garrett and Theodore Allen; (3) Dorothea Green and Milton Wood; (4) Royce Wallace and Lonny Reed; (5) Gwendolyn Hale and Norman DeJoie; (6) Enid Williams and George Thomas; (7) Pearl Bailey and Fayard Nicholas; and (8) Ruby Hill and Harold Nicholas)
Act Two: "Come Rain or Come Shine" (Ruby Hill, Harold Nicholas); "Easy Rider" (Ruby Hill); "Chinquapin Bush" (Children); "We Shall Meet to Part, No Never" (Herbert Coleman); "Lullaby" ("Peekin' around the Chinquapin Bush") (Ruby Hill); "Sleep Peaceful, Mister Used-to-Be" (June Hawkins); Funeral Scene: "Leavin' Time" (Choral Group)
Act Three: "Come Rain or Come Shine" (reprise) (Ruby Hill); "A Woman's Prerogative" (Pearl Bailey); "Ridin' on the Moon" (Harold Nicholas, Ensemble); "Least That's My Opinion" (Robert Pope); "Racin' Forms" (Juanita Hall); "Come On, Li'l Augie" (Ruby Hill, Pearl Bailey, Herbert Coleman, Ensemble); Finale (Entire Company)

Just days before rehearsals of *St. Louis Woman* began, co-librettist Countee Cullen suddenly died, and his passing seemed to hover over the musical like a bad omen. The tryout was chaotic, and Lemuel Ayers, who was both the director and designer, was replaced by Rouben Mamoulian as director, and choreographer Antony Tudor was replaced by Charles Walters. When the musical began its tryout, it was presented in two acts, which Mamoulian reconfigured into three, and at least six songs which were listed in tryout programs were cut: "A Man's Gotta Fight," "Talkin' Glory," "Sow the Seed an' Reap the Harvest," "High, Low, Jack, and the Game," "'S One Thing (Somethin') You Gotta Find Out for Yourself," and "I Wonder What Became of Me." If all this weren't enough, Mamoulian fired Ruby Hill and hired Muriel Rahn (who had alternated in the title role for the original production of **Carmen Jones**), and the cast refused to go on for the New York opening night unless Hill was reinstated (and, of course, she was).

When the musical opened on Broadway, it received a few good notices. But the production couldn't overcome the mostly negative and indifferent reviews, and as a result the musical closed after a little more than three months. Most of the critics panned the book, and some noted Harold Nicholas (Little Augie) lacked the necessary acting skills to create a viable character; they also said he and his brother Fayard (Barney) weren't given enough dancing; after all, when you've got the legendary Nicholas Brothers in your show, don't you devise some great dances for them? In fact, there was only one main dance sequence, "Cakewalk Your Lady," a show-stopper that brought down the house and the first act curtain. Of the cast members, Rex Ingram (as the sadistic Biglow Brown) was killed off early on, and one or two critics felt his villainous character was sorely missed for the rest of the evening (despite Ingram's well-known singing voice, it's curious he was given no songs; apparently one of the numbers eventually cut during the tryout was temporarily transferred to his character, but by New York he was song-less). Pearl Bailey (Butterfly) walked away with the reviews; she had a relatively minor role, but she owned the stage whenever she appeared, and her two comedy songs "Legalize My Name" and "A Woman's Prerogative" were show-stoppers.

The most surprising aspect of the reviews was the critics' mostly indifferent and negative comments about Harold Arlen's and Johnny Mercer's glorious songs, some of the finest ever heard on the Broadway stage. The score has yielded such standards as "Come Rain or Come Shine" and "Any Place I Hang My Hat Is Home"; and "I Had Myself a True Love," "Ridin' on the Moon," "Leavin' Time," "Cakewalk Your Lady," and Bailey's two comedy songs are Broadway gold. And best of all was "Lullaby" (aka "Peekin' around the Chinquapin Bush"), one of the most exquisite theatre songs ever written. It was a touching and heartbreaking lament for things past and gone forever, and its haunting music and yearning lyric were poignant and filled with bittersweet sadness. Like Arlen's other masterwork *House of Flowers* (1954), the critics generally overlooked the music. And, incredibly, one or two reviewers said Arlen's **Bloomer Girl** score was superior. While the latter has its moments, the two scores aren't remotely in the same league: **Bloomer Girl** is watered-down iced tea, and **St. Louis Woman** is rich red wine.

The story dealt with successful jockey Little Augie (Harold Nicholas) and his attraction to St. Louis Woman Della Green (Ruby Hill), a free spirit who is casually involved with tough saloon owner Biglow Brown (Rex Ingram), a cruel man who pines for Della and has dumped Lila (June Hawkins), who nonetheless continues to carry a torch for him. When Della and Augie begin to live together, Biglow becomes furious and beats Della. Lila and Augie discover that Della has been roughed up by Biglow, and Augie goes for a gun; but suddenly a shot is fired from somewhere and Biglow falls, mortally wounded. Thinking Augie has shot him, Biglow puts a curse on him before he dies. It's eventually revealed that Lila killed Biglow, but Augie believes the curse has taken hold and he fears his days as a winning jockey are over; because Della truly believes she's brought on Augie's bad luck, she leaves him. Ultimately, his luck changes for the better, he starts winning races, and he and Della are reunited. A comic subplot dealt with Butterfly (Pearl Bailey), who works as a barmaid in Biglow's saloon and who occasionally steps out with jockey Barney (Fayard Nicholas), whom she won't have much to do with until he legalizes her name.

Robert Garland in the *New York Journal-American* said the book was the musical's "worst opponent, a tactless tripper-upper," and while the show was "all dressed up and rarin' to go" its unfortunate destination was "downhill." According to Garland, Arlen's music and Mercer's "literate" lyrics couldn't save the evening, but he noted Pearl Bailey received "ovations" for her songs, and he praised the "infant phenomenon" (Herbert Coleman) who sang "We Shall Live to Part, No Never." Howard Barnes in the *New York Herald Tribune* admitted the musical offered "moments of exciting theatrical alchemy," but ultimately the show reneged on its promises. The score didn't have "musical buoyancy," and the Nicholas Brothers and Ruby Hill lacked the dramatic know-how to put over their roles. But he noted Pearl Bailey "pulls the show up by its shoestrings every time she makes an entrance."

Lewis Nichols in the *New York Times* suggested that both Little Augie and *St. Louis Woman* were the victims of curses, and in the latter's case it was the plot. He felt the evening wavered between serious folk opera and standard musical comedy and was thus a "hybrid affair." Arlen's score was "not his best," and while an "occasional air" was "catchy," there were no "great novelties." Ward Morehouse in the *New York Sun* said the score was only "fair" (and complained that Arlen's music didn't match the score of **Bloomer Girl**), the book was "laggard and frequently tiresome," and the cast was not "overpowering"; further, when Rex Ingram's Biglow Brown was killed, "a lot of the show died with him." But Pearl Bailey was "zestful" and the evening's "outstanding" sequence was "Cakewalk Your Lady," which was "exhilarating."

However, Vernon Rice in the *New York Post* said that despite being sometimes "hokey," the musical was "colorful, fast-moving and never dull." Mamoulian had "whittled" down the book in order to provide a general framework for the story and to stage his "directorial feats" of "rhythm and picturizations." He mentioned that Bailey "stole the show," and that Arlen had written everything from "low-down torch" to "good old-fashioned Negro spiritual" to love ballads. He also mentioned that "Cakewalk Your Lady" was "breath-taking" in its "design, movement and tempo." The dance number was comprised of eight couples, each one succeeding the other, in a dance competition to win a cake. Burton Rascoe in the *New York World-Telegram* said the (sixth) cakewalk couple were Enid Williams and George Thomas, and Williams danced in "sensational dead-pan" which was "hilarious in the extreme." Louis Kronenberger in *PM* said her "dead-pan look and wonderful motions" were a "high point" of the evening, and Barnes also noted that Williams "quite takes over" the cakewalk with her "dead-pan pantomime." Whatever Williams specifically did to win over the critics is now lost in time and forever hidden within the walls and spaces of the Martin Beck Theatre, but she must have been wonderfully ingratiating.

Kronenberger suggested the overall evening failed because it aimed for a "certain folk-operatic flavor" which was "glazed with musical comedy icing." He suggested better music could have wielded the disparate elements together, but that Arlen hadn't provided a "first-rate" score. Incredibly, he stated the "songs and orchestral tags and tidbits" were "second-rate" and lacked "distinction," "melodic urgency," "excitement," and "cohesive power."

However, Rascoe said as soon as the final curtain had fallen on opening night, he was ready to see the musical again. Only two other musicals during the season had so "thrilled" him (and they were the revivals of **The Red Mill** and **Show Boat**), and as far as "comparisons" go, he felt *St. Louis Woman* was a better musical than **Porgy and Bess** and **Carmen Jones**. Every aspect of the musical was "contagiously delightful," including Pearl Bailey, who "tore the house down" with her two numbers. Harold Arlen had "done very well by himself" and Leon Leonardi's orchestra knew how to play "real music." John Chapman in the *New York Daily News* said *St. Louis Woman* was not only the "best Negro musical in many seasons," it was so far the best new musical of the 1945–1946 season. He praised the "lively" and "smartly staged" show, and said Arlen's music was "infectious" and Mercer's lyrics were "just right." He also mentioned "a very small boy" (Herbert Coleman) who sang a "very small song" ("We Shall Meet to Part, No Never") and earned "rousing applause." In fact, that's what he liked best about the musical: every scene and every song had been staged "as though it were designed to be the best of the evening."

The cast album was recorded by Decca Records (LP # DW-2742; later issued on CD by Broadway Angel # ZMD-7-64662-2-4 and then by DRG/EMI # 19078; the latter is paired with the 1955 Capitol album of *Harold Arlen and His Songs*, in which he performs "Come Rain or Come Shine"). The script was published in hardback in the 1971 collection *Black Theatre* (compiled and with an introduction by Lindsay Patterson, and published by Dodd, Mead & Company), and in 1973 the collection was published in paperback (by New American Library). The lyrics for the used and cut songs are included in *The Complete Lyrics of Johnny Mercer*.

MGM bought the film rights, and for a while a film version was on Arthur Freed's docket (Hugh Fordin in *The Movies' Greatest Musicals* reports that in 1953 Fred Finklehoff wrote a first-, second-, and final-draft screenplay and that Helen Deutsch wrote a continuity script).

In the mid-1950s, Arlen reworked the score, and in 1957 part of it was recorded as *Blues Opera*; in 1959, the work was briefly seen as *Free and Easy*. The recording of *Blues Opera* was released by Columbia Records (LP # CL-1099; issued on CD by DRG # 19044, which also includes Hugh Martin's *The Grandma Moses Suite*). *Free and Easy* premiered at the Theatre Carre in Amsterdam during December 1959, and was then seen in Paris during January 1960 for nine performances; after that, it completely disappeared. The final version apparently included much of the original score of *St. Louis Woman*, along with at least one deleted number ("I Wonder What Became of Me") and some new music. Arlen also utilized fragments of some of his popular songs, such as "Blues in the Night" (from the 1941 film of the same title; lyric by Johnny Mercer). Since the *Blues Opera* recording was released two years before the final version of the opera, the recording isn't complete and includes only highlights from the score.

On April 30, 1998, a concert production was presented at City Center by Encores! for five performances; the cast included Vanessa Williams (Della), Stanley Wayne Mathis (Little Augie), Victor Trent Cook (Barney), Helen Goldsby (Lila), Charles S. Dutton (Biglow), Yvette Cason (Butterfly), and Chuck Cooper (Badfoot). The concert was presented in two acts, and included the cut "I Wonder What Became of Me"; the music of "We Shall Meet to Part, No Never" seems to be lost, and so of course it wasn't part of the concert (its lyric is included in the published script and in the collection of Mercer's lyrics). The concert's recording was released by Mercury CD # 314-538-148-2 and then later by Decca Broadway, which assigned it the same release number as the Mercury CD. A "blues ballet" version of the musical was produced in New York in 2003.

CARMEN JONES

Theatre: City Center
Opening Date: April 7, 1946; *Closing Date*: May 4, 1946
Performances: 32
Book and *Lyrics*: Oscar Hammerstein II
Music: Georges Bizet (new orchestrations by Robert Russell Bennett)
Based on the 1875 opera *Carmen Jones* (music by Georges Bizet, libretto by Henri Meilhac and Ludovic Halevy), which in turn was based on the 1845 story *Carmen* by Prosper Merimee.
Direction: Staged by Hassard Short and book directed by Charles Friedman; *Producer*: Billy Rose; *Choreography*: Eugene Loring; *Scenery*: Howard Bay; *Costumes*: Raoul Pene du Bois; *Lighting*: Hassard Short; *Musical Direction*: David Mordecai; *Choral Direction*: Robert Shaw
Cast: Robert Clarke (Corporal Morrell, Soldier), George Willis (Foreman, Soldier, Bullet Head), Elton J. Warren (Cindy Lou; Coreania Hayman, alternate), Jack Carr (Sergeant Brown, Mr. Higgins), Napoleon Reed (Joe; Le Vern Hutchinson, alternate), Muriel Smith (Carmen Jones; Urylee Leonardos, alternate); Sibol Cain (Sally, Card Player), Edward Roche (T-Bone), James May (Tough Kid), Oliver Coleman (Drummer), Andrew J. Taylor (Bartender), Edward Christopher (Waiter), Ruth Crumpton (Myrt), Theresa Merritte (Frankie), John Bubbles (Rum), Ford Buck (Dink), Bill O'Neil (Boy), Erona Harris (Girl), Glenn Bryant (Husky Miller), Randall Steplight (Soldier), Elijah Hodges (Soldier), Freyde Marshall (Mrs. Higgins, Card Player), Harold Taylor (Photographer), Doris Brown (Card Player), Richard de Vaultier (Waiter), Audrey Vanterpool (Dancing Girl), Frank Palmer (Poncho), Sheldon B. Hoskins (Dancing Boxer), Randolph Sawyer (Dancing Boxer), George Spelvin (Referee); Soldiers, Factory Workers, Socialites: Anne Dixon, Etta May Curry, Fredye Marshall, Doris Brown, Ida Johnson, Mattie Washington, Margaret Eley, Elsie Kennedy, Mary Graham, Sibol Cain, Adelaide Boatner, Lee Allen, Robert Clarke, Elijah Hodges, Randall Steplight, Audrey Vanterpool, John Kelly, Chauncey Reynolds, Edward Roche, Richard de Vaultier, George Willis, Clarence Jones, Andrew J. Taylor, Harold Taylor; Dancers: Evelyn Pilcher, Edith Ross, Dorothy McDavid, Hedye Brown, Posie Flowers, Audrey Graham, Erona Harris, Rita Christiani, Margaret Scott, Mable Hart, Rhoda Johnson, Vera McNichols, Edith Hurd, Randolph Sawyer, Alonzo Hodo, Lester Goodman, Rudolph Crier, Edward Christopher, Ivan Gittens, Albert Rivera, Clifton Gray, Sheldon B. Hoskins, Joseph Noble, Bill O'Neil, James Truitte, Edmond Woodard; Children: Jenkins Hightower, Payton Hightower, James May, Albert Smith, Ralph May, Jack Hightower, Bobby May, Roger Smith
The musical was presented in two acts.
The action takes place during the present time in a Southern town and in Chicago.

This was the third time Oscar Hammerstein II's modern-day adaptation of George Bizet's opera *Carmen* was presented in New York. The original production of *Carmen Jones* opened at the Broadway Theatre on December 2, 1943, and played for 503 performances. Some three months after the production closed, producer Billy Rose brought it back for an additional limited run of 21 performances at City Center prior to the musical's national tour of twenty-six cities. The current production also played at City Center, this time as the musical's last stop of that one-year tour. A few months later, the musical began a second tour which played in thirty-five cities within a four-month period.

The cast of the current revival included Muriel Smith, the original Carmen Jones; Glenn Bryant was again Husky Miller; and Napoleon Reed, who had alternated as Joe in the original production, reprised his role. For more information about the 1943 and 1945 productions, see separate entries (the entry for the 1943 premiere includes a list of the musical numbers).

CALL ME MISTER
"A MUSICAL REVUE"

Theatre: National Theatre (during run, the musical transferred to the Majestic Theatre and then to the Plymouth Theatre)
Opening Date: April 18, 1946; *Closing Date*: January 10, 1948
Performances: 734

Sketches: Arnold Auerbach
Lyrics and *Music*: Harold Rome
Direction: Robert H. Gordon; *Producers*: Melvyn Douglas and Herman Levin; *Choreography*: John Wray; *Scenery*: Lester Polakov; *Costumes*: Grace Houston; *Lighting*: Uncredited; *Musical Direction*: Lehman Engel
Cast: Betty Garrett, Jules Munshin, Bill Callahan, Lawrence Winters, George Hall, Harry Clark, Paula Bane, Maria Karnilova, Alan Manson, Danny Scholl, Betty Lou Holland, David Nillo, Chandler Cowles, George (S.) Irving, Glenn Turnbull, Ruth Feist, Kate Friedlich, Virginia Davis, Alvis Tinnin, Joe Calvin, Steve Allison, Robert Baird, Henry Lawrence, Sid Lawson, Howard Malone, Ward Garner, Eugene Tobin, Francis Dometrovich, Tommy Knox, Peter Fara, William Mende, Edward Silkman, Roy Ross, Alex Dunaeff, Bettye Durrence, Shellie Filkins, Darcy Gardner, Betty Lorraine, Rae MacGregor, Patricia Penso, Evelyn Shaw, Fred Danieli, Kevin Smith, Joan Bartels, Betty Gilpatrick, Bruce Howard, Marjorie Oldroyd, Doris Parker, Paula Purnell
The revue was presented in two acts.

Sketches and Musical Numbers

Act One: Opening Number: "The Jodie Chant" (Sergeant: Jules Munshin; Soldiers: Bill Callahan, Harry Clark, Chandler Cowles, Ward Garner, George Hall, Alan Manson, Danny Scholl, Lawrence Winters; Sailors: Robert Baird, Alex Dunaeff, Henry Lawrence, Sid Lawson, William Mende, Edward Silkman, Alvis Tinnin, Eugene Tobin; Canteen Girls: Bettye Durrence, Kate Friedlich, Shellie Filkins, Darcy Gardner, Betty Lorraine, Rae MacGregor, Patricia Penso, Evelyn Shaw; Marines: Joe Calvan, Fred Danieli, Tommy Knox, Howard Malone, David Nillo, Roy Ross, Kevin Smith, Glenn Turnbull); "Going Home Train" (Ex-G.I.'s: Bill Callahan, Harry Clark, Chandler Cowles, Ward Garner, George Hall, Alan Manson, David Nillo, Danny Scholl, Lawrence Winters, Robert Baird, Henry Lawrence, Sid Lawson, William Mende, Edward Silkman, Alvis Tinnin, Eugene Tobin, Glenn Turnbull, Joe Calvan, Fred Danieli, Alex Dunaeff, Tommy Knox, Roy Ross); "Welcome Home" (Bill Willson: Glenn Turnbull; A Soldier: Harry Clark; Mr. Charles Wilson: George Irving; Mrs. Josephine Wilson: Betty Garrett; Lottie: Evelyn Shaw; Wally Wilson: Joe Calvan); "Love Story, Chapter I: Three-Thousand Miles Apart": "Along with Me" (The Boy: Danny Scholl; His Mates: Robert Baird, Henry Lawrence, Sid Lawson, William Mende, Edward Silkman, Alvis Tinnin, Eugene Tobin; The Girl: Paula Bane; Her Co-Workers: Joan Bartels, Virginia Davis, Ruth Feist, Betty Gilpatrick, Bruce Howard, Marjorie Oldroyd, Doris Parker, Paula Purnell); "The Army Way" (Sam: Alan Manson; Soldier: Tommy Knox; Captain Baines: George Irving; Paul Revere: George Hall; Master Sergeant: Harry Clark; Corporal: Bill Callahan; Dental Officer: Sid Lawson; Insurance Officer: Glenn Turnbull; Hygiene Officer: Roy Ross); "Surplus Blues" (aka "Little Surplus Me") (Betty Garrett); "Love Story, Chapter II: He Remembers": "The Drug Store Song" (The Boy: Danny Scholl; Ballet—The Girl: Maria Karnilova; The Boy: David Nillo; Pop Higgins: Glenn Turnbull; First Couple: Betty Lorraine, Howard Malone; Second Couple: Kate Friedlich, Fred Danieli; Trio: Shellie Filkins, Patricia Penson, Joe Calvan); "Off We Go" (sketch by Arnold Auerbach and Arnold B. Horwitt) (Ted: Roy Ross; Lou: George Irving; Mulvey: Harry Clark; Grover: Jules Munshin; Dover: Alan Manson; Stover: George Hall; Menu Girl: Marjorie Oldroyd; Canape Girl: Betty Gilpatrick; Cigarette Girl: Joan Bartels; Mac: Sid Lawson; Merryweather: Chandler Cowles; Plover: Glenn Turnbull; General: Ward Garner); "The Red Ball Express" (Truck Driver: Lawrence Winters; Other Truck Drivers: Robert Baird, William Mende, Edward Silkman, Alvis Tinnin; Foreman: Roy Ross); "Military Life" (The Sailor: Harry Clark; The Soldier: Chandler Cowles; The Marine: Jules Munshin; The WAVE: Betty Garrett; The WAC: Betty Gilpatrick; The Tenderneck: Evelyn Shaw); "Call Me Mister" (The Marine: Bill Callahan; Floorwalker: Jules Munshin; Customers: Betty Garrett, Betty Lou Holland; Sales Clerks: Joan Bartels, Virginia Davis, Ruth Feist, Betty Gilpatrick, Bruce Howard, Marjorie Oldroyd, Doris Parker, Paula Purnell, Robert Baird, George Irving, Henry Lawrence, Sid Lawson, William Mende, Edward Silkman, Alvis Tinnin, Eugene Tobin; Underwear Models: Bettye Durrence, Shellie Filkins, Rae MacGregor, Patricia Penso; The WACS: Kate Friedlich, Darcy Gardner, Betty Lorraine, Evelyn Shaw; The G.I.'s: Joe Calvan, Tommy Knox, Howard Malone, Roy Ross; The Civilians: Fred Danieli, Alex Dunaeff, Kevin Smith, Peter Fara)

Act Two: "Yuletide, Park Avenue" (The Grandmother: Betty Garrett; The Butler: William Mende; The Uncle: George Irving: The Sister: Marjorie Oldroyd; Her Husband: Eugene Tobin; The Brother: Robert Baird; His Wife: Betty Gilpatrick; The Father: Edward Silkman; The Mother: Virginia Davis; The Young Sister: Betty Lou Holland; The Lieutenant, J.G.: Chandler Cowles); Jules Munshin (monologue); "Love Story, Chapter III: She Dreams": "When We Meet Again" (Paula Bane; Ballet—The Girl: Maria Karnilova; The Boy: David Nillo; The Girls: Kate Friedlich, Shellie Filkins, Darcy Gardner, Betty Lorraine, Rae MacGregor, Patricia Penso; The Boys: Joe Calvan, Fred Danieli, Alex Dunaeff, Howard Malone, Roy Ross); "Once Over Lightly" (sketch by Arnold Auerbach and Arnold B. Horwitt) (Mike: Jules Munshin; Ted: Ward Garner; Barber: Harry Clark); "The Face on the Dime" (A Man: Lawrence Winters); "A Home of Our Own" (Mrs. Winthrop: Betty Garrett; Arthur Benson: Sid Lawson; A Soldier: Alan Manson; A Young Husband: George Irving; A Young Wife: Betty Gilpatrick; A Captain: Chandler Cowles; Lucille: Betty Lou Holland; Bill: Bill Callahan; Lucille's Mother: Virginia Davis; Lucille's Father: Harry Clark; Applicants: Joan Bartels, Ruth Feist, Bruce Howard, Marjorie Oldroyd, Doris Parker, Paula Purnell, Robert Baird, Henry Lawrence, William Mende, Edward Silkman, Alvis Tinnin, Eugene Tobin); Dance Specialty: Betty Lou Holland, Bill Callahan; "Love Story, Chapter IV: Together": "His Old Man" (The Girl: Paula Bane; The Boy: Danny Scholl); "South America, Take It Away" (The Hostess: Betty Garrett; Her Partners: Chandler Cowles, Fred Danieli, Howard Malone, Alan Manson); "South Wind" (Senator Burble: Jules Munshin; Representative Snide: Harry Clark; Representative Gumble: George Hall; Senator Dibble: George Irving; G.I. Joe: Chandler Cowles); "The Senators' Song" (Harry Clark, George Hall, Jules Munshin); Finale: "Call Me Mister" (reprise) (The Veteran: Chandler Cowles; The *Call Me Mister* Company)

Throughout the war years, shows such as **This Is the Army**, **Winged Victory**, and **Tars and Spars** celebrated and honored American servicemen in wartime. Now that the war was over, *Call Me Mister* decided to look at postwar America through the prism of former servicemen who are back home and adjusting to civilian life. With its focused through-line of veterans re-entering the civilian world, the evening was friendly and easy-going and had no particular axe to grind (although there was a gratuitous swipe at Southern politicians). As a result, the revue was one of the most successful of the era. It played on Broadway for almost two years, offered the hit song "South America, Take It Away," enjoyed a national tour (which included such cast members as Bob Fosse, Carl Reiner, Buddy Hackett, William Warfield, Jane Kean, and Edmund Lyndeck), and was even filmed (albeit in name-only) with a newly created plot that retained just three songs from the stage production.

Early in the first act, "Going Home Train" captured the homeward-bound excitement of mustered-out soldiers heading for home and a new life; and later on the title song (which took place in a department store) was a joyous romp that depicted the soldiers turning in their uniforms for civilian clothes. One sketch ("The Army Way") kidded bureaucratic red-tape as it imagined what Paul Revere had to go through in order to requisition a horse for his midnight ride; another ("Welcome Home") satirized civilians who have read all the wrong magazines about returning veterans and thus think all of them are one step away from the psycho ward; "A Home of Our Own" wryly looked at the housing shortage; and another ("Off We Go") was the typical soldier's attitude that a member of the Air Force has a lush and lovely life akin to spending all one's time at the Stork Club.

The song "Surplus Blues" (aka "Little Surplus Me") found Betty Garrett as a waitress in a diner who used to serve soldiers from a nearby, and now closed, military base, and who misses the excitement of the war years; and later Garrett stopped the show with "South America, Take It Away," in which she portrayed a canteen hostess who is sick and tired of the conga and the samba.

There were also the songs "The Red Ball Express," which saluted the black American convoy truck drivers in Europe, and "The Face on the Dime" which honored the late FDR. As a running thread through the evening, there were four "chapters" of a wartime "Love Story," which followed a sailor and his wife (played by Danny Scholl and Paula Bane) throughout the war, from his being stationed some three-thousand miles from her ("Along with Me") to his memories of his hometown main street ("The Drug Store Song") to her dreams ("When We Meet Again") and finally to his return home when he joins his wife and sees his child for the first time ("His Old Man").

Howard Barnes in the *New York Herald Tribune* praised the "vitality and finesse" of the new revue, and found Harold Rome's score "excellent"; as for Arnold Auerbach's sketches, not all of them were perfect but his "batting average" was "way up there." John Chapman in the *New York Daily News* said the "grand" revue was "funny" and "well-paced," and singled out a number of sketches and songs, including "Going Home Train," "Surplus Blues," and the title number. Louis Kronenberger in *PM* liked the "gay" and "springy" revue, and particularly enjoyed "Off We Go" (in which the Army envisions Air Force life as "all Hollywood luxury and Mayfair toniness") and "South America, Take It Away" (and he praised Betty Garrett's canteen hostess, who is "half dead and half disjointed" from too many rhumbas and sambas).

Robert Garland in the *New York Journal-American* said *Call Me Mister* was the town's best new musical; and "South America, Take It Away" was a "classic" song that was "projected classically" by Garrett. Vernon Rice in the *New York Post* said the revue "can't miss," and he praised Rome's "stirring" score, Bill Callahan and Mary Lou Holland's "good old-fashioned" tap dancing, and, like everyone, hailed Betty Garrett ("there is practically nothing the gal can't do"). Ward Morehouse in the *New York Sun* said the "really good" revue offered "excellent" songs and dances and a cast that was "enormously talented." Producers Melvyn Douglas and Herman Levin's "bright, gingery and good-looking" show also offered sketches that were "far better" than those found in most topical revues, and Betty Garrett had outdone herself as a "singing comedian."

William Hawkins in the *New York World-Telegram* said *Call Me Mister* was the "rare" revue that didn't have one bad number, and while it was difficult to single out one special element in the evening, he guessed "nothing in the show is more lionized by the audience than Betty Garrett's farewell to Latin dancing." Lewis Nichols in the *New York Times* said the revue was "one of the cheerful musicals of the year," and he liked the "fresh and engaging" cast. He noted that some of the sketches "quietly" dug themselves into "foxholes" from which they couldn't emerge, and the lyric of "The Face on the Dime" failed to be as "stirring" as Rome's earlier "F.D.R. Jones" (from *Sing Out the News*; 1938). But even so, the revue was "engaging" and a "credit" to the Selective Service.

When Jules Munshin left the revue, his monologue was replaced by the sketch "America's Square Table on the Air."

The original cast recording was issued by Decca (LP # DL-7005). The CD was issued by Decca Broadway (# B0000831-02), which also includes the cast recordings of **This Is the Army** and **Winged Victory**); Jasmine Records (CD # JASCD-115) offers the pairing of the cast albums of *Call Me Mister* and **This Is the Army**); and Sepia Records (CD # 1005) includes the cast albums of *Call Me Mister*, **This Is the Army**, and **Texas, Li'l Darlin'**.

A 1951 film version was released by Twentieth Century-Fox; directed by Lloyd Bacon and scripted by Albert E. Lewin and Burt Styler, the film's cast included Betty Grable, Dan Dailey, Danny Thomas, Dale Robertson, Benay Venuta, Bobby Short, Frank Fontaine, Harry Von Zell, Richard Boone, Jeffrey Hunter, and the Dunhill Dance Trio. Set during the Korean War, the plot revolved around a show business couple who have separated because of his romantic affairs; now in the Army, he goes AWOL in order to try and reconcile with his wife, who is with the USO. Three songs were retained from the stage version ("Call Me Mister," "Military Life," and "Going Home Train," the latter sung by Bobby Short); songs added for the film were "Japanese Girl Like American Boy," "Love Is Back in Business," and "I Just Can't Do Enough for You, Baby" (lyrics by Sammy Fain, music by Mack Gordon); "Lament to the Pots and Pans" (lyric and music by Jerry Seelen and Earl K. Brent); and "I'm Gonna Love That Guy" (lyric and music by Frances Ash). The film's ads quoted Jack Benny as saying "I don't expect to see its equal again—not if I live to be 40!" The DVD was released by Twentieth Century-Fox Cinema Archives.

Like Nanette Fabray, Betty Garrett had popped up during the early years of the decade in various revues and had created a featured role in a Cole Porter musical, and like Fabray it wasn't until the middle of the decade that she came into her own. *Call Me Mister* was a smash hit, and her show-stopping "South America, Take It Away" became one of the era's most popular songs. Garrett had first appeared in New York in the revues **Of 'V' We Sing** and **Let Freedom Ring**, and from there had featured roles in Cole Porter's **Something for the Boys** and Vernon Duke's **Jackpot**. She later had a leading role in Ole Olson and Chic Johnson's revue **Laffing Room Only**, and then came *Call Me Mister*. Her next original Broadway musical role didn't occur until 1960 when she starred in *Beg, Borrow or Steal* with her husband Larry Parks. Prior to that, she and Parks had briefly replaced Judy Holliday and Sydney Chaplin in *Bells Are Ringing* (1956), and in later years Garrett appeared in *Meet Me in St. Louis* (1989) and the 2001 revival of *Follies* where she memorably sang a refreshingly understated "Broadway Baby" to the accompaniment of an equally understated shimmy. Among her other Broadway productions were *Spoon River Anthology* (1963), a reading of poems by Edgar Lee Masters that included occasional songs, and the comedies *A Girl Could Get Lucky* (1964) and *The Supporting Cast* (1981). She also appeared in films and television, including four MGM musicals from the late 1940s, *Words* *and Music* (1948), *On the Town* (1949), *Take Me Out to the Ball Game* (1949), and *Neptune's Daughter* (1949); for the latter, she was one of the quartet who introduced the Academy Award–winning song "Baby, It's Cold Outside." Among her television appearances was a recurring role on the CBS series *All in the Family*, in which she portrayed Archie Bunker's neighbor Irene Lorenzo, who seemed to exist for no other reason than to irk Archie with her unending series of dead-pan put-downs.

ANNIE GET YOUR GUN
"A New Musical"

Theatre: Imperial Theatre
Opening Date: May 16, 1946; *Closing Date*: February 12, 1949
Performances: 1,147
Book: Herbert Fields and Dorothy Fields
Lyrics and *Music*: Irving Berlin
Direction: Joshua Logan; *Producers*: Richard Rodgers and Oscar Hammerstein II; *Choreography*: Helen Tamiris; *Scenery* and *Lighting*: Jo Mielziner; *Costumes*: Lucinda Ballard; *Musical Direction*: Jay S. Blackton
Cast: Clifford Sales (Little Boy), Mary Ellen Glass (Little Girl), Marty May (Charlie Davenport), Daniel Nagrin (Iron Tail, Wild Horse), Walter John (Yellow Foot, Pawnee's Messenger), Cliff Dunstan (Mac), Rob Taylor (Cowboy, John, Mr. Clay), Bernard Griffin (Cowboy, Dr. Percy Ferguson), Jack Pierce (Cowboy), Mary Grey (Cowgirl, Girl in White), Franca Baldwin (Cowgirl), Art Barnett (Foster Wilson), Beau Tilden (Coolie), Lea Penman (Dolly Tate), Betty Anne Nyman (Winnie Tate), Kenny Bowers (Tommy Keeler), Ray Middleton (Frank Butler), Katrina Van Oss (Girl with Bouquet), Ethel Merman (Annie Oakley), Nancy Jean Raab (Minnie), Camilla De Witt (Jessie), Marlene Cameron (Nellie), Bobby Hookey (Little Jake), Don Liberto (Harry, Mr. Schuyler Adams), Ellen Hanley (Mary), William O'Neal (Colonel William F. Cody aka Buffalo Bill), Alma Ross (Mrs. Little Horse), Elizabeth Malone (Mrs. Black Tooth), Nellie Ranson (Mrs. Yellow Foot), John Garth III (Trainman, Major Domo), Leon Bibb (Waiter, Second Waiter), Clyde Turner (Porter, First Waiter), Lubov Roudenko (Riding Mistress), George Lipton (Major Gordon Lillie aka Pawnee Bill), Harry Bellaver (Chief Sitting Bull), Mary Woodley (Mabel), Ostrid Lind (Louise), Dorothy Richards (Nancy, Mrs. Schuyler Adams), Earl Sauvain (Andy Turner), Victor Clarke (Clyde Smith), Robert Dixon (Freddie), Marietta Vore (Mrs. Percy Ferguson), Ruth Vrana (Debutante), Art Barnett (Mr. Ernest Henderson), Truly Barbara (Mrs. Ernest Henderson), Marjorie Crossland (Sylvia Potter-Porter), Fred Rivett (Mr. Lockwood), Christina Lind (Girl in Pink); Singing Girls: Mary Woodley, Christina Lind, Dorothy Richards, Ruth Vrana, Ostrid Lind, Ellen Hanley, Katrina Van Oss, Truly Barbara, Marietta Vore, Ruth Strickland; Singing Boys: Marvin Goodis, Victor Clarke, Jack Byron, Rob Taylor, Vincent Henry, Robert Dixon, Earl Sauvain, Don Liberto, Bernard Griffin, Fred Rivitt; Dancing Girls: Cyprienne Gabelman, Harriet Reeder, Evelyn Giles, Mary Grey, Franca Baldwin, Tessie Carrano, Barbara Gaye, Madeleine Detry; Dancing Boys: Duncan Noble, Parker Wilson, Ken Whelan, John Begg, Michael Maule, Jack Beaber, Paddy Stone, Jack Pierce
The musical was presented in two acts.
The action takes place during the mid-1880s in various locales throughout the United States, including Cincinnati, Ohio, Minneapolis, Minnesota, and New York City.

Musical Numbers

Act One: "Colonel Buffalo Bill" (Marty May, Ensemble); "I'm a Bad, Bad Man" (Ray Middleton, Girls; danced by Duncan Noble, Paddy Stone, Parker Wilson, Ensemble); "Doin' What Comes Naturally" (Ethel Merman, Nancy Jean Raab, Camilla De Witt, Marlene Cameron, Bobby Hookey, Art Barnett); "The Girl That I Marry" (Ray Middleton); "You Can't Get a Man with a Gun" (Ethel Merman); "(There's No Business Like) Show Business" (William O'Neal, Marty May, Ray Middleton, Ethel Merman); "They Say It's Wonderful" (Ethel Merman); "Moonshine Lullaby" (Ethel Merman, Trio); "I'll Share It All with You" (tap dance devised by Harry King) (Betty Anne Nyman, Kenny Bowers); "Ballyhoo" (dance) (Lubov Roudenko, Show People); "(There's No Business Like) Show Business" (reprise) (Ethel Merman); "My Defenses Are Down"

(Ray Middleton, Boys); "Wild Horse Ceremonial Dance" (Daniel Nagrin, Braves, Maidens); "I'm an Indian, Too" (Ethel Merman); "Adoption Dance" (Ethel Merman, Daniel Nagrin, Braves)

Act Two: "(I Got) Lost in His Arms" (Ethel Merman); "Who Do You Love, I Hope?" (Betty Anne Nyman, Kenny Bowers; danced by Betty Anne Nyman, Kenny Bowers, Ensemble); "(I Got the) Sun in the Morning" (Ethel Merman, Ensemble; danced by Lubov Roudenko, Daniel Nagrin, Show People); "They Say It's Wonderful" (reprise) (Ethel Merman, Ray Middleton); "The Girl That I Marry" (reprise) (Ray Middleton); "Anything You Can Do" (Ethel Merman, Ray Middleton); "(There's No Business Like) Show Business" (reprise) (Entire Company)

Irving Berlin's *Annie Get Your Gun* was his biggest hit. It became the season's longest-running musical, with a final tally of 1,147 performances, and Berlin's music box offered an incredible number of songs that became popular standards, including "They Say It's Wonderful," "The Girl That I Marry," "I Got Lost in His Arms," "I Got the Sun in the Morning," "Anything You Can Do," "You Can't Get a Man with a Gun," "Doin' What Comes Naturally," and the now evergreen salute to show business, "There's No Business Like Show Business." Ethel Merman was of course Annie Oakley, and the musical was another feather in her cap; and it was her longest-running show too.

Produced by Richard Rodgers and Oscar Hammerstein II, the musical belatedly opened on May 16, 1946, at the Imperial Theatre where it was directed by Joshua Logan, choreographed by Helen Tamiris, and sumptuously designed by Jo Mielziner and Lucinda Ballard. Dorothy Fields and Herbert Fields' slight but serviceable book dealt with the rivalry between sharp-shooters Annie Oakley and Frank Butler (Ray Middleton) and their on-again, off-again romance. By the final curtain they are reconciled and Annie has learned that you can't get a man with a gun. The musical's world premiere took place on March 28, 1946, at the Shubert Theatre in New Haven, and then was scheduled to play in Boston at the Shubert Theatre for three weeks beginning on April 2 before opening in New York. But the Imperial Theatre's electrical tower and roof area suddenly had to undergo emergency repair work, and so the musical added a last-minute stop at the Shubert Theatre in Philadelphia for two weeks beginning on April 30 before moving on to Broadway.

Most of the critics raved; they enjoyed the lighthearted, entertaining, and unpretentious evening, and Ethel Merman received the best notices of her career (so far; *Gypsy* was still thirteen years away). And while many of the reviewers praised Irving Berlin's greatest score, a few were strangely deaf to its classic songs. The now-iconic show business anthem "There's No Business Like Show Business" was mentioned in passing by some of the critics, but except for Robert Garland in the *New York Journal-American* (who said it "stems straight from Broadway's bathetic heart"), the rest didn't seem to realize that Berlin, who had written classic Christmas ("White Christmas"), Easter ("Easter Parade"), and patriotic ("God Bless America") songs had now created the ultimate Broadway salute to show business and its performers.

Lewis Nichols in the *New York Times* said the evening was a "good professional" one with a book "which doesn't get anywhere in particular." But Merman was "heaven's gift" to musical comedy, and if the show sometimes had "abrupt pauses" that was because Merman had to occasionally change costumes. As for Berlin's score, it was "good" and "steady" but offered nothing in the class of "Easter Parade" and "White Christmas." Louis Kronenberger in *PM* found the musical "in many ways routine," and except for Merman the "formula" show was "competent enough of its kind." Berlin's score was "musically not exciting," and of its "real" songs only "one or two are tuneful." And Ward Morehouse in the *New York Sun* said Berlin's score wasn't "notable"; he also found the book "flimsy" and "listless," and said it was lucky Merman was in her "best form" since *Anything Goes* in 1934 and thus she came to the aid of the "sagging" book.

But Howard Barnes in the *New York Herald Tribune* stated Berlin had created a "fascinating web of wit and melody" and the Fields' book was "lively and funny." Further, Mielziner's décor was in "superb taste" and Ballard's costumes dressed the company "to the teeth." The show was "fresh as a daisy" and "certain to become a hardy Broadway perennial." John Chapman in the *New York Daily News* said Merman sang with the "zing, the punch and the instinct" of great showmanship, and here she was also proving herself a better comedienne than ever before. The entertainment wasn't "the greatest show in the world," but it was a "good, standard, lavish big musical." Vernon Rice in the *New York Post* said the musical (which was "on every count an excellent" one) would "probably run for a lifetime." Merman was "the supreme artist" of musical comedy, and Berlin had "outdone himself this time" because all the songs were "hits."

William Hawkins in the *New York World-Telegram* said that for "verve and buoyancy, unslackening, there had seldom" been a show like *Annie Get Your Gun*, and although everyone connected with it deserved praise, the evening was decidedly "Ethel's party." Berlin's music was "lilting and effective" and his lyrics were "delightfully comical." Garland said his review was a "rave" because the new show was "far and away the best musical in town," and not since *Oklahoma!* had he experienced "so high a musical time on Broadway." Merman was now a performer who was an actress, comedienne, and singer "rolled quite magically into one," and Berlin's music was "rich" and "melodious" with "brilliant" lyrics.

Songs written but not used in the musical were "Take It in Your Stride (Whatever the Fates Decide)" (intended for Annie); "Partners" (for Annie and Frank); and "Something Bad's Gonna Happen ('Cause I Feel So Good)" (probably for Annie). Part of the lyric for the latter song was revised and used in "You're Just in Love" (*Call Me Madam*, 1950).

The musical has been revived in New York three times. On February 18, 1958, the New York City Center Light Opera Company production played for a limited engagement of sixteen performances; the cast included Betty Jane Watson (Annie), David Atkinson (Frank), Jack Whiting (Charlie), Margaret Hamilton (Dolly Tate), Edward Villella (Yellow Foot), Richard France (Tommy), Rain Winslow (Winnie), and, reprising his original role of Chief Sitting Bull, Harry Bellaver.

The next revival was produced by the Music Theatre of Lincoln Center at the New York State Theatre on May 31, 1966, for a limited run of forty-seven performances; Ethel Merman returned in the role of Annie (and again Harry Bellaver reprised his Chief Sitting Bull), and Berlin wrote a new song for the revival, the knock-out show-stopper "An Old-Fashioned Wedding" which Annie and Frank (Bruce Yarnell) sang in counterpoint. (Berlin also wrote another new song, "Who Needs the Birds and Bees?," which was dropped during the revival's tryout.) The book for the production was revised and eliminated the Tommy-Winnie subplot as well as their songs "I'll Share It All with You" and "Who Do You Love, I Hope?" The revival briefly toured, and then returned to New York on September 21 at the Broadway Theatre for a limited run of seventy-seven performances.

A popular but misguided revival with a revised book by Peter Stone opened on March 4, 1999, at the Marquis Theatre for a surprising run of 1,046 performances. Tom Wopat made a fine Frank, but Bernadette Peters was a disappointing Annie and the production bowed to political correctness. The revival included "An Old-Fashioned Wedding," and retained the Tommy-Winnie subplot and their two songs. But "I'm an Indian, Too" was banished from the show. During the run, Susan Lucci and Cheryl Ladd portrayed Annie, and when Reba McEntire took over the role, she received rave reviews. There was brief talk of a television adaptation of the musical with McEntire in the lead, but nothing came of it.

There were, however, two television versions of the show. The first was telecast by NBC on November 27, 1957, with Mary Martin and John Raitt (Martin had toured in the production during the late 1940s), and the second was shown by NBC on March 19, 1967, and was based on the Lincoln Center revival and starred Merman. Unfortunately, no tape is known to exist of the second production and it's presumed lost.

The original London production opened at the Coliseum on June 7, 1947, for a long run of 1,304 performances, which surpassed the Broadway edition. Dolores Gray received raves for her performance, and she was supported by Bill Johnson.

The lively 1950 film version was released by MGM and starred Betty Hutton (who replaced Judy Garland soon after filming began) and Howard Keel. The DVD on Warner Brothers Video (# 65438) includes four outtakes: the cut song "Let's Go West Again" (performed by Betty Hutton, the number had been written by Berlin especially for the film); two numbers with Judy Garland ("Doin' What Comes Naturally" and "I'm an Indian, Too"); and one song ("Colonel Buffalo Bill") for Frank Morgan and Geraldine Wall. Morgan died soon after production began, and was replaced by Louis Calhern. Besides the firing of Judy Garland and the death of Frank Morgan, Howard Keel broke his leg soon after filming began. But for all the turmoil surrounding the production (which Hutton described as the unhappiest experience of her career), the film is colorful and entertaining.

The script was published in paperback twice, first by Emile Littler/Chappell & Co. (London) in 1952, and then in 1967 by the Irving Berlin Music Corporation (the latter script reflects the revised version of the musical that opened in 1966). As of this writing, the script of the original production is scheduled to be published in paperback by Applause Books in 2015. The lyrics of all the score's songs are included in *The Complete Lyrics of Irving Berlin*.

There are numerous recordings of the score, but Decca's original cast album is still the best (LP # DL-8001; issued on CD by Decca Broadway # 012-159-243-2 with various bonus tracks). The Lincoln Center revival was recorded by RCA Victor (LP # LOC/LSO-1124) and includes the terrific "An Old-Fashioned Wedding"; the CD (RCA Victor #1124-2-RC) includes a previously unreleased and extended version of "An Old-Fashioned Wedding." The most complete recording of the score was released by EMI (CD # CDC-7-54206-2); conducted by John McGlinn and with Kim Criswell and Thomas Hampson in the leading roles, the album offers "I'll Share It All with You," "Who Do You Love, I Hope?," "An Old-Fashioned Wedding," and all the dance music (including "Ballyhoo," "Wild Horse Ceremonial Dance," and "Adoption Dance"). The unused song "Take It in Your Stride" is included in the collection *Lost in Boston* (Varese Sarabande CD # VSD-5475).

AROUND THE WORLD IN EIGHTY DAYS
"A Musical Extravaganza"

Theatre: Adelphi Theatre
Opening Date: May 31, 1946; *Closing Date*: August 3, 1946
Performances: 75
Book: Orson Welles
Lyrics and *Music*: Cole Porter
Based on Jules Verne's 1873 novel *Around the World in Eighty Days*.
Direction: Orson Welles; *Producer*: A Mercury Theatre Production; *Choreography*: Nelson Barclift; *Scenery*: Robert Davison; *Costumes*: Alvin Colt; *Lighting*: Peggy Clark; *Musical Direction*: Harry Levant
Cast: Brainerd Duffield (A Bank Robber, Benjamin Cruett-Spew, A Second Arab Spy, Oka Saka, Sol), Guy Spaull (A Police Inspector, Ralph Runcible, Maurice Goodpile), *Orson Welles* (Dick Fix), Nathan Baker (London Bobby, A Sinister Chinese, Father Clown), Jack Pitchon (London Bobby, Roustabout), Myron Speth (London Bobby, A Dancing Fella, Assistant), Gordon West (London Bobby, Fireman), Genevieve Sauris (A Lady), Arthur Margetson (Phileas Fogg), Stefan Schnabel (Avery Jevity, An Arab Spy, Mother Clown, Medicine Man), Julie Warren (Molly Muggins), Larry Laurence (aka Enzo Stuarti) (Pat Passepartout, Clown Groom), Bernard Savage (Sir Charles Mandiboy, The British Counsel), Billy Howell (Lord Upditch, A Station Attendant, A Sinister Chinese, Assistant, Sam, Medicine Man), Bruce Cartwright (A Servingman, Fireman, Mexican Dancer), Gregory McDougall (Another Servingman, Assistant), Dorothy Bird (Meerahlah, Mexican Dancer), Lucas Aco (A Dancing Fella, A Fakir, A Sinister Chinese, Assistant), Eddy Di Genova (Snake Charmer, Monkey Man, Bartender), Victor Savidge (Snake Charmer), Stanley Turner (Snake Charmer, Attendant), Spencer James (A Sikh), Mary Healy (Mrs. Aouda), Arthur Cohen (A High Priest, Minister Clown), Phil King (A Sinister Chinese), Jackie Cezanne (Lee Toy), Lee Morrison (A Daughter of Joy), Nancy Newton (A Daughter of Joy), The Three Kanasawa (The Foot Jugglers), Adelaide Corsi (The Rolling Globe Lady), Miss Lu (The Contortionist), Ishikawa (The Hand Balancer), Mary Broussard (Aerialist), Lee Vincent (Aerialist), Patricia Leith (Aerialist), Virginia Morris (Aerialist), Ray Goody (The Slide for Life), Tony Montell (Roustabout), Bernie Pisarski (Child Clown), Cliff Chapman (Bride Clown), Jack Cassidy (Policeman Clown), Alan Lowell (Kimona Man, Jail Guard), Daniel DePaolo (Dragon), Victoria Cordova (Lola), James Aco (Jim), Spencer James (Jake), George Spelvin (Medicine Man); Singing Gentlemen: Kenneth Bonjukian, Jack Cassidy, Arthur Cohen, Eddy Di Genova, Allan Lowell, Tony Montell, Daniel DePaolo, Jack Pitchon, Victor Savidge, Stanley Turner; Dancing Gentlemen: Lucas Aco, Nathan Baker, Bruce Cartwright, Billy Howell, Phil King, Gregory McDougall, Myron Speth, Gordon West; Singing Ladies: Florence Gault, Natalie Greene, Arline Hanna, Marion Kohler, Rose Marie Pantane, Genevieve Sauris, Gina Siena, Drucilla Strain; Dancing Ladies: Mary Broussard, Jackie Cezanne, Elinor Gregory, Patricia Leith, Virginia Morris, Lee Morrison, Nancy Newton, Miriam Pandor, Virginia Sands, Lee Vincent
The musical was presented in two acts.
The action takes place around the world during 1873.

Musical Numbers

Act One: "Look What I Found" (Julie Warren, Larry Laurence, Singers); "There He Goes, Mister Phileas Fogg" (Arthur Margetson, Larry Laurence); "There He Goes, Mister Phileas Fogg" (reprise) (Arthur Margetson, Larry Laurence, Dancers, Singers); "Meerahlah" (Singing Boys); "Dance" (Dorothy Bird, Dancers); "Suttee

Procession" (Mary Healy, Dancers, Singers); "Dance" (Dancers); "Sea Chanty" (Singing Boys); "Should I Tell You I Love You?" (Mary Healy); "Pipe-Dreaming" (Larry Laurence, Singing Chorus); Oka Saka Circus (Circus Performers)

Act Two: "Dance" (Dorothy Bird, Bruce Cartwright, Jackie Cezanne, Dancers); "If You Smile at Me" (Victoria Cordova); "Pipe-Dreaming" (reprise) (Larry Laurence); "If You Smile at Me" (reprise) (Julie Warren); "Wherever They Fly the Flag of Old England" (Arthur Margetson, Singing Girls); "The Marine's Hymn" (traditional) (Mary Healy, Singing Boys); "Should I Tell You I Love You?" (reprise) (Mary Healy); Finale (Entire Company)

"Wellesapoppin'" was how *Variety* summed up Orson Welles's stage adaptation of Jules Verne's novel *Around the World in Eighty Days*, and it was a perfect description. The musical was a huge free-for-all, and boasted one of the largest casts of the era. Welles pulled out every stop in his bag of tricks to bring the fanciful novel to the musical stage, and so frames, screens, curtains, and even an interior stage (which had been constructed on the main stage) were used to tell the story. And occasionally the action moved into the auditorium in Olsen and Johnson fashion where U.S. Marine soldiers came marching down the aisle to the tune of "The Marine Hymn" and where Welles performed magic tricks (he even snatched a duck out of the vest pocket of a hapless ticket holder, and Howard Barnes in the *New York Herald Tribune* reported that both duck and patron were not amused).

But that wasn't all. There was a huge papier-mâché elephant and an enormous stuffed flying eagle that carried a cast member aloft and offstage. There was a miniature train crossing a bridge, which depicted a sequence from one of the legs of Phileas Fogg's journey, and as the train reached the mainland, the miniature bridge collapsed. There were even silent movies (filmed by Welles especially for the musical) which depicted Fogg's travels, not to mention a spoof of old-time melodramas, clowns, jugglers, contortionists, hand balancers, acrobats, tightrope walkers, and more magic tricks (in which ducks, geese, and chickens suddenly materialized and then just as quickly disappeared). There were exploding firearms, snake charmers, a fakir, an Indian Princess, sinister Chinese, Wild West Indians, and a Japanese circus (the circus closed the first act).

Along with Phileas, the audience traveled from London to Arabia and Egypt and the Suez Canal, and on to India, the Himalayas, the China Seas, Hong Kong, Japan, Northern Mexico, San Francisco, the Rocky Mountains, and then back to London. And along the way there were visits to opium dens, pagodas, canals, forests, the high seas, lakes, swamps, marshes, mountains, forests, and bawdy houses. And if all these weren't enough, there were songs by Cole Porter. A short score to be sure (just eight songs, along with dance and background music), but one with some pleasant numbers, such as the sinuous "Pipe-Dreaming," the joyously exultant "Look What I Found," and the critics' favorite, the lovely, understated ballad "Should I Tell You I Love You?" By and large, the reviewers were dismissive of Porter's score, but it's notable that of the eight songs, six were singled out by the critics as outstanding.

The critics were impressed with the vastness of it all, but in the long run the musical's overpowering effects also revealed that for all the sound and fury there wasn't really much going on. Welles had indulged himself, and his ego had overpowered good old-fashioned story-telling. With cool reviews, there wasn't any way the musical could bring in the crowds and meet its enormous weekly payroll (there were sixty cast members, and reportedly fifty-five stagehands), let alone pay back its investment of approximately $320,000. As a result, the musical collapsed after two months and was never heard from again. (But since the presumed lost silent footage Welles created for a 1938 stage adaptation of *Too Much Johnson* has recently surfaced, maybe someday the *Around the World* footage will show up, too.)

The familiar story centered on Phileas Fogg (Arthur Margetson), who makes a bet that he can travel around the world in eighty days. So he and his manservant Pat Passepartout (Larry Laurence) take off on their great adventure. But they're not quite alone in their travels because they're secretly tailed by Scotland Yard Detective-Inspector Dick Fix (Orson Welles) who mistakenly believes Fogg is a bank robber.

Barnes found the evening more "exhibitionistic" than "entertaining," and suggested that what was a "field day" for Welles wasn't much of one for the audience. Louis Kronenberger in *PM* said Welles had concentrated too much on "showmanship" and less on "show"; as a result, the evening "didn't make the grade" and Welles's "cutting up" became "tiresome." He noted that "it would be one hell of an entertainment if only it were more entertaining." Lewis Nichols in the *New York Times* said the musical was only "fitfully amusing." It offered the promise of a "hilarious" evening but failed because it lacked "unity" and there were "too many styles fighting among themselves."

William Hawkins in the *New York World-Telegram* felt the musical came across like a British Christmas pantomime; but it lacked humor and was overwhelmed by "extraneous vaudeville." He mentioned that Alvin Colt's costumes were sometimes designed awkwardly "to the point of being ugly, and the colors have a way of disliking each other's company." Robert Garland in the *New York Journal-American* said the "hodge-podge" on the Adelphi stage signified "nothing in particular"; Welles was good at magic tricks and making animals disappear, but unfortunately he had made the plot disappear and without a plot there was no show.

Vernon Rice in the *New York Post* reported that the evening was "mammoth," "gigantic," "lavish" . . . and "dull." The musical was "always on the move," but went nowhere; and although Welles had presented an "overpowering and overwhelming colossus," it turned on itself and thus the performers and the production were "so weighed down by the show's own over-sized proportions that nothing seems to register."

But John Chapman in the *New York Daily News* found the show "wonderful, exciting and funny" and said it was the "most thorough and individual example of showmanship" since Billy Rose had presented *Jumbo* eleven years earlier. And while Herrick Brown in the *New York Sun* admitted there were occasional "lapses" during the evening, he said the "theatrical high-jinks" were enough to carry the musical.

As for Porter's score, six of the eight reviewers singled out "Should I Tell You I Love You?" and Hawkins predicted it would soon be hummed on the streets. He also praised Victoria Cordova's "haunting" "If You Smile at Me"; Brown liked the "lively foot-tapper" "Look What I Found" (this joyously exultant number is perhaps the score's best song) and noted "There He Goes, Mister Phileas Fogg" was in both lyric and melody one of the musical's "assets" (and Hawkins said it boasted an "excellent" lyric). As for Nichols, he considered "Should I Tell You I Love You?" and "Pipe-Dreaming" the best of the show's songs.

Brown liked the "delightful" "Wherever They Fly the Flag of Old England," which Barnes said was "magnificent." It was sung in counterpoint with "The Marine Hymn," as British soldiers marched down one side of the Adelphi's aisle while the U.S. Marines came down the other.

Although Garland found Porter's contributions "friendly and familiar," Rice felt the music "didn't sound like top-drawer Porter" and Barnes said the songs were "not in the finest Porter tradition." On the other hand, Brown noted that all the stage business tended to "submerge" the score, and Rice stated that because "so many things" were always happening on the stage "one scarcely had time to listen" to Porter's music.

During the tryout, Fix was performed by Alan Webb, who was succeeded by Welles; and the song "Missus Aouda" was cut. Dropped in preproduction were "Slave Auction" and "Snagtooth Gertie."

A number of songs from the musical have been recorded, including four by cast member Larry Laurence (who later changed his name to Enzo Stuarti): "Look What I Found," "Should I Tell You I Love You?," "Pipe-Dreaming," and "If You Smile at Me"; these are included in the collection *Cole Porter Volume 4* (Pearl Records CD # GEM-0195). The collection *Cole Porter Revisited Volume V* (Painted Smiles CD # PSCD-122) includes "Should I Tell You I Love You?" and "Look What I Found." The used and unused lyrics are included in *The Complete Lyrics of Cole Porter*.

Early on, Welles and Michael Todd were to have coproduced the musical, but Todd pulled out. However, after the musical collapsed, Todd bought the rights from Welles and ten years later produced his own (non-musical) film version of the story, and it won five Oscars, including Best Picture. The musical's theme song "Around the World" (lyric by Harold Adamson, music by Victor Young) was enormously popular, and Young won a posthumous Oscar for Best Music (Scoring of a Dramatic or Comedy Picture).

There have been other musical adaptations of Verne's novel, including one that opened at Jones Beach Marine Theatre on June 22, 1963, for seventy-three performances; the book was by Sig Herzig, the lyrics by Harold Adamson, and the music by Sammy Fain (the world premiere of the musical had taken place at the Municipal Opera in St. Louis during the previous year).

The producer for the Jones Beach production was Guy Lombardo, who was credited as presenting "Michael Todd's *Around the World in Eighty Days*." The cast included Fritz Weaver (Fogg), Robert Clary (Passepartout), and Elaine Malbin (Aouda). While the program credited Fain with the music, a special note indicated some of the music was by Victor Young; later productions credited both Fain and Young with the score. The film's popular song "Around the World" was heard during the first act finale (performed by the ensemble), and then later in a second act reprise by Weaver. There was no cast recording, but a studio cast album (Everest Records LP # SDBR-1020) was released a few years prior to the stage production and included songs later heard in the stage version. The musical returned to Jones Beach in 1964 for an additional seventy performances (David Atkinson was Fogg), and eventually the musical played in summer stock with such performers as José Ferrer and Cyril Ritchard portraying Fogg. And of course earlier in the season *Nellie Bly* (which had also played at the Adelphi) had dealt with an around-the-world theme inspired by the fictitious journey of Phileas Fogg.

LOVE IN THE SNOW
"A New Musical Romance"

Theatres and *Performance Dates*: The musical opened at the Bushnell Memorial Theatre in Hartford, Connecticut, on March 15, 1946; opened on March 19 at the Shubert Theatre, Boston, Massachusetts, for a two-week engagement; and then played at the Forrest Theatre, Philadelphia, Pennsylvania, where it permanently closed on April 6, 1946.

Book and *Lyrics*: Rowland Leigh
Music: Ralph Benatzky
Direction: John Baird; *Producers*: The Messrs. Shubert; *Choreography*: Myra Kinch; *Scenery*: Lawrence Goldwasser; *Costumes*: Jac-Lewis; *Lighting*: Uncredited; *Musical Direction*: Pierre De Reeder
Cast: Jay Rogers (Kurt Remsen), Betty Luster (Ingrid Remsen), Maria Allyn (Ballerina), Normand Anthony (Dancer), Robert Douglas (Hendrick Van Rhyn), Nancy Donovan (Princess Martha), Ellen Love (Mrs. Siebert), Arthur Mack (Frank), Charlotte Lansing (Miss Swanstrom), Lola Kendrick (Griselda), Robert Pitkin (Leif Hansen), Nan Shanon (Cordelia Hansen), Raymond Bailey (Crown Prince Paul), Le Roi Operti (Count Remsen), Stephen Douglas Fitch (Ski Instructor), Rochelle Carlay (Collette Palerme), Peter Preses (Caretaker), Virginia Stanton (Maid), Allegra Varron (Rosella Picelli), Paul Kaye (The Duke of Parthay), Charles Dubin (The Court Photographer), Lee Lindsey (Ballet Master); The Corps de Ballet: Pat Clancy, Rusha Hojson, Rhoda Johannson, Althea Kedrick, Virginia Lee, Rosalie Lynn, Elaine Meredith, Virginia Stanton, Louise Lewis; Singers: Ella Belkin, Virginia Buch, James Cosenza, Kathryn Daye, Stephen Douglas Fitch, Gerta Koblitz, Mary Lundon, Pierre de Reeder Jr., Sue Yager; Show Girls: Baranova, Lola Kendrick, Angela Lapart, Marion Neumark; Boys: Bernard Carson, Lee Lindsey, Roger Stark, Richard Rapp, Rudy Tone, Norval Tormson
The musical was presented in three acts.
The action takes place in 1872 in the mythical Scandinavian country of Olafland.

Musical Numbers

Act One: "Half-Way Chalet" (Ensemble); "When We're Together" (Betty Luster, Jay Rogers); Dance Specialty (Maria Allyn, Normand Anthony); "Love in the Snow" (Nancy Donovan, Robert Douglas); Interlude (Ensemble); "First Love" (Nancy Donovan); "Once in a Lifetime" (Nancy Donovan, Robert Douglas); "Make Up Your Mind" (Betty Luster, Jay Rogers, Ensemble); "Twilight" (Stephen Fitch, Robert Douglas); "First Love" (reprise) (Nancy Donovan); "Winter Ballet" (Corps de Ballet); "Love in the Snow" (reprise) (Nancy Donovan, Robert Douglas)
Act Two: "Party Dress" (Charlotte Lansing, Betty Luster, Maids); "Farewell Letter" (Nancy Donovan); *Queen of Sheba* (Excerpt) (Allegra Varron); "Savoire Faire" (Rochelle Carlay); "Serenade" (Robert Douglas); "Court Ballet" (Corps de Ballet); Finale: "Serenade" (reprise) (Robert Douglas, Entire Company)
Act Three: "Portrait for Posterity" (Charles Dubin, Betty Luster, Jay Rogers, Maids); Dance Specialty (Maria Allyn, Normand Anthony); *La Traviata* (Excerpt) (Rochelle Carlay, Allegra Varron); "Collette" (Rochelle Carlay); "Ballet Rehearsal" (Lee Lindsey, Corps de Ballet); Dance Specialty (Maria Allyn, Normand Anthony); "Farewell Letter" (reprise) (Robert Douglas); Finale (Entire Company)

No doubt the Shuberts mounted *Love in the Snow* in the hope of adding another stalwart operetta to their repertoire of Broadway and touring productions. But the new work closed permanently in Philadelphia just three weeks into its pre-Broadway tryout.

Love in the Snow utilized the old-hat operetta formula in which a member of royalty falls in love with a commoner. Clearly, the rules of operetta don't allow for any such nonsense, and had the characters seen *The Student Prince* they could have saved themselves a lot of heartache. In this case, Princess Martha (Nancy Donovan) falls in love with opera singer Hendrick Van Rhyn (Robert Douglas), but her father the king has arranged for her marriage to the Duke of Parthay (Paul Kaye). It turns out the Duke ain't so bad, and so Martha agrees to marry One of Her Own and leaves poor Henrick out in the snow.

Variety criticized the tired plot, but praised a "breathtaking" scene set in a winter woodland; and although the music was "tuneful" ("but not outstanding"), the operetta wasn't of Broadway caliber. *Billboard* liked the "clever" touches in the script as well as the "good" score (with a "fair share of remembered tunes"); but the reviewer didn't care for the "undistinguished" dances and the somewhat bizarre skiing outfits worn by some of the characters.

The score included operatic sequences from Karl Goldmark's *Queen of Sheba* and Giuseppe Verdi's *La Traviata* (the former's interpolation is quite a mystery because *Love in the Snow* took place in 1872, and *Sheba*'s world premiere didn't occur until 1875).

Soon after the operetta opened in Hartford, the dancers Maria Allyn and Normand Anthony joined the company and performed three dance specialties throughout the evening. For part of the tryout, Eleanor McCabe was credited for choreography.

THE PASSING SHOW
"THE SENSATIONAL NEW REVUE" / "THE NEW MUSICAL COMEDY REVUE"

Theatres and *Performance Dates*: The revue opened on November 9, 1945, at Bushnell Memorial, Hartford, Connecticut; among other venues, it played at the National Theatre, Washington, D.C., on November 12; at the Cass Theatre, Detroit, Michigan, on December 30; and at the Erlanger Theatre, Chicago, Illinois, where it opened on January 7, 1946, and permanently closed on February 16.

Sketches: Uncredited

Lyrics and *Music*: Ross Thomas, Will Morrissey, Irving Actman, Eugene Burton, and Dana Slawson

Direction: Russell Mack; *Producer*: The Messrs. Shubert; *Choreography*: dances by Carl Randall and ballets by Mme. Kamarova; *Scenery*: Watson Barratt; *Costumes*: Stage Costumes, Inc., and Mme. Veronica; *Lighting*: Uncredited; *Musical Direction*: Alfred Evans

Cast: *Willie Howard, Sue Ryan, Bobby Morris, Richard* (Dick) *Buckley, Bob Russell,* (John) *Masters and* (Rowe) *Rollins, Betty Luster, Mimi Kellerman, Ruth Davis, Ruth Clayton, Gil Johnson, Sylvia Russell,* Diane March; Show Girls: June Dahl, Barbara Leslie, Marion Newmark, Geraldine Noonan, Judy Smith, Tahme Farrell, Barbara Leonard, Patricia Flynn, Patricia Withington, Jean Mode, Anne Benson; Dancing Girls: Patricia Birkenhead, Betty Brosh, Doris Clar, Betty Lou Carrier, Patricia Clancey, Virginia Lee, Rosalie Lynn, Elaine Meredith, Virginia Stanton, Doris Avery, Althea Kendick, Rusha Hojson; Dancing Boys: Gene Aquino, Rudy Capitolo, Wallace Gilbert, Bert Longworth, Jeffrey Long, John Lanvin, Roger Stack, Denis Smith, Rudy Tone

The revue was presented in two acts.

Musical Numbers

Act One: Introduction (Richard Buckley); "The Passing Show" (Bob Russell, Show Girls); "Bobby Socks Convention" (Gil Johnson, Diane Marsh; Old Producer: Al Klein; Rag Cutter: Gil Johnson; First Hep: Pat Birkenhead; Second Hep: Diane Marsh; Third Hep: Patricia Clancy; Fourth Chick: Virginia Stanton; Fifth Jit: Betty Lou Carrier; Star: Willie Howard; Friend: Mathew Smith; Three in One Trio: Al Klein, Al Kelly, and John Masters); "Could You Use a New Friend" (Ruth Davis, John Masters)" and "Flower Ballet" (Mimi Kellerman, Dancing Girls); "Two Cups of Coffee" (Waiter: Willie Howard; Salesman: Mathew Smith; Buyer: Al Klein); "Then There's Romance" (Sue Ryan, Bobby Morris); "You Are the Jury" (Horace: Mathew Smith; Violet: Ruth Clayton; Guy: Richard Buckley); "You're My Kind of Ugly" (John Masters, Rowena Rollins); "Doughnuts" (Counter Girl: Sue Ryan; Customer: Richard Buckley; Wife: Ruth Clayton); "Chinese Ballet" (Narrator: Bobby Morris; Show Girls, Diana Marsh, Gil Johnson, Roger Stark, Dancing Boys and Girls); "Lonely Hearts" (Policeman: Bob Russell; "Eugenic" Klein: Willie Howard; Doctor: Mathew Smith; Sergeant: Al Kelly; Miss Geit: Rowena Rollins); "The Avenue of the Americas" (Bob Russell, Ensemble); "Transformer" (Scientist: John Masters; Nurse: Sue Ryan; Dummy: Bobby Morris; First Patient: Al Kelly; Second Patient: Al Klein; Third Patient: Mimi Kellerman); "Pantomimic Illusion" (Richard Buckley); "Living in a Brand New Day" (Bob Russell, Company)

Act Two: Opening: "Crazy Rhapsody" (Dancing Boys and Girls, Gil Johnson, Diana Marsh, Betty Luster); "How Long Will It Be?" (Bob Russell, Ruth Davis); "Back in the Kitchen Again" (Sue Ryan); "Psychoanalyst" (Dr. Zoopf: Willie Howard; Secretary: Betty Luster; Subject: Rowena Rollins); "A Song Is Born" (Bob Russell, Betty Luster); "Kid's First Fight" (Candy Butcher: Bobby Morris; Kid McCoy: Al Kelly; Trainer and Manager: Sue Ryan: Fight Promoter: Bob Russell; Referee: Mathew Smith; Killer Popo: Fred Canania; Second: Al Klein); "It Seems Like Yesterday" (Elizabeth Wainwright: Ruth Clayton; Senator: Bob Russell); "Come on Over and Dance" (John Masters and Rowena Rollins); "His First Case" (Secretary: Pat Withington; Barrister: Willy Howard; Client: Bobby Morris; Interpreter: Al Kelly); "The Lady Who Sits at the Ritz" (Ruth Davis); "The Girl from *Oklahoma* Meets the Boy from *Carousel*" (Sue Ryan, Willie Howard; danced by Gil Johnson, Diane Marsh, Sylvia Russell); "Mr. Whiskers" (Uncle Sam: Mathew Smith; Lord Leslie Lease: Richard Buckley; Count Chainouir: Fred Cantania; Monsieur Beguile: Al Kelly; Tovorich Ramioff: Bob Russell; Song High Chick: Gene Aquino); "Skyhook" (Ruth Clayton; danced by Gil Johnson and Sylvia Russell); "Mister Coward" (Sue Ryan and Richard Buckley); "White Rhapsody" (Mimi Kellerman, Dancing Girls); Willie Howard; "Along the South American Coast Line" (Bob Russell, Company)

The Shuberts' *The Passing Show* played for three months on the road, but never risked Broadway. During the run, the team of Myrtill and Pacaud joined the revue and performed "Rhapsody in Diamonds" (which was probably a revised version of "White Rhapsody"). Early in the tour's run the song "Living in a Brand New Day" was deleted. *Variety* reported the evening showed "insufficient preparation," and John Maynard in the *Washington Times Herald* said he hadn't seen "a more frightful violation of taste in years." Claudia Cassidy in *Best Plays* pronounced the revue "mournful." The program for the National Theatre run in Washington, D.C., gave the revue's title as *The Passing Show*, but for the souvenir program the show was titled *The Passing Show 1946*.

The revue included two numbers with interesting titles, the apparent spoof "The Girl from *Oklahoma* Meets the Boy from *Carousel*" and the presumably friendly insult-duet "You're My Kind of Ugly."

The first revue of the *Passing Show* series opened in 1912, and for almost every year through 1924 a new edition was produced on Broadway (there were eleven in all). (An 1894 revue shared the same title, but otherwise wasn't connected with the later series.) The series was never in the class of the *Ziegfeld Follies* and the *Music Box* revues, and generally speaking never enjoyed numerous hit songs or memorable sketches. But a number of notable performers appeared in the various editions, including Fred Allen, Fred and Adele Astaire, James Barton, Marie Dressler, Mary Eaton, Charlotte Greenwood, George Jessel, Marilyn Miller, Ethel Shutta, Charles Winninger, and the team of (Joe) Smith and (Charles) Dale. Willie Howard, who appeared in the current and final edition of the series, had been in five of the original editions with his brother Eugene.

SHOOTIN' STAR
"THE MUSICAL STORY OF BILLY THE KID"

Theatres and *Performance Dates*: The musical opened on April 4, 1946, at the Shubert Theatre, New Haven, Connecticut, and closed there on April 6; the production also played at the Shubert Theatre, Boston, Massachusetts, where it opened on April 23 and permanently closed on April 27, 1946.
Book: Walter Hart, Lewis Jacobs, and Halsted Welles
Lyrics: Bob Russell
Music: Sol Kaplan
Direction: Halsted Welles; *Producers*: Max Liebman and Joseph Kipness; *Choreography*: Lester Horton; *Scenery*: Frederick Fox; *Costumes*: Kenn Barr; *Lighting*: Uncredited; *Musical Direction*: Pembroke Davenport
Cast: Susan Reed (Folk Singer), Lee Fairfax (Beaver), Marco Rosales (Curley), Larry Stewart (Hank), Art Smith (Cash Claghorne), Margaret Irving (Sarilla), Richard Gibbs (Windy), Howard da Silva (Ross Dixon), Edward Andrews (Fancy), Doretta Morrow (Amy), Everett Gammon (Mr. Barry), Walter Stane (Soldier), Elliott Sullivan (Buckshot), Rex King (Chuck Wagner, Bartender), James Moore (Sheriff Brody, Raphael Ventura), Aldo Cadena (Willy), Peter Gray (Spike), Emily Earle (Lola, Maria Ventura), David Brooks (Billy), Bernice Parks (Lorraine), Sandra Grubel (Teaser), Ruth K. Hill (Paradise), Elline Walther (Velvet), Jean Olds (Saddle Jane), Nelle Fisher (Sally), Ray Harrison (Jerry), Thom Conroy (Mr. Eliot), Jock MacGraw (Mr. MacDonald), Howard Cullen (Mr. Adams), Clay Clement (Francis T. Corey), Larry Anderson (Olie), Larry Gray (Luke),

Sonia Shaw (Conchita), Nathan Kilpatrick (Pedre), Bram Nossen (General Wallace); Singers: Sandra Grubel, Eileen Ayers, Christine Scoville, Mollie Cousely, Ethel Madsen, Jean Olds, Helene Whitney, Elline Walther, Ruth K. Hill, Everett Gammon, Richard Anderson, Lawrence Gray, Larry Anderson, Jerry Bercier, Alan Leonard; Dancers: Barbara Steele, Nancy Lang, Doris Ebener, Patricia Schaffer, Nona Schurman, Billie Kirpich, Lavinia Nielsen, Edythe Uden, Jimmy Kirby, Aldo Cadena, Forrest Bonshire, Francisco Moncion, Herbert Ross, Walter Stane, David Ahdar
The musical was presented in two acts.
The action takes place in Lincoln, New Mexico, around 1880.

Musical Numbers

Act One: "Saga of Billy the Kid" (Susan Reed); "Footloose" (David Brooks, Singers); "Kid Stuff" (Ray Harrison, Nelle Fisher; danced by Ray Harrison, Nelle Fisher, The Four Kids); "Friendly Country" (David Brooks, Doretta Morrow, Singers); "Payday" (Lee Fairfax, Larry Stewart, Edward Andrews, Singers); "What Do I Have to Do?" (Bernice Parks); "Mighty Big Dream" (David Brooks, Howard da Silva); "He'll Make Some Girl a Wonderful Husband" (Doretta Morrow, Girls); "Sometime Tomorrow" (David Brooks, Doretta Morrow); "Saga of Billy the Kid" (reprise) (Susan Reed); "It's a Cold Cruel World" (Bernice Parks, Girls)
Act Two: "Music to a Dancing Bird" (David Brooks); "Chin-Che" (Marco Rosales, Singers and Dancers); Dance (Sonia Shaw, Girls); "Free" (Doretta Morrow); "Nothin'" (Art Smith, Margaret Irving); "I'm Payin' You" (David Brooks); "Saga of Billy the Kid" (reprise) (Susan Reed); "Hip-di-di-otee" (Edward Andrews, Lee Fairfax, Art Smith, Margaret Irving, Ray Harrison, Nelle Fisher); Finale (Company)

Shootin' Star told the story of Billy the Kid, and although this was the era when musicals were knee-deep in Americana, the sad saga of Billy never made it to New York. The musical seems to have "explained" Billy motivations, but whether his criminal bent was understandable or not, he was still an outlaw. Further, the musical ended on a sour note when its leading character is shot to death by his boyhood pal Ross Dixon (Howard da Silva), who is now a sheriff.

During the tryout, the songs "Payday," "He'll Make Some Girl a Wonderful Husband," and "Hip-di-di-otee" were dropped, and "Party Dance" was added for the first act. The New Haven program listed "No Ross Dixon, Lincoln Plaza Saloon" as the final number in the first act, but this looks like a printer's error (and it's not listed in the Boston program). But both programs indicate the final scene in the first act takes place at the Ross Dixon Lincoln Plaza Saloon, and so it seems that the locale of the first act's final scene was inadvertently picked up as the first act's final song number.

Had *Shootin' Star* been successful, it would have been a feather in David Brooks's cap, as he had just wound up a successful run as the leading man of **Bloomer Girl** (and with Celeste Holm had introduced two of that musical's popular songs, "Evelina" and "Right as the Rain"). *Shootin' Star* provided Brooks with a starring role as a colorful American folk legend, but in hindsight one wonders if he was right for the character. His stage persona was one of dapper sophistication, and it's somewhat difficult to envision him as Billy the Kid. At any rate, the musical closed prior to its scheduled Broadway opening, and during the following season Brooks enjoyed a successful run as the leading man in Alan Jay Lerner and Frederick Loewe's **Brigadoon**, where he introduced one of the finest of all theatre ballads, "Almost Like Being in Love."

Shootin' Star was composer Sol Kaplan's one shot at the big time; his only other New York musicals were seen Off-Broadway: *The Banker's Daughter* (1962) and *The Big Winner* (1974). The former was a reunion of sorts for Kaplan and Brooks, as the latter was the musical's director.

SONG WITHOUT WORDS
"A Light Opera"

Theatres and *Performance Dates*: The musical opened on August 20, 1945, at the Philharmonic Auditorium in Los Angeles, California, and a few weeks later permanently closed after its engagement at the Curran Theatre, San Francisco, California.
Book: Frederick Jackson

Lyrics: Forman Brown
Music: Peter Illytch Tschaikowsky (music adapted by Franz Steininger)
Based on a story by Monroe Bachman.
Direction: William Alland; *Producers*: Theodore Bachenheimer and James A. Doolittle; *Choreography*: Anton Dolin; *Scenery*: Harry Dworkin; *Costumes*: Alvin Colt; *Lighting*: Uncredited; *Choral Direction*: Hugo Strelitzer; *Musical Direction*: Franz Steininger
Cast: Allan LeClair (Artist), Leonore Ray (Sonja Korasov), Emerson Trent (Guest), John Pell (Ivan Petrovski), John Maxwell Hayes (Peter Illytch Tschaikowsky), James Newell (Lieutenant Count Steffan Gregorovitch), Della Lind (Princess Katherine Dolgoruki), Margit Bokor (Desiree Artot), Eric Blore (Charles Mannering), George Spelvin (Messenger), Jessica Faulds (First Ballet Dancer), Gretl Schubert (Second Ballet Dancer), Gloria Martin (Third Ballet Dancer), Max Willens (Aristide Le Maitre), Eugene Dorian (Count Vladimir Voronski), Peter Keys (Boris), Paul Craik (Paul), Katherina Baker (Countess Anna Ostrovitch), Michael Stevens (Court Chamberlain), Monroe Manning (Czar Alexander II), Mia Slavenska (Premiere Danseuse), Ivan Kirov (Premiere Danseur); Corps de Ballet: Esther Worthy, Joan Larkin, Beverlee Bower, Marilyn March, Lyn Stephens, Evelyn Torino, Mitzi Gerber (Gaynor), Jo Ann Merritt, Grace Carol Mann, Nina Haven, Jerry Wyss, Dorothy Schloderer, Ceia Karina, David Carlin, Nicky Nadean, Richard Thomas, Derek Low; Singers: Warren Tippie, Harry Humphrey, Richard Scott, Allan LeClair, Gloria Marlon, Etta Prince, Jessica Foulds, Gretl Schubert, Marjorie Wright, Patricia Saunders, Lorraine Gale, Soneva Wedding, Alice Bryant, Emerson Trent, Joseph Edison, Karl Bongfeldt, Paul Craik, Warren Myles
The musical was presented in two acts.
The action takes place during 1870 in St. Petersburg, Russia.

Musical Numbers

Note: Following song title and name of performer is the original source music for each number.
Act One: Opening (Leonore Ray, Ensemble) ("Mazurka" from *Swan Lake* Suite and "Humoresque"); "Come and Do the Polka" (Leonore Ray, Ivan Kirov, Ensemble) ("Mazurka" and theme from the Last Movement of the Fourth Symphony); "Love Is a Game for Soldiers" (James Newell, Chorus) (Theme from *1812 Overture* and Third Movement of Sixth Symphony); "Kiss Me Tonight" (Della Lind, James Newell) ("Andante Cantabile" from String Quartette and Waltz from *Swan Lake* Suite); "Desiree's Entrance" and "Lisa by the Window Stood" (Margit Bokor) ("Melodie" and "Chanson Triste"); "Once upon a Time" (Margit Bokor, James Newell) (Second Movement of Piano Concerto in B Flat Minor and the *Sleeping Beauty* Waltz); Finale of First Act: (1) "Entrance of Ensemble" (Leonore Ray, Ivan Kirov) ("Mazurka" and Theme from Fourth Symphony); (2) "Balalaika Serenade" (performers not credited in program) ("June," "Barcarole," and "Romance"); (3) "Trepak" (Corps de Ballet) ("Trepak"); (4) "Entrance of Royal Courtier" (performer not credited in program) (Theme from *1812 Overture*); (5) Musical Themes under Dialogue ("Flower Waltz" and Themes from Fifth Symphony and "Chanson sans paroles"); and (6) "Am I Enchanted" (Margit Bokor, Entire Ensemble) (Fifth Symphony [program noted this was "quoted exactly as in original"])
Act Two: Opening (Ivan Kirov, Girls) ("Romance"); "Three Is a Crowd" (Margit Bokor, Della Lind, James Newell) (Waltz from "Serenade for Strings" and "Waltz" from *Swan Lake* Ballet); "Night Wind" (Margit Bokor, John Maxwell Hayes) ("Chanson sans paroles"); Interlude: "Night Wind" and "Balalaika Serenade" (Orchestra); "The Song of the Troika" (Leonore Rae, Ivan Kirov, Singing Ensemble) ("Troika"); "The Spook Ballet" (Corps de Ballet) (Pizzicato Movement of Fourth Symphony); "So Strong Is My Love for You" (James Newell) (Theme from opera *Iolantha*); "Polonaise" (Ensemble) ("Polonaise" from opera *Onegin*); "Hail to Our Czar!" (Ensemble) (Theme from Last Movement of the Fifth Symphony); "Fanfare" (Orchestra) (First Movement of Fourth Symphony); "The Imperial Ballet" (Mia Slavenska, Ivan Kirov, Corps de Ballet) (Selected movements from various ballet suites); "Night Wind" (Margit Bokor) ("Chanson sans paroles"); "Love Is the Sovereign of My Heart" and "Why" (Margit Bokor, James Newell) (First Movement of Sixth Symphony); Scene between Tschaikowsky and Katherine (Underscoring of dialogue based on themes from the Sixth Symphony); "None but the Lonely Heart" (Singers) (source uncredited); "Music Divine" (Singers) (First Piano Concerto in B Flat Minor)

As also noted in the later entry for **Music in My Heart**, there were three related attempts to successfully bring Tschaikowsky's life to the musical stage, and all were huge failures: the first was *Song without Words*, which collapsed after its tryout engagements in Los Angeles and San Francisco; it was followed by **Music in My Heart**, which managed to eke out 125 performances on Broadway in 1947; and then finally *The Lady from Paris* imploded after a handful of performances during its Philadelphia tryout in 1950. The adaptations were clearly inspired by the success of **Song of Norway**, the long-running Broadway hit that was first produced on the West Coast and told the story of Edvard Grieg's life through the use of his music.

The book of *Song without Words* was by Frederick Jackson, the lyrics by Forman Brown, and the musical adaptation by Franz Steininger; for *Music in My Heart*, the respective lyrics and musical adaptation were again by Brown and Steininger, and the book was by Patsy Ruth Miller; and for *The Lady from Paris* the lyrics and musical adaptation were again by Foreman and Steininger, and the book was credited to Miller with additional dialogue by Jose Ruben. For all three productions, Steininger was the musical director, and for *The Lady from Paris* he was also the producer. For *Song without Words* and *Music in My Heart*, Alvin Colt was credited with the costume designs; the hand-out program for *The Lady from Paris* didn't list a designer, but its souvenir program gave Colt's name as the designer of record. The three leads in *Song without Words* were John Maxwell Hayes (Tschaikowsky), Margit Bokor (Desiree), and James Newell (Steffan, or Stefan); for *Music in My Heart*, the roles were played by Robert Carroll (Tschaikowsky), Martha Wright (Desiree), and Charles Fredericks (here, the character of Steffan was named Nikki); and for *The Lady from Paris* Helmut Dantine (Tschaikowsky), Martha Errolle (Desiree), and Charles Fredericks was again Nikki.

The plot centered on the fabricated story of Tschaikowsky's unrequited love for French opera singer Desiree Artot, who loves another, and, wouldn't you know it, the another is Nikki, Tschiakowsky's best friend. But all ends well: Tschaikowsky may suffer in affairs of the heart, but he rushes off to the piano to dash off an immortal masterpiece or two. The musical proclaimed that it was "based on a romantic episode" from Tschaikowsky's life, but it really centered on Desiree and Nikki. In fact, the twosome shared a total of nine songs, while Tschiakowsky got just one. And for **Music in My Heart** and *The Lady from Paris* he was given nothing to sing: his musical stage time was relegated to piano solos (it seems Robert Carroll did his own playing in the former, and for the latter Helmut Dantine simulated while Edmund Horn played). And, of course, even the title of *The Lady from Paris* seemed all wrong for a musical "based on the life" of Tschaikowsky. Incidentally, the three productions couldn't agree on how to spell the composer's name: he was Peter Illytch Tschaikowsky in *Song without Words*, Peter Ilych Tchaikovsky in **Music in My Heart**, and Peter Ilyich Tchaikovsky in *The Lady from Paris*.

A look at the programs for all three musical adaptations indicates they were deep into clichéd operetta territory, and the following reflects one or more examples from each of the three productions: There was the exotic Old World locale (of St. Petersburg); unrequited love; characters with names like Nicholai and Tatiana but who of course are called Nikki and Tanya; military officers and their orderlies, ladies in waiting for the czarina, and members of the secret police; a member or two of royalty; and stock comic characters of the S. Z. "Cuddles" Sakall variety (for *Song without Words* there was Eric Blore, for *The Lady from Paris* Sig Arno). There were songs with such titles as "Balalaika Serenade," "Love Is a Game for Soldiers," "Come and Do the Polka," "The Song of the Troika," "Song of the Sleigh Bells," "While There's a Song to Sing," "Kiss Me Tonight," "Am I Enchanted," "So Strong Is My Love for You," "Music Divine," "Three's a Crowd," "None but the Lonely Heart," "Hail to Our Czar!," and, best of all, "Love Is the Sovereign of My Heart." There was also a gypsy in the proceedings; a couple of celebrity walk-ons (Victor Herbert and Andrew Carnegie); and *The Lady from Paris* used a favorite device of the operetta format, the flashback (the prologue was set in the New York City of 1891, and the following two acts took place in the St. Petersburg of 1869). Only the merry villagers seem to be missing from the standard stew of operetta seasoning.

In *Best Plays*, Edwin Schallert of the *Los Angeles Times* reported that although *Song without Words* tried to find the **Song of Norway** "trail," it "missed the right landmarks"; and Fred Johnson in the *San Francisco Call-Bulletin* noted the musical was a "futile attempt" to capture the success of **Song of Norway** because the book and musical adaptation were "insufficient." *Variety* said the musical "fell flat on its face."

SPRING IN BRAZIL
"A MUSICAL PLAY" / "THE SUPERB NEW MUSICAL"

Theatres and *Performance Dates*: The musical opened on October 1, 1945, at the Shubert Theatre, in Boston, Massachusetts, where it played for three weeks; among other venues, it played at the Nixon Theatre in Pittsburgh, Pennsylvania, beginning on November 13, 1945, and also in Philadelphia, Pennsylvania; its final tryout stop was in Chicago, Illinois, where it opened at the Great Northern Theatre on December 28 and permanently closed there on January 12, 1946.

Book: Philip Rapp

Lyrics and *Music*: Robert Wright and George Forrest

Direction: Book staged and directed by Philip Rapp; production staged by John Murray Anderson; *Producer*: The Messrs. Shubert in association with Monte Proser; *Choreography*: Dances staged by Marjery Fielding; ballet and native dances staged by Esther Junger; *Scenery* and *Lighting*: Howard Bay; *Costumes*: Ted Shore and Mary Schenck; *Musical Direction*: Anthony B. Morelli

Cast: Roger Ohardieno (High Priest of Arupa, Tapirape Chief), Gene Blakeley (Roland Peoples [as a young man], Robert Harkness), Ray Arnette (Justin Lake [as a young man]), Christine Ayers (The Amazon Queen), Kent Edwards (John Randall), Joseph Macaulay (Colonel Roland Peoples), Jack McCauley (Bill McEvoy), Jack Kerr (Rafferty), Harry Klein (Tamamint), Jay Brennan (Addison), Charles Hart (Patterson), Harold Crane (Watterson), William Quentmayer (Clump), Rose Marie (Katie Warren), John Cherry (Lucius Sneed), Morton J. Stevens (Honorable Justin Lake), *Milton Berle* (Walter Gribble Jr.), Dee Turnello (Dancing Guest), Don Roberts (Martin Graham), Silas Engum (Samuel Prouty), Bernice Parks (Anya Veranda), Rita Angel (Divine Delight), Danny Hoctor (Pilot), Don Arres (Beniamino), Randolph Symonette (Police Officer), Russo de Pandeiro (Pablo), Gordon Gains (Pedro), Walter Gonsalves (Pancho), James Flash Riley (Fazendoros), Talley Beatty (Fazendoros), LaVerne French (Fazendoros), Wilson W. Woodbeck (Walter's Guide), Ray Long (Jongo), Joe Burns (Lana); Singers: Judith Kean, Frances Joslyn, Mildred Nespor, Betty Baker, Donna Gardner, Helen Ward, Dorothy DeWinter, Marjorie Hudson, Donna Louise, Tom Bowman, Walter Rinner, Gordon Gains, Howard Hoffman, Jack Collin, Jack Cassidy, Dean Campbell, Silas Engum; Dancers: Mary Alice Bingham, Grace DeWitt, Gay Hess, Elana Keller, Candace Montgomery, Janie New, Mary Jane Peiter, Edna Ryan, Dee Turnelle, Gloria Sicking, Evelyn Ward, Lillian Wells, Ray Arnette, Bill Dres, Jim Elsegood, Dan J. Hoctor, Bill McNie, Joseph Pas, Jack Purcell, Eric Shepard, James Flash Riley, Al Bledger, Moore Carson, George Thomas, Walter A. Smith, LaVerne French, Talley Beatty

The musical was presented in two acts.

The action takes place both twenty years ago in Arupa, Brazil, and in 1945 in New York City and Brazil.

Musical Numbers

Act One: Untitled musical number (Roger Ohardieno, Gene Blakeley, Ray Arnette, Christine Ayers, Tribal Dancer); "Fall in Manhattan" (Kent Edwards, Brooklyn Girls, Bobby Soxers, Manhattanites); "Explorers' March" (Joseph Macaulay, Jack McCauley); "Explorers' Lament" (Jack Kerr, Harry Klein, Jay Brennan, Charles Hart, Harold Crane, William Quentmayer); "Little Ol' Boy" (Rose Marie); "Little Ol' Boy" (dance reprise) (Harry Klein, Rose Marie, Jack Kerr, Jay Brennan, Charles Hart, Harold Crane, William Quentmayer); "Our Day" (Milton Berle, Rose Marie); "Explorers' Waltz" (Jack Kerr, Harry Klein, Jay Brennan, Charles Hart, Harold Crane, William Quentmayer, Dancing Guests); "A Star Isn't Born" (Bernice Parks); "I Envy You Rio" (Kent Edwards, Pilots, Mechanics, Stewardesses, Travellers); "Consolation" (Jack Kerr, Harry Klein, Jay Brennan, Charles Hart, Harold Crane, William Quentmayer); "Hymn to Jongo" (Don Arres and unidentified performer); "Spring in Brazil" (Rose Marie, Kent Edwards, Composers, Policemen, Explorers, Celebrants); "Frenetica" (The Jivaros); "Noe' Noe'" (Don Arres, Celebrants); "Chi-ri-qui-chi" (Milton Berle); Finale

Act Two: "Samba at Daybreak" (Don Arres, three unidentified performers [probably James Flash Riley, Talley Beatty, and LaVerne French], Plantation Workers); "The Bean of the Coffee Tree" (Bernice Parks; danced by Plantation Workers and by James Flash Riley, Talley Beatty, and LaVerne French); "Explorers' March" (reprise) (William Quentmayer, Jack Kerr, Harry Klein, Jay Brennan, Charles Hart, Harold Crane); "Jongo at Home" (Ray Long); "New Worlds" (Rose Marie, Ray Long); "Ritual Dance" (Roger Ohardieno); "The Great God Booge" (Milton Berle, Rose Marie, Bernice Parks, Jack McCauley, Wilson W. Woodbeck; danced by Christine Ayers, Subjects); "Rough, Rugged and Robust" (Milton Berle); "Carnival in Rio" (Entire Company)

Spring in Brazil was one of the era's biggest flops. For months, ads for the musical appeared in New York programs as a forthcoming new Broadway musical, but it closed on the road after three-and-a-half months of a tumultuous tryout. The musical reportedly lost over $300,000, and even during tryout performances its star Milton Berle would kid the show. At one performance, he spoke directly to the audience and said, "Look out, we outnumber you." Years later in his nightclub act he'd refer to the musical, telling patrons that on some nights the producers would send the entire audience home in a taxi.

The free-for-all plot dealt with librarian Walter Gribble Jr. (Berle), who somehow ends up in Brazil to locate a white boy (Jongo, played by Ray Long) who has been found in a jungle. It turns out that Walter's late explorer father sired Jongo, and so both Walter and Jongo happily discover they are half-brothers. But that's not before Walter almost ends up as cannibal stew and has to pose as a medicine man in order to avoid being someone's dinner.

Robert Wright and George Forrest had enjoyed considerable success with their lyrics and their adaptation of Edvard Grieg's music for *Song of Norway*, and of course Milton Berle had starred in the long-running 1943 edition of the *Ziegfeld Follies*. But everyone went down in flames with the new musical. *Variety* reported the show "fell as flat as a tortilla" and that the book "flew apart like a 30-year-old-flivver."

During the run, many performers left the musical and were replaced by others: Christine Ayers was succeeded first by Dorothy De Winter and then by Diosa Costello; Rose Marie by Mary Healy; John Cherry by Harry Sothern; Bernice Parks by Marion Colby; Gene Blakeley by Jack Collins; Don Arres by Dean Campbell; and Randolph Symonette by Howard Hoffman. During the tryout, the following numbers were added to the show: "Fernando," "Riot in Rio," and "Arupan Ballet."

The song "Fall in Manhattan" is included in Wright and Forrest's *A Bag of Popcorn and a Dream* (Original Cast Records CD # OC-8801); the song had first been heard in *The Copacabana Revue of 1943*.

WINDY CITY
"A PLAY-WITH-MUSIC"

Theatres and *Performance Dates*: The musical opened on April 18, 1946, at the Shubert Theatre, New Haven, Connecticut, where it closed on April 20; it also played at the Shubert Theatre, Boston, Massachusetts, where it opened on April 30; and then opened on May 16 at the Great Northern Theatre, Chicago, Illinois, where it permanently closed on June 5, 1946.

Book: Philip Yordan

Lyrics: Paul Francis Webster

Music: Walter Jurmann; ballet music composed and adapted by Dorothea Freitag in collaboration with Walter Jurmann

Direction: Direction by Edward Reveaux and co-staging by Katherine Dunham and Edward Reveaux; *Producer*: Richard Kollmar; *Choreography*: Katherine Dunham; *Scenery* and *Lighting*: Jo Mielziner; *Costumes*: Rose Bogdanoff; *Musical Direction*: Charles Sanford

Cast: Kay Stewart (Mac), John Conte (Danny O'Brien), Grover Burgess (Bartender), Susan Miller (Lola), Ralph Hertz (Frankie Keaton), Jack Diamond (Sam), Joey Faye (Ruby), Loring Smith (Martin O'Brien), Al Shean ("Gramps" O'Brien), Norma Vaslavina (A Little Girl), James Russell (A Young Boy), Robert Berry (Louie), Mickey Cochran (Fats), Tom Pedi (Stony), Anna Mitten (A Burlesque Girl), Frances Williams (Patsy), Georgetta Spelvin (Gladys [The Voice in the Juke Box]), Hal Loman (Messenger Boy, Musician), Irene Hawthorne (Helen), George Spelvin (Church Janitor), Stephen Chase (Jimmy Casino), Betty Jane Smith (Gloria), Owen Hewitt (Officer Casey), Betty Lind (Another Burlesque Girl), John C. McCord (George), Jerry Ross (A Reefer Man), Harry Day (Musician); Vocal Ensemble: Martha Burnett, Patricia Neway, Elizabeth Pritchett, Shirley Sudock, Ray Bessmer, Ray Cook, Michael Kozak, Morris Gedzell

The musical was presented in a prologue, two acts, and an epilogue (as the tryout progressed, the epilogue was eventually dropped).

The action takes place in Chicago; the prologue and the epilogue take place in the present time and both acts occur in 1933.

(*Note*: The credits and song list reflect information from the first week of performances given in Chicago, which was the musical's final tryout stop.)

Musical Numbers

Act One: "State Street" (Vocal Ensemble); "Don't Ever Run Away from Love" (Susan Miller, John Conte); "The Little Girl" (dance) (The Little Girl: Norma Vaslavina; Betty Lind, James Russell); "Gambler's Lullabye" (Loring Smith, Al Shean, John Conte); "As the Wind Bloweth" (Susan Miller); "It's the Better Me (That Belongs to You)" (Frances Williams); "Out on a Limb" (Susan Miller); "Nightfall on State Street" (dance) (performers unknown); "It's Time I Had a Break" (John Conte)

Act Two: "Mrs. O'Leary's Cow" (Frances Williams, Jack Diamond, Joey Faye); "Where Do We Go from Here?" (Susan Miller, John Conte); "As the Wind Bloweth" (reprise) (Robert Berry); "The Reefer Man" (dance) (Jerry Ross; Musicians: Harry Day, Hal Loman); Finaletto (Entire Ensemble)

Early ads for *Windy City* proclaimed that the show would "reach and stir your heart" in its story of Chicago gambler Danny O'Brien (John Conte), who must choose between his obsession for cards or the love of his girl Lola (Susan Miller). The ads further proclaimed that among the musical's "unusual features" were choreographer Katherine Dunham's dances (which "have been woven into the plot"); the use of a chorus of female singers performing from the orchestra pit; and a chorus line of all-blonde dancers (because brunettes are "barred by a twist of the plot").

The musical's prologue and epilogue were set in the present day of 1946 as Danny looks back on his past. In 1933, he, his father Martin (Loring Smith), and his grandfather Gramps (Al Shean) were compulsive gamblers. Sometimes they won, sometimes they lost, and a general atmosphere of unhappiness hovered over their lives. Ultimately, Danny loses everything: Gramps has died, his father has moved on to Florida in search of new victims to con, and Lola has married someone else.

During the course of the tryout, the songs "Lady of the Evening," "The Beggar," and "Frankie's Wife" were cut, and the first act dance "The Little Girl" was added. Early ads featured Rose Perfect as one of the featured players, but either her role was eliminated or she was replaced by another performer. Strip tease queen Lily St. Cyr was part of the cast (as "A Stripper") during early tryout performances, but she was succeeded by Anna Mitten (who played the role of "A Burlesque Girl").

Variety noted that the story was essentially written along "drab and somewhat unsavory lines," and mentioned the sets and costumes "mirror effectively the sometimes tawdry, sometimes shoddy foundation" of the work. William Torbert Leonard in *Broadway Bound* reports that in the original script Danny commits suicide, but the book was re-worked to reflect a less downbeat ending. Claudia Cassidy in *Best Plays* commented that the musical had "imagination" as well as "more possibilities than it had been able to exploit."

Windy City seems to have rung down the curtain on Susan Miller's brief career. A comely blonde with a reportedly fine voice, she had been seen on Broadway in the revues **Earl Carroll Vanities** and **For Your Pleasure**, and had the leading female role in **Beat the Band**. Perhaps the succession of flops discouraged her. But *Windy City* was one of the earliest professional appearances by Patricia Neway, who was one of the vocal ensemble; she of course went on to a long and distinguished career in both opera and musicals, and in 1959 won the Tony Award for Best Featured Actress in a Musical for her performance as the Mother Abbess in *The Sound of Music*.

The collection *You Can't Put Ketchup on the Moon* (Rialto CD # SLRR-9201) includes three songs written for the score: "Don't Ever Run Away from Love," "Lucky Duck," and "Harry Is Only Physical"; the last two numbers were probably heard at one time or another during the tryout, but aren't listed in the program for the musical's last tryout stop in Chicago. Paul Francis Webster's lyric for the latter number is somewhat similar to his "'Tis Harry I'm Planning to Marry" (music by Sammy Fain; from the 1953 film musical *Calamity Jane*, which also included the song "Just Blew in from the Windy City"). Pianist Alex Hassan's collection *Beyond My Fondest Dreams: The Enchanting Melodies of Walter Jurmann* (Operetta Archives Foundation CD # OA-1016) includes an eighteen-minute medley of nine songs from the musical: "Don't Ever Run Away from Love," "Serenade of the Street," "Gambler's Lullabye," "Out on a Limb," "Where Do We Go from Here?," "It's Time I Had a Break," "Harry Is Only Physical," "Lucky Duck," and "As the Wind Bloweth" ("Serenade of the Street" might be an alternate title for "State Street" or "Nightfall on State Street").

Windy City shouldn't be confused with the later musical of the same title that opened in London at the Victoria Palace on July 20, 1982, and was based on the 1928 play *The Front Page* by Ben Hecht and Charles McArthur (the musical's book and lyrics were by Dick Vosburgh; the music was by Tony Macaulay; and the cast included Dennis Waterman, Anton Rodgers, Diane Langton, and Victor Spinetti).

1946–1947 Season

ICETIME

Theatre: Center Theatre
Opening Date: June 20, 1946; *Closing Date*: April 12, 1947
Performances: 405
Lyrics and *Music*: James Littlefield and John Fortis
Direction: Catherine Littlefield; *Skating Direction*: May Judels; *Producers*: Sonja Henie and Arthur M. Wirtz (A Sonart Production; Arthur M. Wirtz, Executive Director; William H. Burke, Production Director); *Choreography*: Catherine Littlefield (Dorothie Littlefield, Assistant Choreographer); *Scenery*: Edward Gilbert; *Costumes*: Lou Eisele and Billy Livingston; *Lighting*: Eugene Braun; *Musical Direction*: David Mendoza
Cast: Joan Hyldoft, Freddie Trenkler, The Three Bruises (Monty Stott, Geoffe Stevens, and Sid Spalding), The Brandt Sisters (Helga and Inge), Bob and Florence Ballard, (Buster) Grace and (Charlie/Charles) Slagle, Fritz Dietl, Paul Castle, Claire Dalton, James Caesar, Jack Reese, Patrick Kazda, James Carter, Cissy Trenholm; Singers: Jay Martin, Denise Briault, Shirley Weber, Richard Craig; Ensemble: Ellen Barkey, Kay Corcoran, Helen Dutcher, Babette George, Gloria Haupt, Walli Hackman, Edith Kandel, Patricia Lemaire, Marvette Mosic, Sharlee Munster, Ann Michel, Berenice Odell, Blanch Poston, Theresa Rothacker, Beth Stevens, Eileen Thompson, Edward Brandstetter, Edward Berry, Gere Decker, Robert Fitzgerald, Dan Hurley, Buddy Jones, Garry Kerman, William Knapp, Kenneth Leslie, Edward McDonald, Arthur Meehan, Jack Millikan, Gus Patrick, Kenneth Parker, Leonard Stofka, James Trenholm; also, Bing Stott, Jinx Clark, John Walsh, Grace Church, Charles Cavanaugh, Jean Sakovich, Jimmie Sisk, Helen Carter, John Kasper, Florence Ballard, Robert Ballard, Buck Pennington, Joe Shillen, Patrick Kazda, Grace Bleckman, Marian Lulling, Lela Rolontz, Ragna Ray, Sally Tepley, Ray Blow, Charles Caminiti (aka Carminiti), James Kenny, Evelyn Kenny, Jack Strand, Fred Thompson, Wallace Van Sickle, Gordon Holley, Evelyn Smith, Jerry Rehfield, Jack Strand, Lucille Risch
The revue was presented in two acts.

Skating and Musical Numbers

Act One: Overture (Orchestra); "Winter Holiday" (Ensemble) and "Song of the Silver Blades" (Singers: Richard Craig, Denise Briault, Shirley Weber); "Holiday Inn Octette" (Instructor and Partner: Fritz Dietl and Cissy Trenholm; Bing Stott, James Carter, Jinx Clark, John Walsh, Grace Church, Charles Cavanaugh, Jean Sakovich, Jimmie Sisk); "Mary, Mary, Quite Contrary" (Butterfly: Helen Carter; Cat: Jack Reese; Mary's Mother: John Kasper; Mary: Florence Ballard; Rabbit: Buck Pennington; Bee: Joe Shillen; Boy with Flowers: Patrick Kazda) and "Mary, Mary" (Singer: Richard Craig); "Setting the Pace" (Ellen Barkey, Grace Bleckman, Grace Church, Kay Corcoran, Helen Dutcher, Babette George, Gloria Haupt, Walli Hackman, Edith Kandel, Patricia Lemaire, Marian Lulling, Marvette Mosic, Sharlee Munster, Ann Michel, Berenice Odell, Blanch Poston, Lela Rolontz, Ragna Ray, Theresa Rothacker, Bing Stott, Beth Stevens, Cissy

Trenholm, Eileen Thompson, Sally Tepley, Edward Berry, Edward Brandstetter, Ray Blow, Charles Cava-naugh, Charles Caminiti, Gere Decker, Robert Fitzgerald, Dan Hurley, Buddy Jones, Garry Kerman, James Kenny, William Knapp, Kenneth Leslie, Edward McDonald, Arthur Meehan, Jack Millikan, Gus Patrick, Kenneth Parker, Jack Strand, Leonard Stofka, James Trenholm, Fred Thompson, Wallace Van Sickle, Gordon Holley; "Precision Plus" (Fritz Dietl and James Carter); "Old King Cole" (Footmen: John Walsh, Charles Cavanaugh; King: John Kasper; First Fiddler: Buck Pennington; Second Fiddler: Claire Dalton; Third Fiddler: Paul Castle) and "Ole King Cole" (Singers: Richard Craig, Denise Briault, Shirley Weber); "Light and Shadow" (Helga and Inge Brandt); "Zouaves" (Buster Grace, Charlie Slagle. Jimmie Sisk, Joe Shillen); "Sherwood Forrest" (Robin Hood's Band: Jinx Clark, Jean Sakovich, Grace Church; Robin Hood: James Caesar; Cavalier: Robert Ballard; Countess: Bing Stott); "The Nutcracker" (Father: Charles Cava-naugh; Mother: Kay Corcoran; Children: Berenice Odell, Evelyn Smith, Kenneth Leslie; Nutcracker: Paul Castle; Candy Prince: Jerry Rehfield; Tutu Girls: Grace Bleckman, Ellen Barkey, Helen Dutcher, Edith Kandel, Gloria Haupt, Patricia Lemaire, Marian Lulling, Marvette Mosic, Blanch Poston, Lela Rolontz, Ragna Ray, Theresa Rothacker, Beth Stevens, Cissy Trenholm, Eileen Thompson, Sally Tepley; Candy Fairy: Joan Hyldoft; Edward Berry, Edward Brandstetter, Ray Blow, Charles Cavanaugh, Charles Cami-niti, Gere Decker, Robert Fitzgerald, Garry Kerman, James Kenny, Kenneth Leslie, Jack Millikan, Gus Patrick, Jack Strand, Fred Thompson, Wallace Van Sickle, Gordon Holley; Dance Chinoise: Lucille Risch, Helen Carter, Buck Pennington; Trepak: Jack Reese; Waltz of the Flowers: Tutu Girls, Kay Corcoran, Walli Hackman, Sharlee Munster, Ann Michel); "Bouncing Ball of the Ice" (Freddie Trenkler; Policeman: Joe Shillen; Nursemaid: Jinx Clark); "When the Minstrels Come to Town" (Drummer Boy: Edward Mc-Donald; Banner Bearers: Dan Hurley, Garry Kerman; Head Interlocutor: John Walsh; Interlocutors: John Kasper, James Carter, Patricia Kazda, Jerry Rehfield; Sambo, Bones, Tambo, Jones: Buster Grace, Charles Slagle, Jimmie Sisk, Buck Pennington; Banjo Boys: Edward Berry, Edward Brandstetter, Ray Blow, Charles Cavanaugh, Charles Caminiti, Gere Decker, Robert Fitzgerald, William Knapp, Kenneth Leslie, Arthur Meehan, Jack Millikan, Gus Patrick, Kenneth Parker, Jack Strand, Fred Thompson, Walter Van Sickle; Tambourine Girls: Ellen Barkey, Grace Bleckman, Grace Church, Babette George, Gloria Haupt, Walli Hackman, Patricia Lemaire, Marian Lulling, Sharlee Munster, Berenice Odell, Blanch Poston, Theresa Ro-thacker, Jean Sakovich, Cissy Trenholm, Beth Stevens, Sally Tepley; Lillian Russell: Claire Dalton; Can-Can Girls: Grace Bleckman, Ellen Barkey, Grace Church, Kay Corcoran, Helen Dutcher, Edith Kandel, Patricia Lemaire, Marian Lulling, Marvette Mosic, Sharlee Munster, Ann Michel, Berenice Odell, Blanch Poston, Lela Rolontz, Ragna Ray, Bing Stott, Jean Sakovich, Cissy Trenholm, Eileen Thompson, Sally Tepley) and "Mandy" (from *Ziegfeld Follies of 1919*; lyric and music by Irving Berlin) and "Cuddle Up" (probably "Cuddle Up a Little Closer, Lovey Mine" from *Three Twins*, 1908; lyric by Otto A. Harbach, music by Karl Hoschna) (Singers: Richard Craig, Denise Briault, Shirley Weber)

Act Two: Entr'acte (Overture); "Cossack Lore" (Princes: Patrick Kazda, Jerry Rehfield; Nobles: Ray Blow, Charles Caminiti, Gere Decker, Robert Fitzgerald, Dan Hurley, Buddy Jones, William Knapp, Jack Mil-likan, Leonard Stofka, James Trenholm; Court Pages: Helen Carter, Lucille Risch; Grooms: Jinx Clark, Ragna Ray, Bing Stott, Jean Sakovich; Cossacks: Jimmie Carter, John Kasper, Buck Pennington, John Walsh; Gypsy Girls: Ellen Barkey, Kay Corcoran, Helen Dutcher, Babette George, Walli Hackman, Edith Kandel, Patricia Lemaire, Marian Lulling, Marvette Mosic, Sharlee Munster, Ann Michel, Berenice Odell, Blanch Poston, Lela Rolontz, Theresa Rothacker, Beth Stevens, Eileen Thompson, Sally Tepley; Ivan: James Caesar) and "Cossack Lore" (Singers: Richard Craig, Denise Briault, Shirley Weber); "Divertise-ment" (Evelyn Kenny, James Kenny); "Lovable You" (Jinx Clark, Kay Corcoran, Helen Dutcher, Marian Lulling, Sharlee Munster, Jean Sakovich, Eileen Thompson, Sally Tepley, Joan Hyldoft) and "Lovable You" (Singer: Jay Martin); "Double Vision" (Helga and Inge Brandt; Escorts: John Walsh, Jerry Rehfield); "Garden of Versailles" (Les Faunes: John Kasper, Buck Pennington, Jack Reese, Paul Castle; Peintre: Patrick Kazda; Mademoiselle: Claire Dalton; Madame Jeanne: Fritz Dietl; Academy of Madame Jeanne: Ellen Barkey, Grace Bleckman, Grace Church, Jinx Clark, Kay Corcoran, Helen Dutcher, Babette George, Gloria Haupt, Walli Hackman, Edith Kandel, Patricia Lemaire, Marian Lulling, Marvette Mosic, Sharlee Munster, Ann Michel, Berenice Odell, Blanch Poston, Lela Rolontz, Theresa Rothacker, Jean Sakovich, Beth Stevens, Cissy Trenholm, Eileen Thompson, Sally Tepley; Les Amoureux: Florence Ballard, Robert Ballard); "Those Good Old Days" (Lucille Risch, Jimmie Sisk, Jinx Clark, John Walsh, Claire Dalton, Jerry Rehfield, Helen Carter, James Carter; The Sport: Jack Reese); "Higher and Higher" (Buster Grace and Charles Slagle); "The Dream Waltz" (Jivers: Berenice Odell, Ragna Ray, James Kenny, Buck Pennington,

John Kasper; Dream Girl: Joan Hyldoft; Hussars: James Carter, Patrick Kazda, Jerry Rehfield, John Walsh; Waltz Girls: Ellen Barkey, Grace Bleckman, Grace Church, Kay Corcoran, Jinx Clark, Helen Dutcher, Babette George, Walli Hackman, Edith Kandel, Patricia Lemaire, Marian Lulling, Marvette Mosic, Sharlee Munster, Ann Michel, Blanch Poston, Lela Rolantz, Ragna Ray, Theresa Rothacker, Bing Stott, Jean Sakovich, Beth Stevens, Cissy Trenholm, Eileen Thompson, Sally Tepley; Yellow Hussars: Edward Brandstetter, Ray Blow, Charles Cavanaugh, Charles Caminiti, Gere Decker, Robert Fitzgerald, Garry Kerman, William Knapp, Jack Millikan, Gus Patrick, Jack Strand, Leonard Stofka, James Trenholm, Fred Thompson, Wallace Van Sickle, Gordon Holley; Her Dream Man: Fritz Dietl) and "The Dream Waltz" (Singers: Jay Martin, Denise Briault, Shirley Weber); The Three Bruises (Monty Stott, Geoffe Stevens, Sid Spalding); Finale

Icetime ran out the season, and was quickly followed by ***Icetime of 1948***, which included many of the songs and skating sequences from *Icetime*. For all purposes, ***Icetime of 1948*** was a second edition of *Icetime*.

As usual, in his annual summary of the season George Jean Nathan bemoaned the continuance of the series. He said the current production was a "cheap duplication" of earlier mountings with a lack of imagination that combined Rockettes-styled numbers and a "dialogueless version of some such turkey musical as ***The Girl from Nantucket***" on skates." The evening of "metronomic refrigeration" offered such novelties as "Mary, Mary, Quite Contrary" and "Old King Cole," both of which were "evidently designed for the rapture of children." But if children enjoyed these numbers, then they "must be very backward" these days.

TIDBITS OF 1946
"An Intimate Musical Entertainment" / "An Intimate Diversified Revue"

Theatre: Plymouth Theatre
Opening Date: July 8, 1946; *Closing Date*: July 13, 1946
Performances: 8
Sketches: Sam Locke
Direction: Sam Locke; *Producers*: Arthur Klein in association with Henry Schumer (a Youth Theatre presentation); *Scenery, Costumes*, and *Lighting*: Uncredited; *Musical Direction*: Phil Romano
Cast: Joey Faye, Muriel Gaines, Lee Trent, Josef Marais and Miranda, Carmen and Rolando (with Candido), Eddy Manson, Robert Marshall, Joshua Shelley, Josephine Boyer, Jack Diamond, The Debonairs, Sherry Williams, The Mack Triplets
The revue was presented in two acts.

Sketches and Musical Numbers

Act One: "Apologia" (Lee Trent); "Harmonica Days" (Eddy Manson); "Hi, Havana!" (Carmen and Rolando; Bongo Boy: Candido); "On the Veld" (Josef Marais and Miranda); "Psychiatry in Technicolor" (Dr. Serutan Pimento: Joey Faye; Miss Fortescue Wimpy: Josephine Boyer; The Oedipus Rex: Jack Diamond; Mr. Pickling: Joshua Shelley); "So It Goes at the Met" (Robert Marshall); "In a Jeep" (Joey Faye, Jack Diamond); "I'm the Belle of the Ballet" (Josephine Boyer); "Step This Way" (The Debonairs)
Act Two: "On the Way to Sloppy Joe's" (Carmen, Rolando, Candido); "A Few Moments with Lee Trent"; "The Man Who Came to Heaven" (The Angel: Joey Faye; The Congressman: Joshua Shelley); "Capetown Capers" (Josef Marais and Miranda); "Never Kill Your Mother on Mother's Day" (sketch by Mel Tokin) (Lee Trent and Joshua Shelley) (This sketch was scheduled for this spot and was listed in the program, but wasn't performed on opening night.); "The Lass with the Delicate Air" (Muriel Gaines); "Meet Me on Flugle Street" (Joey Faye, Jack Diamond); Finale

The revue *Tidbits of 1946* was a fast-folding flop which lasted just one week and went down in the record books as the season's shortest-running musical. Much of the material had been presented at the Barbizon-Plaza Theatre with a mostly different cast for five performances during the week of May 20, 1946, but even this "tryout" didn't help. Howard Barnes in the *New York Herald Tribune* said the evening was "a random assortment of vaudeville canapés, with an abundance of crumbs." He wondered how the earlier performances at the Barbizon-Plaza "could have fooled" the producers into thinking the presentation was ready for Broadway.

The revue offered comedians Joey Faye, Joshua Shelley, Jack Diamond, Josephine Boyer, and Lee Trent (the latter also served as master of ceremonies); harmonica player Eddy Manson; singer Robert Marshall; the singing team The Mack Triplets; Cuban dancers Carmen and Rolando (and Candido, their bongo player); and the dancing team The Debonairs. Of the remaining cast members, singer Muriel Gaines and the South African folk-singing team of Josef Marais and Miranda were holdovers from the earlier production.

According to Lewis Funke in the *New York Times*, the evening was an "uneven affair saved by an occasional high spot," and he noted most of the routines would have been more at home in a nightclub setting. Vernon Rice in the *New York Post* had found the revue's spring presentation a "simple and modest" affair with a "great deal of charm." But with all its changes the evening was now just a "slow-moving" revue that lacked "distinction."

Robert Sylvester in the *New York Daily News* mentioned that one might have longed for the return of vaudeville, but *Tidbits of 1946* "cured you" of both "vaudeville" and "longing." Robert Bagar in the *New York World-Telegram* noted the sketch "Psychiatry in Technicolor" was a spoof of Alfred Hitchcock's recent film *Spellbound*, but apparently the sketch wasn't spell-binding. Even the classic burlesque sketch "Meet Me on Flugle Street" didn't go over well.

Herrick Brown in the *New York Sun* stated the revue was an "amateurish hodgepodge" that had "precious little to offer in the way of distinction and entertainment." Robert Garland in the *New York Journal-American* described the revue as a "mistake-with-music" and a "varicose vaudeville." He noted that Robert Marshall sang "Vesti la Gubba" in the style of Willie Howard; that Josephine Boyer burlesqued ballet with "L'apres-midi d'un faun" in the style of Imogene Coca; that Eddy Manson played the harmonica in the style of Borrah Minnevitch; and that Carmen and Rolando danced the samba in the style of Betty Garrett. Among the songs performed by Muriel Gaines was "To Keep My Love Alive" from **A Connecticut Yankee**, and he noted that the Mack Triplets were "non-Andrews Sisters" who sang a number "about Central Park and its nocturnal goings-on." As for poor Joey Faye, he had suffered through **Allah Be Praised!**, **The Duchess Misbehaves**, and now *Tidbits of 1946* (but he didn't have to suffer for long).

Garland reported that "Never Kill Your Mother on Mother's Day" (which was listed in the opening night program) wasn't performed, and Bagar noted that Lee Trent told the audience that the Mack Triplets had joined the cast at the last minute (they weren't listed in the opening night program). Bagar also mentioned that the unbilled Sherry Williams ("an Eiffel Tower of a girl") occasionally participated in some of the sketches.

YOURS IS MY HEART
"An Operetta"

Theatre: Shubert Theatre
Opening Date: September 5, 1946; *Closing Date*: October 5, 1946
Performances: 36
Book and *Lyrics*: Ira Cobb and Karl Farkas
Music: Franz Lehar; musical adaptation by Felix Guenther
Direction: Entire production staged by Theodore Bache and dialogue directed by Monroe Manning; *Producer*: Arthur Spitz; *Choreography*: Henry Shwarze; *Scenery* and *Costumes*: H. A. Condell; *Lighting*: Milton Lowe; *Musical Direction*: George Schick
Cast: Monroe Manning (Guy), Helene Whitney (Lucille), Jane Mackle (Lou), Harold Lazaron (Pierre), Alexander D'Arcy (Fernand D'Orville), Natalye Greene (Yvonne), Dorothy Karrol (Fifi), Jean Heisey (Marie), Sammy White (Archibald Mascotte), Stella Andreva (Claudette Vernay), Harvey Kier (Butler), *Richard Tauber* (Prince Sou Chong), Edward Groag (Huang Wei), Arnold Spector (Prince Tschang), Fred Keating (His Fueng), Lillian Held (Princess Mi), Albert Shoengold (Master of Ceremonies), Fred Briess (High Priest), Beatrice Eden (Li Tsi); Solo Dancers: Trudy Goth, Henry Shwarze, Wayne Lamb, Alberto Feliciano; Dance Ensemble: Helen Farrell, Eleanore Gregory, Mary Kane, Athena Kellar, Sonia Levanskaya, Sondra Lipton, Margaret McCallion, Carol Percy, Gloria Stevens, Estelle Tamus, Edythe A. Uden, Joanna Vischer, Geraldine Wyss; Singing Ensemble: Natalye Greene, Jean Heisey, Julie Jefferson, Dorothy Karrol, Phyllis

Lockard, Jane Mackle, Helene Whitney, Isabella Wilson, Fred Briess, Edwin Budana, Harry Kiery, Harold Lazaron, Scotty Miller, Albert Shoengold

The musical was presented in three acts.

The action takes place in Paris and Peiping around 1900.

Musical Numbers

Act One: "Music Box" and "Waltz" (Ensemble); "Goodbye, Paree" (Alexander D'Arcy, Ensemble); "Free as the Air" (Stella Andreva, Ensemble); "Chinese Melody" (Stella Andreva); "Patiently Smiling" (Richard Tauber), "A Cup of China Tea" (Stella Andreva, Richard Tauber); "Upon a Moonlight Night in May" (Richard Tauber, Ensemble); Finale (Stella Andreva, Richard Tauber)

Act Two: "Chinese Ceremony" (Entire Ensemble): (1) Master of Ceremonies (Henry Shwarze); (2) "Sword Dance" (Wayne Lamb, Alberto Feliciano); (3) "Dance of the Girls" (Dance Ensemble); and (4) "Chinese Puppet Dance" (Trudy Goth, Dance Ensemble); "Love, What Has Given You This Magic Power?" (Stella Andreva, Richard Tauber); "Men of China" (Lillian Held, Dance Ensemble); "Chingo-Pingo" (Lillian Held, Alexander D'Arcy, Dance Ensemble); "Yours Is My Heart Alone" (Richard Tauber); "Wedding Ceremony" (Entire Ensemble); Finale (Stella Andreva, Richard Tauber)

Act Three: "Upon a Moonlight Night in May" (reprise) (Stella Andreva, Ensemble); "Paris Sings Again" (Stella Andreva); "Ma Petite Cherie" (Lillian Held, Alexander D'Arcy); "Chingo-Pingo" (reprise) (Lillian Held); Finale (Stella Andreva, Lillian Held, Richard Tauber, Sammy White, Alexander D'Arcy)

The operetta *Yours Is My Heart* was the first Broadway production of Frank Lehar's *Das Land des Lachelns* (*The Land of Smiles*), which in its revised and final version had premiered on October 10, 1929, at the Metropol Theatre in Berlin, Germany, with Richard Tauber in the leading role. The original libretto was by Ludwig Herzer and Fritz Lohner-Beda, and for the New York premiere it was adapted by Ira Cobb and Karl Farkas, with Felix Guenther providing the musical adaptation.

The operetta had been seen in the United States in at least two other adaptations, one as *Prince Chu Chang* and one as *The Land of Smiles*. The Broadway premiere offered no less than Richard Tauber, the star of the original 1929 production.

The story begins in Paris where opera star Claudette Vernay (Stella Andreva) meets and falls in love with Chinese Prince Sou Chong (Richard Tauber). She agrees to go with him to China, where they'll be married. But royal custom decrees that Sou Chong must first marry a girl to whom he was engaged at the age of twelve; and once that marriage has taken place, he can marry Claudette, who, understandably, doesn't go along with the marriage practices in Old Peiping. Because Sou Chong is so in love with Claudette that he can't bear for her to leave China, he keeps her prisoner in the royal palace (William Hawkins in the *New York World-Telegram* described her "prison" as a "sort of Coney Island version of a sing song house"). But Vernon Rice in the *New York Post* noted that Claudette is allowed to return to Paris . . . "but not until 11:30 and the end of the third act."

Robert Garland in the *New York Journal-American* said *Yours Is My Heart* was an "unhappy hodgepodge" with a few "lesser" songs ("especially 'Chingo-Pingo'"), and suggested the musical died of "book complaint," or "libretitis." Louis Kronenberger in *PM* found the "hell of a yarn" both "dreary" and "moldy"; the plot was "benumbing," the libretto "excruciating," the Chinese maidens went "pit-pat," there were "weird" dances, and some of the comics escaped torture on the stage by "inflicting" it on the audience.

Howard Barnes in the *New York Herald Tribune* said the evening's "witless book" and "random nonsense" resulted in a "tuneful bore," and suggested Lehar's score was better enjoyed on the phonograph player than in the theatre. Like Brooks Atkinson in the *New York Times* and John Chapman in the *New York Daily News*, he felt the music might be better served on the concert stage. The librettists didn't offer a "fragment of regaling entertainment," and while Tauber's voice still retained much in the way of a "rich and controlled instrument," his acting was "straight from grand operatic posturing." Atkinson said the production was a "tarnished valentine" and described one sequence that in typical operetta fashion built up the entrances of the principals. Prior to Stella Andreva's entrance, someone asks, "Is Claudette here yet?" and Atkinson noted you could sure "bet" she wasn't here yet. At least, not until someone else "shouts" the "great news" that "Madame has arrived!" (Atkinson then reported that "the joy is tremendous"). But this was "nothing" in comparison to a butler's "obsequiousness" when Tauber made his first appearance. The butler "croons" "Oh, Your Highness!" in a "decent and reticent passion" and states that "I will announce you immediately."

Chapman said the operetta was "uncomfortably dull" and "most clumsily staged." Although Tauber now had the "shape of a penguin," he was an artist and a "skilled trickster" whose voice underwent "graceful little stunts" which might have been "unmusicianly" but were "theatrically effective." He also noted the evening involved much in the way of "Chinese nonsense" with the chorus girls wearing "pagodas or kimonos or something." Ward Morehouse in the *New York Sun* mentioned that Fred Keating performed a few magic tricks by pulling rabbits and canaries out of his sleeve, and he wished the performer could have made the plot disappear.

Garland reported that as the book "grew thinner and thinner" so did the audience. But like the rest of the critics, he noted the evening's high point was Tauber's rendition of "Yours Is My Heart Alone," the operetta's most famous song. Tauber performed it as if he were singing it for the first time, and offered numerous encores (in all, he sang two English versions plus ones in German, French, and Italian).

In considering Tauber's performance, two or three critics mentioned Jan Kiepura, whose leading roles opposite his wife Marta Eggerth in both the 1943 revival of **The Merry Widow** and in the previous season's **Polonaise** had caused them a certain amount of angst. Hawkins said Tauber's "spider-web pianissimo" was more "secure" than the "loudest bellow of a Kiepura." And Kronenberger noted that while Tauber's performance "vies at some points" with Kiepura's, he preferred the former because Tauber gave the impression he was having a wonderful time *up here* on the stage performing for the audience, while Kiepura suggested the audience *down there* was having a wonderful time only because of his presence on the stage.

The Broadway production was brought to a sudden halt by Tauber's health. Two weeks after the opening, laryngitis caused him to miss performances, and between September 20 and the closing of the musical on October 5 he appeared just three times (during his illness, John Hendrick sang the role of Sou Chong).

There have been at least four film versions of the operetta, all produced in Germany; two were theatrical films, the first released in 1930 with Tauber re-creating his role of Sou Chong, and the second released in 1952 with Marta Eggerth, and, yes, Jan Kiepura. A 1961 adaptation was produced for German television; and a 1974 production (apparently first seen on German television) was released on DVD by Deutsche Grammophon. There are numerous recordings of the score, including versions released by Telarc (on one CD) and another on Warner Classics (in a two-CD set). And during his career Tauber recorded songs from the operetta.

A FLAG IS BORN

Theatre: Alvin Theatre (during run, the work transferred to the Adelphi, Music Box, and Broadway Theatres)
Opening Date: September 5, 1946; *Closing Date*: December 15, 1946
Performances: 120
Play: Ben Hecht
Music: Kurt Weill
Direction: Luther Adler; *Producer*: The American League for a Free Palestine; *Choreography*: Zamira Gon; *Scenery*: Robert Davison; *Costumes*: John Boyt; *Lighting*: Supervised by George Gebhardt; *Musical Direction*: William Tarrasch
Cast: Quentin Reynolds (Speaker), *Paul Muni* (Tevya), Celia Adler (Zelda), Marlon Brando (David), Mario Berini (The Singer), George David Baxter (Saul), Morris Samuylow (Old One), David Manning (Middle-Aged One), John Baragrey (Young One), William Allyn (David the King), Gregory Morton (Solomon), Jonathan Harris (American Statesman, Second Soldier), Yasha Rosenthal (Russian Statesman), Tom Emlyn Williams (First English Statesman), Jefferson Coates (Second English Statesman), Frederick Rudin (French Statesman), Steve Hill (First Soldier), Harold Gary (Third Soldier); Supers: William Berg, Randolph Jones, Nick Ferber, Jack Wesley, Allen Lindstrom, Vincent Beck, Jo Davidson, Charles Feurman, George Anderson, Martin Leavitt, Solomon Goldstein, Jack Sloane, Harry Moses, Gilbert Leigh, Jack Buxbaum, Jim Flynn, Norman Kilroy, Jules Preuss, Thomas Arena, Rudolph McKool, Joe Bernard, Daniel Moskowitz, Carl Shelton, Robert Weston, Bill Reid, Ray Johnson, Jim Davidson, Paul Sugerman, Natalie Norwick, Rona Christie, Selma Stern, Michael Kazaras, Terry Becker, Paul Firestone, Peggy Strange, Steve Graves, Dan Sacks, Eileen Ayers; Dancers: Evangeline Collis, Anne Wayne, Lillian Ekman, Evelyn Leeds, Anne Widman, Ruth Harris, Audrey Eden, Pearl Borchard, Lee Morrison, Lillian Fisher, Maybelle Lama, Sophia

Babert, Virginia Gilchrist, Shirley King, Rosalind Posnick, Jeanne Belkin, Miriam Levy; Choir: Paul Mario, Elton Plowman, Joseph Hill, William Durkin, Carl Manning, Allen Lowell, Nicholas Torzs, Richard Monte

The pageant was presented in one act.

The action takes place during the present time somewhere in Europe.

Note: The program didn't list musical numbers.

Instead of a traditional out-of-town tryout, Ben Hecht's pageant *A Flag Is Born*, which was produced by the American League for a Free Palestine, gave a handful of previews before opening on Broadway for a limited run of four weeks. Because the work proved popular, it extended the run and played for two extra months (at a total of four theatres, the Alvin, Adelphi, Music Box, and Broadway). Because of contractual commitments, Paul Muni wasn't able to remain with the production for more than his originally scheduled four weeks, and was succeeded by Luther Adler. The production later toured with Sidney Lumet. Others in the Broadway production were Stella Adler and Marlon Brando.

A Flag Is Born was a plea for establishing a homeland in Palestine for the European Jews who survived World War II. The setting was a graveyard in Europe where elderly couple Tevya (Paul Muni) and his wife Zelda (Celia Adler) seek the road to Palestine. Because of the war, they've lost everything and hope to find peace and security in Palestine during their remaining years. In the graveyard they meet young David (Marlon Brando) who is also looking for the road to Palestine. In their visions, the three look back at their Jewish heritage with glimpses of Saul, Solomon, and David, and also see current politicians who argue over the viability of Palestine as a free Jewish state. Zelda succumbs to illness, and Tevya soon follows her; but David is shown the "bridge" to Palestine and when he arrives there he raises Tevya's prayer shawl on a staff as the flag of the new Jewish homeland.

John Chapman in the *New York Daily News* noted Hecht's writing was sometimes "purple" and that the work was like a "pamphlet" set upon the stage or a radio script laid out in theatrical format. But the evening was indeed a reminder that theatre can sometimes be a "forum, a pulpit and a platform." In this case, Hecht demanded the right of the Jewish people to a homeland, and he criticized the British for trying to thwart their efforts (all profits from the production went to the American League for a Free Palestine, which helped Jewish European refugees move from Europe to Palestine).

Like fellow critic Chapman, Louis Kronenberger in *PM* noted the propaganda piece was sometimes the victim of purple prose; and while Hecht wrote with "great sincerity," the work by its very nature was "loosely" presented in a series of shifting tableaux. Sometimes the "fire" of Hecht's "wrath" blazed, but generally it never ignited and thus "the fingers never close into a fist." Howard Barnes in the *New York Herald Tribune* said that as a dramatic work the show was "distinctly dubious" with its "quality of a soapbox harangue." The production was "slipshod and rather wearisome" and he felt Hecht had used a "rocket gun" for his message when a "single clean shot" would have been more effective.

While Brooks Atkinson in the *New York Times* suggested the evening's cause deserved a "finer" script than the one written by Hecht, he noted that Paul Muni was "giving one of the great performances of his career." Atkinson reported that Hecht accused the Jews in the audience for remaining "comfortably silent" while their European brothers were slaughtered by Hitler. (And of course Hecht criticized the British for hindering the efforts for the establishment of a Jewish homeland, and he further complained that the nations of the world hadn't stepped up to face the issue.) But Atkinson muddied the waters by claiming that "everyone in the world is guilty." Guilty of what? Of the holocaust? Of the problems in establishing a Jewish homeland in the Middle East? He wasn't quite clear. But as a war correspondent during World War II, one wonders just what Atkinson meant. The "everyone-is-guilty" syndrome is surely too sophomoric a belief for the distinguished journalist, who of course knew that approximately 420,000 American soldiers lost their lives during the war.

Robert Garland in the *New York Journal-American* noted that young Marlon Brando was the evening's "bright particular star"; after *Truckline Café* in 1946, the 1946 revival of *Candida*, and now *A Flag Is Born*, he was "rapidly fulfilling the brilliant promise" he made during his Broadway debut in *I Remember Mama* in 1944. But after *A Streetcar Named Desire* in 1947, he never again appeared on the Broadway stage.

Kurt Weill's incidental music was praised by the critics: it was "beautiful" (Atkinson); "heart-felt" (Garland); "effective" (Barnes); "dramatically helpful" (Chapman); "suitable" (Kronenberger); "appropriate" (Ward Morehouse in the *New York Sun*); and a "dramatically appropriate score which speaks in emotional moods"

(William Hawkins in the *New York World-Telegram*). In his *Kurt Weill: A Handbook*, David Drew reports that some of Weill's music had been heard in the 1936 pageant *The Eternal Road*, including "Opening," "Temple Music," and "Interlude." Other material in *A Flag Is Born* includes dance music, chants, fanfares, and various background musical themes.

GYPSY LADY
"A Period Piece" / "A Gay New Operetta"

Theatre: New Century Theatre
Opening Date: September 17, 1946; *Closing Date*: November 23, 1946
Performances: 79
Book: Arthur Kay
Lyrics: Robert Wright and George Forrest
Music: Victor Herbert; musical adaptation by Arthur Kay
Direction: Robert Wright and George Forrest; vocal numbers staged by Lew Kesler; *Producer*: Edwin Lester; *Choreography*: Aida Broadbent; *Scenery*: Boris Aronson; *Costumes*: Miles White (costumes executed by Walter J. Israel); *Lighting*: Adrian Awan; *Musical Direction*: Arthur Kay
Cast: Clarence Derwent (Baron Pettibois), Kaye Connor (Yvonne), Jack Goode (Fresco), Helena Bliss (Musetta), Edmund Dorsay (Sergeant of Gendarmes), John Tyers (The Great Alvarado), Doreen Wilson (Valerie), Val Valentinoff (Imri), William Bauer (Rudolfo), Melville Cooper (Boris), Patricia Sims (Roszika), George Britton (Sandor), Gilbert Russell (Andre), Joseph Macaulay (Stephan), Suzette Meredith (The Undecided Mademoiselle), Bert Hillner (M. Guilbert Armand), Harvey Shahan (Majordomo); Young Ladies of the Academy, Gypsies, Guests, Maids, and Mannikins: Jeanne Bal, Phyllis Bateman, Mardi Bayne, Betty Brusher, Marydee Buscher, Dorothy Coulter, Beth Alba Cushing, Betty Galavan, Florette Hillier, Rosemary Liesen, Suzette Meredith, Dani Nelson, Bernice Saunders, Nelda Scarsella, Peggy Weakland, Helen Wysatt; Gypsies, Gentlemen, Bellboys, and Waiters: James Andrews, George Dempsey, Paul De Poyster, Ray Drakely, Dean Etmund, Max Hart, Bert Hillner, Elton Howard, William James, Dale Johnson, Richard Scott, Robert Searles, Harvey Shahan, Ray Smith, John Stamford, Stanley Wolfe; Dancing Gypsies and Ballet Dancers: Barbara Bailey, Lyza Baugher, Donna Biroc, Florence Brundage, Jean Marie Caples, Kathleen Cartmill, Elaine Corbett, Marietta Elliott, Mitzi Gerber (Gaynor), Irene Hall, Judy Landon, Joan Larkin, Betty Orth, Patricia Sims, Betty Slade, Maria Taweel
The musical was presented in two acts.
The action takes place in France around 1900.

Musical Numbers

Act One: "On a Wonderful Day Like Today" (Young Ladies of the Academy); "The Facts of Life Backstage" (Jack Goode, Kay Connor, Young Ladies); Serenade: "I Love You, I Adore You" (John Tyers, Doreen Wilson); "Interlude" (Helena Bliss, John Tyers); "On a Wonderful Day Like Today" (reprise) (Young Ladies); "Life Is a Dirty Business" (Gypsy Men); "My Treasure" (George Britton, Gypsy Men); "Romany Life" (Helena Bliss, Gypsies); "Pantomime" (Jack Goode); "The World and I" (Gilbert Russell, John Tyers, Girls from Paris); "Piff Paff" (Joseph Macaulay, Doreen Wilson, Gilbert Russell); "Andalusia Bolero" (Val Valentinoff, Patricia Sims, Gypsies); "Keepsakes" (John Tyers, Doreen Wilson); Finale (John Tyers, Helena Bliss, Clarence Derwent, Jack Goode, George Britton, Gypsies)
Act Two: "Young Lady a la Mode" (John Tyers, Helena Bliss, Jack Goode, Kaye Connor, Bert Hillner, Bellboys, Maids, Mannikins); "Springtide" (Gilbert Russell, Helena Bliss); "Ballet Divertissement" (Ballet Dancers); "My First Waltz" (Helena Bliss, Gilbert Russell, John Tyers, Jack Goode, Ensemble); "Reality" (Melville Cooper, Jack Goode, Clarence Derwent); "Gypsy Love Song" (George Britton); "Piff Paff" (reprise) (Joseph Macaulay, John Tyers, Gilbert Russell, Doreen Wilson, Jack Goode, Guests)

West Coast producer Edwin Lester and lyricists and musical adaptors Robert Wright and George Forrest were among the creators of the popular musical *Song of Norway*, which had been based on the life and music of Edvard Grieg; this time around, Wright and Forrest utilized music from two Victor Herbert operettas, *The Serenade* (1897) and *The Fortune Teller* (1898). The songs (most with new lyrics by Wright and Forrest, and with Herbert's original music adapted by Arthur Kay) were grafted into a new book by Henry Myers, one which purported to be a "period piece" that would reintroduce Herbert's music to the public and offer a "tongue-in-cheek treatment of the stock period operetta story." Like **Song of Norway**, *Gypsy Lady* was first produced in Los Angeles and San Francisco, but instead of a two-year run in New York the new offering lasted just two months.

Helena Bliss, who had starred in **Song of Norway**, here played the title role. The plot revolved around a would-be merry scheme to pass off young gypsy woman Musetta (Bliss) as a princess. It seems that handsome young actor The Great Alvarado (John Tyers) is deemed a mere commoner by the Duke of Roncevalle (Joseph Macaulay) who considers him unsuitable for the hand of his daughter Valerie, the Marquise (Doreen Wilson). For revenge, Alvarado hopes the Duke's son the Marquis Andre (Gilbert Russell) will fall in love with Musetta. Vernon Rice in the *New York Post* asked, "Won't that be a very funny joke? Oh yes indeed it will!" Not only does Andre fall for Musetta, but so does her Henry Higgins–like Alvarado; and it turns out Musetta is a princess after all, a *gypsy* princess! And she returns to her tribe and marries her true love and fellow gypsy Sandor (George Britton).

Brooks Atkinson in the *New York Times* detested operettas, and in viewing the "dead gaiety" of *Gypsy Lady* he wondered "what year is this anyway," because the plot depended on social snobberies; dialogue that could come only from an operetta ("Romance is piff-paff"); and such clichés as an artist depicted in "regulation" smock and tam as he paints a "spurious" picture on a "prop" easel. Because so many operettas loved to dwell on the differences between royals and commoners, the thrust of the plot emphasized this theme. In fact, Atkinson noted that the "odor" of *The Student Prince* permeated the proceedings.

Rice mentioned that besides the two leading men who were after the gypsy lady's favors, it seemed that "all the basses, baritones and tenors for miles around" were, too. And so the stage became a "veritable land of chests out" in "deep breathing" with "mouths opened" in song. He heartily wished that Lester would never again appropriate the music of a well-known composer and then set the music to a new plot, and suggested this "urge" on Lester's part must be stopped before it became a "mania." (But little did Rice know that Lester's *Kismet* was just a few seasons away.)

Ward Morehouse in the *New York Sun* noted the music was presented "engagingly and tunefully," but its idea of humor was "tormentingly unfunny throughout." As a result, the "delightful" music couldn't overcome the "gawky" script. Howard Barnes in the *New York Herald Tribune* found the book "remarkably inoffensive," and since the décor and costumes were "traditional and rather tasteful," he decided those adjectives described the musical as well. And William Hawkins in the *New York World-Telegram* said the show was "lusty" and "vigorous," and with its "vitality, beauty and wit" it stood head and shoulders above recent contenders in the operetta field.

John Chapman in the *New York Daily News* found the musical "pretty solemn" and thought it needed more humor, but noted that Melville Cooper as the king of the gypsies could make an article on medicine sound funny; all in all, the singers were good and the evening was "quite pleasant." But Robert Garland in the *New York Journal-American* said the musical's book belonged in the dustbin; the plot was "plodding," the humor was "hapless," and the evening was "endless"; and Louis Kronenberger in *PM* remarked that as he sat through the production with "drooping spirits and eyelids" he came to the conclusion that "human nature will change before operetta-writing does" because the plot of *Gypsy Lady* was the same one "that grandpa saw on his twelfth birthday."

The original book and lyrics of *The Serenade* and *The Fortune Teller* were by Harry B. Smith. The former had premiered in New York on May 22, 1897, at the Knickerbocker Theatre for seventy-nine performances, and the latter on September 26, 1898, at Wallack's Theatre for forty performances.

Gypsy Lady was first produced as *The Fortune Teller* at the Curran Theatre in San Francisco on July 1, 1946, and after the Broadway production closed the work was presented in London as *Romany Life* at His Majesty's Theatre on March 7, 1947, with Helena Bliss and Melville Cooper reprising their Broadway roles (the production played for approximately ninety-six performances). Incidentally, Wright and Forrest wrote new lyrics for all the songs in *The Fortune Teller/Gypsy Lady/Romany Life* except for "Gypsy Love Song" and "Romany Life." For these numbers, the original lyrics by Harry B. Smith were retained.

Note that one of the musical's chorus dancers was Mitzi Gerber, who later changed her last name to Gaynor.

PARK AVENUE
"A New Musical Comedy"

Theatre: Shubert Theatre
Opening Date: November 4, 1946; *Closing Date*: January 4, 1947
Performances: 72
Book: Nunnally Johnson and George S. Kaufman
Lyrics: Ira Gershwin
Music: Arthur Schwartz
Direction: Book directed by George S. Kaufman and production supervised by Arnold Saint-Subber; *Producer*: Max Gordon; *Choreography*: Helen Tamiris; *Scenery* and *Lighting*: Donald Oenslager; *Costumes*: The program noted that except for Leonora Corbett's gowns (which were created by Mainbocher), all other gowns were designed by Tina Leser; *Musical Direction*: Charles Sanford
Cast: Byron Russell (Carlton), Ray McDonald (Ned Scott), Martha Stewart (Madge Bennett), *Arthur Margetson* (Ogden "Oggie" Bennett), *Leonora Corbett* (Mrs. Sybil Bennett), Robert Chisholm (Charles Crowell), Martha Errolle (Mrs. Elsa Crowell), Charles Purcell (Reggie Fox), Ruth Matteson (Mrs. Myra Fox), Raymond Walburn (Richard Nelson), Mary Wickes (Mrs. Betty Nelson), Harold Mattox (Ted Woods), Dorothy Bird (Mrs. Laura Woods), William (Bill) Skipper (James Meredith), Joan Mann (Mrs. Beverly Meredith), David Wayne (Mr. Meachem), Watson Smith (Freddie Coleman), Virginia Gordon (Carole Benswanger), Adelle Rasey (Brenda Stokes), Sherry Shadburne (Brenda Follansbee), Carol Chandler (Brenda Follansbee-Stokes), Betty Ann Lynn (Brenda Follansbee-Stokes-Follansbee), Kyle MacDonnell (Brenda Cadwallader), Eileen Coffman (Brenda Stuyvesant), June Graham (Brenda Cathcart), Betty Low (Brenda Cathcart-Cartcath), Virginia Morris (Brenda Kerr), Judi Blacque (Brenda Ker-Ker-Ker), Gloria Anderson (Brenda Quincy Adams), Margaret Gibson (Brenda Wright Jr., Sr., 3rd)
The musical was presented in two acts.
The action takes place in the mansion of Mrs. Ogden Bennett in Long Island.

Musical Numbers

Act One: "Tomorrow Is the Time" (Bridesmaids); "For the Life of Me" (Ray McDonald, Martha Stewart)/"Dance" (Ray McDonald, Martha Stewart, William Skipper, Harold Mattox, Bridesmaids); "The Dew Was on the Rose" (Leonora Corbett, Arthur Margetson, Charles Purcell, Raymond Walburn, Robert Chisholm); "Don't Be a Woman If You Can" (Mary Wickes, Martha Errolle, Ruth Matteson); "Sweet Nevada" (Leonora Corbett, David Wayne); "In the Courtroom" (dance) (Plaintiffs: Dorothy Bird, Joan Mann, Betty Low; Judge: David Wayne; Court Attendants: William Skipper, Harold Mattox; Other Plaintiffs: All Brendas); "There's No Holding Me" (Martha Stewart, Ray McDonald); "The Dew Was on the Rose" (reprise) (Leonora Corbett, Arthur Margetson); "There's Nothing Like Marriage for People" (Entire Company)
Act Two: "Hope for the Best" (Bridesmaids, Martha Stewart, Martha Errolle, Mary Wickes, Ruth Matteson); "My Son-in-Law" (Leonora Corbett, Martha Stewart, Ray McDonald); "The Land of Oportunitee" (Arthur Margetson, Raymond Walburn, Charles Purcell, Robert Chisholm)/"Dance" (Dorothy Bird, Joan Mann, All Brendas); "Goodbye to All That" (Martha Stewart, Ray McDonald) and Dance: "Echo" (Harold Mattox, Dorothy Bird, William Skipper, Joan Mann, Bridesmaids); Finale (Entire Company)

With George S. Kaufman, Ira Gershwin, and Arthur Schwartz at the helm, *Park Avenue*, which dealt with marriage and divorce among the tony set, promised to be a smart and witty musical. But despite clever material, the musical wilted after two months. Perhaps the subject of divorce turned off potential ticket-buyers in much the same way that some audience members in 1970 found Stephen Sondheim's ground-breaking *Company* a bit too brittle in its cynical views of marriage and divorce. The author recalls that at an early New York performance of *Company* two people sitting next to him mentioned they had friends and relatives, some of whom decided not to see the show and others who had left during intermission because the subject matter hit too close to home. Perhaps *Park Avenue*'s blithe and cynical views of marriage and divorce account for its short run.

On the other hand, perhaps *Park Avenue* never quite got off the ground, geographically and otherwise. Despite its title, the musical took place at a Long Island mansion (John Chapman in the *New York Daily News* said the show was "somewhat confusedly" titled). And perhaps the musical's notions of satire were a bit too obvious (all the dozen debutantes share the then-trendy first name of "Brenda," and their full names brought to mind the level of humor more appropriate to a varsity show, names such as Brenda Ker-Ker-Ker, Brenda Wright Jr., Sr., 3rd, and Brenda Cathcart-Cartcath). Moreover, the constant turnover of marriages among the social set might have made for an amusing sketch, but the book couldn't sustain a full evening of what was essentially a one-joke show.

The slender plot centered on Sybil Bennett (Leonora Corbett) who is married to her fourth husband Oggie (Arthur Margetson) and is now considering taking a fifth; as she notes in song, it's better to shed a husband while the dew is still on the rose. Among those in Sybil and Oggie's set are her three former husbands Richard, Robert, and Reggie (Raymond Walburn, Robert Chisholm, and Charles Purcell), all of whom have been married and divorced and are now with their current wives. Everyone has gathered at Sybil and Oggie's Long Island estate to celebrate the upcoming marriage of Sybil and Richard's daughter Madge (Martha Stewart), who is engaged to Southern ex-G.I. Ned Scott (Ray McDonald), a chap who actually holds to the quaint notion that marriage should be for keeps (one character isn't quite sure where Ned is from, and suggests it might be from a state called "West Carolina").

Ira Gershwin's lyrics were amusing, and what has emerged from Arthur Schwartz' score is pleasant (here is another of the era's musicals that deserves a studio cast album). Not all the songs were plot driven, and some were instead pleasant interludes, including the calypso-inflected quartette "The Land of Oportunitee," in which Sybil's four husbands salute the capitalist system; "Don't Be a Woman If You Can," in which a group of bored ladies-who-lunch-styled wives catalog the daily *horreurs* of having to choose the right nail polish, perfume, hair-do, and fur coat; and "Sweet Nevada," an ode to the State of Instant Divorce.

"My Son-in-Law" was a sly wink at **Carousel**'s "Soliloquy" in which the parents of the bride rhapsodize over their hopes and expectations for their future son-in-law; and other cynical numbers were "There's Nothing Like Marriage for People," "The Dew Is on the Rose," and "For the Life of Me." In the latter, a bride tells the groom that her "taste may be queer" because he (and not a celebrity such as Van Johnson) is the man of her dreams. The score also offered the affecting torch song "Goodbye to All That."

Brooks Atkinson in the *New York Times* said the "imposing" creators of *Park Avenue* had offered an "unimposing" musical; he felt Schwartz' score was more "orchestration than singing" and what could be heard over the loud orchestra suggested the music was "hardly distinguished"; but Donald Oenslager's mansion looked "impossibly expensive" and Tina Leser's gowns offered a "splendid fashion show," and thus their contributions made the musical a "many-hued delight." Howard Barnes in the *New York Herald Tribune* found the evening an "extended skit" that lacked the "spontaneous combustion" required of a memorable musical; as a result, the material lacked "definition" and was "somewhat disappointing." Louis Kronenberger in *PM* said the new musical was "pretty flat and tiresome" in its constant back-and-forth about marriage and divorce; as a result, the show's one joke was served "hot and cold, creamed and fricasseed," and in both soup and salad servings, and thus his view of the show was similar to his feeling about turkey three days after Thanksgiving.

Chapman liked some of the "excellent" songs and Helen Tamiris's "deft and out-of-the-ordinary" dances, but otherwise the evening offered "endless" and "repetitive" variations on the theme of divorce and marriage. Robert Garland in the *New York Journal-American* was surprised that Kaufman and co-librettist Nunnally Johnson weren't able to come up with "fresher and firmer" material, and suggested that Random House publisher Bennett Cerf, who was sitting in the row behind him, could probably have devised a "million" jests to dress up the plot of *Park Avenue*. William Hawkins in the *New York World-Telegram* said the evening's "lonely" one-joke gag was "tossed in the air, kicked under foot, slammed against the wall and generally clubbed to death." And so the characters became "trifling bores" and the show evolved into a "distasteful" and ultimately "utterly unsavory" evening.

Herrick Brown in the *New York Sun* found the new musical "lavish and smartly dressed," but the one-note evening wore itself out and didn't add up to a satisfying show. He felt that Gershwin's lyrics rather than Kaufman and Johnson's book gave the musical its real "fun."

But Richard Watts in the *New York Post* said the musical was "bright and amusing" and "frequently witty"; he admitted the book was a "trifle slender" and tended to overdo its main theme a "bit insistently," but overall it was a "likeable and lively" entertainment with "gay and colorful" décor and a "bright and smart" score.

During the tryout, choreographer Eugene Loring was succeeded by Helen Tamiris; Ralph Riggs originally was set to play the role of Mr. Meachem, and was succeeded by Jed Prouty who in turn was followed by David Wayne (and when Wayne left the musical about half-way through its two-month run, he was replaced by George Keane); and "Stay as We Are" was cut. Incidentally, a few months later both Wayne and Keane appeared in the season's two biggest hits, the former in **Finian's Rainbow** and the latter in **Brigadoon**.

A few songs from the production have been recorded. "Don't Be a Woman If You Can" is included in the collection *Lyrics by Ira Gershwin* (Harbinger CD # HCD-2502); *Arthur Schwartz Revisited* (Painted Smiles CD #PSCD-137) includes "There's No Holding Me" and "Goodbye to All That"; and *Keep Your Undershirt On!* (Rialto CD) also includes "There's No Holding Me."

The Complete Lyrics of Ira Gershwin includes all the songs heard in the musical as well as the cut "Stay as We Are" and the three unused numbers "The Future Mrs. Coleman," "Remind Me Not to Leave Town," and "Heavenly Day." The collection notes that "Remind Me Not to Leave Town" anticipated Gershwin's lyric for the song "A Weekend in the Country" (from the 1949 film *The Barkleys of Broadway*) and the music for "Heavenly Day" was recycled by Schwartz for an unidentified song in **Inside U.S.A.**

BAL NÈGRE
"THE SENSATIONAL REVUE"

Theatre: Belasco Theatre
Opening Date: November 7, 1946; *Closing Date*: December 21, 1946
Performances: 52
Direction and *Choreography*: Katherine Dunham; *Producers*: Nelson L. Gross and Daniel Melnick (A Katherine Dunham Production); *Scenery*: Uncredited; *Costumes*: John Pratt; *Lighting*: Uncredited; *Musical Direction*: Gilberto Valdes
Cast: *Katherine Dunham*; Dancers: Lucille Ellis, Lenwood Morris, Lawaune Ingram, Vanoye Aikens, James Alexander, Ronnie Aul, Wilbert Bradley, Byron Cuttler, Eddy Clay, Roxie Foster, Dolores Harper, Jesse Hawkins, Richardena Jackson, Eartha Kitt, Gloria Mitchell, Eugene Robinson, Othella Strozier; Guest Artist: Syvilla Fort; Sans-Souci Singers: Jean Leon Destine, Eartha Kitt, Rosalie King, Mary Lewis, Mariam Burton, Gordon Simpson, Ricardo Morrison; Drummers: La Rosa Estrada. Candido Vicenty, Julio Mendez
The revue was presented in three acts.

Musical Numbers

Act One: Overture: (1) "Ylenko-Ylembe" (music by Gilberto Valdes) (Eartha Kitt, Jean Leon Destine, Mariam Burton, Sans-Souci Singers); and (2) "Congo Paillette" (traditional) (Katherine Dunham, with Lenwood Morris and Company); "Motivos": (1) "Rhumba" (music by Gilberto Valdes) (Lucille Ellis, Eartha Kitt, Othella Strozier); (2) "Son" (traditional) (Possessed Dancer: Dolores Harper; Singer: Jesse Hawkins); (3) "Nanigo" (music by Gilberto Valdes) (La Rosa Estrada, Vanoye Aikens, Company); (4) "Choro" (music by Osvaldo Gogliano) (Gloria Mitchell, Richardena Jackson, Wilbert Bradley, Ronnie Aul); and (5) "La Comparsa" (music by Ernesto Lecuona) (Katherine Dunham, with Vanoye Aikens, Byron Cuttler, and James Alexander); "Haitian Roadside" (music by Gilberto Valdes and Paquita Anderson) (Peddler with Guitar: Candido Vicenty; Other Peddlers: La Rosa Estrada, Byron Cuttler, Julio Mendez, James Alexander; Traveling Priest: Jean Leon Destine; Market Girls: Lawaune Ingram, Gloria Mitchell; Carnival Kings: Lenwood Morris, Jean Leon Destine; Chacoon: Katherine Dunham); the "Haitian" sequence included three native songs: "Soleil, O" (Jean Leon Destine, Male Quartet); "Apollon" (aka "Carnival Meringue") (Jean Leon Destine); and "Chocounne" (Katherine Dunham); "Shango" (music by Baldwin Bergerson) (The Shango Priest: La Rosa Estrada; The Boy Possessed by a Snake: Jean Leon Destine; The Leaders of the Shango Dancers: Lucille Ellis, Eddy Clay; Dancers)
Act Two: "L'Ag'ya" (music by Robert Sanders) (Loulouse: Katherine Dunham; Alcide: Vanoye Aikens; Julot: Wilbert Bradley; Roi Zombie: Lenwood Morris; Dancers)

Act Three: Nostalgia: (1) "Ragtime" (Rosalie King with the Sans-Souci Singers; Dancers: Lucille Ellis, Lenwood Morris, Company; dances in sequence included the waltz, fox-trot, ballin' the jack, tango, maxixe, and turkey trot); the ragtime sequence included "Chong"; "Under the Bamboo Tree" (lyric and music by Bob Cole and J. Rosamund Johnson); "Ragtime Cowboy Joe" (lyric by Grant Clarke, music by Lewis F. Muir and Maurice Abrahams); "Oh, You Beautiful Doll" (lyric by Seymour Brown, music by Nat D. Ayer); and "Alexander's Ragtime Band" (lyric and music by Irving Berlin); (2) "Blues" (music by Floyd Smith) (Katherine Dunham and Vanoye Aikens); (3) "Flaming Youth 1927" (music by Brad Gowans) (Blues Singer: Rosalie King; Kansas City Woman: Lucille Ellis; Dancers: Lawaune Ingram, Wilbert Bradley, and Company; dances in sequence included the Charleston, black bottom, mooch, fishtail, and snake hips); Finale: (1) "Havana 1910" (music by Mercedes Novarro) and (2) "Para que tu veas" (music by Bobby Capo) (Jean Louis Destine; Entertainer: Katherine Dunham; Two Lady Tourists: Richardena Jackson and Dolores Harper; Sans-Souci Singers and Katherine Dunham Dancers)

Bal nègre was yet another of Katherine Dunham's dance revues, which were now running into all too familiar patterns with similar subject matter and dance styles as well as material that had been seen in her earlier works. *Bal nègre* borrowed freely from her two previous productions of **A Tropical Revue** and from **Blue Holiday**, **Concert Varieties**, and **Carib Song**. In one form or another, approximately half the numbers in *Bal nègre* had been presented in the earlier shows, including the entire second act ("L'Ag'ya"), which had been seen in the second **A Tropical Revue**. Her later revues (two versions of *Katherine Dunham and Her Company* in 1950 and 1955 and 1962's *Bamboche!*) continued to offer recycled material. Of her six dance revues (not counting the book musical **Carib Song** and the revues in which she and her company had made guest appearances), the average run for each production was forty performances, with the shortest playing for one week and the longest for eight.

For the revue's tour, its flyer proclaimed the evening starred the "incomparable" Katherine Dunham and her "company of 50" in "a brand new hurricane of torrid dances from voodoo to jive! Havana to the South Pacific! Martinque to Brazil!"

In his seasonal summary, George Jean Nathan noted that Dunham's dance programs were becoming "familiar enough" with their borrowings from earlier efforts. He also felt the program offered too many dances of the same variety, and so monotony soon set in. Further, sexuality played a major role in the dances, and he suggested this stemmed less from "authentic choreographic art" and more from "palpable box-office politics."

Note that Eartha Kitt made one of her earliest Broadway appearances in *Bal nègre* (she had also been seen in **Blue Holiday** and **Carib Song**).

IF THE SHOE FITS
"THE CINDERELLA STORY GAILY SET TO MUSIC"

Theatre: New Century Theatre
Opening Date: December 5, 1946; *Closing Date*: December 21, 1946
Performances: 21
Book: June Carroll and Robert Duke
Lyrics: June Carroll
Music: David Raksin
Direction: Book directed by Eugene Bryden and production supervised by Leonard Sillman; *Producer*: Leonard Sillman; *Choreography*: Charles Weidman; tap routines by Don Liberto; *Scenery*: Edward Gilbert; *Costumes*: Kathryn Kuhn; *Lighting*: Carlton Winckler, Lighting Consultant; *Musical Direction*: Will Irwin
Cast: Robert Penn (Town Crier), Eugene Martin (Singing Attendant), Billy Vaux (Dancing Attendant), Jack Williams (Broderick), Jane Vinson (Acrobatic Attendant), Paula Dee (Acrobatic Attendant), Leila Ernst (Cinderella), Jody Gilbert (Mistress Spratt), Marilyn Day (Delilah), Sherle North (Thais), Richard Wentworth (The Butcher Boy, Third Troubadour), Don Mayo (First Undertaker), Walter Kattwinkel (Second Undertaker), Gail Adams (Loreli), Eileen Ayers (Lilith), Harvey Braun (First Lawyer), Stanley Simmonds (Second Lawyer), Florence Desmond (Lady Eve), Joe Besser (Herman), Four Sprites: Vincent Carbone, Harry Rogers, Allen Knowles, and Fred Bernaski, William Rains (First Troubadour), Ray Morrissey (Second Troubadour), Fin Olsen (The Troubadours' Arranger), Youka Troubetzkoy (Major Domo), Eleanor

Jones (Lady Guinevere), Dorothy Karroll (Lady Persevere), Chloe Owen (Dame Crackle), Ray Cook (The Baker), Joyce White (Dame Crumple), Jean Olds (Dame Crinkle), Edward Dew (Prince Charming), Adrienne (Widow Willow), Barbara Perry (Kate), Edward Lambert (King Kindly), Frank Milton (His Magnificent the Wizard), Vincent Carbone (Court Dancer), Richard D'Arcy (Sailor), Marcia Miller (The Sailor's Sweetheart), Marybly Harwood (The Sailor's Sweetheart); Corps de Ballet: Paula Dee, Yvette Fairhill, Jean Harris, Marybly Harwood, Marcia Maier, Ruth Ostrander, Audrey Peters, Gloria Smith, Jane Vinson, Fred Bernaski, George Drake, Vincent Carbone, Allen Knowles, Roy Marshall, Harry Rogers, Billy Vaux
The musical was presented in two acts.
The action takes place during the Middle Ages in The Kingdom of Nicely.

Musical Numbers

Act One: "Prologue" (Robert Penn); "Start the Ball Rollin'" (Jack Williams; danced by Jack Williams and the Corps de Ballet); "I Wish" (Leila Ernst); "Start the Ball Rollin'" (reprise) (Jody Gilbert, Marilyn Day, Sherle North); "I Wish" (reprise) (Leila Ernst); "In the Morning" (Florence Desmond); "Come and Bring Your Instruments" (Fin Olsen, William Rains, Richard Wentworth, Ray Morrissey); "Night After Night" (Eleanor Jones; danced by Barbara Perry and the Corps de Ballet); "Every Eve" (Edward Dew, Eddie Lambert); "With a Wave of My Wand" (Florence Desmond, Leila Ernst; danced by Good Girls [Jean Harris, Marybly Harwood, Audrey Peters] and Bad Girls [Marcia Maier, Yvette Fairhill, Gloria Smith]; "Am I a Man or a Mouse?" (Joe Besser); "I'm Not Myself Tonight" (Leila Ernst and Edward Dew, Barbara Perry and Jack Williams, Florence Desmond); "Three Questions" (Florence Desmond, Leila Ernst, Frank Milton; danced by Barbara Perry and Vincent Carbone)

Act Two: "Entr'acte" (Eleanor Jones, Eugene Martin); "If the Shoe Fits" (Frank Milton, Citizens; danced by the Corps de Ballet); "I Wish" (reprise) (Edward Dew); "In the Morning" (reprise) (Florence Desmond, Joe Besser, Leila Ernst); "What's the Younger Generation Coming To?" (Eddie Lambert, Entourage); "Have You Seen the Countess Cindy?" (Edward Dew, Citizens); "This Is the End of the Story" (Leila Ernst; danced by Richard D'Arcy, Marcia Maier, Marybly Harwood); "I Took Another Look" (Barbara Perry, Jack Williams); "I Want to Go Back to the Bottom of the Garden" (Florence Desmond); "This Is the End of the Story" (reprise) (Edward Dew, Jack Williams); "My Business Man" (Adrienne); Finale (Entire Company)

If the Shoe Fits was a failed tongue-in-cheek look at the traditional Cinderella story that reportedly lost $300,000 during its brief stay on Broadway. Produced by *New Faces'* Leonard Sillman, the musical was the only Broadway score written by the renowned film composer David Raksin, whose haunting, shimmering theme music for *Laura* (1944) is one of the great achievements in screen music. He also wrote the equally ethereal background music for *The Bad and the Beautiful* (1952). The critics had almost nothing good to say about his contributions to *If the Shoe Fits*; however, those few songs that have surfaced are quite notable, including the touching, understated ballad "This Is the End of the Story."

A program note stated the action took place during the Middle Ages in The Kingdom of Nicely, "one of those mythical kingdoms known only to writers of musical comedies." The show utilized the main elements of the traditional Cinderella story, but added a skewed perspective by making British music-hall performer Florence Desmond a match-making fairy godmother who does impersonations of Tallulah Bankhead and who at one point temporarily toys with appropriating Prince Charming for herself. Comedian Joe Besser played the role of Herman, a mouse turned into a man, and he raised eyebrows with his apparently over-the-top impersonation of a rather gay mouse. In his seasonal summary, George Jean Nathan suggested Besser's mincing-hand-on-the-hip impersonation of the "Ecce Homo" added "to the Cinderella story one more fairy than it originally bargained for." And Howard Barnes in the *New York Herald Tribune* commented on Besser's "camping routine" as he "effeminately" waved his hands and scampered about the stage. And if all this wasn't enough, there were even back-and-forth, would-be humorous jokes on the question of whether or not Cinderella is a virgin.

The critics didn't quite know what to make of the evening, and further noted the book and score were lacking. But they praised Edward Gilbert's eye-popping sets, literally eye-popping because each scene began with a depiction of a huge page from a children's story book; as the page was turned, the decor for the upcoming scene popped up from the page and revealed castle turrets, banners, and whatever else was pictorially appropriate for the particular sequence. Richard Watts in the *New York Post* said the scenic device was "ingenious"; John Chapman in the *New York Daily News* praised the "delightfully decorative" and "mechanically ingenious" décor; and William Hawkins in the *New York World-Telegram* found the scenery "delightful" and noted Kathryn Kuhn provided a "riot of color" with her "kaleidoscope" of costumes.

Watts noted that after the "notorious horrors" of **The Girl from Nantucket** and **The Duchess Misbehaves**, *If the Shoe Fits* was probably not as "terrible" as it seemed. But the musical lacked style, the jokes were so bad he almost felt sorry for the writers, and the lyrics and music were "exceptionally uninteresting." Brooks Atkinson in the *New York Times* said the book was "bankrupt in ideas," was "vulgar" but unfunny, and the constant interruptions for "low-comedy interpolations" were no doubt "good enough" for a musical comedy "in the stream of unconsciousness school." Hawkins found the score "undistinguished" and wryly noted that the "flavorless Mother Gooseburger" book so drove away his "concentration" that he was "frequently uncertain" as to what was actually happening on the stage.

Hawkins singled out the fairy godmother's song "I Want to Go Back to the Bottom of the Garden," and some of the other critics praised "This Is the End of the Story," "I Wish," and "In the Morning." Otherwise, Barnes said the "dull" score "almost defies humming," and while Louis Kronenberger in *PM* noted that a couple songs were "pleasant enough" the score wasn't hummable and "never in a million years" would he ever be able to recognize the music. He also noted the dialogue was given to arch lines of the "I'll be with you in a minute or three" variety.

Chapman commented that among those in the musical who committed "misdemeanors" were Florence Desmond ("a low comedienne resembling a poor man's Beatrice Lillie") and Joe Besser as the mouse-man. Chapman denounced producer Leonard Sillman as an "incurable amateur" who should be "spanked, made to wash his mouth out with soap, put to bed" and then never allowed "to go near the professional theatre again."

During the tryout, Ethel Levey was succeeded by Jody Gilbert, and the songs "Three Chances" (not to be confused with "Three Questions"), "Entrances and Exits," and "Recitative" were cut.

The song "My Business Man" is included in the collection *You Can't Put Ketchup on the Moon* (Rialto CD # SLRR-9201), and the lovely "This Is the End of the Story" is included in *Life's a Funny Present* (Rialto CD # SLRR-9306). "Come and Bring Your Instruments" can be heard in the collection *Lost Broadway and More: Volume Two* (Original Cast Records CD # OC-6830).

Awards

Tony Awards: A special Tony Award was given to P. A. MacDonald "for intricate construction for the production *If the Shoe Fits*."

BEGGAR'S HOLIDAY
"A New Musical in the American Idiom (Based on John Gay's *Beggar's Opera*)"

Theatre: Broadway Theatre
Opening Date: December 26, 1946; *Closing Date*: March 29, 1947
Performances: 108
Book and *Lyrics*: John LaTouche
Music: Duke Ellington
Based on the 1728 opera *The Beggar's Opera* by John Gay.
Direction: Book directed by Nicholas Ray; *Producers*: Perry Watkins and John R. Sheppard Jr.; *Choreography*: Valerie Bettis; *Scenery*: Oliver Smith; *Costumes*: Walter Florell; *Lighting*: Peggy Clark; *Musical Direction*: Max Meth
Cast: Tommy Gomez (The Pursued, The Other Eye), Archie Savage (Cop, Gunsel), Herbert Ross (Policeman, Bartender), Lucas Hoving (Policeman, Strip), Albert Popwell (Plainclothesman, Slam), Marjorie Belle (aka Marjorie Bell, Marjorie Beecher, and Marge Champion) (The Lookout, The Girl), *Alfred Drake* (Macheath), Marie Bryant (The Cocoa Girl), Bernice Parks (Jenny), Lavina Nielsen (Dolly Trull), Leonne Hall (Betty Doxy), Tommie Moore (Tawdry Audrey), Doris Goodwin (Mrs. Trapes), Royce Wallace (Annie Coaxer), Claire Hale (Baby Mildred), Nina Korda (Minute Lou), Malka Farber (Trixy Turner), Elmira Jones-Bey

(Bessie Buns), Enid Williams (Flora), Bill Dillard (The Horn), Jack Bittner (Highbinder), Gordon Nelson (O'Heister, Customer, Black Marketeer), Perry Bruskin (The Foot, Mooch), Stanley Carlson (Fingersmith), Pan Theodore (The Eye, Blenkinsop), Paul Godkin (Wire Boy, The Boy), Douglas Henderson (The Caser), Hy Anzel (Customer), Lewis Charles (Drunk), Avon Long (Careless Love), Jet MacDonald (Polly Peachum), Dorothy Johnson (Mrs. Peachum), Zero Mostel (Hamilton Peachum), Rollin Smith (Chief Lockit), Mildred Smith (Lucy Lockit); Dancers: Paul Godkin and Marjorie Belle (aka Marjorie Bell, Marjorie Beecher, and Marge Champion), Malka Farber, Doris Goodwin, Claire Hale, Elmira Jones-Bey, Lavina Nielsen, Royce Wallace, Enid Williams, Tommy Gomez, Lucas Hoving, Albert Popwell, Herbert Ross, Archie Savage; Mac's Gang: Stanley Carlson, Lewis Charles, Gordon Nelson, Bill Dillard, Jack Bittner, Perry Bruskin

The musical was presented in two acts.

The action takes place during the present time in New York City.

Musical Numbers

Act One: "Inbetween" (Mildred Smith); "The Chase" (Tommy Gomez, Herbert Ross, Lucas Hoving); "When You Go Down to Miss Jenny's" (Citizens, Girls); "I've Got Me" (Alfred Drake); "TNT" (Marie Bryant); "Take Love Easy" (Bernice Parks); "I Wanna Be Bad" (Avon Long); ""Rooster Man" (Bernice Parks); "When I Walk with You" (Jet MacDonald, Alfred Drake); "Wedding Ballet"; "I've Got Me" (reprise) (performer uncredited; possibly Marjorie Belle); "The Scrimmage of Life" (Dorothy Johnson, Zero Mostel, Rollin Smith); "Ore from a Gold Mine" (Dorothy Johnson, Zero Mostel); Finaletto (Jet MacDonald, Dorothy Johnson, Zero Mostel); "When I Walk with You" (reprise) (Alfred Drake, Jet MacDonald); "Tooth and Claw" (Stanley Carlson, Lewis Charles, Gordon Nelson, Bill Dillard, Jack Bittner, Perry Bruskin); "Maybe I Should Change My Ways" (Alfred Drake); "The Wrong Side of the Railroad Tracks" (Marie Bryant, Avon Long, Bill Dillard); "Tomorrow Mountain" (Alfred Drake, Ensemble)

Act Two: "Brown Penny" (Mildred Smith); "Chorus of Citizens" (Ensemble); "Tooth and Claw" (reprise) (Zero Mostel, Reporters); "Lullaby for Junior" (Bernice Parks); "Quarrel for Three" (Jet MacDonald, Mildred Smith, Alfred Drake); "Fol-de-rol-rol" (Alfred Drake); "Women, Women, Women" (Prisoners); "When I Walk with You" (reprise) (Alfred Drake); "Ballet"; "The Hunted" (Alfred Drake); Finale (Alfred Drake, Bernice Parks, Jet MacDonald, Mildred Smith)

An early tryout program of *Twilight Alley* credited Duke Ellington with the book and lyrics, and John LaTouche with the music, and while a special program insert quickly reflected the correct information, it seems that right at the very beginning *Twilight Alley*, which soon changed its name to *Beggar's Holiday*, got off on the wrong foot and never quite recovered.

John Houseman was originally credited for staging the production and Nicholas Ray for the direction of the book, but by New York Houseman's name was no longer in the program (moreover, George Abbott had redirected as well as rewritten the book, but he didn't receive credit in the New York program; and Dale Wasserman, who two decades later wrote the book for *Man of La Mancha* [1965], also worked on the script, without official credit). Moreover, Libby Holman was succeeded by Bernice Parks, and at least eleven songs were cut: "Gumshoe Ballet," "Get Out," "He Makes Me Believe," "Let Nature Take Its Course," "Loose Living," "Bible of My Days," "My Reward," "Jailhouse Lament," "Girls Want a Hero," "How Could I Be Happy with Either," and "Live for the Moment." For Broadway, a few numbers underwent minor title changes ("When You're Down by Miss Jenny's" became "When You Go Down to Miss Jenny's" and "Bridal Ballet" became "Wedding Ballet").

The musical used the basic plot and atmosphere of John Gay's *The Beggar's Opera* in its emphasis on heel-hero Macheath (Alfred Drake) and his criminal gang, here transposed from the streets of eighteenth-century London to the back alleys and hobo jungles of modern-day Manhattan. And of course the ladies are drawn to Macheath, and so he enjoys the attentions of brothel-madame Jenny (Bernice Parks), lady-of-the-evening Lucy Lockit (Mildred Smith), and innocent Polly Peachum (Jet MacDonald), the daughter of political boss Hamilton Peachum (Zero Mostel). Avon Long played the role of Careless Love, a character who was a kissing cousin to Sportin' Life, which Long had memorably portrayed in the 1942 revival of *Porgy and Bess*. In Gay's original, Macheath almost Gets His via the hangman's noose, but a *deus ex machina* device saves him; similarly, in *Beggar's Holiday*, Macheath narrowly escapes electrocution, almost at the very last minute.

But for all the musical's out-of-town problems and its short three-month Broadway run, it received a number of surprisingly good reviews, including a near rave from Brooks Atkinson in the *New York Times*. Atkinson urged that "appropriate salutes be fired" in honor of Ellington and LaTouche's "flaring" musical, which offered an "eloquent" score, "brisk" dances, and an excellent cast, including Alfred Drake as the leading figure in a "gutter gavotte" set to the music of an "original, fresh and animated score," one which Broadway "can be proud of." John Chapman in the *New York Daily News* said *Beggar's Holiday* was the "most interesting" musical seen on Broadway since the premiere of *Porgy and Bess* in 1935. Although the plot was sometimes confusing, here was a show that deserved "extraordinary consideration" because of its score, cast, dances, décor, and direction. The music was a "delight" that refused to follow the clichés of Tin Pan Alley, and thus was "extraordinarily interesting." He noted that if Nicholas Ray was responsible for the staging, then his handling of the evening's "colorful patterns" and his manipulation of the stage crowds was the best since Rouben Mamoulian's direction of the original *Porgy and Bess*.

Robert Bagar in the *New York World-Telegram* noted that Ellington's music and LaTouche's adaptation and lyrics were a combination that resulted in the most "felicitous wedding" Broadway had seen in months. The evening was a "remarkable fusion" of cast and writers.

Although Howard Barnes in the *New York Herald Tribune* admitted the musical was "quite an entertainment," it was nonetheless "fragmentary" at best. The evening's "lively accents" were too frequently balanced with sometimes tiresome and "undramatic" elements. Most of the critics felt the musical's finest moments occurred during the latter part of the first act, especially the scene in the hobo jungle. They noted the second act bogged down when Zero Mostel took over. During this era, Mostel was often dismissed for his comic shtick, and many critics felt he was better suited to the nightclub floor than the Broadway stage. In fact, Robert Garland in the *New York Journal-American* said Mostel was a "funny fellow" in the "small closed spaces of Café Society" but was "nothing of the kind" in a large Broadway theatre. Louis Kronenberger in *PM* felt Mostel "absolutely mauled" the character of Peachum with his "intemperate practices," and Atkinson complained of his "grotesque and sweaty posturing."

Richard Watts in the *New York Post* felt that despite its strengths the musical was a "disappointment" that never quite jelled. The script never found a point of view, and so it was a sometimes uneasy combination of social satire, "melodramatic burlesque," and "just plain" musical-comedy "extravaganza." He mentioned the sometimes confusing book took a while to get started, but said Alfred Drake (who "looks even more like Orson Welles than ever") "disarmingly" played the leading role, and suggested Mostel might have been enjoyable had he not worked with "such fatiguing effort."

Kronenberger noted the musical was "praiseworthy" because it travelled its "own road"; unfortunately, the road never had a specific "destination" and thus left the audience "stranded." It seemed that *Beggar's Holiday* kept *The Beggar's Opera* "in its head" but not in "its veins." But he liked Ellington's score, which was "nervous, rhythmic and individual" and a "pleasant relief from stock musical-comedy 'tunes.'" The critics singled out a number of songs, including "I Wanna Be Bad," "Tooth and Claw," "I've Got Me," "When I Walk with You," "The Wrong Side of the Railroad Tracks," and, especially, Drake's rendition of the joys of "Tomorrow Mountain" (where "every kitchen I think is lined with mink"). Lena Horne reportedly turned down a leading role in the production because she felt the story was demeaning to her race, but she later recorded a voluptuous version of "Tomorrow Mountain."

The lyric of "Brown Penny" was based on a poem by William B. Yeats.

The week following the Broadway closing, the musical played in Chicago for two weeks; it opened at the Shubert Theatre on April 5, 1947, with many of the original Broadway cast members (Alfred Drake, Zero Mostel, Avon Long, Mildred Smith, Marie Bryant, and Jet MacDonald). The production omitted "Inbetween" and "Rooster Man," and reinstated "Girls Want a Hero," which had been deleted during the pre-Broadway tryout.

Director Nicholas Ray later helmed such films as noir favorites *They Live by Night* (1949) and *In a Lonely Place* (1950), the latter with Humphrey Bogart and Ray's wife Gloria Grahame; and the iconic *Rebel without a Cause* (1955) with James Dean. He also directed two camp classics, *Born to Be Bad* (1950) and *Johnny Guitar* (1954). The former featured Joan Fontaine as an outwardly sweet but inwardly vicious vixen who will do anything and everything to have her own way (the film was memorably spoofed as *Raised to Be Rotten* on Carol Burnett's television variety show), and the latter starred Joan Crawford as a hard-as-nails saloon keeper in the Old West who apparently downs testosterone cocktails for breakfast.

Note that one of the production's leading dancers was Marjorie Belle; she had appeared in **The Little Dog Laughed** as Marjorie Bell and in **What's Up** as Marjorie Beecher. She later married and teamed with Gower

Champion, and changed her professional name to Marge Champion. She and Gower Champion appeared together in six film musicals between 1951 and 1955, and in 1955 they were one-third of the musical revue *3 for Tonight*.

A demo recording of the score performed by original cast members Alfred Drake, Avon Long, Bernice Parks, Mildred Smith, Jet MacDonald, and Dorothy Johnson was released by Blue Pear Records (LP # BP-1013), and includes eleven songs ("Inbetween," "I've Got Me," "Take Love Easy," "I Wanna Be Bad," "When I Walk with You," "The Scrimmage of Life," "Ore from a Gold Mine," "Tooth and Claw," "The Wrong Side of the Railroad Tracks," "Brown Penny," and "Lullaby for Junior"). The liner notes indicate the recording was made during pre-rehearsals, and so it's unclear why Bernice Parks is on the recording since she didn't join the musical until after the tryout began when she replaced Libby Holman. The recording includes two versions of "Inbetween," the demo version by Alfred Drake and a later one which was recorded by Holman. The recording was paired with the London cast album of the 1952 British musical *Bet Your Life* (which starred Julie Wilson and Sally Ann Howes). The collection *Everybody Else Revisited* (Painted Smiles CD # PSCD-146) includes "The Wrong Side of the Railroad Tracks," "Brown Penny," and "I've Got Me"; and Richard Rodney Bennett's *Take Love Easy: The Lyrics of John LaTouche* (Audiophile LP # AP-206) includes "Take Love Easy." The latter song can also be heard in the collection *Introducing Janice Mars* (Bac Room Records CD).

A recording of the score was also released by DOM (CD # DOM-1233); the cast included David Serero in the role of The Beggar/Happy Mac, with the book and lyrics credited to Dale Wasserman and other lyrics credited to John LaTouche. The album includes eight songs heard in the Broadway production: "Inbetween," "Rooster Man," "Take Love Easy," "The Scrimmage of Life," "Tomorrow Mountain," "Maybe I Should Change My Ways," "Quarrel for Three," "I've Got Me"; two which were deleted during the tryout : "I Want a Hero" (aka "Girls Want a Hero") and "Live for the Moment"; and four songs that seem to have been written by Wasserman and were possibly revised versions of songs deleted during the tryout or otherwise not used: "Time to Take a Holiday," "No One but You," "But He So Charmed Me," and "Elegy to an Honest Crook."

TOPLITZKY OF NOTRE DAME
"A NEW MUSICAL COMEDY" / "THE ALL-AMERICAN MUSICAL"

Theatre: New Century Theatre
Opening Date: December 26, 1946; *Closing Date*: February 17, 1947
Performances: 60
Book and *Lyrics*: George Marion Jr.; additional dialogue and lyrics by Jack Barnett
Music: Sammy Fain
Direction: Jose Ruben; *Producer*: William Cahn; *Choreography*: Robert Sidney; *Scenery*: Edward Gilbert; *Costumes*: Kenn Barr; *Lighting*: Uncredited; *Musical Direction*: Leon Leonardi
Cast: Phyllis Lynne (Army Angel, Patti), Candace Montgomery (Recording Angel), Harry Fleer (Lionel), Warde Donovan (Angelo), Doris Patston (Mrs. Strutt), Marion Colby (Betty), Estelle Sloan (Dodo), Gus Van (McCormack), Walter Long (Roger), J. Edward Bromberg (Toplitzky), Betty Jane Watson (A Girl [Bobby]), Robert Bay (Mailman), Frank Marlowe (Leary); Male Quartet: Oliver Boersma, John Frederick, Eugene Kingsley, Chris Overson; Dancers: Priscilla Callan, Ann Collins, Helen Devlin, Cece Eames, Jessie Fullum, Joan Kavanagh, Pat Marlowe, Mollie Pearson, Frances Wyman, George Andrew, Gene Banks, Charles Dickson, Casse Jaeger, Thomas Kenny, Anthony Starman, Rodney Strong, Joe Wagner, John Wilkins
The musical was presented in two acts.
The action takes place during the present time in Heaven and in New York City.

Musical Numbers

Act One: Overture (Orchestra); "Let Us Gather at the Goal Line" (Warde Donovan, Company); "Baby, Let's Face It" (Walter Long); "Dance" (Walter Long, with Estelle Sloan and Boys and Girls); "Let Us Gather at the Goal Line" (reprise) (J. Edward Bromberg, Gus Van); "I Want to Go to City College" (Frank Marlowe, Marion Colby, Boys and Girls); "Love Is a Random Thing" (Betty Jane Watson); "Common Sense" (J. Edward Bromberg); "Love Is a Random Thing" (reprise) (Warde Donovan); "A Slight Case of Ecstasy" (Walter

Long and Estelle Sloan, Frank Marlowe and Phyllis Lynne); "Dance" (Walter Long with Girls and Boys); Finale (Betty Jane Watson, Company)

Act Two: Entr'acte (Orchestra); "Wolf Time" (Marion Colby, Phyllis Lynne; danced by Estelle Sloan, with Boys and Girls); "McInerney's Farm" (Gus Van); "You Are My Downfall" (Warde Donovan, Betty Jane Watson; danced by Boys and Girls, and by Walter Long and Estelle Sloan); "All-American Man" (Phyllis Lynne, Estelle Sloan, Marion Colby, Frank Marlowe, Candace Montgomery, Gus Van, J. Edward Bromberg; danced by Robert Bay, Boys and Girls); Finale (Entire Company)

Whenever book writer and lyricist George Marion Jr. was associated with a musical, you could be almost certain the evening would be a lighthearted and lavish carnival with a splashy and colorful atmosphere. His first major effort was the book for Richard Rodgers and Lorenz Hart's 1939 college football musical *Too Many Girls*, and it was followed by **Beat the Band**, **Early to Bed**, and **Allah Be Praised!** (only the operetta **Marinka** didn't fall into his usual pattern of contemporary stories with saucy plots). With his final musical *Toplitzky of Notre Dame*, he returned to a college-themed musical, but unlike the hit *Too Many Girls* his new show lasted just seven weeks before it folded. As far as Broadway was concerned, his career was over after *Toplitzky*, but more than thirty years later two of his lyrics turned up in the hit 1978 "Fats" Waller tribute revue *Ain't Misbehavin'* ("When the Nylons Bloom Again" and "The Ladies Who Sing With a Band," both from **Early to Bed**).

Toplitzky (J. Edward Bromberg), a Jewish tavern owner whose establishment is directly across the street from Saint Patrick's Cathedral, regularly prays at his synagogue that the Fighting Irish will win against Army. To further this end, he had adopted a child, hoping the boy would grow up to attend Notre Dame, join the football team, and beat Army. But he discovers the adopted child Bobby (played by Betty Jane Watson) is a girl, not a boy, and so that scotches any hope of a Toplitzky beating Army. But wait. It seems the angels in heaven are also big Notre Dame fans, and so they send to Earth one of their own (Angelo, played by Warde Donovan) so that he can play in the Big Game and beat Army. Angelo's stay is for just ninety days, and so he has a lot to do. And musical-comedy complications ensue when he finds himself falling in love with the mortal Bobby. By the finale, the Army–Notre Dame game is played at Yankee Stadium, Notre Dame wins, and it appears Angelo is allowed to remain on Earth so that he and Bobby can marry, or . . .

"Or something like that," commented a somewhat confused Jim O'Connor in the *New York Journal-American*; and when Lewis Funke in the *New York Times* tried to describe the plot to his readers he concluded, "There it is," as "simple" as he could make it. William Hawkins in the *New York World-Telegram* said the story was "highly complicated" with a "baffling lack of motivation," and suggested his readers "forget it" and concentrate on the performers. One or two of the critics were confused about Betty Jane Watson's character, and so she was described as both Toplitzky's daughter and his niece. To further muddy the waters, there was a secondary plot that John S. Wilson in *PM* said didn't quite make sense, and so he decided it was just "thrown in as a bonus."

H.E.S. in the *New York Sun* found the musical "less than exciting" and felt the cast was "handicapped" by the weak material; Otis L. Guernsey Jr. in the *New York Herald Tribune* said the "mediocre" show was "wan and colorless" and lacked an "inner sparkle" to put it across; Wilson noted the "big, gaudy musical of the Before Ballet school" offered tap dancers, comics, and "several characters whose presence is rather inexplicable"; Vernon Rice in the *New York Journal-American* felt nothing was "particularly bad" about the musical, but there wasn't anything "particularly good," either; and Funke felt Marion's book "complicates matters no end" (but he praised dancers Estelle Sloan and Walter Long, and noted that veteran Gus Van played the part of a recently immigrated Irishman).

However, Robert Sylvester in the *New York Daily News* said the "fresh and pleasant" new musical was "real good fun" and hoped it would be around for a "long while"; and Hawkins said the evening was a "very pleasant holiday surprise" and he was glad to report there was "nothing even vaguely approaching a ballet"; he also noted the dances were "lively and gay" and the décor was "substantial and bright."

H.E.S. found Sammy Fain's score "undistinguished" (but singled out "Love Is a Random Thing," "I Want to Go to City College," and "McInerny's Farm") and Rice didn't think the music was "outstanding"; but Sylvester said "Love Is a Random Thing" (which was praised by six of the opening night reviewers) and "You Are My Downfall" were Hit Parade material and three or four "novelty" numbers kept the show moving. O'Connor liked "Common Sense"; Guernsey praised the "snappy" "Wolf Time" and "Let Us Gather at the Goal Line"; and Wilson especially enjoyed "Love Is a Random Thing" and "A Slight Case of Ecstasy."

During the musical's finale sequence "The Notre Dame Victory March" (lyric by John F. Shea, music by the Reverend Michael J. Shea) and "The Notre Dame Hike Song" (lyric and music by Joseph Casastana and Vincent F. Fagan) were performed. During the tryout, director Earl McGill was succeeded by Jose Ruben; Vivienne Segal was succeeded by Doris Patston; Bonita Primrose and her successor Margaret Phelan were finally replaced by Betty Jane Watson; and the songs "I Like It Here" and "The Schedule" were cut. A later post-Broadway tour (with Julie Oshins, Gus Van, Edward Roecker, and Victoria Schools) added the song "Philadelphia Feeling."

During the tryout, Earle McGill (as book director) was succeeded by Jose Rubin.

The collection *You Can't Put Ketchup on the Moon* (Rialto CD # SLRR-9201) includes "Wolf Time" and "You Are My Downfall," and *Keep Your Undershirt On!* (Rialto CD) offers "Love Is a Random Thing."

Both *Toplitzky of Notre Dame* and **Beggar's Holiday** premiered on the same evening (December 26), and so most of the leading critics attended the Duke Ellington and John LaTouche musical and the second-stringers covered *Toplitzky*.

BLOOMER GIRL
"THE MUSICAL SUCCESS"

Theatre: City Center
Opening Date: January 6, 1947; *Closing Date*: February 15, 1947
Performances: 48
Book: Sig Herzig and Fred Saidy
Lyrics: E. Y. Harburg
Music: Harold Arlen
Based on an unproduced play by Lilith and Dan James.
Direction: Book directed by William Schorr and production staged by E. Y. Harburg; *Producers*: John C. Wilson in association with Nat Goldstone; *Choreography*: Agnes De Mille; *Scenery* and *Lighting*: Lemuel Ayers; *Costumes*: Miles White; *Musical Direction*: Jerry Arlen
Cast: Mabel Taliaferro (Serena), Holly Harris (Octavia), Ellen Leslie (Lydia), Dorothy Cothran (Julia), Claire Stevens (Phoebe), Claire Minter (Delia), Peggy Campbell (Daisy), Matt Briggs (Horatio), John Call (Gus), Nanette Fabray (Evelina), Wilfred Thrush (Byron Milligan), Joshua Dingle (Carlos Sherman), Lester Towne (Ebenezer Mimms), Victor Bender (Herman Brasher), Walter Russell (Hiram Crump), Olive Reeves-Smith (Dolly), Dick Smart (Jeff Calhoun), Lily Pagent (Paula), Noella Pelloquin (Prudence), Alice Ward (Hetty), Hubert Dilworth (Pompey), Joe E. Marks (Sheriff Quimby), Edward Chapel (First Deputy), Ralph Sassano (Second Deputy), Donald Green (Third Deputy), John Byrd (Hamilton Calhoun, State Official), Sidney Bassler (Governor Newton), Arthur Lawson (Augustus); Vocal Ensemble: Lily Pagent, Noella Pelloquin, Gloria Rudsdil, Alice Ward, Elaine Harrington, Claudia Campbell, Edward Chapel, Donald Green, Robert Patterson, Richard Spencer, Hugh Holt, Ralph Sassano; Dancers: Margit Dekova, Emy St. Just, Virginia Bosler, Patricia O'Byrne, Jean Kinsella, Ruth Mitchell, Susan Stewart, Cecile Bergman, Eleanor Synder, Ruthanne Welsh, Patricia Gianinoto, Scott Merrill, Arthur Grahl, Paul Olsen, Frank Reynolds, John Martin, Ray Johnson
The musical was presented in two acts.
The action takes place during spring 1861 in the small Eastern manufacturing town of Cicero Falls.

Musical Numbers

Act One: "When the Boys Come Home" (Mabel Taliaferro, Holly Harris, Ellen Leslie, Dorothy Cothran, Claire Stevens, Claire Minter); "Evelina" (Nanette Fabray, Dick Smart); "Welcome Hinges" (Mabel Taliaferro, Holly Harris, Ellen Leslie, Dorothy Cothran, Claire Stevens, Claire Minter, Byron Milligan, Carlos Sherman, Lester Towne, Victor Bender, Walter Russell, Nanette Fabray, Dick Smart); "The Farmer's Daughter" (Byron Milligan, Carlos Sherman, Lester Towne, Victor Bender, Walter Russell); "It Was Good Enough for Grandma" (Nanette Fabray, Bloomer Girls); "Dance Specialty" (Peggy Campbell, Dancers); "The Eagle and Me" (Hubert Dilworth); "Right as the Rain" (Dick Smart, Nanette Fabray); "T'morra',

T'morra'" (Peggy Campbell); "The Rakish Young Man with the Whiskers" (Nanette Fabray, Dick Smart); "Pretty as a Picture" (Male Ensemble); "Waltz" (Dancers; The Waltzers: Margit Dekova and Scott Merrill, Cecile Bergman and Paul Olsen, Ruthanne Welsh and David Raher, Susan Stewart and Frank Reynolds, Virginia Bosler and Arthur Grahl); "Style Show Ballet" (Principals and Dancers)

Act Two: "Sunday in Cicero Falls" (Principals and Company); "I Got a Song" (Hubert Dilworth, with Arthur Lawson); "Lullaby" (aka "Satin Gown and Silver Shoe") (Evelina); "Simon Legree" (Donald Green); "Liza Crossing the Ice" (Ensemble; danced by Emy St. Just); "I Never Was Born" (Peggy Campbell); "Man for Sale" (Joshua Dingle); "Civil War Ballet" (Dancers; Woman in Black and Red: Emy St. Just; Girl in Rose: Margit Dekova; Her Soldier: Scott Merrill); "The Eagle and Me" (reprise) (Ensemble); "When the Boys Come Home" (Entire Company)

The current production of *Bloomer Girl* was a limited-run return engagement that played at City Center by the national touring company. Nanette Fabray had succeeded Celeste Holm in the role of Evelina in the original 1944 Broadway production, played the part on tour, and was here reprising the role. She made her New York debut in the revue **Meet the People**, had succeeded Constance Moore in **By Jupiter**, and had originated featured-player roles in **Let's Face It!**, **My Dear Public**, and **Jackpot**. After **Bloomer Girl**, she created leading roles in five Broadway musicals over a fourteen-year period: Jule Styne's **High Button Shoes**, Alan Jay Lerner and Kurt Weill's **Love Life** (for which she received the Tony Award for Best Leading Actress in a Musical), Morton Gould's *Arms and the Girl* (1950), Hugh Martin's *Make a Wish* (1951), and Irving Berlin's *Mr. President* (1962). She also appeared in the classic 1953 MGM film musical *The Band Wagon* and with Fred Astaire and Jack Buchanan introduced Arthur Schwartz and Howard Dietz's "That's Entertainment," which with Berlin's "There's No Business Like Show Business" and Cole Porter's "Another Op'nin', Another Show," rounds out a memorable triptych that salutes show business.

For more information about *Bloomer Girl*, see entry for the 1944 production.

STREET SCENE
"A Dramatic Musical"

Theatre: Adelphi Theatre
Opening Date: January 9, 1947; *Closing Date*: May 17, 1947
Performances: 148
Book: Elmer Rice
Lyrics: Langston Hughes and Elmer Rice
Music: Kurt Weill
Based on the 1929 play *Street Scene* by Elmer Rice.
Direction: Charles Friedman; *Producers*: Dwight Deere Wiman and The Playwrights' Company; *Choreography*: Anna Sokolow; *Scenery* and *Lighting*: Jo Mielziner; *Costumes*: Lucinda Ballard; *Musical Direction*: Maurice Abravanel
Cast: Irving Kaufman (Abraham Kaplan), Helen Arden (Greta Fiorentino), Wilson Smith (Carl Olsen), Hope Emerson (Emma Jones), Ellen Repp (Olga Olsen), Norma Chambers (Shirley Kaplan), Creighton Thompson (Henry Davis), Peter Griffith (Willie Maurrant), Polyna Stoska (Anna Maurrant), Brian Sullivan (Sam Kaplan), Remo Lota (Daniel Buchanan), Norman Cordon (Frank Maurrant), David E. Thomas (George Jones), Lauren Gilbert (Steve Sankey), Sidney Rayner (Lippo Fiorentino), Beverly Janis (Jennie Hildebrand), Zosia Gruchala (Second Graduate), Marion Covey (Third Graduate), Juliana Gallagher (Mary Hildebrand), Bennett Burrill (Charlie Hildebrand), Elen Lane (Laura Hildebrand), Helen Ferguson (Grace Davis), Ernest Taylor (First Policeman), Anne Jeffreys (Rose Maurrant), Don Saxon (Harry Easter), Sheila Bond (Mae Jones), Danny Daniels (Dick McGann), Robert Pierson (Vincent Jones), Edwin G. O'Connor (Dr. John Wilson), Norman Thomson (Officer Harry Murphy), Russell George (Milkman), Joyce Carrol (Music Pupil), Randolph Symonette (City Marshall James Henry), Paul Lilly (Fred Cullen), Edward Reichert (Old Clothes Man), Roy Munsell (Interne), John Sweet (Ambulance Driver), Peggy Turnley (First Nursemaid), Ellen Carleen (Second Nursemaid), Betty Van and Joseph E. Scandur (Married Couple); Passersby, Neighbors, Children, etc.: Aza Bard, Ellen Carleen, Joyce Carrol, Marion Covey, Diana Donne, Bessie Franklin, Zosia Gruchala, Juanita Hall, Beverly Janis, Elen Lane, Marie Leidal, Sasha Pressman, Biruta Ramoska, Peggy

Turnley, Bette Van, Larry Baker, Tom Barragan, Mel Bartell, Victor Clarke, Russell George, Bobby Horn, Bernard Kovler, Roy Munsell, Edwin G. O'Connor, Edward Reichert, Joseph E. Scandur, John Sweet, Ernest Taylor, William Woodbeck

The musical was presented in two acts.

The action takes place on the stoop and front sidewalk of a New York City tenement during a period of twenty-four hours in June.

Musical Numbers

Note: Unless otherwise noted, all lyrics are by Langston Hughes.

Act One: "Ain't It Awful, the Heat?" (lyric by Langston Hughes and Elmer Rice) (Helen Arden, Hope Emerson, Ellen Repp, Irving Kaufman, Wilson Smith, Neighbors); "I Got a Marble and a Star" (Creighton Thompson); "Get a Load of That" (lyric by Langston Hughes and Elmer Rice) (Hope Emerson, Helen Arden, Ellen Repp); "When a Woman Has a Baby" (lyric by Langston Hughes and Elmer Rice) (Remo Lota, Helen Arden, Hope Emerson, Polyna Stoska); "Somehow I Never Could Believe" (Polyna Stoska); "Get a Load of That" (reprise) (Hope Emerson, Helen Arden, David E. Thomas, Ellen Repp); "Ice Cream" (lyric by Langston Hughes and Elmer Rice) (Sydney Rayner, Hope Emerson, Helen Arden, Creighton Thompson, David E. Thomas, Wilson Smith, Ellen Repp); "Let Things Be Like They Always Was" (Norman Cordon); "Wrapped in a Ribbon and Tied in a Bow" (lyric by Langston Hughes and Elmer Rice) (Beverly Janis, Neighbors); "Lonely House" (Brian Sullivan); "Wouldn't You Like to Be on Broadway?" (lyric by Langston Hughes and Elmer Rice) (Don Saxon); "What Good Would the Moon Be?" (Anne Jeffreys); "Moon-Faced, Starry-Eyed" (Danny Daniels, Sheila Bond); "Remember That I Care" (Brian Sullivan, Anne Jeffreys)

Act Two: "Catch Me If You Can" (aka "Children's Game") (lyric by Langston Hughes and Elmer Rice) (Bennett Burrill, Juliana Gallagher, Peter Griffith, Children); "There'll Be Trouble" (lyric by Langston Hughes and Elmer Rice) (Norman Cordon, Polyna Stoska, Anne Jeffreys); "A Boy Like You" (Polyna Stoska); "We'll Go Away Together" (Brian Sullivan, Anne Jeffreys); "The Woman Who Lived Up There" (Ensemble); "Lullaby" (lyric by Elmer Rice) (Peggy Turnley, Ellen Carleen); "I Loved Her, Too" (lyric by Langston Hughes and Elmer Rice) (Norman Cordon, Anne Jeffreys, Ensemble); "Don't Forget the Lilac Bush" (lyric by Langston Hughes and Elmer Rice) (Brian Sullivan, Anne Jeffreys); "Ain't It Awful, the Heat?" (Helen Arden, Hope Emerson, Ellen Repp, Irving Kaufman)

Street Scene was based on Elmer Rice's Pulitzer Prize-winning play of the same name, which opened on Broadway at the Playhouse Theatre on January 10, 1929, and ran for 601 performances. Both the drama and the musical took place on the stoop and front sidewalk of a New York City tenement during the twenty-four-hour period of a miserably hot and humid day in June. The story depicted both the trivialities and tragedies of the people who live in the tenement, and centered on the Maurrant family. The doomed Anna (Polyna Stoska) is unhappily married to the insanely jealous Frank (Norman Cordon), and their daughter Rose (Anne Jeffreys) seems prey to the bitterness and futility of the hardscrabble underside of Manhattan life, a world far removed from the gaiety of the fantasyland tourist world of **On the Town** and the tony cocktail set of **Park Avenue** (which actually took place on a Long Island estate).

Street Scene played for just over four months, and while it was not a financial success it is frequently produced by opera companies and its score is one of the glories of American musical theatre. Kurt Weill's music and the lyrics by Langston Hughes and Elmer Rice (and with an occasional assist from Walt Whitman in the songs "Remember That I Care" and "Don't Forget the Lilac Bush") perfectly capture both the tragic and mundane worlds of the tenement dwellers. Anna's intensely powerful aria "Somehow I Never Could Believe" is one of the crown jewels of lyric theatre, one of the most introspective character studies ever composed for the musical stage. Frank's "I Loved Her, Too," was a gripping musical self-analysis in which he explains but doesn't justify himself after he has murdered Anna; and "The Woman Who Lived Up There" was a chilling choral number in which the neighbors sing of the murder victim who used to live on one of the upper floors of their building. Another tenant is Sam (Brian Sullivan), a young man who loves Rose, and his poignant "Lonely House" exposed his intense loneliness, while the janitor Henry (Creighton Thompson) went about his daily chores set to the irresistible if brooding blues of "I Got a Marble and a Star."

But many of the songs looked at the lighter side of tenement life, including the gossips with their "Ain't It Awful, the Heat?" and "Get a Load of That" (these biddies are surely related to the Dublin gossips and their "You Poor Thing" from *Juno* [1959]); an ode to the joys of "Ice Cream" on a hot summer's day; the sardonic "Lullaby" for two nursemaids; and the crowd-pleaser "Moon-Faced, Starry-Eyed" in which neighborhood bobby-soxers Dick (Danny Daniels) and Mae (Sheila Bond) jitterbugged as if there were no tomorrow.

Brooks Atkinson in the *New York Times* praised the "magnificence and glory" of the new "sidewalk opera" with its "fresh and eloquent" score that revealed the "humanity under the argot of the New York streets." He also said the "down-beat" and "hot" "Moon-Faced, Starry-Eyed" was a "superb American apache" that "outranks any of the current show tunes on Broadway." Many of the critics couldn't decide if the work was a musical or an opera or a folk opera (but it seems clear the work is just what its creators called it, a "dramatic musical"), but John Chapman in the *New York Daily News* dubbed it a "metropolitan opera" which was "moving" and "remarkable." The "excellent" lyrics and the "richly colored, effective" music created a "far from ordinary event in the theatre" in its depiction of a "grim Knickerbocker holiday."

Robert Garland in the *New York Journal-American* liked the "always interesting, frequently moving" evening, but felt it somehow failed to "synchronize into an inspired harmonic whole." He said the work wasn't drama, traditional musical comedy, or "out-and-out" grand opera, and in a reference to **Lady in the Dark** suggested the production could never make up its mind what it wanted to be. Richard Watts in the *New York Post* admitted the evening was an "adventurous endeavor" but felt it was most musically successful when it depicted the lighter side of tenement life (the jitterbug, the children's games, the graduation sequence, and the numbers for the gossips), and faltered when the serious elements of the story were set to music.

Although Louis Kronenberger in *PM* had qualifications about *Street Scene*, he nonetheless said it was the "first effective musical" of the season. He felt some of the music was "pretentious," some of it "facilely florid" in movie-music style, and some was of "dubious operatic value." But for all this, the choral music and the underscoring were effective, and the "lighter" songs ("Ice Cream," "Moon-Faced, Starry-Eyed," "Lullaby," and "Wrapped in a Ribbon and Tied in a Bow") were "quite successful." Howard Barnes in the *New York Herald Tribune* said the "uneven" work wasn't a *Porgy and Bess* but was still a "generally exciting folk opera" that was "something to see" for its "electric theatrical quality." He noted Polyna Stoska was a "rare artist for the theatre" with a "controlled and infinitely appealing voice" and acting skills that lacked nothing. He singled out her "Somehow I Never Could Believe" and "A Boy Like You"; and also mentioned he enjoyed the lullaby, children's game, and jitterbug numbers.

Ward Morehouse in the *New York Sun* said the new musical was "highly impressive" and "worth seeing"; Weill's music was "good," but sometimes he wished the drama could have gone "unimpeded by song." William Hawkins in the *New York World-Telegram* found the work "intensely interesting," and praised "Moon-Faced, Starry-Eyed" (a "down-to-earth modern dance tune"), "Ice Cream" (so "rich and full" it could have been composed by Verdi), and "Wrapped in a Ribbon and Tied in a Bow" (a "catchy rhythmic item"). Further, some of the score offered melodies in "opulent" operetta style while the second-act trio ("There'll Be Trouble") brimmed with "ominous grandeur." He noted Polyna Stoska performed "Somehow I Never Could Believe" with "infinite feeling" and a "free soaring vocal treatment" that provided a "thrilling emotional quality." He concluded that despite its "glowering" and "undulating" aspects, the musical was an "experience to be mulled over and remembered."

During the tryout, Richard Manning was succeeded by Brian Sullivan. Four songs in the second act were cut: "She's a Gemini Girl" (for the gossips); "Bon Giorno, Signore" (for a neighbor and the iceman); "Italy in Technicolor" (for Rose and one of the neighbors); and "I'll Live for That Day" (for Rose and Sam).

The cast album was recorded by Columbia (LP # OL-4139; later issued on CD by CBS Masterworks # MK-44668); for the album, the role of Frank Maurrant is sung by Randolph Symonette, who was Norman Cordon's understudy and who eventually assumed the role in the Broadway production. A 1949 radio broadcast from the Hollywood Bowl was released by Naxos (CD # 8-120885) with Polyna Stoska and Brian Sullivan from the original Broadway cast along with Dorothy Sarnoff (Rose) and Norman Atkins (Frank). Both the 1947 and 1949 recordings are abridged, but there are two complete versions that were released on two-CD sets. The English National Opera recording (That's Entertainment CD # CDTER-2-1185) is based on a production that opened on October 13, 1989, with Kristine Ciesinki (Anna), Janis Kelly (Rose), Bonaventura Bottone (Sam), Richard van Allen (Frank), and Catherine Zeta-Jones (Mae); Carl Davis conducted. The other recording (Decca # 433-371-2) includes Josephine Barstow (Anna), Samuel Ramey (Frank), Angelina Reaux (Rose), and Jerry Hadley (Sam); John Mauceri conducted. The cut number "Italy in Technicolor" is included in two collections, *Kurt Weill Revisited* (Painted Smiles CD # PSCD-108) and *Lost in Boston II* (Varese Sarabande CD # VSD-5485).

The musical was revived eight times by the New York City Opera Company: April 2, 1959 (two performances); September 17, 1959 (two performances); February 13, 1960 (three performances); April 26, 1963 (three performances); February 24, 1966 (six performances), all performed at City Center; the final three revivals were seen at the New York State Theatre on October 8, 1978 (four performances), October 13, 1979 (five performances), and September 7, 1990 (six performances).

City Opera's 1979 revival was shown on public television on October 27, 1979, and a joint production by the Houston Grand Opera, the Theatre im Pfalzbau Ludwigshafen, and the Theatre des Westens, Berlin, was released on DVD by Image Entertainment (# ID924-ORADVD).

All lyrics, spoken dialogue, and music were included in an undated softback script published by Chappell & Co.

The musical opened almost eighteen years to the day of the original drama's premiere, and for both the nonmusical and musical versions the scenic design of the tenement's façade was created by Jo Mielziner.

Awards

Tony Awards: Best Score (**Kurt Weill**); Best Costumes (**Lucinda Ballard** for her costume designs for the entire season, which included **Street Scene**, *Happy Birthday*, *Another Part of the Forest*, *John Loves Mary*, and **The Chocolate Soldier**)

FINIAN'S RAINBOW
"A New Musical" / "A Musical Satire"

Theatre: 46th Street Theatre
Opening Date: January 10, 1947; *Closing Date*: October 2, 1948
Performances: 725
Book: E. Y. Harburg and Fred Saidy
Lyrics: E. Y. Harburg
Music: Burton Lane
Direction: Bretaigne Windust; *Producers*: Lee Sabinson and William R. Katzell; *Choreography*: Michael Kidd; *Scenery* and *Lighting*: Jo Mielziner; *Costumes*: Eleanor Goldsmith; *Musical Direction*: Milton Rosenstock
Cast: Sonny Terry (Sunny [The Harmonica Player]), Eddie Bruce (Buzz Collins), Tom McElhany (Sheriff), Alan Gilbert (First Sharecropper), Robert Eric Carlson (Second Sharecropper, Second Deputy), Anita Alvarez (Susan Mahoney aka Susan the Silent), Augustus Smith Jr. (Henry), Maude Simmons (Third Sharecroper), Albert Sharpe (Finian McLonergan), Ella Logan (Sharon McLonergan), Donald Richards (Woody Mahoney), William Scully (Fourth Sharecropper), David Wayne (Og), William Greaves (Howard), Robert Pitkin (Senator Billboard Rawlins), Nathaniel Dickerson (First Geologist), Lucas Aco (Second Geologist), Diane Woods (Diana), Jane Earle (Jane), Roland Skinner (John), Arthur Tell (Mr. Robust), Royal Dano (Mr. Shears), Jerry Laws (First Passion Pilgrim Gospeleer), Lorenzo Fuller (Second Passion Pilgrim Gospeleer), Louis Sharp (Third Passion Pilgrim Gospeleer), Michael Ellis (First Deputy), Harry Day (Third Deputy); Other Children: Norma Jane Marlowe, Elayne Richards; Dancers: Freda Flier, Annabelle Gold, Eleanore Gregory, Ann Hutchinson, Erona Harris, Anna Mitten, Kathleen Stanford, Lavinia Williams, Lucas Aco, Harry Day, Daniel Floyd, J. C. McCord, Frank Neal, Arthur Partington, James Flash Riley, Don Weissmuller; Singers: Arlene Anderson, Connie Baxter, Carroll Brooks, Lyn Joi, Mimi Kelly, Delores Martin, Marijane Maricle, Maude Simmons, Robert Eric Carlson, Ralph Waldo Cummings, Nathaniel Dickerson, Alan Gilbert, Theodore Hines, Morty Rappe, William Scully, Roland Skinner
The musical was presented in two acts.
The action takes place in and around Rainbow Valley, Missitucky.

Musical Numbers

Act One: "This Time of the Year" (Singing Ensemble) and "Dance" (Anita Alvarez, Dancers); "How Are Things in Glocca Morra?" (Ella Logan); "Look to the Rainbow" (Ella Logan, Singers); "Old Devil Moon" (Ella Logan, Donald Richards); "How Are Things in Glocca Morra?" (reprise) (Ella Logan); "Something Sort of Grandish" (Ella Logan, David Wayne); "If This Isn't Love" (Ella Logan, Donald Richards, Singers) and "Dance" (Anita Alvarez; Two Couples: Anna Mitten and J. C. McCord and Annabelle Gold and Lucas Aco; The Uninitiated: Eleanore Gregory and Arthur Partington; The Tentative Two: Ann Hutchinson and Harry Day; The Intense Pair: Annabelle Gold and J. C. McCord; The Exuberant Ones: Freda Flier and Don Weissmuller; Triangle: Kathleen Stanford, James Flash Riley, and Lavinia Williams; Another Couple: Erona Harris and Frank Neal); "Something Sort of Grandish" (reprise) (David Wayne); "Necessity" (Dolores Martin and Maude Simmons, Arlene Anderson, Connie Baxter, Lyn Joi, Mimi Kelly, Carroll Brooks, Marijane Maricle, Alan Gilbert); "(That) Great Come-and-Get-It Day" (Ella Logan, Donald Richards, Singers) and "Dance" (Dancers)

Act Two: "When the Idle Poor Become the Idle Rich" (Ella Logan, Singers; danced by J. C. McCord, Kathleen Stanford, Frank Neal and Lavinia Williams, Ann Hutchinson, Freda Flier and Arthur Partington, James Flash Riley, Don Weissmuller, Annabelle Gold and Lucas Aco, Anna Mitten); "Old Devil Moon" (reprise) (Ella Logan, Donald Richards); "Dance o' the Golden Crock" (Anita Alvarez, accompanied by Sonny Terry); "The Begat" (Robert Pitkin, Jerry Laws, Lorenzo Fuller, Louis Sharp); "Look to the Rainbow" (reprise) (Ella Logan, Donald Richards, Singers); "When I'm Not Near the Girl I Love" (David Wayne, Anita Alvarez); "If This Isn't Love" (reprise) (Entire Ensemble); "How Are Things in Glocca Morra?" (reprise/finale) (Ella Logan, Entire Ensemble)

The 1946–1947 season was a popular one for musical fantasies, and *Finian's Rainbow* enjoyed the longest run of the crop and was in fact the longest-running of all the season's musicals. But another fantasy, **Brigadoon**, has eclipsed it in terms of revivals and general popularity. *Brigadoon* was a lush and romantic operetta, while *Finian's Rainbow* was a satiric and sly old-fashioned musical comedy about Irishman Finian McLonergan (Albert Sharpe), who has stolen a pot of gold from the leprechaun Og (David Wayne). Finian travels to the United States with his daughter Sharon (Ella Logan), and hides the gold somewhere in the state of Missitucky; but Og has followed him and is determined to retrieve his fortune. The amusing fantasy also includes an array of black and white sharecroppers; the hero Woody Mahoney (Donald Richards), who falls in love with Sharon; and the bigoted Senator Billboard Rawlins (Robert Pitkin), whom Og turns into a black in order to give the prejudiced senator some hands-on experience with racism.

Burton Lane's richly melodic score and E. Y. Harburg's alternately romantic and satiric lyrics gave Broadway one of its finest scores and solidified the period as one of the golden eras of the Broadway musical. The memorable ballads included the delicate "Look to the Rainbow" and the jubilant "If This Isn't Love," and with "Old Devil Moon" and "How Are Things in Glocca Morra?" the score reached musical theatre nirvana. "Old Devil Moon" offered a joyous, insinuating, and expansive melody, and the haunting folk-like "Glocca Morra" would have been at home in a concert of old Irish favorites by John McCormack. The comedy songs (such as "Something Sort of Grandish" and "When I'm Not Near the Girl I Love") offered Harburg's famous verbal pyrotechnics; and there were clever social- and political-styled novelties ("Necessity" and "When the Idle Poor Become the Idle Rich") and rousing revival-inspired numbers ("That Great Come-and-Get-It Day" and "The Begat").

Brooks Atkinson in the *New York Times* praised the "highly original" work, which brought the American musical "several steps forward" with its imaginative writing and performances. The "clarion" music by Burton Lane offered "rapturous Irish songs," of which "How Are Things in Glocca Morra?" was one of the "most beguiling." In a prescient note, Atkinson said if the American musical stage continued on its course, then dialogue wouldn't be necessary and "everything essential" could be told through music and dance.

Ward Morehouse in *PM* said the evening was "fresh and jubilant and imaginative" and "something not to miss"; John Chapman in the *New York Daily News* praised the "pleasant" music, "top-grade" lyrics, and Michael Kidd's choreography. He noted that "next to the atom bomb," whimsy was "the most dangerous stuff to fool with." But David Wayne as the sprightly Og was "quite magical" and "cast a spell" with his performance. William Hawkins in the *New York World-Telegram* liked Kidd's "air-borne dances" and Lane's "eminently singable tunes," and noted that "How Are Things in Glocca Morra?" had "already been recorded by every self-respecting singer in the business."

Richard Watts in the *New York Post* said the season's "liveliest and most tuneful" musical possibly had "the most elaborate plot since *War and Peace*," and while the script was probably not quite so "rich" and "biting in its editorial comment" as the librettists wished, the story was nonetheless a "proper springboard" for the "excellent" songs and dances. And Robert Garland in the *New York Journal-American* said *Finian's Rainbow* "has everything a grand new musical should have."

But Howard Barnes in the *New York Herald Tribune* said the direction was "labored" and the evening lacked the "pace and sustained mood" that the story required. He mentioned that David Wayne's Og was a performance of "true brilliance" that revealed what a "wonderful melodic fable" *Finian's Rainbow* could have been had it been better written and directed. Louis Kronenberger in *PM* recognized that the musical's creators were "trying for something different and original," but he felt the evening lacked the "taste and integrity" to overcome its penchant for "harrowing cuteness" and "cheap and even outhouse humor." It was as if the creators wanted to run away from the "standard Broadway scene" but couldn't control themselves and thus were "continually sneaking back for another glimpse."

The script was published in hardback by Random House in 1947 and was also published in the January 1949 issue of *Theatre Arts* magazine. The script was published in hardback in 2014 by the Library of Congress in a collection that includes the scripts of fifteen other musicals.

The cast album was released by Columbia (LP # ML-4062 and # OS-2080). The CD was issued by Sony Classical/Columbia/Legacy (# SK-89208) and includes bonus tracks of Harburg discussing and singing "How Are Things in Glocca Morra?," "When I'm Not Near the Girl I Love," and the unused song "Don't Pass Me By" as well as an alternate take of "(That) Great Come-and-Get-It Day" featuring Donald Richards instead of Ella Logan.

The London production opened at the Palace Theatre on October 21, 1947, for a disappointing run of fifty-five performances; the cast included Patrick J. Kelly (Finian), Alfie Bass (Og), Beryl Seton (Sharon), and Alan Gilbert (Woody). A faithful if belated film version was released by Warner Brothers in 1968 and except for "Necessity" retained the entire score; directed by Francis Ford Coppola, the cast included Fred Astaire (Finian), Tommy Steele (Og), Petula Clark (Sharon), and Don Francks (Woody), who had created the title role in the legendary 1965 Broadway flop *Kelly*. As the years go by, the film looks better and better and is a refreshing break from the generally bloated and overproduced film musicals of the era. The soundtrack was released by Warner Brothers (LP # BS-2550) and includes the cut "Necessity"; the CD was issued by Warner Brothers/Rhino (# RHM2-7852) and includes the previously unissued tracks of the overture, the entr'acte, and exit music. The DVD was released by Warner Brothers (# 11208). (Years before the film's release, a cartoon version of the musical was announced for production but never materialized.)

The first New York revival was presented by the New York City Center Light Opera Company at City Center on May 18, 1955, for fifteen performances; the cast included Will Mahoney (Finian), Donn (aka Don and Donald) Driver (Og), Helen Gallagher (Sharon), and Merv Griffin (Woody). The company next revived the work at City Center on April 27, 1960, for fifteen performances; the production then transferred to the 46th Street Theatre, the home of the original 1947 production, where it played for twelve more performances; the cast included Bobby Howes (Finian; Howes, the father of Sally Ann Howes, was here making his New York debut), Howard Morris (Og), Jeannie Carson (Sharon), Biff McGuire (Woody), and, for the City Center run, Anita Alvarez reprised her original role of Susan the Silent. The production was recorded by RCA Victor (LP # LOC/LSO-1057; the CD release (# 1057-2-RG) includes the previously unissued track of the reprise/finale of "How Are Things in Glocca Morra?"

The company's third and final revival of the musical was seen at City Center on April 5, 1967, for twenty-three performances; the cast included Frank McHugh (Finian), Len Gochman (Og), Nancy Dussault (Sharon), Stanley Grover (Woody), and Sandy Duncan (Susan).

For a number of years the work was deemed unrevivable because of the use of blackface to depict the prejudiced Southern senator who is turned into a black by Og. But the 2009 Broadway revival solved the problem in a manner that should have been obvious to everyone for years: both a white and a black actor who bore a basic resemblance to one another depicted the "before" and "after" senator. This revival was first seen in a concert presentation by Encores! on March 26, 2009, for five performances, and then opened at the St. James Theatre on October 2, 2009, for ninety-two showings; the cast included Jim Norton (Finian), Christopher Fitzgerald (Og), Kate Baldwin (Sharon), and Cheyenne Jackson (Woody). The cast album was released by PS Classics (CD # PS-1088).

An Off-Off-Broadway revival was produced by the Irish Repertory Theatre on April 15, 2004. Its cast album by Ghostlight (CD # 4402-2) marks the musical's third of four New York cast recordings; the performers included Jonathan Freeman (Finian), Malcolm Gets (Og), Melissa Errico (Sharon), and Max Von Essen (Woody), and the album includes a bonus track of E. Y. Harburg singing "Old Devil Moon."

Awards

Tony Awards: Best Featured Actor in a Musical (**David Wayne**); Best Choreographer (**Michael Kidd**, in a tie with Agnes De Mille for *Brigadoon*). *Note*: For the *following* season's Tony Awards, Max Meth was given the Tony for Best Conductor and Musical Director for *Finian's Rainbow* (during the run of the musical, Meth had succeeded Milton Rosenstock as musical director).

SWEETHEARTS

Theatre: Shubert Theatre
Opening Date: January 21, 1947; *Closing Date*: September 27, 1947
Performances: 288
Book: Harry B. Smith and Fred De Gresac; revised book by John Cecil Holm
Lyrics: Robert B. Smith
Music: Victor Herbert
Direction: John Kennedy; *Producers*: Paula Stone and Michael Sloane; *Choreography*: Ensembles by Catherine Littlefield and choreography by Theodore Adolphus; *Scenery*: Peter Wolf; *Lighting*: Uncredited; *Costumes*: Michael Lucyk; *Musical Direction*: Edwin McArthur
Cast: The Daughters: Marcia James (Doreen), Nony Franklin (Corinne), Janet Medlin (Eileen), Betty Ann Busch (Pauline), Martha Emma Watson (Kathleen), and Gloria Lind (Nadine); Eva Soltesz (Gretchen), Muriel Bruenig (Hilda), Robert Shackleton (Lieutenant Karl), Marjorie Gateson (Dame Lucy), Robert Reeves (Peasant), Raynor Howell (Peasant), June Knight (Liane), *Bobby Clark* (Mike Mikeloviz), Gloria Story (Sylvia), Mark Dawson (Prince Franz), Richard Benson (Peter), Ken Arnold (Hans), Paul Best (Baron Petrus Von Tromp), Anthony Kemble-Cooper (Hon. Butterfield Slingsby), Janice Cioffi (Prima Ballerina), John Anania (Adolphus), Cornell MacNeil (Homberg), Robert Feyti (Ambassador), Louis De Mangus (Ambassador), Tom Perkins (Captain Laurent); Singers: Ella Mayer, Florence Gault, Peggy Gavan, Gertrude Hild, Nora Neal, Lillian Shelley, LaVernn Yotti, Alice Arnold, Marjorie Wellock, Richard Benson, Phil Crosbie, Louis DeMangus, Arnold Knippenburg, Wilbur Nelson, Robert Reeves, Charles Wood, Raynor Howell, Robert Feyti, Tom Perkins, Frank Whitmore; Dancers: Jeanette Tannan, Aura Vainio, Bernice Brady, Ingrid Secretan, Connie Wege, Marie Louise Forsythe, Olivia Cardone, Jeanne Lewis, Dorothea Weidner, Alma Lee, Sally Sorvo, James Russell, Bruce Cartwright, Peter Holmes, John Ward
The musical was presented in two acts.
The action takes place during the fifteenth century in Bruges, Belgium, and in the country of Zilania.

Musical Numbers

Act One: Opening: "Iron, Iron, Iron" (Daughters) and "On Parade" (Robert Shackleton, Singers, Ballet Dancers); "Sweethearts" (Gloria Story, Daughters, Singers); "For Every Lover Must Meet His Fate" (Mark Dawson, Daughters, Singers); "Lorelei" (Robert Shackleton, June Knight); "The Angelus" (Gloria Story, Singers); "Jeanette and Her Little Wooden Shoes" (Bobby Clark, Gloria Story, Anthony Kemble-Cooper, Paul Best, Ballet Dancers); Act One Finale (Mark Dawson, Gloria Story, Bobby Clark, June Knight, Robert Shackleton, Paul Best, Marjorie Gateson, Daughters, Singers)
Act Two: "Opening" (danced by Janice Cioffi); "Pretty as a Picture" (Bobby Clark, Male Chorus, Ballet Dancers); "Land of My Own Romance" (Gloria Story, Mark Dawson); "I Might Be Your Once-in-a-While" (June Knight, Robert Shackleton; Dancing Lieutenant Karl: Jimmie Russell; Dancing Von Tromp: Bruce

Cartwright; Dancing Slingsby: Peter Holmes); "Pilgrims of Love" (aka "Monks' Quartette") (Bobby Clark, Robert Shackleton, Paul Best, Anthony Kemble-Cooper, John Anania, Cornell MacNeil); Finale (Entire Company)

Producers Paula Stone and Michael Sloane hit pay dirt with their surprisingly successful revival of Victor Herbert's operetta **The Red Mill**, but their production of the composer's *Sweethearts* received a much cooler reception. However, on the strength of Bobby Clark's free-for-all performance the musical played over nine months on Broadway and then enjoyed a national tour.

Louis Kronenberger in *PM* said the work was already "dull and dated" when he'd seen a revival in 1925; he noted: "Act I—Village Square in Zilania. Act II—The Palace. There you have all you need to know about the vintage, and virtually all you need to know about the plot." Otherwise, the evening was a "one-man show," thanks to Bobby Clark and his shenanigans. Richard Watts in the *New York Post* said Clark's "comic virtuosity" was "nothing short of epic"; Ward Morehouse in the *New York Sun* found him "immense"; and Brooks Atkinson in the *New York Times* said the "genius" was the "funniest man in America," and at the final curtain the audience was "more exhausted" than the "illustrious clown" who had kept them in stitches with "abdominal laughter."

The musical had first been produced on September 8, 1913, for 136 performances at the New Amsterdam Theatre, and was later revived at Jolson's Theatre on September 21, 1929, for seventeen performances. The 1938 MGM film musical *Sweethearts* with Jeanette MacDonald and Nelson Eddy borrowed the operetta's title and a handful of songs but otherwise the story was completely different from the stage version; the film included three songs from the original production ("Jeanette and Her Little Wooden Shoes," "Every Lover Must Meet His Fate," and the title number), all of which had revised lyrics by Robert Wright and George Forrest.

The plot of *Sweethearts* centered on the romance between commoner Sylvia (Gloria Story) and Prince Franz (Mark Dawson). The rigid rules of operetta ordained that a commoner and a member of royalty must never wed, but all is not lost because it turns out Sylvia . . . is of royal blood! That, in a nutshell, was the plot, but no one cared about it as long as Bobby Clark was romping about the stage and the cast was singing Herbert's familiar songs.

For the current revival, John Cecil Holm's revised book gave Bobby Clark enough space to cavort about with his merry bag of tricks. Again present were his painted-on glasses, his glowing cigar, his oversized coat, his walking stick, and his endearing smirks, grimaces, leers, and ogles. At one point, he mumbled to himself and then informed the audience this was simply an "old operetta custom." And when later seen pulling a two-wheeled cart, he asked the audience if they'd seen a horse roaming down the aisles of the Shubert Theatre. The book also provided opportunities for him to don an assortment of costumes and disguises, including one in which he dressed in washerwoman-drag and carelessly tossed wet laundry about; at other times, he impersonated an officer of the French Foreign Legion, a wooden-shoe-wearing Dutchman, a royal courtier, and a monk. For the latter, he and a five-man chorus sang "Pilgrims of Love"; according to William Hawkins in the *New York World-Telegram*, Bobby conducted the number with "idiotic intensity" and blew "the roof off the house" with his "mad miming" which was a "triumph of efficient absurdity." Atkinson said the sequence was a "masterpiece" and the audience would have been happy had Clark gone on performing the number "until two tomorrow morning."

Howard Barnes in the *New York Herald Tribune* felt without Clark's "irrepressible presence" there was "scant excuse" for the revival; but he noted the book accommodated Clark by tailoring it to his "brilliant clowning" skills. Robert Garland in the *New York Journal American* said Clark had himself a "clambake" as he "riotously" clowned about in his "rough and ready way." Clark took hold of the "preposterous," "ancient," and "dishonorable" libretto in the "only way it could be treated": "He tossed it right out into Messrs. Shuberts' Alley." John Chapman in the *New York Daily News* said the evening was a case of "waiting for Bobby," and his "ebullience" made him the "sweetheart of *Sweethearts*."

Admittedly, there *were* other performers in the show, but with Bobby around it was probably easy to overlook them. Mark Dawson was the prince, and is now perhaps best remembered as Floyd the cop in *Fiorello!* (1959), who was the subject of Pat Stanley's memorable "I Love a Cop"; Robert Shackleton was a good-looking singer who never broke into the ranks of the era's leading men, but later appeared in the film version of *Where's Charley?* and sang "My Darling, My Darling"; Gloria Story as the commoner-who-is-really-a-princess appeared in a few musicals during the middle of the decade, including **Rhapsody** and

The Firebrand of Florence; sardonic Marjorie Gateson was a good comic match for Bobby; and June Knight was fondly remembered from *Jubilee* (1935) where she had introduced Cole Porter's "Begin and Beguine" and, with future choreographer Charles Walters, "Just One of Those Things" and "A Picture of Me without You."

The current revival retained eight songs from the original 1913 production ("Iron, Iron, Iron," "On Parade," "Sweethearts," "For Every Lover Must Meet His Fate," "The Angelus," "Jeanette and Her Little Wooden Shoes," "Pretty as a Picture," and "Pilgrims of Love") and omitted nine ("There Is Magic in a Smile," "Mother Goose," "Waiting for the Bride," "The Game of Love," "Cricket on the Hearth," "I Don't Know How I Do It, but I Do" [lyric by Harry B. Smith], "What She Wanted, and What She Got," "Talk about This, Talk about That" and the intriguingly titled "In the Convent They Never Taught Me That").

The revival interpolated three numbers: "Lorelei," "Land of My Own Romance," and "I Might Be Your Once-in-a-While." The latter was from *Angel Face* (1919), but the sources of the two other songs are unclear. The 1929 revival included "The Girl of My Dreams" and "The Garden of Roses," both of which seem to be interpolations (sources unknown).

After the Broadway opening, "Lorelei" was dropped, and "The Game of Love," which had been performed during the revival's tryout, was reinstated. The tryout had also included "There Is Magic in a Smile," but it wasn't used during the Broadway run.

The most complete recording of the score was released by Albany Records (CD # TROY-546/547) on a two-CD set recorded live from a production by the Ohio Light Opera. Another recording (by the Gregg Smith Singers and the Lake Placid Sinfonietta) was released by MMG Records (LP # 1129).

Incidentally, the revival's opening night program was off by a year; it was dated January 21, 1946, instead of January 21, 1947.

MAURICE CHEVALIER—SONGS AND IMPRESSIONS

Theatre: Henry Miller's Theatre
Opening Date: March 10, 1947; *Closing Date*: April 19, 1947
Performances: 46
Producer: Arthur Lesser; *Draperies*: Kaj-Velden Studios; *Lighting*: Century Lighting, Inc.
Cast: *Maurice Chevalier*, Irving Actman (Piano)
The revue was presented in two acts.

Musical Numbers

Note: All songs performed by Maurice Chevalier.
Act One: "La marche de Ménilmontant" (lyric by Maurice Vandair and Maurice Chevalier, music by Borel-Clerc); "La leçon de piano" (lyric by Maurice Vandair and Charlys, music by Henri Betti); American Medley; "Vingt ans" (lyric by Maurice Chevalier and Marc Fontenoy, music by Marc Fontenoy); "A Barcelone" (lyric by Maurice Chevalier, music by Henri Betti)
Act Two: "Weeping Willie" (lyric by Robert Piroshe and Maurice Chevalier, music by Revil); "Quai de Bercy" (lyric by Louis Poterat and Maurice Chevalier, music by Alstone); "Mandarinade" (lyric by Pierre Gilbert and Maurice Chevalier, music by Henri Betti); "Place Pigalle" (lyric by Robert Piroshe and Maurice Chevalier, music by Alstone); "La symphonie des semelles de bois" (lyric by Albert Willemetz and Maurice Chevalier, music by Vincent Scotto)

The current New York visit by legendary French entertainer Maurice Chevalier was his third of seven limited-engagement one-man Broadway concerts over a period of thirty-five years. His Broadway debut occurred on March 30, 1930, at the Fulton Theatre for fifteen performances and was followed by another booking at the Fulton on February 9, 1932, for seventeen performances; after the current production at Henry Miller's Theatre, Chevalier returned to Broadway the next year on March 28, 1948, for forty-six showings at the John Golden Theatre (see entry). His next appearance was at the Lyceum Theatre for forty-six performances beginning on September 28, 1955; at the Ziegfeld Theatre on January 28, 1963, for twenty-nine performances; and then his final New York appearance in *Maurice Chevalier at 77*, which opened at the Alvin Theatre on April 1, 1965, for thirty-one performances. All of Chevalier's New York engagements were one-man concerts, and he never appeared on Broadway in a book musical.

Chevalier had had a remarkable early career in nightclubs and recordings, and starred in a number of memorable films, including Richard Rodgers and Lorenz Hart's *Love Me Tonight* (1932), one of the greatest of all film musicals in which he introduced "Mimi" and "Isn't It Romantic?" In the late 1950s, his popularity enjoyed a second flowering when he appeared in Alan Jay Lerner and Frederick Loewe's hit 1958 film musical *Gigi* which won a then-record eight Academy Awards including Best Picture (Chevalier also won a special honorary Oscar that year). In the film, Chevalier introduced "Thank Heaven for Little Girls," "I'm Glad I'm Not Young Anymore," and, with Hermione Gingold, "I Remember It Well" (the lyric was reworked from a song of the same title that had been sung by Nanette Fabray and Ray Middleton in Lerner and Kurt Weill's **Love Life**). Chevalier also appeared in the film versions of the Broadway musicals *Can-Can* (1960) and *Fanny* (1961).

For the "American Medley" sequence in act one and for the encores at the end of the evening, Chevalier sang a number of songs associated with his career, including the above-cited "Mimi," "You Brought a New Kind of Love to Me" (from the 1930 film *The Big Pond*; lyric by Irving Kahal and Pierre Norman, music by Sammy Fain), and "Louise" (lyric by Leo Robin, music by Richard A. Whiting) and "Valentine" (lyric by Herbert Reynolds, music by Henri Christine), both from the 1929 film *Innocents of Paris*.

THE CHOCOLATE SOLDIER

Theatre: New Century Theatre
Opening Date: March 12, 1947; *Closing Date*: May 10, 1947
Performances: 70
Book and *Lyrics*: Rudolf Bernauer and Leopold Jacobson; American version by Stanislaus Stange; revised book by Guy Bolton; revised and additional lyrics by Bernard Hanighen
Music: Oscar Straus
Based on the 1894 play *Arms and the Man* by George Bernard Shaw.
Direction: Felix Brentano; *Producers*: J. H. Del Bondio and Hans Bartsch (for the Delvan Company); *Choreography*: George Balanchine; *Scenery* and *Lighting*: Jo Mielziner; *Costumes*: Lucinda Ballard; *Musical Direction*: Jay Blackton
Cast: Frances McCann (Nadina), Gloria Hamilton (Mascha), Muriel O'Malley (Aurelia), Keith Andes (Bumerli), Henry Calvin (Massakroff), Billy Gilbert (Popoff), Ernest McChesney (Alexius), Michael Mann (Stefan), Anna Wiman (Katrina), Mary Ellen Moylan (Premiere Danseuse), Francisco Moncion (Premiere Dancer); Ensemble: Elizabeth Bockoven, Eileen Coffman, Catherine Chambers, Peggy Ferris, Adah Friley, Lucy Hillary, Frances Joslyn, Jeanne Koumrian, Josephine Lambert, Terry Saunders, Grace Varik, Evelyn Wick, Jack Anderson, John Duffy, Craig Reynolds, Walter Kelvin, Allan Lowell, Richard Monte, Richmond Page, Harvey Sauber, Stan Simmonds, Karl Sittler, King Taylor, Bill E. Thompson; Ballet Dancers: Barbara (Babs) Heath, Lillian Lenase, Eleanor Miller, Virginia Poe, Yvonne Tiber, Anna Wiman, Marjorie Winters, Hubert Bland, Harold Haskin, Brooks Jackson, Michael Mann, Shaun O'Brien, George Reich, Walter Stane
The musical was presented in three acts.
The action takes place in Bulgaria around 1885.

Musical Numbers

Act One: Overture (Orchestra); "We Are Marching through the Night" (Gentlemen of the Ensemble); "Lonely Women" (Frances McCann, Muriel O'Malley, Gloria Hamilton); "My Hero" (aka "Come, Come, I Love You Only") (Frances McCann); "The Chocolate Soldier" (Frances McCann, Keith Andes); "Sympathy" (Keith Andes, Frances McCann); "Seek the Spy" (Henry Calvin, Frances McCann, Gloria Hamilton, Muriel O'Malley, Keith Andes, Gentlemen of the Ensemble); Act One Finale (Muriel O'Malley, Gloria Hamilton, Frances McCann)

Act Two: Entr'acte (Orchestra); "Bulgaria Victorious" (Singing Ensemble); "Thank the Lord the War Is Over" (Ernest McChesney, Gloria Hamilton, Billy Gilbert, Muriel O'Malley, Singing Ensemble); "Slavic Dance" (Mary Ellen Moylan, Francisco Moncion, Ballet Dancers); "After Today" (Ernest McChesney, Frances McCann); "Forgive" (Frances McCann, Keith Andes); "Tale of the Coat" (Billy Gilbert, Frances McCann, Muriel O'Malley, Gloria Hamilton, Ernest McChesney, Keith Andes); "Falling in Love" (Keith Andes, Frances McCann); Act Two Finale (Entire Company)

Act Three: Entr'acte (Orchestra); "Waltz Ballet" (Mary Ellen Moylan, Francisco Moncion, Ballet Dancers); "Just a Connoisseur" (Billy Gilbert, Karl Sittler, Jack Anderson, Eileen Coffman, Terry Saunders, Barbara Heath, Marjorie Winters); "The Letter Song" (Frances McCann, Keith Andes); "After Today" (reprise) and "That Would Be Lovely" (Ernest McChesney, Gloria Hamilton); "After Today Gala Polka" (Mary Ellen Moylan, Francisco Moncion, Ballet Dancers); Finale (Entire Company)

Oscar Straus's 1908 operetta *The Chocolate Soldier* had most recently been produced in New York at Carnegie Hall in 1942. See that entry for more information regarding the operetta's Viennese and New York premieres, its Broadway revivals, various recordings, and virtually in-name-only film version.

The current (and to date most recent) revival received many favorable notices along with some indifferent ones, but the naysayers prevailed, and the production closed after two months. Brooks Atkinson in the *New York Times* noted that old-fashioned operetta was one of the "more frightful hazards" of Broadway theatergoing, and so he was glad to say the current production was "beautiful and likable." "My Hero" (aka "Come, Come, I Love You Only") was the score's "masterpiece," and the rest of the music had a "pleasant and succulent summer-garden flavor." The production was "magnificent" to look at, and the décor and costumes created a "superb stage picture." Howard Barnes in the *New York Herald Tribune* said the production was a "good conventional" revival with "charming" songs, spirited dances, and "handsome" scenery. Richard Watts in the *New York Post* found the evening one of the season's "pleasant events"; Frances McCann was a "romantically pretty heroine" and Keith Andes in the title role made a "commendably human hero" (and looked like a "younger" Alfred Drake).

John Chapman in the *New York Daily News* found the revival "ingratiating," and he liked the "grand" tunes; he mentioned that some of the dance numbers utilized music from other operettas by Oscar Straus, and noted the interpolations must be "all right" because Straus himself was in attendance for the opening night performance and seemed "pleased and touched" by the production.

Robert Garland in the *New York Journal-American* said that whenever a revival of *The Chocolate Soldier* was sung properly, the operetta was "irresistible." And in this case, the revival was "as good as the memorable original." Louis Kronenberger in *PM* praised the "fresh, jolly and melodious" score, and if the music was somewhat "dated" it had dated in a "pleasant" way. And while the book was "in no way awful," he felt it was "extremely ordinary"; but Keith Andes had a "pleasant" voice, Frances McCann a "nice" one, and as for comic Billy Gilbert, he was "once or twice comical."

William Hawkins in the *New York World-Telegram* said the production lacked "refreshment and excitement" and only occasionally drew sparks; he also noted that the cast seemed to be afflicted with "brain fag," as if they'd just finished a twenty-four-hour rehearsal. But Keith Andes was the evening's "leading personality"; he looked like a "romantic juvenile" version of James Cagney, brought humor to his role, and sang well. Robert Coleman in the *New York Daily Mirror* felt the cast had "opening night jitters," and suggested the musical would play better once they settled into the run. He noted that Andes was "good looking," possessed a "he-man" voice, and like Watts thought Andes looked like Alfred Drake.

A couple of the critics couldn't agree if the interpolated songs were new ones or old ones that had been borrowed from other operettas by Straus. A note buried in the program indicated "After Today," "Just a Connoisseur," "Slavic Dance," and "After Today Gala Polka" had been arranged and adapted by Jay Blackton from various melodies by Straus.

Despite his good looks and powerful voice, Keith Andes created just two roles on Broadway: he starred in *Maggie* (1953) and opposite Lucille Ball in *Wildcat* (1960). He was also Marilyn Monroe's romantic interest in the 1952 film *Clash by Night*.

Awards

Tony Award: Best Costumes (**Lucinda Ballard** for her costume designs for the entire season, including *The Chocolate Soldier*, *Happy Birthday*, *Another Part of the Forest*, **Street Scene**, and *John Loves Mary*)

BRIGADOON
"A New Musical" / "A New Musical Play"

Theatre: Ziegfeld Theatre
Opening Date: March 13, 1947; *Closing Date*: July 31, 1948
Performances: 581
Book and *Lyrics*: Alan Jay Lerner
Music: Frederick Loewe
Direction: Robert Lewis; *Producer*: Cheryl Crawford; *Choreography*: Agnes De Mille; *Scenery*: Oliver Smith; *Costumes*: David Ffolkes; *Lighting*: Peggy Clark; *Musical Direction*: Franz Allers
Cast: David Brooks (Tommy Albright), George Keane (Jeff Douglas), Elliott Sullivan (Archie Beaton), James Mitchell (Harry Beaton), Bunty Kelley (Fishmonger), Walter Scheff (Angus MacGuffie), Hayes Gordon (Sandy Dean), Edward Cullen (Andrew MacLaren), Marion Bell (Fiona MacLaren), Virginia Bosler (Jean MacLaren), Pamela Britton (Meg Brockie), Lee Sullivan (Charlie Dalrymple), Lidija Franklin (Maggie Anderson), William Hansen (Mr. Lundie), Roland Guerard (Sword Dancer), George Drake (Sword Dancer), John Paul (Frank), Frances Charles (Jane Ashton), James MacFadden (Bagpiper), Arthur Horn (Bagpiper), Paul Anderson (Stuart Dalrymple), Earl Redding (MacGregor); Townsfolk of Brigadoon: Singers—Kay Borron, Wanda Cochran, Lois Eastman, Lydia Fredericks, Jeanne Grant, Margaret Hunter, Linda Mason, Virginia Oswald, Eleanore Parker, Shirley Robbins, Faye Elizabeth Smith, Betty Templeton, Delbert (Del) Anderson, Arthur Carroll, Hayes Gordon, Michael Raymond, Mark Kramer, Robert Lussier, Tommy Matthews, Kenny McCord, Earl Redding, John Schmidt, Paul Valin, Jeff Warren; Dancers—Ann Friedland, Helen Gallagher, Phyllis Gehrig, Lidija Franklin, Dorothy Hill, Bunty Kelley, Ina Kurland, Olga Lunick, Mary Martinet, Kirsten Valbor, Forrest Bonshire, George Drake, Richard D'Arcy, Roland Guerard, Kenneth LeRoy, Charles McCraw, Stanley Simmons, Alan Waine, William Weber, Nathan Baker
The musical was presented in two acts.
The action takes place in Brigadoon (a village in the Scottish highlands) and in New York City during May.

Musical Numbers

Act One: "Once in the Highlands" (Chorus); "Brigadoon" (Chorus); "Down on MacConnachy Square" (Hayes Gordon, Pamelia Britton, Townsfolk); "Waitin' for My Dearie" (Marion Bell, Girls); "I'll Go Home with Bonnie Jean" (Lee Sullivan, Townsfolk) and "Dance" (Lidija Franklin, James Mitchell, Fishmongers, Dancers); "The Heather on the Hill" (David Brooks, Marion Bell); "The Love of My Life" (Pamela Britton); "Jeannie's Packin' Up" (Girls); "Come to Me, Bend to Me" (Lee Sullivan) and "Dance" (Virginia Bosler, Dancers); "Almost Like Being in Love" (David Brooks, Marion Bell); "The Wedding Dance" (Virginia Bosler, Lee Sullivan, Dancers); "Sword Dance" (James Mitchell, Roland Guerard, George Drake, Dancers)
Act Two: "The Chase" (Men of Brigadoon); "There but for You Go I" (David Brooks); "My Mother's Weddin' Day" (Pamela Britton, Townsfolk); "Funeral Dance" (Lidija Franklin); "From This Day On" (David Brooks, Marion Bell); "Come to Me, Bend to Me" (reprise) (Marion Bell); "The Heather on the Hill" (reprise) (Marion Bell); "I'll Go Home with Bonnie Jean" (reprise) (Lee Sullivan); "From This Day On" (reprise) (David Brooks, Marion Bell); "Down on MacConnachy Square" (reprise) (Townsfolk); Finale

The charming fantasy *Brigadoon* was the story of an enchanted Scottish village that comes to life every one hundred years (during each night of the town's existence, a century passes by in the real world). By not remaining too long in any one century, the townsfolk remain untouched (and untainted) by any one period of time. But the magic spell will be broken if any villager steps beyond the prescribed boundaries of the town. Everyone seems happy with this arrangement, with the notable exception of Harry Beaton (James Mitchell), who feels Brigadoon is his personal brig. When present-day New Yorkers Tommy Albright (David Brooks) and Jeff Douglas (George Keane, in a non-singing role) stumble upon Brigadoon during a vacation, Tommy is immediately attracted to both the village and Fiona MacLaren, whose sister Jean (Virginia Bosler) is betrothed to Charlie Dalrymple (Lee Sullivan), much to the consternation of Harry, who loves Jean. Harry attempts to destroy Brigadoon by breeching its boundaries, but is inadvertently killed by Jeff. Tommy and Jeff leave Brigadoon, but upon their return a miracle occurs when the town awakens from its night's sleep and Tommy is forever united with Fiona. (Some unromantic wags have remarked that upon Tommy's vanishing into the otherworldly Brigadoon, Jeff is going to have some serious explaining to do when the authorities question him about his friend's mysterious disappearance.)

Among the townsfolk of Brigadoon is Meg Brockie, a musical cousin to Ado Annie and a lassie who has her sights set upon a man (*any* man). The musicals of the post-**Oklahoma!** era were awash with these Jejune Allyson types (Daisy in **Bloomer Girl**, Hildy in **On the Town**, Carrie in **Carousel**, Lois in **Kiss Me, Kate**, Cissy in *A Tree Grows in Brooklyn*, Lola in *Seventeen*, Hilda in *Plain and Fancy*, among many others). Even the 1946 film musical *Three Little Girls in Blue* gave Celeste Holm a variation of "I Cain't Say No" with "Always a Lady."

Besides the charm of its unusual story, Alan Jay Lerner and Frederick Loewe's score for *Brigadoon* was one of the era's most lush and romantic ones. There were six lovely ballads ("Almost Like Being in Love," "The Heather on the Hill," "Come to Me, Bend to Me," "Waitin' for My Dearie," "There but for You Go I," and "From This Day On"), and there were also many highly charged dance numbers, including the wedding, sword, and funeral dances. Other highlights of the score included the irresistible male chorus of "I'll Go Home with Bonnie Jean" and "The Chase," the latter a swirling montage that depicted the villagers' search for Harry Beaton.

Brooks Atkinson in the *New York Times* said *Brigadoon* was one of the "major achievements" of the Broadway stage, and noted that all the theatre arts had "been woven into a singing pattern of enchantment"; John Chapman in the *New York Daily News* said the "enchanting" musical was a "work of imagination and beauty," and Lerner and Loewe's "lovely" songs were "exceptionally good." He also liked an exchange between a Brigadoon villager and Jeff; the former asks if Russia is in Europe, and Jeff replies, "More and more. You just cross the Channel and turn left."

Ward Morehouse in the *New York Sun* said *Brigadoon* was among the best musicals he had ever seen, and he praised Loewe's "exhilarating" music and Agnes De Mille's choreography, which he felt offered the best Broadway dancing since **Oklahoma!** Robert Garland in the *New York Journal-American* stated that his was a "rave review"; the musical had "everything" with its "romance, beauty, originality, excitement and distinction." Robert Coleman in the *New York Daily Mirror* said it took courage for Cheryl Crawford to produce such an "unconventional" musical, but in this case "courage will be richly rewarded."

Coleman also noted that George Keane was "one of the most ingratiating comedians to enliven a musical in the past few seasons." Keane's character of Jeff is somewhat enigmatic. The man-hungry Meg throws herself at him in the hope he'll seduce her, but Jeff is simply not interested. Coleman said Jeff was "flip"; Garland found him "ironic"; and William Hawkins in the *New York World-Telegram* noted Keane played the role in a "telling" manner (for the film version, Van Johnson almost walked away with the movie with a deft portrayal that seemed loaded with subtext).

Richard Watts in the *New York Post* said the "brilliant and beautiful" musical told its story in "literate and intelligent fashion," and while Lerner and Loewe's songs were "attractive," he felt their score for **The Day before Spring** was better. Howard Barnes in the *New York Herald Tribune* praised the "felicitous" songs and "entrancing" choreography, and said the new musical was a reason for theatergoers "to toss tamoshanters in the air."

Hawkins said the musical was "absolute enchantment," and noted Lerner's book had "strength and sentiment and a nice pinch of cutting humor" and Loewe's "ingenious" music was "permeated with Scottish flavor" but wisely avoided the overuse of "bagpipe scales and fling rhythms." Louis Kronenberger in *PM* noted that the musical's creators showed a "good deal of independence" and thus their show called its own tune. As a result, *Brigadoon* was an "engaging" evening in which music, choreography, and décor worked in tandem to create a distinct mood and atmosphere. He almost apologized for a few quibbles, such as the final two scenes, which lost their way and were an "outright blunder." He suggested that musicals should "run like hell" from scenes that offered "gauze-curtain visions of one's lost love standing forlornly on a hill top." But these minor annoyances were forgivable because *Brigadoon* was "so obviously the season's freshest musical."

During the tryout, the role of Kate MacQueen (played by Margaret Hunter) was eliminated, but Hunter remained with the musical as a chorus singer.

The musical has been revived in New York ten times. The first was a return engagement by the national touring company, which opened at the City Center on May 2, 1950, for twenty-four performances (Phil Hanna and Virginia Oswald, who appeared in the singing chorus of the original production, were the leads, and Susan Johnson was Meg Brockie). There were then five revivals at City Center that were produced by the New York City Center Light Opera Company. The first opened on March 27, 1957, and then transferred to the Adelphi Theatre, for a total of forty-seven performances (David Atkinson and Virginia Oswald were the leads, Robert Rounseville was Charlie, and Helen Gallagher, who had appeared in the dancing chorus of the original production, was now Meg Brockie). The next revival opened on May 30, 1962, for sixteen performances (Peter Palmer and Sally Ann Howes; Farley Granger was Jeff, and Edward Villella was Harry); then January 30, 1963, for fifteen performances (again with Palmer, Howes, and Villella); and December 23, 1964, for seventeen performances (Palmer, Villella, and Linda Bennett). The fifth and final NYCCLOC production opened on December 13, 1967, for twenty-three performances (Bill Hayes and Margot Moser; Karen Morrow was Meg Brockie, and Villella appeared as Harry Beaton for the fourth time).

On October 16, 1980, a lavish revival was seen at the Majestic Theatre for a disappointing 133 performances; the cast included Martin Vidnovic and Meg Bussart (John Curry was Harry Beaton). The production was beautifully mounted and thrillingly sung, but sadly didn't leave behind a cast recording.

On March 1, 1986, the New York City Opera Company revived the work at the New York State Theatre for forty performances (Richard White and John Leslie Wolfe alternated in the role of Tommy, and Sheryl Wood and Beverly Lambert alternated as Fiona). The company revived the musical two more times: on November 7, 1991, for twelve performances (John Leslie Wolfe and George Dvorsky, and Michele McBride and Elizabeth Walsh), and on November 13, 1996, for fourteen performances (Brent Barrett and Rebecca Luker, with Judy Kaye as Meg Brockie).

The musical premiered in London on April 14, 1949, at His Majesty's Theatre for 685 performances, a run that was some three months longer than the Broadway production. The cast included Phil Hanna (Tommy), Patricia Hughes (Fiona), Noele Gordon (Meg Brockie), James Jamieson (Harry Beaton), and Hiram Sherman (Jeff).

The film version was released by MGM in 1954; Vincente Minnelli directed, and the cast included Gene Kelly (Tommy), Cyd Charisse (Fiona), and Van Johnson (Jeff). The character of Meg Brockie was all but eliminated, and her saucy songs "The Love of My Life" and "My Mother's Weddin' Day" were omitted. "Come to Me, Bend to Me," "From This Day On," "Sword Dance," and "There but for You Go I" were filmed but cut prior to the film's premiere; the first three numbers are included in the DVD release (Warner Brothers # 67239) along with an audio outtake of the latter.

An ABC television version was seen on October 15, 1966; Ernest Kinoy adapted the script, and the cast included Robert Goulet (Tommy), Sally Ann Howes (Fiona), Edward Villella (Harry Beaton), Marilyn Mason (Meg Brockie), and Peter Falk (Jeff).

The script of *Brigadoon* was published in hardback by Coward-McCann in 1947, and an undated softcover edition was issued in Great Britain by Chappell & Co. The script is also included in the hardback collection *Ten Great Musicals of the American Theatre* (1973), published by Chilton Book Company (the collection isn't identified as volume one, but there was a later second volume in this series).

The original Broadway cast album was recorded by RCA Victor (LP # LOC/LSO-1001; later issued by RCA on CD # 1001-2-RG). There are numerous recordings of the score, and perhaps the best of them all is a studio cast album released by Columbia (LP # CL-1132, later reissued on # OL-7040, and then on CD by DRG # 19071) with Jack Cassidy and Shirley Jones, Susan Johnson (Meg Brockie), and Frank Porretta (Charlie). Beautifully sung, this version is more complete than the Broadway cast album and includes the previously unrecorded numbers "The Love of My Life," "Jeannie's Packin' Up," and "The Chase."

Although the plot of *Brigadoon* is original and not based on any specific source material, the musical's basic premise is somewhat similar to Friedrich Gerstacker's 1862 short story "Germelshausen."

The 1946–1947 season offered eight new book musicals, four of which in one way or another utilized elements of fantasy in their plots; besides *Brigadoon*, the others were **If the Shoe Fits**, **Toplitzky of Notre Dame**, and **Finian's Rainbow** (a fifth fantasy, **Sweet Bye and Bye**, closed on the road).

Awards

Tony Award: Best Choreographer (**Agnes De Mille**, in a tie with Michael Kidd for *Finian's Rainbow*)
New York Drama Critics' Circle Award (1946–1947): Best Musical (***Brigadoon***)

BAREFOOT BOY WITH CHEEK
"A NEW MUSICAL COMEDY ABOUT THE LUNACIES OF CAMPUS LIFE"

Theatre: Martin Beck Theatre
Opening Date: April 3, 1947; *Closing Date*: July 5, 1947
Performances: 108
Book: Max Shulman
Lyrics: Sylvia Dee
Music: Sidney Lippman
Based on the 1944 novel *Barefoot Boy with Cheek* by Max Shulman.
Direction: George Abbott; *Producer*: George Abbott; *Choreography*: Richard Barstow; *Scenery* and *Lighting*:
    Jo Mielziner; *Costumes*: Alvin Colt; *Musical Direction*: Milton Rosenstock
Cast: Jack Williams (Roger Hailfellow), Red Buttons (Shyster Fiscal), Ben Murphy (Van Varsity), Loren Welch
    (Charlie Convertible), Patrick Kingdon (Freshman), Billy (William) Redfield (Asa Hearthrug), Benjamin
    Miller (Eino Ffllikkiinnenn), Billie Lou Watt (Noblesse Oblige), Ellen Hanley (Clothilde Pfefferkorn),
    Nancy Walker (Yetta Samovar), Philip Coolidge (Professor Schultz), Shirley Van (Peggy Hepp), Jerry Aus-
    ten (Kermit McDermott), Solen Burry (Boris Fiveyearplan), Marten Sameth (Playwright), James Lane (Bar-
    tender), Tommy Farrell (Muskie Pike), Harris Gondell (First Band Member), Nathaniel Frey (Second Band
    Member); Dancers: Jean Marie Caples, June Graham, Mary Bly Harwood, Louisa Lewis, Marcia Maier,
    Audrey Peters, Doris York, Leonard Claret, Douglas Deane, Ray Kirchner, John Laverty, David Neuman,
    Tommy Randall; Singers: Betty Abbott, Adrienne Aye, Mary Lee Carrell, Carol Coleman, Beverly Fite,
    Nell Foster, Marion Kohler, Gay Laurence, Abbe Marshall, Ellen Martin, Jean Sincere, Pamela Ward,
    James Bowie, Harvey Braun, Dean Campbell, Robert Edwin, Nathaniel Frey, Harris Gondell, John Leslie,
    Ray Morrissey, Robert Paul Neukum, Alfred Porter, Walter Rinner, Marten Sameth
The musical was presented in two acts.
The action takes place during the present time at the University of Minnesota.

Musical Numbers

Act One: "A Toast to Alpha Cholera" (Fraternity Men); "We Feel Our Man Is Definitely You" (Red Buttons,
    Jack Williams, Fraternity Men); "The Legendary Eino Ffllikkiinnenn" (Benjamin Miller, Billy Redfield,
    Fraternity Men); "(It's) Too Nice a Day to Go to School" (Jerry Austen, Shirley Van, Loren Welch, Ben
    Murphy, Students); "Specialty Dance" (June Graham, Leonard Claret); "Puppy Love" (dance) (Ellen
    Martin, John Laverty); "I Knew I'd Know" (Ellen Hanley); "I'll Turn a Little Cog" (Nancy Walker, Billy
    Redfield; also sung by Loren Welch, Ben Murphy, John Leslie, Robert Neukum, Students; danced by June
    Graham, Mary Bly Harwood, Leonard Claret, Douglas Deane, Ray Kirchner); "Who Do You Think You
    Are?" (Jerry Austen, Billy Redfield, Students); "Everything Leads Right Back to Love" (Ellen Hanley, Billy
    Redfield); "Little Yetta's Gonna Get a Man" (Nancy Walker); "Alice in Boogieland" (Tommy Farrell, Shir-
    ley Van, Red Buttons, Jack Williams; Quartet: Beverly Fite, Harvey Braun, Dean Campbell, Betty Abbott;
    danced by Students; dance specialty by Shirley Van and Leonard Claret)
Act Two: "After Graduation Day" (Loren Welch, Students); "There's Lots You Can Do with Two (but Not
    with Three)" (Nancy Walker, Red Buttons, Billie Lou Watt, Jack Williams, Billy Redfield, Tommy Far-
    rell, Leonard Claret, Douglas Deane, Mary Bly Harwood, Students); "The Story of Carrot" (Billy Redfield,
    Benjamin Miller); "Dance" (Jack Williams); "Star of the North Star State" (Students); "I Knew I'd Know"
    (reprise) (Ellen Hanley); "It Couldn't Be Done (but We Did It)" (Entire Company)

Max Shulman wrote the book of *Barefoot Boy with Cheek*, which he adapted from his 1944 novel of the same name. It took place at the University of Minnesota, but beyond its realistic setting the musical was a free-wheeling spoof of campus life where the Greeks are known as the Alpha Cholera Fraternity and the Beta Thigh Sorority and the characters sport such names as Roger Hailfellow, Shyster Fiscal, Noblesse Oblige, Boris Fiveyearplan, and Yetta Samovar. The last two are fellow travelers among the campus radicals (Nancy Walker played Yetta; the musical's flyer said she was a "Marx-mad co-ed who uses the proletariat for a baton" and "has her malevolent eye fixed on Asa Hearthrug, a freshman who flouts the campus codes" and *Best Plays* described her character as the "reddest of the pinks"). The scattershot plot spoofed campus Commies and campus politics, particularly the "class war" when the somewhat nerdy barefoot-boy-with-cheek freshman Asa (Billy Redfield) runs against smug and smooth upperclassman Kermit McDermott (Jerry Austen) for president of the student council. Meanwhile, Yetta, campus siren Noblesse Oblige (Billie Lou Watt), and nice girl Clothilde Pfefferkorn (Ellen Hanley) all set their sights on Asa, but it's Clothilde who ultimately wins him.

Prior to Asa's choice of Clothilde, both Yetta and Noblesse think they're the ones with the best chance of being pinned by him, and so they decide a contest or two should determine who will be the winner. Yetta suggests contests to see who can sing the most movements from Shostakovich's symphonies, who can spout the most quotes from Karl Marx, and who can list the most names of the jury members on the Sacco-Vanzetti trial, while Noblesse recommends contests to determine who can sing the most popular song hits, who can provide the most quotes from Emily Post, and who can list the most names of sterling silver patterns.

By the musical's finale, it seems Yetta has thrown over her errant political views. But there's one aspect of communism she'll follow: since she and Noblesse lost Asa, they agree to communally share any future available campus men.

Although the reviews were mildly favorable, they weren't overly enthusiastic about the new musical; but the critics hailed Nancy Walker's performance. They also singled out Philip Coolidge in his brief but hilarious role as a professor who hates teaching (he tells his students that all he's required to tell them is his name, the title of the course, and the required textbooks); hates his fellow faculty members; and, most of all, hates his students (the "damn campus is overrun" with them). The critics were disappointed with the score, but singled out a few numbers, including Ellen Hanley's ballad "I Knew I'd Know," Walker and Redfield's ode to communism "I'll Turn a Little Cog" (factory work will be gay, and they'll dine on "beet-blood borscht and baked black bread"), and the students' salute to their college ("Star of the North Star State").

Brooks Atkinson in the *New York Times* suggested the plot was no doubt "less uproarious" than director George Abbott wanted, and so Abbott had to ensure the cast created the "impression of high spirits." But he liked Philip Coolidge and praised Nancy Walker. With her "crisp timing," "quick" gestures, her hilarious way with a dead-pan look, and her eloquent way of shrugging her shoulders, she brought a "sardonic jauntiness" that was the musical's "freshest" element. William Hawkins in the *New York World-Telegram* said that except for the satire on communism (he enjoyed seeing the young communists "toasted on their own grill"), the musical was reminiscent of numerous other college musicals. As for Nancy Walker, he mentioned that with a single shrug of her shoulders she could outperform every cast member on the stage.

Robert Garland in the *New York Journal-American* found the evening "more forced than funny, more collegiate than charming, more anachronistic than necessary," and got tired of an "awful lot" of youth on the stage; as a result, he enjoyed Philip Coolidge's professor "to end all professors." Louis Kronenberger in *PM* felt Abbott's many plays and musicals about student life were becoming a bit "too familiar"; the book was sometimes "bright" but also occasionally "cheesy" and the score was "glaringly mediocre." But Nancy Walker was blessed with "brilliant timing," and he enjoyed her "good-humored toughness," "expressive shrugs," and "aggressive stride."

Richard Watts in the *New York Post* felt the evening was sometimes "fatiguing," and noted that Nancy Walker usually intimidated him. But this time around she was a bit "less frightening" and "more amusing" than usual. Howard Barnes in the *New York Herald Tribune* said the musical substituted "exuberance and ribaldry" for "originality and style," and that Sidney Lippman's score was mostly "pedestrian" (but noted "I Knew I'd Know" was the "loveliest" song in the show). Robert Coleman in the *New York Daily Mirror* said the "fresh and lively" musical provided "plenty of rousing, irresistible hilarity" and that the score "should spell treasure for recording, radio and juke box tycoons." He noted Abbott was a "master at campus capers" (Abbott's earlier visits to high schools, prep schools, and colleges included *Brother Rat* (1936), *What a Life* (1938), *Too Many Girls* (1939), and **Best Foot Forward**).

John Chapman in the *New York Daily News* said the Broadway stage had recently promoted too much in the way of "pinko brotherhood of man stuff," and so it was nice to see the "commy movement" kidded. He singled out a few songs ("I Knew I'd Know," "I'll Build a Little Cog," and "Star of the North Star State"), and while the latter wasn't quite up to "Buckle Down, Winsocki" and *Barefoot Boy with Cheek* wasn't the equal of **Best Foot Forward**, the new musical did "well enough to get a passing grade."

During the tryout, "When You're Eighteen" (for Ellen Hanley) was cut. The script was published in paperback by The Dramatic Publishing Company in 1947; one song from the show ("After Graduation Day") enjoyed some currency, but by and large the score fell by the wayside due to the lack of a hit song and a cast recording. The collection *Lost Broadway and More: Volume 3* (unnamed company and unnumbered CD) includes "I Knew I'd Know" and "It's Too Nice a Day to Go to School."

In January 2011, a "special exploratory reading" of the musical was presented under the aegis of Unsung Musicals, which included the cut "When You're Eighteen" and the apparently heretofore unused "Don't Spoil the Party."

ALICE IN WONDERLAND AND THROUGH THE LOOKING GLASS

Theatre: International Theatre (during run, the musical transferred to the Majestic Theatre)
Opening Date: April 5, 1947; *Closing Date*: June 28, 1947
Performances: 100
Play: Eva Le Gallienne and Florida Friebus
Music: Richard Addinsell
Based on the novels *Alice's Adventures in Wonderland* (1865) and *Through the Looking Glass* (1872) by Lewis B. Carroll (Carroll was a pseudonym for Charles Lutwidge Dodgson).
Direction: Eva Le Gallienne; *Producers*: Rita Hassan and the American Repertory Theatre (Cheryl Crawford, Managing Director); *Choreography*: Ruth Wilton; *Scenery*: Robert Rowe Paddock; *Costumes*: Noel Taylor; *Masks* and *Marionettes*: Remo Bufano; *Musical Direction*: Tibor Kozma
Cast: Act One—*Bambi Linn* (Alice), William Windom (White Rabbit; Julie Harris, alternate), Henry Jones (Mouse), John Straub (Dodo, Seven of Clubs), Angus Cairns (Lory, Mock Turtle), Arthur Keegan (Eaglet, March Hare), Don Allen (Crab, Cook), Eli Wallach (Duck, Two of Spades), Theodore Tenley (Caterpillar, Dormouse), Ed Woodhead (Fish Footman), Robert Rawlings (Frog Footman, Five of Spades), Raymond Greenleaf (Duchess), *Margaret Webster* (Cheshire Cat), *Richard Waring* (Mad Hatter), Donald Keyes (Seven of Spades), John Becher (Queen of Hearts), Eugene Stuckmann (King of Hearts), Frederick Hunter (Knave of Hearts), Jack Manning (Gryphon), John Behney (Three of Clubs), Bart Henderson (Five of Clubs), Thomas Grace (Nine of Clubs); Hearts: Don Allen, Robert Carlson, Michel Corhan, Will Davis, Robert Leser, Gerald McCormack, Walter Neal, James Rafferty, Dan Scott, Charles Townley
Cast: Act Two—*Margaret Webster* (Red Chess Queen), John Straub (Train Guard), William Windom (Gentleman Dressed in White Paper), Don Allen (Goat), Donald Keyes (Beetle Voice), Cavada Humphrey (Gnat Voice), Angus Cairns (Gentle Voice), Mary Alice Moore and Eli Wallach (Other Voices), Robert Rawlings (Tweedledum), Jack Manning (Tweedledee), *Eva Le Gallienne* (White Chess Queen), Theodore Tenley (Sheep), Henry Jones (Humpty Dumpty), *Philip Bourneuf* (White Knight), Will Davis (Front Legs of Horse), Charles Townley (Back Legs of Horse), Eloise Roehm (Singer), Rae Len (Singer); *Note*: Marionettes worked by, and under the direction of, A. Spolidoro: Michael Corhan, Thomas Grace, Bart Henderson, Cavada Humphrey, Robert Leser, Mary Alice Moore, Walter Neal, James Rafferty, Charles Townley
The play with music was presented in two acts.
The action takes place during the late Victorian era in England and Wonderland.

Scenes and Musical Sequences

Note: The programs for the original December 11, 1932, dress rehearsal performance; the programs for the 1932–1933 Civic Repertory and New Amsterdam Theatre showings; and the programs for the current and 1982 revivals all listed the story sequences but not the specific musical numbers.

Act One: "Alice at Home"; "The Looking Glass House"; "White Rabbit"; "Pool of Tears"; "Caucus Race"; "Caterpillar"; "Duchess"; "Cheshire Cat"; "The Mad Tea Party"; "Queen's Croquet Ground"; "By the Sea"; "The Trial"

Act Two: "Red Chess Queen"; "Railway Carriage"; "Tweedledum and Tweedledee"; "White Chess Queen"; "Wool and Water"; "Humpty Dumpty"; "White Knight"; "Alice Crowned"; "Alice with the Two Queens"; "The Banquet"; "Alice at Home Again"

Eva Le Gallienne and Florida Friebus's adaptation of Lewis Carroll's *Alice in Wonderland* and *Through the Looking Glass* was first produced on Broadway at the Civic Repertory on December 12, 1932, for 127 performances; Le Gallienne played the role of the White Chess Queen, and others in the cast were Josephine Hutchinson (Alice), Joseph Schildkraut (Queen of Hearts), Burgess Meredith (Tweedledee), Florida Friebus (Cheshire Cat), and Howard da Sylva in a minor role. The adaptation dramatized the most famous characters and incidents in Carroll's stories, including the Mad Tea Party, Alice's Trial, the White Rabbit, the Cheshire Cat, Humpty Dumpty, Tweedledum and Tweedledee, and of course the White Queen's existential promise of jam yesterday and jam tomorrow but never jam today.

While the work wasn't a full-fledged musical, the score by Richard Addinsell included incidental and dance music as well as the occasional song. The production utilized marionettes, and the scenery and costumes were in the style of John Tenniel's drawings for the original stories.

The 1932 production had a disappointing run, and the current revival was even shorter. Le Gallienne reprised her role of the White Chess Queen, and Broadway dancer Bambi Linn was Alice, William Windom and Julie Harris alternated as the White Rabbit, Margaret Webster was both the Cheshire Cat and the Red Chess Queen, and Eli Wallach and Henry Jones had assorted roles; in what became a tradition for the production, the role of the Queen of Hearts was played by an actor in drag (John Becher for this production). Le Gallienne revived the play one more time, when it opened at the Virginia Theatre on December 23, 1982, for just twenty-one performances; Le Gallienne was again the White Queen, and the Queen of Hearts was played by Brian Reddy; others in the cast were Kate Burton (Alice), Mary Louise Wilson (Red Chess Queen), and Mary Stuart Masterson (White Rabbit).

Brooks Atkinson in the *New York Times* found the adaptation a "little masterpiece of humorous fantasy," and he praised Addinsell's "sparkling" score, which transcended mere musical accompaniment and soared into the "sphere of creative interpretation." It included "lovely" arias, and "light orchestral music" that captured the "fairy-story quality" of the evening. Robert Coleman in the *New York Daily Mirror* said the "superlative" revival was a "Walt Disney cartoon, with point, come to life on the stage." (In 1951, Disney's cartoon version of the story was released; a somewhat chilly adaptation, it was nonetheless a colorful and surreal excursion into the world of Lewis Carroll, and Bob Hilliard and Sammy Fain's delightful score included, for Alice's pre-Wonderland adventures, the delicate and dreamy "All in a Golden Afternoon," and, for Wonderland, such amusing songs as the White Rabbit's worrisome frolic "I'm Late" and, for the human playing-cards, "Painting the Roses Red," in honor of the decree by the Queen of Hearts, who just hates white roses.)

Louis Kronenberger in *PM* enjoyed the "pleasant" evening, and noted that Bambi Linn *was* Alice and evoked "a child's innocence, curiosity and charm." Richard Watts in the *New York Post* liked the "delightful if somewhat specialized" production, and predicted his readers would find it "gay, humorous and strangely touching." He wrote that if your children didn't like the production, then you should "drop them immediately." He said Bambi Linn was "complete perfection," and in comparing the current with the original version he noted just one change: when the mock turtle begins crooning, he does so with a seashell-shaped microphone.

Ward Morehouse in the *New York Sun* found the production a "complete delight," and noted it even offered live kittens and pigs; William Hawkins in the *New York World-Telegram* reported that the work held him in a "kind of gentle delirium" that swept him along in an enchanted state of near-subconscious as it brought forth a world of "fantastic shapes" and "irrational reason." John Chapman in the *New York Daily News* said Addinsell's score was a "work of art" that was as "funny," "gay," and "whimsical" as the story itself, and there was "nothing" on Broadway the equal of the "amusing" and "schmaltzy waltz" of "Beautiful, Beautiful Soup" for the Mock Turtle. Robert Garland in the *New York Journal-American* also praised the song, which he said was one of the evening's high spots; but he felt the revival didn't quite have the "freshness, funniness and charm" of the original, and curiously suggested that "maybe that atom bomb has cast its hellish spell" upon the show.

Howard Barnes in the *New York Herald Tribune* admitted the evening was "enchanting," but nonetheless felt the project was a "somewhat dubious undertaking." For all the "brilliant conceits," *Alice in Wonderland* was occasionally "tiresome."

There have been numerous musical adaptations of Carroll's *Alice* stories, including *Alice with Kisses* (1964; closed during previews), *Alice in Wonderland* (1975; Bil Baird's marionette version), *For the Snark Was a Boojum, You See* (1977), *The Passion of Alice* (1977), *Alice in Concert* (1980; adaptation by Elizabeth Swados), and *Alice* (1995; adapted by Robert Wilson and music cowritten by Tom Waits), all Off- or Off-Off-Broadway productions. An excitingly choreographed and imaginatively designed Broadway-bound version called *Alice* premiered in Philadelphia in 1978, and closed there almost as soon as it opened, and the following year *But Never Jam Today* lasted on Broadway for just one week. An "adult" musical version of the material (as *Alice in Wonderland*) opened Off-Off Broadway in 2007; set in a trailer park in Weehawken, New Jersey, the musical's flyer proclaimed that Alice finds herself in an "erotic Wonderland." The most recent musical adaptation opened on Broadway in 2011 as *Wonderland* (lyrics by Jack Murphy and music by Frank Wildhorn).

Incidentally, co-adaptor Florida Friebus is probably best remembered as Dobie Gillis's mother in the popular CBS television series *The Many Loves of Dobie Gillis* (1959–1963).

THE TELEPHONE (or L'AMOUR A TROIS)
"A Curtain Raiser"

and

THE MEDIUM
"A Tragedy"

Theatre: Ethel Barrymore Theatre
Opening Date: May 1, 1947; *Closing Date*: November 1, 1947
Performances: 212
Book, *Lyrics*, and *Music*: Gian-Carlo Menotti
Direction: Gian-Carlo Menotti; *Producers*: Chandler Cowles and Efrem Zimbalist Jr., in association with Edith Lutyens (A Ballet Society Production); *Scenery* and *Costumes*: Horace Armistead; *Lighting*: Jean Rosenthal; *Musical Direction*: Emanuel Balaban
The Telephone (*Note*: Musical sequences weren't listed in the program.)
Cast: Marilyn Cotlow (Lucy), Frank Rogier (Ben)
The opera was presented in one act.
The action takes place during the present time in New York City, in Lucy's apartment, and in a nearby telephone booth.
The Medium (*Note*: Musical sequences weren't listed in the program.)
Cast: Evelyn Keller (Monica), Leo Coleman (Toby), Marie Powers (Madame Flora aka Baba), Beverly Dame (Mrs. Gobineau), Frank Rogier (Mr. Gobineau), Virginia Beeler (Mrs. Nolan)
The opera was presented in two acts.
The action takes place "in our time" in Madame Flora's parlor.

The current productions of *The Medium* and *The Telephone* marked their Broadway premieres; they had previously been seen in New York in non-Broadway presentations. *The Medium* had first been produced by Columbia University at the Brander Matthews Theatre May 8–11, 1946, with Claramae Turner in the role of Madame Flora (Turner is best remembered today for the 1956 film version of *Carousel* in which she played Nettie Fowler and sang "June Is Bustin' Out All Over" and "You'll Never Walk Alone").

Both *The Medium* and the twenty-minute "curtain-raiser" *The Telephone* were seen at Columbia's Heckscher Theatre during February 18–20, 1947, and then in May premiered on Broadway for 212 performances, a remarkable run for two operas. For the next decade or so, Menotti himself had a remarkable run: in 1950, *The Consul* played for 269 performances, and won the New York Drama Critics' Circle Award for Best Musical of 1949–1950 and the 1950 Pulitzer Prize for Best Music; in 1951, *Amahl and the Night Visitors* premiered on NBC, and for many years was a holiday perennial in its various television versions; in 1954, *The Saint of Bleecker Street* played for ninety-two performances and won the New York Drama Critics' Circle Award for Best Musical of 1954–1955 and the 1955 Pulitzer Prize for Best Music; in 1958, *Maria Golovin* played for five performances; and in 1958 Menotti wrote the libretto for Samuel Barber's *Vanessa*, which premiered at the Metropolitan Opera.

The Telephone was a short comic piece that many reviewers likened to a revue skit. But at twenty minutes it was overlong and might have been more effective had it been trimmed to half that length. The two-character opera centered on the talkative Lucy (Marilyn Cotlow), who likes nothing better than to chat with friends all day on the phone, much to the chagrin of Ben (Frank Rogier), who has been trying to propose to her. But he can't get in a word edgewise because Lucy's always on the phone for another round of gabbing with her girlfriends. Soon Ben gets an inspiration; he leaves Lucy's apartment, walks around the corner to a telephone booth, calls her, and finally gets her undivided attention and proposes to her. (But it's worth noting that in the 1944 film *Meet Me in St. Louis*, the Smith's cook Katie [played by Marjorie Main] states she'd never consider marriage to a man who proposed to her over an *invention*.)

In stark contrast to the frivolous curtain-raiser, *The Medium* was a dark and spooky opera about Madame Flora, a phony medium assisted by her daughter Monica and deaf-mute Toby. She cons bereaved parents into believing she's contacted the spirits of their children, but one evening she feels a ghostly hand at her throat. She goes mad and murders Toby, whom she has mistaken for a ghost.

Brooks Atkinson in the *New York Times* noted that for **Street Scene** "the music illustrates the drama," but for *The Medium* "the drama is the music." The score was "dramatic" and brilliantly sung, and Marie Powers was "superb"; the décor was appropriately "macabre," and Jean Rosenthal lighted the set with a "stage sorcerer's distinction." But he concluded that "less distinguished" music had struck "brighter sparks" on Broadway, such as *Porgy and Bess* and **Street Scene**, and seemed to feel *The Medium* would have been more at home in the opera house.

Otis L. Guernsey Jr. in the *New York Herald Tribune* found *The Medium* a "gripping" and "almost terrifying ghost story," and said Menotti's lyrics, music, and stage action were "perfect"; Louis Kronenberger in *PM* saw "genuine melodramatic power" in *The Medium*, and said it told an "exciting" story through music that had "very dramatic climaxes" and "genuinely lyrical episodes"; he suggested Menotti's work was "more intimate and better integrated" than traditional opera, and said it was "fresh and interesting."

William Hawkins in the *New York World-Telegram* said *The Medium* had the "eerie fascination of the most macabre thriller" and was in fact the "only successful horror play" of the 1946–1947 season (incidentally, Hawkins noted that the first-nighters included Arturo Toscanini, Gladys Swarthout, and Libby Holman). John Chapman in the *New York Daily News* found that both "musically and dramatically" *The Medium* was a "tersely and excitingly" written opera with "simple and highly effective" lyrics and a "melodic and theatrical" score. Robert Garland in the *New York Journal-American* said *The Medium* was a "taut and tingling killer-diller" that Menotti must have devised with the help of Charles Addams.

Robert Coleman in the *New York Daily Mirror* said *The Medium* was "sung and acted to the hilt" by Marie Powers, and he noted Menotti was "amazing" in his "versatility" as librettist, lyricist, and composer; and while he didn't think the evening would prove commercially successful, he hoped it would pave the way for similar (and hopefully "profitable") works in the future.

Richard Watts in the *New York Post* found *The Medium* and *The Telephone* "disappointing" and felt Menotti had been "far from successful"; the former's ending was a "most melancholy let-down" and the latter wasn't "witty" and "inventive" enough; and Ward Morehouse in the *New York Sun* felt the evening came up short theatrically because *The Medium* was "pretty flat at the finish" and *The Telephone* was a "flimsy farcical playlet."

As for *The Telephone*, the critics were generally mixed in their assessments: "a rather tedious joke" (Atkinson) and "not very original" in story and music (Garland); but on the other hand, it was a "satirical little piece" that was presented with "musical and verbal wit" (Guernsey); a bit of "musical fun" that needed to be shortened (Kronenberger); and "apt and witty" with "sprightly gaiety" in the music (Hawkins).

About a year after the double bill closed, it was revived at City Center for forty performances beginning on December 7, 1948 (see entry). The works were later revived on Broadway at the Arena on July 19, 1950, for 110 performances; for *The Medium*, Evelyn Keller and Leo Coleman reprised their original roles, and Zelma George was Madame Flora. The New York City Opera Company revived *The Medium* twice at City Center; the first production (presented on a double bill with Menotti's *The Old Maid and the Thief*) opened on April

20, 1958, for three performances, and the second (on a double bill with Norman Dello Joio's *The Triumph of St. Joan*) opened on April 16, 1959, for two performances; for both the 1958 and 1959 revivals, Claramae Turner re-created her original 1946 role of Madame Flora.

The scripts of *The Medium* and *The Telephone* were published separately in paperback by G. Schirmer in 1947.

The cast recordings of the 1947 productions of the operas were released by Columbia (LP # SL/OSL-154; later, # OL-4174-75); the CD was released by Pearl (# 122) and includes excerpts from Menotti's 1937 opera *Amelia Goes to the Ball*. Other recordings of *The Medium* include a production by the Chicago Opera Theatre (Cedille CD # CDR-9000-034) and an Italian version, *La Medium*, which was released on CD by G.O.P. Records.

A CD of an Italian version of *The Telephone* was issued by Nuova Era; and Video International Artists released a DVD (# 4374) of both *The Telephone* and, appropriately, Francis Poulenc's *La voix humaine*, another "telephone" opera. These two operas, along with Jack Beeson's 1999 lyric adaptation of *Sorry, Wrong Number*, would make an interesting triple bill.

In 1951, the film version of *The Medium* was released by Transfilm; directed by Menotti and produced by Walter Lowenthal, the film starred original cast members Marie Powers and Leo Coleman. Others in the cast included Anna Maria Alberghetti and Belva Kibler, and Thomas Schippers conducted the Symphony Orchestra of Rome. The film was released on DVD by Video Artists International, and the same company also released a CD of a 2004 Stratford Opera Ensemble production.

In his fascinating *Gian Carlo Menotti on Screen: Opera, Dance and Choral Works on Film, Television and Video*, Ken Wlaschin reports that twelve versions of *The Medium* were televised between 1948 and 1981. There were two different telecasts in 1948, one on NBC on October 3 with Mary Davenport (who had performed the role of Madame Flora during the run of the 1947 Broadway production) and Leo Coleman, and one on CBS on December 12 with Marie Powers and Coleman. A BBC adaptation with Powers (Elaine Malbin was Monica) was seen on November 1, 1953, and a French telecast (also with Powers) was shown on June 5, 1956. A 1959 version was presented on NBC's *Omnibus* on February 15 with Claramae Turner. Other telecasts were produced in Australia (1960), Austria (1961), Holland (1966), Italy (1969), Canada (1975), Austria (1981), and Italy (1981). Wlaschin also reports that a 1991 American Chamber Opera production seen at Columbia University was privately filmed for the University's archives.

Awards

Tony Award: Best Scenic Designer (**Horace Armistead**, for *The Medium*)

UP IN CENTRAL PARK

Theatre: City Center
Opening Date: May 19, 1947; *Closing Date*: May 31, 1947
Performances: 16
Book: John Kennedy and Sammy Lambert; *Producer*: Michael Todd; *Choreography*: Helen Tamiris; *Scenery*: Howard Bay; *Costumes*: Grace Houston and Ernest Schraps; *Lighting*: Uncredited; *Musical Direction*: William Parson
Cast: Oren Dabs (Laborer), Walter Burke (Danny O'Cahane), Russ Brown (Timothy Moore), Betty Bruce (Bessie O'Cahane), Maureen Cannon (Rosie Moore), Earle MacVeigh (John Matthews), Guy Standing Jr. (Thomas Nast), James Judson (Andrew Munroe), John Quigg (William Dutton, Head Waiter), Paul Reed (Vincent Peters), Rowan Tudor (Mayor A. Oakey Hall, George Jones), George Lane (Richard Connolly), Harry Meehan (Peter Sweeney), Malcolm Lee Beggs (William Marcey Tweed), Dick Hughes (Butler), Louise Holden (Maid, Governess), Eve Harvey (Second Maid), Lillian Withington (Mildred Wincor), Jack Stanton (Joe Stewart), John Thorne (Porter), June MacLaren (Lotta Stevens), Janet Roland (Fanny Morris), Lilas MacLellan (Clara Manning), Jack Howard (James Fisk Jr.), George Bockman (George), Kenneth Owen (The Gnome, Organ Grinder), Joanne Lally (First Child), Janet Lally (Second Child), Wally Coyle (Arthur Finch), Hobart Streiford (Newsboy), Edward Pate (Organ Grinder); *Dancing Ensemble*: Betty Lou

Bolles, Marjory Bradford, Rita Charise, Isabelle Chase, Virginia Conwell, Spicy Gillen, Ruth Lowe, Gloria Michaels, Sheila Reilly, Joanne Stone, Patsy Wymore, George Bockman, Robert Billheimer, Ray Arnett, Wally Coyle, Kenneth Owen, Dick Trevorrah, Louis Yetter; Singing Ensemble: Mary Allen, Eloise Anderson, Betty Halperin, Eve Harvey, Shirley Neumann, Janet Roland, Lillian Withington, Mary Jane Woerner, Martha Wright, Will Bigelow, Oren Dabbs, Joseph Fazio, Dick Hughes, Russ Jondreau, Calvin Marsh, William Nuss, Edward Pate, Sidney Paul, Hobart Streiford, John Throne, Bernard Zwang
The musical was presented in two acts.
The action takes place in New York City during the years 1870–1872.

Sigmund Romberg's hit musical *Up in Central Park* had closed on Broadway about fourteen months earlier; producer Michael Todd brought it back for a limited run of two weeks at City Center with the national touring company, which included Maureen Cannon and Betty Bruce from the original cast. For the current production, the leading male roles (of John Matthews, William Marcy Tweed, and Thomas Nast) were played by Earl MacVeigh, Malcolm Lee Beggs, and Guy Standing Jr., respectively. For more information about the musical (including a list of musical numbers), see entry for the original production.

ICETIME OF 1948
"A Musical Icetravaganza"

Theatre: Center Theatre
Opening Date: May 28, 1947; *Closing Date*: April 3, 1948
Performances: 422
Lyrics and *Music*: James Littlefield and John Fortis
Direction: Catherine Littlefield; *Skating Direction*: May Judels; *Producers*: Sonja Henie and Arthur M. Wirtz (Produced by Sonart Productions; Arthur M. Wirtz, Executive Director; William H. Burke, Production Director); *Choreography*: Catherine Littlefield (Dorothie Littlefield, Assistant); *Scenery*: Bruno Maine and Edward Gilbert; *Costumes*: Lou Eisele, Billy Livingston, and Katherine Kuhn; *Lighting*: Eugene Braun; *Musical Direction*: David Mendoza
Cast: Lloyd "Skippy" Baxter, Joan Hyldoft, Freddie Trenkler, Joe Jackson Jr., The Three Bruises (Monte Stott, Geoffe Stevens, and Sidney Spalding), Fritz Dietl, The Brandt Sisters (Helga and Inge), James Caesar, James Carter, Claire Dalton, Paul Castle, (Buster) Grace and (Charles) Slagle, Jimmie (James) Sisk, Lou Folds, Jerry Rehfield, John Walsh, Grace Bleckman, Jean Sakovich, Cissy Trenholm, Lucille Risch, Charles Cavanaugh, Joe Shillen, John Kasper, Fred Griffith, Rose Holder, Buck Pennington; Singers: Nola Fairbanks, Richard Craig, and Melba Welch; Ensemble: Pauline Beevor, Ann Boykin, Kay Corcoran, Helen Dutcher, Peggy Fisher, Babette George, Gloria Haupt, Sue Holder, Walli Hackman, Sheri Lynn, Patricia Lemaire, Chris Linden, Marge Mahne, Marvette Mosic, Doris Nelson, Berenice Odell, Blanch Poston, Rusty Rodgers, Ruth Russell, Lela Rolontz, Sonia Rashkoff, Ragna Ray, Theresa Rothacker, Beth Stevens, Eileen Thompson, Janet Van Sickle, Julian Apley, Edward Berry, Edward Brandstetter, Ray Blow, William Carvel, Charles Caminiti (aka Carminiti), Nicholas Dontos, Arthur Erickson, Louis Glessmann, Dan Hurley, Garry Kerman, Kenneth Leslie, Ernest Mann, Robert Martina, Edward (Eddie) McDonald, John Melendez, Arthur Meehan, Gus Patrick, Ken Parker, Sandy Quitne, Leonard Stofka, Steve Stokfa, James Toth, James Trenholm, Walter Van Sickle
The revue was presented in two acts.

Skating and Musical Numbers

Act One: Overture (Orchestra); "Breaking the Ice" (lyric by Al Stillman, music by Richard Craig) (Nola Fairbanks, Richard Craig, and Melba Welch; Ensemble); "Precision Plus" (James Carter, Jerry Rehfield, John Walsh, Charles Caminiti, Claire Dalton, Grace Bleckman, Jean Sakovich, Cissy Trenholm); "Goldilocks and the Three Bears" (Goldilocks: Lucille Risch; Papa Bear: Charles Cavanaugh; Mama Bear: Joe Shillen; Baby Bear: Paul Castle); "Mountain Echoes" (Kay Corcoran, John Kasper); "Cossack Lore" (Tartar Princess: Cissy Trenholm; Princes: Jerry Rehfield, John Walsh; Cossacks: James Carter, Fred Griffith, Charles Caminiti, Walter Van Sickle; Nobles: Julian Apley, William Carvel, Nicholas Dantos, Arthur Erickson, Dan Hurley, Ernest Mann, Gus Patrick, Sandy Quitne, Leonard Stofka, Steve Stofka; Gypsy Girls: Pauline Beevor, Ann Boykin, Helen Dutcher, Peggy Fisher, Babette George, Rose Holder, Walli Hackman, Sheri Lynn, Patricia Lemaire, Chris Linden, Marvette Mosic, Bernice Odell, Blanch Poston, Ruth Russell, Lela Rolontz, Sonia Rashkoff, Theresa Rothacker, Beth Stevens, Eileen Thompson, Janet Van Sickle; Court Pages: Grace Bleckman, Lucille Risch); "Zouaves" (Buster Grace, Paul Castle, Buck Pennington, James Sisk); "Bit of Old Erin" (Colleens: Grace Bleckman, Jean Sakovich, Cissy Trenholm, Janet Van Sickle; Carpenter: Edward Berry; Bricklayer: Edward Brandstetter); "Light and Shadow" (Helga and Inge Brandt); "Toss-Up" (Lou Folds); "The Nutcracker" (Father: Charles Cavanaugh; Mother: Kay Corcoran; Children: Berenice Odell, Beth Stevens, Kenneth Leslie; Nutcracker: Paul Castle; Tutu Girls: Ann Boykin, Helen Dutcher, Peggy Fisher, Babette George, Gloria Haupt, Walli Hackman, Patricia Lemaire, Marge Mahne, Marvette Mosic, Blanch Poston, Rusty Rodgers, Lela Rolontz, Ragna Ray, Theresa Rothacker, Eileen Thompson, Janet Van Sickle; Prince: Lloyd "Skippy" Baxter; Candy Fairy: Joan Hyldoft; Boys: Julian Apley, William Carvel, Louis Glessmann, Dan Hurley, Garry Kerman, Ernest Mann, Robert Martina, Edward McDonald, John Melendez, Arthur Meehan, Gus Patrick, Ken Parker, Sandy Quitne, Leonard Stofka, James Toth, Walter Van Sickle; Dance Chinoise: Lucille Risch, Berenice Odell, Buck Pennington; Waltz of the Flowers: Kay Corcoran, Eileen Thompson, Lela Rolontz, Ann Boykin, Walli Hackman, Marvette Mosic, Babette George, Sonia Rashkoff, Peggy Fisher, Gloria Haupt, Blanch Poston, Chris Linden, Patricia Lemaire, Sheri Lynn, Doris Nelson, Ragna Ray, Rusty Rodgers, Grace Bleckman, Marge Mahne, Theresa Rothacker); "Bouncing Ball of the Ice" (Freddie Trenkler; Policeman: Joe Shillen; Nursemaid: Cissy Trenholm); "When the Minstrels Come to Town" (Drummer Boy: Eddie McDonald; Banner Bearers: Garry Kerman, James Trenholm; Head Interlocutor: John Walsh; Interlocutors: John Kasper, Wally Van Sickle, Charles Caminiti, Jerry Rehfield; Sambo, Bones, Tambo, Jones: Edward Brandstetter, Edward Berry, Buster Grace, James Sisk; Banjo Boys: Julian Apley, Ray Blow, William Carvel, Nicholas Dontos, Louis Glessmann, Dan Hurley, Kenneth Leslie, Ernest Mann, Robert Martina, John Melendez, Arthur Meehan, Gus Patrick, Ken Parker, Leonard Stofka, Steve Stofka, James Toth; Tambourine Girls: Pauline Beevor, Grace Bleckman, Ann Boykin, Peggy Fisher, Gloria Haupt, Sue Holder, Sheri Lynn, Patricia Lemaire, Chris Linden, Marge Mahne, Doris Nelson, Berenice Odell, Blanch Poston, Ruth Russell, Sonia Rashkoff; Lillian Russell: Claire Dalton; Can-Can Girls: Pauline Beevor, Ann Boykin, Kay Corcoran, Helen Dutcher, Rose Holder, Sheri Lynn, Patricia Lemaire, Chris Linden, Marvette Mosic, Doris Nelson, Berenice Odell, Blanch Poston, Rusty Rodgers, Ruth Russell, Lela Rolontz, Sonia Rashkoff, Ragna Ray, Jean Sakovich, Cissy Trenholm, Janet Van Sickle; Singers: Richard Craig, Nola Fairbanks, Melba Welch)

Act Two: Entr'acte (Orchestra); "The Dream Waltz" (Jivers: Berenice Odell, Ragna Ray, Joe Shillen, John Kasper, Edward Brandstetter; Dream Girl: Joan Hyldoft; Hussars: James Carter, Jerry Rehfield, John Walsh, Charles Carminiti; Waltz Girls: Pauline Beevor, Ann Boykin, Kay Corcoran, Helen Dutcher, Peggy Fisher, Babette George, Sue Holder, Walli Hackman, Sheri Lynn, Patricia Lemaire, Chris Linden, Marge Mahne, Marvette Mosic, Doris Nelson, Blanch Poston, Rusty Rodgers, Ruth Russell, Lela Rolontz, Theresa Rothacker, Beth Stevens, Eileen Thompson, Janet Van Sickle; Yellow Hussars: Julian Apley, Ray Blow, William Carvel, Nicholas Dontos, Arthur Erickson, Louis Glessmann, Dan Hurley, Garry Kerman, Ernest Mann, Edward McDonald, John Melendez, Gus Patrick, Sandy Quitne, Leonard Stofka, Steve Stofka, James Trenholm; Her Dream Man: Lloyd "Skippy" Baxter; Singer: Richard Craig); "Higher and Higher" (Buster Grace, Charles Slagle); "Man of Distinction" (Joe Jackson Jr.); "Setting the Pace" (Ensemble; Singers: Nola Fairbanks, Richard Craig); "Design in Rhythm" (Fritz Dietl, James Carter); "Double Vision" (Helga and Inge Brandt, John Walsh and Charles Caminiti); "Over the Top" (James Caesar, Jean Sakovich); "Garden of Versailles" (Le Faun: Paul Castle; Les Amoureux: Claire Dalton and Fred Griffith; Court Ladies: Pauline Beevor, Grace Bleckman, Ann Boykin, Peggy Fisher, Babette George, Gloria Haupt, Sue Holder, Walli Hackmann, Sheri Lynn, Patricia Lemaire, Chris Linden, Marge Mahne, Marvette Mosic, Doris Nelson, Berenice Odell, Blanch Poston, Rusty Rodgers, Ruth Russell, Sonia Rashkoff, Ragna Ray, Lucille Risch, Theresa Rothacker, Beth Stevens, Janet Van Sickle; Singer: Nola Fairbanks); "Lovable You" (Kay Corcoran, Helen Dutcher, Babette George, Walli Hackman, Lela Rolontz, Jean Sakovich, Cissy Trenholm, Eileen Thompson; Singer: Richard Craig); "Style on Steel" (Lloyd "Skippy" Baxter); The Three Bruises (Monte Stott, Geoffe Stevens, Sid Spalding); Finale (Entire Company)

The 1946–1947 musical theatre season began with *Icetime*, which played for 405 performances, and ended with *Icetime of 1948*, which topped out at 422 showings. The popularity of the ice revues was waning, and while this season's two shows were successful, each one played for about half the length of its predecessors. The series had kept the Center Theatre busy for almost a decade, but after *Icetime of 1948* there would be just one more entry, **Howdy, Mr. Ice of 1950** (which opened in 1949 and played for 430 performances).

The current production included many of the songs and skating sequences from *Icetime*, and for all purposes was a second edition.

In his seasonal summary, George Jean Nathan complained about the "refrigerated ennui" of the evening and said the "glaciated mediocrity" was "as dull as yesterday's razor blades."

BARBARA
"A New Dance-Comedy"

Theatre: Ziegfeld Theatre
Opening and *Closing Date*: April 20, 1947
Performances: 2
Ballet Story: Trudi Schoop
Music: Nico Kaufman
Direction and *Choreography*: Trudi Schoop; *Producer*: S. Hurok; *Scenery* and *Costumes*: Irene Zurkinden
Cast: Lukas Ammann, Blanche Aubry, Herta Bamert, Werner Belmont, Hanny Bouman, Lisa Czobel, Manuela Espada, Voli Geiler, Rosmarie Knoepfli, Elisabeth Mayen, Jack Menn, Marti Muffler, Robert Rosselat, *Trudy Schoop*, Alfons Vischer, Richard Wyatt; Pianos: Nico Kaufman and Kurt Sulger
The "dance comedy" was presented in two acts.

Musical Numbers

Act One: "The Railroad Station" (Barbara: Trudi Schoop; Travelers, Passers-by, Waiting Persons, Soldiers, The Railroad Station Personnel: Ensemble); "The Fashion Salon" (The Salesladies: Hanny Bouman, Liza Czobel, Trudi Schoop; The Manager: Werner Belmont; Three Ladies: Manuela Espada, Voli Geiler, Elisabeth Mayen; The Couple: Marti Muffler and Robert Rosselat; Joe: Blanche Aubry; Jim: Lukas Ammann); "Noblesse in a 'Furnished Room'" (Joe: Blanche Aubry; Jim: Lukas Ammann; Barbara: Trudi Schoop; The Landlady: Marti Muffler); "Behind Tenement Walls" (The Mothers: Herta Bamert, Lisa Czobel, Elisabeth Mayen, Marti Muffler; The Children: Blanche Aubry, Hanny Bouman, Manuela Espada, Voli Geiler, Rosmarie Knoepfli; The Lieutenant: Lukas Ammann; The Soldiers: Werner Belmont, Jack Menn, Robert Rosselat, Alfons Vischer, Richard Wyatt; Barbara: Trudi Schoop; Jim: Lukas Ammann); "The Party for the 'Poor Children'" (Ladies of the Society: Herta Bamert, Hanny Bouman, Lisa Czobel, Manuela Espada, Elisabeth Mayen; Gentlemen of the Society: Jack Menn, Marti Muffler, Robert Rosselat, Richard Wyatt; A Waiter: Alfons Vischer; The Jazz Orchestra: Herta Bamert, Werner Belmont, Rosmarie Knoepfli, Marti Muffler, Robert Rosselat; The Ballroom Dance Team: Jim—Lukas Ammann, Joe's Understudy—Trudi Schoop, Joe—Blanche Aubry)
Act Two: "Home Again" (The Mother: Elisabeth Mayen; The Father: Robert Rosselat; Barbara: Trudi Schoop; The Sister: Voli Geiler; The Fiancé: Lukas Ammann; The Maid: Rosmarie Knoepfli); "Youth in White" (Youth in White: Ensemble; Barbara: Trudi Schoop; The Painter: Werner Belmont); "The Studio" (The Painter: Werner Belmont; Barbara: Trudi Schoop); "In Vaudeville": (1) "Eternal Spain" (Manuela Espada, Robert Rosselat); (2) "The Haep-Heap Family and Their Wonderchild" (The Father: Werner Belmont; The Mother: Marti Muffler; The Wonderchild: Rosmarie Knoepfli); (3) "O-lala" (Titine: Blanche Aubry); (4) "Barbara, The Dancing Clown" (Barbara: Trudi Schoop; Dick, The Strong Man: Richard Wyatt; Lilly, The Ballerina: Hanny Bouman; Pleasant Dreams: Ensemble); and (5) "Before the Curtain" (Lilly: Hanny Bouman)

On *Brigadoon*'s day off, S. Hurok presented on April 20, 1947, a special Sunday matinee and evening performance of Trudi Schoop's *Barbara*, a self-described "new dance comedy" with her comic ballet troupe. The program noted the performers would "talk little, sing sometimes and dance a great deal."

The storyline followed Barbara (Trudi Schoop) from a railroad station where she waits in vain for a return-ing soldier; her adventures in a fashion salon where she's given a mysterious card that leads her to a furnished room where she meets a dance team; and then to a society party where her performing debut meets with "bitter disappointment." From there, she returns to her family home, but realizes she can't remain there and soon becomes involved in new adventures, including one with a portrait painter. Ultimately she finds her niche as a dancing clown in vaudeville.

Schoop had presented a similar evening at the Longacre Theatre on April 27, 1937, when S. Hurok pro-duced her *Blonde Marie*, which played for eight performances. For that "dance comedy," Schoop starred in the title role of a young woman who becomes involved in a variety of escapades, including one in which she gets a job in the chorus of an upcoming operetta titled *Blonde Marie*; the star gets sick, Marie goes on in her place, and becomes a big star. Like Barbara, Marie also finds adventure when she meets a portrait painter.

EVERYTHING'S ON ICE

Theatre and *Performance Dates*: The ice revue opened on April 8, 1947, at the Center Theatre, Boston, Mas-sachusetts, for four weeks. It's unclear if the production played elsewhere.
Lyrics and *Music*: Lee Morris and Selene Harmon
Cast: Maribel Vinson, Guy Owen, Lillian Tribby, Heinie Brock, Chet Nelson, Jimmy Kelly, Ronny and Boots Roberts, Valerie Fortune-East, Spic and Span, Buddy Lalonde, Ralph Emory

Since ice revues were the rage in New York, perhaps the producers of *Everything's on Ice* thought they could get on the ice-show bandwagon. But the obscure "musical comedy on ice" seems to have disappeared after its Boston engagement. The show offered new songs by Lee Morris and Selene Harmon, and also included standards by George Gershwin, Cole Porter, and Vincent Youmans.

IN GAY NEW ORLEANS
"A CARNIVAL OF GAIETY, ROMANCE AND MUSIC"

Theatre and *Performance Dates*: The musical opened on December 25, 1946, at the Colonial Theatre, Boston, Massachusetts, and permanently closed there on January 31, 1947.
Book and *Lyrics*: Forbes Randolph
Music: Carl Frederickson
Direction: Forbes Randolph; *Producer*: Forbes Randolph; *Choreography*: Felicia Sorel; *Scenery*: Watson Bar-ratt; *Costumes*: Mary Grant; *Lighting*: Leo Kerz; *Musical Direction*: Ray Kavanaugh
Cast: Pat Meaney (Peppi), Maria Gambarelli (Suzanne, Siren), Glenn Martin (Stage Door Johnny, Charles Blau-velt, Second), Keny McCord (Stage Door Johnny, Proprietor), Bernard Sloane (Stage Door Johnny, Second), Al Stewart (Stage Door Johnny, Director, Stage Door Man), Bertha Powell (Agatha), Monica Coryeo (Lu-cinda Bonnet), John Cherry (George Monteux), Jeanne Grant (Annette, Belle of Basin Street), Betty O'Rear (Queenie, Charwoman), Katherine Barlow (Dora, Belle of Basin Street), Ruth Shor (Clara, Belle of Basin Street), Charles Julian (Page Boy, Waiter), Richard Oneto (Maurice), Tom Fletcher (Phillip), Betty Vorhees (Marie), Marek Windheim (Maestro), Helen Raymond (La Duchesse), Gilbert Russell (Robert Randall), R. Davis Williams (Blackamoor), Richard Williams (Blackamoor), Clifford Jackson (Spanish Singer, Second), Rhoda Boggs (Colored Woman, Another Colored Woman), Jean Johnson (Colored Woman), Delphine Roach (Colored Woman), Charles Colman (George), Louvinia White (Mary Lou), Nat Dano (Merrymaker), Janie Javier (Michelle, Belle of Basin Street, Charwoman), Penny Carroll (Julie Le Blanc, Belle of Basin Street), Teresa Castagna (Belle of Basin Street), Patricia Hall (Belle of Basin Street), Leona Vanni (Belle of Basin Street, Charwoman), Charles Welch (Stephen), Berton Davis (Second, Theatre Manager), Catherine Ayers (Conjure Woman), John Diggs (Colored Man); Singing Ensemble: Catherine Ayers, Katherine Bar-low, Rhoda Boggs, Lucille Burney, Penny Carroll, Teresa Castagna, Anne Francis, Jeanne Grant, Patricia Hall, Alma Hubbard, Janie Janvier, Jean Johnson, Bertha Powell, Delphine Roach, Ruth Shor, Donna Tol-bert, Leona Vanni, Betty Voorhees, Leontyne Watts, Louvinia White, Isabella Wilson, Charles Colman, Berton Davis, John Diggs, Melvyn Howard, Glenn Martin, Keny McCord, William McDaniel, Richard

Oneto, Alford Pierre, Bernard Sloane, Leon Smith, Al Stewart, Charles Welch; Corps de Ballet: Marjorie Backus, Barbara Bailey, Lysa Baugher, May Block, Phyllis Gehrig, Anzia Kubicek, Marilyn March, Jeanne Mikuta, Marilyn Pendry, Janith Robinson, Sally Sorvo, Ronny Chetwood, Nat Dano, Charles Julian, Ray Kirchner, Lee Lindsey, Gene Wilson

The musical was presented in two acts.

The action takes place in New Orleans in 1829 and 1835.

Musical Numbers

Act One: "New Orleans" (Singing Ensemble); "New Orleans Saga" (Maria Gambarelli, Pat Meaney); "Don't Pull the Wool Over My Eyes" (Maria Gambarelli, Pat Meaney, Corps de Ballet); "Just to Say That I Love You" (Monica Coryeo, Glenn Martin, Keny McCord, Bernard Sloane, Al Stewart); "Just to Say That I Love You" (reprise) (Monica Coryeo, Singing Ensemble); "Concert Waltz" (Monica Coryeo); "Madame La Duchesse" (Helen Raymond); "Just to Say That I Love You" (reprise) (Monica Coryeo); "Music at Night" (Clifford Jackson); "What Would You Do" (Maria Gambarelli); "Now and Forevermore" (Monica Coryeo, Gilbert Russell); "Heavens Declare" (Vieux Carre Ensemble); "House on a Cloud" (Monica Coryeo, Gilbert Russell); "Ballet" (Maria Gambarelli, Corps de Ballet); "Wind from the Bayou" (Louvinia White); "Forever Spring" (Monica Coryeo, Gilbert Russell); "In a Hundred Years from Now" (John Diggs, Tom Fletcher, Vieux Carre Ensemble); "Lonely Straggler" (Louvinia White); "Love Came By" (Monica Coryeo); "Belles of Basin Street" (Katherine Barlow, Penny Carroll, Teresa Castagna, Jeanne Grant, Patricia Hall, Janie Janvier, Ruth Shor, Leona Vanni); "If He Hollers" (Janie Janvier); "Carnaval" (Entire Company)

Act Two: "When the Weddin' March Is Ended" (Maria Gambarelli, Pat Meaney, Dancing Ensemble); "Barcarolle" from *Anthony & Cleopatra* (Monica Coryeo); "What Kind of Noise Annoys an Oyster" (R. Davis Williams, Richard Williams); "Sky of Stars" (Gilbert Russell); "Is You Happy-Go-Lucky" (Bertha Powell, Charles Welch); "Love Came By" (reprise) (Monica Coryeo); "Charwomen's Song" (Janie Janvier, Betty O'Rear, Leona Vanni); "Barcarolle" (reprise) (Monica Coryeo); "Forever Spring" (Monica Coryeo, Gilbert Russell); "Don't Break the Spell" (Gilbert Russell); "Concert Waltz" (reprise) (Monica Coryeo)

In case its title wasn't enough to let you know where the musical took place, *In Gay New Orleans* offered such songs as "New Orleans," "New Orleans Saga," "Wind from the Bayou," and "Belles of Basin Street." And other song titles seemed to emphasize that we were also in deep operetta territory ("Music at Night," "Sky of Stars," "Now and Forevermore," "Forever Spring," "Don't Break the Spell," "Love Came By," and "Just to Say That I Love You"; the latter was apparently the musical's hoped-for song hit because it was performed three times in the first act). As for "What Kind of Noise Annoys an Oyster," perhaps that song was in a category all by itself.

The musical lasted a month in Boston before permanently closing. The plot dealt with aspiring opera singer Lucinda Bonnet (Monica Coryeo), and the men in her life, Maestro (Marek Windheim), who supports her career, and her husband Robert (Gilbert Russell), who apparently does not (or at least he doesn't approve of Maestro's interest in Lucinda). Annoyed with both of them, Lucinda takes off solo for Europe, becomes a famous prima donna, and then returns to New Orleans as the star of the New Orleans Opera Company. If the plot sounds somewhat familiar, it's because the earlier **Sunny River**, which also took place in Old New Orleans, centered on a bordello singer in the early 1800s who goes to Europe, becomes a famous prima donna, and then returns to New Orleans as a celebrated opera star.

The musical's promotional flyer reported that the show had been in the planning and preparation stages for three years, and that its gestation had begun in England where librettist and lyricist Forbes Randolph "conceived" the idea of the show when composer Carl Frederickson was visiting him. It's no doubt miraculous that their ideas about the musical "matched and blended perfectly," and thus their aim was to present to the public "the most colorful visually and most entrancing musically of any musical production in the history of the American Theatre." Further, *In Gay New Orleans* had its locale and story in the "roots" of "American soil" and its music was "true to American themes and American inspirations."

Variety said *In Gay New Orleans* was a "stupendous Christmas turkey," and *Billboard* stated the musical was "the most fantastically expensive and colossal bore within memory" (in *Broadway Bound*, William Torbert Leonard reports the show lost $300,000).

Although *In Gay New Orleans* never made it to New York, its scenery and costumes did. Early in the following season, the producers of **Louisiana Lady** bought the décor and costumes for their new musical, which also took place in New Orleans, a notoriously unlucky geographical locale for musical comedies (almost three-dozen musicals that took place in that city and its environs have been failures). Along with **Sunny River** and *In Gay New Orleans*, **Louisiana Lady** proudly took its place in the New Orleans Musical Comedy Hall of Flops after giving just four performances on Broadway.

Incidentally, not only did the producers of **Louisiana Lady** buy the sets and costumes of *In Gay New Orleans*; they also purchased the promotional artwork, and thus the artwork for both the window cards and flyers of *In Gay New Orleans* and **Louisiana Lady** are the same.

In Gay New Orleans shouldn't be confused with Michael Todd's revue **Gay New Orleans**, which was performed at the 1940 New York World's Fair and then later on tour.

SWEET BYE AND BYE
"A New Musical Comedy"

Theatres and *Performance Dates*: The musical opened on October 10, 1946, at the Shubert Theatre, New Haven, Connecticut, and closed there on October 12; it then opened on October 21 at the Forrest Theatre, Philadelphia, Pennsylvania, transferred to the Erlanger Theatre, and permanently closed there on November 5, 1946.

Book: S. J. Perelman and Al Hirschfeld
Lyrics: Ogden Nash
Music: Vernon Duke
Direction: Directed by Curt Conway and production staged by Nat Karson; *Producer*: Nat Karson; *Choreography*: Fred Kelly; *Scenery*: Boris Aronson; *Costumes*: Nat Karson; *Lighting*: Uncredited; *Musical Direction*: Charles Blackman
Cast: Robert Strauss (Grover Slump, Mr. Twenty-Four, J. Walter Noodnik), Le Roy Operti (Don Fox, Dr, Cody), Jack Blair (Cameraman), Billy Parsons (Workman, Dancer, Eskimo), Fred Hearn (Diver, Borvis, Executive, Eskimo), Leonard Stocker (Dr. Moon, Mr. Flack, Bundy's Double), Kay Rich (Miss Parker, Kimona), Sandra Grubell ("Secretary in Television," Department Store Executive), Doris York and Joey Thomas (Lovers), Gene Sheldon (Solomon Bundy), Jennie Lewis (Policewoman, Stevedore), Nevada Smith (Policewoman, Stevedore), Leonard Claret (Pedestrian), Rosemary Schaefer (Pedestrian), George O'Leary (Pedestrian), Gretchen Houser (Pedestrian), Jay Lloyd (Pedestrian), Charlotte Bergmeier (Pedestrian), Walter O'Keefe (Egon Pope), Percy Helton (Brimmer), Stella Anderson (Executive), Kay Borron (Executive, Mrs. Flack), Arthur Carroll (Executive, Magazine Editor), Kenneth Bonjukian (Executive), Eddy Di Genova (Executive), Walter Holland (Executive), Dolores Gray (Diana Janeway), Nat Dano (Mr. Fugazy), Joanne Jaap (Joan), Betty Bartley (Bubbles), Jack Blair (Stoat, Eskimo), Eleanor French (Miss Pittman), Jerry Boyar (Neon Flack), Miriam Lavelle (Nora), A. Winfield Hoeny (Dr. Knife), Tom Glazer (Tramp); Dancing Ensemble: Daurine Andrews, Charlotte Bergmeier, Jackie Dodge, Beverly Griffith, Gretchen Houser, Lee Morrison, Rosemary Schaefer, Doris York, Estelle Young, Leonard Claret, Nat Dano, Fred Hearn, Lee Ketcham, John Laverty, Jay Lloyd, George O'Leary, Joey Thomas, Gene Wilson; Singing Ensemble: Stella Anderson, Kay Borron, Ann Browning, Sandra Grubell, Kenneth Bonjukian, Arthur Carroll, Eddy Di Genova, Walter Holland
The musical was presented in two acts.
The action takes place in New York City and environs, in outer space, and in Alaska during the year 2076.

Musical Numbers

Act One: "Sweet Bye and Bye" (Entire Ensemble); "Texas, Brooklyn and Love" (Kay Rich, Leonard Stocker, Robert Strauss); "Old-Fashioned Tune" (Gene Sheldon; danced by Billy Parsons and Pedestrians); "Yes, Yes" (Walter O'Keefe, Percy Helton, Executives); "Diana" (Dolores Gray); "Good Deed for Today" (Gene Sheldon, Walter O'Keefe, Percy Helton); "Factory Ballet" (Gene Sheldon, Walter O'Keefe, Percy Helton, Dancing Ensemble); "Low and Lazy" (Gene Sheldon, Dolores Gray); "I Says to Him" (Eleanor French,

Betty Bartley); "Crispy and Crunchy" (Jack Blair, Miriam Lavelle; danced by Miriam Lavelle and Jack Blair); "Let's Be Young" (Dolores Gray; danced by Leonard Claret, George O'Leary, Dancing Ensemble); "Roundabout" (Gene Sheldon)

Act Two: "Hymn" (A. Winfield Hoeny, Executives); "My Broker Told Me So" (A. Winfield Hoeny, Executives); "Just Like a Man" (Dolores Gray); "It's Good" (Gene Sheldon, Tom Glazer); "Where Is Bundy?" (Jack Blair, Ensemble); "We Love Us" (Gene Sheldon, Dolores Gray); "Eskimo Bacchante" (Ensemble; danced by Miriam Lavelle); Finale (Entire Company)

Sweet Bye and Bye was an ambitious musical by S. J. Perelman, Al Hirschfeld, Ogden Nash, and Vernon Duke. Set in 2076, the musical's main target was a look at capitalism in the future (and, of course, it wasn't all that different from capitalism in the twentieth century). At a celebration of the nation's tricentennial, a time capsule from the 1939 New York World's Fair is opened, and among other things it reveals that meek and mild-mannered Prospect Park tree surgeon Solomon Bundy (Gene Sheldon) has inherited the Futurosy Candy Company, which a century-and-a-half later has become one of the most powerful and profitable companies in the country. A group of handlers, including personality consultant Diana Janeway (Dolores Gray), transform the likable Solomon into an unpleasant caricature of an overbearing corporate baron, and Diana, who had fallen in love with him, is turned off by his love of self. Ultimately, she realizes she had a hand in his transformation, and when Solomon gets wise to himself he returns to Prospect Park and his former occupation of tree surgeon, and he and Diana are reunited.

The musical's tryout was one of the most chaotic on record, and the writers, lyricist, and composer were at odds as to what kind of musical they had created. As a result, the evening varied wildly in style and in point of view. Despite rewriting, nothing helped, and so the musical closed without ever reaching Broadway. Among the changes made during the tryout were the deletion of at least two songs ("Texas, Brooklyn, and Love" and "I Says to Him") and the addition of at least three others ("Breakfast in Bed," "The Sea-Gull and the Ea-Gull," and "Ham That I Am"). As for "Born Too Late," it isn't listed in three different programs (from New Haven and Philadelphia as well as a one-sheet "corrected" program from the Philadelphia run), but it seems to have been performed at some point during the tryout. Soon after the New Haven opening, Gene Sheldon was replaced by Erik Rhodes, and just prior to the opening, leading lady Pat Kirkwood withdrew from the production because of medical reasons and was replaced by Dolores Gray.

Max de Schauensee in the *Philadelphia Evening Bulletin* said the musical amounted to almost three hours of "unadulterated tedium"; *Billboard* said the show was miscast (hence, Sheldon's quick departure from the show) and the book "very dull," but noted the musical had lavish production values and a "lovely" score; and Samuel L. Singer in the *Philadelphia Inquirer* said that despite "good" dressing, "a bit of sage," and a "little meat," the musical was nonetheless a "turkey."

In 1952, two songs from the musical ("Just Like a Man" and "Roundabout") appeared in Duke and Nash's revue *Two's Company*, which starred Bette Davis; the revue lasted just three months, but the songs were preserved on RCA Victor's cast album (LP # LOC-1009; reissued on RCA Red Seal LP # CBM1-2757; and on Sepia CD # 1047). In 1956, "Born Too Late" was heard in the Off-Broadway revue *The Littlest Revue*, and was recorded for that show's cast album (Epic Records LP # 3275; later reissued by Painted Smiles CD # PSCD-112). Over the years, other songs from the score surfaced, such as "Low and Lazy," "Just Like a Man," and "Roundabout" (*Vernon Duke Revisited*; Painted Smiles CD # PSCD-138) and "The Sea-Gull and the Ea-Gull," "Born Too Late," "Roundabout," and "Low and Lazy" (*Dawn Upshaw Sings Vernon Duke*; Nonesuch CD # 79531-2).

In 2011, PS Classics (CD # PS-1198) surprised everyone with a full-length studio cast recording of the delightful lyrics and music. The liner notes indicate there were many variations of the score, and as a result the album's producers decided to re-create the score as Duke and Nash had first "envisioned" it, and thus the album's producers allowed for only those "improvements" that the composer and lyricist had officially sanctioned. The result is a bountiful recording that includes dance music, reprises, and short scenes, not to mention the deleted number "I Says to Him," such added ones as "Ham That I Am" and "The Sea-Gull and the Ea-Gull," and at least two ("Too Enchanting" and "Our Parents Forgot to Get Married") that may have been heard during the tryout but weren't listed in the New Haven and Philadelphia programs (including the special "corrected" from Philadelphia). Songs not included on the recording are "Texas, Brooklyn and Love," "Old-Fashioned Tune," "Low and Lazy," "Good Deed for Today," "Crispy and Crunchy," and "We Love Us." The album includes "Executives Anonymous," which is probably a later title for "Hymn," which had been performed at the beginning of the second act by the executives.

1947–1948 Season

LOUISIANA LADY

"A New Musical Comedy" / "A Carnival of Gaiety, Romance and Music" / "A Lavish, Colorful and Hilarious Musical Comedy"

Theatre: New Century Theatre
Opening Date: June 2, 1947; *Closing Date*: June 4, 1947
Performances: 4
Book: Isaac Green Jr., and Eugene Berton
Lyrics and *Music*: Monte Carlo and Alma Sanders
Based on the 1927 play *Creoles* by Samuel Shipman and Kenneth Perkins.
Direction: Edgar MacGregor; *Producer*: Hall Shelton; *Choreography*: Felicia Sorel; *Scenery*: Watson Barratt; *Costumes*: Mary Grant (Frank Thompson also credited as costume designer); *Lighting*: Leo Kerz; *Musical Direction*: Hilding Anderson
Cast: Ray Jacquemot (El Gato), Lou Wills Jr. (Joe), Val Buttignol (Michel), Tina Prescott (Sarah), Ann Lay (Corrine), Patti Hall (Germaine), Angela Carabella (Annette), Patti Kingsley (Suzanne), Ann Viola (Yvonne), Edith Fellows (Marie-Louise), Howard Blaine (Charley), Bert Wilcox (Christophe, Judge Morgan), Lee Kerry (Hugh), Isabella Wilson (Genevieve), Monica Moore (Madam Corday), Gil Cass (Pierre), Robert Kimberly (Marquet), George Baxter (Merluche), Charles Judels (Alphonse), Bertha Powell (Celeste), George Roberts (A Drunk), Berton Davis (Hoskins), Frances Keyes (Janet), Victoria Cordova (Golondrina), Patrick Meany (Lieutenant Mason); Singers: Angela Carabella, Patti Hall, Frances Keyes, Patti Kingsley, Ann Lay, Tina Prescott, Ann Viola, Isabella Wilson, Gil Cass, Berton Davis, Ken Emery, Gerald Griffin Jr., George Roberts, Robert Kimberly, Michael Landau, Patrick Meany; Ballet Dancers: Aleta Buttignol, Karlyn De Boer, Louise Harris, Anzia Kubicek, Terry Miele, Nancy Milton, Helen Osborne, Ruth Ostrander, Daniel Buberniak, Val Buttignol, Kenneth Davis, Robert De Voye, Tony Matthews, Ralph Williams, Raoul Celeda
The musical was presented in two acts.
The action takes place in New Orleans during April 1830.

Musical Numbers

Act One: Overture (Orchestra); "Gold, Women and Laughter" (Ray Jacquemot, Men); "That's Why I Want to Go Home" (Edith Fellows); "Men About Town" (Monica Moore, Ensemble); "That's Why I Want to Go Home" (reprise) (Edith Fellows); "Just a Bit Naïve" (Edith Fellows, Ray Jacquemot); "The Cuckoo-Cheena" (Victoria Cordova, Lou Wills Jr., Ensemble); "The Cuckoo-Cheena Dance" (Helen Osborne, Louise Harris, Tony Matthews, Ensemble); "I Want to Live—I Want to Love" (Edith Fellows); "I Want to Live—I Want to Love" (ballet) (Ballet Dancers); "I Want to Live—I Want to Love" Classic Trio (Ruth Ostrander, Kenneth Davis, Robert De Voye); "The Night Was All to Blame" (Ray Jacquemot); "Beware of Lips That Say 'Cherie'" (Monica Moore); "Louisiana's Holiday" (Ray Jacquemot, Victoria Cordova, Ensemble); Act One Finale (Company)

Act Two: "It's Mardi Gras" (Ensemble, Ballet Dancers; Dance Specialty: Kenneth Davis); "No, No, Mam'selle" (Ray Jacquemot, Girls); "When You Are Close to Me" (Edith Fellows, Ray Jacquemot); "When You Are Close to Me" (reprise) (Edith Fellows); "Mardi Gras Dance" (Lou Wills Jr.); "No One Cares for Dreams" (Monica Moore); "Mammy's Little Baby" (Bertha Powell); Finale (Company)

Louisiana Lady was one of the biggest duds of the decade; it closed after four performances, and had the shortest run of all the season's musicals. Robert Garland in the *New York Journal-American* memorably summed up the proceedings as a "mild mixture of muck, music and magnolias." And it's no wonder the musical received some of the worst notices of the decade: it was set in the generally unfriendly musical-comedy territory of New Orleans and environs, the location of some three-dozen musicals that flopped in New York or on the road.

Such song titles as "Louisiana's Holiday," "It's Mardi Gras," and "Mardi Gras Dance" revealed we were in forbidden musical comedy territory; "Beware of Lips That Say 'Cherie'" and "No, No, Mam'selle" promised ooh-la-la French-flavored exotique; "The Cuckoo-Cheena" gave us the latest musical comedy dance craze; and "Gold, Women and Laughter," "I Want to Live—I Want to Love," "The Night Was All to Blame," "When You Are Close to Me," and "No One Cares for Dreams" promised typical musical comedy clichés. As for "Mammy's Little Baby," well, who knows what that promised because according to Garland it was performed by Bertha Powell as a "feminine Al Jolson" who sang about "mammy's little white-faced baby."

During the tryout, Olga Baclanova (who during rehearsals had replaced Irene Bordoni) and Henry Lascoe were succeeded by Monica Moore and Robert Kimberly; the dancing team of The Hotshots was written out of the musical; and two songs ("In Gay Paree" and "Nothing but Love on My Mind") were deleted.

Like **Early to Bed**, the story revolved around a bordello-in-finishing-school drag. Madame Corday (Monica Moore) runs the brothel Casino De Luxe, but only because she owes money to the evil Merluche (George Baxter), who makes his fortune in the slave trade. When Madame's innocent daughter Marie-Louise (Edith Fellows) arrives from boarding school a day early, the Madame and everyone in the establishment pretend it's a finishing school. In the meantime, Marie-Louise falls in love with noble rouge pirate El Gato (Ray Jacquemot), who wears evening clothes and is otherwise all-gentleman in his Robin-Hood-like mission to scuttle Merluche's slave ships and send the slaves to Haiti and freedom. Meanwhile, Merluche dumps his girlfriend Golondrina (Victoria Cordova) and hopes to force Marie-Louise into marriage; but the innocent girl is saved from a fate almost worse than death by El Gato and his fellow pirates.

Brooks Atkinson in the *New York Times* said the musical utilized "stock" conventions from "odds and ends of yesterday's theatre"; the music was "uninspired" (with equally "suitable" lyrics), the "teetering artistic" dances verged on "burlesque," and there was even a magnolia number. Robert Coleman in the *New York Daily Mirror* stated the opening night audience had come to the New Century Theatre in order "to be bored" by the "inept" musical. The "maze of musical comedy errors" had an "amateurish" and "dull" book, "undistinguished" music, and "pedestrian" direction.

John Chapman in the *New York Daily News* suggested *Louisiana Lady* was so completely "undistinguished" that it "must have been done on purpose." He noted the musical's top ticket price was $3.60, which was "low" for a musical but unfortunately "not low enough." William Hawkins in the *New York World-Telegram* said the "ordinary" musical's most "marked talent" was its ability to inspire the audience to seek "fleet exodus" from the theatre. Once the evening settled into its plot, "what remained of the audience sighed and surged toward the doors."

Louis Kronenberger in *PM* found the "trite" and "tedious" show awash in "particularly moronic double-entendres" and "sad, sickly, stunted little jokes." Ward Morehouse in the *New York Sun* said the "pretty sorry affair" wasn't "the worst" of musicals but was definitely one of the "dullest." The sometimes "fairly pleasant" score couldn't make up for the "awful" book, "witless" dialogue, and "routine" performances; the "very long" evening was "well-intentioned and expensive . . . and beyond all hope."

Richard Watts in the *New York Post* suggested if theatre audiences had suddenly developed a "passion" for "outmoded" musicals, then here was their show; further, the dialogue was so "incredible" it was actually "funny"; and Howard Barnes in the *New York Herald Tribune* called *Louisiana Lady* a "comatose carnival."

If the New Orleans' setting wasn't enough to send *Louisiana Lady* into theatrical oblivion, its appropriation of the scenery and costumes from another flop musical set in that city (**In Gay New Orleans**) should have cinched it. The creators of *Louisiana Lady* should have known that the producers of the earlier flops **The**

Lady Comes Across (1942, three performances) and ***Hairpin Harmony*** (1943, and also three performances) had purchased their scenery from two *other* earlier flops (the former bought the scenery from ***She Had to Say Yes***, the latter the scenery from a 1941 comedy titled *Pie in the Sky*). As for ***In Gay New Orleans*** (not to be confused with Michael Todd's 1940 World's Fair revue ***Gay New Orleans***), it had closed on the road about six months before *Louisiana Lady* opened on Broadway; besides the scenery and costumes, *Louisiana Lady* also bought the rights for the advertising artwork of the earlier musical (and so the flyers and window cards of ***In Gay New Orleans*** and *Louisiana Lady* used the same design).

MUSIC IN MY HEART
"A ROMANTIC MUSICAL PLAY WITH MELODIES OF TCHAIKOVSKY"

Theatre: Adelphi Theatre
Opening Date: October 2, 1947; *Closing Date*: January 24, 1948
Performances: 125
Book: Patsy Ruth Miller
Lyrics: Forman Brown
Music: Peter Ilych Tschaikovsky (music adapted by Franz Steininger)
Direction: Hassard Short; *Producer*: Henry Duffy; *Choreography*: Ruth Page; *Scenery* and *Costumes*: Alvin Colt; *Lighting*: Hassard Short; *Musical Direction*: Franz Steininger
Cast: Harold Norman (Stage Manager), Vivienne Segal (Tatiana Kerskaya), George Lambrose (Mischa), Robert Carroll (Peter Ilych Tchaikovsky), Allan Lowell (Stage Doorman), Martha Wright (Desiree Artot), Jan Murray (Maurice Cabanne), Charles Fredericks (Captain Nicholas "Nikki" Gregorovitch), James Starbuck (Ivan Petrofski), Dorothy Etheridge (Natuscha), Jean Handzlik (Gypsy), Robert Hayden (Joseph), Della Lind (Princess Katherine Dolgoruki), Martha Flynn (Lady in Waiting), Pauline Goddard (Olga), Edward White (Messenger of the Tsar), Jeanne Shelby (Sonya), Olga Suarez (Vera Remisova, Prima Ballerina), Ralph Glover (Lord Chamberlain), Nicholas Magallanes (Premier Danseur); Ballet Dancers: Dorothy Bauer, Iris Burton, Barbara Cole, Francy Falk, Mary Haywood, Clara Knox, Sheila Lawrence, Nanon Millis, Carol Nelson, Nina Popova, Yvonne Tibor, Marjorie Winters, James Barron, Robert Cadwallader, Ronald Chetwood, Charles Dickson, Charles L. Grasse, Jack Miller, Nicolai Polajenko; Vocal Ensemble: Dorothea Berthelsen, Anne Marie Biggs, Audrey Dearden, Jane Flynn, Martha Flynn, Joyce Homiere, Joan Kibrig, Barbara Weaver, Kathleen Zaranova, Jack Cassidy, Peter Hagen, Bernie Koveler, Allan Lowell, Harold Norman, Robert Rippy, Michael Risk, John Vanderhoof, Frank Whitmore; Stage Hands, Footmen, Claque, and Others: Jack Cassidy, Peter Hagen, Bernie Koveler, Robert Rippy, Michael Risk
The musical was presented in two acts.
The action takes place in 1869 in and around St. Petersburg, Russia.

Musical Numbers

Act One: "Unrequited Love," or "The Storm" (ballet) (music by Gioachino Rossini) (Ballet Dancers; Girl: Barbara Cole; Boy: Nanon Millis; Ballet Dancers); "Flower Waltz" (Martha Wright); "Natuscha" (James Starbuck, Dorothy Etheridge, Ensemble); "Love Is a Game for Soldiers" (Charles Fredericks); "Stolen Kisses" (Della Lind, Charles Fredericks); "No! No! No!" (Vivienne Segal, Jan Murray); "While There's a Song to Sing" (Martha Wright, Ensemble); "The Balalaika Serenade" (Jean Handzlik); "Trepak" (Ensemble); "Am I Enchanted" (Martha Wright, Charles Fredericks, Ensemble)
Act Two: "Gossip" (James Starbuck, Dorothy Etheridge, Ballet Dancers); "Once Upon a Time" (Martha Wright, Charles Fredericks); "Three's a Crowd" (Martha Wright, Della Lind, Charles Fredericks); "Song of the Troika" (Martha Wright, Charles Fredericks); "The Ballerina's Story" (Vivienne Segal); "Song of the Claque" (Jan Murray); "Beauty and the Beast" (ballet) (Beauty: Olga Suarez, The Beast: Nicholas Magallanes; Ballet Dancers); "Love Song" (Martha Wright); "Love Is the Sovereign of My Heart" (Martha Wright, Charles Fredericks); Finale

As noted in the entry for ***Song without Words***, there were three related attempts to bring Tchaikovsky's life to the musical stage, and all of them were huge failures. ***Song without Words*** collapsed during its West

Coast tryout in 1945, the current *Music in My Heart* received scathing reviews but somehow managed to hang on for a few months on Broadway, and **The Lady from Paris** closed in Philadelphia after two weeks of performances in 1950.

Blossom Time (1921) and **Song of Norway** told the stories of Franz Schubert and Edvard Grieg, and enjoyed long and profitable runs, but attempts to depict the romantic goings-on of Frederic Chopin in **Polonaise** and Richard Strauss in **The Waltz King** and **Mr. Strauss Goes to Boston** were quick failures. An examination of the three Tchaikovsky-related musicals indicates they were sunk in a swamp of operetta's most tired and shopworn clichés (for examples, see **Song without Words**), and when the critics reviewed the stultifying languor of *Music in My Heart*, they had a field day quoting the dreary dialogue that coursed throughout the tedious and fabricated story about Tchaikovsky (Robert Carroll) and his unrequited love for French opera star Desiree Artot (Martha Wright, who replaced Marguerite Piazza shortly before the New York opening), who loves Another . . . the Another being not Just Another but also Tchaikovsky's Best Friend, Captain Nicholas Gregorovitch (Charles Fredericks). But all ends well: Tchaikovsky may suffer in affairs of the heart, but he rushes off to the piano to dash off an immortal masterpiece or two.

And thanks to Brooks Atkinson in the *New York Times*, Louis Kronenberger in *PM*, and George Jean Nathan in his seasonal summary, we have a catalog of some of the choicest bits of dialogue heard in the musical:

- "You are a genius, and some day everybody will know it!"
- "She's lovely . . . like a flower."
- "Ah, Paris! What memories it holds for me!"
- "I've been a prima ballerina since I was sixteen." "Prima ballerina? Why, I thought you were a dancer."
- "I am mistress of the ballet. That's the only kind of mistress I can still be."
- "I might have worn sables and mink, but I ended with squirrel and skunk."
- "Do you recall that wonderful night when I came to your room and we loved each other?" "Oh, was that you?"

William Hawkins in the *New York World-Telegram* said the creators of *Music in My Heart* had undertaken "one of the greatest research jobs in the history of the theatre" because "there is not an original idea in it." And Kronenberger was amazed how the musical never once missed a chance "to go wrong on the biggest scale." If the authors had a "choice of two or more ways of being trite," they always picked the tritest. If there were various ways to be "trashy," they always chose the trashiest. As he watched the production, he began to mentally *dare* the writers to offer the clichés he just knew would be forthcoming. Would they dare have snow fall during the troika scene? Yes, snow fell. Would they dare use the first-movement theme of *Pathetique* as the basis of a love song? Yes, they did. When the hero gets thrown over by his girl, would they dare depict him "ripping the guts out of his concert grand" in order to write a masterpiece? Yes, they certainly did.

Ward Morehouse in the *New York Sun* found the "dreary" book "tormentingly dull" and "generally lifeless"; Robert Garland in the *New York Journal-American* said the libretto was "lackluster" as it plodded along in its "pedestrian" way; and Richard Watts in the *New York Post* said the "strangely tedious nonsense" reduced the "great" Tchaikovsky to "pigmy proportions."

Howard Barnes in the *New York Herald Tribune* found the lyrics "ungainly" and the book "two-dimensional" with a "woeful lack of dramatic conviction"; Atkinson said the evening of "grab-bag Tchaikovsky" had "debased" some of the world's "grandest" music, and he suggested that "even" the radio and the jukeboxes gave the composer "more honorable treatment."

But perhaps Robert Coleman in the *New York Daily Mirror* summed it up best: *Music in My Heart* was a "musical bowwow."

UNDER THE COUNTER
"A COMEDY WITH MUSIC"

Theatre: Shubert Theatre
Opening Date: October 3, 1947; *Closing Date*: October 25, 1947
Performances: 27

Play: Arthur Macrae
Lyrics: Harold Purcell
Music: Manning Sherwin
Direction: Jack Hulbert; *Producers*: Lee Ephraim in association with the Messrs. Shubert; *Choreography*: Jack Hulbert and John Gregory; *Scenery*: Clifford Pember; *Costumes*: Jacqmar, Lorian, Honore, Therese, B.J. Simmons & Co., Ltd., James & James, Ltd., and J.P. Anderson, Ltd.; *Lighting*: Uncredited; *Musical Direction*: Harry Levant
Cast: Winifred Hindle (Eva), Francis Roberts (Detective Inspector Baxter), Ballard Berkeley (Mike Kenderdine), Thorley Walters (Tim Garret), *Cicely Courtneidge* (Jo Fox), George Street (Mr. Burroughs), Glen Alyn (Zoe Tritton), Ingrid Forrest (Kitty), Wilfred Hyde-White (Sir Alec Dunne), John Gregory (Lieutenant Commander Hugo Conway, RNVR), Frederick Farley (Mr. Appleyard)
The comedy with music was presented in three acts.
The action takes place at the present time in London.

Musical Numbers

The following songs were performed during the play:
"Everywhere" (The Girls); "No-one's Tried to Kiss Me" (Thorley Walters, Girls); "The Moment I Saw You" (Cicely Courtneidge, Thorley Walters); "Let's Get Back to Glamour" (Cicely Courtneidge, Girls); "Ai Yi Yi" (Cicely Courtneidge, John Gregory, Girls); "The Moment I Saw You" (reprise) (Cicely Courtneidge, Thorley Walters)

Under the Counter had been a great success in London, where it opened at the Phoenix Theatre on November 22, 1945, for 665 performances with Cicely Courtneidge in the leading role. She and a few of the other West End cast members reprised their performances for New York, but the Broadway production received cool notices and closed after little more than three weeks.

In many respects, the evening was a one-woman *tour de force* in which Courtneidge played the irrepressible take-no-prisoners Jo Fox, an actress who is determined to get her way when it comes to her career and to men. To that end, she rehearses her new musical show in her living room; manipulates her contacts in the government to ensure that an old boyfriend is transferred from overseas to a job in Britain; and, despite postwar rationing, she cleverly obtains whatever she needs in the way of clothes through the black market (that is, under the counter).

Brooks Atkinson in the *New York Times* said *Under the Counter* was "not one of England's most durable export articles"; its humor was the kind you had to "be in at the beginning and go with it all the way," and he could not join in the fun. As for its star, he was "not her audience." Howard Barnes in the *New York Herald Tribune* said the evening amounted to little more than an extended revue sketch, and soon the plot fell "as flat as a popover which refuses to rise." Courtneidge worked "valiantly" and there were a few "pleasant" songs, but otherwise "tedium" prevailed.

Ward Morehouse in the *New York Sun* praised the "cyclonic" Courtneidge, a "skillful buffoon" who was "amusing," reminiscent of Beatrice Lillie, and "all over the stage with the energy of Bobby Clark." But her vehicle was "very flimsy" and the script was "feeble-minded." Richard Watts in the *New York Post* found the star "skillful and inventive," but the evening soon fell into the "doldrums" and wore thin; further, the show suffered from "excessive length." Robert Coleman in the *New York Daily Mirror* said Courtneidge was "one of the world's funniest women," and the producer shouldn't have burdened her with such an "anemic" show when only a "top flight musical" was her proper due.

The headline of Louis Kronenberger's review in *PM* called the production "quite anemic," and the critic said that while the script was timely in its allusions to the black market, it was "well-nigh prehistoric in its general structure." It went from "agreeable" to "agreeably silly" to "uncomfortably silly" to "quite oppressively" silly. Courtneidge had her "amusing" moments, and while she was "inexhaustible" she was also "exhausting." He concluded that she may not be an "event," but was nonetheless an "experience."

Robert Garland in the *New York Journal-American* hated *Under the Counter* and said, "Perfidious Albion, take it away!" He also made it clear that Courtneidge was "most certainly not for" him, but admitted that not even Beatrice Lillie could have put across the show. William Hawkins in the *New York World-Telegram* noted the evening was built around Courtneidge, who made her entrance "with all guns blazing" and throughout the evening she sang, danced, emoted, and clowned; he suggested the show would have been more successful had it jettisoned the book and let Courtneidge loose in a one-woman show.

Only John Chapman in the *New York Daily News* gave the offering a good review, saying the Shuberts had brought in a hit. The book was "high-spirited" and the star was a combination of the "low comedy talents" of Beatrice Lillie and Bobby Clark; further, in comparison Courtneidge made Betty Hutton "look like a promising candidate for the role of Camille."

HIGH BUTTON SHOES
"A NEW MUSICAL COMEDY"

Theatre: New Century Theatre (during run, the musical transferred to the Shubert Theatre and then to the Broadway Theatre)
Opening Date: October 9, 1947; *Closing Date*: July 2, 1949
Performances: 727
Book: Stephen Longstreet
Lyrics: Sammy Cahn
Music: Jule Styne
Based on the 1946 novel *The Sisters Liked Them Handsome* by Stephen Longstreet.
Direction: George Abbott; *Producers*: Monte Proser and Joseph Kipness; *Choreography*: Jerome Robbins; *Scenery*: Oliver Smith; *Costumes*: Miles White; *Lighting*: Peggy Clark; *Musical Direction*: Milton Rosenstock
Cast: Phil Silvers (Harrison Floy), Joey Faye (Mr. Pontdue), Paul Godkin (Uncle Willie), Jack McCauley (Henry Longstreet), Johnny Stewart (Stevie Longstreet), Lois Lee (Fran), Nanette Fabray (Sara Longstreet), Helen Gallagher (Nancy), Mark Dawson (Hubert "Oggie" Ogglethorpe), Carole Coleman (Shirley Simpkins), Nathaniel Frey (Elmer Simpkins), Donald Harris (Elmer Simpkins, Sr.), Tom Glennon (Coach), William David (Mr. Anderson), Arthur Partington (A Boy at the Picnic), Sondra Lee (The Boy at the Picnic's Playmate), Jacqueline Dodge (A Popular Girl), George Spelvin (A Betting Man), Howard Lenters (Another Betting Man); Corps de Ballet: Jean Marie Caples, Jacqueline Dodge, Virginia Gorski (Gibson), June Graham, Christine Karner, Elena Lane, Sondra Lee, Kay Lewis, Louisa Lewis, Audrey Peters, Gloria Smith, Toni Stuart, Eleonore Treiber, Vincent Carbone, Raul Celada, Lenny Claret, Evans Davis, Fred Hearn, Ray Kirchner, Tommy Morton, Arthur Partington, William Pierson, William Sumner, Don Weissmuller; Singers: Nancy Babcock, Gloria Casper, Estelle Gardner, Ronnie Hartmann, Dorothy Karrol, Hannah O'Leary, Fay Moore, Helene Whitney, Edward (Ed) Cole, Ray Cook, Erno Czako, John Dennis, Nathaniel Frey, Neil Harwood, Edward Hayes, Ben Murphy
The musical was presented in two acts.
The action takes place during 1913 in Kokomo "and points East," and in both New Brunswick and Atlantic City, New Jersey.

Musical Numbers

Act One: "He Tried to Make a Dollar" (Ed Cole, Ray Cook, John Dennis, Edward Hayes); "Can't You Just See Yourself in Love with Me?" (Mark Dawson, Lois Lee); "There's Nothing Like a Model 'T'" (Phil Silvers, Company); "Next to Texas, I Love You" (Mark Dawson, Lois Lee; danced by Girls and Boys); "Security" (Nanette Fabray, Lois Lee, Singing Girls); "Tango" (Helen Gallagher, Paul Godkin); "The Bird Watcher's Song" (Nanette Fabray, Singing Girls); "Get Away for a Day in the Country" (Jack McCauley, Johnny Stewart, Singers); "A Summer Incident" (dance) (A Boy: Arthur Partington; His Playmate: Sondra Lee; A Popular Girl: Jacqueline Dodge; Her Friend: Raoul Celada); "Papa, Won't You Dance with Me?" (Nanette Fabray, Jack McCauley, Girls and Boys); ""Can't You Just See Yourself in Love with Me?" (reprise) (Phil Silvers, Lois Lee); Finaletto (Entire Company)
Act Two: "On a Sunday by the Sea" (Singers); "Mack Sennett Ballet" (aka "Keystone Kops' Ballet" and "Bathing Beauty Ballet") (Bathing Beauties: Audrey Peters; and Jean Marie Caples, Virginia Gorski, June Graham, Elena Lane, Gloria Smith, Eleonore Treiber; Life Guard: Evans Davis; The Twins: Kay Lewis and Louisa Lewis, and Fred Hearn and Don Weissmuller; Crooks: Raul Celada, Jacqueline Dodge, Sondra Lee;

Chief of Police: William Sumner; Cops: Vincent Carbone, Lenny Claret, Ray Kirchner, Tommy Morton, William Pierson); "You're My Girl" (Mark Dawson, Lois Lee); "I Still Get Jealous" (Nanette Fabray, Jack McCauley); "You're My Boy" (Phil Silvers, Joey Faye); "Nobody Ever Died for Dear Old Rutgers" (Phil Silvers, Mark Dawson, Singing Boys); "Castle Walk" (Nanette Fabray, Jack McCauley); "He Tried to Make a Dollar" (reprise) (Entire Company)

High Button Shoes has for all purposes become a forgotten hit. It ran on Broadway for almost two years, enjoyed a national tour and London production, and was seen in four different television adaptations over an eighteen-year period. Further, the musical represented Jule Styne's first Broadway score (his earlier **Glad to See You** had closed during its tryout) and included three song hits, "I Still Get Jealous," "Papa, Won't You Dance with Me?," and "Can't You Just See Yourself in Love with Me?," and Jerome Robbins's legendary "Mack Sennett Ballet" was a show-stopper of the first order. But by and large the musical has faded away and now is virtually never produced.

The nostalgic story looked back at small-town New Jersey in the early years of the twentieth century and centered on the calm, easy-going Longstreet family, including Papa (Jack McCauley), Mama (Nanette Fabray), their son Stevie (Johnny Stewart), Mama's brother Willie (Paul Godkin), Mama's sister Fran (Lois Lee), and their maid Nancy (Helen Gallagher). Into their placid world explodes the fast-talking con man Harrison Floy (Phil Silvers) and his stooge Pontdue (Joey Faye). Floy ingratiates himself with the Longstreets and promises to sell their useless family property (which is basically swampland). Once the property is sold, Floy and Pontdue take off for Atlantic City with the proceeds; and when they're tracked down by the police, soon everyone on the beach becomes involved in the proceedings, including bathing beauties and life guards, a Gloria Swanson lookalike, the cops and the crooks, and the Longstreet family members. When the money is returned, Floy unveils his latest scheme, to sell the mud in the swampland because it's a gold mine, or, rather a mud mine, which is sure to rake in the dollars when it's manufactured as a beauty cream for mud baths. But when Floy discovers the police are still on his trail, he decides to quickly move on to new ventures and bids the Longstreets goodbye with a promise (or perhaps a threat) to one day return.

High Button Shoes opened the night before the season's most anticipated musical **Allegro**, which enjoyed an enormous advance sale, loads of publicity, and a few sterling reviews. While some of the critics viewed *High Button Shoes* as an also-ran, it became the season's longest-running musical and more than doubled the run of the Rodgers and Hammerstein show.

Robert Coleman in the *New York Daily Mirror* said the new musical didn't "add up," and Longstreet's book was "ineptly" written; but Nanette Fabray's performance was the "best" of her career and here she flowered as a "delightful personality" and a "resourceful artist," and Jerome Robbins's choreography was the most "enjoyable" seen on Broadway in a long time. But Phil Silvers was "handicapped by mediocre material and a bad throat" and his part "cried for the vitality of Bobby Clark." Robert Garland in the *New York Journal-American* said the musical had good and bad material, with Silvers and Joey Faye's "You're My Boy" the "low-spot" of the evening. Although at times the musical came across as a "straight play being rehearsed in a night club while the floor show's going on," Fabray was "lovely" and the "Mack Sennett Ballet" was "beautifully batty." Howard Barnes in the *New York Herald Tribune* liked the "lilting" score and "brilliant" choreography, but otherwise felt the evening often lagged and came across as a "conglomeration of night-club antics."

Like Garland, Barnes also disliked "You're My Boy" and stated Silvers and Faye were "guilty of atrocious taste in consenting" to sing it. It took George Jean Nathan in his annual seasonal summary to shed some light on just what offended the two critics. Nathan reported that Silvers and Faye offered a "funny act out of burlesque" that followed "the homosexual comedy pattern of that bygone art." He also noted that those in the audience who "severely criticized" the "highly objectionable" sequence also "burst their sides laughing at it."

Louis Kronenberger in *PM* said that for a musical that wasn't all that good, *High Button Shoes* was often "wonderful" and "gay." It was an "upsy-downsy" show that at its best allowed Fabray to emerge as "a real and thoroughly vivacious personality" and in Robbins's "Mack Sennett Ballet" it offered "one of the comic glories of the age."

Ward Morehouse in the *New York Sun* praised the "sprightly and exuberant" musical, and besides the "wonderful" beach ballet he also liked Helen Gallagher and Paul Godkin's tango sequence. William Hawkins in the *New York World-Telegram* said the ballet should eventually find its way into Ballet Theatre's repertoire; moreover, he liked the "politely humorous" soft-shoe dance that accompanied Fabray and McCauley's

"I Still Get Jealous"; the "sardonic" tango; and the "charming" polka "Papa, Won't You Dance with Me?" John Chapman in the *New York Daily News* said the ballet was a "masterpiece" that had the first-nighters "paralyzed with delight." Otherwise, much of the musical was not all that "socko" but was nonetheless an "amiable affair" with "handsome" décor and a "good enough" score. But it was Robbins who "cops the evening."

Richard Watts in the *New York Post* said *High Button Shoes* would be the first musical hit of the season, and he praised Robbins's ballet ("a genuine masterpiece"), the score ("lively"), and Phil Silvers ("a truly funny fellow"). Brooks Atkinson in the *New York Times* found the show an "immensely likeable" one and praised the "hilarious" ballet that was "swift and insane, like a jiggly old film" and an "inspired bit of animated entertainment." He also liked the tango (a "brief cartoon") and the score ("simple in style and very pleasant to hear, like a well-oiled hurdy-gurdy").

During the tryout the role of Gramps (General Longstreet), which was played by Clay Clement, was eliminated, and the songs "She's Right" (for Nanette Fabray, Lois Lee, and the female chorus) and "Too Soon" (for Clay Clement) were cut. During preproduction "Betwixt and Between" was eliminated; with a new lyric by Stephen Sondheim, the song was later heard as "Everything's Coming Up Roses" in *Gypsy* (1959).

The cast album was recorded by RCA Victor (first issued on LP by RCA Camden # CAL-457, and then by RCA on LP # LOC-1107/LSO-1107c), and includes eight songs from the production; the CD was released by RCA/BMG Direct/Camden/Special Music Company (# CAD1-457). Under the overall title of "On a Sunday by the Sea," the "Mack Sennett Ballet" was recorded for the two-CD cast album of *Jerome Robbins' Broadway* (RCA Victor # 60150-2-RC), which also includes the song and the accompanying soft-shoe dance of "I Still Get Jealous." The overture of *Lost Broadway and More Volume 5* (unnamed company and unnumbered CD) is based on "He Tried to Make a Dollar," the opening number of *High Button Shoes*. *Forgotten Broadway* (unnamed company; LP # T-101) includes "The Bird Watcher's Song" performed by Nanette Fabray and chorus (source unknown, but probably from the 1956 television adaptation of the musical [see below]).

Librettist Stephen Longstreet adapted the script into a straight play version (also called *High Button Shoes*), which includes the cast and credits from the musical production; this version was published in hardback by Samuel French in 1949.

The London production opened at the Hippodrome on December 22, 1948, for 291 performances; the cast included Lew Parker (Harrison Floy), Kay Kimber (Mama), Sidney James (Papa), and, in the dancing chorus, Audrey Hepburn.

There have been four television adaptations. The first was seen on April 20, 1948, as an episode on the CBS series *Tonight on Broadway*, which consisted of interviews with the cast as well as musical excerpts. The next was a ninety-minute version seen on *Saturday Spectacular* in 1956; Nanette Fabray and Joey Faye reprised their Broadway roles, and others in the cast were Hal March (Harrison Floy) and Don Ameche (Papa). The third version was an abridged one (of about twenty minutes) seen as part of the segment "That Wonderful Year" on the CBS series *The Garry Moore Show*. And the fourth adaptation was also seen on *The Garry Moore Show* in a one-hour version presented on November 20, 1966; the cast included Jack Cassidy (Harrison Floy) as well as Carol Lawrence, Maureen O'Hara, Jerry Lanning, Garry Moore, and Durward Kirby.

The musical was revived by the Equity Library Theatre for the period March 2–6, 1955, and by Goodspeed Opera House, East Haddam, Connecticut, during the period June 16–September 11, 1982; both productions included a first-act song for the football players ("On the Banks of the Old Raritan").

Awards

Tony Award: Best Choreography (**Jerome Robbins**)

ALLEGRO
"A New Musical Play"

Theatre: Majestic Theatre
Opening Date: October 10, 1947; *Closing Date*: July 10, 1948
Performances: 315

Book and *Lyrics*: Oscar Hammerstein II
Music: Richard Rodgers
Direction and *Choreography*: Agnes De Mille; *Producer*: The Theatre Guild; *Scenery* and *Lighting*: Jo Miel-
ziner; *Costumes*: Lucinda Ballard; *Musical Direction*: Salvatore Dell'Isola
Cast: Annamary Dickey (Marjorie Taylor), William Ching (Dr. Joseph Taylor), Edward Platt (Mayor, Minis-
ter), Muriel O'Malley (Grandma Taylor), Ray Harrison (Joey's Friend), Frank Westbrook (Joey's Friend),
Roberta Jonay (Jennie Brinker), Robert Byrn (Principal, Biology Professor), Evelyn Taylor (Mabel), Stanley
Simmons (Bicycle Boy), Harrison Muller (Georgie), Kathryn Lee (Hazel), John Conte (Charlie Townsend),
John Battles (Joseph Taylor Jr.), Susan Svetlik (Miss Lipscomb, Shakespeare Student), Charles Tate (Cheer
Leader), Sam Steen (Cheer Leader), Wilson Smith (Coach, Buckley), Paul Parks (Ned Brinker), David
Collyer (English Professor), William McCully (Chemistry Professor), Raymond Keast (Greek Professor),
Blake Ritter (Philosophy Professor), Ray Harrison (Bertram Woolhaven), Katrina Van Oss (Molly), Gloria
Wills (Beulah), Julie Humphries (Millie), Sylvia Karlton (Dot), Patricia Bybell (Addie), Lawrence Fletcher
(Dr. Bigby Denby), Frances Rainer (Mrs. Mulhouse), Lily Paget (Mrs. Lansdale), Bill Bradley (Jarman), Jean
Houloose (Maid), Lisa Kirk (Emily), Tom Perkins (Doorman). Stephen Chase (Brooks Lansdale); Singers:
Mary O'Fallon, Charlotte Howard, Lily Paget, Helen Hunter, Sylvia Karlton, Priscilla Hathaway, Gay
Lawrence, Josephine Lambert, Julie Humphries, Patricia Bybell, Yolanda Renay, Devida Stewart, Nanette
Vezina, Mia Stenn, Lucille Udovick, Glen Scandur, Gene Tobin, Walter Kelvin, Bernard Green, David
Collyer, Joseph Caruso, Tommy Barragan, Victor Clarke, Edward Platt, Robert Reeves, Wilson Smith,
Tom Perkins, James Jewell, David Poleri, Robert Neukum, Raymond Keast, Wesley Swails, Clarence
Hall, Blake Ritter, Ralph Patterson, Robert Byrn, William McCully, Robert Arnold; Dancers: Jean Tachau,
Evelyn Taylor, Mariane Oliphant, Patricia Gianinoto, Andrea Dowling, Jean Houloose, Therese Miele,
Frances Rainer, Susan Svetlik, Ruth Ostrander, Patricia Barker, William Bradley, Daniel Buberniak, Bob
Herget, John Laverty, Ralph Linn, Harrison Muller, Stanley Simmons, Charles Tate, Frank Westbrook,
Ralph Williams, Sam Steen
The musical was presented in two acts.
The action takes place during the years 1905–1940 in a small town, a college town, and a big city.

Musical Numbers

Act One: "Joseph Taylor Jr." (Entire Ensemble); "I Know It Can Happen Again" (Muriel O'Malley); "One
Foot, Other Foot" (Singing Ensemble); "One Foot, Other Foot" (dance) (aka "Children's Dance") (Ballet
Dancers; Specialties: Kathryn Lee, Patricia Barker, and Ray Harrison); "The Winters Go By" (Ensemble);
"Poor Joe!" (Ensemble); "A Fellow Needs a Girl" (William Ching, Annamary Dickey); "Freshman Dance"
(the dance incorporates the music of Richard Rodgers's "Mountain Greenery" from *The Garrick Gaieties*
[1926]): (a) "As They Are" (Dancers) and (b) "As They Imagine They Are" (Dancers); "One Foot, Other
Foot" (reprise) (Ensemble); "It's a Darn Nice Campus" (John Battles); "The Purple and Brown" (aka "Wild-
cats") (Freshmen); "She Is Never Away" (Ensemble); "So Far" (Gloria Wills); "You Are Never Away" (John
Battles, Ensemble); "What a Lovely Day for a Wedding" (Ensemble, Paul Parks); "It May Be a Good Idea
for Joe" (John Conte); "The Wedding": (a) "To Have and to Hold" (Ensemble) and (b) "Wish Them Well"
(Ensemble)
Act Two: "Money Isn't Everything" (Roberta Jonay, Kathryn Lee, Patricia Bybell, Julie Humphries, Sylvia
Karlton); "Hazel Dances" (dance) (Kathryn Lee); "Poor Joe!" (reprise) (Male Ensemble); "You Are Never
Away" (reprise) (John Battles); "A Fellow Needs a Girl" (reprise) (Annamary Dickey); "Yatata, Yatata,
Yatata" (John Conte, Ensemble); "The Gentleman Is a Dope" (Lisa Kirk); "Allegro" (Lisa Kirk, John Conte,
John Battles, Ensemble); "Allegro" (dance) (Kathryn Lee, Dancers); "Come Home" (Annamary Dickey);
"Yatata, Yatata, Yatata" (reprise) (Ensemble); Finale (reprises of "Come Home" and "One Foot, Other
Foot") (Entire Company)

Allegro is the most problematic musical by Richard Rodgers and Oscar Hammerstein II. Including its tryout, Broadway run, and post-Broadway tour, it played for eighteen months but never recouped its investment,
and since its inception has been generally misunderstood and misinterpreted.

Originally envisioned as a musical analysis of a man's entire life from birth to death, Hammerstein's libretto instead followed its central character Joseph Taylor Jr. (John Battles) from his birth to his thirty-fifth year. He's a small-town boy who becomes a big-city doctor where he's enmeshed in hospital politics, rich patients who are little more than hypochondriacs, and an unfaithful wife, Jennie (Roberta Jonay). He ditches Jenny, is clearly destined for a romantic relationship with his faithful nurse Emily (Lisa Kirk), and moves back to his hometown to join his father's practice.

Much has been made of Hammerstein's alleged big-city-bad, small-town-good plot, and due to fuzzy writing in the second act, it's easy to understand this interpretation. But what Hammerstein really seems to be saying is that one shouldn't stray too far from one's roots. If Joe had been a big-city boy living unhappily in a small town, presumably Hammerstein would have had Joe return to the city sidewalks.

It's a given that the script's second act lacks clarity. But even if Hammerstein's intentions had been crystal clear, the musical suffers from a leading character who lacks characterization. There's absolutely no one to care about in this musical, especially Joe, who is a cipher without personality and dramatic depth. The audience is told how special he is, but in fact he's just a blank slate lacking flesh and blood. Rodgers and Hammerstein should have given Joe one or two introspective character songs to explore his thoughts and feelings. But musically the leading character is given just one solo in a score that includes thirty-one separate musical sequences, and that one number is sung early in the first act when he's in college. Otherwise, he shares a lovely (if someone generic) late first-act ballad (and a later reprise) with the musical's oppressive and omnipresent chorus, and toward the evening's conclusion is part of a trio (with chorus) which performs the title song. But Joe is never given a song (such as Billy Bigelow's "Soliloquy" [*Carousel*] or even Doc's "The Man I Used to Be" [*Pipe Dream*, 1955]) to show what makes him tick and reveal his thoughts about his life, relationships, and choices.

Further, most of the remaining songs were parceled out singly to other characters who come across as walk-ons. Joe's best friend Charlie (John Conte) has one solo ("It May Be a Good Idea for Joe"); his college would-be girl friend Beulah (Gloria Wills) has another ("So Far"); his grandmother (Muriel O'Malley) another one ("I Know It Can Happen Again"); his mother (Annamary Dickey) had her solo ("Come Home"); and Joe's nurse Emily (Lisa Kirk) has her specialty ("The Gentleman Is a Dope"). Further, just twelve of the thirty-one numbers were solos; the remaining nineteen were performed by anonymous singing and dancing choruses (which were sometimes dominated by a minor character), and for the most part these sequences seemed impersonal and generic.

The script and score never coalesced into what should have been a touching story about a man who makes consistently wrong choices but ultimately finds his heart and makes the necessary decisions to enable him to enjoy a satisfying and fulfilling life. Even the title song was misguided. It's one of the best in the Rodgers and Hammerstein canon, an upbeat, driving, and jingly melody that in fact turns on itself. The song, a criticism of a fast-paced lifestyle, is joyfully fast-paced with irresistible melody. Here was the evening's take-home tune, the most enjoyable one in the score, and the song's mission is to tell you that its liveliness is all wrong.

Besides the title number, the score offered the shimmering ballad "You Are Never Away," the touching "A Fellow Needs a Girl," the torch song "The Gentleman Is a Dope," and the upbeat and expectant yet yearning "So Far." Otherwise, the evening was awash in generic and flavorless choral numbers (such as "Joseph Taylor Jr.," "One Foot, Other Foot," "To Have and to Hold," and "Wish Them Well"), and the would-be comedy songs ("Money Isn't Everything" and "Yatata, Yatata, Yatata") lacked genuine humor and lyrically were painfully obvious.

Prior to the Broadway opening, the public's enthusiasm for the first new Rodgers and Hammerstein musical following *Oklahoma!* and *Carousel* and the hit 1945 film *State Fair* was intense. The advance sale broke records, and the early performances were sell-outs. Despite a few good reviews, there was a general lack of critical enthusiasm for the show, and while the score yielded some popular numbers, they didn't equal the appeal of "People Will Say We're in Love," "Oh, What a Beautiful Mornin'," "If I Loved You," and "It Might as Well Be Spring."

There was also much talk about the musical's innovative staging techniques, which were indeed unusual for the era. Instead of lavish scenery, Hammerstein's script, Agnes De Mille's staging, and Jo Mielziner's décor emphasized scrims, drapes, lantern slides, occasional touches of suggestive scenery, moving platforms, and intricate lighting techniques. Further, an intrusive and pretentious Greek chorus accompanied much of the action and, annoyingly, got in the way of the narrative. The over-use of the chorus was all too obvious and all too arty; it contributed nothing to the story and was an example of overreach on the part of the creators.

And if the alienating chorus wasn't enough, at times the voice of an offstage Joe was heard commenting on the action in the manner of a choral voice-over.

Hammerstein's lyrics and libretto also overreacted to Joe; they shouted that he was special, but there was no supporting evidence. Joe remained a blank all evening. In fact, the opening sequence seemed close to ridiculous: Joe's birth is treated by the townsfolk as if it were the Second Coming, and the omnipresent choral group chimes in as well. The town aldermen, the mayor, and even the town drunks treat the event like a royal birth, although admittedly the script suggests the folderol about Joe's birth is part of his father's imagination (but did the father imagine the chorus, too?). Moreover, the wedding sequence was overblown and seemed to take up more stage time than was warranted. And Hammerstein's way with "homey" dialogue became somewhat tiresome and even condescending to his "simple" characters: Joe's father was particularly trying with his references to Baby Joe as "Old Skeezicks," and when Dad leaves for his office he says he has to go and "kill a few patients." If dear old Dad always talks this way, no wonder Joe heads off to the big city.

But for all its many faults and its few charms, *Allegro* is important because it was the first major concept musical in Broadway history. Here was an attempt to create a mood and an atmosphere to tell a somewhat abstract story, and while *Allegro* and the following season's **Love Life** (and the earlier opera *Paul Bunyan* [1941]) didn't quite make their marks with the era's audiences and critics, they set into motion and created the format for the concept musicals that began to flower in the late 1960s with Galt MacDermot's *Hair* (1967), Al Carmines' *Promenade* (1969), Tom Jones and Harvey Schmidt's *Celebration* (1969), Leonard Bernstein's *Mass* (1971), Al Carmines' *A Look at the Fifties* (1971), John Kander and Fred Ebb's *Chicago* (1975), Marvin Hamlisch's *A Chorus Line* (1975), Leonard Bernstein's *1600 Pennsylvania Avenue* (1976), Alfred Uhry and Robert Waldman's *Swing* (1980), Maury Yeston's *Nine* (1982), Philip Glass's *The Voyage* (1992), and, of course, Stephen Sondheim's *Company* (1970), *Follies* (1971), *Pacific Overtures* (1976), *Sunday in the Park with George* (1984), *Into the Woods* (1987), and *Assassins* (1991).

For the concept musical, the story and characters are less important than the mood, atmosphere, and viewpoint of the production. A linear storyline with well-defined characters and a clear beginning, middle, and end is less important than an overall pattern in which book, lyrics, music, direction, choreography, visual design, and performance style tell an essentially abstract story that avoids a traditional narrative and a clear-cut conclusion.

In concept musicals we meet restless and discontented singles and married couples seeking *Company* in Manhattan; we regret the *Follies* of lost youth, ideals, and innocence; we witness a priest's loss of faith while celebrating *Mass*; and we discover that long *Hair* is a means of protesting the status quo. At the end of **Oklahoma!**, Jud Fry dies, Curly and Laurey marry, and Oklahoma becomes a brand-new state. But what happens to birthday-boy Bobby in *Company* when his friends throw a surprise party for him at the end of the show? Or is that party really the same party that began at the onset of the first act? Was everything in between an introspective review of his relationships? And at the end of *Follies*, will Ben and Phyllis reconcile and accept their essentially loveless marriage for what it is? And will Sally and Buddy adapt to the reality of their empty lives and unhappy marriage?

And what about Claude in *Hair*? At the end of the musical, the young anti-war protestor is drafted into the Army. Plays and films that depict a military misfit traditionally use this situation as the starting point of the plot. But *Hair* presents a full evening of Claude, his cronies, and their rebelliousness in the free-wheeling anything-goes world of the East Village in the mid-1960s, and then suddenly catapults him into the conservative military world of tradition, rules, and obedience, a culture in which *you cut your hair*. How in the world will Claude adapt to his new environment? The inherent conflict in his situation takes place after the final curtain because the concept musical presents situations and asks questions for which there are perhaps no neat resolutions and answers.

And so while *Allegro* is in many ways a concept musical, its style is also embedded in the traditional Broadway musical style of the 1940s. It could have gotten by with its unusual staging techniques and its innovative use of décor; but the era demanded a fully rounded character in the leading role of a serious musical, and there was the expectation that songs were the major way to explain that character. And so for all its daring techniques, the failure of *Allegro* was the wraith-like depiction of the leading character and the unwillingness to give him enough music to explain himself.

The critical reaction to *Allegro* was decidedly split. Robert Coleman in the *New York Daily Mirror* seemed to go overboard with his assessment that the musical was a "great" one that lent "new stature to the American musical stage." It was a "stunning" evening of "beauty, integrity, intelligence, imagination, taste and skill." If all these weren't enough, the musical "races the pulses and puts lumps in the throat." Richard Watts in the *New York Post* said the work pushed "back the frontier of the American music drama." Ward Morehouse in the *New York Sun* stated the musical was one of "beauty and dignity," and he found the "distinguished" production one of "taste, imagination and showmanship." And Howard Barnes in the *New York Herald Tribune* said the "memorable" work was one of "rare distinction" and a "boldly exciting and original show."

But John Chapman in the *New York Daily News* noted Rodgers and Hammerstein had "gone philosophical" and even "sententious" with the "pretty solemn" goings-on, and he wondered why the musical seemed to sell a "sobersided" look at life when at the same time it offered "grand dances, pretty girls and good jokes." William Hawkins in the *New York World-Telegram* found the musical a "vast disappointment" and its "Doctor Kildare narrative" was "painfully obvious." And Louis Kronenberger in *PM* said the work was a "grave disappointment" and an "out-and-out failure" that was not so bad as boring, and its "earnestness bordering on solemnity" was "about as morally impressive as most high deeds of operetta."

Brooks Atkinson in the *New York Times* found the first half of *Allegro* one of "great beauty and purity," as if *Our Town* (1938) had been transformed into a musical. The work had "the lyric rapture of a musical masterpiece," and if the second half was "commonplace," it was only because the early scenes were so "overwhelming." As a result, *Allegro* "just missed the final splendor of a perfect work of art."

During the tryout, "Sitting on the Porch by the Moonlight," "Two Short Years," and the pantoum version of "What a Lovely Day for a Wedding" (all three for the singing chorus) were cut, and "So Far" and "Come Home" were respectively titled "We Have Nothing to Remember" and "Come Home, Son, Come Home."

The original cast album was recorded by RCA Victor on a 78 RPM set, and the first LP release didn't occur until 1965 (# LOC-1099/LSO-1099e, and later reissued on # CMB1-2758; the CD was issued on # 07863-52758-2); the recording included twelve songs, for a total of about thirty-four minutes of music. In 2009, Masterworks Broadway (# 88697-41738-2) issued a complete recording of the score on a two-CD set of over eighty minutes of music; the studio cast included Patrick Wilson (Joseph Taylor Jr.), Norbert Leo Butz (Charlie), Laura Benanti (Jennie), Judy Kuhn (Beulah), Nathan Gunn (Dr. Joseph Taylor), and Marni Nixon (Grandma Taylor). "So Far" was interpolated into the 1996 stage version of *State Fair* and is included on the cast album (DRG Records CD # 94765).

The script was published in hardback by Alfred A. Knopf in 1948, and was included in Random House's 1959 hardback collection *Six Plays by Rodgers and Hammerstein*. The lyrics for the used and cut songs are included in *The Complete Lyrics by Oscar Hammerstein II*.

Allegro was revived by the Equity Library Theatre for the period January 12–29, 1978; at St. Bart's Playhouse May 3–19, 1984; and by Encores! at City Center on March 2, 1994, for five performances (Stephen Bogardus was Joseph Taylor Jr.).

EDITH PIAF AND HER CONTINENTAL ENTERTAINERS

Theatre: Playhouse Theatre
Opening Date: October 30, 1947; *Closing Date*: December 6, 1947
Performances: 44
Direction: Edward Lewis; *Producer*: Clifford C. Fischer; *Musical Direction*: Lou Forman
Cast: *Edith Piaf*, Les Compagnons de la Chanson, Georges Andre Martin (Conferencier), George and Tim Dormonde, Les Canova, Lyda Alma and Vanni Fleury, The Winter Sisters, Dorritt Merrill (Announcer)
The revue was presented in two acts.

Musical Numbers

Act One: Les Canova ("Poetry in Motion" from Italy); Lyda Alma and Vanni Fleury ("Hellenic Dancers" from Greece); George and Tim Dormonde ("Scientific Nonsense" from Sweden); Georges Andre Martin ("Digital Dancing"); Les Compagnons de la Chanson ("French Voices in Satiric Ballads") (Joseph Frachon, Guy Bourguignon, Hubert Lancelot, Gerard Sabbat, Paul Buissonneu, Jean Albert, March Herrand, Fred Mella, and Jean-Louis Jaubert, Director): "Song about the Bear"; "My Lover Must Stay in Bed or He May Catch a Cold"; "The Duel" ("an opera in two acts"); "Au claire de la lune" (as performed by a jazz band, a Russian choir, and a symphony orchestra)

Act Two: Edith Piaf ("Chanteuse"): "De l'autre côté de la rue"; "La marice"; "Je n'en connais pas la fin"; "L'accordeoniste" (lyric and music by Michel Emer); "Monsieur St. Pierre" (lyric by Henri Contet, music by J. Hesse); "C'est toujours la meme histoire" (lyric by Henri Contet, music by D. White); "J'ai danse avec l'amour"; "Mon homme" (lyric by Albert Willemetz and Jacques Charles, music by Maurice Yvain); "Mon Legionnaire" (lyric by R. Asso and music by Marguerite Monnot); and "Les cloches" (lyric by De-caye and music by Vincent Scotto)

There's probably no middle ground concerning Edith Piaf (1915–1963), aka the "Little Sparrow"; either she's the finest interpreter of melancholy, heartbroken ballads or she's impossibly arch and calculated in her persona of the singing waif done wrong by life.

In his annual summary of the season, George Jean Nathan was clear about his vote. He reported that Piaf sang all her numbers in the same manner. She barely changed her "emotional pattern," "expression," and "projection"; each song began in a low key and climaxed with a "terrific abdominal, chest and laryngeal explosion" which was always accompanied by her "pointing" an index finger at the audience or by extending her arms "laterally"; and all this was "sold" with the same "woebegone look" and the same "air of heartbroken but brave defeat."

As for the others on the bill, the "alleged" Greek dancers Lyda Alma and Vanni Fleury performed "less well" than those in the chorus of any Jerome Robbins or Agnes De Mille show. He also noted that one male performer gave the impression that "homosexual conduct is amusing," and two other male performers ("with nude, thickly powdered bodies") engaged in a routine in which they took turns lifting one another other up and down, and all with "a great deal of muscle quivering."

During the run, Lyda Alma and Vanni Fleury, George and Tim Dormonde, Dorritt Merrill, and The Winter Sisters left the production and were not replaced.

Works about Piaf have amounted to a cottage industry: the Off-Off-Broadway *Dear Piaf* (1975); three Off-Broadway productions *Piaf* (1977), *Piaf Remembered . . .* (1993), and *Piaf: Love Conquers All* (2007); another *Piaf* (by Pam Gems) that first opened in London and then later on Broadway in 1981 (and won Jane Lapotaire the Tony Award for Best Leading Actress in a Play); and the 2007 film *La vie en rose* (for which Marion Cotillard won the Academy Award for Best Actress).

CARIBBEAN CARNIVAL

"The First Calypso Musical Ever Presented" / "A New Caribbean Dancing and Mirth Revue"

Theatre: International Theatre
Opening Date: December 5, 1947; *Closing Date*: December 13, 1947
Performances: 11
Lyrics and *Music*: Samuel L. Manning and Adolph Thenstead
Direction: Samuel L. Manning; Colonel John J. Hirshman, Associate Director; *Producer*: Adolph Thenstead; *Choreography*: Choreography for "Rookombay" by Pearl Primus; additional choreography by Claude Marchant; *Scenery*: Uncredited; *Costumes*: Lou Eisele; *Lighting*: Uncredited; *Musical Direction*: Ken Macomber
Cast: Pearl Primus, Josephine Premice, Claude Marchant, The Duke of Iron (aka Cecil Anderson), Sam Manning, The Smith Kids, Pamela Ward, Pat Hanson, The Trio Cubana, Peggy Watson; Calypso Dancers: Gem Bolling, Dorothy Graham, Eloise Hill, Curtis James, Andre (Andrew) King, Paul Meeres, Lillie Peace, Charles Queenan, Bernard Taylor, Mildred Thomas, Alex Young; Claude Marchant Dance Group: Billie Allen, Jacqueline Hairston, Marjorie James, Donald Curtis, James Brown; Ensemble: Clifton Gray, Clara Hubbard, Dorothy McDavid, Louis Sterling, Wahne Ha San, Helen Tinsley, Fannie Tucker (possibly Turner); Other Dancer: Padjet Fredericks; Other Singers: Helen Carr, Fred Thomas
The revue was presented in two acts.

Musical Numbers

Act One: Overture: "Fantasia Calypso" (Orchestra); "Carnival in Trinidad" (Sergeant Squashie: Sam Manning; Press Photographer: Pat Hanson; A Native: Eddie Talifferro); "America, The Great" (Duke of Iron), "Marabella" (Peggy Watson), and "Pretty" (Josephine Premice, Eddie Talifferro) (all three numbers accompanied by Ensemble); Native Songs (The Smith Kids); The Claude Marchant Group, featuring Claude Marchant and Billie Allen (choreography by Claude Marchant): (a) "Enlloro" ("Voodoo Moon") (music by Morales-Blanco) and (b) "Canto de las palmas" ("Chant of the Palms") (music by Paquita Anderson); The Trio Cubana; Scene (Sam Manning and Pat Hanson); "Firefly Dance" (Eloise Hill, Dancers); Comedy Skit (Sam Manning, Eddie Talifferro, Josephine Premice); "Love, Love, Love" (Josephine Premice, Candido Antomattei, Ensemble); Scene (Sam Manning, Eddie Talifferro, Pat Hanson); Duke of Iron; "Market Scene": (a) "Native Song" (Ensemble); (b) "Washer Woman" (The Smith Kids); (c) "Chant" (Peggy Watson); and (d) Claude Marchant Group

Act Two: "Rookombay" ("Voodoo Night") (choreographed by Pearl Primus) (Pearl Primus) (possibly presented as the entr'acte); "Don't Stop the Carnival" (Calypso Dance) (Company); "Hold 'Em, Joe" (Calypso) (Fat Woman: Peggy Watson; Donkey: Alex Young; Singers: The Smith Kids); "Rookombay" (choreographed by Pearl Primus) (chant music by Duke of Iron) (Shango Calypso) (Serpent Totem: Curtis James; Guards: Alex Young, Curtis James, Padjet Fredericks; Singer: Fred Thomas; Shango Woman: Pearl Primus; Dancers: Gem Bolling, Dorothy Graham, Eloise Hill, Lillie Peace, Mildred Thomas, Curtis James, Andre King, Charles Queenan, Alex Young, Padjet Fredericks; Singers: Helen Carr, Clara Hubbard, Dorothy McDavid, Wahne Ha San, Fannie Turner, Clifton Gray, Louis Sterling, Fred Thomas); "Cleaning-Up Song" (Helen Carr, Fred Thomas, Company); "Tease for Two" (Gem Bolling, Curtis James); "Tamboule" (Stick Fight) (Alex Young, Curtis James); "Exultation" (Shango Woman: Pearl Primus); "At Bay" (music by Camilla DeLeon) (Guards: Alex Young, Curtis James, Padjet Fredericks; Shango Woman: Pearl Primus); "Celebration" (Women Possessed: Eloise Hill, Dorothy Graham; Man Possessed: Charles Queenan; Shango Woman: Pearl Primus; Drummers: Alphonse Cimber, Bernard Taylor, Paul Meeres); Josephine Premice; Sam Manning and Eddie Talifferro; Native Café Scene (Entire Company)

The revue's tag line stated *Caribbean Carnival* was "The First Calypso Musical Ever Presented," and surely such a tag deserved an exclamation point. The 1947 dance revue was certainly ahead of its time, because it wasn't until the mid-1950s that the American Nation underwent a calypso craze that led to the seminal 1957 film *Bop Girl Goes Calypso* (aka *Bop Girl*), in which a college professor's scientific analysis of popular music proves that rock-and-roll is on its way out and calypso music will be forever in. (The camp classic is truly a relic of its age, and Broadway fans will note that the title role was played by *Pipe Dream*'s Judy Tyler.)

As for *Caribbean Carnival*, which was *not* another in the series of Katherine Dunham's seemingly endless excursions into West Indies' *danse exotique*, it apparently underwent a series of identity crises. Before it shuttered on Broadway after eleven performances, it had toured under three other titles, *S.S. Calypso*, *Calypso*, and *Bongo* (during its Philadelphia tryout engagement it was titled *Calypso*, and its tag was "A New Caribbean Dancing and Mirth Revue").

During the tryout, Samuel L. Manning and Adolph Thenstead were credited with sketches, lyrics, and music, but by New York there were no credited sketch writers; and while Thenstead was the producer of record for New York, the tryout listed him as well as Manning and the Messrs. Shubert. Moreover, the Broadway production didn't cite scenic and lighting designers, but during the tryout Herbert Brodkin was credited. Deleted during the tryout was a two-part sequence titled "The Bridal Shop," which included the song "Money Power"; other cut numbers were the songs "African Chant," "Love, Plaything of Fate," "Zinge," "Nite Scene," "Mother and I," "Ice Cream Brick," "Love Me Little, Love Me Long," and "Caribbean Conga" as well as the sketch "Pele and Her Jackass." For Broadway, the "Market Scene" included a sequence with a washer woman that probably included the song "Delia Gone," which had been heard during the tryout. Finally, the tryout's opening number "Mardi Gras in Trinidad" became "Carnival in Trinidad" for New York.

Brooks Atkinson in the *New York Times* praised the performers and noted Pearl Primus and Claude Marchant deserved a show of "triumphant showmanship" and shouldn't be "wasted on this feeble assembly of odds and ends." The evening never decided if it was a traditional musical or a dance recital, and thus the production was unorganized and "rudderless"; he also mentioned the calypso music was too "monotonous" for an entire show. Ward Morehouse in the *New York Sun* echoed these sentiments: the revue was "shapeless" and there was a "great sameness and monotony to it all." He mentioned that the evening was so haphazard that even the program didn't reflect what was being performed on stage.

John Chapman in the *New York Daily News* said he left the theatre with a "throbbing" head, for calypso music was "about as interesting as a stuck phonograph needle" that "goes on and on." He admired the cast, but after ten minutes their "irresistible" material soon became boring. Clearly, the evening was too one-note for its own good. William Hawkins in the *New York World-Telegram* seconded Chapman's comments. A full evening of calypso music led to "incredible monotony" which no one should be asked to sit through, and the "constant drumming" of calypso rhythms was one of the "most nerve wracking of theatrical experiences." He also noted the evening had a tiny thread of plot that attempted to hold together the songs and dances when it introduced a white journalist (Pamela Ward) who tries to gain access to secret voodoo rituals in Trinidad.

Richard Watts in the *New York Post* said the production wasn't "well-organized" and it "refused absolutely to adhere to its printed program"; Louis Kronenberger in *PM* found the material "mediocre," "monotonous," and "entirely" lacking in variety and showmanship. It was "tough to sit through," and its "sloppy and soggy and any-which-way presentation" even had its program "constantly jumping the track."

Robert Coleman in the *New York Daily Mirror* worried that Josephine Premice's normally "saucy" and "dead-pan" style was veering in the direction of Gertrude Lawrence's "cutie-pie method." For all that, Premice never made a "superfluous motion," gave meaning to every movement, and was a true "artist." Robert Garland in the *New York Journal-American* felt the evening held promise with its dancing and music ("lively, if repetitious") but collapsed when Pamela Ward came on stage in an "oh-so-Nordically" way in her quest to report on voodoo rituals. He made the curious comment that if the musical's creators had kept "the poor white trash" out of the production the evening might have succeeded; but once the journalist was introduced the evening lost its bearings with embarrassing attempts at humor (one example of a would-be comic moment occurred when Napoleon's last name is pronounced "Bones-Apart").

ANGEL IN THE WINGS
"A NEW INTIMATE MUSICAL REVUE"

Theatre: Coronet Theatre
Opening Date: December 11, 1947; *Closing Date*: September 4, 1948
Performances: 308
Sketches: Hank Ladd, Ted Luce, and Grace and Paul Hartman
Lyrics and *Music*: Bob Hilliard and Carl Sigman
Direction: John Kennedy; *Producers*: Marjorie and Sherman Ewing; *Choreography*: Edward Noll; *Scenery* and *Lighting*: Donald Oenslager; *Costumes*: Julia Sze; *Musical Direction*: Phil Ingalls
Cast: *Grace* and *Paul Hartman*, Hank Ladd, Nadine Gae, Peter Hamilton, Robert Stanton, Viola Roche, Johnny Barnes, Elaine Stritch, Eileen Barton, Patricia Jones, Bill McGraw, Janet Gaylord, Alan Green
The revue was presented in two acts.

Sketches and Musical Numbers

Act One: The Hartmans; Hank Ladd; "Long Green Blues" (Hank Ladd; Dancers: Nadine Gae and Peter Hamilton); "Up Early with the Upjohns" (Nettie: Grace Hartman; Horace: Paul Hartman; Wilford: Robert Stanton; Charlie: Johnny Barnes; Lula Belle: Elaine Stritch); "Holler Blue Murder" (Eileen Barton); "Reminiscences" (Hank Ladd); "Professor De Marco and Company" (Grace and Paul Hartman); "Breezy" (Patricia Jones, Bill McGraw; danced by Nadine Gae and Peter Hamilton); "Swingeasy" (The Killer: Hank Ladd; Lefty: Robert Stanton; The Kid: Johnny Barnes; The Stranger: Paul Hartman; Three Gone Cats: Viola Roche, Janet Gaylord, Alan Green); "Civilization" (aka "Bongo, Bongo, Bongo") (Elaine Stritch); "Apoliagia" (Hank Ladd); "The Glamorous Ingabord" (Headwaiter: Bill McGraw; Mrs. Tidworth: Viola Roche; Mr. Tidworth III: Robert Stanton; Mrs. Blodgett: Grace Hartman; Mr. Blodgett: Paul Hartman; Waiter: Johnny Barnes; Ingabord: Elaine Stritch)

Act Two: "Tambourine" (Eileen Barton; danced by Johnny Barnes, assisted by Hank Ladd); "Trailer Trouble" (George: Paul Hartman; Charlie: Johnny Barnes; Ruth: Grace Hartman; Milly: Elaine Stritch; Lieutenant Jackson: Robert Stanton; Joe: Bill McGraw); "If It Were Easy to Do" (Eileen Barton; danced by Nadine Gae and Peter Hamilton); "The Serious Note" (Hank Ladd); "The Thousand Islands Song" (Hank Ladd; Florence: Nadine Gae); "The Salina Select Garden Club" (Mrs. Schultz: Viola Roche; Mrs. Hutchinson: Grace Hartman; Dr. Hutchinson, W.T.: Paul Hartman); "The Big Brass Band from Brazil" (Entire Company)

Grace and Paul Hartman had been supporting-role favorites in such Broadway musicals and revues as *Red Hot and Blue!*, **Keep 'Em Laughing**, and **Top-Notchers**, but with the revue *Angel in the Wings* they came into their own. One of their comic specialties was to spoof all kinds of dances; and for their comic personas he was always constantly puzzled, flustered, bemused, dazed, and confused over what the world threw at him, and she in humorous but dead-pan style seemed to apologize to the audience for taking up its time while she was up there on the stage, but her job was to get on with it and entertain everybody, damn it. The critics always adored them, but wondered if the two weren't perhaps best in supporting roles and suggested they probably weren't able to carry an entire show. But *Angel in the Wings* settled this question for all time. The Hartmans were brilliant comedians of the first order, and they not only carried their show, they were even able to take occasionally weak material and send it flying into the comic stratosphere. They received valentines from all the critics, and won Tony Awards for Best Actor and Actress in a Musical. The revue played over 300 performances, and closed in the profit column.

The intimate revue included Hank Ladd as the evening's host; he in essence played the title role because he took on the character of the revue's producer; he chatted with the audience (and noted the typical heroine of a Tennessee Williams play is one who complains because she has two ears) and sometimes joined in a song or a sketch. While the critics felt most of the score was a let-down (but Elaine Stritch's "Civilization" was already on the Hit Parade, and "The Thousand Islands Song" had its adherents), they enjoyed the sketches. The Hartmans scored in "Up Early with the Upjohns," in which they portrayed a husband-and-wife radio-breakfast-show team; two explorers who enact a perhaps too-too exotic native dance for the ladies of a very proper garden club; and played victims of the postwar housing shortage who decide to enroll in college and take advantage of not only the G.I. bill but of off-campus trailer housing for married couples (the matter of off-campus trailers for G.I.s also figured into the plot of **Hold It!**, which opened later in the season).

Another successful sketch was "The Glamorous Ingabord," in which Elaine Stritch kidded Hildegarde (although Richard Watts in the *New York Post* noted it was impossible to do a malicious impersonation of the chanteuse because no impersonation could be as "incredible" as the original). Robert Garland in the *New York Journal-American* noted the "one-and-that's-enough" Hildegarde received a "ribald ribbing" from Stritch, and John Chapman in the *New York Daily News* said Stritch's portrayal was "excellent satire."

Brooks Atkinson in the *New York Times* found the Hartmans "hilarious" as well as "disarming and captivating"; their "special brand of crack-brained merriment" was put to good use in the "devastatingly humorous" garden-party lecture sketch, and throughout the evening the "wonderful" pair offered their nonsense with "grace and drollery" in what amounted to a "capital" revue. Watts said the Hartmans were now "important candidates for the select company of the top-rank clowns"; they were "superior" comedians who were "wonderfully hilarious." Robert Coleman in the *New York Daily Mirror* found the team "gorgeously wacky," and when they struck a comic blow it was "beautifully aimed" and flew "unerringly to its mark."

Louis Kronenberger in *PM* found the material a bit "skimpy" and even on the "sad side," but the Hartmans and Hank Ladd made the evening work with their special talents; William Hawkins in the *New York World-Telegram* said the revue was the "most amiable way" to "spend an evening laughing yourself silly" and the Hartmans were so funny they could "ruin stomach muscles and mascara." Ward Morehouse in the *New York Sun* noted that the sometimes "skimpy" revue was lacking as "full-measure entertainment," but the "goofy and vastly entertaining" Hartmans were "funny" and "demented and exhilarating." Howard Barnes in the *New York Herald Tribune* also used the S-word when he noted the revue was "skimpy" and "uneven"; but the Hartmans were "at the top of their form"; they were "wonderfully funny" and collaborated "brilliantly" in their sketches. Chapman said the intimate revue was a "cozy affair" that was "very funny." The sketches were enjoyable, and the garden-club lecture in particular was "deliciously" amusing, but he wished the score had been stronger. However, the Hartmans were "real humorists" and when they appeared in a show it was "bound to be funny." He noted that one sequence ("Swingeasy") had a "good enough idea" but "didn't work out" (the number was soon dropped from the production and was replaced by an untitled monologue for Hank Ladd).

During the tryout, Connie Baxter was succeeded by Eileen Barton; the songs "Wanderlust" and "Funny Papers" were cut as well as the Hartmans' sequence "By Request"; and "The Salina Select Garden Club" was titled "The Kansas Salina Select Garden Club." As *Heaven Help the Angels*, the revue had been first presented at Bucks County Playhouse, New Hope, Pennsylvania, beginning on June 23, 1947.

For *Make Mine Manhattan and Great Revues Revisited* (Painted Smiles CD # PSCD-119), Elaine Stritch re-created her show-stopping "Civilization."

Awards

Tony Awards: Best Leading Actor in a Musical (**Paul Hartman**); Best Leading Actress in a Musical (**Grace Hartman**)

THE CRADLE WILL ROCK
"A PLAY IN MUSIC"

Theatre: Mansfield Theatre (during run, the musical transferred to the Broadway Theatre)
Opening Date: December 26, 1947; *Closing Date*: January 11, 1948
Performances: 21
Book, *Lyrics*, and *Music*: Marc Blitzstein
Direction: Howard da Silva; *Producer*: Michael Myerberg (during Broadway run, the rights to the revival transferred to David Lowe); *Scenery*: The production didn't utilize scenery; *Costumes* and *Lighting*: Uncredited; *Musical Direction*: Leonard Bernstein on opening night, and Howard Shanet thereafter
Cast: Estelle Loring (Moll), Edward S. Bryce (Gent, Bugs), Jesse White (Dick), Taggard Casey (Cop), Harold Patrick (Reverend Salvation), Brooks Dunbar (Editor Daily), Jack Albertson (Yasha), Chandler Cowles (Dauber), Howard Blaine (President Prexy), Leslie Litomy (Professor Trixie), Edmund Hewitt (Professor Mamie), Ray Fry (Professor Scoot), Robert Pierson (Doctor Specialist), David Thomas (Harry Druggist), Will Geer (Mr. Mister), Vivian Vance (Mrs. Mister), Dennis King Jr. (Junior Mister), Jo Hurt (Sister Mister), Stephen West Downer (Steve), Marie Leidal (Sadie Polock), Walter Scheff (Gus Polock), Alfred Drake (Larry Foreman), Muriel Smith (Ella Hammer), Hazel Shermet (Attendant's Voice), Rex Coston (First Reporter), Gil Houston (Second Reporter), Howard Shanet (Clerk; the role was played by Leonard Bernstein on opening night); Chorus: Lucretia Anderson, Robert Burr, John Fleming, Michael Pollock, Germaine Poulin, Napoleon Reed, Gwen Ward
Note: At the beginning of the revival's run, the musical was in one act and song titles weren't listed in the program; during the run, the revival was presented in two acts and song titles were listed.
The action takes place in Steeltown, U.S.A., on the night of a union drive.

Musical Numbers

Act One: "I'm Checkin' Home Now" (Estelle Loring); "So That's the Way" (Estelle Loring); "Hurry Up and Telephone" (Liberty Committee); "Hard Times" (Vivian Vance); "Chorale"/"Chorale Variation" (Harold Patrick); "War! War!" (Vivian Vance, Harold Patrick, Ensemble); "Croon-Spoon" (Dennis King Jr., Jo Hurt); "Freedom of the Press" (Will Geer, Brooks Dunbar); "Let's Do Something" (Dennis King Jr., Jo Hurt); "Honolulu" (Dennis King Jr., Jo Hurt, Will Geer, Brooks Dunbar); "Summer Weather" (David Thomas, Stephen West Downer, Edward S. Bryce); "Gus and Sadie Love Song" (Walter Scheff, Marie Leidal); "The Rich" (Jack Albertson, Chandler Cowles); "Ah, There You Are" (Vivian Vance); "Art for Art's Sake" (Jack Albertson, Chandler Cowles, Vivian Vance)
Act Two: "Nickel under the Foot" (Estelle Loring); "Leaflets" (Alfred Drake); "The Cradle Will Rock" (Alfred Drake); "Lovely Morning" (Howard Blaine, Will Geer); "Triple Flank Maneuver" (Edmund Hewitt); "Do I Have to Say?" (Ray Fry); "Listen, Fellas!" (Leslie Litomy); "Joe Worker" (Muriel Smith); "Stuck Like a

Sandwich" (Alfred Drake, Liberty Committee); "Ex-Foreman" (Alfred Drake, Will Geer); "Polyphonic" (Alfred Drake, Will Geer, Estelle Loring, David Thomas, Liberty Committee); Finale (Ensemble)

The original production of Marc Blitzstein's *The Cradle Will Rock* was produced under the aegis of the Works Progress Administration/Federal Theatre Project, and was scheduled to open at Maxine Elliott's Theatre on June 16, 1937. But on June 10 the WPA announced that funding cuts precluded the opening of any new FTP productions before July 1, including *The Cradle Will Rock*. The cuts are clearly documented, but the "street" interpreted the cancellation as evidence that the government was repressing Blitzstein's left-leaning so-called "labor opera."

As befits the capitalist system, nothing precluded the musical's creators from raising private money to finance the production, but over the decades the contretemps has served to bolster opinions from a number of sides, including those who view the matter as government censorship and repression, those who choose to deify the musical as a martyred masterpiece, and those who feel the issue is a prime example why the government shouldn't spend taxpayers' money on arts projects that may offend other taxpayers.

On the night of June 16, ticket-holders for the world premiere performance of *The Cradle Will Rock* found the Maxine Elliott closed. But the creators were determined their show would go on and soon found an empty theatre (the Venice), and so the cast and audience members marched uptown for a decidedly one-of-a-kind opening-night performance. As detailed in Eric A. Gordon's masterful biography of Blitzstein (*Mark the Music: The Life and Work of Marc Blitzstein*), the performers couldn't appear on the stage of the Venice because they were still technically under the employ of the FTP, but nothing prevented them from performing in the auditorium itself. The last-minute acquisition of a piano allowed Blitzstein to play the score while the actors, scattered across the theatre, performed their roles as if they were on stage. The original cast members included Howard da Silva (Larry Foreman) and Olive Stanton (Moll).

The musical was given for a total of 14 performances at the Venice (some sources cite 19), and on June 27 a sequence from the production was broadcast on national radio. On December 5, the work was presented over four consecutive Sunday nights at the Mercury Theatre and then on January 3, 1938, the musical "officially" premiered on Broadway, playing first at the Windsor Theatre and then returning to the Mercury for the final weeks of the run for a total of 108 performances. All these performances were privately produced (that is, in the traditional manner by private investors and not by the federal government). Early programs give the following production credits at the Windsor: "Sam H. Grisman presents The Mercury Theatre Production"; and later ones were slightly altered to "The Mercury Theatre in Association with Sam H. Grisman."

The script was published by Random House in 1938, and was one of the first musicals to be issued commercially in hardback; it's noteworthy that the first published hardback musical scripts were all in one way or another political in nature: *Of Thee I Sing* (1931), *Let 'Em Eat Cake* (1933), *Johnny Johnson* (1936), *I'd Rather Be Right* (1937), *The Cradle Will Rock* (1937), and *Knickerbocker Holiday* (1938).

The original cast album was recorded in April 1938 by Musicraft Records on seven twelve-inch 78 RPM records (# 18, with the individual records numbered 1075–1081). The release marks the first time an American musical received a full-length Broadway cast recording. (A few Broadway musicals had previously been recorded in London with their original West End casts, and of course occasionally a cover version of a song from a Broadway musical was recorded by one of its cast members, such as Helen Morgan's "Bill" from *Show Boat* [1927]). The *Cradle* recording was later released in a limited-edition LP of one thousand copies by American Legacy Records (# T-1001).

The current 1947 revival was inspired by a "complete concert performance" that had taken place at City Center a month earlier. On November 24 and 25, 1947, Leonard Bernstein conducted the New York City Symphony for two performances; Howard da Silva and Will Geer reprised their original respective roles of Larry Foreman and Mr. Mister, and Estelle Loring was Moll; other cast members were Shirley Booth (Mrs. Mister), Robert Chisholm (Reverend Salvation), Jack Albertson, Muriel Smith, and Jo Hurt. When the concert transferred to the Mansfield (now Brooks Atkinson) Theatre a month later, Booth and Chisholm were succeeded by Vivian Vance and Harold Patrick, and da Silva was succeeded by Alfred Drake. After playing a few performances at the intimate Mansfield, the production transferred to the large Broadway Theatre, and there it expired after a total of twenty-one performances.

But it wasn't the cavernous theatre that did in the revival; instead, many of the critics refused to indulge the musical's outdated polemics and its chip-on-the-shoulder attitude of all things establishment. Further, the production was still presented in a somewhat stiff concert format, and instead of naturalistic staging the orchestra was placed on the stage, the cast members sat in three rows of chairs and stepped forward on cue to speak their lines and sing their numbers, and there was no scenery. In an era of fully designed musicals that utilized modern staging techniques, perhaps audiences were unwilling to pay full Broadway prices in order to sit in a lecture-hall environment and be hectored about the evils of capitalism. (One or two critics also noted that considering the musical's for-the-people message, it seemed incongruous that for the opening night Leonard Bernstein conducted the work in full-evening dress, and there was a snide comment or two about his "boiled" shirt.)

Louis Kronenberger in *PM* said the musical was still "serviceable" but had never seemed all that "distinguished"; as a result, only the song parodies still worked. Robert Coleman in the *New York Daily Mirror* considered the musical "dated" in its view that all businessmen were "villains" who lacked even a "single virtue" and that its heroes couldn't "have a single fault." He noted that Blitzstein "throws rocks" at the medical and newspaper professions, at college professors, and at businessmen and artists; in fact, anyone with "folding money" is no good. Ward Morehouse in the *New York Sun* felt the work had "lost a good deal of its timeliness" and was "less impressive" than it had been a decade earlier. He too noted that the author attacked "the press, the pulpit, the police, and men of medicine." Robert Garland in the *New York Journal-American* said there was only one way to enjoy and understand the musical: everyone with a bank balance is "stupid and shortsighted, venal and vindictive" while everyone without an account is "bright and farsighted, honest and forgiving."

Although Robert Sylvester in the *New York Daily News* noted the musical was "lusty and vigorous," he stated he didn't like it in 1937 and still didn't; moreover, the work was now "outdated" and came across as a parody of itself; and Richard Watt in the *New York Post* said the work was "frankly and proudly propaganda," but admitted the passage of years had "deprived it of some of its topical bite."

Howard Barnes in the *New York Herald Tribune* found the revival "savagely arresting" and said the "proletarian cartoon" had a strong score; but he noted some of the "soap box perorations" were now "dated"; William Hawkins in the *New York World-Telegram* said the musical was "fresh and vigorous theatre with a punch"; and Brooks Atkinson in the *New York Times* called the work "the most vivid proletarian drama ever written in this country" which was "no less militant and exciting" than it had been a decade earlier. But he also said the storyline now came across as an "old-fashioned model," the emphasis was "dated," and the "echoes" from a decade before were now "hackneyed."

The musical was next revived at City Center on February 11, 1960, by the New York City Opera Company for a limited engagement of four performances; the cast included David Atkinson (Larry Foreman), Tammy Grimes (Moll), Ruth Kobart (Mrs. Mister), Nancy Dussault (Sister Mister), and Frank Porretta (Steve); like the 1947 production, the revival was directed by Howard da Silva.

On April 19, 1964, the work was revived in an abridged version as part of the Marc Blitzstein Memorial Concert (Blitzstein had been murdered three months earlier); the cast included Howard da Silva (Larry Foreman) and Barbara Harris (Moll), with Leonard Bernstein at the piano.

On November 8, 1964, the musical was revived Off-Broadway at Theatre Four for eighty-two performances; the work was again directed by da Silva, and the cast included Jerry Orbach (Larry Foreman), Lauri Peters (Moll), Clifford David (Dauber and Professor Trixie), Nancy Andrews (Mrs. Mister), Joseph Bova (Junior Mister), Rita Gardner (Sister Mister), Micki Grant (Ella Hammer), and Gershon Kingsley (Clerk). The production was recorded on a two-LP set by MGM Records (# SE-4289-2-OC), although early programs featured a full-page ad for a forthcoming cast album by Columbia Records.

On September 12, 1978, a revival was produced Off-Off Broadway at the Eighteenth Street Playhouse for four performances. On May 9, 1983, an Off-Broadway revival opened at the American Place Theatre, and on July 12 it reopened at the Douglas Fairbanks Theatre for a total of sixty-four performances; the American Place Theatre cast included Patti LuPone (Moll) and Randle Mell (Larry Foreman), and for the reopening Lisa Banes succeeded LuPone. The American Place Theatre production was shown on public television in 1985. (An earlier televised look at the musical was seen on CBS's *Camera Three* on November 29, 1964, and included interviews with and performances by the 1964 Off-Broadway cast.)

On August 5, 1985, a London production opened at the Old Vic with LuPone and Mell, and was recorded by Polydor Records (LP # 827-937-1-Y-1), and the complete cast recording was later issued on a two-CD set by That's Entertainment Records (# CDTEM2-1105).

A later Los Angeles production from 1994 was recorded by Lockett Palmer Records (CD # LPR-940411). *Marc Blitzstein Presents 'The Cradle Will Rock' 'No for an Answer' 'Regina'* (Spoken Arts LP # 717) is a discussion by Blitzstein of the three works and is accompanied by occasional songs; for *The Cradle Will Rock* sequence, two songs are included: "Nickel under the Foot" and "Hotel Lobby" (performed by Evelyn Lear, Roddy McDowall, Jane Connell, and Alvin Epstein).

A few songs from the musical were included in *Cradle Will Rock*, a 1999 film that dealt with the opening of the 1937 production; the soundtrack was released by RCA Victor/BMG Records (CD # 09026-635772), and a coffee-table book about the film (which includes the screenplay by Tim Robbins and lyrics by Blitzstein) was published by Newmarket Press in 2000.

Jason Sherman's play *It's All True*, which opened at the Terragon Theatre in Toronto on January 6, 1999, took another look at the musical's famous 1937 premiere.

Blitzstein's *No for an Answer* is another look at labor and management issues, but this time around he was in an even more bitter mood and was less satiric about this seemingly eternal conflict. The work premiered at the Mecca Auditorium (now City Center) for a limited engagement of three performances beginning on January 5, 1941. The cast included Carol Channing, and the cast recording was issued by Keynote Records on a 78 RPM set, later released on LP by Theme Records (# 103), then by JJA Records (# JJA-19772A/B), and then later by AEI Records (LP # 1140; CD issued by AEI on # AEI-CD-031). For more information about the production, see the author's *Off-Broadway Musicals, 1910–2007*.

MAKE MINE MANHATTAN
"A NEW MUSICAL REVUE"

Theatre: Broadhurst Theatre
Opening Date: January 15, 1948; *Closing Date*: January 8, 1949
Performances: 429
Sketches and *Lyrics*: Arnold B. Horwitt
Music: Richard Lewine
Direction: Staged by Hassard Short and sketches directed by Max Liebman; *Producer*: Joseph M. Hyman; *Choreography*: Lee Sherman; *Scenery*: Frederick Fox; *Costumes*: Morton Haack; *Lighting*: Hassard Short; *Musical Direction*: Charles Sanford
Cast: Sid Caesar, David Burns, Sheila Bond, Joshua Shelley, Kyle MacDonnell, Jack Kilty, Danny Daniels, Nelle Fisher, Ray Harrison, Eleanor Bagley, Max Showalter; Dancers: Anne Feris, Annabelle Gold, Rhoda Johannson, Phyllis Mayo, Marta Nita, Dolores Novins, Willis Brunner, Tony Charmoli, Hal Loman, Tommy Morton, Skip Randall, Rudy Tone, Betty Lind, Wayne Lamb; Singers: Stephanie Augustine, Joy Carroll, Jean Jones, Barbara Weaver, Larry Carr, Ed Chappel, Biff McGuire; Others: Perry Bruskin, Joseph Melvin, Sterling Mace
The revue was presented in two acts.

Sketches and Musical Numbers

Act One: "Anything Can Happen in New York" (Max Showalter, Eleanor Bagley, Stephanie Augustine, Joy Carroll, Jean Jones, Larry Carr, Ed Chappel, Biff McGuire; danced by Nelle Fisher and Hal Loman, and Anne Feris, Louise Ferrand, Annabelle Gold, Rhoda Johannson, Betty Lind, Phyllis Mayo, Dolores Novins, Willis Brunner, Tony Charmoli, Wayne Lamb, Tommy Morton, Skip Randall, Rudy Tone); "First Avenue Gets Ready" (sketch by Arnold B. Horwitt and Max Liebman) (Kelly: David Burns; Mamie: Sheila Bond; A Delegate: Sid Caesar; His Aide: Perry Bruskin; Another Delegate: Sid Caesar; Still Another Delegate: Sid Caesar; Ukranian: Richard Arnold; Slovanian: Ed Chappel; Roumanian: Joseph Melvin); "Phil the Fiddler" (Jack Kilty; Passersby: Biff McGuire, Dolores Novins, Betty Lind, Anne Feris, Annabelle Gold; Ballroom Dancers: Stephanie Augustine, Rhoda Johannson, Phyllis Mayo, Willis Brunner, Skip Randall, Rudy Tone; The Heroine: Nelle Fisher; The Villain: Tommy Morton; The Horses: Tony Charmoli, Hal Loman; The Billionaire: Joshua Shelley; The Lackeys: Larry Carr, Biff McGuire, Max Showalter); "Movie House in Manhattan" (Eleanor Bagley); "Any Resemblance . . ." (Blodgett: Sid Caesar; Bassett: David Burns; Jukes: Joshua Shelley); "Talk to Me" (Sheila Bond, Danny Daniels); "Traftz" (Joshua Shelley); "I Don't Know His Name" (The Boy: Jack Kilty; The Girl: Kyle MacDonnell); "The Good Old Days" (Sid Caesar and David

Burns; The Girls: Sheila Bond, Eleanor Bagley); "Once Over Lightly" (In Front of the Theatre: David Burns, Eleanor Bagley, Dancers; Mother: Phyllis Mayo; Father: Perry Bruskin; Mother-in-Law: Jean Jones; Great Aunt: Rhoda Johannson; Second Cousin: Eleanor Bagley; Herman W. Willoughby Jr.: Sid Caesar; Bessie Bricker: Sheila Bond; Nurse: Nelle Fisher; Patient: Max Showalter; The Choir: Joshua Shelley, Jack Kilty, Kyle MacDonnell, Stephanie Augustine, Joy Carroll, Barbara Weaver, Bill McGuire, Ed Chappel, Larry Carr; The Dancers: Anne Feris, Annabelle Gold, Betty Lind, Dolores Novins, Tony Charmoli, Tommy Morton, Skip Randall, Rudy Tone); "Penny Gum Machine" (sketch by Allan Roberts, Sid Caesar, and Max Liebman) (Sid Caesar); "Saturday Night in Central Park" (Kyle MacDonnell, Jack Kilty, Eleanor Bagley, Max Showalter, Singers; Dance Variations: Annabelle Gold, Tony Charmoli, Rudy Tone, Hal Loman; Phyllis Mayo, Dolores Novins, Willis Brunner; Sheila Bond, Nelle Fisher, Danny Daniels, Ray Harrison)

Act Two: "Ringalevio" (Joshua Shelley; First Ringleader: Tommy Morton; Second Ringleader: Rudy Tone; Sissy: Danny Daniels; Dancers); "Noises in the Street" (lyric by Peter Barry, David Gregory aka Greggory, and Arnold B. Horwitt) (Taxi Driver: David Burns; Milkman: Max Showalter; Street Cleaner: Sid Caesar; Street Digger: Perry Bruskin; Newsboy: Joshua Shelley); "I Fell in Love with You" (Kyle MacDonnell, Jack Kilty; danced by Nelle Fisher and Ray Harrison); "My Brudder and Me" (Sheila Bond, Danny Daniels); "Hollywood Heads East" (sketch by Arnold B. Horwitt and Max Liebman) (The Mayor: Max Showalter; Eddie: Joshua Shelley; Mr. Bigelow: Sid Caesar; The Actress: Kyle MacDonnell; The Actor: Jack Kilty; Photographer: Biff McGuire; Assistant Photographer: Perry Bruskin; Make-Up Girl: Stephanie Augustine; Mr. Rappaport: David Burns); "Gentleman Friend" (Sheila Bond, Hal Loman, Dancers); "Subway Song" (Joshua Shelley; The Girl: Rhoda Johannson); "Full Fathom Five" (sketch by Arnold B. Horwitt and Sylvia Rosales) (The Salesman: Max Showalter; The Customer: David Burns; The Model: Jean Jones; The Clerks: Larry Carr, Ed Chappel, Sterling Mace, Biff McGuire); "A Night Out" (sketch by Max Liebman) (Sid Caesar); "Glad to Be Back" (Entire Company)

The late 1940s and early 1950s marked the last hurrah of the traditional Broadway revue, and *Make Mine Manhattan* was one of the most successful; the evening's point of view was from the perspective of life in Manhattan, and even if the material wasn't all that "New York" (presumably the pen shop sketch "Full Fathom Five" could have taken place in a store in Chicago or Boston), the evening nonetheless offered a basic unity of songs, sketches, and dances that occurred in New York's shops, streets, parks, and theatres.

One song demolished the craze for quaint tea-room-styled restaurants ("Traftz" [as in Schraft's]); another kidded movie theatres so luxurious that the films themselves are incidental ("Movie House in Manhattan"); there was a look at the new United Nations building (the sketch "First Avenue Gets Ready," in which Sid Caesar impersonated three different U.N. delegates at virtually the same moment); the sketch "Hollywood Heads East" was a humorous comment about the current trend of on-location shooting in New York City; and there were songs about Central Park ("Saturday Night in Central Park"), the city streets ("Noises in the Street"), a comparison of prices in the New York of 1938 and 1948 (the sketch "A Night Out"), Grand Central Station ("Glad to Be Back"), and the subway ("Subway Song," in which a boy from 242nd Street in the Bronx is dating a girl from New Lots Avenue) as well as a sketch about the snacks for sale in subway stations ("Penny Gum Machine"). The song "Gentleman Friend" took place at Union Square, "I Fell in Love with You" was set near the East River, and "I Don't Know His Name" was performed on a Manhattan rooftop.

The theatre was spoofed in three sketches. "Any Resemblance . . ." looked at the incompetence of theatre critics (an applicant who positively hates the theatre is the one who gets the position of drama critic). "Once Over Lightly" kidded the recently opened Richard Rodgers and Oscar Hammerstein II's musical **Allegro**. Instead of doctor Joseph Taylor Jr., the hero is now Herman W. Willoughby Jr., a dentist (played by Sid Caesar), who undergoes the angst of professional and personal crises, all to the accompaniment of an omnipresent choir that comments on the action and is backed by a group of dancers. And "Ringalevio" spoofed the Agnes De Mille school of choreography.

Dancers Sheila Bond and Danny Daniels had scorched the sidewalks in **Street Scene**, and they did so again with their numbers "Talk to Me" and "My Brudder and Me."

Brooks Atkinson in the *New York Times* found the revue "fresh and buoyant" and "affectionate and knowing," and praised the "good-humored" sketches, "droll" lyrics, and "beguiling hurdy-gurdy" music. He also liked the **Allegro** spoof (a stout and "gutsy parody") in which dentist Sid Caesar must make "grotesque moral choices." Robert Coleman in the *New York Daily Mirror* said the evening was "breezy, speedy and intimate"; it moved "like a whirlwind" and was "packed with laughs" (he also noted that fellow first-nighter

Beatrice Lillie "roared lustily" at the proceedings). Richard Watts in the *New York Post* said the "resounding" hit didn't include one dull moment, and he praised Hassard Short's smooth, imaginative, and beautiful staging. He also noted that the *Allegro* sketch was more devastating in its criticism of the Rodgers and Hammerstein musical than those critics who originally panned it.

Ward Morehouse in the *New York Sun* liked the "brisk, exuberant and delightful" revue; and Louis Kronenberger in *PM* said *Make Mine Manhattan* was so far the season's "brightest and liveliest" musical, and he particularly liked its fast pace (Morehouse noted the two directors had insisted that encores would not be permitted, and that the final curtain must come down before eleven o'clock); he also suggested the revue itself was the best reason to see *Allegro* because the parody would be all the more enjoyable. John Chapman in the *New York Daily News* said the revue provided "one of the best times" ever at the theatre. He praised the evening's two "first class" comedians Sid Caesar and David Burns, and said the Rodgers and Hammerstein spoof was "splendid." He also noted the revue moved with the pace of "Ben Hur winning the big chariot race"; he too noted there were no bows and encores after the numbers, and as soon as one sequence was over the next one was "whisked" on. Robert Garland in the *New York Journal-American* said the revue deserved a "grand and glorious send-off," and he enjoyed the "run around" given to *Allegro* and the "nose-thumbing" given to Agnes De Mille.

William Hawkins in the *New York World-Telegram* gave the evening a curious review. While he found the sketches "uproariously funny," he felt the show was "uneven" and lacked "originality." But he admitted the direction provided "continuity with rising momentum" and noted it was staged "with speed." Howard Barnes in the *New York Herald Tribune* felt the production was mostly "frenetic and pointless," and said the revue's "clumsiness" was best indexed by the Rodgers and Hammerstein and Agnes De Mille spoofs (the revue set them up as sitting ducks "and then missed them by a mile"). He concluded by noting the program thanked Moss Hart for his "valued suggestions," and then suggested that Hart "take a bow very quietly."

During the tryout, Gloria Wills left the show and her material was assigned to Eleanor Bagley; "Take It Back, We're Through" (for Biff McGuire and Gloria Wills) was cut; "Glad to Be Back" was titled "Grand Central Station"; and "Once Over Lightly" was titled "Matinees—Thursday and Saturday." "Noises in the Street" had a busy life in and out of various revues; for more information, see *The Shape of Things!*

The post-Broadway tour starred Bert Lahr, and the cast included Jack Albertson, Bob Fosse, his then-wife Mary Ann Niles, and Peter Gennaro. The sketches "Doctors Don't Tell" (by Matt Brooks) and "Income Tax" (by David Freedman) and the song "Manhattan in the Spring" were added, and "Song of the Woodman" (lyric by E. Y. Harburg, music by Harold Arlen), that Lahr had introduced in the 1937 revue *The Show Is On*, was interpolated into the score.

The collection *Make Mine Manhattan and Great Revues Revisited* (Painted Smiles CD # PSCD-119) includes nine numbers from the revue ("Anything Can Happen in New York," "Gentleman Friend," "Noises in the Street," "My Brudder and Me," "Subway Song," "Phil the Fiddler," "I Fell in Love with You," "Traftz," and "Saturday Night in Central Park") as well as "Manhattan in the Spring," which had been added for the national tour.

On May 4, 1948, the production was the subject of CBS's *Tonight on Broadway*, which featured interviews with the cast as well as selections from the revue. The sketch "Full Fathom Five" (as "Fountain Pen Sketch") was included in the 1949 film *Always Leave Them Laughing*.

Sid Caesar and sketch director Max Liebman teamed up a few years later for NBC's classic comedy series *Your Show of Shows*; Caesar was of course the star, and Liebman served as the producer and director.

LOOK, MA, I'M DANCIN'!
"A NEW MUSICAL COMEDY"

Theatre: Adelphi Theatre
Opening Date: January 29, 1948; *Closing Date*: July 10, 1948
Performances: 188
Book: Jerome Lawrence and Robert E. Lee
Lyrics and *Music*: Hugh Martin; dance music for "Mademoiselle Marie" Ballet and "Pajama Dance" by Trude Rittman

Direction: George Abbott and Jerome Robbins; *Producer*: George Abbott; *Choreography*: Jerome Robbins; *Scenery*: Oliver Smith; *Costumes*: John Pratt; *Lighting*: Uncredited; *Musical Direction*: Pembroke Davenport

Cast: Don Liberto (Wotan), Loren Welch (Larry), Alice Pearce (Dusty Lee), Janet Reed (Ann Bruce), Virginia Gorski (Gibson), Harold Lang (Eddie Winkler), Tommy Rall (Tommy), Robert H. Harris (F. Plancek), Katharine Sergava (Tanya Drinskaya), Alexander March (Vladimir Luboff), *Nancy Walker* (Lily Malloy), James Lane (Mr. Gleeb), Eddie Hodge (Mr. Ferbish), Raul Celada (Tanya's Partner), Dean Campbell (Bell Boy), Dan Sattler (Stage Manager), Sandra Deel (Suzy); Members of the Russo-American Ballet Company: Margaret Banks, Forrest Bonshire, Mary Broussard, Dean Campbell, Bruce Cartwright, Raul Celada, Leonard Claret, Virginia Conwell, Julie Curtis, Richard D'Arcy, Charles Dickson, Clare Duffy, June Graham, Nina Frenkin, Marybly Harwood, Priscilla Hathaway, Eric Kristen, Ina Kurland, Douglas Luther, Bettye McCormick, Gloria Magginetti, Gloria Patrice, James Pollack, Dorothy (Dottie) Pyren, Walter Rinner, Herbert Ross, Marten Sameth, Walter Stane, Gisella Svetlik, Robert Tucker

The musical was presented in two acts.

The action takes place during the present time in New York City; Joplin, Missouri; Amarillo, Texas; Phoenix, Arizona; Los Angeles, California; Glendale, California; and Des Moines, Iowa.

Musical Numbers

Act One: "Gotta Dance" (Harold Lang, Company); "I'm the First Girl" (Nancy Walker, Corps de Ballet); "I'm Not So Bright" (Loren Welch; danced by Janet Reed and Harold Lang); "I'm Tired of Texas" (Nancy Walker, Company); "Tiny Room" (Loren Welch); "The Little Boy Blues" (Virginia Gorski, Don Liberto); "Mademoiselle Marie" (ballet) (aka "Mme. Scandal Ballet") (music by Trude Rittman) (Mademoiselle Marie: Nancy Walker; Her Beloved: Herbert Ross; Attendants: Virginia Gorski, Gisella Svetlik; Messenger: Tommy Rall; Innkeeper: Eric Kristen; Servant: Walter Stane; Jacques: Charles Dickson; Igor: Richard D'Arcy; Adolph: Raul Celada; Archie: Forrest Bonshire; Serfs: Leonard Claret, Bruce Cartwright, Ina Kurland, Marybly Harwood, Virginia Conwell, Corps de Ballet)

Act Two: "Jazz" (Don Liberto, Nancy Walker, Company); "The New Look" (Alice Pearce); "If You'll Be Mine" (Nancy Walker, Dean Campbell, Priscilla Hathaway, Sandra Deel, Loren Welch, Alice Pearce, James Pollack); "Pajama Dance" (aka "The Sleep-Walking Ballet" (music by Trude Rittman) (Company); "Shauny O'Shay" (Virginia Gorski, Don Liberto); "Pas de deux" from *Swan Lake* (music by Peter Illyitch Tschiakowsky) (Janet Reed, Harold Lang); "The Two of Us" (Nancy Walker, Harold Lang, Co-workers)

Look, Ma, I'm Dancin'! provided Nancy Walker with another in her career of seemingly sure-fire starring roles, and while she always garnered praise for her performances, the musicals themselves were often disappointing and most never attained classic status. She had featured roles in her first two musicals (the hits **Best Foot Forward** and **On the Town**), but most of her shows had short runs on Broadway or closed out of town. In 1960, she played the role of Kay Cram opposite Phil Silvers in *Do Re Mi*, her final Broadway musical. It received mostly rave reviews, won five Tony nominations (including nominations for Best Musical, and, for Walker, Best Leading Actress in a Musical), and enjoyed the hit song "Make Someone Happy"; considering the show's rave reviews, the year's run was a disappointment and it didn't quite turn a profit. Walker was one of the great clowns of Broadway, but unlike Ethel Merman, Mary Martin, and Carol Channing, she unfortunately never left behind an array of classic roles in long-running hits (however, in the 1970s she had supporting roles in three television series, as Rhoda Morgenstern's long-suffering Jewish mother Ida in both *The Mary Tyler Moore Show* and *Rhoda* and as Rock Hudson's wise-cracking housekeeper Mildred in *McMillan and Wife*; and for years she appeared in a series of prominent television commercials as the spokeswoman for Bounty paper towels).

For *Look, Ma, I'm Dancin'!*, Walker portrayed brewery heiress Lily Malloy, who bankrolls the Russo-American Ballet Company in order to ensure she gets leading roles despite the fact she has absolutely no dancing talent whatsoever. The first scene of the musical was set on a train platform in Pennsylvania Station where the ballet company is waiting for their new owner's arrival before they all take off on a national tour. Walker made her grand entrance swathed in furs off her shoulder; an almost indescribable feathered hat of global proportion that was twice the size of her head; high heels with straps winding around her ankles and lower legs; and on a leash a Russian wolfhound half her size. The central gimmick of no-talent dancer Walker buying a ballet company was genuinely funny, and a secondary plot revolved around the company's leading choreographer and male dancer Eddie Winkler (Harold Lang) who hopes to introduce modern jazz ballet into the company's standard repertoire of such classics as *Swan Lake*.

The musical managed to run almost six months and even turned a small profit, thus placing it in the hit column. And while the critics adored Walker and praised Jerome Robbins's choreography, they felt Jerome Lawrence and Robert E. Lee's book never quite reached its potential and Hugh Martin's score was less than memorable.

Brooks Atkinson in the *New York Times* liked the "good knockabout" and "top-drawer" musical and said the "hilarious" Walker was "the best slap-stick comedian of her generation"; Robert Coleman in the *New York Mirror* praised Walker, who was "terrific" and a "one-woman show all by herself"; William Hawkins in the *New York World-Telegram* said she was "one of that half handful of the world's funniest people"; and Robert Sylvester in the *New York Daily News* liked the "comical brat" who was "loaded with talent" and had all the comic authority of Bobby Clark and Frank Fay. Ward Morehouse in the *New York Sun* noted that the musical had "book trouble," but praised the "fast and furious" ballet "Mademoiselle Marie" which kidded the French bedroom farce school and found Walker portraying a femme fatale in a negligee; he compared the sequence to Robbins's classic "Mack Sennett Ballet" (aka "Keystone Kops' Ballet" and "Bathing Beauty Ballet") in **High Button Shoes**, and also commended the "original and imaginative" "Pajama Dance." Sylvester found "Mademoiselle Marie" a "very funny" spoof, and noted the "Pajama Dance" was the evening's "highlight," for here "in practically no stage space at all" Robbins devised a dance that "builds to a really stirring conclusion."

Atkinson liked Martin's "cheerful" music, which was accompanied by "the most imaginative lyrics of the season" (and singled out "I'm Tired of Texas," "I'm Not So Bright," "The Little Boy Blues," and "Shauny O'Shay"). Hawkins suggested that at first hearing, the score didn't seem "sensational," but he liked "I'm Tired of Texas" and "Shauny O'Shay"; and Morehouse found the book "generally lifeless" and the songs "on the routine side" (but said "I'm Tired of Texas" was a "good and hearty" number). Louis Kronenberger in *PM* felt the idea behind the book was a "bright" one that unfortunately never reached its potential. Further, the score wasn't "good enough" and the book was "not good at all" (but the opening "Gotta Dance" got the show off to a great start with its "potpourri of dance styles," and "Pajama Dance" was "fresh," "original," and served as a "real oasis in the second-act desert").

Richard Watts in the *New York Post* had to deal with the horror of the show's title, which he complained was "difficult to write, what with its commas, apostrophes, exclamation points and all." Once he got beyond that, he reported that the musical was "steadily disappointing" and suggested it was more "wonderful" in theory than in execution. Martin's score was "fairly routine" (but like most of the critics he praised "I'm Tired of Texas" and "Shauny O'Shay"), "Mademoiselle Marie" was "very funny," and "Pajama Dance" was an "engagingly delightful sleepwalking dance."

Walter Terry in the *New York Herald Tribune* perhaps best described Walker's special genius as the talent-free ballet dancer when he reported that she did "everything wrong so perfectly." She "persecuted" a pirouette "unmercifully," she "mangled" entrechats, in the jete position her leg was like a "pile-driver," and her "balletic-line" was "beyond description." Walker was especially sparkling in her introductory number "I'm the First Girl," in which she explained that she was "the first girl in the second row of the third scene in the fourth number in fifth position at ten o'clock on the nose."

During the tryout, "Horrible, Horrible Love" and "Let's Do a Ballet" were cut; and it appears the following songs were dropped either in preproduction or during rehearsals: "The Way It Might Have Been," "Lost in This Town," "Lullaby," "The Toast," and a title song. George Schaff was credited for the lighting design, but for New York there was no official credit (but the Broadway program notes that Peggy Clark was Oliver Smith's assistant, and perhaps she and Smith created the lighting). Hugh Martin reworked "Horrible, Horrible Love" and "Let's Do a Ballet" and both emerged respectively as "Who Gives a Sou?" and "The Tour Must Go On" for *Make a Wish* (1951). Martin had originally written "I'm Tired of Texas" and "I'm the First Girl" (as "I'm the First Man") in 1944 for a Special Services revue while he was in the Army.

Because of the ASCAP musicians' strike there was no regular cast recording; but in anticipation of the impending strike, a number of songs from the musical were recorded by Decca six weeks before the Broadway opening (78 RPM set # DA-637; then issued on ten-inch LP # DL-5231, which was later issued on a pairing with the 1950 musical *Arms and the Girl* by MCA/CSP/CBS # X-14879; the CD was later released by Decca

Broadway # B0003571-02). The following list includes the names of the performers on the album, which are followed by the names of the cast members who sang the songs on Broadway: "Gotta Dance" (Harold Lang and Chorus; Harold Lang and Chorus); "I'm the First Girl" (Nancy Walker; Nancy Walker); "I'm Not So Bright" (Harold Lang; Loren Welch); "I'm Tired of Texas" (Nancy Walker and Chorus; Nancy Walker and Chorus); "Tiny Room" (Bill Shirley; Loren Welch); "The Little Boy Blues" (Hugh Martin and Sandra Deel; Don Liberto and Virginia Gorski); "If You'll Be Mine" (Nancy Walker and Bill Shirley; Nancy Walker, Dean Campbell, and various members of the company); and "Shauny O'Shay" (Sandra Deel and Chorus; Virginia Gorski and Don Liberto). The CD release also includes two cut songs, "Let's Do a Ballet" (Loren Welch, Sandra Deel, Nancy Walker, Bill Shirley, Harold Lang, and Chorus) and "Horrible, Horrible Love" (Sandra Deel, Nancy Walker, and Chorus), and alternate versions of "Gotta Dance" (Harold Lang and Chorus) and "Shauny O'Shay" (Sandra Deel and Chorus). As the "Mme. Scandal Ballet," the "Mademoiselle Marie" ballet was recorded for the collection *Ballet on Broadway* (Painted Smiles CD # PSCD-149).

The musical was featured on the May 25, 1948, episode of the CBS series *Tonight on Broadway*, which included interviews with cast members and songs from the show.

On March 7, 2000, Musicals Tonight! produced a limited-run engagement of the musical for sixteen performances at the 14th Street Y; the revival was recorded by Original Cast Records (unnumbered CD) and includes "Jazz," "The Two of Us," and "The New Look" (the CD's liner notes indicate the latter was "extensively re-written" by Martin for the revival). The album also includes an interpolated number by Martin, "All My Life."

TONIGHT AT 8:30

Theatre: National Theatre
Opening and *Closing Dates*: Under the umbrella title of *Tonight at 8:30*, the first group of three one-act plays (*Ways and Means*, *Family Album*, and *Red Peppers*) opened on February 20, 1948; the second group (*Hands Across the Sea*, *Fumed Oak*, and *Shadow Play*) opened on February 23; and then all six were performed in repertory until they closed on March 13, 1948.
Performances: 26
Plays, *Lyrics*, and *Music*: Noel Coward
Direction: Noel Coward; *Producers*: Homer Curran, Russell Lewis, and Howard Young; *Choreography*: Richard Barstow; *Scenery* and *Costumes*: George Jenkins; Gertrude Lawrence's gowns by Hattie Carnegie; *Lighting*: Uncredited (possibly by George Jenkins); *Musical Direction*: Frank Tours

Group One:

Ways and Means

"A Light Comedy in Three Scenes"

The action takes place on the Côte d'Azure at the present time.
Cast: *Gertrude Lawrence* (Stella Cartwright), Graham Payn (Toby Cartwright), Booth Colman (Gaston), William Roerick (Lord Chapworth aka Chaps), Sarah Burton (Olive Lloyd-Ransome), Valerie Cossart (Princess Elena Krassiloff), Philip Tonge (Murdoch), Norah Howard (Nanny), Rhoderick Walker (Stevens)

Family Album

"A Victorian Comedy with Music"

The action takes place in Kent during 1860.
Cast: Graham Payn (Jasper Featherways), *Gertrude Lawrence* (Jane), Sarah Burton (Lavinia), Norah Howard (Harriet), Valerie Cossart (Emily), William Roerick (Richard), Rhoderick Walker (Charles Winter), Booth Colman (Edward Valance), Philip Tonge (Burrows)

Musical Numbers
"Drinking Song" (aka "Here's a Toast"); "Music Box"; "Princes and Princesses"; and "Hearts and Flowers" (all songs performed by the entire cast)

Red Peppers

"An Interlude with Music"

The action takes place in a small English provincial town during the present time.
Cast: *Gertrude Lawrence* (Lily Pepper), Graham Payn (George Pepper), Booth Colman (Alf), Rhoderick Walker (Bert Bentley), Philip Tonge (Mr. Edwards), Norah Howard (Mabel Grace)
Musical Numbers
"Has Anybody Seen Our Ship?" and "Men About Town" (both songs performed by Gertrude Lawrence and Graham Payn)

Group Two:

Hands Across the Sea

"A Light Comedy in One Scene"

The action takes place in London at the present time.
Cast: Sarah Burton (Walters), *Gertrude Lawrence* (Lady Maureen Gilpin aka Piggie), Graham Payn (Commander Peter Gilpin, R.N.), William Roerick (Lieutenant Commander Alastair Corbett, R.N.), Valerie Cossart (Mrs. Wadhurst), Philip Tonge (Mr. Wadhurst), Booth Colman (Mr. Burnham), Norah Howard (The Honorable Clare Wedderburn), Rhoderick Walker (Major Gosling aka Bogey)

Fumed Oak

"An Unpleasant Comedy in Two Scenes"

The action takes place in London at the present time.
Cast: *Gertrude Lawrence* (Doris Gow), Norah Howard (Mrs. Rockett), Valerie Cossart (Elsie), Philip Tonge (Henry Gow)

Shadow Play

"A Fantasy with Music"

The action takes place in London at the present time.
Cast: Valerie Cossart (Lena), *Gertrude Lawrence* (Victoria Gayforth), Norah Howard (Martha Cunningham), Graham Payn (Simon Gayforth), Booth Colman (Hodge), Sarah Burton (Sibyl Heston), William Roerick (Michael Doyle), Rhoderick Walker (A Young Man), Philip Tonge (George Cunningham)
Musical Numbers
"Then"; "Play, Orchestra, Play!"; and "You Were There" (all songs performed by Gertrude Lawrence and Graham Payn)

Noel Coward's *Tonight at 8:30* premiered in London on January 6, 1936, at the Phoenix Theatre for 157 performances with Coward and Gertrude Lawrence in the leading roles; they later appeared in the New York production, which opened on November 24, 1936, at the National Theatre for 118 showings. The work was comprised of a series of nine short plays, a few of which contained songs, and all were presented in repertory, with each performance offering three of the plays (for New York, *Hands Across the Sea*, *The Astonished Heart*, and *Red Peppers* opened on November 24; *We Were Dancing*, *Fumed Oak*, and *Shadow Play* on the 27th, and *Ways and Means*, *Still Life*, and *Family Album* on the 30th). The current Broadway production, which also played at the National and starred Lawrence (and was again directed by Coward), included six plays (noted above) and omitted three (*We Were Dancing*, *Still Life*, and *The Astonished Heart*).

Graham Payn, here making his American debut, played Coward's roles; over a twenty-eight-year period, Payn appeared in the original London productions of seven works by Coward: *Words and Music* (1932), *Sigh No More* (1945), *Pacific: 1860* (1946), *Ace of Clubs* (1950; in which he introduced "Sail Away," which with a slightly altered lyric was heard in Coward's 1961 New York musical *Sail Away*), *The Globe Revue* (1952), *After the Ball* (1954), and *Waiting in the Wings* (1960).

The critics had been charmed by *Tonight at 8:30* when it opened a dozen years earlier. But now, and despite Lawrence reprising her original roles, the critics were mostly in a sour mood and felt the frivolity of the prewar playlets was out of date in the postwar years. As a result, the revival could do no better than three weeks of performances.

In reviewing the first group of plays, Brooks Atkinson in the *New York Times* said the intervening twelve years hadn't been "much good for any of us" and time had "passed by" Coward's plays. But Gertrude Lawrence outdazzled her material, and in *Red Peppers* ("the liveliest of the lot," which "sprinkles a few brisk dashes of vitality into a slow and decorous evening") she happily whooped it up and larded "the vulgarity on thick"; William Hawkins in the *New York World-Telegram* was shocked that the "chic froth" from an earlier day was now "dated and lackadaisical"; Louis Kronenberger in *PM* said the work hadn't "mellowed" like wine but was instead "puckered and wrinkled" like cocoa; and Howard Barnes in the *New York Herald Tribune* noted that what had once been "wonderful" was now "flat and disappointing"; further, even if Graham Payn had been good ("which he isn't") the evening would still have needed Coward's special touch.

In looking at the second group of plays, Robert Garland in the *New York Journal-American* said Lawrence was in need of "less outmoded material," and commented that Payn was "the Noel Coward of the road"; John Chapman in the *New York Daily News* said Coward's "champagne" had gone flat, and it was no longer amusing to watch plays in which characters were nicknamed "Piggie" and "Bogey"; but Lawrence continued to prove she was a star of "charm and accomplishment" and Payn could "wear a dressing gown more stylishly than anybody this side of Clifton Webb"; Ward Morehouse in the *New York Sun* mentioned that Payn "dances well and knows how to wear his evening clothes," and reported that fellow audience-member Coward appeared to enjoy the second group of plays more than the first round; Robert Coleman in the *New York Daily Mirror* liked the "bitter, wry, yet amusing" *Fumed Oak*, and said the Coward plays were worth reviving because "Broadway is a bright place" with Lawrence around; and Richard Watts in the *New York Post* thought the second grouping of plays was "considerably more effective" than the first; all three playlets were "little masterpieces," Lawrence was "a joy in everything she does," and Payn, who had been "rather severely criticized for not being Noel Coward," found his best role in *Shadow Play*. Watts also noted the latter offered "You Were There," and he rightly suggested it could take its place among such Coward standards as "Someday I'll Find You" and "I'll See You Again."

The overture for the production offered the following songs: "Dance, Little Lady" and "A Room with a View" (*This Year of Grace!*; London and New York, 1928); "Someday I'll Find You" (*Private Lives*; London, 1930; New York, 1931);"You Were There" (*Red Peppers*/*Tonight at 8:30*; London and New York, 1936); and "I'll Follow My Secret Heart" (*Conversation Piece*; London and New York, 1934).

The 1952 British film *Meet Me Tonight* (released in the United States in 1953 as *Tonight at 8:30*) included three of the short plays (*Red Peppers*, *Fumed Oak*, and *Ways and Means*); the cast included Valerie Hobson, Nigel Patrick, Martita Hunt, and Stanley Holloway.

"Play, Orchestra, Play!," "You Were There," "Has Anybody Seen Our Ship?," and "Men About Town" were recorded by Lawrence and Coward at the time of the original British production and are available on various LP and CD collections. The collection *Gertrude Lawrence* (EMI/Regal LP # REG-110) includes Lawrence and Coward in a sequence from *Family Album*.

The texts of all nine plays in *Tonight at 8:30* are included in *The Collected Plays of Noel Coward: Play Parade Volume Four* which was published in hardback by William Heinemann in 1954.

MAURICE CHEVALIER IN AN EVENING OF SONGS AND IMPRESSIONS

Theatre: John Golden Theatre
Opening Date: February 29, 1948; *Closing Date*: March 28, 1948
Performances: 33
Producer: Arthur Lesser; *Lighting*: Duwico; *Musical Direction*: Irving Actman
Cast: *Maurice Chevalier*; Irving Actman (piano)
The revue was presented in two acts.
Musical Numbers (*Note*: All songs and impressions performed by Maurice Chevalier.)
Act One: "J'ai du ciel dans mon chapeau" (lyric by Maurice Chevalier, music by Alstone); "It's Good to Fall in Love" (lyric by Robert Piroshe, music by George Van Parys); "George Bernard Shaw"—"Just Talk"; "Mimi" (1932 film *Love Me Tonight*; lyric by Lorenz Hart, music by Richard Rodgers); "A Barcelone" (lyric by Maurice Chevalier, music by Henri Betti)
Act Two: "Fox a poil dur" (lyric and music by Fred Pearly); "Quai de Bercy" (lyric by Louis Poterat and Maurice Chevalier, music by Alstone); "Weeping Willie" (lyric by Robert Piroshe and Maurice Chevalier, music by Revil); "Prière" (lyric by Maurice Chevalier, music by Alstone); "Place Pigalle" (lyric by Robert Piroshe, music by Alstone); "Le symphonie des semelles de bois" (lyric by Maurice Chevalier, music anonymous; when Chevalier sang this number in previous concert engagements, the lyric was attributed to both Chevalier and Albert Willemetz, and the music to Vincent Scotto)

A year after his previous Broadway visit, Maurice Chevalier returned for another limited run of songs and patter. For more information about the singer and his seven New York engagements during the period 1930–1965, see entry for the 1947 production.

For encores, Chevalier sang "Louise" (lyric by Leo Robin, music by Richard A. Whiting) and "Valentine" (lyric by Herbert Reynolds, music by Henri Christine), both from the 1929 film *Innocents of Paris*, and "Just a Bum" (lyricist and composer unknown). During the run, the George Bernard Shaw sequence was replaced by "Mandarinade" (lyric by Pierre Gilbert and Maurice Chevalier, music by Henry Betti).

HOLIDAY ON BROADWAY

Theatre: Mansfield Theatre
Opening Date: April 27, 1948; *Closing Date*: May 1, 1948
Performances: 6
Producer: Al Wilde
Cast: Billie Holiday, Wyatt and Taylor (Piano and Organ), The Slam Stewart Trio (John Collins, Guitar; Beryl Booker, Piano; Slam Stewart, Bass), The Bobby Tucker Quintet, Cozy Cole
The revue was presented in two acts.

Musical Numbers

Act One: Wyatt and Taylor (Piano and Organ): Their selections included "I Got Rhythm" (1930 musical *Girl Crazy*; lyric by Ira Gershwin, music by George Gershwin); "Lover" (1932 film *Love Me Tonight*; lyric by Lorenz Hart, music by Richard Rodgers); and "You Were Meant for Me" (1929 film *The Broadway Melody*; lyric by Arthur Freed, music by Nacio Herb Brown); The Slam Stewart Trio: Their selections included "Play, Fiddle, Play"; Billie Holiday and The Bobby Tucker Quintet: Their selections included "Easy to Love" (1936 film *Born to Dance*; lyric and music by Cole Porter); "Lover Man" (lyric and music by Jimmy Davis, Roger "Ram" Ramirez, and Jimmy Sherman); "Lover, Come Back to Me" (1928 musical *The New Moon*; lyric by Oscar Hammerstein II, music by Sigmund Romberg); "Them There Eyes" (lyric and music by Maceo Pinkard, William Tracey, and Doris Tauber) and "Strange Fruit" (lyric and music by Lewis Allan).
Act Two: Cozy Cole (Drums); Wyatt and Taylor; The Slam Stewart Trio; Billie Holiday and The Bobby Tucker Quintet: Their selections included "You're Driving Me Crazy" (lyric and music by Walter Donaldson); "I Cover the Waterfront" (lyric by Edward Heyman, music by Johnny Green); and "Billie's Blues"; Finale

Legendary blues singer Billie Holiday (1915–1959) made her only Broadway appearance in *Holiday on Broadway*, which was a concert-like evening in which she sang a number of songs associated with her career (including "Lover Man," "Strange Fruit," and "Them There Eyes"). But despite her presence, and since she wasn't then quite the legend she was to become, the production closed after just six performances.

The Off-Broadway musical *Lady Day: A Musical Tragedy* was based on Holiday's life and career; it opened at the Brooklyn Academy of Music on October 17, 1972, for twenty-four performances with Cecelia Norfleet in the title role. Although Holiday's standard "God Bless the Child" was included in the score, most of the songs were written especially for the production. Coincidentally, the film *Lady Sings the Blues* was released during *Lady Day*'s run; Diana Ross gave a memorable performance as the doomed singer, and the film included a number of songs associated with Holiday.

On September 7, 1986, Lanie Robertson's play-with-music *Lady Day at Emerson's Bar & Grill* opened at the Westside Theatre (Upstairs) for 281 performances; Lonette McKee played the leading role, and the production included various standards associated with Holiday. On April 13, 2014, the work was revived on Broadway at the Circle in the Square.

INSIDE U.S.A.
"A New Musical Revue"

Theatre: New Century Theatre (during run, the musical transferred to the Majestic Theatre)
Opening Date: April 30, 1948; *Closing Date*: February 19, 1949
Performances: 399
Sketches: Arnold Auerbach, Moss Hart, and Arnold B. Horwitt; additional sketch material by Arnold Auerbach
Lyrics: Howard Dietz
Music: Arthur Schwartz; incidental dance music by Genevieve Pitot
Based on the 1947 book *Inside U.S.A.* by John Gunther.
Direction: Robert H. Gordon; *Producer*: Arthur Schwartz; *Choreography*: Helen Tamiris; *Scenery*: Lemuel Ayers; *Costumes*: Eleanor Goldsmith and Castillo; *Lighting*: Uncredited; *Musical Direction*: Jay Blackton
Cast: *Beatrice Lillie*, *Jack Haley*, Valerie Bettis, John Tyers, Thelma Carpenter, Herb Shriner, Estelle Loring, Eric Victor, Jane Lawrence, Lewis (Louis) Nye, Joan Mann, Carl Reiner, William LeMassena, Albert Popwell, J. C. McCord; Ensemble: Rod Alexander, Talley Beatty, Mary Lou Boyd, Beverlee Bozeman, Jack Cassidy, Michael Charnley, Ronald Chetwood, Jacqueline Fisher, Court Fleming, Robert (Bob) Hamilton, Holly Harris, Jim Hawthorne, Randell Henderson, Alfred Homan, Pat Horn, Norma Larkin, Mara Lynn, Dorothy MacNeil, Nanon Mills, John Mooney, Betty Nichols, Hilde Palmer, Richard Reed, George Reich, Ricky Riccardi, Thomas Rieder, Michael Risk, Boris Runanin, Dorothy Scott, Sherry Shadburne, Raymond (Ray) Stephens, Gloria Stevens, Royce Wallace
The revue was presented in two acts.

Sketches and Musical Numbers

Act One: "Inside U.S.A." (Entire Company); "Leave My Pulse Alone" (sketch) (Lottie: Estelle Loring; First Pollster: Carl Reiner; Mrs. Jones: Jane Lawrence; Mr. Jones: Jack Haley; Second Pollster: Lewis Nye; Mary: Beverlee Bozeman; Third Pollster: William LeMassena); "(Come, O Come to) Pittsburgh" (Choral Director: Beatrice Lillie; Pittsburgh Choral Society: Singers); "Forty Winks" (sketch by Arnold B. Horwitt and Arnold Auerbach) (Mr. Bemis: Jack Haley; Hotel Manager: William LeMassena; Bellboy: Lewis Nye; Professor Poultergeist: Carl Reiner); "Blue Grass (of Kentucky)" (Thelma Carpenter; danced by Her Boy Friend: Albert Popwell; and danced by His Friend: Bob Hamilton; Bookies, Spectators, Jockeys: Rod Alexander, Talley Beatty, Beverlee Bozeman, Michael Charnley, Ronald Chetwood, Jacqueline Fisher, Holly Harris, Pat Horn, Norma Larkin, Mara Lynn, Dorothy MacNeil, Joan Mann, Nanon Mills, John Mooney, Betty Nichols, Richard Reed, George Reich, Ricky Riccardi, Thomas Rieder, Boris Runanin, Dorothy Scott, Sherry Shadburne, Gloria Stevens, Royce Wallace); "A Song to Forget" (sketch by Arnold Auerbach) (Miss Twitchell: Beatrice Lillie; Frederic Chopin: Carl Reiner; A Butler: William LeMassena;

Mme. Lapis de Lazuli: Beatrice Lillie; Franz Liszt: John Tyers; Peter Ilyitch Tschaikowsky: Lewis Nye); "Rhode Island Is Famous for You" (Jack Haley, Estelle Loring); "Haunted Heart" (John Tyers; danced by Valerie Bettis with Bob Hamilton, George Reich, and Rod Alexander); "Massachusetts Mermaid" (Beatrice Lillie); "A Feller from Indiana" (Herb Shriner); "First Prize at the Fair" (Ticket Seller: William LeMassena; First Couple: Jane Lawrence and Ray Stephens; Second Couple: Estelle Loring and Jim Hawthorne; Third Couple: Beatrice Lillie and Jack Haley; Caller: Eric Victor; Contestants and Spectators: Entire Company)

Act Two: "At the Mardi Gras" (Beatrice Lillie; Six Swains: Jack Cassidy, Jim Hawthorne, Alfred Homan, Thomas Rieder, Michael Risk, Raymond Stephens; Dancers: Rod Alexander, Talley Beatty, Ricky Riccardi, Beverlee Bozeman, Michael Charnley, Ronald Chetwood, Robert Hamilton, Pat Horn, Mara Lynn, Joan Mann, J. C. McCord, Betty Nichols, Albert Popwell, Richard Reed, George Reich, Boris Runanin, Dorothy Scott, Gloria Stevens, Royce Wallace); "School for Waiters" (sketch by Arnold Auerbach; suggested by George S. Kaufman) (Girl: Joan Mann; Man: Carl Reiner; Professor: Jack Haley; Herman: Lewis Nye; Girl Diner: Jane Lawrence; Her Escort: William LeMassena; Another Diner: Carl Reiner; His Companions: Holly Harris and Hilde Palmer; Captain of Waiters: Ronald Chetwood; Student Waiters: Rod Alexander, Court Fleming, Richard Reed, George Reich, Boris Runanin); "My Gal Is Mine Once More" (Groom: John Tyers; Bride: Estelle Loring; Minister: Carl Reiner; Cowboy with Rope: Rod Alexander; Townspeople: Mary Lou Boyd, Beverlee Bozeman, Jack Cassidy, Jim Hawthorne, Norma Larkin, Mara Lynn, Dorothy MacNeil, Joan Mann, J. C. McCord, John Mooney, Thomas Rieder, Michael Risk, Dorothy Scott, Sherry Shadburne, Raymond Stephens, Gloria Stevens); "Better Luck Next Time" (sketch by Moss Hart) (Mary Shelton: Jane Lawrence; Her Maid: Beatrice Lillie; The Stage Manager: Randell Henderson); "Tiger Lily" ("a tabloid ballet conceived by Helen Tamiris") (Tiger Lily: Valerie Bettis; Doctor Zilmore: Eric Victor; Detectives: Rod Alexander, Robert Hamilton, J. C. McCord, Richard Reed; Prosecuting Attorney: Rod Alexander; Defense Attorney: Ronald Chetwood; Jury: Talley Beatty, Gloria Stevens, Robert Hamilton, Joan Mann, J. C. McCord, Boris Runanin; Judge: Carl Reiner; Newspaper Readers and Spectators: Beverlee Bozeman, Jack Cassidy, Jacqueline Fisher, Court Fleming, Holly Harris, Jim Hawthorne, Alfred Homan, Pat Horn, Norma Larkin, William LeMassena, Mara Lynn, Nanon Mills, John Mooney, Betty Nichols, George Reisch, Richard Reed, Thomas Rieder, Michael Risk, Dorothy Scott, Sherry Shadburne, Raymond Stephens, Gloria Stevens, Royce Wallace); "We Won't Take It Back" (Beatrice Lillie, Jack Haley; Tourists: Alfred Homan, Jane Lawrence, William LeMassena, Carl Reiner, Lewis Nye, Hilde Palmer); Finale (Entire Company)

Inside U.S.A. wasn't the first time Howard Dietz and Arthur Schwartz took a musical trip. Their 1935 revue *At Home Abroad* (which also starred Beatrice Lillie) took place in such spots as London, the Riviera, Spain, Brussels, Vienna, Russia, and Jamaica, and there was even a "third" Dietz and Schwartz travel revue when *Bon Voyage* (advertised as an "Exciting Musical Journey") opened at the Versailles supper club during Fall 1954 (one assumes the evening was a compendium of the team's earlier travel revues). Moreover, their 1961 book musical *The Gay Life* offered two opposing views of travel by the hero Anatol's two amours: the world-weary Helene asks him "Why Go Anywhere at All?" and gypsy hellcat Magda entices him to "Come A-Wondering with Me."

Inside U.S.A. traveled around the country, looking at horse-racing at Churchill Downs ("Blue Grass of Kentucky"), the spurious joys of living in Pittsburgh ("Come, O Come to Pittsburgh"), a Miami Beach hotel loaded with sleep-inducing aids designed to keep its customers awake ("Forty Winks"), a lonely wharf in San Francisco ("Haunted Heart"), a quirky mermaid on the (Plymouth) rocks ("Massachusetts Mermaid"), a Kenosha County fair ("First Prize at the Fair"), Mardi Gras time in New Orleans ("At the Mardi Gras"), restaurants in Manhattan where waiters are taught to despise and ignore their customers ("School for Waiters"), a decidedly western wedding in Wyoming ("My Gal Is Mine Once More"), a sensational murder trial in Chicago that centers on a beautiful murderess ("Tiger Lily," a self-described "tabloid ballet"), and a delightful novelty song ("Rhode Island Is Famous for You") that cataloged famous products of various states. At the end of the musical, New Mexican Indians made an irrevocable decision ("We Won't Take It Back," which was an answer of sorts to Richard Rodgers and Lorenz Hart's "Give It Back to the Indians" from 1939's *Too Many Girls*).

One sketch ("A Song to Forget") didn't seem to have much to do with general theme of life in the U.S.A., but it sure sounds amusing. This was the era of Great Composer musicals both on stage (***Polonaise*** [Chopin], ***The Waltz King*** [Richard Strauss], ***Mr. Strauss Goes to Boston*** [Richard], ***Music in My Heart*** [Tschiakowsky], and the revival of ***Blossom Time*** [Schubert]) and screen (***A Song to Remember*** [Chopin]), and so here we had

Chopin (Carl Reiner), Franz Liszt (John Tyers), and Tschiakowsky (Louis Nye) all enamored of Mme. Lapis de Lazuli (Beatrice Lillie), and, due to her inspiration, all write a variant of a song titled "Burning Lips" in her honor.

The revue received mostly favorable reviews, and returned a profit. It played on Broadway almost a full year, and then toured with Lillie and Jack Haley. "Haunted Heart" became one of the most enduring of all Broadway ballads (Jo Stafford's version is particularly memorable, and the song was the main musical theme for the 1999 film *The End of the Affair*), and "Rhode Island Is Famous for You" still enjoys currency among today's saloon singers.

Brooks Atkinson in the *New York Times* praised the "enormously enjoyable" revue, and singled out "Tiger Lily" ("swift and vivid"), "My Gal Is Mine Once More" (one of the "best" songs in the show), "First Prize at the Fair" ("jubilant"), and the title number (a "roaring serenade"). As for Lillie, she had "never been more brilliant" and was "the most deliberate and intelligent wit that illuminates the musical stage of our day."

Ward Morehouse in the *New York Sun* liked the "new and solid hit," praised the "dead-pan" Jack Haley, and said Lillie could "stop a show by lifting an eyebrow." Robert Garland in the *New York Journal-American* suggested had Ziegfeld been alive *Inside U.S.A.* would have been his *Ziegfeld Follies of 1948*, and the critic noted "such a comparison is praise, indeed!" Robert Coleman in the *New York Daily Mirror* liked the "breezy, amusing and handsome" revue and noted that the score had already "become the delight of nitery and radio bands." Richard Watts in the *New York Post* said the revue's "chances of a smash success are almost certain," and he liked Dietz's "skillful" lyrics and Schwartz' "attractive" music (and singled out seven songs). Lillie was an "incomparable" and complete "delight" while Haley was "one of the best and least appreciated" of Broadway comedians.

Howard Barnes in the *New York Herald Tribune* praised the "joyous entertainment"; the choreography was "first-rate," the "repetitive" score was nonetheless "witty and sophisticated," and Lillie and Haley "brilliantly" romped through the evening. John Chapman in the *New York Daily News* said the country needed Beatrice Lillie and should make her the forty-ninth state; the "great" clown and humorist could "make anything funny," including *Medea*. Chapman said "Haunted Heart" was the best song in the score, praised the "handsome" décor, and found dancer Valerie Bettis "slinky, sexy and agile."

William Hawkins in the *New York World-Telegram* said the "lush, bright, beautiful" revue was "full of song hits," offered "luxurious and bright" scenery and costumes, and presented dances that were "alive and fresh." Lillie was at her "handsome best" and had many opportunities to bring down the house "with a faint smirk or twitch"; and Haley was "most ingratiating." The critic singled out over a half-dozen numbers, including "Haunted Heart," which was "lovely." But he concluded his favorable review with the strange observation that while *Inside U.S.A.* "might run three years," he wasn't certain it would return a profit.

Because of the impending ASCAP musicians' strike, there wasn't a regular cast recording; but prior to the revue's opening, RCA recorded a number of songs from the production with Beatrice Lillie and Jack Haley as well as Perry Como, Billy Williams, and Russ Case (78 RPM # 6371-B); and Columbia issued an album of songs performed by Pearl Bailey and Buddy Clark (78 RPM # C-162). A combination of both recordings was released on CD by Sepia (# 1056), and include: "Come, O Come to Pittsburgh," "At the Mardi Gras," and "Atlanta" (all performed by Beatrice Lillie; the latter song was dropped in preproduction); "Rhode Island Is Famous for You" and "First Prize at the Fair" (Jack Haley); "Blue Grass of Wyoming" and "Protect Me" (Pearl Bailey; the latter song was also dropped in preproduction); "My Gal Is Mine Once More" (Billy Williams); "Haunted Heart" (Perry Como); "Rhode Island Is Famous for You," "Haunted Heart," "First Prize at the Fair," and "My Gal Is Mine Once More" (Buddy Clark); and the title song (Chorus with Russ Case and His Orchestra).

During the tryout, "If We Had a Little More Time" was cut; and Allen Boritz was credited as one of the revue's sketch writers.

Moss Hart's sketch "Better Luck Next Time" found Lillie as a dressing-room maid from hell who ruins a star's opening night. She had earlier appeared in a somewhat similar sketch in Robert MacGunigle's "The Girl Friend" from the 1932 revue *Walk a Little Faster* in which she played Nancy Fixit, a decidedly unhelpful "friend" who manages to wreck a star's opening night, and she reprised this sketch for her 1952 revue *An Evening with Beatrice Lillie* (this time around the sketch was titled "A Star's First Night").

For the national tour, Herb Shriner's monologue "A Feller from Indiana" was omitted and a sketch titled "All Over the Map" (by Joseph Stein and Will Glickman) was added for Jack Haley.

With its story about a sensational Chicago trial of a beautiful murderess, Helen Tamiris's "Tiger Lily" (a self-described "tabloid ballet" with music by Arthur Schwartz) certainly anticipates Bob Fosse's *Chicago*

(1975), which of course was based on the 1926 play of the same name by Maurine Watkins. And Fosse seems to have anticipated *Chicago* with his 1962 musical *Little Me*; its song "Dimples" by Cy Coleman and Carolyn Leigh describes the sensational Chicago murder trial of a cold-blooded murderess and the attendant show business-related publicity surrounding the event.

"Tiger Lily" is part of a small genre of Broadway and film murder-mystery and suspense ballets. The granddaddy of them all is of course Richard Rodgers's "Slaughter on Tenth Avenue" from *On Your Toes* (1936), which was choreographed by George Balanchine. The 1940 revue **Keep Off the Grass** included the ballet "Raffles," about a society thief who confounds Scotland Yard (music by Vernon Duke, and, like "Slaughter on Tenth Avenue," danced by Ray Bolger), and the 1964 revue *Zizi* offered Zizi Jeanmaire in "La Chambre," which was choreographed by Roland Petit and focused on a detective who tries to solve a murder before the murderess does him in (the ballet's text was by no less than celebrated mystery writer Georges Simenon, and the music was by Georges Auric). Tamiris herself also choreographed "Detective Specs" (described as "A Radio Mystery Ballet," with music by Genevieve Pitot), which was deleted during the tryout of **Touch and Go**. And of course the 1953 MGM musical *The Band Wagon* offered the classic "The Girl Hunt" ballet for Fred Astaire and Cyd Charisse, which was choreographed by Michael Kidd. It was a spoof of the hard-boiled Mickey Spillane school of murder mysteries (the text was by Alan Jay Lerner, and Roger Edens adapted musical themes that Arthur Schwartz had composed especially for the ballet). Hugh Fordin in *The Movies' Greatest Musicals* reports that Howard Dietz and Schwartz had written the song "The Private Eye" for a murder mystery sequence in the film, but the song was jettisoned once "The Girl Hunt" ballet was conceived.

HOLD IT!
"A New Musical Comedy"

Theatre: National Theatre
Opening Date: May 5, 1948; *Closing Date*: June 12, 1948
Performances: 46
Book: Matt Brooks and Art Arthur
Lyrics: Sam Lerner
Music: Gerald Marks; music for "Hollywood Sequence" by Irma Jurist
Direction: Robert E. Perry; *Producer*: Sammy Lambert; *Choreography*: Michael Kidd; *Scenery*: Edward Gilbert; *Costumes*: Julia Sze; *Lighting*: Uncredited; *Musical Direction*: Clay Warnick
Cast: Usherettes: Wana Allison, Gloria Benson, Janet Bethel, Penny Carroll, Kathryne Mylroie, and Helena Schurgot; Bob (Robert) Shawley (Rodney Trent), Ruth Saville (Mrs. Simpkins, Mrs. Jollop, Anne Green), Douglas Rutherford (Mr. Simpkins, Headwaiter), Helen Wenzel (Mrs. Blandish), Budd Rogers (Mr. Blandish, Budd, Reporter), Larry Douglas ("Sarge" Denton), Johnny Downs (Bobby Manville), Helen Wenzel (Helen), Jack Warner (Jack), Robert (Bob) Evans (Chuck), Kenny Buffett ("Judge" Rogers), Sid Lawson (Sid, Reporter), Jet McDonald (Jessica Dale), Patricia Wymore (Pamela Scott), Ada Lynne (Millie Henderson), Bib Bernard (Bernie), Red Buttons ("Dinky" Bennett), Paul Lyday (Paul), Douglas Chandler (George Monopolis), Penny Carroll (Penny), Paul Reed (Mr. Jenkins), Tom Bowman (Joe), Pat McVey (Charlie Blake), Scott Lewis (O'Brien), Martin Kraft (Martin), Helena Schurgot (Reporter), John Kane (Felix Dexter); Singing Ensemble: Gloria Benson, Penny Carroll, Kathryne Mylroie, Helena Schurgot, Tom Bowman, Sid Lawson, Budd Rogers, Frank Stevens; Dancing Ensemble: Onna White, Wana Allison, Janet Bethel, Margit DeKova, Helen Kramer, Barbara McCutcheon, Elena Salamatova, Yvonne Tibor, Helen Wenzel, John Begg, Bob Bernard, Jack Claus, Robert Cadwallader, Robert (Bob) Evans, Martin Kraft, Vernon Lusby, Paul Lyday
The musical was presented in two acts.
The action takes place during the present time in and around the campus of Lincoln University, and in Hollywood.

Musical Numbers

Act One: Opening (Usherettes); "Heaven Sent" (Larry Douglas, Johnny Downs, Boys) and "Dance" (Dancing Ensemble); "Buck in the Bank" (Johnny Downs, Jet McDonald, Singing Ensemble) and "Dance" (Johnny

Downs); "Always You" (Johnny Downs); "About Face" (Larry Douglas, Johnny Downs, Red Buttons, Kenny Buffett, Singing Ensemble) and "Dance" (Johnny Downs, Red Buttons, Kenny Buffett, Singing Ensemble); "Fundamental Character" (Ada Lynne, Red Buttons); "Hold It!" (Johnny Downs, Jet McDonald, Red Buttons, Ada Lynne, Patricia Wymore, Kenny Buffett, Singing Ensemble) and "Dance" (Patricia Wymore); "Nevermore" (Jet McDonald); "Hollywood Sequence": (1) "Roll 'Em" (Larry Douglas, Jet McDonald, Ada Lynne, Patricia Wymore, Singing Ensemble); (2) *Continued Next Week* (Star: Jet McDonald; Stand-In: Ada Lynne; Director: Larry Douglas); (3) *Operation 'X'* (Doctor: Vernon Lusby; Patient: Jack Claus; Nurses: Elena Salamatova, Janet Bethel, Wana Allison, and Helen Kramer); (4) *Saga of Roaring Gulch* (The Kid: Jack Warner; The Gal: Margit DeKova; The Boss: Martin Kraft; Bartender: Paul Lyday; Dance Hall Girls: Barbara McCutcheon, Yvonne Tibor; Cowboys: Robert (Bob) Evans, Robert Cadwallader, Bob Bernard; and (5) *Arsenic and Old Araby* (Sultan: Budd Rogers; Favorite: Jet McDonald; Out-of-Favor Trio: Wana Allison, Helen Wenzel, Onna White; Out-of-Favor Duo: Margit Dekova, Barbara McCutcheon; Vessel Bearers: Elena Salamatova, Yvonne Tibor; Message Bearers: Jack Claus, Bob Bernard; Attendants: Helen Kramer, Janet Bethel; Sinbad: Martin Kraft)

Act Two: "So Nice Having You" (Ada Lynne, Entire Ensemble) and "Dance" (Dancing Ensemble); "Down the Well" (Larry Douglas, Jet McDonald); "You Took Possession of Me" (Patricia Wymore, Kenny Buffett) and "Dance" (Dancing Ensemble); "Always You" (reprise) (Johnny Downs); "Friendly Enemy" (Ada Lynne, Red Buttons); "Hold It!" (reprise) (Entire Company); Finale (Entire Company)

Hold It! dealt with campus capers, but unlike the hits *Good News* (1927), *Too Many Girls* (1939), and **Best Foot Forward**, it went the way of such also-rans as **Toplitzky of Notre Dame**, **Barefoot Boy with Cheek**, and *All American* (1962). The musical played for just five weeks and reportedly lost $300,000 (prior to the Broadway tryout, the flyer proclaimed the cost to mount the show was $200,000).

The plot revolved around Bobby Manville (Johnny Downs), who has appeared in drag at the college's annual varsity show; as a joke, a classmate snaps his photo and submits it to a Hollywood studio that is holding a contest to choose an ingénue for its next picture (along with a movie role, the contest also awards a prize of $5,000). Of course, Bobby's photo is chosen, and the timing couldn't be better because he's misplaced $3,000 that he and his friends have raised to buy off-campus trailers as homes for former soldiers while they attend college under the G.I. Bill.

The critics liked the game cast, but otherwise felt the promising book missed most of its comic opportunities and that Gerald Marks and Sam Lerner's score was underwhelming (although a number of songs were singled out, including "Friendly Enemy," "Fundamental Character," "Down the Well," "Buck in the Bank," and "Always You"). Michael Kidd contributed some lively dance sequences, and the reviewers were happy to note he was in the Jerome Robbins tradition and not an acolyte of Agnes De Mille. Robbins had of course wowed the critics earlier in the season with his "Mack Sennett Ballet" from **High Button Shoes**, and Kidd created a somewhat similar sequence at the end of the first act in a roundelay that kidded clichéd movie plots (the musical created four mini-movies, *Continued Next Week*, *Operation 'X'*, *Saga of Roaring Gulch*, and *Arsenic and Old Araby*).

Of the cast members, future Academy Award winner Red Buttons was singled out, along with tap dancer Patricia Wymore and singer Larry Douglas. The musical marked another early appearance by future choreographer Onna White, who was a chorus member as well as the musical's dance captain. In 1949, she appeared in **Pretty Penny**, in which Kidd both choreographed and starred, and when Kidd was signed to choreograph *Guys and Dolls* two years later, White was among the dancers in the new show. She continued to perform in such musicals as **All for Love** (in which Wymore also appeared), **Regina**, and *Silk Stockings* (1955), but by the late 1950s she was established as a Broadway choreographer, and among the musicals for which she created dances and musical staging were *The Music Man* (1957), *Take Me Along* (1959), *Irma La Douce* (1960), *Half a Sixpence* (1965), *Mame* (1966), and *1776* (1969). She was nominated eight times for a Tony Award as Best Choreographer, and in 1968 won an Honorary Academy Award for her choreography for the film version of *Oliver!* White and Douglas married, and he later created the role of Lun Tha in the original production of Richard Rodgers and Oscar Hammerstein II's *The King and I* (1951), and with Doretta Morrow introduced the ballads "We Kiss in a Shadow" and "I Have Dreamed." Despite good reviews, Wymore appeared in just one more musical (the aforementioned **All for Love**) and soon became Mrs. Errol Flynn.

Robert Coleman in the *New York Daily Mirror* said the songs were orchestrated at "too uniform a tempo" and so even the ballads came across as "hot" numbers. He felt that many of the songs would sound better once they made the rounds of the radio and nightclubs. He noted that Kidd's dances had "zip and zing," and while the musical moved along at "express-train speed" and was one of the "fastest" to ever hit Broadway, it lacked the "laughs, originality and class for a click." Richard Watts in the *New York Post* complained that an "aura of the commonplace" hung over the evening, and except for "Friendly Enemy" and "Fundamental Character" the songs were "singularly mediocre." Brooks Atkinson in the *New York Times* said *Hold It!* suffered from a "case of arrested musical comedy development," and while the musical moved along at "high speed" it should also be removed at high speed.

Herrick Brown in the *New York Sun* said the musical offered "youthful exuberance" and an "undistinguished" score that nonetheless offered a few "catchy" tunes, but suggested many college varsity shows were probably more entertaining. Howard Barnes in the *New York Herald Tribune* warned that the new musical was "dull stuff" and its "tasteless tedium" resulted in an evening that was "labored and somewhat soporific." But Kidd's choreography provided "excitement" and "superior hoofing," and "Down the Well" was the show's best song.

John Chapman in the *New York Daily News* felt that with the right touches the musical could have been a "knockout," but even so it offered the audience a number of "enticements." Kidd's contributions were "lively, attractive and clever," the Hollywood sequence was "funny and well-staged," and he was "particularly charmed" by Patricia Wymore. Robert Garland in the *New York Journal-American* said the musical was at its "zestful" best when it sang and danced, and the score was from the "sunny side of Tin Pan Alley." Johnny Downs was "young, likeable and danceful," and Patricia Wymore was a "delight" for both ear and eye. William Hawkins in the *New York World-Telegram* said *Hold It!* would never make "history," but was certainly a "good-humored, vivacious prism." He noted that Red Buttons had a "wry and brittle" comedic style and an "instinct" for timing because he could "dress up" a comedy line and make it "punch." In her tap numbers, Patricia Wymore was a "menace to equilibrium" and when she and Kenny Buffett joined forces in their dance routines they were "just plain Hell on wheels."

During the tryout, "Courage" was deleted; and Jet McDonald succeeded Jean Darling.

SALLY

Theatre: Martin Beck Theatre
Opening Date: May 6, 1948; *Closing Date*: June 5, 1948
Performances: 36
Book: Guy Bolton
Lyrics: P. G. Wodehouse and Clifford Grey
Music: Jerome Kern
Direction: Billy Gilbert; *Producers*: Hunt Stromberg Jr., and William Berney; *Choreography*: Richard Barstow; *Scenery* and *Lighting*: Stewart Chaney; *Costumes*: Henry Mulle; *Musical Direction*: David Mordecai
Cast: Gloria Sullivan (Nadina), Charles Wood (The Young Waiter), Holger Sorenson (The Old Waiter), Jack Goode (Otis Hooper), Kay Buckley (Rosie), Bibi Osterwald (Lily Bedlington), Henry Calvin (Shendorf), Robert Shackleton (Mickey Sinclair), Bambi Linn (Sally), *Willie Howard* (The Grand Duke Constantine aka Connie), Kathryn Cameron (Mrs. Vischer Van Alstyn), Lucy Hillary (Toto), Andrea Mann (Olga); Singers: Lucy Hillary, Ruth Johnston, Andrea Mann, Audrey Guard, Jean Olds, Eila Brynn, Gloria Haydn, Gloria Sullivan, Charles Wood, John George, Lynn Alden, Richard Oneto, Holger Sorenson, Steve Coleman, Hank Roberts, Brian Otis; Dancers: Aura Vainio, Marcella Dodge, Mary Alice Bingham, Carmina Cansino, Gretchen Houser, Karlyn DeBoer, Carol Lee, Marcia Maier, Dolores Nevins, Jo McCann, Tommy Randall, Lee Lindsey, Dusty McCaffrey, Joe Vilane, Frank Reynolds, Garry Fleming, Jack Miller, Jimmy Russell
The musical was presented in two acts.
The action takes place during the early 1920s in Greenwich Village and Long Island.

Musical Numbers

Act One: "Down Here in Greenwich Village" (Ensemble); "Bungalow in Quoque" (Kay Buckley, Jack Goode); "Look for the Silver Lining" (Bambi Linn, Robert Shackleton); "Looking All Over for You" (Principals,

Ensemble); "Tulip Time in Sing-Sing" (Willie Howard, Waiters); "The Whippoorwill Waltz" (aka "Whip-Poor-Will") (Ensemble; Principal Dancers: Jimmy Russell and Aura Vainio); "The Siren (Siren's) Song" (Bambi Linn, Robert Shackleton, Ensemble); "Cleopatra" (aka "Cleopatterer") (Bibi Osterwald); "Wild Rose" (Bambi Linn, Robert Shackleton, Male Ensemble)

Act Two: "The Church 'round the Corner" (Kay Buckley, Jack Goode; Sailors: Tommy Randall, Dusty McCaffrey; Sailors' Girl Friend: Carmina Cansino; Old Man: Joe Vilane; His Bride: Gretchen Houser; Lovesick Couple: Mary Alice Bingham, Jack Miller); "Dear Little Girl" (Robert Shackleton, Bambi Linn); "Look for the Silver Lining" (reprise) (Bambi Linn, Willie Howard); "Reaching for Stars" (Bambi Linn, Ensemble); Finale

Jerome Kern's *Sally* was one of the biggest hits of the 1920s; with the legendary Marilyn Miller in the title role, a score that included the evergreen "Look for the Silver Lining," and a lavish Ziegfeld production, the musical opened on December 21, 1920, at the New Amsterdam Theatre for 570 performances. But its only Broadway revival floundered after a month on the boards. The years had been kind to Kern's score but not Guy Bolton's book, and despite the talent and loveliness of Bambi Linn in the title role, she lacked the star quality to make critics forget the evanescence of Marilyn Miller's fondly remembered performance.

The Cinderella-like story centered on Sally (Bambi Linn), a slavey who works in a restaurant's kitchen down in Greenwich Village; she dreams of romance and show business splendor as the star of the *Ziegfeld Follies*, and in true musical comedy tradition finds both. She meets young, handsome, and rich Long Island society heir Mickey Sinclair (Robert Shackleton) *and* becomes the toast of Broadway. The story was somewhat similar to *Irene* (1919), which also offered a Cinderella-inspired story of a shop girl who finds love with a rich boy who lives on a Long Island estate.

Brooks Atkinson in the *New York Times* noted that *Sally* was no "hand-me-down" revival; it was "colorful," but unfortunately its book and performance style were now "counterfeit." He complained that Bambi Linn was "no singer" and lacked the "clean-cut" dancing style of Marilyn Miller, and felt that comic Willie Howard was all but wasted (and noted the comedian offered a series of impersonations during the second act, including those of George Jessel, Eddie Cantor, Al Jolson, and Maurice Chevalier). William Hawkins in the *New York World-Telegram* found the evening "lackadaisical" with no "imagination" and "punch," but Vernon Rice in the *New York Post* said the "routine" revival offered the "wonderfully funny" Willie Howard triumphing over indifferent material, and while Bambi Linn was "sweet and girlish" she seemed more comfortable with choreography by Agnes De Mille. Joseph Mackey in the *New York Sun* found the evening an uneasy combination of "streamlined nostalgia and dubious topicality," and commented that Willie Howard was "richly comic" despite his weak material and that Bambi Linn came across as "somewhat peevish" in the title role. John Chapman in the *New York Daily News* said the revival was "rather dull."

But Robert Coleman in the *New York Daily Mirror* had a "delightful" time, and praised the producers for their "wonderful job" in mounting the revival; Robert Garland in the *New York Journal-American* said the production was a "great success"; and Howard Barnes in the *New York Herald Tribune* found the musical "as fresh and captivating as ever" with "gaiety" and "enchantment."

Most of the lyrics were by Clifford Grey, but a few were by other lyricists, including "Look for the Silver Lining" and "Whip-Poor-Will" (Buddy B. G. De Sylva), "The Lorelei" (Anne Caldwell), and "The Little Church 'round the Corner" (P. G. Wodehouse). The original production also included the lavish "Butterfly Ballet," with music by Victor Herbert. The revival retained four songs from the original: "Look for the Silver Lining," "The Wild Rose," "Whip-Poor-Will," and "The Little Church 'round the Corner"; and omitted seven: "Way Down East," "On with the Dance," "Joan of Arc" (aka "You Can't Keep a Good Girl Down"), "The Social Game," "(On the Banks of) The Schnitza-Kommisski (Where the Schnitza Flows Down to the Sea)," "The Lorelei," and the title song. The revival's "Dear Little Girl" was probably "This Little Girl," which had been heard in the original production.

The revival also included interpolations from other musicals by Kern, all with lyrics by P. G. Wodehouse: "Down (Here) in Greenwich Village" (aka "Greenwich Village" and "Something in the Air") (*Oh, Lady! Lady!*, 1918), "Bungalow in Quoque" (*The Riviera Girl*, 1917), "Tulip Time in Sing-Sing" (aka "Dear Old-Fashioned Prison of Mine"; *Sitting Pretty*, 1924), "Looking All Over for You" (*The Cabaret Girl*, 1921), and both "The Siren (Siren's) Song" and "Cleopatra" ("Cleopatterer") were from *Leave It to Jane* (1917). The source of "Reaching for Stars" is unclear; it may have been an older Kern song with a new lyric written especially for the revival.

The first London production of *Sally* opened at the Winter Garden on September 10, 1921, for 387 performances with Dorothy Dickson in the title role; another London mounting opened at the Prince's Theatre on August 6, 1942, for 205 performances with Jesse Matthews (who seems to have quickly bounced back from the debacle of **The Lady Comes Across**).

In 1929, Marilyn Miller reprised her stage role in a Technicolor film version released by Warners-First National. The cast included Alexander Gray, Joe E. Brown, Pert Kelton, and three songs from the original Broadway production were retained ("Look for the Silver Lining," "Wild Rose," and the title song). The film has been released by Warner Brothers' Archive Collection; the color print of the film has been lost, but a Technicolor fragment of the "Wild Rose" number has happily surfaced. In 1925, First National released a silent version of the musical; Colleen Moore played the title role, and from the original 1920 stage production Leon Errol reprised his role of Connie.

The original London production was recorded, and offers a generous sampling of the score: "You Can't Keep a Good Girl Down," "Look for the Silver Lining," "On with the Dance," "Sally," "Wild Rose," "The Schnitza Kommisski," "Lorelei," "Whip-Poor-Will," "The Church 'round the Corner," "Butterfly Ballet," and "Sally (in Our Alley)". A 2005 concert recording by the Comic Opera Guild (located in Ann Arbor, Michigan) as part of its Kern Festival was released on an unlabeled and unnumbered CD by the Guild with singers and a two-piano duo; it includes songs from the original production (and "Nerves," which was cut prior to the New York opening) as well as interpolations from other Kern musicals.

Bambi Linn had created dancing roles in the original Broadway productions of **Oklahoma!** and **Carousel**, but after playing the title roles in two failed revivals (**Alice in Wonderland** and **Sally**), she created just two more roles in musicals, *Great to Be Alive!* (1950) and *I Can Get It for You Wholesale* (1962).

BALLET BALLADS

Theatre: Maxine Elliott's Theatre
Opening Date: May 9, 1948; *Closing Date*: May 16, 1948
Performances: 7
Theatre: Music Box Theatre
Opening Date: May 18, 1948; *Closing Date*: July 10, 1948
Performances: 62
Texts: John LaTouche
Music: Jerome Moross
Direction: Mary Hunter; *Producers*: T. Edward Hambleton and Alfred R. Stern (A Production for the Benefit of the American National Theatre and Academy) (The Experimental Theatre's Production); also produced by Nat Karson; *Scenery, Costumes*, and *Lighting*: "Production scheme devised, designed and lighted by Nat Karson"; *Musical Direction*: Hugh Ross (Gerard Samuel, Associate Conductor; Pianist: John Lesko Jr., and Mordecai Sheinkman)
The dance revue was presented in three acts; for each act, a "ballet ballad" was performed, all of which were sung-through and danced-through. The sequences were story ballets with lyrics that accompanied the music and the dances.

Act One

Susanna and the Elders

Choreography: Katherine Litz
The action takes place at a revival meeting in which the congregation's parson takes his sermon from the story of Susanna and the Elders as found in the *Apocrypha*.
Cast: Richard Harvey (The Parson), Katherine Litz (Dancing Susanna), Sheila Vogelle (Singing Susanna), Sharry Traver (The Cedar from Lebanon), Ellen R. Albertini (The Little Juniper Tree), Margaret Cuddy (Handmaiden), Barbara Downie (Handmaiden), Frank Seabolt (The Elder [Moe]). Robert Trout (The Elder [Joe]), James R. Nygren (The Angel); The Singing Ensemble (The Ladies and Gentlemen of the Congregation)

Act Two

WILLIE THE WEEPER

Choreography: Paul Godkin

The action takes place "in Willie's untidy mind" and covers seven episodes in his life after an Introduction, "Did You Ever Hear about Willie the Weeper?"; the episodes were: (1) "Rich Willie" ("Has a Million Cattle"); (2) "Lonely Willie" ("I'm Mister Nobody"); (3) "Famous Willie" ("He's Wonderful"); (4) "Baffled Willie" ("No Thoroughfare"); (5) "Super-Willie" ("They Can't Scare Me"); (6) "Self-Sufficient Willie" ("I've Got Me"); and (7) "Lover Willie" ("Introducin' Yuh to Cocaine Lil" and "Oh Baby and Gee Baby"); and the seven episodes were followed by a finale ("Poor Dreamy Willie").

Cast: Sono Osato (Cocaine Lil), Robert Lenn (Singing Willie), Paul Godkin (Dancing Willie); The Singing Ensemble; Dancers: Cecile Bergman, Nora Bristow, Mary Ann Cousins, Sandra Lipton, Iona McKenzie, Rosa Rolland, Jack Warren Kozal, James R. Nygren, William Weaver, Walter Stane, Richard Goltra, Charles Yongue

Act Three

THE ECCENTRICITIES OF DAVEY CROCKETT (AS TOLD BY HIMSELF)

Choreography: Hanya Holm

From a program note: "The People assemble to celebrate the memory of Davey Crockett. In the terms of his own tall tales they recall his exploits; his youth, courtship, and marriage; how he built a living room in the wilderness; how he fought the Indian Wars; how he hooked a Mermaid; how he saved the world from Halley's Comet; how he went to Congress and left it; how he died at the Alamo and became a legend."

Musical sequences: Introduction: The People Gather to Celebrate the Memory of Davey Crocket—"Oh, the Western Star Is Riding Low"; Young Davey in the Backwoods—"Funny Kind of Lad Is Davey"; The Courtship of Davey—"Young Women"; Davey Meets Sally Ann—"Sally Ann"; They Journey to the Frontier, They Build a House in the Wilderness—"Peace Be on This House of Logs"; The Indian War—"Cherokee, Choctaw, Shawanoe"; On the Banks of the Tennessee River—"You're My Yaller Flower"; Davey Catches a Mermaid in the River—"I Swam Upstream This Morning"; Davey Saves the World from Halley's Comet—"There's a Comet A-Comin'"; Davey Goes on a Bear Hunt—"Oh, Davey Would A-Huntin' Ride"; Davey in the Haunted Cave—"Brave Hunter"; Davey Goes to Congress—"Maybe I Should Cut Some Public Capers" and "Ridin' on the Breeze"; Finale—"They Journeyed to the Alamo"

Cast: Ted Lawrie (Davey Crockett), Barbara Ashley (Sally Ann), Lorin Barrett (Indian Chief), Carl Luman (General Andrew Jackson), Betty Abbott (The Mermaid), Olga Lunick (The Comet), William A. Myers (Brown Bear), Robert Bear (Ghost Bear), William Ambler (Singing John Oldham), John Castello (Dancing John Oldham), Gertrude Lockway (Singing Ann Hutchinson), Sharry Traver (Dancing Ann Hutchinson), Eddie Varrato (Singing Nathaniel Bacon), Frank Seabolt (Dancing Nathaniel Bacon), Arlouine Goodjohn (Singing Grace Sherwood), Barbara Downie (Dancing Grace Sherwood), Arthur Friedman (Singing Nathaniel Turner), Beau Cunningham (Dancing Nathaniel Turner), Harold Michener (President Andrew Jackson); The Singing Ensemble; Dancers: Ellen R. Albertini, Margaret Cuddy, Barbara Downie, Sharry Traver, Beau Cunningham, John Castello, Frank Seabolt, Robert Trout, Spencer Teakle

Singing Ensemble: Sopranos—Arlouine Goodjohn, Barbara Lewis, Frances Joslyn, Marian C. Covey, Dee Carrol, Manya Kanty; Altos—Carol Nason, Ethel Madsen, Gertrude Lockway, Jane Flynn, Estelle Moss, Joan Bartels, Betty Abbott; Tenors—Harold Michener, M. R. Alch, Farrold Stevens, Eddie Varrato, Douglas Martin, Kenneth Renner; Basses—Bernard Zwarg, Robert Baird, David Vogel, Lorin Barrett, Arthur Friedman, William Ambler

John LaTouche and Jerome Moross's ambitious *Ballet Ballads* was comprised of three stories told exclusively through dance, lyrics, and music; there was no dialogue, and all the sequences were sung-through and danced-through. *Susanna and the Elders* was a version of the biblical story as depicted by a parson's sermon at a revival meeting; *Willie the Weeper* was an original story of a cocaine addict's fantasies; and *The*

Eccentricities of Davey Crockett (as told by himself) was a tall tale on the order of Paul Bunyan, John Henry, and other (fictional or otherwise) American folk heroes.

The dance revue was performed for one week at Maxine Elliott's Theatre, and then transferred to the Music Box for a total of sixty-nine performances. The run was disappointing, but perhaps potential ticket-buyers were turned off by the title, which may have sounded too arty and seemed to belong in the concert hall. And it didn't help that the revue lacked name performers and opened at the tail end of the season when the hot weather was beginning to set in.

In reviewing *Ballet Ballads*, Brooks Atkinson in the *New York Times* said he was "thoroughly delighted" with the three "spinning and singing whimsies," which were "original in theme as well as form." He noted that the original content of the stories of Susanna and Davey Crockett were essentially "literary" and "abstract," but when set to music and dance there was "something exhilarating" about them.

While the *Times'* dance critic John Martin found the material mostly "unchoreographic," he noted the bear hunt in *Davey Crockett* was a "quite delightful dance." And although *Susanna* offered "quiet humor," the stage was too "crowded" with singers; further, LaTouche's lyrics were so "clever" it was easy to concentrate on the words and overlook the "slender" dance movements. As for *Willie the Weeper*, Paul Godkin danced "valiantly," and Sono Osato was a "really low-down" Cocaine Lil whose "beauty" and "electric style" gave the piece a "radiant flash of life." LaTouche's lyric noted that Cocaine Lil lived on Cocaine Hill with her cocaine dog and her cocaine cat and the cocaine rats. Moross's score for *Willie* was a "beautiful job" of blues and boogie-woogie, and Martin suggested the sequence would work well as a choral number sans dance.

Richard Watts in the *New York Post* found the evening a "happy" blend of the "gayest features of ballet, music, and folk drama," and said nothing during the season matched it in terms of "imagination, creative freshness, and theatrical intelligence." In his seasonal summary, George Jean Nathan said *Ballet Ballads* was "novel, witty, and engrossing." He noted that Moross's score offered an "uncommon range and ability" and LaTouche's lyrics had "humor, wit, delicacy" and the necessary "dramatic force." As a result, the evening was a "successful adventure in a synthesis of several of the theatrical arts." In his accompanying seasonal "Honor List," Nathan named Paul Godkin as the season's Best Choreographer for *Willie the Weeper*.

Robert Sylvester in the *New York Daily News* said *Ballet Ballads* was the best musical of the Broadway season, and *Willie the Weeper* was one of the season's "most exciting pieces of theatre." As for Sono Osato, he maintained she could do more "real" dancing "with her hands than most dancers could with their feet." Robert Garland in the *New York Journal-American* found the evening "fresh and exciting" and "as American as a hot dog spiked with mustard"; he noted that the Ballet Theatre wasted one's time with *Fall River Legend* "and other over-de-Mille-to-the-storehouse-ballets" and the Experimental Theatre enriched one's time with *Ballet Ballads*.

The entire *Willie the Weeper* sequence was recorded by Naxos (CD # 8-559086) in the collection *Moross: Frankie and Johnny*; the album identified *Willie* as a "dance cantata," and the thirty-five-minute sequence provided the titles of "Introduction," "Rich Willie," "Lonely Willie," "Famous Willie," "Baffled Willie," "Big Willie," "Contented Willie," and "Sexy Willie." The Moross collection *Windflowers* (PS Classics CD # 0307-01022) includes "You're My Yaller Flower" and "Ridin' on the Breeze" from *Davey Crockett* and "I've Got Me" and "Oh Baby and Gee Baby" from *Willie*. The collection also offers "Come Live with Me," which isn't on the Naxos recording or in the published script but is attributed to *Ballet Ballads*.

The 2000 Off-Broadway tribute *Taking a Chance on Love: The Lyrics & Life of John LaTouche* included four songs from *Davey Crockett* ("Opening," "You're My Yaller Flower," "Ridin' on the Breeze," and "Finale") and two from *Willie* ("Oh Baby and Gee Baby" and "I'm Mister Nobody"); these songs are included in the revue's cast album, which was released by Original Cast Records (CD # OC-4444).

The script of *Ballet Ballads* was published in softcover by Chappell & Co. in 1949; all three sequences were published separately as well as together in one volume (the lyrics, stage directions, and piano score are included).

A revival of *Ballet Ballads* was presented Off Broadway on January 3, 1961, for forty performances at the East 74th Street Theatre. In his review in the *New York Times*, Howard Taubman said he hoped the "curiosity of venturesome theatergoers" would give the musical a "new lease on life." Unfortunately, the revival was gone in five weeks and except for the occasional recordings cited above the work seems to be ignored by dance companies.

The revival retained *Davey* (now *Davy*) *Crockett* (with new choreography by Glen Tetley; the title role was performed by Jack Mette) and *Willie* (new choreography by John Butler; Glen Tetley was Willie and Carmen de Lavallade was Cocaine Lil). *Susanna* was replaced by *Riding Hood Revisited* (choreography by Mavis Ray), a sequence that had been intended for the 1948 production as *Red Riding Hood* but hadn't been completed in time for the premiere. It may be that *Susanna* wasn't retained because Carlisle Floyd's 1956 opera *Susannah* was also based on the biblical story and had achieved popularity in New York and other cities.

In 1954, LaTouche and Moross wrote the sung-through *The Golden Apple*, a masterpiece of the American musical theatre that combined music (in the style of American turn-of-the-twentieth-century songs) and rhymed couplets to tell a home-grown version of the Trojan War set during the time of the Spanish-American War. In 1963, the New York City Opera Company presented Moross's *Gentlemen, Be Seated!*, which used the framework of the traditional minstrel show to tell the story of the Civil War (the lyrics were by Edward Eager, and the book by Moross and Eager).

ALLEY MOON
"A New Musical"

Theatre and *Performance Dates*: The musical was presented at the University Theater, Catholic University, Washington, D.C., during the period May 2–15, 1948, for fourteen performances.
Book and *Lyrics*: Walter Kerr
Music: Stephan Allers
Direction: Walter Kerr; *Producer*: The Catholic University of America (Speech and Drama Department, The Reverend G. V. Hartke, O.P., Head); *Choreography*: Evelyn Davis; *Scenery* and *Costumes*: Don Gilman; *Lighting*: James Waring; *Musical Direction*: Musical arrangements for two pianos by Bernard Mikolitsky; *Choral Direction*: Nick Wandmacher
Cast: Meredith Schoonover (Keys), Louis Camuti (Owl), Robert Moore (Buddy), James M. Langan (Ace), Jack Carr (Slap), Alice McGrattan (Kid), John Walsh (Weasel), Nadya Grushetzky (Ma), Anne Chodoff (Marjorie), Tony Donadio (Punchy), Dan Rodden (Bert Burns), Rickey Rudell (Carol), Arthur Conescu (Cop), Nick Wandmacher (Tim Harris), J. Robert Dietz (Skippy), Irene Eckmann (Mrs. Galloway), Anthony Brink (Henry), Joe Mayer (Hotel Proprietor), Arch Lustberg (Soft Drink Man); Singers: George Beebe, James Buckley, Frank Dolan, Janice Driscoll, Mary Ellen Fitzgerald, Joe Garvey, Margery Hunter, Robert Kirby, Edward Kozumplik, Jill Leahy, Joseph Lewis, John Mahoney, Ionia Manley, Joan Mohler, Hugh Palmerston, Byron Rash, Ronnie Simpson, Naomi Vincent, Joan Walsh, Herman Weiss; Dancers: Anthony Brink, Janice Driscoll, Jacqueline Egan, Mary Ellen Fitzgerald, Joe Garvey, Lucille Hake, Jean Heller, Margery Hunter, Robert Kirby, George La Buda, Joseph Lewis, Ionla Manley, Russell McBride, Betty Moeslein, Bob O'Connor, Maureen O'Malley, David Pritchard, Byron Rash, Beverly Shaffer, Naomi Vincent, Joan Walsh
The musical was presented in two acts.
The action takes place in locations throughout a city, including a street, an all-night parlor, a greenhouse, a reform school, a hotel, and a marriage license bureau.

Musical Numbers

Act One: "Keys to the Street" (Meredith Schoonover, Robert Moore, James M. Langan, Louis Camuti, Jack Carr); "Alley Moon" (Nadya Grushetzky); "Reefer" (Dancers); "A Man's Time" (Anne Chodoff); "Goin' Places" (Meredith Schoonover); "All Night" (Tony Donadio); "Dames" (Dan Rodden); "You Know" (Meredith Schoonover, Anne Chodoff); "While We Work" (Louis Camuti, Jack Carr, James M. Langan); "What Do You Do in the Morning" (Alice McGrattan, Meredith Schoonover, Chorus); "Someday" (Alice McGrattan); "Dance of the Dandelions" (Rickey Rudell, Boys); "It's a Lousy World" (Meredith Schoonover, Robert Moore, James M. Langan, Louis Camuti, Jack Carr); "All Night" (reprise) (Tony Donadio, Chorus)
Act Two: "State Reform" (Meredith Schoonover, Robert Moore, James M. Langan, Louis Camuti, Jack Carr); "Buggy with the Boogie" (Rickey Rudell); "A Man's Time" (reprise) (Chorus); "Today" (Rickey Rudell, Company, Tony Donadio); "Pursuit" (Robert Moore, Dancers); "Stranger" (Meredith Schoonover); "Lament" (Nadya Grushetsky); "Shy Guy" (Chorus); "This Is the Way the Day Ends" (Chorus)

Before he became one of Broadway's premier theatre critics, Walter Kerr was a professor of speech and drama at Catholic University in Washington, D.C., during the 1940s. He was associated with four productions at Catholic University that were later presented on Broadway: the book musical **Count Me In** (1942; coauthor); the semi-revue **Sing Out, Sweet Land!** (1944; author); the drama *The Song of Bernadette* (1946; director and coauthor); and the revue **Touch and Go** (1949; director and coauthor of sketches and lyrics).

A fifth production, *Alley Moon*, for which Kerr wrote the book and lyrics and also directed, was produced at Catholic University in 1948 but was never seen in New York. The musical is included in this volume since it fills in the gap of Kerr's playwriting years at Catholic University.

Note that future Broadway and Off-Broadway director Robert Moore is included in the cast of *Alley Moon*. He directed dramas, comedies, mysteries, and musicals, including the original productions of *The Boys in the Band* (1968; 1,000 performances), *Promises, Promises* (1968; 1,281), *The Last of the Red Hot Lovers* (1969; 706), *The Gingerbread Lady* (1970; 193), *Lorelei* (1974; 320), *Deathtrap* (1978; 1,793), *They're Playing Our Song* (1979; 1,082), and *Woman of the Year* (1981; 770).

BONANZA BOUND!
"A NEW MUSICAL COMEDY"

Theatre and *Performance Dates*: The musical opened on December 26, 1947, at the Shubert Theatre, Philadelphia, Pennsylvania, and permanently closed there on January 3, 1948.
Book and *Lyrics*: Betty Comden and Adolph Green
Music: Saul Chaplin
Direction: Charles Friedman; *Producers*: Herman Levin, Paul Feigay, and Oliver Smith; *Choreography*: Jack Cole; *Scenery*: Oliver Smith; *Costumes*: Irene Sharaff; *Lighting*: Peggy Clark; *Musical Direction*: Lehman Engel
Cast: Sidney Melton (Chokkilok), Tina Prescott (Chokkilok's Wife), Ted Thurston (First Prospector), George Coulouris (Waldo Cruikshank), Ben Miller (Hunk), Robert Penn (Larsen), Hal Hackett (Peter Fleet), John Mooney (Second Prospector), Johnny Silver (Third Prospector), Vici Raaf (Clarabelle), Adolph Green (Leonardo [Leonard] Da Vinci), Betty Lou Barto (Toodles Da Vinci), Carol Raye (Belinda Da Vinci), Allyn (Ann) McLerie (Eustasia), Zamah Cunningham (Mrs. Cornelia Van Rensselaer), Sydney Arnold (Digby), Sven Holst (Croupier), Ken Foley (Croupier); Singers: Jeanne Anderson, Mary Alice Barker, Mardi Bayne, Abbe Marshall, Shirley Neuman, Tina Prescott, Helen Stanton, Bette Van, Neil Chirico, Ken Foley, Herbert Greene, Jim Hawthorne, Sven Holst, John Mooney, Ray Morrisey, Johnny Silver, Ted Thurston, Phil Waters; Dancers: Eleanor Fairchild, Louise Ferrand, Pat Horne, Maura Lynn, Marian McPherson, Iona McKenzie, Barbara McCutcheon, Rosa Rolland, Janith Robinson, Mary Statz, Aura Vainio, Gwenn Verdun (Gwen Verdon), Lee Ballard, Robert Evans, Hugh Ellsworth, Paul Godkin, Wayne Lamb, Remi Martel, Tony Matthews, Richard Reed, John Ward
The musical was presented in two acts.
The action takes place in Alaska during 1898.

Musical Numbers

Act One: "Little Fish" (Sidney Melton); "The Vein of Gold" (George Coulouris, Hal Hackett, Ensemble); "No Mind of Your Own" (Carol Raye, Adolph Green, Betty Lou Barto); "Dance in the Snow" (Allyn McLerie; First Girl in Green: Gwenn Verdun; Second Girl in Green: Pat Horne; Third Girl in Green: Maura Lynn; Three Prospectors: Remi Martel, Robert Evans, Hugh Ellsworth); "Tell Me Why" (Hal Hackett, Carol Raye); "Fill 'Er Up" (sung and danced by Entire Ensemble); "The Versatile Da Vinci's" (sung and danced by Carol Raye, Adolph Green, Betty Lou Barto); "Tell Me Why?" (reprise) (Carol Raye); "Misunderstood" (George Coulouris); "Up in Smoke" (Hal Hackett, Carol Raye); "Gambling Dance" (Gwenn Verdun); "Bonanza" (Carol Raye, Ensemble); "Bonanza Bound" (First Siren: Maura Lynn; Second Siren: Pat Horne; Third Siren: Mary Statz); "Wind" (Gwenn Verdun, Marian McPherson, Entire Company)
Act Two: "Totem Dance" (White Foxes: Richard Reed, Wayne Lamb; Sea Lion: Paul Godkin; "Cruikshank March" (Singing Ensemble); "Somewhere in the Snow" (Carol Raye, Betty Lou Barto); "True" (Hal Hack-

ett, Carol Raye); "Spring" (Sidney Melton, Carol Raye, Hal Hackett, Allyn McLerie, Adolph Green, Betty Lou Barto); "This Was Meant to Be" (George Coulouris); "Waltz" (danced by Carol Raye, Paul Godkin, Richard Reed); "It Was Meant to Be" (reprise) (Zamah Cunningham); "Inspiration" (Adolph Green, Allyn McLerie); "True" (reprise) (Carol Raye, Hal Hackett, Allyn McLerie, Adolph Green, Zamah Cunningham, Sydney Arnold, Betty Lou Barto)

Bonanza Bound! collapsed after one week of tryout performances in Philadelphia. *Variety* said it would be "hard to figure how this one can ever be whipped into shape for any real degree of success" and Edwin H. Schloss in the *Philadelphia Evening Bulletin* found the book "dull" and the lyrics "ailing."

The plot took place in the Alaska of 1898 and revolved around greedy Waldo Cruikshank (George Coulouris) who devises a phony gold strike in order to gull innocent prospectors. Cruikshank is attracted to dance-hall entertainer Belinda Da Vinci (Carol Ray), who loves prospector Peter Fleet (Hal Hackett), and others in the story included Belinda's brother Leonardo (Adolph Green) and sister Toodles (Betty Lou Barto), and Cruikshank's daughter Eustasia (Allyn Ann McLerie), who loves Leonardo. When Belinda, Peter, Leonardo, Toodles, and Eustasia take refuge in a cave in order to escape from Cruikshank, the villain throws a bomb inside their cave (nice guy, he even tries to murder his own daughter). But Peter tosses the bomb outside the cave, where it explodes and reveals a literal mountain of gold.

The musical clearly meant to be lighthearted, but perhaps the villain was too villainous. Maybe the book would have been more successful had it been written in the style of a Gay Nineties' melodrama and Cruikshank had been Eustasia's cousin or uncle instead of her father.

The musical's program included a full-page ad by RCA Victor touting the cast albums of **Allegro**, **High Button Shoes**, **Brigadoon**, **Finian's Rainbow**, and *Bonanza Bound!* Yes, "all the hit music" from the latter would "soon appear in a great new album. Ask your dealer to let you know when it's ready!" As the years passed, many would-be cast albums received full-page program ads for recordings that were never made due to short Broadway runs or out-of-town closings (*The Conquering Hero*, *Nowhere to Go but Up*, and *Hot September*, for example).

But perhaps in anticipation of the impending ASCAP musicians' strike, *Bonanza Bound!* was actually recorded by RCA on December 28, 1947, two days after the Philadelphia opening. Of course, the company never released the album, and when RCA rereleased a batch of their earlier cast albums in 1965, musical theatre and film historian Miles Kreuger wrote that the "bright, vivacious" score was a deserving candidate for release. He noted "it could be the most talked-about show album of the season, a kind of reclaimed treasure." Unfortunately, RCA never issued the recording, but in 1976 Box Office/JJA Records issued the album (LP # JJA-19764A/B) of eight songs (along with material recorded by The Revuers between 1938–1944; The Revuers were of course the nightclub team comprised of Betty Comden, Adolph Green, Judith Tuvum [Judy Holliday], John Frank, and Alvin Hammer). The collection *Lost Broadway and More: Volume Two* (Original Cast Records CD # OC-6830) includes "I Know It's True"; *Lost Broadway and More: Volume 5* (unnamed company and unnumbered CD) includes "Misunderstood"; and both collections offer different recordings of "Fill 'Er Up."

In Comden and Green's retrospective revue *A Party with Betty Comden and Adolph Green* (John Golden Theatre; December 23, 1958; eighty-two performances; revived and slightly revised at the Morosco Theatre on February 10, 1977, for ninety-two performances), the team performed the song "Inspiration" from *Bonanza Bound!* (the musical wasn't listed by name, but as "A Show"). "Inspiration" was recorded for two cast albums of *A Party*: both the original (released by Capitol Records LP # SWAO-1197) and a 1977 production seen at Arena Stage in Washington, D.C., which was recorded there live (a two-LP set by Stet Records # S2L-5177).

Although co-librettist and co-lyricist Betty Comden didn't appear in *Bonanza Bound!*, Adolph Green did, along with his then wife Allyn Ann McLerie, who later created the role of Amy in **Where's Charley?** and the title role in **Miss Liberty**; and Betty Lou Barto was Nancy Walker's sister.

Bonanza Bound! is also notable as the first professional theater appearance by Gwen Verdon; it appears to be her likeness on the show's artwork logo as the dance-hall girl being carried on the back of a burly gold miner. She was then known as Gwenn Verdun; in her early years, she was associated with choreographer Jack Cole (who devised the dances for *Bonanza Bound!*) and after the current musical she appeared in various stage and film productions that he choreographed. Her breakthrough role was in *Can-Can* (1953), which was choreographed by Michael Kidd, and then of course in 1955 she joined professional forces with Bob Fosse (whom she later married) and together they created one of musical theatre's most legendary partnerships in a series of musicals in which she starred and he choreographed (and most often directed): *Damn Yankees* (1955), *New Girl in Town* (1957), *Redhead* (1959), *Sweet Charity* (1966), and *Chicago* (1975).

As for gold-rush musicals, they seem to be under one of those musical comedy curses. *Bonanza Bound!* closed during its tryout, and while Alan Jay Lerner and Frederick Loewe's *Paint Your Wagon* (1951) ran out the season and offered one of the era's finest scores, it lost money. The 1964 *Foxy* (based on *Volpone* by Ben Jonson) floundered after seventy-two performances despite a delightful score by Johnny Mercer and Robert Emmet Dolan and a Tony Award for Best Leading Actor in a Musical for Bert Lahr. There was also the gold-rush-musical-on-ice **Alaskan Stampede**, which played in Chicago during the 1944–1945 season (*Chicago Tribune* critic Clauda Cassidy called it a "cold storage turkey"). However, gold-rush musicals on film seem to have fared somewhat better: *Belle of the Yukon* (1945) offered a Johnny Burke-Jimmy Van Heusen score that included the lovely ballads "Like Someone in Love" and "Sleigh Ride in July"; and the Bob Hope and Bing Crosby "road" movie *Road to Utopia* (1946) included Burke and Van Heusen's saucy "Personality" for Dorothy Lamour and the "insult" duet "Put It There, Pal" for the boys; the latter was kissing cousin to Cole Porter's "Friendship" from *DuBarry Was a Lady* (1939) and Richard Rodgers and Lorenz Hart's "Ev'rything I've Got" from **By Jupiter**.

LAFFACADE

Theatre and *Performance Dates*: The revue seems to have played for just one week in September 1947 at the Oriental Theatre, Chicago, Illinois, before permanently closing there.

Cast: Ole Olsen and Chic Johnson, The Roxyettes, J. C. Olsen and Jane Johnson, The Salici Puppets, Michael Edwards, Shorty Renna, Patricia Basso, Don Tompkins [*sic*] (Tomkins), Marvel, Shannon Dean, The Pitchmen, Eddie Franklin, Billy Young, Charles Senna, Al Cook, Leonard Sues and His Orchestra

The glory days for the comedy shtick of Ole Olsen and Chic Johnson were fast receding. *Hellzapoppin'* (1938; 1,404 performances) and **Sons o' Fun** (1941; 742 performances) had been long-running hits, and **Laffing Room Only** (1944; 233 performances) managed to play out the season. But *Laffacade* never made it to New York, and **Funzapoppin** lasted for one month at Madison Square Garden in 1949 (37 performances). In 1950, *Pardon Our French* played for three months on Broadway, for a total of one hundred performances; from there, the duo and some of their cronies were on a Palace bill in 1952 for four weeks, and their revue *Pardon Our Antenna* collapsed on the road in 1954.

PARIS SINGS AGAIN

Theatre and *Performance Dates*: The revue opened on December 25, 1947, at the Majestic Theatre, Boston, Massachusetts, and permanently closed there on January 3, 1948.

Direction: Jo Bouillon; *Producer*: Aaron H. Payne; *Musical Direction*: Irving Klase

Cast: *Josephine Baker*, Hurtado de Cordoba, Roland Gerbeau, Jo Bouillon and His Internationally Famous Orchestra

The revue was presented in two acts (division of acts unknown).

Musical Numbers

Numbers Sung by Josephine Baker: "Vereda Tropical" (lyric and music by Carlo Curiel); "Mama"; "Parlez moi d'amour" (lyric and music by Jean Lenoir); "Dans moi village" (lyric and music by Francis Lopez); Potpourri of Songs from 1900; "Mon triste coeur" (lyric and music by Jo Bouillon and Pierre Guillermin); "Hortensia" (lyric and music by Louiguy); "Zoubida" (lyric and music by J. Tranchant); "J'ai deux amours" (lyric and music by Vincent Scotto)

Numbers Sung by Roland Gerbeau: "La mer" (lyric and music by Charles Trenet); "Maitre Pathelin"

Numbers Danced by Hurtado de Cordoba: "Cordoba" (music by Isaac Albenitz); "Farruca" (music by Manuel de Falla)

Numbers Played by Jo Bouillon and His Internationally Famous Orchestra: Potpourri of French Songs; "Humoresque" (music by Antonin Dvorak); "Three Waltzes—España"; "Sous les ponts de Paris"; "Le beau Danube bleu" (music by Richard Strauss); "L'abeille" (music by Franz Schubert); Introduction for Miss Baker; "Vous qui passez sans me voir" (music by Misraki); "Varsovie" Concerto (music by d'Addincel); "Trois jeunes tambours"; "Noce Bretonne" (music by Jean Vuillaume)

Josephine Baker (1906–1975) hadn't been seen on Broadway since the 1936 *Ziegfeld Follies*, and her current Broadway-bound vehicle never made it beyond one week in Boston. But she was later seen on Broadway in her revue *Josephine Baker and Her Company*, which opened in 1964 for two slightly separate engagements that totaled forty performances, and in 1973 made her final New York appearance in *An Evening with Josephine Baker*.

Born in Missouri, Baker was first seen on Broadway in *Chocolate Dandies* in 1924; she later relocated to Paris where she became a superstar, a French citizen, and the toast of the continent. Irving Berlin's 1933 revue *As Thousands Cheer* paid homage to her in the sequence "Josephine Baker Still the Rage of Paris" in which Ethel Waters portrayed the wealthy international headliner who confesses that for all her fame she still has "Harlem on My Mind."

Christmas week of December 1947 was not a good one for pre-Broadway tryouts. *Paris Sings Again* opened in Boston on Christmas Day and permanently closed on January 3. Similarly, **Bonanza Bound!** opened in Philadelphia on December 26, and it too was gone on January 3. In reviewing *Paris Sings Again*, *Variety* said it was a "creaking vehicle" that would "never do as it stands." In *Broadway Bound*, William Torbert Leonard reports that Jo Bouillon's "Internationally Famous Orchestra" was in fact a group of union musicians who were Boston and New York City locals. Incidentally, at the time of the production, Bouillon was Josephine Baker's husband.

The biographical film *The Josephine Baker Story* was shown on Home Box Office in 1991 (Lynn Whitfield played the title role). And there have been at least five musicals written about Baker's life and career, four of them produced: *Josephine* was seen in a showcase production in London in the 1980s at the Fortune Theatre with Heather Gillespie in the title role and a score by Michael Wild; *Looking for Josephine* was produced in U.S. regional theatre; Wally Harper and Sherman Yellen's *Josephine Tonight* (which focused on her early years) was also seen in regional theatre; and *The Sensational Josephine Baker*, written and performed by Cheryl Howard, opened Off-Broadway at the Beckett Theatre on June 26, 2012, for a scheduled run of twelve weeks. The one as-yet-unproduced musical is untitled but was once mentioned for a New York production. The London *Josephine* was recorded, and the *Washington Post* praised the score for *Josephine Tonight* ("the ragtime-and-blues inspired songs often sparkle with wit, melodiousness and infectious rhythm").

THE SHAPE OF THINGS!
"A NEW MUSICAL REVUE"

Theatre and *Performance Dates*: The revue played in summer stock venues during Summer 1947, including the week of July 28 at the John Drew Theatre in East Hampton, Long Island, New York.
Lyrics: James Shelton; additional lyrics by Carly Mills, Ted Fetter, David Gregory (sometimes cited as David Greggory), Arnold B. Horwitt, Peter Barry, and Eddie De Lange
Music: James Shelton; additional music by Richard Lewine, Carly Mills, and Clay Boland
Sketches: James Sheldon, George Hall, Leslie Stevens, Irving Wexler, and Sally Humason
Direction: Lew Kesler; *Producer*: Francis I. Curtis; *Choreography*: William (Billy) Skipper; *Scenery*: Frederick Stover; *Costumes*: Uncredited; *Lighting*: Uncredited; *Musical Direction*: Bud Gregg and Randy Kraft, Pianists
Cast: George Hall, William (Billy and Bill) Skipper, Joan Mann, Elaine Stritch, Eleanor Bagley, Ray Long, Neetza Arden, Tommy Morton, Larry Baker, Marie Foster, Jimmy Carr, Tommy Randall, Bibi Osterwald, Lois Bolton, Elna Anderson, Harry Fleer, Mavis Mims, Betty Lou Barto, Helen Ferguson, Andrea Mann, Ray Arnett, Pat Horn, Margie Gaye, Arthur Devlin, Frederick Ross
The revue was presented in two acts.

Sketches and Musical Numbers

Act One: "Curtain Time" (sketch by James Shelton) (He: George Hall; She: Lois Bolton); "Opening Number" (lyric and music by James Shelton) (Show Girls: Neetza Arden, Andrea Mann, Eleanor Bagley, Elaine Stritch; Dancing Girls: Margie Gaye, Pat Horn, Marie Foster; Dancing Boys: Ray Arnett, Tommy Randall; Chef: Harry Fleer; Tycoon: Tommy Morton); "How to Write a Play" (sketch writer uncredited) (The Playwright: John Barker; He: George Hall; She: Elaine Stritch); "Gertrude, You and Me" (lyric and music by Carly Mills) (Sailor: William Skipper; The Girl: Joan Mann); "The Harem" (lyric and music by James Sheldon) (Mamie: Bibi Osterwald; The House Boy: Ray Long; Ladies of the Harem: Elna Anderson, Neetza Arden, Andrea Mann, Eleanor Bagley; Dancing Girls: Marie Foster, Margie Gaye, Pat Horn; Dancing Boys: Tommy Randall, Ray Arnett, Tommy Morton); "Men of Distinction" (sketch by Leslie Stevens and Irving Wexler) (Calvert: George Hall; Lady Seagram: Elaine Stritch; Russell: Larry Baker; Carstairs: Frederick Ross; Schenley: Art Devlin); "Once" (lyric and music by James Sheldon) (The Boy: Harry Fleer; The Girl: Elna Anderson; Dancers: William Skipper and Joan Mann); "Mama at the Bar" (lyric and music by James Shelton) (Betty Lou Barto); "Street Noises" (lyric by David Gregory, Arnold B. Horwitt, and Peter Barry, music by Richard Lewine) (Street Cleaner: George Hall; Doorman: Harry Fleer; Musician: Larry Baker); "Heaven Scent" (sketch by Leslie Stevens and Irving Wexler) (Helena: Bibi Osterwald; Mrs. Delilac: Lois Bolton; Miss Yardley: Andrea Mann); "That's Love" (lyric and music by James Shelton) (Organ Grinder: Larry Baker: Organ Grinder's Assistant: Jimmie Carr; Singer: Eleanor Bagley; Cupid: Betty Lou Barto; Dancers: Pat Horn, Marie Foster, Marjorie Gaye, Tommy Randall, Tommy Morton, Ray Arnett; Sailor: Ray Long; Sailor's Girl Friend: Neetza Arden; Specialty Dance: Mavis Mims); "This Is Heaven" (lyric and music by James Sheldon) (Helen Ferguson); "Come Home and Get Cozy with Me" (lyric and music by Carly Mills) (He: George Hall; She: Lois Bolton; Kitty's Room-Mate: Bibi Osterwald; Lovers: William Skipper and Joan Mann; Life Guard: Ray Long; Carrie: Mavis Mims; Mary: Elna Anderson; Bill: Harry Fleer; The Vacationeers: Neetza Arden, Andrea Mann, Eleanor Bagley, Elaine Stritch, Betty Lou Barto, Margie Gaye, Pat Horn, Marie Foster, Ray Arnett, Tommy Randall, Tommy Morton)

Act Two: "As We Told You" (lyric and music by James Sheldon) (Show Girls: Eleanor Bagley, Andrea Mann, Neetza Arden, Elaine Stritch; Dancing Boys and Girls: Margie Gaye, Marie Foster, Pat Horn, Ray Arnett, Tommy Randall; Chef: Harry Fleer; Tycoon: Tommy Morton); "Lydia" (sketch writer uncredited) (Lecturer: George Hall); "I'm the Girl" (lyric and music by James Sheldon) (Elna Anderson); "Coronet" (sketch by George Hall) (He: George Hall; She: Bibi Osterwald); "Susie's Back in Town" (lyric and music by James Sheldon) (Susie: Elaine Stritch; First Cowboy: Harry Fleer; Second Cowboy: Ray Long; Dancers: Marie Foster, Pat Horn, Margie Gaye, Ray Arnett, Tommy Morton, Tommy Randall; Bartender: Larry Baker; Visitors: Neetza Arden, Eleanor Bagley, Andrea Mann); "Mama, What's Love?" (lyric by Eddie De Lange, music by Clay Boland) (Betty Lou Barto and Jimmie Carr); "Good Morning" (sketch writer uncredited) (Mrs.: Lois Bolton; Mr.: George Hall); "Is It You or the Cocktail?" (lyric and music by James Sheldon) (Harry Fleer and Elna Anderson; The Cocktail: Eleanor Bagley; The Lobster: Elaine Stritch; The Salad: Andrea Mann; The Dessert: Neetza Arden: Head Waiter: Ray Long; Waiter: Larry Baker; Cigarette Girl: Joan Mann; Page Boy: William Skipper; Waitresses and Waiters: Pat Horn, Marie Foster, Margie Gaye, Tommy Morton, Ray Arnett, Tommy Randall; The Check: Mavis Mim); Specialty (Mavis Mim); "Life of the Party" (lyric by Ted Fetter, music by Richard Lewine) (Bibi Osterwald, George Hall, Larry Baker); Finale (lyric and music by James Sheldon) (Entire Company)

James Sheldon's revue *The Shape of Things!* played in summer stock venues during the summer of 1947, and included early appearances by Elaine Stritch and Bibi Osterwald. In 1950, Sheldon's revue *Dance Me a Song* opened on Broadway and included one number from *The Shape of Things!*, the lovely understated blues "I'm the Girl."

Another number from the revue, "Street Noises" (lyric by David Gregory [aka Greggory], Arnold B. Horwitt, and Peter Barry, music by Richard Lewine) never became a well-known song but nonetheless managed to float in and out of revues for a period of nineteen years. As "Noises in the Street" (with lyric credited to Peter Barry and David Gregory), the song was first heard in the 1940 summer stock revue **Two Weeks with Pay** where it was introduced by Earl Oxford, Hiram Sherman, Pat Harrington, Julian Olney Jr., and Lawrence Weber. From there, it was included in the 1940 flop revue **'Tis of Thee**, which played for one performance; and then in 1942 it was heard in preview performances of **Star and Garter**; it resurfaced in the current revue, and here Arnold B. Horwitt was included as one of the three lyricists. It was then performed in the successful 1948 revue **Make Mine Manhattan**, where it was sung as a quintet that included Sid Caesar, David Burns, and Max Showalter. In the 1956 *Ziegfeld Follies*, which closed prior to its Broadway opening, Horwitt and Levine contributed a song titled "Noises in the Theatre," which was later heard during the tryout of the team's short-lived 1959 revue *The Girls Against the Boys*. "Noises in the Street" was recorded for the collection *Make Mine Manhattan and Other Great Revues Revisited* (Painted Smiles CD # PSCD-119).

SPIKE JONES AND HIS MUSICAL DEPRECIATION REVUE

Theatres and *Performance Dates*: The revue played at various theatres during the 1947–1948 season, including ten weeks at the Studebaker Theatre, Chicago, Illinois, and for a week and a half at the National Theatre, Washington, D.C., beginning on March 14, 1948.
Direction: Spike Jones; *Producer*: Spike Jones (An Arena Stars Production); *Scenery*: Phil Raiguel (special cartoon curtain designed by Milt Gross); *Costumes*: Jack's of Hollywood, Max Koltz, and Ethel Mattison; *Lighting*: Carlton Winckler; *Musical Direction*: Overture conducted by Edward Pripps
Cast: *Spike Jones*, The City Slickers, The Slickerettes, Frank Little, Doodles Weaver, Dr. Horatio Q. Birdbath, Bettyjo Huston, Freddie Morgan, George Rock, Sir Frederick Ham, Dick Morgan, Bill King, Robert Perry, Renee Paul, Helen Grayco, Dick Gardner, Ina Souez
The revue was presented in two acts.

Sketches and Musical Numbers

Act One: Overture (Orchestra); Introduction: "Der Feuhrer's Face" (lyric and music by Oliver Wallace) (The City Slickers); "Greetings" (The Slickerettes); "Hot-Cha Cornya" (The City Slickers, with Frank Little on the rope); "Chloe" (The City Slickers, featuring Doodles Weaver); "Barnyard Roundup" (Dr. Horatio Q. Birdbath); "Some New Twists in Dancing" (Bettyjo Huston); "You Always Hurt the One You Love" (lyric by Allan Roberts, music by Doris Fisher) (The City Slickers, featuring Freddie Morgan and Doodles Weaver); "Minka" (George Rock); "That Old Black Magic" (1942 film *Star-Spangled Rhythm*; lyric by Johnny Mercer, music by Harold Arlen) (The City Slickers, and "one or two Hams"); "A One-Act Play" (Sir Frederick Gas); "Holiday for Strings" (The City Slickers, featuring Dick Morgan, Dr. Birdbath, and Bill King); "Our Distinguished Visitor" (Freddie Morgan); "Take Me Out to the Ballgame" (lyric by Jack Norworth, music by Albert Von Tilzer; special lyric by Edward Brandt) (The Benchwarmers, and Doodles Weaver); "The Ups and Downs" (Robert Perry, Renee Paul); "I'm Forever Blowing Bubble Gum" ("Master" George Rock); "Liebestraum" (The City Slickers, featuring Dick Morgan with Bill King; and Doodles Weaver in the box)
Act Two: "Laura" (heard as instrumental background music in the 1944 film *Laura*; music by David Raksin; lyric written by Johnny Mercer in 1945) (The City Slickers); "Catch as Catch Can" (Bill King); "Flashbulb Freddie" (sketch by Freddie Morgan; lyric and music by Edward Brandt) (Freddie Morgan); "The Sheik of Araby" (lyric by Harry B. Smith and Francis Wheeler, music by Ted Snyder) (The City Slickers, featuring Dick Morgan and Dr. Birdbath); "Ca Ca Carumba" (lyric and music by Rene Tuzete and Edward Brandt) (Helen Grayco); "Nonce and Stuff Sense" (Doodles Weaver); "Czardas" (Dick Gardner, The Lease Breakers); "Hawaiian War Chant" (original lyric and music by Prince Leleiohoku; English lyric by Ralph Freed, new musical adaptation by Johnny Noble) (The City Slickers, featuring Doodles Weaver and The Slickerettes); "Glow Worm" (1902 musical *Lysistrata*; lyric by Heinz Bolten-Backers, music by Paul Lincke; English lyric by Lilla Cayley Robinson; and later new English lyric by Johnny Mercer) (Ina Souez and Dick Morgan, assisted by The City Slickers); "Ah! Sweet Mystery of Life" (1910 operetta *Naughty Marietta*; lyric by Rida Johnson Young, music by Victor Herbert) (Sir Frederick Gas); "Cocktails for Two" (1934 film *Murder at the Vanities*; lyric by Arthur Johnston, music by Sam Coslow) (Entire Company)

Spike Jones and his band The City Slickers made a career of spoofing popular songs with strange vocal sounds, the use of intrusive horns and various rude noises, and, in general, cutting up whenever possible and taking nothing seriously. In the early war years, they recorded the song "Der Feuhrer's Face," which became a popular hit and was included in the current revue.

1948–1949 Season

SLEEPY HOLLOW
"AN ENCHANTING NEW MUSICAL" / "A MUSICAL PLAY"

Theatre: St. James Theatre
Opening Date: June 3, 1948; *Closing Date*: June 12, 1948
Performances: 12
Book and *Lyrics*: Russell Maloney and Miriam Battista; additional lyrics by Ruth Hughes Aarons
Music: George Lessner
(A note in the program indicated the production was "suggested" by Nicholas Bela; another note stated "The management gratefully acknowledges the assistance of Marc Connelly." *Best Plays* noted that the book and lyrics were by "the late Russell Maloney and Miriam Battista [Mrs. Maloney]").
Based on the 1820 story *The Legend of Sleepy Hollow* by Washington Irving.
Direction: John O'Shaughnessy; *Producer*: Lorraine Lester; *Choreography*: Anna Sokolow; *Scenery* and *Lighting*: Jo Mielziner; *Costumes*: David Ffolkes; *Musical Direction*: Irving Actman
Cast: William Ferguson (Ike), Larry Robbins (Roelf), Laura Pierpont (Mrs. Van Brunt), Ruth McDevitt (Mrs. Van Tassel), Jean Handzlik (Mrs. Van Ripper), Ellen Repp (Wilhelmina), Bert Wilcox (Mr. Van Brunt), Tom Hoier (Mr. Van Tassel), Morley Evans (Mr. Van Ripper), Bobby White (Jacob Van Tassel), Walter Butterworth (Willie Van Twiller), Alan Shay (Hans Van Ripper), Richard Rhoades (Martin Van Horsen), Lewis Scholle (Stuyveling Van Doorn), Doreen Lane (Teena), Robin Lane (Hilda), Sylvia Lane (Greta), Hayes Gordon (Brom "Bones" Van Brunt), Betty Jane Watson (Katrina Van Tassel), Ward Garner (Henrick), Mary McCarty (Eva), Russell George (Luther), Gil Lamb (Ichabod Crane), Margery Oldroyd (Annie), Peggy Ferris (Lena), Franklin Wagner (Nick), Shaun O'Brien (Piet), Ray Drakeley (Balt), James Starbuck (Walt), John Ward (Chris), Margaret Ritter (Bertha), Jo Sullivan (Margaret), Kaja Sumdsten (Elizabeth), Ann Dunbar (Jenny), Ken Foley (Mr. Van Hooten), John Russel (Joost), Ty Kearney (Conscience), Kenneth Remo (Indian), William Mende (Cotton Mather), Dorothy Bird (The Lady from New Haven); Dancers: Aza Bard, Clara Courdery, Ann Dunbar, Kate Friedlich, Saida Gerrard, Carmella Guiterrez, Margaret McCallion, Kaja Sumdsten, Alex Dunaeff, Don Farnworth, Jay Lloyd, Remi Martel, Joseph Milan, Shaun O'Brien, Franklin Wagner, John Ward; Singers: Ilona Albok, Joan Barrett, Peggy Ferris, Deda La Petina, Margery Oldroyd, Margaret Ritter, Janice Sprei, Jo Sullivan, Ray Drakeley, William Ferguson, Ken Foley, Russell George, Vincent Lubrano, William Mende, Larry Robbins, John Russel; Children: Walter Butterworth, Doreen Lane, Sylvia Lane, Richard Rhoades, Lewis Francis Scholle, Alan Shay, Robin Sloan
The musical was presented in two acts.
The action takes place during the autumn of 1795 in the village of Sleepy Hollow, up by the Tappan Zee on the east bank of the Hudson River.

Musical Numbers

Act One: "Time Stands Still" (Villagers); "I Still Have a Lot to Learn" (Hayes Gordon); "Ask Me Again" (Betty Jane Watson); "I Still Have a Lot to Learn" (reprise) (Hayes Gordon, Betty Jane Watson); "Never Let Her Go" (Villagers); "There's History to Be Made" (lyric by Russell Maloney, Miriam Battista, and Ruth Hughes Aarons) (Gil Lamb); "Here and Now" (Hayes Gordon, Betty Jane Watson); Dance (Dorothy Bird, James Starbuck); "Why Was I Born on a Farm?" (lyric by Ruth Hughes Aarons) (Mary McCarty); "If" (Gil Lamb, Betty Jane Watson); "My Lucky Lover" (Betty Jane Watson, Ellen Repp, Mary McCarty, Sleepy Hollow Girls); "A Musical Lesson" (Gil Lamb); "You've Got That Kind of a Face" (lyric by Russell Maloney, Miriam Battista, and Ruth Hughes Aarons) (Ward Garner, Mary McCarty); "Couple Dance" (First Couple: Clara Courdery and Jay Lloyd; Second Couple: Aza Bard and Joseph Milan; Third Couple: Kate Friedlich and Alex Dunaeff; Girl with a Flower: Kaja Sumdsten); "I'm Lost" (lyric by Ruth Hughes Aarons) (Hayes Gordon); "Goodnight" (Villagers); "The Englishman's Head" (Ellen Repp, Hayes Gordon, Villagers)

Act Two: "Pedro, Ichabod" (Hayes Gordon, James Starbuck, Village Boys); "Poor Man" (lyric by Russell Maloney, Miriam Battista, and Ruth Hughes Aarons) (Gil Lamb); "The Things That Lovers Say" (Betty Jane Watson); "I'm Lost" (reprise) (Hayes Gordon); "Ichabod" (Ty Kearney, Kenneth Remo, William Mende); Dance (Dorothy Bird); "Bouree" (dance) (Village Dancers); "Headless Horseman Ballet" (Gil Lamb, Village Dancers); "The Gray Goose" (Bobby White, Ensemble)

Sleepy Hollow was the first production to play at the St. James Theatre following its marathon run of **Oklahoma!** But Americana didn't strike twice, and *Sleepy Hollow* was gone after twelve performances (it tied with **Heaven on Earth** as the season's shortest-running musical).

Washington Irving's story centered on the hapless but smug school master Ichabod Crane (Gil Lamb) and his overreaching social ambitions when he sets his sights on the coy and flirtatious Katrina Van Tassle (Betty Jane Watson). She's the daughter of the town's richest and who loves local town hunk Brom "Bones" Van Brunt (Hayes Gordon). The story was alternately romantic and haunting, the basic storyline offered a sturdy plot and a variety of colorful characters, and the Halloween-flavored setting was rich in mood and atmosphere. But despite good performances, colorful decor, and what appears to have been a melodic and original score, the musical quickly faltered.

Brooks Atkinson in the *New York Times* said the book and staging were lacking, but he was enthusiastic about the score and the cast. The evening was "unhackneyed" and often captured the "artless and joyous" quality of Irving's story. George Lessner's "fresh and exhilarating" score was "distinguished" in its use of a folk-music-like quality at its foundation, and the "delightful" duets for Betty Jane Watson and Hayes Gordon represented the evening's "best" melodies. Gordon was a "superb" baritone and Watson possessed a "rich" voice and was a "delightful" actress; Gil Lamb was "droll and inventive," his characterization was "fresh," and he scored with the "humorous rhythms" of "Poor Man"; and Mary McCarty was notable as a "hot-tempered hussy."

But the other critics were less than impressed. Although Richard Watts in the *New York Post* liked Anna Sokolow's choreography (the "Headless Horseman Ballet" was one of the show's liveliest moments) and felt the score was cheerful and occasionally charming, he felt the musical came across like a college show that had "unfortunately got itself entangled in the mazes of Broadway." Robert Coleman in the *New York Daily Mirror* said the production bored "the heck" out of the first-nighters who were caught in a "booby trap"; the musical was "hollow" and sleep-inducing, and while there was probably a "good folk operetta" in the material, *Sleepy Hollow* wasn't it.

William Hawkins in the *New York World-Telegram* found the score "pleasant" if "undistinguished," liked the "Couple Dance" (which "stopped the show"), and said Mary McCarty made a "distinctly favorable impression." Otherwise, the musical had "the air of having been written and restaged yesterday afternoon." John Chapman in the *New York Daily News* said Gil Lamb was an "ideal" Ichabod Crane, the musical itself was "handsome," and David Ffolkes's costumes were the "most attractive" he'd seen in months; but the evening never really moved, and it kept snoozing. Herrick Brown in the *New York Sun* felt the musical was "inept and tedious," but noted the score was "delightfully tuneful" and he particularly liked the three-part song sequence that ended the first act ("I'm Lost," "Goodnight," and "The Englishman's Head").

Howard Barnes in the *New York Herald Tribune* said the "moribund" musical was "intermittently zestful," and he praised the "stylish" décor, the "energetic" dances, and the "pleasant" score (he singled out "I'm

Lost" and "Here and Now"). Robert Garland in the *New York Journal-American* called the musical a "mistake" that fell "flat on its fantasy."

During the tryout, "Hereabouts," "Alone," "In the Hay," and a danced prologue (for the village children) were deleted.

Jo Sullivan made her Broadway debut in the musical's singing chorus, and a few years later created the role of Amy/Rosabella in *The Most Happy Fella* (1956); and Mary McCarty in a supporting role later appeared in the original productions of Irving Berlin's **Miss Liberty**; Stephen Sondheim's *Follies* (1971; where she introduced "Who's That Woman?"); and John Kander and Fred Ebb's *Chicago* (1975; as Matron Mama Morton, she introduced "When You're Good to Mama" and, with Chita Rivera, the amusingly classless "Class").

Other musical versions of Washington Irving's story include: the 1966 Off-Broadway *Autumn's Here!* (book, lyrics, and music by Norman Dean; the first production to play at the Bert Wheeler Theatre, it opened on October 25, 1966, for eighty performances); *Ichabod* (book and lyrics by Gene Traylor, music by Thomas Tierney; Town Hall on January 12, 1977, for a limited engagement of one performance in which Tommy Tune performed all the roles); and *The Legend of Sleepy Hollow* (book by Robert Stempin, lyrics and music by James Crowley; a limited engagement of one performance at the York Theatre on June 27, 2000, which was recorded on a two-CD set released by CE/Crowley Entertainment Records).

Awards

Tony Awards: Best Scenic Designer (**Jo Mielziner** for his scenic designs for the entire season, including **Sleepy Hollow**, *Summer and Smoke*, *Anne of the Thousand Days*, *Death of a Salesman*, and **South Pacific**) (*Note*: **South Pacific** was awarded other Tony Awards, which were given during the 1950 award year.)

HOWDY, MR. ICE
"A Musical Icetravaganza"

Theatre: Center Theatre
Opening Date: June 24, 1948; *Closing Date*: April 23, 1949
Performances: 406
Lyrics: Al Stillman
Music: Alan Moran
Direction: Staged by Catherine Littlefield; William H. Burke, Production Director; *Producers*: Sonja Henie and Arthur M. Wirtz (Sonart Productions, Inc.; Arthur M. Wirtz, Executive Director); *Choreography*: Catherine Littlefield; Dorothie Littlefield, Assistant Choreographer; *Skating Direction*: May Judels; Scenery: Bruno Maine; *Costumes*: Billy Livingston and Katherine Kuhn; *Lighting*: Eugene Braun; *Musical Direction*: David Mendoza
Cast: Lloyd "Skippy" Baxter, Eileen Seigh, Freddie Trenkler, Cissy Trenholm, Jinx Clark, Harrison Thomson, Rudy Richards, Paul Castle, James Sisk, Fred Werner, Buster Grace, Snookums and Buck Pennington, The Three Bruises (Monte Scott, Sidney Spalding, Geoffe Stevens), The Prestons (Mickee and Paul), Trixie, John Kasper, John Walsh; Singers: Nola Fairbanks, Dick Craig, Fred Martell, William (Bill) Douglas; Girls: Margaret Barry, Peggy Bauer, Josephine Belluccia, Dorothy Bergmann, Evelyn Biderman, Ann Boykin, Bernice Deane, Helen Dutcher, Walli Hackman, Pat Harrington, Gloria Haupt, Lynne Immes, Joan King, Pat Lemaire, Ann Liff, Marjorie Mahne, Marvette Mosic, Doris Nelson, Priscilla Paulson, Ragna Ray, Gerri Richardson, Rusty Rodgers, Lela Rolontz, Theresa Rothacker, Betty Smith, Beth Stevens, Catherine Webber, Eileen Thompson, Catherine Webber; Boys: Julian Apley, Eddie Berry, Ray Blow, Charles Caminiti, Nicholas Dantos, Gerry Decker, Arthur Erickson, John Farris, Kurt Fischman, Louis Glessman, Ray Hendrickson, Dan Hurley, George Kramser, Gene Leff, Kenneth Leslie, Robert Lewis, Ernest Mann, Mickey Meehan, John Melendez, Ken (Kenneth) Parker, Gus Patrick, James Paul, Sandy Quitne, Leonard Stofka, Stephen Stofka, William Taft, James Toth, Wally (Walter) Van Sickle, William Waldron, Harvey Weber
The revue was presented in two acts.

Skating and Musical Numbers

Act One: Overture (Orchestra); "In the Pink" (Girls: Peggy Bauer, Josephine Belluccia, Evelyn Biderman, Ann Boykin, Bernice Deane, Walli Hackman, Gloria Haupt, Joan King, Pat Lemaire, Marjorie Mahne, Marvette Mosic, Doris Nelson, Priscilla Paulson, Ragna Ray, Gerri Richardson, Rusty Rodgers, Theresa Rothacker, Beth Stevens, Catherine Webber; Boys: Ray Blow, Gerry Decker, Kurt Fischman, Louis Glessman, Ray Hendrickson, Dan Hurley, James Paul, Sandy Quitne, Leonard Stofka, Stephen Stofka, William Taft, James Toth, Wally Van Sickle, William Waldron; Show Girls: Margaret Barry, Dorothy Bergmann, Helen Dutcher, Pat Harrington, Lela Rolontz, Eileen Thompson) and "In the Pink" (Nola Fairbanks, Richard Craig, Bill Douglas, Fred Matell); "Dynamic Duo" (Cissy Trenholm and John Walsh); "Landscape Artists" (Eddie Berry, John Melendez); "Celebration"—(a) "Easter" (Lilies: Margaret Berry, Dorothy Bergmann, Helen Dutcher, Walli Hackman, Lela Rolontz, Eileen Thompson; Daffodils: Peggy Bauer, Evelyn Biderman, Ann Boykin, Bernice Deane, Pat Harrington, Joan King, Pat Lemaire, Ann Liff, Marvette Mosic, Doris Nelson, Gerri Richardson, Theresa Rothacker; Chicks: Josephine Belluccia, Gloria Haupt, Lynne Innes, Marjorie Mahne, Priscilla Paulson, Rusty Rodgers, Betty Smith, Catherine Webber); (b) "Fourth of July" (Yankee Doodle Dandies: Ray Blow, Gerry Decker, Nicholas Dantos, Kurt Fischman, Louis Glessman, Ray Henrickson, Dan Hurley, George Kramser, Robert Lewis, Mickey Meehan, James Paul, Sandy Quitne, Leonard Stofka, Stephen Stofka, James Toth, William Waldron); (c) The Prestons; (d) "Thanksgiving" (Pilgrims: Eileen Thompson, John Kasper; Turkeys: Kenneth Leslie, Ken Parker, Gus Patrick, William Taft); and (e) "Yuletide" (Townsfolk: Margaret Barry, Peggy Bauer, Dorothy Bergmann, Evelyn Biderman, Ann Boykin, Bernice Deane, Helen Dutcher, Walli Hackman, Pat Harrington, Lynne Innes, Joan King, Pat Lemaire, Marvette Mosic, Doris Nelson, Ragna Ray, Gerri Richardson, Lela Rolontz, Theresa Rothacker, Betty Smith, Ray Blow, Gerry Decker, Nicholas Dantos, Kurt Fischman, Louis Glessman, Ray Hendrickson, Dan Hurley, George Kramser, Robert Lewis, Ernest Mann, Mickey Meehan, James Paul, Sandy Quitne, Leonard Stofka, Stephen Stofka, James Toth, Wally Van Sickle, William Waldron; Santa Claus: Arthur Erickson); Vocals: Nola Fairbanks, Richard Craig, Bill Douglas, Fred Martell); "Precision Plus" (Harrison Thomson and Rudy Richards); "Safari" (Hunters: Buster Grace, Buck Pennington, James Sisk; Lion: Eddie Berry); "Trinidad Wharf" (Calypso Pete: Rudy Richards; Tropical Siren: Cissy Trenholm; Islanders: Margaret Barry, Peggy Bauer, Josephine Belluccia, Dorothy Bergmann, Ann Boykin, Bernice Deane, Helen Dutcher, Walli Hackman, Pat Harrington, Lynne Innes, Joan King, Pat Lemaire, Marjorie Mahne, Marvette Mosic, Doris Nelson, Priscilla Paulson, Ragna Ray, Rusty Rodgers, Theresa Rothacker, Beth Stevens, Ray Blow, Charles Caminiti, Gerry Decker, Nicholas Dantos, Arthur Erickson, Kurt Fischman, Louis Glessman, George Kramser, Kenneth Leslie, Robert Lewis, Ernest Mann, John Melendez, Ken Parker, James Paul, Gus Patrick, Sandy Quitne, Leonard Stofka, Stephen Stofka, James Toth, William Waldron) and "Plenty More Fish in the Sea" (Nola Fairbanks, Richard Craig, Bill Douglas, Fred Martell); "Mercury" (Mercury: Lloyd "Skippy" Baxter; Pandora: Jinx Clark; Maidens: Walli Hackman, Lela Rolontz, Eileen Thompson); Trixie (Assistant: Leonard Stofka); "48 States" (Inquiring Reporter: Richard Craig; Matron: Nola Fairbanks; School Girls: Doris Nelson, Theresa Rothacker; Newsboy: Paul Castle; Ladies and Gentlemen of the Ensemble: Margaret Barry, Peggy Bauer, Josephine Belluccia, Dorothy Bergmann, Evelyn Biderman, Grace Bleckman, Ann Boykin, Bernice Deane, Helen Dutcher, Walli Hackman, Pat Harrington, Gloria Haupt, Lynne Innes, Joan King, Ann Liff, Pat Lemaire, Marjorie Mahne, Marvette Mosic, Priscilla Paulson, Ragna Ray, Gerri Richardson, Rusty Rodgers, Lela Rolontz, Betty Smith, Eileen Thompson, Catherine Webber, Julian Apley, Ray Blow, Charles Caminiti, Gerry Decker, Nicholas Dantos, Arthur Erickson, Kurt Fischman, Louis Glessman, Ray Hendrickson, Dan Hurley, Kenneth Leslie, Robert Lewis, Ernest Mann, Mickey Meehan, John Melendez, Ken Parker, James Paul, Gus Patrick, Sandy Quitne, Leonard Stofka, Stephen Stofka, William Taft, James Toth, Wally Van Sickle, William Waldron; Golden Eagle: Eileen Seigh; Pilots: Buster Grace, John Kasper, James Sisk, John Walsh) and "48 States" (Dick Craig, Fred Martell, Bill Douglas)

Act Two: Entr'acte (Orchestra); "The Sleeping Beauty"—(1) "The Princess' Birthday" (Princess Aurora: Jinx Clark; King: Arthur Erickson; Queen: Eileen Thompson; Maids of Honor: Josephine Belluccia, Evelyn Biderman, Bernice Deane, Gloria Haupt, Lynne Innes, Joan King, Marvette Mosic, Doris Nelson, Priscilla Paulson, Ragna Ray, Rusty Rodgers, Theresa Rothacker; Prince from the East: Rudy Richards; Prince from the West: Buck Pennington; Prince from the North: John Farris; Prince from the South: John Walsh; Guards: John Melendez, James Toth); (2) "A Remote Tower" (Wicked Fairy: John Kasper; Good Fairy:

Cissy Trenholm); (3) The Forest" (Prince Desire: Harrison Thomson; The Archers: Julian Apley, Ray Blow, Charles Caminiti, Ernest Mann, James Paul, Gus Patrick); and (4) "The Sleeping Castle" (Ladies in Waiting: Margaret Barry, Helen Dutcher, Walli Hackman, Pat Harrington, Betty Smith, Eileen Thompson; Courtiers: Peggy Bauer, Dorothy Bergmann, Ann Boykin, Pat Lemaire, Marjorie Mahne, Gerri Richardson, Lela Rolontz, Catherine Webber, Gerry Decker, Kurt Fischman, Louis Glessman, Dan Hurley, Robert Lewis, Leonard Stofka, Stephen Stofka, Wally Van Sickle); "Highland Laddies" (Paul Castle, Buster Grace, Buck Pennington, James Sisk); "The Bluebirds" (Eileen Seigh and Lloyd "Skippy" Baxter); "The Cradle of Jazz" (Rhythm Man: Rudy Richards; Cocottes: Evelyn Biderman, Ragna Ray, Rusty Rodgers; Blues Boys and Girls: Josephine Belluccia, Ann Boykin, Pat Lemaire, Marvette Mosic, Priscilla Paulson, Gerri Richardson, Ray Blow, Louis Glessman, Dan Hurley, Ernest Mann, Gus Patrick, Leonard Stofka; Cakewalkers: Peggy Bauer, Theresa Rothacker, Charles Caminiti, John Farris; Strutters: Kurt Fischman, Robert Lewis, James Paul, Stephen Stofka, Wally Van Sickle, William Waldren; Mr. Strut: John Walsh; Flappers: Joan King, Ann Liff, Doris Nelson, Catherine Webber; Kampus Kids: Ragna Ray, John Kasper; Boogie Woogie: Margaret Barry, Dorothy Bergmann, Helen Dutcher, Walli Hackman, Lela Rolontz, Eileen Thompson, Gerry Decker, Nicholas Dantos, George Kramser, Ken Parker, Sandy Quitne, James Toth; Jitterbugs: Marjorie Mahne, Gloria Haupt, Eddie Berry, Arthur Erickson) and "Cradle of Jazz" (Richard Craig, Bill Douglas, Nola Fairbanks, Fred Martell); "Flirtation Lesson" (Mam'zelle: Mickee Preston; Bellhop: Paul Preston); "In the Dark" (Sweethearts: Jinx Clark, Lela Rolontz, Cissy Trenholm, John Farris, Harrison Thomson, John Walsh; Ladies of the Ensemble: Margaret Barry, Peggy Bauer, Josephine Belluccia, Dorothy Bergmann, Evelyn Biderman, Bernice Deane, Helen Dutcher, Walli Hackman, Pat Harrington, Gloria Haupt, Joan King, Pat Lemaire, Ann Liff, Marjorie Mahne, Doris Nelson, Priscilla Paulson, Ragna Ray, Gerri Richardson, Rusty Rodgers, Lela Rolontz, Theresa Rothacker, Betty Smith, Eileen Thompson, Catherine Webber) and "I Only Wish I Knew" (Nola Fairbanks, Fred Martell); "Variations on a Romantic Theme" (Beguine: Lloyd "Skippy" Baxter; Valse: Eileen Seigh); "Fireman, Save That Tramp" (Chief: Arthur Erickson; Firemen: Buster Grace, Buck Pennington, James Sisk; Tramp: Freddie Trenkler) (*Note*: Shortly after opening, The Three Bruises [Monte Stott, Geoffe Stevens, and Sid Spalding] joined the production, and the "Fireman" number was replaced by an unnamed sequence by the comic skating trio); "The World's Greatest Show" (Ringmaster: Harrison Thomson; Clowns: Nicholas Dantos, Kurt Fischman, Louis Glessman, Ray Henrickson, George Kramser, Kenneth Leslie, John Melendez, Ken Parker, Stephen Stofka, William Taft, James Toth, William Waldren; Elephant Girls: Peggy Bauer, Josephine Belluccia, Gloria Haupt, Priscilla Paulson, Ragna Ray, Catherine Webber; Tumblers: Ray Blow, Charles Caminiti, Ernest Mann, Mickey Meehan, James Paul, Gus Patrick; Trainer: Cissy Trenholm; Gold Leopards: Evelyn Biderman, Bernice Deane, Pat Harrington, Joan King, Doris Nelson, Gerri Richardson; Trainer: John Walsh; Black Panthers: Margaret Barry, Dorothy Bergmann, Walli Hackman, Marvette Mosic, Theresa Rothacker, Eileen Thompson; Giant: Buster Grace; Giantess: Rusty Rodgers; Mammy Mine: Paul Castle; Ranee: Peggy Bauer, Marjorie Mahne; Rajah: Rudy Richards; Aerialists: Jinx Clark, Ann Boykin, Helen Dutcher, Pat Lemaire, Lynne Innes, John Farris, John Kasper; Acrobats: Mickee and Paul Preston; Trixie; Equestrienne: Eileen Seigh; Horses: Gerry Decker, Dan Hurley, Robert Lewis, Sandy Quitne; Cowboys: Eddie Berry, Buck Pennington; Billy the Kid: Lloyd "Skippy" Baxter; Strongman: Arthur Erickson) and "World's Greatest Show" (Nola Fairbanks, Richard Craig, Bill Douglas, Fred Martell); Finale (Entire Company)

Howdy, Mr. Ice ran out the season for a total of 406 performances; a few weeks after its closing, it was revised as **Howdy, Mr. Ice of 1950** and played for 430 performances (with the latter's closing, the highly successful ice revue series at the Center Theatre came to an end after almost a full decade of performances that topped the four-thousand mark).

In his seasonal summary, George Jean Nathan stated there had been no good reason for him to see the new ice revue because it was assuredly the same as those that had preceded it. He admitted that occasionally new material was added: for example, a bottle-green costume might be substituted for one of pale green, and sometimes a skater jumped over four hurdles instead of three. Otherwise, the ice sequences were "slight variants" of one another, and it would be lost on him if a skater of "incredible genius" whirled around on the ice thirty times instead of twenty-nine. In fact, all skaters of "any proficiency" looked alike to him, and while they might be "extremely skilful in their idiotic way," one a shade more skilful than the others would probably be lost on him. He concluded his essay by telling his readers they could congratulate themselves that he didn't attend the latest ice show and thus spared them of having to read his review.

SHOW BOAT

Theatre: City Center
Opening Date: September 7, 1948; *Closing Date*: September 19, 1948
Performances: 15
Book and *Lyrics*: Oscar Hammerstein II
Music: Jerome Kern
Based on the 1926 novel *Show Boat* by Edna Ferber.
Direction: Staged by Hassard Short and book directed by Oscar Hammerstein II; *Producers*: Jerome Kern and Oscar Hammerstein II; *Choreography*: Helen Tamiris; *Scenery* and *Lighting*: Howard Bay; *Costumes*: Lucinda Ballard; *Musical Direction*: David Morde
Cast: George Spellman (Windy), Fred Brookins (Steve), Gerald Prosk (Pete, Jeb), Helen Dowdy (Queenie), Ruth Gates (Parthy Ann Hawks), Billy House (Captain Andy), Clare Alden (Ellie), Sammy White (Frank), Gordon Alexander (Rubber Face), Carol Bruce (Julie), Norwood Smith (Gaylord Ravenal), Fred Ardath (Vallon), Pamela Caveness (Magnolia), William C. Smith (Joe), Howard Frank (Backwoodsman), La Verne French (Sam, Dahomey King), Gloria Smith (Sal), Walter Russell (Barker, Drunk), Sylvia Myers (Fatima), Robert Fleming (Sport), Sara Floyd (Landlady), Assota Marshall (Ethel), Lorraine Waldman (Mother Superior), Danice Dodson (Kim [as a child]), King Brill (Jake), Seldon Bennett (Jim), Albert McCary (Man with Guitar), Walter Mosby (Doorman at Trocadero), Sara Dillon (Lottie), Elaine Hume (Dolly), Janet Van Derveer (Sally), Ann Lloyd (Old Lady on Levee); Singers: Sybol Cain, Clarice Crawford, Sara Dillon, Betty Graeber, Marion Hairston, Kate Hall, Elaine Hume, Charlotte Junius, Assota Marshall, Sylvia Myers, Eleyn Paul, Eulabel Riley, Dee Sherman, Janet Vanderveer, Lorraine Waldman, Jerome Addison, Gilbert Adkins, Gordon Alexander, Ivory Bass, Henry Davis, William Cole, Clarence Jones, Albert McCary, Walter Mosby, Walter Russell, William Sol, Charles Welch, Leo Norman, Robert Flavelle, Francis Fleming, Henry Hamilton; Dancers: Eloise Hill, Evelyn Pilcher, Gloria Smith, Alma Sutton, Isaiah Clark, James Hunt, Reginald Ridgley, George Thomas, James Fields
The musical was presented in two acts.
The action takes place from the 1880s to the 1920s, principally in Mississippi and Chicago.

The 1946 revival of Oscar Hammerstein II and Jerome Kern's *Show Boat* had played on Broadway for 418 performances from January 5, 1946, to January 4, 1947. The national touring company visited fourteen cities from October 20, 1947, to June 26, 1948; and a second tour of forty-five cities began with the current two-week engagement, which opened at City Center on September 7, 1948; the tour closed on April 30, 1949.

For the 1946 revival, Buddy Ebsen portrayed Frank, but for the current session Frank was played by Sammy White, who had created the role in the original 1927 production. With Sammy White now in the show, the revival underwent some alterations from the 1946 showing. "Life upon the Wicked Stage" (for Ellie and the chorus) was dropped in favor of "I Might Fall Back on You" for Frank and Ellie, which had been performed in the 1927 production by Sammy White and Eva Puck and which had been cut for the 1946 mounting. A special "Olio Dance" was added for White as well; and the production was shortened with the omission of the dance "Congress of Beauties," the background music for the "Service and Scene Music at St. Agatha's Convent" sequence, the "Dance 1927" number, and "Nobody Else but Me," which had been written especially for the 1946 revival. This revised version of the revival also seems to have completely eliminated the character of the older Kim.

In their reviews of the touring production, Brooks Atkinson in the *New York Times* said the revival was "admirable"; Otis L. Guernsey Jr. in the *New York Herald Tribune* found it "mechanical"; and while Arthur Bronson in *Variety* felt the musical was too large for the small City Center stage, the revival was nonetheless "just right" and was as "fresh and melodious as ever."

For more information about *Show Boat* and a complete list of its musical numbers, see entry for the 1946 revival.

MOREY AMSTERDAM'S HILARITIES

Theatre: Adelphi Theatre
Opening Date: September 9, 1948; *Closing Date*: September 18, 1948

Performances: 14
Sketches: Sidney Zelinka, Howard Harris, and Morey Amsterdam
Lyrics and *Music*: Buddy Kaye, Stanley (Stan) Arnold, and Carl Lampl
Direction: Production supervised by Mervyn Nelson; *Producers*: Ken Robey and Stan Zucker; *Choreography*: George Tapps; *Scenery*: Crayon; *Costumes*: Uncredited; *Lighting*: Uncredited; *Musical Direction*: Ruby Zwerling
Cast: *Morey Amsterdam*, George Tapps, Betty Jane Watson, Gali Gali, Mitzi Novelle, Larry Douglas, Gerald Austen, Connie Stevens, The Calgary Brothers (Andre and Steve Calgary), Enid Williams, Raul and Eva Reyes, Sid Stone, Connie Sawyer, Nancy Andrews, The Holloway Sisters, Victoria Crandall, Moreland Kortkam, Al Kelly, The Herzogs, Gil Maison, Harold and Lola
The revue was presented in two acts.

Sketches and Musical Numbers

Act One: "Showtime" (Betty Jane Watson, Mitzi Novelle, Larry Douglas, Gerald Austen, Connie Stevens, Andre and Steve Calgary, Raul and Eva Reyes, Entire Company); Your Host, Morey Amsterdam, and Others; "The Man with the Snake" (Harold and Lola); "The Pitchman" (Sid Stone); "Rise and Shine" (Gerald Austen, Connie Stevens, Connie Sawyer, Nancy Andrews, Mitzi Novelle, Morey Amsterdam); The Holloway Sisters; Gali Gali; "The Bridegroom" (Morey Amsterdam, Larry Douglas, Gerald Austen, Andre and Steve Calgary); "Where in the World" (Betty Jane Watson, Larry Douglas, George Tapps); "The Lost Weekend" (Andre and Steve Calgary); George Tapps, assisted by Victoria Crandall and Moreland Kortkam; Morey Amsterdam and His Cello
Act Two: "About Politics" (Morey Amsterdam and Al Kelly); "'Tis the Luck of the Irish" (Betty Jane Watson, Gerald Austen, Nancy Andrews, Mitzi Novelle, Larry Douglas, George Tapps, The Holloway Sisters); The Herzogs; "Vaudeville Hoofer" (George Tapps); "Great New Talent" (Connie Sawyer); "One Man's Menagerie" (Gil Maison); "Rio de Janeiro" (Nancy Andrews, Gerald Austen, Larry Douglas, The Holloway Sisters, Raul and Eva Reyes); "The Entrance of the Adelphi Theatre" (Morey Amsterdam, Entire Company)

Morey Amsterdam's Hilarities (aka *Hilarities*) was a vaudeville-like revue with songs, dances, and comedy skits. But it couldn't overcome mostly negative reviews and so was gone in less than two weeks. Amsterdam served as the evening's master of ceremonies and told jokes, and the other performers included magician Gali Gali; tap dancer George Tapps; the acrobatic comedy team of the Calgary Brothers; the snake-dancers Harold and Lola; straight singer Betty Jane Watson; dead-pan torch singer Enid Williams; comedy singer Connie Sawyer; more tap-dancers with the Holloway Sisters; Gil Maison and his animal act; the trapeze artists the Herzogs; Latin-styled dancers Raul and Eva Reyes; and pitchman Sid Stone.

Brooks Atkinson in the *New York Times* said "even a little" of Morey Amsterdam would "be quite a lot in the happiest circumstance" because the comedian was a "mediocre wag" of "tiresome persistence." But the evening offered two compensations, Gali Gali and the Calgary Brothers. Robert Coleman in the *New York Daily Mirror* said the revue was an attempt to bring back vaudeville, but "vaudeville still remains to be brought back." The show wasn't entertaining and it wasn't hilarious, and some of the good acts (the Calgary Brothers, Gil Maison and his "menagerie of blasé animals," and the Herzogs) came on so late that many of the first-nighters and critics had gone home.

The headline of John Lardner's review in the *New York Star* proclaimed "Few Hits, Many Duds." The few hits were the Calgary Brothers, Enid Williams (who had scored positive notices with her dead-pan cakewalk in **St. Louis Woman**), and Gali Gali, and one of the major errors was George Tapps (who is a "minority group who considers himself the best hoofer in the world"). Robert Garland in the *New York Journal-American* noted that Morey Amsterdam's name was plastered throughout the regular program, and the souvenir program (which cost a quarter) was "profusely illustrated" with Amsterdam's photos, alone, with family, and with various celebrities. *Hilarities* was his show and he was "welcome to it."

Ward Morehouse in the *New York Sun* noted that if vaudeville wasn't dead, then it was certainly "half-dead" if *Hilarities* was any indication. Most of it was "definitely mediocre" and "dreary," and Amsterdam was not a performer to "enchant" one. John Chapman in the *New York Daily News* said the show's title was heroic, and most of the evening gave proof "why vaudeville committed suicide."

William Hawkins in the *New York World-Telegram* said the evening had "first-rate" acts as well as "too many ordinary" ones. A show that charged a top ticket price of $2.40 on weeknights required "smart routing, cutting and pacing." He noted that Gil Maison's animal act was "fresh and one of the best of its kind"; it included a Saint Bernard "with a punch drunk disposition" and a monkey who was a jitterbugging fool. Richard Watts in the *New York Post* said the revue was "happy in spots," but there weren't enough of those happy spots to fill out the evening. But he praised Enid Williams (who burlesqued torch songs with "dead-pan boredom" and was "something of a personality") and the animal act (he noted that on cue the jitterbugging monkey became "violent" the moment the name "Frank Buck" was spoken).

Howard Barnes in the *New York Herald Tribune* said there was an "amiable and unpretentious quality" about the revue but noted the acts varied in their "entertainment voltage"; he mentioned that Enid Williams was a "fresh and dynamic performer" and the Calgary Brothers contributed the evening's "brightest interlude."

As for Morey Amsterdam, he later found television immortality as a second-banana on the long-running CBS television series *The Dick Van Dyke Show*; he played the role of television script writer Buddy Sorrell, a wise-cracking master of the put-down and the sardonic insult; on the show, his writing partner-in-crime was Rose Marie, and their back-and-forth banter was honed to a sharp edge of take-no-prisoners comic hostility.

SMALL WONDER
"A NEW MUSICAL REVUE"

Theatre: Coronet Theatre
Opening Date: September 15, 1948; *Closing Date*: January 8, 1949
Performances: 134
Sketches: Charles Spalding, Max Wilk, George Axelrod, Louis Laun, and Richard F. Maury
Lyrics: Phyllis McGinley, Billings Brown (pseudonym for Burt Shevelove), Albert Selden, and Mark Lawrence
Music: Baldwin Bergersen, Albert Selden, and Mark Lawrence
Direction: Burt Shevelove; *Producer*: George Nichols 3rd; *Choreography*: Gower Champion; *Scenery* and *Lighting*: Ralph Alswang; *Costumes*: John Derro; *Musical Direction*: William Parson
Cast: Tom Ewell, Alice Pearce, Mary McCarty, Marilyn Day, Hayes Gordon, Tommy Rall, J. C. McCord, Joan Mann, Jonathan Lucas, Kate Friedlich, Chandler Cowles, Alan Ross, Mort Marshall, Virginia Oswald, Jack Cassidy, Joan Diener, Evelyn Taylor, Bill Ferguson, Devida Stewart
The revue was presented in two acts.

Sketches and Musical Numbers

Act One: "Count Your Blessings" (lyric by Phyllis McGinley, music by Baldwin Bergersen) (Entire Company); "The Normal Neurotic" (Tom Ewell); "The Commuters' Song" (lyric by Phyllis McGinley, music by Baldwin Bergersen) (Marilyn Day, Alan Ross); "Ballad for Billionaires" (lyric by Billings Brown, music by Albert Selden) (Junior: Chandler Cowles; Pop: Mort Marshall; Louise van Steele: Mary McCarty; Clint LaRue: Hayes Gordon); "No Time" (lyric by Phyllis McGinley, music by Baldwin Bergersen) (First Variation: Jonathan Lucas and Kate Friedlich; Second Variation: Tommy Rall and Evelyn Taylor; Third Variation: J. C. McCord and Joan Mann); "The Human Body" (Tom Ewell); "Flaming Youth" (lyric by Billings Brown, music by Albert Selden) (Mary McCarty); "D-e-m-ocracy" (The Normal Neurotic: Tom Ewell; The Wife: Alice Pearce; The Husband: Mort Marshall); "The Show-Off" (lyric and music by Albert Selden) (Tommy Rall, Marilyn Day); "I Could Write a Book" (The Normal Neurotic: Tom Ewell; (1) Mom: Alice Pearce; Joey: Jonathan Lucas; Gabby: Joan Mann; (2) Eddie: Chandler Cowles; Dolores: Marilyn Day; and (3) Joy Polloi: Mary McCarty; Czar Nicholas: Mort Marshall); "Badaroma" (lyric by Billings Brown, music by Billings Brown) (J. C. McCord, Entire Company)
Act Two: "Nobody Told Me" (lyric by Phyllis McGinley, music by Baldwin Bergersen) (The Bride: Joan Diener; The Groom: Hayes Gordon; The Maid of Honor: Devida Stewart; The Best Man: Alan Ross; The Mother: Alice Pearce; The Bridesmaids: Mary McCarty, Marilyn Day, Virginia Oswald; The Ushers: Jonathan Lucas, Jack Cassidy, Bill Ferguson); "The Civilized Thing" (sketch by Richard F. Maury) (Tom Ewell);

"Pistachio" (lyric and music by Mark Lawrence) (Alice Pearce, Mort Marshall); "When I Fall in Love" (lyric and music by Albert Selden) (Marilyn Day; danced by Jonathan Lucas and Kate Friedlich, assisted by Joan Mann, Evelyn Taylor, Tommy Rall, and J. C. McCord); "(This Is an Adv.)" (The Normal Neurotic: Tom Ewell); "Saturday's Child" (lyric by Phyllis McGinley, music by Baldwin Bergersen) (Mary McCarty); "William McKinley High" (lyric by Billings Brown, music by Albert Selden) (Marilyn Day, Jonathan Lucas, Tommy Rall, Jack Cassidy, Chandler Cowles, Mort Marshall, Alan Ross); "The Happy Ending" (1—Small Boy: Tom Ewell; Nina: Joan Mann; 2—Maurice: Tom Ewell; Beryl: Alice Pearce; Elvira: Kate Friedlich; and 3—Nick: Tom Ewell; The Kid: Mary McCarty; Her Brother: Tommy Rall; Tony Akimbo: Jack Cassidy) (Note: "The Happy Ending" sketch included the song "From A to Z," lyric by Billings Brown, music by Albert Selden; it was sung by The Kid: Mary McCarty; Tony Akimbo: Jack Cassidy; and the Megalo-Golden-Mania Girls); "Just an Ordinary Guy" (lyric by Phyllis McGinley and Billings Brown, music by Albert Selden) (Virginia Oswald, Entire Company)

The revue *Small Wonder* is mostly notable for the performers and creative staff who went on to make names for themselves in future musicals: cast members Mary McCarty, Tommy Rall, Jonathan Lucas, Mort Marshall, Jack Cassidy, and Joan Diener; choreographer Gower Champion, who later in the season created the staging and dances for the hit revue **Lend an Ear**; and director Burt Shevelove, who made his mark as the co-librettist for *A Funny Thing Happened on the Way to the Forum* (1962) and directed and adapted the book for the 1971 revival of *No, No, Nanette*.

The cast also included Alice Pearce, who had made a memorable impression in **On the Town**, and Tom Ewell; the latter and *Small Wonder* sketch writer George Axelrod later joined forces in 1952 when Ewell starred in Axelrod's hit comedy *The Seven Year Itch*, which was memorably filmed by Billy Wilder in 1955 with Ewell reprising his role of the hapless summer bachelor who meets a curvaceous blonde (Marilyn Monroe) who always recognizes classical music because it doesn't have any words. The revue was also notable because the well-known poet Phyllis McGinley was one of its lyricists.

Small Wonder received mild reviews, but managed to last four months before closing in the red.

Brooks Atkinson in the *New York Times* liked the bright cast, but felt their material needed sharpening. The revue kidded wealthy Texans ("Ballad for Billionaires"), popular novels (and how to avoid reading them) ("I Could Write a Book"), Madison Avenue ("This Is an Adv."), Hollywood ("The Happy Ending"), the radio ("D-e-m-ocracy" spoofed *Voice of America*–styled broadcasts by offering its commentary in the mode of afternoon soap operas), and commuting ("The Commuters' Song"), but Atkinson felt the satire was "uniformly small" and "monotonous"; Richard Watts in the *New York Post* said the revue was "so-so," lacked "sharpness and humor," and had a score that was "neither tuneful nor interesting." Tom Ewell served as a kind of master of ceremonies as the "normal neurotic" who muses upon the passing scene of popular culture; but his comments about trends, fads, and foibles weren't "very pointed" and needed more "satirical thrusts." As for Mary McCarty, she was a comedienne of "talent and intelligence," and she shined in "The Happy Ending," a sequence that spoofed Hollywood in which she mocked the acting styles of Lana Turner, Betty Grable, Lauren Bacall, Lizabeth Scott, Joan Caufield, and Dorothy Lamour.

Robert Garland in the *New York Journal-American* found the revue "slick" as well as "intimate and intelligent"; he liked Tom Ewell, and noted that Mary McCarty "walks, sings and dances away with secondary honors" and her "Saturday's Child" was the "top song of a none too tuneful score." Ward Morehouse in the *New York Sun* said the revue "never gets going" and "doesn't come off," the score was "decidedly unexciting," and the evening required "more distinctive material"; for him, the most "zestful" moments were provided by Mary McCarty. William Hawkins in the *New York World-Telegram* said the revue was often "collegiate" and "amateurish," and while there were some "sharp and witty" moments, much of the evening was "uninspired and lackadaisical."

Although Robert Coleman in the *New York Daily Mirror* generally liked the new revue, he felt the six-dollar top was too high and was a "big mistake" on the part of the producer; he could easily recommend *Small Wonder* if its ticket prices were $4.80 or under, but $6.00 was just too much. But Tom Ewell was an "ingratiating emcee," next best was Mary McCarty, and the lyrics were "more intelligent" than those usually heard in the typical revue.

But John Lardner in the *New York Star* liked most of the sketches (at least half were successful, which he noted was a "very fair average") and singled out such songs as "Flaming Youth," "Saturday's Child," "Ballad for Billionaires," and "The Commuters' Song." John Chapman in the *New York Daily News* praised the "amiable" company and liked the sketches, but noted the music was "scarcely deserving" of the superior lyrics. Like Lardner, he enjoyed the "wise and critical and very funny" spoof of Hollywood, and noted that the skit's heroine is "a worse actress than Betty Grable and Judy Garland combined, if that is a human possibility."

During the tryout, "I Like a Man Around the House" and "Things" were dropped.

The songs "The Show-Off" and "Saturday's Child" are included in the collection *Make Mine Manhattan and Great Revues Revisited* (Painted Smiles CD # PSCD-119), and "Nobody Told Me" and "No Time" are performed in the collection *Everyone Else Revisited* (Painted Smiles CD # PSCD-146). *Introducing Janice Mars* (Bac Room Records CD) includes "The Commuters' Song" and "Nobody Told Me."

The song "When I Fall in Love" is not the standard "When I Fall in Love" ("it will be forever"), which became popular a few years later when it was first heard in the 1952 film *One Minute to Zero* (lyric by Edward Heyman, music by Victor Young).

HEAVEN ON EARTH
"A NEW MUSICAL COMEDY"

Theatre: New Century Theatre
Opening Date: September 16, 1948; *Closing Date*: September 25, 1948
Performances: 12
Book and *Lyrics*: Barry Trivers; additional lyrics by Norman Zeno
Music: Jay Gorney
Direction: Production supervised by Eddie Dowling and directed by John Murray Anderson; *Producers*: Monte Proser in association with Ned C. Litwack; *Choreography*: Nick Castle; *Scenery* and *Costumes*: Raoul Pene du Bois; *Lighting*: John Murray Anderson; *Musical Direction*: Clay Warnick
Cast: Peter Lind Hayes (James Aloysius McCarthy), Dorothy Jarnac (Friday), Danny Drayson (Punchy), Caren Marsh (Fannie Frobisher), Ruth Merman (Florabelle Frobisher), Nina Varela (Mrs. Frobisher), Irwin Corey (Commissioner Frobisher), Claude Stroud (Officer Clabber), Robert Dixon (John Bowers), Barbara Nunn (Mary Brooks), June Graham and Richard D'Arcy (aka Darcy) (The Lovers), Wynn Murray (Lieutenant Sullivan), Dorothy Keller (Officer Jonesy), Betty George (Officer Blandings), Billy Parsons (Sailor), David Burns (H. H. Hutton), Dick Bernie (Magistrate Kennedy), Steve Condos (Sailor with Trumpet), Bert Sheldon (Officer O'Brien), Jack Russell (Radio Engineer, Dippy), Remi Martel (Slim), Bill Hogue (Butch); Dancers: Lisa Ayers, Cece Eames, Babette George, Gretchen Houser, Marguerite James, Carol Lee, Dorothy Love, Caron Marsh, Ruth Merman, Gloria Sickling, Alice Swanson, Evelyn Ward, Harold Drake, Ernie DiGennaro, Dente DiPaolo, Ray Johnson, Red Knight, Remi Martel, Jack Mattis, Don Powell, Frank Reynolds, Jack Whitney, Jack Wilkins; Singers: Angela Castle, Julie Curtis, Betty George, Pearl Hacker, Ellen McCown, Jean Olds, Dottie Pyren, Lucille Udovick, Dean Campbell, John Gray, Bill Hogue, Doug Luther, Vincent Van Lynn, Jack Russell, Bert Sheldon, Curt Stafford
The musical was presented in two acts.
The action takes place in New York City on the first day of spring.

Musical Numbers

Act One: Overture (Orchestra); "In the Back of a Hack" (Peter Lind Hayes, Betty George, Pearl Hacker, Doug Luther, Dean Campbell); "Anything Can Happen" (Full Company); "So Near and Yet So Far" (Barbara Nunn, Robert Dixon); "Lovers' Dance" (June Graham and Richard D'Arcy); "Don't Forget to Dream" (Peter Lind Hayes); "Bench in the Park" (Wynn Murray, Dorothy Keller, Billy Parsons, Danny Drayson, Dancing Ensemble); "The Letter" (Peter Lind Hayes, Dorothy Jarnac); "Push a Button in a Hutton" (David Burns, Jack Whitney, Singing and Dancing Ensemble); "Home Is Where the Heart Is" (Barbara Nunn, Robert Dixon, Singing Ensemble); "Apple Jack" (Wynn Murray, Steve Condos, Dorothy Keller, Dorothy Jarnac, Singing and Dancing Ensemble); "Wedding in the Park" (Peter Lind Hayes, Barbara Nunn, Robert Dixon); "Heaven on Earth" (Barbara Nunn, Robert Dixon, June Graham, Richard D'Arcy); Finale (Full Company)

Act Two: Entr'acte (Orchestra); "What's the Matter with Our City?" (Peter Lind Hayes, Full Company); "So Near and Yet So Far" (reprise) (Barbara Nunn, Robert Dixon); "First Cup of Coffee in the Morning" (Wynn Murray, Claude Stroud, Dorothy Keller, Billy Parsons, Steve Condos, Singing and Dancing Ensemble); "Gift Number" (Peter Lind Hayes, Claude Stroud, Jack Whitney Quartette, Ensemble); "Musical Tour of the City" (Peter Lind Hayes, Claude Stroud); Finale (Peter Lind Hayes, Entire Company)

Heaven on Earth was another of the new season's fast flops. Its leading pair of lovers were John (Robert Dixon) and Mary (Barbara Nunn), whose names brought to mind the recent Broadway hit comedy *John Loves Mary*; the musical's locale was Central Park, which of course was the setting for **Up in Central Park** and for part of **Make Mine Manhattan**; and the characters played by nightclub performer Peter Lind Hayes (as the "leprechaun-like" James Aloysius McCarthy) and dancer Dorothy Jarnac (as a pixie named Friday who is Aloysius's secretary and dances rather than speaks her dialogue) were reminiscent of Og and Susan the Silent in **Finian's Rainbow**. But the conglomeration of current and recent hit shows didn't help, and like **Sleepy Hollow** and **Morey Amsterdam's Hilarities**, *Heaven on Earth* was gone in two weeks and tied with **Sleepy Hollow** as the season's shortest-running musical.

Aloysius is a genial cabbie who hangs around Central Park and performs good deeds for his fellow New Yorkers. When he discovers that homeless and jobless ex-G.I. John has neither the prospects of a job nor a permanent home and is thus unable to wed Mary, Aloysius encourages them to get married anyway. He then moves them into a pre-fabricated house that is on display in the park, much to the consternation of the builder (David Burns) and a New York housing commissioner (Irwin Corey). But all ends well, and by the final curtain it appears that Aloysius and the pixie are also headed for the altar. Other Central Park types peppered throughout the evening were Wynn Murray (as a lady cop) and Charles Stroud (as another policeman, but one who hates his job). As the evening progressed, things grew so desperate that Hayes performed some of his nightclub routines, including one of his comic personas (Callahan, a punch-drunk boxer) as well as his celebrity impersonations (of such Hollywood types as Peter Lorre and Ronald Coleman); and John Chapman in the *New York Daily News* reported that Irwin Corey repeated a comic shtick twice during the evening.

The critics were unhappy with the musical, and were disappointed with Jay Gorney's score. The composer had of course written the classic "Brother, Can You Spare a Dime?" for the 1932 revue *New Americana*, but unfortunately *Heaven on Earth* yielded no standards. Even some of the song titles were unimaginative and overly familiar, such as "Home Is Where the Heart Is," "Anything Can Happen," "Don't Forget to Dream," and, especially, "So Near and Yet So Far," a title Cole Porter had used for his beguiling and popular number, which Fred Astaire had introduced in the 1941 film *You'll Never Get Rich*; further, "You're Far Too Near Me" was heard in **The Firebrand of Florence** and "You're Near and Yet So Far" was sung during tryout performances of **My Romance**.

Howard Barnes in the *New York Herald Tribune* thought "So Near and Yet So Far" was "engaging," and Robert Garland in the *New York Journal-American* "supposed" it was "intended" to become the show's hit song, but commented that the score was "lively without being actually alive." William Hawkins in the *New York Post* mentioned the score contained "a number of cheery tunes," and singled out "Apple Jack" and "First Cup of Coffee in the Morning," both of which were introduced by Wynn Murray. But Brooks Atkinson in the *New York Times* found the music "remarkably undistinguished," Ward Morehouse in the *New York Sun* said the songs were "dreary," and Richard Watts in the *New York Post* said the music was "all right, if far from memorable."

Atkinson noted that *Heaven on Earth* set a "very high standard for mediocrity"; Hayes was a "monotonous" leading man, the two directors (Eddie Dowling and John Murray Anderson) made "gaiety unbearable," the usually dependable Raoul Pene du Bois created décor that a "honky-tonk might not willingly accept," and in general the cast was forced to "stomp" around in "slush"; Hawkins said the show lacked "glamour" and needed "a course at a charm school"; and Watts stated the "top-heavy fantasy" rarely managed "to be anything but earthbound."

The headline in Robert Coleman's review for the *New York Daily Mirror* proclaimed that *Heaven on Earth* was "hardly that"; and while the book bogged down and du Bois's décor was "amazingly disappointing," he noted the songs sounded "like candidates for the Hit Parade" and the choreography avoided "phony musical comedy ballet" and instead favored "some good old-fashioned time-stepping and acrobatic antics." He also used one of his favorite verbs when he noted that the first-nighters "blistered" their palms in praise of Dorothy Jarnac's performance.

Garland said *Heaven on Earth* was "nothing of the kind"; Barnes noted the book was "uninspired," the score "ordinary," the décor "somewhat frightening," and although the evening was "colorful" it was also "strenuous" and "tedious"; Morehouse found the "labored" musical a "clamorous and aimless" one with a "shoddy" book; and Chapman said the "lead-footed" musical never jelled and poor David Burns got himself into "book trouble" with his role (which he nonetheless played "with a fine W. C. Fields air").

John Lardner in the *New York Star* said the show was a "stiff," but a "bargain" too because the producers were "practically giving away the biggest sleeping pill in town." The creators of the musical seemed to "pass the opium and tuck you in, and the next thing you know, it's a week from Tuesday."

Jackie Gleason had left **The Duchess Misbehaves** during its tryout, and did the same with *Heaven on Earth*. It appears his role of a New York City cop morphed into a lady cop that was then played by Wynn Murray.

MAGDALENA
"A ROMANCE OF THE MAGDALENA RIVER JUNGLE" / "A MUSICAL ADVENTURE"

Theatre: Ziegfeld Theatre
Opening Date: September 20, 1948; *Closing Date*: December 4, 1948
Performances: 88
Book: Frederick Hazlitt Brennan and Homer Curran
"Pattern" and *Lyrics*: Robert Wright and George Forrest
Music: Heitor Villa-Lobos
Direction: Jules Dassin; *Producer*: Homer Curran and Edwin Lester; *Choreography*: Jack Cole (Dance Captain, Matt Mattox; Assistants to Jack Cole, Gwyneth Verdun [Gwen Verdon] and George Martin); *Scenery* and *Lighting*: Howard Bay; *Costumes*: Sharaff (Irene Sharaff); *Choral Direction*: Robert Zeller; *Musical Direction*: Arthur Kay
Cast: Gerhard Pechner (Padre Josef), Peter Price (Manuel), Melva Niles (Solis), Henry Reese (Ramon), Dorothy Sarnoff (Maria), John Raitt (Pedro), Ferdinand Hilt (Major Blanco), Carl Milletaire (Doctor Lopez), Hugo Haas (General Carabana), Betty Huff (Chanteuse), Christine Matsios (Cigarette Girl), John Schickling (Zoggie), Lorraine Miller (Danseuse), Irra Petina (Teresa), Gene Curtsinger (The Old One), Patrick Kirk (Chico), Leonard Morganthaler (Juan), Betty Brusher (Conchita), Roy Raymond (Major Domo), Marie Groscup (Bailadora), Matt Mattox (Bailador); Singers: Lucy Andonian, Marion Begin, Jean Bishop, Betty Brusher, Trudy De Luz, Sofia Derue, Jeanne Eisen, Vera Ford, Martha Flynn, Audrey Gardner, Audrey Guard, Betty Flannagan, Phyllis Kramer, Gwenn LaKind, Christine Matsios, Theresa Piper, Mary Wood, Rolph Angell, Arthur Brey, Stephen Esail, Kahler Flock, Tommy Gleason, John Huck, Robert Hudson, John King, Ross Lynch, Joseph Mazzolini, Roy Raymond, Stanley Rose, Leonard Taylor; Dancers: Libby Burke, Rita Charise, Norma Doggett, Marie Groscup, Judy Landon, Mary Menzies, Lorraine Miller, Joan Morton, Sue Remos, Dale Lefler, Matt Mattox, Bill Miller, Verne Miller, Michael Sandin, Michael Scrittorale, Ralph Smith, Paul Steffen, Robert Thompson; Children: Fred Cuelar, Peter De Bear, Patrick Kirk, Rosarita Varela; Soldiers and Servants: Ralph Graves, Robert Meser, Maurice Monte, Arthur Viega
The musical was presented in two acts.
The action takes place around 1912 in the environs of the Magdalena River and in Paris.

Musical Numbers

Act One: "The Jungle Chapel": (1) "Women Weaving" (Ensemble, Gerhard Pechner); (2) "Peteca!" (Melva Niles, Henry Reese, Dancers, Ensemble); and (3) "The Seed of God" (Gerhard Pechner, Dancers, Ensemble); "The Omen Bird" ("Teru, Teru") (Dorothy Sarnoff, Dancers, Ensemble); "My Bus and I" (John Raitt, Ensemble); "The Emerald" (aka "The Emerald Song") (Dorothy Sarnoff, John Raitt);"The Civilized People" (Hugo Haas, Lorraine Miller, John Schickling, Ensemble); "Food for Thought" (aka "Teresa's Song") (Irra Petina, Ensemble); "Colombia Calls": (1) "Come to Colombia" (Irra Petina, Hugh Haas, Ferdinand Hilt); (2) "Plan It by the Planets" (Irra Petina, John Schickling, Ensemble); (3) "Bon soir, Paris" (Irra Petina); and (4) "Travel, Travel, Travel" (Irra Petina, Hugo Haas, Ferdinand Hilt, John Schickling, Ensemble);

"Magdalena": (1) "Magdalena" (Gene Curtsinger) and (2) "The Broken Pianolita" (danced by Matt Mattox, Norma Doggett, Ensemble); "The Festival": (1) "Greeting" (Children); (2) "River Song" (Dorothy Sarnoff, Ensemble); and (3) "Chivor Dance" (Dancers); "My Bus and I" (reprise) (John Raitt, Irra Petina, Ferdinand Hilt, Children); "The Forbidden Orchid" (Dorothy Sarnoff, John Raitt)

Act Two: "Ceremonial" (danced by Men, Marie Groscup, Norma Doggett, Lorraine Miller, Gene Curtsinger, Ensemble); "The Singing Tree" (Henry Reese, Melva Niles, Ensemble); "Lost" (Dorothy Sarnoff, John Raitt); "Freedom!" (John Raitt, Ensemble); "Vals de España" (Dancers, Marie Groscup, Matt Mattox); "The Emerald" (reprise) (John Raitt); "Piece de Resistance" (Irra Petina, Hugo Haas); "The Broken Bus" (John Raitt); "The Seed of God" (reprise) (Gerhard Pechner, Dorothy Sarnoff, John Raitt, Henry Reese, Melva Niles, Ensemble)

Like *Florodora* (which opened in London in 1899, and in New York the following year), *Magdalena*'s title would seem to be the name of the heroine of an operetta. But Florodora and Magdalena were places, not people: the former was a fictitious island in the Philippines, and the latter is the river that courses through Colombia. Robert Wright and George Forrest had adapted Edvard Grieg's music into the hit **Song of Norway**, and for their latest venture hoped to adapt themes by South American composer Heitor Villa-Lobos for a new musical. When they approached Villa-Lobos, he suggested that he compose an entirely new musical score for the show, and so he and the lyricists collaborated on one of the most expensive musicals of the decade, which reportedly cost (and lost) $360,000. Although the expansive score was attractive, the décor lavish, and the cast appealing, the musical's plot travelled down two completely different roads, neither of which quite met: part of the work was a musical play that examined religious faith from the perspectives of the devout Catholic Maria (Dorothy Sarnoff) and the atheist bus driver Pedro (John Raitt), and the other offered clichéd operetta shenanigans that focused on vixenish Teresa (Irra Petina) who's determined to kill off her rich playboy lover Carabana (Hugo Hass) by preparing overly rich foods for him (a kind of death by hollandaise). The evening wavered between the majestic and the madcap, the two stories never jelled, and *Ol' Man Magdalena* went dry after less than three months on Broadway.

Set mostly in the area surrounding the Magdalena, the plot centers on an emerald mine that is temporarily managed by Maria in the absence of the local padre. Her religious beliefs are an integral part of her life, but her love for Pedro is problematic because he scorns religion and is only interested in running his run-down bus (or "gasolina"). Because of religious differences, their romance never quite blossoms, but once Pedro realizes the importance of religion he finally embraces God and looks to a future with Maria.

In the meantime, a strike by the Indian mine workers sets into motion the secondary plot. Although most of the story takes place along the Magdalena, a lengthy Paris scene (which included six songs) in the middle of the first act introduced absentee mine-owner Carabana and his greedy mistress Teresa (who has only visions of emeralds dancing in her head). Carabana suffers from high blood pressure (and also apparently from gout and heart problems), but when he's told of the strike he decides to travel to Colombia; the sequence therefore included the beckoning call of "Come to Colombia," the idea of "Travel, Travel, Travel," and Teresa's good-bye to gay old Paree ("Bon soir, Paris"). The scene also included a song which seems to be a career summing-up of Wright and Forrest's idea of amusing linguistic wordplay ("Plan It by the Planets"). Teresa is especially interested in traveling to Colombia if the trip can yield her a legendary necklace made of one hundred perfect emeralds (she eventually gets her gems, but the headline of Howard Barnes's review in the *New York Herald Tribune* proclaimed "Colombia—No Gem").

When Carabana and Teresa arrive in Colombia, he soon becomes romantically interested in Maria, and Teresa, quickly sizing up the situation, decides that while jewels are a girl's best friend, sometimes a girl has to be proactive in getting them. So she prepares a lavish feast for the gourmand Carabana by serving him the richest foods from her culinary cunning (two of her songs were "Food for Thought" and "Piece de Resistance," and Carabana himself sang of the glories of fine wine in "The Civilized People"). With Carabana dead, Teresa takes off with the jewels, Maria and Pedro unite, and the workaday world of the Magdalena River inhabitants goes on. (The title of this last song was appropriated by Wright and Forrest for their 1961 musical *Kean*; as a catty trio for Alfred Drake, Lee Venora, and Joan Weldon, "Civilized People" was one of the highlights of *Kean*'s lush and romantic score.)

The critics praised Villa-Lobos's score, although they were quick to note it wasn't aimed for the jukeboxes and the Hit Parade (John Chapman in the *New York Daily News* said he wasn't able to assimilate the music in one sitting, and so planned to go back for one or two more visits, and Robert Garland in the *New York*

Journal-American mentioned that he was looking forward to hearing the score again). The reviewers were also impressed with Howard Bay's gargantuan production designs and with the talented cast. They noted in particular that Petina was not only a fine singer but a good comedienne, and mentioned that Raitt's acting skills had greatly improved since his days in **Carousel**. But the musical's book was the problem.

Brooks Atkinson in the *New York Times* found the plot "unintelligible" with "stock" characters, and thus the "profoundly" and "overpoweringly" dull story set back "the art of music drama" by "several generations"; Barnes said the evening was "top-heavy" with "general tedium" and a "rambling" story; Ward Morehouse in the *New York Sun* noted the "heavy-footed" and boring musical was "cumbersome and pretentious" with its "awkward and ponderous" book; John Lardner in the *New York Star* said the new musical opened in a "blaze of lights, color, melody and dramatic torpor," and if one attended the show with eyes and ears but without one's brain it just might be possible to enjoy it (he also noted the characters spoke in the special kind of "foreign" English so dear to the hearts of show folk, such as "I do not care" instead of "I don't care"); and Richard Watts in the *New York Post* also used the phrase "heavy-footed" to describe the proceedings, which moreover were "ponderous, fatiguing and steadily laborious" in their "boredom."

Robert Coleman in the *New York Daily Mirror* found the score sometimes "rich" and "lush," but noted the book was "dull" and "nothing better than serviceable." He was skeptical that the evening's "high purpose and virtue" could overcome its "towering" investment, its "staggering" weekly expenses, and its top-ticket price of six dollars. Chapman said the work was a "bold and stunning departure" from the typical musical, and was "flaming, opulent, disturbing and imaginative." Although the evening was sometimes "overly solemn" and took its time getting started, he felt audiences would be "rewarded" if they "gave" in to the musical's special charms (but they would "have to do a lot of giving"). He praised the "splendid" cast (and noted Irra Petina was a "wonderful lowdown comedian" with a "fine voice"), and said Howard Bay's décor, Irene Sharaff's costumes, and Jack Cole's choreography were "turbulent and ablaze with color."

Watts noted that Villa-Lobos was "clearly the star" with his score of "power and originality" and "striking austerity," and like most of the critics he singled out "The Broken Pianolita" (Garland said it was a "show-stopper," Atkinson enjoyed the "amusingly orchestrated burlesque" of the broken mechanical piano, and William Hawkins in the *New York World-Telegram* liked the "startling conflicts" of its musical styles).

As for the murder scene, Watts found it a "rather dubious episode": Teresa serenades Carabana while he dines, he "writhes over the table," begins a series of convulsions, and then dies (and all of this is presented in "much detail").

Because of the ASCAP musicians' strike, there was no chance of a cast album, but years later a special one-performance concert version at Lincoln Center's Alice Tully Hall on November 23, 1987 (with Raitt, Judy Kaye, Faith Esham, Keith Curran, Charles Repole, Kevin Gray, and George Rose) led to a CD recording issued two years later (CBS # MK-44945) with Kaye, Esham, Gray, Rose, and Jerry Hadley. In May 2010, the Theatre du Chatelet's production was broadcast on MusiqueFrance radio, and a pirated recording of the complete two-act performance has made the rounds of theatre-music collectors. Judy Kaye's collection *Where, Oh Where: Rare Songs of the American Theatre* (Premier Recordings CD # PRCD-1001) includes a "fantasy-medley" of four songs from *Magdalena* ("Magdalena," "The Omen Bird," "Bon Soir, Paris," and "Food for Thought").

LOVE LIFE
"A VAUDEVILLE"

Theatre: 46th Street Theatre
Opening Date: October 7, 1948; *Closing Date*: May 14, 1949
Performances: 252
Book and *Lyrics*: Alan Jay Lerner
Music: Kurt Weill
Direction: Elia Kazan; *Producer*: Cheryl Crawford; *Choreography*: Michael Kidd; *Scenery*: Boris Aronson; *Costumes*: Lucinda Ballard; *Lighting*: Peggy Clark; *Musical Direction*: Joseph Littau
Cast: Nanette Fabray (Susan Cooper), Ray Middleton (Sam Cooper), Johnny Stewart (Johnny Cooper), Cheryl Archer (Elizabeth Cooper), Jay Marshall (Magician), Johnny Thompson (Hobo), Elly Ardelty (Trapeze Artist), Lyle Bettger (William Taylor), Victor Clarke (Interlocutor); Children (The Three Tots): Rosalie Alter, Glenn Dale, Vincent Gugleotti; The Quartette: John Diggs, Joseph James, James Young, William Veasey;

The Go-Getters: David Collyer, Victor Clark, David Thomas, Robert Byrn, Jules Racine, Gene Tobin, Mark Kramer, Larry Robbins; Singers: Holly Harris, Josephine Lambert, Peggy Turnley, Marie Leidal, Sylvia Stahlman, Carol Maye, Lily Paget, Dorothea Berthelson, Faye E. Smith, David Collyer, Victor Clarke, David Thomas, Robert Byrn, Evans Thornton, Gene Tobin, Mark Kramer, Larry Robbins; Dancers: Paula Lloyd, Melissa Hayden, Pat (Patricia) Hammerlee, Wanna Allison, Virginia Conwell, Barbara McCutcheon, Ed Philips, Bill Bradley, Frank Westbrook, Arthur Partington, Forrest Bonshire, Michael Maule, Veda Brown, Robert Tucker

The musical was presented in two acts.

The action takes place mostly in Mayville, Connecticut, and New York City during the period from 1791 to the present.

Musical Numbers

Act One: "Who Is Samuel Cooper?" (Holly Harris, David Thomas, Gene Tobin, Robert Byrn, Women); "My Name Is Samuel Cooper" (Ray Middleton); "Here I'll Stay" (Nanette Fabray, Ray Middleton); "Progress" (The Go-Getters); "I Remember It Well" (Nanette Fabray, Ray Middleton); "Green-Up Time" (Nanette Fabray, Men and Women); "Green-Up Time" (dance) (Arthur Partington, Dancers); "Economics" (The Quartette); "Mother's Getting Nervous" (The Three Tots); "My Kind of Night" (Ray Middleton); "Women's Club Blues" (Nanette Fabray, Women); "Women's Club Blues" (dance) (Dancers); "Love Song" (Johnny Thompson); "I'm Your Man" (Ray Middleton, Larry Robbins, Victor Clarke, David Thomas, David Collyer)

Act Two: "Ho, Billy, O!" (David Thomas, Madrigal Singers); "I Remember It Well" (reprise) (Ray Middleton, Nanette Fabray); "Is It Him or Is It Me?" (Nanette Fabray); "Punch and Judy Get a Divorce" (ballet) (Dancers); "This Is the Life" (Ray Middleton); The Minstrel Show: (1) "Here I'll Stay" (reprise) (Victor Clarke); (2) "Minstrel Parade" (Minstrels); (3) "Madame Zuzu" (Holly Harris, Carolyn Maye); (4) "Taking No Chances" (David Thomas); and (5) "Mr. Right" (Nanette Fabray, Sylvia Stahlman)

Alan Jay Lerner and Kurt Weill's *Love Life* was one of the most ambitious musicals ever seen on Broadway. It was truly groundbreaking in its attempt to examine marriage and family life in the United States from colonial times to the present day; in its use of two characters, husband Sam Cooper (Ray Middleton) and wife Susan (Nanette Fabray), who never age as they personify a couple who live through the dynamics of a changing economy and the nation's shifting mores, morals, and values; and in its use of various forms of entertainment styles to tell its vaudeville-like story (magic, old-fashioned dances, singing quartettes, trapeze artists, a Charles Addams–styled children's trio, a mild strip tease, radio programs, madrigals, a Punch and Judy ballet, and a minstrel show).

Here was one of the first concept musicals in which every facet of the production was used to tell an essentially abstract story in order to convey the atmosphere and mood of American marriage and family life. And like the concept musicals that came after it, there was no clear-cut ending (as the curtain falls, Sam and Susan are teetering on a tightrope in an attempt to meet one another halfway and try to mend their marriage, but there's no assurance they'll do so). (For more information about the history and conventions of the concept musical, see **Allegro**.)

Love Life received mixed reviews; about half the critics were enthusiastic, but the others were disappointed. The show lost money, but the public was interested enough to allow it to play out the season for a total of 252 performances, and Nanette Fabray won a Tony Award for Best Leading Actress in a Musical. Because of the ASCAP musicians' strike, there was no cast recording, but over the years two songs ("Here I'll Stay" and "Green-Up Time") have enjoyed a certain amount of popular currency.

Kurt Weill's score was one of his best, and clearly the performances of Nanette Fabray and Ray Middleton, Michael Kidd's choreography, Elia Kazan's direction, and the lavish décor by Boris Aronson and Lucinda Ballard were all on target. It was unfortunately Lerner's book that caused the major problems. His concept was admirably ambitious but fuzzy in execution, and one could never be certain what he was trying to say. Was economic progress detrimental to marriage? Was the shift from an agricultural to an industrialized society a bad thing? Were politically empowered women who join the work force the reason for the downfall of marriage?

Major cultural, social, political, and economic changes are always challenging, and since time began one assumes every age had specific outside factors that threatened the stability of the family. Life couldn't have been easy in London during the plague years; the American pioneers certainly faced unimaginable hardships; and throughout the ages war, famine, disease, and natural disasters must have seemed almost insurmountable to those who lived through them. But they all coped, they all got through their trials, and we're all still here. So why did Lerner think the relatively easy life of Sam and Susan was emblematic of the instability of marriage? Did he really believe progress was detrimental to happiness? Maybe not—but his libretto wasn't fully realized and whatever points he was trying to make were unclear. In many ways, his book suffered the fate of Oscar Hammerstein II's script for **Allegro**: Hammerstein probably didn't mean to contrast city and small town life in order to reach the conclusion that the Big City is Bad (it seems more likely Hammerstein was trying to say that one has to get closer to one's roots in order to find happiness, and thus even an unhappy city boy in the country might find a more fulfilling life if he returned to the city), and perhaps Lerner didn't mean to condemn progress as the root of the nation's marital problems. But unfortunately his script came across as somewhat sophomoric in its criticisms and conclusions.

But Lerner's script and lyrics were often genuinely amusing. When listening to the radio, Sam's complaining teenage daughter wonders who to believe, Louella Parsons or Hedda Hopper? Sam shuts her up with his reply: "Walter Winchell." And Lerner's lyric for the madrigal "Ho, Billy, O!" wasn't traditional; it was a "modern" one in which the hero is a neurotic manic depressive who is sexually maladjusted. Lerner's book also provided a framework that allowed for ample opportunities to tell the story through musical sequences, and Weill provided a glorious score overflowing with memorable songs. "Green-Up Time" was an insinuating melody of the joys of spring (and a kissing cousin to "June Is Bustin' Out All Over"); "Here I'll Stay" was a delicately hopeful if moody blues; "Economics" and "Progress" were wry and comic looks at two of Lerner's major themes; Sam's "This Is the Life" was a sweepingly bravura statement of his newfound independence when he tries to assert his freedom from marital bonds; and Susan's devastating "Mr. Right" was a show-stopper in which she described her ideal man: when she makes mistakes ("as whom doesn't?"), he'll just smile and nod and indulge her.

Brooks Atkinson in the *New York Times* found *Love Life* "cute, complex and joyless—a general gripe masquerading as entertainment." The evening was an "intellectual idea" turned "bitter" and "gone wrong," and the story soon became lost in a "strange, cerebral labyrinth." But he said Weill had never before written such a "versatile" and "agreeable" score, and he singled out six numbers. John Lardner in the *New York Star* felt the evening began well, and noted that the first act included the "best" of Weill's "tuneful and ingenious" score (he mentioned four songs), but when the second act offered such numbers as a divorce ballet and a "painfully sophisticated" minstrel show, the musical went "kerplop." William Hawkins in the *New York World-Telegram* felt the musical tried "too hard to be different" and switched moods so frequently that it seemed "ashamed" of them. But the evening offered "plenty of entertainment," and the show-stopper "Mr. Right" was to Nanette Fabray what "The Saga of Jenny" had been to Gertrude Lawrence in **Lady in the Dark**. Howard Barnes in the *New York Herald Tribune* noted the musical had a "fresh and stimulating approach" to its subject but was unfortunately more "approach" than "accomplishment." And while he found the score "fair to middling," he nonetheless praised nine songs, including Fabray's "triumphant" and "fetching" "Mr. Right."

But Richard Watts in the *New York Post* said *Love Life* had "excitement, distinction and style," Lerner's lyrics were "varied, intelligent and amusing," and Weill's score was "striking, lively and tuneful." He noted he'd never before quite appreciated Fabray, but was now ready to proclaim her "enchanting" with a "spirit and sparkle" that were "irresistible." Ward Morehouse in the *New York Sun* found the "distinctive" work "thoroughly stimulating" in an "experimental and imaginative mood," and John Chapman in the *New York Daily News* said that in "conception and performance" *Love Life* was a "superb" musical with "original and quite witty" sequences.

Robert Garland in the *New York Journal-American* found the musical "elegant" and "unusual," singled out seven songs, and said Cheryl Crawford had given *Love Life* a "smart" production; and Robert Coleman in the *New York Daily Mirror* said the new work was a "superlative entertainment" that set a "new high standard" for the Broadway musical; it was an "adroit" blend of story and vaudeville and its "great achievement" was its ability to be "constantly entertaining" as "wonderful theatre" while it still made its points about American family life. He also praised Fabray's "electric delivery" of "Mr. Right," and said the number was "one of the theatre's all-time tops in torch songs."

During the tryout, Jay Marshall succeeded Robert Strauss in the role of the magician. The following numbers were cut: "Susan's Dream," "You Understand Me So" (once this trio was dropped, it left Lyle

Bettger with a non-singing role), "The Locker Room," and the dance "Puppet Show." Incidentally, Lerner later reworked the lyric of "I Remember It Well" for his and Frederick Loewe's 1958 film musical *Gigi* where it was memorably sung by Maurice Chevalier and Hermione Gingold.

Over the years, most of the *Love Life* score has been recorded, but what is essential is a complete studio cast recording to fully preserve one of the most important musicals and scores in the history of American theatre. In the late 1980s, it was rumored that John McGlinn was planning to assemble singers and orchestra for a studio cast album of the score. He, Kim Criswell, Davis Gaines, and the National Symphony Orchestra presented two performances of theatre music on November 23 and 24, 1990, at the Kennedy Center, and the program included four selections from *Love Life*: the overture, "Here I'll Stay," "Love Song," and "Mr. Right." And in 1996, McGlinn's *Kurt Weill on Broadway* (Angel CD # 7243-5-55563-2-5) featured Thomas Hampson, Jeanne Lehman, and other singers in a twenty-plus-minute sequence of five songs from the musical ("Who Is Samuel Cooper?," "My Name Is Samuel Cooper," "Here I'll Stay," "I Remember It Well," and "This Is the Life"). But unfortunately a full-fledged recording of the score never happened.

Many songs from the score have surfaced on other recordings. The collection *Alan Jay Lerner Revisited* (Painted Smiles CD # PSCD-141) includes "Progress," "Love Song," "Economics," "Mr. Right," "This Is the Life," and "I'm Your Man" sung by a number of Broadway stalwarts including Jerry Orbach, Dorothy Loudon, and Nancy Walker; and *Alan Jay Lerner Performs His Own Songs: Lyrics by Lerner* (DRG CD # 5246) includes "Love Song," "Economics," "Here I'll Stay," "Green-Up Time," "Progress," "Mr. Right," and the deleted "Susan's Dream."

Other recordings include "Here I'll Stay" (Julie Andrews, *Broadway: Here I'll Stay: The Words of Alan Jay Lerner*; Philips CD 446-219-2); "Green-Up Time" and "Economics" (Brent Barrett, *The Alan Jay Lerner Album*; Fynsworth Alley CD # 302-062-161-2); "Here I'll Stay" and "This Is the Life" (Bryn Terfel, *If Ever I Would Leave You*; Deutsche Grammophon CD # 289-457-628-2); "Here I'll Stay" (Barbara Brussell, *Lerner in Love*; LML Music [unnumbered CD]); "This Is the Life" (*Kurt Weill: This Is the Life and Other Unrecorded Songs*; Arabesque Recordings CD # Z6579); "Green-Up Time" (*Kurt Weill: Life, Love and Laughter: Dance Arrangements, 1927–50*; RCA/BMG CD # 09026-63513-2); "This Is the Life" and "Here I'll Stay" (*Kurt Weill on Broadway*; Koch/Schwann CD # 3-1416-2); "Green-Up Time," "Love Song," and "Here I'll Stay" (*Kurt Weill in America*; LML Music CD # AND-07); "Economics" and "Here I'll Stay" (*Lerner, Loewe, Lane & Friends*; Varese Sarabande 2-CD set # VSD2-5917); "Ho, Billy, O!" (*Songs of Humor and Satire* by The Gregg Smith Singers; Premier CD # PRCD-1030); "Love Song" (*You Can't Put Ketchup on the Moon*; CD # SLRR-9201); "My Kind of Night" (*Kurt Weill Revisited II*; CD # PSCD-109); and the deleted "The Locker Room" (*Kurt Weill Revisited: Volume I*; CD # PSCD-108).

A major revival of *Love Life* was presented at the Walnut Street Theatre in Philadelphia, Pennsylvania, on June 6–24, 1990; the cast include Debbie Shapiro (Gravitt) as Susan and Richard Muenz as Sam; the production was directed by Barry Harman, choreographed by Christopher Chadman, and "additional book materials" were written by Thomas Babe. The production was a rare opportunity to hear the score in context, but unfortunately the weaknesses of Lerner's original conception still had to be dealt with. The revival omitted "My Name Is Samuel Cooper" and "Ho, Billy, O!," but reinstated "Susan's Dream."

The deleted "The Locker Room" was a paean by Sam to the all-male camaraderie of the locker room, and makes an interesting companion piece to Leonard Bernstein's "There's a Law about Men" from *Trouble in Tahiti* (1952; first performed on Broadway in 1955) in which another character (also named Sam, and who is also undergoing a midlife crisis) sings of his frustrations in the exclusively male environment of the locker room.

Awards

Tony Award: Best Leading Actress in a Musical (**Nanette Fabray**)

WHERE'S CHARLEY?
"A NEW MUSICAL COMEDY"

Theatre: St. James Theatre
Opening Date: October 11, 1948; *Closing Date*: September 9, 1950

Performances: 792
Book: George Abbott
Lyrics and *Music*: Frank Loesser
Based on the 1892 play *Charley's Aunt* by Brandon Thomas.
Direction: George Abbott; *Producers*: Cy Feuer and Ernest H. Martin in association with Gwen Rickard (Mrs. Ray Bolger); *Choreography*: George Balanchine; *Scenery* and *Costumes*: David Ffolkes; *Lighting*: Uncredited; *Musical Direction*: Max Goberman
Cast: John Lynds (Brassett), Byron Palmer (Jack Chesney), *Ray Bolger* (Charley Wykeham), Doretta Morrow (Kitty Verdun), Allyn (Ann) McLerie (Amy Spettigue), Edgar Kent (Wilkinson), Paul England (Sir Francis Chesney), Horace Cooper (Mr. Spettigue), Jack Friend (A Professor), Jane Lawrence (Donna Lucia D'Alvadorez), James Lane (Photographer), Marie Foster (Patricia), Douglas Deane (Reggie); Dancers: Mary Alice Bingham, Vicki Barrett, Geraldine Delaney, Marge Ellis, Marie Foster, Marcia Maier, Nina Starkey, Susan Stewart, Toni Stuart, Douglas Deane, George Enke, John Friend, Bobby Harrell, Dusty McCaffrey, Walter Rinner, Bill Weber, Gordon West, Ken Whelan; Singers: Rae Abruzzo, Jane Judge, Ruth McVane, Betty Oakes, Eleanor Parker (not the film actress with the same name), Katharine Reeve, Gloria Sullivan, Irene Weston, Robert Baird, James Bird, Dan Gallagher, Bob Held, Cornell MacNeil, Stowe Phelps, William Scully, Ernest Taylor
The musical was presented in two acts.
The action takes place at Oxford University in 1892.

Musical Numbers

Act One: "The Years Before Us" (Students); "Better Get Out of Here" (Ray Bolger, Allyn McLerie, Doretta Morrow, Byron Palmer); "The New Ashmolean Marching Society and Students' Conservatory Band" (Byron Palmer, Allyn McLerie, Doretta Morrow, Bobby Harrell, Students and Young Ladies); "My Darling, My Darling" (Byron Palmer, Doretta Morrow); "Make a Miracle" (Ray Bolger, Allyn McLerie); "Serenade with Asides" (Horace Cooper); "Lovelier Than Ever" (Jane Lawrence, Paul England, Students and Young Ladies); "The Woman in His Room" (Allyn McLerie); "Pernambuco" (ballet) (danced by Ray Bolger, Allyn McLerie, The Pernambucans)

Act Two: "Where's Charley?" (Byron Palmer, Cornell MacNeil, Stowe Phelps, Students and Young Ladies); "Once in Love with Amy" (Ray Bolger); "The Gossips" (Jane Judge, Marie Foster, Rae Abruzzo, Betty Oakes, Katharine Reeve, Gloria Sullivan, Eleanor Parker, Mary Alice Bingham, Irene Weston, Ruth McVane, Geraldine Delaney); "At the Red Rose Cotillion" (Byron Palmer, Doretta Morrow, Guests; danced by Ray Bolger and Allyn McLerie); Finale

Based on Brandon Thomas's 1892 farce *Charley's Aunt*, Frank Loesser's *Where's Charley?* revolves around the shenanigans at Oxford University when students Charley Wykeham (Ray Bolger) and Jack Chesney (Byron Palmer) devise a scheme for Charley to impersonate his rich aunt, Donna Lucia D'Alvadorez (Jane Lawrence), so that "she" can chaperone Amy Spettigue (Allyn McLerie) and Kitty Verdun (Doretta Morrow) when they visit Charley and Jack in their rooms for lunch. Soon Charley is darting in and out of the rooms in Aunt Lucia drag and later is amorously pursued by both Amy's uncle, Mr. Spettigue (Horace Cooper), and Jack's father, Sir Francis (Paul England). And just when the confusion couldn't get any more confused, in walks the real Aunt Lucia from Brazil ("where the nuts come from").

The musical ran for two years, won Ray Bolger a Tony Award for Best Leading Actor in a Musical, enjoyed two hit songs ("Once in Love with Amy" and "My Darling, My Darling"), and was made into a faithful film version. But surprisingly the show received many indifferent reviews. Bolger and the cast were praised, but the critics felt George Abbott's book was flat, unfunny, and missed the inherent charms of Thomas's farce, and some were less than impressed with Frank Loesser's score, which marked his first full-length Broadway musical. Loesser had written many popular hits, either independent songs or ones from films, and some reviewers felt his numbers for the musical were a bit of a let-down.

Brooks Atkinson in the *New York Times* said Bolger was "great enough" to make the "mediocre" musical with its "rusty plot" seem "thoroughly enjoyable," and he liked the "lively" score (and noted Loesser had the "most acceptable notion" of combining songwriting with composing). John Chapman in the *New York Daily*

News said without Bolger the musical wouldn't be "engaging," and while he found Loesser's score "pleasant," he felt the book was on the "slow side." Richard Watts in the *New York Post* found the goings-on "strangely dreary" because the "routine and spiritless effort" lacked "humor, style and high spirits" and Loesser's contributions were "pleasant" but "commonplace and unexhilarating." John Lardner in the *New York Star* felt that while most of the performers were "handcuffed" to the plot, the usually "knock 'em dead" Loesser "leaves you slightly more conscious with his gentle score" (and he noted that "Once in Love with Amy" allowed Bolger to "wrap up the whole art of comic dancing in one big package").

Howard Barnes in the *New York Herald Tribune* said the "heavy-handed and witless entertainment" was "rarely funny" with its "bad" book and "lumbering" direction, and while he liked the "fairish tune" of "Make a Miracle" and the "good march" "The New Ashmolean Marching Society and Students' Conservatory Band," the score was otherwise "unimaginative." Ward Morehouse in the *New York Sun* said the "lackadaisical" show was "humorless" and he couldn't advise his readers to "go hurtling" toward the St. James box office because the score was "routine" and the "superior" Bolger needed "better songs, a better book, and a better show." And Robert Coleman in the *New York Daily Mirror* stated Bolger made a "triumphant" return to Broadway in a "mediocre" musical, and although the show had its "hilarious moments" they weren't enough to warrant a top ticket price of six dollars. Coleman and about half his colleagues ignored "Once in Love with Amy," which proved to be one of the most memorable show-stoppers of its era (Coleman felt that Bolger had been denied "a truly sock number designed to send the first-nighters out cheering").

William Hawkins in the *New York World-Telegram* found the "sublimely satisfactory" musical the "sort of show you fall in love with, and go back to see over and over again." Abbott's book was "humorous and concise," Loesser's score was "brisk and fresh," and Bolger's "Once in Love with Amy" was infused with such "jubilance" that it alone was "worth the whole evening." Robert Garland in the *New York Journal-American* said that thanks to Bolger the evening was occasionally "amusing"; and he noted the star danced "most rapturously" and "flawlessly" when he took over the stage with "Once in Love with Amy." Incidentally, Coleman made a curious comment about the audience, noting that "thanks to somebody" the opening night was free "of the hoodlums in mink and tails who have been cheapening the recent openings with Mayfairy misdemeanors."

Because of the ASCAP musicians' strike, there was no cast album, but Bolger recorded "Once in Love with Amy." The script was published in softback by Samuel French (London; undated edition circa 1958), and the lyrics for all the used and unused songs are included in the collection *The Complete Lyrics of Frank Loesser* ("Saunter Away" was cut during the tryout, and the following were dropped in preproduction: "Culture and Breeding," "Your Own College Band," "The Train That Brought You to Town," and "Don't Introduce Me to That Angel").

After *Where's Charley?* closed, Bolger took a short vacation and then headlined a brief national tour that began in Boston in December 1950, continued on to New York for a brief return engagement, and then played in other cities such as San Francisco and Los Angeles. The New York visit opened at the Broadway Theatre on January 29, 1951, for forty-eight performances, and in some respects the tour served as a tryout for the upcoming film version in which Bolger, McLerie, Cooper, and England reprised their original roles (Robert Shackleton performed the part of Jack Chesney both on tour and in the film).

Produced by Warner Brothers, the film was made in England (one of the dancers is future *Upstairs Downstairs* creator and star Jean Marsh); directed by David Butler and choreographed by Michael Kidd, the adaptation is surprisingly faithful to its source and is thus a solid re-creation of the show and its performance style. Because of rights issues, the film has unfortunately not been seen in public for decades.

The London production opened at the Palace Theatre on February 20, 1958, for 404 performances; Norman Wisdom was Charley, and this time around the dances were created by Hanya Holm. Happily, the London version was recorded by Columbia (LP # 33SX1085), and the CD was issued by EMI/West End Angel (# 0777-7-89058-2-0). The CD was later reissued and paired with the 1959 London cast of *Chrysanthemum* on *Must Close Saturday* (# MCSR-3044). A college revival (probably produced at the University of Vermont) was recorded and privately issued during the early 1960s. The unused "Your Own College Band" is included in the collection *Lost in Boston III* (Varese Sarabande CD # VSD-5563) along with "The Bee," which may or may not have been intended for *Where's Charley?*

The musical was included as part of the New York City Center Light Opera Company's 1966 tribute to Frank Loesser (which also offered *Guys and Dolls*, *The Most Happy Fella*, and *How to Succeed in Business without Really Trying*); the revival opened on May 25, 1966, for fifteen performances and was again directed by Abbott; the cast included Darryl Hickman (Charley), Susan Watson (Amy), David Smith (Jack), Karen Shepard (Kitty), Mort Marshall (Mr. Spettigue), and Eleanor Steber (Donna Lucia); in the singing chorus was Nina Hirschfeld, forever immortalized by her father Al Hirschfeld, who hid the letters of her first name in each and every one of his famed caricatures. The next revival occurred on December 19, 1974, when the musical opened at the Circle in the Square (Uptown) for seventy-six performances; among the cast members were Raul Julia (Charley), Marcia McClain (Amy), Jerry Lanning (Jack), and Taina Elg (Donna Lucia).

The musical was revived in concert by Encores! for a limited run of five performances at City Center beginning on March 17, 2011, with Rob McClure (Charley), Lauren Worsham (Amy), Sebastian Arcelus (Jack), Rebecca Luker (Donna Lucia), and Howard McGillin (Sir Francis). In his review for the *New York Times*, Charles Isherwood noted the concert was "impeccable on every level" and praised Loesser's songs, all of which "emerge from the dramatic moment at hand and precisely reflect the period and place."

Awards

Tony Award: Best Leading Actor in a Musical (**Ray Bolger**)

MY ROMANCE
"A New Musical Play"

Theatre: Shubert Theatre (during run, the musical transferred to the Adelphi Theatre)
Opening Date: October 19, 1948; *Closing Date*: January 8, 1949
Performances: 95
Book and *Lyrics*: Rowland Leigh
Music: Sigmund Romberg
Based on the 1913 play *Romance* by Edward Sheldon.
Direction: Rowland Leigh; *Producers*: The Messrs. Shubert; *Choreography*: Frederic N. Kelly; *Scenery*: Watson Barratt; *Costumes*: Lou Eisele; *Lighting*: Uncredited; *Musical Direction*: Roland Fiore
Cast: Lawrence Brooks (Bishop Armstrong aka Tom), Joan Shepard (Suzette Armstrong), Marion Bradley (Alice), Hildegarde Halliday (Miss Potherton), William Berrian (Harry Armstrong), Melville Ruick (Cornelius van Tuyl), Hazel Dawn Jr. (Susan van Tuyl), Tom Bate (Percival Hawthorne-Hillary), Barbara Patton (Mrs. DeWitt), Gail Adams (Veronica DeWitt), Luella Gear (Octavia Fotheringham), Rex Evans (Sir Frederick Putman), Doris Patston (Lady Putman), Melton Moore (Rupert Chandler), Nat Burns (Vladimir Luccachevitch), Natalie Norman (Miss Joyce), Lawrence Weber (Bertie Wessel), Verna Epperly (Georgianna Curtright), Mary Jane Sloan (Margaret Pears), Andy Aprea (Lawrence Riley), Lou Maddox (Thyra Winslow), Donald Crocker (Dewitt Bodeen), Allegra Varron (Rosella), Anne Jeffreys (Mme. Marguerita Cavallini aka Rita), Madeline Holmes (Charlotte Armstrong), Tito Coral (Tosatti), Edith Lane (First Maid), Patricia Boyer (Second Maid), Norval Tormsen (Page Boy); Other Guests: Martha Burnett, June Reimer, Muriel Birkhead, Harold Ronk, LeRoy Bush
The musical was presented in three acts.
The action takes place in New York City during the present time and in 1898.

Musical Numbers

Act One: Overture (Orchestra); "Souvenir" (Lawrence Brooks); "1898" (Ensemble); "Debutante" (Hazel Dawn Jr., Gail Adams, Ensemble); "Written in Your Hand" (Hazel Dawn Jr., Lawrence Brooks); "Millefleurs" (Anne Jeffreys); "Love and Laughter" (Anne Jeffreys, Lawrence Brooks); "From Now Onward" (Anne Jeffreys, Lawrence Brooks); "Little Emmaline" (Luella Gear); "Aria" (Anne Jeffreys)
Act Two: "Desire" (Lawrence Brooks); "Polka" (Gail Adams, Barbara Patton, Ensemble); "If Only" (Anne Jeffreys); "Bella Donna" (Tito Coral, Anne Jeffreys, Ensemble); "Paradise Stolen" (Anne Jeffreys, Lawrence Brooks); "In Love with Romance" (Anne Jeffreys, Lawrence Brooks); Finaletto (Lawrence Brooks)

Act Three: "Waltz Interlude" (Allegra Varron); "Musical Scene" (Anne Jeffreys, Lawrence Brooks); "Prayer" (Anne Jeffreys); Finale (Anne Jeffreys, Lawrence Brooks)

The Shuberts' lugubrious operetta *My Romance* received scathing reviews, but with some forcing it managed to run for almost three months. Based on Edward Sheldon's popular 1913 play *Romance*, the clichéd story centered on Italian-opera-star-with-a-Past Rita, otherwise known as Mme. Marguerita Cavallini (Anne Jeffreys), and her fluctuating on-again, off-again romance with staid Episcopalian priest Tom (Lawrence Brooks). Of course, Romance between two of such different backgrounds can Never Be, and so the would-be lovers Must Part. The musical used a number of clichés from the operetta grab bag, including a story which was told in flashback (it began and ended in 1948 with Tom, now a bishop, Looking Back on three acts that took place during the year 1898); the musical employed the hoary humors of old-hat operetta, and here the would-be bon mots were given to comedian Luella Gear (perhaps her best line was that her next husband must have one foot in the grave and the other at Tiffany's); and there were song titles which seemed to say it all, including "Souvenir," "Written in Your Hand," "Millefleurs," "Love and Laughter," "Desire," "Polka," "Paradise Stolen," "In Love with Romance," "Waltz Interlude," "Prayer," and perhaps the best title of them all, "From Now Onward." There were no merry villagers (although Manhattan society types perhaps served this function) and there were no gypsies (but there was an organ-grinder named Tosatti); shockingly, there seems to have been no hushed and solemn obeisances to royalty during the entire course of the prologue, three acts, and epilogue (one critic noted that not counting two intermissions, the playing time was a full two hours and forty-five minutes).

The lovely Anne Jeffreys came in for a good deal of criticism. Robert Garland in the *New York Journal-American* said her singing and speaking bespoke a "dialect such as never was on land or sea"; noted she sang Sigmund Romberg's music with "harsh correctness"; and then mentioned her "Italian-American dialect" was "no comfort to my ear." John Lardner in the *New York Star* assumed that despite her "Romberg-Italian accent and all" she was a better singer than Doris Keane (who had originated the role of the opera singer in the 1913 production), but cautioned that because Jeffreys was so "handsome and tuneful" she might inspire more such operettas, and that would "be a heavy load for her lovely conscience to bear."

William Hawkins in the *New York World-Telegram* mentioned the "brazenly lovely looking" Jeffreys "wrestles with a kittenish accent and some hefty melodrama"; Howard Barnes in the *New York Herald Tribune* said her accent wavered among "Russian, Italian and Hottentot"; and Richard Watts in the *New York Post* found the "handsome" performer too "arch and metallic." John Chapman in the *New York Daily News* wryly noted that the "lovely" Jeffreys made for an "enchanting operetta heroine" who sang Romberg's songs "as though they meant something."

Perhaps some of the critics were snappish with Jeffreys because they were annoyed with her almost overbearingly coy and arch program biography. It stated that her personal notices for **Street Scene** included "all of Mr. Roget's glowing synonyms for 'magnificent'"; that in her recent film *Return of the Badmen*, she played a "hard-riding gun-gal"; that she had "six pet cats and a couple of dozen pet hats"; and that she was born in "Goldsboro, N.C., suh."

Brooks Atkinson in the *New York Times* stated the musical was "pretentious fiddle-faddle"; Watts said *My Romance* demonstrated that operetta "can be the most tedious form of dramatic art" because most of the evening resulted in "almost epoch-making dullness" and the "emotional claptrap" was "so unexhilarating," he wondered if perhaps he'd been "too hard" on **Where's Charley?**; Robert Coleman in the *New York Daily Mirror* said the evening was a "disappointment," but noted the audience's applause was "appreciative and robust" (he usually reported that first-nighters "blistered" their palms with applause, but this time around said they gave "salvos of palm pats"); Ward Morehouse in the *New York Sun* said the "entirely lifeless" and "poky and ponderous" musical was one of "almost overpowering dullness"; and Hawkins noted the term "Shubert musical" was a definition unto itself, and thus for those who liked a "Shubert musical" *My Romance* would give them a "perfectly wonderful time"; as for the others, they would have only themselves to blame if they attended the show.

Barnes found the music "dreary," the lyrics "witless," the performances a "dither of period posturing," the plot "ponderous," and the dialogue "stilted." Apparently even the direction was slipshod because the critic reported Jeffreys made an entrance with her pet monkey, proceeded to sing "Bella Donna" to the accompaniment of the organ-grinder, and then promptly made her exit, "quite forgetting her simian pet."

Earlier in the year, Garland had seen the musical's tryout when it had a completely different score (see below), and he had been "less unhappy" with that production than with the current one. As for Lardner, he noted there was a special place in purgatory that Dante had never written about: it was a special ring where "people are forced to play comedy roles in Shubert musicals" as punishment for their worldly sins.

As mentioned, the tryout of *My Romance* had been seen earlier in the year, when it opened on February 12, 1948, at the Shubert Theatre, New Haven, Connecticut; it played in such venues as the Forrest Theatre, Philadelphia, Pennsylvania, beginning on March 8; and opened on April 19 at the Great Northern Theatre in Chicago, Illinois, and closed there on May 9. For the tryout, the book and lyrics were by Rowland Leigh, but the score was by Denes Agay, with additional music by Philip Redowski; this production took place during the years 1947 and 1897, while the New York version (with music by Sigmund Romberg) took place in 1948 and 1898. Anne Jeffreys appeared in both the tryout and Broadway versions, but for Broadway Charles Fredericks was replaced by Lawrence Brooks.

When Romberg wrote an entirely new score, he apparently set to music some of the lyrics that had been heard during the tryout version with music by Agay or Redowski. The song titles "Souvenir," "Written in Your Hand," "Millefleurs," "Bella Donna," and "Prayer" were used in both versions; but the following were dropped between the tryout and the New York productions: "Fancy Free," "With You," "Entre Nous," "Laugh at Life," "Come Farfalle," "Nothing Like a Cup of Tea," "First Bouquet," "Romance," "Food for Thought," "Magic Moment," "The Vision," "Tingle," "Ev'ry Time I Dance the Polka," and, most importantly, "You're Near and Yet So Far." The latter's title was an all too familiar one, and it and its variations popped up throughout the decade in various musicals (see **Heaven on Earth**).

For years, rumors have persisted that a private original cast album of *My Romance* was recorded and is in the Shubert Archives. It makes sense, given that the Shuberts were the force behind the production, that Sigmund Romberg was in many ways their "house" composer, and that the ongoing ASCAP musicians' strike sadly ensured that many shows of the era were never commercially recorded (otherwise, it seems certain that **Inside U.S.A.**, **Love Life**, **Where's Charley?**, and **As the Girls Go** would have enjoyed cast recordings; happily, the strike was over by the end of 1948, and so the season's biggest hits, **Kiss Me, Kate** and **South Pacific**, were recorded). So perhaps the Shuberts wanted to ensure that Romberg's score for *My Romance* was preserved for posterity; unfortunately, if the recording exists, the public can't access it, and one can only hope that someday a limited edition CD might be made available.

AS THE GIRLS GO
"THE MUSICAL COMEDY"

Theatre: Winter Garden Theatre (during run, the musical transferred to the Broadway Theatre)
Opening Date: November 13, 1948; *Closing Date*: January 14, 1950
Performances: 420
Book: William Roos
Lyrics: Harold Adamson
Music: Jimmy McHugh
Direction: Howard Bay; *Producer*: A Michael Todd Production; *Choreography*: Hermes Pan; *Scenery* and *Lighting*: Howard Bay; *Costumes*: Oleg Cassini; *Musical Direction*: Max Meth
Cast: Bobby Clark (Waldo Wellington), Irene Rich (Lucille Thompson Wellington), Bill Callahan (Kenny Wellington), Betty Lou Barto (Mickey Wellington), Donny Harris (Tommy Wellington), John Sheehan (Guard), Betty Jane Watson (Kathy Robinson), Hobart Cavanaugh (Barber), John Brophy (White House Visitor), Cavada Humphrey (Miss Swenson), Curt Stafford (Butler), Daughters of the Boston Tea Party: Claire Grenville, Claire Louise Evans, Lois Bolton, and Marjorie Leach, Douglas Luther (Floyd Robinson, President of Potomac College), Mildred Hughes (Diane), Kenneth Spaulding (Photographer), Jack Russell (Ross Miller), Dorothea Pinto (Daphne), William Reedy (Another Photographer), Dick Dana (Blinky Joe), Rosemary Williamson (Darlene), Secret Service Women: Gregg Sherwood and Truly Barbara, Children: Marlene Cameron, Pauline Hahn, Norma Marlowe, Jonathan Marlowe, Clifford Sales, and Eugene Steiner, Ruth Thomas (Secretary), Kathryn Lee (Premiere Danseuse); Dancing Ensemble: Jeanette Aquillina, Carmina Cansino, Arline Castle, Babs Claire, Jessie Elliott, Yvette Fairhill, Christina Frerichs, Patty Ann Jackson, Margaret Jeanne Klein, Frances Krell, Pat Marlowe, Ila McAvoy, Toni Parker, Joyce Reedy, Diane Sinclair,

Norma Thornton, James Brock, Charles Chartier, Peter Conlow, James Elsegood, William Reedy, Bobby Roberts, Joseph Schenck, Eugene Schwab, Kenneth Spaulding, Larry Villani; Singing Ensemble: Barbara Davis, Lydia Fredericks, Betty George, Pearl Hacker, Abbe Marshall, Ellen McCown, Judy Sinclair, Jo Sullivan, Bob Burkhardt, Dean Campbell, John Gray, Douglas Luther, George Morris, Jack Russell, John Sheehan, Curt Stafford; Show Girls: Truly Barbara, Pat Gaston, Mildred Hughes, Mickey Miller, Dorothea Pinto, Gregg Sherwood, Ruth Thomas, Rosemary Williamson

The musical was presented in two acts.

The action takes place during 1953 in Washington, D.C.

Musical Numbers

Act One: "As the Girls Go" (Bobby Clark, Girls); "Nobody's Heart but Mine" (Betty Jane Watson, Bill Callahan); "Brighten Up and Be a Little Sunbeam" (Bobby Clark, Children); "Rock, Rock, Rock" (Bill Callahan, Betty Jane Watson); "It's More Fun Than a Picnic" (Betty Lou Barto, Children); "American Cannes" (Bobby Clark, Girls); "You Say the Nicest Things, Baby" (Betty Jane Watson, Bill Callahan, Singing Girls); "I've Got the President's Ear" (Bobby Clark, Girls); "Holiday in the Country" (Entire Company)

Act Two: "There's No Getting Away from You" (Bill Callahan, Singing and Dancing Ensembles); "Dance" (Kenneth Spaulding, Kathryn Lee, Dancing Ensemble); "Lucky in the Rain" (Bill Callahan, Betty Jane Watson, Ensemble; danced by Kathryn Lee and Bill Callahan); "Father's Day" (Bobby Clark, Irene Rich, Bill Callahan, Betty Lou Barto, Donny Harris); "It Takes a Woman to Get a Man" (Bobby Clark, Ensemble); "You Say the Nicest Things, Baby" (reprise) (Bobby Clark, Irene Rich); Finale (Entire Company)

Michael Todd's lavish musical *As the Girls Go* was a madcap merry-go-round that allowed Bobby Clark, the maddest comic of them all, a chance to cavort and frolic about in a free-wheeling plot as the nation's First Gentleman Waldo Wellington who is married to the first woman president of the United States Lucille Thompson Wellington (Irene Rich). As far as Bobby is concerned, living in the White House has one singular advantage: it gives him free rein to ogle and leer at amply endowed young lovelies who might happen to be about the premises, and, this being a musical comedy, there's plenty of feminine pulchritude in this White House.

Yes, Bobby and his famous leer, his painted-on glasses, his glowing cigar, his trick cane, his ambling gait, and his strange array of costumes were back in full glory. At one point, he made an entrance carrying a fur umbrella, and, perhaps as an homage to his former partner Paul McCullough, a fur coat. Following him is an assortment of flunkeys who tote his luggage, which includes scuba-diving equipment, skis, snow shoes, and golf clubs. When asked where he's going, Bobby replies that he has absolutely no idea.

The story's basic premise of the nation's first woman president was essentially over almost as soon as the show began; the evening wasn't intended as political satire (one critic noted that the president wondered if she could win a battleship on a radio quiz program, and that just about took care of the political jokes), and instead was an old-fashioned jamboree designed to give Bobby a series of wild comic turns.

And so Bobby gets mixed up with a group of kids visiting the White House, and in the Rumpus Room (which is perhaps down the hall from the Chartreuse Room) he gives them marching orders via the song "Brighten Up and Be a Little Sunbeam" (unfortunately, his idea of marching instructions is relegated to the announcement of "Forward . . . *Halt!*"). In another sequence he appeared in drag as a manicurist and barber in order to overhear the president's enemies conspire against her, and of course with Bobby in charge the manicure turns into a massacre and his tonsorial skills proceed to give Sweeney Todd a run for his money. Moreover, he makes mincemeat of an elegant White House tea for The Ladies of the Boston Tea Party, causes comic chaos at a university when he's awarded an honorary degree, and at one point he seems a one-man embodiment of the Marx Brothers as he dons a series of beards in order to disguise himself.

The critics described the musical as a *carnival*, a *festive carousel*, a *full cornucopia*, an *extravaganza*, a *romp*, and a *frolic*. For here was old-time musical comedy with nothing on its mind but fun. Brooks Atkinson in the *New York Times* said the musical was "bountiful and uproarious" and "gay and rowdy," and McHugh's score was "lively and melodious." He noted there was "hardly a corner of the script into which" Bobby Clark had "neglected to poke his gleaming impishness," and concluded there might be "many" presidents but there was "only one master of the revels."

Robert Coleman in the *New York Daily Mirror* said "human cyclone" Bobby Clark was "the funniest man in the world" in a "fast, furious, immensely funny frolic"; Richard Watts in the *New York Post* stated the "great, magnificent and incomparable" Clark was a "comic genius"; Ward Morehouse in the *New York Sun* liked the "strident and opulent" extravaganza and noted that the "demented" and "incomparable" Clark was at "his best," which meant "something wonderful in the American theatre"; Robert Garland in the *New York Journal-American* said Clark was "rough, ready and uproarious," and in the barber shop scene was at his funniest (Garland also noted the "American Cannes" lyric seemed to have "been dry-cleaned for Broadway"); and William Hawkins in the *New York World-Telegram* found Clark "wonderfully hilarious" in scenes of "wonderful" and "grand" nonsense; in short, there was "nothing in his kind of theatre that can top him."

John Lardner in the *New York Star* felt the show's book was a "spare part," but thanks to the "smilingly cynical" and "iconoclastic drollery" of Clark the "threadbare" plot was tolerable; and Howard Barnes in the *New York Herald Tribune* said without Clark the musical would have been a "haphazard and laggard entertainment" and a "downright bore."

John Chapman in the *New York Daily News* said the political humor was "slight," and beyond remembering that the songs contained "notes and music" he had "no memory" of them. But Clark took care of the show, and with him it couldn't have been in "better custody"; he was as "inexhaustible" as his wardrobe and he kept chasing the chorus girls all over the stage (Chapman feared if the girls stepped outside the theatre they'd "catch their deaths," and Morehouse noted the production offered the most nudity since Michael Todd's **Star and Garter**).

Because of the ASCAP musicians' strike, there was no cast album, but happily Bobby Clark recorded two numbers from the production, "Father's Day" and the rousing title song; these are included in the JJA collection *Four Cast Recordings: Arms and the Girl, As the Girls Go, Texas, Li'l Darlin'*, and *Meet the People* (LP # JJA-1975-2A/B). The musical's ballads have been widely recorded, and "Lucky in the Rain" is included in the collection *Mike Todd's Broadway* (Everest Records LP # LPBR-5011).

On July 9, 1997, Goodspeed Opera House, East Haddam, Connecticut, presented *Lucky in the Rain*; the book by Sherman Yellen utilized songs by Jimmy McHugh to tell its story (the only number borrowed from *As the Girls Go* was "Lucky in the Rain").

Because of Bobby Clark's health, *As the Girls Go* suspended performances for over two months during the middle of its Broadway run. The musical was capitalized at $340,000 and charged a then unheard-of top-ticket price of $7.20 (opening night seats were $12.00 apiece), and while the final number of showings tallied 420, this was the first time in Broadway history that a run of over four-hundred performances didn't guarantee financial success. This was a depressing omen of things to come, and within the next two decades musicals with runs of over five-hundred performances closed in the red (such as *Milk and Honey* and *What Makes Sammy Run?*), and soon even a run of one thousand performances couldn't ensure a profit.

As the Girls Go marked Bobby Clark's final appearance on Broadway. In 1950, he directed *Michael Todd's Peep Show* and contributed some sketches, and just prior to the New York opening the street swarmed with rumors that Bobby would appear in the show. But after *As the Girls Go*, his last stage appearances were in the mid-1950s when he starred in the national tour of *Damn Yankees* as Applegate (the devil).

Awards

Tony Award: Best Conductor and Musical Director (**Max Meth**)

LEND AN EAR
"AN INTIMATE MUSICAL REVUE"

Theatre: National Theatre (during run, the musical transferred to the Broadhurst, Shubert, and Mansfield Theatres)
Opening Date: December 16, 1948; *Closing Date*: January 21, 1950
Performances: 460
Sketches, Lyrics, and *Music*: Charles Gaynor; additional sketch by Joseph Stein and Will Glickman

Direction: Production directed by Hal Gerson and staged by Gower Champion; *Producers*: William R. Katzell, Franklin Gilbert, and William Eythe; *Choreography*: Gower Champion; *Scenery, Costumes*, and *Lighting*: Raoul Pene du Bois; *Musical Direction*: George Bauer

Cast: Yvonne Adair, Anne Renee Anderson, Dorothy Babbs, Carol Channing, Al Checco, Robert Dixon, William Eythe, Nancy Franklin, Antoinette Guhlke, George Hall, Gloria Hamilton, Bob Herget, Beverly Hosier, Jenny Lou Law, Arthur Maxwell, Tommy Morton, Gene Nelson, Bob Scheerer, Jeanine Smith, Lee Stacy, Larry Stewart; Duo Pianists: George Bauer and Dorothy Freitag

The revue was presented in two acts.

Sketches and Musical Numbers

Act One: "After Hours" (Company); "Give Your Heart a Chance to Sing" (The Girl: Dorothy Babbs; The Boys: Robert Dixon, Arthur Maxwell, Bob Herget, Tommy Morton, Bob Scheerer); "Neurotic You and Psychopathic Me" (The Nurse: Lee Stacy; The Patient: Anne Renee Anderson; The Doctor: William Eythe); "I'm Not in Love" (The Boss Who Dictates: Arthur Maxwell; The Secretary Who Sings: Yvonne Adair; The Bosses Who Dance: Gene Nelson, Tommy Morton, Bob Scheerer); "The Power of the Press" (sketch by Joseph Stein and Will Glickman) (Husband: George Hall; Wife: Carol Channing); "Friday Dancing Class" (Gloria Hamilton, Beverly Hosier, Jeanine Smith, Arthur Maxwell, Robert Dixon, Larry Stewart; Henry Jones: Bob Scheerer; Henry's Mother: Carol Channing; Henry's Friends: Al Checco, Bob Herget; Miss Bridey: Jenny Lou Law; The Girl: Dorothy Babbs; The Dancing Class: Lee Stacy, Antoinette Guhlke, Nancy Franklin, Gene Nelson, Bob Herget, Tommy Morton); "Ballade" (Anne Renee Anderson); "When Someone You Love Loves You" (Gloria Hamilton, Robert Dixon; danced by Antoinette Guhlke and Gene Nelson); and

"The Missing Road Company" (Announcer: William Eythe, who introduced the first act finale [the minimusical *The Gladiola Girl*])

The Gladiola Girl

Cast: Gloria Hamilton (Rosalie), William Eythe (Larry Van Patten), Yvonne Adair (Ginger O'Toole), George Hall (Skiddy Tyres), Bob Herget (Policeman); Girls: Dorothy Babbs, Anne Renee Anderson, Carol Channing, Lee Stacy; Boys: Bob Scheerer, Al Checco, Tommy Morton, Arthur Maxwell

The Gladiola Girl was presented in two acts; the first takes place in a garden in Bronxville, the second at Skiddy Tyres's estate on Long Island.

Act One: "Join Us in a Cup of Tea" (Boys and Girls); "Where Is the She for Me" (William Eythe, Girls); "I'll Be True to You" (Gloria Hamilton, William Eythe); "Doin' the Old Yahoo Step" (Yvonne Adair, Chorus); Finaletto

Act Two: Opening: "A Little Game of Tennis" (Boys and Girls); "In Our Teeny Little Weeny Nest" (Gloria Hamilton, William Eythe); Finale

Act Two: "Santo Domingo" (The Travel Agent: Arthur Maxwell; The Tourist: Yvonne Adair; Santo Domingans: Company); "I'm on the Lookout" (Gloria Hamilton); "Three Little Queens of the Silver Screen" (Lee Stacy, Anne Renee Anderson, Carol Channing); "Molly O'Reilly" (Jeanine Smith, Gloria Hamilton, Beverly Hosier, Robert Dixon, Arthur Maxwell, Larry Stewart; danced by Bob Scheerer and Dorothy Babbs); "All the World's" (Announcer: Arthur Maxwell; Mr. Playgoer: William Eythe; Mrs. Playgoer: Carol Channing; A Bartender: George Hall); "Who Hit Me?" (Yvonne Adair; danced by Gene Nelson); "Words without Song" (Announcer: Arthur Maxwell; The Countess: Carol Channing; Mathilda: Anne Renee Anderson; Alberto: George Hall; The Count: William Eythe; The Chorus: Antoinette Guhlke, Lee Stacy, Beverly Hosier, Jenny Lou Law, Bob Herget, Al Checco, Tommy Morton, Larry Stewart); Finale (Company)

Charles Gaynor's intimate *Lend an Ear* was one of the high water marks of the era's revues; with a small cast and modest scenery, the revue managed to be more entertaining than many that opened at three or four times its cost. The evening's songs and sketches were amiable, and many are among the most fondly remembered from the postwar period. Moreover, *Lend an Ear* put Carol Channing on the map. She had appeared in a handful of shows during the decade, but it was here that she made her mark, and a year later she starred in

Gentlemen Prefer Blondes and made the cover of *Time* magazine with her iconic interpretation of gold-digger Lorelei Lee. Also in the cast of *Lend an Ear* was Gene Nelson, who soon became a fixture of Warner Brothers' musicals, later played the role of Will Parker in the 1955 film version of *Oklahoma!*, and in 1971 starred in Stephen Sondheim's *Follies*, arguably the towering achievement of American musical theatre.

Lend an Ear was director and choreographer Gower Champion's second musical of the season (he had earlier choreographed **Small Wonder**, which was still playing when *Lend an Ear* opened). As a film and stage performer and choreographer he would stay busy for the next decade, but it wasn't until the 1960s that he came into his own as one of the foremost director-choreographers of the era with a string of hits: *Bye Bye Birdie* (1960; 607 performances), *Carnival!* (1961; 719), *Hello, Dolly!* (1964; 2,844; here Champion was of course memorably reunited with Carol Channing), and *I Do! I Do!* (1966; 560). In 1980, he directed and choreographed the stage version of the 1933 film musical *42nd Street*, which at 3,486 performances was his longest-running show (its 2001 revival chalked up an additional 1,524 showings). Sadly, Champion didn't enjoy his final triumph: in a twist that would have been criticized as too melodramatic had it occurred in the plot of a show, Champion died hours before the opening night curtain of his greatest hit, and his unexpected death made the front pages.

Charles Gaynor had written *Lend an Ear* during the early 1940s, and on and off throughout the decade the revue played the straw-hat circuit as well as in some of the larger cities (it premiered in Pittsburgh, Pennsylvania, in 1941). Its Los Angeles premiere at Las Palmas Theatre was a long-running West Coast hit, and when the show opened in New York for a full year's run, a second company was still playing in Los Angeles.

The most memorable sequence from *Lend an Ear* was *The Gladiola Girl*, a two-act mini-musical that brought down the first act curtain and was an affectionate tribute to the clichés of 1920s musicals (a few years later, Sandy Wilson's *The Boy Friend* covered the same territory with its tongue-in-cheek look at the songs, dances, acting techniques, and staging conventions of 1920s musical comedies). Other highlights of the revue were: the sketch "The Power of the Press," in which husband George Hall and wife Carol Channing read their morning newspaper and feel obliged to follow the advice and admonishments of every columnist (if a gossip columnist says *Mister Roberts* is worth seeing once a week, then the couple will buy tickets for every week of the show's run); the sketch "All the World's" in which moviegoers William Eythe and Channing emerge from three different movies, each time affecting the tone, accent, and style of the movie they've just seen (after a Shakespearian film, they speak in iambic pentameter and use such words as "zounds" and "prithee"); in the sketch "Words without Song," an opera company has an opera (*In Flagrante Delictu*), a prima donna (Channing), and a full singing company but unfortunately no orchestra to play the music; but since the show must go on, the singers speak the words of the libretto in the manner in which they would have been sung, and so the world "close" is spoken as "clo-ho-ho-hose"; and the song "Three Little Queens of the Silver Screen" was a gay and cynical romp in which Lee Stacy, Anne Renee Anderson, and Channing respectively portrayed Mary Pickford, Pearl White, and Theda Bara, three movie queens of yesteryear who bemoan the current screen products of Grables and Disney fables, none of which can hold a candle to their "silence-was-golden" days of celluloid glory (Channing revisited silent cinema when she appeared as another pre-talkie star in 1955's *The Vamp*).

Other delights in the revue were: "Santo Domingo," the de rigueur South American song-and-dance tribute (but here the "gay little isle" is in truth "dirty, dismal and drab," a place where tourists are insulted, attacked, robbed, knifed, or shot during a dance sequence in which a street fight morphs into a full-scale banana-republic-styled revolution); the song "Neurotic You and Psychopathic Me," a bit of madness in which a doctor and patient discover they're both awash in complexes and neuroses and thus can look forward to a happy life of "sharing abnormality" together; and the song "Ballade," which kidded sixteenth-century-styled folk ballads in its tale of Sir Richard, who loved to run his toes through the golden locks of Lady Alyce (*Vintage '60* explored the same territory with its "ballade" spoof "Dublin Town"). "Molly O'Reilly" was a nostalgic Irish number set in a turn-of-the-century beer garden, and the sketch "Friday Dancing Class" explored one of the "tragedies" of youth, the obligatory weekly dancing class (the 1957 Off-Broadway revues *Well I Never!* and *Take Five* offered a similarly themed number in "The Pro Musica Antiqua," which sympathized with prep school and finishing school students who are required to attend pompous musical "evenings").

Brooks Atkinson in the *New York Times* found the "band-box" revue a "model of skill and taste," and although it was "thoroughly professional" it nonetheless still offered "the genuine light-heartedness of an amateur carnival"; Howard Barnes in the *New York Herald Tribune* said the "superior" revue was "gay and refreshing" with talented performers and "exciting" choreography; Robert Garland in the *New York Journal-American* liked the "zestful" and "good-looking" show, and because of the "brilliance of the dancing" he suggested the title could have been *Lend an Eye* (and he especially enjoyed "Friday Dancing Class," which in "good mean fun" took swipes at Agnes De Mille in **Allegro** mode); and John Chapman in the *New York Daily News* praised the "original" dances, said the songs had "melody and bounce," and the overall production was "as friendly as a pup and as smart as a cat."

Richard Watts in the *New York Post* said the "bright and entertaining" evening was "so unaffectedly high-spirited that there is no resisting its appeal," and noted Channing was priceless in "All the World's" (after seeing Lawrence Olivier's *Hamlet*, she and her date stop at a bar for a drink, and when she accidentally spills wine on her clothes she says in plumy British tones, "Horror! Horror! Horror!," and then of course utters, "Out, damned spot!"). William Hawkins in the *New York World-Telegram* praised the "gay, exuberant and endearing" show, and noted that Channing was a "remarkable personality" and one of "the funniest people extant" who could be "ecstatically idiotic or viciously sophisticated in a twinkling." Herrick Brown in the *New York Sun* liked the revue's "most engaging air of freshness" and praised Champion's "excellent" dances. And Robert Coleman in the *New York Daily Mirror* noted that the entertainment sent the audience "into something closely resembling hysterics," and he felt the evening was like a party in which the "talented guests work themselves into a tizzy to entertain each other."

Unlike his colleagues, John Lardner in the *New York Star* was cool to the revue, and felt some of its targets were handled better in **Small World** and **Love Life**. But he noted the evening had "several assets," that Gaynor's material was often "glib and witty," and that *The Gladiola Girl* was a "triumph" well worth "the lofty price of admission" in its "grotesque and marvelous reproduction" of an authentic 1920s musical.

During the revue's pre-Broadway performances, a number of sketches and songs were cut, including the songs "Hard to Get," "Who Knows," "The Old McGinty Place," and "Romantic'ly Inclined" and the sketches "The Message," "Treatment," and "Science for Sale." The pre-Broadway sketch "After the Theatre" may have been an earlier version of "All the World's." For *The Gladiola Girl*, the song "Rough Stuff" was dropped. Late during the tryout, William Tabbert joined the production and was with the show during the early weeks of December and just prior to the Broadway opening; but he left the revue at some point during the month and didn't open in New York. Because the first tryout performances of **South Pacific** were scheduled for the first week of March 1949, Tabbert was no doubt already contracted to appear in the role of Lieutenant Cable and it's likely rehearsals for the Richard Rodgers and Oscar Hammerstein II musical began soon after the opening of *Lend an Ear*.

There was no cast album, but three songs ("Join Us in a Cup of Tea," "Doin' the Old Yahoo Step," and "In Our Teeny Little Weeny Nest") from *The Gladiola Girl* were included in Charles Gaynor's 1961 Broadway revue *Show Girl*, which starred Carol Channing. The cast recording, which was released by Roulette Records (LP # 80001; issued on CD by Kritzerland # KR-20012-9), included "Join Us in a Cup of Tea" and "Doin' the Old Yahoo Step." The collection *Make Mine Manhattan and Great Revues Revisited* (Painted Smiles CD # PSCD-119) includes a medley of "After Hours," "When Someone You Love Loves You," and "Molly O'Reilly."

The script was published in softcover by Samuel French in 1971 and includes "Do It Yourself" (from the 1959 Off-Broadway revival [see below]) and omits "The Power of the Press."

The revue was the subject of the October 2, 1949, telecast of CBS's *Tonight on Broadway* which included sequences from the show as well as cast interviews.

The Off-Broadway revival opened on September 24, 1959, at the Renata Theatre for ninety-four performances; two members from the original Broadway company (Jenny Lou Law and Al Checco) reprised their roles (the former also directed and coproduced the revival) and others in the cast were Susan Watson, June Squibb, Bob Fitch, Charles Nelson Reilly, and Elizabeth Allen. The sketch "The Power of the Press" (by Joseph Stein and Will Glickman) was deleted from the revival, and "Do It Yourself" (by Charles Gaynor) was added. Atkinson noted *The Gladiola Girl* was the evening's "most priceless" sequence, and he praised Squibb (who in order to "denote daring and abandon" kept her mouth wide open), Watson ("impossibly arch"), and Reilly ("dashing" in a "stalwart and grand" way).

Awards

Tony Awards: Best Choreography (**Gower Champion**)

THE TELEPHONE (or L'AMOUR A TROIS)
"A Curtain Raiser"

and

THE MEDIUM
"A Tragedy"

Theatre: City Center
Opening Date: December 7, 1948; *Closing Date*: January 9, 1949
Performances: 40
Direction: Gian-Carlo Menotti; *Producers*: The New York City Center by arrangement with Chandler Cowles, Efrem Zimbalist Jr., Edith Luytens (A Ballet Society Production); *Scenery* and *Costumes*: Horace Armistead; *Lighting*: Jean Rosenthal; *Musical Direction*: Emanuel Balaban
The Telephone (*Note*: Musical sequences weren't listed in the program.)
Cast: Marla d'Attili (Lucy), Paul King (Ben)
The opera was presented in one act.
The action takes place during the present time in New York City, in Lucy's apartment and in a nearby telephone booth.
The Medium (*Note*: Musical sequences weren't listed in the program.)
Cast: Evelyn Keller (Monica), Leo Coleman (Toby), Madame Flora (Marie Powers), Derna de Lys (Mrs. Gobineau), Paul King (Mr. Gobineau), Virginia Beeler (Mrs. Nolan)
The opera was presented in two acts.
The action takes place "in our time" in Madame Flora's apartment.

Gian-Carlo Menotti's double bill of the operas *The Telephone* and *The Medium* premiered on Broadway at the Ethel Barrymore Theatre for 212 performances beginning on May 1, 1947. The New York City Center produced the current revival by arrangement with the operas' original producers Chandler Cowles, Efrem Zimbalist Jr., and Edith Luytens, and cast members Marie Powers, Evelyn Keller, Virginia Beeler, and Leo Coleman reprised their original roles. The limited engagement marked the first New York showings of the two operas since the originals had closed in late 1947. For more information, see entry for the 1947 production.

For certain performances, Derna de Lys sang the role of Monica, Margery Mayer the role of Madame Flora, and Maria d'Attili the role of Mrs. Gobineau. It appears that for some performances, William McDermott was the musical director.

THE RAPE OF LUCRETIA
"A Music Drama"

Theatre: Ziegfeld Theatre
Opening Date: December 29, 1948; *Closing Date*: January 15, 1949
Performances: 23
Book (*Libretto*): Ronald Duncan
Music: Benjamin Britten
Based on the 1931 play *Le viol de Lucrece* by Andre Obey (produced on Broadway as *Lucrece* in 1932 in an adaptation by Thornton Wilder).

Direction: Agnes De Mille; *Producers*: Marjorie and Sherman Ewing, and Giovanni Cardelli; *Scenery* and *Costumes*: John Piper (Costume Supervision by Frank Thompson); *Lighting*: Peggy Clark; *Musical Direction*: Paul Breisach
Cast: Edward Kane (The Male Chorus), Brenda Lewis (The Female Chorus), Holger Sorenson (Collatinus), Emile Renan (Junius), George (Giorgio) Tozzi (Tarquinius), Kitty Carlisle (Lucretia), Vivian Bauer (Bianca), Marguerite Piazza (Lucia), Lidja Franklin (Roman Woman), Kazimir Kokic (Etruscan Soldier), Lucas Hoving (Etruscan Soldier), Robert Pagent (Roman Man), Stanley Simmons (Roman Youth), Bunty Kelley (Prostitute) (*Note*: The cast list represents the singers who performed on opening night; there were alternates throughout the run, including Patricia Neway, who sang the role of the Female Chorus at certain performances.)
The opera was presented in two acts.
The action takes place during 509 BC in Rome
Note: The program didn't list musical numbers.

Benjamin Britten's chamber opera *The Rape of Lucretia* was a brave undertaking for Broadway. The work had first been produced at the Glyndebourne Festival on July 12, 1946, and ultimately enjoyed a consecutive run of 150 performances in Britain. It played in numerous world capitals, and the United States premiere by the Opera Theatre of Chicago took place in Spring 1947. The Broadway premiere included a fourteen-member cast and a twelve-piece orchestra, and while the work was advertised as a "musical drama," no one was fooled. This was an opera, but like others produced on Broadway the word *opera* was assiduously avoided lest it scare off potential ticket buyers. Whether it was called a musical drama or an opera, however, the piece was perhaps too rarified and cerebral for the Broadway marketplace, and so it lasted less than three weeks.

The libretto was by British poet Ronald Duncan, who had based his text on Andre Obey's 1931 play *Le viol de Lucrece*, which had been produced on Broadway as *Lucrece* the following year in an adaptation by Thornton Wilder. The New York production of the opera was staged by Agnes De Mille, and the scenery and costumes were by British painter John Piper, whose designs had originally been used for the British production. It was De Mille and Piper who walked away with the best reviews. De Mille's fluid, stylized stage movement led one or two critics to suggest the work might have been more effective as a dance piece, and according to Robert Coleman in the *New York Daily Mirror* Piper's contributions were "magnificent," "the hit of the evening," and "nothing less than stunning." In fact, Coleman felt De Mille and Piper provided "one of the most effective and stirring pictorial masterpieces of our time."

Although the action took place some five hundred years before Christ, the work nonetheless fused pagan and Christian philosophies, and audiences may have been confused when they heard Christ's name invoked. And perhaps the Male Chorus and the Female Chorus didn't help to clarify matters; these roles were sung by one male and one female performer, and at times they voiced the respective thoughts and actions of the male and female characters. The plot dealt with the conquest of Rome by the Etruscans, including the hedonistic Etruscan prince Tarquinius (George Tozzi) who has heard of the chastity of Lucretia (Kitty Carlisle), the wife of the Roman Collatinus (Holger Sorenson), who is encamped at a nearby battlefield. Unlike other wives whose husbands are at war, Lucretia has remained faithful to her spouse and thus becomes an obsession for Tarquinius, who is determined to bed her. He steals into her home and rapes her, although the text hints that he believes (or at least wants to believe) the sex was consensual. The next day Lucretia sends for Collatinus and tells him what happened, and even apologizes; and then she kills herself. The personal tragedy gives Collatinus the impetus to fight even harder to rid Rome of the hated Etruscans, and the Male and Female Chorus sing a hymn in which Christ's crucifixion is invoked as the means for all sinners to find redemption.

Virgil Thomson in the *New York Herald Tribune* found the opera's theme (that "rape requires co-operation" from the victim and that rape is a "form of unchastity" on the victim's part which justifies suicide) "thoroughly silly and without reality." And in his annual seasonal summary, George Jean Nathan scoffed at the notion that purports that "virtue in women is merely lack of opportunity or that women are all whores by nature."

The critics also took aim at Duncan's writing style: both Olin Downes in the *New York Times* and Coleman used the words "high-falutin'" to describe the text. Thomson found it "pompous, wandering and incredibly garrulous," and Richard Watts in the *New York Post* said the "fairly routine" book lacked "lyric beauty" and was "about as poetic as Maxwell Anderson" (which he noted some might assume was a "neat compliment"). Robert Bagar in the *New York World-Telegram* felt the book suffered from an "epic detachment from anything like naturalness" and the words were in the "grandiose manner" and weighed down by imagery. But Watts credited the libretto for being "direct and unpretentious," and John Chapman in the *New York Daily News* said the text had "intelligence and grace."

As for Britten's score, Coleman found it "often exciting" but "seldom really singable"; Robert A. Hague in the *New York Star* said the music was "infinitely skillful and inventive" but felt the composer had been "unable to give it more than passing life and fitful power" in its "series of monochromatic and unmelodic recitatives." Downes suggested the score was occasionally "thin" but overall was "far and away" Britten's "most mature, flexible and distinguished" lyric work. Many of the critics praised various set pieces in the opera, including the Male Chorus's description of Tarquinius's ride to Rome as well as the "linen" trio and "flower" duet for Lucretia's servants.

Bagar found George (later Giorgio) Tozzi "especially good vocally" as Tarquinius; Hague said Carlisle was "lovely to look at" and sang "pleasingly," Coleman said she was "admirably dramatic," and Robert Garland in the *New York Journal-American* praised her singing and acting; William Hawkins in the *New York World-Telegram* liked her "dignity and bearing" but suggested she was a bit "too cool and aloof" in her characterization. Brenda Lewis was singled out for her Female Chorus, and Marguerite Piazza for her role of Lucia, Lucretia's maid.

The libretto was published in paperback by Boosey & Hawkes. A complete recording was issued on a two-CD set by Chandos Records (# CHAN-9254/5); conducted by Richard Hickox for the City of London Sinfonia, the cast includes Jean Rigby (Lucretia), Alastair Miles (Collatinus), and Donald Maxwell (Tarquinius). A DVD by the English National Opera was released by Kultur (# D-2929); the conductor was Lionel Friend, and the cast includes Jean Rigby (Lucretia), Richard Van Allen (Collatinus), and Russell Smythe (Tarquinius).

Britten's opera *Paul Bunyan* (with libretto by W. H. Auden) had premiered in New York at Columbia University's Brander Matthews Hall on May 5, 1941, and this innovative and fascinating work, which predates **Allegro** and **Love Life** by a few years, is a legitimate and forceful argument for being the first concept musical. Britten's *Let's Make an Opera* received its American premiere on Broadway at the John Golden Theatre on December 13, 1950.

KISS ME, KATE
"A New Musical Comedy"

Theatre: New Century Theatre (during run, the musical transferred to the Shubert Theatre)
Opening Date: December 30, 1948; *Closing Date*: July 28, 1951
Performances: 1,077
Book: Sam and Bella Spewack
Lyrics and *Music*: Cole Porter
Based on the play *The Taming of the Shrew* (written approximately 1594) by William Shakespeare.
Direction: John C. Wilson; *Producers*: (Arnold) Saint Subber and Lemuel Ayers; *Choreography*: Hanya Holm; *Scenery* and *Costumes*: Lemuel Ayers; *Lighting*: Al Alloy; *Musical Direction*: Pembroke Davenport
Cast: *Alfred Drake* (Fred Graham, Petruchio), Thomas Hoier (Harry Trevor, Baptista), Lisa Kirk (Lois Lane, Bianca), Don Mayo (Ralph), *Patricia Morison* (Lilli Vanessi, Katharine aka Kate), Annabelle Hill (Hattie), Lorenzo Fuller (Paul), Harold Lang (Bill Calhoun, Lucentio), Harry Clark (First Man), Jack Diamond (Second Man), Bill Lilling (Stage Doorman), Denis Green (Harrison Howell), Edwin Clay (Gremio), Charles Wood (Hortensio), John Castello (Haberdasher), Marc Breaux (Tailor); Specialty Dancers: Fred Davis and Eddie Sledge; Singing Ensemble: Peggy Ferris, Christine Matsios, Joan Kibrig, Gay Laurence, Ethel Madsen, Helen Rice, Matilda Strazza, Tom Bole, George Cassidy, Herb Fields, Noel Gordon, Allan Lowell, Stan Rose, Charles Wood; Dancing Ensemble: Ann Dunbar, Shirley Eckl, Jean Houloose, Doreen Oswald, Janet Gaylord, Gisella Svetlik, Jean Tachau, Marc Breaux, John Castello, Victor Duntiere, Tom Hansen, Paul Olson, Glen Tetley, Rudy Tone
The musical was presented in two acts.
The action takes place during the present time in and around Ford's Theatre in Baltimore, Maryland.

Musical Numbers

Act One: "Another O'p'nin', Another Show" (Annabelle Hill, Singing Ensemble; danced by Dancing Ensemble); "Why Can't You Behave?" (Lisa Kirk); "Wunderbar" (Patricia Morison, Alfred Drake); "So in Love" (Patricia Morison); "We Open in Venice" (Alfred Drake, Patricia Morison, Lisa Kirk, Harold Lang); "Dance" (Dancing Ensemble); "Tom, Dick or Harry" (Lisa Kirk, Harold Lang, Charles Wood, Edwin Clay); Specialty Dance (aka "Rose Dance") (Harold Lang); "I've Come to Wive It Wealthily in Padua" (Alfred Drake, Singing Ensemble); "I Hate Men" (Patricia Morison); "Were Thine That Special Face" (Alfred Drake; danced by Shirley Eckl and Dancing Girls); "I Sing of Love" (Lisa Kirk, Harold Lang, Singing Ensemble); Finale: "Kiss Me, Kate" (Patricia Morison, Alfred Drake, Singing Ensemble) and "Tarantella" (danced by Lisa Kirk, Harold Lang, Dancing Ensemble)

Act Two: "Too Darn Hot" (Lorenzo Fuller, Fred Davis, Eddie Sledge; danced by Fred Davis, Eddie Sledge, Harold Lang, Dancing Ensemble); "Where Is the Life that Late I Led?" (Alfred Drake); "Always True to You (in My Fashion)" (Lisa Kirk); "Bianca" (Harold Lang, Singing Girls; danced by Harold Lang and Dancing Girls); "So in Love" (reprise) (Alfred Drake); "Brush Up Your Shakespeare" (Harry Clark, Jack Diamond); "I Am Ashamed That Women Are So Simple" (Patricia Morison); "Pavane" (Dancing Ensemble); Finale (Alfred Drake, Patricia Morison, Company)

The dozen or so years prior to the opening of *Kiss Me, Kate* had been artistically lean ones for Cole Porter. During the late 1930s and early 1940s, six of his musicals (*Leave It to Me!* [1938], *DuBarry Was a Lady* [1939], **Panama Hattie**, **Let's Face It!**, **Something for the Boys**, and **Mexican Hayride**) had been financial successes, five had run more than a year, five had been made into films, and all had offered an array of amusing comedy songs and beguiling ballads, but the street felt his best days were behind him and his scores no longer matched the glory days of *Gay Divorce* (1932) and *Anything Goes* (1934). Then in the mid-1940s two of his shows (**Seven Lively Arts** and **Around the World in Eighty Days**) had failed with the critics and the public and weren't able to recoup their enormous production costs. So when *Kiss Me, Kate* was announced for production, there was a certain blasé, so-what attitude about the event. But Porter surprised everyone and outdid himself with *Kate*: the score is his masterpiece and one of the greatest in all American musical theatre. The show was a blockbuster that played over a thousand performances; it became Porter's longest-running musical and engendered a London production, a lengthy U.S. tour, a radio version, a lavish film version, three television versions, endless revivals in summer stock and community theatre, and numerous recordings. There were four later productions in New York: a return engagement by the national touring company, two institutional revivals at City Center, and a 1999 Broadway revival that played over two years.

Porter's score offered an incredible array of songs. It was his score of scores, and each and every number was top-drawer Porter: the haunting ballad "So in Love"; the theatre anthem "Another Op'nin', Another Show"; the torch song "Why Can't You Behave?"; the saucy comedy song "Always True to You (in My Fashion)"; the mock-operetta number "Wunderbar"; and the sizzling ode to cold-weather sex, "Too Darn Hot." For the "Shakespearean" numbers there was the emphatic statement of "I've Come to Wive It Wealthily in Padua"; the insinuating beguine "Were Thine That Special Face"; the jaunty "Where Is the Life That Late I Led?"; the joyously expectant "We Open in Venice"; the carefree nonchalance of the roundabout quartet "Tom, Dick or Harry"; and Kate's riveting damn-'em-all "I Hate Men."

And the score contained what is perhaps the naughtiest musical comedy song of all time. For "Brush Up Your Shakespeare," two hoodlums advised that quoting Shakespeare was a sure-fire means of laying the groundwork for sex. Porter worked in the titles of fifteen plays and poems by Shakespeare, and virtually all were doused in double-entendre (*Measure for Measure, Coriolanus*, etc.). Brooks Atkinson in the *New York Times* noted that some of Porter's lyrics "would shock the editorial staff of *The Police Gazette*."

Reportedly inspired by the backstage bickering of Lynn Fontanne and Alfred Lunt when they appeared on Broadway in a 1942 revival of *The Taming of the Shrew*, the musical took place at Ford's Theatre in Baltimore where the once-married Fred Graham (Alfred Drake) and Lilli Vanessi (Patricia Morison) are starring in the pre-Broadway tryout of a new musical version of *Shrew*. And of course their backstage battles mirror their onstage antics as Petruchio and Kate. The plot's secondary couple was Lois Lane (Lisa Kirk) and Bill Calhoun (Harold Lang), who play Bianca and Lucentio in the musical-within-the-musical, and on the periphery of the story were Harrison Howell (Denis Green), a rich Texan who has financed the *Shrew* musical and is courting

Lilli, and two gangsters (Harry Clark and Jack Diamond) who threaten Bill because of his unpaid gambling debts.

Needless to say, the critics were beside themselves with praise. Atkinson: "Terribly" and "thoroughly" enjoyable with a "remarkable melodious score"; Robert Garland in the *New York Journal-American*: If it "isn't the best musical-comedy I ever saw, I don't remember what the best musical-comedy I ever saw was called"; Richard Watts in the *New York Post*: "A smash hit of epic proportions"; John Chapman in the *New York Daily News*: "The sprightliest, handsomest and most tuneful musical imaginable"; Howard Barnes in the *New York Herald Tribune*: "It is difficult to catalogue all the virtues of this lavish and memorable musical"; John Lardner in the *New York Star*: "With fine songs, good singing, dancing and playing," it "amounts to quite a show"; Ward Morehouse in the *New York Sun*: *Kate* "struck gold" and is one of "the best Broadway has had in ten years"; William Hawkins in the *New York World-Telegram*: *Kate* "strains a reviewer's supply of adjectives. It is gay, beautiful, tuneful, funny" with one of Porter's "all-time best scores"; Robert Coleman in the *New York Daily Mirror*: a "rousing triumph" and Porter's score was his "best to date."

Kate opened during the golden era of Broadway musicals, and if the critics thought the season hit its pinnacle with Porter's masterpiece they didn't know that four months later they'd again be blown away with the opening of **South Pacific**. It was that kind of era, with hit after musical hit: **Cabin in the Sky**, **Pal Joey**, **Lady in the Dark**, **Oklahoma!**, **One Touch of Venus**, **Bloomer Girl**, **On the Town**, **Carousel**, **Annie Get Your Gun**, **Finian's Rainbow**, **Brigadoon**, **High Button Shoes**, and **Where's Charley?** Even the failures were ambitious and chock-full of gorgeous music: **The Firebrand of Florence**, **The Day before Spring**, **St. Louis Woman**, **Beggar's Holiday**, **Street Scene**, **Allegro**, **Ballet Ballads**, **Magdalena**, and **Love Life**. And in the waning months of the decade there was an old-fashioned musical comedy hit to come (**Gentlemen Prefer Blondes**) and two ambitious musical dramas (**Lost in the Stars** and **Regina**).

For at least part of *Kate*'s tryout, "Too Darn Hot" was titled "Too Damn Hot"; Bella Spewack was the sole credited book writer; and some of the songs had slight title variations ("Wunderbar, Wunderbar," "So in Love Am I," and "Women Are So Simple").

Five months after the Broadway production closed, the national touring company played a one-week engagement at the Broadway Theatre, opening on January 13, 1952, for eight performances; the cast included Robert Wright (Fred) and Holly Harris (Lilli). There were two revivals by the New York City Center Light Opera Company, both of which played at City Center for twenty-three performances apiece. The first opened on May 6, 1956, with David Atkinson (Fred), Kitty Carlisle (Lilli), Barbara Ruick (Lois), and Richard France (Bill); the future celebrated saloon singer Bobby Short was also in the cast. The second revival opened on May 12, 1965, with Robert (now Bob) Wright reprising his role of Fred, and, from the original production, Patricia Morison as Kate; others in the cast were Nancy Ames (Lois) and Kelly Brown (Bill), and from the original 1948 production Hanya Holm re-created her choreography and musical director Pembroke Davenport again took up the baton.

The most recent revival opened on November 18, 1999, at the Martin Beck (now Hirschfeld) Theatre for 881 performances; the cast included Brian Stokes Mitchell (Fred), Marin Mazzie (Lilli), Amy Spangler (Lois), Michael Berresse (Bill), Ronald (Ron) Holgate, and Lee Wilkof. The book was slightly revised (by an uncredited John Guare) and included one interpolation, "From This Moment On" (for Holgate); the song had originally been heard during the tryout of Porter's 1950 musical *Out of This World*, was cut before the New York opening, and was later used in the 1953 MGM film version of *Kiss Me, Kate*. The rather tiresome revival never quite overcame the inherent weaknesses of the original book by Sam and Bella Spewack, and the two leads seemed somewhat uncomfortable playing over-the-top hammy roles. The production was eventually shown on public television with Brent Barrett, Rachel York, Nancy Anderson, and Michael Berresse and was released on DVD by Image Entertainment (# ID0180WNDVD).

The original London production opened at the Coliseum on March 8, 1951, for 501 performances with Bill Johnson (Fred), Patricia Morison (Lilli), Julie Wilson (Lois), Walter Long (Bill), Adelaide Hall, and Archie Savage.

The film adaptation (which was released "flat" and in 3-D format) was a mixed blessing. The leading roles were solid: Howard Keel was a virile Fred, Ann Miller made a saucy Lois, the three suitors were no less than Bob Fosse (Hortensio), Bobby Van (Gremio), and Tommy Rall (Bill/Lucentio), and Carol Haney appeared in a minor dancing role. Even Kathryn Grayson was good; this was her finest screen performance, and she never looked so chic and lovely. The direction was by George Sidney, and the choreography by Fosse and Hermes Pan. Given the censorship codes of the era, it's understandable that some of Porter's lyrics had to be laundered; but the screenplay was sometimes rather slow-going and there was some strange business with a new character, a songwriter named "Cole Porter" (played by Ron Randell). The soundtrack was issued on MGM (LP # 2353-062), and the DVD was released by Warner Brothers Home Video (# 65088).

Besides the above-mentioned public television version, there were two earlier televised productions. The cast of the November 20, 1958, NBC *Hallmark Hall of Fame* presentation included Drake, Morison, and Lorenzo Fuller from the original cast as well as Julie Wilson, Bill Hayes, Harvey Lembeck, Jack Klugman, Lee Cass, Eva Jessye, and Lee Richardson; Franz Allers conducted, George Schaefer directed, and Ernest Flatt choreographed. The color telecast inspired a new recording that reunited the original four Broadway leads as well as Fuller (Capitol LP # STAO-1267). A black-and-white copy survives and was released on DVD by Video Artists International (# 4535).

Another television version was seen on March 25, 1968, on ABC's *Armstrong Circle Theatre*. Directed by Paul Bogart and choreographed by Lee (Becker) Theodore and with costumes by Alvin Colt, the cast included Robert Goulet (Fred), Carol Lawrence (Lilli), Jessica Walter (Lois), and Michael Callen (Bill); other cast members were Jules Munshin, Marty Ingels, Russell Nype, Tony Hendra, and David Doyle. The soundtrack was released by Columbia Records (LP # CSS-645; in 2014, the CD was issued by BroadwayMasterworks on a pairing with the 1966 television adaptation of *Brigadoon*, which also starred Goulet).

In the early 1950s, a radio adaptation was heard on *The Railroad Hour* with a cast that included Gordon MacRae and Patrice Munsel.

The script was first published in hardback by Alfred A. Knopf in 1953, and then later in the January 1955 issue of *Theatre Arts* magazine. The script is also included in the hardback collection *Ten Great Musicals of the American Theatre* (1973), published by Chilton (the collection isn't identified as volume one, but there was a later second volume in this series). The lyrics for the used and unused songs are included in *The Complete Lyrics of Cole Porter*. The script was published in hardback in 2014 by the Library of Congress in a collection that includes the scripts of fifteen other musicals.

There are numerous recordings of the score, some of which are more complete than the original cast album. But no matter: the only one you really want is the indispensible original, recorded by Columbia (LP # ML-4140; issued on CD by Sony Classical/Columbia/Legacy # SK-60536). The most complete recording is the two-CD studio cast album by EMI (# CDS-7-54033-2), which offers all the dance music (including "Rose Dance," "Tarantella," and "Pavane"), the entr'acte, and "I Sing of Love" as well as six unused songs ("It Was Great Fun the First Time," "A Woman's Career," "We Shall Never Be Younger," "I'm Afraid, Sweetheart, I Love You," "If Ever Married I'm," and "What Does Your Servant Dream About?").

To summarize Patricia Morison's appearances in the musical: besides creating the title role in 1948, she was in the original 1951 London production, the 1958 television version, and the 1965 City Center revival. She recorded the score twice (the original cast album and the 1958 studio cast album).

Awards

Tony Awards: Best Musical (**Kiss Me, Kate**); Best Producers of a Musical (**Saint Subber** and **Lemuel Ayers**); Best Authors of a Musical (**Sam** and **Bella Spewack**); Best Composer and Lyricist (**Cole Porter**); Best Costumes (**Lemuel Ayers**)

ALONG FIFTH AVENUE
"THE NEW MUSICAL REVUE"

Theatre: Broadhurst Theatre (during run, the revue transferred to the Imperial Theatre)
Opening Date: January 13, 1949; *Closing Date*: June 18, 1949
Performances: 180
Sketches: Charles Sherman and Nat Hiken; additional sketches by Mel Tolkin and Max Liebman
Lyrics: Tom Adair; additional lyrics by Nat Hiken, Milton Pascal, Rick French, and Thomas Howell
Music: Gordon Jenkins; additional music by Richard Stutz, Mel Pahl, and Philip Kadison
Direction: Uncredited (A note in the program stated "The management acknowledges the assistance of Charles Friedman"); *Producer*: Arthur Lesser; *Choreography*: Robert Sidney; *Scenery*: Oliver Smith; *Costumes*: David Ffolkes; *Lighting*: Peggy Clark; *Musical Direction*: Irving Actman

Cast: Nancy Walker, Jackie Gleason, Hank Ladd, Carol Bruce, Donald Richards, Viola Essen, Johnny Coy, Virginia Gorski (Gibson), Judyth Burroughs, Joyce Mathews, Dick Bernie, George S. Irving, Zachary Solov, Lee Krieger, Wallace Seibert, Louise Kirtland; Singers: Joan Coburn, Gloria Hayden, Candace Montgomery, Tina Prescott, Dorothy Pyren, Lucille Udovick, Ted Allison, Leonard Claret, Bob Neukum, Ken Renner, Bert Sheldon; Dancers: Franca Baldwin, Tessie Carrano, Shellie Farrell, Marian Horosko, Gretchen Houser, Carol Nelson, Janet Sayers, Harry Asmus, Ted Cappy, Dante Di Paolo, Howard Malone, Wallace Seibert, Zachary Solov, Walter Stane
The revue was presented in two acts.

Sketches and Musical Numbers

Act One: "Fifth Avenue" (lyric by Tom Adair, music by Gordon Jenkins) (Virginia Gorski, Company); "Sweet Surrender" (sketch by Nat Hiken) (Miss Heerkimer: Nancy Walker; Mr. Farquahar: George S. Irving; Mr. Higgins: Dick Bernie); "The Best Time of Day" (lyric by Tom Adair, music by Gordon Jenkins) (Carol Bruce, Dante Di Paolo, Bob Neukum, Ken Renner, Bert Sheldon); "A Window on the Avenue" (music by Gordon Jenkins) (Window Dresser: Zachary Solov; Girls: Shellie Farrell, Marian Horosko, Gretchen Houser; Boys: Harry Asmus, Howard Malone, Wallace Seibert); "If This Is Glamour!" (lyric by Rick French, music by Richard Stutz) (Nancy Walker); "The Fifth Avenue Label" (sketch by Charles Sherman) (Nurse: Joyce Matthews; Doctor: Dick Bernie; Ambulance Driver: Lee Krieger; Patient: Jackie Gleason; Insurance Adjuster: George S. Irving; Models: Ted Allison, Ken Renner, Walter Stane); "Skyscraper Blues" (lyric by Ted Adair, music by Gordon Jenkins) (Donald Richards; Girl: Viola Essen; Boy: Zachary Solov; Lovers: Marian Horosko, Wallace Seibert; Young Girls: Franca Baldwin, Shellie Farrell; Street Walkers: Tessie Carrano, Gretchen Houser, Janet Sayers; Men: Harry Asmus, Dante Di Paolo, Walter Stane); Hank Ladd; "I Love Love in New York" (lyric by Tom Adair, music by Gordon Jenkins) (Hurdy-Gurdy Man: Lee Krieger; First Couple: Carol Bruce and Donald Richards; Second Couple: Virginia Gorski and Johnny Coy; Girls: Franca Baldwin, Shellie Farrell, Marian Horosko, Gretchen Houser, Carol Nelson, Janet Sayers; Boys: Harry Asmus, Dante Di Paolo, Howard Malone, Wallace Seibert, Zachary Solov, Walter Stane); "The Fugitive from Tenth Avenue" (lyric by Nat Hiken, music by Richard Stutz) (Captain: Lee Krieger; Legionnaires: Ted Allison, Dick Bernie, George S. Irving; The Fugitive: Jackie Gleason); Hank Ladd; "Santo Dinero" (lyric by Milton Pascal, music by Richard Stutz) (Nancy Walker, Viola Essen, Zachary Solov, Wallace Seibert, Lee Krieger, Singing and Dancing Ensembles)
Act Two: "In the Lobby" (lyric by Tom Adair, music by Gordon Jenkins) (Singing and Dancing Ensembles); "What's in the Middle?" (sketch by Charles Sherman) (Counter Girl: Nancy Walker; Customer: Jackie Gleason; Other Customers: Dick Bernie, Leonard Claret, Lee Krieger; Manager: George S. Irving; Assistant Counter Girl: Joyce Matthews; Assistant Manager: Bert Sheldon); "Weep No More" (lyric by Tom Adair, music by Gordon Jenkins) (Carol Bruce); "Mr. Rockefeller Builds His Dream House" (sketch by Mel Tolkin and Max Liebman) (Guide: Lee Krieger; Visitors: Singing Ensemble; Gentleman: Hank Ladd); "Challenge" (dance) (music by Mel Pahl and Richard Stutz) (Hoofer: Johnny Coy; Ballerina: Viola Essen); "Chant d'amour" (lyric by Nat Hiken, music by Gordon Jenkins) (Nancy Walker); "Vacation in the Store" (lyric by Tom Adair, music by Gordon Jenkins) (Trio: Gloria Hayden, Candace Montgomery, Tina Prescott; Nancy Walker, Jackie Gleason, Carol Bruce, Donald Richards, Johnny Coy, Virginia Gorski, Zachary Solov, Lee Krieger, Wallace Seibert, Company); Hank Ladd; "Call It Applefritters" (lyric by Milton Pascal, music by Richard Stutz) (Boy: Hank Ladd; Girl: Carol Bruce); "Murder on Fifth Avenue" (sketch by Charles Sherman) (Detective: Dick Bernie; Philip Ashton: Donald Richards; Mrs. Schuyler: Joyce Matthews; Butler: Ted Allison; Inspector Mahoney: Jackie Gleason; Daisy: Nancy Walker; Mrs. Ashton: Carol Bruce; Dr. Brown: George S. Irving); "A Trip Doesn't Care at All" (lyric by Thomas Howell, music by Philip Kadison) (Pam: Judyth Burroughs; Chris: Donald Richards); Finale: "Fifth Avenue" (reprise) (Entire Company)

The sketch surely defines musical comedy heaven. It was the tenth scene of the second act of the revue *Along Fifth Avenue,* and its title was "Murder on Fifth Avenue." Pint-sized, dead-pan, seen-it-all Nancy Walker is Daisy, a murder victim (of sorts) who has accidentally taken poison intended for another. The docs and the cops say the only antidote for the poison is to jump around and dart about until the poison wears off.

One critic said Walker became a human seismograph, and so while the police and the doctors seriously went about their business of investigating the crime scene and interviewing the suspects (including . . . a butler) in a stately Fifth Avenue mansion, Walker single-mindedly hopped and jiggled and bounced about the stage like a whirling dervish, or maybe like the jitterbugging monkey in **Morey Amsterdam's Hilarities**. The *idea* of Nancy Walker was funny, and when her material matched her talents, there was no stopping her from stopping the show.

Along Fifth Avenue gave her another memorable moment in "Chant d'amour," in which she demolished torch songs of the "Bill" and "My Man" variety as she warbled about her love for the one and only man in her life . . . Irving. John Lardner in the *New York Star* said the sequence was "one of the fine moments in the history of musical shows," and Walker's performance "ranks alongside Fannie Brice's 'Rose of Washington Square'."

Besides Walker, the revue offered another capital clown in Jackie Gleason as well as the amiable master of ceremonies Hank Ladd, who had impressed everyone when he performed similar duties in **Angel in the Wings**; singers Carol Bruce (who had recently scored a major success as Julie in the revival of **Show Boat**) and Donald Richards (the romantic lead of **Finian's Rainbow**); and dancers Johnny Coy and Viola Essen, who provided a memorable "Challenge" dance in which they contrasted old-fashioned hoofing and the ballet. By today's standards of theatrical weak tea, the revue seems like ambrosia. This era marked the last stand of the old-fashioned musical comedy revue, and while some (like **Make Mine Manhattan**) were hits, others, such as *Along Fifth Avenue*, meandered along for a few months without breaking even. The era also offered an amazing number of headliners, clowns both old and new, and so theatergoers had the chance to see Bert Lahr, Nancy Walker, Jackie Gleason, Beatrice Lillie, Sid Caesar, Carol Channing, Grace and Paul Hartman, Ray Bolger, Elaine Stritch, David Burns, Jack Haley, Jack Gilford, Carl Reiner, and Dolores Gray in a series of revues that played on Broadway during the late 1940s and early 1950s.

Like **Make Mine Manhattan**, the theme of *Along Fifth Avenue* was New York, and in keeping with the spirit of its title most of the songs and sketches took place in such locales as chic Fifth Avenue shops ("A Window on the Avenue," "Vacation in the Store," "Sweet Surrender"), a Fifth Avenue skyscraper ("Skyscraper Blues"), a Fifth Avenue mansion ("Murder on Fifth Avenue"), a restaurant ("What's in the Middle?"), a New York hospital ("The Fifth Avenue Label"), Washington Square ("I Love Love in New York"), Rockefeller Center ("Mr. Rockefeller Builds His Dream House"), Harlem ("A Trip Doesn't Care at All"), and the avenue itself ("Fifth Avenue").

But the era's musicals all but demanded a South American number, and so the first act finale sang and danced the praises of "Santo Dinero." Other musicals in the season that offered similar numbers were **Howdy, Mr. Ice** and **Howdy, Mr. Ice of 1950** ("Plenty More Fish in the Sea"), **Morey Amsterdam's Hilarities** ("Rio de Janeiro"), **Small Wonder** ("Badaroma"), **Lend an Ear** ("Santo Domingo"), and even the 1892 Oxford University setting of **Where's Charley?** managed to work in a first-act finale with a Brazilian tribute ("Pernambuco"). And of course **Magdalena** took place in Colombia, and one of its numbers was "Vals de España."

As the evening's host, comic Hank Ladd noted the revue might be the first of a series of similarly themed revues (*Along Sixth Avenue, Along Seventh Avenue*, etc.) and commented that this was an awfully round-about way of trying to get to New Jersey. Besides the above-noted performers, songs, and sketches, there was also some lively dancing by Judyth Burroughs, an off-the-cuff sketch ("The Fugitive from Fifth Avenue") in which Jackie Gleason portrayed a Damon Runyon type who ends up in the French Foreign Legion, and a Fifth Avenue perfume shop sketch ("Sweet Surrender") in which an unwitting male customer is inadvertently sprayed with an alluring perfume and immediately finds himself romantically pursued by another male shopper.

Brooks Atkinson in the *New York Times* noted that some places along the avenue were better than others; as a result, he praised Nancy Walker's "Chanson d'amour" and "Murder on Fifth Avenue," the dance "Challenge," and a few songs such as "A Trip Doesn't Care at All" (an "enchanting caprice"), "Call it Applefritters" ("a gay little tune"), and "Skyscraper Blues" ("a torch ballet of quality"). Otherwise, the revue failed to provide Walker and Jackie Gleason with enough good material. John Lardner in the *New York Star* had seen better and worse revues, and thus placed *Along Fifth Avenue* "somewhere between *The Bandwagon* and *Morey Amsterdam's Hilarities*." Besides Walker, he praised the "pretty nifty" dances and noted "A Trip Doesn't Care at All" was "whimsical but pleasant."

William Hawkins in the *New York World-Telegram* felt Nancy Walker's material came off best; otherwise, Jackie Gleason made "more of his comic material than anyone could expect" and Donald Richards sang a "pretty dull" number "as if he really cared." Howard Barnes in the *New York Herald Tribune* said the "rambling and rowdy" revue lacked style, but noted Walker and Gleason provided "fugitive fun," she particularly in the murder sketch and he in the restaurant scene in which a pie is thrown in his face. John Chapman in the *New York Daily News* felt the material was there to make a good revue, and if the evening had had a firm hand to pull it all together the "ordinarily" pleasant show could have been "extraordinarily" pleasant.

Robert Coleman in the *New York Daily Mirror* thought the "smart" revue was "one of the brightest and most amusing musicals of recent seasons" and noted that Walker and Gleason "romped merrily" throughout their sketches. Robert Garland in the *New York Journal-American* mentioned that the revue was always "good and danceful," that Oliver Smith's sets were "imaginative," and such songs as "Chanson d'amour," "A Trip Doesn't Care at All," and "The Fugitive from Tenth Avenue" were pleasing.

Richard Watts in the *New York Post* said the revue had "pace, good humor and high spirits" and thus was one of the most "entertaining" shows of the season. He noted that the "Challenge" dance was "particularly disarming" and one of the evening's "high points." Herrick Brown in the *New York Sun* praised the "jaunty style" of the "very funny" revue; Walker was a "hilarious delight" in "Chanson d'amour," Gleason was amusing in the "laugh-provoking" "Fugitive from Tenth Avenue," and the "Challenge" dance went over "most charmingly."

During the tryout, Willie Howard became ill and left the show (he died the day after the New York opening) and was succeeded by Jackie Gleason; Robert H. Gordon was the director of record; and the following numbers were cut: the songs "If" and "With You So Far Away" (both with lyrics by Tom Adair and music by Gordon Jenkins) as well as "Crème de la Crème" (lyric by Milton Pascal, music by Richard Stutz); the dance "Echoes in the Night" (music by Richard Stutz); and the sketches "Will It Come to This?," "Juvenile Delinquency," and "Miss Fifth Avenue" (all by Charles Sherman). For the tryout, the sketch "The Fugitive from Fifth Avenue" was titled "The Foreign Legion."

The collection *The Broadway Musicals of 1949* (Bayview CD # RNBW-035) includes three songs from the revue ("Skyscraper Blues," "Call It Applefritters," and "Santo Dinero").

ALL FOR LOVE
"A NEW MUSICAL REVUE"

Theatre: Mark Hellinger Theatre
Opening Date: January 22, 1949; *Closing Date*: May 7, 1949
Performances: 141
Sketches: Jane Bishir, Billy K. Wells, Ted Luce, Grace and Paul Hartman, and Max Shulman (all sketches edited by Max Shulman)
Lyrics and *Music*: Allan Roberts and Lester Lee
Direction: Edward Reveaux; *Producers*: Sammy Lambert and Anthony B. Farrell; *Choreography*: Eric Victor; *Scenery*: Edward Gilbert; *Costumes*: Billy Livingston; *Lighting*: Uncredited; *Musical Direction*: Clay Warnick
Cast: *Grace* and *Paul Hartman*, *Bert Wheeler*, Patricia Wymore, Milada Mladova, Dick Smart, Leni Lynn, Kathryne Mylroie, Milton Frome, Paul Reed, Budd Rogerson, June Graham, Richard D'Arcy; Singers: Gloria Benson, Ann Blackburn, Ruth Edberg, Arlyne Frank, Marilyn Frechette, Janie Janvier, Helen Schurgot, Thomas (Tom) Bowman, Arthur Carroll, Carl Conway, John Henson, Sid Lawson, Frank Stevens; Carol Lee, Prue Ward, Jack Warner, Sid Lawson, Eric Kristen, Tiny Shimp, Peter Gladke, Onna White, Bill Thompson, Bob Shawley, Yvonne Tibor, Helen Wenzel, Janet Bethel, Norma Doggett, Jean Handzlik, Verne Rogers
The revue was presented in two acts.

Sketches and Musical Numbers

Act One: "All for Love" (Singers and Dancers); "Fashion Expert" (sketch by Jane Bishir) (Department Store Manager: Milton Frome; Renee Mulfinger: Grace Hartman; Signor Pignatelli: Paul Hartman); "My Baby's Bored" (Patricia Wymore, Budd Rogerson); "Morris, My Son" (sketch by Billy K. Wells) (Foreward: Bert

Wheeler; Withers: Milton Frome; Ivy: Janie Janvier; Lord Malcolm Twonkey: Bert Wheeler; Olive: Patricia Wymore); "The Big Four" (music "paraphrased" by Peter Howard Weiss) (Producer: Milton Frome; First Secretary: Carol Lee; Second Secretary: Prue Ward; Office Boy: Jack Warner; Agents: Frank Stevens, Carl Conway, Sid Lawson, and Tom Bowman; Jerry Redbreast: Eric Kristen; Aggie Dee: Tiny Shimp; Mr. X. Jackson: Peter Gladke; Ellen LaMouris: Onna White; Dancers); "Isolde" (sketch by Ted Luce, and Grace and Paul Hartman) (Treadwell: Paul Hartman; Barton: Bert Wheeler; Isolde: Grace Hartman; Wagernick: Dick Smart); "Why Can't It Happen Again" (lyric by Sammy Gallop, music by Michel Emer) (Kathryne Mylroie); "My Heart's in the Middle of July" (Dick Smart and Leni Lynn; Specialty Dancers: Patricia Wymore and Budd Rogerson; Dancers and Singers); "Lament" (Bert Wheeler); "It's a Living" (Grace and Paul Hartman); "Benjamin O'Dell" (Boy: Dick Smart; Girl: Leni Lynn; Policeman: Milton Frome; Captain: Bert Wheeler; Chambermaid: Grace Hartman; Purser: Paul Hartman; Sailors: Bill Thompson, Peter Gladke; Balloon-Man: Bob Shawley; Little Girl: June Graham; Little Boy: Richard D'Arcy); with Patricia Wymore, Milada Mladova, Kathryne Mykroie, Budd Rogerson, Dancers, Singers)

Act Two: "Prodigal Daughter" (ballet music by Peter Howard Weiss) (Dorothy and Crystal: June Graham; First Man in Her Life: Richard D'Arcy; Honky-Tonk Girls: Yvonne Tibor, Helen Wenzel, Tiny Shimp, Janet Bethel, Norma Dogett; Jewel: Milada Mladova; Shadow: Onna White; Singers and Dancers); "Message to Our Sponsor" (Bert Wheeler); "Sea Diver" (sketch by Jane Bishir) (Professor Pisces Beebe: Paul Hartman; Mrs. Beebe: Grace Hartman; Sailor: Dick Smart); "Run to Me, My Love" (Leni Lynn, Dick Smart); "Mary Maggie McNeil" (sketch by Ted Luce, and Grace and Paul Hartman) (Make-Up Girls: Janie Janvier and Marilyn Frechette; Chief Peterson: Bert Wheeler; Sonya: Jean Handzlik; LeRoy: Milton Frome; Mary Maggie McNeil: Grace Hartman; Cameramen: Carl Conway and Sid Lawson; Hobart Havermill: Paul Hartman; Wardrobe Man: John Henson; Boy: Bob Shawley); "No Time for Love" (Patricia Wymore, Be-Bop Boys); "Flying Mare" (sketch by Max Shulman) (Gus: Paul Reed; Al: Arthur Carroll; McNulty: Milton Frome; Harold Minafee: Bert Wheeler; Georgeius Georgia: Verne Rogers; Referee: Richard D'Arcy; Seconds: John Henson and Bob Shawley); "Dreamer with a Penny" (Dick Smart); "The Farrell Girl" (Budd Rogerson, Boys); "Oh, How Fortunate You Mortals Be" (Kathryne Mylroie); Finale (Entire Company)

The revue *All for Love* was greeted with unanimously negative reviews, and for any other show such notices would have meant a quick closing. But *All for Love* dragged on for the remainder of the season and chalked up the surprising number of 141 showings, no doubt thanks to its wealthy coproducer Anthony B. Farrell who kept the show going in his determination to bankroll a big Broadway hit (he hadn't had much luck with his first venture **Hold It!**, and in fact one critic suggested *All for Love* should be retitled *Drop It!*). Farrell had just bought (and refurbished) the glorious Hollywood Theatre, which he now renamed the Mark Hellinger in honor of the late producer.

As a producer as well as owner and operator of the Mark Hellinger, Farrell ensured that the venue remained a viable house during his tenure, and so he booked (and sometimes coproduced) a number of musicals that played there during the late 1940s and the first half of the 1950s (but most were financial failures with relatively short runs): **Texas, Li'l Darlin'**, *Tickets, Please!, Bless You All, Two on the Aisle, Three Wishes for Jamie, Hazel Flagg, The Girl in Pink Tights, Hit the Trail, Plain and Fancy* (the one out-and-out hit), and *Ankles Aweigh*. But in 1956 Farrell booked one of the greatest musicals of them all into the Hellinger, and when *My Fair Lady* closed it was the longest-running musical in Broadway history. (Farrell also enjoyed considerable success as the coproducer of the long-running 1952 revival of *Pal Joey*, which played at the Broadhurst Theatre.)

Normally, the Hartmans could do no wrong, but Richard Watts in the *New York Post* said *All for Love* might force him to reassess his belief that they belonged in the pantheon of great musical comedy performers; he noted their material was among the "dullest and most vulgar known to mankind" and it was "pathetic" to watch Bert Wheeler "battling hopelessly" against the ineptitude of it all. He stated that *All for Love* was a "calamity of epic proportions" and the "epoch-making disaster" included just two performers who weren't "destroyed in the general massacre," ballet dancer Milada Mladova and singer and tap dancer Patricia Wymore; and Ward Morehouse in the *New York Sun* said the evening was "as tasteless and witless as anything the New York stage has had during the past half century." The Hartmans were "painfully unfunny" in a production of "unlimited expenditure, overpowering ineptitude, and unfathomable dullness." Only Patricia Wymore survived the wreckage, and her commendable performance never once gave hint that she was trapped in a "hopeless cause."

Howard Barnes in the *New York Herald Tribune* said the revue was "badly seasoned goulash"; Robert Coleman in the *New York Daily Mirror* found the evening "dull and pedestrian"; and John Chapman in the *New York Daily News* said the spoof of the recent play *Edward, My Son* (as "Morris, My Son") should have been "amusing" but was just "ordinary," and that Bert Wheeler was "laughable and lowdown" in the sketch "Flying Mare" which spoofed the world of wrestling (one wrestler was named "Georgeius Georgia") in which he donned drag as a lady wrestler.

William Hawkins in the *New York World-Telegram* said the Hartmans were experts in satiric dancing, but they gave it short shrift in their new revue; if they were going to concentrate on sketches rather than dancing, they needed "much sharper material"; as for Bert Wheeler, he was "pretty much lost" during the evening, and his resurrection of what appeared to be some of his old material reeked of "desperation." Robert Garland suggested that "*All for Love, Drop It!, Farrell's Folly* or whatever you choose to call" the "handsome mishap" proved that "ardent amateurs" were sometimes no better than the professionals when it came to producing Broadway shows.

Brooks Atkinson in the *New York Times* said the Hartmans' sketches were not yet "ready for the paying public," and noted the team hadn't even mastered their props or their timing and thus had never before looked like such "shoddy workmen." The revue had "very little" to recommend it, and in general the evening was "overwhelmed by the general lack of taste, design and knowledge of modern theatre." John Lardner in the *New York Star* said he'd have had a better time if the Hellinger's stage had been turned over to a troop of Boy Scouts giving a "good, brisk exhibition of building a fire without matches."

A few routines in the revue are worth noting. Grace Hartman's "The Farrell Girl" was a spoof of a former *Ziegfeld Follies* star who is bedecked beyond belief with diamonds (including a large diamond denture), and "The Big Four" kidded current Broadway choreographers Jerry Redbreast (Jerome Robbins), Aggie Dee (Agnes De Mille), Ellen LaMouris (Helen Tamiris), and Mr. X. Jackson (Jack Cole). According to Lardner, the ballad "Dreamer with a Penny" was a "burden" sung by Dick Smart to the effect that he'd rather be a poor man with dreams rather than a rich one without them; Barnes found the song "rather dull," and Watts said the "terribly serious" number was "one of the low points in revue history."

During the run, the sketches "Fashion Expert," "Message to Our Sponsor," and "Flying Mare" and the song "Run to Me, My Love" were dropped; and the number "O Gentle Sleep" was added.

The collection *The Broadway Musicals of 1949* (Bayview CD # RNBW-035) includes "No Time for Love" (as "No Time for Nothin' but You").

CAROUSEL
"THE MUSICAL PLAY"

Theatre: City Center (during run, the musical transferred to the Majestic Theatre)
Opening Date: January 25, 1949; *Closing Date*: March 5, 1949
Performances: 48
Book and *Lyrics*: Oscar Hammerstein II
Music: Richard Rodgers
Based on the 1909 play *Liliom* by Ferenc Molnar (as adapted by Benjamin F. Glazer).
Direction: Rouben Mamoulian; *Producer*: The Theatre Guild; *Choreography*: Agnes de Mille; *Scenery*: Jo Mielziner; *Costumes*: Miles White; *Lighting*: Uncredited; *Musical Direction*: Frederick Dvonch
Cast: Margot Moser (Carrie Pipperidge), Iva Withers (Julie Jordan), Louise Larabee (Mrs. Mullin), Stephen Douglass (Billy Bigelow), Kenneth Knapp (First Policeman, Principal), Ross Chetwynd (David Bascombe), Christine Johnson (Nettie Fowler), Mavis Ray (June Girl), Eric Mattson (Enoch Snow), Mario De Laval (Jigger Craigin), Dusty Worrall (Hannah), Kenneth MacKenzie (Boatswain, Carnival Boy), Bobra Suiter (Arminy), Evelyne Ross (Penny), Audrey Sabetti (Jennie), Jean Rogers (Virginia), Ruth Devorin (Susan), Richmond Page (Second Policeman), Warren Harr (Captain), Jay Velie (Heavenly Friend, Brother Joshua), Calvin Thomas (Starkeeper), Diane Keith (Louise), Anthony Aleo (Enoch Snow Jr.); Singers: Donna Phillips, Jean Rogers, Edith Fitch, Evelyne Ross, Audrey Sabetti, Grace Bruns, Bobra Suiter, Ruth Devorin, Robert Davis, Richmond Page, Jerry Lucas, Warren Harr, Kenneth E. Knapp, Joseph Milly, Charles Scott, Anthony Aleo, Charles E. Wood Jr.; Dancers: Karel Krauter, Lila Popper, Hazel Patterson, Shirley Andahazy, Jane Burroughs, Mildred Ferguson, Virginia Harris, Hilda Wagner, Meredith Baylis, Yolanda Novak,

Lorand Andahazy, Stanley Herbert, Hubert Bland, Raymond Dorian, Joseph Camiolo, Martin Schneider, Marvin Krauter

The musical was presented in two acts.

The action takes place in Maine during the period 1873–1888.

Musical Numbers

Act One: "Waltz Suite: Carousel" (Orchestra; pantomimed by principals); "You're a Queer One, Julie Jordan" (Margot Moser, Iva Withers); "When I Marry Mister Snow" (Margot Moser); "If I Loved You" (Stephen Douglass, Iva Withers); "June Is Bustin' Out All Over" (Christine Johnson, Margot Moser, Ensemble; danced by June Girl: Mavis Ray; and Dancing Ensemble); "When I Marry Mister Snow" (reprise) (Margot Moser, Eric Mattson, Girls); "When the Children Are Asleep" (Eric Mattson, Margot Moser); "Blow High, Blow Low" (Mario de Laval, Stephen Douglass, Male Chorus); "Hornpipe" (dance) (Dusty Worrall, Kenneth MacKenzie, Dancers); "Soliloquy" (Stephen Douglass); Finale

Act Two: "This Was a Real Nice Clambake" (Margot Moser, Christine Johnson, Iva Withers, Eric Mattson, Ensemble); "Geraniums in the Winder" (Eric Mattson); "What's the Use of Wond'rin'" (Iva Withers); "You'll Never Walk Alone" (Christine Johnson); "The Highest Judge of All" (Stephen Douglass); "Ballet" (Louise: Diane Keith; A Younger Miss Snow: Dusty Worrall; The Brothers and Sisters Snow: Lila Popper, Hazel Patterson, Hilda Wagner; Badly Brought-Up Boys: Hubert Bland, Stanley Herbert; A Young Man Like Billy: Kenneth MacKenzie; A Carnival Woman: Mildred Ferguson; Members of the Carnival Troupe: Shirley Andahazy, Lorand Andahazy, Marvin Krauter, Jane Burroughs, Meredith Baylis, Raymond Dorian, Yolanda Novak, Martin Schneider); "If I Loved You" (reprise) (Stephen Douglass); "You'll Never Walk Alone" (reprise) (Company)

The current production of *Carousel* was the final stop of the musical's national touring company, which had opened almost two years earlier at the Shubert Theatre in Chicago, Illinois, on May 29, 1947, for a fifty-five city tour. The limited New York engagement began performances at City Center on January 25, 1949, played there until February 20, and then on February 22 transferred to the Majestic Theatre, the home of the original production; the musical played there through March 5, and the performances at both theatres totaled forty-eight showings.

The program didn't list "There's Nothin' So Bad for a Woman" (aka "Stonecutters Cut It on Stone"); either the omission was inadvertent or the song was dropped at some point during the national tour.

The London production opened at the Drury Lane on June 7, 1950, for 566 performances, and included most of the leads from the current New York visit (Stephen Douglass, Iva Withers, Margot Moser, and Eric Mattson) as well as Bambi Linn from the original 1945 Broadway cast who reprised her role of Louise.

SOUTH PACIFIC
"A New Musical Play"

Theatre: Majestic Theatre (during run, the musical transferred to the Broadway Theatre)

Opening Date: April 7, 1949; *Closing Date*: January 16, 1954

Performances: 1,925

Book: Oscar Hammerstein II and Joshua Logan

Lyrics: Oscar Hammerstein II

Music: Richard Rodgers

Based on James A. Michener's 1947 collection of short stories *Tales of the South Pacific* (two of the stories, "Our Heroine" and "Fo' Dolla'," were the main basis for the musical).

Direction: Joshua Logan; *Producers*: Richard Rodgers and Oscar Hammerstein II in association with Leland Hayward and Joshua Logan; *Choreography*: Joshua Logan; *Scenery* and *Lighting*: Jo Mielziner; *Costumes*: Motley; *Musical Direction*: Salvatore Dell'Isola

Cast: Barbara Luna (Ngana), Michael DeLeon (Jerome), Richard Silvera (Henry), *Mary Martin* (Ensign Nellie Forbush), *Ezio Pinza* (Emile de Becque), Juanita Hall (Bloody Mary), Musa Williams (Bloody Mary's

Assistant), Archie Savage (Abner), Henry Slate (Stewpot), Myron McCormick (Luther Billis), Fred Sadoff (Professor), William Tabbert (Lieutenant Joseph Cable, U.S.M.C.), Martin Wolfson (Captain George Brackett, U.S.N.), Harvey Stephens (Commander William Harbison, U.S.N.), Alan Gilbert (Yeoman Herbert Quale), Thomas Gleason (Sergeant Kenneth Johnson), Dickinson Eastham (Seabee Richard West), Henry Michel (Seabee Morton Wise), Bill Dwyer (Seaman Tom O'Brien), Biff McGuire (Radio Operator Bob McCaffrey), Jim Hawthorne (Marine Corporal Hamilton Steeves), Jack Fontan (Staff Sergeant Thomas Hassinger), Beau Tilden (Seaman James Hayes), Jacqueline Fisher (Lieutenant Genevieve Marshall), Roslyn Lowe (Ensign Dinah Murphy), Sandra Deel (Ensign Janet MacGregor), Bernice Saunders (Ensign Cora MacRae), Pat Northrop (Ensign Sue Yaeger), Gloria Meli (Ensign Lisa Minelli), Mardi Bayne (Ensign Connie Walewska), Evelyn Colby (Ensign Pamela Whitmore), Helena Schurgot (Ensign Bessie Noonan), Betta St. John (Liat), Richard Loo (Marcel), Don Fellows (Lieutenant Buzz Adams); Islanders, Sailors, Officers: Mary Ann Reeve, Chin Yu, Eugene Smith, Richard Loo, William Ferguson

The musical was presented in two acts.

The action takes place on two islands in the South Pacific during World War II.

Musical Numbers

Act One: "Dites-moi (pourquoi)" (Barbara Luna, Michael DeLeon); "A Cockeyed Optimist" (Mary Martin); "Twin Soliloquies" (Mary Martin, Ezio Pinza); "Some Enchanted Evening" (Ezio Pinza); "Bloody Mary (Is the Girl I Love)" (Sailors, Seabees, Marines); "There Is Nothin' Like a Dame" (Myron McCormick, Sailors, Seabees, Marines); "Bali Ha'i" (Juanita Hall); "I'm Gonna Wash That Man Right Outa My Hair" (Mary Martin, Nurses); "(I'm in Love with) A Wonderful Guy" (Mary Martin, Nurses); "Bali Ha'i" (reprise) (French and Native Girls); "Younger Than Springtime" (William Tabbert); Finale: (1) "Twin Soliloquies" (reprise) (Mary Martin, Ezio Pinza); (2) "A Cockeyed Optimist" (reprise) (Mary Martin, Ezio Pinza); (3) "I'm Gonna Wash That Man Right Outa My Hair" (reprise) (Ezio Pinza); and (4) "Some Enchanted Evening" (Ezio Pinza)

Act Two: "Soft Shoe Dance" (Nurses and Seabees); "Happy Talk" (Juanita Hall, Betta St. John, William Tabbert); "Honey Bun" (Mary Martin, Myron McCormick); "You've Got to Be Carefully Taught" (aka "Carefully Taught") (William Tabbert); "This Nearly Was Mine" (Ezio Pinza); "Some Enchanted Evening" (reprise) (Mary Martin); Finale: "Dites-moi (pourquoi)" (Mary Martin, Ezio Pinza, Barbara Luna, Michael De Leon)

Richard Rodgers and Oscar Hammerstein II's *South Pacific* was the right show at the right time. It opened during the years immediately following World War II, and it resonated with postwar audiences in its bittersweet and adult look at young Americans who find themselves almost over their heads in the confusion of war, foreign lands and customs, and the threat of imminent death. The musical theater was now presenting more and more works with adult and adventuresome themes and seemed ready for almost any challenge. And the drama and the innovative writing and staging of *South Pacific* were perfect for the zeitgeist. For here the theatrical arts blended into a smooth production that utilized traditional musical comedy songs with a frank and adult plot; and in keeping with its inherent realistic tone there was no formal dancing; heretofore, all the previous Rodgers and Hammerstein musicals had been choreographed by Agnes De Mille, but for *South Pacific* there was just an impromptu bit of dancing on the beach for Nellie and the nurses as they sang "I'm in Love with a Wonderful Guy," some throwaway jokey dance movements for the sailors in "There Is Nothing Like a Dame," and the purposely amateurish bit of soft shoe dancing for *The Thanksgiving Follies*.

Further, Joshua Logan's innovative staging techniques blended one scene into another; there were no stage waits, no in-front-of-the-curtain "in one" scenes to mark time while the stagehands shifted scenery. An authorized private film taken from a complete performance at the Drury Lane during the musical's London run (which starred Mary Martin and Wilbur Evans) is a perfect visual record of what director Logan and co-librettists Logan and Hammerstein devised: smooth interlocking scenes that unfold in an almost surreal manner. For example, the first scene ends on the terrace with de Becque and his children. As they sing a reprise of "Dites-moi (pourquoi)" and start to walk off stage, the sailors in the second scene have suddenly materialized on the terrace and are singing "Bloody Mary." For a few moments the characters in both scenes share the same space in a stage limbo of both terrace and beach; then de Becque, the children, and the terrace are suddenly gone and the stage is full of servicemen on the beach finishing their musical salute to Bloody Mary (the stage directions state that all scene transitions in the musical "are achieved in this manner" in order to provide the effect that each scene dissolves into the next one).

The story focused on Nellie Forbush (Mary Martin) and Joseph Cable (William Tabbert), two young Americans caught up in the South Pacific war theatre where they encounter racial and romantic challenges in a world radically different from Nellie's hometown of Little Rock, Arkansas, and Cable's background of Philadelphia, Pennsylvania, and Princeton, New Jersey. Nellie has fallen in love with Emile de Becque (Ezio Pinza), a wealthy and older French émigré planter who has two children by his late Polynesian mistress (Nellie has assumed the children are the offspring of a servant), and Cable falls in love with native Tonkinese girl Liat (Betta St. John), daughter of the boisterous Bloody Mary (Juanita Hall), the island's jill-of-all-trades who sells everything from grass skirts to shrunken heads. For Nellie and Cable, the Polynesian children and Liat are their first exposures to other races, and while they at first recoil in confusion from this new experience, they learn to accept and embrace it. When de Becque goes on a secret war mission, Nellie befriends the children and is ready to become their surrogate mother if and when de Becque returns. Cable also realizes that Liat is his only love, and decides that once the war is over he'll live on the island and marry her. But it's too late for Cable, and he's killed in the war.

The musical's characters are so well written that almost seventy years after the musical's premiere there are still debates about the nature of their motives and feelings. In trying to marry off Liat, is Bloody Mary no less than a procurer? Does she condone Liat and Cable's sexual encounters because she's convinced he'll eventually marry her daughter? As for Cable, there's the school of thought that he "deserves" to die because he's a racist. Of course, he's not. He's simply a bewildered young man who has never dated any girl outside his world of Princeton and Philadelphia mainline society, and so his feelings for Liat almost overwhelm him as they seem to go against everything his background taught him. Racist? Hardly, because it is Cable who sings "You've Got to Be Carefully Taught," the musical theatre's seminal song about racial tolerance and acceptance. Those who accuse Cable of racism have simply not listened to his dialogue: toward the end of the musical he tells de Becque that after the war he's going back to the island because all he cares about is "right here" and "to hell with the rest."

All but one of the reviews were unanimous raves, and *South Pacific* became the season's longest-running musical and immediately took its place as one of the classics of musical theatre. It won numerous Tony Awards, including Best Musical, and, after George and Ira Gershwin's *Of Thee I Sing* (1931), was the second musical to win the Pulitzer Prize for drama. Brooks Atkinson in the *New York Times*: A "magnificent" and "thoroughly composed musical drama"; Robert Garland in the *New York Journal-American*: The musical has "pretty nearly everything," and "nearly everything" means it is "always good, often better, frequently best"; Howard Barnes in the *New York Herald Tribune*: "A show of rare enchantment . . . a musical play to be cherished"; Robert Coleman in the *New York Daily Mirror*: "A truly great musical . . . beguiling, heart-warming, amusing and rewarding"; Ward Morehouse in the *New York Sun*: "Stunning . . . a thrilling and exultant musical play"; William Hawkins in the *New York World-Telegram*: The "almost terrifyingly enthusiastic advance reports" were on target because the new musical "soared exquisitely" over the stage of the "blessedly enchanted" Majestic Theatre; and Richard Watts in the *New York Post*: "Few shows" had been so "handicapped" by "advance reports" from their out-of-town tryouts, but *South Pacific* was an "utterly captivating work of theatrical art" which "lived up so handsomely" to its pre-Broadway "superlatives."

Although John Chapman in the *New York Daily News* liked the "good show" and noted it was both an ambitious and "remarkable venture," it was not "the greatest thing since the invention of the wheel or even since **Kiss Me, Kate**." He concluded his review with the curious comment that ticketholders should read Michener's book before seeing the show.

During the New Haven tryout, Betta St. John was known as Betta Striegler. "Now Is the Time" (for de Becque); "My Girl Back Home" (for Cable); and "Will My Love Come Home to Me?" (aka "Loneliness of Evening") (for Nellie and de Becque) were cut. When "My Girl Back Home" was reinstated for the 1958 film version, it was sung by Cable and Nellie, and some sources assume the number had been performed as a duet by them during the pre-Broadway tryout; but three different tryout programs (one from the Shubert Theatre in New Haven and two from the Shubert in Boston) indicate that only Cable sang the number.

For the tryout, "Honey Bun" was titled "A Hundred and One Pounds of Fun." Songs cut in preproduction were: "Bright Canary Yellow" (for Nellie); "My Friend" (for Cable and Liat); "Bright Young Executive of Today" (for Harbison, Cable, and de Becque); and "In a Slender Beam" (for Nellie and de Becque). Also dropped in preproduction were "Suddenly Lucky" and its variant "Suddenly Lovely" (both for Cable); the song was later reworked as "Getting to Know You" for *The King and I* (1951).

As of this writing, the musical has been revived in New York seven times. The first four revivals were produced by the New York City Center Light Opera Company at City Center. The first opened on May 4, 1955, for fifteen performances; the cast included Sandra Deel (Nellie), Richard Collett (de Bacque), Herb Banke (Cable), Sylvia Sims (Bloody Mary), Henry Slate (Billis), and Carol Lawrence (Liat); Deel had played one of the nurses in the original production. The next revival opened on April 24, 1957, for twenty-three performances with Mindy Carson (Nellie), Robert (Bob) Wright (de Becque), Allen Case (Cable), Juanita Hall (Bloody Mary), Harvey Lembeck (Billis), and Imelda de Martin (Liat); here Hall reprised her original role, and Carson had played Nellie during the original New York run. The third revival opened on April 26, 1961, for twenty-three performances with Allyn Ann McLerie (Nellie), William Chapman (de Becque), Stanley Grover (Cable), Rosetta Le Noire (Bloody Mary), Dort Clark (Billis), and Coco Ramirez (Liat); and the fourth opened on June 3, 1965, for fifteen performances with Betsy Palmer (Nellie), Ray Middleton (de Becque), Richard Armbruster (Cable), Honey Saunders (Bloody Mary), Alan North (Billis), and Eleanor Calbes (Liat); Middleton had succeeded Pinza during the original run, and in this production Brackett was played by Murvyn Vye, who had created the role of Jigger in the original production of **Carousel** (he was also the original Kralahome in *The King and I*, but as the tryout progressed his role was considerably reduced and so he left the musical prior to the New York opening).

Two more non-commercial revivals followed, both at the New York State Theatre. On June 12, 1967, the Music Theatre of Lincoln Center's production ran for 104 performances; the cast included Florence Henderson (Nellie), Giorgio Tozzi (de Becque), Justin McDonough (Cable), Irene Byatt (Bloody Mary), David Doyle (Billis), and Joyce Maret (Liat); for the 1958 film version, Rossano Brazzi's singing voice had been dubbed by Tozzi. On February 27, 1987, the New York City Opera Company presented the work for sixty-eight performances; Susan Bigelow and Marcia Mitzman alternated in the role of Nellie, and Justino Diaz and Stanley Wexler in the role of de Becque; others in the cast were Cris Groenendaal (alternating with Richard White as Cable), Muriel Costa-Greenspon (alternating with Camille Saviola as Bloody Mary), Tony Roberts (Billis), and Ann Yen (alternating with Adrienne Telemaque as Liat).

The first commercial revival was presented at the Vivian Beaumont Theatre on April 8, 2008, for 996 performances with Kelli O'Hara (Nellie), Paulo Szot (de Becque), Matthew Morrison (Cable), Loretta Ables Sayre (Bloody Mary), Danny Burstein (Billis), and Li Jun Li (Liat). This production included "My Girl Back Home" (for both Cable and Nellie), which had been dropped during the 1949 tryout but had been included for the 1958 film version. The production won seven Tony Awards: Best Revival of a Musical; Best Leading Actor in a Musical (Szot); Best Direction of a Musical (Bartlett Sher); Best Scenic Design of a Musical (Michael Yeargan); Best Costume Design of a Musical (Catherine Zuber); Best Lighting Design of a Musical (Donald Holder); and Best Sound Design of a Musical (Scott Lehrer).

The musical was also twice presented at nearby Jones Beach on Long Island. The first revival opened on June 27, 1968, with Kathleen Nolan (Nellie), Jerome Hines (de Becque), and Barney Martin (Billis); the second opened on June 3, 1969; Nancy Dussault was Nellie and Hines was again de Becque.

The original London production opened at the Drury Lane on November 1, 1951, for 802 performances with Mary Martin and Betta St. John reprising their original roles of Nellie and Liat; others in the cast were Wilbur Evans (de Becque), Peter Grant (Cable), Muriel Smith (Bloody Mary), and Ray Walston (Billis). Martin's son Larry Hagman was one of the Seabees, and during the run Sean Connery appeared as a Seabee. As mentioned, the musical was privately filmed during one of the Drury Lane performances.

The 1958 film version was released by Twentieth Century-Fox and was directed by Joshua Logan; the screenplay was by Paul Osborn, and the cast included Mitzi Gaynor (who is perhaps the definitive Nellie Forbush), Rossano Brazzi (de Becque), John Kerr (Cable), Juanita Hall (Bloody Mary), Ray Walston (Billis), and France Nuyen (Liat); others in the cast were Mr. **Viva O'Brien** himself, Russ Brown, as well as Tom Laughlin, Ron Ely, Doug McClure, and James Stacy. Although Hall had created the role of Bloody Mary on Broadway, her singing voice was dubbed by Muriel Smith, who had played the role in London. The singing voice of de Becque's daughter Ngana was dubbed by Betty Wand, who during the same year dubbed Leslie Caron's singing voice in *Gigi*. The film reinstated "My Girl Back Home" (for Cable and Nellie) and part of the lyric for the deleted song "Loneliness of Evening" was briefly spoken as words in a letter.

A most misguided 2003 television adaptation was presented by CBS with a miscast Glenn Close (Nellie); others in the production were Rade Sherbedgia (de Becque) and Harry Connick Jr. (Cable); the soundtrack was issued by Columbia/Sony Music (# CK-85684) and includes a bonus track of "My Girl Back Home," which was filmed but not used for the showing; the DVD released by Buena Vista Home Entertainment (# 23248) includes the deleted scene. There was also a 2005 concert version of the musical presented at Carnegie Hall which was later telecast on public television; it was released on DVD (Rhino # R2-971631) and CD (Decca # B0006462-02); the cast included Reba McEntire (Nellie) and Brian Stokes Mitchell (de Becque).

The original cast album was recorded by Columbia (LP # ML/OL-4180 and # OS-2040), and was the first Broadway musical to be issued on the new LP format. The CD was released by Sony Classical/Columbia/Legacy (# SK-60722) and includes such bonus tracks as "My Girl Back Home" and "Loneliness of Evening" (both sung by Mary Martin) and "Bali Ha'i" (Pinza).

The script was published in hardback by Random House in 1949, and three books have been written about the musical. *The Tale of "South Pacific"* is an account of the film version published by Lehmann Books in 1958 (edited by Thana Skouras and designed by John De Cuir and Dale Hennesey); *The "South Pacific" Companion* by Lawrence Masion (Fireside Books, 2008) explores the musical's various incarnations; and *"South Pacific": Paradise Rewritten* by Jim Lovensheimer (Oxford University Press, 2010) looks at the racial and social context in which it was created. The lyrics for used, unused, and cut songs are included in *The Complete Lyrics of Oscar Hammerstein II*. Two editions of the script were published in 2014: one in paperback by Applause Books and the other in a hardback edition by the Library of Congress in a collection that includes the scripts of fifteen other musicals.

Among the replacements during the original Broadway run were Cloris Leachman (Nellie Forbush), Patricia Marand (Lieutenant Genevieve Marshall), Billie Worth (Ensign Janet MacGregor), Virginia Martin (Ensign Bessie Noonan), and Shirley Jones (Ensign Sue Yaeger).

Awards

Tony Awards: Best Musical (**South Pacific**); Best Leading Actor in a Musical (**Ezio Pinza**); Best Leading Actress in a Musical (**Mary Martin**); Best Featured Actor in a Musical (**Myron McCormick**); Best Featured Actress in a Musical (**Juanita Hall**); Best Director of a Musical (**Joshua Logan**); Best Producers of a Musical (**Richard Rodgers**, **Oscar Hammerstein II**, **Leland Hayward**, and **Joshua Logan**); Best Composer (**Richard Rodgers**); Best Scenic Designer (**Jo Mielziner**) (*Note*: During the previous Tony Award season, Jo Mielziner had also received the Tony for Best Scenic Designer for the body of his work during the season, including his designs for **South Pacific**.)
New York Drama Critics' Circle Award (1948–1949): Best Musical (**South Pacific**)
Pulitzer Prize: Best Drama (**South Pacific**)

HOWDY, MR. ICE OF 1950
"A Musical Icetravaganza"

Theatre: Center Theatre
Opening Date: May 26, 1949; *Closing Date*: April 15, 1950
Performances: 430
Lyrics: Al Stillman
Music: Alan Moran
Direction: Staged by Catherine Littlefield; William H. Burke, Production Director; *Producers*: Sonja Henie and Arthur M. Wirtz (Sonart Productions, Inc.; Arthur M. Wirtz, Executive Director); *Choreography*: Catherine Littlefield; Dorothie Littlefield, Assistant Choreographer; *Skating Direction*: May Judels; *Scenery*: Bruno Maine; *Costumes*: Grace Huston, Billy Livingston, and Katherine Kuhn; *Lighting*: Eugene Braun; *Musical Direction*: David Mendoza
Cast: Lloyd "Skippy" Baxter, Eileen Seigh, Harrison Thomson, The Three Bruises (Monte Scott, Sidney Spalding, Geoffe Stevens), The Prestons (Mickee and Paul), Jinx Clark, Edward (Eddie) Berry, Sid Krofft, Paul Castle, Trixie, Buster Grace, John Kasper, Buck Pennington, Cissy Trenholm, Arthur (Art) Erickson, John Walsh, Vaughn Pipes, Howard Brand; Singers: Nola Fairbanks, Dick Craig, Fred Martell, Bill Douglas; Girls: Margaret Barry, Peggy Bauer, Josephine Belluccia, Dorothy Bergman, Evelyn Biderman, Ann Boykin,

Bernice Deane, Helen Dutcher, Pat Harrington, Gloria Haupt, Lynne Immes, Joan King, Pat Lemaire, Ann Liff, Marjorie Mahne, Marvette Mosic, Doris Nelson, Priscilla Paulson, Gerri Richardson, Lela Rolontz, Theresa Rothacker, Betty Smith, Jean Sturgeon, Eileen Thompson, Catherine Webber; Boys: Stanley Belliveau, Fred Brennan, Gerry Decker, Nicholas Dantos, Ralph Evans, Kurt Fischman, Peter Fernandez, Louis Glessman, Ray Henderson, Dan Hurley, John Kasmarsik, Jimmy (James) Kelly, Gary Kerman, Ed McDonald, F. Meyer, Ken (Kenneth) Parker, James Partridge, Gus Patrick, Stephen Stofka, William Taft, James Toth, Dan Touhey, William Waldren, W. Wellenborn; Others: Grace Bleckman, Walli Hackman, Ragna Ray, Wally Van Sickle, Rusty Rodgers, Leonard Stofka, Kenneth Leslie, John Melendez, Hugh Pope
The revue was presented in two acts.

Skating and Musical Numbers

Act One: Overture (Orchestra); "Big City" (Nola Fairbanks, Bill Douglas, Dick Craig, Fred Martell; Girls and Boys [as above]); "At Your Service" (Doormen: Buster Grace, Buck Pennington, John Farris) and "We're the Doormen of New York" (Dick Craig, Fred Martell, Bill Douglas); "Man about Town" (Man: Edward Berry; Policeman: Arthur Erickson); "Hearts Aglow" (Pair: Cissy Trenholm and John Walsh; Cupids: Margaret Barry, Evelyn Biderman, Grace Bleckman, Helen Dutcher, Walli Hackman, Lela Rolontz, Theresa Rothacker, Eileen Thompson; Desires: Peggy Bauer, Josephine Belluccia, Pat Harrington, Gloria Haupt, Lynne Immes, Joan King, Pat Lemaire, Ann Liff, Marjorie Mahne, Marvette Mosic, Doris Nelson, Priscilla Paulson, Ragna Ray, Gerri Richardson, Betty Smith, Catherine Webber; Beaux: Gerry Decker, Nicholas Dantos, Louis Glessman, Ray Henderson, Dan Hurley, John Kasmarsik, James Kelly, Gary Kerman, James Partridge, Gus Patrick, Leonard Stofka, Stephen Stofka, James Toth, Dan Touhey, Wally Van Sickle, William Waldren; Singers: Nola Fairbanks, Bill Douglas, Dick Craig, Fred Martell; Puppet Artistry (Sid Krofft); The Prestons (Mickee and Paul Preston); "On High" (Buster Grace, Jean Sturgeon, Rusty Rodgers) and "You Was" (Nola Fairbanks and Fred Martell); "Trinidad Wharf" (Calypso Pete: John Walsh; Tropical Siren: Cissy Trenholm; Islanders: Margaret Barry, Peggy Bauer, Josephine Belluccia, Dorothy Bergman, Ann Boykin, Bernice Deane, Helen Dutcher, Pat Harrington, Lynne Immes, Joan King, Pat Lemaire, Marjorie Mahne, Marvette Mosic, Doris Nelson, Priscilla Paulson, Ragna Ray, Rusty Rodgers, Theresa Rothacker, Betty Smith, Catherine Webber, Stanley Belliveau, Gerry Decker, Nicholas Dantos, Kurt Fischman, Peter Fernandez, Louis Glessman, James Kelly, Garry Kerman, Kenneth Leslie, Kenneth Parker, James Partridge, Gus Patrick, Leonard Stofka, Stephen Stofka, William Taft, James Toth, Dan Touhey, Wally Van Sickle, William Waldren) and "Plenty More Fish in the Sea" (Nola Fairbanks, Bill Douglas, Dick Craig, Fred Martell); "Mercury" (Mercury: Lloyd "Skippy" Baxter; Pandora: Jinx Clark; Maidens: Walli Hackman, Lela Rolontz, Eileen Thompson); The Three Bruises (Monte Scott, Geoffe Stevens, Sid Spalding); "48 States" (Inquiring Reporter: Dick Craig; Matron: Nola Fairbanks; School Girls: Doris Nelson and Theresa Rothacker; Newsboy: Paul Castle; Ladies and Gentlemen of the Ensemble: Margaret Barry, Peggy Bauer, Josephine Belluccia, Dorothy Bergman, Evelyn Biderman, Ann Boykin, Bernice Deane, Helen Dutcher, Walli Hackman, Pat Harrington, Gloria Haupt, Lynne Immes, Joan King, Ann Liff, Marjorie Mahne, Marvette Mosic, Priscilla Paulson, Ragna Ray, Gerri Richardson, Rusty Rodgers, Lela Rolontz, Betty Smith, Eileen Thompson, Catherine Webber, Stanley Belliveau, Fred Brennen, Gerry Decker, Nicholas Dantos, Kurt Fischman, Peter Fernandez, Louis Glessman, Ray Henderson, Dan Hurley, John Kasmarsik, James Kelly, Garry Kerman, Kenneth Leslie, Ed McDonald, Kenneth Parker, James Partridge, Gus Patrick, Stephen Stofka, William Taft, James Toth, Dan Touhey, Wally Van Sickle, William Waldren, W. Wellenborn; Golden Eagle: Eileen Seigh; Pilots: Buster Grace, John Kasper, John Walsh) and "48 States" (Dick Craig)

Act Two: Entr'acte (Orchestra); "The Sleeping Beauty": (1) "The Princess' Birthday"—Princess Aurora: Jinx Clark; King: Arthur Erickson; Queen: Eileen Thompson; Maids of Honor: Josephine Belluccia, Bernice Deane, Gloria Haupt, Lynne Immes, Joan King, Ann Liff, Marvette Mosic, Doris Nelson, Priscilla Paulson, Ragna Ray, Rusty Rodgers, Theresa Rothacker; Prince from the East: Wally Van Sickle; Prince from the West: Buck Pennington; Prince from the North: John Farris; Prince from the South: John Walsh; Guards: John Melendez, Hugh Pope; (2) "A Remote Tower"—Wicked Fairy: John Kasper; Good Fairy: Cissy Trenholm; (3) "The Forest"—Prince Desire: Harrison Thomson; The Archers: Dan Hurley, James Paul, Gus Patrick, Stephen Stofka, William Waldren, Wally Van Sickle; and (4) "The Sleeping Castle"—Ladies in Waiting: Margaret Barry, Helen Dutcher, Walli Hackman, Pat Harrington, Betty Smith, Jean Sturgeon;

Courtiers: Peggy Bauer, Dorothy Bergman, Ann Boykin, Pat Lemaire, Marjorie Mahne, Gerri Richardson, Lela Rolontz, Catherine Webber, Fred Brennen, Gerry Decker, Peter Fernandez, Louis Glessman, Jimmy Kelly, Leonard Stofka, William Taft, Dan Touhey; "In Every Port" (Sailors: Buster Grace, Edward Berry, Buck Pennington; Mermaid: Rusty Rodgers; Little Brown Girl: Jean Sturgeon; Monkey: Ken Leslie); Trixie (Assisted by Leonard Stofka); "The Bluebirds" (Eileen Seigh and Lloyd "Skippy" Baxter); "The Cradle of Jazz" (Rhythm Man: Buck Pennington; Cocottes: Evelyn Biderman, Doris Nelson, Rusty Rodgers; Blues Boys and Girls: Josephine Belluccia, Ann Boykin, Pat Lemaire, Marvette Mosic, Priscilla Paulson, Gerri Richardson, Dan Hurley, John Kasmarsik, Gus Patrick, Leonard Stofka, William Taft, Dan Touhey; Cake-walkers: Peggy Bauer, Theresa Rothacker, John Farris, Louis Glessman; Strutters: Kurt Fischman, Ray Henderson, James Partridge, Stephen Stofka, Wally Van Sickle, William Waldren; Mr. Strut: John Walsh; Flappers: Bernice Dean, Pat Harrington, Joan King, Ann Liff, Betty Smith, Catherine Webber; Kampus Kids: Ragna Ray, John Kasper; Boogie Woogie: Margaret Barry, Dorothy Bergman, Helen Dutcher, Walli Hackman, Lela Rolontz, Eileen Thompson, Gerry Decker, Nicholas Dantos, James Kelly, Kenneth Leslie, Kenneth Parker, James Toth; Jitterbugs: Gloria Haupt, Marjorie Mahne, Eddie Berry, Arthur Erickson) and "Rocked in the Cradle of Jazz" (Bill Douglas, Dick Craig); "Flirtation" (Mam'zelle: Mickee Preston; Bellhop: Paul Preston); "Net Wizardry" (Vaughn Pipes vs. Howard Brand; Commentator: Fred Martell); "Reflections in the Dark"—"If I Only Knew" (Nola Fairbanks, Fred Martell; Ladies of the Ensemble); "Romantic Variations" (Valse: Eileen Hugh; Beguine: Lloyd "Skippy" Baxter); "Mountain Mirth" (Monte Stott, Sid Spalding, Geoffe Stevens, Paul Castle); "The World's Greatest Show" (Ringmaster: Harrison Thomson; Clowns: Stanley Belliveau, Nicholas Dantos, Kurt Fischman, Louis Glessman, Ray Henderson, Jimmy Kelly, Gary Kerman, Ken Parker, Leonard Stofka, Stephen Stofka, William Taft, William Waldren; Elephant Girls: Gloria Haupt, Pat Lemaire, Ann Liff, Priscilla Paulson, Ragna Ray, Catherine Webber; Tumblers: Gerry Decker, Ralph Evans, Peter Fernandez, James Paul, James Partridge, Gus Patrick, Dan Touhey; Trainer: Cissy Trenholm; Gold Leopards: Evelyn Biderman, Bernice Deane, Pat Harrington, Joan King, Doris Nelson, Gerri Richardson; Trainer: John Walsh; Black Panthers: Margaret Barry, Dorothy Bergman, Walli Hackman, Marvette Mosic, Theresa Rothacker, Eileen Thompson; Giant: Buster Grace; Giantess: Rusty Rodgers; Mammy Mine: Paul Castle; Ranee: Peggy Bauer, Marjorie Mahne; Rajah: Rudy Richards; Aerialists: Jinx Clark, Josephine Belluccia, Betty Smith, Helen Dutcher, Lynne Immes, John Farris, John Kasper; Acrobats: Mickee and Paul Preston; Trixie; Equestrienne: Eileen Seigh; Horses: Dan Hurley, James Toth; Cowboys: Eddie Berry, Buck Pennington, James Sisk; Billy the Kid: Lloyd "Skippy" Baxter; Strongman: Arthur Erickson) and "World's Greatest Show" (Nola Fairbanks, Bill Douglas, Dick Craig, Fred Martell); Finale (Entire Company)

Howdy, Mr. Ice of 1950 was a revised version of **Howdy, Mr. Ice**, which had opened earlier in the season. The latest ice revue was also the last in the Center Theatre's series of seven successful ice shows which had kept the theatre filled for an entire decade. This book contains separate entries for all seven productions, and the first in the series (**It Happens on Ice**) includes a complete list of all the shows, which played for a total of 4,043 performances.

The current edition included a few of the skating sequences that had been performed in **Howdy, Mr. Ice**. As usual, George Jean Nathan in his seasonal summary groaned about the lack of variety in the revues and noted that except for a puppet sequence, a skater who whirled on her head, a skating juggler, and some costumes decorated with tiny mirrors, the rest of the production amounted to "new titles attached to the old spectacular numbers." He mentioned that the show's press agent reported that eight and one-half million customers had seen the previous six ice shows, and that during one week all box-office records had been broken when ticket sales totaled $69,000.

The production was featured on the October 30, 1949, episode of the CBS series *Tonight on Broadway*.

ED WYNN'S LAUGH CARNIVAL

Theatres and *Performance Dates*: The revue opened on November 7, 1948, at the Curran Theatre in San Francisco, California, and played there for one month, toured for a few weeks, and then permanently closed at the American Theatre, St. Louis, Missouri, on January 22, 1949.
Producer: Paul Small; *Musical Direction*: Jay Freeman

Cast: *Ed Wynn*, Phil Baker, Allan Jones, Pat Rooney, Sr., Betty Reilly, Sid Silvers, Dick and Dottie Remey, Marion Harris Jr., The Hermanos Williams Trio, Lola Kendrick, Zell Russell, Texas Kendrick, Jean Spangler
The revue was presented in two acts.

Ed Wynn's Laugh Carnival was a vaudeville-styled revue that included the star's lovable and familiar shtick of ambling through the evening with his befuddled enjoyment of the evening's various acts, and, of course, he brought along one or two of his Rube Goldberg-like inventions (no doubt his famous bicycle-cum-piano made an appearance). Vaudevillian Phil Baker provided patter and songs; singer Allan Jones offered a number of standards, including "The Donkey Serenade," which he had introduced in the 1937 film *The Firefly*; and Pat Rooney Sr., sang and danced, including his rendition of "The Daughter of Rosie O'Grady," which he had previously performed in **Take a Bow** (two years later, Rooney created the role of Arvide Abernathy in the original production of *Guys and Dolls* and introduced "More I Cannot Wish You").

Variety reported that San Francisco "laughed itself silly" with the vaudevillian antics of Wynn's "comic wizardry." But the revue closed on the road, and marked Wynn's last stage performances. He soon became popular on television, and in the late 1950s starred in two episodes of *The Twilight Zone*. In 1959, he was nominated for a Best Supporting Actor Academy Award for his performance in *The Diary of Anne Frank*.

THE FOOLIES OF 1949
"A MYSTERY REVUE"

Theatres and *Performance Dates*: The revue opened on January 1, 1949, at the Geary Theatre, San Francisco, California, played at the Studebaker Theatre in Chicago, Illinois, for five weeks, and then permanently closed at the Shubert-Lafayette Theatre in Detroit, Michigan, on February 26, 1949.
Producer: Dante (aka Harry A. Jansen); *Musical Direction*: Alvin Jansen
Cast: Dante (aka Harry A. Jansen), Moi-Yo Miller and Her 50 Mystery Girls, Victoria Lopez
The revue was presented in two acts.

The Foolies of 1949 was a self-described "mystery revue" which included acts of magic and illusion by the celebrated magician Dante, otherwise known as Harry A. Jansen.
William Leonard in *Theatre World Season 1948–1949* noted that the revue was "allegedly Broadway-bound," but Dante was unable to magically materialize his show onto a New York stage.

RAZE THE ROOF

Theatres and *Performance Dates*: The revue opened on September 17, 1948, at the Curran Theatre, San Francisco, California; it played in various venues, including six weeks at the Great Northern Theatre in Chicago, Illinois; and closed permanently at the American Theatre in St. Louis, Missouri, on March 12, 1949.
Direction: Jerry Lester and Maurice Duke; *Producer*: Stage Productions, Inc., and Maurice Duke; *Choreography*: Ray Malone; *Scenery*: Matty Frei; *Costumes*: Jack's of Hollywood, Ada Leonard, and Adrian; *Lighting*: Uncredited; *Musical Direction*: Bobby Sherwood
Special Songs and *Material*: Snag Werris
Cast: *Jerry Lester*, The Wiere Brothers (Herbert, Sylvester, and Harry), Chili Williams, Bobby Sherwood and His Orchestra, Ada Leonard, Ray Malone, Cecil Stewart's Royal Rogues, The Golden Gate Girls, Richard Stauff, Mark Cook, Alan Egan, Roland Hughston, Clifford Orr
The revue was presented in two acts.

Sketches and Musical Numbers

Act One: Overture: California Medley (Bobby Sherwood and His Orchestra); "An Odd Moment" (Jerry Lester); "Hey, Look, I'm Dancin'" (Ray Malone, The Golden Gate Girls); "Spots Before Your Eyes" (Chili

Williams, with assistant); "Continental Pandemonium" (The Wiere Brothers, accompanied by Richard Stauff); "Call for Herbert Tillson" (Herbert Tillson: Jerry Lester; Bill: Bobby Sherwood; Announcer: Mark Cook); Cecil Stewart's Royal Rogues (featuring Mark Cook)

Act Two: "Royal Garden Blues" (Bobby Sherwood and His Orchestra); "Pardon Me, Pretty Baby" (Bobby Sherwood, Jerry Lester, Chili Williams); "Rhythmic Charm" (Ada Leonard); "Poono in Persia" (Ali Ben Poono: Jerry Lester; Hareenie La Hay: Chili Williams; Punjab: Allen Egan; Moolah: Roland Hughston; Tahoe: Clifford Orr); "Dancing Feet" (Ray Malone); "Rum-Rum-Rumba Fantasy" (The Golden Gate Girls); "The House of Sherwood" (Bobby Sherwood, Entire Cast, "and, incidentally" Jerry Lester)

The revue *Raze the Roof* didn't, and never made it to New York. *Variety* was optimistic about the show's chances and suggested that with some tightening the evening "may yet prove a payoff." But in *Best Plays*, *Chicago Tribune* critic Claudia Cassidy called the revue a "shoddy little horror" and noted that special songs and material were "gravely attributed to one Snag Werris."

During the early part of the run, Joe Pasco, Lita Terris, and Hector and His Pals were seen in the production.

THAT'S THE TICKET!
"A NEW MUSICAL COMEDY"

Theatre and *Performance Dates*: The musical opened on September 24, 1948, at the Shubert Theatre, Philadelphia, Pennsylvania, and permanently closed there on October 2, 1948.
Book: Julius and Philip G. Epstein
Lyrics and *Music*: Harold Rome
Direction: Jerome Robbins; *Producers*: Joseph Kipness, John Pransky, and Al Beckman; *Choreography*: Paul Godkin; *Scenery*: Oliver Smith; *Costumes*: Miles White; *Lighting*: Peggy Clark; *Musical Direction*: Lehman Engel
Cast: Edna Skinner (Patricia Vale-Waterhouse), Dudley Sadler (Rex, Photographer, Second Republican, Delegate-at-Large, Second Knight), John Gorrin Jr. (Frog), Loring Smith (Robert Vale-Waterhouse), Ralph Hertz (Whyte), Jesse M. Cimberg (Browne), Bobby Vail (Greene), Jack C. Carter (Joe Tompkins), Byron Russell (Meadows, Druid), Leif Erickson (Alfred, Lord of Nottingwood aka Alfred the Average), Art Carroll (First Reporter, California Delegate, Supreme Court Justice), Sven Holst (Second Reporter, Delegate-at-Large, Supreme Court Justice), Sam Kirkham (Third Reporter, Delegate-at-Large, First Announcer), Bob Neukum (Fourth Reporter, New York Delegate, Supreme Court Justice), John M. Backus (First Newsboy, Frog Leg Salesman, Supreme Court Justice), Douglas Martin (Second Newsboy, Delegate-at-Large, Supreme Court Justice), Rufus Norris (Third Newsboy, Footman, Delegate-at-Large, Supreme Court Justice), Blake Ritter (Fourth Newsboy, Third Democrat, Florida Delegate), Harry Clark (Commentator, First Democrat, Second Announcer), Mia Stenn (Mabel, Druid's Handmaiden), Joan Coburn (Millie, Florida Delegate), George S. Irving (Wholesaler, First Republican, Announcer, Analyst, First Night), Rolly Beck (Wholesaler's Partner, Second Democrat, Knight on Horseback, Supreme Court Justice), Mary Statz (Fashion Editor, Druid's Handmaiden), Jenny Lewis (Foundation Model, Texas Delegate, Carrie Nation), Eileen Jenkins (Fan Model, Virgin Islands Delegate, Pocahontas), Candace Montgomery (Shield Model, Florida Delegate, Dolly Madison), Marion Richards (Umbrella Model, Alaskan Delegate, Daughter of the American Revolution), Kaye Ballard (Marcia LaRue), Gisella Svetlik (Nora, California Delegate), Gloria Patrice (Bobby Soxer, Drum Majorette), Royal Dano (Third Republican, Idaho Delegate, Supreme Court Justice, Kansas Farmer, Third Knight), Kasimir Kokic (Oklahoma Indian, Indian), Herbert Ross (Texas Cowboy, Supreme Court Justice, Fourth Knight), Gay Laurence (Florida Delegate), Audrey Peters (Florida Delegate), Shellie Farrell (Drum Majorette), Isabel Mirrow (Drum Majorette), Marijane Maricle (Gypsy), Bonnie Blair (New York Delegate), Joyce Homier (New York Delegate), Rhoda Luscomb (New York Delegate), Eleanor Boleyn (California Delegate), Shirley Eckl (California Delegate), Nancy Eliot (Club Woman Delegate), Julia Humphries (Club Woman Delegate), James Nygren (Uncle Sam), Harry Asmus (Delegate-at-Large, Southern Colonel), Marx Breaux (Delegate-at-Large), Jack Miller (Delegate-at-Large, Indian), Wallace Seibert (Delegate-at-Large), Stanley Simmons (Delegate-at-Large), Carlos Valenzuela (Delegate-at-Large, Indian); Singers: Bonnie Blair, Joan Coburn, Nancy Eliot, Joyce Homier, Julia Humphries, Gay Laurence,

Rhoda Luscomb, Marijane Maricle, Mia Stenn, John M. Backus, Art Carroll, Sven Holst, Sam Kirkham, Douglas Martin, Bob Neukum, Rufus Norris, Blake Ritter; Dancers: Eleanor Boleyn, Shirley Eckl, Shellie Farrell, Gloria Patrice, Audrey Peters, Isabel Mirrow, Mary Statz, Gisella Svetlik, Harry Asmus, Marc Breaux, Kasimir Kokic, Jack Miller, James Nygren, Wallace Seibert, Stanley Simmons, Carlos Valenzuela

The musical was presented in two acts.

The action takes place in New York City and North Shamokin, Pennsylvania.

Musical Numbers

Act One: "How Peaceful Is the Evening" (Singers; danced by Shirley Eckl, Shellie Farrell, Isabel Mirrow, Gisella Svetlik, Harry Asmus, Jack Miller, Wallace Seibert, Stanley Simmons); "Looking for a Candidate" (Loring Smith, Jesse M. Cimberg, Ralph Hertz, Bobby Vail); "Read All About It" (Ensemble); "Chivalry Reel" (Rod Alexander, Ensemble); "The Ballad of Marcia LaRue" (Kaye Ballard, Jack C. Carter, Ensemble); "Take Off the Coat" (Kaye Ballard; danced by Rod Alexander and Shirley Eckl); "The Fair Sex" (Kaye Ballard, Jack C. Carter, Rolly Beck, Harry Clark, Royal Dano, George S. Irving, Blake Ritter, Dudley Sadler, Dancers); "Dost Thou" (Edna Skinner, Leif Erickson); "The Money Song" (aka "Money, Money, Money") (Jack C. Carter, Jesse M. Cimberg, Leif Erickson, Ralph Hertz, Loring Smith, Bobby Vail, Joan Coburn, Nancy Eliot, Gay Laurence); "You Never Know What Hit You—When It's Love" (aka "What Hit You") (Kaye Ballard); "We're Going Back" (Entire Company)
Act Two: Newsreel; "Cry, Baby" (aka "Cry, Baby, Cry") (Jack C. Carter); "I Shouldn't Love You" (Edna Skinner); "Gin Rummy Rhapsody" (Jack C. Carter); "Political Lady" (Harry Clark; Quartet: John M. Backus, Sam Kirkham, Bob Neukum, Blake Ritter; danced by Kaye Ballard and Ensemble); "A Determined Woman" (Kaye Ballard, Leif Erickson, Royal Dano, George S. Irving, Dudley Sadler, Herbert Ross); Finale (Singers)

The ambitious political satire and fantasy *That's the Ticket!* (also advertised without the exclamation point) closed prematurely during its Philadelphia tryout. The score was by Harold Rome, who had recently written the score for the long-running hit revue **Call Me Mister**, the book was by Julius J. and Philip G. Epstein (who with Howard Koch had written the screenplay for *Casablanca*), Jerome Robbins directed the production, Oliver Smith designed it, Miles White costumed it, and Paul Godkin, who had created the choreography for the well-received *Willie the Weeper* sequence in **Ballet Ballads**, provided the dances. But *That's the Ticket!* collapsed after just one week of performances, lost an estimated $215,000, and disappeared for over fifty years.

The story looked at the Democrats and Republicans who for the first time in history share a common cause, their dislike of the two other major political parties, one of which is known as the Feudals. One night in Central Park, Patricia (Edna Skinner), the daughter of Feudal Party political boss Robert Vale-Waterhouse (Loring Smith), meets a knight who had been turned into a frog and who's now a knight again. Alfred, Lord of Nottingham, otherwise known as Alfred the Average (Leif Erickson), and Patricia immediately fall in love, and Robert decides he's found the perfect candidate to run for president. Meanwhile, the witch Marcia LaRue (Kaye Ballard) who originally placed the frog-curse on Alfred and is now a famous Hollywood star, is determined to become the first female president. The Democrats and Republicans unite and become the Republicrats with Marcia as their candidate against Alfred. Marcia turns Alfred back into a frog, but ultimately all her powers fail her and Alfred is elected president.

Rome's score was fresh and melodic, with a number of outstanding songs, including "Political Lady," "A Determined Woman," "Gin Rummy Rhapsody," "The Ballad of Marcia LaRue," "Cry, Baby," and "You Never Know What Hit You—When It's Love." In a score filled with highlights, perhaps the finest numbers were the sinuous and seductive "Take Off the Coat" and the comic calypso salute to "Money, Money, Money," which became a popular hit.

E. P. Sensenderfer in the *Philadelphia Evening Bulletin* noted the musical was a reversal of the story of **A Connecticut Yankee**, and so instead of a modern-day American journeying back to medieval times there was now a knight thrust into the present day. And so what happens? Sensenderfer replied, "Nothing much." And *Variety* felt the musical's problems were "seemingly insurmountable."

Despite the failure of the musical, Rome recycled a number of its songs. "You Never Know What Hit You—When It's Love" was heard the following summer in the straw-hat circuit revue **Pretty Penny** and then later in the 1950 Broadway revue *Bless You All*, which also included "Take Off the Coat" in its score. "Cry, Baby" was also used in **Pretty Penny**, and was heard in the 1950 Broadway revue *Alive and Kicking*, and "I Shouldn't Love You" was rewritten for *Fanny* (1954) as "I Have to Tell You."

On April 19, 2002, Musicals Tonight! revived *That's the Ticket!* at the 14th Street Y for nineteen performances. The production was recorded by Original Cast Records (CD # OC-6038); "We're Going Back" was heard as "Campaign Song"; the dance number "Chivalry Reel" was omitted; and "Couplet for Alfred," "Fa-La-La," and "Love is Still Love" were added. The recording features George S. Irving, who had appeared in the original 1948 production (for the recording, he sings the role of Robert Vale-Waterhouse).

1949 Season

FUNZAPOPPIN
"A MUSICAL CARNIVAL"

Theatre: Madison Square Garden
Opening Date: June 30, 1949; *Closing Date*: July 31, 1949
Performances: 37
Lyrics and *Music*: Ole Olsen, Chic Johnson, Chuck Gould, and Perry Martin
Direction: Ole Olsen and Chic Johnson; *Producers*: Arthur M. Wirtz, Ole Olsen, and Chic Johnson; *Choreography*: Catherine Littlefield (Carl Littlefield, Assistant Choreographer); *Scenery*: Becker Brothers Studio; *Costumes*: Uncredited; *Lighting*: Uncredited; *Musical Direction*: Jack Pfeiffer
Cast: Ole Olsen, Chic Johnson, Marty May, June Johnson, J. C. Olsen, The Six Mighty Atoms, The P. L. Taylor Trio, Gloria Gilbert, The Berry Brothers, Baron Hopper, Gloria Short, William (Bill) Hayes, Frank Cook, Andy Ratouscheff, Shirley Ann Basso, Andy Woolandi, Helen Magna, Shorty Renna, Nirska, The Clark Brothers, Ray Dorian, The Three Jigsaws, Lee Berrie, Lou Barrison, Irene Billings, Chiampi, Red Breen, Eugenie Carlson, Frank Cook, Dixon and Dugan, Frank Harty, John Howes, Jack Joyce, Billy Kay, The Happy Kellems, Joe Madden, Maurice Millard, Pat Moran, Russ Sobey, Georges Suzanne; The Choraleers: Andrey Calib, Mignon Chappell, Nora Dee, Norma Hawkins, Jacqueline Paul, Rita Stevans, Carl Bryson, Lynford Cautz, Ward Ohrman, Fred Smythe, Alan Stone, John Tantillo; Ensemble: Anna Andrews, Shirley Ann Basso, Sonya Besant, Iris Burton, Marie Camadeca, Connie Codilis, Celeste Cowan, Georgine Darcy, Juanita M. Eastman, Norma Ek, Dolores Frazzini, Juanita Given, Caroline Grant, Barbara C. Greaves, Joyce Harley, Nancy Heck, Jeanette Heller, Betty Kallas, Dorothy Kallas, Marion Kallas, Joy Kerber, May Kirby, Florence Leighton, Eleanor Lynne, Dorothy Macy, Beverly McNichols, June Miller, Candace Monte, Sharon O'Neill, Joyce O'Rourke, Nancy O'Rourke, Billy Partridge, Victoria Risch, Inger Van Jepmond, Dawn Zarlinga, Raymond Dorian, Albert Fiorella, Phillip Gerard, Joseph Kaminski, Neil Peters, Jack Tygett
The revue was presented in two acts.

Sketches and Musical Numbers

Act One: Prelude (J. C. Olsen, Marty May); "Oh, What a Night (Nite) for a Party" (lyric and music by Ole Olsen, Chic Johnson, and Chuck Gould) (William Hayes, The Choraleers, J. C. Olsen, Ole Olsen, Chic Johnson); "Bedlam" (Ole Olsen, Chic Johnson, Company); "Dancing Feet" (The Berry Brothers); "Men about Town" (Ole Olsen, Chic Johnson); "Jungle Rhythm" (William Hayes, The P. L. Taylor Trio, The Six Mighty Atoms, The Choraleers, Dancers and Singers); "Perjury in Pittsburgh" (Ole Olsen, Chic Johnson, Marty May, June Johnson, John Howes); "Daisies Won't Tell" (Dancers [The 36 Precisionists]); "Baby Sitters" (sequence included song "I'd Like to Be a Sitter for a Baby Like You," lyric and music by Ole Olsen, Chic Johnson, and Perry Martin) (Ole Olsen, Chic Johnson, June Johnson, J. C. Olsen, The Six Mighty

Atoms); "Here Comes Cookie" (Frank Cook); "It's a Great Wide Wonderful World": (1) "Bridal Party" (June Johnson, William Hayes); (2) "Venice" (The Choraleers); (3) "East India" (Gloria Short, Ray Dorian); and (4) "The Berry Brothers in Harlem"; "Swing on the Corner" (lyric and music by Ole Olsen, Chic Johnson, and Chuck Gould)/Finale (Ole Olsen, Chic Johnson, Entire Company)

Act Two: "Six-Gun Joe from Cicero" (lyric and music by Ole Olsen, Chic Johnson, and Chuck Gould) (Ole Olsen, Chic Johnson, Marty May, J. C. Olsen, June Johnson, Company); Marty May; "The Barber Shop" (Ole Olson, Chic Johnson, Marty May, June Johnson, Company); "Ballet Beautiful" (Gloria Gilbert); "The Escape Artist" (Chic Johnson); "Foolin' Around" (Ole Olsen, Chic Johnson, J. C. Olsen); "Hoe Down" (Company [with audience interaction]); Give-Away Time; "Jam Session" (Frank Cook, Russ Sobey, The Berry Brothers, Helen Magna, J. C. Olsen, Andy Ratouscheff, Pat Moran, Lou Barrison, Jack Joyce); "Funzapoppin" (lyric and music by Ole Olsen, Chic Johnson, and Chuck Gould) (Ole Olsen, Chic Johnson, Entire Company)

Funzapoppin was another free-for-all from Ole Olsen and Chic Johnson's smorgasbord of lowbrow comedy antics. The revue had been produced in such cities as Indianapolis and Chicago (where it played for three weeks at the Chicago Stadium) and then opened at Madison Square Garden for a limited engagement of five weeks. But the team's popularity was on the wane, and there wouldn't be any more long-running successes like *Hellzapoppin'*, **Sons o' Fun**, and **Laffing Room Only**. (The revue's souvenir program referred to the show's title as *Funzapoppin*, but sometimes the show is referenced as *Funzapoppin'*.)

Later in the season their *Tsk! Tsk! Tsk! Paree* played on the West Coast, and picked up a few performers and songs from a revue called **A la Carte**, which had shuttered in Los Angeles on its aborted route to Broadway. *Tsk! Tsk! Tsk! Paree* and **A la Carte** then morphed into *Pardon Our French*, which opened in New York in 1950 for a three-month run; from there, the team appeared on a Palace bill in the early 1950s, and their final venture *Pardon Our Antenna* closed on the road in 1954. But for many years they had a good run, the word *hellzapoppin'* soon defined a certain style of free-wheeling comedy, and their farcical brand of comic bedlam was unique to Broadway (and their audience participation format foreshadowed theatregoing of later decades when many audience members became obsessed with being part of the theatergoing experience by ecstatically applauding, whistling, and hooting after every song and giving every production an obligatory standing ovation; the Olsen and Johnson shows would have been theatrical nirvana for this type of audience member).

Funzapoppin offered all the usual Olsen and Johnson antics. Audiences were greeted by clowns as they entered the theatre, were guided to the wrong seats, and in some cases were forced to walk across the stage in order to reach their seats. And once seated they were met by performers in gorilla and polar bear outfits, were showered by beans, corn, bananas, eggs, and rubber ducks and spiders, and a prop stork circled above their heads. They were also accosted by cast members who encouraged them to dance in the aisles and then on the stage itself, and there were giveaways, too, including refrigerators, blocks of ice, and a live pig. There were midgets who cavorted about, and there were tap dancers, a tumbler, a stilt dancer, and even a one-legged dancer. There were blood-curdling screams from every direction, guns were fired throughout the performance, and there were the usual bathroom jokes (Richard Watts in the *New York Post* noted that without cap pistols and bathroom fixtures Olsen and Johnson would be left "virtually bound and gagged"). There was even a prop airplane that took to the air with June Johnson and Bill Hayes. The revue also revived one of the most popular routines from earlier Olsen and Johnson shows: a picture of a battleship suddenly starts to fire at the audience, cast members fire back, and then within the frame the battleship sinks.

Brooks Atkinson in the *New York Times* noted that "not since the hot war stopped have so many shots been fired in public," Watts suspected there were fewer gunshots fired during the Spanish-American War, and Robert Coleman in the *New York Daily Mirror* said World War II munitions factories would stay in business as long as Olsen and Johnson kept producing revues. Atkinson described the show as a "gargantuan honky-tonk" in which one out of every ten gags was really funny; Watts said Olsen and Johnson were fundamentally "minor" comedians who had devised a popular formula that made them "unique and triumphant"; and while their jamboree of jokes was "incessant, thunderous, and rather harrowing," their humor was occasionally "pretty funny"; and William Hawkins in the *New York World-Telegram* found the "cheerful nightmare" a "spangled meatloaf made of a history of show business."

In his review, Robert Garland in the *New York Journal-American* reported that a "sneak preview" of *Funzapoppin* had been recently seen on television.

The program said that "Marty May, or he may not," that Gloria Short was a "pulchritudinous pretzel," that Irene Billings was "tall, blonde and sexciting," and Helen Magda was a "teenie weenie ballerweenie." The program further noted that the three-hour evening was a "howling hooligan hilarity reminiscent of New Year's Eve, Custer's Last Stand, VJ Day, Charge of the Light Brigade, the End of the World, Ringling Brothers Circus, the Metropolitan Opera, Truth and Consequences, Stop the Music, the County Fair, and Frankenstein's Bride." And, imagine, all this for a top ticket price of $3.00.

For *Funzapoppin*, a huge stage was erected at the west end of Madison Square Garden (the Ninth Avenue side, from 49th Street to 50th Street). Joe Pihodna in the *New York Herald Tribune* suggested the revue would have been better suited had it played in the round in arena fashion with the audience sitting on all four sides of the playing area. By utilizing a stage at one end of the arena, visibility and audibility were diminished. But he quickly noted that not being able to hear the gags wasn't "the worst punishment in the world."

CABALGATA
"SPANISH MUSICAL CAVALCADE"

Theatre: Broadway Theatre
Opening Date: July 7, 1949; *Closing Date*: September 10, 1949
Performances: 76
Direction and *Choreography*: Daniel Cordoba; *Producers*: S. Hurok and Daniel Cordoba; *Scenery*: Luis Marquez; *Costumes*: Daniel Cordoba; *Lighting*: Uncredited; *Musical Direction*: Ramon Bastida
Cast: Dancers: Carmen Vazquez, Pepita Marco, Floriana Alba, Pilar Calvo, Aurea Reyes, Jose Toledano, Paco Fernandez, Julio Toledo, Sebastian Castro, Fernando Vargas, Violeta Carrillo, Maria Castan, Pepita Durango, Conchita Escobar, Carmen Gamez, Luisa Garcia, Paloma Larios, Zenia Lopez, Teresa Martinez, Catalina Maytorena, Elba Ocaiza, Pepita Ramirez, Gracia Rios, Rocio Stantisteban, Malena Telmo, Armonia Villa, Andres Aguirre, Carlos Castro, Gustavo Delgado, Raul Izquierdo, Gustavo Garzon, Guillermo Marin, Fernando Marti, Rene Ochoa, Luis Riestra, Ricardo Solano, Jose Valois, Juan Villarias; Singers: Miguel Herrero, Rosa De Avila, Enrique Barrera, Victor Torres, Rafael Hernan; Concert Pianist: Jose Cortes; Guitars: Manuel Medina and Paco Millet
The revue was presented in two acts.

Act One: Overture: "The Wedding of Luis Alonso" (music by Gimenez) (Orchestra); "A Garden in Valencia": (1) "Song of Valencia" (music by Giner); (2) "Women of Valencia" (music by Bastida); and (3) "Regional Dances" (music from popular songs) (Dancers: Pepita Marco, Floriana Alba, Aurea Reyes, Jose Toledano, Julio Toledo, Sebastian Castro, Corps de Ballet; Singers: Rosa de Avila, Enrique Barrera and Rafael Hernan); "Zambra" (Gypsy Dance) (music by Soutullo and Vert) (Pilar Calvo and Paco Fernandez); "Petenera" (Dancer: Carmen Vazquez; Singer: Miguel Herrero; Guitars: Paco Millet and Manuel Medina); "Salmantina" (Provincial Dance) (Pepita Marco); "Dance School" (music by Latorre) (Floriana Alba, Pilar Castro, Corps de Ballet); "Tanguillo"—"Three Flamenco Boys" (music of unidentified popular song) (Dancers: Jose Toledano, Julio Toledo, Fernandez Vargas; Guitars: Paco Millet and Manuel Medina); "Asturias" (music by Albeniz) (Castanet Dance) (Carmen Vazquez); "Three Popular Songs" (music by Manuel de Falla): (1) "Castellana" (Fernando Vargas and Luisa Garcia); (2) "La Nana" (Floriana Alba); and (3) "El Pano Muruno" (Jose Teledano and Paco Fernandez) (these three songs were performed by Rosa De Avila, who was accompanied by Jose Cortes on the piano); "Rondalla Aragonesa" (Vignette): (1) Popular Songs; (2) "Serenaders" (music by Monreal); (3) "Dance of "The Ribbon Pole"; and (4) "Jota" (music by Breton) (Dancers: Pepita Marco, Aurea Reyes, Julio Toledo, Sebastian Castro, Corps de Ballet; Singers: Enrique Barrera, Victor Torres, Rafael Hernan; Guitars: Paco Millet and Manuel Medina)
Act Two: Overture: "La Revoltosa" (music by Chapi) (Orchestra); "Glory and Blood": (1) "Arrival at the Bull Ring"; (2) "Girls and Toreadors"; (3) "The Bullfight"; (4) "Tragedy"; and (5) "Road to Glory" (Dancers: Pepita Marco, Aurea Reyes, Jose Toledano, Paco Fernandez, Julio Toledo, Sebastian Castro, Fernando Vargas, Corps de Ballet; Singers: Miguel Herrero, Rosa de Avila, Enrique Barrera, Victor Torres, Rafael Hernan); "Zapateado" (Flamenco) (music of unidentified popular song) (Carmen Vazquez; Guitars: Paco Millet and Manuel Medina); "Jota" (music by Larregla) (piano solo by Jose Cortes); "Los Piconeros" ("Andalucia") (music by Quiroga) (Singer: Miguel Herrero; Dancers: Pilar Calvo, Jose Toledano, Paco Fernandez); "Galician Airs" (Vignette): (1) "Dawn" (music by Caballero); (2) "Song of the Washerwomen" (music

of unidentified popular song); (3) "Farewell of the Emigrant" (music by Vives); (4) "Song of the Fisherman" (music of unidentified popular song); and (5) "La Muneira" (Dance) (music by Vives) (Dancers: Floriana Alba, Pepita Marco, Aurea Reyes, Julio Toledo, Sebastian Castro, Fernando Vargas, Corps de Ballet; Singers: Rosa de Avila, Enrique Barrera); "Andaluza" (music by Granados) (Carmen Vazquez, Jose Toledano, Paco Fernandez); "Madrid—1900": "Mazurka" (music by Chueca and Valverde) (Floriana Alba, Julio Toledo); "Classic Bolero—18th Century" (music of unidentified popular song) (Aurea Reyes, Sebastian Castro); "An Inn in Seville" (Vignette): (1) "Fandangos" (music of unidentified popular song) (Pilar Calvo, Fernando Vargas, Corps de Ballet); (2) "Jealousy" (music by Quiroga) (Carmen Vazquez, Miguel Herrero); (3) "The Shellfish Vendor" (music of unidentified popular song) (Paco Fernandez); (4) "La Chunga" (music by Monreal) (Pepita Marco, Julio Toledo); (5) "The Bootblack" (music of unidentified popular song) (Jose Toledano); (6) "Espanola" (music by Luna) (Rosa de Avila); and (7) "Alegrias" ("Dance of Cadiz") (music of unidentified popular song); Finale

Cabalgata (which means "cavalcade") was an evening of Spanish dances that had first been produced in 1942 by Daniel Cordoba at the Fontalba Theatre in Madrid; according to the program, the revue gave seven years of consecutive performances in Spain, Latin America, and the West Coast prior to the Broadway production. The revue was advertised as a "Spanish Musical Cavalcade," but for the post-Broadway tour was touted as "The Musical Extravaganza." During the Broadway run, the title was altered to *A Night in Spain: "Cabalgata,"* but for the tour was titled *A Night in Spain* in which "The Cabalgata Company" appeared.

The reviews were generally positive, although two or three critics noted the dancing was somewhat one-note and thus became monotonous. The evening offered boleros and mazurkas as well as flamenco and castanet dances and numerous songs, and clearly the star of the show was Carmen Vazquez, who received glowing notices for her dancing. The production managed a nine-week run, and then embarked on a national tour.

Lewis Funke in the *New York Times* said a full program of Spanish dances at first seemed to offer "the prospect of monotony," but the revue offered "ample variety" and was thus a "pleasant surprise." The highlight was "Rondalla Aragonesa," and he also singled out the ribbon dance and "Jota." As for Carmen Vazquez, she danced with "infectious zest and spirit," and had "wit and delicacy" and a warm personality. Robert Coleman in the *New York Daily Mirror* said the "spirited and colorful" revue moved "with express-train speed and admirable precision"; and William Hawkins in the *New York World-Telegram* praised the "refreshing, animated, unpretentious and unique" revue and said Vazquez stood "in a class by herself" with a "willowy grace" that earned her "repeated vociferous accolades."

Robert Garland in the *New York Journal-American* found the evening "colorful, exciting, authentic" . . . and "repetitious"; but he enjoyed the show and said Vazquez was "the heroine" of his review. He concluded that with Spanish music it was "too easy" to add "too much" garlic and onions, and so he praised Ramon Bastida's "expert" conducting. The last line of his review unfortunately contained an indelicate word choice: "Spick and Spanish, the spick part of *Cabalgata* is well controlled." Walter Terry in the *New York Herald Tribune* said the "pleasant diversion" lacked distinguished material because the choreography was merely "serviceable" instead of "brilliant" (and what brilliance there was stemmed from the performers themselves). Robert Sylvester in the *New York Daily News* reported the revue started off well but soon bogged down, and suggested that with judicious tweaking the production could find great success in New York. He noted the production had met with favor everywhere it played including Havana (where Sylvester had seen it two years previously and where it had run for many months) and the West Coast (where it surprised everyone with "highly successful grosses").

Although Ward Morehouse in the *New York Sun* found "pleasant interludes" throughout the evening and said the "outstanding" Vazquez had "style, spirit and looks" and stopped the show with her castanet dance, the evening was nonetheless "monotonous." And Richard Watts in the *New York Post* said the "bright, lively, good-looking" show was "given to monotony" and lacked "excitement." But the revue's qualities were not "inconsiderable ones" and offered a "field day" for fans of Spanish dancing; and if the production included one "outstanding personal success" that success belonged to Carmen Vazquez. Watts noted *Cabalgata* brought to mind another Latin dance revue, 1939's *Mexicana*, which was "one of the most enchanting shows" he'd ever seen.

In later seasons, occasional Latin dance-styled evenings popped up on Broadway, including *Fiesta in Madrid* (1969), *Tango Argentino* (1986 and 1999), *Flamenco Puro* (1986), *Oba Oba* (1988), *Oba Oba '90* (1990), *Oba Oba '93* (1993), *Gypsy Passion* (1992), *Tango Pasion* (1993), and *Forever Tango* (1997, 2004, and 2013).

MISS LIBERTY
"THE NEW MUSICAL COMEDY"

Theatre: Imperial Theatre
Opening Date: July 15, 1949; *Closing Date*: April 8, 1950
Performances: 308
Book: Robert E. Sherwood
Lyrics and *Music*: Irving Berlin
Direction: Moss Hart; *Producers*: Irving Berlin, Robert E. Sherwood, and Moss Hart; *Choreography*: Jerome Robbins; *Scenery* and *Lighting*: Oliver Smith; *Costumes*: Motley; *Musical Direction*: Jay Blackton
Cast: Mary McCarty (Maisie Dell), Rowan Tudor (The Herald Reader), Charles Dingle (James Gordon Bennett), Eddie Albert (Horace Miller), Evans Thornton (Police Captain, The Policeman, Immigration Officer), Donald McClelland (The Mayor, Richard K. Fox), Emile Renan (French Ambassador), Sid Lawson (Carthwright), Philip Bourneuf (Joseph Pulitzer), Bill Bradley (Shark), Allen Knowles (Shark, Reception Delegate), Kazimir Kokic (Shark, Strong Man), Robert Pagent (Shark), Herbert Berghof (Bartholdi), Stephanie Augustine (Model), Trudy DeLuz (Model), Marilyn Frechette (Model, A Socialite), Allyn (Ann) McLerie (Monique Dupont), Tommy Rall (The Boy, Another Lamplighter, The Dandy), Maria Karnilova (The Girl, Ruby), Virginia Conwell (Acrobat, Reception Delegate), Joe Milan (Acrobat, Train), Eddie Phillips (Acrobat, Train, A Sailor), Ethel Griffies (The Countess), Ed Chappel (A Lover, A Minister), Helene Whitney (His Girl, An Actress), Robert Penn (A Gendarme), Johnny V. R. Thompson (A Lamplighter), Robert Patterson (An Admiral, A Policeman), Bob Kryl (Boy), Ernest Laird (Boy, Another Boy), Elizabeth Watts (The Mother), Lewis Bolyard (Brother), David Collyer (Brother), Erik Kristen (Train, The Judge), Dolores (Dody) Goodman (Reception Delegate, Sailor's Girl), Fred Hearn (Reception Delegate), Bob Tucker (Reception Delegate), Gloria Patrice (A Maid); Singers: Stephanie Augustine, Irene Carroll, Trudy DeLuz, Marilyn Frechette, Estelle Gardner, Norma Larkin, Marilyn O'Connor, Yolanda Renay, Helene Whitney, Lewis Bolyard, Ed Chappel, David Collyer, Billy Hogue, Sid Lawson, Robert Patterson, Robert Penn, John Sheehan, Evans Thornton; Dancers: Virginia Conwell, Coy Dare, Norma Doggett, Dolores (Dody) Goodman, Patricia Hammerlee, Norma Kaiser, Gloria Patrice, Janice Rule, Tiny Shimp, Bill Bradley, Fred Hearn, Allen Knowles, Kasimir Kokic, Erik Kristen, Joe (Joseph) Milan, Robert Pagent, Eddie Phillips, Bob Tucker; Newsboys: William Calhoun, Ronald Kane, Bob Kryl, Ernest Laird, Kevin Mathews, Rusty Slocum
The musical was presented in two acts.
The action takes place during 1885 in Paris and New York City.

Musical Numbers

Act One: "Extra! Extra!" (William Calhoun, Ronald Kane, Bob Kryl, Ernest Laird, Kevin Mathews, Rusty Slocum, Ensemble); "What Do I Have to Do to Get My Picture Took?" (aka "I'd Like My Picture Took") (Mary McCarty, Eddie Albert, Dancers); "The Most Expensive Statue in the World" (Philip Bourneuf, Charles Dingle, Donald McClelland, Singers, Dancers); "A Little Fish in a Big Pond" (Eddie Albert, Mary McCarty, Bill Bradley, Allen Knowles, Kazimir Kokic, Robert Pagent); "Let's Take an Old-Fashioned Walk" (Eddie Albert, Allyn McLerie, Singers, Dancers); "Homework" (Mary McCarty); "Paris Wakes Up and Smiles" (Johnny V. R. Thompson, Allyn McLerie, Ensemble); "Only for Americans" (Ethel Griffies, Eddie Albert, Singers, Dancers); "Just One Way to Say I Love You" (Eddie Albert, Allyn McLerie)
Act Two: "Miss Liberty" (Entire Company); "The Train" (Allyn McLerie, Eddie Phillips, Erik Kristen, Joe Milan); "You Can Have Him" (Mary McCarty, Allyn McLerie); "The Policemen's Ball" (Mary McCarty, Tommy Rall, Ensemble); "Homework" (reprise) (Mary McCarty); "Follow the Leader Jig" (Ensemble); "Me and My Bundle" (Eddie Albert, Allyn McLerie, Company); "Falling Out of Love Can Be Fun" (Mary McCarty); "Give Me Your Tired, Your Poor" (lyric by Emma Lazarus) (Allyn McLerie, Singers)

Miss Liberty was one of those can't-miss musicals: the lyrics and music were by Irving Berlin, the book by three-time Pulitzer Prize-winning playwright Robert E. Sherwood, the direction by Moss Hart, and the choreography by Jerome Robbins. But the show ran for just a little over 300 performances, toured briefly, and closed without recouping its reported investment of $175,000. Ethel Griffies and Robbins walked away with the best notices. The seventy-two-year-old Griffies stopped the show with her caustic comedy song "Only for Americans" and Robbins's inventive dances were highly praised. Otherwise, the critics were disappointed. Some found Berlin's songs less than inspired, but his score was generally pleasant. The ballads "Let's Take an Old-Fashioned Walk" and "Just One Way to Say I Love You" were among his best, and "Homework," "You Can Have Him," "Falling Out of Love Can Be Fun," and "Only for Americans" were tuneful and enjoyable. Unfortunately, one or two numbers (such as "The Most Expensive Statue in the World") were tiresome, and the hoped-for "God Bless America"–inspired "Give Me Your Tired, Your Poor" (which was based on Emma Lazarus's poem) was leaden and ponderous.

The less-than-exciting plot brought down the lavish production values, congenial score, game cast, and lively dances. Like **Nellie Bly**, the story revolved around two feuding newspapers that hope to scoop the other. James Gordon Bennett (Charles Dingle) of the *New York Herald* and Joseph Pulitzer (Philip Bourneuf) of the *New York World* hope to capitalize on the public's excitement surrounding the Statue of Liberty by French sculptor Bartholdi (Herbert Berghof). Newspaper photographer Horace Miller (Eddie Albert) goes to Paris in search of the statue's model, and in Monique Dupont (Allyn McLerie) he unwittingly believes he's found her. Because she's not the real model, a scandal erupts; but all ends well when the public forgives Monique and she attends the unveiling of the statue.

Also figuring into the plot was *Police Gazette* reporter Maisie Dell (Mary McCarty) whose love for Horace goes unrequited. It was the secondary character of Maisie who shouldered most of the musical's songs (seven sequences in all), and McCarty was a stand-out in such numbers as "Homework" and "Falling Out of Love Can Be Fun." Despite impressing the critics in **Small Wonder** and *Miss Liberty*, McCarty disappeared from the musical stage for almost two decades, but in the early and mid-1970s she created two memorable roles. In Stephen Sondheim's *Follies* (1971) she was Stella Deems and introduced "Who's That Woman?," and as Matron Mama Morton in John Kander and Fred Ebb's *Chicago* (1975) she made emphatic musical statements with "When You're Good to Mama" and "Class."

Brooks Atkinson in the *New York Times* found the "routine" musical a "disappointing" one, and while "Let's Take an Old-Fashioned Walk" was the evening's "best" number, the score wasn't Berlin's " most memorable"; Richard Watts in the *New York Post* said the musical was "only pretty fair," and although it wasn't a "botch" or a "bore," it was "surprisingly commonplace"; Howard Barnes in the *New York Herald Tribune* found the book "random and tedious," felt Berlin and Hart had failed to keep the show "properly defined and engaging," and noted the evening lacked comedy; but Robbins's choreography was "captivating" (especially the "wonderful brawl" of "Follow the Leader Jig" and the "nicely paced rhythmical pattern" of "Only for Americans").

Ward Morehouse in the *New York Sun* said the "sharp" but "gravely" disappointing production lacked humor and Berlin's score wasn't one of his best (but was nonetheless "creditable"); Robert Sylvester in the *New York Daily News* found the book "confusing" and noted Sherwood vacillated between a "serious" story and one that was gagged up; but whenever Ethel Griffies was on the stage, "things picked up immediately and stayed picked up" (he noted she "ought to be arrested just for the way she leers at an audience"); and an unsigned review in the *New York World-Telegram* found the musical "bright" in its dancing but disappointing in its lack of humor.

Robert Garland in the *New York Journal-American* liked the new musical and suspected it would "be around for quite some time"; Griffies's "Only for Americans" was a "show-stopper," and Robbins provided "attabouyant" dances. But he felt sorry for the Mary McCarty character and suggested Sherwood's book failed "to do right" by her and left her in the lurch without the hero (but Berlin came to her rescue with a "face-saving" song, "Falling Out of Love Can Be Fun"). Robert Coleman in the *New York Daily Mirror* predicted the musical would be a hit, and while Berlin's score was not his best it was still "sprightly, tuneful and infectious"; Sherwood's book was only "serviceable," but Robbins's dances were "clever" and "swiftly-paced."

Atkinson noted that Motley had "dressed the show beautifully" and Watts said the costumes had "color and beauty"; but Sylvester reported the costumes ranged from the "spectacular" to the "just plain ugly," and said Mary McCarty had so many costume changes that "for a while you thought she must be trying to find a dress that looked good."

During the tryout, "The Hon'rable Profession of the Fourth Estate," "What Do I Have to Do to Get My Picture in the Paper?" (not the same song as "What Do I Have to Do to Get My Picture Took?" aka "I'd Like My Picture Took"), "Mrs. Monotony," and "I'll Know Better Next Time" were cut. Unused songs were: "Business for a Good Girl Is Bad," "For a Good Girl It's Bad," "The Pulitzer Prize," "Sing a Song of Sing Sing," "The Story of Nell and the *Police Gazette*," "A Woman's Place Is in the Home," and "Only in America" (the music for the latter was used for "Only for Americans").

"Mrs. Monotony" had originally been written as "Mr. Monotony" for Judy Garland in the 1948 MGM musical *Easter Parade*, and although the number was filmed it was cut prior to release (the outtake is included in the film's DVD which was issued by Warner Home Video # 67072). For *Miss Liberty*, "Mrs. Monotony" was performed by Mary McCarty and the singing and dancing chorus, but was cut during the tryout. The song next surfaced (as "Mr. Monotony") in the tryout of *Call Me Madam* (1950) where it was sung by Ethel Merman, Muriel Bentley, Tommy Rall, and Arthur Partington; it was again cut during the pre-Broadway engagement (and was replaced by "Something to Dance About"). In 1954, the song was set for the Twentieth Century-Fox film *There's No Business Like Show Business* (which starred Merman), but the number was never filmed. The song never made it into *Easter Parade* and *There's No Business Like Show Business* and of course never got to the Imperial Theatre, which was the home of both *Miss Liberty* and *Call Me Madam*. But the song seems to have been destined for the Imperial because four decades later it was performed there by Debbie Shapiro (Gravitte) in the 1989 dance retrospective *Jerome Robbins' Broadway* (the two-CD cast album recorded by RCA Victor # 60150-2-RC includes the complete song and dance music, a sequence of about ten minutes).

The original cast album of *Miss Liberty* was released by Columbia Records (LP # ML-4220; issued on CD by Sony Broadway # SK-48015). With the advent of the LP format and the huge success of the **South Pacific** recording, cast albums and cover recordings were now as firmly institutionalized as the process of the out-of-town tryout and the sales of tryout souvenir programs (which included rehearsal photographs) and then later souvenir programs which included photos of fully staged scenes. In the same way, many musicals made the cover of *Life* magazine, were published in book format (usually by Random House), and excerpts from the shows were featured on *The Toast of the Town* (later known as *The Ed Sullivan Show*).

The program for the first week of *Miss Liberty*'s tryout advertised the "soon to be released" cast album (the ad also touted the cast recordings of **Kiss Me, Kate** and **South Pacific**), and there were two other advertisements announcing single recordings already on sale: "Let's Take an Old-Fashioned Walk" (Frank Sinatra and Doris Day); "Just One Way to Say I Love You" (Sinatra); "You Can Have Him" (Dinah Shore and Doris Day); "Homework" (Shore); "A Little Fish in a Big Pond" (Shore and Buddy Clark); "Paris Wakes Up and Smiles" (Clark); "Homework" (Fran Warren); "You Can Have Him" (Warren); "Just One Way to Say I Love You" (Perry Como); and "Let's Take an Old-Fashioned Walk" (Como).

Another recording of the score was issued by RCA Victor (LP # LK-1009); the studio cast included Al Goodman and His Orchestra along with Wynn Murray, Martha Wright, Bob Wright, Sandra Deel, and Jimmy Carroll. Besides the cast album of *Jerome Robbins' Broadway*, "Mr. Monotony" is also included in the collection *The Broadway Musicals of 1949* (Bayview CD # RNBW-035) and in Kim Criswell's *Something to Dance About: The Music of Irving Berlin* (Jay Records CD # CDJAY-1381). The collection *Irving Sings Berlin* (Koch International Classics CD # 3-7510-2-111) has Berlin himself performing "Let's Take an Old-Fashioned Walk," "Paris Wakes Up and Smiles," "Just One Way to Say I Love You," and "The Policemen's Ball"; the cut songs "The Hon'rable Profession of the Fourth Estate" and "What Do I Have to Do to Get My Picture in the Papers?"; and the unused "Business for a Good Girl Is Bad," "Sing a Song of Sing Sing," and "The Story of Nell and the *Police Gazette*."

The script was published in paperback by Samuel French in 1977. The lyrics for the used, cut, and unused songs are included in *The Complete Lyrics of Irving Berlin*.

The musical was revived at the Goodspeed Opera House, East Haddam, Connecticut, for the period June 22–September 16, 1983; the following songs were omitted: "The Most Expensive Statue in the World," "The Train," and "Follow the Leader Jig."

Awards

Tony Award: Best Stage Technician (**Joe Lynn**)

KEN MURRAY'S BLACKOUTS OF 1949

Theatre: Ziegfeld Theatre
Opening Date: September 6, 1949; *Closing Date*: October 15, 1949
Performances: 51

Direction: Ken Murray; *Producer*: Ken Murray and David W. Siegel; *Scenery*: Ben Tipton and Leo Atkinson; *Costumes*: Uncredited; *Lighting*: Uncredited; *Musical Direction*: Bert Shefter

Cast: *Ken Murray*, Nick Lucas, Owen McGiveney, Harris and Shore, Shelton Brooks, Dot Remy, Crystal White, Danny Duncan, Mabel Butterworth, Pat Williams, D'Vaughn Pershing, Les Zoris (Claudine Baudin and Robert Gross), Charles Nelson, Elizabeth Walters, Robert Hightower and Betsy Ross (some sources give her last name as Roos), Danny Alexander, Milton Charleston, George Burton (and birds), Jack Mulhall, Peg Leg Bayes, Alphonse Berge, Irene Kaye, Al Mardo (and dog), Joe Wong; The Enchanters: Darla Hood, Bob Decker, Val Grund, Sheldon Disrud, Bob Wollter; The Glamourlovelies: Lorayne Anderson, Phyllis Applegate, Consuelo Cezon, Bettye Meade, Jean Marshall, Joan Morley, Crystal White, Joy Windsor, Jean Corbett, JoAnn Corbett; The Elderlovelies: Rose DeHaven, Ethel Getty, Mabel Hart, Sue Kelton, Perle Kincaid, Mattie Kennedy, Julia Wright, Mabel Butterworth

The revue was presented in two acts.

Sketches and Musical Numbers

Act One: "Hollywood and Vine" (lyric by Royal Foster, music by Charles Henderson) (Movie Extra: Joan Morley; Woman in Slacks: Mabel Hart; Twins: Jean Corbett and JoAnn Corbett; Peter the Hermit: Danny Duncan; Newsboy: Bob Decker; Broadway Playboy: Bob Wollter; Maharajah: Val Grund; Prospector: Sheldon Disrud; Miss Iowa: Darla Hood; Veronica: Irene Kaye; Plaza Doorman: Shelton Brooks; Bette Davis: Consuelo Cezon; Chinese Laundryman: Joe Wong; Shoe Shine Boy: Danny Alexander; Strolling Couple: Betsy Ross and Milton Charleston; Sailor: Robert Hightower); "Now and Then" (The Glamourlovelies and The Elderlovelies; the latter performed such songs as "Silver Threads among the Gold" and "Put on Your Old Gray Bonnet"); "Introducing Your Host, Ken Murray"; Pat Williams; "Three Idle Rumors"; "Ecstasy in F" (Harris and Shore); Shelton Brooks (who performed his own compositions "The Darktown Strutters' Ball" and "Some of These Days," among others); "Bridal Night" (Groom: Jack Mulhall; Bride: Jean Marshall; Bell Hop: Danny Alexander; Bridesmaids: Irene Kaye, Betsy Ross, Joan Morley; Hotel Guest: Ken Murray); "Jungle Fantasy" (Vocal Specialty: The Enchanters; Dance Specialty: Crystal White; Jungle Man: Robert Gross; Leopard: Claudine Baudin; Girls of the Forest: The Glamourlovelies); D'Vaughn Pershing; Charles Nelson; "Burton's Birds" (George Burton)

Act Two: Al Mardo (and dog); "*Blackouts'* Television Newsreel"; "The New Look" (Models: Lorayne Anderson, Joan Morley, Crystal White, Consuelo Cezon, Joy Windsor, Jean Marshall, Bettye Meade, Phyllis Applegate, Jean Corbett, JoAnn Corbett; Maid: Elizabeth Walters); Nick Lucas (his repertoire included "Tiptoe Through the Tulips," which he had introduced in the 1929 film *Gold Diggers of Broadway*; lyric by Al Dubin and music by Joe Burke); "A Page from *Oliver Twist*" (Monks, Nancy, Fagin, Bill Sikes, The Artful Dodger: Owen McGiveney); "Nautical Moments" (Pirates: The Glamourlovelies; Long John Silver: Peg Leg Bates); "*Blackouts of 1949* Sports Parade" (Archery: Betty Meade; Ice-Skating: Darla Hood; Cowgirl: Lorayne Anderson; Golf: Joan Morley; Baseball: Consuelo Cezon; Hunting: Jean Corbett and JoAnn Corbett; Skiing: Jean Marshall; Swimming: Phyllis Applegate; Fishing: Joy Windsor); Finale

One of the jokes in *Ken Murray's Blackouts of 1949* was the one about marriage being a fine institution, but who wants to live in a . . . Yes, it was that kind of evening, and it prompted one to wonder how a series of the *Blackouts* revues could have played for more than seven years at the El Capitan Theatre in Los Angeles (Brooks Atkinson in the *New York Times* decided Los Angeles businessmen were more tired than the ones in New York).

The evening was a mélange which included animal acts (Al Mardo and the most bored dog of all time as well as George Burton and his trained birds); singer and guitarist Nick Lucas (who had originally introduced the hit song "Tiptoe Through the Tulips"); composer Shelton Brooks (who had written the lyrics and music of "The Darktown Strutters' Ball" and Sophie Tucker's signature song "Some of These Days"); Owen McGiveney (a quick-change artist who presented a five-character mini-version of *Oliver Twist*); Peg Leg Bates (the second one-legged tap dancer of the season [see **Funzapoppin**]); Les Zoris (Claudine Baudin and Robert Gross, an adagio team); Hightower and Shore (who burlesqued ballroom dancing); teenaged pianist D'Vaughn Pershing; and teenaged baritone Charles Nelson. There were also a bevy of young chorines (The Glamourlovelies) and a group of seasoned ones (The Elderlovelies), and throughout the evening Murray chatted up the audience and served as master of ceremonies.

Atkinson found the evening "routine music-hall," but devoted an entire paragraph to a sequence in the opening number in which an unnamed performer (probably Betsy Ross, or Roos) bent over backward and retrieved a handkerchief with her teeth; he noted that only a diagram could really capture this "practically supernatural" and "astounding achievement." In fact, the routine left him so "dazed" he found the remainder of the revue anti-climactic. John Chapman in the *New York Daily News* liked Al Mardo and his "hideous fat slob of a bulldog" who was determined to do no tricks (Richard Watts in the *New York Post* said the unnamed pooch was "splendidly ugly," and Robert Coleman in the *New York Daily Mirror* found him the "most blasé bulldog this side of Yale"). The bulldog clearly had much in common with Bob Williams's red setter Red Dust in ***Show Time***, another canine completely uninterested in becoming the toast of Broadway and winning Tony Awards.

William Hawkins in the *New York World-Telegram* said the revue was an "amiable grab-bag" and Coleman thought it was a "real entertainment bargain" (at a $3.60 top on weekdays and $4.80 on weekends). But Watts found it "pretty dismal" and both he and Ward Morehouse in the *New York Sun* suggested Murray should have stayed in Hollywood (Morehouse found Murray "painfully unfunny"). Howard Barnes in the *New York Herald Tribune* said the production was a "hodge-podge" in which "exuberance is not matched by artistry."

Besides the uncooperative canine, the revue also offered a flock of birds. But these were extremely willing to dutifully follow the instructions of their trainer George Burton. Hawkins said the lovebirds literally played with fire, turned somersaults, and juggled, and Chapman found them "remarkable" and praised their "astounding stunts." However, Watts, Barnes, and Morehouse thought the bird act would have been more effective had the routine been shortened. Incidentally, Burton's birds were featured in the 1948 film *Bill and Coo*, which was produced by Ken Murray; the film won an honorary Oscar.

During the run, Nick Lucas, D'Vaughn Pershing, and Peg Leg Bates left the show, the sequence "Three Idle Rumors" was cut, and the sketch "Saturday Night Card Game" was added.

The decision to close the revue seems to have been a sudden one. The revue shuttered on October 15, but the programs for the week of October 17 had already been printed.

Ken Murray returned to Broadway on May 10, 1965, when *Ken Murray's Hollywood* opened at the Royale Theatre for sixteen performances. The evening consisted of commentary by Murray (with piano accompaniment by Armin Hoffman) while highlights of his home movies of Hollywood stars taken over a thirty-year period were shown. The production also included a film sequence titled "Backstage with *Bill and Coo*."

TOUCH AND GO

Theatre: Broadhurst Theatre (during run, the revue transferred to the Broadway Theatre)
Opening Date: October 13, 1949; *Closing Date*: March 18, 1950
Performances: 176
Sketches and *Lyrics*: Jean Kerr and Walter Kerr
Music: Jay Gorney; ballet music by Genevieve Pitot
Direction: Walter Kerr; *Producer*: George Abbott; *Choreography*: Helen Tamiris; *Scenery* and *Costumes*: John Robert Lloyd; *Lighting*: Peggy Clark; *Musical Direction*: Antonio Morelli
Cast: Kyle MacDonnell, Dick Sykes, Jonathan Lucas, Daniel Nagrin, Nancy Andrews, Muriel O'Malley, Helen Gallagher, George Hall, Peggy Cass, Pearl Lang, Lewis Nye, Mary Anthony, Eleanor Boleyn, Art Carroll, Lydia Fredericks, Arlyne Frank, Nat (Nathaniel) Frey, Pearl Hacker, David Lober, Greb Lober, Ilona Murrai, Carl Nicholas, Ray Page, Beverly Purvin, Merritt Thompson, Dorothy Scott, Richard Reed, George Reich, Larry Robbins, William Sumner, Beverly Tassoni, Bobby Trelease, Parker Wilson, Mara Lynn
The revue was presented in two acts.

Sketches and Musical Numbers

Act One: "An Opening for Everybody" (George Hall, Helen Gallagher, Jonathan Lucas, Company); "This Had Better Be Love" (Nancy Andrews, Dick Sykes); "Gorilla Girl" (Director: George Hall; Assistant Director: Art Carroll; Miss Hilton: Kyle MacDonnell; Skeets: Jonathan Lucas; Trainer: Lewis Nye; Cameraman: Nat Frey); "American Primitive" ("Funny Little Old World") (Muriel O'Malley; Father: Art Carroll; Daughter: Helen Gallagher; danced by Pearl Lang and Daniel Nagrin, and by Greb Lober, David Lober, Richard Reed, William Sumner, Beverly Tassoni, Merritt Thompson, Dorothy Scott, Parker Wilson); "Highbrow, Lowbrow" (Dick Sykes, Jonathan Lucas, Larry Robbins); "Disenchantment" (Muffins: George Hall; Old Gent aka Pippy: Dick Sykes; Moonbeam: Peggy Cass; Newsboy: William Sumner; Papa: Lewis Nye; Pilgrim: Larry Robbins); "Easy Does It" (The Girl: Helen Gallagher; The Man: Daniel Nagrin; The Other Man: David Lober; The Girl Friends: Eleanor Boleyn, Greb Lober; Company); "Be a Mess" (Olivia: Peggy Cass; Barbara: Nancy Andrews; Jane: Kyle MacDonnell); "Broadway Love Song" (Pearl Lang, Jonathan Lucas); "It'll Be All Right in a Hundred Years" (Boy: Art Carroll; Girl: Kyle MacDonnell); "Great Dane A-Comin'" (King: Ray Page; Queen: Nancy Andrews; Hamlet: Dick Sykes; Laertes: Daniel Nagrin; Ophelia: Kyle MacDonnell; Polonius: George Hall; Company)

Act Two: "Wish Me Luck" (Nancy Andrews; Croupier: David Lober; danced by Company); "What It Was Really Like" (First Aide: Nat Frey; Second Aide: Lewis Nye; General: Dick Sykes; Malloy: Larry Robbins; C.O.: George Hall; Kerrigan: Jonathan Lucas); "Under the Sleeping Volcano" (The Singers: Pearl Hacker, Lydia Fredericks, Arlyne Frank, Beverly Purvin; Carita's Sister: Ilona Murrai; Carita: Pearl Lang; Felipe: Daniel Nagrin; Francesco: David Lober; Villagers: Dorothy Scott, Eleanor Boleyn, Beverly Tassoni, Greb Lober, William Sumner, Parker Wilson, Merritt Thompson, Richard Reed, George Reich); "Men of the Water-Mark" (Art Carroll, Nat Frey, George Hall, Carl Nicholas, Louis Nye, Larry Robbins); "Mr. Brown, Miss Dupree" (Miss Dupree: Kyle MacDonnell; Mama: Muriel O'Malley; Mr. Brown: Jonathan Lucas; danced by Mary Anthony, Ilona Murrai, Beverly Tassoni, Dorothy Scott, David Lober, Richard Reed, George Reich, Merritt Thompson); "Miss Platt Selects Mate" (Nancy Andrews); "Cinderella" (Stepmother: Muriel O'Malley; Neighbor: Helen Gallagher; First Sister: Nancy Andrews; Second Sister: Peggy Cass; Cinderella: Kyle MacDonnell; Newsboy: Jonathan Lucas; Prince: Lewis Nye; Page: Larry Robbins); Finale (Company)

Like Walter Kerr's other Broadway shows of the era (**Count Me In**, **Sing Out, Sweet Land!**, and *The Song of Bernadette* [1946]), *Touch and Go* was first produced at Catholic University in Washington, D.C. (as *Thank You, Just Looking*). George Abbott saw it in Washington, was impressed with the material by Kerr and his wife Jean, and brought it to New York where he directed it. The revue managed to run over five months, but lost money; two months after its closing, it opened in London where it doubled the run of the New York production.

The critics were mixed in their opinions of the new revue, but most agreed there were many outstanding numbers, most of them having to do with spoofs of the entertainment industry. Everyone loved "Be a Mess," in which Peggy Cass (as Olivia de Havilland), Nancy Andrews (as Barbara Stanwyck), and Kyle MacDonnell (as Jane Wyman) emphasized the importance of portraying characters with afflictions in order to receive Oscar recognition. In 1948, all three had been nominated for Best Actress: de Havilland for the mental patient in *The Snake Pit*; Stanwyck for the neurotic hypochondriac in *Sorry, Wrong Number*; and the year's winner Wyman for the deaf-mute rape victim in *Johnny Belinda*.

The first act finale ("Great Dane A-Comin'") was a spoof of *Hamlet* in the style of Rodgers and Hammerstein (the inhabitants of Elsinore sing of their real nice castle, and in song Hamlet informs Ophelia that she's a queer one); and for a further musical comedy touch, Polonius is depicted in Bobby Clark drag. The second act finale ("Cinderella") laughed at the classic fairy tale by presenting it as an Elia Kazan production in the style of *A Streetcar Named Desire* (1947) and *Death of a Salesman* (1949), and even kidded Jo Mielziner's scenery for those dramas (among the sketch's "realistic" touches: when the wicked stepmother and stepsisters tell the prince they're the only inhabitants of the house, the sound of a flushing toilet alerts the prince otherwise).

Another sketch ("What It Was Really Like") spoofed the trend of realistic World War II novels and memoirs; in this case, the soldiers are so busy writing away in the trenches they have no time to fight the war (one of their titles is *The Bloody and the Sweaty*, and Robert Garland in the *New York Journal-American* noted these warriors are afraid of nothing but Simon and Schuster); "Gorilla Girl" looked at the rehearsals of a Hollywood jungle epic in which the gorilla is more intelligent than the leading lady; for "Broadway Love Song," a swain serenades his love with words and phrases in the manner of critical quotes used in theatre advertisements, even to the point of mentioning the names of current Broadway newspaper critics; and "Disenchantment" was a take-off on films that over-utilize flashbacks in order to tell their stories.

And this being a 1940s musical, there was the required South American dance salute, in this case one depicting a romantic triangle set in Mexico ("Under the Sleeping Volcano"). There was also a Grandma Moses-styled dance ("American Primitive," or "Funny Little Old World"). For her dances, Helen Tamiris won the Tony Award for Best Choreography.

Brooks Atkinson in the *New York Times* noted the "literate" Kerrs had written a "capital" revue with "skill and wit"; their satire skewed "intelligent" topics "with swift dexterity" and thus provided a "friendly evening in the theatre." William Hawkins in the *New York World-Telegram* said the revue was "energetic" and "up to the minute in its spoofing." "Be a Mess" was the "most outrageously funny thing of its kind" since **Lend an Ear**'s "Three Little Queens of the Silver Screen," and the Cinderella spoof was in its way as "shocking" as *A Streetcar Named Desire*. John Chapman in the *New York Daily News* praised the topical attitude of the evening, and singled out "Be a Mess," "Cinderella," and especially "Great Dane A-Comin'"; and noted he was "almost always amused" whenever Nancy Andrews was on stage.

Richard Watts in the *New York Post* generally liked the "pleasant, lively and good-looking" revue and its "likeable and wholesome" cast; he was particularly enamored of "Cinderella," "Be a Mess," and "Gorilla Girl," but felt the *Hamlet* spoof wasn't particularly funny. Herrick Brown in the *New York Sun* liked "Be a Mess" and the *Hamlet* parody but otherwise found the material "heavy handed"; he also mentioned that Jay Gorney's score was "pleasant" but not "outstanding." Howard Barnes in the *New York Herald Tribune* said the revue was generally "amateurish when not plain dull," but noted the evening achieved "high hilarity" in "Be a Mess." Robert Coleman in the *New York Mirror* said the evening offered a few "tremendously funny sketches" but overall lacked "wallop." It was often "fresh, youthful and ingratiating" but too many targets missed their marks and thus there wasn't "quite enough entertainment for a completely satisfying evening." He noted the "best" sequences were "Be a Mess" and "Great Dane A-Comin'," and praised Kyle MacDonnell for her contributions to "Gorilla Girl" and "Cinderella."

During the tryout, an elaborate dance sequence with music by Genevieve Pitot called "Detective Specs" (subtitled "A Radio Mystery Ballet") was cut.

The collection *Broadway Musicals of 1949* (Bayview CD # RNBW-035) includes "This Had Better Be Love" and "It Will Be All Right in a Hundred Years"; and *Make Mine Manhattan and Great Revues Revisited* (Painted Smiles CD # PSCD-119) includes original cast member Nancy Andrews singing "This Had Better Be Love" and "Miss Platt Selects Mate."

The London production opened at the Prince of Wales Theatre on May 19, 1950, for 348 performances; original Broadway cast members Helen Gallagher, Jonathan Lucas, and David Lober appeared in the production, and Kaye Ballard joined the cast. Added to the revue were: the production number "The Little Bar Off Times Square" (written by Happy Felton and Mack Perrin); the sketch "Never Felt Better" (by Joseph Stein and Will Glickman); "The Shoe Song" (by John Tore); and the sketch "Any Resemblance" (by Arnold Horwitt), which originally had been seen in **Make Mine Manhattan**; and two numbers (writers unknown), "Shore Leave" and "Machine Age," both sung by The Debonairs. Kaye Ballard had two monologues ("Kaye Ballard Tells You about Ben" and "Kaye Ballard Discusses Albert"). During the run, the sketch "See It from the Beginning" was added (writers unknown). Omitted from the London production were: "This Had Better Be Love," "Gorilla Girl," "Highbrow, Lowbrow," "Disenchantment," "Easy Does It," "Broadway Love Song," "It'll Be All Right in a Hundred Years," "What It Was Really Like," and "Men of the Water-Mark."

Awards

Tony Award: Best Choreographer (**Helen Tamiris**)

LOST IN THE STARS
"A MUSICAL TRAGEDY"

Theatre: Music Box Theatre
Opening Date: October 30, 1949; *Closing Date*: July 1, 1950

Performances: 273
Book and *Lyrics*: Maxwell Anderson
Music: Kurt Weill
Based on the 1948 novel *Cry, the Beloved Country* by Alan Paton.
Direction: Rouben Mamoulian; *Producer*: The Playwrights' Company (Maxwell Anderson, Elmer Rice, Robert
    E. Sherwood, Kurt Weill, and John F. Wharton); *Scenery*: George Jenkins; *Costumes*: Anna Hill Johnstone;
    Lighting: Uncredited; *Musical Direction*: Maurice Levine
Cast: Frank Roane (Leader), Joseph James (Answerer), Elayne Richards (Nita), Gertrude Jeannette (Grace
    Kumalo), Todd Duncan (Stephen Kumalo), Lavern French (The Young Man), Mabel Hart (The Young
    Woman), Leslie Banks (James Jarvis), Judson Rees (Edward Jarvis), John Morley (Arthur Jarvis), Warren
    Coleman (John Kumalo), Charles McRae (Paulus), Roy Allen (William), William C. Smith (Jared), Herbert
    Coleman (Alex), Jerome Shaw (Foreman, The Guard), Georgette Harvey (Mrs. Mkize), William Marshall
    (Hlabeni), Charles Grunwell (Eland), Sheila Guyse (Linda), Van Prince (Johannes Pafuri), William Greaves
    (Matthew Kumalo), Julian Mayfield (Absalom Kumalo), Gloria Smith (Rose), Inez Matthews (Irina), Robert
    Byrn (Policeman), Biruta Ramoska (White Woman), Mark Kramer (White Man), John W. Stanley (Burton),
    Guy Spaull (The Judge), Robert McFerrin (Villager); Singers: Sibol Cain, Alma Hubbard, Elen Longone,
    June McMechen, Biruta Ramoska, Christine Spencer, Constance Stokes, Lucretia West, LaCoste Brown,
    Robert Byrn, Joseph Crawford, Russell George, Joseph James, Mark Kramer, Moses LaMar, Paul Mario,
    Robert McFerrin, William C. Smith, Joseph Theard
The musical was presented in two acts.
The action takes place during the present time in South Africa, in the small village of Ndotsheni and in Jo-
    hannesburg.

Musical Numbers

Act One: Opening: "The Hills of Ixopo" (Frank Roane, Singers); "Thousands of Miles" (Todd Duncan); "Train
    to Johannesburg" (Frank Roane, Singers); "The Search" (Todd Duncan, Frank Roane, Singers); "The Little
    Grey House" (Todd Duncan, Singers); "Who'll Buy?" (Sheila Guyse; danced by Lavern French and Mabel
    Hart); "Trouble Man" (Inez Matthews); "Murder in Parkwold" (Singers); "Fear" (Singers); "Lost in the
    Stars" (Todd Duncan, Singers)
Act Two: Opening: "The Wild Justice" (Frank Roane, Singers); "O Tixo, Tixo, Help Me" (Todd Duncan); "Stay
    Well" (Inez Matthews); "Cry, the Beloved Country" (Frank Roane, Singers); "Big Mole" (Herbert Cole-
    man); "A Bird of Passage" (Robert McFerrin, Singers); "Thousands of Miles" (reprise) (Singers)

Lost in the Stars took place during the apartheid era of South Africa, and centered on village preacher
Stephen Kumalo (Todd Duncan) who travels to Johannesburg and discovers that his son Absalom (Julian
Mayfield) has been arrested for the murder of a white man named Arthur Jarvis (John Morley) during a rob-
bery. Ironically, Arthur was an activist for the civil rights of blacks. Absalom admits his guilt and is executed.
When Stephen meets the victim's father James Jarvis (Leslie Banks), the two men who are separated by the
law of apartheid are united in the bond of personal tragedy which has claimed the lives of their sons.
    Based on Alan Paton's 1948 novel *Cry, the Beloved Country*, the musical was curiously dry and remote.
Maxwell Anderson's book and lyrics never quite captured the personal tragedies of the two main characters
and the larger tragedy of apartheid, and Kurt Weill's music was too often emotionally detached from the characters and the action. This is arguably his weakest and most uninteresting Broadway score, although some
have made a case for the title song.
    A major failing of the adaptation is that two of the three main characters are given nothing to sing, and
thus Jarvis and Absalom are musical bystanders in their own musical. Stephen is given five songs, and the
remaining eleven numbers are divided among amorphous singing groups and minor characters: six of these
are performed by a generic Greek chorus (which includes a "Leader" and an "Answerer") and various choral
groups, and five are sung by relatively minor characters. Moreover, one or two songs in the score are time-
fillers which are almost completely extraneous to the action, and the use of the abstract Greek chorus with
its leader and answerer further contributed to the emotional detachment of the narrative.

Robert Coleman in the *New York Daily Mirror* said the musical wasn't off Anderson's "top shelf," and while the adaptation tried for "simplicity" all it achieved was a "pretentious simplicity" that never tugged at the emotions. William Hawkins in the *New York World-Telegram* stated that Anderson had "simplified" the original novel, and "not always with felicitous results." Robert Garland in the *New York Journal-American* noted the musical's "mislaid simplicity" and complained there was "too much" in the way of "words and music, production and direction, scenery and costume. And group singing!"

Richard Watts in the *New York Post* said Anderson's attempt at "simplicity" was "rather unpersuasive," and Weill's score wasn't "particularly interesting or distinguished." And while Brooks Atkinson in the *New York Times* found the work "memorable" and "illuminating," he noted Anderson and Weill had adapted the novel not "without obvious difficulty" and thus the "literal and skimming" narrative sometimes led to "patchy" results.

But Howard Barnes in the *New York Herald Tribune* said the "soaring musical tragedy" brought "great honor to the season" (although Weill's score was not "overly distinguished"); Ward Morehouse in the *New York Sun* found the evening "beautiful and frequently enthralling"; and John Chapman in the *New York Daily News* pronounced the musical a "work of art."

The script was published in hardback by Anderson House/William Sloane Associates in 1950, and is also included in the hardback collection *Great Musicals of the American Theatre Volume Two* (1976), published by Chilton. The script was also published in the December 1950 issue of *Theatre Arts* magazine.

The original cast album was released by Decca Records (LP # DL-8028); a 1968 revival produced by Tougaloo College (Tougaloo, Mississippi) was recorded by Word Records (LP # CS-5117); and a 1992 studio cast recording (issued by MusicMasters Classics CD # 01612-67100-2) by the Orchestra of St. Luke's and the Concert Chorale of New York was conducted by Julius Rudel and includes "Little Tin God," a song dropped prior to the 1949 New York premiere.

The musical was revived by the New York City Opera Company at City Center on April 10, 1958, for fourteen performances; the cast included Lawrence Winters (Stephen Kumalo), and others in the company were Patti Austen, Rosetta Le Noire, Nicholas Joy, John Irving, Frederick O'Neal, Louis Gossett, Eva Jessye, Olga James, Conrad Bain, Godfrey Cambridge, and Douglas Turner. An uninvolving and emotionally arid Broadway revival at the Imperial Theatre on April 18, 1972, lasted for just thirty-nine performances; the cast included Brock Peters (Stephen Kumalo), Jack Gwillim (James Jarvis), Gilbert Price (Absalom), Rosetta Le Noire, and Staats Cotsworth. This revival omitted "Who'll Buy?" and "A Bird of Passage," and in order to provide a musical number for Absalom, Irina's "Stay Well" was reassigned to him.

A belated film version was released in 1974 as part of the short-lived American Film Series; directed by Daniel Mann, the cast included Brock Peters, Raymond St. Jacques, Clifton Davis, Melba Moore, and Paula Kelly. The complete AFS collection of fourteen filmed plays and musicals was released on a fourteen-DVD set by Kino (besides *Lost in the Stars*, the set includes one other musical, the 1968 Off-Broadway revue *Jacques Brel Is Alive and Well and Living in Paris*).

REGINA
"A MUSICAL DRAMA"

Theatre: 46th Street Theatre
Opening Date: October 31, 1949; *Closing Date*: December 16, 1949
Performances: 56
Libretto and *Music*: Marc Blitzstein
Based on the 1939 play *The Little Foxes* by Lillian Hellman.
Direction: Robert Lewis; *Producers*: Cheryl Crawford in association with Clinton Wilder; *Choreography*: Anna Sokolow; *Scenery*: Horace Armistead; *Costumes*: Aline Bernstein; *Lighting*: Charles Elson; *Musical Direction*: Maurice Abravanel
Cast: Lillyn Brown (Addie), William Warfield (Cal), Priscilla Gillette (Alexandra Giddens [Zan]), Philip Hepburn (Chinkypin), William Dillard (Jazz [Trumpet]), Angel Band Members: Bernard Addison (Banjo), Buster Bailey (Clarinet), Rudy Nichols (Traps), and Benny Morton (Trombone), Jane Pickens (Regina Giddens), Brenda Lewis (Birdie Hubbard), David Thomas (Oscar Hubbard), Russell Nype (Leo Hubbard), Donald

Clarke (Marshall), George Lipton (Ben Hubbard), Clarisse Crawford (Belle), Marion Carley (Pianist), Alfred Bruning (Violinist), William Wilderman (Horace Giddens), Lee Sweetland (Manders), Peggy Turnley (Ethelinda); Townspeople: Ellen Carleen, Earl McDonald, Robert Anderson, Kay Borron, Kayton Nesbitt, Sara Carter, Keith Davis, Barbara Moser, Karl Brock, Isabelle Felder, Derek MacDermot; Dancers: Wana Allison, Joan Engel, Barbara Ferguson, Kate Friedlich, Gisella Weidner, Onna White, Leo Guerard, Robert Hanlin, Regis Powers, Boris Runanin, Walter Stane, John Ward

The opera was presented in two acts.

The action takes place in the Giddens's home in Bowden, Alabama, during Spring 1900.

Musical Numbers

Note: Musical numbers weren't listed in the program; the following list is taken from the libretto and recordings and juxtaposed with the names of the original cast members. Since Blitzstein had to trim his original score prior to the Broadway production, the list doesn't reflect what was necessarily heard at the premiere but does show who would have performed the deleted musical sequences had they been restored for the opening, including the veranda music and some of the party music.

Act One: Prologue—The Veranda: "Want to Join the Angels" (Lillyn Brown, William Warfield, Priscilla Gillette, Jane Pickens, Chorus); Introductory Music (Orchestra); "Oh, Cal" (Lillyn Brown, Brenda Lewis); "Now, Mr. Marshall" (Jane Pickens, Brenda Lewis, Donald Clarke, Russell Nype, George Lipton, David Thomas); "The Children Will Drive You" (David Thomas, Jane Pickens, Brenda Lewis, Russell Nype); "Ya Ta Tum" (aka "Big Rich") (George Lipton, David Thomas, Jane Pickens, Brenda Lewis); "Regina, We Are Ready" (David Thomas, George Lipton, Jane Pickens); "I've Asked Before" (David Thomas, George Lipton, Brenda Lewis, Jane Pickens, Priscilla Gillette, Russell Nype, Lillyn Brown); "You Are to Say You Miss Him" (Jane Pickens, Priscilla Gillette); "You Know, If You Want" (aka "The Best Thing of All") (Jane Pickens, Brenda Lewis, George Lipton, David Thomas, Russell Nype); "Zan! Zan!" (Brenda Lewis, Priscilla Gillette, David Thomas); "Oh, Addie" (Jane Pickens); "Deedle Doodle" (Russell Nype, William Warfield, David Thomas, Brenda Lewis, Jane Pickens); "Careful, Papa" (Priscilla Gillette, William Wilderman, Brenda Lewis); "The Bottle of Medicine" (Priscilla Gillette, Brenda Lewis, Jane Pickens, Lillyn Brown, William Wilderman, George Lipton, Russell Nype); "Well? Well?" (Jane Pickens, William Wilderman, George Lipton); "For Us, Too" (Jane Pickens, Priscilla Gillette, William Wilderman, Russell Nype, George Lipton, David Thomas); "Regina Does a Lovely Party" (Chorus); "Evening, Manders" (William Wilderman, Priscilla Gillette, Jane Pickens, Brenda Lewis, Donald Clarke, Russell Nype, George Lipton, David Thomas); "Night Could Be Time to Sleep" (Lillyn Brown, Brenda Lewis); "Oh, There You Are" (Jane Pickens, William Wilderman); "There's Mister Marshall" (Jane Pickens, Brenda Lewis, Priscilla Gillette, George Lipton, Russell Nype, Donald Clarke); The Party: (1) "Chinkypin" (William Dillard); (2) "Blues" (Lillyn Brown, Brenda Lewis); (3) "Waltz" (Jane Pickens); and (4) "Gallop" (Party Guests)

Act Two: Introductory Music (Orchestra) and "Isn't This Nice?" (aka "Rain Quartet") (Brenda Lewis, Priscilla Gillette, Lillyn Brown, William Wilderman); "Miss Birdie" (aka "Lionnet" and "Birdie's Aria") (Lillyn Brown, Brenda Lewis); "Addie! Take Zan Away" (William Wilderman, Lillyn Brown, Jane Pickens); "As Long as You Live" (Jane Pickens, Priscilla Gillette, William Wilderman, William Warfield, Russell Nype); "Where Is He?" (George Lipton, David Thomas, Russell Nype, Jane Pickens); "You Don't Yet" (aka "Greedy Girl") (Jane Pickens, George Lipton); "I'm Smiling, Ben" (Jane Pickens, Priscilla Gillette, George Lipton, David Thomas); "What Do You Want to Talk to Me About, Alexandra?" (Jane Pickens, Priscilla Gillette); "Certainly, Lord" (Chorus)

Lillian Hellman's powerful 1939 melodrama *The Little Foxes* centered on a family of vipers who will do anything for power and money, including murder. And Regina Giddens (portrayed by Jane Pickens in the opera) is the deadliest of all. It is she who commits murder by denying her husband, Horace (William Wilderman), the medicine he needs; she tries to force her daughter Zan (Priscilla Gillette) into a loveless marriage with her sleazy cousin Leo (Russell Nype); and in order to wrest control of the family business she blackmails her brothers, Ben (George Lipton) and Oscar (David Thomas). At the end of the play and the opera, Regina is rich and powerful but has been abandoned by Zan and must necessarily form an unholy alliance with her brothers, who suspect but can't quite prove she was the cause of Horace's death.

It's understandable how the emotions of the intense drama inspired Marc Blitzstein to adapt the material into his opera *Regina* (which he called a "musical drama"). When the work premiered on Broadway, it received respectful but somewhat cool notices and many critics felt the music didn't enhance Hellman's play. Three reviewers used the word "experiment" to define the evening, including Robert Coleman in the *New York Daily Mirror* who felt the opera was "uneven" and lost its way with extraneous jazz interludes by a "hot band" as well as a polka sequence (for the party sequence, Blitzstein had also composed a gallop, and, for a black child, music for a tap dance). John Chapman in the *New York Daily News* felt the music got in the way of *The Little Foxes*; as for Blitzstein's music, he said he couldn't "remember any of the tunes" and suggested "maybe there weren't any." Howard Barnes in the *New York Herald Tribune* found the opera "exceedingly disappointing" and said the visceral impact of Hellman's story was "vitiated in stylized situations and jangling moods."

Brooks Atkinson in the *New York Times* reported that Blitzstein had unfortunately "softened" a "hard" play and that his score didn't "compensate for the loss in force, belligerence and directness," and Richard Watts in the *New York Post* said the music was inadequate to meet the urgent demands of the powerful story (and he was happy when the libretto allowed for brief periods of spoken dialogue).

But Robert Garland in the *New York Journal-American* said *Regina* was a "real achievement" in which music added a third dimension to the story, and William Hawkins in the *New York World-Telegram* proclaimed the work as the "most exciting musical theatre" since *Der Rosenkavalier*. Among the highlights of the score were "The Best Thing of All," "Lionnet," "Night Could Be Time to Sleep," "Rain Quartet," and "Greedy Girl."

On November 13, 1949, the opera was the subject of CBS's *Tonight on Broadway*, which included interviews with cast members as well as excerpts from the production.

The opera played for just seven weeks on Broadway, but on April 2, 1953, the New York City Opera Company revived the work at City Center for three performances. Four of the original cast members returned: Priscilla Gillette, William Wilderman, William Dillard (Jazz), and Brenda Lewis, who had played Oscar's pathetic wife Birdie in the 1949 production but who now assumed the title role. The revival restored the opera to three acts (as had been Blitzstein's original intention before producer Cheryl Crawford had insisted he compress the action into two) and included music written for but not used in the Broadway production.

City Opera revived the work four more times: at City Center on October 9, 1953 (two performances; with Lewis and Wilderman); on April 17, 1958 (three performances; Lewis); on April 19, 1959 (two performances; Lewis); and at the New York State Theatre on October 9, 1992 (four performances; Leigh Munroe).

There were also two limited-engagement New York revivals; the first opened Off-Off-Broadway on October 19, 1978, at the Encompass Theatre for twenty-three performances, and the second on May 9, 1984, for eight performances by the Opera Ensemble of New York at the Lillie Blake School Theatre.

There have been two recordings of the score. City Opera's 1958 revival inspired the first, which was released by Columbia Records on a three-LP boxed set (# 031-260 and # 03S-202; the CD was issued by Sony Masterworks Broadway/ArkivMusic # 72912); the cast includes Lewis, Elisabeth Carron, Carol Brice, and Joshua Hecht (Samuel Krachmalnick, who had conducted the original Broadway production of *Candide*, was the conductor for the 1958 and 1959 revivals as well as for the recording). The most complete recording is the two-CD London Records set (# 433-812-2) that includes the opening veranda sequence as well as the entire party scene; the cast includes Katherine Ciesinski, Samuel Ramey, Angelina Reaux, and Sheri Greenawald, and John Mauceri conducts the Scottish Opera Orchestra and Chorus. The LP and CD releases include the libretto of the opera.

Marc Blitzstein Presents 'The Cradle Will Rock' 'No for an Answer' 'Regina' (Spoken Arts LP # 717) is a discussion by Blitzstein of the three works and is accompanied by occasional songs; for *Regina*, Brenda Lewis performs "Birdie's Aria" (aka "Lionnet").

Awards

Tony Awards: Best Costume Designer (**Aline Bernstein**); Best Conductor and Musical Director (**Maurice Abravanel**)

TEXAS, LI'L DARLIN'
"A NEW MUSICAL COMEDY"

Theatre: Mark Hellinger Theatre
Opening Date: November 25, 1949; *Closing Date*: September 9, 1950
Performances: 293
Book: John Whedon and Sam Moore
Lyrics: Johnny Mercer
Music: Robert Emmett Dolan
Direction: Paul Crabtree; *Producers*: Studio Productions, Inc., and Anthony Brady Farrell Productions; *Choreography*: Al White Jr.; *Scenery* and *Lighting*: Theodore Cooper; *Costumes*: Eleanor Goldsmith; *Musical Direction*: Will Irwin
Cast: Loring Smith (Harvey Small), Charles Bang (John Baxter Trumbull, Texas Ranger, Radio Announcer), Alden Aldrich (Parker Stuart Eliot, Engineer), Edward Platt (William Dean Benson Jr., Texas Ranger, The Voice of *Trend*), Ned Wertimer (Frothingham Fry), Fredd Wayne (Brewster Ames II), The Texas Rhythm Boys (The Three Coyotes—Bunkhouse: Eddy Smith; Muleshoes: Bill Horan; Fred: Joel McConkey), Kenny Delmar (Hominy Smith), Betty Lou Keim (Dogie Smith), Dante Di Paolo (Amos Hall, Cowboy), Cameron Andrews (Sherm, Joe Raker), William Ambler (Duane Fawcett, Texas Ranger), Ray Long (Branch Pedley, Cowboy, Guard), Ronnie Hartmann (Delia Pratt, *Trend* Secretary), Merrill Hilton (Red, Cowboy), Elyse Weber (Jo Ann Woods, One Little Maid, Cheer Leader, *Trend* Secretary), Dorothy Love (Calico Munson, One Little Maid), Carol Lee (Rebecca Bass, One Little Maid, Oil Worker), Ruth Ostrander (Sally Tucket), Doris Schmitt (Sue Crocket), Aileen Ethane (Sarah Boone), Yvonne Tibor (Belle Cooper), Mary Hatcher (Dallas Smith), Danny Scholl (Easy Jones), Jared Reed (Sam), Kate Murtah (Melissa Tatum), Elliott Martin (Prospector, Neighbor), Edmund Hall (Prospector, Stan, Football Player), Carl Conway (Prospector, Neighbor), Ralph Patterson (Herb, Texas Ranger), Bob Bernard (Jack Prow), Joey Thomas (Harry Stern), Jack Purcell (Oil Worker), Tommy Maier (Oil Worker), Jacqueline James (Drum Majorette, *Trend* Secretary), Dorothy Mary Richards (*Trend* Secretary), Marion Lauer (*Trend* Secretary), B. J. Keating (*Trend* Secretary), Patricia Jennings (Neighbor), Lloyd Knight (Neighbor), Jo Gibson (Neighbor), Muriel Bullis (Neighbor)
The musical was presented in two acts.
The action takes place during the present time in New York City and Texas

Musical Numbers

Act One: "Whoopin' and a-Hollerin'" (Betty Lou Keim, Kenny Delmar, Eddy Smith, Bill Horan, Joel McConkey, Ensemble); "Texas, Li'l Darlin'" (Kenny Delmar, Ensemble); "They Talk a Different Language" (aka "The Yodel Blues") (Mary Hatcher, Kenny Delmar, Eddy Smith, Bill Horan, Joel McConkey); "A Month of Sundays" (Mary Hatcher, Danny Scholl); "Down in the Valley" (Elyse Weber, Carol Lee, Dorothy Love, Elliott Martin, Edmund Hall, Carl Conway); "Hootin' Owl Trail" (Danny Scholl, Betty Lou Keim, Ensemble); "They Talk a Different Language" (aka "The Yodel Blues") (reprise) (Mary Hatcher, Ensemble); "The Big Movie Show in the Sky" (Danny Scholl, Ensemble); "Horseshoes Are Lucky" (Danny Scholl); "The Big Movie Show in the Sky" (reprise) (Jared Reed, Danny Scholl, Friends); "Love Me, Love My Dog" (Kenny Delmar, Danny Scholl, Ensemble)
Act Two: "Take a Crank Letter" (Jacqueline James, Ronnie Hartmann, Elyse Weber, Dorothy Mary Richards, Marion Lauer, B. J. Keating); "Politics" (Kenny Delmar, Loring Smith); "Ride 'em, Cowboy" (Mary Hatcher); "Square Dance" (Ray Long, Kenny Delmar, Mary Hatcher, Ensemble); "Take a Crank Letter" (reprise) (Fredd Wayne, Jacqueline James, Ronnie Hartmann, Elyse Weber, Dorothy Mary Richards, Marion Lauer, B. J. Keating); "Affable, Balding Me" (Mary Hatcher, Fredd Wayne); "A Month of Sundays" (reprise) (Mary Hatcher, Danny Scholl); "Whichaway'd They Go?" (Mary Hatcher, Jared Reed, Betty Lou Keim, Friends); "It's Great to Be Alive" (Danny Scholl, Ensemble)

Texas, Li'l Darlin' was perhaps too scattershot in its plot to be a completely satisfying and unified musical. There seems to have been three spoofs going on all at once: a general satiric look at the so-called Texas lifestyle; another on American politics; and still another that kidded the Henry Luce magazine empire (here, Harvey Small [Loring Smith] publishes the influential weekly *Trend*).

The basic plot surrounded Small's attempt to sponsor a presidential candidate, and grassroots Texas state senator Hominy Smith (Kenny Delmar) seems a likely candidate until war veteran Easy Jones (Danny Scholl) runs against him. Easy's campaign flyer (which was inserted into the theatre programs) stated he wasn't "such a wonderful candidate, but he's sure a lot better than that slippery old crook Hominy Smith." The flyer also listed Easy's stands on vital issues of the day, such as: "Garbage Disposal—Hell yes." Romantic complications ensue when Easy's old flame Dallas (Mary Hatcher) reenters the picture: the fly in the ointment is that she's Hominy's daughter. But all ends well when Hominy decides to run for sheriff instead of senator, Easy and Dallas make plans for the altar, and Easy's political future looks assured.

The reviews were mixed, but overall the critics were indulgent with the lighthearted spoof, and most were enthusiastic about Robert Emmett Dolan's music and particularly Johnny Mercer's playful lyrics. The score included the spoof "The Big Movie Show in the Sky," a critical favorite that soon became popular on the radio; "Affable, Balding Me," a love ballad flavored with *Time*-speak phraseology; "Take a Crank Letter," a tongue-in-cheek lament for Small's secretaries; the sparkling "They Talk a Different Language" (aka "The Yodel Blues"), a Texan's bemused appraisal of how New Yorkers speak; and "Politics," a cynical duet for Small and Smith. The critics liked Bostonian Kenny Delmar, who specialized in Southern-styled politicians; earlier, he had created the successful radio personality of Senator Claghorn.

Anthony Farrell had bought the Mark Hellinger Theatre, and *Texas, Li'l Darlin'* was his third attempt to produce a successful musical for the house; **Hold It!** and **All for Love** had been quick failures, and although *Texas, Li'l Darlin'* lost money, at least it received some favorable notices, enjoyed a hit song, and ran for almost 300 performances. But *The Complete Lyrics of Johnny Mercer* reports the initial investment of $100,000 ballooned into a loss of $150,000.

Brooks Atkinson in the *New York Times* noted that Texas was a "large area" that was "considerably better organized" than *Texas, Li'l Darlin'*. The book never settled on its satiric points, the music was "commonplace," and the lyrics were "in a similar vein" (but he noted "The Big Movie Show in the Sky" had "considerable gusto and imagination"). In the long run, it was the book that did in the "cheerful-looking show." Richard Watts in the *New York Post* reported that the satire wasn't "always properly pointed" and the book collapsed during the second act, but he nevertheless enjoyed the show. Dolan's music was "lively and tuneful" and Mercer's lyrics were "fresh" and had a "highly agreeable air of mockery about them" (he singled out "The Big Movie Show in the Sky," "Affable, Balding Me," and "Politics").

Robert Garland in the *New York Journal-American* recalled that the score of **Look, Ma, I'm Dancin'!** had included the song "I'm Tired of Texas," and noted that after a while the audience of *Texas, Li'l Darlin'* was also "pretty tired" of the Lone Star State. The would-be political satire got lost somewhere in the plot and soon the material became "more and more pedestrian." But A.C. in the *New York World-Telegram* said the "whale of an evening" was a "sparkling combination" of political and topical satire and each of Mercer's lyrics was "a small masterpiece of mirth" (he noted that the "sly" "Politics" had the "customers clamoring for more," and Kenny Delmar and Loring Smith "must have been ready to drop").

John Chapman in the *New York Daily News* found the musical "amiable" with "pleasant" music, "intelligent" lyrics, and an "engaging" cast; but the "modest and fairly pictorial" show was sometimes slow as it "dawdled along" (he noted Mercer's lyrics packed "more punch and stings" than the book, and Dolan's score offered "nice melodies"). But Robert Coleman in the *New York Daily Mirror* said the songs were "run-of-the-mill" and the book was "wheezy" (but noted Johnny Mercer's lyrics were the "best thing" about the evening, and he praised "Politics" and "The Big Movie Show in the Sky").

Ward Morehouse in the *New York Sun* found the musical "good-natured and unoffending" with more dull spots than bright ones. It was "affable, ingenuous—and negligible." Howard Barnes in the *New York Herald Tribune* said the show was more exuberant than inspired, but the company was "amiable," there were "flashes of hilarious satire," and Mercer's lyrics were "first-rate." He noted the "bountiful musical carnival" lacked "wit and musical felicity" and thus its "enjoyable interludes" grew "less and less beguiling" as the evening progressed.

During the tryout, Lenore Lonergan was succeeded by Kate Murtah; "Family Tree" and "Little Bit o' Country" were cut; and "Just to Keep the Record Straight," "He Threw Me a Curve," and "The Way You Fall in Love" were dropped in preproduction.

The cast album was released by Decca Records (LP # DL-5188; issued on CD by Decca Broadway # B0003437-02 on a pairing with the soundtrack of the 1956 film *You Can't Run Away from It*, a musical version of *It Happened One Night* with lyrics by Johnny Mercer and music by Gene De Paul). The collection *The Broadway Musicals of 1949* (Bayview CD # RNBW-035) includes "The Big Movie Show in the Sky" and "It's Great to Be Alive." The lyrics for the used, cut, and unused songs are included in *The Complete Lyrics of Johnny Mercer*.

On December 4, 1949, the musical was featured on CBS's series *Tonight on Broadway*, which included interviews with cast members and selections of songs from the show.

In 1964, Johnny Mercer and Robert Emmett Dolan's musical *Foxy* opened on Broadway for a short run of nine weeks; like their score for *Texas, Li'l Darlin'*, there were a number of delightful songs, including the double-edged ballad "Talk to Me, Baby," the sly and insinuating "Everything's Easy when You Know How," the blues "I'm Way Ahead of the Game," and the irresistible "Bon Vivant," one of musical theatre's great comedy songs (for his performance in the title role, Bert Lahr won the Tony Award for Best Leading Actor in a Musical).

GENTLEMEN PREFER BLONDES
"A New Musical Comedy"

Theatre: Ziegfeld Theatre
Opening Date: December 8, 1949; *Closing Date*: September 15, 1951
Performances: 740
Book: Joseph Fields and Anita Loos
Lyrics: Leo Robin
Music: Jule Styne
Based on the 1925 novel *Gentlemen Prefer Blondes: The Intimate Diary of a Professional Lady*, by Anita Loos (the book had been previously serialized in *Harper's Bazaar*); in 1926, a nonmusical stage adaptation by Loos and her husband John Emerson opened on Broadway.
Direction: John C. Wilson; *Producers*: Herman Levin and Oliver Smith; *Choreography*: Agnes De Mille; *Scenery*: Oliver Smith; *Costumes*: Miles White; *Lighting*: Peggy Clark; *Musical Direction*: Milton Rosenstock
Cast: Yvonne Adair (Dorothy Shaw), Jerry Craig (Steward), Carol Channing (Lorelei Lee), Jack McCauley (Gus Esmond), Robert Cooper (Frank), Eddie Weston (George), Pat Donohue (Sun Bather), Marjorie Winters (Sun Bather), Reta Shaw (Lady Phyllis Beekman), Rex Evans (Sir Francis Beekman), Alice Pearce (Mrs. Ella Spofford), Bob Burkhardt (Deck Steward), Shelton Lewis (Deck Steward), Eric Brotherson (Henry Spofford), Curt Stafford (An Olympic), George S. Irving (Josephus Gage), Fran Keegan (Deck Walker), Junior Standish (Deck Walker), Peter Birch (Bill), Anita Alvarez (Gloria Stark), Bob Neukum (Pierre), Kazimir Kokic (Taxi Driver, Headwaiter), Peter Holmes (Leon), Mort Marshall (Robert Lemanteur), Howard Morris (Louis Lemanteur), Nicole France (Flower Girl), Crandall Diehl (Maitre d'Hotel), Judy Sinclair (Zizi), Hope Zee (Fifi), Honi Coles (as himself), Cholly Atkins (as himself), William Krach (The Tenor), William Diehl (Policeman), Irving Mitchell (Mr. Esmond, Sr.); Show Girls: Pat Donohue, Anna Rita Duffy, Fran Keegan, Annette Kohl, Junior Standish, Marjorie Winters; Singers: Angela Castle, Joan Coburn, Ellen McCown, Candy Montgomery, Judy Sinclair, Lucille Udovick, Beverly Jane Weston, Hope Zee, Bob Burkhardt, Jerry Craig, William Diehl, William Krach, Shelton Lewis, Bob Neukum, Curt Stafford, David Vogel; Dancers: Suzanne Ames, Florence Baum, Nicole France, Pauline Goddard, Patty Ann Jackson, Alicia Krug, Mary Martinet, Caren Preiss, Evelyn Taylor, Norma Thornton, Polly Ward, Prue Ward, Helen Wood, Charles Basile, Bill Bradley, Rex Cooper, Robert Cooper, Crandall Diehl, Aristide J. Ginoulias, Peter Holmes, John Laverty, Eddie Weston
The musical was presented in two acts.
The action takes place during 1924 in New York City, at sea aboard the *Ile de France*, and in Paris.

Musical Numbers

Act One: "It's High Time" (Yvonne Adair, Ensemble); "Bye, Bye, Baby" (Jack McCauley, Carol Channing); "Bye, Bye, Baby" (reprise) (Jack McCauley, Ensemble); "A Little Girl from Little Rock" (Carol Channing);

"I Love What I'm Doing" (Yvonne Adair); Dance (Peter Birch, Yvonne Adair, Ensemble); "Just a Kiss Apart" (Eric Brotherson); "The Practice Scherzo" (dance) (Anita Alvarez); "It's Delightful Down in Chile" (Rex Evans, Carol Channing, Show Girls, Male Ensemble); "Sunshine" (Eric Brotherson, Yvonne Adair); "In the Champ de Mars" (aka "Park Scene") (Ensemble); Dance (aka "Pas de Deux") (Anita Alvarez, Kazimir Kokic); "Sunshine" (reprise) (Ensemble); "I'm A'Tingle, I'm A'Glow" (George S. Irving); "A House on Rittenhouse Square" (Yvonne Adair); "You Say You Care" (Eric Brotherson); Finaletto (Carol Channing, Ensemble)

Act Two: "Bye, Bye, Baby" (reprise) (Dancing Ensemble); "Mamie Is Mimi" (Anita Alvarez, with Honi Coles and Cholly Atkins); "Coquette" (William Krach, Show Girls); "Diamonds Are a Girl's Best Friend" (Carol Channing); "You Say You Care" (reprise) (Yvonne Adair, Eric Brotherson); "Gentlemen Prefer Blondes" (Carol Channing, Jack McCauley); "Homesick Blues" (Carol Channing, Yvonne Adair, Jack McCauley, Eric Brotherson, Alice Pearce, George S. Irving); "Keeping Cool with Coolidge" (Yvonne Adair, Peer Birch, Ensemble); "Button Up with Esmond" (Carol Channing, Show Girls, Ensemble); Finale: "Gentlemen Prefer Blondes" (reprise) (Carol Channing, Jack McCauley, Ensemble) and "Bye, Bye, Baby" (reprise) (Entire Company)

The revue **Lend an Ear** had included the mini-musical *The Gladiola Girl*, a parody of 1920s musicals that featured Yvonne Adair and Carol Channing as two flappers. *Gentlemen Prefer Blondes* was a full-fledged Broadway musical set in the same era and was based on Anita Loos's 1925 novel of the same name. The story focused on diamonds-in-her-eyes Lorelei Lee (Channing) and her more practical girlfriend Dorothy Shaw (Adair) who willingly accepts the proposition that romance is possible with a guy without a simoleon. But not Lorelei, who combines the traits of a coldly calculating diamond hunter (of the tiara variety) and a dizzy innocent who really needs diamonds in order to be truly happy. The slight plot was an excuse for an evening of lighthearted merriment and offered a number of colorful characters (but none of course more colorful than Channing's Lorelei), a lavish production, old-fashioned dances created by Agnes De Mille, and a lively and tuneful score with music by Jule Styne and lyrics by Leo Robin. De Mille's dances were particularly welcome because they concentrated on hot dance routines rather than expository and serious ballets. The musical was the longest-running of the season (the shortest was *Happy as Larry*, which opened a month later and played for three showings).

With the exception of Richard Watts in the *New York Post*, the critics adored the show and showered Channing's legendary comic performance with the kind of valentines most performers can only dream of. Brooks Atkinson in the *New York Times*: A "fabulous comic creation," which Channing glided through like a "dazed automaton" (there has "never been anything like this before in human society"); John Chapman in the *New York Daily News*: "The funniest female to hit the boards since Fannie Brice and Beatrice Lillie"; Howard Barnes in the *New York Herald Tribune*: Channing was "enchanting" and had "few peers among musical comedy actresses"; Ward Morehouse in the *New York Sun*: The "pretty wonderful" Channing of the "vacuous stare and the mincing steps" was as "helpless as a fretful boa constrictor"; William Hawkins in the *New York World-Telegram*: Channing is one "of the most extraordinary people in the entertainment world today"; and Robert Coleman in the *New York Daily Mirror*: With her "artful pretense, gravelly voice and mincing walk," Channing was a "triumph." Watts found Channing a "shrewd and effective comedienne of great force, skill and originality" whose "position in the theatre is already an assured one," but said she was more awesome than delightful; both the reason for her being cast as Lorelei, and her interpretation of the role, "eluded" him.

But with Channing's performance, the high spirits of the show's comic plot and eccentric characters, and the lively dances (mostly headed by Anita Alvarez), the musical became one of the blockbusters of the era and played on Broadway for almost two years. The melodic score included the ballad "Bye, Bye, Baby," Channing's two comic show-stoppers "A Little Girl from Little Rock" and "Diamonds Are a Girl's Best Friend," the ingratiating Charleston "Keeping Cool with Coolidge," and the celebratory "It's High Time" (in the vein of "It's Today," from *Mame* [1966]). The score also included two particularly outstanding songs, a nightclub sequence in which Honi Coles and Cholly Atkins smoothly sang the sizzling and insinuating saga of "Mamie Is Mimi" (a gal of dubious virtue who is undoubtedly related to such famous musical comedy dames as Edie, Katie, and Jenny) and the leading characters' lament of having the "Homesick Blues" (Styne's irresistible melody was perfectly matched by Robin's Porterish-styled list song of what Americans miss when they're in France, such as old-fashioned kissing and modern plumbing).

Gentlemen Prefer Blondes was the decade's final musical, and it's somehow appropriate that it included yet another South American number (in this case, the rhumba "It's Delightful Down in Chile," for Channing, Rex Evans, and the ensemble). South American songs and dances (with a few thrown in from Spain) dominated the era's revues and musicals, and of the total number of 262 shows that opened during the decade (including revivals, imports, personality revues, ice shows, return engagements, and pre-Broadway closings), fifty (almost 25 percent) offered South-of-the-Border or Spanish songs and dances.

During the tryout, Muriel Bentley was succeeded by Anita Alvarez. The original cast album was released by Columbia Records (LP # ML-4290; issued on CD by Sony Broadway # SK-48013).

In 1973, the musical was revised as *Lorelei*, or *Gentlemen Still Prefer Blondes*. With a new book by Kenny Solms and Gail Parent and with some new songs by Styne (with lyrics by Betty Comden and Adolph Green), the musical starred Carol Channing. It began a year-long national tour in early 1973, and opened on Broadway at the Palace Theatre on January 27, 1974, for 321 performances. The prologue and epilogue were set in 1944, with Lorelei reminiscing about her conquests of men and jewels back in the 1920s. The cast included Tamara Long (Dorothy), Peter Palmer (Gus Esmond), Dody Goodman (Mrs. Ella Spofford), and Lee Roy Reams (Henry Spofford); the new songs were "Looking Back," "I Won't Let You Get Away," "Men," and "Miss Lorelei Lee." Retained from the original production were: "Bye, Bye, Baby," "A Little Girl from Little Rock," "I Love What I'm Doing," "It's Delightful Down in Chile," "Keeping Cool with Coolidge," "Coquette," "Mamie Is Mimi," "Diamonds Are a Girl's Best Friend," "Homesick Blues," and "Button Up with Esmond." During the tour, "I'm A'Tingle, I'm A'Glow," "Just a Kiss Apart," and "Sunshine" (as "Paris, Paris") were dropped as well as the new song "A Girl Like I" for Channing. For much of the tour, Joe Layton was the director and choreographer of record, and Ernie Flatt was credited for additional choreography; by the time the musical reached New York, Robert Moore was the director and Flatt the choreographer.

Channing was a delight, and knocked out audiences all over again with "A Little Girl from Little Rock" and "Diamonds Are a Girl's Best Friend," and she made a great comic impression with the new song "Men," which literally brought down the curtain on both her and the first act. During the tryout, John Mineo and Bob Fitch were an ingratiating duo in "Mamie Is Mimi," as were Fitch and Ian Tucker for the New York version.

There were two cast albums of *Lorelei*. The national tour was recorded by MGM/Verve (LP # MV-5097-OC), and includes "I'm A'Tingle, I'm A'Glow," "Just a Kiss Apart," "Paris, Paris," and Palmer's easy-listening version of the title song. The Broadway cast album (MGM LP # M3G-55) includes the previously recorded tracks for the touring version as well as new ones, such as "It's Delightful Down in Chile," "Men," and the title song version by Channing and the chorus. The CD (released by Decca Broadway # B0001407-02) includes all the songs from both LPs as well as both overtures (the first overture included "A Girl Like I," which had been dropped at some point during the national tour).

On April 10, 1995, *Gentlemen Prefer Blondes* was revived (and revised, but with uncredited revisions) on Broadway at the Lyceum Theatre for twenty-four performances; the cast included K. T. Sullivan (Lorelei), Karen Prunzik (Dorothy), George Dvorsky (Henry Spofford), and Jamie Ross (Josephus Gage). The production omitted two dance sequences ("The Practice Scherzo" and "In the Champ de Mars"), "Button Up with Esmond," "A House on Rittenhouse Square," "Coquette," and "Sunshine" (although the latter's music was retained for the newly created "Sunshine Montage" number). "A Ride on a Rainbow" was interpolated into the revival; it had first been heard in Styne and Robin's 1957 NBC television musical *Ruggles of Red Gap* where it was sung by Jane Powell (the soundtrack recording was issued by Verve LP # 1500, and the CD was released by Stage Records # 9004). *Ruggles* is also notable for its song "I'm in Pursuit of Happiness"; with a new lyric by Stephen Sondheim, it was heard two years later as "You'll Never Get Away from Me" in *Gypsy*. The CD of the 1995 revival of *Gentlemen Prefer Blondes* was released by DRG Records (# 94762).

The musical was presented in concert format in a well-received production by Encores!, where it played at City Center for seven performances beginning on May 9, 2012. The cast included Megan Hilty (Lorelei) and Rachel York (Dorothy), and the presentation was recorded by Masterworks Broadway (CD # 88725-44451-2). The album includes a number of sequences that weren't recorded for the 1949 cast album, including "In the Champ de Mars" (here, "Park Scene"), the untitled dance sequence for Gloria and the taxi driver (here, "Pas de Deux"), "Coquette," and "Button Up with Esmond"; the production seems to have given short shrift to "A House on Rittenhouse Square."

The London production opened at the Princes Theatre on August 20, 1962, for 223 performances; the cast included Dora Bryan (Lorelei), Anne Hart (Dorothy), and early-talkie film favorite Bessie Love as Ella Spofford. The production included revised versions of "Coquette" and the second-act reprise of "Bye, Bye, Baby" (as

"You Kill Me" and "Au Revoir, Babies," respectively). The cast recording was released by HMV Records (LP # 1464), and reissued by That's Entertainment Records (LP # TER-1059).

The 1953 film version released by Twentieth Century-Fox may not have been a faithful adaptation, but the splashy Technicolor-drenched production kept the essential plot and spirit of the original and put Marilyn Monroe on the map as the screen's one-and-only sex kitten. Her "Diamonds Are a Girl's Best Friend" is probably as iconic as Channing's, and the number practically defines the look of the lavish 1950s film musical production number (note that Monroe is flanked by a number of chorus boys, including George Chakiris and Larry Kert). The film was directed by Howard Hawks, choreographed by Jack Cole, and scripted by Charles Lederer. Monroe was second-billed after Jane Russell, who played Dorothy, and others in the cast included Charles Coburn (Sir Francis Beekman), Tommy Noonan (Gus Esmond), Norma Varden (Lady Beekman), and Elliott Reid as Malone, a new character created for the film. The adult role of Henry Spofford was reconceived as Henry Spofford III, and was memorably performed by George "Foghorn" Winslow, who in the time-honored tradition of child performers almost managed to steal the show, even from Monroe. The film retained three numbers from the stage production ("Bye, Bye, Baby," "A Little Girl from Little Rock," and "Diamonds Are a Girl's Best Friend") and added two memorable songs with lyrics by Harold Adamson and music by Hoagy Carmichael, "When Love Goes Wrong" and "Ain't There Anyone Here for Love?" The former was a bluesy shuffle for Monroe and Russell, and the latter was a sardonic lament sung by Russell in the ship's gymnasium and swimming pool where she's surrounded by dozens of scantily clad muscle men going through their workout routines with one another and showing absolutely no interest whatsoever in her.

A LA CARTE
"New Intimate Revue"

Theatre and *Performance Dates*: The revue was performed for approximately two months during the 1949–1950 season at the El Capitan Theatre in Los Angeles, California.
Sketches: Hal Fimberg, Henry Piffl, and Ernst Matray
Lyrics: Edward Heymann
Music: Victor Young
Direction and *Staging*: Ernst and Maria Matray; *Producers*: Ernst Matray, Maria Matray, and Edward Heymann; *Choreography*: Ernst and Maria Matray; *Scenery*: Karin; *Costumes*: Fini; *Lighting*: Uncredited; *Musical Direction*: Harry Sukman
Cast: Gale Robbins, Bill Shirley, George Zoritch, Patricia Denise, Hawthorne, Helene Stanley, Joseph Warfield, Gisela Werbezirk, Erika Lund, Eddie Robertson, Dolores Boucher, John Perri, Priscilla Allen, Felice Basso, Sherree Bessire, Richard Cahill, Gloria DeWerd, Robert Rosselat, Marilyn Russell, Phil Terry, Gloria Stone, Bill Tremaine, Angela Velez, Dick (Richard) Wyatt
The revue was presented in two acts.

Sketches and Musical Numbers

Act One: "Prologue" (Grandma: Gisela Werbezirk; Dad: Joseph Warfield; Gale: Gale Robbins); "Opening" (Chefs: Robert Rosselat, Dick Wyatt, Bill Tremaine, Felice Basso; Usherettes: Gloria DeWerd, Priscilla Allen, Sherree Bessire, Gloria Stone, Marilyn Russell, Angela Velez; Producer: Hawthorne; Composer: John Perri; Lyricist: Eddie Robertson; Singer: Dolores Boucher; Director: Phil Terry; Critics: Dick Wyatt, Richard Cahill, Joseph Warfield; Choreographer: George Zoritch); "A Face in the Crowd" (Bill Shirley); "Sweetheart Semicolon" (Gale Robbins, Bill Shirley, Hawthorne, John Perri, Eddie Robertson); "Citizen Schmidt" (Mrs. Schmidt: Gisela Werbezirk; Man: Hawthorne; Judge: Joseph Warfield; Bailiff: Phil Terry; Miss Smith: Dolores Boucher); "There's No Man Like a Snowman" (sung and danced by Helene Stanley; School Girls: Priscilla Allen, Sherree Bessire, Gloria DeWerd, Marilyn Russell, Angela Velez; Snowmen: Felice Basso, Richard Cahill, John Perri, Robert Rosselat, Bill Tremaine, Dick Wyatt); "Life of a Salesman" (Bill Shirley, Joseph Warfield, Hawthorne); "Folk Song 1950" (Erika Lund); "Cat Party" (The Kitten: Helene Stanley; Cats: Sherree Bessire, Gloria DeWerd, Angela Velez, Priscilla Allen, Marilyn Russell, Gloria Stone; Tom Cat: Dick Wyatt); "I Oughta Know More About You" (Gale Robbins, Bill Shirley);

"The Virtuoso" (Dolores Boucher); "Half of Me" (Larry: Bill Shirley; Harry: John Perri; The Girl Friend: Gale Robbins; The Dancers: Gloria DeWerd, Angela Velez, Felice Basso, Richard Cahill, Robert Rosselat); "Beastly Luck" (Narrator: Bill Shirley; Secretary: Marilyn Russell; Producer: Hawthorne; Agent: Joseph Warfield; Wardrobe Man: John Perri); "The Poker Polka" (a. Dolores Boucher, Eddie Robertson; b. Felice Basso, Richard Cahill, John Perri, Robert Rosselat, Bill Tremaine, Dick Wyatt; c. Priscilla Allen, Sherree Bessire, Gloria DeWerd, Marilyn Russell, Gloria Stone, Angela Velez; d. Patricia Denise, George Zoritch; e. Gale Robbins, Bill Shirley)

Act Two: "Venezia and Her Three Lovers" (ballet written and choreographed by Ernst Matray) and "Bella Signora" (Eddie Robertson) (First Lover: George Zoritch; Second Lover: Bill Tremaine; Third Lover: Richard Cahill; Venezia: Patricia Denise; Tailor: Robert Rosselat; Drunkard: Phil Terry); "Folk Song 1950 Sequel" (Erika Lund); "Food for Thought" (Bertha: Gisela Werbezirk; June: Gail Robbins; Jim: Bill Shirley; Mr. Schlickenbacker: Hawthorne); "In the Arty Manner" (The Speaker: Helene Stanley; She: Dolores Boucher; The Company: Sherree Bessire, Gloria DeWerd, Angela Velez, Priscilla Allen, Marilyn Russell, Gloria Stone, Felice Basso, Richard Cahill, John Perri, Robert Rosselat, Bill Tremaine, Dick Wyatt); "Until Tonight" (Boy: Bill Shirley; Girl: Gale Robbins; Flamenco Singer: Erika Lund; Dancer: George Zoritch); "Clara the Divine" (Gisela Werbezirk); "I'm Gonna Make a Fool Out of April" (Gendarmes: Felice Basso, Robert Rosselat, Dick Wyatt, Bill Tremaine; Boy: John Perri; Girl: Helene Stanley; Midinettes: Priscilla Allen, Sherree Bessire, Gloria DeWerd, Angela Velez); "The Flower Song" (Hawthorne, Joseph Warfield); "The Wedding" (finale) (Cook: Helene Stanley; Bride: Gale Robbins; Mother: Erika Lund; Father: Phil Terry; Sister: Dolores Boucher; Brother: Eddie Robertson; Groom: Bill Shirley; Wedding Party: Sherree Bessire, Gloria DeWerd, Angela Velez, Priscilla Allen, Marilyn Russell, Gloria Stone, Felice Basso, Richard Cahill, John Perri, Robert Rosselat, Bill Tremaine, Dick Wyatt); Dancing Cook: Patricia Denise; Dancing Chef: George Zoritch; Guests: Hawthorne, Gisela Werbezirk, Joseph Warfield)

A note in the souvenir program of the revue *A la Carte* reported that lyricist Edward Heyman had taken "a leaf" from Oscar Hammerstein II, who always wrote his lyrics before submitting them to Richard Rodgers to set to music; and thus Heyman wrote the revue's lyrics before giving them to composer Victor Young; once the score was in place, the producing team stated they "started on the thousand-and-one details that go with producing and presenting a revue of this magnitude."

But it appears the revue never got beyond its two-month run in Los Angeles at the El Capitan Theatre, which had recently played host to the seven-year engagement of **Ken Murray's Blackouts**. *Best Plays* indicated *A la Carte* was "attractive" but "lacked the zest of entertainment."

Also playing in Los Angeles during the same season as *A la Carte* was Ole Olsen and Chic Johnson's new revue *Tsk! Tsk! Tsk! Paree*, and upon the closing of *A la Carte*, some of its sketches and musical numbers as well as a few of its cast members turned up in *Paree*. Olsen and Johnson's revue later opened in New York as *Pardon Our French* on October 5, 1950, for one-hundred performances at the Broadway Theatre.

Cast members of *A la Carte* who appeared in *Pardon Our French* were: Bill Shirley, Helene Stanley, Patricia Denise, George Zoritch, Robert Rosselat, Richard Cahill, Richard Wyatt, and Gloria Stone.

The following numbers from *A la Carte* were held over for *Pardon Our French*: "There's No Man Like a Snowman," "Life of a Salesman," "I Oughta Know More About You," "Venezia and Her Three Lovers," "A Face in the Crowd," "I'm Gonna Make a Fool Out of April," "The Flower Song," and "The Poker Polka."

A la Carte shouldn't be confused with two other revues with the same title. The first played on Broadway in 1927; and the second was given for three performances at Princeton University's McCarter Theatre beginning on September 21, 1956, with Jimmy Savo and Vera Brynner in the leading roles (Savo appeared in the spoof "L'apres-midi d'un Bum," and the evening included "Giselle's Revenge," which kidded the ballet *Giselle* and was presented "after the manner of Charles Addams").

PRETTY PENNY
"A New Revue"

Theatres and *Performance Dates*: The revue played in summer stock venues during the summer of 1949, including a one-week engagement of eight performances at the Bucks County Playhouse, New Hope, Pennsylvania, beginning on June 20.

Sketches: Jerome Chodorov
Lyrics and *Music*: Harold Rome
Direction: George S. Kaufman; *Producer*: Leonard Field; *Choreography*: Michael Kidd; *Scenery*: Paul Morrison; *Costumes*: Kenn Barr; *Lighting*: Uncredited; *Musical Direction*: Harold Rome
Cast: George Keane, Marilyn Day, Ken Spaulding, Peter Gennaro, Jay Lloyd, Wana Allison, Phyllis Gehrig, Diane Sinclair, Wayne Lamb, Barbara McCutcheon, Evelyn Taylor, Robert Morrow, Onna White, William (Bill) Skipper, Barbara Martin, Carl Reiner, Lenore Lonergan, David Burns, Walter Scheff, Michael Kidd, John Henson, Bud Sweeney, Florence Henson, Barbara Weaver; Pianists: George Davis and Joseph Antman
The revue was presented in two acts.

Sketches and Musical Numbers

Act One: Introduction: George Keane (Impresario); "Small World" (Teacher: Marilyn Day; American: Ken Spaulding; Russians: Peter Gennaro, Jay Lloyd; Spanish: Wana Allison, Phyllis Gehrig; Hawaiians: Diane Sinclair, Wayne Lamb; Chinese: Barbara McCutcheon, Evelyn Taylor, Robert Morrow; Balinese: Onna White, William Skipper); "Meet the Authors" (Chairwoman: Barbara Morris; Dr. Flick: Carl Reiner; Miss Tremaine: Lenore Lonergan; Dr. Drawbridge: David Burns); "What Hit You?" (Marilyn Day); "Gin Rummy Rhapsody" (Carl Reiner, Barbara Martin, Lenore Lonergan, Bud Sweeney); "A Visit to the Doctor" (Doctor: William Skipper; Patient: David Burns); "The Fair Sex" (David Burns, Walter Scheff, Carl Reiner, George Keane, Dancers); "Death with Father" (Father: David Burns; Mother: Barbara Martin; Clarence: Carl Reiner; Girl: Lenore Lonergan; Harlan: Walter Scheff; Uncle Ben: Bud Sweeney; Willie: William Skipper; Junior: Michael Kidd); "Stop Walking Around in My Mind" (Marilyn Day; danced by Diane Sinclair and Ken Spaulding); "I'll Trade My Dreams" (David Burns, Barbara Martin, Bud Sweeney); "French with Tears" (Lenore Lonergan); "Rome Rides Again" (Producer: David Burns; Writer: John Henson; Cass Cassius: Carl Reiner; Bill Brutus: Walter Scheff; Two-Gun Caesar: Bud Sweeney; Mark Anthony: George Keane; Gambling Girl: Barbara Martin; Portia: Lenore Lonergan; Barroom Girls: Marilyn Day, Florence Henson, Barbara Weaver)

Act Two: "I Never Learned to Waltz" (Walter Scheff; A Ballroom: William Skipper, Wana Allison; A Bistro: Wayne Lamb, Phyllis Gehrig; A Café: Ken Spaulding, Diane Sinclair; A Drugstore: Peter Gennaro, Evelyn Taylor, Jay Lloyd, Onna White; A Village Square: Michael Kidd, Barbara McCutcheon; A Waiter: John Henson); "Investigation" (George Keane, David Burns, Bud Sweeney, Carl Reiner); "The Electric Age" (Mrs.: Barbara Martin; Mr.: Bud Sweeney); "Libido" (George Keane); "Up North American Way" (Marilyn Day; danced by Michael Kidd, Barbara McCutcheon, Dance Ensemble); "Life of a Salesman" (The Little Man: David Burns; Salesmen: Carl Reiner, George Keane, Bud Sweeney; The Girl: Onna White); "Cry, Baby" (Barbara Martin, Lenore Lonergan, Marilyn Day); "Operation Television" (Director: George Keane; Assistant: Carl Reiner; Cameraman: John Henson; Doctor: Bud Sweeney; Mr. Kraus: David Burns; Make-Up Man: Wayne Lamb; Anesthetist: Walter Scheff; First Nurse: Barbara Weaver; Second Nurse: Florence Henson; Orderlies: Jay Lloyd, Ken Spaulding; Trio: Lenore Lonergan, Marilyn Day, Barbara Martin); "The Ballad of Marcia La Rue" (Ronald: Carl Reiner; Marcia La Rue: Lenore Lonergan; Agent: David Burns); Finale (Entire Company)

The revue *Pretty Penny* had an impressive line-up of creators and cast members. Harold Rome wrote the songs, Jerome Chodorov the sketches, Michael Kidd provided the choreography, and George S. Kaufman directed; the cast included David Burns and Carl Reiner, and Kidd was one of the principal dancers (others in the dancing chorus were future choreographers Peter Gennaro and Onna White).

Four of *Pretty Penny*'s songs had first been introduced in Rome's book musical **That's the Ticket!**, which had closed on the road a year earlier: "What Hit You?" (aka "You Never Know What Hit You—When It's Love"), "Gin Rummy Rhapsody," "Cry, Baby" (aka "Cry, Baby, Cry"), and "The Ballad of Marcia La Rue." These numbers are included on the cast album of the 2002 revival of **That's the Ticket!** by Musicals Tonight!

Although the revue never reached New York, a number of its songs and sketches were heard in later Broadway productions. "What Hit You?" was used in the 1950 Broadway revue *Bless You All* and "Cry, Baby" was heard the same year in the revue *Alive and Kicking*.

"French with Tears," a spoof of the Edith Piaf school of torching, was also recycled for *Alive and Kicking*; and the sardonic "I'll Trade My Dreams" (as "Pocketful of Dreams") turned up in the 1950 revue *Michael Todd's Peep Show* ("Dreams" was recorded by Rome for his collection *Rome-Antics*, released by Heritage Records LP # H-0063). The sketch "Meet the Authors" was added to *Bless You All* during its Broadway run.

Pretty Penny included Chodorov's sketch "A Visit to the Doctor" (William Skipper was the doctor and David Burns the patient); for *Bless You All*, Arnold Auerbach's sketch "The Cold War" looked at a druggist and a customer. Further, Chodorov's *Pretty Penny* sketch "Operation Television" seems to have inspired "Hippocrates Hits the Jackpot" which Will Glickman and Joseph Stein wrote for *Alive and Kicking*. Other medical-themed sketches during the era were "Painless Distraction" (**Two for the Show**); "Have You Had Any Good Dreams Lately?" (**Meet the People**); "The Great Man Speaks" (**Seven Lively Arts**); "Doctors Don't Tell" (**Make Mine Manhattan**); "Neurotic You and Psychopathic Me" (**Lend an Ear**); and "Dentist" (*Michael Todd's Peep Show*).

This was also the era of sketches and songs about politics and politicians (especially senators), and so *Pretty Penny* included "Investigation"; *Tickets, Please!* (1950) looked at "A Senate Investigation"; **Meet the People** looked at "Senate in Session"; Rome's **Call Me Mister** included "The Senators' Song"; Zero Mostel kidded senators in **Keep 'Em Laughing**, **Top-Notchers**, and **Concert Varieties**; *Texas, Li'l Darlin'* sang of "Politics"; and various revues on the order of **Of "V" We Sing**, **Morey Amsterdam's Hilarities**, and **Up to Now** also offered comments about elected officials.

Besides medical and political songs and sketches, the era saw spoofs of *Life with Father* and *Death of a Salesman*, and *Pretty Penny* offered both "Death with Father" and "Life of a Salesman." **Keep Off the Grass** included "Life with Mother"; the first edition of **Crazy with the Heat** offered "Life without Father"; and **Seven Lively Arts** kidded *Life with Father*, *Angel Street*, and *Tobacco Road* in "Heaven on Angel Street."

The above-mentioned "French with Tears" satirized Edith Piaf, and "Up North American Way" seems to be a variation of Rome's "South America, Take It Away" from **Call Me Mister**. The sketch "Rome Rides Again" sounds pretty funny: it depicted Shakespeare's *Julius Caesar* in the style of a typical Hollywood Western (with such characters as Two-Gun Caesar, Cass Cassius, and Bill Brutus). (Perhaps "Rome Rides Again" wasn't so far off the mark: in 1955, Paul Douglas and Ruth Roman starred in the film *Joe Macbeth*, which told the familiar story against the background of big-city gangsters.)

UP TO NOW
"A NEW MUSICAL REVUE"

Theatres and *Performance Dates*: The revue played the summer stock circuit during Summer 1949, including stops at the Olney Theater, Olney, Maryland, and the Ivoryton Playhouse, Ivoryton, Connecticut (the latter for the week of August 29).
Sketches: Harry Herrmann, Ed Rice, and Jack Roche
Lyrics and *Music*: Mostly by Clay Warnick
Direction: Harry Herrmann; *Producer*: Milton Stiefel; *Choreography*: Uncredited; *Scenery*: Don Finlayson; *Costumes*, *Lighting*, and *Musical Direction*: Uncredited
Cast: *Grace* and *Paul Hartman*, Jack Albertson, Johnny Barnes, Bud Rogerson, Merle Meier, Ted Luce
The revue was presented in two acts.

Sketches and Musical Numbers

Act One: Prologue (Eve: Grace Hartman; Adam: Paul Hartman); "They Started It" (Johnny Barnes, Bud Rogerson, Merle Meier, Ted Luce); "At the Roller Derby" (Budd Rogerson, Merle Meier); "92nd Armory" (The Gabber: Jack Albertson; Poil: Grace Hartman); "Just a Boy and a Girl" (lyric by Barrie O'Daniels) (Bud Rogerson, Merle Meier); "Just a Boy and a Girl" (reprise) (Grace and Paul Hartman); "The Psychiatrist" (Dr. Wolfgang Platzsitzen: Jack Albertson; Nurse: Merle Meier; Dr. Bombinder: Johnny Barnes); "Dance, Don't Run to the Nearest Exit" (lyric by Walter Nones) (Johnny Barnes); "The Drama" (Grace and Paul Hartman, Jack Albertson, Johnny Barnes, Merle Meier, Ted Luce)

Act Two: "Pals at the Palace" (lyric by Jack Fox) (Paul Hartman, Jack Albertson); "Mista Electric Storm" (Bud Rogerson; ballet danced by Grace and Paul Hartman and Company); "Clichés" (Jack Albertson); "Design for Loving" (music by Don Walker) (Bud Rogerson, Merle Meier); "I Do a Little Peel" (lyric by Jack Fox) (Hunsbuns Laverne: Grace Hartman; Greasy: Jack Albertson; Cop: Paul Hartman); "It Didn't Get Me Anywhere" (lyric and music by Leroy Hale) (Budd Rogerson); "Book Review" (Mrs. Wigglesworth: Grace Hartman; Mr. Proggle: Paul Hartman); "Boing Boy" (Johnny Barnes); "Another Investigation" (Senator Diddlesnooper: Budd Rogerson; Madame Senator: Merle Meier; Senator Potts: Jack Albertson; Professor Brainstein: Paul Hartman; Mrs. Brainstein: Grace Hartman); Finale (Entire Company)

As *Heaven Help the Angels*, Paul and Grace Hartman's revue played the summer stock circuit during Summer 1947 before going on to New York later in the year as **Angel in the Wings**, where it played for a profitable 308 performances. Their next revue **All for Love** struggled along for 121 showings in early 1949, and then that summer they were back on the straw-hat circuit with a new revue *Up to Now*, which featured Jack Albertson.

In October 1950, they brought a variation of *Up to Now* to New York under the title *Tickets, Please!* (at the beginning of the evening they noted their show had much in common with **South Pacific** because prior to the performance of each show, the ticket-takers called out, "Tickets, please!"). *Tickets, Please!* ran for 245 performances and probably showed a small profit.

A few numbers from *Up to Now* were retained for *Tickets, Please!*: "At the Roller Derby" became "Roller Derby"; "Another Investigation" became "A Senate Investigation"; "The Drama" became "Drama—The Plot Is Always the Same"; and "Book Review" became "Mr. Proggle." The summer revue had included a second-act opening called "Pals at the Palace" for Hartman and Albertson (lyric by Jack Fox, music by Clay Warnick); the song was revised for *Tickets, Please!* as "Back at the Palace," a second-act opener for Hartman and Albertson (lyric and music credited to Mel Tolkin, Lucille Kallen, and Clay Warnick, with additional lyric by Jack Fox).

Appendix A: Chronology (by Season)

The following is a seasonal chronology of the 273 productions discussed in this book. Musicals that closed during their pre-Broadway engagements are marked with an asterisk (*) and are listed alphabetically at the end of the season in which they were produced.

Following each title is a classification that describes the nature of each musical (book musical with new music, book musical with preexisting music, revue, import, etc.). For more information on classifications, see appendix B, "Chronology (by Classification)."

1940
John Henry (book musical with new music)
Earl Carroll Vanities (revue)
Two for the Show (revue)
Reunion in New York (revue)
Theatre of the Piccoli (revue)
Higher and Higher (book musical with new music)
American Jubilee (revue)
Keep Off the Grass (revue)
Russian Bank (play with incidental songs)
Louisiana Purchase (book musical with new music)
* *Tropical Pinafore* (book musical with preexisting music)
* *The White Plume* (aka *A Vagabond Hero*) (book musical with new music)

1940–1941
Walk with Music (book musical with new music)
Gay New Orleans (revue)
Sim Sala Bim (revue)
Hold on to Your Hats (book musical with new music)
Boys and Girls Together (revue)
It Happens on Ice (includes second edition) (ice revue)
Cabin in the Sky (book musical with new music)
'Tis of Thee (revue)
Panama Hattie (book musical with new music)
Mum's the Word (personality revue)
Meet the People (revue)
Pal Joey (book musical with new music)
All in Fun (revue)
Night of Love (book musical with new music)

Crazy with the Heat (includes revised edition) (revue)
Lady in the Dark (book musical with new music)
Liberty Jones (play with incidental songs)
* *La belle Helene* (revival; book musical; revised version of 1864 operetta)
* *Hi Ya, Gentlemen* (book musical with new music)
* *Hot from Harlem* (revue)
* *The Little Dog Laughed* (book musical with new music)
* *Rhapsody in Black* (revue)
* *She Had to Say Yes* (book musical with new music)
* *Two Weeks with Pay* (revue)

1941–1942

Best Foot Forward (book musical with new music)
Viva O'Brien (book musical with new music)
Let's Face It! (book musical with new music)
High Kickers (book musical with new music)
La vie Parisienne (revival; book musical; revised version of 1866 operetta)
Sons o' Fun (revue)
Sunny River (book musical with new music)
Banjo Eyes (book musical with new music)
The Lady Comes Across (book musical with new music)
Porgy and Bess (revival; book musical)
Of "V" We Sing (revue)
Priorities of 1942 (revue)
Johnny 2 x 4 (play with incidental songs)
Keep 'Em Laughing (revue)
Harlem Cavalcade (revue)
Top-Notchers (revue)
* *American Sideshow* (revue)
* *Dansation* (revue)
* *Jump for Joy* (revue)
* *Patricia* (book musical with new music)
* *They Can't Get You Down* (book musical with new music)

1942–1943

By Jupiter (book musical with new music)
Laugh, Town, Laugh (revue)
The Chocolate Soldier (revival; book musical)
Star and Garter (revue)
Stars on Ice (includes second edition) (ice revue)
This Is the Army (revue)
The Merry Widow (revival; book musical)
The New Moon (revival; book musical)
New Priorities of 1943 (revue)
Show Time (revue)
Wine Women and Song (revue)
Let Freedom Sing (revue)
Count Me In (book musical with new music)
Oy is dus a leben! (play with incidental songs)
Beat the Band (book musical with new music)
The Time, the Place and the Girl (revival; but with mostly new music)
Rosalinda (book musical; revival of and revised version of *Die Fledermaus*)

La vie Parisienne (book musical; revival of and revised version of 1866 operetta)
Once Over Lightly (book musical with preexisting music; revised version of *The Barber of Seville*)
New Faces of 1943 (revue)
You'll See Stars (book musical with new music)
Something for the Boys (book musical with new music)
For Your Pleasure (revue)
Lady in the Dark (return engagement)
Oklahoma! (book musical with new music)
Ziegfeld Follies (revue)
* *Adamant Eve* (play with incidental songs)
* *Cocktails at 5* (book musical with new music)
* *Dancing in the Streets* (book musical with new music)
* *The Firefly* (revival; book musical)
* *Full Speed Ahead* (book musical with new music)
* *Headliners of '42* (revue)
* *Life of the Party* (book musical with new music)
* *Merry-Go-Rounders* (aka *The Merrymakers*) (revue)
* *Sugar 'n' Spice* (revue)

1943–1944
The Student Prince (revival; book musical)
Early to Bed (book musical with new music)
The Vagabond King (revival; book musical)
The Merry Widow (revival; book musical)
Run Little Chillun (revival; book musical)
Chauve-souris of 1943 (revue)
Blossom Time (revival; book musical)
Laugh Time (revue)
My Dear Public (book musical with new music)
Porgy and Bess (return engagement)
Bright Lights of 1944 (revue)
A Tropical Revue (revue)
Hairpin Harmony (book musical with new music)
One Touch of Venus (book musical with new music)
Artists and Models (revue)
What's Up (book musical with new music)
A Connecticut Yankee (revival; book musical)
Winged Victory (play with incidental songs)
Carmen Jones (book musical with preexisting music; revised version of *Carmen*)
Jackpot (book musical with new music)
Mexican Hayride (book musical with new music)
Porgy and Bess (two return engagements in two slightly separated bookings)
Follow the Girls (book musical with new music)
Allah Be Praised! (book musical with new music)
Helen Goes to Troy (book musical with preexisting music)
Tars and Spars (revue)
The New Moon (revival)
Dream with Music (book musical with mostly preexisting music)
* *Big Time* (revue)
* *Curtain Time* (revue)
* *Marching with Johnny* (revue)
* *Marianne* (book musical with new music)
* *The Rose Masque* (book musical; revival of and revised version of *Die Fledermaus*)

* *Stovepipe Hat* (book musical with new music)
* *Vincent Youmans' "Fiesta"* (revue)
* *The Waltz King* (book musical with preexisting music)

1944–1945

Take a Bow (revue)
Hats Off to Ice (ice revue)
Song of Norway (book musical with preexisting music)
Star Time (revue)
Bloomer Girl (book musical with new music)
The Merry Widow (book musical; revival)
Robin Hood (revival; book musical)
The Gypsy Baron (revival; book musical)
Sadie Thompson (book musical with new music)
Rhapsody (book musical with preexisting music)
Seven Lively Arts (revue)
Laffing Room Only (revue)
A Tropical Revue (return engagement)
Sing Out, Sweet Land! (book musical with mostly preexisting music)
On the Town (book musical with new music)
A Lady Says Yes (book musical with new music)
La vie Parisienne (revival; book musical; revised version of 1866 operetta)
Up in Central Park (book musical with new music)
The Firebrand of Florence (book musical with new music)
Carousel (book musical with new music)
Carmen Jones (return engagement)
Blue Holiday (revue)
Memphis Bound (book musical with preexisting music)
Hollywood Pinafore (book musical with preexisting music)
* *Alaskan Stampede* (ice revue)
* *Glad to See You* (book musical with new music)
* *Watch Out, Angel!* (book musical with new music)

1945–1946

Concert Varieties (revue)
Marinka (book musical with new music)
Mr. Strauss Goes to Boston (book musical with mostly new music)
Carib Song (book musical with new music)
Polonaise (book musical with mostly preexisting music)
The Gypsy Baron (revival; book musical)
The Red Mill (revival; book musical)
The Girl from Nantucket (book musical with new music)
Are You With It? (book musical with new music)
The Day before Spring (book musical with new music)
Billion Dollar Baby (book musical with new music)
Show Boat (revival; book musical)
The Desert Song (revival; book musical)
Nellie Bly (book musical with new music)
Lute Song (play with incidental songs)
The Duchess Misbehaves (book musical with new music)
Three to Make Ready (revue)
St. Louis Woman (book musical with new music)
Carmen Jones (return engagement)

Annie Get Your Gun (book musical with new music)
Call Me Mister (revue)
Around the World in Eighty Days (book musical with new music)
* *Love in the Snow* (book musical with new music)
* *The Passing Show* (revue)
* *Shootin' Star* (book musical with new music)
* *Song without Words* (book musical with preexisting music)
* *Spring in Brazil* (book musical with new music)
* *Windy City* (book musical with new music)

1946–1947
Icetime (ice revue)
Tidbits of 1946 (revue)
Yours Is My Heart (import; book musical)
A Flag Is Born (play with incidental songs)
Gypsy Lady (book musical with preexisting music)
Park Avenue (book musical with new music)
Bal nègre (revue)
If the Shoe Fits (book musical with new music)
Toplitzky of Notre Dame (book musical with new music)
Beggar's Holiday (book musical with new music)
Bloomer Girl (return engagement)
Street Scene (book musical with new music)
Finian's Rainbow (book musical with new music)
Sweethearts (revival; book musical)
Maurice Chevalier—Songs and Impressions (personality revue)
The Chocolate Soldier (revival; book musical)
Brigadoon (book musical with new music)
Barefoot Boy with Cheek (book musical with new music)
Alice in Wonderland (revival; play with incidental songs)
The Telephone and *The Medium* (new operas)
Up in Central Park (return engagement)
Icetime of 1948 (ice revue)
Barbara (revue)
* *Everything's on Ice* (ice revue)
* *In Gay New Orleans* (book musical with new music)
* *Sweet Bye and Bye* (book musical with new music)

1947–1948
Louisiana Lady (book musical with new music)
Music in My Heart (book musical with preexisting music)
Under the Counter (import; play with incidental songs)
High Button Shoes (book musical with new music)
Allegro (book musical with new music)
Edith Piaf and Her Continental Entertainers (personality revue)
Caribbean Carnival (revue)
Angel in the Wings (revue)
The Cradle Will Rock (revival; book musical)
Make Mine Manhattan (revue)
Look, Ma, I'm Dancin'! (book musical with new music)
Tonight at 8:30 (revival; includes two double bills, each with three short one-act plays, some with incidental
    songs)
Maurice Chevalier in an Evening of Songs and Impressions (personality revue)

Holiday on Broadway (personality revue)
Inside U.S.A. (revue)
Hold It! (book musical with new music)
Sally (revival; book musical)
Ballet Ballads (three short one-act book musicals with new music: *Susanna and the Elders; Willie the Weeper;* and *The Eccentricities of Davey Crockett [as told by himself]*)
* *Alley Moon* (book musical with new music)
* *Bonanza Bound!* (book musical with new music)
* *Laffacade* (revue)
* *Paris Sings Again* (personality revue)
* *The Shape of Things!* (revue)
* *Spike Jones and His Musical Depreciation Revue* (personality revue)

1948–1949

Sleepy Hollow (book musical with new music)
Howdy, Mr. Ice (ice revue)
Show Boat (return engagement)
Morey Amsterdam's Hilarities (personality revue)
Small Wonder (revue)
Heaven on Earth (book musical with new music)
Magdalena (book musical with new music)
Love Life (book musical with new music)
Where's Charley? (book musical with new music)
My Romance (book musical with new music)
As the Girls Go (book musical with new music)
Lend an Ear (revue)
The Telephone and *The Medium* (return engagement)
The Rape of Lucretia (import; opera)
Kiss Me, Kate (book musical with new music)
Along Fifth Avenue (revue)
All for Love (revue)
Carousel (return engagement)
South Pacific (book musical with new music)
Howdy, Mr. Ice of 1950 (ice revue)
* *Ed Wynn's Laugh Carnival* (revue)
* *The Foolies of 1949* (revue)
* *Raze the Roof* (revue)
* *That's the Ticket* (book musical with new music)

1949

Funzapoppin (revue)
Cabalgata (import; revue)
Miss Liberty (book musical with new music)
Ken Murray's Blackouts of 1949 (revue)
Touch and Go (revue)
Lost in the Stars (book musical with new music)
Regina (new opera)
Texas, Li'l Darlin' (book musical with new music)
Gentlemen Prefer Blondes (book musical with new music)
* *A la Carte* (revue)
* *Pretty Penny* (revue)
* *Up to Now* (revue)

Appendix B: Chronology (by Classification)

Each of the following 273 productions is listed chronologically within its specific classification. For more information, see appendix A, "Chronology (by Season)" as well as the specific entry for a particular production.

Some productions were revived one or more times during the decade, and so their titles are followed by the particular year in which they were produced.

A musical's classification status can sometimes be ambiguous. It's clear that *Oklahoma!* is a "book musical with new music" and that *Song of Norway* is a "book musical with preexisting music." However, *Rosalinda* is a revival of *Die Fledermaus* with a revised book, lyrics, and even musical score; while it could technically be considered a book musical with preexisting music, for the purposes of this book its revival status trumps any other classification category. On the other hand, while *Carmen Jones* is based on *Carmen* and *Once Over Lightly* on *The Barber of Seville*, these are radically revised productions that are less out-and-out revivals than they are book musicals with preexisting music. And the 1943 production of *The Time, the Place and the Girl* is technically a revival because the basic plot of the book remains the same as the original 1906 production, and the overture utilizes music from the original; but the songs performed during the show were written especially for the revival. For the purposes of this book, the production is classified as a revival, but with the caveat that with the exception of the book and the overture, all the musical numbers are new.

BOOK MUSICALS WITH NEW MUSIC (80)
The following book musicals offered new lyrics and music.

John Henry
Higher and Higher
Louisiana Purchase
Walk with Music
Hold on to Your Hats
Cabin in the Sky
Panama Hattie
Pal Joey
Night of Love
Lady in the Dark
Best Foot Forward
Viva O'Brien
Let's Face It!
High Kickers
Sunny River
Banjo Eyes
The Lady Comes Across
By Jupiter

Count Me In
Beat the Band
You'll See Stars
Something for the Boys
Oklahoma!
Early to Bed
My Dear Public
Hairpin Harmony
One Touch of Venus
What's Up
Jackpot
Mexican Hayride
Follow the Girls
Allah Be Praised!
Bloomer Girl
Sadie Thompson
On the Town
A Lady Says Yes

Up in Central Park
The Firebrand of Florence
Carousel
Marinka
Mr. Strauss Goes to Boston
Carib Song
The Girl from Nantucket
Are You With It?
The Day before Spring
Billion Dollar Baby
Nellie Bly
The Duchess Misbehaves
St. Louis Woman
Annie Get Your Gun
Around the World in Eighty Days
Park Avenue
If the Shoe Fits
Toplitzky of Notre Dame
Beggar's Holiday
Street Scene
Finian's Rainbow
Brigadoon

Barefoot Boy with Cheek
Louisiana Lady
High Button Shoes
Allegro
Look, Ma, I'm Dancin'!
Hold It!
Ballet Ballads (Susanna and the Elders; Willie the Weeper; and The Eccentricities of Davey Crockett [as told by himself])
Sleepy Hollow
Heaven on Earth
Magdalena
Love Life
Where's Charley?
My Romance
As the Girls Go
Kiss Me, Kate
South Pacific
Miss Liberty
Lost in the Stars
Texas, Li'l Darlin'
Gentlemen Prefer Blondes

BOOK MUSICALS WITH PREEXISTING MUSIC (12)

The following musicals had new books, with scores drawn from mostly preexisting music (many of these were not revivals *per se* because their new books were radical departures from the original libretti).

Once Over Lightly (Gioachino Rossini)
Carmen Jones (Georges Bizet)
Helen Goes to Troy (Jacques Offenbach)
Dream with Music (Various classical composers)
Song of Norway (Edvard Grieg)
Rhapsody (Fritz Kreisler)

Sing Out, Sweet Land! (Various composers)
Memphis Bound (Arthur Sullivan)
Hollywood Pinafore (Arthur Sullivan)
Polonaise (Fredric Chopin)
Gypsy Lady (Victor Herbert)
Music in My Heart (Peter Ilyich Tschiakovsky)

OPERAS (3)

The Telephone
The Medium

Regina

PLAYS WITH INCIDENTAL SONGS (7)

This list includes plays that utilized songs and incidental music.

Russian Bank
Liberty Jones
Johnny 2 x 4
Oy is dus a leben!

Winged Victory
Lute Song
A Flag Is Born

REVUES (57)
The following revues were mostly traditional in nature (and thus included sketches, songs, and dances).

Earl Carroll Vanities
Two for the Show
Reunion in New York
Theatre of the Piccoli
American Jubilee
Keep Off the Grass
Gay New Orleans
Sim Sala Bim
Boys and Girls Together
'Tis of Thee
Meet the People
All in Fun
Crazy with the Heat
Sons o' Fun
Of "V" We Sing
Priorities of 1942
Keep 'Em Laughing
Harlem Cavalcade
Top-Notchers
Laugh, Town, Laugh
Star and Garter
This Is the Army
New Priorities of 1943
Show Time
Wine Women and Song
Let Freedom Sing
New Faces of 1943
For Your Pleasure
Ziegfeld Follies

Chauve-souris of 1943
Laugh Time
Bright Lights of 1944
A Tropical Revue (1943)
Artists and Models
Tars and Spars
Take a Bow
Star Time
Seven Lively Arts
Laffing Room Only
Blue Holiday
Concert Varieties
Three to Make Ready
Call Me Mister
Tidbits of 1946
Bal nègre
Barbara
Caribbean Carnival
Angel in the Wings
Make Mine Manhattan
Inside U.S.A.
Small Wonder
Lend an Ear
Along Fifth Avenue
All for Love
Funzapoppin
Ken Murray's Blackouts of 1949
Touch and Go

PERSONALITY REVUES (6)
The above-listed revues were traditional in nature and included sketches, songs, and dances. Their casts included such well-known names as Ray Bolger, Jack Haley, Bert Lahr, and Beatrice Lillie, but the revues weren't so star-driven they couldn't have been performed by other entertainers.

   The personality revues listed below are more in the nature of concert-like personal appearances by Maurice Chevalier, Billie Holiday, Edith Piaf, and Jimmy Savo. In some instances, other performers were on the bills, but it's clear the productions were designed to showcase the special skills and talents of specific entertainers.

Mum's the Word (Jimmy Savo)
Maurice Chevalier—Songs and Impressions
Edith Piaf and Her Continental Entertainers
Maurice Chevalier in an Evening of Songs and Impressions

Holiday on Broadway (Billie Holiday)
Morey Amsterdam's Hilarities

ICE REVUES (7)

It Happens on Ice (includes two editions)
Stars on Ice (includes two editions)
Hats Off to Ice
Icetime

Icetime of 1948
Howdy, Mr. Ice
Howdy, Mr. Ice of 1950

IMPORTS (4)

Yours Is My Heart (book musical)
Under the Counter (play with incidental songs)

The Rape of Lucretia (opera)
Cabalgata (revue)

REVIVALS (29)

La vie Parisienne (1941) (book musical; revised version of 1866 operetta)
Porgy and Bess (1942) (book musical)
The Chocolate Soldier (1942) (book musical)
The Merry Widow (1942) (book musical)
The New Moon (1942) (book musical)
The Time, the Place and the Girl (book musical)
Rosalinda (book musical; revised version of *Die Fledermaus*)
La vie Parisienne (1942) (book musical; revised version of 1866 operetta)
The Student Prince (book musical)
The Vagabond King (book musical)
The Merry Widow (1943) (book musical)
Run Little Chillun (book musical)
Blossom Time (book musical)
A Connecticut Yankee (book musical)
The New Moon (1944) (book musical)

The Merry Widow (1944) (book musical)
Robin Hood (book musical)
The Gypsy Baron (1944) (book musical; revised version of 1885 operetta)
La vie Parisienne (1945) (book musical; revised version of 1866 operetta)
The Gypsy Baron (1945) (book musical; revised version of 1885 operetta)
The Red Mill (book musical)
Show Boat (book musical)
The Desert Song (book musical)
Sweethearts (book musical)
The Chocolate Soldier (1947) (book musical)
Alice in Wonderland (play with incidental songs)
The Cradle Will Rock (book musical)
Tonight at 8:30 (six short one-act plays on two bills, some with incidental songs)
Sally (book musical)

RETURN ENGAGEMENTS (12)

In contrast to a revival, a return engagement is usually a limited booking of a musical's touring company. Because the run isn't open-ended, the Broadway engagement is usually another stop of the road tour, most often at the beginning or the end of the tour.

Lady in the Dark (1943)
Porgy and Bess (1943)
Porgy and Bess (1944, in two slightly separated runs)
A Tropical Revue (1944)
Carmen Jones (1945)
Carmen Jones (1946)

Bloomer Girl (1946)
Up in Central Park (1947)
Show Boat (1948)
The Telephone and *The Medium* (1948)
Carousel (1949)

PRE-BROADWAY CLOSINGS (56)

Tropical Pinafore (book musical with preexisting music [Arthur Sullivan])

The White Plume (aka *A Vagabond Hero*) (book musical with new music)

La belle Helene (revival; book musical; revised version of 1865 operetta [Jacques Offenbach])

Hi Ya, Gentlemen (book musical with new music)

Hot from Harlem (revue)

The Little Dog Laughed (book musical with new music)

Rhapsody in Black (revue)

She Had to Say Yes (book musical with new music)

Two Weeks with Pay (revue)

American Sideshow (revue)

Dansation (revue)

Jump for Joy (revue)

Patricia (book musical with new music)

They Can't Get You Down (book musical with new music)

Adamant Eve (play with incidental songs)

Cocktails at 5 (book musical with new music)

Dancing in the Streets (book musical with new music)

The Firefly (revival; book musical)

Full Speed Ahead (book musical with new music)

Headliners of '42 (revue)

Life of the Party (book musical with new music)

Merry-Go-Rounders (aka *The Merrymakers*) (revue)

Sugar 'n' Spice (revue)

Big Time (revue)

Curtain Time (revue)

Marching with Johnny (revue)

Marianne (book musical with new music)

The Rose Masque (book musical; revival and revised version of *Die Fledermaus* [Johann Strauss])

Stovepipe Hat (book musical with new music)

Vincent Youmans' "Fiesta" (revue)

The Waltz King (book musical with preexisting music [Johann Strauss])

Alaskan Stampede (ice revue)

Glad to See You (book musical with new music)

Watch Out, Angel! (book musical with new music)

Love in the Snow (book musical with new music)

The Passing Show (revue)

Shootin' Star (book musical with new music)

Song without Words (book musical with preexisting music [Peter Ilyich Tschiakowsky])

Spring in Brazil (book musical with new music)

Windy City (book musical with new music)

Everything's on Ice (ice revue)

In Gay New Orleans (book musical with new music)

Sweet Bye and Bye (book musical with new music)

Alley Moon (book musical with new music)

Bonanza Bound! (book musical with new music)

Laffacade (revue)

Paris Sings Again (personality revue [Josephine Baker])

The Shape of Things! (revue)

Spike Jones and His Musical Depreciation Revue (personality revue)

Ed Wynn's Laugh Carnival (revue)

The Foolies of 1949 (revue)

Raze the Roof (revue)

That's the Ticket (book musical with new music)

A la Carte (revue)

Pretty Penny (revue)

Up to Now (revue)

Appendix C: Discography

The following two lists are of cast recordings, studio cast recordings, or recordings that were released in song collections or in pop (or "cover") versions for the musicals discussed in this book. The first list represents those musicals that were first produced in the 1940s, and the second reflects those that were produced prior to 1940 but were revived during the decade.

For specific information about these recordings, see entries for particular shows. The criterion for inclusion in these lists is that the recordings were officially on sale to the public at one time or another.

Of the eighty new book musicals to premiere on Broadway during the decade, most were recorded in one way or another via cast albums, studio cast albums, album collections, and commercial (or cover) recordings, such as Bing Crosby's "Just My Luck" from *Nellie Bly*. But twelve book musicals seem to have gone unrecorded (although there may have been contemporary commercial recordings from some of them): *John Henry*, *Night of Love*, *Viva O'Brien*, *High Kickers*, *Count Me In*, *You'll See Stars*, *My Dear Public*, *Hairpin Harmony*, *A Lady Says Yes*, *The Duchess Misbehaves*, *Sleepy Hollow*, and *Heaven on Earth*. A thirteenth musical, *My Romance*, may have been privately recorded (for more information, see entry for the production).

RECORDINGS OF MUSICALS THAT FIRST OPENED IN THE 1940S

Allah Be Praised!
Allegro
All for Love
All in Fun
Along Fifth Avenue
American Jubilee
Angel in the Wings
Annie Get Your Gun
Are You With It?
Around the World in Eighty Days
As the Girls Go
Ballet Ballads
Banjo Eyes
Barefoot Boy with Cheek
Beat the Band
Beggar's Holiday
Best Foot Forward
Billion Dollar Baby
Bloomer Girl
Bonanza Bound!
Boys and Girls Together

Brigadoon
By Jupiter
Cabin in the Sky
Call Me Mister
Carib Song
Carmen Jones
Carousel
Dancing in the Streets
The Day before Spring
Dream with Music
Early to Bed
Finian's Rainbow
The Firebrand of Florence
Follow the Girls
Gentlemen Prefer Blondes
The Girl from Nantucket
Glad to See You
High Button Shoes
Higher and Higher
Hold on to Your Hats
Hollywood Pinafore

If the Shoe Fits

Inside U.S.A.

Jackpot

Jump for Joy

Keep Off the Grass

Kiss Me, Kate

The Lady Comes Across

Lady in the Dark

Lend an Ear

Let Freedom Sing

Let's Face It!

The Little Dog Laughed

Look, Ma, I'm Dancin'!

Lost in the Stars

Louisiana Purchase

Love Life

Lute Song

Magdalena

Make Mine Manhattan

Marching with Johnny

Marinka

The Medium

Meet the People

Mexican Hayride

Miss Liberty

Mr. Strauss Goes to Boston

Nellie Bly

Oklahoma!

One Touch of Venus

On the Town

Pal Joey

Panama Hattie

Park Avenue

Polonaise

Pretty Penny

The Rape of Lucretia

Regina

Sadie Thompson

Seven Lively Arts

The Shape of Things!

Sing Out, Sweet Land!

Small Wonder

Something for the Boys

Song of Norway

South Pacific

Spring in Brazil

Star and Garter

Stars on Ice

St. Louis Woman

Street Scene

Sunny River

Sweet Bye and Bye

The Telephone

Texas, Li'l Darlin'

That's the Ticket

They Can't Get You Down

This Is the Army

Three to Make Ready

Toplitzky of Notre Dame

Touch and Go

Two for the Show

Two Weeks with Pay

Up in Central Park

Walk with Music

What's Up

Where's Charley?

The White Plume (aka A Vagabond Hero)

Windy City

Winged Victory

Ziegfeld Follies

RECORDINGS OF MUSICALS PRODUCED IN THE 1940S BUT ORIGINALLY PRODUCED BEFORE 1940

Blossom Time

The Chocolate Soldier

A Connecticut Yankee

The Cradle Will Rock

The Desert Song

The Firefly

The Gypsy Baron

La belle Helene

La vie Parisienne

The Merry Widow

The New Moon

Porgy and Bess

The Red Mill

Robin Hood

Rosalinda (as Die Fledermaus)

Sally

Show Boat

The Student Prince

Sweethearts

Tonight at 8:30

The Vagabond King

Yours Is My Heart

Appendix D: Gilbert and Sullivan Operettas

The following is a chronological list of all operettas by W. S. Gilbert and Arthur Sullivan that were revived on Broadway during the period January 1, 1940, through December 31, 1949. Following each title is the opening date, number of performances, name of theatre, and name of producer.

Of the fourteen major works by Gilbert and Sullivan, the decade saw nine produced in New York: *The Gondoliers*, or *The King of Barataria*; *The Mikado*, or *The Town of Titipu*; *Trial by Jury*; *The Pirates of Penzance*, or *Love and Duty*; *H.M.S. Pinafore*, or *The Lass That Loved a Sailor*; *Iolanthe*, or *The Peer and the Peri*; *Patience*, or *Bunthorne's Bride*; *Ruddigore*, or *The Witch's Curse*; and *The Yeomen of the Guard*, or *The Merryman and His Maid*.

The Gondoliers (September 30, 1940; 7 performances; 44th Street Theatre; The Lyric Opera Company [LOC], Joseph S. Daltry and Herman Levin)

The Mikado (October 3, 1940; 11 performances; 44th Street Theatre; LOC)

Trial by Jury (October 7, 1940; 6 performances; 44th Street Theatre; LOC)

The Pirates of Penzance (October 7, 1940; 6 performances; 44th Street Theatre; LOC)

H.M.S. Pinafore (January 21, 1942; 18 performances; St. James Theatre; Boston Comic Opera Company [BCOC])

The Mikado (February 3, 1942; 19 performances; St. James Theatre; BCOC)

The Pirates of Penzance (February 17, 1942; 11 performances; St. James Theatre; BCOC)

Iolanthe (February 23, 1942; 5 performances; St. James Theatre; BCOC)

Trial by Jury (February 28, 1942; 7 performances; St. James Theatre; BCOC)

The Gondoliers (March 3, 1942; 3 performances; St. James Theatre; BCOC)

The Mikado (February 11, 1944; 6 performances; Ambassador Theatre; The Gilbert and Sullivan Opera Company [GSOC]; R. H. Burnside, Director)

Trial by Jury (February 14, 1944; 7 performances; Ambassador Theatre; GSOC)

H.M.S. Pinafore (February 14, 1944; 7 performances; Ambassador Theatre; GSOC)

The Pirates of Penzance (February 17, 1944; 8 performances; Ambassador Theatre; GSOC)

The Gondoliers (February 21, 1944; 4 performances; Ambassador Theatre; GSOC)

Iolanthe (February 22, 1944; 6 performances; Ambassador Theatre; GSOC)

Patience (February 25, 1944; 4 performances; Ambassador Theatre; GSOC)

Ruddigore (March 2, 1944; 3 performances; Ambassador Theatre; GSOC)

Yeomen of the Guard (March 3, 1944; 1 performance; Ambassador Theatre; GSOC)

The Mikado (December 29, 1947; 40 performances; Century Theatre; D'Oyly Carte Opera Company [DCOC])

Trial by Jury (January 5, 1948; 16 performances; Century Theatre; DCOC)

The Pirates of Penzance (January 5, 1948; 16 performances; Century Theatre; DCOC)

Iolanthe (January 12, 1948; 16 performances; Century Theatre; DCOC)

H.M.S. Pinafore (January 19, 1948; 16 performances; Century Theater; DCOC)

The Gondoliers (January 26, 1948; 16 performances; Century Theatre; DCOC)

The Yeomen of the Guard (February 2, 1948; 16 performances; Century Theatre; DCOC)

Patience (February 9, 1948; 16 performances; Century Theatre; DCOC)

The Mikado (October 4, 1949; 7 performances; Mark Hellinger Theatre; S. M. Chartock, Producer)

The Pirates of Penzance (October 10, 1949; 8 performances; Mark Hellinger Theatre; Chartock)

Trial by Jury (October 17, 1949; 8 performances; Mark Hellinger Theatre; Chartock)

H.M.S. Pinafore (October 17, 1949; 8 performances; Mark Hellinger Theatre; Chartock)

Appendix E: Filmography

The following are two lists of film, television, video, and radio versions of musicals discussed in this book. The first list represents those musicals that were first produced in the 1940s, and the second reflects musicals that were originally produced prior to 1940 but were revived during the decade. In some cases, a musical was the subject of a television show that included excerpts from the musical and interviews with cast members. For more information about a specific film, television, video, or radio version, see entry for specific musical.

FILM VERSIONS OF MUSICALS THAT OPENED IN THE 1940S

Annie Get Your Gun
Are You With It?
Beat the Band
Best Foot Forward
Bloomer Girl
Brigadoon
Cabin in the Sky
Call Me Mister
Carmen Jones
Carousel
Finian's Rainbow
Funzapoppin
Gentlemen Prefer Blondes
High Button Shoes
Higher and Higher
Howdy, Mr. Ice of 1950
Kiss Me, Kate
Lady in the Dark
Lend an Ear
Let's Face It!
Look, Ma, I'm Dancin'!
Lost in the Stars
Louisiana Purchase
Magdalena

Make Mine Manhattan (As "Fountain Pen Sketch," the sketch "Full Fathom Five" was included in the film *Always Leave Them Laughing*)
The Medium
Meet the People
Mexican Hayride
Oklahoma!
One Touch of Venus
On the Town
Pal Joey
Panama Hattie
The Rape of Lucretia
Regina
Something for the Boys
Song of Norway
South Pacific
Street Scene
Tars and Spars
The Telephone
Texas, Li'l Darlin'
This Is the Army
Up in Central Park
Where's Charley?
Winged Victory

FILM VERSIONS OF MUSICALS THAT WERE REVIVED DURING THE 1940S

The Chocolate Soldier
A Connecticut Yankee
The Cradle Will Rock
The Desert Song
The Firefly
La belle Helene
La vie Parisienne
The Merry Widow
The New Moon

Porgy and Bess
The Red Mill
Sally
Show Boat
The Student Prince
Tonight at 8:30
The Vagabond King
Yours Is My Heart

Appendix F: Other Productions

The following selected productions played in New York (or closed during their pre-Broadway tryouts) during the 1940s and in one way or another utilized music via songs, dances, or background music.

1939–1940
Mamba's Daughters by Dorothy and DuBose Heyward (Broadway Theatre; March 23, 1940; 17 performances)

Mamba's Daughters had originally opened at the Empire Theatre on January 3, 1939, for 162 performances; the production starred Ethel Waters and included the song "Lonesome Walls" (lyric by DuBose Heyward and music by Jerome Kern). The revival also starred Waters, and like the original production the song was heard over a radio broadcast as part of the play (and was sung by Anne Brown, who created the role of Bess in the original 1935 production of *Porgy and Bess* and reprised that role for the 1942 revival); it seems likely that Waters also sang the number in both the original and revival productions of *Mamba's Daughters*. The script of the play was published in hardback by Farrar & Rinehart in 1939. For the revue **Blue Holiday**, Waters reprised a sequence from *Mamba's Daughters*.

1940–1941
The Time of Your Life by William Saroyan (Guild Theatre; September 23, 1940; 32 performances)

William Saroyan's drama *The Time of Your Life* originally opened at the Booth Theatre on October 25, 1939, for 185 performances and won the Pulitzer Prize for drama (an award that Saroyan declined). Gene Kelly appeared in the production, and created the incidental choreography, which he re-created for the revival.

The play was filmed in 1948, and there were television versions in 1958 and 1976. Besides the current revival, there have been three other Broadway revivals (1955, 1969, and 1975) as well as an Off-Broadway production in 1985.

Incidentally, Saroyan wrote the lyric of "Come on-a My House," which was recorded by Rosemary Clooney in 1951 and became one of the era's hit songs (the music was by Ross Bagdasarian, Saroyan's cousin).

My Sister Eileen by Joseph A. Fields and Jerome Chodorov (Biltmore Theatre; December 26, 1940; 865 performances)

The comedy's famous conga sequence was choreographed by Paul Seymour; the comedy was adapted into two musicals, *Wonderful Town* (1953, Winter Garden Theater; lyrics by Betty Comden and Adolph Green, music by Leonard Bernstein) and the 1955 film musical *My Sister Eileen* (lyrics by Leo Robin, music by Jule Styne).

1941–1942
The Pirate by Ludwig Fulda, as adapted by S. N. Behrman (Martin Beck Theatre; November 25, 1942; 177 performances)

The incidental music was by Herbert Kingsley, and the dance sequences were choreographed by Felicia Sorel. In 1948, the play was adapted into the MGM film musical *The Pirate* (lyrics and music by Cole Porter).

1943–1944
South Pacific by Howard Rigsby and Dorothy Heyward (Cort Theatre; December 29, 1943; 5 performances)

The incidental music was by Paul Bowles.

Jacobowsky and the Colonel by Franz Werfel, as adapted by S. N. Behrman (Martin Beck Theatre; March 14, 1944; 417 performances)

The incidental music was by Paul Bowles. In 1979, the play was adapted as the musical *The Grand Tour* (lyrics and music by Jerry Herman).

The Maid as Mistress and *The Secret of Suzanne*

Giovanni Battista Pergolesi's 1733 opera *La serva patrona* (*The maid as mistress*) and Ermanno Wolf-Ferrari's 1909 opera *Il segreto di Susanna* (*The secret of Suzanne*) were revived on a double bill by the New Opera Company at the Alvin Theatre on May 14 and May 21, 1944, for two performances.

The cast members of the former included Melville Cooper, Ralph Dumke, and Virginia MacWatters; the direction was by Felix Brentano, the choreography by Joan Woodruff, and the musical direction by Isaac Van Grove. The action took place in Naples, Italy, during 1733.

The cast members of the latter opera were Hugh Thompson, Brenda Lewis, and Anne MacQuarrie; the direction was by Felix Brentano.

The lyrics and dialogue for both operas were adapted by Marion Farquhar.

1944–1945
Spook Scandals (President Theatre; December 8, 1944; limited engagement of two performances)

Best Plays reported that The Michael Todd Midnight Players (who were cast members of the currently running productions of *Catherine Was Great*, **Mexican Hayride**, and *Pick-Up Girl*) presented a limited two-performance engagement of this variety revue, which included three one-act plays along with comic and musical acts. The production was conceived and directed by Jerry Sylvon; original music was by Sergio De Karlo; and the choreography was by Paul Haakon, Marta Nita, and Paul Reyes. Among the cast members were Don de Leo, Gedda Petry, Al Henderson, Dean Myles, Mila Niemi, Eva Reyes, and Kendal Bryson.

Dark of the Moon ("A Legend with Music") by Howard Richardson and William Berney (46th Street Theatre; March 14, 1945; 320 performances)

The production included incidental songs and music by Walter Hendl, and the choreography was by Esther Junger; Hershy Kay was the musical director.

The Glass Menagerie by Tennessee Williams (Playhouse Theatre; March 31, 1945; 561 performances)

The incidental music was by Paul Bowles.

1945–1946
The Would-Be Gentleman by Moliere (aka Jean-Baptiste Poquelin), as adapted by Bobby Clark (Booth Theatre; January 9, 1946; 77 performances)

Bobby Clark adapted and starred in Michael Todd's revival of Moliere's *Le bourgeois gentilhomme*. The music was adapted by Jerome Moross from the original score by Jean-Baptiste Lully, and the production also included music by Cosme McMoon. The incidental dances were staged and performed by Ruth Harrison and Alex Fisher, and the singers were Constance Brigham, Mary Godwin, and Lewis Pierce.

The revival marked the fourth of six collaborations between Todd and Clark: the others were *The Streets of New York* (1939); **Star and Garter** (1942); **Mexican Hayride** (1944); **As the Girls Go** (1948); and *Michael Todd's Peep Show* (1950). Clark starred in the first five productions and directed the sixth.

A Gift for the Bride by Andrew Solt and S. Bekeffi, as adapted by Rowland Leigh (opened at the Park Theatre, Youngstown, Ohio, December 1, 1945; closed at the Royal Alexandra Theatre, Toronto, Ontario, January 12, 1946)

The pre-Broadway closing included three songs with lyrics by Rowland Leigh and music by Jean Schwartz ("Charm," "All the Time," and "Home from Home") and one song with lyric and music by Jay Rogers ("See You in the Morning"). The three Leigh and Schwartz songs had previously been heard in **Cocktails at 5**.

Crescendo by Ramon Romero and Harriet Hinsdale (opened at the Bushnell Memorial Theatre, Hartford, Connecticut, January 18, 1946; closed at the Shubert Theatre, Philadelphia, Pennsylvania, February 16, 1946)

The murder mystery utilized music by Sigmund Romberg, Frederic Chopin, and Claude Debussy. As *Swan Song*, the play was revised by Ben Hecht and Charles MacArthur; it opened on Broadway at the Booth Theatre on May 15, 1946, for 158 performances and included "Dance of the Buffaloes" (music by Lou Cooper).

1946–1947
Hamlet by William Shakespeare, adapted by Maurice Evans (City Center; June 3, 1946; 16 performances)

This so-called "G.I version," was a shortened version of the play. The incidental music for the revival was by Roger Adams.

The Dancer by Milton Lewis and Julian Funt (Biltmore Theatre; June 5, 1946; 5 performances)

The mystery included incidental music by Paul Bowles.

Cyrano de Bergerac by Edmund Rostand, adapted by Brian Hooker (Alvin Theatre; October 8, 1946; 193 performances)

The incidental music for the revival was by Paul Bowles. (There have been at least sixteen musical adaptations of Rostand's classic; for more information, see ***The White Plume***, aka ***The Vagabond Hero***, which closed during its pre-Broadway engagement in the 1939–1940 season.)

The Duchess of Malfi by John Webster, as adapted by W. H. Auden (Ethel Barrymore Theatre; October 15, 1946; 38 performances)

The incidental music for the revival was by Benjamin Britten.

Happy Birthday by Anita Loos (Broadhurst Theatre; October 31, 1946; 564 performances)

This forgotten hit comedy starred Helen Hayes and included the song "I Haven't Got a Worry in the World" by Richard Rodgers and Oscar Hammerstein II, who produced the show. The production also included incidental music by Robert Russell Bennett.

Henry VIII by William Shakespeare (International Theatre; November 6, 1946; 40 performances)

The incidental music for the revival was by Lehman Engel.

John Gabriel Borkman by Henrik Ibsen, as adapted by Eva Le Gallienne (International Theatre; November 12, 1946; 21 performances)

The incidental music for the revival was by Lehman Engel.

Another Part of the Forest by Lillian Hellman (Fulton Theatre; November 20, 1946; 182 performances)

Lillian Hellman's prequel to *The Little Foxes* included incidental music by Marc Blitzstein.

Androcles and the Lion by George Bernard Shaw (International Theatre; December 19, 1946; 40 performances)

The incidental music for the revival was by Marc Blitzstein. A musical adaptation of the play was produced for television by NBC in 1967 with lyrics and music by Richard Rodgers.

Burlesque by George Manker Watters and Arthur Hopkins (Belasco Theatre; December 25, 1946; 439 performances)

The revival of the 1927 comedy outran the original's run of 372 performances; Bert Lahr starred in the current production, which was choreographed by Billy Holbrook and included various popular songs ("Rhapsody in Blue," "The Man I Love," "Hallelujah," "Hindustan," "Peggy O'Neal," "Hold That Tiger," "He's Got to Get Under, Get Out and Get Under," "Just Around the Corner," "Put Your Arms Around Me," "The Sheik of Araby," "There's Something About a Soldier," and "The Daughter of Rose O'Grady").

Lovely Me by Jacqueline Susann and Beatrice Cole (Adelphi Theatre; December 25, 1946; 37 performances)

The comedy included songs by Arthur Siegel and Jeff Bailey.

Yellow Jack by Sidney Howard in collaboration with Paul de Kruif (International Theatre; February 27, 1947; 21 performances)

The incidental music for the revival was by Lehman Engel.

Love for Love by William Congreve, as adapted by John Gielgud (Royale Theatre; May 26, 1947; 48 performances)

All the songs and incidental music for the revival were by Leslie Bridgewater (the lyrics for the songs "A Nymph and a Swain," "Cynthia," and "Charmion" were by William Congreve).

The Alchemist by Ben Jonson (City Center; May 6, 1948; 14 performances)

The incidental music for the revival was by Deems Taylor.

A Lady Passing Fair by Harry Wagstaff Gribble (opened at the Lyric Theatre, Bridgeport, Connecticut, January 3, 1947; closed at the Newark Opera House, Newark, New Jersey, January 11, 1947)

The production included "Sensemaya" (original lyric by Nicolas Guillen, English lyric by Ben Frederic Carruthers, music by Heitor Villa Lobos). The choreography was by Claude Marchand.

1947–1948
Our Lan' by Theodore Ward (Royale Theatre; September 27, 1947; 41 performances)

The production included the musical numbers "Hoe, Boy, Hoe" (lyric by Theodore Ward and music by Joshua Lee) and "Cotton Song" (according to the program, this song was "paraphrased from slave secular" by Ward and Lee). The choral direction and arrangements were by Lee.

Dear Judas by Robinson Jeffers, as adapted by Michael Myerberg (Mansfield Theatre; October 5, 1947; 17 performances)

The production included music by Johann Sebastian Bach, as arranged by Lehman Engel.

Galileo by Bertolt Brecht as adapted by Charles Laughton (Maxine Elliott's Theatre; December 7, 1947; 6 performances)

The lyrics were by Albert Brush and the music by Hans Eisler. The choreography was by Lotte Gosler, and was executed by Joan McCracken.

Me and Molly by Gertrude Berg (Belasco Theatre; February 26, 1948; 156 performances)

Music for the production was arranged by Lehman Engel.

A Temporary Island by Halsted Welles (Maxine Elliott's Theatre; March 14, 1948; 6 performances)

The original songs were by Lorenzo Fuller. Lehman Engel wrote the calliope music.

Macbeth by William Shakespeare (National Theatre; March 31, 1948; 29 performances)

Alan Bush wrote the music for the revival, and the production's musical director was Lehman Engel.

1948–1949
The Insect Comedy by Karel Capek, as adapted by Owen Davis (City Center; June 3, 1948; 16 performances)

The production's choreography was by Hanya Holm.

Summer and Smoke by Tennessee Williams (Music Box Theatre; October 6, 1948; 100 performances)

The incidental music for the production was by Paul Bowles.

Anne of the Thousand Days by Maxwell Anderson (Shubert Theatre; December 8, 1944; 286 performances)

The incidental music for the production was by Lehman Engel.

Death of a Salesman by Arthur Miller (Morosco Theatre; February 10, 1949; 742 performances)

The incidental music for the production was by Alex North; the score was released by Kritzerland (CD # KR-20012–1) on a pairing with Laurence Rosenthal's background music for the 1959 Broadway production *Rashomon*.

Exodus by Herbert Cobey and Abby Mann (Brighton Theatre, Brighton Beach, Brooklyn, New York; April 14–24, 1949)

The production included incidental songs (music by Lawrence Chaiken, with additional music by Joseph Rumshinsky and lyrics by Nick Kenny).

1949–1950
I Know My Love by Marcel Achard, as adapted by S. N. Behrman (Shubert Theatre; November 2, 1949; 246 performances)

Based on Archard's play *Aupres de ma blonde*, Behrman's adaptation included an untitled Christmas carol written by Stephen Sondheim, which was sung offstage (the program and the published script didn't credit Sondheim and didn't reference the song). The script was published in both hardback and paperback editions by Samuel French, in 1949; the first scene of the first act takes place on Christmas Day, and the stage directions indicate that Christmas carols are performed offstage ("outdoors"), including "Adeste Fideles." *I Know My Love* is the play Holden Caulfield saw in J. D. Salinger's *The Catcher in the Rye*.

Caesar and Cleopatra by George Bernard Shaw (National Theatre; December 21, 1949; 149 performances)

The incidental music for the revival was by Irma Jurist. In 1968, Shaw's play was adapted as the musical *Her First Roman* with lyrics and music by Ervin Drake.

Signor Chicago by Edward Chodorov (opened at the Shubert Theatre, New Haven, Connecticut, November 3, 1949; closed November 19, 1949, at the Locust Theater, Philadelphia, Pennsylvania)

The program noted that the play was "based on the Granville-Barker version of a play by the Quinteros." The incidental music was by Lehman Engel.

Note: During the decade, the following operas (along with one Off-Broadway musical comedy revival) had their New York premieres. In chronological order, they are: Marc Blitzstein's *No for an Answer* (1941), Benjamin Britten and W. H. Auden's *Paul Bunyan* (1941), Gian-Carlo Menotti's *The Island God* (1942), *Naughty-Naught '00* (1946 revival of 1937 musical), Norman Corwin and Bernard Rogers's *The Warrior* (1947), and Gertrude Stein, Maurice Grosser, and Virgil Thomson's *The Mother of Us All* (1947). These works are discussed in my reference book *Off-Broadway Musicals, 1910–2007: Casts, Credits, Songs, Critical Reception and Performance Data of More Than 1,800 Shows*.

Appendix G: Published Scripts

Following are two lists of published scripts for the musicals discussed in this book The first represents those musicals that were first produced in the 1940s, and the second gives those produced prior to 1940 but revived during the decade.

The criterion for these lists is that the scripts were officially on sale to the public at one time or another; entries in this book occasionally refer to unpublished scripts, and these aren't included in the appendix.

For more information about a script (such as publication date and publisher), see the entry for the specific musical.

SCRIPTS OF MUSICALS FIRST PRODUCED IN THE 1940S

Allegro
Annie Get Your Gun
Ballet Ballads
Barefoot Boy with Cheek
Best Foot Forward (published as nonmusical version)
Brigadoon
Carmen Jones
Carousel
Finian's Rainbow
High Button Shoes (published as nonmusical version)
John Henry
Kiss Me, Kate
La vie Parisienne
Lady in the Dark
Lend an Ear
Liberty Jones
Lost in the Stars
Lute Song

The Medium
Miss Liberty
Oklahoma!
One Touch of Venus
On the Town
Pal Joey
The Rape of Lucretia
Regina
St. Louis Woman
Sing Out, Sweet Land!
Song of Norway
South Pacific
Street Scene
The Telephone
Three to Make Ready (as *Three to One*)
Two for the Show (as *Three to One*)
Where's Charley?
Winged Victory

SCRIPTS OF MUSICALS PRODUCED PRIOR TO 1940 BUT REVIVED DURING THE 1940S

The Cradle Will Rock

The Desert Song

La vie Parisienne

The New Moon

Porgy and Bess

Show Boat

Tonight at 8:30

The Vagabond King

Appendix H: Theatres

For the productions in this book, the New York theatres where they played are listed in alphabetical order. Following the name of each theatre is a chronological list of the productions that played there (for those shows that had more than one production during the decade, the entry is identified by year).

Many productions transferred to other theatres, and entries are so noted. If a production transferred once, the notation "transfer" follows the name of the show; if a production transferred to more than one theatre, notations such as "first transfer" and "second transfer" are given.

Perhaps not surprisingly, the geographically desirable Shubert Theatre topped out with seventeen bookings. But it's noteworthy that the luckless Adelphi Theater (which had perhaps the most undesirable location of all the theatres and was the venue that William Gaxton once called "the dump of dumps") ran a close second, with sixteen musicals.

Adelphi Theatre

Allah Be Praised!
Robin Hood
On the Town
Carib Song
Polonaise (transfer)
The Girl from Nantucket
Nellie Bly
The Duchess Misbehaves
Three to Make Ready
Around the World in Eighty Days
A Flag Is Born (first transfer)
Street Scene
Music in My Heart
Look, Ma, I'm Dancin'!
Morey Amsterdam's Hilarities
My Romance (transfer)

Alvin Theatre

Lady in the Dark (1941)
Laugh, Town, Laugh
Once Over Lightly
Something for the Boys
Jackpot
Helen Goes to Troy

Sadie Thompson
The Firebrand of Florence
Hollywood Pinafore
Polonaise
Billion Dollar Baby
A Flag Is Born

Ambassador Theatre

Wine Women and Song
Blossom Time
Laugh Time (transfer)

Belasco Theatre

Blue Holiday
Memphis Bound (transfer)
Bal nègre

Belmont Theatre

Mum's the Word

Booth Theatre

Two for the Show

Broadhurst Theatre

Keep Off the Grass
Boys and Girls Together
High Kickers
Show Time
Early to Bed
Follow the Girls (second transfer)
Take a Bow
A Lady Says Yes
Three to Make Ready (transfer)
Make Mine Manhattan
Lend an Ear (first transfer)
Along Fifth Avenue
Touch and Go

Broadway Theatre

This Is the Army
La vie Parisienne (1942)
Lady in the Dark (1943)
The Student Prince
Artists and Models
Carmen Jones (1943)
Song of Norway (transfer)
Up in Central Park (transfer)
Memphis Bound
A Flag Is Born (third transfer)
Beggar's Holiday
High Button Shoes (second transfer)
The Cradle Will Rock (transfer)
As the Girls Go (transfer)
Cabalgata

Carnegie Hall

The Chocolate Soldier (1942)
The Merry Widow (1942)
The New Moon (1942)

Center Theatre

It Happens on Ice
Stars on Ice
Hats Off to Ice
Icetime
Icetime of 1948
Howdy, Mr. Ice
Howdy, Mr. Ice of 1950

City Center

Porgy and Bess (two engagements, both February 1944)
The New Moon (1944)

The Merry Widow (1944)
The Gypsy Baron (1944)
La vie Parisienne (1945)
Carmen Jones (1945)
The Gypsy Baron (1945)
The Desert Song (1946)
Carmen Jones (1946)
Bloomer Girl (1947)
Up in Central Park (1947)
Show Boat (1948)
The Telephone and *The Medium* (1948)
Carousel (1949)

Concert Theatre

Of "V" We Sing

Ethel Barrymore Theatre

Walk with Music
Pal Joey
Best Foot Forward
Count Me In
Marinka (transfer)
The Telephone and *The Medium*

Forrest Theatre (later renamed Coronet Theatre)

Bright Lights of 1944 (Forrest)
A Tropical Revue (1943; transfer) (Forrest)
Angel in the Wings (Coronet)
Small Wonder (Coronet)

44th Street Theatre

John Henry
Crazy with the Heat
La vie Parisienne (1941)
The Lady Comes Across
Keep 'Em Laughing
Top-Notchers
Rosalinda
Rosalinda (second transfer; the musical first opened at the 44th Street Theater, transferred to the Imperial, then returned to the 44th Street, and finally transferred to the 46th Street Theatre)
Porgy and Bess (1943)
Winged Victory
Follow the Girls (first transfer)
On the Town (first transfer)

46th Street Theatre

Panama Hattie
Sons o' Fun (transfer)

Priorities of 1942
New Priorities of 1943
Beat the Band
Rosalinda (third transfer)
My Dear Public
One Touch of Venus (transfer)
The Red Mill
Finian's Rainbow
Love Life
Regina

Henry Miller's Theatre

Maurice Chevalier—Songs and Impressions

Hollywood Theatre (later renamed Mark Hellinger Theatre)

Banjo Eyes (Hollywood)
All for Love (Mark Hellinger)
Texas, Li'l Darlin' (Mark Hellinger)

Hudson Theatre

Night of Love
Run Little Chillun

Imperial Theatre

Louisiana Purchase
Let's Face It!
Rosalinda (first transfer)
One Touch of Venus
Song of Norway
Annie Get Your Gun
Along Fifth Avenue (transfer)
Miss Liberty

International Theatre

Sing Out, Sweet Land!
Alice in Wonderland
Caribbean Carnival

John Golden Theatre

Maurice Chevalier in an Evening of Songs and Impressions

Little Theatre

Reunion in New York

Longacre Theatre

Johnny 2 x 4
Let Freedom Sing

Madison Square Garden

Funzapoppin

Majestic Theatre

Theatre of the Piccoli
All in Fun
Viva O'Brien
Porgy and Bess (1942)
The Merry Widow (1943)
Mexican Hayride (transfer)
Dream with Music
Star Time
Carousel (1945)
Call Me Mister
Alice in Wonderland (transfer)
Allegro
Inside U.S.A. (transfer)
Carousel (1949; transfer)
South Pacific

Mansfield Theatre

Meet the People
The Time, the Place and the Girl
For Your Pleasure
The Cradle Will Rock
Holiday on Broadway
Lend an Ear (third transfer)

Martin Beck Theatre

Cabin in the Sky
A Tropical Revue (1943)
A Connecticut Yankee
On the Town (second transfer)
St. Louis Woman
Barefoot Boy with Cheek
Sally

Maxine Elliott's Theatre

'Tis of Thee
You'll See Stars
Ballet Ballads

Molly Picon Theatre

Oy is dus a leben!

Morosco Theatre

Sim Sala Bim

Music Box Theatre

Star and Garter
A Flag Is Born (second transfer)
Lost in the Stars

National Theatre

Hairpin Harmony
What's Up
The Day before Spring
Call Me Mister
Tonight at 8:30
Hold It!
Lend an Ear

New Century Theatre

Follow the Girls
Rhapsody
A Tropical Revue (1944)
Up in Central Park
Mr. Strauss Goes to Boston
Are You With It?
Gypsy Lady
If the Shoe Fits
Toplitzky of Notre Dame
The Chocolate Soldier (1947)
Louisiana Lady
High Button Shoes
Inside U.S.A.
Heaven on Earth
Kiss Me, Kate

Playhouse Theatre

Edith Piaf and Her Continental Entertainers

Plymouth Theatre

Lute Song
Call Me Mister (second transfer)
Tidbits of 1946

Ritz Theatre

Harlem Cavalcade
New Faces of 1943

Royale Theatre

Chauve-souris of 1943

St. James Theatre

Earl Carroll Vanities
Russian Bank
Pal Joey (second transfer)
Sunny River
Oklahoma!
Sleepy Hollow
Where's Charley?

Shubert Theatre

Higher and Higher
Hold on to Your Hats
Pal Joey (first transfer)
Liberty Jones
By Jupiter
The Vagabond King
Laugh Time
Bloomer Girl (1944)
Are You With It?
Yours Is My Heart
Park Avenue
Sweethearts
Under the Counter
High Button Shoes (first transfer)
My Romance
Lend an Ear (second transfer)
Kiss Me, Kate (transfer)

Strand Theatre

Tars and Spars

Winter Garden Theatre

Sons o' Fun
Ziegfeld Follies
Mexican Hayride
Laffing Room Only
Marinka
As the Girls Go

Ziegfeld Theatre

Seven Lively Arts
Concert Varieties
The Red Mill
Show Boat (1946)
Brigadoon
Barbara
Magdalena
The Rape of Lucretia
Ken Murray's Blackouts of 1949
Gentlemen Prefer Blondes

Productions that played at the New York World's Fair:

American Jubilee
Gay New Orleans

Bibliography

For the productions discussed in this book, I used source materials such as programs, souvenir programs, flyers, window cards (posters), sheet music, published and unpublished scripts, and recordings. In addition, many reference books were helpful in providing both information and reality checks, and these are listed below.

Asch, Amy, ed. *The Complete Lyrics of Oscar Hammerstein II*. New York: Alfred A. Knopf, 2008.

The Best Plays. As of this writing, the most recent edition of the venerable series is *The Best Plays Theater Yearbook of 2007–2008* (Jeffrey Eric Jenkins, editor; New York: Limelight Editions, 2009).

Bloom, Ken. *American Song: The Complete Musical Theatre Companion, Second Edition*. New York: Schirmer Books, 1996.

Drew, David. *Kurt Weill: A Handbook*. Berkeley: University of California Press, 1987.

Duke, Vernon. *Passport to Paris*. Boston: Little, Brown and Company, 1955.

Fordin, Hugh. *The Movies' Greatest Musicals: Produced in Hollywood USA by the Freed Unit*. New York: Frederick Ungar, 1975.

Gordon, Eric A. *Mark the Music: The Life and Works of Marc Blitzstein*. New York: St. Martin's Press, 1989.

Green, Stanley, ed. *Rodgers and Hammerstein Fact Book: A Record of Their Works Together and with Other Collaborators*. New York: The Lynn Farnol Group, 1980.

Hart, Dorothy, and Robert Kimball, eds. *The Complete Lyrics of Lorenz Hart*. New York: Alfred A. Knopf, 1986.

Hughes, Elinor. *Passing Through to Broadway*. Boston: Waverly House, 1948.

Kimball, Robert, ed. *The Complete Lyrics of Cole Porter*. New York: Alfred A. Knopf, 1983.

———. *The Complete Lyrics of Frank Loesser*. New York: Alfred A. Knopf, 2003.

———. *The Complete Lyrics of Ira Gershwin*. New York: Alfred A. Knopf, 1993.

———. *The Complete Lyrics of Irving Berlin*. New York: Alfred A. Knopf, 2001.

Kimball, Robert, Barry Day, Miles Kreuger, and Eric Davis, eds. *The Complete Lyrics of Johnny Mercer*. New York: Alfred A. Knopf, 2009.

Leonard, William, ed. *Chicago Stagebill Yearbook 1947*. Chicago: Chicago Stagebill, 1947.

Leonard, William Torbert. *Broadway Bound: A Guide to Shows That Died Aborning*. Metuchen, NJ: The Scarecrow Press, 1983.

Nathan, George Jean. *The Theatre Book of the Year* (Volumes 1942–1943 through 1949–1950). New York, Alfred A. Knopf.

Norton, Richard C. *A Chronology of American Musical Theatre* (Three Volumes). New York: Oxford University Press, 2002.

Suskin, Stephen. *Show Tunes: The Songs, Shows, and Careers of Broadway's Major Composers* (revised and expanded third edition). New York: Oxford University Press, 2000.

———. *Opening Nights on Broadway: A Critical Quotebook of the Golden Era of the Musical Theater, "Oklahoma!" (1943) to "Fiddler on the Roof" (1964)*. New York: Schirmer Books, 1990.

Theatre World. As of this writing, the most recent edition of this important annual is *Theatre World, Volume 68, 2011–2012* (Ben Hodges and Scott Denny, editors; Milwaukee, WI: Theatre World Media, 2013).

Wlaschin, Ken. *Gian Carlo Menotti on Screen: Opera, Dance and Choral Works on Film, Television and Video*. Jefferson, NC: McFarland & Company, 1999.

Note: Virtually all the brief newspaper quotes in this book come from the annual series *New York Theatre Critics' Reviews*. Each volume includes the complete newspaper reviews of all plays and musicals (along with the names of the critics and their newspapers) to open on Broadway during a calendar year (for example, the 1943 volume includes reviews of all the shows that opened on Broadway during calendar year 1943, and not the traditional Broadway seasons of 1942–1943 or 1943–1944).

Index

A. C., 509
Aarons, Alex A., 69
Aarons, Ruth Hughes, 443
Abbott, Betty, 433
Abbott, Bud, 32, 211
Abbott, George, 20, 54, 77–78, 92, 103, 115, 139, 261, 309, 364, 383–84, 402, 419, 460, 501–2
Abravanel, Maurice, 63, 153, 192, 251, 271, 307, 369, 505, 507
Actman, Irving, 160, 163–64, 341, 377, 424, 443, 475
Adair, Ted, 69
Adair, Tom, 475
Adair, Yvonne, 467, 510
Adamant Eve, 159–60
Adams, Frank R., 142
Adams, Margret, 15
Adams, Stanley, 265
Adamson, Harold, 15, 69, 92, 151, 339, 464
Addinsell, Richard, 385–86
Addis, Jus, 123
Addison, Bernard, 505
Adler, Bruce, 156
Adler, Celia, 354
Adler, Charles, 102
Adler, Larry, 17
Adler, Luther, 354–55
Adler, Stella, 298
Adolphus, Theodore, 165, 375
Adrian, 488
Adrian, Henry, 303, 305
Agay, Denes, 464
Ahdar, David, 228
Ahern, Will, 166
Ahlert, Fred E., 39
Aikens, Vanoye, 360
A la Carte, 513–14
Alaskan Stampede, 284
Alba, Floriana, 495
Alba, Raoul, 73
Alberghetti, Anna Maria, 389
Albert, Eddie, 201, 497
Albert, Irving, 123

Albertini, Ellen R., 432
Albertson, Frank, 23, 52
Albertson, Jack, 51, 214, 265, 413, 516
Alden, Clare, 448
Aldrich, Alden, 508
Alexander, Alex, 176
Alexander, Carlos, 146
Alexander, Cris, 261–62
Alexander, Fay, 218
Alexander, James, 360
Alexander, Rod, 66, 202
Alfano, Franco, 27
Alice in Wonderland and Through the Looking Glass, 385–87
Alison, David, 286
Allah Be Praised!, 214–16
Allan, Lewis, 99
Alland, William, 344
Allegro, 404–8
Allen, Betty, 221
Allen, Don, 385
Allen, Earl, 123
Allen, Elizabeth, 469
Allen, Lewis, 134
Allen, Robert, 312
Allers, Franz, 380, 475
Allers, Stephan, 435
Alley Moon, 435–36
All for Love, 478–80
All in Fun, 57–59
Allison, Wana, 428, 515
Alloy, Al, 187, 197, 472
Allyn, Maria, 340
Allyn, William, 354
Allyson, June, 15, 49, 53, 78–79
Alma, Lyda, 408–9
Alma, Richard, 9
Along Fifth Avenue, 475–78
Alswang, Ralph, 450
Alton, Robert, 6, 12, 14, 46, 48, 54–55, 87, 113, 136–37, 157, 161, 171, 254
Alvarez, Anita, 59, 372, 374, 511

Alvers, Zinaida, 179
Alyn, Glen, 401
Amato, Pasquale, 27
Amaya, Carmen, 115–17
Amdurs, Sam, 261
Ameche, Don, 404
Amend, 142
American Jubilee, 15–17
American League for a Free Palestine, 354–55
American Negro Light Opera Association, 24
American Repertory Theatre, 385
American Revue Theatre, 109
American Sideshow, 108
American Viennese Group, Inc., 9
American Youth Theatre, 99–100
Ames, April, 225
Ames, Nancy, 474
Ammann, Lukas, 392
Ammons, Albert, 290
Amsterdam, Morey, 448–50
Anderson, Alan, 123
Anderson, Anne Renee, 467
Anderson, Arthur, 144
Anderson, Bette, 307
Anderson, Cecil, 409
Anderson, George, 123
Anderson, Georgia, 111
Anderson, Hilding, 397
Anderson, Ivy, 109–10
Anderson, John, 60, 62–63, 65, 78, 81, 83, 85, 89, 91, 93,
    95–96, 99, 101, 103–5, 114, 117, 120, 125, 130–31, 133,
    135, 137–38, 141, 143–44, 159, 170, 175
Anderson, John Murray, 6, 57, 90, 157, 254, 271, 324, 346,
    452
Anderson, Maxwell, 504–5
Anderson, Nancy, 474
Anderson (J. P.), Ltd., 401
Andes, Keith, 243, 378–79
Andreas, Christine, 156
Andreva, Stella, 353
Andrews, Edward, 303
Andrews, Herbert, 97, 134, 186
Andrews, Nancy, 501–2
Angel in the Wings, 411–13
Angelus, Muriel, 90
Angoletta, Bruno, 11
Annie Get Your Gun, 334–37
Anstey, F., 192
Anthony, Norman, 187
Anthony, Normand, 340
Antoine, Robert, 236
Antrum, Harry, 165
Apollon, Dave, 36, 38
Apus, 70
Arbuckle, Roscoe "Fatty," 303
Arcelus, Sebastian, 462
Archer, Cheryl, 456
Archer, Jeri, 312
Archer, John, 307

Archibald, William, 8, 59, 295
Ardelty, Elly, 456
Arden, Eve, 6, 8, 82–84, 195
Arden, Helen, 369
Arden, Neetza, 439
Arena Stars, 441
Are You With It?, 305–7
Argentinita, 102, 107
Arkuss, Albert, 189
Arlen, Harold, 118, 240, 242, 327–29, 368
Arlen, Jerry, 368
Armbruster, Richard, 484
Armin, Walter, 317
Armistead, Horace, 387, 389, 470, 505
Armstrong, Louis, 44
Arnette, Ray, 346
Arno, Sig, 238–39
Arnold, Ainswirth, 90
Arnold, Stanley, 449
Aronson, Boris, 42, 197, 246, 316, 356, 395, 456
Aronson, James, 215–16, 257, 269
Around the World in Eighty Days, 337–40
Arthur, Art, 428
Arthur, Helen, 163–64, 181
Arthur, Jack, 102
Arthur, Jean, 138
Arthur, Robert, 212
Arthur, Zinn, 123
Artists and Models, 195–97
Ashley, Barbara, 433
Ashley, Clayton, 265
Askam, Perry, 163
Askey, Arthur, 214
Asner, Edward, 205
Asquith, Ruby, 226
Astaire, Fred, 342, 369, 374, 428
As the Girls Go, 464–66
Atkins, Arthur, 123
Atkins, Cholly, 511
Atkins, Norman, 371
Atkins, Van, 146
Atkins, Zoe, 31
Atkinson, Betty, 41–42
Atkinson, Brooks, 2–3, 5, 7, 10–12, 14, 17, 19, 21, 23, 30,
    35–36, 38, 41, 43–44, 46, 48, 50, 55, 58–60, 62, 64–65,
    67, 79, 81, 83, 85, 89, 91, 93, 95–96, 99–100, 102–3, 105,
    129–33, 137, 139–41, 143, 163, 200, 353, 355, 357, 359,
    363, 365, 371, 373, 376, 379, 381, 384, 386, 388, 398,
    400–401, 404, 408, 410–12, 415, 417, 420, 423, 427,
    430–31, 434, 444, 448–49, 451, 453, 456, 458, 460, 463,
    465, 468–69, 473–74, 477, 480, 483, 494, 498, 500–501,
    503, 505, 507, 509, 511
Atkinson, David, 277, 336, 382, 415, 474
Atkinson, Leo, 500
Attles, Joseph, 1, 3, 68
Aubry, Blanche, 392
Auden, W. H., 2, 472
Audre, 324
Auer, John H., 141, 332

Auer, Mischa, 66, 95–96
Auerbach, Arnold, 331, 425
Auerbach, Boris, 138
Augustine, Stephanie, 65–66
Aul, Ronnie, 360
Aurthur, Robert Alan, 303
Austen, Gerald, 449
Austen, Patti, 505
Avery, Phyllis, 202
Avory, Don, 91
Awan, Adrian, 230, 301, 356
Axelrod, George, 450–51
Ayers, Catherine, 97, 186
Ayers, Christine, 265, 346
Ayers, Lemuel, 154–55, 236, 240, 327, 368, 425, 472, 475

Babbs, Dorothy, 467
Babe, Thomas, 459
Bacall, Betty, 104
Bache, Theodore, 352
Bachelor, Stephanie, 159
Bachenheimer, Theodore, 230, 344
Bachman, Monroe, 344
Bacior, Charles, 123
Baclanova, Olga, 398
Bacon, Glen, 57
Bacon, Lloyd, 333
Baer, Max, 70
Bagar, Robert, 352, 365, 471–72
Bagley, Eleanor, 418, 439
Bailey, Buster, 505
Bailey, Pearl, 98, 207, 327–28
Baird, John, 340
Baker, Belle, 167
Baker, Benny, 209
Baker, Herbert, 216
Baker, Josephine, 438–39
Baker, Kenny, 192
Baker, Nathan, 337
Baker, Phil, 101–2, 488
Balaban, Emanuel, 387, 470
Balanchine, George, 17, 21–22, 42, 44, 94, 143–44, 176–77, 197, 220, 236, 238, 243, 293, 378, 460
Baldwin, Kate, 375
Balieff, Nikita, 180
Balin, Edmund, 195
Ball, Lucille, 53, 79, 93
Ballard, Bob, 349
Ballard, Florence, 349
Ballard, Kaye, 503
Ballard, Lucinda, 12, 15, 30, 120, 184, 227, 258, 280, 312, 314, 334, 369, 372, 378, 380, 405, 448, 456
Ballard, Roy, 267
Ballero, Marc, 218
Ballet Ballads, 432–35
Ballet Society, 387, 470
Bal Nègre, 360–61
Balsam, Martin, 205
Balzer, George, 305

Bamert, Herta, 392
Bane, Paula, 331–32
Bang, Charles, 508
Banjo Eyes, 91–94
Bank, Xenia, 243
Banke, Herbert, 156
Bankhead, Tallulah, 248, 362
Banks, Leslie, 504
Banner, Jimmy, 73
Bannister, Georgiana, 179
Banton, Travis, 284
Baragrey, John, 354
Barbara, 392–93
Barbier, Henri Auguste, 274
Barclift, Nelson, 123, 337
Barefoot Boy with Cheek, 383–85
Barker, Albert, 280
Barnes, Charles, 101
Barnes, Howard, 130–31, 135, 137, 141, 143–44, 149, 151–52, 155, 159, 170, 173, 175, 178–79, 181, 189, 192, 194, 197–98, 201, 205, 207, 211, 213, 217, 222, 234, 238, 240, 242, 245, 247–48, 251, 253, 257, 260, 263, 266, 272–73, 280–81, 290, 292, 294–97, 299–300, 305, 309, 314, 319, 321, 323, 326, 328–29, 332, 335, 338, 351–53, 355, 357, 362, 365, 374, 376, 379, 381, 384, 387, 398, 400–401, 403, 408, 412, 415, 418, 423, 427, 430–31, 444–45, 450, 453–54, 456, 458, 461, 463, 468–69, 474, 478, 480, 483, 498, 501, 503, 505, 507, 509, 511
Barnes, Johnny, 411, 516
Barnett, Jack, 366
Baron, Al, 36
Baronova, Irina, 212
Barr, Kenn, 224, 342, 366, 515
Barratt, Watson, 25, 29, 31, 59, 157, 169, 181, 195, 265, 341, 393, 397, 462
Barrett, Betty, 254, 331
Barrett, Brent, 474
Barrett, Lorin, 433
Barrett, Sondra, 54, 197
Barrie, Gracie, 61
Barrie, Lee, 99
Barry, Elaine, 138
Barry, Fred, 138
Barry, Gene, 112, 127, 143, 176, 285
Barry, Peter, 9, 45, 439
Barry, Philip, 66–67
Barstow, Josephine, 371
Barstow, Richard, 383, 421, 430
Barto, Betty Lou, 437, 464
Barton, Charles T., 211
Barton, Eileen, 413
Barton, James, 187, 189, 304
Bartsch, Hans, 117, 126, 378
Bartsch, Rudolf Hans, 182
Barzman, Ben, 50
Barzman, Sol, 50
Bass, Alfie, 374
Bassman, George, 51
Basso, Patricia, 438

Bastida, Ramon, 495–96
Bate, Tom, 462
Bates, Peg Leg, 500
Battista, Miriam, 443
Battles, John, 261–62
Bauer, George, 467
Bauer, Rollin, 84
Bauer, Vivian, 471
Bauman, Mordecai, 134–35
Baxter, Connie, 413
Baxter, George David, 354
Baxter, Gladys, 26
Baxter, Lloyd, 39, 41–42, 121, 390, 445, 485
Baxter, Warner, 66
Bay, Howard, 102–3, 136, 150, 176, 192, 205, 212, 225,
    236, 243, 268–70, 277, 284, 291, 298–99, 312, 314, 330,
    346, 389, 448, 454, 456, 464
Bayliss, Fene, 148
Bayne, Mardi, 301
Beal, John, 66
Beane, Reginald, 183
Bear, Robert, 433
Beat the Band, 139–41
Beatty, Talley, 257
Beavers, Dick, 56
Becker Brothers Studio, 493
Beckman, Al, 489
Beckwith, Reginald, 17
Beebe, Lucius, 19, 48, 55, 60, 110
Beecher, Marjorie (Bell; Belle; Champion), 71, 199, 363,
    365–66
Beeler, Virginia, 387, 470
Beery, Lee, 156
Beery, Noah, Sr., 268–69
Beggar's Holiday, 363–66
Behymer, L. E., 226
Bela, Nicholas, 443
Belafonte, Harry, 207, 243
Belasco, Jacques, 303
Belasco, Leon, 230
Bel Geddes, Norman, 39, 41, 251
Belita, Maria, 25
Bell, Marion, 380
Bell, Marjorie (Beecher; Belle; Champion), 71, 199, 363,
    365–66
Bell, Stanley, 224
Bellaver, Harry, 336
Belle, Gwendolyn, 207
Belle, Marjorie (Beecher; Bell; Champion), 71, 199, 363,
    365–66
La Belle Helene, 68
Belmont, Werner, 392
Belmont Opera Company, 220
Belmore, Bertha, 114–15, 249, 251
Benanti, Laura, 408
Benatzky, Ralph, 340
Benchley, Robert, 200
Bennett, Harry Gordon, 138
Bennett, Helen, 214

Bennett, Linda, 382
Bennett, Richard Rodney, 242
Bennett, Robert Russell, 70, 205, 242, 277, 330
Bennett, Russell, 249
Bennett, Seldon, 312
Benny, Jack, 333
Benson, Gloria, 428
Benson, Lucille, 307
Benson, Sally, 280
Bentley, Muriel, 262
Benton, Marguerite, 82
Benz, Hamilton, 220
Berens, Fritz, 230
Berg, Gene, 39
Bergasse, Joshua, 264
Bergdorf Goodman, 131
Berger, Ludwig, 175
Bergersen, Baldwin, 8, 57, 99, 157, 171, 214, 295, 450
Berghof, Herbert, 9
Bergman, Cecile, 433
Berini, Mario, 354
Berkeley, Ballard, 401
Berkeley, Busby, 284
Berle, Milton, 157–59, 346–47
Berlin, Irving, 21–23, 118, 123, 125, 136, 158, 334–36,
    497–98
Berlioz, Hector, 50, 274
Bernard, Robert, 238
Bernardi, Roberto, 80
Bernauer, Rudolf, 117, 378
Berney, William, 430
Bernier, Buddy, 31
Bernstein, Aline, 505, 507
Bernstein, Leonard, 261, 263, 413–15
Berresse, Michael, 474
Berrian, William, 462
Berry Brothers, 32, 131–32, 239, 493
Bert, Flo, 166
Berte, Heinrich, 181–82
Bertens, Serge, 230
Berton, Eugene, 274, 397
Besser, Joe, 362–63
Best, Paul, 143
Best Foot Forward, 77–80
Bethea, David, 171
Bethel, Janet, 428
Bettger, Lyle, 456
Bettis, Valerie, 284, 363, 425, 427
Bevan, Frank, 249
Biancolli, Louis, 11–12
Big Boy, 254, 256
Bigelow, Joe, 322
Bigelow, Susan, 484
Big Time, 223
Billion Dollar Baby, 309–12
Binyon, Claude, 126
Birdbath, Horatio Q., 441
Bishir, Jane, 478
Bishop, Adelaide, 181, 303

Bissell, Whit, 138
Bizet, Georges, 9, 205, 277, 330
Bizzelle, George, 24
Black, Frank, 322
Blackford, G. E., 152, 173, 177
Blackman, Charles, 220, 395
Blackton, Jay, 334, 378, 425, 497
Blackwell, Carlyle, 190
Blaine, Vivian, 84, 151
Blair, Anthony, 171
Blair, Betsy, 49
Blair, Jack, 59–60, 395
Blair, Janet, 195, 219
Blair, Sandy, 201
Blake, Doris, 216
Blake, Eubie, 70, 107
Blake, George, 187
Blake, Robert (Bobby), 53
Blakeley, Gene, 346
Blane, Ralph, 30, 77–78, 94
Blankfort, Henry, 50, 109
Blazer, Judy, 23, 202
Bleyer, Archie, 51, 77, 139, 171
Bliss, Helena, 82, 236, 239, 356–57
Blitzstein, Marc, 134, 413–16, 505, 507
Bloch, Stella, 225
Block, Hal, 87
Bloom, Ruby, 72
Bloomer Girl, 240–43, 368–69
Bloomfield, Harry, 298
Bloomingdale, Alfred, 84, 157, 165, 171, 214–15
Blossom, Henry, 301
Blossom Time, 181–83
Blue, Ben, 49
Blue Holiday, 278–80
Blunkall, E. J., 92
Blyer, Archie, 3
Blyth, Ann, 171
Bogart, Paul, 276, 475
Bogdanoff, Rose, 102, 225, 347
Bois, Curt, 298–99
Bokor, Margit, 231, 344
Boland, Clay, 439
Bolen, Virginia, 74
Boles, John, 192, 317
Boleslavsky, Natasha, 20
Bolger, Ray, 7, 17, 19, 113–15, 324–26, 460–62
Bolton, Guy, 29, 31, 33, 36, 207, 212, 378, 430
Bolton, Lois, 82
Bonanza Bound!, 436–38
Bond, Ridge, 156
Bond, Ruth, 160, 163–64
Bond, Sheila, 214, 416–17
Bonelli, Richard, 230–31
Bonnell, Sam, 192
Bontemps, Arna, 327
Booker, Beryl, 424
Booth, John N., Jr., 80, 228
Booth, Shirley, 282, 284, 414

Borde, Albert, 212, 214
Bordman, Gerald, 229
Bordoni, Irene, 22–24, 398
Borge, Victor, 15
Boris, Ruthanne, 169
Borne, Hal, 109
Bosler, Virginia, 380
Bostock, Kenneth, 30
Boswell, Connee, 223
Bottone, Bonaventura, 371
Bouillon, Jo, 438
Bouman, Hanny, 392
Bourneuf, Philip, 385
Bova, Joe, 264
Bower, William, 316
Bowers, Kenneth, 77, 79
Bowers, Kenny, 284
Bowers, William, 15
Bowles, John, 175
Bowles, Paul, 66–67
Bowman, Patricia, 249
Box, Sydney, 183
Boyd, Edith, 322
Boyd, Elena, 322
Boyd, Mildred, 322
Boyd, Sydney, 305
Boyer, Charles, 105
Boyer, Josephine, 351–52
Boys and Girls Together, 36–38
Boyt, John, 354
Bradford, Roark, 1–3
Bradley, Marion, 462
Bradley, Wilbert, 360
Brady, Leo, 136
Brady, Patti, 236
Braggiotti, Stiano, 94
Brainin, Jerome, 31
Brancato, Rosemarie, 249
Brander, Margot, 254
Brando, Marlon, 354–55
Brandon, Johnny, 68
Brandt, Helga and Inge, 121, 234, 349, 390
Braun, Jerry, 117
Brastoff, Sascha, 205
Braun, Eugene, 120, 234, 349, 390, 445, 485
Brazzi, Rossano, 484
Brecher, Irving, 79
Bree, Chet, 160
Breisach, Paul, 145, 471
Bremer, Lucille, 17, 49
Brendel, El, 166–67
Brennan, Frederick Hazlitt, 454
Brennan, J. Keirn, 111
Brent, Romney, 94
Brentano, Felix, 86, 126–27, 143, 145, 176, 243, 267, 293, 378
Brian, Donald, 111
Brian, Mary, 30
Brice, Fannie, 30

Bricklayers, 104–5, 107, 129–30, 183–84
Bricusse, Leslie, 27
Bridges, Kenneth, 65
Brigadoon, 380–83
Briggs, Matt, 240, 368
Bright Lights of 1944, 187–89
Brill, Klaus, 9
Brink, Robert, 221
Bristow, Nora, 433
Britten, Benjamin, 2, 470–72
Broadbent, Aida, 286, 301, 316, 356
Brock, Heinie, 393
Brodkin, Herbert, 410
Brodney, Oscar, 212, 307
Brodsky, Irving, 74
Bromberg, J. Edward, 366
Bromberg, Louis, 20
Bronson, Arthur, 448
Brookins, Fred, 448
Brooks, David, 167–68, 225, 343, 380
Brooks, Evelyn, 146
Brooks, Lawrence, 236, 462, 464
Brooks, Matt, 33, 428
Brooks, Shelton, 500
Brooks Costume Company, 127, 220
Brotherson, Eric, 17, 153
Brown, Ada, 280
Brown, Anne, 68, 97, 99
Brown, Anthony, 3, 102
Brown, Billings, 450
Brown, Forman, 301, 344, 399
Brown, Herrick, 33, 52, 117, 119, 125, 135, 170, 173, 207, 222, 234, 279, 281, 284, 290, 306, 339, 352, 359, 430, 444, 469, 478, 503
Brown, Isabelle, 132
Brown, Joe E., 158, 432
Brown, John Mason, 12, 14, 17–18, 23, 30, 38, 41, 43–44, 46, 48, 50, 55, 58–60, 62, 65, 78, 81, 83, 85, 89–91, 93, 96, 101–5, 107, 130–31, 133, 135, 137–38
Brown, Kelly, 474
Brown, Lew, 62
Brown, Lillyn, 505
Brown, Nacio Herb, 3
Brown, Rowland, 102
Brown, Russ, 81–82, 282, 389, 484
Brown, Thelma Waide, 24
Browne, Roscoe Lee, 27
Bruce, Betty, 17, 20, 150, 268, 270, 389
Bruce, Carol, 22, 56, 129–30, 314, 476–78
Bruce, Eddie, 372
Bruce Dancers, 32
Bruenig, Muriel, 375
Brulatour, Jules, 130
Bryan, Dora, 512
Bryant, Glenn, 278, 330
Bryant, Marie, 363
Bryant, Willie, 278
Bryce, Edward S., 413
Bryden, Eugene, 159, 361

Brynner, Yul, 320–21
Buckley, Kay, 430
Buckley, Richard, 341
Buckmaster, John, 186
Bufano, Remo, 385
Buffett, Kenny, 430
Buka, Donald, 216
Bunker, Ralph, 71, 139, 171
Burgess, Anthony, 27
Burgess, Grover, 347
Burke, Georgia, 42
Burke, Johnny, 66, 108, 129–30, 138, 201, 317, 319
Burke, Maurice, 268
Burke, Virginia, 45
Burke, Walter, 268, 389
Burke, William H., 120, 234, 349, 390, 445, 485
Burnett, Martha, 113
Burns, David, 184, 312, 416, 418, 454
Burns, Larry, 218
Burns, Nat, 167
Burnside, R. H., 29, 244
Burnson, George, 226
Burr, Donald, 31, 145
Burr, Raymond, 63
Burrill, Ena, 91
Burton, Eugene, 341
Burton, George, 500–501
Burton, Sarah, 421–22
Burtson, Bud, 157
Busch, Betty Ann, 375
Bussart, Meg, 382
Butler, Billy, 70, 278
Butler, David, 461
Butler, John, 435
Butterworth, Charles, 136–37
Buttignol, Val, 397
Buttons, Red, 202, 205, 383, 429–30
Butz, Norbert Leo, 408
Buzzell, Edward, 79
Byers, Trudy, 165
By Jupiter, 113–15
Byrd, Joe, 72, 105
Byrd, Sam, 1
Byrn, Robert, 200, 274, 405

Cabalgata, 495–96
Caballos, Larry, 166
Cabin in the Sky, 42–44
Caesar, Irving, 20, 136, 184–85
Caesar, Sid, 218–19, 261, 416–18, 441
Cahn, Sammy, 219, 284–85, 402
Cahn, William, 366
Cain, Henri, 11
Cairns, Angus, 385
Caley, Dorothy, 121, 234
Caley, Hazel, 234
Caley Sisters, 39
Calgary Brothers, 449–50
Callahan, Bill, 331, 333, 464

Callan, Chris, 317
Callanan, William, 146
Callen, Michael, 475
Call Me Mister, 330–34
Calloway, Cab, 98
Calvin, Henry, 378, 430
Calvo, Pilar, 495
Campbell, Paul, 291
Campbell, Peggy, 368
Camuti, Louis, 435
Canarutto, Angelo, 11
Cannon, Maureen, 78, 80, 190, 268, 270, 389
Canova, Les, 408
Cantor, Eddie, 92–93, 317, 319, 431
Carabella, Angela, 397
Caramba, 11
Card, Virginia, 145, 230
Cardelli, Giovanni, 471
Cardinale, Frank, 228
Carell, Victor, 231
Caribbean Carnival, 409–11
Carib Song, 295–98
Carlisle, Kevin, 238–39
Carlisle, Kitty, 14, 29, 471–72, 474
Carlisle, Una Mae, 105
Carlo, Monte, 397
Carlson, Robert Eric, 372
Carlson, Stanley, 145, 245
Carlton, Sam, 148
Carmen Jones, 205–7, 277–78, 330
Carmichael, Hoagy, 29–31
Carnegie, Hattie, 63, 153, 421
Carney, Art, 49
Carol, Judy, 110
Carousel, 274–77, 480–81
Carpenter, Carleton, 66
Carpenter, Constance, 202
Carpenter, Thelma, 280, 425
Carr, Jack, 205, 278, 330, 435
Carrol, Sidney, 146
Carroll, David James, 136
Carroll, Diahann, 98, 207
Carroll, Earl, 3–5
Carroll, Georgia, 21
Carroll, Joan, 48
Carroll, June, 146, 361
Carroll, Lewis, 385
Carroll, Pat, 79, 264
Carroll, Penny, 428
Carroll, Renee, 188
Carroll, Robert, 399
Carroll, William, 236
Carson, Jeannie, 79, 374
Carson, Mindy, 484
Carter, Dixie, 56
Carter, Jack C., 489
Carter, Maggie, 177
Carter, Marion, 267
Casazza, Yolanda, 108, 152

Case, Allen, 484
Case, Evelyn, 142
Casey, Stuart, 200
Casey, Taggard, 413
Casher, Izidor, 138
Casher, Jennie, 138
Cass, Lee, 475
Cass, Peggy, 502
Cassel, Walter, 238, 316
Cassidy, Claudia, 190, 342, 348, 438, 489
Cassidy, Jack, 249, 382, 404
Cassini, Oleg, 464
Castillo, 425
Castle, Gene, 79
Castle, Nick, 109, 452
Castle, Paul, 445
Castle, William, 31
Casto, Jean, 274
Catholic University of America, 435
Catlett, Walter, 307
Cato, Minto, 1
Caton, Edward, 246, 295, 317
Caulfield, Joan, 139
Cavanaugh, Hobart, 464
Caveness, Pamela, 448
Cavett, Dick, 27
Caymmi, Dorival, 118
Ceeley, Leonard, 163–64
Cellini, Benvenuto, 272, 274
Century Lighting, 80, 102, 377
Cerf, Bennett, 359
Chadman, Christopher, 56, 459
Chakiris, George, 513
Chambers, Norma, 369
Chambers, Ralph, 102
Champion, Gower, 71, 95–96, 136–37, 218, 365–66, 450, 467–68, 470
Champion, Marge (Beecher; Bell; Belle), 71, 199, 363, 365–66
Chandler, Evelyn, 284
Chaney, Stewart, 68, 73, 90, 94, 220, 222, 226, 254, 293, 430
Channing, Carol, 311, 416, 467–69, 510–12
Channing, Stockard, 56
Chaplin, Saul, 436
Chapman, John, 17, 177, 182–83, 185, 189, 191, 194, 197, 199, 201, 205, 207, 209, 211, 213, 215–16, 218, 222, 234, 238, 240, 242, 245, 247–48, 251, 253, 256–57, 263, 267, 269, 272–73, 276, 280–82, 284, 290, 294–95, 297, 299, 302, 305, 309, 311, 314, 319, 321, 323, 325–26, 329, 332–33, 335, 339, 353–55, 357, 359, 363, 365, 371, 373, 376, 379, 381, 385–86, 388, 398, 402, 404, 408, 411–12, 418, 427, 430–31, 444, 449, 451–54, 456, 460–61, 463, 466, 469, 472, 474, 478, 480, 483, 501, 505, 507, 509, 511
Chapman, William, 484
Charig, Phil, 195, 212
Charisse, Cyd, 382, 428
Charles, Richard, 316

Chase, Ilka, 17
Chauve-Souris of 1943, 179–81
Chayres, Nestor, 290
Checco, Al, 467, 469
Chenoweth, Kristin, 312
Cherry, John, 126, 200, 249
Chetwynd, Ross, 480
Cheu, Byron, 33
Chevalier, Maurice, 127, 377–78, 424, 431
Child, Alan, 144
Chilton, Nola, 159
Ching, William, 405
Chisholm, Robert, 12, 15, 59, 181, 200, 310, 358, 414
The Chocolate Soldier, 117–18, 378–80
Chodorov, Jerome, 23, 515
Chopin, Frederic, 298
Chotzinoff, Samuel, 99
Christensen, Lew, 66
Christensen, William, 226
Christie, Ken, 15
Christy, Anna, 273
Christy, Eileen, 277
Church, George, 33
Ciesinki, Kristine, 371
Cimberg, Jesse M., 489
City Slickers, 441
Clark, Bobby, 118–20, 210–11, 375–76, 464–66, 502
Clark, Buddy, 187
Clark, Harry, 192, 331
Clark, Jinx, 445, 485
Clark, Lyle, 261
Clark, Peggy, 337, 363, 380, 402, 436, 456, 471, 475, 489, 501, 510
Clark, Petula, 374
Clark, Victoria, 273
Clarke, Robert, 205, 278, 330
Clary, Robert, 339
Clay, Edwin, 154, 218
Clayton, Jan, 112, 274, 312, 314
Clayton, Ruth, 80, 341
Clements, Dudley, 165
Cleveland, Jean, 210
Cleveland, John, 63
Clift, Montgomery, 218
Cline, Edward, 254
Close, Glenn, 484
Clutsam, G. H., 183
Clyde, June, 92
Cobb, Daniel, 246
Cobb, Ira, 352
Cobb, Lee J., 205
Coburn, Charles, 513
Coca, Imogene, 57–58, 289–90
Cochran, Dorcas, 3
Cocktails at 5, 160–61
Cocrell, Eustace, 44
Cohen, Alexander H., 99–100, 187
Colby, Marion, 52, 366
Cole, Beatrice, 94

Cole, Doris, 278
Cole, Jack, 104, 150, 157, 214–15, 219, 436–37, 454, 456, 480, 513
Coleman, Emil, 115
Coleman, Herbert, 328–29
Coleman, Leo, 387, 389, 470
Coleman, Nancy, 66
Coleman, Robert, 17, 139, 379, 381, 384, 386, 388, 398, 400–401, 403, 407–8, 411–12, 415, 417–18, 420, 423, 427, 429–31, 444, 449, 451, 453, 456, 458, 461, 463, 466, 469, 471–72, 474, 478, 480, 483, 494, 496, 498, 501, 503, 505, 507, 509, 511
Coles, Honi, 72, 511
Colin, Saul, 146
Colleano, Con, 131–32, 223
Collett, Richard, 484
Collins, Charles, 111, 165, 302–3
Collins, John, 424
Colman, Booth, 421–22
Colt, Alvin, 261, 337, 339, 344, 383, 399, 475
Colt, Phyllis, 38
Colton, John, 246
Comden, Betty, 261–62, 264–65, 309, 311, 436–37
Comic Opera Theatre, 226
Committee to Defend America by Aiding the Allies, 136
Como, Perry, 151
Comstock, Frances, 7, 117
Concert Varieties, 289–91
Conchita, 47
Condell, H. A., 245, 300, 352
Condon, Eva, 12
Conklin, Hal, 167
A Connecticut Yankee, 199–202
Connelly, Marc, 44, 114, 443
Connery, Sean, 484
Connick, Harry, Jr., 484
Connolly, Bobby, 69
Connor, Kaye, 356
Connors, Barry, 111, 165
Conoway, Charles, 284
Conrad, Eugene, 254
Conrad, Karen, 190
Constant, Benoit, 27
Constant, Marius, 27
Conte, John, 202, 277, 347
Conway, Curt, 99, 395
Conway, Shirl, 8
Conway, Tom, 195
Cook, Alton, 207, 306
Cook, Barbara, 156, 243, 277, 315
Cook, Joe, 38–39, 41
Cook, Victor Trent, 329
Cooke, Marjorie, 230–31
Cooke, Martin, 298
Coolidge, Edwina, 73
Coolidge, Philip, 258, 260, 384
Cooper, Horace, 460
Cooper, Hy, 303
Cooper, Jerry, 36

Cooper, June, 159
Cooper, Lew, 177
Cooper, Lou, 99
Cooper, Marilyn, 264
Cooper, Melville, 176, 216, 271, 273, 357
Cooper, Robert, 510
Cooper, Theodore, 508
Copeland, Joan, 56
Copeland, William, 225
Coppola, Francis Ford, 374
Corbett, Leonora, 358
Cordoba, Daniel, 495
Cordon, Norman, 369
Cordova, Victoria, 80, 104
Corey, Irwin, 146, 148, 452
Corey, Wendell, 209
Corwin, Jonathan, 503
Corwin, Norman, 99
Coryeo, Monica, 393
Cossart, Ernest, 161
Cossart, Valerie, 421–22
Costello, Diosa, 63, 223, 347
Costello, Lou, 32, 211
Cothran, Dorothy, 368
Cotillard, Marion, 409
Cotlow, Marilyn, 387
Coudy, Douglas, 282
Coulouris, George, 436
Count Me In, 136–38
Courtneidge, Cicely, 401–2
Cousins, Mary Ann, 433
Covert, Earl, 284
Coward, Noel, 110, 125, 421, 423
Cowles, Chandler, 387, 413, 470
Coy, Johnny, 476–77
Coyle, Jack, 160
Crabtree, Don, 508
The Cradle Will Rock, 413–16
Craig, Helen, 320
Craig, Jerry, 510
Craig, Reginald, 111
Crain, Jeanne, 205
Crane, David, 136
Crater, Aline, 303
Crawford, Cheryl, 11, 97, 99, 186–87, 192, 380–81, 385, 456, 505, 507
Crawford, Joan, 248, 365
Crayon, 449
Crazy with the Heat, 60–63
Crooker, Earle, 165
Cropper, Roy, 181
Crosby, Bing, 201, 242, 438
Cross, Alan, 223, 233
Crowley, Bob, 277
Cryer, David, 317
Cuddy, Margaret, 432
Cukor, George, 205
Cullen, Countee, 327
Cullen, Edward, 380

Cummings, Irving, 23
Cummings, Robert, 79
Cummings, Vickie, 142
Cunningham, George, 301
Cunningham, John, 27
Curcio, Frank, 33
Curran, Homer, 236, 421, 454
Curry, John, 382
Curtain Time, 223–24
Curtis, Francis I., 439
Curtiz, Michael, 126, 175
Cutler, Robert F., 7
Czettel, Ladislas, 143, 216, 267
Czobel, Lisa, 392

Dabs, Oren, 389
Dache, Lily, 131
Da Costa, Morton, 227
Dahl, Arlene, 219
Dahlman, Lou, 148
Dailey, Dan, 49, 265
Daily, Dan, 333
Dale, Charles, 115, 117, 187
Dale, Margaret, 63, 153
Dali, Salvador, 252
Dall, Evelyn, 214
Daly, James, 66
Daly, Lou, 167
Dame, Beverly, 387
Damrosch, Walter, 27
Dancing in the Streets, 161–63
Dandridge, Dorothy, 98, 109–10, 207
Dane, Faith, 249
Daniel, Billy, 83
Daniels, Billy, 280
Daniels, Dan, 166
Daniels, Danny, 77–79, 138, 312, 416–17
Daniels, Marc, 9
Daniels, Mark, 202
Dansation, 108
Dante, 33, 488
Dantine, Helmut, 345
Da Pron, Louis, 307
D'Arcy, Alexander, 352
Dare, Danny, 50–51, 111
Darian, Anita, 315
Darian, Joe, 99–100
Darling, Jean, 224, 274
Da Silva, Howard, 154, 342, 413–14
Dassin, Jules, 454
d'Attili, Marla, 470
Davenport, Mary, 389
Davenport, Pembroke, 42, 225, 289, 295, 342, 419, 472, 474
David, Mack, 187
David, William, 309
Davidson, John, 156
Davidson, Ken, 115, 117
Davies, Marion, 303

Davis, Andrew, 273
Davis, Benny, 233
Davis, Bette, 158
Davis, Blevins, 249
Davis, Bus, 146
Davis, Carl, 371
Davis, Diane, 146
Davis, Eddie, 33, 36, 212, 284–85
Davis, Henry, 97, 186
Davis, Luther, 63
Davis, Mack, 61
Davis, Maude, 17
Davis, Meyer, 177, 282
Davis, Nancy, 320
Davis, Ruth, 341
Davis, Sammy, Jr., 98
Davis, Warren, 218
Davison, Robert, 236, 337, 354
Davison, Robert H., 307
Dawn, Hazel, Jr., 462
Dawn, Isabel, 286
Dawson, Mark, 113, 376
Day, Edith, 91, 317
Day, Marilyn, 450, 515
The Day before Spring, 307–9
Dean, Douglas, 102
Dean, Jo Ann, 39
Deane, Douglas, 309
de Cordoba, Hurtado, 438
De Cordova, Fred, 17, 30, 157
Dee, Paula, 361
Dee, Sylvia, 383
Deel, Sandra, 24, 484
Deering, Jane, 324
de Falla, Manuel, 291
De Gresac, Fred, 375
DeHaven, Gloria, 79
de Havilland, Olivia, 502
DeKoven, Reginald, 244
De Lange, Eddie, 439
de Lange, Eddie, 286–87
de Lantz, Virginia, 29, 31
de Lappe, Gemze, 86
DeLaria, Lea, 264
de Lavallade, Carmen, 435
Del Bondio, J. H., 378
DeLeon, Michael, 481
Dell'Isola, Salvatore, 405, 481
Delmar, Harry, 212
Delmar, Kenny, 509
Del Ruth, Roy, 49
Delvan Company, 378
de Lys, Derna, 470
De Marco, Renee, 36, 38
De Marco, Sally, 38, 92–93, 131, 239
De Marco, Tony, 36, 38, 92–93, 131, 239
De Martin, Imelda, 484
De Mille, Agnes, 154–55, 192, 194, 208–9, 240, 242, 274,
    276, 325, 368, 380–81, 383, 405–6, 418, 469, 471, 480,
    510–11

De Molas, Nicholas, 70
de Najac, Emile, 159
Dengate, Dennis, 169, 243, 293
Denise, Patricia, 513
Dennis, Dorothy, 146
Dennis, Paul, 245
Dennis, Shirley, 239–40
Denny, Reginald, 312
de Paul, Gene, 70
de Paur, Leonard, 1, 202
de Reeder, Pierre, 169, 181, 340
De Rose, Peter, 3, 39
Derro, John, 450
Derwent, Clarence, 320–21, 356
de Schauensee, Max, 396
The Desert Song, 316–17
Desjardins, Pete, 81
Desmond, Florence, 362–63
De Sylva, B. G. (Buddy), 21–22, 46, 48
Deutsch, Helen, 329
Devlin, Helen, 82
Devon, Shirley, 167
de Wailly, Leon, 274
De Winter, Dorothy, 347
De Wit, Jacqueline, 159
DeWood, Loraine, 160
Diamond, Harold, 80
Diamond, Hugh, 80
Diamond, Jack, 347
Diamond, Tom, 80
Diaz, Justino, 484
DiChiera, David, 27
Dick, Richard, 77
Dickey, Annamary, 250, 282, 405
Dickson, Artells, 174
Dickson, Dorothy, 432
Dietl, Fritz, 390
Dietrich, Marlene, 7
Dietz, Howard, 17, 19, 161–62, 207, 218, 246–48, 425, 427
Di Gatano, Adam and Jane, 183, 223
Digges, Dudley, 161
Dillard, William, 505, 507
Dilworth, Gordon, 243, 300
Dingle, Charles, 497
Dix, Tommy, 77, 79
Dixon, Harland, 136
Dixon, Lee, 12, 15, 36, 154
Dixon, Mort, 50
Dixon, Robert, 467
Dodgson, Charles Lutwidge, 385
Dolan, Frank, 102
Dolan, Robert Emmett, 21, 508–10
Dolin, Anton, 29, 251, 344
Dolinoff, Alexis, 169
Don, Karl, 9
Donaldson, Walter, 49
Donan, Stanley, 54
Donen, Stanley, 78–79, 265
Donnelly, Dorothy, 169, 181
Donohue, Jack, 79, 251, 305

Donohue, Pat, 510
Donovan, Nancy, 340
Donovan, Warde, 366
Doolittle, James A., 344
Dorati, Antal, 86, 267
Dorfman, Nat, 72
Dormonde, George and Tim, 408
Dorsay, Edmund, 356
D'Orso, Wisa, 264, 312
Doucet, Catherine, 111
Douglas, Betty, 94
Douglas, Bob, 113
Douglas, Larry, 199, 322, 429, 449
Douglas, Melvyn, 59–60, 331, 333
Douglas, Robert, 340
Douglass, Nancy, 240
Douglass, Stephen, 276, 480
Dowd, Harrison, 59
Dowdy, Helen, 97, 257, 312, 448
Dowling, Doris, 146
Dowling, Eddie, 70, 452
Dowling, Edward Duryea, 17, 87
Downes, Olin, 86, 144, 471–72
Downie, Barbara, 432
Downs, Johnny, 305, 428
Doyle, Michael, 52
Drake, Alfred, 6–7, 154, 219, 258, 260, 363, 365, 472, 475
Drake, Dona, 23
Drake, Tom, 15
Draper, Josef, 298
Draper, Paul, 71, 101
Dratler, Jay, 15
Drayson, Danny, 452
Dream with Music, 220–22
Dresselhuys, Lorraine Manville, 249
Drew, David, 356
Drinkwater, John, 183
Driver, Donn, 374
Drury, Charles, 317
Dubin, Al, 17, 73, 118, 257
The Duchess Misbehaves, 322–24
Dudley, Alice, 30
Duffield, Brainerd, 337
Duffy, Henry, 111, 165–66, 399
Duke, Maurice, 488
Duke, Milton, 44
Duke, Robert, 361
Duke, Vernon, 17, 19, 25–27, 39, 42, 92–94, 161–62, 207, 218, 246–49, 395
Duke of Iron, 409
Dulo, Jane, 305
Dumke, Ralph, 176, 216, 246, 293, 312
Dumont, Margaret, 166
Dunbar, Brooks, 413
Duncan, Augustin, 320
Duncan, Danny, 500
Duncan, Ronald, 470
Duncan, Sandy, 374
Duncan, Todd, 44, 97, 99, 504

Dunham, Katherine, 24–25, 42–44, 189–90, 257, 278, 289–90, 295–97, 347, 360
Dunkel (E. B.) Studios, 117
Dunlap, Florence, 192
Dunn, Henry, 223, 233
Dunne, Irene, 315
Dunning, Phillip, 103
Dunnock, Mildred, 320
Dunstan, Cliff, 334
DuPont, Bob, 223
du Pont, Paul, 97, 117, 134, 142, 186, 192
DuPree, William, 207
Durant, Jack, 19, 305
Durante, Jimmy, 17–20, 56, 105
Durbin, Deanna, 270
Dussault, Nancy, 277, 374, 415, 484
Dutton, Laura Deane, 146
Duweco, 223
Duwico, 127, 424
Dvonch, Frederick, 480
Dvorkin, Judith, 27
Dworkin, Harry, 344

Eager, Edward, 220, 260
Eager, Helen, 260–61
Earl Carroll Vanities, 3–5
Early to Bed, 171–74
Eastley, William, 33
Easton, Sid, 72
Eaton, Dorothy, 167
Eaves Costume Company, 126–27, 148
Ebersole, Christine, 156, 202
Ebsen, Buddy, 312
Eckels, Lew, 102
Eckl, Shirley, 262
Eckley, Dan, 134, 187, 225
Eddy, Nelson, 118, 129, 317, 376
Edens, Roger, 264
Edith Piaf and Her Continental Entertainers, 408–9
Edwards, Gus, 149
Edwards, Kent, 146, 236, 346
Edwards, Lee, 267
Edwards, Leo, 148
Edwards, Michael, 438
Edwards, Penny, 322
Edwards, Ralph, 141
Ed Wynn's Laugh Carnival, 487–88
Eggerth, Marta, 12, 14, 177, 243, 298–300, 354
Eichberg, Richard, 126–27
Eisele, Lou, 212, 265, 303, 349, 390, 409, 462
Elder, Althea, 208
Elg, Taina, 24, 462
Elinson, Izzy, 92
Eliscu, Edward, 50–51, 53, 111, 134, 225–26, 274
Ellington, Duke, 109–10, 363, 365
Ellington, Mercer, 109
Elliott, Leonard, 202, 291
Ellis, Elaine, 126
Ellis, Evelyn, 278

Ellis, Lucille, 189, 257, 360
Ellis, Margie, 214
Ellis, Maurice, 171
Ellstein, Abraham, 224
Elson, Charles, 505
Elzy, Ruby, 1, 3
Emerson, Edward, 111
Emerson, Hope, 369
Emerson, John, 510
Encore Studio, 127
Engel, Lehman, 70, 331, 436, 489
Engels, Jeanne, 248
Engeran, Virgil, 274
England, Paul, 460
Ephraim, Lee, 401
Epstein, Julius, 489–90
Epstein, Philip G., 489–90
Erens, Joseph, 157, 187
Ermoloff, George, 174
Ernie, Val, 84
Ernst, Leila, 54, 361
Errico, Melissa, 248, 375
Errol, Leon, 432
Errolle, Martha, 59, 345, 358
Espada, Manuela, 392
Essen, Viola, 476–77
Estrelita, 70
Evans, Alfred, 341
Evans, Byron, 218
Evans, Fred, 166
Evans, Greek, 170
Evans, Margie, 82
Evans, Ray, 94
Evans, Wilbur, 127, 145, 211, 268, 482, 484
Evenson, Billy, 108
Everett, Francine, 248
Everything's on Ice, 393
Ewell, Tom, 66, 90, 450–51
Ewing, Marjorie and Sherman, 411, 471
Experimental Theatre, 432
Eythe, William, 467

Fabray, Nanette, 51, 53, 82, 184, 208–9, 243, 256, 368–69, 402–4, 456–59
Fadiman, Clifton, 19
Fain, Sammy, 36, 53, 73, 87, 339, 366–67, 386
Fairfax, Lee, 342
Falk, Peter, 382
Falkenburg, Jinx, 33
Family Album, 421–22
Farell, Marita, 226
Farkas, Karl, 243, 291, 293, 352
Farquhar, Marion, 86, 145, 267
Farrar, Tony, 146, 148
Farrell, Anthony B., 478–79, 508–9
Farrell, Eileen, 270
Farrell, Frank, 244
Farrell (Anthony Brady) Productions, 508
Faulkner, Virginia, 57

Fay, Frank, 183
Faye, Alice, 46
Faye, Frances, 195
Faye, Herbie, 132
Faye, Joey, 53, 214–15, 322, 347, 351, 402–4
Fazenda, Louise, 303
Feder, 33
Feder, Abe, 202
Feigay, Paul, 261, 309, 436
Feld, Eliot, 264
Fellows, Edith, 293
Ferber, Edna, 312, 448
Ferguson, William, 443
Fernandez, Paco, 495
Ferova, Nina, 230
Ferraro, Buddy, 322
Ferrel, Frank, 24
Ferrer, Gregory, 33
Ferrer, Jose, 27, 84, 249, 339
Ferrer, Mel, 145
Fetchit, Stepin, 29–30
Fetter, Ted, 44, 74, 439
Feuer, Cy, 460
Ffolkes, David, 380, 443–44, 460, 475
Field, Leonard, 515
Field, Robert, 176, 244
Field, Ron, 264
Fielding, Marjery, 57, 101, 233, 346
Fields, Benny, 240
Fields, Dorothy, 9, 82–83, 150–51, 187, 210, 267–69, 334–35
Fields, Gracie, 107–8
Fields, Herbert, 46, 48, 82–83, 150–51, 199, 210, 267, 269, 334–35
Fields, Joseph, 23, 162, 510
Fiffi, Mme., 131
Fiffl, Henry, 513
Fillmore, Russell, 111, 165
Fimberg, Hal, 109, 513
Fine, Sylvia, 83
Fini, 513
Finian's Rainbow, 372–75
Finklehoff, Fred F., 183, 223, 329
Finklehoffe, Fred F., 69, 79, 131
Finlayson, Don, 516
Finn, Frank, 293
Finnell, Carrie, 118
Fiore, Roland, 462
The Firebrand of Florence, 271–74
The Firefly, 163
Fischer, Clifford C., 101, 104, 107, 129, 408
Fischer, Loretta, 101
Fiser, Don, 293
Fisher, Nelle, 270, 416
Fiske, Louise, 184
Fitch, Bob, 469
Fitzgerald, Christopher, 374–75
Fitzgerald, Lillian, 278
Fitzgerald, Neil, 126

Fitzhugh, Ellen, 136
Fitzmaurice, Michael, 117, 126
A Flag Is Born, 354–56
Flatt, Ernest, 475, 512
Fleer, Harry, 366
Fleury, Vanni, 408–9
Flick, Pat C., 36
Flippen, Jay C., 167, 233–34
Floetman, Lucille, 307
Florell, Walter, 176, 243, 293–94, 363
Florman, Irving, 179
Follow the Girls, 212–14
Fontaine, Joan, 365
Fontanne, Lynn, 118, 125, 473
The Foolies of 1949, 488
Foran, Dick, 200
Forbes, Brenda, 6–7, 324
Forbes, Kenneth, 202
Forde, Hal, 25
Fordin, Hugh, 309, 329
Forgie, Hugh, 117
Forkins, Marty, 70
Forman, Lou, 101, 129, 183, 408
Forrest, George, 27, 236, 238–39, 346–47, 356–57, 454
Forrest, Ingrid, 401
Forshew, Robert Pierpont, 145
Fort, Syvilla, 189
Fortier, Robert, 66
Fortis, John, 234, 349, 390
Fortune-East, Valerie, 393
For Your Pleasure, 151–53
Fosse, Bob, 56, 311, 332, 427–28, 437–38, 474
Foster, Nannie, 146
Fox, Franklyn, 274
Fox, Frederick, 132, 224, 342, 416
Fox, Harry, 202
Foy, Eddie, Jr., 285, 301–2
France, Richard, 336, 474
Francine, Ann, 167–68
Franck, Nelly, 9
Francks, Don, 374
Frank, Melvin, 17
Franklin, Ann, 167
Franklin, Nancy, 467
Franklin, Nony, 375
Franklin, Stanley, 33
Franklin, William, 187, 295
Franzell, Carlotta, 205, 278
Fraser, Jane, 167
Fredericks, Charles, 312, 314, 345, 399, 464
Frederickson, Carl, 393–94
Freed, Arthur, 44, 49, 79, 329
Freed, Bert, 271, 307
Freed, Ralph, 53
Freedley, Vinton, 42, 82, 161, 208–9, 280
Freeman, Charles K., 108, 236
Freeman, Howard, 66
Freeman, Irving, 148
Freeman, Jay, 487

Freeman, Jonathan, 375
Frei, Matty, 488
Freitag, Dorothea, 347
French, Lavern, 504
French, Laverne, 189
French, Rick, 475
Frenkin, Nina, 228
Friebus, Florida, 385, 387
Friedberg, William, 317
Friedlander, William B., 142
Friedman, Charles, 3, 205, 277, 330, 369, 436, 475
Friedman, Murray, 132
Friml, Rudolf, 163, 174–75
Froman, Jane, 17, 20, 56, 115–16, 195, 197
Fuller, Lorenzo, 472, 475
Fuller, Lori Ann, 273
Full Speed Ahead, 164
Fumed Oak, 422
Funke, Lewis, 306–7, 352, 367, 496
Funzapoppin, 493–95
Furness, Betty, 84
Futral, Elizabeth, 273

Gable, Clark, 158
Gable, June, 139
Gabowitz, Martin, 257
Gabrielle, Josefina, 156
Gae, Nadine, 6, 47, 157, 411
Gaige, Truman, 26–27
Gaines, Davis, 248
Gaines, Muriel, 351–52
Gainsworth, Marjore, 60
Gali, Gali, 449
Gallagher, Helen, 55, 156, 309, 311–12, 374, 382, 402–3, 501, 503
Galli, Augusto, 11
Galli, Eola, 166
Galvin, Gene, 321
Gambarelli, Maria, 393
Ganz, Al, 87
Garbo, Greta, 30, 52, 110
Garde, Betty, 154, 156
Gardella, Tess, 71
Garden, Louis, 145
Gardiner, James W., 305
Gardner, Ava, 195, 313
Gardner, Lynn, 197
Gardner, Rita, 56, 415
Garland, Judy, 155, 336
Garland, Robert, 182–83, 185, 188, 192, 194, 197, 199, 201, 207, 209, 213–15, 218, 222, 234, 238, 240, 244, 247–48, 251, 253, 257, 260, 263, 266–67, 269, 273, 276, 279–80, 282–84, 290, 292, 295–96, 299–300, 302, 305, 309, 311, 314–15, 318–19, 321, 323, 325, 328, 333, 335–36, 339, 352–55, 357, 359, 365, 371, 374, 376, 379, 381, 384, 386, 388, 398, 400–401, 403, 411–12, 415, 418, 423, 427, 430–31, 434, 445, 449, 451, 453–55, 458, 461, 463–64, 466, 469, 474, 478, 480, 483, 494, 496, 498, 502, 505, 507, 509

Garr, Eddie, 127
Garrett, Betty, 53, 99, 134–35, 150–51, 209, 256, 264, 332–33
Garris, John, 226
Gary, Bill, 152
Gary, Ted, 218
Gates, Ruth, 448
Gateson, Marjorie, 377
Gatts, George M., 152
Gauld, Carlton, 245
Gaxton, William, 21–22, 24, 79, 104–5, 136, 282–83, 317–19, 325
Gay, John, 363
Gaynes, George, 195
Gaynes, Kathy, 304
Gaynes, Kim, 304
Gay New Orleans, 31–33
Gaynor, Charles, 466, 468
Gaynor, Gay, 190
Gaynor, Mitzi, 357, 484
Gear, Luella, 61–63, 66, 136–37, 463
Gebhardt, George, 354
Gee, Parker, 286
Gehrig, Phyllis, 515
Geiler, Voli, 392
Geleznova, Katia, 228
Genee, Richard, 143
Gennaro, Peter, 515
Gentlemen Prefer Blondes, 510–13
Gentner, Norma, 271
George, Helen, 300
George, Phillip, 267
George, Vicki, 160
George, Zelma, 388
Gerard, Adele, 63
Gerbeau, Roland, 438
Gerber, Mitzi, 357
Gering, Marion, 224
Gerrits, Paul, 57
Gerry, Roger, 47
Gersene, Georges D., 142
Gershwin, Arthur, 265–66
Gershwin, George, 72, 97, 99, 186
Gershwin, Ira, 63–64, 66, 97, 153, 186, 271–73, 358–59
Gerson, Hal, 467
Geto, Al, 99, 134
Gets, Malcolm, 375
Gibbs, Richard, 342
Gibbs, Wolcott, 17
Gibson, Millard, 246
Gibson, Virginia, 202
Gifford, Gordon, 163–64
Gilbert, Alan, 372, 374
Gilbert, Billy, 301, 378–79, 430
Gilbert, Edward, 57, 146, 349, 361–62, 366, 390, 428, 478
Gilbert, Franklin, 467
Gilbert, Gloria, 93, 493
Gilbert, Jody, 361, 363
Gilbert, Larry, 293

Gilbert, Mercedes, 295
Gilbert, Robert, 176, 243
Gilbert, W. S., 24–25, 280, 282, 533–34
Giler, Berne, 303
Gilford, Jack, 50–51, 53, 138
Gilfry, Rodney, 273
Gilkey, Stanley, 6, 324
Gillespie, Heather, 439
Gillette, Priscilla, 505, 507
Gilman, Toni, 139
Gingles, Keith, 316
Giovonelli, Rosa, 11
The Girl from Nantucket, 303–5
Girvin, Ramon B., 24
Givot, George, 21, 210
Glad to See You, 284–86
Glass, Mary Ellen, 334
Glazer, Benjamin, 274
Glazer, Benjamin F., 480
Gleason, Helen, 59–60, 117, 127
Gleason, Jackie, 18, 195, 197, 212–14, 322–23, 454, 476–78
Gleason, Thomas, 187
Glenn, Wilfred, 244
Glickman, Will, 317, 466
Glover, Ernest, 159
Glyn, Elinor, 317
Gobel, George, 94
Goberman, Max, 228, 261, 309
Gochman, Len, 374
Godfrey, Arthur, 324, 326
Godkin, Paul, 402–3, 433–34, 489–90
Gold, Leon, 138
Goldemberg, Rose Leiman, 139
Golden, Annie, 264
Golden, Ray, 51, 109
Goldmark, Karl, 341
Goldsmith, Beatrice, 99
Goldsmith, Eleanor, 372, 425, 508
Goldstein & Co., 226
Goldstone, Nat, 240, 368
Goldwasser, Lawrence, 74, 340
Goldwyn, Samuel, 98
Gomez, Tommy, 189, 257, 363
Gomez, Vincente, 108, 152
Gon, Zamira, 354
Good, Jack, 160, 163–64
Goode, Jack, 316, 356, 430
Goodhart, Ernest, 212
Goodman, Al, 12, 33, 499
Goodman, Benny, 251, 253
Goodman, Dody, 17
Goodrich, William B., 303
Gordon, Eric A., 414
Gordon, Harold, 220
Gordon, Hayes, 380, 443–44, 450
Gordon, Irving, 118
Gordon, Mack, 50
Gordon, Max, 90, 271, 282, 358
Gordon, Noel, 291

Gordon, Noele, 382
Gordon, Robert H., 146, 197, 214, 225, 331, 425, 478
Gorin, Igor, 146
Gorney, Jay, 51–53, 111, 225–26, 452–53, 501
Gorrin, John, Jr., 489
Gorski, Virginia, 202, 419, 476
Goslar, Lotte, 9–10
Gossett, Louis, 505
Gottesfeld, Charles, 184
Gould, Berni, 111, 134
Gould, Chuck, 493
Gould, Edward, 167
Gould, Elliott, 264
Gould, Morton, 39, 291, 309, 311
Goulet, Robert, 276, 382, 475
Grable, Betty, 333
Grace, Buster, 349
Grady, Blanche, 265
Graf, Herbert, 216
Graham, Irvin, 61
Graham, Ronald, 94–96, 114, 221
Grahame, Gloria, 156, 365
Grainger, Peter, 70
Grandee, George, 111
Grant, Cary, 144
Grant, John, 212
Grant, Mary, 210, 251, 270, 291, 298, 393, 397
Grant, Peter, 484
Gravitte, Debbie, 24
Gray, Alexander, 181, 432
Gray, Dolores, 252, 254, 265, 306–7, 336, 396
Grayson, Kathryn, 175, 313, 317, 474
Greanin, Leon, 179–81
Green, Adolph, 65, 261–62, 264–65, 309, 311, 436–37
Green, Alfred E., 219
Green, Donald, 25
Green, Eddie, 161
Green, Isaac, Jr., 397
Green, Jackie, 148
Green, Johnny, 69, 113, 139–40
Green, Mitzi, 29–30, 134–35, 186, 311
Green, Natalye, 352
Greene, Herbert, 261
Greene, Mort, 141, 230
Gregg, Bud, 439
Greggory, David, 9, 45, 134, 439
Gregory, John, 401
Grever, Maria, 80
Grey, Clifford, 430
Grey, Virginia, 211
Grieg, Edvard, 222, 236, 238
Griffies, Ethel, 497–98
Griffin, Bernard, 227, 334
Griffin, Merv, 374
Griffith, Billy, 301
Griffith, Linda, 47
Griffith, Peter, 369
Grimes, Tammy, 415
Grisman, Sam H., 414

Groenendaal, Cris, 484
Groener, Harry, 156
Grosch (R. L.) & Sons, 183
Grosh (R. L.) & Sons, 223, 239
Gross, Edward, 327
Gross, Milt, 441
Gross, Nelson L., 360
Grossman, Larry, 136
Grover, Mary, 276
Grover, Stanley, 374, 484
Grubell, Sandra, 395
Gruenwald, Alfred, 293
Grushetzky, Nadya, 435
Guare, John, 474
Guelis, Jean, 228, 271
Guenther, Felix, 352
Guernsey, Otis T., 269, 276, 306, 367, 388, 448
Guidi, Agostino, 11
Guiterson, Waldemar, 239
Guittard, Laurence, 156
Gunn, Nathan, 273, 408
Gunther, John, 425
Gunther, Mizzi, 127
Guster, Al, 109
Guterson, Waldemar, 223, 316
Guthrie, Thomas Anstey, 192
Guttler, Archie, 72
Guy, Bessie, 177
Guys, Sheila, 280
The Gypsy Baron, 245–46, 300
Gypsy Lady, 356–57

Haack, Morton, 416
Haakon, Paul, 15, 210
Haas, Dolly, 320–21
Haber, Louis, 72
Hack, Monroe B., 278–79
Hackett, Buddy, 332
Hackett, Hal, 436
Hackett, Jeanette, 190
Hackley, Bland "Crack Shot," 72
Hadley, Jerry, 171, 315, 371
Haffner, Karl, 143
Haggott, John, 271
Hagman, Larry, 484
Hague, Robert A., 307, 472
Hairpin Harmony, 190–92
Halasz, Laszlo, 145–46, 245, 300
Hale, Chester, 70, 80
Hale, George, 33, 80, 94
Hale, Richard, 153
Halevy, Ludovic, 205, 216, 277, 330
Haley, Jack, 12–15, 131, 425, 427
Hall, Adelaide, 474
Hall, Cliff, 167
Hall, George, 331, 439, 501
Hall, Jon, 66
Hall, Juanita, 258, 481, 484–85
Hall, Patti, 397

Hall, Teddy, 187
Halliday, Hildegarde, 462
Halliday, Robert, 129, 317
Halligan, Tom, 301
Halouze, Edouard, 129
Hambleton, John, 1
Hambleton, T. Edward, 432
Hamer, Janet, 236
Hamill, John, 249
Hamilton, Gloria, 378
Hamilton, Margaret, 156, 336
Hamilton, Nancy, 6, 324–25
Hamilton, Peter, 260, 411
Hammerstein, Oscar II, 15, 50, 89–90, 127, 154, 205, 219, 274, 276–77, 312–13, 316, 330, 334, 405–7, 448, 480–81, 485
Hammond, Virginia, 202
Hampson, Texas, 273
Hands Across the Sea, 422
Handzlik, Jean, 323, 443
Haney, Carol, 287, 474
Hanighen, Bernard, 320, 378
Hanley, Ellen, 384
Hanna, Phil, 382
Hannan, Walter F., 227
Hanson, Clarence, 167
Hanson, Pat, 409
Harbach, Otto, 163, 316
Harburg, E. Y., 33, 36, 49, 53, 240, 368, 372, 375
Hare, Marilyn, 286
Hargrave, Roy, 208
Hargreaves, John, 239
Harkrider, John, 82
Harlan, Ken, 169
Harlem Cavalcade, 105–7
Harline, Leigh, 141
Harman, Barry, 459
Harmon, Selene, 393
Harnick, Sheldon, 27, 136
Harper, Herbert, 29
Harper, Leonard, 105
Harrell, Bobby, 77
Harrington, Hamtree, 68
Harrington, Pat, 47, 74, 118
Harris, Barbara, 415
Harris, Donny, 464
Harris, Holly, 368, 474
Harris, Howard, 15, 449
Harris, Jed, 279
Harris, Jonathan, 227
Harris, Julie, 385
Harris, Leland, 33
Harris, Natalie, 20
Harris, Robert H., 419
Harris, Sam H., 63, 153
Harris and Shore, 500
Harrison, Ray, 405
Harriton, Maria, 309
Harrod, Ben, 218

Harrold, John, 243, 300
Hart, Anne, 512
Hart, Lorenz, 12, 15, 50, 54, 113–14, 127, 200, 202
Hart, Mabel, 504
Hart, Margie, 55, 132–33, 197
Hart, Moss, 63–65, 153, 158, 202, 205, 251, 418, 425, 427, 497–98
Hart, Teddy, 127, 192
Hart, Toni, 240
Hart, Walter, 342
Hartke, G. V., 138, 435
Hartman, Grace, 15, 30, 104, 107, 411–13, 478–80, 516–17
Hartman, Paul, 15, 30, 104, 107, 411–13, 478–79, 516–17
Hartt, Sherle, 45
Harvey, Georgette, 97–99, 186
Harvey, Richard, 432
Harvey, Robert, 1, 177
Harvey, Roslyn, 99, 134
Hassan, Rita, 385
Hatch, Eric, 229
Hatfield, Lansing, 248
Hathaway, Charles, 286
Hats Off to Ice, 234–36
Hatten, Lennie, 99
Hatton, Fanny and Frederic, 59
Hatvany, Lili, 59
Havoc, June, 54–55, 210, 246, 248–49
Hawkins, June, 327
Hawkins, William, 159, 333, 335–36, 339, 353, 355–57, 359, 363, 367, 371, 373–74, 376, 379, 381, 384, 386, 388, 398, 400–403, 408, 411–12, 415, 418, 420, 423, 427, 430–31, 444, 450–51, 453, 456, 458, 461, 463, 466, 469, 472, 474, 477–78, 480, 483, 494, 496, 501, 503, 505, 507, 511
Hawks, Howard, 513
Hawthorne, 513
Hawthorne, Irene, 261
Hayden, Michael, 277
Haydn, Richard, 6–7
Hayes, Alfred, 45, 99
Hayes, Bill, 382, 475
Hayes, John Maxwell, 344
Hayes, Laurence, 220
Hayes, Peter Lind, 452–53
Hayle, Grace, 322
Hayman, Coreania, 330
Haymes, Dick, 195, 270
Hayward, Leland, 481, 485
Hayward, Marjorie, 224
Hayward, Susan, 20, 197
Hayworth, Rita, 56, 249
Headley, George L., 303
Headliners of '42, 165
Healey, Eunice, 6, 36, 139
Healy, Mary, 136, 347
Hearn, Fred, 395
Heathen, Boyd, 271
Heaven on Earth, 452–54
Hecht, Ben, 251, 354–55

Heckart, Eileen, 56
Heisey, Jean, 352
Helavy, Ludovic, 86, 145, 267
Helburn, Theresa, 258, 274
Helen Goes to Troy, 216–18
Hellman, Lillian, 158, 505, 507
Helm, Litzie, 231
Hemingway, Ernest, 158
Henderson, Florence, 156, 239, 484
Henderson, Horton, 210
Henderson, Ray, 157
Hendrick, John, 354
Henie, Sonja, 39, 46, 120, 234, 349, 390, 445, 485
Henley, Bob, 72
Hepburn, Audrey, 404
Hepburn, Katharine, 30, 52, 110, 114, 158
Hepburn, Philip, 505
Herbert, A. P., 68
Herbert, Evelyn, 129
Herbert, Glenn, 187
Herbert, Ralph, 144, 267
Herbert, Victor, 27, 301, 356–57, 375
Herbert, Walter, 226
Herczeg, Geza, 293
Herk, I. H., 133
Herlick, Edith, 244
Herman, Jerry, 139
Hermann, Harry, 516
Herold, Don, 61
Hersholt, Jean, 46
Hertz, Ralph, 347, 489
Herwood, Marion, 74
Herzig, S. M., 53
Herzig, Sig, 240, 319, 339, 368
H.E.S., 367
Heyman, Edward, 227, 513–14
Heyward, Dorothy, 97, 186
Heyward, DuBose, 97, 99, 186
Hickey, William, 80, 264
Hickman, Darryl, 462
High Button Shoes, 402–4
Higher and Higher, 12–15
High Kickers, 84–85
Hightower, Robert, 113
Hiken, Nat, 475
Hildegarde, 104, 412
Hilgenberg, Katherine, 277
Hill, Annabelle, 472
Hill, Phyllis, 216
Hill, Ruby, 327
Hillary, Lucy, 243
Hilliard, Bob, 386, 411
Hilliard, Mack, 190
Hilt, Ferdinand, 454
Hilty, Megan, 512
Hindle, Winifred, 401
Hindus, Milton, 9
Hines, Jerome, 484
Hinnant, Bill, 27

Hirschfeld, Al, 395
Hirschfeld, Nina, 462
Hirshman, John J., 409
Hirst, George, 164, 282
Hively, Jack, 307
Hi Ya, Gentlemen, 69–70
Hobson, Valerie, 423
Hodge, Edward, 309
Hodge, Martha, 66
Hodges, Joy, 221, 317, 319
Hoff, Fred, 169
Hoffman, Jane, 45–46
Hogan, Dick, 202
Hoier, Thomas (Tom), 443, 472
Holbrook, William, 200
Holden, Richard, 9
Holder, Donald, 484
Hold It!, 428–30
Hold on to Your Hats, 33–36
Holgate, Ronald, 474
Holiday, Billie, 424–25
Holiday, Hope, 79
Holiday on Broadway, 424–25
Holland, Joseph, 25
Holland, Mary Lou, 333
Holliday, Judy, 205
Holloway, Stanley, 423
Holloway, Sterling, 316
Hollywood Pinafore, 282–84
Hollywood Theatre Alliance, 51
Holm, Celeste, 154, 240, 242, 270
Holm, Hanya, 175, 433, 472, 474
Holm, John Cecil, 77, 80, 92, 161, 375
Holman, Libby, 364, 388
Holmes, Taylor, 291
Holt, Ethelyne, 176
Holt, Henry, 159
Holtz, Lou, 101, 239–40
Homolka, Oscar, 239
Honore, 401
Hooker, Brian, 174
Hope, Bob, 23, 84, 438
Hopwood, Avery, 31
Horan, Bill, 508
Horn, Edmund, 345
Hornaday, Frank, 59, 169
Horne, Lena, 44, 49, 313
Horne, Marilyn, 207
Horne, William, 216, 245
Horner, Harry, 9, 63, 65, 82–83, 92, 118, 153, 202, 205
Horton, Edward Everett, 277
Horton, Lester, 342
Horwitt, Arnold, 416
Horwitt, Arnold B., 305, 425, 439
Hot from Harlem, 70
Hough, Will M., 142
House, Billy, 448
Houseman, John, 66, 320, 364
Houston, Elizabeth, 126, 220

Houston, George, 25–27, 268
Houston, Grace, 197, 234, 269, 331, 389, 485
Houston, Josephine, 20–21
Hoving, Lucas, 363
Howard, Bruce, 68
Howard, Cheryl, 439
Howard, Eugene, 61, 342
Howard, Harry, 291
Howard, Joe, 142
Howard, Marcella, 221
Howard, Norah, 421–22
Howard, Sidney, 320
Howard, Warda, 73
Howard, Willie, 61, 63, 102, 184–86, 341–42, 430–31, 478
Howdy, Mr. Ice, 445–47
Howdy, Mr. Ice of 1950, 485–87
Howell, Harry, 286
Howell, Thomas, 475
Howes, Bobby, 374
Howes, Sally Ann, 382
Howland, Alice, 245
Hoysradt, John, 215
Hubert, Rene, 109
Hudson, Barclay, 114
Huey, Richard, 90
Hughes, Elinor, 162, 228
Hughes, Langston, 109, 369
Hughes, Patricia, 382
Hulbert, Jack, 401
Hull, Lytle, 143
Humans, Maria, 61
Humason, Sally, 439
Humphrey, Doris, 258
Humphreys, Kalita, 82
Hunnicut, Arthur, 71
Hunt, Martita, 423
Hunter, Margaret, 382
Hunter, Mary, 295, 432
Hurdle, Laurence, 146
Hurlbut, Gladys, 12
Hurok, S., 189, 257, 392–93, 495
Husmann, Ron, 264
Huston, Bettyjo, 441
Hutcherson, LeVern, 98, 207, 278, 330
Hutton, Betty, 6–8, 48, 84, 336
Hyde-White, Wilfred, 401
Hyers, Frank, 47
Hyldoft, Joan, 349, 390
Hyman, Joseph M., 416
Hynda, Harry and John, 108
Hynter, Nicholas, 277
Hyrt, Nell, 9

Icetime, 349–51
Icetime of 1948, 390–92
If the Shoe Fits, 361–63
Ingalls, Phil, 411
In Gay New Orleans, 393–95
Inghram, Rose, 113, 216, 300, 324–25

Ingram, Lawaune, 360
Ingram, Rex, 42, 44, 327–28
Inside U.S.A., 425–28
Iolas, Alexander, 228
Irving, George S., 23, 491
Irving, Margaret, 33, 342
Irving, Washington, 443, 445
Irwin, Charles, 268, 508
Irwin, Will, 57, 88, 146, 197, 212, 305, 320, 361
Isherwood, Charles, 462
Israel, Walter, 236, 301, 356
It Happens on Ice, 38–42
Ives, Burl, 125, 258, 260–61

J. P., 52
Jackman, Hugh, 156
Jackpot, 207–9
Jack's of Hollywood, 441, 488
Jackson, Andrew, 109
Jackson, Arrin, 33
Jackson, Cheyenne, 375
Jackson, Danny, 286
Jackson, Frederick, 343
Jackson, Harriet, 295
Jackson, Harriett, 97, 186
Jackson, Joe, 15
Jackson, Joe, Jr., 390
Jackson, Margie, 134
Jackson, Richard, 286, 301
Jackson, Warren, 183
Jac-Lewis, 340
Jacobs, Lewis, 342
Jacobson, Leopold, 117, 378
Jacqmar, 401
Jacquemot, Ray, 397
James, Dan, 240, 368
James, Harry, 79
James, Ida, 280
James, Inez, 307
James, Joseph, 504
James, Lilith, 240, 368
James, Marcia, 375
James, Olga, 207
James, Sidney, 404
James & James, Ltd., 401
Jamieson, James, 382
Janney, Russell, 174–75
Jansen, Alvin, 488
Jansen, Harry A., 33, 488
Jarnac, Dorothy, 452–53
Jarrett, Art, 29
Jarvis, Louise, 171
Jeannette, Gertrude, 504
Jefferson, Lauretta, 195, 208
Jeffreys, Anne, 369, 462–64
Jeffries, Herb, 109
Jenkins, Allan, 150
Jenkins, George, 171, 210, 214, 280, 305, 421, 504
Jenkins, Gordon, 475

Jerome, Adele, 99
Jessel, George, 84–85, 131, 177, 431
Jessye, Eva, 97, 280, 505
Jocelyn, Mildred, 249
John, Walter, 334
John Henry, 1–3
Johnny 2 X 4, 102–4
Johnson, Albert, 1, 15, 61, 184, 258, 303
Johnson, Arte, 79
Johnson, Bill, 8, 27, 59, 75, 92, 150, 307, 336, 474
Johnson, Bobbie, 68
Johnson, Bobby, 73
Johnson, Chic, 87–89, 136, 158, 254, 256–57, 438, 493–94, 514
Johnson, Christine, 274, 480
Johnson, Eddie, 51–52, 111
Johnson, Fred, 345
Johnson, Gil, 77, 190, 341
Johnson, Hall, 177–79, 278
Johnson, Harriet, 217–18
Johnson, Harriett, 292
Johnson, J. Rosamond, 42
Johnson, James P., 187
Johnson, Jane, 438
Johnson, June, 493
Johnson, Nunnally, 358–59
Johnson, Susan, 382
Johnson, Van, 381–82
Johnson, Walter, 169
Johnson, Willie, 152
Johnston, Johnny, 111
Johnston, Roy M., 126
Johnstone, Anna Hill, 504
Johnstone, Jane, 134
Jokai, Mor, 245–46, 300
Jolson, Al, 33, 35–36, 431
Jonay, Roberta, 405
Jones, Allan, 26, 117, 163, 208–9, 315, 488
Jones, George, Jr., 1
Jones, Geraldine, 32
Jones, Henry, 385
Jones, Robert Edmond, 161, 208, 216, 320–21
Jones, Sabra, 248
Jones, Shirley, 156, 276, 303, 382, 485
Jones, Spike, 53, 441
Jones, T. C., 209
Jordan, Claudia, 240
Jordan, Jack, Jr., 77, 79
Jordan, Jackson, 265
Journet, Marcel, 127
Joyce, Janice, 82
Judels, May, 120, 234, 349, 390, 445, 485
Judson, James, 389
Julia, Raul, 462
Jump for Joy, 108–10
Junger, Esther, 45, 346
Jurist, Irma, 428
Jurmann, Walter, 109, 347

Kadison, Philip, 475
Kahal, Irving, 36, 73
Kaj-Velden Studios, 377
Kalich, Jacob, 138–39
Kalman, Emmerich, 291
Kalmar, Bert, 84
Kaltenborn, H. V., 96
Kamarova, Natalie, 25, 195, 265, 341
Kane, Edward, 471
Kao-Tong-Kia, 320
Kaper, Bronislaw, 298
Kaplan, Sol, 342–43
Kappeler, Alfred, 69
Karin, 513
Karinska, 68
Karle, George, 174
Karloff, Boris, 201
Karnilova, Maria, 331
Karrol, Dorothy, 352
Karson, Nat, 17, 84, 165, 200, 317, 395, 432
Kasia, 278
Kasten, Sam, 138
Kasznar, Kurt, 61
Katsaros, Doug, 136
Katzell, William R., 372, 467
Katzman, Louis, 142
Kauffman, Marta, 136
Kaufman, George S., 22, 25, 251, 282–83, 358, 515
Kaufman, Harry, 87, 136, 157, 254
Kaufman, Irving, 369
Kaufman, Nico, 392
Kaufman, S. Jay, 17
Kavanaugh, Ray, 6, 57, 80, 166–67, 233, 291, 324, 393
Kay, Arthur, 356, 454
Kay, Beatrice, 225
Kay, Kenneth, 200
Kaye, Alma, 258
Kaye, Arthur, 236
Kaye, Buddy, 449
Kaye, Danny, 63, 65–66, 82–83
Kaye, Mary, 63
Kazan, Elia, 192, 194, 456
Kazounoff, Berenece, 9
Kean, Betty, 61
Kean, Jane, 69, 303, 305, 332
Keane, Doris, 463
Keane, George, 360, 380–81, 515
Keane, Teri, 190
Kearney, Ty, 160
Keating, Fred, 167, 354
Keaton, Douglas, 167
Keegan, Arthur, 385
Keel, Howard, 156, 276–77, 313, 336, 474
Keeler, Ruby, 36
Keep 'em Laughing, 104–5
Keep off the Grass, 17–20
Keith, Sally, 129
Keller, Evelyn, 387, 470

Keller, Leonard, 225
Kellerman, Mimi, 341
Kelley, Barry, 154
Kelley, Bunty, 380
Kelly, Emmet, 17–18
Kelly, Fred, 395
Kelly, Frederic N., 462
Kelly, Gene, 54–55, 74–75, 77–78, 264–65, 382
Kelly, George, 102
Kelly, Janis, 371
Kelly, Jimmy, 393
Kelly, Maurice, 74
Kelly, Patrick J., 374
Kelly, Terry, 212
Kelton, Pert, 57, 432
Ken Murray's Blackouts of 1949, 499–501
Kennedy, Bob, 303
Kennedy, Jack, 195, 210
Kennedy, John, 268, 375, 389, 411
Kenney, Kay, 63
Kent, Carl, 45, 61, 236
Kent, Edgar, 460
Kent, Lennie, 190
Kerby, Paul, 143
Kermoyan, Michael, 277
Kern, Jerome, 50, 312–13, 430, 448
Kerr, Jack, 346
Kerr, Jean, 501–3
Kerr, John, 484
Kerr, Walter, 136, 258, 260, 297, 435–36, 501–3
Kerry, Addison, 70
Kert, Larry, 513
Kerz, Leo, 393, 397
Kesler, Lew, 356, 439
Kibler, Belva, 389
Kidd, Michael, 17, 265, 291, 372–73, 375, 428, 430, 456, 461, 515
Kiepura, Jan, 14, 177, 243, 298–300, 354
Kilgallen, Dorothy, 67, 220, 222
Kilty, Jack, 161, 416
Kim, Willa, 305, 322
Kimber, Kay, 113, 404
Kimberly, Robert, 398
Kinch, Myra, 340
King, Carlotta, 317
King, Dennis, 73, 175, 317
King, Marjorie, 245
King, Paul, 470
King, Rosalie, 177
King, Rose, 166
Kingdon, Patrick, 383
Kingsford, Guy, 159
Kingsley, Herbert, 49, 68
Kingsley, Patty, 397
Kinoy, Ernest, 382
Kipness, Joseph, 187, 342, 402, 489
Kirby, Durward, 404
Kirby, John, 187–88
Kirk, Lisa, 472

Kirk, Van, 45
Kirkland, Jack, 111
Kirkwood, Pat, 396
Kirov, Ivan, 228
Kirtland, Louise, 165
Kiss Me, Kate, 472–75
Kitt, Eartha, 361
Kiviette, 161, 208
Klase, Irving, 438
Klein, Arthur, 351
Klein, Harry, 346
Kleinsinger, George, 45–46, 99
Klugman, Jack, 475
Knapp, Kenneth, 480
Knight, Felix, 126, 146
Knight, June, 284–86, 377
Kobart, Ruth, 156, 415
Koch, Howard, 490
Koenig, John, 54, 123
Kogan, Zinovy, 20
Kolar, Charles, 108
Kollmar, Richard, 61, 113, 171, 220, 222, 305, 347
Koltz, Max, 441
Komack, Jimmie, 79
Komisarjevsky, Theodore, 20
Korngold, Erich Wolfgang, 68, 143, 216
Kozma, Tibor, 385
Kraft, Beatrice, 246
Kraft, Randy, 439
Krakeur and Schmidlapp, 136
Kramer, Dave, 148
Kramer, Sam, 227
Kramer, Searle, 225
Krauss, Charlotte, 10
Kreig, Frank, 212
Kreisler, Fritz, 9, 249–51
Kreuger, Miles, 437
Kristen, Eric, 271
Kriza, John, 262
Kronenberger, Louis, 60, 62, 67, 78, 81, 83, 85, 91, 93, 95–96, 99, 101, 103, 105–6, 115, 117, 120, 125, 130–31, 133, 135, 137, 140–41, 143–44, 149, 151–52, 155, 158, 170, 173, 175, 177–78, 181–82, 185, 188, 191, 194, 197–98, 201, 205, 207, 209, 211, 213, 218, 222, 234, 238, 240, 242, 245, 247, 250, 253, 257, 260, 263, 266, 269, 272–73, 275–76, 280, 284, 290, 292, 294–96, 299, 302, 305, 308–9, 311, 314, 319, 321, 323, 325–26, 329, 333, 335, 338, 353–55, 357, 359, 363, 365, 371, 374, 376, 379, 381, 384, 386, 388, 398, 400–401, 403, 408, 412, 415, 418, 420
Krupa, Gene, 141
Krupska, Dania, 179
Kuhn, Judy, 408
Kuhn, Katherine, 152, 390, 445, 485
Kuhn, Kathryn, 195, 282, 361, 363
Kuhnly, Fred, 142
Kuller, Sid, 51, 109–10
Kurer, Vilma, 9
Kurnitz, Harry, 195

Kusmiak, Eugene, 320
Kwartin, Paul, 145

L. N., 33, 52, 107
La Belle Helene, 68
Lackland, Ben, 208
Ladd, Cheryl, 336
Ladd, Hank, 129–30, 165, 411–12, 476–77
The Lady Comes Across, 94–96
Lady in the Dark, 63–66, 153–54
A Lady Says Yes, 265–67
Laffacade, 438
Laffing Room Only, 254–57
LaGuardia, Fiorello, 119, 133
Lahr, Bert, 53, 84, 165, 251, 253, 438, 510
Lake, Florence, 74
Lake, Veronica, 79
Lamb, Gil, 33, 443–44
Lambert, Beverly, 382
Lambert, Sammy, 389, 428, 478
Lamberti, Professor, 3, 118–19
Lambrose, George, 399
Lamour, Dorothy, 438
Lampl, Carl, 449
Landau, Irving, 216, 267, 298
Landin, Nils, 243
Landis, Carole, 265–66
Landis, Jessie Royce, 245
Landry, Clarence, 109
Lane, Burton, 33, 36, 49, 254, 372–73
Lane, Fred, 169
Lane, James, 139
Lane, Rosemary, 78
Lanfield, Sidney, 84
Lang, Harold, 55, 262, 264, 294, 324, 419, 472
Langan, James M., 435
Langford, Frances, 126, 141
Langley, Stuart, 150
Langner, Lawrence, 68, 144, 258, 274
Lanning, Jerry, 404, 462
Lanza, Mario, 171, 205
Larabee, Louise, 480
Lardner, John, 449, 451, 454, 456, 458, 461, 463–64, 466, 469, 474, 477, 480
Lascoe, Henry, 398
LaTouche, John, 42, 44, 68, 92–94, 249, 298–99, 363, 365, 432, 434–35
Lattauda, Emma, 11
Laugh, Town, Laugh, 115–17
Laugh Time, 183–84
Laun, Louis, 450
Laurence, Larry, 339
Laurence, Paula, 150, 192
La Varre, Paul, 223
La Vie Parisienne, 86, 145, 267
Law, Jenny Lou, 469
Lawford, Betty, 29, 31
Lawrence, Bert, 50
Lawrence, Bob, 90

Lawrence, Brian, 267
Lawrence, Carol, 404, 475, 484
Lawrence, Gertrude, 7, 63–66, 153, 421–23
Lawrence, Jane, 166
Lawrence, Jerome, 418, 420
Lawrence, Lester, 157
Lawrence, Mark, 450
Lawrence, Norman, 3, 246
Lawrie, Ted, 433
Laws, Jerry, 186
Laws, Sam, 44
Lawson, Kate, 51
Lawson, Sid, 497
Lawson, Sidney, 298
Lay, Ann, 397
Laye, Evelyn, 91, 129
Layton, Joe, 264, 512
Lazaron, Harold, 352
Lazarus, Milton, 236
Lazarus, Paul, 136
Leach, Archie, 144
Leachman, Cloris, 485
Leavitt, Doug, 181
LeBerthon, Helene, 265
LeClair, Allan, 344
Lecuona, Ernesto, 228
Lederer, Charles, 513
Lee, Ann, 63, 119, 153
Lee, Gypsy Rose, 32, 55, 118, 120, 125, 133, 197, 249
Lee, Jackie, 236
Lee, Kathryn, 228
Lee, Lester, 118, 129, 138, 157, 478
Lee, Lois, 402
Lee, Pinky, 132
Lee, Robert E., 418, 420
Lee, Sammy, 53
Lee, Tom, 21, 29, 69
Lee, William A., 210
Leeds, Phil, 99, 134
Lefebre, Hans, 9
Le Gallienne, Eva, 385
Le Gon, Jeni, 171
Lehack, Ned, 99
Lehar, Franz, 126, 176, 243, 352–53
Lehrer, Scott, 484
Leibert, Dick, 187
Leigh, Rowland, 29, 59–60, 160, 164, 340, 462
Leighton, Isabel, 274
Leisen, Mitchell, 66
Leiser, Henry, 146
Lend an Ear, 466–70
Lenn, Robert, 433
Le Noire, Rosetta, 44, 68, 225, 484, 505
Lenters, Howard, 309
Lenya, Lotte, 271, 273
Leon, Victor, 126, 176, 243
Leonard, Ada, 488
Leonard, Charles, 109
Leonard, George, 127

Leonard, Jack, 49
Leonard, William, 488
Leonard, William Torbert, 228–29, 286, 348, 439
Leonardi, Leon, 240, 327, 366
Leonardos, Urylee, 207, 330
Leoncavallo, Ruggero, 11
Leonidoff, Leon, 15, 39, 258
Lerner, Alan Jay, 165–66, 197, 199, 307–9, 380–81, 456–58
Lerner, Sam, 184, 428
le Roux, Madeleine, 248
LeRoy, Hal, 136–37
Leser, Tina, 358–59
Le Seyeux, Jean, 3, 129
Lesko, John, Jr., 432
Leslie, Edgar, 72
Leslie, Ellen, 368
Leslie, Joan, 126
Leslie, Lew, 72
Lessac, Arthur, 258
Lesser, Arthur, 377, 424, 475
Lessner, George, 443–44
Lester, Alan, 148
Lester, Edwin, 236, 356–57, 454
Lester, Jerry, 3, 5, 139, 209, 488
Lester, Ketty, 44
Lester, Lorraine, 443
Le Tang, Henry, 184, 220
Let Freedom Sing, 133–36
Let's Face It!, 82–84
Levant, Harry, 54, 184, 210, 303, 337, 401
Leve, Sam, 139, 141
Leveen, Raymond, 80
Leven, Boris, 230
Levene, Sam, 94
Leventhal, Jules J., 291
Le Verne, 39, 41
Levey, Ethel, 90
Levey, Harold, 61
Levin, Herman, 331, 333, 436, 510
Levine, Bert, 230
Levine, Maurice, 504
Levinson, Leonard L., 249, 293
Levy, Parke, 17, 29
Lewin, Albert E., 333
Lewine, Richard, 45, 74, 416, 439
Lewis, Albert, 42, 92
Lewis, Ann, 32
Lewis, Brenda, 300, 471, 507
Lewis, Edward, 408
Lewis, Jerry, 84
Lewis, Joe E., 94–96, 165
Lewis, Martin, 298
Lewis, Mary, 295
Lewis, Michael J., 27
Lewis, Morgan, 6, 324–25
Lewis, Mort, 17
Lewis, Robert, 380, 505
Lewis, Russell, 316, 421
Leyden, Norman, 202

Liberto, Don, 167–68, 361, 419
Liberty Jones, 66–67
Libuse, Frank, 87, 254
Lichine, David, 139, 141, 230, 249, 298
Lichtman, Nat, 45–46
Liebman, Max, 61, 66, 83, 132–33, 218–19, 342, 416, 418, 475
Liebowitz, Sam, 21
Life of the Party, 165–66
Lilley, Edward Clarke, 30, 58, 69, 303
Lillie, Beatrice, 251, 253, 418, 425, 427
Lime Trio, 15
Lincoln, Arthur, 298
Lind, Della, 344
Lind, Gloria, 375
Lind, Monica, 228
Linden, Robert, 39
Lindenberg, Paul, 9
Lindfors, Viveca, 56
Ling, Ming, 166
Linn, Bambi, 66, 202, 274, 276–77, 385–86, 430–32, 481
Linz, Joe, 42
Lippman, Sidney, 383–84
Lipscott, Alan, 17, 29
Lipton, Ann, 86
Lipton, George, 244, 300
Lipton, Sandra, 433
Lishner, Leon, 86
Littau, Joseph, 59, 205, 274, 456
Little, Frank, 441
The Little Dog Laughed, 70–71
Littlefield, Carl, 493
Littlefield, Catherine, 15, 33, 39, 61, 120, 212, 214, 234, 271, 349, 375, 390, 445, 485, 493
Littlefield, Dorothie, 234, 349, 390, 445, 485
Littlefield, James, 234, 349, 390
Litwack, Ned C., 452
Litz, Katherine, 432
Livesey, Sam, 202
Livingston, Billy, 150, 254, 349, 390, 445, 478, 485
Livingston, Jay, 94
Livingston, Jerry, 187
Lloyd, George, 45–46
Lloyd, Jay, 515
Lloyd, John Robert, 501
Lloyd, Norman, 225
Lobel, Adrianne, 264
Lober, David, 503
Locke, Charles O., 25–26
Locke, Sam, 45, 99, 134, 351
Lockridge, Richard, 2, 5, 8, 12, 14, 19–21, 23, 31, 35, 38, 41, 43–44, 46, 48, 50, 55, 58, 60, 62, 65, 67, 78, 81, 83, 85, 89, 91, 93, 95–96, 99, 103–6, 114, 130–31, 133, 137–38, 140, 143, 149, 151
Loeb, Philip, 71, 225, 251
Loesser, Frank, 257, 460, 462
Loew, E. M., 195
Loewe, Frederick, 165–66, 197, 199, 307, 309, 380–81
Logan, Ella, 69–70, 87, 131–32, 372

Logan, Joshua, 6, 12, 113, 123, 334, 481–82, 484–85
Lombardo, Guy, 339
Lonergan, Arthur, 301
Lonergan, Lenore, 509
Lonergan, Lester, Jr., 102
Long, Avon, 68, 97, 99, 186, 281–82, 295, 297, 364
Long, Nick, Jr., 26
Long, Ray, 439
Long, Tamara, 512
Long, Walter, 36, 367, 474
Longstreet, Stephen, 402–4
Look, Ma, I'm Dancin'!, 418–21
Loos, Anita, 510
Loper, Don, 59
Lopez, Pilar, 107
Lopez, Victoria, 488
Loraine, Karol, 307
Lord, Bruce, 268
Lorenz, Fred, 9
Lorian, 401
Loring, Estelle, 413, 425
Loring, Eugene, 205, 277, 330, 360
Lost in the Stars, 503–5
Louisiana Lady, 397–99
Louisiana Purchase, 21–24
Love, Bessie, 512
Love, Ellen, 340
Love, Kermit, 192
Love in the Snow, 340–41
Lovelace, Henrietta, 1
Love Life, 456–59
Lowe, David, 413
Lowe, Milton, 352
Lowell, Allan, 399
Lowenthal, Walter, 389
Lubitsch, Ernest, 127, 160, 171
Lubritzky, David, 138
Lucas, Jonathan, 501, 503
Lucas, Nick, 500
Lucci, Susan, 336
Luce, Ted, 411, 478, 516
Luckey, Susan, 276
Lucyk, Michael, 375
Luker, Rebecca, 462
Luman, Carl, 433
Lumet, Sidney, 355
Luna, Barbara, 481
Lund, John, 146, 148, 171
Lunick, Olga, 433
Lunt, Alfred, 118, 125, 473
LuPone, Patti, 415
Luster, Betty, 340–41
Lute Song, 320–22
Luther, Frank, 195
Lutyens, Edith, 387, 470
Lyndeck, Edmund, 332
Lynds, John, 460
Lynn, Billy, 304
Lynn, Joe, 499

Lynn, Leni, 478
Lynn, William, 66
Lynne, Carol, 121, 234
Lynne, Phyllis, 366
Lyons, Colette, 195, 312

Macaulay, Joseph, 284, 286, 346
MacColl, James, 322
MacDonald, Jeanette, 127, 129, 163, 175, 376
MacDonald, P. A., 363
MacDonnell, Kyle, 416, 501–3
MacFarlane, Carol, 240
MacGregor, Edgar, 21, 33, 46, 58, 82, 161, 184, 267, 317, 397
MacGregor, Rae, 212
Mack, Arthur, 340
Mack, Cecil, 72
Mack, Johnny, 233
Mack, Russell, 341
Mackey, Joseph, 431
Mackle, Jane, 352
MacLaine, Shirley, 243
MacMillan, Kenneth, 276
Macomber, Ken, 409
Macon, Sarah, 197
Macrae, Arthur, 401
MacRae, Gordon, 156, 276, 317, 324–25, 475
MacVeigh, Earle, 270, 389
MacWatters, Virginia, 143, 224, 293
Macy, Gertrude, 6
Madison, Rosalind, 174
Magdalena, 454–56
Magelssen, Ralph, 86
Mahieu, 70, 129, 167, 190
Mahler, Fritz, 249
Mahler, Myron, 9
Mahoney, Francis X., 313
Mahoney, Will, 374
Mainbocher, 192, 358
Maine, Bruno, 120, 234, 390, 445, 485
Maison, Gil, 118, 449–50
Majer, Joseph, 174
Make Mine Manhattan, 416–18
Malas, Spiro, 156
Malbin, Elaine, 339, 389
Malcolm-Smith, George, 305
Malden, Karl, 205
Malina, Luba, 102, 211, 292–93
Malloy, Francetta, 165
Malone, Ray, 488
Maloney, Russell, 443
Maltby, Richard, Jr., 27
Maltz, Maxwell, 265
Mamoulian, Rouben, 154, 246–47, 274, 327–28, 480, 504
Mandel, Frank, 127, 219, 316
Mann, Delbert, 303
Mann, Joan, 312, 439, 450
Mann, Michael, 378
Mann, Terrence, 273

Manners, Jayne, 113, 187, 215
Manners, Loraine, 181
Manning, David, 354
Manning, Irene, 307, 317
Manning, Monroe, 352
Manning, Richard, 371
Manning, Samuel L., 409
Mansfield, Richard, 27
Manson, Eddy, 351–52
Mantle, Burns, 2–3, 5, 7, 10, 12, 14, 19, 22–23, 30, 35, 38, 41, 44, 46, 48, 50, 55, 58–60, 64, 67, 78, 81, 83, 89, 91, 93, 95–96, 99, 103, 106–7, 114, 116–17, 120, 125, 130–31, 133, 135, 137, 139–41, 143–44, 148–49, 152, 155, 159, 170, 173, 175
Manulis, Martin, 322
Manville, Tommy, 5, 130, 158, 209
Mapes, Bruce, 284
Marais, Josef, 351
Marand, Patricia, 485
March, Hal, 404
Marchant, Claude, 189, 257, 409–10
Marching with Johnny, 225–26
Marco, Pepita, 495
Marcy, Everett, 57
Mardo, Al, 500–501
Margetson, Arthur, 337, 358
Marianne, 224–25
Marinka, 291–93
Marion, George, Jr., 139, 143–44, 171, 214, 291, 293, 366–67
Marion, Sid, 167
Markey, Gene, 15
Marko, Robert, 61
Markova, Alicia, 251
Marks, Gerald, 184, 428
Marks, Joe, 84
Marks, Sylvia, 99
Marlow, Mary-Robin, 84
Marlowe, Anthony, 230
Marquez, Luis, 495
Marrero, Estelle, 32
Marsh, Caren, 452
Marsh, Carolyn, 38
Marsh, Howard, 170
Marsh, Jean, 461
Marshall, Armina, 68
Marshall, Don, 271
Marshall, Everett, 169–70
Marshall, Jack, 225
Marshall, Jay, 456
Marshall, Mort, 462
Marshall, Pat, 197, 199
Marshall, Patricia, 308
Marshall, Red, 57–58, 142
Marshall, Robert, 351–52
Martin, Barney, 484
Martin, Dean, 84
Martin, Ernest H., 460
Martin, Eugene, 361

Martin, George, 454
Martin, Georges Andre, 408
Martin, Glenn, 393
Martin, Hugh, 22, 30, 77–78, 94, 418, 420
Martin, John, 434
Martin, Linton, 72, 226
Martin, Mary, 104, 161–63, 192–94, 320–21, 336, 481, 484–85
Martin, Perry, 493
Martin, Thomas, 226
Martin, Thomas Philipp, 245
Martin, Tony, 313
Martin, Virginia, 485
Martin, Walter, 9
Martingale, 286
Martini, Lola, 108
Marvenga, Ilse, 170–71
Marx, Chico, 223, 233
Marx, Harpo, 303
Marx, Louis, 130
Mason, Marilyn, 276, 382
Mason, Melissa, 60
Massenet, Jules, 11
Massey, Ilona, 157, 159
Massine, Leonide, 216, 228, 267
Masters, John, 341
Mathews, Christine, 56
Mathews, Jessie, 95
Mathews, Joyce, 84
Mathis, Stanley Wayne, 329
Matray, Ernst and Maria, 513
Mattern, Katherine, 9
Matteson, Ruth, 176, 293, 358
Matthews, Edward, 97, 186
Matthews, Inez, 207, 278
Matthews, Joyce, 33
Mattison, Ethel, 441
Mattox, Matt, 454
Mattson, Eric, 27, 274, 276, 480
Mature, Victor, 219
Mauceri, John, 371
Maugham, Dora, 190
Maugham, W. Somerset, 246
Maurice Chevalier in an Evening of Songs and Impressions, 424
Maurice Chevalier—Songs and Impressions, 377–78
Maurstad, Toralv, 239
Maury, Richard F., 450
Maxey, Paul R., 111
Maxwell, Arthur, 265
Maxwell, Donald, 472
Maxwell, Marilyn, 79, 319
May, Elaine, 303
May, Marty, 195, 334, 493
Mayehoff, Eddie, 249, 289–90
Mayen, Elisabeth, 392
Mayer, Edwin Justus, 271
Mayer, Ray, 21
Mayfield, Julian, 504

Mayfield, Kathryn, 111
Maynard, John, 342
Mayo, Don, 472
Mayo, Virginia, 92–93
Mazzie, Marin, 474
McArthur, Edwin, 312, 375
McCabe, Eleanor, 341
McCallister, Lon, 205
McCandless, Stanley, 249
McCann, Frances, 175, 378–79
McCarthy, Justin Huntley, 174
McCarty, Mary, 112, 444–45, 450–51, 497–98
McCauley, Jack, 258, 286, 346, 402, 510
McChesney, Ernest, 143, 378
McClain, John, 139
McClain, Marcia, 462
McClarney, Pat, 303
McClelland, Donald, 497
McClure, Rob, 462
McConkey, Joel, 508
McCord, J. C., 450
McCord, Keny, 393
McCormick, Myron, 485
McCracken, Joan, 240, 242, 310–11
McDaniel, Hattie, 315
McDevitt, Ruth, 443
McDonald, Ray, 69, 358
McDonough, Justin, 484
McElhany, Tom, 372
McEntire, Reba, 336, 485
McGee, Truly, 129, 132, 187
McGeoy, Carrie Nye, 27
McGill, Earl, 368
McGillin, Howard, 462
McGinley, Phyllis, 450–51
McGiveney, Owen, 500
McGlinn, John, 273, 315, 459
McGowan, Juanita, 32
McGrane, Paul, 120
McGrath, Michael, 23
McGrattan, Alice, 435
McGuire, Biff, 374
McHale, Duke, 305
McHugh, Frank, 374, 465
McHugh, Jimmy, 15, 17, 118, 151, 187, 464
McKechnie, Donna, 264
McKee, Lonette, 425
McKenna, Boots, 30, 160, 163–64, 265
McKenzie, Iona, 433
McLauchlin, Russell, 166
McLennan, Rodney, 102
McLeod, Norman Z., 49
McLerie, Allyn Ann, 437, 460, 484
McMahon, Jere, 200–201, 251
McManus, John, 17, 36, 87, 136, 157, 254
McNeil, Claudia, 70
McVeagh, Eve, 111
McVeigh, Earl, 25
Mead, George, 145, 245, 300

Meade, Claire, 197
Meader, George, 301
Meaney, Pat, 393
Medcraft, Russell, 82
Medford, Kay, 56, 277
Medina, Benigno, 107
The Medium, 387–89, 470
Medlin, Janet, 375
Meehan, John, Jr., 143, 216
Meeropol, Abel, 134
Meet the People, 50–53
Meier, Merle, 516
Meilhac, Henri, 86, 145, 205, 216, 267, 277, 330
Meiser, Edith, 83, 210
Mell, Randle, 415
Melnick, Daniel, 360
Melton, Sidney, 436
Meltzer, Robert, 225
Memphis Bound, 280–82
Mendel, Ross, 108
Mendelsohn, Daniel, 66
Mendoza, David, 39, 120, 234, 349, 390, 445, 485
Menendez, Nilo, 159
Menken, Alan, 136
Menn, Jack, 392
Menotti, Gian-Carlo, 387–89, 470
Mercer, Johnny, 29–31, 72, 118, 327–29, 508–10
Mercer, Ruby, 25, 27, 86
Mercury Theatre Production, 337
Merimee, Prosper, 205, 277, 330
Merlin, Ving, 214, 265
Mermaid Theatre, 48
Merman, Ethel, 47, 150, 247, 334–36
Merman, Ruth, 452
Meroff, Diane, 271
Mero-Irion, Yolanda, 143, 176, 216, 243, 267
Merrill, Blanche, 58
Merrill, Dorritt, 408
Merrill, Gary, 205
Merrill, Joan, 101–2
Merry-Go-Rounders, 166–67
The Merrymakers, 166–67
The Merry Widow, 126–27, 176–77, 243
Meth, Max, 42, 55, 82, 161, 187–88, 195, 197, 208–9, 220, 268, 284, 363, 375, 464, 466
Mette, Jack, 435
Metzl, Beatrice, 224
Metzl, Lothar, 9–11, 224
Mexican Hayride, 210–12
Meyers, Henry, 134
Meyers, Joe, 167
Meyers-Foster, Wilhelm, 169
Michaels, Beverly, 284
Michaels, Jackie, 148
Michaels, Sidney, 276
Michel, Werner, 9–11
Michener, James A., 481
Michon, Michel, 179
Middleton, Ray, 15, 49, 205, 334, 456, 484

Middleton, Tony, 44
Mielziner, Jo, 12, 54, 70, 77, 113, 271, 273–74, 282–84,
    295, 297, 334, 347, 369, 372, 378, 383, 405–6, 443, 445,
    480–81, 485, 502
Mikolitsky, Bernard, 435
Miles, Alastair, 472
Miles, William, 73
Milland, Ray, 66
Millar, Virginia, 104
Miller, Ann, 264, 474
Miller, Ben, 436
Miller, Benjamin, 383
Miller, Flournoy, 105–7
Miller, Marian, 132–33
Miller, Marilyn, 431–32
Miller, Moi Yo, 33, 488
Miller, Patsy Ruth, 399
Miller, Sidney, 109, 307
Miller, Susan, 3, 141, 152–53, 347–48
Milletaire, Carl, 454
Mills, Carly, 439
Milton, Frank, 261
Milton, Robert, 80
Mimi, 284
Mims, Stuart, 20
Minnelli, Liza, 79
Minnelli, Vincente, 44, 49, 382
Minter, Claire, 368
Miquel, Pablo, 107
Miranda, Carmen, 87, 89, 151, 205
Miss Liberty, 497–99
Mr. Strauss Goes to Boston, 293–95
Mitchell, Brian Stokes, 474, 485
Mitchell, Fanny Todd, 144
Mitchell, Fred, 1
Mitchell, George, 126, 220
Mitchell, James, 312, 380
Mitchell, Norma, 82
Mitten, Anna, 348
Mitzman, Marcia, 484
Mladova, Milada, 478–79
Moldow, Edwin Bruce, 90
Molnar, Ferenc, 118, 274, 480
Monahan, Dick, 84
Monks, John, Jr., 69
Monroe, Lucy, 15
Monroe, Marilyn, 451, 513
Monroe, Vaughn, 53
Monte, Joseph, 293
Montedoro, Marco, 86, 145
Montgomery, Candace, 366
Montgomery, David, 301–2
Monti, Mili, 71
Montoya, Carlos, 107–8
Mooney, John, 436
Moore, Adrienne, 153
Moore, Colleen, 432
Moore, Constance, 114
Moore, Dennie, 71

Moore, Garry, 404
Moore, Grace, 129
Moore, Jann, 174
Moore, Melba, 505
Moore, Monica, 113, 398
Moore, Owen, 303
Moore, Paulina, 32
Moore, Phil, 225
Moore, Robert, 435–36
Moore, Sam, 508
Moore, Scott, 312
Moore, Tim, 72, 105
Moore, Victor, 21–22, 24, 104–5, 282–83, 317–19
Moran, Alan, 74, 445, 485
Moran, Dick, 201
Moran, Lois, 318
Morde, David, 448
Mordecai, David, 134, 277, 330, 430
Morehouse, Ralph, 20
Morehouse, Ward, 152, 159, 177–78, 180, 182–83, 185,
    188, 191–92, 194, 197–98, 201, 205, 209, 211, 215, 238,
    240, 242, 247–48, 250, 253, 256–57, 260, 263, 267, 269,
    276, 292–93, 295–96, 299–300, 302, 305, 309, 311, 314,
    319, 321, 323, 325–26, 328, 333, 335, 354–55, 357, 371,
    373, 376, 381, 386, 398, 400–401, 403, 408, 411–12, 415,
    418, 420, 423, 427, 449, 451, 454, 456, 458, 461, 463,
    466, 474, 479, 483, 496, 498, 501, 505, 509
Morelli, Anthony B., 346
Morelli, Antonio, 501
Moreno, Rita, 175
Morey Amsterdam's Hilarities, 448–50
Morgan, Frank, 336
Morgan, Freddie, 441
Morgan, Helen, 315
Morgan, Johnny, 220
Morgan, Mme., 70
Morison, Patricia, 215, 472, 474–75
Moritz, Al, 278
Moross, Jerome, 68, 432, 434–35
Morris, Amarilla, 54
Morris, Bobbie, 160
Morris, Bobby, 265, 341
Morris, David, 57
Morris, Howard, 374
Morris, Lee, 393
Morris, Lenwood, 360
Morrison, Matthew, 484
Morrison, Paul, 515
Morrissey, Will, 142, 341
Morros, Boris, 230
Morrow, Doretta, 460
Morrow, Karen, 156, 382
Morton, Tommy, 439
Moser, Margot, 276, 382, 480
Moss, Al, 45
Moss, Paul, 119, 133
Mostel, Zero, 104–5, 107–8, 289–90, 364–65
Motley, 246, 295, 481, 497–98
Muenz, Richard, 459

Muffler, Marti, 392
Mulcay, Jimmy and Mildred, 239
Mulle, Henry, 430
Mulligan, Robert J., 54
Mum's the Word, 49–50
Muni, Paul, 354–55
Munroe, Leigh, 507
Munroe, Walter, 127
Munsel, Patrice, 127, 475
Munshin, Jules, 156, 264, 331, 475
Munson, Jerry, 45
Murphy, Ben, 383
Murphy, Dean, 157
Murphy, George, 126
Murray, Harold, 317
Murray, Honey, 197
Murray, Jan, 399
Murray, Ken, 499–501
Murray, Ted, 233
Murray, Wynn, 15, 57, 59, 89, 95–96, 452–53, 499
Murtah, Kate, 509
Muse, Clarence, 177
Music in My Heart, 399–400
My Dear Public, 184–86
Myerberg, Michael, 320–21, 413
Myers, Henry, 50–51, 111, 225
Myers, William A., 433
Mylroie, Kathryne, 428, 478
My Romance, 462–64
Myrow, Josef, 286–87

Nagler, A. N., 249
Nagrin, Daniel, 270, 334, 501
Naldi, 63, 234
Narciso, Grazia, 246
Nash, Marie, 13, 57, 61–62, 74, 223
Nash, Ogden, 192–94, 248, 395
Nast, Thomas, 269
Nathan, George Jean, 41, 118, 122, 127–28, 138–39, 143, 146, 155, 191, 236, 253, 290, 294, 296, 305, 307, 317, 323, 351, 361–62, 392, 400, 403, 409, 434, 447, 471, 487
National Congress of Industrial Organizations War Productions, 225
Neff, John, 142
Nelles, Arthur, 39
Nellie Bly, 317–19
Nelson, Barry, 205
Nelson, Carl, 127, 220
Nelson, Charles, 501
Nelson, Chet, 393
Nelson, Gene, 84, 156, 468
Nelson, Mervyn, 45, 225, 449
Nelson, Stanley, 227
Neway, Patricia, 145, 276–77, 348
New City Opera, 243
Newdahl, Clifford, 86
Newell, Billy, 195
Newell, James, 344
New Faces of 1943, 146–48

Newill, James, 246
Newman, Azadia, 246
Newman, Lionel, 3
Newman, Phyllis, 264
The New Moon, 127–29, 219–20
New Opera Company, 86, 143, 145, 176, 216, 267
New Priorities of 1943, 129–31
New York City Center, 470
New York City Center Opera Company, 245, 300
Nicholas, Eden, 286
Nicholas, Fayard, 327
Nicholas, Harold, 327
Nichols, Barbara, 56, 94
Nichols, George III, 450
Nichols, Lewis, 114, 117, 119, 125, 149, 151–52, 155, 159, 172, 175, 177, 179, 181–82, 184–85, 188, 192, 194, 197, 199, 201, 205, 207, 209, 214–15, 217, 222, 238, 240, 242, 245, 247–48, 251, 253, 257, 260, 263, 266, 269, 273, 276, 280–81, 283, 290, 292, 294–96, 299, 302, 304, 309, 311, 314, 321, 323, 325, 328, 333, 335, 338
Nichols, Mike, 303
Nicodemus, 21
Nielson, Lavina, 261
Niesen, Gertrude, 126, 213–14
Night of Love, 59–60
Niles, Eleanor, 223
Niles, Marion, 303
Niles, Mary-Ann, 311
Niles, Melva, 454
Nimura, Yeichi, 320
Nirska, 5
Nixon, Marni, 408
Noble, Dennis, 91
Nolan, Jim, 286
Nolan, Kathleen, 484
Noll, Edward, 411
Nones, Walter, 61
Noonan, Tommy, 513
Norfleet, Cecelia, 425
Norman, Harold, 399
Norman, Marsha, 227
Norris, McKay, 320
North, Alex, 45, 99
Northrop, Patricia, 55, 156
Norton, Barry, 159
Norton, Dean, 165
Norton, Elliot, 228
Norton, Jim, 374
Norville, Hubert, 300
Norworth, Jack, 136
Novak, Kim, 56
Novarro, Ramon, 171
Novelle, Mitzi, 449
Novotna, Jarmila, 216–18
Nurok, Robert, 111
Nype, Russell, 195, 277, 475, 505

Obey, Andre, 470
O'Brady, Hope, 301

O'Brien, Chester, 123
O'Brien, Chet, 322
O'Brien, Edmond, 205
O'Brien, Lois, 156
O'Brien, Virginia, 19–20, 49, 53, 313
O'Connor, Donald, 303, 307
O'Connor, Jim, 242, 306, 367
O'Daniels, Barry, 59, 163–64
O'Dea, Sunnie, 83
Oenslager, Donald, 190, 192, 324, 358–59, 411
Offenbach, Jacques, 51, 68, 86, 145, 216–17, 267
Offner, Mortimer, 50–51
Of "V" We Sing, 99–100
O'Hara, John, 54, 114
O'Hara, Kelli, 484
O'Hara, Maureen, 404
Ohardieno, Roger, 189, 257, 346
O'Keefe, Walter, 102
Oklahoma!, 154–57
Olsen, Heidi, 286
Olsen, J. C., 438, 493
Olsen, Ole, 87–89, 136, 158, 254, 257, 438, 493–94, 514
O'Malley, Muriel, 378, 405, 501
O'Mara, Brian, 293
Once Over Lightly, 145–46
O'Neal, William, 334
O'Neil, Guy, 108
O'Neill, Eugene, 3
One Touch of Venus, 192–95
On the Town, 261–65
Operti, Le Roy, 395
Orbach, Jerry, 277, 415
Oreste, 175
Orlob, Harold, 190–92
Orondenker, M. H., 71
O'Rourke, Betty, 81
Osato, Sono, 194, 263, 433–34
Osborn, Paul, 484
O'Shaughnessy, John, 443
O'Shay, William, 317
O'Shea, Michael, 151, 301
O'Shea, Patsy, 284
Oshins, Julie, 126
Osterwald, Bibi, 258, 324, 430
Ostrander, A. A., 227, 322
Oswald, Virginia, 382
Otero, Emma, 163–64
Owen, Ethel, 254, 312
Owen, Guy, 393
Oxford, Earl, 30, 74, 126
Oy Is Dus a Leben!, 138–39

Paddock, Robert Rowe, 385
Padula, Edward, 307
Page, Lucille, 234
Page, Ruth, 399
Pahl, Mel, 475
Paiva, Jararaca, 3
Paiva, Vicente, 3

Pal Joey, 54–56
Palmer, Betsy, 484
Palmer, Byron, 460
Palmer, Frank, 24
Palmer, Jeanne, 20
Palmer, Peter, 156, 382, 512
Pan, Hermes, 464, 474
Panama, Norman, 17
Panama Hattie, 46–49
Panvini, Grace, 146
Parent, Gail, 512
Parish, Mitchell, 38
Paris Sings Again, 438–39
Parkas, Karl, 176
Park Avenue, 358–60
Parker, Eleanor, 56
Parker, Frank, 212
Parker, Lew, 305, 307, 404
Parker, Mary, 83
Parks, Bernice, 366
Parks, Larry, 333
Parrish, Mitchell, 3
Parson, William, 389, 450
Parsons, Billy, 395
Parsons, William, 150
Pascal, Milton, 195, 212, 475
The Passing Show, 341–42
Paton, Alan, 504
Patricia, 111
Patrick, Harold, 244, 413–14
Patrick, Nigel, 423
Patston, Doris, 117, 127, 246, 366
Pavlovska, Vera, 179
Payn, Graham, 421–23
Payne, Aaron H., 438
Payne, Barbara, 7, 324
Pearce, Alice, 148, 262, 264, 419, 450–51
Pearce, John, 126
Pearson, Bud, 38
Pearson, Eppy, 47, 118
Pechner, Gerhard, 226, 454
Pell, John, 344
Pember, Clifford, 401
Pendleton, Austin, 27
Pene du Bois, Raoul, 6, 33, 46, 48, 66, 87, 167, 205, 207, 271, 273, 277, 305, 330, 452–53, 467
Penn, Robert, 258, 361, 436
Pennington, Ann, 170–71
Penzner, Seymour, 227
Perelman, S. J., 192, 395
Perez, Rosario, 87, 289
Perkins, Kenneth, 397
Perrin, Sam, 305
Perry, Barbara, 286
Perry, Mitzi, 184, 197
Perry, Robert E., 428
Pershing, D'Vaughn, 501
Peters, Bernadette, 264, 336
Peters, Block, 98

Peters, Brock, 207, 505
Peters, Elsie, 45
Peters, Fred, 317
Petersen, Nels, 316
Petina, Irra, 230, 236, 238–39, 456
Petry, Gedda, 153
Pevney, Joseph C., 134, 186
Pfeiffer, Jack, 493
Pharr, Kelsey, 68
Phelan, Margaret, 368
Philbrick, Will H., 174
Phillips, H. I., 61, 118
Phillips, James, 142
Piaf, Edith, 408–9, 516
Piazza, Marguerite, 245, 400, 471–72
Pickens, Jane, 36
Picon, Molly, 138–39
Pierce, John, 117, 127
Pierpont, Laura, 443
Pierson, Arthur, 157, 197
Pierson, Don, 24
Pihodna, Joseph, 139, 495
Pincus, Irvin, 12
Pinkham, Daniel, 72
Pinto, Thea, 33
Pinza, Ezio, 481, 485
Piper, John, 471
Pitchon, Jack, 337
Pitkin, Robert, 21
Pitot, Genevieve, 425, 501
Pitt, Merle, 102
Pitts, ZaSu, 84
Platova, Helene, 245
Platt, Edward, 59, 405, 508
Platt, Marc, 95, 219
Playwrights' Company, 369, 504
Plummer, Christopher, 27
Pobers, Tatiana, 179
Podrecca, Lia, 11
Podrecca, Vittorio, 11–12
Poitier, Sidney, 98
Pokrass, Samuel D., 25–26
Polakov, Lester, 9, 61, 331
Polk, Oscar, 90–91
Poll, Martin, 187
Polonaise, 298–300
Pope, Robert, 327
Poppen, Detmar, 117
Popwell, Albert, 363
Porgy and Bess, 97–99, 186–87
Porretta, Frank, 239, 382, 415
Porter, Cole, 23, 46, 48–49, 82–83, 150–51, 158, 194, 210–
    11, 251, 253, 337–39, 472–75
Potter, Lois, 301
Povah, Phyllis, 84
Powell, Bertha, 177, 393
Powell, Dawn, 94
Powell, Dick, 53
Powell, Michael, 145

Power, Tyrone, 46, 55
Powers, Marie, 277, 387–89, 470
Powys, Stephen, 29, 31
Pransky, Al, 489
Pratt, John, 24, 189, 257, 360, 419
Preisser, June, 136, 138
Premice, Josephine, 409, 411
Preminger, Otto, 98
Prescott, Alan, 29
Prescott, Tina, 397, 436
Pressburger, Emeric, 145
Preston, Mickee and Paul, 485
Pretty Penny, 514–16
Previn, Andre, 265
Price, Dennis, 145
Price, Hal, 301
Price, Leontyne, 98
Price, Naomi, 70
Price, Peter, 454
Price, Vincent, 270
Primrose, Bonita, 368
Primus, Pearl, 409–10
Prince, Hughie, 303
Pringle, William, 169
Prinz, Eddie, 3
Prinz, LeRoy, 126
Prior, Allan, 171
Priorities of 1942, 101–2
Pripps, Edward, 441
Producers Associates, Inc., 164
Proser, Monte, 346, 402, 452
Prosk, Gerald, 448
Prouty, Jed, 111, 150, 360
Provost, William, 61
Prunzik, Karen, 512
Purcell, Charles, 358
Purcell, H. V., 183
Purcell, Harold, 401
Purdom, Edmund, 171

Quaglia, Antonio, 11
Quayle, Anthony, 145
Quigg, John, 268
Quillan, Joe, 92, 317
Quin, Mike, 50

Rabiroff, Jacques, 73, 94
Rae, Nan, 17
Ragland, Rags, 47, 49, 53
Rahn, Muriel, 327
Raiguel, Phil, 441
Raines, Ron, 248
Raitt, James, 276–77
Raitt, John, 274, 315, 336, 454
Raksin, David, 361–62
Rall, Tommy, 419, 450, 474
Ramey, Samuel, 371
Ramirez, Carlos, 63
Ramsay, Remak, 264

Rand, Ayn, 20
Rand, Sally, 55
Randall, Carl, 21, 61, 84, 90, 142, 186, 300, 341
Randell, Pamela, 240
Randell, Ron, 475
Rando, John, 264
Randolph, Clemence, 246
Randolph, Donald, 63
Randolph, Forbes, 393–94
The Rape of Lucretia, 470–72
Rapp, Erno, 39
Rapp, Philip, 346
Rappaport, N. H., 159
Rapps and Tapps, 304–5
Rasch, Albertina, 36, 63, 153, 291
Rascoe, Burton, 143, 148–49, 152, 155, 159, 170, 173, 175,
    177, 179–80, 183, 185, 192, 194, 197–98, 201, 205, 209,
    211, 214–15, 218, 222, 234, 238, 240, 242, 244–45, 247,
    250, 253, 256–57, 260, 263, 266, 269, 273, 280–81, 284,
    290, 292, 294–95, 297, 299–300, 302, 304, 308–9, 311,
    314, 319, 321, 323, 325, 329
Rasely, George, 86, 216, 282
Raset, Val, 303
Rasumny, Mikhail, 20
Ravel, Maurice, 228
Ray, Alan, 148
Ray, Aldo, 249
Ray, Leonore, 344
Ray, Mavis, 435, 480
Ray, Nicholas, 363, 365
Raye, Martha, 33, 35–36
Raye, Mary, 234
Raymond, Helen, 161, 165, 303
Raze the Roof, 488–89
Reagan, Ronald, 126
Reams, Lee Roy, 156
Reardon, John, 65
Reaux, Angelina, 371
Redfield, Billy (William), 383–84
Redgrave, Michael, 145
The Red Mill, 301–3
Redowski, Philip, 464
Red Peppers, 422
Redstone, Michael, 195
Reed, Janet, 262, 291, 419
Reed, Napoleon, 24–25, 205, 207, 278, 330
Reed, Paul, 127, 145, 224, 389
Reed, Susan, 342
Rees, Roger, 273
Reese, Henry, 454
Reeves, Peter, 27
Reeves-Smith, Olive, 163–64
Regan, Sylvia, 224
Regina, 505–7
Reichert, Heinz, 182
Reid, Elliott, 513
Reilly, Betty, 488
Reilly, Charles Nelson, 469
Reiner, Carl, 332

Reinhardt, Gottfried, 143, 216, 298
Reinhardt, Max, 143
Relkin, Edwin A., 138
Remey, Dick and Dottie, 488
Remos, Susanne, 99
Remy, Dot, 500
Renan, Emile, 471, 497
Rene, Otis, 109
Renee, Carol, 90
Renna, Shorty, 438
Rennie, James, 20–21
Repp, Ellen, 369, 443
Reunion in New York, 9–11
Reveaux, Edward, 305, 347, 478
Revel, Harry, 50, 305
Revil, Ruth, 61
Rey, Federico, 107
Reyes, Aurea, 495
Reynolds, James, 174
Reynolds, Quentin, 354
Rhapsody, 249–51
Rhapsody in Black, 72
Rhea, La Julia, 24
Rhodes, Erik, 69, 396
Rice, Ed, 516
Rice, Elmer, 369, 504
Rice, Vernon, 319, 321, 323–24, 326, 328–29, 333, 335,
    339, 352–53, 357, 367, 431
Rich, Irene, 464
Rich, Kay, 395
Richards, Donald, 476–77
Richards, Elayne, 504
Richards, Houston, 208
Richards, Jess, 264
Richards, Rudy, 445
Richman, Harry, 129–30
Richmond, June, 307
Rickard, Gwen, 460
Riddick, Clyde, 152
Riesner, Charles, 53
Rigaud, George, 293, 295
Rigby, Jean, 472
Riggs, Lynn, 154
Riggs, Ralph, 21, 360
Riley, Eulabel, 295
Rimsky-Korsakov, Nikolai, 228
Ring, Carl E., 227–28
Risch, Matthew, 56
Riskin, Leo, 145
Rissman, Herbert, 154
Ritchie, Robert G., 69
Ritter, Tex, 228
Rittman, Trude, 418
Roane, Frank, 504
Robbins, Gale, 513
Robbins, Jerome, 18, 236, 261–63, 289, 291, 309–11, 402–4,
    419, 480, 489, 497–98
Robbins, Jerry, 244–45
Robbins, Larry, 443

Rober, Richard, 92
Roberts, Allan, 31, 478
Roberts, Ben, 127, 176, 207, 220, 222, 243
Roberts, Boots, 393
Roberts, Eric, 210, 284
Roberts, Francis, 401
Roberts, Henry, 109
Roberts, Joan, 90, 154, 292–93, 305–6
Roberts, Lee, 77
Roberts, Pernell, 276
Roberts, Ronny, 393
Roberts, Thayer, 316
Robertson, Lanie, 425
Robeson, Paul, 1–3, 315
Robey, Ken, 449
Robin, Leo, 510
Robin Hood, 243–45
Robins, Edward H., 21, 317
Robins, Gregory, 224
Robinson, Ann, 148, 280
Robinson, Bill "Bojangles," 25, 57–58, 70, 280–81
Robinson, Casey, 126
Robinson, Chris, 277
Robinson, Clark, 80
Robinson, Edward G., 239
Robinson, Freddie, 70
Robinson, Norah, 202
Roche, Jack, 516
Roche, Mary, 197
Roche, Viola, 411
Rockwell, Doc, 251
Rockwell, Don, 251
Rodgers, Eileen, 312
Rodgers, Richard, 12, 15, 50, 54, 113–14, 127, 154–55, 200, 274–76, 334, 405, 480–81, 485
Roecker, Edward, 214, 267
Roerick, William, 421–22
Rogers, Charles R., 94
Rogers, Dick, 303
Rogers, Ginger, 66
Rogers, Hilda, 72
Rogers, Jay, 340
Rogers, Jo Jean, 30
Rogers, Phyllis, 30
Rogers, Timmie, 278
Rogers, Will, 201
Rogerson, Bud, 516
Rogier, Frank, 387
Roland, Dawn, 74
Roland, Howard, 169
Roland, Norman, 293
Rollins, Rowe, 341
Romano, Phil, 104, 351
Romanoff, Boris, 179
Romberg, Sigmund, 89, 127, 169, 181–82, 219, 268–69, 316, 462, 464
Rome, Harold, 70–71, 118, 120, 134–35, 331–32, 489, 515
Ronell, Ann, 136–37
Rooney, Mickey, 15, 109

Rooney, Pat, 233
Rooney, Pat, Sr., 488
Roos, William, 464
Roosevelt, Eleanor, 52, 256
Roosevelt, Franklin, 18–19, 158
Root, Lynn, 42–43
Rosales, Marco, 342
Rosalinda, 143–45
Rose, Billy, 205, 207, 251–53, 277, 289–90, 330
Rose, Lewis, 224
The Rose Masque, 226–27
Rosenberg, Ben, 306
Rosenberg, J. B., 146
Rosenstock, Milton, 123, 372, 383, 402, 510
Rosenthal, Jean, 143, 387–88, 470
Rosoff, Charles, 3
Ross, Adrian, 126–27, 176, 243
Ross, Arthur, 50
Ross, Don, 195
Ross, Emily, 309
Ross, George, 10, 52, 67, 119, 125, 141
Ross, Herbert, 363
Ross, Hugh, 432
Ross, Jerry, 250–51
Ross, Robert, 97, 136, 186, 227, 280
Ross, Shirley, 12, 14
Rosselat, Robert, 392
Rossini, Gioachino, 11, 146
Rostand, Edmond, 25
Rostova, Luba, 61
Roth, Lillian, 175
Rotov, Alex, 221
Rounseville, Robert, 15, 276, 382
Rox, John, 57–58
Ruben, Jose, 117, 220, 366
Ruby, Harry, 84
Rudel, Julius, 245, 300, 505
Rudie, Evelyn, 303
Ruggles, Charles, 166, 276
Ruick, Barbara, 276, 474
Ruick, Melville, 462
Ruiz, Antonio, 87, 289
Rumshinsky, Joseph, 138
Run Little Chillun, 177–79
Ruskin, Coby, 225
Russell, Bob, 341–42
Russell, Byron, 358
Russell, Gail, 66
Russell, Gilbert, 282
Russell, Jane, 513
Russell, Renee, 184
Russell, Sylvia, 341
Russell, Zella, 25
Russian Bank, 20–21
Ryan, Peggy, 51
Ryan, Sheila, 151
Ryan, Sue, 157, 265, 341
Rychtarik, Richard, 146, 267
Ryskind, Morrie, 21–22, 94

Sabinson, Lee, 372
Sacher, Toby, 99
Sachs, Dorothy, 146
Sachse, Leopold, 300
Sacks, Dorothy, 72
Sadie Thompson, 246–49
Sadler, Dudley, 489
Saidy, Fred, 53, 240, 368, 372
St. Cyr, Lili, 55, 348
St. Elmo Johnson Choir, 32
St. John, Betta, 483–84
St. Louis Municipal Opera Company, 26
St. Louis Woman, 326–29
Saint-Subber, Arny, 257, 282, 358
    See also Subber, Saint
Saks Fifth Avenue, 115
Sales, Clifford, 334
Sally, 430–32
Saltman, Phil, 167
Saltzman, Esta, 138
Salzer, Gene, 46
Sameth, Marten, 261
Samuel, Gerard, 432
Sanders, Alma, 397
Sanford, Charles, 280, 322, 347, 358, 416
Sanford, Charles G., 246
Sanford, Charles S., 148
San Juan, Olga, 195, 307
Santiago, 230
Sardou, Victorien, 159
Sargent, Dorothy, 59
Sargent, Mary, 224
Sarnoff, Dorothy, 143–44, 371, 454
Saron, Alex, 45
Saroyan, William, 10, 55, 132–33, 148, 158
Saunders, Jack, 316
Saunders, Wardell, 177
Sauris, Genevieve, 337
Sava, Marusia, 179
Savage, Archie, 42, 363, 474, 482
Saville, Ruth, 428
Savo, Jimmy, 49, 59, 132–33, 198–99
Sawyer, Wilson, 284
Saxon, Luther, 25, 205
Schaefer, George, 475
Schaeffer, George, 195
Schafer, Natalie, 63
Schaff, George, 309
Schallert, Edwin, 112, 345
Scharff, Mickey, 108
Scheff, Walter, 380
Schenck, Mary, 346
Schenck, Mary Percy, 282
Schere, Loretta, 267
Schick, George, 352
Schippers, Thomas, 389
Schloss, Edwin H., 437
Schmidt, John V., 298
Schnitzer, Ignaz, 245, 300

Schofield, Al, 167, 187
Scholl, Danny, 332
Schollin, Christina, 239
Schoonover, Meredith, 435
Schoop, Paul, 159
Schoop, Trudi, 392–93
Schorr, William, 240, 368
Schrank, Joseph, 44, 70
Schrappro, Ernst, 25
Schraps, Ernest, 59, 115, 132, 268–69, 389
Schubert, Franz, 11, 181–82
Schulberg, B. P., 224
Schumer, Henry, 351
Schunzel, Reinhold, 226
Schurgot, Helena, 428
Schwab, Laurence, 127, 219
Schwartz, Arthur, 15, 358–59, 425
Schwartz, Jean, 160, 164
Schwartz, Stephen, 136
Schwartzdorf, Jacob, 90, 154
Schwezoff, Igor, 86
Scofield, Al, 167, 187
Scott, Clement, 244
Scott, Hazel, 101–2
Scott, Ivy, 66–67, 90
Scott, Raymond, 39, 320–21
Scully, Barbara, 181–82, 244–45
Seabolt, Frank, 432
Seabra, Nelson, 94
Sedan, Rolfe, 142
Seelen, Jerry, 118, 129, 138, 157
Segal, Alex, 243
Segal, Vivienne, 55, 201, 317, 368, 399
Segrera, Carolina, 86, 145
Seigh, Eileen, 445, 485
Seiter, William A., 195, 270
Selden, Albert, 450
Sell, Janie, 56
Seltzer, Leo A., 284
Selwyn, Ruth, 29
Sensenderfer, E. P., 490
Serangeli, Mario, 11
Seton, Beryl, 374
Seven Lively Arts, 251–54
Seven Studio, 70
Shackleton, Robert, 375–76, 430, 461
Shadow Play, 422
Shafer, John, 226, 231
Shafer, Robert, 236, 239
Shakespeare, William, 472
Shanet, Howard, 413
The Shape of Things!, 439–41
Shaper, Hal, 27
Shapiro, Dan, 195, 212
Shapiro, Debbie, 459, 499
Shapiro, Irvin, 278
Shapiro, Lillian, 138
Sharaff, Irene, 31, 36, 57, 63, 90, 92, 113, 118–19, 136, 153, 309, 436, 454, 456

Sharkey, 13
Sharp, Louis, 42, 327
Sharpe, Albert, 270, 372
Sharron, Robert, 99
Shaw, Bob, 84
Shaw, George Bernard, 117–18, 378
Shaw, Hollace, 15, 63
Shaw, Len G., 166
Shaw, Robert, 205, 251, 277, 330
Shaw, Wini, 284
Shawley, Bob, 428
Shearer, Norma, 171
Sheehan, John, 464
Sheekman, Arthur, 61
Sheffer, Jonathan, 136
Shefter, Bert, 500
She Had to Say Yes, 72–74
Sheinkman, Mordecai, 432
Shelby, Jeanne, 63, 153
Shelby, Laurel, 195
Sheldon, Edward, 462
Sheldon, Gene, 101, 233–34, 396
Sheldon, Reid, 277
Sheldon, Sidney, 127, 176, 207, 209, 220, 222
Shelley, Gladys, 228, 322–23
Shelley, Joshua, 351, 416
Shelton, Hall, 397
Shelton, James, 439
Shelton, Jerry, 108, 152
Shelton, Marla, 228
Shelton, Sidney, 243
Shepard, Joan, 462
Shepard, Karen, 462
Sheperd, Joan, 90
Sheppard, John R., Jr., 363
Sher, Bartlett, 484
Sherbedgia, Rade, 484
Sherman, Charles, 57, 146, 167, 187, 251, 475
Sherman, Harold, 284, 303
Sherman, Hiram, 49–50, 74–75
Sherman, Jason, 416
Sherman, Lee, 317, 416
Sherrock, Irene E., 267
Sherwin, Julie, 111
Sherwin, Manning, 401
Sherwood, Bobby, 488
Sherwood, Gale, 201, 317
Sherwood, Robert E., 497–98, 504
Shevelove, Burt, 450
Shipman, Samuel, 397
Shire, David, 27
Shirley, Bill, 513
Shootin' Star, 342–43
Shore, Ted, 346
Short, Bobby, 253, 333, 474
Short, Hassard, 31, 63, 92–93, 118, 150, 153, 205, 210, 251, 277, 291, 293, 312, 330, 399, 416, 418, 448
Shoup, Howard, 202
Show Boat, 312–25, 448

Show Time, 131–32
Shriner, Herb, 425
Shubert, J. J., 164, 169, 181, 265
Shubert, Lee, 133
Shubert, Messrs., 17, 25, 27, 29, 59, 87, 101, 104, 107, 129, 136, 157, 160, 163, 169, 181, 254, 340–41, 346, 401, 410, 462
Shulman, Max, 383, 478
Shutta, Ethel, 184–85
Shwarze, Henry, 352
Sidney, George, 474
Sidney, Robert, 123, 126, 324, 366, 475
Siegel, David, 500
Siegmann, George, 303
Siegmeister, Elie, 258, 261
Sigman, Carl, 411
Sillman, Leonard, 57, 146, 361, 363
Silvera, Richard, 481
Silvers, Phil, 151, 159, 285, 402–4
Silvers, Sid, 19, 69, 84, 488
Simenon, Georges, 428
Simmons, Georgia, 227
Simmons, Maude, 372
Simmons (B. J.) & Co., Ltd., 401
Simon, Neil, 79, 139, 202, 317
Simon, Robert A., 144
Simon, Simone, 30
Sim Sala Bim, 33–34
Sinatra, Frank, 15, 56, 135, 155, 264, 276, 286
Sinatra, Ray, 92, 118
Sinclair, Diane, 54, 515
Singer, Andre, 9
Singer, Samuel L., 396
Sing Out, Sweet Land!, 258–61
Sissle, Noble, 105–7, 136
Six Mighty Atoms, 493
Skelton, Red, 49
Skinner, Edna, 489
Skipper, William, 270, 439
Slagle, A. Russell, 117
Slawson, Dana, 341
Sleepy Hollow, 443–45
Slickerettes, 441
Sloan, Estelle, 366–67
Sloane, Bernard, 393
Sloane, Michael, 375
Small, Jack, 214
Small, Paul, 183, 223, 239–40, 487
Smallens, Alexander, 97, 99, 186
Small Wonder, 450–52
Smart, Dick, 478, 480
Smart, Jack, 161
Smith, Al, 88, 117
Smith, Art, 342
Smith, Augustus, Jr., 372
Smith, Betty, 213
Smith, Betty Jane, 69
Smith, Cecil, 25, 112
Smith, Cyril, 80

Smith, David, 462
Smith, Eddy, 508
Smith, Harry B., 244, 375
Smith, Joe, 115, 117, 186–87
Smith, Kate, 125–26, 286
Smith, Loring, 347, 489, 508
Smith, Mildred, 278
Smith, Muriel, 205, 207, 278, 330, 484
Smith, Norwood, 448
Smith, Oliver, 143, 220, 249, 251, 261, 264, 309, 363, 380, 402, 419, 436, 475, 489, 497, 510
Smith, Pete Kite, 61
Smith, Robert, 6
Smith, Robert B., 375
Smith, William C., 280
Smith, Wilson, 369
Smith Kids, 409
Smythe, Russell, 472
Sobel, Louis, 179, 181
Sobol, Edward, 84
Sokolow, Anna, 369, 443–44, 505
Solms, Kenny, 512
Soltesz, Eva, 375
Somerville, Phyllis, 49
Something for the Boys, 149–51
Sonart, 120, 234, 349, 390, 445, 485
Song of Norway, 236–39
Song Without Words, 343–45
Sons o' Fun, 86–89
Sorel, Felicia, 68, 177, 184, 393, 397
Sorenson, Holger, 430, 471
Sothern, Ann, 49, 66
Sothern, Georgia, 118–20, 197
Sothern, Harry, 347
Soudeikine, Jeanne and Serge, 179
Sour, Robert, 293
Sour, Robert B., 224
South Pacific, 481–85
Sovey, Raymond, 174, 208
Soyfer, Jura, 9
Spalding, Charles, 450
Spalding, Sid, 39, 349, 390, 485
Spangler, Amy, 474
Spaulding, Ken, 515
Spaull, Guy, 337
Spectorsky, Auguste, 9
Spellman, George, 448
Spelvin, George, 59
Spence, Ralph, 15
Spencer, Kenneth, 314
Spencer, Margaret, 226, 284
Speth, Myron, 337
Spewack, Bella, 472, 475
Spewack, Sam, 472, 475
Spialek, Hans, 70
Spielman, Fred, 265
Spike Jones and His Musical Depreciation Revue, 441
Spina, Harold, 227–28
Spitainy, H. Leopold, 164

Spitz, Arthur, 352
Sponder, Wanda, 108
Spong, Hilda, 12
Spring in Brazil, 345–47
Sprinzena, Nathaniel, 300
Squibb, June, 469
Squire, Katherine, 66
Stafford, Jo, 427
Stage Costumes, Inc., 160, 169, 181, 341
Stage Productions, Inc., 488
Stander, Arthur, 61
Standing, Guy, Jr., 389
Stanford, Paul, 303
Stang, Arnold, 148
Stange, Stanislaus, 117, 378
Stanley, Bert, 174
Stanley, Helene, 513
Stanton, George, 295
Stanton, Olive, 414
Stanton, Robert, 411
Stanwyck, Barbara, 502
Star and Garter, 118–20
Stars on Ice, 120–22
Star Time, 239–40
Stauffer, Aubrey, 230
Stearns, Johnny, 305
Steber, Eleanor, 462
Steele, Tommy, 374
Steifel, Milton, 516
Steiger, Rod, 156
Stein, Joseph, 466
Stein, Leo, 126, 176, 243
Steininger, Franz, 344, 399
Sterbini, Cesare, 146
Stern, Alfred R., 432
Stevens, Claire, 368
Stevens, Connie, 449
Stevens, Frank W., 104, 115
Stevens, Geoffe, 349, 390, 485
Stevens, George, 162
Stevens, Leslie, 243, 439
Stevens, Morton L., 94, 208
Stevens, Rise, 65, 118
Stewart, Al, 393
Stewart, Cecil, 488
Stewart, Johnny, 402, 456
Stewart, Kay, 347
Stewart, Larry, 342
Stewart, Martha, 307, 358
Stewart, Slam, 424
Stillman, Al, 3, 38, 118, 120, 445, 485
Stocker, Leonard, 143, 395
Stockwell, Harry, 291–93
Stodelle, Ernestine, 20
Stoltz, Robert, 59–60, 176–77
Stolz, Robert, 176, 243, 293–94
Stone, Andrew L., 239
Stone, Carol, 159–60
Stone, Dorothy, 111, 165, 301–3

Stone, Ezra, 9, 123, 126
Stone, Fred A., 301–3
Stone, Gary, 3
Stone, Paula, 73, 301, 303, 375
Stone, Peter, 336
Stone, Sid, 214
Stoner, Joe, 195
Stoner, Lou, 195
Story, Gloria, 249, 375–77
Stoska, Polyna, 245, 369, 371
Stothart, Herbert, 127
Stott, Monte, 349, 390, 485
Stovepipe Hat, 227–28
Stover, Frederick, 51, 111, 439
Strasfogel, Ignace, 298
Stratas, Teresa, 315
Stratton, Chester, 200–201
Stratton, Gil, Jr., 78
Stratton, Mike, 45
Straub, John, 385
Straus, Oscar, 117, 378
Strauss, Johann, 11, 143, 226, 230–31, 245, 294, 300
Strauss, Robert, 317, 395
Stravinsky, Igor, 251
Street, George, 401
Street Scene, 369–72
Strelitzer, Hugo, 230, 344
Striegler, Betta, 483
Stritch, Elaine, 303, 412, 439
Stromberg, Hunt, Jr., 301, 430
Stroud, Claude, 452
Strudwick, Shepperd, 66
Stuarti, Enzo, 339
The Student Prince, 169–71
Studio Productions, Inc., 508
Stutz, Richard, 475
Styler, Burt, 333
Styne, Jule, 219, 284–85, 311, 402–3, 510, 512
Subber, Saint, 18, 472, 475
    See also Saint-Subber, Arny
Sues, Leonard, 141
Sugar 'n' Spice, 167–68
Sukman, Harry, 513
Sullivan, Arthur, 24–25, 280, 282–83, 533–34
Sullivan, Barry, 66
Sullivan, Brian, 371
Sullivan, Ed, 62, 105–6
Sullivan, Elliott, 380
Sullivan, Gloria, 430
Sullivan, Jo, 277, 445
Sullivan, Joseph, 226
Sullivan, K. T., 512
Sullivan, Lee, 29, 134, 142, 380
Sundgaard, Arnold, 249
Sundstrom, Florence, 293
Sunny River, 89–91
Supreme Scenery Studio, 127
Susann, Jacqueline, 92, 94, 163–64, 208–9, 265
Sutcliffe, Steven, 202

Sutherland, Victor, 24
Swanson, Gloria, 248
Swarthout, Gladys, 388
Sweet Bye and Bye, 395–96
Sweethearts, 375–77
Sykes, Dick, 501
Sylvester, Robert, 53, 101, 105, 306, 352, 367, 415, 420, 434, 496, 498
Symonette, Randolph, 230, 271, 371
Szandrowsky, Myron, 146
Szantho, Enid, 300
Sze, Julia, 411, 428
Szot, Paulo, 484

Tabbert, William, 199, 212, 254, 312, 469
Take a Bow, 233–34
Talbot-Martin, Elizabeth, 51–52
Taliaferro, Mabel, 240, 368
Tallchief, Maria, 239
Tallchief, Marjorie, 231
Talma, Zolya, 246
Tamberg, Enio, 27
Tamiris, Helen, 224, 227, 268–70, 312, 334, 358–59, 389, 425, 428, 448, 480, 501, 503
Tapps, George, 322, 449
Tapps, Georgie, 184
Tarrasch, William, 354
Tars and Spars, 218–19
Tashamire, 117
Tashlin, Frank, 195
Tauber, Doris, 118
Tauber, Richard, 352–54
Taubman, Howard, 434
Taylor, Deems, 289–90
Taylor, Don, 202
Taylor, Matt, 161
Taylor, Noel, 385
Taylor, Rob, 334
Tcherina, Ludmilla, 145
Teed, Rose, 84
The Telephone (or L'Amour a Trois), 387–89, 470
Terris, Norma, 314
Terry, Phillip, 141
Terry, Renee, 69
Terry, Sonny, 372
Terry, Walter, 420, 496
Testa, Mary, 264
Tetley, Glen, 435
Texas, Li'l Darlin', 508–10
Thaell, Cliff and Edwina, 121
That's the Ticket!, 489–91
Theatre Guild, 66, 154, 258, 274, 405, 480
Theatre of the Piccoli, 11–12
Thenstead, Adolph, 409
Theodore, Lee Becker, 239, 475
Therese, 401
They Can't Get You Down, 111–12
This Is the Army, 123–26
Thomas, Brandon, 460

Thomas, Danny, 333
Thomas, Irene, 286
Thomas, Ross, 341
Thompson, Creighton, 369
Thompson, Dorothy, 58
Thompson, Elsie, 61
Thompson, Frank, 397, 471
Thompson, Fred, 94, 212, 284, 303
Thompson, Hugh, 86, 145
Thompson, Johnny, 456
Thompson, Julian F., 113
Thompson, Oscar, 217
Thompson, Woodman, 228
Thomson, Arline, 174
Thomson, Harrison, 445, 485
Thomson, Virgil, 144, 471
Thornton, Evans, 497
Thorpe, Richard, 171
Three to Make Ready, 324–26
Thurston, Ted, 436
Tibbett, Lawrence, 129
Tidbits of 1946, 351–52
Tilden, Martha, 55–56
Timberg, Herman, 148
The Time, the Place, and the Girl, 141–43
Tingey, Cynthia, 264
Tipton, Ben, 500
'Tis of Thee, 45–46
Todd, Michael, 31–32, 118–20, 150, 210–11, 268–70, 339, 389, 464
Toledano, Jose, 495
Toledo, Julio, 495
Tolkin, Mel, 99, 475
Tomkins, Don, 89, 438
Tonge, Philip, 421–22
Tonight at 8:30, 421–23
Toplitzky of Notre Dame, 366–68
Top-Notchers, 107–8
Topsy, 3
Torloff, Frank, 145
Tormé, Mel, 15
Toscanini, Arturo, 388
Touch and Go, 501–3
Tours, Frank, 421
Towers, Constance, 277
Toy, Noel, 132–33
Tozzi, Giorgio, 471–72, 484
Traver, Sharry, 432
Travilla, 230
Travolta, John, 248
Treacher, Arthur, 157, 159
Trenholm, Cissy, 445
Trenkler, Freddie, 42, 234, 236, 349, 390, 445
Trent, Emerson, 344
Trent, Lee, 351–52
Treumann, Louis, 127
Tribby, Lillian, 393
Trivers, Barry, 452
Tropical Pinafore, 24–25

A Tropical Revue, 189–90, 257–58
Trout, Robert, 432
Truex, Ernest, 218, 224
Tschaikowsky, Peter Illytch, 344, 399
Tucker, Sophie, 85
Tudor, Antony, 282, 307, 327
Tudor, Rowan, 497
Tugend, Harry, 84
Tunberg, Karl, 270
Tune, Tommy, 445
Turnbull, Glenn, 111
Turner, Claramae, 387, 389
Turner, Joe, 110
Tushinsky, Joseph S., 117, 126–28
Twain, Mark, 199
Twardy, Ray, 81
Tweed, Boss, 268
Two for the Show, 6–8
Twomey, Kay, 303, 305
Two Weeks with Pay, 74–75
Tyers, John, 86, 146, 205, 356, 425
Tyler, Beverly, 271
Tyler, Jeanne, 95–96, 136–37
Tyler, Judy, 8, 410

Uggams, Eloise, 177
Ulisse, Arthur, 245
Under the Counter, 400–402
Unger, Gladys, 144
United States Army Air Forces, 202
United States Coast Guard, 218
United Studios, 244
Up in Central Park, 267–70, 389–90
Up to Now, 516–17

The Vagabond King, 174–74
Vail, Bobby, 489
Valdes, Gilberto, 360
Vale, Sonny, 108
Valentina, 115, 161, 251, 320–21
Valentinoff, Val, 356
Van, Bobby, 474
Van, Gus, 366–67
Van, Shirley, 309
Van Allen, Richard, 371, 472
Vance, Jerri, 183
Vance, Vivian, 83, 414
Vandair, 61
Vanderneers, Gloria, 51
Van Dijk, Ad, 27
Van Dijk, Koen, 27
Van Grona, Eugene, 228
Van Heusen, James (Jimmy), 66, 201, 317, 319
Van Horn & Son, 245, 300
Varden, Norma, 159, 513
Varela, Nina, 452
Vaudeville 1942, 115–17
Vaughan, Alan, 243
Vaughan, Eva, 177

Vaughn, Walter, 24
Vaux, Billy, 361
Vazquez, Carmen, 495–96
Veiller, Anthony, 298
Velden, Kaj, 70, 131, 233
Velez, Lupe, 286
Veloz, Frank, 108, 152
Vene, Roger P., 244
Venuta, Benay, 114, 277, 317, 319, 333
Vera-Ellen, 15, 49, 114, 201, 264
Verdi, Giuseppe, 51, 341
Verdon, Gwen, 311, 437–38, 454
Vereen, Ben, 254
Verne, Jules, 337
Verneuil, Louis, 86, 145, 267
Veronica, 105, 244, 341
Versailles Beauties, 101
Victor, Eric, 148, 425, 478
Victor, Lucia, 68
Victoria, Halina, 239
Vidnovic, Martin, 156, 382
La Vie Parisienne, 86, 145, 267
Vilan, Demetrios, 68
Villa, Danny, 382
Villa-Lobos, Heitor, 454
Villella, Edward, 56, 276, 336, 382
Villon, Francois, 175
Vincent, Romo, 139, 141, 165, 291
Vincent Youmans' "Fiesta," 228–30
Vine, Billy, 84, 102
Vinson, Jane, 361
Vinson, Maribel, 393
Vitale, Joseph, 71
Viva O'Brien, 80–82
Vodery, Bill, 105
Vogelle, Sheila, 432
Von Essen, Max, 375
Von Stade, Frederica, 315
von Zell, Harry, 136
Voorhees, Don, 1, 15
Vroom, Lodewick, 143
Vye, Murvyn, 17, 484

Wagner, Albert Richard, 227
Wainer, Lee, 146
Waits, Tom, 387
Waldorf, Wilella, 3, 8, 10, 20–21, 33, 42, 52, 67, 78, 81, 83–85, 89, 91, 93, 95–96, 99, 101–2, 104–6, 114, 116, 120, 125, 130–33, 135, 137–40, 143, 148, 151, 153, 155, 159, 170, 173, 175, 177, 179–82, 184–85, 189, 191–92, 194, 197, 199, 201, 205, 207, 209, 211, 213–14, 222, 234, 238, 240, 242, 245, 247–48, 250, 253, 260, 263, 266, 272–73, 276, 280–81, 283, 290, 294, 297, 299–300, 302, 304, 309, 314–15
Walken, Christopher, 79
Walken, Glenn, 79
Walker, Don, 70, 136, 138, 214, 281–82
Walker, Nancy, 78–79, 262–64, 384, 419–20, 476–78
Walker, Ray, 219

Walker, Rhoderick, 421–22
Walker, Robert, 195
Walk with Music, 29–31
Wallace, Ben, 233
Wallach, Eli, 385
Waller, Oden, 36
Waller, Thomas "Fats," 171–74
Walsh, John, 435
Walsh, Mary Jane, 82, 84, 214, 224
Walston, Ray, 484
Walter, Jessica, 475
Walters, Charles, 53, 73, 79, 82–83, 92, 327
Walters, Lou, 157, 195, 233
Walters, Thorley, 401
Walther, Elline, 291
The Waltz King, 230–31
Wand, Betty, 484
Wandmacher, Nick, 435
Wanger, Wally, 233
Ward, Ada, 70
Ward, Edward, 301
Ward, Pamela, 409, 411
Warfield, Joseph, 513
Warfield, William, 313, 315, 332, 505
Waring, Richard, 385
Warner, Ardelle, 146
Warnick, Clay, 66, 220, 280–82, 428, 452, 478, 516
Warnow, Mark, 197
Warren, Elton J., 205, 278, 330
Warren, Julie, 201
Wasserman, Dale, 189, 257, 364
Watch Out, Angel!, 286–87
Waters, Ethel, 42–44, 183, 278–80, 439
Waters, Jimmy, 97
Watkins, Perry, 148, 177, 187, 278, 363
Watson, Betty Jane, 156, 336, 367, 443–44, 449, 464
Watson, Martha Emma, 375
Watson, Milton, 80
Watson, Susan, 156, 277, 462, 469
Watt, Billie Lou, 383
Watts, Richard, 2, 5, 7, 10, 12, 14, 17, 19–21, 23, 30, 35, 38, 41, 44, 46, 48, 50, 55, 58–60, 62, 64, 67, 78, 81, 83, 85, 89, 91, 93, 95–96, 99, 101, 103, 105–6, 114, 117, 120, 125, 359–60, 363, 365, 371, 374, 376, 379, 381, 384, 386, 388, 398, 400–401, 404, 408, 411–12, 415, 418, 420, 423, 427, 430, 434, 444, 450–51, 453, 456, 458, 461, 463, 466, 469, 471–72, 474, 478–79, 483, 494, 496, 498, 501, 503, 505, 507, 509, 511
Watts, Twinkle, 121
Waxman, A. P., 246, 322
Wayne, David, 360, 373–75
Wayne, Fredd, 508
Wayne, Jerry, 224, 293
Wayne, Paula, 79
Ways and Means, 421
Weaver, Doodles, 51, 441
Weaver, Fritz, 339
Webb, Alan, 339
Webb, Ruth, 171, 291

Webster, Margaret, 324, 385
Webster, Paul Francis, 109, 347
Weidler, Virginia, 79
Weidman, Charles, 146, 208–9, 220, 225, 258, 361
Weil, Richard, 109
Weiler, Erich, 226
Weill, Kurt, 63–65, 153, 192, 194, 271, 273, 354–56, 369, 371–72, 456–58, 504–5
Weissmuller, Don, 198
Welch, Loren, 383, 419
Welchman, Harry, 317
Welles, Halsted, 342
Welles, Orson, 67, 148, 337–39
Wellman, Edward, 316
Wells, Billy K., 478
Wells, Eleanor, 80
Wells, William K., 80
Wences, Senor, 115–17
Wentworth, Richard, 146
Werbezirk, Gisela, 513
Werris, Sam E., 61
Werris, Snag, 488
Wertimer, Ned, 508
Wesson Brothers, 132–33
West, Everett, 143
West, Gordon, 337
West, Mae, 318
West, Willie, 254
Westbrook, Frank, 405
Westerfield, James, 258
Western Costume Co., 159, 230
Weston, Eddie, 510
Weston, Ruth, 96
Wexler, Irving, 439
Wexler, Stanley, 484
Wharton, John F., 504
What's Up, 197–99
Whedon, John, 508
Wheeler, Bert, 129–30, 165, 183, 478–80
Whelan, Ken, 134
Whelen, Tim, 15
Where's Charley?, 459–62
Whipple, Sidney B., 5, 7, 14, 19–21, 23, 30–31, 33, 35, 38, 41–44, 46, 48, 50, 55, 58–60, 62, 64
Whitcup, Leonard, 284
White, Al, Jr., 118, 200, 280, 508
White, Crystal, 500
White, Dan, 157
White, George, Jr., 200
White, Jesse, 413
White, Jon, 207
White, Josh, 278, 280
White, Joshua, 1–2
White, Kenneth, 224
White, Lester, 38
White, Miles, 77, 154, 157, 171, 214, 220, 240, 274, 307, 356, 368, 402, 480, 489, 510
White, Onna, 227, 429

White, Richard, 382
White, Roger, 65
White, Sammy, 448
The White Plume, 25–27
Whitfield, Lynn, 439
Whiting, Jack, 29, 31, 33, 36, 139, 141, 336
Whitman, Walt, 370
Whitney, Helene, 352
Wick, Evelyn, 174
Wickes, Mary, 156, 161, 208, 282
Wiere Brothers, 488
Wilcox, Bert, 443
Wildberg, John, 186, 192, 280
Wilde, Al, 424
Wilde, Cornell, 25, 27
Wilder, Billy, 451
Wilder, Clinton, 505
Wilder, Thornton, 148, 470
Wilderman, William, 507
Wildhorn, Frank, 27
Wile, Everett, 109
Wilenski, Michael, 138
Wilk, Max, 450
Wilkof, Lee, 474
Willenz, Max, 230
Williams, Bob, 131–32
Williams, Chili, 488
Williams, Enid, 329, 450
Williams, Frances, 29–31
Williams, Jack, 51–53, 361, 383
Williams, Lavinia, 189, 257
Williams, Mary Lou, 278
Williams, Musa, 1, 186, 481
Williams, Sherry, 352
Williams, Tom Emlyn, 321
Williams, Vanessa, 329
Williamson, Robert, 73
Willis, George, 205, 278, 330
Willkie, Wendell, 158
Willner, Alfred M., 182
Willner, Sis, 118
Wills, Gloria, 418
Wills, Lou, Jr., 305, 397
Wilson, Burt, 303
Wilson, Dooley, 42, 44
Wilson, Doreen, 356
Wilson, Edith, 70, 72, 280
Wilson, Eileen, 195
Wilson, John C., 200, 240, 307, 368, 472, 510
Wilson, John S., 367
Wilson, Julie, 474–75
Wilson, Marjorie, 111
Wilson, Orlandus, 152
Wilson, Patrick, 156, 408
Wilson, Robert, 387
Wilton, Burt, 304
Wilton, Ruth, 385
Wiman, Dwight Deere, 12, 111, 113, 369

Winckler, Carlton, 51, 146, 289, 322, 361, 441
Windom, William, 385
Windsor, Marie, 167
Windust, Bretaigne, 372
Windy City, 347–48
Wine Women and Song, 132–33
Winged Victory, 202–5
Winninger, Charles, 314
Winslow, George "Foghorn," 513
Winslow, Rain, 336
Winters, Lawrence, 331, 505
Winters, Marjorie, 510
Winters, Shelley, 143, 161
Winter Sisters, 408
Wirtz, Arthur, 39, 120, 234, 349, 390, 445, 485
Withers, Iva, 276, 480
Withers, Jane, 284–86
Witherspoon, Cora, 161, 186
Wittop, Freddy, 139, 141
Witty, Don, 190
Wodehouse, P. G., 315, 430
Wolf, Peter, 375
Wolfe, Jacques, 1–2
Wolfe, John Leslie, 382
Wolfe, Karin, 79
Wolper, David, 212, 284
Wonder, Tommy, 157
Wood, Charles, 430
Wood, Sheryl, 382
Woods, Harry, 50
Woods, Johnny, 3
Wopat, Tom, 336
Worsham, Lauren, 462
Worster, Howett, 129
Worth, Billie, 12, 162–63, 208, 485
Wray, John, 146, 331
Wray, John, Jr., 73
Wright, Bob, 127, 474, 484
Wright, Martha, 399
Wright, Robert, 27, 236, 238–39, 346–47, 356–57, 454, 474
Wrightson, Earl, 220, 271, 273
Wyatt and Taylor, 424
Wyckoff, Evelyn, 63, 94–96, 103, 304
Wyman, Jane, 502
Wymetal, William, 245
Wymore, Patricia, 429–30, 478–79
Wyner, Yehudi, 102
Wynn, Ed, 36, 38, 115–17, 223, 487–88

Wynn, Keenan, 6–8
Wynn, Nan, 251

Yablon, Irene, 108
Yarnell, Bruce, 156, 277, 336
Yarus, Buddy, 99
Yeargan, Michael, 484
Yeats, William B., 365
Yellen, Jack, 36, 87, 157
Yellin, Gleb, 179
Yeo, Mary Jane, 39, 121
Ygor and Tanya, 3
Yordan, Philip, 347
York, Chick, 166
York, Doris, 395
York, Rachel, 474, 512
You'll See Stars, 148–49
Youmans, Vincent, 228
Young, Harry, 146
Young, Howard, 316, 421
Young, Keith, 264
Young, Victor, 339, 513–14
Youngman, Henny, 53, 129–30
Yours Is My Heart, 352–54
Youth Theatre, 134, 351

Zagnit, Stuart, 139
Zani, Dario, 11
Zaret, Hy, 134
Zelinka, Sidney, 449
Zelinka, Sydney, 61
Zeller, Robert, 454
Zeno, Norman, 167, 187, 452
Zeta-Jones, Catherine, 371
Ziegfeld, Billie Burke, 157
Ziegfeld, Florenz, 314
Ziegfeld Follies, 157–59
Zimbalist, Efrem, Jr., 387, 470
Zinnemann, Fred, 218
Zipser, Arthur, 99
Zolotow, Sam, 192
Zorina, Vera, 21, 125, 221–22
Zoritch, George, 513
Zuber, Catherine, 484
Zucker, Stan, 449
Zurkinden, Irene, 392
Zweig, Fritz, 243
Zwerling, Ruby, 449

About the Author

Dan Dietz was a Woodrow Wilson Fellow at the University of Virginia, and the subject of his graduate thesis was the poetry of Hart Crane. He taught English and the history of modern drama at Western Carolina University, and then later served with the U.S. Government Accountability Office and the U.S. Education Department. He is the author of *Off-Broadway Musicals, 1910–2007: Casts, Credits, Songs, Critical Reception and Performance Data of More Than 1,800 Shows* (2010); this book was selected as one of the outstanding reference sources of 2011 by the American Library Association. He is also the author of *The Complete Book of 1950s Broadway Musicals* and *The Complete Book of 1960s Broadway Musicals* (both published in 2014 by Rowman & Littlefield).